RICHARD MILHOUS NIXON

RICHARD MILHOUS NIXON

The Rise of an American Politician

ROGER MORRIS

HENRY HOLT AND COMPANY • NEW YORK

PUBLISHED BY HENRY HOLT AND COMPANY, INC.,
115 WEST 18TH STREET, NEW YORK, NEW YORK 10011.
PUBLISHED IN CANADA BY FITZHENRY & WHITESIDE LIMITED,
195 ALLSTATE PARKWAY, MARKHAM, ONTARIO L3R 4T8.

LIBRARY OF CONGRESS CATALOGING-IN-PUBLICATION DATA
MORRIS, ROGER.
RICHARD MILHOUS NIXON : THE RISE OF AN AMERICAN POLITICIAN /
ROGER MORRIS. —1ST ED.
P.   CM.
ISBN 0-8050-1121-8
1. NIXON, RICHARD M. (RICHARD MILHOUS), 1913- . 2. PRESIDENTS—
UNITED STATES—BIOGRAPHY.   3. UNITED STATES—POLITICS AND
GOVERNMENT—1945-1953.   4. CALIFORNIA—POLITICS AND
GOVERNMENT—1850-1950.   I. TITLE.
E856.M67   1990
973.924'092—DC20
[B]   89-7451
CIP

HENRY HOLT BOOKS ARE AVAILABLE AT SPECIAL DISCOUNTS
FOR BULK PURCHASES FOR SALES PROMOTIONS, PREMIUMS,
FUND-RAISING, OR EDUCATIONAL USE. SPECIAL EDITIONS
OR BOOK EXCERPTS CAN ALSO BE CREATED TO SPECIFICATION.
FOR DETAILS CONTACT:
SPECIAL SALES DIRECTOR, HENRY HOLT AND COMPANY, INC.,
115 WEST 18TH STREET, NEW YORK, NEW YORK 10011.

FIRST EDITION

Book Design by Claire M. Naylon
PRINTED IN THE UNITED STATES OF AMERICA
1   3   5   7   9   10   8   6   4   2

Grateful acknowledgment is given for permission to reprint excerpts from the following:
"Richard Nixon: A Mother's Story," by Hannah Nixon as told to Flora Rheta Schrieber, Good
Housekeeping (June 1960), copyright © 1960, reprinted by permission of The Hearst Corporation;
Hide and Seek: A Continuing Journey, copyright © 1973 by Jessamyn West, reprinted by permission
of Harcourt Brace Jovanovich, Inc.; Nixon vs. Nixon, copyright © 1977 by David Abrahamsen,
reprinted by permission of Farrar, Straus and Giroux, Inc.; Pat Nixon: The Untold Story, copyright
© 1986 by Juldee, Inc., A Delaware Corporation, reprinted by permission of Simon & Schuster, Inc.;
RN: The Memoirs of Richard Nixon, copyright © 1978 by Richard Nixon, reprinted by permission
of Warner Books/New York; Six Crises, by Richard M. Nixon, copyright © 1962 by Richard M.
Nixon, reprinted by permission of Doubleday, a division of Bantam, Doubleday, Dell Publishing
Group, Inc.; Southern California: An Island on the Land, copyright © 1983 by Carey McWilliams,
reprinted by permission of Peregrine Smith Books.

For Kathrin and Paul Morris
Velma and John Erickson
Mary Ann Morris
and in memory of William Clinton Morris, 1928–87

for their loving support, inspiration, example

CONTENTS

Contents

III.   Congress and the Hiss Case

IV.   Senate Race

V.   Running Mate

Contents

Photographs follow page 496.

ACKNOWLEDGMENTS

No conventional acknowledgment—nor, for that matter, anything I write here—can adequately recognize the role of my wife, Kathy, in the writing of this book. This is, quite simply and in so many ways, her book—though she has typically refused to be named formally as the coauthor. It is not just that she was there every inch and mile, every archive and interview, every paragraph of the way, sharing fully the thought and work, shaping the conception in her own creativity, and enduring well more than half the considerable sacrifice. It is her intellect and intrepid political wisdom that informs whatever is good or insightful here; her sensibility, understanding, and compassion that unfold whatever is to be learned about the people, the essential human reality of the history. Any lasting achievement in these pages is unimaginable without her, and everyone should know who really accomplished this book, whatever the cover says.

This biography owes a primary debt to Nat Sobel, who is in every sense its godparent. Nat has been a creative and enterprising literary agent. His intellect, sensibility, and support have been constant—and, as he knows so well, nothing less than saving. He has believed in this undertaking through trials of fire and ice, just as he believes in and maintains an agency of unique substance and seriousness amid the fashionable fluff of contemporary publishing. He is truly a man of parts. As one of his writers and friends, I am fortunate, grateful, admiring.

I am indebted as well to many others. At the Sobel-Weber Literary Agency, James Cassese was always there with his patience and steadfastness when we needed him most. At Henry Holt, Jack Macrae has been an inspired and inspiring editor, graciously adding his own accomplished prose and store of knowledge about California and America in general. Jamie Friddle has been yet another Holt stalwart, shepherding the book to completion. From the beginning, for this biography as for earlier work, there was the professional excellence and buoyant encouragement of the staff of the New Mexico State Library, especially Sandra Esquibel, Sandy Faull, Peggy Medina Giltrow, Penny Grigsby, Norma McCallan, Michael Miller, Orlando Romero, Kathleen Schumpert, Susie Sonflieth, Robert Upton, and Ingrid Vollnhofer. At crucial points in the research, Joe Lennihan and John McClements gave brilliant and devoted aid, as did my children, Zoe and David Hammer. And John Hammer and Peter Klempay generously sheltered me in Washington during several trips.

Though most are duly recognized in the notes, I owe special gratitude to several whose cooperation was significant and unstinting: to Leslie Baird for showering me with his exceptional experience and personal papers; to John Rothmann for his unique insights, and in particular for rare and crucial materials authored by Murray Chotiner; to Richard Kiefer and John J. Irwin for their thorough, painstaking recollections; to Max McPherson, husband of the late Jessamyn West, who candidly gave me his intimate perspective; to Harlan Vinnedge for making available his knowledge of a dramatic juncture in the Hiss Case; to Mac and Dick St. Johns, and to Paul Keye, for their invaluable, often sparkling memories, genuine reflections of the integrity and sophistication of Adela Rogers St. Johns; to Pierce Butler III, who so forthrightly discussed with a stranger the hitherto secret political activities of his father and other Stassen agents; to Richard Norton Smith for insights and guidance drawn from his own fine biographies of Herbert Hoover and Thomas Dewey; to Amelia Fry and Richard Arena for sharing the wisdom of their own extraordinary experience in oral history interviews at Bancroft and Whittier College, encounters with many sources who had passed away or were incapacitated by the time this book began. There is, in that respect, no acknowledgment sufficient to the service performed for us all by the oral history programs at California State, Fullerton, Bancroft, UCLA, the Claremont Colleges, the Presidential Libraries, and elsewhere. Their work is the living, pulsing plasm of our recent political heritage.

I have been continually thankful for the remarkable scholarship that has gone before, notably to the family of Fawn Brodie for steering me toward her rich collection of research materials gathered for her 1980 book, *Richard M. Nixon: The Shaping of His Character*, a work tragically cut short by Professor Brodie's illness and death. While I do not share many if not most of Fawn Brodie's conclusions, or her approach to politics and history, hers is far and away the most impressive intellectual spadework on the subject of Nixon's childhood and youth, and I have drawn gratefully— albeit with rather different results—on her own oral history archives as it were, taped interviews done in the mid–1970s, many with figures no longer available by the mid–1980s. Other distinguished scholars were also generous: among them, Athan Theoharis of Marquette University, who shared with me scores of FBI documents gathered for his own biography of J. Edgar Hoover; Peter Irons of San Diego State University, who lent his thoughtful perspective on Father John Cronin; Rick Frederick of the University of Pittsburgh, who passed along his interesting discoveries in the correspondence of George Creel. Allen Weinstein was similarly thoughtful in guiding me to the voluminous collection of FBI documents now housed at the Truman Library and to other benefits of his work on the Hiss-Chambers affair. Mike Riccards, formerly president of St. John's College of Sante Fe and now president of Shepherd College, read the entire manuscript, issuing in much inspiration as well as typically erudite commentary. And I must thank in particular two friends and colleagues, Jim Hill and Frank Clifford of the *Los Angeles Times*, for their indispensable help with the archives of their newspaper.

Throughout the nation, there have been gifted, dedicated archivists and librarians who have made our research not only possible and productive but often joyous: David Haight, our ever-thorough, ever-stimulating mentor at the Eisenhower Library; Shirley E. Stephenson and Harry Jeffrey, curators of the priceless Young Nixon collection of California State University, Fullerton, who so skillfully started and followed us on our way; John M. Caldwell, who masterfully presides over the Helen Gahagan Douglas Papers at the Carl Albert Center at the University of Oklahoma; Dennis Bilger of the Truman Library, who led us through the maze of FBI documents as well as other key materials; Fred Klose and his colleagues at the National Archives at Laguna Niguel who were constantly solicitous and skillful with the Nixon Pre-Presidential Papers; Jerry Wallace in Washington whose ready expertise in the National Archives brought alive Richard Nixon the young and the zealous OPA bureaucrat; Dwight Miller of the Hoover Library who unearthed crucial materials on the hidden relationship between "The Chief" and his young California protégé; Edwin Southern of Duke University who was most helpful with law school records and correspondence; Pearl Hefte of the Karl E. Mundt Library at Dakota State University, much in command of her extraordinary collection and most accommodating; Nancy Bressler of the Princeton University Library and Mrs. James H. Chadbourn of Harvard Law Library for their assistance in utilizing the John Foster and Allen Dulles Collections and the Alger Hiss

RICHARD MILHOUS NIXON

If thee had gone up as
thee came down, thee would
have come down
as thee went up.

—Almira Burdg Milhous

Prologue

"ITS ROOTS AND MENTOR"

The power began gently, silently, far away.

It came in the darkness of an autumn night, the snowflakes swirling suddenly and insistently. That first white coverlet was only a premonition. In a few weeks the skies grew leaden and close, and the snow fell through long surging storms until it buried the valleys and drifted man-high among the slopes. Crystalline and still, it lay there through the winter in the thin alpine air. Then, as swiftly and quietly as it began, the warmth of an early spring day unleashed it.

In countless small torrents, in icy roaring streams, the Colorado rose at the Continental Divide, northwest of Denver. After a first rush out of the mountains, the river seemed to descend from that altitude almost casually, winding south and west across the Colorado plateau. The tributaries it emptied—the Yampa, Gravel, and Gunnison, the Green, Snake, Elk, and Muddy—joined it in the same deceptive cadence. But beneath the meandering lines on the map was a geologic wonder, a primeval precondition that was to shape the history of the land and the nation.

Imperceptibly, relentlessly, vast forces in the earth's crust long ago elevated the plate of land drained by the Colorado. As the plateau massif slowly rose, the river ate ever deeper into the shale and limestone along its ancient path, striking for the sea. In time, there was a fateful parting of the stream and its old basin. The highlands were left dry and barren while the Colorado cut away through plunging flayed canyons. Prodigal and strangely free, the river became a thing of extraordinary beauty and might. It would fall steeply, over twelve thousand feet in less than fifteen hundred miles, and a third of the descent came after it had taken in most of the tributaries, giving it an enormous, majestic strength.

Yet for better or worse, for all its sinew and richness, the old river was never to escape the parched wilderness. Deserting the high plateau of its headwaters, the Colorado negotiated the yawning stone chasms it had carved for itself—Glen Canyon in Utah, farther downstream in Arizona the Grand Canyon, and eventually Black Canyon at the southern tip of Nevada. Then due south, out of the Black, it ran a gauntlet of desolate mountains on the California-Arizona border, the Sacramento and Mojave and Whipple, and before it could reach the sea it plummeted onto the floor of the Great American Desert. Once the northern depths of a prehistoric gulf of California, the dry wasteland was a mocking end to the West's wild river. Rainfall was scarcely more than three inches a year. The Colorado's own annual surge, sweeping down out of its great canyon sluice, dropped a rich alluvial deposit on the old ocean bed, what one writer called the river's "chocolate flood." But the empty desert lowland, much of it beneath sea level, simply took in the river, absorbed its fury and expanse. When the Colorado retreated, as it always did, when in its caprice the flow could vary tenfold from the swollen spring runoff to the shriveled stream of winter, the rich soil was left alone to the constant, merciless sun. Looking back on his crossing of the land, the first Spanish explorer called it *la jornada de los muertos*, "the journey of the dead."

It was there that frontier America found the Colorado at the end of the nineteenth century, ferocious, erratic, wondrous, an ultimately spent river that rose amid one desert and emptied through another. Vainly, settlers and private development companies, even the formidable Southern Pacific Railroad, tried makeshift irrigation projects in the desert valley to extract at least a portion of the river's profligate life. The venture ended in 1904 in bankruptcy for the developers and a man-made flood more destructive than nature's.

Some years before, there had been a warning of sorts against taking such liberties with the Colorado. One-armed (the other lost at Shiloh), Major John Wesley Powell had twice conducted government surveys down the Colorado: once, during the first run through the Grand Canyon, he was seated magisterially in a captain's chair strapped to the wildly pitching deck of a small wooden boat. Powell delivered his verdict eight years later in 1877: "I want to say to you . . . there is not sufficient water to supply these lands." At that, the Major spoke only of the Colorado's own arid basin south of the canyons, the silted but bleached shores of the fitful river, where the enduring American frontier dream of a yeoman farmstead now required an irrigation ditch at the least.

Still, the thirst for the river on a grander scale persisted. And as Powell lay dying at the turn of the century, it came in voices not from the river's canyons and banks but farther west. "What is the key that will unlock the door to modern enterprise and human genius?" the writer William Smythe asked. "It is the Rio Colorado. Whoever shall control the right to divert these turbid waters will be master of this empire."

It was a purpose not even the worldly Major Powell comprehended, much less the audacity and force that lay behind it.

A hundred miles west of the old desert Colorado, the tides of the prehistoric gulf had lapped against its far shores, etching their geologic watermark on the rocky foothills. There the land rose again up the San Bernardino and San Jacinto ranges, then fell sharply onto a great coastal basin and into a different world.

A semi-desert, treacherous and demanding under a relentless sun, the remarkable contour of the country hid its harshness. Cradling mountains not only offered a shield from the forbidding wasteland on the east, but also turned and trapped sea winds from the Pacific to condense a precious margin of rainfall and humidity. Together, the basin and wind and sunlight created a climate men had long associated with the hereafter, or at least with no other locale in America—a constant, bright, gentle mildness, an eternal spring and summer without extremes. "The visible wrath of God is not to be found here," one visitor recorded solemnly. "No one ever froze or roasted to death." The weather dressed the region in a seductive beauty; the seasons seemed always to rescue it just in time from its desert provenance. Bald brown hills, glaring and naked in the sun, were softened in a moment by ocean mist, and alternated between a tawny drought and a brilliant emerald lushness. There were visible defects in the country— dubious soil, no forest or mineral riches, no natural harbor, an arid fastness for a hinterland—but the climate canceled out doubt or limits. What was lacking could somehow be supplied, the omissions of the miracle filled in.

It was a love affair from the beginning, between the Anglo voyager by land or sea and this Mediterranean Eden on the edge of a wasteland. Rounding the point north of San Diego that would bear his name, Richard Henry Dana recorded in 1836 a common sense of awe: "There was a grandeur in everything around, which gave a solemnity to the scene, a silence and solitariness . . . no sound heard but the pulsations of the great Pacific . . . as refreshing as a great rock in a weary land." The Spanish were the first Europeans to rule, putting down rancheros and a string of missions that doubled as profitable ecclesiastical sweatshops for their Indian wards. The American declaration of war on Mexico in 1846 would have other pretexts, but California was the real prize luring President James Polk and Congress, both assured by a New York newspaper of Washington's "manifest destiny" to govern the entire North American continent. Defeated repeatedly in the Far West in a theater of the war its historians would discreetly ignore, the United States finally won a decisive battle near Los Angeles. The Americans marched methodically toward the city in a square of volleying troopers, their withering grapeshot cutting a fearful toll among the mounted Californians, who attacked the formation from all sides in charge after desperate charge.

The conquerors wasted no time taking hold of their spoil. What had been a trickle of Yankee settlers in old Los Angeles, men who often married into Spanish families and blended into the colonial repose, now became a horde of frontier immigrants. The population of the basin exploded 1,200 percent between 1860 and 1900, Los Angeles swelling from a small pueblo to more than a hundred thousand. Even by America's motley pioneer standards, the sociology of the settlement was remarkable. "Take a sprinkling of sober-eyed, earnest, shrewd, energetic New England businessmen," a contemporary described the influx,

> mingle them with a number of rollicking sailors, a dark band of Australian convicts and cutthroats, a dash of Mexican and frontier desperadoes, a group of hardy backwoodsmen, some professional gamblers, whiskey dealers, general swindlers . . . and having thrown in a promiscuous crowd of broken-down merchants, disappointed lovers, black sheep, unfledged dry-goods clerks, professional miners from all parts of the world . . . stir up the mixture, season strongly with bad liquors, faromonte, *rouge et noir*, quarrels, oaths, pistols, knives, dancing and digging, and you have something approximating California society in early days.

Januslike, southern California faced both the ocean and the filling continent behind, vaguely promising the fortunes of yet another inexhaustible frontier, beckoning to the East as the final El Dorado of climate and opportunity. Knowing a sure thing, a legion of professional boosters and real-estate hustlers, their persuasive skills honed in land bubbles in Chicago or the plains, came to tout and entice. But here they were less important than an even more enterprising institution, the American railroad. Having pushed their tracks and stockholders' capital across the nation only to find themselves in a desert, the houses of Santa Fe and Southern Pacific promptly set to work to make the trip, and the investment, worthwhile. With the completion of the Santa Fe's line to Los Angeles in 1886, the giddy cycle of booms began. Crawling at little more than twenty miles an hour, taking five days and nights from Missouri River departures, the excursion and emigrant trains were packed by an elaborate campaign of railroad publicity and promotion resounding across America and into Europe. They arrived three and four a day, some with a hundred cars of eager settlers. At first, the $125 fare tended to determine the class of migrants, but a rate war between the Southern Pacific and Santa Fe drove the ticket price to one dollar early in 1887, and a deluge followed.

The new arrivals found a raucous, vibrant scene, the basin convulsed by the boom. Gamblers flourished with impunity. Prostitutes rode Los Angeles boulevards in expensive carriages, passing out engraved cards. The region saw its first wave of murder, theft, and highway robbery. And everywhere were the speculators and their eager customers, the ox roasts and sales of guaranteed ocean-view properties, albeit some at a distance. In the last half of the 1880s over a hundred new towns were laid out in the region, more than sixty in a two-year period. They appeared, remembered one witness, "like scenes conjured up by Aladdin's lamp—out of the desert, in the river wash or a mud flat, upon a barren slope or hillside." Then, almost overnight, in the suddenness of the region's pseudo seasons, in 1889 it was gone. More than half the platted towns disappeared forever. Fortunes were lost, thousands of ordinary settlers broken, the rotten tissue of the speculative economy exposed. "I had half a million dollars wiped out in the crash," says a character of the era in a California novel, "and what's worse, $500 of it was cash."

Nonetheless, the bravado that underwrote the boom remained, along with stranded tourists. In fifteen years a new surge of growth had begun, this time less blustering if equally predatory, and more controlled by the region's increasingly powerful civic leaders and businessmen. Eloquent of the ardor and pretense, the new Los Angeles Chamber of Commerce publicly resolved that the city annex Baja California from Mexico, an excess of boosterism that precipitated in the 1890s a diplomatic incident between Washington and Mexico City.

For all the tumult and sharp practices, the region continued to exert its charm and pull on Americans. Part of the marvel, like the shifting light and shadow tempering the basin's hills, was that there always seemed yet another texture and meaning to this sensuous place, something to be felt and found by almost any seeker, and often a civility and grace beyond the coarse huckstering of the land and weather. On the eve of the boom of the eighties, Miriam Leslie of New York's *Leslie's Illustrated*, attended by half a dozen friends and staff, her Skye terrier, and survival rations of canned oysters and vintage champagne, ventured on tour into raw Los Angeles only to discover a "quaint, uneventful little city, with its lingering flavor of Spanish and monastic domination, its fruit and flowers, its sweet and fragrant atmosphere." Another author amid the booms saw southern

California in the comfortable, bucolic hue of a midwestern county seat. "It is pleasant to note that beautiful homes and high average prosperity," he recounted, "have not spoiled the democratic simplicity of these communities."

The setting imparted all visions to all men. It was, above everything else perhaps, a matter of pure physical pleasure, which in turn came back to the singular geography. "Here in the Southwest," as a Los Angeles editor rhapsodically described the historic event, "we have the Saxon transplanted to a livable climate . . . where he dares to go out and enjoy himself." And out of the sheer self-consciousness and hedonism, there grew about the place a unique theology of deliverance, the frontier as shrine. "My first impression was such as one might receive on arriving in a city of refuge, or alternatively on a religious retreat," wrote one pilgrim. "Here, it seems, is the place where harassed Americans come to recover the joy and serenity which their manner of life denies them elsewhere, the place, in short, to study America in flight from herself." Implicit from the beginning, alongside the immigrant's common nostalgia for home, was the sense of escape from a less hospitable America, as often a matter of society as of climate—and the seeds of a historic regional rivalry.

Inevitably, the country drew from its special natural gifts, its clamorous growth and chauvinism, an identity that was to form into a concerted presence and political power. "When I am in California," President Theodore Roosevelt told an appreciative Los Angeles audience in 1905, "I am not in the West. I am west of the West." The growing particularism was reflected in the very look of the country, in a public ethic of gigantic improvisation. To the advertised promised land the settlers and civic fathers simply added the absent elements, importing grass, plants, flowers, eucalyptus, acacia and pepper trees, along with sparrows, pheasants, the rat, the house mouse, and ordinary weeds. Crossing the desert and mountains, an early migrant found suddenly in Los Angeles lawns of unearthly richness, "the kind of green that seems as though it might rub off on your hands," he wrote, "a theatrical green, a green that was not quite real."

Yet in the midst of the gathering beauty and fulfillment there was, in the end, an ominous secret, a flaw seen clearly by only a few in the euphoria of the half century of growth after the American conquest. For beneath the temperate air and winds and protecting mountains, there was not a single river, not a natural lake, not even a creek in the entire basin with a truly reliable year-round supply of water. By 1910, they had sunk over 1,500 artesian wells, but in the profligacy of the time the earliest wells, drilled forty years before, had been allowed to spray uncapped into the air, and the artesian water supply was largely dissipated in a generation.

As the headlong growth continued, the available water gradually, invisibly receded. Los Angeles at the turn of the century still had enough water for a population of a hundred thousand, though shortages were already known. Instead of conserving what was left, reservoirs were built and pumps installed, even one drilled into the bedrock beneath the Los Angeles River, the city's lifeblood. These would not be enough.

In the looming specter of drought and stagnation, there was suddenly the echo of haunting, early chronicles of Spaniards who saw the basin before civilization had created a tropical fantasy out of what little water there was, before investment and migration and deliverance.

"A wretched land," one of those first explorers recorded the scene; it is "barren and bereft."

At this juncture the civic fathers of Los Angeles reached out with a vengeance to make whole their paradise. Beyond the craven press and authorized histories of the era, what really happened in the water wars that followed would for a time belong only to the folklore of the country, to murmured accounts in discreet clubs and boardrooms and on shaded patios. A frontier expedient, it was not the sort of thing even rowdy boosters advertised, a morganatic marriage between villainy and vision, between private greed and grand public purpose. On September 7, 1905, the voters of Los Angeles gratefully approved a $35 million bond issue to build an aqueduct to secure a new water supply for the region, and hidden in the election was a remarkable scandal.

Watered by the slopes of the great Sierra Nevada 250 miles north-northeast of the southern California basin, the Owens Valley at the turn of the century was a sylvan string of pioneer farming communities beginning to prosper along their mountain river. In 1903, the U.S. Reclamation Service was planning a federal irrigation project and dam at the valley's northern end, and local ranchers had already in good faith signed over water storage rights to the government. But then, J. B. Lippincott, a reclamation service engineer who was mapping the valley hydrology, told his Los Angeles friends about the irrigation scheme, and together they plotted a sweeping fraud. Among Lippincott's powerful basin cronies was Fred Eaton, a former water superintendent and future mayor of Los Angeles, who moved quietly and quickly to collect options on 12,000 acres of headwater property in the Owens Valley, including the proposed dam site for which the valley ranchers had already ceded their water storage rights.

Now on the Los Angeles city payroll as well as reclamation's chief engineer for the region, Lippincott solemnly recommended against building the project, the irrigation plans were duly canceled by the Department of the Interior in 1904, and Eaton exercised his options and bought up the water rights

7

from the bewildered settlers. In July 1905, the *Los Angeles Times* announced with suitable fanfare the acquisition of the water rights and plans for an aqueduct, a virtual edict and first news of the project for the Los Angeles City Council, whose members, unlike the *Times* management, had not been privy to the conspiracy. Finally, to forestall any awkward last-minute questions or doubts from the electorate, which had to approve a bond issue to finance the aqueduct, precious Los Angeles water was secretly dumped into sewers to create an artificial reservoir shortage on the eve of the vote.

The next stage of the theft was hatched by a syndicate of financial giants, including Henry Huntington the banker and promoter, rail tycoon E. H. Harriman, General Harrison Grey Otis of the *Los Angeles Times*, and, not least, Otis's former circulation clerk become dynastic-minded son-in-law, Harry Chandler. To exploit the water still further, the syndicate first bought 16,000, then 45,000 acres of barren, waterless land in the San Fernando Valley in the northeast of the basin at about $30 an acre. The plan was simple. When the publicly financed aqueduct would come down from the Owens Valley, it would spill not in Los Angeles proper but at the edge of the San Fernando, raising acreage values two-hundred fold and giving the providential syndicate more than $100 million in profits. It would be the basis of Harry Chandler's fortune, making his family southern California's biggest landowners.

As politics, it was a portent of the future. There were few heroes, save perhaps a lone journalist named Samuel Clover, who wrote briefly about the swindle and was promptly driven into bankruptcy. When Owens Valley ranchers protested, they were coerced and financially crushed. When San Fernando Valley bankers tried to carry the few small farmers squeezed by the syndicate, Los Angeles found prosecutors and juries to send the creditors to San Quentin for purported violations of banking laws. Meanwhile, Gifford Pinchot, the progressive head of the U.S. Forest Service and renowned for his devotion to conservation, was enlisted by the syndicate to keep more troublesome settlers out of the valley by declaring the surrounding land a federal preserve.

With similar alacrity the U.S. Congress enacted special legislation to clear the way for the municipal aqueduct to cross federal land. While the right-of-way bill was being introduced by Frank Flint, the Republican senator from California, an amendment was offered in the House to reinstate the original Reclamation Service plan, which had proposed that the water be available to the city only when there was an excess and only for domestic use. Though Pinchot's initial support of the amendment gave the conspirators a scare, the measure was defeated and the syndicate rescued by the forceful intervention of another well-known champion of conservation, Theodore Roosevelt, who declared that the need for water in

Los Angeles must, unfortunately, take precedence over the interests of the few.

In the 1920s, sections of the aqueduct would be dynamited and control gates sabotaged. But such resistance was quickly trampled, and the ruined valley became a virtual desert. For their part, Harry Chandler and his syndicate partners, their corruption politely obscured, went on to unparalleled power and enormous wealth. In mocking irony, the small farmers used their last money to purchase an ad that Los Angeles papers readily ran in characteristic hubris. It began, "We, the farming communities of Owens Valley, being about to die, salute you."

At the heart of the tragedy was not only avarice and deception but an engineering blunder of some magnitude. In the nearby Long Valley was a potential storage basin ample to have gathered and dispensed enough water for both the valley and Los Angeles. But the original scheme included no storage dam, and the stream was directly flushed into the pipeline. Then as later, hydrology was even more obscure than politics. The aqueduct snaked down from the valley and across the desert as a feat of man's dominion over the austere nature of the West.

When the Owens water first gushed into the basin in 1913, its channel was dubbed "Mulholland's Ditch" for the imperious and visionary Los Angeles water superintendent, Eaton's hand-picked successor, who became the official patron saint of the project. A formidable, almost ascetic Irish roustabout, William Mulholland rose through the infant Los Angeles water bureaucracy to become the gruff, thick-mustachioed *zanjero* of the system and, more important, vassal to the new businessmen of power. He embodied the region's bravura. Not a man to ponder flaws in his considerable prowess, he was once asked in court to testify to his engineering credentials. "Well, I went to school in Ireland when I was a boy," he replied, "learned the three R's and the Ten Commandments—or most of them—made a pilgrimage to the Blarney Stone, received my father's blessing, and here I am." Mulholland would be the basin's answer to the Colorado's Major Powell.

Both engineering legend and political act, the Owens Valley depredation would become an example and a spur to other, far vaster plans. The basin's thirst, like its appetite for profitable growth, was unappeasable. Over the next decade, inevitably, Mulholland and the multiple powers he represented would turn toward the ever-beckoning Colorado. With lobbying and maneuver reminiscent of the Owens Valley tactics, the Boulder Dam Act was passed by Congress at the end of 1928. Public utility champions were cheered by federal proprietorship. Conservatives would be quietly contented with the new California model of business profit from public enterprise.

And if a one-armed, bearded ghost waved a warning from his tossing little boat, no one seemed to notice.

Their purpose was nothing less than to break the old Colorado, to strangle the flood in its canyon cradle, to give a desert empire its water. "Henry, it sounds a little ambitious," W. A. "Dad" Bechtel said to Henry J. Kaiser, his partner in the Six Companies consortium that got the contract. So it was. The methods, like the men, were suntanned and strapping, not the sallow disciplines of the laboratory but engineering on a gargantuan scale by a nation already begun to worship itself and its technology, and sometimes unable to distinguish between the two. They blasted and tore at Black Canyon, and heaved in thousands of tons of rock to raise the river toward its cage. Taut-stomached men from Oklahoma and Texas and the plains with the telltale sunburn along the hatline, scrubbed young surveyors in Stetsons and high-laced boots, the pale, thin, pinched women among the camp followers—a reporter for *Harper's* named Theo White found them in 1935. "It is an extraordinary existence out there," he wrote. "All is extreme. The men work with an enforced intensity and play with a hilarious looseness. Their existence is a continual thrill, centered about the callous, cruel lump of concrete at the bottom of the canyon."

They would pour concrete twenty-four hours a day for two years, enough to pave a highway sixteen feet wide from San Francisco to New York. The $48 million contract for the dam and powerhouse was the largest ever offered by the U.S. government, and there was an added toll in 110 dead, labor unrest, discrimination, and bitter resentment. But like the Owens Valley, the history of Boulder Dam was less in statistics and flesh than in the mythic symbolism, and, of course, in the sequel. Boulder was only the beginning. Downstream they built Parker Dam and behind it took out the aqueduct to Los Angeles, ran it sixteen hundred feet off the floor of the desert, over the San Jacintos, and ended in 1939 nearly four hundred miles away in a basin reservoir. Still farther along the Colorado's barren course, they placed another dam and a canal, resurrecting the Southern Pacific's washed-away dream to irrigate the wasteland, watering thousands of fertile acres of sun-baked silt into an agricultural oasis that would be called, aptly enough, the Imperial Valley.

The sheer dominance, governments and businessmen having their way with nature, became infectious. "We build dams the way the Aztecs built pyramids," wrote a California author. It was always more than the water. Boulder Dam was brought to completion under the New Deal and a Democratic administration, but it had begun with the blessing of the Republicans, under Herbert Hoover, whose name it would finally bear after

Franklin Roosevelt's death. The structure spanned ideology as it spanned Black Canyon, joining public purpose and private enrichment in a marriage the West, and Los Angeles in particular, took for granted. The Six Companies made only $10.4 million at Boulder, but they went on to similarly heroic federal and state projects, and astronomical profits. For Kaiser and Bechtel and others, Boulder Dam was the beginning of a commercial leviathan, and the portent of a giant military-government industrial complex spawned by public money and policy.

As vital and historic as the sleek aqueducts were the gawky circuit transmission lines that carried the hum of Boulder's hydroelectric power to southern California. From 1936 to 1942, the first four generators at Black Canyon gave Los Angeles 98 percent of its electricity. It was all in time to ignite the enormous boom of World War II in the basin, to fuel the military plants so crucial to the outcome of the war, and to the burgeoning economy, sociology, and politics of the postwar era. In the war years five thousand new factories rose in the region with $800 million in new investments. Production went from $5 billion to $12 billion, and southern California's share of national manufacturing and defense contracts more than doubled overnight. Population in the basin soared by over a million, and more than tripled between 1920 and the end of the war.

By 1945 the soft flakes of snow falling on the Colorado's headwaters had propagated a wealth and power in the Los Angeles basin no turn-of-the-century booster or syndicate, however greedy, could have imagined. There was a hidden price here, too—the congestion and poisoned air, the unnecessary dams and bureaucratic tyranny, a free river transformed into plumbing and retaliating with destructive silt and salination and critical water loss in the desert reservoirs by evaporation. Ultimately, all the water and hydroelectricity could not seem to sate the appetites long ago accustomed to excess. Some believed God would eventually exact retribution for the sin in the Owens Valley, and many were simply struck with the precariousness of the old, enduring miracle. "There is something disturbing about this corner of America, a sinister suggestion of transience," thought J. B. Priestley, the distinguished English writer who had come to Hollywood in the 1930s to write films. "There is a quality hostile to men in the very earth and air here. As if we were not meant to make our homes in this oddly enervating sunshine. . . . California will be a silent desert again. It is all as impermanent and brittle as a reel of film."

But in the rash, exhilarating spiral that came with the conquered water, such reckonings, if ever, lay in a seemingly far distant future. It was instead a time to flex the new, charged strength. "The idea is held by everybody in southern California," novelist and film writer James M. Cain concluded, "that some sort of destiny awaits the place."

The Owens Valley, then the Colorado River, made possible a churning new metropolitan society in southern California on the foundation of the old frontier booms. America in flight now turned and half-faced the gallery, its features composed in part out of the past, in part out of the teeming, uprooted present. Observers were always struck by how much this place of fresh promise, this haven, merely transferred to a more congenial climate what had been left behind, what the migrants were supposedly escaping. In the mid-twenties, Louis Adamic, a sociologist and novelist, thought Los Angeles still "the enormous village." Surrounding the local Babbitts and promoters and parasites had come tide after tide of what Adamic called "the folks," the retired farmers or grocers, former Ford agents or merchants, people who had sold out homesteads and businesses in Illinois or Ohio, Iowa or Missouri to live in the basin's palm-tree-fronted little bungalows. After them came waves of laborers from the drudgery of Pennsylvania or New York factories, ranch hands and sharecroppers from Oklahoma and Texas, blacks from the Deep South.

Yet for all its growing variety, the settlement would remain overwhelmingly from the Midwest, and in its majority a fugitive lower middle class. With the radical act of migration, they tended to bring, like an old quilt, the comforting traditions, values, root conservatism of their origins, what one onlooker scorned as "the mode of existence they learned elsewhere, and have not the imagination to transcend." Abandoning the prairie freeze and swelter, they reproduced in the temperate basin the neat flat hamlets of the prairies. Earthquake ordinances and real-estate predators helped stretch the metropolis into its sprawl, but habit and nostalgia stunted the skyline no less. The arrangement of small-town America was stamped indelibly on what would be the West's greatest city.

They brought, too, other relics. Alongside ambition, conviction, and pioneer confidence traveled homespun priggishness, religiosity, and intolerance. "A glacial dullness engulfed the region," one chronicler wrote about the years after 1900 and the colorful early booms. "Every consideration was subordinated to the paramount concern of attracting church-going Middle Westerners to Southern California." Immigrant religion did carry its own color and bombast. The basin became fertile ground for evangelists and their crusades, well attended by those with the hearty evangelical strains of Protestantism and precarious sense of salvation the settlers so largely brought with them. But when the tents were folded and the revivalist temples emptied, inspiration could decline here also into routine sanctimony. "Hypocrisy, like a vast fungus, has spread over the city's surface," wrote art critic Willard Wright in a book published the year the Owens

Valley water came to the basin. The scourge, he thought, was the immigrants' "complete stock of rural beliefs, pieties, superstitions and habits—the Middle West bed hours, the Middle West love of corned beef, the church bells . . . union suits and missionary societies."

It was to be an orderly, peaceful, reverent paradise—for some. Southern California's Indian population, many effectively detribalized by the missions and passed on as wards from the exploitative but comparatively benign Spanish, were soon decimated under U.S. rule by disease, starvation, and outright genocide. Eminent historian Hubert Howe Bancroft called it "one of the last human hunts of civilization, and the basest and most brutal of them all." Settlers promptly extended the custom of bigotry and racial harassment to succeeding minorities, Asian, Mexican, black. "California was willing to have free nonwhites," concluded a later scholar studying racial attitudes in the booms, "but only if they had few or no human rights and if they could be considered without argument to be born inferiors." Europeans were encouraged to immigrate and in some cases given free housing in the bargain. Racial minorities were greeted with exclusionary alien land laws, cordoned-off slums, and frequent violence.

The migrant prejudice festered from fear of competition in the new refuge as well as from the ingrained prejudices of their origins. With the immigration of Chinese and then Japanese in the thousands, anti-Orientalism flourished. So bitter was the animus that the Chinese, who were all but driven out of the area by the early decades of the century, even returned at one later point to disinter their dead from the basin's ground. In their wake, the Japanese stoically adapted to the discriminatory order, prospered in business by their gifts and industry, and began to educate an American-born and equally apt generation of children. They accomplished each against great odds, to face not only unacceptance but often mounting hatred. For the Japanese it was to climax in a half-fabricated hysteria in the weeks after the outbreak of World War II, and a harsh deportation from their California homes to inland concentration camps. "Racism," a local historian would judge later, "has been as deep and pervasive in the history of California as in that of any state outside the South." And as elsewhere in the country, the contagion spread inevitably and instantly into politics. Robert Kenny, a Democratic Party leader for decades, former state attorney general, and later a Los Angeles judge, would say of the period 1914–40, "A California politician who wanted to get elected had to be just as racist on the Japanese as a Democratic politician in the South had to be on the Negro."

In the 1920s and 1930s, it would be the Mexicans' turn, segregated in their "Jimtown" cabins, consigned to separate schools and churches, movie balconies, "Mexican Day" at the local swimming pools, and, finally, cem-

13

eteries—all in a society boastfully advertising its opportunities and progress. Like the Japanese, Mexican immigrants were to face the full fury of bigotry during World War II in the infamous Zoot Suit Riots in which roving bands of white servicemen and local vigilantes murdered and tortured Los Angeles Hispanics caught on the streets.

Yet if the explosive growth carried with it old-fashioned sanctimony and prejudice, the sheer size and ferment of it all produced as well the unprecedented and the bizarre. In the 1920s—which saw a bonanza of real estate, oil, and the motion picture industry—over a million and a half people moved into southern California, the largest internal migration in American history. In 1923 and 1924 their rattletrap cars were an endless caravan westward on the narrow highways that ran over planks thrown across the desert sand, curling into the basin past the little ranches and tourist camps on the outskirts of the promised land. Wealth could be fabulous, from the oil strikes to local commerce to millionaire expatriots. Social classes in the towns were often uniquely silhouetted, the rich ensconced on the hillside heights, the well-to-do on the sloping approaches, the middle class and laborers farther down, ending with railroad tracks or dry riverfront and the Mexican fieldhands and black servants. Throughout the region were fragrant belts of citrus, a carefully tended and guarded empire within the empire.

At the heart was the squat city. "As New York is the melting pot for the peoples of Europe," Sarah Comstock wrote from her vantage point as a Californian and Manhattan editor, "so Los Angeles is the melting pot for the peoples of the United States." Into the melt coursed not only the stolid migrant burghers or farmers lately foreclosed, but also charlatans and cultists, canary and rabbit breeders, storefront saviors, invalids and the wan, healers of exotic means, pet morticians, heretics, fixers, palm readers and parvenus of every description. While climate and opportunity were marvelous and small-town values to be sternly preserved, the city from the 1920s also far exceeded the national average in divorces and suicides, and led the country in embezzlement, bank robberies, narcotics addiction, and society murders. The grasping could be charted, too, in a parade of sensational commercial scandals, with casts of suckers and conmen from every class, and in local courtrooms crowded with fraud litigation. "Incessant migration has made Los Angeles a vast drama of maladjustment," Los Angeles writer and social activist Carey McWilliams reflected in 1945, a place "where perversion is perverted and prostitution prostituted." Emblematic of the disillusion, a real-estate memoir of 1930 was entitled *Sunshine and Grief in Southern California*.

Economics and politics both created and mirrored the tumult. A great migration meant at once a ceaseless demand for labor, a surplus of immigrants desperate for work, and in the coincidence an irresistible temptation for the basin's employers and capitalists. Owners and boosters kept wages low and unions out to attract more capital and to compete industrially with relatively high-wage San Francisco. At the same time, migrants struggling to meet the rent or mortgage and stay in paradise could scarcely organize or strike amid the continuing influx of homeseekers ever eager to take a protester's job. The result was a virulent exploitation and bitterness that made prewar Los Angeles the national epitome of the open shop and labor strife.

The languid, tepid climate seemed to breed political extremes—May Day parades in contrast to roaming Red Squads burning "un-American" books, the basin's own collective farm on the model of a worker's soviet next to a closed guild of merchants and manufacturers. The guild, as a congressional committee once put it, was given to "a conspiratorial pattern of malfeasance . . . accompanied by occasional outbursts of class violence and a constant undercurrent of class hostility." Behind the cameras and glittering public façade, Hollywood and the motion picture business in the 1930s were wracked by their own bloody and venomous industrial civil war, a clash that would have a later reckoning played out before the nation.

The larger dispossession fed in the 1930s a series of utopian political and economic schemes and movements, usually plans to provide guaranteed income or pension payments. Now one more pitchman's mirage or cult fad, now with the dark cast of social fascism, the movements were invariably paid for and peopled by the lower middle class and the apprehensive, struggling elderly who had become the political tinder of the basin. The schemes petered out by the beginning of World War II, and the promoters tended to disappear with the era. But they left an uneasy political legacy, the glimpse of a society confident but fearful, at home while uprooted, conservative of the past and cheated by the pallor of the present, an exuberance yet despair.

At the top politics remained starkly conventional, the essence of power little moved by the social ferment. Controversy softened the frightening edges of popular resentment by settling on personalities. At center stage was the *Los Angeles Times*'s General Otis, a volatile, vengeful robber baron of the old school who was said to possess, as one editor expressed it, "the fixed idea that he owned Los Angeles, in fee simple, and that he alone was destined to lead it to greatness." As an epigram on the *Times*'s power and the Otis-Chandler family interests, as well as the general's megalomania, the description was not idle. Otis found his most conspicuous adversary in Hiram Johnson, the California progressive and renegade Republican senator. "He sits there," Johnson once said of Otis in an age of rather more florid political rhetoric, "in senile dementia with gangrene

15

heart and rotting brain, grimacing at every reform, chattering impotently at all things that are decent, frothing, fuming, violently gibbering, going down to his grave in snarling infamy." It was flamboyant theater. But Johnson's malediction did not alter the fact that Los Angeles from the 1890s through World War II remained, of all America's great cities, perhaps the least reformed, the least touched by currents of civic housecleaning that elsewhere revitalized parties and rendered both government and its silent partners more accountable.

Confronted in a pivotal mayoral election in 1911 by progressive reformers and a militant labor movement astride a growing socialist party—both obviously anathema—Otis and his colleagues of power simply chose the lesser of evils. They proceeded to finance, publicly support, and quietly coopt the progressives. After the election, more polite reformers did inject efficiency and economy into government and managed to eliminate the most visible excesses of the old municipal machine but left the base control of urban and regional politics intact. "The main qualification for public office in Los Angeles," a political observer wrote in the mid-forties, "has been a pleasant and easily remembered name."

For their part, the Progressives proved more adaptable to the subtle coalition than their subsequent image of enlightenment and independence would reveal. Regarded by later scholars as wisely prescient in their opposition to American expansion and belligerence abroad, California Progressives tended to make discreet exceptions in their wisdom. With an eye on social tastes at home, they voted determinedly for embargoes against Japan or punitive expeditions against Mexico. Politicians perforce learned early in southern California what a later era would call pragmatism. "The bitter lessons of politics," said Johnson, applying his customary similes, "have taught our people that regularity is a fetish for the mentally weak and halt and lame . . . the last refuge of the political moron." As if in agreement with Johnson, the Democratic Party nominated for Congress during the 1940s an ostensibly liberal candidate later exposed as an active leader of the Ku Klux Klan.

The critics relished it all—the social anomalies, the inequities, the contortions of politics. "Los Angeles represents the ultimate segregation of the unfit," pronounced Britain's prodigal socialist and scientist Bertrand Russell. Substantially to Russell's right, American columnist Westbrook Pegler thought a guardian should be appointed for the region, and the whole basin declared politically incompetent. "I saw one colossal swindle after another perpetrated on the public, and for every official who was sent to jail I knew a thousand were hiding with their loot," remarked Upton Sinclair, the legendary muckraker who in his outrage vainly ran for governor of California in 1934. "It is absolutely selfish, very empty, but not false, and at least, not full of false effort," D. H. Lawrence wrote of the region not long before Sinclair's run. "I don't want to live here, but a stay here rather amuses me. It's sort of crazy-sensible." Carey McWilliams, whose friends numbered among the social and intellectual elite of the basin and whose legal clients included Mexican victims of race riots, believed by the mid-forties that, "Here the defeat of the American dream has been most recent in point of time, most widely sensed, most sharply experienced."

Yet the strength of the place was irrepressible. The new power pulsed, then throbbed. There was a sense as World War II ended that some latent force was in the offing, like an old Colorado flood pounding down through the canyons. "The air is fresh here, but the real twang of it is the foretaste of coming change," thought the *New York Post* columnist Samuel Grafton, who reported on the "hungry, questing crowd" in the heady boom of wartime California. "That really makes men's nostrils flare, and their eyes look round."

From what Lord Bryce called the "mixed multitude" of the Los Angeles basin emerged a nation in microcosm. It was more than Bryce's vision of a single region of the Pacific coast with the "character of a great country, capable of standing alone in the world," though that was true enough. Far more important, the place had become, for its kinship, a laboratory and litmus test, a foreword, for the rest of the United States. Culture, manners, architecture, furniture, clothes, tastes and trends, images and advertising, not least the chimerical hybrid art of politics—the future would be visible on this coveted and much imitated frontier. The influence grew not only from Hollywood and its hall of mirrors refracting and inventing national life. It was lodged in the nature and essence of the entire migration, who they were and what they were becoming. "The region manifests in many ways a remarkable exaggeration of all those things," noted one Hollywood writer, "which we are wont to call typically American."

By the end of the war, the sanctuary with its fleeing pilgrims, the contrived paradise with its expropriated water and electricity, at last turned its face fully toward the continent behind. It presented, for those who would see, a familiar reflection.

"Here American institutions sharpen into forces so startling as to give the effect, sometimes, of caricature," wrote Farnsworth Crowder, who knew the setting vividly as a journalist and social critic. "What America is, California is, with accents, in italics . . . all richly, pungently American and not to be disowned, out of embarrassment and arrogance, by the rest of the nation which is in fact its parental flesh and blood, its roots and mentor."

I

ORIGINS

1

Families, 1878–1912

I see there is a people risen," Oliver Cromwell once said of the Quakers, "that I cannot win either with gifts, honors, offices, or places." Born amid the sectarian turmoil, civil war, and regicide of seventeenth-century England, the movement began as a radical Puritanism. "The most protestant of Protestants," as one historian called them, the Quakers rooted their new theology in a fierce individualism and democracy of faith, the innate conscience and grace of every believer's "inner light" or "the light of Christ within." "There was that of God in every man," went a basic maxim. So vehement was their anticlerical urge that they declared in effect a universal priesthood, each man and woman communing personally with the Deity without intercession, life itself the sacrament. Fortified by scriptural authority, they worshiped prayerfully in silent meetings, anyone free to speak as and when the spirit moved them, unencumbered by ritual or even a preacher's homilies. Pastors might emerge as spiritual leaders, be "recognized," though never "ordained" or with special prerogative. If sin were inherent in mankind, they believed, so too was the capacity to apprehend God untranslated. They would carry the Reformation to a conclusion of mute spiritual autonomy.

Their apostle was George Fox, "dear George . . . a new and heavenly minded man," as William Penn saw him. "The most awful, living, reverent frame I have ever felt or beheld." Fox had left home at nineteen at the command of God to find "a way," and only six years later, in 1650, had become a new religious leader. On a Yorkshire hill he stood before three thousand people for three hours in utter silence, and held his audience. "I famished them for words," he said later.

When Fox did speak, it was not only to the ecclesiastical oppression of an English church still heavy with incense and authority, but also to the social inequities and injustice of the era. It was a singular strength of the movement, especially among the young, that Fox and his converts confronted openly the hypocrisies they saw in both clerical and secular England, frequently to the point of sedition and imprisonment. Oddities to a later age, their habits and acts of nonconformity were at their inception vivid symbols of defiance and reform. The recoil from official oaths as an affront to the Christian's intrinsic truthfulness; the unwillingness to wear powdered wigs or to remove hats in the presence of upper classes; the simple dress and use of the plain speech, "thee" and "thy," for commoners and gentry alike; not least the insistent refusal to bear arms or join in violence however prominently blessed—all struck at a caste-ridden society and the epoch's virulent political or military ambition in the garb of piety.

They took the name Society of Friends from John 15:14, "Ye are my friends, if ye do whatsoever I command you." Yet they would be more widely known as Quakers, after Fox's ringing rejoinder to a British court "to tremble at the word of the Lord." Set against an opposition given to flamboyance in manners and dress as well as ceremony, they soon acquired in addition to rebellious simplicity a reputation for the dour, austere, and even astringent. Quakers were thus said to object to "bells, games, festivals, May poles and Roman Catholics," though not always in that order. More enduring and significant than the defiant gestures of their emergence was the application of their primal Christianity to what they termed wider "social concerns"—peace, antislavery, prison and asylum reform, racial equality, the abolition of capital punishment, the extension of scriptural morality to economic and business ethics. Their unshrinking involvement in such temporal issues, far ahead of its time, would come to distinguish the movement long after insurgent clothes or speech had lost their meaning.

But at the heart of the teaching was a spiritual introspection in a sense equally modern and formidable, presaging what later theology would variously approach as a Christian existentialism. In their silence they drew a quiet, self-effacing inner strength and tolerance, and a fierce privacy that marked the sanctity of the ordinary layman's access to the Holy Spirit. Corporately and individually, Quakers "waited on God" for inspiration and guidance, charged when the answers came to concern themselves personally with politics and society, to respond to "the burden of the world's suffering" as well as their own.

With the clannishness and fervor of those possessing a new religious insight, they were equipped for martyrdom, and soon found opportunities. Quakers in the thousands crowded English jails, saw their nonclerical marriages declared illegal and their sons designated bastards, watched their dead denied burial in hallowed ground. For their nonconformity and the disturbing mirror they held before current mores, they were rejected initially in the American Colonies. The first Friends in the New World were promptly expelled for witchcraft. Successors were flogged and imprisoned. "The persecutor's pillory," a religious historian wrote of later colonists, "became the Quaker's pulpit." Not until William Penn established his Pennsylvania colony as a "holy experiment" in 1682 was their immigration free and secure, a development that prompted Samuel Pepys to console the elder Penn on the news that young William "had fallen into some such melancholy state." By the American Revolution there were over fifty thousand Friends in the country. The sect seemed to be flourishing in its Pennsylvania haven and elsewhere, and the Quakers had already begun what would be a century of agitation against slavery.

On the pattern of the Catholicism they quietly abhorred, the movement's crisis came not from persecution and its moral *élan* but rather from acceptance. Behind the ministry to society's outcasts—convicts, the insane, Indians, and black slaves—Quakerism by 1825 had become as a religious impulse what one of its historians called "static and exclusive." Filled with "birthright" Friends, only those born of Quaker parents, membership was all but stagnant. Blanched of the founding zeal, worship often lapsed into total silence. In this brittle state the sect felt the great waves of evangelical Christianity out of England in the second quarter of the nineteenth century, and the new ardor struck American Quakerism with much the same force Fox had hurled at the Anglicans two centuries earlier.

With fresh emphasis on personal conversion, pastors, missionaries, and more structured, traditional Protestant services, the evangelical appeal reached suddenly beyond the old Quaker fold and onto the American frontier. There, hardship and daily preoccupation with survival left little time for silent introspection and tended to produce instead a hunger for pastoral exhortation and more palpable inspiration. Evangelical influences produced three great "Separations" in the movement between 1827 and 1854, splitting Quakers not only on doctrinal lines but also, equally historic, by class and region. The urban, relatively affluent, and educated Quakers largely remained in their hushed orthodox meetings. The agrarian, comparatively poor, and unschooled followed the evangelical impulse into more conventional church services, and eventually into the noisy emotionalism and group compulsion of camp meeting and revival. "The old sense of awe and restraint gave way to an era of freedom and spontaneity," wrote one observer, "[and] nothing stemmed the current." Quaker meetings on the raw frontier west of Pennsylvania were now given to music and singing and fervid public testimony. A Friends mother in Iowa reportedly purchased an organ just to keep her children from defecting to the Methodists. Even a pastoral "system" was evolved to meet the growing demand for ministers, an event hardly envisioned by George Fox and his patient company long ago in the Yorkshire stillness.

But the more lasting casualty would be the movement's remarkable secular activism. Identified with the dwindling orthodox remnant, diluted in the din and doling of the new vocal clergy, the original pacifism and social reform of the religion would lose their force in the evangelical congregations. As Quakerism migrated westward with its freshly rousing preachers and music, it grew increasingly withdrawn from the old social concerns and ever more conservative politically. The schism invariably brought its tragedies. Meetings were shattered in chaos, families riven. Gentle Quaker women were often heard, according to a contemporary account, "to weep long into the night."

The profound changes among nineteenth-century American Friends swept over the Society's old families with effects now subtle, now dramatic. The Milhous ancestors of Richard Nixon were of German descent, fought for Cromwell's Roundheads, and were rewarded for their services by the Lord Protector with land in Ireland, where they were swiftly converted to Quakerism and renounced their military heritage. Irish Quakers, it was said, amounted to a contradiction in terms, though the faith survived despite the anomaly and a generation of persecution. Having been "educated from their childhood by their religion," according to a certificate of the Dublin Friends meeting, Thomas Milhous and his wife, Sarah, left Timahoe County, Ireland, in May 1729 to settle in William Penn's new colony. They bought two hundred acres scarcely ten miles from where a Nixon ancester homesteaded two years later across the Delaware border at Brandywine Hundred. In 1805 the family moved to a Friends settlement close to the Ohio River, where they felt the first tremors of separation that would so deeply divide their church, and recorded at the same time the coming of the implacable national crisis of slavery. "I have got to be almost an Abolitionist," wrote a Milhous in the 1830s.

The fourth generation in America, Richard Nixon's great-grandparents, Joshua Vickers Milhous and his wife, Elizabeth, again migrated in 1854, this time to land near Butlerville in Jennings County, in the southeastern quarter of Indiana, a rich forested plain beside the Muscatatuck River midway between Indianapolis and Louisville. They were an extraordinary pair. Elizabeth was a trained teacher and like her mother a Quaker minister, Joshua the stubbornly independent, modern, music-loving model for the hero of *Friendly Persuasion*, a novel by a great-granddaughter, Jessamyn West. During the next forty years he became one of the more prosperous nurserymen in southern Indiana, while Elizabeth helped found local Friends congregations. Together they cultivated not only faith and stock for farmers' orchards but also five children, the eldest of whom, Franklin, Richard Nixon's grandfather, was to join the family nursery business with similar success.

"The Milhouses believed . . . that handsome was as handsome did," a family chronicler noted. "As a result they tried even harder, even when handsome, which wasn't often." Franklin presented at least a partial exception to the rule, with deep-set eyes, a sensuous mouth, and a head of dark hair discreetly maintained by a toupee in old age. Almost rakish for a Quaker gentleman, he sported muttonchops, a top hat, and moccasins as a young man posing jauntily against a photographer's pseudo pillar. He was at any rate a family favorite, "open and enthusiastic," a relative remembered. "The second child of necessity plays second fiddle," Jessamyn West wrote about her own grandfather, Franklin's younger brother, adding of Franklin, "This task is more onerous when the first fiddle turns out to be virtuoso and would have been first no matter what his position in the birthing program." Sharing his father's affection for music, given to sucking peppermint and to a certain wanderlust, tastes he kept throughout life, Franklin went off in 1865 to Moore's Hill College, fifty-five miles away in Cincinnati, where he finished his studies and for a year taught German. He returned to Jennings County and his nursery inheritance a man of talents, though none, with Quaker restraint, destined to be carried too far.

The family practiced a stout, unquestioned tribal closeness. In part it was kindred tradition and the Quaker bond long cemented by shared revelation and ostracism, in part the custom of the times and rural society. To those ties, though, the Milhouses added an almost peremptory lineal pride, made all the more exclusive for being couched in piety, and easily larded with snobbery or arrogance. "The Milhouses thought highly of the Milhouses," said Max McPherson, who married into the family two generations later and shared the perception of most in-laws. "If we were without fault," wrote a daughter down the line, "we were wholly Milhous." Jessamyn West would later entertain audiences with lore of the family self-esteem, a trait that was far more serious and oppressive in the event. On more than one occasion, for example, the family was known simply to change unilaterally a first name it thought somehow improper for a daughter-in-law, elevating a Dollie to a Mollie or a Lima to a Dorothy. "It was rather a pity," West recalled the family airs, "that there had to be for biological reasons an admission of non-Milhous blood into our life-stream." It was also never quite clear what unique virtue or feat lay behind the pretense. Intelligent, well off, reverent, but no more so than many diligent Quaker families, the Milhouses were without conspicuous achievement through the nineteenth century and well into the next.

At twenty-three Franklin wed a local Quaker girl who would bear him two children, but who less than five years later died in childbirth. In April 1879 he married Almira Park Burdg, whose Quaker family had settled in Jennings County a year before his. Thirty, plain, a strong, ambitious woman on the verge of spinsterhood, Allie, as she was called as a girl, had been a teacher for ten years, riding to the schoolhouse on horseback and nurturing what would be a lifelong fondness for writing verse. Fifty years afterward, she recorded their wedding.

> *In old Grove Church, near the tall beech trees.*
> *Any eye, a setting like that, should please . . .*
> *Then we journeyed to the Burdg home, a few rods from the door,*
> *Where a company was gathered, numbers nearing four score.*
> *There was a sumptuous wedding dinner, and a table long indeed*
> *Filled with the best of eats, plenty, all the guests to feed.*

They settled hard by his parents' home, which by now had become noteworthy both for Joshua Milhous's relative affluence and for his penchant for the modern. First among local Friends to buy a carriage, install a telephone (connecting his house and Franklin's), and build an indoor bathroom, the father also had an imposing library and an organ, the latter an instrument of potential levity and scandal that had been delivered from the depot under cover of darkness. In the sixteen years after her marriage, Almira had six girls and a boy. The third, a daughter born on March 7, 1885, would be Richard Nixon's mother; they named her Hannah after a Milhous aunt and for the devout mother of Samuel in the Old Testament.

Seen through the gauze of memory, the childhood of Hannah and the others took on a simple, lost charm. A long lane bordered by pine trees wound down from the house on the hill, ending at a big red gate at the pike where swarms of children greeted visitors. They went to classes at "Harmony Hill," a little red schoolhouse built on a corner of the farm. In the evenings Franklin read aloud his own favorite stories by James Whitcomb Riley. They were "comfortably very well off," a daughter described them, and had a "colored girl" who lived in. There were trips to Niagara Falls, the World's Fair, Mammoth Cave, Philadelphia, and voyages down the Ohio River.

"Father and mother never talked loud—never yelled orders," Hannah recounted. "I was one of a large family and father never paddled us. Mother switched my ankles once with an apple twig. I was about five. . . . The switching didn't amount to anything but I felt terrible about it." Edith,

Hannah's elder sister, recalled the switches, and Franklin as "a very methodical, austere type of man. He expected the truth and all that was in us to help make it the truth." Yet Edith remembered, too, harsher moments, Franklin whipping Ezra, the boy two years younger than Hannah, until Edith wept watching it. "He made the law and order. . . . He wasn't what you'd call a loving tender-hearted type," she said later of their father.

They were steeped in religion. Beyond the Sunday services, the family sang hymns after supper, had communal Bible readings and prayers, and witnessed both Joshua and Elizabeth work and travel in the grandmother's countryside pastorate. Quakerism both tempered and confined the lives of the children. "Father and Mother were full of love, faith and optimism," Hannah said, remembering her father more benignly than Edith had seen him in Ezra's whipping. "I don't recall ever seeing them in despair." At the same time, as older girls grew into their teens, there were strictures against parties or even chaperoned square dances. "Mama didn't want us to go," Edith said. "She thought it would be too much for our morals."

Still severe in matters of personal conduct, their church had become steadily more evangelical in tenor and theology. Franklin's own sister had married a Friends revival preacher, who, by one account, "sang, stamped, pranced, tossed his songbook to the ceiling, tossed his great mane of white hair, sweated, reminded us that this might be our last chance." Equally clear was the evangelical effect on the sect's original social concerns. Anti-slavery Friends had separated from the Indiana church in the 1840s when the larger meeting refused to take a stand on the question. "That Friends of Indiana were too overbearing and treated the subject of abolition as well as those who advocated it with too much contempt," a relative had written when it happened, "who will deny?" The Milhouses never sided with the abolitionists. Though Indiana remained a free state, fugitive slave laws were hardened after 1850 and Quakers in Jennings County largely refused to help runaway blacks on grounds that it was illegal, a reason George Fox and his young adherents who streamed into London jails on lesser ordinances would have thought uncompelling. The underground railroad continued until 1861 to run in and around the county, one of its busy terminals a black settlement called "Africa" scarcely five miles from Franklin's nursery, though with no trace of any Milhous involvement. Not even military service was still anathema for frontier Quakers. Franklin at thirteen was too young for the Civil War, and Joshua in his forties too old, but an Ohio Milhous first cousin became a captain in the Union Army and spent much of the war in a Confederate prison camp. When slavery gave way to other social issues after 1865, western meetings went on similarly uninvolved in prisons, asylums, and other causes that still engaged traditional Quakers in the East.

By the late 1880s J. V. Milhous and Sons nursery had given them, by one account, "capital to spare." Franklin now began a search for land investments and a potential new home and nursery, drawn away in part by a mounting concern for the education of his growing children. There were no schools both Quaker and close enough to keep the children at or very near home, conditions that Franklin and Almira seemed to have given equal weight. At the climax of the great boom of the eighties he visited a tiny settlement being devoutly if somewhat speculatively founded by Friends twenty miles east of Los Angeles. The new town was christened for the most famous Quaker poet. Seventy-nine and still a bachelor, John Greenleaf Whittier quickly composed a maudlin verse dedicated to his unexpected namesake.

> *A life not void of pure intent,*
> *With small desert of praise or blame,*
> *The love I felt, the good I meant,*
> *I leave thee with my name.*

The Whittier Franklin Milhous found was a dusty mix of piety and profiteering. Only a few years before it had been tranquil, vacant land, falling gently from the Puente Hills and covered in tall, stately wild mustard. The last Mexican governor of California, Pio Pico, once possessed large holdings nearby and would live to wander as an impoverished oddity through the dirt streets of the new town. A Chicago railroad man of impressive goatee and nose to match, Aquilla Pickering and his wife had been planning a Quaker colony in California since the early eighties, animated by salvation no less than settlement. "A strong community of Friends would doubtless assist in bringing about much needed reforms," he thought of the raucous frontier. "Many localities were without schools and churches . . . the Sabbath was poorly observed . . . the need of moral and Christian influence was everywhere apparent." His purchase of the town site, he added later, was made "with much prayer, seeking to know the mind of the Master, and with a fervent desire that our Heavenly Father's blessing should rest with the undertaking."

The Pickering Land and Water Company swiftly proved half a misnomer. Like the rest of the basin, the tract in its virgin setting had no ready supply of water before artesian wells were finally sunk at the turn of the century. Yet just as typically, the lack of water, politely ignored or concealed, did not delay the land rush. Surveyors drove down the towering mustard stalks and laid out town lots spread across thirty-two blocks. On the first day of sales, May 19, 1887, clerks wrote land contracts from morning into the night. Non-Quakers were welcomed as well. "There is no intention to make it narrow or sectarian so that it will exclude fair-minded people of other denominations," read a company prospectus. "To them also we say come."

The developers also denied any speculative practices, "wholly concerned," a Quaker historian wrote, "in providing the economic advantages and privileges of colonization for Friends of like mind and spirit." But the boom would also have what a later city history called "men of no conscience, tricky, smooth oily tongues—professional land sharks." And they found in Whittier, the history conceded, "an over-ripe crop of suckers." While the Friends erected their first meetinghouse, lot prices spiraled from $100 to $300, then suddenly to $500 and on to $2,000. It was all, thought one observer, "beyond the ken of normalcy." So, too, was the bust by 1888 and afterward. Land that sold for $7,000 went for $700 a year later, and soon for $100. A boom population that had pushed past one thousand plunged to four hundred in the 1890s. "Those who remained," a municipal historian said of the hard times that followed, "were . . . the heroes of their day." Slowly the town took shape on the wreckage of the land bubble. A Quaker academy, a secondary school that would grow into a college, was begun in 1891. A year earlier a state reformatory for boys with its helpful payroll was placed nearby. The father of Lou Henry, a student at the academy and later to be Mrs. Herbert Hoover, started and soon abandoned the first bank, but laid the foundation for other banks and for a small, solid, two-story business district that descended from the hills by 1900.

"All welcome," said a sign along the main boulevard, or nearly so. The town bore unmistakably the imprint of its Quaker colonization. There were no saloons, dance halls, or theaters, nor would there be for generations. When a contingent of Coxey's Army, a protest march on Washington of jobless men in the depression of the nineties, camped near Whittier in 1894, Quaker founders benevolently gave them loaves of bread, a hundred pounds of beef, and a religious service in the bargain. Community leaders would duly volunteer for health and welfare work in nearby Picoville, later Jimtown, the impoverished Mexican settlement that squatted to the west along the San Gabriel River. Yet when starving children from Los Angeles and other towns tried to pick walnuts or citrus from Whittier's groves, farmers here as elsewhere in the basin organized armed patrols to keep the urchins at a profitable distance. Along with the patrols came, too, an original Whittier ordinance against nonwhites buying lots in what Quaker brochures described as "the ideal city of dreams." It was, as one resident said later, "pure bigotry on the part of the early founders."

When Joshua Milhous's death released the family from Indiana, Franklin began plans for a large Whittier house. In 1897, complete with black servants, he moved the entire family and their possessions in chartered railroad cars, taking a carriage, horses and livestock, along with lumber, door frames, windows, and a fireplace mantle. Their new home would be on the south side of Whittier Boulevard, the old Camino Real, standing almost alone hardly a mile down the slope from the academy and the First Friends Church. It was a spacious two-story frame house of simple Victorian design with five bedrooms and a balcony over the porch. Behind he set out the seedlings for his new Milhous Nursery.

With a continuing bustle of the clan, relatives sojourned often at the Whittier home during the next decade. Two brothers and two sisters eventually followed him to Whittier, and his mother, Elizabeth, came in 1906, producing, as one family observer put it, an "astounding" number of aunts, uncles, and cousins frequently assembled "down home," as the Whittier Boulevard house came to be known. Meals were now a solemn ritual in which a bell was rung, Franklin, Almira, or Elizabeth read a chapter from the Bible, and each person at the table joined by reciting a verse or prayer. At home the children still addressed their parents with the traditional plain Quaker speech. The dinner table might also include the black servants, hired hands, or even occasional passersby asking a handout, vivid instances of Friends tolerance and egalitarianism that stood out in family memory. "She was always taking care of every tramp that came along the road," Richard Nixon, her grandson, said of Almira. "At her house no servant ever ate at a separate table. They always ate with the family. There were Negroes, Indians, and people from Mexico—she was always taking somebody in."

About Whittier Franklin became known as "Mr. Rancher," respected for his readiness to replace questionable nursery stock, and generally thought to enjoy, in the words of a family friend, "a comfortable living." Yet the children also remembered working hard to add to household money. "The main thing was to make myself an asset to the family, and if there was any financial help we furnished it if we could," recounted Edith. She and her sisters tended the nursery and picked beans and other crops for Whittier farmers. Hannah sometimes hired out as a housemaid or cook for five dollars a week.

Twelve at the time of the move to California, Hannah Milhous was a placid, shy, dutiful girl who grew in Whittier into an equally gentle young woman of wasp waist and serious countenance, marked by thick raven hair and eyebrows above dark, limpid eyes. Of the busy houseful of girls she was especially adept and conscientious in the kitchen and came to be relied upon. "She liked to cook," a sister said. "She was our mainstay on the cooking line, and especially if we wanted something happy and kind of a surprise, we'd turn it over to her." At the same time an apt student, she finished grammar school with good marks and walked the still muddy streets up the hill to the Quaker academy that would become Whittier College.

At fifteen she had what she and her sisters called a "spiritual awakening," a public conversion before an evangelist at their small clapboard church. "The revival fervor that had swept the Midwest earlier was at that time laying California Quakers low in the aisles of their spiritless little wooden buildings," a memoirist recorded. "Hands were laid on then as now, confessions were made, tears shed, songs sung, bodies put in a weaving way," Jessamyn West depicted the scene. "Grudges and animosities long cherished were admitted and discarded." It was an emotional event, sometimes traumatic. A non-Milhous relative elsewhere, having publicly declared her sin of sexual intercourse out of wedlock, went home from a revival and slit her own throat. The more common result among Friends was a rededication to their faith, "centered down" in Quaker terms. "I remember Hannah encouraging me to go forward and accept the Lord," her younger sister Jane recalled of the night in 1900, "and she said that I would feel so much stronger and feel such wonderful release from any feeling, guilty conscience, or anything like that."

For her own part, Hannah practiced her religion in utter seriousness then and later. Taking literally the instruction from the Sermon on the Mount "when thou prayest, enter into thy closet," she was in the habit of going into a darkened clothes closet for her nightly prayers. "I think it was just really her life," a sister said of Hannah's faith. Others found in her even as a girl a strength of character, a self-respect without too visible pretense or pride. If already a "mainstay" to the family, it was a role and stability she would assume much of her life.

She graduated from secondary school in 1905 with superior grades and courses in Latin and French. Telling friends she was thinking of teaching, she went on the next year to four-year-old Whittier College, enrolling as a freshman with the class of '09, and taking during the next two years what she recalled as "quite a bit of German." Over five feet five inches, she was relatively tall among family and friends, meek and retiring, and "gentle, very gentle, soft of voice," an older sister recalled. Typical of Quaker girls her age, her social life was largely limited to the gatherings of Christian Endeavor, a young people's organization of the Friends church. Through high school and the first two years at Whittier College, Hannah had been paired occasionally with one boy in group outings, a nameless "beau" her sisters would vaguely recollect. But at nearly twenty-three, shy and sheltered, she had never had a date.

"NOTHING BUT STRUGGLE AND HARDSHIP"

Of the myriad pioneer legends, Samuel Brady's had an authentic starkness. To avenge the murder of his father, they said, Brady had become a

31

vigilante Indian killer in the old Ohio River wilderness in the early nineteenth century. Eventually captured by one tribe and tried for his marauding, he was being led off to be burned at the stake when he grabbed a papoose from a woman who came too near and threw it into the flames of his own pyre. He then made good his escape by running several miles naked while the Indians tried in vain to rescue the burning baby. The exploit remained in local lore, and bodies of water and children were duly named for Brady.

One of those children was Richard Nixon's paternal grandfather, Samuel Brady Nixon, who was born in 1847 in Washington County in southwestern Pennsylvania, his forebears having moved from the Atlantic seaboard two generations before. The family name has been traced to thirteenth-century England with later Scottish and Irish strains. The first ancestor in America appeared in 1731, buying land for a cooperage and homestead at Brandywine Hundred in Delaware's corner of the Piedmont plateau. Nixons variously farmed, fought in the Revolutionary War, and eventually trailed the frontier into Pennsylvania. In 1853 the family migrated west to Vinton County in southeastern Ohio, little more than a hundred miles from where the Milhouses had settled earlier in the century. They were there at the outbreak of the Civil War when Samuel's father, a forty-year-old struggling Methodist farmer with nine children, volunteered to serve in another man's place in the Ohio infantry, and went on in 1863 to be fatally wounded atop Cemetery Ridge on the third day at Gettysburg.

The battlefield death set off in the family a spiral of tragedy and want, bleak even by the harsh standards of the time. Within months his mother was dead as well. Samuel at seventeen toiled to keep the family and fifty-acre farm together, only to see the children scattered among relatives and most of the land go in a sheriff's sale. During his early twenties, he hired out as a fieldhand, acquired something of a reputation as a horsetrader, and aspired to be a self-educated teacher. Then in 1873 he met and married Sarah Ann Wadsworth, already a teacher and the daughter of a local storekeeper. She was a pleasant, open-faced twenty-one-year-old with long wavy hair carefully shaped in Victorian curves about her forehead. At twenty-six he wore an earnest, more mature handsomeness, and the thick eyebrows he would bequeath to his posterity. He called her adoringly "my Sally Ann."

They settled on forty acres around Richland near the original Nixon homestead, not far from the Ohio River. It was soft rolling land, part of the old Hanging Rock Iron Region whose furnaces lit the night sky in a strange auroral glow. He taught in the ridge schools, though none could pay a living wage, and eked out the rest by delivering mail, farming part-time, and selling produce to the nearby colony of iron workers. "Untainted by aristocracy," a later historian wrote of Samuel Nixon, he was "unscarred by worldly success." Pregnant within months of their wedding, Sarah had five children over the next nine years, the middle one on December 3, 1878, a lively boy named Francis Anthony. But by the last birth in 1883, Sarah was visibly ill with tuberculosis.

Samuel now sold the farm and stock, and took the family and their belongings on a desperate exodus to save his young wife. With Sarah's canary and cage, the family Bible, and McGuffey *Readers*, they rode the train as far as the misty West Virginia slopes of the Blue Ridge. There they lived in a primitive cabin. Sarah began the prescribed routine of lengthy walks along the low mountain trails, but returned exhausted and grew no better. Late in 1884, they set off again farther south in search of the phantom remedy of climate, Samuel working where he could. They wandered through the Carolinas and Georgia with the five children and their coughing mother living out of the back of an old wagon. After nearly a year of vagrant poverty, Sarah asked to be taken home to Ohio, where she died in her father's home in January 1886.

The family was now dispersed about Vinton County. "We were so poor," one of the sons remembered, "that all the livestock we had was a setting hen with a dozen eggs." Barely seven, Frank was sent to live with his father's youngest brother. "Here we are," a son quoted Samuel at the time, "and it's root, hog, or die." By 1890, he had married again, and recouped enough to bring the children back together. But the ordeal would take its continuing toll. After the grim odyssey of his mother's illness and death and the foster years with his uncle, Frank at age twelve was by all accounts a wounded, combative child, and he soon clashed with his new stepmother, whom contemporaries described as cruelly punishing. "When she was married to Samuel," a relative recalled with emotion long afterward, "she was hard and beat Frank."

Two months short of his fourteenth birthday and accompanying Ernest, his nine-year-old brother, Frank Nixon was finally sent to a one-room country schoolhouse. It was his first classroom, and his last. He was placed in the fourth grade, "poor, strange, and badly dressed," Ernest remembered. "We were newcomers . . . the big boys would follow us home through the woods to pick a fight. Frank was the more aggressive of us, slow to anger but a wild bull if things went too far." More than eighty years later his son would recount the scene that had become imprinted on family memory, the boy Frank "dressed in ragged clothes . . . taunted by his schoolmates," countering "with a quick tongue and a ready pair of fists." In a few months, he was gone from the schoolhouse.

Over the next few years Frank Nixon drifted through a number of jobs, never lasting long in any one yet winning a reputation for a stern, Protestant industriousness. "In the sweat of thy face shalt thou eat bread," he was given to quoting the scripture. "To him playing was daydreaming," a brother recalled of the boy who had been afforded so little time for either. "Frank believed the invitation to lean on the Lord was intended for the weary and the lazy." In his teens he fired bricks at a nearby works, and made enough profit raising potatotes to be called "The Potato King" of the township. He spent much of what he earned on clothes, still answering the humiliation of the school. "He was a fancy dresser," a brother said. "He seemed to take keen delight in showing his former classmates that he dressed just a bit better and was more mannerly. He acquired a pride that became the armor of his body and soul." Meanwhile, he bought a handsome sorrel, and hearing in 1896 that Presidential candidate and Ohio governor William McKinley was campaigning in the county seat, he rode off in characteristic brashness to join the parade. McKinley was said to have admired the horse, and asked the young owner how he was going to vote. "Republican, of course," Nixon shot back, still more than three years too young to cast a ballot. Within months he was off to Colorado where he sheared sheep, painted Pullman cars, farmed again, installed crank telephones, worked now in a glass factory, now for an electric company, and became a fine carpenter. At the turn of the century, though, he was back home, his skills and energy, as one observer recorded, "cancelled by pride and prickliness." "Some folks said he was quarrelsome," Ernest ruefully admitted, "but they were the ones who hadn't come out too well when they picked a fight with him."

He did not stay long in Vinton County, leaving in 1901 for Columbus, where he went to work for the city's growing trolley and interurban lines. Of the powerful private utilities of the era, the streetcar combine was a model of the benevolent despotism that held organized labor at bay even in a period of rising agitation. Wages for most workers were less than twenty cents an hour for a six-day, fifty-four-hour week. Working conditions were sometimes severe, and strikes put down harshly. In bitter Columbus winters, streetcar passengers and the conductor rode inside stove-heated cars, while the motorman drove from an exposed, open vestibule. Nixon worked in obscurity for the company for five years. Then in 1906, at twenty-seven, he was promoted to motorman, and on a frigid winter night soon afterward, both his feet were severely frostbitten.

"Then and there he swore vengeance against a company that forced its motormen to brave the elements," recounted one local version of the event. There would be less melodrama in what followed, though no lack of the man's temper and tenacity. Frank first went to fellow motormen and convinced them to join him in a concerted complaint to the company. When the management flatly refused to enclose or heat the motormen's cabs, the men asked their union to intercede, but were put off there, too. Thwarted and increasingly angry—"so danged mad," as one account described him— Nixon then turned on his own initiative to a local state senate candidate, offering to organize motormen to help elect him if the new senator would in turn push legislation to heat the vestibules. However traveled or aggressive he had become, it was a rash, remarkable act for a young man from the country with no schooling, much less experience in politics or in organizing employees of a powerful, paternalistic company. But the trolleymen and sympathetic labor were a sizable bloc in the legislative district, and the candidate accepted. Still more remarkable, Nixon organized the votes. Canvassing after a nine-hour day on still painful feet, he rallied both motormen and conductors. In a political result of rare simplicity, the state senator won, and proceeded to sponsor and pass over heavy company opposition a law requiring vestibule doors and heating for the streetcars.

The sequel for Frank Nixon was equally direct. His role in the election and legislation well known, he quit the company before he was fired or forced out. In March 1907 Frank Nixon and a fellow motorman took the train to Los Angeles, carrying a discreet letter of introduction from a union official. "They are both gentlemen of good habits," Brother W. J. Insey wrote with no awkward reference to heated cabs or politics, "and any favors you can show them will be appreciated. They are experienced Street-Car men and the very many fine recommendations they have will no doubt insure them success." Nixon left much as he had come to Columbus six years before, in a dress suit with shirt, socks, and a few other possessions in a bundle. At twenty-eight, a drifting life as child and adult and a dozen unfinished trades behind him, he took to California as well a desolate and abiding sense of his youth. "We had nothing," he later reminisced with a brother, "but struggle and hardship."

"HANNAH IS A BAD GIRL!"

As Los Angeles reached for the Owens Valley water in the first decade of the century, the city also wove an impressive network of interurban transit from beach to mountains. Without wood or coal, the basin used electricity earlier and more lavishly than most urban areas, and one of the results was over a thousand miles of trolley tracks. Before the automobile, tire, and oil industries exerted their influence on public policy and planning, the little red cars of the Pacific Electric crisscrossed the region in a latticework of mass transit that encouraged subdivisions and regional development. So scenic were some routes that the lines became tourist attractions. One ran from the center of Los Angeles south along the ocean to Long

Beach, joining a branch line that led back east to Whittier, "for each cent of the hundred expended," announced one travelogue, "a mile of joy." Frank Nixon became a motorman on the branch soon after he arrived in southern California in 1907. He roomed in a Quaker boardinghouse at his Whittier terminus, and at the urging of acquaintances began to attend Friends services.

He met Hannah Milhous at a Quaker Valentine's party in 1908. "He was lonesome and wanted some recreation in the way of social life and strayed into the Christian Endeavor room," as one of her family described it. "His was love at first sight," thought Edith. "Of course, she let him advance as far as he would, and finally it led into more or less their courtship." He walked her home down the slope to the boulevard. Only four months later they were married.

"I immediately stopped going with five other girls I was dating," Frank said later, "and I saw Hannah every night." By any measure it was an interesting as well as whirlwind match, and all the more so against the backdrop of the Milhouses and the cloistered province of Whittier Quakerism—an outgoing, aggressive young man nearly thirty, with no formal education and a comparatively stark, independent existence since early childhood; a young woman seven years younger whose temperament, family circumstances, and insular social experiences seemed everything his was not. The sharpness of the contrast, though not yet fully seen, moved Hannah's family at the moment and afterward to explanations of the relationship. "He was a fast worker," said Olive, the youngest sister. Frank was "overpowering," wrote a physician after talking to family members about their courtship.

Soon after they met he lost his job with Pacific Electric when his trolley hit an automobile crossing its tracks, and he went to work as a foreman at the nearby Judson Ranch and citrus orchard. The change added to Milhous apprehensions, though at the time they supposed that Frank had at least a high school education. He readily agreed to become a Quaker, removing the only seeming objection to the wedding. They were married in a Friends ceremony on June 2, 1908. She wore a long white Victorian gown of simple beauty, he white tie and a formal suit noticeably too large.

The Milhouses would remain unhappy with the marriage, tending to ignore not only their daughter's love and attraction for Frank Nixon, but also her own urge for independence from the family regime. On reflection Edith believed her "sick of housework" and eager as well to be free of an imposing Franklin Milhous. "She wasn't strong enough to stand up against my father," her sister said later. "Both he and Frank Nixon were too much for her. Frank decided he wanted to get married and Hannah thought that would be a leap out of the fire, and it probably was."

Hannah's education remained a sore point still unresolved after the wedding. Franklin had felt strongly, a neighbor recounted, that his daughters should "stay at home and go to college; that was his idea." Hannah was staying out a year from Whittier College, working as usual for her mother and occasionally for other households, when she met Frank. But she was a serious, good student and had planned to return to the campus in the autumn of 1908. Like one of her sons later, "she would stay up until all times in the night to get her [school] work done," a sister related. But now she was the first to be married, and her family and new husband openly clashed. "We wanted Hannah to go on and finish college and make the best of her education by the teaching . . . Papa and I had thought of as her goal," Edith confided long afterward. "But Frank didn't think that was necessary. Of course, he persuaded her."

On the eve of the wedding, Almira Milhous rued their old domestic reliance on Hannah and the missed year in college that seemed to have such consequences. She wrote in a verse dedicated to her daughter and a neighboring girl being married at the same time:

> *You sure deserve honors, yes, noble and grand,*
> *Who as dutiful daughters by your mother's did stand;*
> *Who sacrificed pleasure, and some college life, too,*
> *To preside in the home, so helpful and true.*

The mother then added a couplet remarkable in its bleakness and other-worldly reference for a young woman about to be married.

> *But you'll get your reward for such service given,*
> *If not here on earth, you'll get it in heaven.*

Four months after their wedding, Hannah was pregnant, and the question of her education sealed. Hearing the family talk about the swift events since February, thirteen-year-old Olive Milhous climbed the pepper tree in the backyard of the boulevard house and on the trunk wrote of her devout, soft-voiced older sister, "Hannah is a bad girl."

In what one account called "a flimsy cottage that came with the job," they lived for the first several months at the Judson Ranch east of Whittier. Her husband was paid little more than the Mexican fieldhands he oversaw, and Hannah was suddenly in and amid a poverty that a school friend thought "another world, going from one world to another." To the hardship and the underlying displeasure of the family was added an even more cruel rejection by girlhood friends and their families. "You were ostracized for marrying a non-Quaker by the community," her bridesmaid told an interviewer sixty years later. "It was a taboo and there were all kinds of problems." Frank's conversion and the church attendance from the ranch did nothing to lift the ban. "She was virtually kicked out of her element," a local scholar concluded after talking with witnesses of the period following the marriage. After several lonely months at the ranch and with her pregnancy well advanced, the Milhouses "insisted" Hannah return "down home" to have her child.

Early in 1909 they came back to a boulevard house teeming with the immediate family and relatives. Frank worked for his father-in-law in the nursery, while they crowded into one of the bedrooms and were absorbed into the religious routine of the household. On Frank Nixon the effect of this retreat to his wife's home after only a brief period of marital independence was plainly mixed. While on the surface he was welcomed into the home and one sister thought him "jolly and . . . nice to the rest of the family," he was visibly ill at ease or worse. "I always felt like he didn't like to join in the family gatherings like all the rest of us did," Jane Milhous observed then and later. "Maybe he didn't want to share Hannah with the rest of us . . . I felt like maybe there was a little bit of jealousy there . . . he was quite possessive." In a sedate, educated, often smug household he was a demonstrative, flinty Irishman, wounded and unforgetting about his past, ever sensitive to slight. Caught in the middle, Hannah characteristically appeased both sides. "She was generous almost to a fault, as you say," Edith recounted. "She was with the rest of us when she could be, she took it out of herself." In June 1909, the month her class graduated from Whittier College, she gave birth to a boy in a difficult, protracted labor. They named him Harold Samuel, after an English king and Frank's father.

They stayed in Whittier for several months with the new baby, who became and remained a favorite with his young aunts and grandparents. "We took him over when he was a baby," Edith said of Harold. "[Later] Harold liked to come to his grandfather's. We made over him!" But the baby also brought moments of tension in Whittier. Hannah's sister Jane remembered with pain Frank bringing Harold, a little over two years old, to a Quaker meeting and spanking the toddler angrily when he cried during the service.

In 1910 Franklin gave them a parcel of property he owned near Lindsay, a small settlement two hundred miles north in the San Joaquin Valley of central California. They homesteaded there and set out the seedlings for an orange grove. But long before the trees were established, Hannah grew disconsolately homesick and lonely. Scarcely a year later they sold the ranch and returned to the basin, moving once more into her parents' Whittier Boulevard house. Frank again staked out land owned by his father-in-law, this time ten acres across a small hillside in Yorba Linda, an empty tract fifteen miles southeast of Whittier. In the closing months of 1911, he began to set out a lemon grove on the hill with Milhous Nursery stock and built by himself at the rear of the lot a sturdy one-story clapboard bungalow in the simple craftsman style of the time, its double gables facing east.

He completed the house by January 1912, in time for an unknown photographer to record it at a distance, standing alone on a deserted hillock silhouetted against the smooth bare hills to the north. That spring Hannah found she was again pregnant.

2

Yorba Linda, 1913–22

he setting of Richard Nixon's
birth was remarkable only for the grit and hue of the place, and for what
it told of the people. In November 1912, the new Yorba Linda Women's
Club considered a surprise party for a charter member who was expecting.
While other children had been born in the newly platted settlement as
early as 1911, Hannah Nixon, Club minutes noted, was "the first one of
our members to have anticipations of a little one in her home." After
reflecting on Mrs. Nixon's well-known shyness, however, and her obvious
embarrassment at being more than seven months pregnant—"the sensitivities of a . . . timid and certainly modest member"—the ladies thoughtfully voted instead to "purchase a book to be presented in some quiet
way."

A month later, what had been advertised as "frostless" Yorba Linda
was in the grip of a record cold wave engulfing the entire basin. By early
January temperatures plunged to twenty-six degrees and to as low as twelve
degrees in the nearby Pomona Valley, where frozen citrus trees burst open
and died. In desperation the small ranchers ran water and kept huge bonfires
blazing to save the infant orange and lemon groves. Most of the Yorba
Linda orchards survived, though hills to the north were white with hail
and thousands of trees suffered damage throughout the basin.

On Thursday morning January 9, 1913, the cold lifted briefly. Frank
left early as usual to work with a crew fighting frost in the groves and
returned late that afternoon. Ella Eidson, a widow with two small daughters
who lived a few yards away, remembered him soon knocking at her door,
"awfully nervous" and asking that she stay with his wife until the doctor

came. Mrs. Eidson followed him back to the Nixon bungalow to find the little clapboard house heated with extra stoves, Harold in tow to Almira Milhous, and Hannah lying in the single small bedroom off the living room, calm yet weary after hours of labor. "She didn't seem to be worried or concerned at all," the neighbor said. "It was all right with her. She was getting along. She had no doubt but what the doctor would get there in time." Yet the pains soon became more frequent and intense into the evening, and Eidson, a schoolteacher with no experience in midwifery, was "very much frightened" the doctor would be too late. Minutes before the 9:35 P.M. birth, "barely . . . in time," the worried neighbor thought, Dr. Horace Wilson and a nurse arrived from Whittier.

The baby was a large eleven-pound boy, "roly-poly" with brown eyes and a thick crop of black hair. Afterward, everyone agreed on what the nurse, Henrietta Shockney, called the infant's "powerful, ringing" cry. Unlike Harold, who had been a smaller, quiet baby, the new son would be known in the family as a "screamer," a stridor his mother came to describe more delicately as his "decided voice." But amid the crying there was obvious delight at a healthy baby. "I told his father," Hannah said, recalling the moment, " 'He's real good looking.' " They named him Richard Milhous, the first name once again Hannah's romantic choice from an English monarch, the twelfth-century Plantagenet whom his French allies called Coeur de Lion, the Lion-Hearted. Hoyt Corbit, a young man who worked in the groves, remembered Frank Nixon coming out the next morning laughing and dancing a little jig. "I've got another boy," he said excitedly. "I've got another boy."

Hannah took weeks to recover from the long labor. Despite her weakness, she managed to breast-feed the new baby, and six months later nursed as well Russell Harrison, Jr., the newborn of her sister Elizabeth, who lived nearby. Yet she was frail throughout Richard's infancy. Edith recalled her coming back briefly to the Milhous home after mastoid surgery at a Whittier hospital late in 1913. She brought Richard with her, and he was still "putting up such a squall and noise," the sister told the story later, that Great-grandmother Elizabeth Milhous noted he "would surely make a good preacher or a good teacher." Soon afterward, the new baby only fourteen months old, Hannah was pregnant again. For the birth of yet another boy, Francis Donald in November 1914, she went back once more to the big boulevard house.

Photographs duly recorded Richard at nine months posed on a child's wooden chair in a delicate baby dress, or later, the autumn Donald was born, placed along with five-year-old Harold amid giant California pumpkins that dwarfed the children. In a formal family portrait of 1916, he is a pretty three-year-old, stylishly dressed with a large bow at his neck, standing in short pants and high-top shoes next to his mother, and wearing the same sober expression the rest of the family struck for the photographer. The child beyond the pictures seemed now quiet and almost solitary, now animated and clamorous. The Eidson daughters, who played with him as a baby—"as young girls like to do," one of them said, "a real live doll"— thought him "a very serious child, not lots of fun." Ollis Burdg, a relative of Almira who began working with Frank in 1913 and took meals regularly with the Nixons the next two years, remembered a placid little boy in a conventional household. "He got along with his dad, he always sat with his dad at the table, and his dad always fed him," Burdg described the family scene. "Hannah was generally always cooking and bringing stuff to the table instead of sitting down and eating with us. She'd get it ready, she'd get us fed, and then she'd feed herself; that was kind of the way she worked it." Silent or briefly spoken, grace was said before each meal, and Burdg recalled that after Donald was born Frank continued to feed the babies while Hannah served them. "They got along swell," he would say of Hannah and Frank, "and I never heard a cross word between the two as long as I was there, two years."

To Burdg, Richard seemed "a very good kid, very quiet, never a crybaby at least around his father." Yet another man who worked with Frank during these years, Ralph Shook, believed him "no less boisterous" than other children. "It would be the other way around. He wanted his way," said Shook. "I can remember he used to cry loud," agreed Paul Ryan, who was six years older and grew up nearby. " 'I was the biggest crybaby in Yorba Linda,' " Ryan recalled Richard reminiscing with him years later. " 'My dad could hear me even with the tractor running.' " His first word, Hannah noted, had been "Bird," the name of Frank's white workhorse, and by several accounts he was a talkative, expressive toddler. When Ollis Burdg brought his fiancée to visit the Nixons in 1916, Richard crawled into the young woman's lap and regaled her with stories of his future exploits. "He was quite a talker," Burdg recounted. "He was telling her about how, when he got big, he was going to kill wild animals, and elephants, and lions and tigers."

Taken along when Hannah visited a friend in Whittier, he was an eager, interested child, fascinated by dolls he did not have at home. "The first thing that little tyke wanted to do was hightail it upstairs and play with my dolls," said the older girl who watched him on those visits. "He liked to play with them better than I did." Yet to others he would seem somehow aloof, apart. "It didn't strike me that he wanted to be hugged. He had a fastidiousness about him," thought his cousin Jessamyn West, then a thirteen-year-old and sometime babysitter. "I saw him and I didn't" because of the difference in their ages, she said, adding, "he was not a little puppy dog, one you wanted to cuddle, though he may have longed for it."

42

His own first memory was of a childhood accident. Hannah had taken them out to pick grapes and drove a buggy while holding Donald on her lap. Eleven-year-old Elizabeth Eidson, Ella's daughter, came along to watch Richard, but on their return he refused to sit on the buggy seat and stood at the dashboard. As the horse rounded a corner sharply he toppled out, the buggy wheel slitting his scalp in a long, angular cut along the left side. "He was up and bawling," Elizabeth remembered, when she ran back to him after Hannah stopped the horse. In the mind's eye of a frightened child who had fallen overboard and was being left behind, he later described the fall himself. "I managed to get up and run after the buggy," he wrote, "while my mother tried to make the horse stop." The Eidson girl held together the profusely bleeding scalp as she walked him back to the buggy. They hurried to Austin Marshburn, a neighbor who drove them in his Ford the few miles to a Fullerton physician to stitch up the gaping but surface wound, reassuring a distraught Hannah on the way that her son's lusty crying was a good sign. To hide the scar he would ever afterward comb his hair straight back, even, as he later rued, "when the vogue of parting hair on the left side came along."

The mishap left no apparent fear or timidity. Following the buggy accident he excitedly rode with the local grocery boy as he made rounds in a buckboard. At home he and Harold rolled down the orchard hillside shrieking in a rickety child's wagon, play that gave their mother, she confessed later, "many a start." Outwardly, it was an ordinary childhood, Shook and others recalled, "just like any other tow-headed boy in Yorba Linda." The only distinction may have been a front-page newspaper photo, by far the first of so many. A wide-eyed baby Donald and a rather skeptical Richard, now nearly four in a velvet-collared coat, peered out with another Yorba Linda youngster from an enscrolled picture in the November 23, 1916, *Los Angeles Evening Herald*, part of a campaign throughout the area to promote children's mites for Germanic relief in a world war in which America was still neutral.

The next year he went through a siege of pneumonia. It was to be his only serious boyhood ailment, though there was already some foreshadowing of the specter that illness would become for the family. From an early age Harold seemed to suffer frequent coughs and colds. Mildred Jackson, the older daughter of one of Hannah's friends, and Phoebe Eidson, Ella's other daughter, both described him as "always sickly" in early childhood. "Harold . . . had been ill a great deal," recalled a woman close to the family in Yorba Linda, and the Nixons seemed "afraid" he might develop something more serious. They were in a sense surrounded by the continuing plague of tuberculosis, still one of the nation's great killers. Believed to be an infection that was not contagious, a predisposition appearing to be hereditary, the disease that took Frank's mother had also killed his sister and stricken one of Hannah's first cousins. Basin mythology held that the climate could cure TB, and the foothills had attracted since the 1880s droves of "lungers," the attendant clinics or hospitals becoming what a Los Angeles writer called "one vast sanitorium," providing if not magical healing then at least "soothing death beds for those who are beyond recovery." Among their closest neighbors, Ella Eidson was convalescing from consumption, and the wife of one of Frank's coworkers was dying of it. A half-dozen more young people in the small settlement would eventually perish from tuberculosis. "Oh, among the beautiful hills," wrote Jessamyn West, who nearly died of the disease herself in the 1920s, "we went around with burning cheeks and hacking coughs."

Of its kind, Yorba Linda followed a classic history among the small outlying settlements of the basin—the colonial decay and dispossession of the old land, the charm and lure, the betrayal, disillusion, and hardpan reality.

The land had been discovered with some portent. "We experienced here a horrifying earthquake which was repeated four times during the day," a friar in the Spanish expedition recorded. A large-eyed don with bushy burnsides and twenty children by three wives, Bernardo Yorba acquired the land in the 1830s, and built a hulking fifty-room hacienda attended by 130 Indian servants and ranch hands. While the first U.S. settlers thought such ranchos a decaying and indolent order, later American accounts came to paint them as an Arcadia of dashing vaqueros and gracious senoritas, "happy tranquil days," as Bret Harte described the era. "A soft-handed Latin race slept and smoked the half year's sunshine away." The romance of the image grew with the remorse of the conquerors at the destruction of a culture, and in an official nostalgia that provided both historical identity and real-estate charm for the rootless new California. In reality, the Californians were neither so decadent nor so picturesque. Yorba and his brothers fell prey to various frauds after the American conquest. A Yorba daughter tried to retrieve some of the acreage in a U.S. court, but like most grantees she was refused a hearing. By the end of the nineteenth century the hacienda had become a derelict, crumbling adobe, and the estate awaited the developers.

The land that would be the town had the intimate, subtle loveliness of much of the basin. Washing up on the hills to the north, it rolled back to the south and to the east, toward the desert, in gentle, shadowed waves. At a distance it was a treeless range with little apparent color or life. Closer, in its midst, there were suddenly sage, cactus and buckbrush, mustard, mariposa lilies, greasewood and vivid yellow violets, wild tobacco and the dense butter-colored spikes of mullen weed. It was a terrain alive, too, with horned toads, rattlesnakes, rabbits, coyotes, and what one settler recalled in awe as "the great black soaring buzzards of Yorba Linda." Dotted with live oaks, holly, and eucalyptus, the foothills were clothed by the seasons in cinnamon or gold or a verdant green, and flushed with bright red and blue wildflowers. Standing visible guard on the east were the Santa Ana Mountains and beyond, the San Bernardinos, snow-capped in winter.

"The sun came up there as I think it always should, from behind a mountain called Old Saddleback," Jessamyn West said of her girlhood home and the setting of some of her novels. "The evening breezes sprang up there as evening breezes always should, fresh and sweet off the blue Pacific." When the land was cultivated, orange and lemon trees planted and manicured in a neat phalanx, row after row marching across the bare wavy landscape, the air was redolent with the young citrus, and the tract took on a graceful symmetry.

In 1908 the land had passed to the Janss Investment Company of Los Angeles, which promptly platted a town site of thirty-five hundred acres. A hale Nebraska physician with an eye for ground and a passion for abstinence, Dr. Peter Janss had founded ten years before a development corporation that was to grow into a real-estate colossus, numbering among its projects a barley field that would become Westwood and UCLA. Characteristically, Janss drew up deeds to the new Yorba Linda district—Yorba for the colonial owners, Linda for "beautiful"—expressly forbidding the sale of alcohol anywhere in the tract, the lots to revert to the developer if the condition were violated. Less exact were the company advertisements, and what purported to be candid photographs of a fruit-laden citrus grove, native walnut trees, and a brimming Santa Ana River. The promotions promised "choice ranches" at $250 an acre and some of "the richest land in California." "The soil is a deep, rich loam, underlaid by a moist subsoil, entirely free from hardpan, alkalai, and adobe," read the announcements. "The rainfall is generous and the irrigation supply is ample. Yorba Linda is in a frostless belt." Most of all, the ads repeated, there was "an inexhaustible amount of pure soft water," the company undertaking to provide 777,600 gallons every thirty days for each ten-acre plot.

Nothing of the bait was altogether true. Much of the soil turned out to be what one pioneer called "loaf sugar," a weak, thin topsoil and a porous substratum that came up in flaky chunks and leached quickly, leaving a dry hardpan surface choking to citrus. The first water had to be carried by the bucket from an old five-mile irrigation ditch run through the tract by the Anaheim Union Water Company. Wells yielded water with deposits "like brick dust," a settler recalled. "The stock could drink it and we would irrigate with it . . . but we couldn't drink it and we couldn't wash in it." It was "very nearly desert land," one writer later described Yorba Linda. At that, it was not even "frostless." Photographs later recorded eighteen-inch icicles hanging from the eucalyptus trees.

It was true enough that frosts were rarer there. The open land west and south of the hills was protected by a warmth that descended across it, but the protection itself was a curse. Its portent was air uncommonly still and clear. "Then, in the east," a witness recounted, "just visible at the pass of San Gorgonio ninety miles away, a smudge the size of a hand would appear." A wall of dust before it, the infamous Santa Ana wind, what the Indians called the Devil Breath, came down on the site from the northeast in all its fury. The Santa Ana screamed and lashed, the desert's hot, fierce reminder of its nearness. On the treeless rises the first Yorba Linda houses swayed and shuddered under the force, beds scudding across rooms, the shower of rocks against siding a frightening din. Cecil Pickering, a young bride who moved to a homestead in 1910, could hardly breathe when the fiery wind penetrated her wooden walls. Sleeping in a room on the east, she awoke the morning after a Santa Ana her hair white with dust. The August before Richard Nixon was born, settlers had desperately carried water to keep citrus seedlings alive in the vicious blow.

In Yorba Linda, as in a dozen other tiny basin settlements of the era, residents dug and oiled their own roads, built their own public structures, took on their own utilities and services in acts of self-reliance born out of the fraud or forfeit of the region's real-estate come-on. Like the torrid, gritty gales off the desert, the business ethics and habits of the boom seemed to come with the land. Here as elsewhere around Los Angeles, the twin results were enterprise as well as cynicism. Their plight provoked an autonomy and independence among the settlers that reenforced and perpetuated the social and political individualism of the age. It gave the area a conservative cast for generations. Yet it also produced a kind of acceptance of the sharp practices that had become so widely the region's regime. The small ranchers of Yorba Linda, like immigrants to southern California before and after, would cling doggedly to the dream, occasionally contest the betrayal, more often step around the large and small deceits to salvage what they could. Salted in the spongy soil was the old basin lure of prosperity and salvation.

Here Frank Nixon built his house less than fifty feet south of the Anaheim ditch. The hill had been in barley when purchased by Franklin Milhous, who now urged his son-in-law to plant a lemon grove. Once in the ground, the lemon trees required at least five years to fruition. On ten acres Nixon's would be a minute yeoman fragment of the basin citrus belt, a society and economy one California writer thought "a kind of outdoor hothouse," its trim and feeding generally tended "as carefully as the diet of a diabetic patient in a Santa Barbara hospital."

The orchards gave the region a lustrous green mask over the semi-desert, and in the first decades of the century a $2 billion industry. No pursuit, save perhaps movie stardom in a later era, more symbolized the California dream. The orange was the popular and profitable jewel of the culture, though lemons were coveted as well. "To own an orange grove in Southern California," wrote Carey McWilliams, "is to live in the real gold coast of American agriculture." As the industry grew apace after 1890, stories of success and wealth were common, but it was an ever more narrow and select "gold coast." Freezes, questionable soil or water, poor culti-vation, harsher-than-usual economies of scale, high-cost marginal produc-tion—each of these factors eliminated hundreds of small ranchers, ceding the industry to large commercial operators. For all the charm and money in citrus, it also rewarded the rich and discouraged the poor. Once more, the place and the chance were not for all what they seemed. Behind the thriving groves were rarely migrant farmers or storekeepers, but far more frequently retired businessmen or professionals who brought with them, one citrus industry authority noted, "the needed capital, commercial habits, and business ability." Placed atop a Yorba Linda hill and stocked with Milhous Nursery seedlings, Frank Nixon would have none of those nec-essary assets.

It was a plain, exacting life. A sparse bungalow neighborhood had begun to grow to the north toward the new Pacific Electric depot. Hannah's younger sister Elizabeth, and Eldo and Grace Milhous West, a first cousin, lived nearby. In its setting the Nixon house was simple but respectable, an ordinary rectangular interior with a living room, kitchen, and small bedroom. Unlike many of the first Yorba Linda homes, it was plastered inside, and had adjoining a small summerhouse storage shed for food, a luxury to some of the early families. The Nixons also had a cow and horse, some chickens and rabbits. After furrowing and planting his own orchard, Frank began late in 1912 to tend other area orchards of absentee owners and to do piecework carpentry to eke out a living while the lemon trees matured. He followed a routine of hard work, accepted sacrifice, and hope typical of the homesteaders. "The area was full of young men on the make who had bought ranches and were looking for ways up," one of them recounted. Yet the severity of the tract was inescapable. Eldo West thought it "not virgin, but . . . mighty raw." Across the ditch Mrs. Pickering feared to let her toddler outside "because the coyotes were thick out there; they'd come right up to the door." Everywhere was the dense powdery dust of the land newly gouged for orchards and houses and roads, "nothing except dust," a neighbor recalled.

A few miles away was the raucous oil camp of Olinda with its bars and dance halls, roustabouts and whores, or Placentia with a large Mexican colony working its orange groves. But Yorba Linda, with little more than two hundred in 1913, began and remained its own quiet, staid world amid the pulsing life of other basin frontiers. While two Japanese farmers, a Basque family, and a handful of Mexican settlers were scattered about the area, the tract would be overwhelmingly what one of its children remembered as "white Anglo." The dirt streets and grassy sidewalks of the small-town center north of the depot had a drug and hardware store, a post office, and later a filling station and bank, but no dance hall or saloon, no pool parlor or theater. The prohibition written into the Janss deeds was fortified by an influx of Quaker settlers who, like the Nixons and Wests, could not afford the higher-priced land in Whittier. So strong was the early Quaker presence that the town's first church, begun in 1911 as a nondenominational community project, soon became solely Friends, over half of the money to build it coming from monied Quaker congregations in Whittier and Pasadena. "They took it away from us," one non-Quaker resident described the episode.

There was no visible pretense to the place, though a propriety and parochialism that left it one more island in the basin's archipelago of towns and villages, together yet distinct and apart. Nine times a day, the Pacific Electric "Peanut Roaster" interurban car went to and from Los Angeles, its conductor, a local rancher, calling out in whimsy as he approached the tiny insular settlement at the end of the line, "Yorba Linda, Yorba Linda, the capital of the world."

Exhausted after nursing Harold through the measles in 1916, Hannah hired a young Quaker woman, Mary Guptill, to help care for the children. On her first visit, Guptill found "a simple home . . . on a rather tight budget," and a pattern of life that was largely constant during the intervals she witnessed it over the next two years. Frank arose at dawn, took his warm cereal from where it had been overnight in a fireless cooker in the fireplace, and left for a long day in the groves, returning wearily at nightfall. "He just wanted to show people that he could, and what he could do," thought Guptill. "The Milhous family was a well-established family and Mr. Nixon was more or less of a Johnny-come-lately in the area. And so, of course, he was very anxious to do well for his family." Hannah, the young woman remembered, had her own household regimen, making the children's clothes to save money and struggling with "a miserable old distillate stove" to cook the meals and bake all their bread.

For her part, the young woman worked for the Nixons "like I would in a home of my own, or in my own folks' home. . . . I was just treated like a guest, almost." She remembered vividly reading to the boys from James Whitcomb Riley's *Songs O'Cheer* a favorite poem, "The Hired Man's Faith in Children."

> *I believe all children's good,*
> *Ef they're only understood,—*
> *Even bad ones, 'pears to me,*
> *'S jes as good as they kin be!*

And Hannah, who had worked in much the same way in other homes a decade before, admonished her sons for then calling Mary Guptill, however fondly, their own "hired girl." "When their mother heard them calling me that, she spoke rather disapprovingly of it," Guptill recounted. "She said I wasn't their hired girl, I was their friend that was helping them out." It was a gesture the young woman thought characteristic of Hannah Nixon, whom she remembered affectionately as "a gentle woman in every sense of the word . . . always quiet-spoken and thoughtful of people."

The three boys slept in a second bedroom Frank had added to the back of the house. Later they moved to a partly finished attic, though the small house was always crowded. They dressed in front of the fireplace on cool, sometimes chill California mornings amid spartan, unupholstered furnishings, "nothing . . . cushioned," as one neighbor put it, "just chairs you sat on." Among the sons, Richard struck Mary Guptill as "a quiet, little round-faced boy with large, dark eyes," who often played contentedly alone. "He was not as outreaching as many children are," she recalled. "He lived more within himself." The boys were accustomed to being read stories or poetry at bedtime, and when Guptill took up the ritual, Richard more than his brothers seemed to delight in the readings, usually from *Songs O'Cheer*, Riley's sentimental poems celebrating the virtues of village America. Following the reading, they said their prayers. "He'd clasp his little hands and close his eyes, and you could just feel it," she remembered Richard's earnestness. "He was really praying instead of just saying his prayers." The well-memorized lines went:

> *Jesus Holy Savior, Hear me while I pray,*
> *Look upon thy little child, help me all the day.*
> *Forgive me when I'm naughty, Take all my sins away,*
> *Help me to love Thee better, Dear Jesus, every day.*

He was often the least noticeable of the children, Guptill thought, "kind of in between" the baby Donald, whom she found "very easy to enjoy and love," and an older Harold whose illnesses had aroused his parents' continuing concern. They seemed to have no particular toys or pets, and few playmates at hand. The sons were still too small to roam the sparsely settled tract and were forbidden to play at other houses without Frank's specific permission. Handsome and outgoing with thick, curly hair and bright eyes, Harold Nixon at seven was already the puckish, fun-loving, playful boy he would be into young manhood. Harold once invited several children to his own birthday party without telling his mother, who learned about it only when another parent asked her what sort of present would be appropriate. Hannah promptly told the invited children "no presents, please," as Guptill recalled the moment, but cheerfully went ahead with a party complete with birthday cake.

Her response to the birthday party seemed typical of the way Hannah Nixon dealt with her growing sons, quietly and gently yet with an abiding firmness. "She never punished them, but she did explain and talk with them," Mary Guptill remembered. The talks were intense and insistent, and usually followed by the child sitting in a chair to reflect on his transgressions. These experiences, which the boys would recall years afterward, produced what Mary thought at the time a formidable authority. "She managed them very well. They seemed to feel that they wouldn't do anything to hurt their mother, rather than that they were afraid of her." The sanctions were sometimes restriction, sometimes a form of restitution, but standards in either case were exacting. When Richard came home with a handful of grapes he had picked from a neighbor's vine without express permission, his mother made him return them along with an earned five cents to pay for what he had eaten. "They were very strict parents and expected them to do right in everything," said Ella Eidson.

Still, beginning in Yorba Linda, and persisting as the boys grew older, there were those who would believe that Hannah's muted strictures were not enough. "Some people thought that she was too permissive," Guptill observed. Among them was Hannah's own family. Almira Milhous thought her "too lenient," Hannah once confessed. "She was a very soft and kind and quiet woman, the angel unaware," said her brother-in-law, Oscar Marshburn, who reflected the misgivings of much of the family. "Sometimes we felt she wasn't exerting her will power over them as far as being strict. She appealed to them by her counselling, that's as far as it went."

"She never left it to Frank to reprimand them," Guptill noted. If the mother was hushed and deliberate, the father was "explosive." She witnessed no spankings by Frank. "He was not unjust; there was nothing unjust about him." Yet he was obviously quick to ire, loud, severe. "They were somewhat in awe of his temper," she remembered of the small boys. "We all were." Like Ollis Burdg before her, however, Mary Guptill saw no conflict between a husband and wife so outwardly different in temperament and manner. When Hannah in her fatigue from nursing Harold through the measles went back to the Milhous home for a rest in 1916, Frank soon grew lonely and took both the children and the young woman to visit her on Whittier Boulevard. Having stayed with her mother and Edith only days, Hannah then became similarly "homesick," as she admitted to Mary, and returned to Yorba Linda. Eight years after their swift courtship and wedding, they were still clearly in love, Hannah's serenity and devotion seeming to absorb between them her husband's volatile bent. "I think she probably had a decisive influence because he practically worshipped her," Guptill came to believe during her stays with the family. "What she wanted was what he wanted eventually." Altogether, the young woman concluded as she left the bungalow in the summer of 1918, "they were a close family."

At nearly forty, Frank Nixon was a still slender, muscular figure whose face bore an angled leanness, a rawboned taper carved by his physical labor. He was by any measure impulsive, excitable, hot-tempered, delighting in combat and contention. Within the family the heat of the man flared with barked orders and impatient blustering at his small sons. Outside, it issued in a pugnacious love of argument. "He'd debate you on any subject and let you choose any side you wanted," said a fellow worker. He could be blunt beyond the point of tactlessness and utterly without embarrassment. Frank's tongue, concluded one observer, "could clip a hedge." His boy Richard might have learned later to concentrate and talk well, Ralph Shook reminisced, "but not lickety-split like his dad."

The eruptions, however, passed as swiftly as they came. "If he thought he had reason to be fired up about something he would get excited real fast," a friend said, "but then he got over it just as fast." To Hoyt Corbit and his wife, "he never seemed to carry any grudges . . . when the argument was over, it was over." Jessamyn West regarded him as a "rough customer," though his truculence was offset by "a boisterous geniality, which none of my Milhous relatives ever evidenced." He was plainly without guile, openly honest and forthright as well as bristling and indiscreet. What remained of the fire and its passage was the ever-stark contrast in style and temperament to his in-laws. "They didn't take a chance on making fools of themselves," West said later of the Milhouses. "But Frank was a different creature. He said what he thought."

In Yorba Linda he moved tirelessly from job to job, chance to chance, piecing together an income while the lemon trees matured. He also had begun to instill in his sons the same sense of work and earning so dominant in his own life from childhood. The boys were expected to do chores around the bungalow as soon as they could, and later, they recalled, to hoe and help manicure the citrus on which the family fortunes depended.

Beyond hard work and its intrinsic virtues, his dual passions were politics and the Bible. "He loved to argue either one or both," said Hoyt Corbit. With typical savor he instigated or quickly joined political conversations after church and threw himself into the local politics of the town, "head over heels," a friend recalled. By 1918 he had been among the leaders in a settlers' legal battle with Janss over water assessments, and was one of a handful who fought doggedly and successfully to keep a pool table out of Yorba Linda. Ollis Burdg believed him "a little radical once in a while." Ralph Shook remembered his stubborn resolve on political matters—"two sledge hammers and a crowbar, you couldn't move him. Translating his attitude on up to now, he might be out on the street corner with a banner."

Having quietly voted for Democrat Woodrow Wilson in 1916, Hannah never forgot her stoutly Republican husband's reaction: "When I told Mr. Nixon afterward he just went pale and white." She had argued with him about Wilson's promise to stay out of war, Hannah went on, "but my husband was a stubborn man, and arguments stiffened him." Yet his taste for native populism was real enough and cut across parties for Frank Nixon as it did for millions in that era. In Yorba Linda he spoke admiringly of Robert La Follette, Sr., the Wisconsin Republican Progressive, and even kept on the living room wall a picture of William Jennings Bryan, the florid, fundamentalist Nebraskan who had been McKinley's Democratic opponent for the Presidency. Part of the paradoxical politics of the basin, small ranchers or businessmen like Frank Nixon larded their Republicanism and enterprise with a fierce sense of their disadvantage before organized power, whatever its stripe. In her autobiography Emma Goldman, the socialist organizer, recorded the small towns around Los Angeles before World War I as doggedly conservative yet "seething with discontent."

The politics were clear also in his religion, and he promptly married the two in Yorba Linda with his habitual vehemence. While Hannah attended services irregularly during her pregnancies and lengthy recoveries, he had gone faithfully since the Quaker church was completed in 1912, taking the boys with him and becoming a stalwart of the congregation. He volunteered to teach Sunday school and soon took on a notoriously unruly class of ten- and eleven-year-old boys. The effect was electric. The incorrigibles became a model, and not alone for their new teacher's stern discipline. By 1917 he had moved on to a class of young people between fourteen and twenty with the same results. So popular was the Nixon group that it outgrew room after room until it overflowed into the main church sanctuary and choir pews. Students would recall admiringly a "firebrand" teacher whose fervor and energy were infectious, and whose message, delivered in the same outspokenness their elders found abrasive, was unashamedly political and, as one said later, "with it."

"His cheeks flamed and his voice trembled. He was the first person to make me understand that there was a great lack of practicing Christianity in civic affairs," Jessamyn West recounted as a member of the class. "Frank was, in his thinking and feeling, a political animal. He cared about what public officials did." The essential moral she thought unmistakable. "I do not remember, though he may have preached them, any partisan politics in Frank's Sunday school classes. I was a socialist, he a Republican, and what Frank had to say about probity in politics pointed, as far as I was concerned, straight to Norman Thomas." Nor was she unique in her thinking. "The entire class," she wrote in 1973, "felt somewhat as Nader's Raiders or a group of Vista volunteers do today. Christianity was not just a matter of the blood of the lamb, but of seeing that that blood had not been shed in vain. . . . All of us who had been in Frank's class had been convinced that Christians should be political, and that politics, if not Christian, should at least be ethical."

His ardor did not stop with flushed Sunday school lectures or politics. "Grace, I swear you get prettier every time I see you. How do you do it?" he would tell Hannah's shy and embarrassed cousin. "I want your recipe. Come here and let me give you a hug." In a culture and family notably reserved physically as well as emotionally—"Quaker families are isolated from touching," said a relative; "there is not much hugging or kissing or daughters sitting on their fathers' knees"—Frank Nixon was a demonstrative, almost sensuous man. One adolescent girl in the extended family saw him as "real manly," and another confided years later that he had been "a pincher and squeezer of his young nieces." Sexual self-consciousness seemed passed down in the Milhous blood, thought one of the recipients, and was preferably to be "lost in bed with a loving man." (Jessamyn West once gently condemned a relative with the judgment that "she probably *was* a Milhous in bed.") The interloper here, too, Frank seemed to suffer no such disabilities. Dancing did not just offend his religious rectitude; it was a veritable risk. "When his arms went around a woman," he admitted to Eldo West, "his amorous propensities were instantly aroused."

There would be about the years in Yorba Linda for Frank Nixon a lightness and flavor, for all the hard work a freshness of opportunities still not closed, a vestige of youth, that set the period apart from what had come before and what followed. Life on the tract, however hardscrabble, was the first relative stability he had known for more than a decade, Hannah and the children the first sustained family life since early childhood. He had responded in characteristic ebullience. His friends recalled him never again so happy.

In Yorba Linda as elsewhere, his wife was always his obvious, softly congenial contrast. Seven years younger, still in her early thirties in this interval before the First World War, Hannah Nixon had largely kept the trim figure and glowing dark eyes of her youth, and had acquired a rich, resonant voice she would carry all her life. Outwardly, she seemed everything Frank was not—calm, retiring, naturally polite and tactful, untroubled. "She was considered in Yorba Linda," said Virginia Shaw, whose family lived across the Anaheim ditch, "a cultured, refined, educated person from a rather superior family in comparison to Mr. Nixon."

Her neighbors and friends remembered her now and later with an almost uniform affection and respect. Another young girl who worked for them briefly after Mary Guptill thought Hannah shy, almost "timid." She was "quite reserved about forming friendships," Blanche McClure remembered, and Ella Eidson saw her as a virtual "stay-at-home" compared to Frank. Yet there were endearing memories of Hannah quietly stealing on errands of mercy. She often visited the deathbed of a friend's tubercular wife, promised the woman she would see to her children's birthdays, and true to her word sent them remembrances faithfully for the next half century. Among neighborhood families stricken with illness, she took in the well children to help their parents. When old Dr. Marshburn, a fellow Quaker and Yorba Linda's lone physician, lost his wife, Hannah walked miles to visit him in consolation for months afterward.

There were those who saw some of her manner as a pretension. "I'm sure she wasn't at the bridge club," Ralph Shook, one of Frank's coworkers, would say of her frequent absences from the house. "There was no such thing. She would have been there if there had been." But such disdain was rare. "She was the kind who would balance the wheel of the whole family," said William Barton, who ran a local garage and knew them both. It remained a subtle balance. Already visible in the bungalow by 1918 was a pattern that would persist—Frank the ostensible master, vocal, flashing, Hannah deferring, placating, on occasion discreetly maneuvering and prevailing. "Nobody could dominate Frank Nixon. Nobody," pronounced Ralph Shook in a common and emphatic judgment of the time. Nonetheless, her influence was clear. Her sister Olive saw plainly enough on the surface that Hannah was "not the dominating one in the family. She wanted to please Frank, that was her nature, but if she thought something ought to be done she would do it. He was the one that made the decisions mostly [and] if she made them she made them quietly and didn't talk about it."

In the end, there would be as well as her discretion and goodness Frank Nixon's own virtual worship of his wife, and so the basis of what became increasingly an intimate, implicit acquiescence and accommodation between them. Mute and fragile, it was an early resolution sensed if not often clearly understood by others, including their young sons, and it left their glaring differences of approach and temperament largely intact. "If she ruled the family," observed Mary Guptill, "she ruled it by love."

Beyond the compassion and conciliation, however, there was also a visibly darker side of these years for Hannah Nixon, an inner disquiet, bouts of exhaustion and dismay that seemed to stem from her daily life in the tract. "She almost went crazy out there if it hadn't been for things like the Women's Club," a family friend said of the period. "She seemed sometimes overwhelmed by the poverty." Again and again the comfort and respite of the old Milhous Whittier home beckoned, the "fire" Edith a decade before thought she married to escape. There she had been sick of housework, her sister recalled, yet now in Yorba Linda Hannah had "run into it more than she ever had to have before, really." Between Richard's birth in January 1913 and her fourth pregnancy in the spring of 1918, she returned repeatedly to Whittier, sometimes, as Mary Guptill remembered, pining for her family and staying only briefly, sometimes pausing longer, but continually fleeing the drudgery of the cramped bungalow, the small children and the dust and wind, her passionate, devoted but hard-bitten husband.

Hannah portrayed starkly the family's poverty during these years. "While we were there, the lemon grove only kept us poor," she would say. "Many days I had nothing to serve but corn meal. I'd bring it to the table and exclaim, 'See what we have tonight—wonderful corn meal!' And they would gobble it up as if it were the most delectable of dishes." Yet their actual poverty was in every sense relative, not least to their surroundings and to the existence Hannah had left behind on Whittier Boulevard. In a settlement of small citrus ranchers and others fashioning a living from the town's start, they were very much like most of their neighbors. "I wouldn't consider them poor at all," said Phoebe Eidson, who at the same time looked on the Milhouses in Whittier as "well-to-do." Next door, Gerald Shaw saw the Nixons "just a shade above what you might want to call the middle income bracket. . . . They were doing reasonably well." Working for Frank, Hoyt Corbit recalled him saying he had to "keep busy to support his family," but that they were "just in very modest circumstances . . . just like my parents." Soon after the Nixons moved to Yorba Linda, a cousin would be taken with the elegance of Hannah's china closet, and by 1918 Frank Nixon had in addition to a tractor an automobile, at that point still a comparative rarity and luxury in the tract. Although Hannah made the children's playsuits, and Richard and Donald wore hand-me-downs like most other children in the area, they continually dressed well enough to impress neighbors. "They always came to church with their ties on, wore their little hats and were very mannerly. Hannah taught them well," recounted Cecil Pickering. Struck by what seemed not merely neat, polite boys but almost a class distinction in their wardrobes, Virginia Shaw believed "the Nixon children dressed well because of Mrs. Nixon's background. . . . I don't know, but you had a feeling that she came from a family that was a little better in culture and money."

To keep up appearances, in fact, the Milhouses gave them financial help during these years well beyond Frank's original land stake or the nursery stock. "There was always some place for the money to come from . . . some of the family could help when necessary," Olive conceded long afterward. The hardship and rawness of the place, Frank's long-drawn labor in the groves and perpetual search for marginal jobs on the side, were real enough. But the well-dressed Nixon children, the tractor and car, the hired help, the china closet—all belied the later, well-publicized images of poverty, and bespoke, for those who knew, both Milhous subsidies and pride. Richard Nixon had not been born or left to the grim impoverishment depicted in his political mythology. The reality seemed very different to others nearby who lived much the same existence, and even in the same larger family. "We had our own good small happy life," Jessamyn West once said of her comparable childhood in Yorba Linda, separated from the Nixons by the irrigation ditch. Measured against the poor-boy origins Richard seemed to claim later, against genuine poverty in the basin and elsewhere, she concluded, "We were the landed gentry."

Their society and diversions in the tract were simple. Old Yorba Lindans remembered going to the Nixons or the Shooks, herding the small children into a group, laying out the babies "in a string on the bed," and having a party. Virginia Shaw and others remembered as vividly the stolid, bedazed stillness of Yorba Linda's Sunday afternoons, the adults napping heavily after church and dinner. "California! What a place to find yourself in while still young and with a means of travel the world had never known before: a mechanical car!" one of the children of the time reflected. Yet despite their own automobile, the Nixons remained for the most part on their small hillside, less from lack of means than lack of interest. Franklin Milhous had purchased a touring car by 1916 and drove an assembled brood of daughters and their families on vacations to Yosemite or even San Francisco. Hannah and Richard or another brother occasionally went along on those excursions, but almost always without Frank.

Tension between Frank and the Milhouses was constant. "I don't think they ever let Hannah forget the fact that she married outside her status," said Max McPherson. "Her marriage always put her in a tough spot," another friend of the family added. The Milhous aversion was only partially Frank Nixon's failure to do more than scratch a living from the tract. Added to the disdain was the old, enduring tribal possessiveness toward the daughters. "There was an arrogance about the Milhouses that tended to swallow up the marriage partners—reinforced by the size of the family and the unrelenting spirit of togetherness," wrote Edwin P. Hoyt, who compiled a genealogical history of the clan. With the marriage and departure from the boulevard house of the last of the daughters in 1918, the plaintive, all but wailful tone in Almira's ubiquitous poetry was telling. "To think thee's gone and left it, thy little bedroom blue," she wrote to Edith, to whom they had planned to bequeath the nursery but who had finally married at thirty-seven, "left it for a whole long year, And left thy mother too." When Olive married Oscar Marshburn, the Yorba Linda doctor's son, in the spring of 1918, the mother's lament seemed funereal.

> *I'd thought the girls I was raising*
> *Would care for me when I am old.*
> *But now they're all gone away*
> *And I'm left in the cold.*
> *Out of the six I have raised*
> *Through ailments great and small,*
> *Yes, out of my six dear girls*
> *There's no one to answer my call.*

Hannah, the dutiful "mainstay," was both drawn back by her parent's overt sense of abandonment and attracted to the boulevard haven to shed her own burdens. Yet her husband remained defiantly "unswallowed." The aloofness and unease Hannah's sister Jane had noticed in Frank amid family gatherings ten years before continued in these years as plainly as ever. "He had a hard time fitting the mold," thought McPherson. "They [the Milhouses] made it pretty difficult for anyone who did not fit the mold. Hannah had quite a problem."

Before World War I was over, Hannah had given birth to her fourth son, Arthur Burdg. As a college student, Richard described the moment at age five when he and his brothers were told by their father about the baby:

> After talking with my grandmother, who was taking care of my two brothers and me while Mother was away on a visit he came over to where we boys were quarreling over some toys and told us there was a little doll over at the hospital for us, a real, live doll! Naturally we then began to quarrel over whose doll it would be, although each of us wished to have it merely to keep one of the others from getting it. My father, however, assured us that our rights would be equal, and then he asked us what name we should give our doll. After learning that

it was not a "girl doll," we finally decided that its name
should be Arthur.

Having been "scrubbed . . . all up" by Almira and told "secretly" by
nine-year-old Harold that the "doll" was in fact a baby, they were bundled
into the "family Ford" and taken to the hospital, where Richard remembered being "rather disappointed in the baby, because, after all, a tiny
baby is not as pretty as a doll, at least in outward appearances."

The "doll" was another beautiful infant, like his brothers, but even
more frail than Harold. Hannah had wanted a daughter, she confessed to
the Shooks, who were expecting at the same time. "I want a girl," Ralph
remembered her telling them. During much of Arthur's childhood she
seems to have treated and dressed him in her disappointed hope. "My
parents had wanted him to be a girl in the first place; consequently they
attempted to make him one as much as possible," Richard wrote in his
college reminiscence, describing his little brother's "grief . . . over his
hair," how Arthur had "begged my mother for a boy's haircut," how he
"disliked" being a ring-bearer in a wedding because he had to walk beside
a little flower girl, and how "my mother had to work with him for hours
to get him to do it."

In the same recollection he also recorded in loving detail his own observations of the growth of the new baby, on whom he obviously doted.
"For example, I remember how his eyes changed from their original baby-
blue to an almost black shade; how his hair, blond at first, became dark
brown; how his mouth, toothless for five months, was filled with tiny, white
teeth which, by the way, were exceedingly sharp when applied on soft
fingers or toes which happened to get within their reach."

On Armistice Day, 1918, Frank drove his family and the neighboring
Shaws all the way into Los Angeles in what Virginia remembered as "this
big old open Ford." She recalled Richard, nearly six, as "withdrawn" on
what may have been his first conscious trip into the city. They passed few
cars and only a random gas station in the gaping open spaces that lay
between the outlying settlements and the old center of Los Angeles, much
of that area that would later be the twelfth congressional district where
Richard Nixon began his political career twenty-seven years later. Nearer
the downtown they could see across the empty fields from Seventh to Ninth
streets, and on the way, a tall tower with a huge "J" atop it, for Janss
Investment. "I bet some day this will all be built up in here," Gerald Shaw
said at one point. They all laughed. "We thought it was awfully funny,"
Virginia recalled.

"PLEASE CALL MY SON RICHARD"

He began school in the autumn of 1919, entering the first grade because Yorba Linda had no kindergarten. Like most other children of the settlement, he went barefoot on the usually mild southern California days, carrying shoes and socks in a sack as he walked less than a mile to the small wooden schoolhouse. On rainy mornings the red clay of the path turned from dust to a slick, gummy mud, and at the school playground, along with a maypole and swings, was a water faucet where the children routinely washed their feet and legs before classes. Rain or shine, he seemed to arrive each day in what a teacher remembered distinctly as "a freshly starched white shirt with a big black bow tie and knee pants." Though he played before school and "joined in heartily" during the recesses, he would appear somehow unsoiled through the day. "He always looked like his mother had scrubbed him from head to toe," said his first teacher, Mary George. "The funny thing is, I can never remember him ever getting dirty."

The day started, as it continued, by rote and ritual, a bell silencing suddenly the noisy playground, the flag saluted at the front of the building, the students solemnly trooping to class to the cadence of a march played by one of their classmates on a piano in the hall. Inside was a setting familiar to generations of students in small-town America. A potbelly stove squatted at the center of each room, blackboards at the front hid cloakrooms, and portraits of George Washington and Abraham Lincoln peered down on rows of old-fashioned slanted wooden desks with inkwells. "Absolutely the three R's. Nothing else," a Yorba Linda teacher of these years described the curriculum. "That's why children learned so much in such a short space of time." Trained at local normal schools, teachers were expected to follow the prescribed course exactly and to conform to even more rigid community standards after school, expressly forbidden to dance or merely be seen talking to a man on town streets.

Soon after classes began, Hannah Nixon visited the school with her own concern for social form. "By the way, Miss George," the teacher remembered her saying, coming politely but insistently to the point, "please call my son Richard and never Dick. I named him Richard." It was the sort of injunction, Mary George said fifty years later, "I never forgot." He was a quiet, serious student and obviously bright, "one of those rare individuals born with knowledge," his teacher thought. "He had only to be exposed or shown, and he never forgot. . . . He absorbed knowledge of any kind like a blotter." By his own account, his mother had taught him to read at home before starting school, though Mary George remembered clearly that "at first, of course, he couldn't read." In any case, he was soon reading avidly. At one point he was sent across the playground and into the main building to recite before the third-graders what one described as "some long verse or some long poem." "It was so amazing," Virginia Shaw said, recalling the performance. "I remember all of us were very, very envious."

Mary George concluded that he had "a photographic mind" and "never had to work for knowledge at all." Others were equally impressed. "Where the rest of them would have to hem and haw, when they'd ask him a question, well, Richard could say it right away," said a neighbor with a daughter in his class. "When they would want the story written, he could write a story in just about a third of the words that the rest of them required." His progress the next year allowed him to jump ahead to the third grade, a move that would make him still eight years old going into the fourth grade the following term, and as much as a year younger than his classmates for the rest of his education.

From the beginning he had "kept mostly to himself . . . was kind of by himself," as Miss George saw him, "a very solemn child [who] . . . rarely ever smiled or laughed." The young teacher, who chafed under the town's prudishness, thought his reserve natural, given his disciplined Quaker home. "He mixed all right when he knew he should," she reminisced afterward. "He was strictly brought up to mind. . . . He understood what he was at school for. He was there to learn and not to play around." The second- and third-grade teacher who advanced him, Ellen Anderson, placed him in the back of the room with the well-behaved students, though she remembered, like Mary George, that he seemed to play easily with the other children despite his quiet manner. In the first-grade photograph he sat soberly to the side in the bow tie his teachers so clearly remembered. By the second- and third-grade picture he had moved to the midst of the group, still in a neat white shirt but now tieless like the other boys, a classmate's arm jauntily around his shoulder.

Yet his sheer ability continued to set him apart. In his second year, he won a children's recitation contest, defeating his brother Harold and other older youngsters on the platform of the Friends Church. "Richard won it," one of the neighboring children said later, "and we were so jealous. We just really thought it was because he was so cute and little and had such a long piece that we were really quite disappointed that he won." There were signs, too, that for all the reserve and obedience he was already growing assertive if not cocky with his academic skill. Cecil Pickering remembered the story making the rounds in the neighborhood that Richard had actually questioned an assignment. "One of the things the teachers wanted him to write about, well, he didn't think it was necessary." Some children would remember him as well for an urge to dominate and control, and a petulance when he could not. An elderly Ralph Shook summed up the reaction when some were more reticent about their famous classmate: "I've been told that he just wanted to run everything. Wasn't happy unless he did."

"He was no child prodigy," Hannah would say candidly when there was a tendency later to exaggerate or read some portent from his early record in school, though his keenness was plain enough and widely noticed at the time. "He was interested in things way beyond the usual grasp of a boy his age," his mother told one of his early biographers. "He was thoughtful and serious. 'He always carried such a weight.' That's an expression we Quakers use for a person who doesn't take his responsibilities lightly." His performance in the early grades traced more to that child's earnestness and conformity than to purely academic or intellectual stimulation at home. There had been the nightly poem-and-story readings, and he would remember fondly magazines and newspapers that came into the small house, the *Saturday Evening Post*, the *Ladies' Home Journal*, the *Los Angeles Times*, the Marshburns' cast-off *National Geographics*. Yet when Jessamyn West, a voracious reader as a girl, visited the Nixons frequently in the years before 1919, she found a pamphlet on sex education discreetly tucked away on a shelf but, unlike in her own home, no books. Mary Guptill and others remembered the well-worn Riley *Songs O'Cheer*, though almost nothing else.

Still, his interest and excellence in school became an added bond between the son and his educated mother. "As a youngster, Richard seemed to need me more than my other sons did," Hannah said later. "As a schoolboy, he used to like to have me sit with him when he studied. . . . It wasn't that Richard needed my help with his work. . . . Rather, it was that he just liked to have me around." Olive and other relatives saw the same intimacy developing from his earliest school days in Yorba Linda. "As a child Richard wanted his mother alone to do things for him, and he asked her rather than his father," his aunt once said. But beyond the quiet evenings of study with his mother, the mark of the father was unmistakably there also. In school discussions, one of his classmates recalled, Richard had "lots to say," much of it about politics. Seven years old, on the way to his second-grade class in the fall of 1920, he had chattered to somewhat bewildered children along the path about candidates in the current national election. "I didn't understand a word he said," one listener remembered. "Where did a boy of seven pick up such ideas?" asked Jessamyn West, who knew the answer well from her own Sunday school. "Frank, of course."

After school, he began to take lessons on a black Starr piano at home. Hannah thought he had a "natural ear" and reported later that at seven "he could play the piano without discord," though it was not always that simple. If talented, he hated practice, and especially musical scales. His mother alternately cajoled and enforced. "I had to think up all kinds of stories about the woods and the birds in the trees to make the scales interesting," she once confessed. On another occasion Virginia Shaw recalled her own "terrible shock" at seeing the usually gentle Hannah "cross," and apparently out of nature stories. Going to the Nixons' screen door one warm summer day in 1920, the girl saw "Richard practicing the piano, and she was sitting on the piano bench with a switch in her hand while he was practicing."

Once freed from piano practice or homework, he spent after-school hours and summer vacations in a neighborhood now, after 1919, teeming with children compared to earlier years. With Gerald and Virginia Shaw; Jessamyn's younger brother, Merle; Floyd Wildermuth, a Nixon family cousin; and his own brothers and others, they played hopscotch, tag, and hockey with a tin can, or threw clods at one another across the ditch. Gerald Shaw long remembered Richard Nixon hitting him in the head with the blunt end of a hatchet when he refused to surrender a jar full of polliwogs. But they became fast friends, eating lunches together, the Shaws taking Richard to an automobile show in the glittering ballroom of the Biltmore Hotel in Los Angeles, the boys spending summer weekends at the Shaw cabin at nearly Barton Flats, where they could hike and swim, fish and spear frogs at Jinx Lake, or capture chipmunks in small cages to keep in Yorba Linda. Back in the tract, he picnicked with Merle West on the reservoir hill to the south and made forays with other children to a "haunted house" in the foothills, "to be viewed with awe," he recalled, "and approached with caution."

"Yorba Linda's roadrunners, horned toads, trap door spiders, and tumbleweeds blowing before the big Santa Anas marked you," recorded one of them who grew up there. Yet it marked Richard Nixon only in part. When he came to write about his life in the tract, he called the setting "idyllic" for a child, but gave barely a page to his memories of it, and wrote most warmly about yearning to leave. The railroad tracks passing only a mile away, he could see the smoke of engines during the day, and was sometimes awakened by train whistles in the night, "the sweetest music I ever heard." Richard thought Everett Barnum, a Santa Fe engineer and family friend who visited them occasionally and regaled the boys with railroad stories, "the best-off man in town," and being an engineer "an awfully good job to have." He dreamed, he would say many times, of "far-off places."

Wanderlust, along with his academic seriousness, was part of the enduring contrast with his brothers. Rotund, mischievous, unremarkable in school, Donald "liked to get out and play with the other boys while Richard would sit at home and read," a friend remembered. Harold had come to write poetry and tinker with a crystal set but remained an indifferent student. "He was a leader but not a serious kind of a person. He liked to play and roughhouse and do things like that," one classmate said of him. Fair-skinned like his father, talkative and likable, Harold "sort of took the stage if he was around, a little bit more than Richard," Edith recalled, at the Milhous family gatherings that were ritual on Whittier Boulevard at Christmas and other occasions. Beside them both, Richard seemed all the more sober-minded and, sometimes, vulnerable for it. "I actually never can recall him laughing and having fun, too much, except whooping it up when we were playing boats or playing cars," said Virginia Shaw. "The older brother, Harold . . . was just full of fun." Floyd Wildermuth told the story of how he and Harold, both eleven and playing in the lemon grove, exploited seven-year-old Richard by betting he could not bring them cookies or milk from the house before they counted to a hundred. As they began the count he eagerly ran off, and they picked up the numbers near the end as he hurried back with the treats. "He was very competitive in fact, so we would always make a game out of this," Wildermuth said. "He'd get in there all puffing, you know, but he'd always win. That way we'd never have a problem with him the next time we wanted him to run an errand." Whether from some sense of slight or plain rivalry, the competitive urge was there early and strong. "When he played, he played hard; he always played to win," thought a cousin who saw Richard often, both "down home" at the Milhouses' and in Yorba Linda. "He was sensitive, very sensitive, but he had a real desire to win."

As the brothers grew older they grew apart and into very different children and adolescents. Family and friends would recall Harold or Don with warmth, affection, closeness, Richard with descriptions of his "seriousness." The exception was always Richard's own loving attention to the baby Arthur. "The first two or three years of my baby brother's life are rather indistinct in my memory," he wrote later, "for I was engrossed in the first years of my grammar school education." But he had spent hours watching the infant and playing with him, and later pushing him in an old wire-wheeled wagon about the small yard and dusty paths around the bungalow. He traced with fascination the physical changes and growth in the new brother, including "how he learned to roll over, then to crawl, and finally to walk." Cecil Pickering remembered that Arthur in Yorba Linda was a "weakly" baby, often ill and "badly spoiled because they didn't want him to cry, you know. . . . He just got terribly spoiled until people didn't like to go around." Yet Richard continued to adore and care for his youngest brother, who between bouts of illness and irritability would come to seem, like him, a distant and solitary child.

Their play at home, like so many children in the tract, centered on the Anaheim canal, "that miserable irrigation ditch," Mary Guptill had called it as she and Hannah were "constantly on the alert" to keep the small Nixon boys from falling in. Little more than three feet deep but ten feet wide with steep dirt sides, it seemed to many a peril. Soon after he got his Ford, Frank backed it out from the garage he built behind the bungalow a few feet from the canal, drew too close to the crumbly bank, and braked helplessly as the car sank into the ditch. Ever afterward, Hannah would wait to seat herself or the boys in the car until he had it well clear of the water. Being in the ditch or the larger reservoir a mile and a half west of the Nixon house was strictly forbidden by the Anaheim Union Water Company, its *zanjero* patrolling the banks on the lookout for drowned cats and squirrels or swimming children. Yet "no child in his right mind ever saw that stream, flowing as it did . . . through a countryside that was still semi-arid," said Jessamyn West, "without thinking of swimming." Despite parents and the water company, they all swam and waded, teaching other children to do the same. "Richard and his older brother Harold defied the law and spent many a happy summer hour floating down that forbidden stream," West remembered.

But the ditch would also be the scene of their harshest encounters with their father's temper. When the ocean breeze was right it brought Frank's hollered orders to neighboring houses. "But he never yelled at them cross," Cecil Pickering recalled the wafting sounds. "Now boys, you know you mustn't do that. . . . Now boys it's time to wash the dishes." Yet he had once whipped Harold so hard that the boy's screaming could be heard through the neighborhood, and as the three older sons grew to school age, spankings and punishments became more common. More than once he angrily pulled them from the ditch. "I have seen Frank mighty upset with the kids when they went swimming in the ditch. He would yank them out pretty severely," Merle West recounted. "This bothered me because it seemed like he was overdoing it a little bit. . . . But he yanked them out mighty fast . . . he sure yanked them out." Hannah's sister Elizabeth Milhous Harrison looked on in alarm as he plucked out the boys and then angrily tossed them back in, yelling, "If you want water I'll give you enough." "Frank, you'll kill them, you'll kill them!" their aunt had screamed at him.

Like the Milhous relatives, Richard was to tell the story of the dousing, making light of it to friends yet writing later of his father, "It was his temper that impressed me most as a small child." To the boys' playmates the scenes at the ditch presented a frightening figure. "As a kid I can definitely remember that we were kind of afraid of Frank, he was quite a disciplinarian," Joe Johnson said. "We knew that we had to behave ourselves or we might get thrashed." Paul Ryan remembered his "awful temper. He was an awful rough guy, but it was just his way." The punishments continued, though less and less for Richard. "I got the strap," he said once. But from the early episodes in the Anaheim ditch he had begun to avoid or deflect his father's wrath. "I learned early that the only way to deal with him was to abide by the rules he laid down," he would say. "Otherwise I would probably have felt the touch of a ruler or the strap as my brothers did." Years afterward, Yorba Linda memories of Frank's temper still vivid, Hannah acknowledged that her husband "would not hesitate using the strap or rod on the boys when they did wrong, although I don't remember that he ever spanked Richard."

While he was beginning school with praise and promotion, their life in Yorba Linda was otherwise ending in failure and hardship. In 1919 Franklin Milhous died, and with his death, almost symbolically, the lemon grove he had given Frank Nixon seven years before came to maturity an obvious failure, the trees and fruit weak and stunted. Many of his friends agreed it was not Frank's fault, that the original rootstock was too frail, that the soil was notoriously bad. There were other poor plots, other failures nearby. "All of us were citrus ranchers with a minimum of citrus knowledge," said Ralph Shook. Frank Nixon had been "intelligently industrious." But others thought the ranch might still have been saved. The Pickerings had poured fertilizer on their land to open the stubborn soil, including manure from their own animals, and urged Frank to do the same. "I won't buy fertilizer until I raise enough lemons to pay for it," Mrs. Pickering heard him say repeatedly. But then he couldn't raise the lemons without the fertilizer. Alarmed at his anemic grove, Frank had asked advice from the local Sunkist packinghouse manager, Stephen Skidmore, who also told him that the hill badly needed fertilizer and nutriments. "I guess Frank Nixon thought that maybe they would grow without all that. He didn't do anything to help the trees," Skidmore's wife recounted. "Mr. Nixon could be a very stubborn man," she thought. "The result was that later he lost his grove." He had ignored the advice, she and her husband concluded, "because he was Mr. Nixon."

Late in 1919 Frank abandoned the orchard and his piecework and became a roustabout for Union Oil in its lucrative new fields in the area. The nearest gushers and pumps could sometimes be heard from Yorba Linda, an audible drum of prosperity and sometimes sudden riches thumping over the quiet tract with its struggling or aborted groves. Like the citrus gold coast, oil seemed a miracle within ordinary reach. The Nixons and Shaws had walked down excitedly one Sunday with the rest of the settlement to see a well sunk inside the town site. Eldo West later sold the rights to one of his orchards for $5,000, and the story would be told, almost certainly apocryphal, that Frank Nixon was offered $45,000 by a driller for the rights to the hillside acreage and turned it down with plans to sink his own well. But no oil was ever found on the West land, or on most of the tract's rolling terrain. "We didn't know the people who struck it rich in oil. That was fairy tale stuff," a Yorba Lindan would say afterward. They were left, as many of them had been from the start, working for someone else.

Out of humiliation and necessity, Hannah went to work at the Sunkist lemon packinghouse in Yorba Linda, at intervals taking Richard or even Donald with her both to be watched and to work as sweepers. Large cavernous buildings crouching among the groves, chilled and dampened by the primitive refrigeration of the time, the basin's packinghouses were an early and visible emblem of its emerging caste economy, the jobs consigned largely to Mexican labor or poorer migrants and divided in a well-known hierarchy from sorters to packers to managers and marketing associations, all seeming to match the social strata in the community outside. Both for the reality and the symbolism, the houses were already the focus of labor agitation. The year Hannah went to work in the lemon house in Yorba Linda, 1920, the town had awakened one morning and buzzed ominously to find a large *IWW* painted during the night on the building wall, the "I Won't Work" slogan and initials of the Wobblies, the era's radical International Workers of the World who were conducting local union organizational campaigns.

Hannah Nixon was now one of the packinghouse laborers, the quiet daughter of Franklin Milhous who dressed her son in bow ties and velvet-collared coats and insisted on his proper Christian name. The hours were long for meager wages, and she returned home in the evenings, past the groves, to face an often fretful Arthur and a messy house. It had been "up to Mr. Nixon and the boys to do the housework," Cecil Pickering remembered, but "Well, you know, they couldn't keep it clean." Mary George recalled that the job gave her no chance for school activities, though she seemed to want to participate. The effect of the packinghouse on Richard was physical revulsion. Already given to motion sickness that would seize him throughout childhood, he frequently became nauseated at the roil and churn of the packing machinery. He remembered one period as "sixteen weeks of misery." He and Donald also worked in 1920 and 1921 as child pickers in bean fields and citrus groves, and talked about it openly afterward. "We would work twelve long hard hours to earn that one dollar," he once told an interviewer, adding with a grin, "I still hate the sight of string beans." But neither he nor the rest of the family spoke about his mother in the packinghouse. In memory and myth, their hard times from 1919 to 1922 would be defined by the respectable failure of the yeoman lemon ranch, and the father who went to work for Union Oil. For the Milhous pretense of the time, as for later political images, the packinghouse, with its sounds and smells and graffiti of another world, did not fit.

He wrote in his memoirs that their life in Yorba Linda had been "hard but happy," and that with a cow and garden "we had plenty to eat despite our low income," but otherwise gave no account of their last years on the tract. They had little help from the Milhouses after Franklin's death, though he left a bequest that would maintain Almira for twenty years as well as other donations, including a $2,000 scholarship fund for Milhous descendants at Whittier College. Hannah struggled to maintain appearances, dressing her boys neatly if only to send them out to play in the dust. "I think of the Nixons as being a spotlessly clean family. I mean morally, too," Virginia Shaw reflected. "Even though we kids played in the dirt, they'd look clean." How much the sons were aware of their circumstances is unclear, though their own work and their mother's resort to the packinghouse marked a decided change. By several accounts Richard was increasingly self-conscious. He was now at pains to close the kitchen blinds to keep from being seen doing the evening dishes. "Richard was ashamed for people to know he had to wash dishes," said a neighbor. "To Harold it didn't make much difference."

Hannah continued to return periodically to the Milhous home in 1921 and 1922, once for a longer interval and appearing "tired to death with her boys," recalled a relative who saw her there. In the spring of 1922 she approached old Whittier friends of the family, the Mundts, about selling a lot on the southeastern corner of Whittier Boulevard and Leffingwell Road in East Whittier, scarcely three miles from her mother's house and the college. For weeks they had discussed trying to run a gasoline station in the area, and Frank had also pondered a site in oil-booming Santa Fe Springs, standing for hours along the street in front of both locations carefully counting the traffic. But the East Whittier property, with no other station along a growing eight-mile stretch, was the busier, and they chose it. They sold the Yorba Linda hillside that May at a loss, borrowed $5,000 from a Whittier bank on Hannah's family backing, and left the bungalow by the ditch when school was out.

Later there were disparaging stories about Frank Nixon's failure in Yorba Linda. Though oil was never discovered on the hill, both Hannah and Richard would tell writers that a strike had come in after they left, and that the family might have been wealthy. Again, when oil was found in fact on the Santa Fe Springs station site they had passed over, there were more tales of Frank Nixon's improvidence and the family's narrowly missed riches, though the decision to choose East Whittier had been Hannah's as well and the initiative on the boulevard property hers to begin with. Frank's friends were always kinder and more accurate. He had "simply starved out," said one. "Practically everybody, everybody in fact that I knew, liked Frank Nixon, liked the whole family you know," said Hoyt Corbit. "It was considered quite a loss to the little town of Yorba Linda at the time they moved away."

After they were gone, the family feelings were ever tangled, sometimes cryptically bitter. When Richard came back to the tract as a young man, he reminisced with old acquaintances about his father's stunted grove and what it had cost. But they were never quite sure whether he was talking about the Janss deception, or some other fraud, or even, for that matter, his Milhous grandfather, "Mr. Rancher," as he was known in Whittier, who had set a stubborn, unschooled Frank Nixon and his lemon trees on the notoriously poor ground of a Yorba Linda hillside. "The rancher," Richard Nixon would say repeatedly, "was a liar."

3

East Whittier, 1922–26

risk cities of the gringo spread their great, wide thoroughfares to the sun" is how a travelogue described Whittier and neighboring towns in the early 1920s, "neatly paved and enlivened with crowds of crisp-looking girls, healthy, fresh and clean as the air itself, and happy in well-starched blouses or clean muslin frocks." Part of the basin's exultant self-promotion at the time, the portrayal was not simply tourist fiction. The Whittier to which the Nixons took their sons in the summer of 1922 held in many ways the sweet-scented promise of the region.

Still largely rural, the settlement had grown into a composed grace and prosperity. Nearly five thousand lived along the leafy, flower-covered blocks leading off the small business district, another twenty-five hundred in outlying areas like East Whittier. "It was one of the prettiest towns in California then," a Los Angeles artist recalled. Tall palms draped the college hillside, and Whittier Boulevard was paved. At dusk a rosy haze hung over the San Gabriel River. Down the slope from the college and town, out the boulevard and the few dirt roads that crossed it, groves of mature citrus and walnuts lined the way mile after mile, broken only by patches of olives or barley or an occasional house and garden. In the pure cool light after a rainstorm, it could all be seen from the heights above the college, the symmetry of the glistening orchards and still-scattered towns, horizon to horizon, east to west, ending at the thin, foamy line of the ocean breakers off Long Beach. At every turn the air was heavy with the perfume of the empire. "In the springtime on a warm evening," a Whittier teacher would remember, "one almost felt like a June bride to go out and get that wondrous odor of orange blossoms."

In 1920 nine packinghouses operated in and about East Whittier, processing as much as $9 million in citrus a year for area growers. Whittier proper stood a few miles apart from the lucrative orchards, and grew slowly up its hillside, building banks and stores, lodges and societies, schools and churches—above all churches. First Friends had long since left the little clapboard building where Hannah felt her spiritual awakening. Its eighteen hundred members now met in an imposing cathedral-like edifice, and continued to dominate the ethos, government, and commerce of the town, standing guard with sixteen other denominations over Whittier's ever rigid civic morals. When returning Whittier doughboys were honored in 1919 with a banquet at the public high school, and in the joy of their homecoming pushed back tables to dance to improvised music, the high school principal had been promptly and roundly condemned from pulpit to school board for allowing such an outrage.

The virtual theocracy of the town fortified as well its bigotry and caste distinctions. At pains to deny that local usage gave any pejorative meaning to the name "Jimtown"—in a sense the basin equivalent to the South's "niggertown"—a Whittier city history at the end of the decade felt constrained to pronounce the Mexican settlement on the San Gabriel "long a rendezvous for bands of Gypsies and undesirables." Mexican laborers or black shoeshine boys worked in Whittier by day and returned at nightfall to Jimtown or Los Angeles. "They just knew they weren't wanted, thank you," recalled Forrest Randall, who grew up in the town in the twenties. In a community where Quaker founders had welcomed "all" twenty-five years earlier, there were still no encroachments on the white heights. Uptown, formal property covenants kept out nonwhites. On the edges of the town, what local bankers and realtors would later call "unwritten agreements" confined Mexican citrus workers to isolated colonies on the large ranches.

Race and class also took their separate church pews. Whittier congregations remained devoutly white, conducting occasional missionary work in Jimtown as if it were a foreign country. Even within the fold, First Friends plainly disdained the poorer, smaller East Whittier Friends church farther down the boulevard and discreetly maintained for years a gold coast of seats for wealthy members. "There was a pecking order also inside the Society of Friends," recounted Paul Smith, then a young Quaker history professor at Whittier College. "You would go to the Quaker meeting in Whittier, for example, and some of the better-to-do would be in one section of the sanctuary, which was theirs. If you got over there, you might be snubbed. . . . So, there was this cleavage within the various classes of people living in the city of Whittier, and even within the Quaker people."

After the flux of the First World War and the distant thunder of revolutions in Europe and Russia, small towns of the basin seemed in the twenties to hive up in their sunny prosperity, inward, jealous, sometimes fearful pockets of the southern California dream. At nearby Anaheim, the municipal pool was ceremoniously drained and filled with fresh water after the one day of the week Mexican children were allowed to swim. There, too, the Ku Klux Klan governed the city during the mid-twenties. Founded in a men's Bible class of a local church, the Anaheim Klavern staged mass rallies for white supremacy and anti-Catholicism and spread the Klan throughout the basin with a recruitment and popular ardor matched only in the Deep South. Like Yorba Linda, Whittier at once belonged to the region, felt those currents, took on some of the cast by sheer proximity, yet in its hardened piety remained insulated and aloof. On the surface, the town was a narrow, simple place, its economy controlled by a few, its churches overflowing, its college sedate, its precincts yet untainted by a movie theater. "There was no particular poverty or disgrace about Whittier at all," Forrest Randall concluded. "We always had the boys' school down there, but that was all right; we were doing good for the poor little criminals." If crosses burned in the darkness close by in Anaheim, Whittier's children of the era remembered more clearly night softball games. Many of them grew up, recalled Hubert Perry, later a classmate of Richard Nixon, "really without a knowledge of what went on fifty miles away."

They stayed for several months with Almira at the old Milhous home in Whittier while Frank began to build a house a few blocks away on South Painter. But he soon abandoned the nearby site, which would have placed them in a pleasant neighborhood just down the hill from the college, and put up instead a small wooden house and garage behind the gas station three miles out the boulevard. His buildings were plain and gray and faced west onto Leffingwell Road, later called Santa Gertrudes. The house had a single small bedroom, a living room, and a kitchen with bare wooden counters. An outside stairway led to a dormitory bedroom over the garage where the boys slept. Some upholstered chairs were now added to the austere wooden furnishings of the Yorba Linda bungalow. Visitors would remember an ordinary middle-class home of the era, plain rugs on the floor, an oilcloth covering a big kitchen table, an upright mahogany piano only Richard would play, Hannah's neatly ironed antimacassars shielding chair backs and arms.

They sat on less than an acre, an islet in the sea of citrus. South sprawled the Leffingwell Ranch, on five hundred acres a model of the basin orange and lemon plantations, complete with its own experimental laboratory, factory for sprays and fertilizers, fire station, and some two hundred Mexican laborers housed in company cabins. From the second-story dormer the boys could see the railroad spur leading into the ordered groves and hear the sharp screech and crack of the cars taking on California's export wealth. To the north was the Murphy Ranch, four times larger than Leffingwell's. Between the great ranches they were nearly alone. Across the street was the East Whittier Friends Church. But the boulevard ran east and west for long deserted stretches of nothing but the groves and ranches. Their three pumps and tire rack, thought Paul Ryan, who visited them from Yorba Linda, were "just like a filling station out in the desert."

With the nearest rival gasoline miles away, Nixon's Service Station prospered from the thickening traffic out the single paved road connecting Whittier and the small settlements to the east. "We used to have the customers lined up waiting for gas," Don would remember. During one two-week period after they opened, Frank recorded some $2,500 in tire sales. Farmers soon left produce and citrus to be sold, and Nixon's began to stock bread, canned goods, even thread and socks, adding an old re- frigerator to hold soda, eggs, and milk. By 1925 it had become almost as much grocery as gas station. When East Whittier Friends decided to build a larger church, Frank purchased the old frame church building and moved it across the boulevard, crafting it onto the façade of the station and con- verting the sanctuary into Frank Nixon's General Merchandise.

In the autumn of 1922, Richard entered the fifth grade at East Whittier School, walking and later bicycling nearly two miles down the boulevard. Classically southern Californian, the school was a handsome Spanish Co- lonial structure with tile roof, graceful portico, and elaborate landscaping by a local Japanese gardener. "I can remember him coming in and getting right to work," said Blanche Burum, Richard's teacher that year who thought him "rather quiet" and a serious, outstanding student "especially interested in history and geography." As in Yorba Linda, his attendance was nearly perfect and seemingly not interrupted by the common childhood illnesses.

The boy he was becoming was etched in two very different letters written within two months surrounding his eleventh birthday in the winter of 1923–24. The first, on November 19, 1923, was addressed to his mother while she was on one of her recurrent retreats to the Milhous family home. Obviously modeled on a children's dog story, it was the pitiable cry and fantasy of a lonely boy.

> My Dear Master:
>
> The two boys that you left me with are very bad to me. Their dog, Jim, is very old and he will never talk or play with me.

One Saturday the boys went hunting. Jim and myself went with them. While going through the woods one of the boys triped and fell on me. I lost my temper and bit him. He kiked me in the side and we started on. While we were walking I saw a black round thing in a tree. I hit it with my paw. A swarm of black thing came out of it. I felt pain all over. I started to run and as both of my eys were swelled shut I fell into a pond. When I got home I was very sore, I wish you would come home right now.

Your good dog
Richard

A few weeks later, he addressed quite another letter to the *Los Angeles Times* in response to a want ad:

Whittier, Calif.
Jan. 24, 1924

Times Office
K. Box 240

Dear Sir

Please consider me for the position of office boy mentioned in the Times paper I am eleven years of age and I am in the Sixth grade of the East Whittier Grammar School

I am very willing to work and would like the money for a vacation trip. I am willing to come to your office at any time and I will accept any pay offered. My address is Whittier boulavard and Leffingwell road. The phone number is 5274. For Reference you can see Miss Flowers princaple of the East Whittier School

Hoping that you will accept me for your service, I am, Yours Truly,

Richard M. Nixon

It was the conventional diligence of the second letter—rather than the dark dismay of the first—that continued to mark his performance in school. In the middle grades he got his first taste of public debate, what would be an almost lifelong avocation, and he excelled from the start. Assigned to uphold that "It is better to rent than to own," he immediately asked advice of his father, who ardently believed just the opposite yet worked late into the evening at the kitchen table helping Richard marshal his case. In another debate, whether insects were more beneficial than harmful, he researched the topic in the Whittier library and on his own initiative tested the points with his uncle, Philip Timberlake, a respected local entomologist.

He began to do his homework back in a small office that had been the bottom of the old church belfry. Friends and family would remember him there throughout his school years, a lone boy off to himself, lost in study. His classes at East Whittier, steeped in the moralism of effort and ambition, reinforced both. In the fall semester of the seventh grade under Lewis Cox, an energetic young instructor, he was taught for the first time the U.S. Constitution and the framework of government and politics. He long remembered the teacher and the first academic exposure to what would be his profession. Yet reflecting years later on what Cox had taught him, he thought not of the subject but rather of "the importance of fighting hard all the time and working hard all the time."

The same ethic dominated his childhood reading. He would remember a particular fondness for Albert Payson Terhune's dog stories, tales of simple heroism and loyalty written in 1919 and 1920. But his favorite author was Clarence Buddington Kelland, whose fiction he read almost in series before 1930. Kelland began writing free-lance in 1915 and made a fortune with sixty novels and more than two hundred short stories, largely in the *Saturday Evening Post* and *The American* magazines. Between 1940 and his death at eighty-two in 1964, Kelland would be a prominent conservative Republican, one of Herbert Hoover's closest friends who denounced the New Deal as a "tapeworm" and "a center of fifth-column activities." Later, in a strange and dramatic irony, he was to cross Richard Nixon's political rise behind the scenes at a historic moment. But the author's far earlier influence was in the model and world he had created for an avid young reader in East Whittier in the 1920s.

A single character underlay Kelland's long and lucrative career. Beginning as Efficiency Edgar, evolving into Mark Tidd, boy sage, and then Scattergood Baines, who first appeared in 1920 and whose stories Nixon remembered in particular, the hero and his moral were plain. A shrewd, thrifty, achieving young Yankee who craftily pretends to a certain ingenuousness, Scattergood invariably triumphed over evil or folly. *The New York Times* called him "a Down East cross between Machiavelli and Confucius." Book after book, crisis after crisis, he was innocent and respectfully self-effacing while canny and astute. In an era of headlong change and increasing complexity, and a full two decades after the passing of Horatio Alger, Kelland still proffered the tried American nostrums of intelligence and persistent application. With both, as one title announced, *Scattergood Baines Pulls the Strings.*

In other books published in the early twenties outside the Scattergood series, novels that were also read behind the Nixon store, Kelland sometimes took his old-fashioned protagonists into the sinister politics and sedition of the new century. In *The Highflyers*, vigilant Potter Waite, the son of a U.S. senator and wealthy auto manufacturer, thwarts a German spy conspiracy in the shadow of World War I and alerts a prosperous, complacent Detroit to the lethal danger in its midst.

> He studied and weighed the manifestations of public consciousness in Detroit, smug, wealthy, inaccessible Detroit. Detroit was on no exposed coast . . . was safe from invasion . . . did not share the fears and the excitement of the seaboard. . . . Submarine sinkings were academic affairs in Detroit: bomb plots, the incitement of labor to violent unrest, the torch of the plotter, were matters that affected her more nearly. There were those in high places who knew that the stealthy eye of Germany's army of moles was on the city: that they tunneled underneath the city's feet, sinister, frightful.

Like Kelland's heroes, Richard continued to win the approval of his elders for his seriousness of purpose and the resulting high grades at East Whittier. His mother and father regularly checked the boys' school papers, Hannah characteristically the more patient but Frank typically emphatic in his encouragement and delight in success. "He always admired educated people. He was more interested in my education than my career," Richard would recall long afterward. "Never a day went by when he did not tell me and my . . . brothers how fortunate we were to be able to go to school," he said of his father in this period. "I was determined not to let him down. My biggest thrill in those years was to see the light in his eyes when I brought home a good report card."

It was a bond that would be his alone. Harold and Don continued to be indifferent students. Richard's resolution and earnestness set him apart more and more, though in these earlier years in East Whittier there was still much of the childhood flavor of Yorba Linda. Together with neighborhood children they carved out a makeshift tennis court on the rest of the lot south of the house along Santa Gertrudes, played football in the road, lay in the hay of a nearby barn swapping stories. Living in La Habra, Lyle Sutton remembered Harold Nixon with Richard and Don and other East Whittier boys organizing sandlot rivalries with La Habra in basketball or baseball, and then the groups meeting in a "clubhouse" that was the Nixon dormitory over the garage. Harold ingeniously rigged a microphone to play through a radio speaker. They put the set in the store, and with Richard playing the piano as background music, staged from the house mock radio programs that fooled customers or delivery men with scripted announcements about the latest lines of meat and bacon at Nixon's.

"They were fond of each other, of course, I suppose," a cousin said of the Nixon brothers, "but I don't think they were ever very, very close." Floyd Wildermuth noticed Harold's relish at getting away from his brothers to rent horses from a Mexican family in La Habra and ride the still-open countryside. Don would recall that "Dick was the peacemaker. When we had fights with neighbor boys, he would step in and talk us out of it. And he did not explode himself." But a year after they had moved to East Whittier, his usually quiet, conciliatory brother had flashed in pent-up anger. "He wouldn't argue much with me, for instance, but once, when he had had just about as much of me as he could take, he cut loose and kept at it for a half to three quarters of an hour. He went back a year or two listing things I had done. He didn't leave out a thing. I was only eight, and he was ten." As in Yorba Linda, Richard's clear favorite was Arthur. He watched the youngest brother in East Whittier continue to rebel against his parents' image of him. When Arthur's long baby hair was finally shorn in a boy's haircut, "there was not a happier boy in the state," Richard remembered. Having learned to read and hating the formal wool suits in which he was dressed, the little boy pored over mail order catalogs, his brother noted, "for suits which weren't sticky." In 1923 as the station had begun to stock extra items, Arthur had filched cigarettes from the counter and tried to smoke one in back of the house. Richard recounted the episode with obvious feeling: "Unfortunately for him, one of our gossipy neighbors happened to see him, and she promptly informed my mother. I have disliked that neighbor from that time."

The bookishness that separated Richard from Harold and Don began to distinguish him as well in the frequent and competitive gatherings of the Milhous clan. Reunions of the daughters, or simply Sundays "down home," took on for the children the qualities and ritual of a court. Diminutive and dominant, Almira would sit in the parlor of her large house in a red velvet dress, addressing her daughters in plain Quaker speech, the grandchildren bringing her presents or performing some recital, this one with a small violin and flattering accompaniment by a mother on the piano, that one tendering a piece of art or some other accomplishment. The little levee was in its way modest and warm, yet symbolic of the heavy presence and authority of the family. "It was a matriarchy," Richard, like the other offspring, saw very clearly. It was also, he neglected to add, an assembly of quiet but strong women among the sisters and a perpetuation of the Milhous pretense and vanity. At ten and older he was both drawn into the circle and moved to pull away. "She seemed to take a special interest in me," he wrote later of his grandmother. "She was his real favorite, and I think he was sort of her favorite. I know that he spent a lot of time talking with her," said Sheldon Beeson, one of his cousins who saw the special bond. "I'm sure that she could soon see that Dick had a keen mind." All the Nixon sons visited their grandmother regularly, but "Richard used to go see her especially," an old family friend, Agnes Brannon, recalled. "He liked to talk to his grandmother and I think she was a religious influence." Beginning a long series of gifts he would remember, Almira gave him for his thirteenth birthday "a very welcome five-dollar bill" along with a portrait of Lincoln, her favorite President, and an inscription in her own hand from Longfellow's *Psalm of Life*, which he hung over his bed.

> *Lives of great men all remind us*
> *We can make our lives sublime,*
> *And, departing, leave behind us*
> *Footprints on the sands of time.*

Yet Olive and others would notice him in these years drifting apart from the throng of relatives, "away by himself." Once at the Milhous home, she had called to him to come in as he lay "stargazing" on the lawn on a summer afternoon and with some irritation had to go shake him to break his reverie. "At family picnics," Don recounted, "he would always go off by himself."

They returned from the reunions down the boulevard to an increasingly oppressive regimen at the grocery. "It was small, dark, and old-fashioned . . . [and] would be lost in the corner of a present supermarket," remembered Irwin Chapman, who shopped there. They drew on La Habra as well as portions of Whittier and particularly on the Mexican labor and Anglo overseers at the Leffingwell and Murphy ranches. But trade along the boulevard was uneven and the work hard. To avoid waste, Hannah began to cull the older, decaying fruit to salvage it for pies, and soon her baking—cakes as well as the fresh fruit pies—became the early store's most popular item, adding to their long day. She got up at five in the morning to bake, making as many as ten pies a day on order, with special mince and pumpkin at holidays. Frank began to bake as well. "Come tomorrow morning. Tonight I'll bake some pies and they'll be ready for you," his friend and neighbor Harry Schuyler recalled him telling customers after they had run out. "And they were marvelous pies," added Schuyler. "He baked as good pies as did Hannah, and was quite renowned for his pies."

Alongside their parents the Nixon sons worked with much the same rigor. "As soon as those boys were able to do anything at all they had to work," Schuyler remembered. Harold and Richard pumped gas at the station, and Don joined them working in the store. "So you'd come home from school and go to work and work 'til the end of the day . . . six o'clock when the store closed and then an hour or so afterwards and then after that, studied," Don once described his routine. "We combined that, too, with work early in the morning. It was mostly study and work." At first the grocery was open every day, and they even worked Sundays between morning and evening church services across the street.

With the store as crucible, Frank Nixon continued for a time the physical punishment neighbors had seen along the ditch in Yorba Linda. He was a "thumper," Don and Richard once said, given to flicking the top of their heads with an index finger. "He could be hard on the children—spank them freely and give them cracks," a family friend would echo. As they grew older the clashes turned to quarreling and shouting, often in front of customers. "His biggest weapon was his big voice, and he had a big voice," Floyd Wildermuth remembered. "He had tempestuous arguments with my brothers Harold and Don, and their shouting could be heard all through the neighborhood," Richard later wrote of scenes in the store, adding, "He was a strict and stern disciplinarian and I tried to follow my mother's example of not crossing him when he was in a bad mood." He recalled telling his brothers, "Just don't argue with him. You'll have a better chance of getting what you want out of him in the long run."

Often he simply fled or evaded the conflict. "I can recall that when we'd want Dick to do something, we could never find him," recounted Wildermuth. "We got so we'd hunt him. Dick would hide out. I remember one time, when they had a pumphouse back there, and we found him up in the pumphouse. They had a little room in there with a bed, and we caught him under the bed with a book." But increasingly the growing boys, including Richard, responded in kind. Merle West would recall vividly going into the store to find young Don Nixon trying to "outshout Frank," and the son and father bellowing at each other "like two bulls." "It got so, to tell the truth," Wildermuth said, "the boys got to be about as big a hollerer back as he was." West added, "Now, I've heard Dick talk loud, I heard Dick talk wild down there." The defiance only deepened Frank's frustration. "Now hush, all of you," a family chronicler quoted Hannah trying to silence a dinner table argument. And then the reply by her "rebuked" husband: "You make them hush and I'll hush."

In the 1920s, Frank Nixon grew into a ruddy, thickened man, a shop-keeper in a string-tied apron, and what one niece thought a "slop Jake" heedless to change clothes bloodied at the butchering block. Beginning to suffer the arthritis that would become a slowly mounting agony the rest of his life, he eventually found it painful to stand, and in his misery would sit behind the counter by the cash register or at the kitchen table when he made his pies. "He was made for towering angers," thought one observer, "then stranded amid lettuce and ground beef."

Stranded or no, he managed on the boulevard the same mix of religious and political ardor that had crowded the Yorba Linda church and provoked his friends to think of him as radical. In East Whittier he worked with the Orange County sheriff to organize a Friends Sunday school class among delinquent teenagers and taught it with his usual zest. Having read Ida Tarbell's 1904 muckraking classic, *History of the Standard Oil Company*, he carried products only from the smaller Richfield Petroleum, railed against larger chain grocers and the emerging oil lease scandal of Teapot Dome, advised shoppers to vote for "Fighting" Bob La Follette when the Wisconsin Progressive bolted the Republicans to run for President in 1924. "He often argued vehemently on almost any subject with the customers he waited on in the store," Richard wrote. "I hate Standard Oil and everybody who works for them," Frank would announce, though a number of Standard employees traded at the store, and some quit in anger. "He . . . put politics ahead of business," said Paul Smith. Hannah and her sons watched for more prickly customers entering the store and hurried to take them in tow before Frank could engage them. In any case, many shoppers came to prefer Hannah and made clear their aversion to Frank. "So they just kept a line of people to see her in the store," her sister Jane recalled with some laughter.

Nonetheless, as in Yorba Linda, there was about the man an irrepressible gusto that many, especially the young, found likable, while his Milhous in-laws reacted with scorn. He was loud, thought Helen Letts, who lived nearby, "and yet he made you feel welcome; you know, he was always glad to see you and called you by name." His sister's son, Floyd Wildermuth, saw Frank as simply a typical Nixon "because all the Nixons that I know are like this. . . . That was my mother." Staying with the family for a short time as a boy, Herman Brannon remembered that "Frank used to holler at me just like he did at Don and Dick. . . . It was just Frank's way. I mean, he just couldn't say something, he hollered it."

Nor were the customers always put off. "For many people in the community," recounted still another cousin, William Milhous, "an interesting aspect of going over to their business was the chance to talk and get involved in a discussion." There were also private acts of compassion and goodwill.

He would carry jobless or sick or straitened customers for months or longer on credit. When long sieges of rain left the Mexican families short of food in the Leffingwell cabins, he took them provisions. "Frank would always put on his big boots, shoulder a sack of beans and other things, walk down the road and into the grove where they had their houses, and see that they all had some food," recounted Dr. I. N. Kraushaar, his physician. "This was taken just for granted. It wasn't something to be talked about or to be explained to someone else."

He shouted as well at his quiet wife, though it was far less in anger than out of a deepening dependence. "Something went wrong," recalled Lucille Harrison, "and you could hear him bellowing clear uptown, 'Hannah up there?!' She couldn't be gone five minutes out of his sight without him yelling, because he didn't like to be left in that store alone." There would never be particular displays of physical affection. Yet in the corner store on Whittier Boulevard, as in the bungalow in Yorba Linda, the feelings seemed obvious. "He used to yell at her, too, but he loved her dearly," Mildred Mendenhall, a Milhous relative, said of Frank and Hannah then and afterward. "I can remember one time when she was quite seriously ill, and he was so worried about her. The tears came to his eyes when he talked about her, so you knew how he depended on her and loved her."

Living all the closer to the Milhouses, Frank Nixon was now visibly more jealous and possessive of his wife. He stayed away from many of the family gatherings where his sons were expected to perform. While uptown in Whittier Hannah would drop by to see her mother, but when Frank was along he stayed in the car, soon sounding his impatience. "And Uncle Frank would be out there honking the horn for her to hurry up," a cousin remembered. "Seemed like he was always waiting for her to get back in the car." She went to showers with her sisters and nieces only to excuse herself early, saying she could not leave Frank alone. When she managed to get away by herself to the boulevard house, there was pressure from both sides in familiar tones. "I know grandmother used to get so mad because she'd say, well, they could at least spend a half hour with her poor old mother," said Lucille Harrison, describing the rivalry. "Aunt Hannah would just be getting there, and Uncle Frank would be calling on the phone for her to come home."

Beyond the horn honking and her mother's persistent lament, Hannah's long hours in the grocery were spent holding restless babies, listening patiently to customers' gossip and tales of woe, conscientiously checking sacks of potatoes to be certain buyers were given full measure or better. She, too, carried forward credit for the needy, repaired her family's clothes and cooked their meals, even for a time taught a Sunday school class herself—all with gentleness and grace, a radiating goodness that was to be remembered in East Whittier as it had been in Yorba Linda. She moved through the grocery aisles to placate, appease, mollify, smoothing Frank's stormy wake. "She would make every attempt to avoid an argument," concluded William Milhous. "My husband himself had talents as a debater and used to turn our store into a kind of club where he debated the customers on political issues" is how she spoke nimbly of it years later, "while I tried to soothe them so they would continue buying from us." At the time, she had been staunchly and silently forbearing. "She never complained," recalled a niece who knew her well. "I never heard that woman say, 'Oh, I'm so tired,' and yet she'd show it and you knew she was."

Only after her husband was dead did Hannah Nixon acknowledge how deeply she had felt about Frank shouting at the boys. "And I tried not to yell at my children," she once said. "It does something to a child." In her rich resonant tones she never spoke loudly. "But like my maternal grandmother," Richard recalled, "she could be immensely effective with that voice." Nearly forty years after he wrote his college essay about Arthur, he added a sequel omitted when his mother was still alive. It had been after the youngest brother was caught smoking behind the house on Santa Gertrudes in 1923.

> And my mother had known about it, and so I went and talked to Arthur about it to ask him whether he had and I remember he said to me . . . "if mother knows, tell her to give me a spanking," he said, "don't let her talk to me . . . I just can't stand it, to have her talk to me." And so we always, in that family, in our family, we would always prefer . . . my mother used to say later on that she never gave any one of us a spanking. I'm not so sure, she might have, but I do know that we dreaded far more than my father's hand, her tongue. Not that it was very sharp, but she would just sit down and she would talk very, very quietly and when you got through, you had been through an emotional experience.

In the end, it was an accommodation, even collaboration, accepted by both parents, Hannah never confronting or openly disagreeing with her husband's anger or impulse, yet quietly deflecting them, Frank Nixon incorrigible in his bluster yet sensing the limit of his noisy writ. Echoing several who knew them, Sheldon Beeson recalled the implicit, unspoken bargain struck between Richard Nixon's mother and father:

I think Frank would never concede but what he was the head of the house and that everything was determined by what he said. But he would just make a point-blank statement that this was the way it was going to be. Aunt Hannah knew that it wasn't the way she would prefer it to be, so she would have to go to many extremes to work around what Frank said. . . . Then finally, Frank would rather ignore the fact that things didn't work out the way he had said it would. He would never admit that things were done differently. . . . But quite frequently things were done differently. He would just tend to rather ignore the fact that here they went against his will. He would rather be ignorant of the fact that they had gone that way than to concede that they had done things contrary to what he said should be done. So, he maintained.

Aunt Hannah would never tend to minimize what Frank said or try to degrade him at all in the eyes of the boys. He was the father of the house, and I know she would say, "That's right, Frank, that's right, Frank." . . . But all the time you knew that she was sort of scheming as to how she could kind of smooth this over and go around and do it some other way. There was never an open conflict of authority in the home. . . . I can never remember but what she'd support Frank in the eyes of the boys, but then she knew she had to plan some way that she could discreetly get around what he said they were going to do, and do it in a little different way.

"So I don't think his disciplinary measures went over very good with the boys," a cousin said after years of working and living near the Nixons. "I don't see how in the world some of them, if he had been the disciplinarian he thought he was, would ever have been able to talk to him like I've heard some of them—all of those boys do."

"SOME KIND OF DIVINE DISPLEASURE"

Richard had continued to take piano lessons, but his progress seemed slow to Hannah, and she talked about more advanced work with her younger sister, Jane Beeson, who had studied piano at the Indianapolis Conservatory and was an accomplished teacher. Jane "convinced" his mother, as he wrote afterward, that he should live with the Beesons for a time to take daily lessons from her, and after Christmas 1924 he was bundled off to the Beeson ranch two hundred miles away in Lindsay. The Lindsay interlude, little more than five months to June 1925, was the only period of his childhood spent away from both his parents and outside southern California and the sole interval after the age of nine when he was not working at a job in addition to school.

The Beesons thought him "quite a normal boy," as Jane said later. He took piano lessons and practiced daily on their shiny George P. Bent upright, had violin instruction in nearby Exeter as well, and walked with his cousins a mile and a half to Sunnyside school for the last semester of the seventh grade. Able to play only "little simple things" when he arrived, his Aunt Jane recalled, he was soon into Chopin, playing Christian Sindling's "Rustle of Spring," and later on Brahms and Bach, realizing a competence and fondness for music he would have the rest of his life. More than fifty years afterward, he still played with evident pleasure some of the compositions he learned in Lindsay. Jane also remembered his remarkable interest in the news and politics. Local California papers in early 1925 were full of the Teapot Dome scandal, including the nearby Elk Hills oil reserve where private interests had tried to exploit public land. Richard lay on the floor of the Beeson ranch, newspapers spread out in front of him. "Of course, he was just a young kid, you know. He didn't like what he was reading," Jane recalled. He had told her then, as he would say to his mother about the scandal as well, "When I grow up, I'm going to be an honest lawyer so things like that can't happen."

Hannah and Frank came to take him back to East Whittier in June, and he noted in particular his reunion with Arthur. When they met, Arthur kissed him "solemnly" on the cheek. "I learned later that he had dutifully asked my mother if it would be proper to kiss me, since I had been away for such a long time," Richard wrote about the moment. "Even at that early age," he added in another account, "he had acquired our family's reticence about open displays of affection." As the little brother grew older, they seemed more and more alike. "He was rather quiet and sort of a loner," Olive recalled Arthur. "He wasn't gregarious like Harold or Don . . . he was keen enough and smart enough but he played by himself." She took pictures at a birthday party at the Milhous home that spring. Like Richard, seven-year-old Arthur was often standing apart, alone.

Later that July, Arthur fell ill, suffering headaches and indigestion. After a week he was no better, had lost his appetite altogether, and told his mother he felt unusually sleepy. Alarmed, they called a doctor, who administered a series of tests. Richard remembered his father coming down the stairs from the boys' bedroom after one of the tests, the tears streaming down his face. It was the first time he had seen his father cry. "The doctors are afraid that the little darling is going to die," Frank told them.

They moved Arthur to the small bedroom in the house, and prayer meetings for the child were held at East Whittier Friends. Richard and Donald were sent to stay with Carrie Wildermuth, who now lived in Fullerton. Before they left, the brothers went in to see Arthur, who had rallied briefly and asked his mother for one of his favorite dishes, tomato gravy over toast. They took him the food. "I remember how much he enjoyed it," Richard wrote afterward. Two days later, Arthur called his mother into the bedroom to say good night. "I wish you had another baby," a family friend remembered him telling her. When she asked why, he answered, "So you would stay home and wouldn't be in the store." They talked briefly and he repeated one of their ritual bedtime prayers, "If I should die before I wake, I pray Thee, Lord, my soul to take." That night, in the early hours of August 19, 1925, their aunt roused Richard and Don in Fullerton and hurried them to East Whittier, though too late. Arthur was dead when they arrived home.

"I can still see Richard when he came back," Hannah later said of that night they returned from Fullerton. "He slipped into a big chair and sat staring into space, silent and dry-eyed in the undemonstrative way in which, because of his choked, deep feeling, he was always to face tragedy." Yet he did shed tears later. They buried the little boy in a family plot in Whittier Heights, near Franklin Milhous. "For weeks after Arthur's funeral," he wrote, "there was not a day that I did not think about him and cry. For the first time I learned what death was like and what it meant."

The mother's own grief ran deep. "It's difficult at times to understand the ways of our Lord, but we know there is a plan and the best happens for each individual," she told a neighbor afterward. But Olive, who helped at the store and house during the ordeal, remembered, too, an inner guilt about all the hours her sister had spent in the grocery. They were all working in the store [and] Hannah had feelings of remorse that she hadn't been right with him, not during the sickness, but other times. . . . She never really neglected him at all but a mother could always have those feelings." With a similar sense of responsibility for his son's death albeit typically unconcealed, Frank Nixon soon came to regard it as the punishment of a God angered by their commercial hours selling gas and groceries. His father "half believed," Richard remembered, "that Arthur's death represented some kind of divine displeasure, and he never again opened the station or the market on a Sunday."

Beyond the sorrow and self-reproach of the moment, the death of the youngest brother was to become one of those pivotal events in their lives, shaping decisions and giving force to influences that might have been quite different had Arthur lived. For a time, the boys were taken in by the larger family, spending much of the remaining weeks of the summer at the Milhous home or with the Harrisons, Hannah's sister and husband who had moved just up the boulevard from the grocery. "Their uncle's home was lively and gay," wrote one family friend, "and the scene of many happy childhood days for Dick." But with the resumption of school, he was soon at the old routine of work and study and threw himself into both with a still more noticeable resolution. "I think it was Arthur's passing that first stirred within Richard a determination to help make up for our loss by making us very proud of him," his mother would say. "Now his need to succeed became even stronger."

In the eighth grade he became the president of the class and was voted its "outstanding member," played soccer for East Whittier, and emerged as the valedictorian at grammar school graduation. Asked to write an autobiography for the occasion, he spelled out for the first time the rather precise educational and political ambitions that had taken shape in his grade school years and an echo of what he had told his aunt Jane in Lindsay about becoming an honest lawyer. "My plans for the future, if I could carry them out," he wrote, "are to finish Whittier High School and College and then to take postgraduate work at Columbia University, New York. I would also like to visit Europe [and] I would like to study law and enter politics for an occupation so that I might be of some good to the people."

He was given a Bible by his mother for graduation, but took with him, too, a sense of still boyish mirth, and even some rare irreverence toward family and personal icons. Assigned to write his class history in the spring of 1926, he shamelessly parodied the Longfellow "Psalm" Almira had given him a few months before.

> *Now the lives of great men all remind us*
> *We can make our lives that sort*
> *And departing, leave behind us*
> *Footprints on the tennis court.*

At home the mood was seldom so light. With Arthur's death, Helen Letts recalled, Frank Nixon "became extremely religious, almost to the point of being fanatic." At the same time giving up his Sunday school class and refusing to attend church suppers, which he now believed sacrilegious, he began to give regular and heated testimony in church, rising during the time allotted in the Quaker service to declare to the congregation his trials and comfort. "He did this frequently right immediately following the death," remembered Letts. Hannah seemed "very, very happy" about her husband's resurgent piety, though she did not follow his example of public profession. "She was not the kind who'd stand up in church and talk about her faith as he did," a member of East Whittier Friends said later.

Even without a new fervor following Arthur's death, the family was immersed in the church. Richard and his brothers were across the boulevard for services four times each Sunday at least and once during the week. In junior high he began to play the piano at some services, led Easter sunrise programs conducted by young people, and had perfect attendance at Sunday school and Christian Endeavor. Of "basic conservative evangelical belief," as one of its pastors described it, East Whittier Friends followed the rousing Protestantism of the southern California Quakers. "I had lived where there was a Quaker church," said Blanche Burum, one of Richard's public school teachers, "but these people seemed just like Methodists to me." To Raymond Burbank, a Sunday school classmate and later a Friends minister, Richard now seemed, in his years just before high school, a devoted and thoroughly orthodox young student of that more muscular wing of the faith. "Dick would be the one who could stand up for the position of the church, and know why. He could set them straight," Burbank recalled. His motto, remembered Burbank, was in an oft-repeated verse: "If God is for us, who can be against us?"

To all this his father now added the fire and brimstone—the fevered salvation—of the latest wave of revivalism washing across the basin. He had taken the family from Yorba Linda once to hear the famous Billy Sunday preach his perspiring, throaty sermon on damnation and rescue. Now, punished and agitated by his little boy's death, Frank Nixon was crying for help. Customers would remember him pounding the counter and shouting—often to the dismay of the most evangelical of his Quaker brethren— "We must have a revival, we must have a revival!"

Wintering in southern California after national junkets or simply headquartered in the region's congenial climate of fundamentalism, the renowned revivalists of the era built their opulent temples, drew their enormous following, wielded their often ominous political and social power in the basin throughout the decade. Invariably, wrote one California historian, they appealed to "mostly lower-middle-class people—small shopkeepers, barbers, beauty-parlor operators, small-fry realtors, and the owners of hamburger joints . . . the uprooted, unhappy, dispirited lumpen proletariat." Arriving in Los Angeles in 1922 with two children, an old car, and a hundred dollars, Aimee Semple McPherson, "Sister Aimee," promptly assembled a million dollars in offerings, another quarter million in property, and her five-thousand-seat Angeles Temple. There she drove an ugly devil around the stage with a pitchfork or took the rather lusty lead in a dramatized sermon on Sodom and Gomorrah, all to the excited deliverance of throngs of the faithful, until a staged kidnapping and rescue began her slow scandal-ridden eclipse in 1926. In the same years, the Reverend Robert Shuler with his Blue Ridge drawl commanded one of the largest radio audiences in the world, while leading successful campaigns to drive from office a mayor, a district attorney, and several police chiefs. From the pulpit, he organized public attacks on the California Institute of Technology for teaching evolution, engineered a southern California vote of three to one making the King James Bible compulsory in public schools, and in the end missed only narrowly being elected to the United States Senate. An erstwhile athletic director and preacher's son named Paul Rader also pioneered radio revivals, presided over his own World Wide Gospel Couriers, and from his opulent Hollywood home directed a suitably modern missionary tour by motorcycle among "primitive tribes" of Africa and Asia.

The Nixons attended them all. "They were both fascinated by the evangelists and revivalists of those times," Richard said of his parents, "and often we drove to Los Angeles to hear Aimee Semple McPherson at the Angeles Temple and Bob Shuler, her great competitor at Trinity Methodist church." Though Hannah would go to the mass meetings on occasion, it was Frank who went "faithfully," as Jane Beeson put it, "and took the boys." The rallies and crusades reached a peak the summer of 1926. Richard wrote later that he "never went to bed at night without reading a few verses" of the Bible his mother had given him that spring for eighth-grade graduation.

On a sultry night after he began high school in September 1926, his father drove Richard, Harold, and Don to Los Angeles to hear Paul Rader. There, with his mother absent but in an episode something like her own a quarter century before in small Whittier First Friends, Richard solemnly and emotionally went through his public conversion and reawakening. On Rader's command, the wide-eyed, sometimes wailing, and almost frantic crowd leapt to its feet and surged in the aisles and about the platform for the cleansing rebirth. "We joined hundreds of others that night," he recounted, "in making our personal commitments to Christ and Christian service."

Well before they stood to be saved at Rader's revival, the religion and its moral austerity had already changed the course of the two older sons. A blithe seventeen, Harold Nixon was sociable and winning, in some ways very like his father, friends thought, without the shrill abrasiveness. "Much more of a swinger with the girls than his younger brother," a relative compared him to Richard, while another close family friend saw him as a "headstrong, devil-may-care Irishman." In three years at Whittier High,

Harold had made only middling, sometimes inferior grades, still writing his own sensitive poetry but remaining jovially indifferent to academics. At home, Harold followed the same monotonous round of work and church, though with little of his younger brother's earnestness and diplomacy, quarreling hotly with Frank and having his mother quietly paper it over. He was always eager to slip away with friends to race his stripped Model T Ford that he rakishly "cut down all the way around," said a classmate, "like a bug." Family and friends saw Harold at once as the favorite yet the problem son of the Nixons after Arthur's sudden, haunting death. He did not quite fit the mold, was not quite under control. Even in high school, concluded one family historian, Harold was "too much like his father to live peacefully in the same house."

In their frustration and anxiety, the parents blamed the school and Harold's friends, though both were tamely Quaker, and they turned to finding a suitably religious and disciplined school for Harold's senior year. "Hannah wasn't too happy with some of the things that were going on at the high school, they were a bit too free, too many liberties . . . moral standards were not quite what she liked so she was looking for something else," Olive Marshburn related. "Then also," the sister added, "she felt he needed discipline." Through church and revivalist sources, they discovered Dwight Moody's Mount Hermon School for boys in Northfield, Massachusetts.

A prosperous traveling shoe salesman become international evangelist, father of the Chicago Bible Institute, Moody had established the school in 1881 on a remote bank of the Connecticut River in north central Massachusetts. When he died at the close of the nineteenth century, reverent students in shifts of ten had carried their 230-pound founder in his coffin a mile across the campus to the chapel in bitter December cold, and "Mr. Moody's school," as it was known by ministers and revivalists throughout the country, had lost none of its original spartan spirtualism. There were several respected Quaker academies in the East they might have chosen, but none more sternly evangelical or fundamentalist than the nondenominational Mount Hermon. So persuasive was Moody's conservative theology that the science department still taught evolution according to Genesis and chapel was compulsory five days out of six, with Sunday devoted entirely to Bible study. As if to underscore the severity of it all, an architectural quirk placed the dormitory baths in the basement. In the twenties they took cold showers at five-thirty in the morning, coming back upstairs outside in New England winter temperatures that plunged to twenty below zero, appearing at breakfast after prayers with icicles in their hair.

Here they enrolled Harold in the autumn of 1926, a boy Richard would describe as "never particularly religious." They readily paid the $300

Mount Hermon tuition. "They weren't strapped for money even in those days . . . even though that has been emphasized so much, that wouldn't have held them back," Olive remembered. "They sent him back East to school because they thought he needed a change from the kids he was running around with," Lucille Timberlake remembered. Their concern now changed Richard's life as well. Refusing to see him go down the boulevard to a corrupted Whittier High where they thought Harold had gone astray, they ironically sent him instead to the larger, more cosmopolitan Fullerton Union High School.

4

Intervals—Fullerton, Prescott, Whittier Union, 1926–30

"WE ALL GREW UP RATHER FAST"

Nearly twice the size of Whittier, Fullerton in the mid-twenties was one of the basin's tinted-picture-postcard towns, basking in the wealth of citrus and oil. Its California tiled roofs of the Spanish Mission Revival period seemed, Frank Lloyd Wright once observed, to "give back the sunshine stained pink." There were Japanese truck gardens nearby, a black family or two, several older Mexican families, including Yorbas. But the bustling community and high school—a union or consolidated school that took students from outlying Orange County settlements as well—remained largely white and determinedly middle class. If Fullerton escaped Whittier's prudishness, it was still unmistakably one of the region's enclaves. In 1922 the school district dutifully but at a distance organized an "Americanization" program for surrounding Mexican labor colonies. Classes in English, cooking, or sewing took place in La Habra or Atwood or the distant La Jolla tract, where the "Americanization buildings," with no evident irony, served as segregated social centers and servants' schools for what were called somewhat hopefully "the foreigners in this district."

The high school, which had more than nine hundred students, was one of the most picturesque in the state. Under an ornate Moorish campanile and a colonnade of graceful arches, students went to classes in a campus cluster of separate buildings like a small well-endowed college, the grounds decorated with bright flowers, eucalyptus trees, tall palms. It was among California's most progressive academically, and graduates commonly went on to college, still a rarity for American high schools at the time. Social codes were strict, the girls required to wear middies, the boys expected to be neat but without uniforms. In mild rebellion, the Fullerton boys made a fad of yellow corduroys, worn "until they got so dirty you just couldn't wear them anymore," said a student. Everyone sported those fashionably soiled cords, they recalled later—everyone, that is, except young Richard Nixon, whom they remembered coming over from East Whittier with a "heavy shock of black curly hair" and neat gray trousers obviously washed once or even twice a week. "He never participated, like the rest of us, in dirty cords," a classmate, James Grieves, recounted. "I don't know whether he didn't want to or if his family just wouldn't let him."

He rode a school bus for an hour each way during his freshman year, and then, during 1927–28, went to live in Fullerton with Aunt Carrie Wildermuth, coming back on weekends, all the while working in the store whenever he was at home. Riding the crowded bus, he was fastidious. Richard took "great pains," his mother recalled, brushing his teeth in the morning, gargling carefully, and then asking her to smell his breath "to make sure he would not offend anyone on the bus." He was soon repelled himself by the less cleanly students on his route. "He once said he didn't like to ride the school bus," a cousin related, "because the other children didn't smell good."

His grades were nearly perfect: A's in English, Latin, algebra, and science the first year, one B and the rest A's as a sophomore. "He always sat in the back and he always knew all the answers," a girl in his English class said. There was a dour fierceness of application and ambition about the record. He found geometry difficult and made only B's the first two quarters. But when the teacher once presented a special problem, promising an A for the next quarter for its solution overnight, he worked until 4:00 A.M., got the grade, and finished the course with an A. Raymond Burbank remembered playing touch football Sunday afternoons on Santa Gertrudes right outside the Nixon house and the "remarks and cracks" made by the players about Dick studying inside. Given the nationally used Otis intelligence test his freshman year, he scored 143 out of 160, far above the norm of 117.

Ironically, he received his lowest grades at the beginning of what would be his most memorable course, oral English and public speaking, taught by a young red-haired Ph.D. named Lynn Sheller. Sheller gave him C's at the outset and thought Richard "a serious shy boy" who was clearly "not a born speaker." Yet the teacher soon found him working doggedly to write out speeches with great care and to memorize them. "Nixon overcame his honest humility and became a pretty good speaker," the coach concluded. Stressing simplicity, economy, and repetition in the persuasive speech,

Sheller taught them "to be convinced in what they have to say," and the "importance of choosing just one point to make." "Otherwise," he told them constantly, "people won't remember what you were talking about."

Losing his first oratorical contest without even placing, he went on to win a school title, and finished second in a larger Orange County meet. Forensic success, like high grades, delighted Frank, who "regarded rhetorical skill as a demonstration of superior education," wrote one observer, and began to accompany him to contests, making copious notes on both Richard and the competition. In his public speeches, thought some who heard them both, the son would sound increasingly like the father. Moreover, there were those who felt that Richard had taken on something of Frank Nixon's sheer verbal sparring, flexing fast words and combativeness, contention without conviction. Coming back from a school picnic in the mountains, Alice Walker found Richard arrogantly taking the opposite side in whatever they discussed. "We argued all the way back about which would be more useful to take with you into the wilds—a goat or a mule. Dick said a goat, and then argued in favor of the mule," she recounted. More and more, Helen Letts remembered similar polemics at Christian Endeavor meetings, where he seemed to disagree or provoke a dispute almost apart from what he believed. "I don't think it was because he wanted to be for or against anything, it was just for the argument, really."

By the beginning of his sophomore year he was five foot seven and one-half and weighed more than one hundred forty-seven pounds, a suddenly bulky, almost stout young man for his age who had spurted and filled out in growth over the past year. Living with the Wildermuths, he went out for Fullerton's junior varsity football team, the lightweight B's, as they were called. Comparable in size to most of his teammates, he was a tackle in the line, and a teammate, Robert McCormack, remembered him as "scrappy." But he played little in games, and practice was often a punishing experience. "He used to be the dummy for everybody to tackle. He wasn't coordinated enough for a football player. He had two left feet, I think," recalled Gerald Shaw, his childhood friend who was also on the team. "I don't know of a guy that took a more terrific beating than Dick did," echoed James Grieves. Yet he seemed as indomitable, as determined to play as he was athletically inept. "He'd get knocked down and come right back up," said Grieves. "He was always there, and always there for every practice," recounted another. "I don't know a guy that ever tried so hard, really." He had come to love the sport, reciting team standings and statistics to friends and fellow players, analyzing games shrewdly from the bench.

Yet he remained forlornly awkward with the team, off the field as on it. Virginia Shaw, Gerald's sister, saw him at the B team banquet that year at the old Grant Hotel, sitting among the other players silent and in a kind of wretchedness. He was not accustomed to eating out like this and seemed alone and ignored amid his celebrating teammates. "I remember walking by," she told the story. "No one knew I knew him because I had passed the era of Yorba Linda and I was in Fullerton. I remember sort of hurting inside for him because he sat there so ill at ease at the table, kind of with his head ducked down. I felt sorry that he was feeling ill at ease."

He would find a respite in music and in the Fullerton High orchestra in which he played violin both years. Uniformed in white flannel pants, dark coat, and red bow tie, Richard "was very much at ease, just correct in his attire," recalled Dick Heffern, who sat beside him. When Heffern forgot his own bow tie and wore a polka dot substitute, the conductor exploded, saying that he stuck out like a "sore thumb." Then, during the performance, Heffern impishly ran his violin bow through Richard's neatly combed hair, pushing it in his face as he played. "Don't do that again!" Nixon implored, but Heffern persisted. "Why, we went through the whole piece with the conductor looking at my spotted tie and at Dick's mussed up hair." They became friends, Heffern taking him to concerts in his Model T, meeting later when their colleges played each other, and still later in local clubs and politics.

As a merchant's son, Nixon was squarely in the middle of the economic scale at Fullerton. Especially in the more rural areas where truly poorer children dropped out of school after the lower grades, simply going to high school in itself created a caste distinction in the basin. "We thought we were grown up," Heffern said, "because a lot of the boys and a lot of the girls would get married at the end of grammar school, or they would be working in the oil fields around Yorba Linda, Placentia, and Richfield." At that, a nucleus of the students at the high school had been raised together in relatively prosperous Fullerton. Forming cliques, they looked down on the bus riders from outlying settlements like La Habra or East Whittier. "We were considered the farmers," Heffern remembered. The orchestra, the football team, and forensics sometimes allowed them to break onto the edges of the school society, yet lines remained rigid. "There was a certain group that always was in everything, you know," Helen Letts described it. "The rest of us sort of were on the outside looking in."

Heffern and others thought Richard "pretty much a loner" and could not remember him dating girls at Fullerton or going to "any of the social functions the rest of us went to." "I never could get up the nerve to ask them for dates," Richard would explain about high school social life. Once he was paired with Harriet Palmer on an outing to an amusement park at Long Beach. Her mother had made her promise not to ride the roller coaster. "All the others went but, even though I wanted to go, Dick made me stay on the ground," she told the story. "True to form, he wouldn't let me disobey my mother. Then, when the others came back, he went for a ride alone." At Fullerton he was still self-consciously, childishly averse to girls, though often in their company to tell them so. "Oh, he used to dislike us girls so!" Harriet remembered. "He would make horrible faces at us. As a debater his main theme . . . was why he hated girls. One thing was strange, though. He said he didn't like us, but he didn't seem to mind arguing with us."

In April 1927, Harold Nixon returned suddenly from Mount Hermon, sick with a cough and sore throat that became the onset of tuberculosis. After an uncertain period in East Whittier, his parents began a fearful, fitful search for treatment in the basin. For the few extra feet of altitude, Hannah first took him to the small guest house of a family friend in the Puente Hills a few miles north of the boulevard, where the two of them lived for a time. There followed a stay at what Richard remembered as "an expensive private sanatorium" at La Crescenta in the San Gabriels northwest of Pasadena. Frank would not consider the basin's public clinic. "My father refused to let him go to the county tuberculosis hospital, one of the best in the country," Richard wrote in his memoirs, "on the ground that going there would be taking charity." He once told an interviewer, "My dad was an individual—he'd go to his grave before he took government help. This attitude of his gave us pride, maybe it was false pride, but we had it." After La Crescenta, they moved Harold again briefly to a cottage in California's Antelope Valley below the Tehachapi Mountains and astride the old Owens River aqueduct.

Between the periods in the sanatorium and cabins, they waged a losing battle to control Harold's own care of himself. In the intervals of apparent remission he was more irrepressible than ever, at one point taking temporary work nearby fumigating citrus groves, a job hazardous even to those with healthy lungs. "Very dangerous work, people died," said a family friend. "He wasn't supposed to fool around with airplanes, but every opportunity he would run off to the airport. Flying airplanes was his passion. He always was hanging around airports very much against his father's orders."

In the spring of 1928 Harold seemed to decline again after a brief recovery. Both to effect a cure and to control him more easily, they decided Hannah would leave the two younger boys with Frank and go to care for Harold more than four hundred miles away at Prescott, Arizona, a small mountain resort then known as a haven for tubercular patients.

More than a mile high in a looming pine forest above the Arizona desert, Prescott at the close of the 1920s was a town of seven thousand, a former territorial capital that had become one of the West's fashionable if out-of-the-way tourist attractions. Its summers were cool and dry, the winter months crisp and bright, children's voices on the shady old streets carrying far in the clear, high air. Seventeen dude ranches served tourists, while conventions met in town and Tom Mix made movies in the scenic Granite Dells nearby. Each Fourth of July, Prescott's Frontier Days rodeo and carnival swelled the population by thousands. Since before the World War, however, there existed another Prescott under the vivid blue sky, less fasionable and quaint and marked by the small signs unknowing vacationers sometimes found cryptically about the central plaza—"Please use cups."

The sputum cups symbolized the town's more discreet industry, the colony of coughing tuberculars and wheezing asthmatics who flocked to its climate for healing. Those who could afford it went into the cabins of one of several sanatoriums tucked away around town. Other consumptives had begun to gather in an area at the outskirts of Prescott called Pinecrest, where businessmen offered free lots or inexpensive rentals. On a steep hillside strewn with volcanic rock and a carpet of pine needles, streets with Indian names wound tightly about small frame cottages or tiny single-room lunger cabins back among the tall evergreens. Hannah settled in Pinecrest early in 1928, moving with Harold first into a cabin down the hillside, then soon up the slope to a corner house on Apache Drive that she rented for twenty-five dollars a month and where she took in as boarders three other tubercular men around her son's age. The small house was rough-hewn, with indoor plumbing and electricity, two screened porches and a modest bedroom for the boys, but no washer, only a wood stove, and a ladder that let down from a close, cramped attic space Hannah used as her own room. Neither Harold nor the others would be under the regular care of a doctor. Struggling to duplicate what she knew of clinic regimen, Hannah cleaned and cared for her four patients, boiling dishes, disposing of the ever-present sputum cups, hauling wood and coal, scrubbing linens on a washboard. Neighbors remembered her slowly climbing the hill from the Piggly-Wiggly store a mile away, bags of groceries carried wearily on each hip.

Richard was to spend the summers of 1928 and 1929 with his mother and tubercular brother. Entrusting the station and store to the Wests or other hired relatives, Frank also took Richard and Don to visit them as regularly as once a month, making the trek to Prescott at every school holiday or even for weekends in their 1924 Packard. They drove more than four hundred miles and fourteen hours, over the old Sunkist Trail out of San Bernardino and Indio across the California line and the still-free Colorado River at Blythe. Not far into Arizona's desert scrub, the gravel and dirt road lifted out of the river valley and angled northeast across the wasteland toward jagged misty peaks on the far horizon. Green and flowering for a moment in the spring, the desert plateau was burned brown again by June, and they climbed onto the conifers and crystalline air of Prescott as a mountain oasis.

For more than two years, Richard Nixon moved in and out of this world of shared affliction and his mother's enduring sacrifice. While there was no quarantine, no clear medical sense of transmittal of the disease, the uncertainty and fear were tangible in the boiled dishes and buried sputum cups. "I hate to say it but it's sort of like leprosy," said the daughter of a Pinecrest consumptive. "You knew how to live with it." Homes up and down Apache Drive hid the stricken. Verna Hough, whose physician-husband had come to Pinecrest on a stretcher two years before, remembered Richard and Don visiting her house "many times" when they came on weekends that spring of 1928. Richard had been visibly uncomfortable. "He seemed to want to keep his distance from his brother, didn't want to get close to him—or anyone," she recounted.

At the same time, he was outgoing and friendly enough in his own way with other well young people in the neighborhood. "Dick was dark and serious like his mother, real serious. He would try to kid but it would fall flat," Helen Lynch recalled. Soon after he first came with his father, he had walked over to talk with her, climbed a tree, and hung from a low branch like a little boy, betting her she would marry Marshall Clough, a Prescott friend. He explained debate, mused about history "and things that bored me to death." Introduced by Harold to Virginia Green, he "chatted and kidded" and wrote in her autograph book, "Yours till the butter butts, Richard Milhous Nixon." But he never danced or dated any of the girls, they remembered, and struck up no more than passing acquaintances. Marshall Clough, who came to know and like him, thought on first appearance in Prescott he had seemed a "square" or even a "sissy," but soon learned he loved football and had a "keen sense of humor." "Dick was a confirmed Quaker," Clough explained later. "He inhibited his real true feeling."

During the summers in Prescott, he took a series of jobs, "a hard-working young man," Budge Ruffner, a local author, recalled him. "He'd be in a different place whenever I'd see him." At one point he plucked and dressed chickens for a local butcher. For a time he was a janitor and pool boy at the posh Hassayampa Country Club. With its stately clubhouse and meticulously rolled oil and sand golf greens high amid the pine trees and reddish rocks, the Hassayampa was a favorite of the Phoenix rich, "the most exclusive country club in Arizona," thought one longtime resident. His more colorful job would be as a barker at the Slippery Gulch carnival, part of the Frontier Days celebration every July. For as much as ninety cents an hour, he became a practiced, successful tout, one of his booths "the most popular in town," as a later account described it. During the crowded event, Prescott's always hearty backroom poker games, bootleg-ging, and prostitution flourished, the cards and liquor sometimes fronted by the concessions. "Slippery Gulch was a basic education in all forms of gambling," remembered Ruffner, whose uncle had been a renowned Pres-cott sheriff.

Richard often recalled the barker's job but never publicly acknowledged any backroom vice, though it had always been an open secret winked at in Prescott. Marshall Clough, who had a job at Slippery Gulch as well, remembered they had worked only the bingo concession for women and children, and was certain at the time that "Dick would never touch alco-hol." If only as an innocent observer—and there is no evidence he was anything else—the raucous, glossy scene at Slippery Gulch, the opulent tile and verandas of the Hassayampa Country Club were a far different universe than any he had known before. It was the stark contrast between comparatively wide-open Prescott and Yorba Linda or Whittier, between the worldiness and affluence he saw in Arizona and the sedate wealth of the Puente Hills or the Shuler revivals with their iron moralism and lower-middle-class crowds.

He would work at Frontier Days the two summers of 1928 and 1929 and then later a third summer during the Depression for reduced wages. Clough and others remembered him in his free hours around the Apache Drive house quiet and withdrawn. He read, listened to the radio, and rehearsed his debate case. "When drying the dishes he would mumble all the time, practicing," Clough recounted. "They'd have to take the glass out of his hand—practicing both sides." Helen Lynch, who also worked at Slippery Gulch, thought him far less titillated or corrupted than somehow weighed down by it all. "Dick had a rather sad life," she and a friend had come to believe.

In the crowded little house on Apache, the closed, foreboding society of young tuberculars was at once invalid and intense. Ambulatory but rarely out of pajamas and robes, the fevered coughing boys carried on dalliances with neighboring girls, some of them consumptive themselves. Across the narrow street Jessie Lynch, a beautiful, frail seventeen-year-old, fell in love with one of Hannah's boarders, Larry Easton, while Harold tried himself to woo doll-like Jessie and wrote her adoring notes. They all signaled each other excitedly at night with flashlights from their screened porches, and at one point Harold climbed into Hannah's attic room to tap the telephone and eavesdrop on a call between Larry and Jessie, repeating the intimate conversation in full to the astonished young lady soon afterward. There was an abandon and courage, even gaity about them, though the disease and death itself were a hovering presence. Often totally bedridden, Jessie Lynch never began a serialized magazine story for fear she might die before the parts were completed. But Harold would characteristically tease his mother as she resolutely took the boys' temperature each day, heating the thermometer over a flame or in hot water when she turned away and then popping it back with his mouth.

"She was cute then, when she found out what he was doing, and would smile," Helen Lynch recalled. But Mrs. Nixon was usually "stern and strict," she thought. "You didn't play around with her." His mother had not approved of Harold's love letters to the pretty girl across Apache Drive. "She scared me to death," Jessie remembered. "She seemed to me to be very cranky, straitlaced." At the same time, Hannah impressed Marshall Clough as "the most wonderful person I think I've ever met. You wanted to do what she wanted you to do." "She was a hard character in that you got the impression that inside this frail, skinny woman . . . inside was pure steel, pure steel," said a California friend of the family familiar with her life in Prescott. "She was a true Quaker."

With his mother anxiously laboring to give him the prescribed climate and regime, Harold Nixon was charmingly defiant and reckless. When Edith Timberlake and her family visited Prescott on a trip east, he had wanted to go with them on a local sightseeing tour and refused to stay down. "He just insisted and did it. He got up out of bed and went with us," Edith said. His East Whittier friend Ralph Palmer drove over one July Fourth weekend and found that "he wasn't taking care of his health. He was living every moment." Harold built model airplanes and wrote poetry in Pinecrest but also begged to go out on horseback and from time to time rode at a local stable. Their childhood playmate from La Habra, Lyle Sutton, was not surprised his old friend was not following the recommended rest, even under his mother's tireless care. "I didn't think he would stay in bed for a year for anybody, for any reason," he said. Harold was too "strong-headed." "None of them," Grace Bumpus reflected afterward, "took care of themselves."

With their mother nursing Harold in Prescott, the burden of the store fell more than ever on the remaining Nixon sons. Returning from Arizona at the end of the summer in 1928, Richard enrolled in Whittier Union—the school his parents had spurned for him and Harold two years before—in order to be nearer home and work at the grocery, where he took over the purchase of produce and arrangement of the vegetable displays. He rose at 4:00 A.M. and drove twelve miles into the Seventh Street market of Los Angeles in their old Ford converted to a makeshift truck, bargaining with the truck farmers and hucksters at their stalls, returning to wash the vegetables in a tub behind the house and then array them in crates near the entrance of the store before leaving for school. Richard always took "great pains cleaning out the decaying produce and ordering each day's fresh display," his mother remembered. Merle West, who had taken over the service station late in 1928, would be opening up as Nixon came back from his morning run to the produce market, and watched him set up the vegetable counter. "Boy, I mean, old Dick could peel those grimed-up leaves off the lettuce and tomatoes and make them look like new again. He would sprinkle them with water out of the sprinkling can and fluff them up and get the good ones on top." But underneath the practiced efficiency was a loathing. "I never drive by a vegetable stand without feeling sorry for the guy who picks out the rotten apples," he said to friends later. "Dick hated it," his college teacher Paul Smith would say of the routine.

He was also plainly embarrassed by the task. "He didn't want anybody to see him go get vegetables, so he got up real early and then got back real quick," remembered his cousin Lucille Parsons, who worked alongside them in the grocery. She and others saw that Richard also found it distasteful to wait on customers, preferring to work on his father's single thick set of grocery books, a chore that often required extra hours on Sunday afternoons toting bills on an old adding machine in the belfry office. Frank and Don Nixon now both unabashedly wore grocer's aprons. No one could recall Richard putting on an apron from the time he took over the vegetables in the autumn of 1928.

If the grocery was oppressive and sometimes humiliating, however, it had also lifted them out of the poverty of the last years in Yorba Linda, even with the added costs of Harold's illness. "That store did pretty good . . . they did well," said Merle West, who knew the size of some of their accounts with the Leffingwell and Murphy ranches as well as other trade. Profits did depend largely on the family's own work. "I'll tell you why they did fairly well," West added. "It's because they didn't have any outside labor." To keep Harold at La Crescenta sanatorium in 1927, Frank had sold a small parcel of his land south along Santa Gertrudes to Harry Schuyler. But in the same period, he had also invested in three small lots down Whittier Boulevard opposite the East Whittier School and planned to put up small rental houses on the property. With the store, they would never truly be poor.

"My father just about made things pay," Richard once reflected. "It's been said our family was poor and maybe it was," he told an interviewer, "but we never thought of ourselves as poor, and we never had to depend on anyone else." Still, the thread of early poverty and deprivation would run through his political memories of the time. As he once told a national audience, "I recall . . . the Fourth of July we were the only ones in the neighborhood who didn't have any—we didn't have the money frankly—

for fireworks." But Mary Jean Marshburn, Olive's daughter, would remember no less vividly the Nixons coming regularly to the Milhous home on the boulevard on the Fourth: "We had a big front yard and the Nixons seemed able to get more fireworks than we did. They would bring them here; my grandmother loved the fireworks." Lucille Parsons recalled there were times "Uncle Frank wouldn't spend a nickel for a firecracker—that was a waste of money." Even then, though, the Nixon sons had fireworks. "We always had firecrackers, so the boys all came up to our house," she reminisced. "Uncle Frank . . . didn't have to be as tight as he was."

Without Hannah, the father and sons took turns preparing meals, though none could cook or apparently bothered to learn. Richard recalled eating canned chili and soup, spaghetti, pork and beans, frequent fried eggs, and hamburgers. "Odd as it may seem," he told the story later, "I still like all of those things." Many mornings, he would say, "I ate nothing for breakfast but a candy bar." In the same period, he was watching his father grow portly and Donald settle into the round-cheeked young man he was becoming, and Richard developed an abiding vanity and watchfulness about his own weight. Almost paunchy at Fullerton, he now trimmed down noticeably. "He has always watched his diet and his weight very carefully, and has little respect for people who overeat," his mother said later, though it had not been true before her absence. "You just can't get a teaspoon of ice cream into him once he's decided that he has had enough." The tension of the interval was clear. Alone with their father, the brothers fought frequently with Frank and one another. Sheldon Beeson, like others, thought "there was always bickering going on, probably more than in the average family . . . a lot of arguing particularly between Don and Dick."

"The very fact of separation from the rest of us was very hard on my mother," Richard would write in his memoirs, burying their own open unhappiness at the time. They all soon vied to have Hannah return, much as Frank pulled at her impatiently during her visits to the Milhouses. And Harold, dependent like the rest of them, tugged back. "The family couldn't get along without her here, and when she was here Harold thought he just couldn't stand to have her away," one of Harold's friends, Edith Brannon, remembered. "I don't know how she survived, but she did." Richard would once describe the years as redeeming after all: "It was a rather difficult time actually, from the standpoint of the family being pulled apart, but looking back, I don't think that we were any the worse for it, because we learned to share the diversity [sic] and you grew stronger for having to take care of yourself . . . not having your mother to lean on." But he had ended his recollection with a passage that more than hinted at the true feelings regarding his mother's absorption with Harold. "We all grew up rather fast in those years," he remarked, adding in pointed qualification, "those of us who remained home."

"I SUFFERED MY FIRST POLITICAL DEFEAT"

Whittier Union High School in 1928 was emblematic of the town. Like other southern California schools of the era, it was airy, sprawling, and stucco. Yet beyond the façade and flowers, there was a heaviness about the place, a squat, bleak sense of the pious Whittier burghers who presided over the business district a few blocks to the east.

It brought together nearly a thousand students from a growing fifty-square-mile area well beyond the Puente Hills. With no Americanization center like Fullerton's to segregate "foreigners," Whittier was also the only high school for the relatively few Mexican children of the district who went beyond the lower grades, and who made up 10 percent of the student body. They came up the slope from Pico Rivera and other settlements in the bottoms, though rarely going out for sports or attending evening events, the streetcars they had to take on the Philadelphia Street hill all but ceasing to run after nightfall. For the rest of the students, most of them from middle-class families, social life was limited in any case. School board policy still prohibited dances. Wealthier students—some from families flush with new oil profits in Santa Fe Springs, others from old Quaker merchant money in the town—discreetly threw their dinner dances at the Hacienda Country Club in the eastern heights. Officially, Whittier Union prescribed more wholesome habits. Girls in the obligatory middies and boys in white shirts passed school bulletin boards emblazoned with Theodore Roosevelt's stirring motto, which not even the gentlest Quaker seemed to find amiss in the robust economic and civic ethic of the twenties. "Don't flinch, don't foul," read the poster, "but hit the line hard."

At first Richard rode a school bus back and forth along the boulevard, going home immediately after classes and giving up both orchestra and football to help mind the grocery. In working, however, he was hardly alone. "Many, many students except the very rich had jobs," one of the girls at the school remembered. "Most worked every afternoon." By his senior year he had at least escaped the hated bus. "Frank was tired of arguing with the boys about the use of his car," a Whittier friend recalled. With Don entering the high school as a freshman in 1929, their father had bought them an old Ford to make the drive together.

At school he moved with the usual intensity, often preoccupied and lost in thought. "He would walk right by and not even see me, when we were kids in high school," remembered Agnes Brannon. Some believed him "uppity" or arrogant. Many would be awed or a little unnerved by the stark concentration and ambition that had begun to hang about him. His grades were excellent, all A's his junior year, as a senior B's in journalism and physics and A's in trigonometry, history, and Latin. When he stood up to dispute a respected teacher in American history and proved her wrong, he "became quite famous overnight," a fellow student recalled.

Nonetheless, the grades and the sometimes brash exhibition of knowledge never came with ease, never seemed to grow simply out of some spontaneous interest or intellectual love apart from the sheer toil and responsibility of academics. Late into the evening in the grocery office, or Sundays between church services and adding store accounts, he continued to pore over assignments and texts. "I always think of him in his free time as never one to just goof around," Sheldon Beeson recalled these years. "He always had a little spot where he could get off and study." "You're lucky, Dick, to get such good grades so easily," a high school classmate once told him. "It isn't luck," he shot back in some irritation. "You've got to dig for them." And he was determined that he or other students should get their due. Roy Newsom remembered once during their junior year when a chemistry exam came back and Nixon discovered that Newsom had a right answer that had been marked wrong. "I could hardly keep him from hauling me over with him to protest—I was bashful and backward and didn't want to go."

With his father's enthusiastic support, he continued extracurricular debate and public speaking. "Of course, he had the bulldog tenacity that his father had," said Ralph Palmer, who thought him still "more of a Milhous" than a Nixon. "It made a wonderful combination. . . . He was more explosive; he was a dynamic individual. He'd pound the table if he was going to make a point, you see." But Richard was no longer the earnest, awkward student struggling against an instinctive shyness Lynn Sheller had watched him overcome at Fullerton or the boy who playfully tried his polemics with the girls on outings or at Sunday school—and the reactions were no longer so admiring or sympathetic. "He had this ability to kind of slide round an argument instead of meeting it head-on," his Whittier debate coach, Mrs. Clifford Vincent, would remember afterward. She was often "disturbed" that he could take any side of a debate with such technical skill. "There was something mean in him," she would relate more than forty years later, "mean in the way he put his questions, argued his points."

Mrs. Vincent was not alone in her disquiet. Though few of his teachers were openly critical at the time, and fewer still when he had become prominent, the other side of his high school debate reputation was there, politely muted in the small town. "He offended some of his Quaker teachers by his willingness to justify bad means by the end. They said he cared too much about winning school contests," revealed a *Whittier Daily News* editor, Loverne Morris, who often heard the private misgivings. "His schoolmates were proud of his winnings but admired rather than liked him." Forrest Randall remembered that it was easy enough to set Dick Nixon talking or arguing, but "it wouldn't be an intellectual discussion, it wouldn't be intriguing or creative. Well, it would be a dogmatic, pedagogical kind of argument that would be no fun at all."

Both years at Whittier he entered the *Los Angeles Times* oratorical contests extolling the virtues of the U.S. Constitution, and the speeches he wrote gave the first hints of his emerging views on politics and government. "They were seeking to promulgate this philosophy of the American Constitution demonstrating that it came down from Mt. Sinai along with the Decalogue . . . whereby all the Founding Fathers were saints and especially ordained by God and had connections with Him," remembered Merton Wray, a Whittier High contestant in 1929 and later a local judge. It was "to give the kids," thought Wray, "the pietistic interpretation of the Constitution." In the event, speeches seldom strayed beyond the understood bounds, and contests were judged as much by orthodoxy of thought as style or eloquence. When Wray spoke in the spring of 1929 on extending the obvious benefits of the Constitution to a worldwide rule of law, with a universal Bill of Rights, two out of the three judges at Whittier Union were outraged at the prospective loss of U.S. sovereignty and placed him last simply because of his theme. "I never realized that I was stepping on a sore point," Wray reminisced later. For the more conventional winners there were community accolades and crowded audiences cheering for them at the widening district competition, the Whittier Parent-Teacher Association patriotically paying expenses to out-of-town contests.

Easily besting Wray and others, the winning Whittier oration of 1929 was Richard Milhous Nixon's "Our Privileges Under the Constitution." It had been written as he was to write all his school speeches, almost entirely alone with little help from teachers or family, drafted on a tablet in the belfry office and then read to his father, whose criticism and suggestions changed the text little. His high school coach polished spelling and punctuation, weaknesses Nixon would carry through college and into law school, but the diction and voice remained very much his own. Most of all, he suffered none of Merton Wray's apparent lapse into world federalism or other heresy. His interpretation of constitutional privileges conformed clearly enough with the prevailing views of his local audience and judges, as well as adopting some favorite editorial canons of the *Los Angeles Times*. "Mr. Nixon has a splendid oration," pronounced the *Whittier Daily News*, "and he delivers it in a forceful and convincing manner."

His main theme was not to expand on Constitutional privileges so much as to warn against their abuse and to set out proper limits against excesses.

In freedom of speech and press, he found inherent dangers to public morality and order, and he devoted the heart of his 1929 oration to a remarkable passage on the hazards of Constitutional rights.

> The framers of the Constitution provided that we, their descendants, need not fear to express our sentiments as they did. Yet the question arises: How much ground do these privileges cover? There are some who use them as a cloak for covering libelous, indecent, and injurious statements against their fellowmen. Should the morals of the nation be offended and polluted in the name of freedom of speech or freedom of the press? In the words of Lincoln, the individual can have no rights against the best interests of society. Furthermore, there are those who, under the pretense of freedom of speech and freedom of the press, have incited riots, assailed our patriotism, and denounced the Constitution itself. They have used Constitutional privileges to protect the very act by which they wished to destroy the Constitution. Consequently laws have justly been provided for punishing those who abuse their Constitutional privileges—laws which do not limit these privileges, but which provide that they may not be instrumental in destroying the Constitution which insures them. We must obey these laws, for they have been passed for our own welfare.

For a sixteen-year-old, it was obviously serious political thought. The text was also rich in ironic portent of his subsequent political career, his views of the press, of conformity and radicalism—even in the strained allusion to Lincoln, an eerie foreshadowing of the concept of national security and executive power that would make his own Presidency the great Constitutional crisis of the century. But when the oration was written in Whittier during the early spring of 1929, the images of sedition and revolt reflected a near and vivid history.

In southern California, where there had been a resurgence of labor protests before and immediately after the First World War, the national Red Scare that followed the Bolshevik revolution had been taken up with a singular vengeance. Proclaiming the basin "the white spot" of the country, local prosecutors sent over a hundred labor organizers to San Quentin penitentiary under a criminal syndicalism act, one of those laws, as Richard wrote, which "provided for punishing those who abuse their Constitutional privileges." At one juncture, a sympathetic local judge summarily suspended trial by jury to speed the process. Meanwhile, Los Angeles police had organized a "Red Squad" and scheduled "shove Tuesdays" to disrupt what were officially called "communist demonstrations" but which usually turned out to be union meetings or parades. The *Nation* and *New Republic* magazines were banished from Los Angeles school libraries, and teachers were fired as Bolsheviks for discussing public ownership of utilities. It had all gone on with the lavish backing and public endorsement of the *Times* and was to reach a climax on a June night in 1924 when a hundred and fifty vigilantes attacked a local IWW meeting with blackjacks, pickaxes, and revolvers, beating both men and women, and then turning on the children to scald them with hot coffee.

On the eve of the Great Depression, the tide of that reaction had left Los Angeles and its surrounding small towns by far the least unionized and most fearfully antiradical of the nation's metropolitan areas. "It is somehow absurd but nevertheless true," wrote one historian of the labor strife, "that for forty years the smiling booming sunshine City of the Angels has been the bloodiest arena in the Western world!" While union organizers defended themselves by claiming Constitutional protections of free speech and assembly, the *Times* and its business allies had branded their opponents with revolution and destruction of the American system. Now, in the spring of 1929, Richard Nixon's schoolboy oration invoked with some skill that historic battle with the frightening, faceless radical bogey. His alarm about legal rights spoke unmistakably to the inbred fear of leftist or alien forces among the small businessmen and merchants of southern California enclaves like Whittier. At heart it was the old festering clash of class and economics among the migrants. Over the musty school auditoriums where he spoke there was still the specter of the Wobblies who had left their initials so ominously scrawled that night on the Yorba Linda packinghouse where he and his mother worked.

The following year, he sounded some of the same ritual warning against enemies of the Constitution. But his oration in the 1930 contest also gave some clue to his knowledge about the world outside and, again, an uncanny intimation of his own policies in the White House. He chose among the prescribed topics "America's Progress—Its Dependence on the Constitution." He defined that progress "by the increase of its wealth, territory and power," and not least by its prestige. "That nation whose government was once the world's laughingstock, and whose power was comparatively futile, now commands the respect of the world's greatest nations." Such "stupendous progress—our present-day worldwide power" traced plainly to matters of national character and geography; it showed "that the people who settled in this country were of a superior type" and "that the tremendous natural resources of the land were especially fitted for the development of a nation."

Most of all, America owed her success to "that powerful instrument, the United States Constitution." The proof, he argued, could be seen clearly in the development of South American nations, whose "wealth, population and power . . . did not approach that of the United States" until recently. "Surely we cannot say that the people who have settled in the southern countries are of an inferior type," he wrote, "for the Latin race, which constitutes the greater part of their population, once ruled the known world." Nor was their backwardness due to a lack of natural resources, which were "inestimable in extent." No, the obstacle had been political, and the engine of growth was a government patterned after the United States. "For since the countries of the south have established governments similar to our own they too have begun to progress and in recent years their wealth, population and power have been increasing at an amazing rate." As history, the analogy ignored altogether the underlying influences of social caste, feudal economics, and colonial policy in the Spanish empire, and the deeper cultural and intellectual roots of Constitutionalism. And it was hardly clear what "amazing" progress in exactly which "governments similar to our own" he had in mind in 1930 in a Latin America still overwhelmingly impoverished and undemocratic. Simplistic and reassuring, his argument mirrored the sombrero images of South America in U.S. school textbooks of the era as well as a native American self-congratulation and naïve idealism vis-à-vis the rest of the world. It was a premonition, too, of a later view of foreign policy in which Latin and other governments would be measured for U.S. help in "progress" by their conformity with the American economic system, if not the Constitution, and social, political, and economic realities remained buried beneath the old caricature.

Still, he managed in the 1930 speech to find perils at home along with heartening imitation abroad. "At the present time," he wrote less than six months after the stock market crash, "a great wave of indifference to the Constitution's authority, disrespect of its law, and opposition to its basic principles threatens its very foundations." In his peroration was yet another irony and premonition, especially when read against the controversy in which his own Presidency would crumble.

> For as long as the Constitution is respected, its laws obeyed and its principles enforced, America will continue to progress. But if the time should ever come when America will consider this document too obsolete to cope with changed ideals in government, then the time will have arrived when the American people as an undivided nation must come back to normal and change their ideals to conform with those mighty principles set forth in our incomparable Constitution.

Both years he won the local contest, with a ten-dollar prize from the town Kiwanis, twenty dollars from the *Times*, and the orations proudly published in the school annual. Each time, though, he lost at a higher level of competition outside Whittier. The family remembered less the merits or substance of the competition than the pressure and hopes that had gathered behind his speaking success, and the community-wide prestige it had brought. Hadley Marshburn recalled how upset Hannah Nixon had been when her son lost in the advanced round in 1930. "His mother didn't like that. She thought he should have scored better," Marshburn said. "I know his mother wasn't a pusher or a driver, but she was always anxious to see him excel and get to the top in whatever he did."

Oratory and debate led to his first political campaign. Debating success, and especially his performance in the *Times* oratorical contest, moved the Whittier Union administration in the spring of 1929 to nominate Richard Nixon for student body president the following year on a faculty-approved slate of candidates. Long the practice at Whittier, the student government election ran one set of candidates nominated by the senior class against another chosen by the juniors, both carefully screened and controlled by teachers and staff. It was all, thought one observer, a Whittier Union High version of "the political machine."

Running on the senior ticket, Nixon was expected to defeat his hand-picked opponent, Roy Newsom. The campaign began uneventfully. Then, within days, there was suddenly a third candidate in the race. A football player and captain of the basketball team, active in both the Varsity Club and the school orchestra, Robert Logue was good looking and popular, a "dark horse" in the race, as his classmates now saw him, challenging tradition and faculty control of school politics with the backing of fellow athletes and other students, especially girls. "Some of the people on the teams really got out and worked for him. He was a very nice person . . . [and] also . . . a good student," one of the girls, Elizabeth Glover, said, recalling Logue. The students were consciously putting forward an athletic candidate that clashed with the fusty administration's mold. "I think they decided that they would run somebody that was out for sports," Glover said later.

"It was quite a hotly contested election," Douglas Ferguson remembered of the campaign after Logue's entry. In place of the usually quiet, *pro forma* electioneering, there were suddenly "sandwich boards and all kinds of signs around." While Nixon and Newsom seemed to rely mainly on their respective class endorsements and faculty support, Logue politicked energetically at breaks and lunch hours, personably shaking hands and asking for an "independent" vote. His volunteers covered the campus with hand-lettered banners and pamphlets carrying the slogan "Stop, Think, and Vote for Bob Logue."

Watching him as an opponent in 1929, Roy Newsom thought Dick Nixon "had to work hard at being a politician. I don't think he ever did have smooth going—not a naturally glad-handing, extroverted politican." Forrest Randall heard him deliver speeches in the race for student body president that seemed both dull and self-righteous. "He was so colorless then. . . . He would have made a wonderful missionary, because he was always right, he knew everything. God was on his side," Randall said afterward. If withdrawn and painfully shy, standoffish to the point of unfriendliness, he appeared at the same time to some students aggressive, wanting it too much. As so often later, his peers would see in the same person two vastly different personalities, two nearly opposite silhouettes of character and purpose. "When he was in Whittier High he was going to be student body president and didn't care whose feet he trampled on," Mildred Jackson Johns, an old Milhous family friend, said later, recalling the race. "The students hated him. He didn't care how he went after it . . . kids in the school would tell me how he would elbow his way right through [to] anything he wanted."

When the student votes were counted, Logue had beaten him decisively, though the rest of the senior ticket won office. "He had something new. He deserved to win," Nixon once said of Logue and the campaign, adding, "There were no hard feelings." But the loss was obviously sharp and scarring. A half century later he still marked the event tersely. "I suffered my first political defeat in my junior year at Whittier High School," he wrote in his memoirs, "when I lost the election for president of the student body." It was to be his last losing campaign for thirty years, until another presidential run when he would again be an administration candidate facing yet another fresh, attractive challenger.

Much of his senior year was spent recouping some of the social and political loss of the election. Appointed student body general manager by the faculty, he plunged into the usually thankless, perfunctory job with conspicuous zeal, overseeing the sale of tickets and the filling of water buckets for football games, selling yearbook advertising to local businessmen. As he would so often in the future, particularly after a setback, he prepared carefully and did the chores others might shirk. "Dick Nixon was the best organizer we ever had," recalled Alvin Whitcomb, the school's director of athletics. "He took care of details."

On the two-thousandth anniversary of Virgil's birth, the Whittier Latin

Club performed a brief dramatization of the *Aeneid*, and Richard was cast in the lead as Aeneas, the legendary Trojan hero who founds Rome. His stage debut he remembered as "sheer torture," the student audience "bored stiff." Boots for his costume were size nine for his eleven-D feet. His Latin teachers labored with him for several minutes just getting them on and off, and he passed the hour on stage as "agony beyond description and almost beyond endurance." The students had no real dramatic coaching, and they never rehearsed the tame but tender love scene at the climax. As he starchly embraced his romantic opposite, Queen Dido, protocol at the usually sedate school broke down altogether. The scene brought "catcalls, whistles and uproarious laughter," he recorded, and the embarrassed players had to wait for the outburst to end before going on. When the performance concluded to what one account called "polite applause," he had been mortified. He rushed up to Jane Steck, one of the Latin instructors, and volunteered to play the piano to entertain the audience further. "I'll do anything," she remembered him blurting out, "to make the party a success."

The Latin Club drama was to be far more important than the pinching boots or catcalls. Playing Dido was Ola Florence Welch, his first girlfriend whom he would date for the next seven years. They had met during an honor society party and began to see each other after the play. "We all wore white gowns," she recalled of their performance. "It was so romantic. It must have been contagious because after that Dick and I started going together." She remembered, too, their dramatic embrace. "We never practiced it. When we came to do it, it was very awkward and the kids went to pieces. I just about died. Neither of us ever said anything to each other about it."

Bright, pretty, vivacious, well-liked, she was from a family of girls and still shy with young men, the daughter of a Whittier deputy police chief once a sheriff in Tombstone, Arizona, and of a modern, intelligent mother whose education had been cut short near the end of medical school. Richard was the first boy Ola had dated, and she thought him "really quite handsome . . . tall and good-looking." She was attracted, too, by his obvious intelligence, and went along to hear him in the *Times* oratorical contests. He talked to her with his deep-felt earnestness about debate and history, and what younger girls in Fullerton and Prescott remembered as boring or aggressive Ola found exciting, an opening onto the world in provincial Whittier. "I just thought that he was the smartest man that ever was," she said later.

Sandy Triggs remembered the two of them at the senior class dress-up day near the end of school in 1930, Ola in an old-fashioned long dress and hat "which brought her out to the best," Richard clowning for her as a bum panhandler. He took her out in the little old Ford he drove to school, and brought her that June to the junior-senior banquet in a gymnasium decorated like a garden of spring flowers, where as president of the honor society he made one of the speeches. Looking back at the final happy weeks of high school, some would remember them "being in love."

At Christmas 1929, Hannah Nixon had unexpectedly come back to East Whittier, leaving Harold in Prescott. Forty-five, she was now pregnant with her fifth child, and the doctor advised her to leave the Pinecrest tubercular colony. Olive Marshburn recalled Frank Nixon blustering after Hannah had been to the doctor and the pregnancy confirmed. Frank "didn't think he knew what he was talking about." She heard him scoffing at the physician, incredulous and upset about their "trailer." "Frank would say anything fast," Olive remembered.

During the holidays Frank Nixon returned to Arizona to build a tiny lunger cabin for Harold on the grounds of the Cloughs' chicken ranch in Cortez Park, another outlying area of Prescott, arranging to pay the family sixty dollars a month to care for his tubercular son. Marshall Clough remembered Frank then and later as "a good father" but unable to console Harold, who was already lonely and restless in his mother's absence.

For Hannah there was little respite. Not long after she returned, Richard contracted undulant fever, his temperature rising to 104 degrees. She nursed him through weeks of recovery, arranging homework from the high school to avoid any loss of credit. As it was, he made up the missed material easily, and in June graduated third in a class of 207. "Richard Nixon," read the class prophecy for the 1950s, "is associated with the *Los Angeles Times*, sponsor of the *Times*'s Oratorical Contests, which are still going strong." Students saw him visibly more relaxed in the last weeks of school, the pressures somehow eased. "Here's to the best artist I have ever known and I don't mean maybe," he scrawled in a friend's yearbook. "Good luck to you and stay away from Brunettes—they aren't your type." He now signed his name "Dick Nixon."

"I had dreamed of going to college in the East," he wrote in his memoirs. At Whittier he won an award as "best all-around student" from the Harvard Club of California, the prize an invitation to apply for a tuition scholarship to the prestigious college. There was also, he remembered, the prospect of a tuition grant to Yale. But he applied for neither. "The enormous expenses of Harold's illness had stripped our family finances," he wrote. "I had no choice but to live at home." Once again, their financial circumstances were never so dire as he depicted them. Frank still held the boulevard property across from the East Whittier School. But the sixty dollars paid each month to the Cloughs for Harold's care would have made it difficult. And the new baby, Edward Calvert, born in May 1930, now added to the uncertainty of Harold's illness and tied Richard to East Whittier. "We needed Richard at home," Hannah said simply about the choice of a school.

He applied to Whittier College, listing as references his uncle Oscar Marshburn and Lewis Cox, the seventh-grade teacher at East Whittier. Marshburn alone responded to the college form, rating his nephew "distinctly above average" in ambition, cooperation, industry, faithfulness, loyalty and straight-forwardness, "markedly above average" in character, "above average" in personality. He added a note that Richard Nixon would be "a fine student and a good citizen." As a Milhous descendant, he was given a $250-per-year full-tuition scholarship from the $2,000 fund bequeathed by his maternal grandfather in 1919. The grant left average added costs of only fifty dollars a year for Whittier students living at home.

That summer he occasionally dated Ola, who would be going to Whittier College as well, and otherwise plodded through the old routine at the grocery. In June he begged his parents excitedly to go along on a trip to the Grand Canyon with a Milhous cousin and her husband, Leonidas Dotson, a recent honors student at Whittier College. "Richard didn't think they'd let him go," Mrs. Dotson remembered, "but they finally did." Touring the canyon with the Dotsons and another cousin, Russell Harrison, he seemed buoyant. "I was not disappointed," he wrote later about giving up Harvard or Yale for Whittier, "because the idea of college was so exciting that nothing could have dimmed it for me."

II

STRIVINGS

5

Whittier College, 1930–34

"YOU GET THERE . . . FAST, IF YOU CAN"

e were cuddled up here on the hill . . . ," a student later said of the college in 1930, "an eddy on the stream of life."

Dappled in vivid shadows of eucalyptus and palms, the campus climbed a steep hill to Founders Hall, an old four-story stucco Gothic building with awninged windows and tower where Hannah Milhous had taken courses, and where the college auditorium, most of the whitewashed classrooms, and somber, walnut-lined administration offices were still housed. Nearby stood two small Spanish Revival dormitories for men and women. Behind the buildings, atop the hill, were the football gridiron, Hadley Field, flanked by weathered wooden bleachers and the new Wardman Gymnasium. Save for the palm fronds and Moorish arches, Whitter might have been any of dozens of small picturesque colleges in the Midwest. Only inside Founders were there visible signs of the laboring ethos of the school denomination and of the historic rent in the Quaker soul. Etched in sandstone over the fireplace in the main hall was a passage from one of John Whittier's more stirring if unanswered poems:

Early hath life's mighty question
Thrilled within the heart of youth
With a deep and strong beseeching
What and where is Truth?

Down the hall two service flags hung unfurled, one commemorating the names of students who had died in World War I, the other with similar starred names for those who had been conscientious objectors. Later, the flag honoring the pacifists would be defaced and eventually removed. But in the early 1930s, when Richard Nixon and other students passed them daily, the two flags hung side by side.

The community embraced the sober little school on one side and spurned it on the other. A student remembered the Whittier slogan: "We invite you down to Quaker Town, for you the light streams out." At one level students mingled freely in the economy and society of the town, went to the new movie theaters, jammed the Roxy Malt Shop, entertained local crowds that thronged college football games. Townspeople bought yearbook ads, gave low-interest loans to impecunious scholars, tirelessly proselytized students with free church suppers on long, tepid California evenings. "They loved us all and we loved them," said William Hornaday, a student in the early thirties. But there was also in Whittier as in other college towns tension and distrust between campus and city. "The students cheated the townspeope," said Osmyn Stout, a student of the same era, "and vice versa."

"Stated in social terms," read the 1933 catalog, "the purpose of Whittier College is education for Christian Democracy." A chapel hour was mandatory for all students. On its masthead the student newspaper, *Quaker Campus*, proclaimed, "Whittier College: Christian Culture Without Sectarian Bias: The Friendly Spirit." Nonetheless, there was an inherent intellectual clash with the town's reactionary politics and primitive evangelism. As a young history professor, Paul Smith once scandalized a local service club with a speech quoting Thomas Jefferson. "He was for more rapid change, you see," Smith explained later about the author of the Declaration of Independence, "than this Whittier Quaker community was willing to go . . . " When *What Price Glory* appeared on Broadway in 1924, its author, Maxwell Anderson, the most famous former faculty member of the college, had been similarly upbraided by the community for the play's pacifist and antinationalist tone.

In that autumn of 1930, Guy Phelps, a fiery revivalist, drew large Whittier crowds at the local Nazarene Church denouncing the "Godless professors" teaching evolution at the college. When a Whittier classics teacher with a divinity degree stood up in the church to reply to Phelps's charges, he was forcibly removed by ushers, much to the approval of the congregation. "Now things smell better," Phelps told them. Invited to speak at the college, Phelps refused in a letter vowing a ceaseless campaign against the institution until "the church of peace has fumigated you infidel vermin out and put real scholars in your stead." In the face of such benighted rancor, the little school stood all but alone. Its trustees, Quaker businessmen and bankers, resisted the worst attacks, yet remained a bit unsure about Darwin themselves and were content to prescribe campus morals in return for continuing contributions.

Of just over four hundred students altogether, most were Methodists and Baptists, and Quakers less than a fifth. Richard Nixon's class of 1934 began with 139 freshmen, fifty-eight of them from Whittier proper, only three from outside California. They were for the most part sons and daughters of shopkeepers and small businessmen, ranchers, and farmers. Only a dozen came from Los Angeles. An occasional black athlete or Japanese student found no overt discrimination on campus or in the town that otherwise barred the family of either from buying property there. But non-white, non-Protestant students were evident oddities.

In the fall of 1930 only a small minority of high school graduates went on to college at all; fewer still would be able to enroll or continue in the looming Depression. Campus society and politics remained dominated by the affluent minority, what poorer Whittier students called caustically the "kite fliers" and "bridge players." Sororities and fraternities were ostensibly outlawed, but the ban was resolved by another of Whittier's discreet accommodations, in the college case "literary societies," exclusive organizations of thirty or less. While dancing on campus was deemed immoral, societies held their posh dinner dances at local clubs or Los Angeles hotels and duly recorded them in school annuals. There were four societies for girls, and only one for boys, the Franklins, known for their tuxedos, formal balls, four-course suppers, and select membership. "They seemed to be the aristocrats of the campus," said Robert Farnham, who enrolled in 1931. William Hornaday remembered how many young men aspired to the Franklins, only to be uninvited or blackballed by a society that "kept out the poor, the unwashed, and the physically strong," as one historian put it. "We felt—and we couldn't have been wrong—that the Franklins were above everyone," Hornaday said, echoing the sentiments of most students. "We didn't think it was democratic."

Richard Nixon stood out from the beginning in the class of 1934, a slight young man with wavy hair combed back in a dark, thick mat, wearing his ever-serious expression and the usual starched white shirts. He was elected freshman class president with 90 percent of the votes; "a popular Whittier High School graduate," the *Quaker Campus* called him, with "considerable experience as an executive" and "well-known among local students for his oratorical ability." At a student body reception at the end of September he had his first brush with wider college politics and with the issue that would be so important in his own campus political career. In a Wardman gym decorated with Hawaiian flowers and leis, President Walter

Dexter and upperclassmen welcomed the new students as freshman president Nixon replied. It began in a grand march but ended in the college's first impromptu dance on campus, delighting the students, scarring the gym floor, and bringing down on Dexter calls from trustees and other outraged community leaders. "I don't think he got an hour's sleep that night for Quakers waking him up saying he was leading the students down the road to hell," Richard Thomson, a freshman at the dance, said of Dexter.

That first year, Nixon plunged into sports as never before, going out for the freshman football team, playing at tackle or guard in every game on the tiny eleven-man squad, winning his first, and last, letter sweater. In playing basketball that winter he lunged for a rebound, took an elbow in the mouth, and acquired what he later called his "only trophy from sports," a porcelain dental bridge. In the spring he ran track, though a fellow squad member thought it clear that "he had no athletic ability whatsoever," and he often finished fifty yards behind the rest of the runners. More than four decades later, on the last night of his Presidency, he would recall those races. "I remember running the mile in track once. By the time we reached the last fifty yards, there were only two of us struggling in for next-to-last place," he said to an aide. "Still, I sprinted those last yards just as hard as if I were trying for the first-place ribbon." At a freshman meet in San Diego in 1931, Ed Wunder, already with two second-place finishes and due to win the next race, saw the leader pulling away and slowed down for Nixon to pass him. "Come on and get your second," Wunder told him. "I can still see that smile of appreciation on his face when he passed me and said, 'Thanks, Wunder.' "

Before the varsity football game with Occidental College that fall, Whittier's arch rival "Oxy," he took charge of the traditional freshman bonfire rally, and drove the old Nixon grocery truck through town alleys scavenging for wood, stealing crates, leaving a trail of littered garbage and angry merchants. Sandy Triggs remembered the police stopping them on their second trip for crates. "Get those crates back! You get those crates back here from that bonfire or we're gonna throw you in!" When they returned to find someone had already lit the stack of wood, Nixon remained cool and simply told the police the crates were gone. He emerged from the episode something of a campus hero, "when he first showed," Triggs recalled it, "some of his ability to get us out of scrapes."

Only weeks into his first college semester he was one of the better known students on the small campus, liked and respected in his sheer fervor and intensity. Yet for all the eagerness, he was not invited into the coveted Franklins, and the rejection promptly opened another social and political opportunity. That autumn a transfer student, Dean Triggs, had approached Whittier English professor Albert Upton about forming a rival men's society. They would appeal directly to a core of freshmen and sophomore athletes excluded from the Franklins. "In the Franklin Society deal," said Murle Marshburn, another organizer, "part of the fellows didn't have invitations, so we knew some of them wouldn't be in." But most of the charter members of the new society were football players with little academic strength, and Upton told them they should recruit something more to match the Franklins. Triggs approached Richard Nixon. "I think we figured that we needed one *student*," he said later. The avid freshman accepted immediately, and volunteered to take over a number of the new group's organizational chores the older students were glad to delegate. Impressed with his ardor and ability, and looking, as Triggs's girlfriend put it, "for somebody that would push and hold things together and really be a pusher," they went even further and elected Nixon their first president.

With a linguistic assist from Upton, Triggs named them Orthogonians, for on-the-square or square-shooters, and their emblems pointedly expressed their differences with their polished rivals. The Orthogonian mascot was the wild boar, their motto "Beans, Brains, Brawn and Bowels." "And we were more the bourgeoisie—is that what they call it?" said Robert Farnham. "The bean boys." While the Franklins appeared for yearbook pictures in tuxedos, the Orthogonians were photographed in simple, open-collared white shirts that were to be their hallmark. Upton puckishly suggested the slogan "*Écrasons l'infame*," or "Crush the infamous," which, with some irony at the little Quaker college, had been one of Voltaire's volleys against the Roman Catholic Church. Richard Nixon quickly drafted the constitution and to a borrowed tune composed the lyrics of the Orthogonian song.

> *All hail the mighty boar*
> *Our patron beast is he*
> *Our aims forevermore*
> *In all our deeds must be*
> *to emulate his might*
> *His bravery and his fight . . .*

> Écrasons l'infame
> *Our battle cry will be*
> *We'll fight for the right*
> *And win victory*
> *We'll raise our standards high*
> *And never let them fall . . .*

My brothers to you
I give my handclasp true
We part now to go
To meet our greatest foe

We'll fight our battles fair
And always on the square
Brothers together we'll travel on
Worthy the name of Orthogonian.

He took special interest, too, in devising initiation rites and unconcealed pleasure in administering them. As charter members, he and fourteen others recruited by Triggs that fall of 1930 never underwent the ceremony, for which some were thankful decades later. The Franklins marched their pledges around campus in dresses, and hazing, including some paddling, was as common at Whittier as at other colleges. To this Nixon and the new Orthogonians now added a series of small tortures purported to build character. At nightlong sessions, accompanied by what one member called "secret ritualistic stuff," initiates were not only paddled but stripped naked, fed spoiled meat and asafetida, a foul-smelling gum resin that stiffened muscles, subjected to various taunting and humiliations, and eventually taken somewhere on the outskirts of the basin and left off in underpants to find their way back to the college. "The initiation was too much. It was just too much and it caused a great deal of repercussion," one of the first pledges recalled. "To my brother Orthogonian, remember the initiation we had together?" Nixon wrote in William Hornaday's yearbook after the first round of initiates. "But all ended well." In Hornaday's annual the following year he was still gleeful about the hazing. "Next year we are really going to do things around the initiation," he wrote. Eventually, the practices were barred altogether by the college when a student and relative of an administrator was seriously injured. "A very tough thing," Dean Triggs remembered the initiation. "Anybody that went through it was basically ready for World War II or Vietnam or North Korea."

Upton, the English professor, soon receded as faculty adviser, and the Orthogonians became increasingly identified with Wallace "Chief" Newman, Whittier's Indian football coach, coming to be known as "the Chief's boys." For their part, the Franklins christened them the "big pigs," and in one campus show a Franklin appeared in a sweatshirt, necktie, and filthy corduroys, announcing he was dressed up to go to an Orthogonian formal. In December 1930 the student-faculty Joint Council at Whittier found it necessary to address the need for "better feelings" between the two men's societies. The Orthogonians had obviously struck a chord of student resentment at the Franklin monopoly, and the raw issues of class and athlete versus nonathlete were near the surface. "The kids disliked them. They wanted to overthrow them, and the ferment was ripe and strong." Merton Wray remembered watching from the sidelines the challenge to the Franklins' campus dominance. "Anyway," he added, "Nixon . . . saw this ferment and decided to take advantage of it." It was a gift of sensing the moment and issue, he thought, that Dick Nixon would display again and again.

By the end of the year, however, the rivalry seemed muted and the new society had taken its place, like the Franklins meeting monthly, if more modestly, for spaghetti-and-bean dinners at the Sanders Café near the campus. "They were the haves and we were the have-nots," Richard Nixon once described the two groups. But there were those who looked back and saw the new society and its ardent president in another light. "I've always . . . felt Dick Nixon was something of an opportunist," Richard Harris, his classmate at both Whittier High and College, said, recalling the Orthogonians. "I think this was a thing that would contribute toward his election as student body president and as a leader on campus," Harris said later. As for the organization itself, what began in an air of democratic and social change on the campus would soon become in its own right a powerful political and social force at the college, electing its own political slate, dominating student activities, and in its studied secret rituals and punishing initiations no less selective than the Franklins. In the thirties the Franklins and Orthogonians together would induct hardly a quarter of the men studying at Whittier College. Scores of athletes as well as serious students were excluded from both. "The Orthogonians," remembered Osmyn Stout, who was asked to join, "were just as vicious as any college fraternity, friends of friends."

In March 1931, the *Quaker Campus* whimsically reported, Richard Nixon staged a mock *coup d'état*, calling a meeting as "acting" student body president, staging a vote of "impeachment" of the real president, and even taking a swipe at Whittier's most sacred institution. "The president," the newspaper said of Nixon, "moved, seconded and carried the motion that chapel be done away with." But such prankish intervals were rare. He continued to apply himself with patent earnestness, though his freshman grades were not high enough for Whittier's demanding Honors, an A in French and B's in English composition and literature, European history, and algebra the first term, B's in all those continuing courses, and a C in journalism the second semester.

"For the first time I met students who were able to get grades without working very hard for them," he wrote about his academic baptism at college, "but I needed the steady discipline of nightly study to keep up with all the courses and reading." On the way home from dates, Ralph Palmer drove down Whittier Boulevard past the store, and "I'd see him at his dining room table there, poring over the books at one-thirty or two o'clock in the morning." Herman Brannon went out with Don Nixon, "and when we would come back in, regardless of what time it was, Dick would still be sitting at the old kitchen table with his books open, studying." The stories were told again and again. Local delivery men coming to the grocery before dawn found him with his light still on after studying all night and ready to go off to the Seventh Street market for the day's produce. On the campus, as Lyle Otterman saw him, "he went from one class to another with his hands full of books and his head down, plodding along, and that was just Dick Nixon, that's all." His history professor, Paul Smith, thought him "always in a hurry to get to the next whatever-it-was. There was a sense of motion about him. He was moving fast physically and mentally, never loafing around, always checking in and checking out." Hubert Perry, who was in the class behind, either saw him at football practice or in the library, where there might be only three or four students but one of them invariably Nixon. "There was an old place back in the corner where we knew we could always find him between three and five P.M. every day except during football season," remembered Osmyn Stout, who thought he was there "religiously every day," just as the how-to-study books prescribed. "I was a freshman and he was a junior," Stout looked back, "and he was very charitable toward me, and would point out how important it was to spend an hour each day."

Whittier had the special strengths and limits of a small denominational college. Grading could be exacting, classes were uncrowded, and students knew the faculty personally, pitching horseshoes with them between lectures, dining with some, listening to them engage in earnest philosophical discussions with one another sitting on a curb in front of the campus. Graduating in the class of 1923, Jessamyn West found her education "superficial" in what she called "the gentle monogamy of Whittier's one-man English department," and went on to Berkeley never having heard of James Joyce, T.S. Eliot, or other prominent writers. Walter Dexter, a dynamic young Quaker minister of cherubic handsomeness and graduate degrees from Columbia and Harvard, had since changed much of that during his presidency, winning national accreditation for the school and instituting one of the earliest liberal arts experimental programs in American colleges. Yet scarcely a quarter of the teachers had Ph.D.s, and the tiny old Redwood Library held fewer than 20,000 volumes.

In 1930 most departments of the college remained one-man affairs, though general quality of the "monogamy" had been improved. Richard

Nixon chose a major in history and government under Paul Smith, a young Quaker and Wisconsin Ph.D. Smith was legendary on the little campus for his absentmindedness and professorial intensity. Putting his beat-up felt fedora on a seat at the front of the classroom, he often became so carried away with a lecture that he stomped on the chair to make a point and put his size-twelve foot in the middle of the hat. Students recalled him almost "climbing" a portable blackboard as he filled it with notes. To bring political oratory alive, he rummaged through old music stores in the summer, found an heirloom recording of William Jennings Bryan's Cross of Gold speech, and played it to classes as they followed the words in their texts. "He made you feel the aliveness of it, the dynamics of it," Ezra Ellis said of Smith. "He did more by his spirit than by his words." William Hornaday remembered, "He didn't care about dates in history, he cared about what was behind it all and what was behind us. . . . He'd inspire you."

In many of the same courses Nixon took, Merton Wray thought Paul Smith "very liberal as a young professor," his teaching a pungent corrective to the idolatry in American history they had imbibed at Whittier High or in the *Los Angeles Times* contests. Smith promptly introduced his pious young Californians to Charles Beard's irreverent *Economic Interpretation of the Constitution*, revealing the sometimes pedestrian politics that went into drafting the document. His basic text in American history was the similarly realistic collegiate standard of that time and long afterward, the two-volume *Growth of the American Republic*, by Samuel Eliot Morison and Henry Steele Commager. As a history major, Nixon was later assigned the monumental but generally uncritical ten-volume biography of Abraham Lincoln by John Hay and John G. Nicolay, Lincoln's former secretaries. Smith recalled checking Nixon's notes turned in after the project: "He had gone assiduously through the longest and most exhaustive biography of that American martyr, and had become deeply, personally involved in what he was reading."

His other notable assignment in the field came in a senior course in which Smith required a detailed analysis of Frederick Teggart's 1925 *Theory of History*. Teggart was a revelation of a different sort. A profound critic of traditonal historiography, he drew unabashedly on Malthus and Darwin and shocked Quaker sensibilities with a view of war and violence as a major catalyst of historical progress. Most significant, Teggart would be one of the first American historians to deplore the then utter ignorance and neglect in U.S. historical studies of non-Western people. "It's a book of caution— the need to hesitate in making a judgment, to take a second and third and fourth look," Smith would say later of Teggart's *Theory*, noting that it "especially impressed young Nixon." It was also to be Richard Nixon's fleeting and only intellectual glimpse of the world outside Western Europe and the United States in his entire formal education.

Smith saw him in his courses on American and English history as "an analytical student, rather than a philosophical student," and "a brute for discipline. He couldn't get enough of it." The young professor gave him all A's except for a B in the course on the Constitution. He was struck, and a little unnerved, by the terseness of Nixon's responses. "In his examination papers, I was nettled because they were always so brief. . . . He went to the heart of things," Smith recounted. "I would read the paper and feel that it wasn't sufficient for the top grading. But, in looking back to what was left out, nothing was left out so far as the examination question itself was asking for something. He gave all of that but he didn't vouchsafe much beyond that." Later, the teacher came to think the answers reflected the utter pragmatism and impatient drive of his student. "You get there . . . fast, if you can, with not too much philosophizing," is how Smith summed up Richard Nixon's approach to learning.

When his student and history major from the class of '34 had become famous, Paul Smith was president of Whittier College and would be reported to have been the principal mentor during Nixon's undergraduate years. Yet as important as Smith and his classes were, Richard Nixon had taken even more courses from, spent far more time with, and been much closer to another young professor, Albert Upton. Named the "Owl" behind his thick horn-rimmed glasses, a slight, natty man given to bow ties and a caustic brilliance, Upton had come to Whittier in 1929 to teach English and coach drama after a hitch in the navy and a doctorate at Berkeley. Dean Triggs remembered him as "pretty salty," Richard Spaulding as "a young sarcastic, sophisticated Ph.D. . . . I and most of us hated the ground he walked on, but he was a most challenging personality." While Smith enthusiastically preached his gentle revisions of popular myths in U.S. history and remained the earnest Quaker, Upton's intellect was traveled, scoffing, profane. "Religion," he laughingly quoted an exchange with Whittier's theology professor, "is something you believe in what you know ain't true." Glad to sponsor the Orthogonians with their preponderance of football players, he was clearly more at home in the classroom or in the theater wings and promptly informed the athletes in his Whittier courses that they would have a tough time getting a good grade. "And we did," remembered one. He taught Nixon as a freshman in journalism in the spring of 1931, giving him one of his few college C's, but beginning what would be a mutually admiring relationship over the next three years. "He and Dick got along very well together," Emmett Ingrum recounted. Dick walked across campus often with Smith, was frequently in his office. But it was Upton he seemed most to seek out. "Upton and Nixon would be together when some of the others of us would be with other professors," Ingrum remembered.

Nixon enrolled in eleven of Upton's courses, three more than with

Smith. He thus had almost as many English as history classes, including two year-long and demanding courses, Great Books and the Philosophy of English Literature. Along with his worldliness and bite, Upton was an ardent disciple of C. K. Ogden and I. A. Richards, the two Cambridge University professors whose work on the force and influence of language was seminal in the 1920s. "The citizen of today is the victim of new forms of word magic so universal and so subtle that he is unable ever to escape their influence," Ogden had written. Upton's students at Whittier were required to read carefully *The Meaning of Meaning*, which probed deeply into the symbolic power of words in human affairs from mathematics to industrial disputes, politics, and wartime propaganda. At Upton's urging Nixon read Tolstoy on his own during a summer; Upton warned him his "education would [otherwise] not be complete." And he also recalled reading "cover to cover" a biography of Gandhi, another gift from Almira Milhous. "At that time in my life," he wrote afterward about his exposure to the giants of nonviolence, "I became a Tolstoyan."

Beyond the lecture rooms, Upton coached and directed Nixon in a series of college dramas that he played with relish and increasing skill. They began in May 1931 with Booth Tarkington's *The Trysting Place* and eighteen-year-old Nixon as "a middle-aged gentleman." Using Richard's deepening voice and sober, dark-haired good looks, Upton cast him repeatedly as an older man, parts invariably of more substance and challenge than the romantic leads most students coveted. "He had a deep voice and an old man's face," another actor recalled, "and he seemed to have physical substance. The effect was more maturity." In John Drinkwater's *Bird in Hand* the autumn of his junior year, Nixon was an elderly country innkeeper losing his daughter to a charmer from the city. Upton "tried to convert a young kid who walked on the balls of his feet to an old man who walked on his heels," the director remembered. "While not a great athlete, he had a springy step and a fine youthful body, and my first problem was to teach him to walk across the stage as if he were at least forty years older."

Upton also taught him to weep openly on stage. "I showed him how to get up a good cry, told him if you got your throat acting up you'd get tears in your eyes," he said later. Actor and director were uncertain of the crying, and it was never rehearsed before opening. But the night of the performance, Richard Nixon sat heavily in a chair, telling the story of his lost daughter while tears rolled down his nose and cheeks and fell in his lap with an emotion and realism those who saw it recalled half a lifetime later. He had given "an outstanding performance" and "carried his part with exceptional skill," said the *Quaker Campus*. "Richard Nixon, playing the heavy role of the English innkeeper," pronounced the yearbook *Acropolis*, "acted with a surety that has been seen far too seldom in Whittier productions!" Afterward, Upton was impressed no less. "Now, there are tricks to this, but people with imagination, and who sympathize with their fellow-man, reach this emotional stage without artificial means," he once said about Nixon's tears. "I was amazed at his perfection." He played in three more college productions over his last two years, all to similarly admiring reviews. "Dick loved the stage," Upton would say later. "Nixon was the easiest person to direct I've ever dealt with. He'd come to class with his lines memorized [and] do what I told him to do." On another occasion the professor said of him, "I've never coached an amateur who responded so quickly and intelligently to suggestions."

He was taut and temperamental before performances. "To the best property mistress W.C. ever had," he wrote in childish hand and green ink in the yearbook of Marjorie Hildreth. "Forgive all my nervous fits and thank you for your soothing words." Answering a fan who years later sent him a souvenir copy of the program from *Bird in Hand*, he self-consciously relived his stage fright as the old proprietor: "I can still remember thinking my legs would give out or I would lose my voice at some crucial moment." Both on stage and from the audience, Ola Welch saw him as "a marvelous actor, quick, perceptive, responsive, industrious," who had "great stage presence and an almost instinctive rapport with his audience." To Upton he was a performer plainly "at home on the platform [who] got a thrill out of getting to an audience." It was all an experience, the director reflected, that "didn't hurt his ego." At the moment, both his drama coach and girlfriend thought him so devoted to acting that he might well go into the theater professionally. "I honestly believe that if he had made the stage his career instead of studying law," Ola once remarked, "I'm sure he would have developed into a top-notch leading man." Upton would conclude decades later and after generations of students that Nixon was "the most competent student I ever had, but I couldn't think of him as a genius or as a boy destined for greatness. . . . I wouldn't have been surprised if, after college, he had gone to New York or Hollywood looking for a job as an actor."

Long afterward, Albert Upton remembered warmly his actor-turned-politician. He had been "a typical American Quaker," he reflected. "One of the pure in heart," he said another time. Looking back when both of them were in retirement, he remarked that among Nixon's college professors "his relation to me was closest." They had seen each other in classes once or twice each day for seven of Nixon's eight semesters at Whittier and for long hours of rehearsals. Yet Richard Nixon never acknowledged their intimacy or the importance of Upton's influence. Recounting college experiences in his memoirs, he called Smith "the greatest intellectual inspiration of my early years," and noted the English teacher and dramatics coach, his crucial courses and plays, only in passing. Albert Upton "was an iconoclast," he wrote. "Nothing was sacred to him, and he stimulated us by his outspoken unorthodoxy."

Nixon continued through college to attend East Whittier Friends four times each Sunday and for Wednesday evening prayer meetings, to play the piano at some services, even to lead the church "gospel team," preaching and debating before youth groups and other congregations with his own revivalist zeal. At home the family maintained their ritual devotions before each meal. But he had also begun to edge away from the old piety. At the end of their freshman year, William Hornaday, like his fellow Orthogonians and others, felt sure that Richard Nixon, imbued with a deep idealism and moral sense, was destined for the Quaker pulpit. "In everything that he did," Hornaday recalled, "it just seemed that what he chose to speak about was, you know, also affirmative about, not only the college, but the country, the universe, this tremendous cooperation, the brotherhood of man." Richard, he thought, would make "a tremendous minister." But when Hannah suggested openly at one point early in college that he might go on to study for the ministry or to be a missionary, she met an icy silence. "He didn't exactly respond favorably," Hannah said. "So I dropped the issue." He would be active in a half-dozen campus organizations, endlessly volunteering to help this group or that event, but students remembered him consistently turning down invitations to join one gathering, the Ethelontair Society, Whittier's religious fellowship.

At college he would travel some distance from the touching essay he wrote in a freshman English course describing his memories of Arthur and the little brother's death. He ended that eulogy with the story of Arthur's bedtime prayer the last night, "If I should die before I awake, I pray Thee, Lord, my soul to take." "There is a growing tendency among college students to let their childhood beliefs be forgotten," he had written.

> Especially we find this true when we speak of the divine creator and his plans for us. I thought I would also become that way, but I find that it is almost impossible for me to do so. . . . And so when I am tired and worried, and am almost ready to quit living as I should, I look up and see the picture of a little boy with sparkling eyes, and curly hair: I remember the child-like prayer; I pray that it may prove true for me as it did for my brother Arthur.

Despite Whittier's religious cast and the fundamentalist pressures of the community, his education in Founders was to be almost entirely secular. The notable exception was a senior course, the Philosophy of Christian Reconstruction, in which students were required to write long introspective essays on "What Can I Believe?" Nixon's October 9, 1933, paper revealed candidly the fundamentalism of his earlier religious indoctrination, his parents' own apprehension about "liberal" influences at the college, and, as they feared, his eventual drift away from a simple, literal Quakerism.

My parents, "fundamental Quakers," had ground into me, with the aid of the church, all the fundamental ideas in their strictest interpretation. The infallibility and literal correctness of the Bible, the miracles, even the whale story, all these I accepted as facts when I entered college four years ago. Even then I could not forget the admonition to not be misled by college professors who might be a little too liberal in their views! Many of those childhood ideas have been destroyed but there are some which I cannot bring myself to drop. To me, the greatness of the universe is too much for man to explain. I still believe that God is the creator, the first cause of all that exists. I still believe that He lives today, in some form, directing the destinies of the cosmos. How can I reconcile this idea with my scientific method? It is of course an unanswerable question. However, for the time being I shall accept the solution offered by Kant, that man can go only so far in his research and explanations; from that point on we must accept God. What is unknown to man, God knows.

He now saw Jesus Christ less as the martial, extraterrestrial figure of Rader revivals than in far more symbolic and sophisticated terms.

He reached the highest conception of God and of value that the world has ever seen. He lived a life which radiated those values. He taught a philosophy which revealed those values to men. I even go so far as to say Jesus and God are one, because Jesus set the great example which is forever pulling men upward to the ideal life. His life was so perfect that he "mingled" his soul with God's. . . . The important fact is that Jesus lived and taught a life so perfect that he continued to live and grow after his death—in the hearts of men. It may be true that the resurrection story is a myth, but symbolically it teaches the great lesson that men who achieve the highest values in their lives may gain immortality. . . . Orthodox teachers have always insisted that the physical resurrection of Jesus is the most important cornerstone in the Christian religion. I believe that the modern world will find a real resurrection in the life and teachings of Jesus.

He would finish college with a B+ average, mostly A's the last two years, the only C's in French and in three semesters of journalism with Upton. It was an impressive record, and he would make the most of the offerings. Only on closer examination was it apparent what a strikingly narrow undergraduate education he had been afforded at the small college. Richard Nixon would graduate with no science courses, only an elementary survey of economics, not even an introductory brush with sociology, psychology, or art. Like most Whittier students at the time, he would be given no real intellectual taste of the thought shaping the world they inherited— Marxism and fascism, the great currents in modern sociology, economics, physics, and government. He could select no classes in Paul Smith's tiny domain in political science or diplomatic history. Of the few courses offered in his major, he chose not to enroll in a history of California or the young professor's popular Representative Americans, a biographical study of "the character and makeup" of notable men and women in government. In both the California history and the biographies, Smith tried to go behind the façade of politics to the moral crises and subtle corruptions of power. One of the special studies was the rise and fall of Pio Pico, the last Mexican governor of California. "I've often thought that it would have been marvelous if . . . he could have had the Pio Pico project, and read the life of that man," Smith said of Nixon decades later. "He would have seen how far up one can go and, after that, how far down one can go. It would be a very sobering study . . . there is a lesson in humility. You have to be darned careful what you're doing in politics."

"YOU MUST GET ANGRY . . . ABOUT LOSING"

More than any academic experience, it was college debating that seemed to foreshadow and ever shape his later entry into national politics. He debated all four years at Whittier, and his triumphs were celebrated by later writers and in part by Nixon himself, who saw in debate the successful campaigner and congressional investigator he would become.

He was painstakingly prepared, keeping on small index cards notes from research or from advice asked of Smith and Upton, little aide-mémoire he stuffed in his suit-coat pocket, a habit he would carry through most of his political life. Despite experience in high school, he was visibly nervous before debates, much as he was tense before walking on stage as an actor. "But as soon as he began to speak," team manager Kenny Ball remembered, "he would always seem to settle down." Having spoken, he wrote furiously as he sat listening to opposing speakers or his teammate, from time to time impatiently thrusting on his partner an attack or rebuttal scribbled in what one of them called his "impossible handwriting and own particular style of condensing words and phrases." "He'd write like mad and hand it to you to read from the scrawls," said Osmyn Stout, who was frequently teamed with him one year. "He always had the answers for everybody and some of the men didn't like this."

His own delivery could be quick and cutting, but his physical gestures awkward and the style broken by stilted phrases. A sometime opponent, William Hornaday, thought him "very astute and serious, no humor, it was to the point," yet given to the "old-time emphasis—'May I make this one thing clear.' " For three years he would be in the shadow of another Whittier debater, Joe Sweeney, a red-haired, confident, and outgoing Irishman who was a Franklin and whom the newspaper pronounced only half in jest Nixon's "deadly rival." "He was not our best debater at all," Osmyn Stout would say of Richard Nixon when asked about his reputation as a college champion. "A fellow named Sweeney was much better."

Arguing tariff policy, the team drove back and forth in 1930–31 among other small schools of the Southern California Debating Conference—California Christian, Cal Tech, La Verne, Redlands, and Pasadena. Kenny Ball remembered Frank Nixon following them avidly, taking notes just as he had done in high school. "And his father would always take us to the debates if we needed transportation. He was very much interested in hearing Dick and how he got along." Nixon became, he wrote later, "a convinced free-trader" as a result of that season, and his victory over perennial conference champion Redlands made him a campus hero. The next year, Frank Nixon loaned the team his big Packard for a thirty-five-hundred-mile trip through the Pacific Northwest, in which they argued the question of government economic controls and won twenty-four of twenty-seven debates.

Away from home or family, nineteen-year-old Richard remembered in some detail a side trip in San Francisco. The worldly Joe Sweeney had gotten a card from a bellboy at their hotel and led them down winding streets to a drugstore, where he showed the card to a man at the counter who dramatically pushed round a fake shelf of drugs to open onto a speakeasy. "It was not a particularly boisterous place," Nixon thought,

> although the smoky air and the casual attitude of the patrons made us feel that we had wandered into a veritable den of iniquity. I did not have the slightest idea what to drink so Sweeney ordered a Tom Collins for me. Except for him, none of us had been in a speakeasy before, and I had never tasted alcohol, so it was a lark just to sit there watching the people, listening to their conversation, and admiring the barmaid who served our drinks.

Afterward, the team teased their devout and sober Quaker colleague about the trip. Richard Nixon had "toured the Northwest with the debate team," said the *Quaker Campus*, "leaving a trail blazed with victories and fluttering feminine hearts."

The next season, 1932–33, was to be Whittier's chance for national acclaim in forensics. For the topic of U.S. cancellation of the Allied war debts, an entire reference room of the city library was turned over to the team, and funds raised for another three-thousand-mile eighteen-day regional tour, this time with Sweeney and Nixon as a single team on both sides of the question. "Blizzards, mix-ups in dates, and hard-headed judges" is how the *Acropolis* would later characterize the trip. More plainly, it was a competitive disaster. Against larger schools, they won only one debate. "Nixon overwhelmed us with his first speech, and won the audience," recalled Weldon Taylor, one of the opponents at Brigham Young, "but we had the data." That spring they lost the championship cup back to Redlands, and the year ended with a dinner at the Nixon home behind the grocery in honor of Joe Sweeney's last season.

His rival graduated, Nixon won the *Reader's Digest* extemporaneous speaking contest among conference colleges in the autumn of 1933, but the debate team, arguing the expansion of Presidential power, entered only two tournaments his senior year and went winless. In the wake of the forlorn 1933 tour there were no more regional trips scheduled, and college appropriations to the program were cut drastically. After a bright beginning, his college debating career would end with little fanfare and two years of consistent defeat, though the actual record remained buried while the legend of his forensic powers grew.

"He was a merciless opponent," concluded one Whittier teacher. Dick's great strength, manager Kenny Ball remembered, "was his ability to get his opponent off-balance. He would so fluster the other speaker with his steady attack that his opposition would become emotional and stop thinking clearly." Ball recounted how Nixon had become angry and ineffectual during the hapless 1933 season, and later guarded against it. "Dick himself lost a debate once against La Verne College because he lost his temper. He learned his lesson, and that never happened again." Another classmate, Louis Valla, thought Nixon debated in his final college years with almost a controlled rage. He once advised Valla, "To be a good debater, you've got to be able to get mad on your feet without losing your head." William Hornaday saw the same anger in the scrawled notes Nixon passed to team-mates. One of them to Hornaday read insistently "Pour it on at this point!" What had begun as suggestions of substantive arguments became in the last two years curt orders about technique—"save your ammunition," "play to the judges, they're the ones who decide."

Kenny Ball and his other partners also watched how he might suddenly depart from the carefully prepared case, perplexing his own team no less than opponents. "I know that a few times when I debated with him even I did not know what he was going to say," Ball recounted. "He would come out suddenly extemporaneously with some ideas that I had not heard before when we were going over the material for the debate." Hornaday remembered, "He never left himself unguarded. Here I'd be opposing him, you know, and . . . we had debated on the same issue before, and I thought he'd used practically the same material as I was. He would come up with something that would just beat us down—oh, my! Always using that ace in the hole. He always looked for that."

One morning late in February 1933, Nixon's team debated Southern California in Founders. Early in the match Nixon seemed relaxed and confident before the home crowd, and he brought down the house with humorous asides. "The world is going to the bow-wows," a girl in the audience remembered him saying. It struck them all as so amusing. But as the contest wore on, USC scored noticeably and Whittier needed a rally in the final rebuttals. The *Quaker Campus* editor, Lois Elliot, was sitting in a balcony just above the debaters. "I remember it clearly," she said long afterward. "It took place in the spring of 1933. I was editor on the school paper covering the debate. I sat in the gallery, and I saw when Nixon spoke in his rebuttal that he quoted from a blank paper. I told it later to my roommate; it was against all regulations, and very cunning. I remember it well."

By his sophomore year he had reached his full height of five feet eleven and still weighed less than one hundred fifty pounds, "all bones and very slender . . . all hair," Jewell Triggs, a junior coed, remembered. Yet he went out for varsity football, and along with debate, drama, and several other activities, intense studying, and work at the grocery, he played football every year at Whittier. It was before the era of the mammoth college football player, and the team had "any number of undersized fellas" like Nixon, coach Wallace Newman recalled. But he was never more than a third-string substitute on the thirty-four man squad, rarely appearing in varsity games, and then for only a few minutes if Whittier were far ahead or hopelessly behind. "He just nearly died, he wanted to be on the team so bad," said Lucille Parsons. "He said they needed bench warmers anyway."

"If he could have run well, we could have used him," Newman said later. "Dick was a pretty awkward kid." For three years he was again, as at Fullerton, the tackle and blocking dummy, the scrimmage cannon fodder for the larger, faster varsity. "Guts. I'll say that for Nixon," recalled Gail Jobe, another substitute. "He had guts." Across the line on the varsity, tackle Clint Harris was six feet four, two hundred eleven pounds, and three years older. "We couldn't let up or the coach would be on us. So I'd have to knock the little guy for a loop. Oh, my gosh, did he take it. The harder you hit him the more he came back at you." Another player thought at the time, "Dick Nixon, I don't know why you do this, but I admire your red-blooded intestinal fortitude to stay with it until the end of the season, or until the end comes otherwise."

When the afternoon sessions did not go well, Newman often kept them into the misty autumn dusk, bringing out an old white football and turning on the weak lights around Hadley Field. In the locker room afterward there was horseplay and comradery, but Nixon never seemed to be part of it. "I can't ever remember Dick in bull sessions in free time," Newman said. Wood Glover, one of the players, described the times after practice: "Dick was just a little remote . . . not the kind of guy who participated in that. I think his purpose was to take his shower, get dressed, go home, and get back to studying and to mind the store."

Often he met his father outside the dressing room. Frank Nixon came to watch practices faithfully. Jewell Triggs, whose boyfriend was on the team, recounted how Frank trudged up the slope to Hadley Field, visibly slowed by his arthritis. "I can remember Dick's father coming up and watching the practices . . . wandering up the hill behind the old athletic building, and he would stand there in the afternoons and watch the boys working out. He was always right there behind him." Frank also asked to go along on the team bus, and sometimes rode with Grace Newman, the coach's wife, who recalled him as "a lot of fun to be with. He was keyed up and having the best time. He said it was no matter whether Dick played or not." "I have a very close memory, an image of the two of them, father and son, walking out together afterwards," said Jewell Triggs. "He was," she thought of Frank Nixon, "very, very close to his son."

As many as six thousand fans streamed onto the bleached wooden stands at Hadley Field to watch the purple and gold Poets play other small colleges. Played in light shoulder pads, thin canvas pants, and stiff leather helmets, it was a bruising, often bloody game fought against bare shins and unprotected bodies. And the somber little Quaker city loved it. Local merchants financed an elaborate water wagon on old Model A wheels and an aging alumnus would dash out at time-out to give the team a drink from separate sprays released from the wagon. When Whittier won, students jumped in jalopies and tore through town with horns squawking. Local movie theaters let the team in without tickets, and drugstore counters fed some players free for the week.

The hero of this small spectacle was Wallace "Chief" Newman, the Indian coach who had been born on the La Jolla reservation, played football at USC, and come to Whittier in 1929. "Pretty much kicked around as a kid," as one of his players described him, Newman was a big swarthy man, nearly six feet three, childless, given to a slight stutter and, when the game went badly, to drinking large quantities of water in nervous gulps. His coaching was rigid and simplistic. "Being willing to pay the price" is how one player summarized his credo. "With him good enough wasn't good enough," recounted Charlie Kendle. "There is only one question, 'Did you get the job done?' . . . and if you didn't, there weren't any excuses. . . . Chief drove the fellows, and he was very demanding." Players remembered his "booming voice . . . urging his men on." "You know who a good loser is?" he mockingly asked them. "It's somebody who hates to lose and who gets up and comes back and fights again." From a core of exceptional talent lured to the small college, Newman produced winning seasons in 1930 and 1931 and a conference championship the next year, but his team Nixon's senior year was mediocre and suffered an ignominious 51–0 defeat at the hands of USC. He rarely praised a boy on a fine play and never consoled his team in a hard-fought defeat. Often he told Nixon and the others, "You must get angry, terribly angry about losing . . . the mark of the good loser is that he takes his anger out on himself and not on his victorious opponents or his teammates." If disgusted at their performance, he gave few pep talks, preferring to walk out with a caustic aside, "I'll leave you girls alone." "He was a football coach. That's all he knew," remembered Emmet Ingrum, a member of the team. "He didn't understand personalities, he could care less, I guess . . . I don't think he'd get along five minutes today."

Richard Nixon never lettered in Whittier football, even in his senior year when he was one of fourteen denied the recognition, most of them underclassmen. When Nixon hesitated to go out his senior year, Newman had appealed to him personally. "You ought to come out," the coach told him. "Really what is wrong is not losing. What is wrong is not making the team." "And once out you can't quit," the coach explained to an interviewer later, "you make a commitment."

About to sit on the bench and play only when it no longer mattered, he was nonetheless so tense before kickoff that he could not eat. Other players jockeyed to sit next to him and eat his steak at the meals Newman had served on game days. Charlie Kendle remembered that "his interest and enthusiasm were just almost contagious. . . . Dick can get pleasure out of putting on a wet uniform." He was at his most vocal when the other side appeared to be cheating or the referees missed a penalty. "See some underhanded act on the field, and no one could yell louder than Dick," Edwin Wunder said. With Whittier well ahead, the student body would set up a chant: "Put Nixon in! Put Nixon in!" "I'll never forget the tremendous roar that went up from the rooting section when Dick got into the lineup for the last few minutes of the game," said a teammate. Charlie Kendle recalled him coming into the huddle and "everybody would attempt to make Dick look good because there was this feeling toward him." But in his eagerness and nervousness he jumped offside on the first play. "I never saw anybody play harder," Ed Wunder said, recalling those moments. "He gave it everything he had, and that's the truth. I can see him yet."

He would recall sports at Whittier as "my happiest memories," games "the most exciting kind of combat imaginable." As for coach Newman, "I think that I admired him more and learned more from him than from any man I have ever known outside my father," Nixon wrote in his memoirs. "There is no way I can adequately describe Chief Newman's influence on me." When Nixon's last season was over he invited the senior players down to the East Whittier house where Hannah and Frank served them a huge meal. "We had a delicious chicken dinner and Dick sat there and played the piano while we all sang," Wood Glover recalled.

Later, reporters were ever puzzled at why he had played football so long and so punishingly at Whittier and, even with the cheers when he finally got in the game, with such failure and humiliation. In the end, thought Wood Glover, "He just enjoyed the game. He enjoyed being around it." He found among the football team, even apart from their locker room bull sessions, the candor and freedom from artifice that he had seen in his father, and that was missing in much of the rest of his universe. If the Milhouses were a tribe of quiet, compelling women, if debate and academics demanded subtlety and maneuver, the football field was a world of men and a kind of raw honesty. "I think he liked the contact with those people," Ingrum said. "And I'm not too sure that he didn't enjoy it more than he did with just the scholar type, because I think he was challenged from a different standpoint. You know, the athletes don't give a hoot what they say or when they say it . . . and I think Dick enjoyed the comradeship and the straightforwardness."

"BY SOME THEY WERE CONSIDERED RICH"

In the early thirties the Depression enveloped Whittier like a chill basin fog, touching a few only lightly, blanketing many more in want and uncertainty. No bread lines curled along the leafy hillside streets or the boulevard. But smaller ranchers and businessmen suffered, jobs were lost, and the visible evidence of the larger disaster was not far away. "A lot of ranchers in the citrus area were all having a rough time," Wood Glover recalled. By 1931, hundreds of migrant families squatted by the roadside in smoking makeshift camps only a few miles beyond Whittier's outskirts, waiting for work as pickers at ten cents an hour. "A dollar for a ten-hour day," Merle West remembered. "There were families all camped around. I don't know what the poor people were living on."

The southern California boom of the twenties had faded slowly, almost invisibly. Ever sensitive to its image and the presence of what papers and politicians called "bums and Reds," local governments commonly swept their streets clean of the unsightly homeless. Los Angeles police arrested over twelve thousand people for "vagrancy" in 1927–28. "Unemployment," observed Louis Adamic bitterly, "is a crime in sunny California." Soon afterward, however, the tide of the dispossessed overwhelmed the civic fiction. As impoverished Okies and Arkies from the Dust Bowl crowded outlying areas, the region's otherwise winsome national advertising began to carry an ominous footnote. "Warning! Come to California for a glorious vacation. Advise anyone not to come seeking employment."

The climate of extremity laid bare old fears. Merle West described Frank nervously transferring money from the cash register to a sack he secreted away in some corner, only to find one day that "a couple of hundred bucks in this paper bag" had been swept up and thrown out by mistake. In a panic, he found the money still intact in the smoldering trash ditch behind the house. Hadley Marshburn remembered his uncle buying a revolver in the early thirties and setting it ominously under the cash register. "Now, it's all right to use that to scare somebody with but don't fire it at anybody," Hannah had told him. "Oh, yes, if anybody tries to rob me," Frank replied, "I'll shoot to kill him." His frightened belligerence was hardly unique in the quiet town. With starving migrants camped only miles away, a local orange rancher, "a good old Quaker," as Paul Smith remembered him, "shouldered his shotgun and marched up and down the row of trees vowing that he would shoot any intruder."

At first the college adopted the graveyard jauntiness of the Hoover administration and local boosters. "Everybody insists that the problem is not all that serious," the student paper commented on a campus topic that October of 1931; "like Free Love or the Depression, perhaps we shouldn't have mentioned it at all." In Founders Hall the reality was far more grim. Fund-raising fell drastically, new campus building ground to a halt for nearly two decades, and the school verged on bankruptcy. William Hornaday remembered Dexter telling him not to worry about being behind in tuition, but adding almost plaintively, "If you can bring in a dollar or two, do it." Ola Welch worked part-time for the college treasurer, where the situation was frequently desperate. "My instructions were first thing in the morning to open the mail and deposit any money," she said. "It was that close."

Most Whittier students worked, struggling to pay fees and subsist. They shared textbooks, negotiated tuition payments by the month, survived on ten-cent tamales, crept into neighboring groves after nightfall to pick avocados. "We weren't the only ones," a student said of the avocados. "There were teachers there, too." Many "smudged" at Leffingwell's or other citrus groves for twenty-five cents an hour, keeping the small smoking pots going on frosty evenings to save the fruit. "We prayed for cold winters," said Wood Glover, who also worked year-round as a milkman. Clint Harris cleaned chicken houses, bartered game tickets for meat from local merchants, and fumigated orange groves to the point of exhaustion. "If you had fifty cents in your pocket," said Ed Wunder, "there was a pretty good chance you had fifty cents more than the guy standing beside you." Ola could afford just one pair of shoes for school every year. "Oh, how we envied the dorm girls who played bridge in the afternoon," she said later.

Though the cash trade diminished, the Nixon grocery continued to return a profit during the depths of the Depression. Ironically, as the boom disappeared, they were better off than ever before. "Dick got what he needed here to go to college," Merle West recalled. Elizabeth Timberlake remembered huge Thanksgiving dinners at the Nixons' where fifty or sixty relatives might gather and Hannah and Frank would cook from the store. They used their margin generously. "Oh, lots of credit [was] extended and I'm sure there must have been lots that was never collected," said Mildred Mendenhall, who helped in the store and sometimes kept books. "We had to carry a lot of people on credit—sometimes for years—and I saw at first hand the problem of people out of a job, who couldn't pay their bills," Richard Nixon once told a reporter. "I remember back in the 1930s how deeply I felt about the plight of those people my own age who used to come into my father's store where they couldn't pay the bill," he said forty years afterward, "because their fathers were out of work, and how this seemed to separate them from the others in our school."

Though there were far wealthier students, he was certainly one of those "others." Merle West went with him into Los Angeles before his junior year to buy a 1930 Model A Ford for $325. "He [was] tickled, he was full of laughs and jokes," West remembered. The price was more than it cost most hometown students for a full year at the college, and the car immediately set him off from the majority of his peers. E. V. Lindstrom, a fellow Orthogonian, thought "one out of fifty students" had an automobile. "We thumbed a lot," he said. "There were only about half a dozen cars in college when we went there," recalled Robert Halliday of the class of '34. Merely to have an automobile, said Hubert Perry, a banker's son who had a car, made them "one of the fortunate few."

If there was a more visible symbol of economic status at the college than a car, it was the tuxedo, the very mark of distinction between the Franklins and Orthogonians. Robert Farnham recounted how the Orthogonians went to dances "in suits and ties because none of us had a tux and we didn't have the wherewithal to rent it. . . . They were the black-tie boys and we were the straight-tie boys." Yet Richard Nixon would have his own tuxedo all four years, and bought a new one as a senior. A Franklin, Dick Spaulding, asked to borrow his tux for a girls' society dance not knowing he had just purchased another, and Nixon was unforgettably gracious and selfless about the newly purchased formal suit. "I caught him loaning me his new tuxedo, and he was going to wear the old one to the dance," said Spaulding, warmly remembering the incident long afterward. "I almost had to fight him to keep him from loaning me his new one and wearing the old himself. That's the Dick Nixon I knew and loved," he wrote.

In his later political career, Nixon frequently spoke and wrote of his own poverty, and occasionally of the hurt and humiliation he witnessed during the Depression among indigent customers, but never of the cars he drove, nor of tuxedos and his own relative affluence among the Whittier students. "The idea that the key to Nixon was his early poverty is ridiculous," Jessamyn West would say. "The Nixons had a grocery store, two cars, and sent their son to college. By some they were considered rich."

Despite their relatively better circumstances and the generosity in the family and store, the Nixons' Depression charity was sometimes strained, and occasioned the first and last open disputes witnesses would record between Hannah and Frank. "She never turned a tramp away from the

door. This was one of the things she and my dad used to argue about,"
Richard Nixon once recalled. "My father thought they ought to be made
to work before helping them out. But mother ran the house like a charitable
operation." While Frank helped "certain families . . . in difficult circumstances . . . with rent, food or a job," an East Whittier Friends minister
recalled years later, he also railed bitterly about local Quakers who boasted
in church of their contributions while running large unpaid bills at Nixon's
across the boulevard.

Once they had discovered a regular customer shoplifting. She was the
Quaker mother of two, and Hannah was distraught about the publicity if
she were arrested. Frank and Don had argued that they should turn her
over to the police, but Richard had said, "Let's drop the whole thing."
When Hannah started to argue that they must report it, he abruptly overrode
her. "You can't let them arrest her," he said. "You know what it will do
to those boys to hear that their mother is a thief. Work it out some other
way." Hannah quietly confronted the woman, who confessed and privately
made amends. "My husband thought the woman would never pay us back,"
Hannah recounted, "but Richard was sure I had done the right thing. It
took months and months, but eventually she paid us every cent. Richard
was right."

He arose at 4:00 A.M. with his mother, who had resumed baking her
popular pies soon after Edward's birth. They continued to be close. He
confided in her and "discussed things" in the predawn hour together, she
would recall, "even though he isn't the gushy type and doesn't pour out
his heart." He asked his mother to shop for his clothes. "He'd get me
to buy it or do without it," she recalled. He insisted, too, that his shirts be
ironed perfectly, and one niece recalled Hannah "always having to press
his shirt at the last minute," frequently because others refused to listen to
his complaints. "Give me anything to iron but Richard's shirts," one of
her sisters told her. "He's too fussy." "Richard was clearly his mother's
favorite," said Verna Hough, watching them all in Prescott. "I felt sorry
for Don. Richard took it for granted that everything was being done for
him. Everything was being done for Richard's education."

Friends recalled no open resentment among the brothers in these college
years, but the tension they all remembered was the continuing, sometimes
venomous shouting between father and sons. Frank Nixon still yelled at
his boys as they matured, and they retaliated with a vengeance. Visiting
the grocery in the early thirties, Eldo West was astounded that the Nixon
boys, as he wrote his daughter Jessamyn, "could be so cruel, so loud-
mouthed, so outspoken, so critical of their father there in the store before
everyone else." West could not understand the anger "unless they felt
they got it when they were young and now they are paying their father

back." Marshall Clough, who thought Dick so quiet and withdrawn in Prescott, visited them in East Whittier at this point and was shocked to overhear him in such an "angry . . . argument with his father."

In the memories of his college years, as so often in his later career, there sometimes seemed two Richard Nixons, the one prominent and familiar, the other almost opaque or unseen. Scores of students knew him as the now imposing, now awkward campus leader, scholar, actor, debater, and football bench warmer, the brisk, intent young man hurrying from activity to activity. Many saw him much closer, behind stage or on the football field or in Orthogonian meetings, as a solitary, shy, painfully uncertain boy amid all the apparent energy and versatility. But a half century afterward, when they all looked with their fragments of view, the observers and the friends, the onlookers and teammates and society brothers in the end had at least one recollection in common. Near or far, they would come to conclude that they had hardly known him at all.

"The sophomore with the intellectual look above the eyebrows," *Quaker Campus* called him in October 1931. The following spring, the paper's gossip column chided him in the wake of his debate successes: "Dick Nixon letting you, sir, and you, know that he is not conceited." On October 21, 1932, the *Campus* profiled him with the first of what would be countless caricatures, a block print by Dick Harris that caught in dark lines the thick hair and heavy eyebrows, the ski nose and rounded cheek of a Nixon not yet twenty, and the intimation of a famous jowl already sensed by the artist. He could seem reserved and utterly distracted and to some coldly aloof. They used almost the same words to describe him. "I wouldn't say Nixon was hail-fellow-well-met," said Regina Dunkin Kemp, who was his academic equal. "Well, he wasn't hail-fellow-well-met by a long shot . . . he became a person people would either intensely dislike or intensely like . . . I think he excited both reactions," said Merton Wray, who had known him also through Whittier High. From Iowa, Ed Wunder had begun the freshman year late and remembered the first time he saw class president Nixon. "So I went up and introduced myself . . . and, as we know, he is not the real friendly type. I didn't get a real royal welcome or anything."

Many saw him as strained and tightly strung, physically as well as in personality. "Dick was a very tense person, always a tense person," Jewel Triggs said, remembering him striding across the shaded hillside at Whittier. "He walked tense, and when he walked he would really take out. I mean he didn't have a leisurely graceful walk." He was a good "listener,"

Hubert Perry thought, "not the kind of individual who would ever monopolize a class or conversation." Yet others found him impatiently cutting them off, and often peremptory. "He had the ability to let you start a sentence and he ended it by the time you got to about the fourth word," said Emmett Ingrum. It was a habit that alienated many students and "didn't permit him to be accepted as well as he might have been." Years later Jewel Triggs could picture him on the steps of Founders "just laying down the line, just talking his head off to three or four people." Working with Nixon in the Poet Theatre, Marjorie Hildreth was not surprised by the resentment at his manner. "Well, he was stuffy, let's face it," she said. In the audiences or on campus, Hubert Perry and other friends watched him act or debate or argue aggressively in an obvious and deliberate effort to overcome his innate shyness and to win the very approval his intensity sometimes prevented. "I think maybe this was a kind of a power attempt," Perry would say of Nixon. "I don't think he ever had self-confidence." To still others, though, the effort was too convincing. "He had an almost ruthless cocksureness about him," said Helen Larson, "which was the reason some students disliked him."

"Nixon did not have any close friends," concluded Kenny Ball, who saw him often and at close range over the four years as a fellow debater, history major, and in other activities. "If Nixon had any close personal friends it was probably me," said Keith Wood. Still, Wood looked back with the same sense so many others felt: "He was a loner." Lorena Yee, a popular, practical-joking freshman when Nixon was a senior, used to borrow his car often and they had an easy, warm friendship. "They were kind of boy-girl pals, you know," recalled Robert Halliday, "just pals." Yet however relaxed, however pleasant, the relationship always remained only on the surface—even, some of them remembered, with the girl he seemed sure to marry.

"A damn strong woman," Edith Gibbons, one of the Milhous cousins, would say of Ola Florence Welch at Whittier College. Despite a continuing shyness, Ola remained consistently popular and accomplished in her own right, elected as a class officer or to the student council three of their four years, active in drama, women's glee club, and the Metaphonian Society, frequently winning academic honors as a music education major. In the early 1930s she was a fashionably plump coed of her era, fresh and attractive, quietly substantial, with dark hair and deep, heavy-lidded eyes that gave her an almost sultry look, and with an uncommon sense of identity and poise her fellow students widely admired. "With the dignity of a true lady," the 1934 *Acropolis* described her in the student government, "Ola Florence

Welch represented the women's point of view toward the difficulties which continually arose."

"I tell you," one of her friends said later of Ola and Richard Nixon, "they made a handsome couple." They seemed paired off from the beginning, from their high school romance, and appeared to date steadily through college. Many who saw them at Whittier assumed they would marry sometime after graduation. "They seemed to be matched intellectually. . . . I think it was mainly because they were both good students and intelligent people that it seemed like a good match," said Byron Netzley. Her friends, though, remained puzzled by the relationship. "The girls used to say, 'Why do you go out with him?' " Ola once recalled. To other women on campus, Nixon would appear dull and often pretentious. "Dick was not a ladies' man," said Jewel Triggs. "He didn't have the glamour about him that attracts the opposite sex. He wasn't sexy." Another friend thought, "He didn't know how to be personable or sexy with girls. He didn't seem to have a sense of fun, you know? I felt a kind of amused affection for him, like 'Oh, Dick, come off it.' " A girl who double-dated with him added, "Sometimes, when he'd be off on cloud nine about some philosophical subject, I'd want to blurt out, 'Oh, for heaven's sake, we're supposed to be having fun.' "

They went to the beach, to movies, to society dances at the Whittier women's club or hotels in the area, usually alone. He occasionally set up double or triple dates with Ed Wunder or Clint Harris but "he had no close boyfriends," Ola remembered, and they never double-dated with her friends. "He didn't like my girlfriends. He would stalk out of the room with his head high. I still remember it, they'd get angry about it. . . . People liked him and didn't like him." But it was not only her snubbed friends who disliked him. Her parents had come to disapprove of Richard Nixon. "My mother was not fond of him from the first," Ola said. "I really don't know why." He picked her up by parking outside the Welch home in Whittier and insistently beeping the horn. "Mother was death against it," Ola recalled. At one point the parents had ordered her not to see Nixon again. "Her father detested him," thought one observer, "and forbade her to go out with him." But the Welches soon relented, and they continued to date.

The disapproval of girlfriends and parents, and a common shyness, worked to keep them together, though the attraction others could not see was always there for Ola. "I am not counting out sex appeal," she answered a question once about their romance, "which as a subject, believe me, we didn't discuss in those days." She confided later that he had been "a perfectly normal young man," but she remembered, too, the sexual strictness and taboos of the moment. "We were very puritanical. There was no hanky-panky." As in high school, her enduring attraction in college was explained by his exceptional intelligence and relative sophistication. "I think most of all it was because of his mind," she reminisced. "He had a fine mind. He read the newspapers. He knew what was going on." "You have no idea," she once said, "how tremendously interesting and engrossing he was to me, the daughter of a small-town police chief. I considered myself provincial and him worldly."

They had "marvelous talks," Ola recalled. "We used to argue politics constantly," she said afterward. "He was a Republican. I thought Roosevelt was wonderful and he detested him." She came to believe his political conservativism was "ingrained in Dick as a boy," and that "he grew up with a strong feeling of individualism, of self-reliance, of not depending upon the government or anyone but yourself. The bureaucracy of the New Deal antagonized him." Later she wondered about their long and often heated discussions. "I don't know why he argued with me. I was not as intelligent as he was. I guess he just tried to show me the way." Yet his own relatives and others saw her as having what one called "an unusual interest in politics" and a home as much or more politically conscious than the East Whittier grocery. "Politics," remarked Olive Marshburn, "were more important in her family than in his. I know that her mother and father felt strongly that way."

Whatever the subject, they argued and fought often during their college years. "We had a very stormy relationship, more stormy than most," Ola would remember it. While friends later described her as "stubborn" and unrelenting in their arguments, what seemed more volatile was his own swift anger beneath the disciplined surface. To many who watched them together, Nixon appeared flinty and sharp. "He was combative rather than conciliatory. He had a nasty temper," said a fellow student. "He seemed to me to lack tenderness and warmth." Ola's own memories of the quarrels were softer but little different. "His face would cloud," she remembered of the beginning, "and he'd make a conscious effort to restrain himself." But the argument soon flashed and followed a familiar sequence. "He'd be harsh and I'd cry," she said. "Then we'd make up."

"He was so changeable," she later reflected. "He had a tendency to downgrade himself." Like some of his male friends who saw him more distantly, she felt an underlying unease and awkwardness, a deeper unfulfilled need. "He seemed lonely and so solemn at school," she thought, watching him so immersed in activities and so often surrounded by people yet somehow isolated. "He didn't know how to mix. He was smart and sort of set apart. I think he was unsure of himself, deep down."

Still, they kept seeing each other, and Ola Welch was through it all his dearest, closest friend. "We did have some good times together," she said afterward. He frequently loaned her the 1930 Ford, a privilege few others got. Ola adored dancing—"I love floating to dreamy music," she would say—but while he took her to off-campus informals, he would never actually get on the ballroom floor. One of his more endearing moments came in May 1933, on the eve of the student body presidential election, when he picked her up for an Orthogonian party. This time he came in the house. "I can dance," she remembered him announcing proudly. He had taken lessons and proceeded to show her simple fox trot and waltz steps in their living room. "Nixon more than enjoying his first dance—Florence Welch must be a good teacher," the *Quaker Campus* recorded the same evening in a later gossip column. But even then Ola had felt afterward a sense of intrusion on his fragile reserve. "I pushed him into it," she would say later about dancing. "Don't think he was ever happy about that."

Dick was "very close-mouthed" about his family, she recounted, and "we didn't talk about our parents." Ola's own reception in East Whittier was warm. "He was nothing but very kind to me," she recalled of her meeting with Frank Nixon. Hannah she thought "a lovely lady, wonderful to me, but an iron fist in a velvet glove," although at the same time it appeared "her husband overpowered her."

From time to time they each dated others at Whittier, usually with Nixon making the break and leaving Ola to discover it afterward in hurt or jealousy. "He went out off on a date but wouldn't tell, and I'd find out about it," she recounted. "I'd go out with others but he always knew." Some of these were what Sheldon Beeson remembered as "an accommodation date." Nixon "would ask a girl to go to something for the sake of being able to go because it was a boy-girl, male-female party . . . he liked to be at places where people were. . . . He wanted to be where the fire was," said Jewell Triggs. But the urge to be part of campus society did not explain the random little rejections and deceits with Ola. On other occasions, when he felt no need to attend, Orthogonians and others remembered almost cajoling him about taking a girl. "All of us would have to needle Dick a little bit to be sure that he came up with a date," Charlie Kendle recalled society dances after ballgames. Besides Ola, there seemed no other visible crush on the Whittier campus despite his prominence and apparent popularity. "He was a poor dancer and not in demand," said Keith Wood. His awkwardness with girls even became the object of a cruel joke. Friends told him they had arranged a date with Elizabeth Rees, an attractive Whittier girl who had gone with Robert Logue at the high school, but when he arrived to pick her up she was not dressed to go out and they both realized the hoax in a mortifying moment. "I probably was as embarrassed as he was, or more so," Elizabeth said.

Beyond the dates, he seemed to have almost no social life at all in college. "He wasn't one you'd find downtown on Saturday night playing around with a bunch of other guys," said Bruce Burchell, who was in the class behind. Friends recalled occasional outings in groups to Corona del Mar or Catalina Island; Nixon was seldom along. Once he had gone with Merle West to the old Follies on Burbank in downtown Los Angeles, where West remembered them hearing "a lot of loud music" and "a lot of semi-dirty jokes" with a "strip-teaser [who] didn't strip too far." He seemed always to return to Ola. "Dick Nixon is going around with a broad smile now that Ola Florence prefers a Ford," the campus gossip column remarked after one spat in the spring of their junior year. "He felt comfortable with her, and he didn't want to start any new relationship . . . he was stiff," one of her friends said later.

"There was a tacit agreement that we would be married some day," Ola would say of their last two years at Whittier. He had asked her to marry him, and they had begun to plan on it, though no date was set. "It was a foregone conclusion," thought Dick Spaulding, who knew them both. "All of us in Whittier expected Richard and Ola Florence to get married," another classmate said. Yet into their senior year, as in the preceding four years of the relationship, there was always something missing, something she felt he held back. "Sometimes I think I never really knew him," Ola would say long afterward, "and I was as close to him as anyone. I still feel some of that—he was a mystery."

His brother Harold was back and forth between Prescott and East Whittier in the winter and spring of 1930–31, home for brief stays and reluctantly, sometimes bitterly returning to Arizona at his parents' insistence when he visibly worsened in California. He continued to defy convalescence. The Timberlakes visited him in 1931, and his young cousins found him with his own horse, which he rode irrepressibly. Hannah returned to Prescott that summer and tried in vain to buy outright the Apache Drive house or property in Cortez Park near the Cloughs, obviously planning a lengthy recovery for Harold in the clear desert air. But with Edward scarcely a year old she could not yet go back to care for Harold full-time, and she spent most of the next year with the rest of the family in East Whittier, Harold coming and going in his homesickness amid the fitful pauses and advance of the disease.

In the summer of 1932 she took Don and her two-year-old with her and once more rented a cottage in Pinecrest, where she had lived with Harold and took in two other consumptives as boarders. Richard had been fighting a sinus infection at the close of school that spring, and his mother anxiously insisted that he join her that summer in Prescott, where he again worked as a barker at Frontier Days. They all drove back to East Whittier at the close of that summer. Then, early in the fall of Richard's junior year at Whittier, Harold again worsened. They moved him briefly back to Prescott, but he soon "insisted on coming home," as a cousin described it, and flatly refused to return to Arizona. His boyhood friend Floyd Wildermuth visited him often in his downstairs bedroom in the house, "begging him to go back there," he remembered. "He told me, and it left quite an impression on me, that he wouldn't go," Floyd said afterward. "He even knew he was going to die, but he would not go back. He just didn't like it down there."

Now twenty-three, at home to stay after more than two years of battle with his parents, Harold seemed to refuse all restraint. He loved to play checkers or simply sit and talk with Merle West at the gas station and struggled, wheezing and coughing with his sputum cup, up the slight incline to the pumps on Whittier Boulevard, taking ten minutes to negotiate the sixty feet from the house behind. "He would just go a little bit, just gasping for breath and sit there," West recalled the scene. Ralph Palmer, another close friend, came to see him that fall and cheerfully, without knowing the fatal flush of the disease, complimented him on the color in his cheeks. "Well, that's the sign of the last stages," Harold replied. The shadows seemed to reach out from the old group of boarders on Apache Drive. "One by one," Richard later recorded, they heard the news of the boys' deaths, which grieved his mother "as deeply as if they had been her own sons."

The end came relatively quickly, with some last spasms of hope and indulgence by the family. Early in 1933 Harold told his father he would like to see the desert beyond the San Bernardinos in spring bloom, and Frank "dropped everything to make plans for the trip," as Richard described it, renting one of the first house trailers, a simple wooden room on a truck chassis, and carefully planning their itinerary together. The family saw them off for what they all assumed would be a month's trip, but they were back in three days, Harold having hemorrhaged on the road. "He loved nature, music and beauty in all its forms," his parents wrote about him later, and Richard remembered clearly his brother's voice as he returned from the abortive trip describing "the wild flowers in the foothills and the striking sight of snow in the mountains." They called in a practical nurse to care for him, "to wait on him hand and foot," Merle West remembered, looking on from the station. "He was up and going until he was down, down, down, where he couldn't move."

On Monday, March 6, 1933, a day before their mother's forty-eighth birthday, Harold asked Richard to drive him downtown to buy Hannah an electric cake mixer he had seen advertised. "He barely had the strength to walk with me into the hardware store," Richard recounted. They had the mixer wrapped as a birthday present and took it home to hide in the closet until they could give it the next day. Early Tuesday morning Harold told his brother he was not feeling well and wanted to wait until that evening to present the mixer. Richard left for college. Soon afterward, Harold called for his mother in a wrenching scene very like Arthur's last night eight years before. " 'Though I do so want to get well I am so glad I am at peace with my maker,' " she quoted him later. "This is the last time I will see you until we meet in heaven." Richard was in Redwood Library when they handed him a note saying to return home at once. He drove back down the boulevard to find the hearse, the same mortician who had taken Arthur, already drawn up on Santa Gertrudes, and his mother and father "crying uncontrollably," as he remembered them, while the undertaker carried out Harold's body. "That night," he wrote, "I got the cake mixer out and gave it to my mother and told her that it was Harold's gift to her."

Ola went with him to the funeral two days later; they buried Harold, like Arthur, near Franklin Milhous in the Whittier Heights plot. "This death had a deep effect on him," Hannah remembered of Richard. But "he didn't let it out." His mother saw him react almost exactly as he had behaved after Arthur's death. "He sank into a deep, impenetrable silence. From that time on, it seemed Richard was trying to be three sons in one, striving even harder than before to make up to his father and me for our loss." In the mute grief there was also renewed fear. "Dick was kind of fatalistic," Ola recounted. "He thought he might get TB, too."

The parents' reaction would be typical as well. "We had high hopes for him," Hannah said later, "but we musn't question God's decision. The months I spent with Harold taught me a lesson in suffering, and helped me to understand the soul a little better. You see, God . . . let me learn understanding and compassion through the suffering of my son." After the death, Frank came with Eldo West to visit Jessamyn in the Altadena sanatorium where she was suffering herself from TB. The grieving father asked them painfully, "Why is it that the best and the brightest are always taken first?" Jessamyn West never forgot the moment. "It was something to have a brother die who was really accounted by his father as the flower of the family," she would say decades later. A small memorial pamphlet prepared after the death tenderly eulogized Harold Nixon. "His desire to create things in these preparatory years manifested itself in his having written many lovely poems to his family and friends," it said. "Harold accomplished as much in his short life in an exemplary way as many others who live their allotted span. His cheerfulness, patience and fortitude in the years of invalidism battling against disease were a constant challenge to those with whom he was in daily contact."

The last tribute was symbolic of the stabbing ironies cloaked in the funereal memories and morals. The "challenge," as the closer family and friends well knew, had been in the unequal struggle between a self-destructive young man and his divided parents, now punitive and commanding, now sacrificial and tragically doting toward their firstborn.

Richard's own memory of the death was telling as well. "He had a desperate will to live," he would write of his brother, ignoring years of behavior and family crises showing just the opposite. "TB was almost always incurable," he wrote, though they all knew that, too, was not the case, and that the genuine prospect of recovery had taken them to Prescott from the beginning. At a distance, he chose to see the death in terms of money. "My older brother . . . had tuberculosis for five years," he once told a Presidential audience. "The hospital, the doctor bills were more than we could afford. In the five years before he died, my mother never bought a new dress. . . . But the wonder of it was that we didn't know it." That version obscured his mother's real and perhaps more painful sacrifice, for all of them—her separation from her husband and sons to care for Harold in Prescott for more than a year and a half.

In the end, there seemed only one epitaph for Harold Samuel Nixon free of the tangled emotions of Yorba Linda and East Whittier. For decades after his death, his old roommate at Mount Hermon would send yearly to that school in Northfield, Massachusetts, a modest check in memory of their friendship there amid the scheduled prayers and cold basement showers of Mr. Moody's school.

"A REAL SMART POLITICIAN"

A few weeks after Harold's burial, Richard was in the midst of a campus campaign for student body president, the culmination of nearly three years of careful, sometimes frenetic preparation and positioning in the politics of the college. Friends like William Hornaday believed afterward that "he didn't care about his popularity, he never tried to be popular at Whittier College." "Even in college, political battles as such never appealed to me," he once said, "but I always seemed to get dragged into them to run for some office or another." Yet the actual sequence that led up to his run for student body president in the spring of 1933 told a very different story. At the time, it seemed that the only obstacle to his success was the very nakedness of his ambition and design. "He was shy," Ola Welch would say of her boyfriend's natural and lifelong diffidence in politics. "Still," she added, "he wanted to be president of the student body."

At the end of his freshman year, he had run for member-at-large on the student council and behind the scenes acted as unofficial campaign manager and adviser to Tolbert Moorhead, the junior opposing the Franklin candidate for the presidency. "I can still see him pacing up and down, jabbing his finger at me and firing instructions on how to deliver an effective speech," Moorhead recalled. "You have to find an issue and concentrate on it—forget yourself completely—think only of that issue!" he told the older student. Moorhead lost the race but remembered vividly the "fireball" walking back and forth across his living room and how Dick Nixon "sure tried" to defeat the Franklin candidate.

Nixon was himself elected to a council seat, but his most renowned act that year came amid a student scandal that rocked the quiet little campus in the autumn of 1931, threatening even the future of Wallace Newman's emerging football glory. Before the big game with Occidental, William Soeberg, Joe Gaudio, William Hornaday, and Charlie Kendle had gone over to the opposing campus at three o'clock in the morning and in a wild prank—"I didn't know one building from another," Soeberg said later—painted "to hell with Oxy" on the steps and columns of the school chapel, where the paint promptly penetrated the masonry and became virtually indelible. Returning to Whittier, they decided to paint their own campus as if Oxy students had retaliated or even struck first, and splashed "Oxy" on Whittier's sacred rock, a relic of the original Quaker Academy campus. "We thought we might as well get both, and create a little bit of fire between the two schools," Soeberg said. "And we did."

The incident set off a furor at both schools, and prominent Quakers called for the expulsion of the guilty Whittier students, who cheerfully admitted their roles. There was even more sensation when Hornaday, a minister's son, confessed to President Dexter that one of the painters had carried a small blackjack to ward off any Occidental student attack. Suddenly Whittier was in danger of being banished altogether from the small college athletic conference, which would have crippled the sports program with its crucial community subsidies and lure to continuing enrollment on which the school's survival depended. For hours the fate of the students was debated in a meeting of faculty, the administration, and the student council, and the nervous young men listening outside in the hallway of Founders remembered how passionately and effectively Dick Nixon, the sophomore member-at-large, had defended them. "In fact it was nip and tuck," Joe Gaudio said, recounting his near expulsion. "And one of the most understanding people . . . was Dick Nixon. . . . He was one of the people . . . to try to have everybody understand . . . that it was wrong, but that we shouldn't be thrown out of the college and the college . . . thrown out of the conference."

He had argued that the fate of the students and the college itself would be the same, a subtle and skillful tactic with a faculty and administration anxiously looking for a way out, and ended up mediating a settlement in which the Whittier students apologized and paid to have the paint at Occidental laboriously removed. The performance again made him a campus hero, particularly among athletes.

Students remembered him clearly as a "liberal" in terms of campus privileges and student rights as against the traditional strictures of the faculty and town. It was a matter not only of smoothing over clashes with Whittier police or merchants over bonfires or defending the Oxy painters, acts uniformly popular among his schoolmates, but also of pushing at the barriers of student society itself. In the Orthogonians he led the group toward its own social and political power on campus, yet also pressed them to pledge Bill Brock, one of Whittier's rare black athletes, from Los Angeles, and at the time with Nixon's sponsorship one of the first blacks to be accepted into a white college fraternity or society in southern California or in the country at large, for that matter. "He was one of the guys that was a believer in bringing a Negro into this group," Dean Triggs recalled. "Dick was one of the guys who felt very strongly that we should have representation from minority groups in our organization." He had also, they remembered, befriended two other black athletes at Whittier over the four years, Nathaniel George and George Venable, who were not Orthogonians. Asked long afterward if he ever knew any blacks growing up, Nixon named the three students at Whittier. "I thought that was quite an honor," Nathaniel George recalled the statement later, "because we were 'friends.' "

In the spring of his sophomore year Nixon ran for student body vice-president for the following academic year. "My policy will be one of impartial cooperation with the president and executive committee in solving student problems," he then described his platform. He defeated a female opponent by almost four to one in a May 1932 election the student paper described as "unusually quiet" with "little enthusiasm . . . aroused by political parties, strikes and campaigning," though "the balloting was heavy." Beneath the surface, however, it was a small *coup d'état* at Whittier. Herschel Daugherty, a handsome football player, theater set designer, and Orthogonian, had defeated Joe Sweeney, the Franklin candidate, by almost two to one for the student body presidency, the beginning of an Orthogonian political dominance on the campus barely two years after the society's founding.

That next year, 1932–33, Nixon was more than ever politically active, a man-about-campus grooming himself to be Daugherty's successor. As chairman of the annual grand bonfire on Fire Hill, he set a school record that became permanent college lore. "It was the duty and privilege of the chairman to top the heap with as large and gaudy a privy as he could steal from the neighboring countryside," Ralph de Toledano wrote, describing the event. The trophy was usually a one- or two-seat outhouse. Scouring the outlying basin ranches to the east in Frank's grocery truck, he grandly crowned the pyre with an ornate four-holer. As a less flamboyant sophomore and junior he was, along with Sweeney and a few others, a College Knight, a small group of men organized by the administration to help maintain student discipline at athletic events or curfews, whom some students disliked as informers and enforcers. "To some of us," William Hornaday said of the Knights, "they were not too popular, because we considered they were going to report anything . . . we felt they were sort of a police force, you know, in a certain way." Selection as a Knight was a mixed blessing and potential political pitfall, yet another honor among faculty and administrators, and resentment of the group was thought to be one of the factors in Sweeney's defeat for student body president. Nixon quickly solved the dilemma by going out of his way to do the group's more obscure jobs, setting up chairs or cleaning, making his fellow Knights grateful for his dedication while avoiding clashes with the students. "For instance, when he was a Knight . . . Dick did a lot of the menial tasks," Charlie Kendle remembered. "He completed them and you'd say, 'Who did that?' 'Well, Dick did it—that's already done.' He didn't seek recognition."

The pattern was rarely so visible at the time, and other students saw it clearly only in retrospect. "I don't know that I would have thought it until he was elected student body president," one of his rivals, Dick Harris, said afterward, "and then looking back [it] looks like logical steps." Then, as later, what seemed so much deliberate maneuvering and ingratiation was also combined with genuine gestures of compassion and generosity, episodes free of ambition. Paul Smith remembered him bringing a five-gallon container of peppermint ice cream from the store to a History Club meeting, and then quietly leaving. "He couldn't stay for the party because he had to get back to the grocery to work," the professor said, describing the moment. "I'll never forget this." At the worst of the Depression he invited the Orthogonians to eat at the old Milhous home at the foot of the hill, where his mother, Olive, and Almira presided over a feast of fried chicken. "They didn't live very high," Olive recalled. "They had enough to eat, such as it was, but he felt that he'd just like to have them for one time to get a real good meal, where they had all they could eat and good food."

In the final weeks before the student body presidential election in the spring of 1933, he seemed indefatigable. Beyond spring football practice, debate, the Knights, student government, and his own theater appearances, he had volunteered to be stage manager of the spring production of *The Mikado*. Only days after Harold's death, he volunteered again to share a fund-raising drive for a student exchange with the University of Hawaii, a position that brought two successive weeks of front-page stories in the college newspaper and in which he raised the money with impressive speed.

"Being quite stubborn as well as unable to do the Poet square dance, the Orthogonians' candidate was coaxed for weeks to run for the merited prexy's stall," read a later *Acropolis* account of his nomination in late April.

He was hardly so reluctant. On the day the nominations were to close, April 21, Nixon was the only candidate in the race for the student body presidency, with the Franklins yet to put forward a nominee. "The Orthogonians have theirs and it's no secret," said "Scoop," the pseudonym for Garland F. Swain, whose column, "As Seen from College Hills," was the lone political commentary in the *Quaker Campus.* "The logical man for them to run is Dick Nixon, already vice president of the student body, and a great many people feel that he has a fine chance of being elected. Dick has many qualifications which in some aspects tower over almost any other candidate I can think of right now. His scholastic plus athletic plus extra curricular activity record for the past three years give him a fine start." For hours that day, almost as at Whittier High four years before, his election seemed *pro forma*, and for the same reasons of political arrangement behind the scenes. Quickly negotiating a division of offices that would give the Orthogonians dominance in student government and the Franklins control over an important student-alumni board, the two societies and their faculty sponsors were near a deal that would allow Nixon to run without opposition. With campus politics in the grip of the two fraternities, the majority of independent students would offer no challenge. "It was a foregone conclusion," Osmyn Stout remembered.

At the last moment, however, the settlement of spoils had collapsed "into a real organized fight for the different positions on the alumni governing board," Ed Wunder recalled. And with the breakdown, the presidential race changed overnight. What seemed Nixon's easy succession and polite praise of his record turned into a heated contest that laid bare deeper feelings on the usually docile little campus. To run against him the Franklins promptly nominated Dick Thomson, a popular cheerleader, and Garland Swain immediately backed Thomson in a *Quaker Campus* endorsement that indirectly but unmistakably criticized Nixon, and even identified Thomson with the popular Orthogonian incumbent, Herschel Daugherty. "It is a likely fact that the students' choice for next year will be Dick Thomson for student body president," wrote "Scoop." "Fully qualified not by promises or any political platform, Thomson would make an outstanding president, one, who like Herschel Daugherty, will grasp the significance of on-campus rather than off-campus relationships. Thomson has a better personality for this than any other student."

Swain's rebuke was scarcely fair, many students felt, in terms of Nixon's own obvious fervor for "on-campus" activities at Whittier. But more telling was the swipe by contrast at his often stilted manner and personality, a point few readers missed. As at Whittier High School with Robert Logue four years before, the office he coveted and seemed certain to inherit suddenly appeared less a matter of conventional hard work or qualification than simple personal popularity. In any case, though his own candidacy remained stronger and better organized than Thomson's last-minute bid, and though Swain's initial column was milder than what was to follow, this first real challenge to his election sent Richard Nixon into a brooding doubt, a moment of self-pity and recoil that was to mark similar experiences of setback or trial in almost every political race he ran from that moment on. At home he was obviously troubled by the political turn at school, and the Franklin opposition loomed large for the family. "Richard was always running for some office, but I suppose his first real test was in 1933," Hannah said of the college election. "I remember he had quite a bit of competition." The week after the column appeared, he went to Annabelle Tupper, Albert Upton's mother, who lived in Whittier and who had become friendly with him after watching his debates and theater performances. He was withdrawing from the student body race, he told her dejectedly, though he did not mention Thomson's opposition or the campus paper. It was the grocery, he said. His work had given him no opportunity for the social life necessary for his popularity, nor would he have enough time to give to the school presidency. "He felt that he had so little extra time to devote to campus social life that he didn't stand a chance of being elected," as Mrs. Tupper told the story afterward. "It was genuine simplicity and humility," she would say. "He took his responsibilities very seriously, and he really didn't have time for social affairs." Like many others at similar junctures afterward, she praised him for his sacrifices, told him how much he was needed, and, as their conversation was later recounted, "despite his protests, talked him out of giving up."

In the last days before the May 8 election, he returned to what the *Quaker Campus* called "heavy campaigning," walking the halls of Founders to solicit votes, his supporters tacking up posters and handing out flyers. His official platform was a detailed and formal statement of how he would save student government money, promote the college among prospective students, and encourage alumni help. But the central plank was the old issue that still agitated the college three years after their controversial welcome reception at Wardman Gym—the prospect of dances on campus. Accepting their nominations in short campaign speeches before a chapel assembly, Thomson had proposed to convert an old building into a student union where dances might be held, but he had only alluded to the actual purpose. "I pledge myself to the benefit of the students if they choose to elect me their president," he said meekly. Nixon followed him with a plain promise. "If elected president," he told the college, "I shall work for strict economy on the executive committee, student body dances on campus, a more systematic use of the facilities within the student body for publicity in high schools and junior colleges, and better relations between the alumni and the student body."

Nixon's open advocacy of dancing marked for many students a clear difference between the candidates. In fact, in the gentle, relatively subdued fashion of Whittier College, students and the *Quaker Campus* had been lobbying for dances on the hill from his first weeks there. As one 1930 editorial put it with the offending word blanked out:

> "There are none so blind as those who won't see" that young people want to ——— and that if they are forbidden to do so on the campus, they will go elsewhere where surroundings are certainly less wholesome . . . Yet we have been taught, I believe, that the nearer home we find entertainment, the better. Are we any finer, any purer, any better than students in our fellow colleges, Occidental, Pomona, and California Christian, because we forgo the pleasure of ———ing? Are we any more likely to be sent hurtling into the black pit on judgment day because of a few innocent ———s?

Richard Nixon would make the same arguments his own three years later. At the time, it was not the issue those who knew him expected Dick to champion. Though he had proudly learned to dance himself that same spring for Ola, he remained a comparative wallflower and outwardly the devout Quaker. As it was, his parents had frowned on his dance lessons and agreed with the college prohibition. "Why, it's terrible," Lucille Timberlake remembered Frank Nixon telling her when she remarked that she saw nothing wrong in school dances. "It's not either, it's just how you look at it," the young niece replied boldly to Frank. "Your mind must be terrible." They "went round and round," as she recalled the argument. Yet Richard now drove down the boulevard to his campus campaign and simply ignored his father's objection.

Above all, dances on campus appealed to the usually voiceless majority of what Merton Wray called the "non-org" students, those who belonged to no society, who did not go to the Franklin or Orthogonian or Metaphonian balls off-campus, and for whom on-campus dances were an important and affordable boon in their social life. In a sense, dancing at the little college opened again the class and clique division that had led to the founding and success of the Orthogonians. It was, once more, an issue to use against the Franklins, who had never been energetic about wider social life at Whittier.

"The platform on which he ran," Ed Wunder said, remembering Nixon's campaign emphasis, "was that there would be some kind of social event every month, where all students could take part, not just the ones that might belong to a society and had all the social life they wanted. There were many of the students that did not belong to anything and that was what he was thinking about. . . . I think he was a very good organizer." "That campaign," Merton Wray would say, repeating his praise of the young politician and his intuition for popular discontent, "was merely . . . a tremendous ability to sense the situation."

Watching from the sidelines, Osmyn Stout thought at first that Nixon was running on "a very dangerous platform" and that the explicit promise of dancing "created quite a consternation" among the alumni. To mollify Dexter and his aides, the candidate shifted his later impromptu campaign speeches around campus from the dancing issue to schemes for increasing college revenue. Kenny Ball remembered him "cleverly making the presentation saying that we would have to have hedges planted around the athletic field so that people would want to come in and see the game rather than stay on the outside and watch through the fence or back of a certain line and be a freeloader." Yet the promise of dance parties on campus, inexpensive and open to all students, continued to be his main appeal, and by the last weekend before the Monday balloting, Nixon seemed clearly ahead. In an effort to rescue Thomson, Swain's final election column appeared on Friday, May 5. He was no longer indirect in attacking the candidate who "has nursed the job since he was a freshman." Of a history later so crowded with commentary about Richard Nixon and in the end with his bitter, ultimately lethal battle with the press, it was the long-forgotten portent and first salvo. "Nixon will be a hard man to beat," Swain began.

> His platform, however, is complicated and would be difficult to realize. He is about the first to ever outline the "how" of things. His prestige will be hard to ride down. He is the quiet, self-contained type who gets others to do things for him . . . a real executive. On the other hand, Thomson has a wider circle of friends. Some say Nixon stole Thomson's platform, or parts of it. Thomson is more amiable and would likely do a job himself rather than depend upon others. . . . People who seem to know, say that Nixon has a two to one chance to win the election. He has nursed the job since he was a freshman and has arisen in chronological fashion to the top. Yet Thomson has proven himself a world-beater at getting jobs done . . . doing things rather than thinking things.

On election day Nixon mobilized the same student strength Bob Logue had used to defeat him four years earlier. This time it was the Orthogonians who were the athletes and campus heroes, with still other varsity players Nixon's teammates, and the lettermen and their girlfriends voted as a block. "Well, we all banded together," Bruce Burchell recalled, "and every Orthogonian got his girlfriend and all his friends to vote for Nixon. We just outdid the Franklins." The dance issue also pitted the less affluent, non-organization students who lived at home against the wealthier dormitory residents. The off-campus students voted in their numbers for Nixon. "There was always a thing between us and the dorm girls," remembered Ola, who ran with him as a student council representative, "and I think it swung [the] election." He won the presidency in what the *Quaker Campus* called "an unusually quiet election" with "approximately 75 percent of the student body voting." But unlike earlier campus elections, the 1933 vote count was never published.

Afterward, the *Acropolis* called it "a fairly quiet political season, and a campaign in which mud-slinging was noticeably lacking." "Although political dictators managed to cause as much trouble as possible," the yearbook added in reference to Swain's biting columns, "Dick Nixon came through the melee unscathed with the title of student body president." From the vantage point of his memoirs, the winner himself recalled the politics as "necessarily low-keyed in a small school where everyone knew one another." His contemporaries remembered it as more serious. "Nixon won because he was smart about campaigning," Marjorie Hildreth said, looking back at the race and the heat of the dance issue. "And this kind of surprised me, because here was a man who was born and raised a . . . Quaker. . . . But here he was going off entirely to the left, so to speak, a liberal," Dick Thomson, the loser, would say of the campaign and Nixon's promise of dancing on campus. "But he knew what issue to use to get support." "I was naïve," he remembered later. "I think he's a real smart politician." The Swain criticism, as so much like it that followed, rankled long afterward. It had been, Nixon related, "a bitter attack," and "the critic could find no specific charges, but had to stick to generalities."

Ironically, Swain ended the year rallying behind the new president. "Nixon has the opportunity of becoming the greatest student body president in the history of Whittier College . . . and it is generally believed that he has the stuff," "Scoop" wrote. "The whole situation will depend upon his nerve, his backbone to ask for his own way and his fortitude. Won't it be a grand and glorious feeling to have a real prom on the campus . . . ?" Like others in the press thirty-five years later when the president of the student body had become the President of the United States, Swain even recommended journalistic support of the new man. "A good one," he said of the *Quaker Campus* editorial policy, "would be to follow right along with Nixon and get public opinion in favor of his program." For his part, the president-elect seemed ready. In keeping with the popular political imagery that spring of 1933, Richard Nixon pledged to Whittier students "a new deal."

His senior year at Whittier was a triumph.

Over the summer he arranged with Dexter and Herbert Harris, a Quaker English professor well liked among the trustees, to meet the board to propose dancing on campus. "I promised the student body this," he told a skeptical Ed Wunder, "so this is what I want to do." "The two of us kind of worked together on it," remembered William Soeberg. "But I give him the credit because, naturally, he knew which ones to contact and how to do it." Early in September 1933, Nixon appeared before the board. "Whether or not one approved of dancing . . . most of the students were going to dance," he recalled telling them. "Surely . . . it would be better to have dances on campus where they could be supervised, rather than off-campus in some second-rate dance hall." The argument was in part spurious; the societies' proms were scarcely held in "some second-rate dance hall" but rather fashionable hotels or resorts. Still, few trustees knew the details of student social life. Nixon knew his audience; his point was decisive. Faced with the specter of Whittier students forced into iniquity, the board submitted.

"Think of the nerve of this lad," Paul Smith said, recalling Nixon's performance, "appearing before the august body, the Board of Trustees at Whittier College, in a plea that that body discontinue the long-standing policy of no dancing. . . . It took a lot of guts and nerve and crust. . . . But he did it, and convinced the board that they ought to modify their policy." Led by Herman L. Perry, a Whittier Quaker banker who had known Frank and Hannah Nixon since their courtship, whose son was a junior at the college, and who would later be a seminal figure in Richard Nixon's political life, the trustees voted in effect to lift the prohibition, though not without a typical Whittier fig leaf. Since the athletic department complained of the expense in protecting the Wardman Gym floor, the board donated $200 to rent the Women's Club for what they decorously termed "large social affairs," avoiding mention of the word "dancing" and keeping the deplorable act still technically off-campus. At that, some Quaker donors soon cut off contributions. "We finally got dancing in school," Nathaniel George recounted, "but we lost a lot of people that supported the college." Dexter had warned Nixon there might be retaliation. "Look, we have three or four people who keep this college open," he said at a meeting before

Nixon's appeal to the board. "We just have to be beholden to them, to a certain extent." Yet the president supported Nixon at the meeting, and the lost gifts were not crippling.

Nixon moved ahead boldly with the trustees' mandate, appointing a "social chairman" to organize nine free, all-student dances. In addition to the dances there was to be an all-college weekend with games, picnics, one-act plays, vaudeville, and off-campus students invited to stay at the dorms. By mid-autumn the dances and other gatherings had begun to democratize campus social life and break down old barriers at Whittier as never before. "President Nixon has literally worked his head off lately . . . his actively successful administration . . . [is] really forging ahead under his admirable leadership," said *Quaker Campus*.

Amid all the campus politics, he seldom talked of his larger political ambitions. Rivals and longtime acquaintances like Merton Wray thought "he never disclosed them [plans], but you knew that he was just driving, that's all." On the Glee Club trips around California, though, he talked openly with Hubert Perry, the trustee's son, about political goals beyond graduation. "So he said that if he ever got into politics," Perry recalled, "he would go into something big." "It's one of my great ambitions," he once told Osmyn Stout, a fellow Glee Club singer as well as sometime debate partner, "to become a congressman." Stout saw Nixon as a "strong Republican," but no one in 1933–34 took the college politician's dreams too seriously. "We all laughed at him," he remembered.

There was a quality of endearment and affection about the impressions of him that last year. "Nothing is funnier than to call Richard Nixon 'Nicky' and watch him bristle," wrote Marjorie Hildreth in her gossip column. "I did it once and he was too surprised to speak, if you can imagine Nixon inarticulate." *Quaker Campus* warmly welcomed him back after an illness with the same teasing nickname. "Nixon, Nicky to those who know him best and the idol of those who would like to know him better, silent for an interim in his otherwise voluble life, glad you're back, Nicky." He became especially friendly with the newspaper's two columnists, Joanne Brown and Marjorie Hildreth, and their shards of campus gossip recorded "the cheese nips supplied by Mr. Magnanimous Nixon" or "Nixon, the Great-Hearted . . . sharing his daily rations of one stick Wrigley's Doublemint." After one student council meeting, friends from the football team rigged the sparkplugs of his Ford for a mock explosion and looked on as it fizzled and he drove away apparently undismayed. "It didn't do anything except make smoke and noise," said one of the saboteurs decades later. "Still don't think he knows what happened." He took the joke good-naturedly. "Dick Nixon, student body prexy and all 'round good fellow," read the identifying notes on another of Richard Harris's cartoons showing him in suit and tie and with an unmistakable ski nose amid other student caricatures on the Whittier hill.

That winter he applied to Duke University Law School. His faculty recommendations were glowing. "I do not wish to badger professional schools on behalf of our students and it is only when I feel that we have an unusually well qualified one that I feel free to write to you as I do," said Paul Smith. Upton told the admissions committee that "during the four years in which I have observed his rather prominent career at Whittier he has displayed a rich sense of humor, human understanding, personal eloquence and a marked ability to lead. He is intellectually honest, modest, and youthfully enthusiastic. If he has any handicap, it is his lack of sophistication." "I cannot recommend him too highly," Walter Dexter wrote grandly from the tiny California campus at the beginning of 1934, adding from some oracular depth, "because I believe that Nixon will become one of American's important, if not greatest, leaders."

The only sour note of the senior year was to be his ever more fitful relationship with Ola. Following his election as student body president, they had grown apart, Ola feeling, as she once told an interviewer, that she "wasn't good enough for him, that he wanted to be free and swinging." At the spring prom he escorted her in only to spend much of the evening away from her talking with other men. They quarreled in a corner of the dance hall, and he angrily left her to find her own way home. "I had to call my folks to come get me," she recalled. Once more, her parents were furious. The next week he dated another girl, and again Ola was hurt. "I didn't like that because we were supposed to be going steady," she said. On the eve of the Metaphonian formal, she still had not asked Nixon, and a girlfriend suggested she invite instead Gail Jobe, a wiry, personable, handsome California farm boy who was Nixon's fellow Orthogonian and football teammate. She waited until the last moment and finally approached Jobe, who immediately asked Nixon why he wasn't taking Ola to the dance. "Well, we aren't going steady," he answered curtly, and then appeared at the prom with Marjorie Hildreth to spite Ola.

In a few weeks he was back with Ola reveling in the most important news of his life thus far. In mid-May Duke notified him that he had been admitted to the law school with a $250 full-tuition scholarship. Elated, he drove to Ola's house and sounded long and loudly the Ford horn her mother despised. "But the night he found out about the scholarship—oh, we had fun that night," Ola recalled. "He was not only fun, he was joyous, abandoned—the only time I remember him that way. He said it was the best thing that ever happened to him. We rode around in his car and just celebrated." For a time, it seemed they were finally reconciled, and in the final days of school he was jubilant. "Where did Nixon get that pink and white disposition he's been flinging around lately?" asked a campus gossip column.

As they were about to graduate, they learned that Walter Dexter had been eased out as college president, a casualty of trustee politics and his reputation for excessive liberalism. "Dexter was more a politician than an administrator, and an honest one," Albert Upton reflected, recalling his fund-raising and campus relations. Yet he had come to be seen as somehow "radical." Some believed that Dexter's support of his bold student body president and the promise of college-approved dancing had been perhaps the last straw in a series of steps that began with curriculum reform and the faculty's relative religious freedom. The Quakers, Upton thought, "digest radicals in a way other religions can't. They put up with them but don't let them lead them too far." In a parting act of tame rebellion, the class of 1934 insisted on Dexter's signature on their diplomas rather than his successor's as some trustees wished.

Richard Nixon finished second in the class, now shrunken to eighty-five from the 139 who had begun at the Wardman Gym reception four years before. He won as well the coveted Dexter Award for "outstanding service to the student body," and a warm, memorable tribute beneath his handsome presidential photo in the *Acropolis*. "After one of the most successful years the college has ever witnessed, we stop to reminisce, and come to the realization that much of the success was due to the efforts of this very gentleman. Always progressive and with a liberal attitude, he has led us through the year with flying colors." "It was one of those times [when we had] a cluster of strong people," Upton recalled, looking back at the class of '34. They went on mostly as they had come, small-town, largely insular young people, many of them struggling in the Depression to get one of the basin's scarce teaching or coaching jobs. Most remembered their years on the hillside fondly. Yet for all their relative conservatism and apparent indifference toward the outside world, they took with them, too, a Depression generation's sense of insecurity, defining success as the safe, stolid middle-class existence the town and school seemed to represent.

They graduated on a sunny, warm June 9, 1934. Unlike most of his classmates, Nixon remembered the strong political legacy of the college. "The populist elements of my father's politics, the progressive influence of Paul Smith, the iconoclasm of Albert Upton, and . . . Christian humanism . . . gave my early thinking a very liberal, almost populist tinge," he wrote in his memoirs. "Thanks to my teachers I studied hard and received a first-rate education at Whittier." Others were less certain. "I didn't know what a prestige college was," Ola Florence Welch said later. Osmyn Stout would come to believe that "education at Whittier College was really pretty second-rate in many, many ways."

When he had announced his law scholarship to Duke, his classmates "were all quite happy for him," Osmyn Stout recalled. The majority of Whittier graduates had little idea of what they would do or where they would now go. Millions of Americans were still jobless, hungry, without decent homes. Osmyn Stout vividly recalled the legion of men down and out on the streets of Los Angeles—though no such vagrants were visible in Whittier—with their pathetic crates of apples selling at two for five cents. But scenes of the Great Depression in the basin were never a part of the landscape of Richard Nixon's memories of college or the era. He prepared to go to Duke with the same intensity and channeled discipline that had brought him to this point. Like Whittier itself, he seemed inured to much of the world around him.

He had been a teenager and young man raised and educated, Hannah once reflected years later, during the "roaring twenties" and the crisis of the Depression, yet remained strangely untouched by his times. She was proud that he did not smoke or drink and that he had not succumbed to the "freedom and license" of the era, but her observations went far deeper. The marks of the age, she thought, had "just passed him by."

6

Duke Law, 1934–37

"AS IF HE MIGHT BE KNOCKED DOWN"

Richard Nixon was exultant that summer of 1934 before going off to law school. Obviously elated to be leaving Whittier, he spoke openly of his ambition as never before. Merle West and his girlfriend arranged a blind date for him on the Fourth of July. The two couples drove to Long Beach where they sat on a wall near the Pike watching fireworks burst and shower in the starry ocean sky off the pier. Dick joked, was warmly personable with everyone, and mused about his future as a successful lawyer. "He had such big plans for himself," said his date, Frances Stanley, remembering the night fondly.

Duke seemed an opportunity for nineteen-year-old Donald Nixon as well. Having dropped out of Whittier High two years before, he was now being sent discreetly to North Carolina with his scholarly brother to finish public high school at Greensboro, not far from the law school campus in Durham. For appearances, friends and Milhous relatives (and later inquiring reporters) would be told that Don was attending a "preparatory school" or a "Quaker college" near Dick. After a last prayerful family supper in the small house behind the store, the two sons left to cross the country early in September.

"Like a medieval cathedral town," Richard Nixon recalled the university in Durham, with "spires and towers and stained glass everywhere." Endowed only a decade before as part of a $40 million philanthropy of tobacco baron James Buchanan Duke, the school rose in clusters of Gothic stone buildings on the edge of the small tobacco and textile town in northeastern North Carolina. Its grounds giving onto the picturesque and still wild beauty of dogwood and tall pines in the seven-thousand-acre Duke Forest, the university had a solemn, almost mythic setting, venerable Eu-

162

ropean towers of learning transplanted to the American South. In the autumn of 1934, the trees on the relatively new campus were still saplings. Duke, thought one of Nixon's classmates, lacked "the one thing money could not buy—age."

Against that backdrop erected by vast wealth, Richard Nixon lived a spartan, austere life. His scholarship paid the full $250 yearly tuition, and he had assumed in his letter of acceptance ("I wish to express my deepest appreciation") that he would occupy a dormitory room. But he soon discovered campus housing was relatively expensive, and took instead a small room in a Durham boardinghouse for five dollars a month, only to have to change to another rented room across town when divinity students at the first house disturbed him with their practiced sermons. "There were fourteen preachers rooming there," he would say. "I had to move because of the noise." Through most of the three years at law school, he boarded without a chest of drawers or even a closet, living out of an old family trunk hauled from California.

Between classes he worked part-time for thirty-five cents an hour in the law school library under a program for student employment funded by the New Deal's National Youth Administration. On occasional afternoons he earned extra money by chauffeuring the invalid wife of law professor John Bradway. As years before when his mother had first left them to take Harold to Prescott, his eating habits now became erratic. Among his relatively few recorded memories of Duke was how often he breakfasted on nothing more than a Milky Way candy bar. Duke friends would remember him having only two meals a day. One fellow student thought him so "extremely poor" that "he did not eat as regularly as most of us think a person has to in order to keep alive." Gone, too, was the fastidiousness that had kept Hannah slavishly ironing the freshly starched white shirts. "I remember he wore a reddish-purple sweater day after day," said a Duke classmate who saw it then as an emblem of his impoverishment. "The image I have of . . . Nixon is that sweater."

One of his fellow students was a Reynolds tobacco heir; a handful were well-off. But most of them went to Duke in the midst of the Depression with the same frugal economy. "None of us had any money," said Edward Rubin, one of three Californians in the school and a class ahead of Nixon. Richard Kiefer, another typical freshman in 1934, came to Durham from a small college in Maryland with forty dollars saved after a summer job, lived out of a foot locker in an unheated, unplumbed house, and worked like many others at an NYA project. They took free cream from one Duke Forest landlady with a cow, ate ten-cent breakfasts at the University Coffee Shop, had boardinghouse dinners for a quarter. "We were all scroungers, all poor and looking for a cheap way to live," Kiefer remembered.

Nixon, meanwhile, received thirty-five dollars a month from his parents in addition to the scholarship and NYA and Bradway jobs. There were periodic gifts of ten dollars and twenty dollars or as much as fifty dollars from Almira Milhous and boxes of citrus fruit or avocados from the store. On their Whittier Boulevard corner, even with their older sons away, the Nixons continued to make a relatively comfortable living. Frank would start in the mid-1930s to build small rental units on the lots he owned across from the East Whittier School, and they began planning a move from the cramped old house behind the grocery to a larger, more respectable home in the fashionable Puente Heights above the college. Don was to leave North Carolina that first winter, having completed only a semester at Grimsley Public High School in Greensboro. Afterward he would ruefully and in some confusion tell reporters he had been forced to come home from "college" so "we could keep Dick at Whittier [sic]," perpetuating what was to be a full-blown family legend of privation and sacrifice. But the younger son's quiet return to the store meat counter in January 1935, as relatives revealed later, was far less from financial need than from Don's continuing and ultimate frustration with formal education. Like Harold, he was never to complete his schooling.

Their circumstances were more plain in a trip the two Nixon brothers took together from North Carolina to New York City at Christmastime 1934. Traveling by car with three Duke classmates, they had decided for some reason to pool their money in one wallet, and then discovered after leaving a drive-in that somehow the billfold had been left behind on a counter, probably to be picked up by the proprietor. While the others argued excitedly how to get the money back, as Don told the story, his brother "sat in deep silence and was gloomier than ever." On returning to the drive-in, Dick strode inside and barked, "Hand over my wallet at once!" to the startled owner, who sheepishly reached in his pocket and gave it back. Don often described the episode to illustrate Dick's decisiveness. Only a quarter century afterward did Hannah Nixon confide the rest of the story of the drive to New York. Her sons had not only found the money for the trip, but in Manhattan had also bought their mother her first fur piece for Christmas.

Richard Nixon's deliberate asceticism at Duke was part of a self-conscious, dogged, ever-anxious drive for grades. Eager to establish a national student body with an academic reputation to match its Gothic spires, the newly endowed law school recruited outstanding college graduates throughout the country and offered full-tuition scholarships to almost half of the forty-four incoming freshmen in the Depression autumn of 1934. Soon after Nixon's arrival in Durham, his California summer sureness seemed to evaporate overnight when he heard the ominous rumor that only a fraction of such first-year grants, dubbed by students as the "meat grinders," would be renewed the second year. In fact, financial aid at Duke was not so stringent, but the anxiety at losing the scholarship gripped Nixon from the start and, at times, drove him to the verge of dropping out in despair.

The competition was real enough. Many of his peers had been at the top of their undergraduate classes in far more distinguished colleges than Whittier. There were thirty-two members of Phi Beta Kappa entering Duke Law that year. And Richard Nixon, graduate of a small Quaker school that did not even qualify for a chapter of the renowned honor society, knew the exact number. With mounting apprehension he had counted their telltale keys at registration and during early classes. One night at the library at the beginning of the semester, he had artlessly confided to a studious senior, William Adelson, "I'm scared . . . I don't believe I can stay up top in that group." But Adelson had assured him with a smile, "You don't have to worry. You have what it takes to learn the law—an iron butt."

It was an apt description of how he would endure and excel over the next three years. At Duke, as before and after, he reacted to challenge, now to a fresh sense of rivalry and disadvantage, with the old single-minded, often fierce diligence. The law school faculty taught by the traditional Harvard case method and so put a premium on the sheer absorption and recital of example after example of litigation and decision, each illustrating the evolution and nuances of legal principles. "My memory was a great asset here," Nixon wrote later about the process in which he was so adept. He was less certain about a deeper understanding of what he was taking in and reproducing. "I sometimes despaired," he admitted long afterward, "of pulling the memorized facts together into any meaningful knowledge of the law." However rote the learning, his persistence was prodigal. When not in class or at a job, he spent hour after hour in the Duke law library, students remembering him there without fail every one of the seven days and five nights a week the building stayed open.

There was an air of combativeness about him these first months at Duke. Douglas Maggs, a brilliant and voluble young Californian on the faculty, habitually intimidated his torts class of freshmen, who felt, said one from 1934–35, "a little like Christian martyrs facing the lions." That fall "Nixon was the first to stand up to Maggs," as Lyman Brownfield, a friend in the class, recalled the morning. "Dick was obviously just as nervous as anyone else, but from the first time he recited . . . I never saw him back down when he thought he was right." Classmates admired and did not forget his example of intellectual bravery and conviction, though they were struck, too, by his tenseness and vulnerability in the act. "I remember the way he stood" is how another law student sitting nearby described the moment in Maggs's course, "flat-footed and feet apart as if he might be knocked down." ·

In addition to the academic fears, he felt an aching homesickness. To Ola Welch, whom he had seen only intermittently over the summer, he soon began to write long, moody, often despondent accounts of his predicament, pouring out the apprehension and discouragement he felt over the initial months in Durham. "He was unhappy at law school in the beginning," she would say afterward. "He wrote me these sad letters. He sounded close to quitting two or three times." Nixon was never to talk openly about how near he came to abandoning law school. Twenty-five years later he did recall his misery in a candid note to a Duke classmate. "I was as confused and homesick as anyone at one time or another," he wrote. "It was the first time I had been so far from home, and more than once I was tempted to head back to the West Coast!"

Like his impulse to quit the student body president's race at Whittier when first stung by public criticism, the abrupt descent into doubt and gloom in the face of the freshman strains in law school was again a portent of what would become a pattern in Richard Nixon's adult political life. Sudden, often unexpected adversity would be met by desolation, near despair, then plaintiveness, the impulse to quit, followed by a grim if still uncertain determination.

Yet it was always a measure of his complexity and strength that while privately enveloped in his own self-pity he could still reach out to others. Oren Mollenkopf had enrolled in Duke in the autumn of 1934 only to discover soon afterward his wife needed surgery that would force him to give up law school. "Without money and without friends," as Mollenkopf described himself, he had sat in utter dejection one day on the entrance steps of the school, ignored by passing students until "one fellow, Richard Nixon, must have sensed my feelings." They had not met before, but Nixon now stopped and struck up a conversation. When Mollenkopf eventually told him his plight, Nixon responded with an impassioned little pep talk about overcoming the setback and starting fresh somewhere else, perhaps in another profession. He spoke "with fire in his eyes about the future," the other student recalled. "A nation as powerful as America will combat her difficulties sooner or later if her citizens keep faith in her." Genuinely stirred and rallied, Mollenkopf took the advice, went home to Ohio to teach school, and a quarter century later as a high school principal in Cincinnati movingly wrote Nixon in gratitude for "a kind word for a confused, homesick, and frightened young man when he needed one the most."

The gesture to Mollenkopf remained private, though there were similar acts of compassion his fellow law students saw openly. Sometimes in locked arms with another man, more often by himself, Nixon carried Fred Cady, a student who had been stunted and crippled by infantile paralysis, up the steep steps of the law school. He befriended Cady as few others, and later campaigned with him in law school politics. Men who watched them would remember vividly how Dick Nixon grunted and staggered as he worked his way with Cady and crutches and books up the slate stairway, how gently he set him down on the landing, and then slowly walked along with the crippled young man as he dragged himself into the classroom.

Edward Rubin saw a similar sensibility as he and Nixon got a ride west with another student at the end of the academic year. Dick was typically pensive and worried about his final grades. But when they came upon a woman hitchhiker on a lonely stretch of road and Rubin and the other student started to pass her by, it had been Nixon who insisted they stop. "Richard was really pushing to help her," Rubin told the story. "He said, 'Here she is out there, and what's going to happen?'" Rubin was impressed by still another incident a few days later when he and Nixon had been left off by their driver in Arizona, had taken the train the rest of the way into Los Angeles, and were having a Coke in the railroad station coffee shop before going their separate ways. Watching intently the Mexican women serving the tables, Nixon talked to Rubin with obvious concern and sympathy about "the plight of the waitresses, working for tips." Mollenkopf, Cady, hitchhiker, and waitresses—the brooding, uncertain first-year law student showed them much the same empathy and tenderness his family and friends always saw in him, the "real Nixon" they would feel was somehow tragically hidden and overlooked in the politician he was to become.

Back on Whittier Boulevard that summer, he waited nervously for his grades. The letter from Dean H. C. Horack came in mid-June, informing him he had achieved an 81.6 or A average, making him third in his class and eligible for one of the full scholarships going automatically to the three top freshmen. Again he was jubilant. Only later did he learn that seventeen out of the forty-four in his class had washed out completely, and several with lesser grades had received continuing grants. "I hope that my work next year will prove myself worthy of the award," he wrote Horack in accepting the second-year aid, adding in a perfunctory but poignant little half-truth, "I greatly enjoyed my first year's work at Duke."

From Durham Richard Nixon had written Ola Welch dozens of letters, confessions not only of his melancholy but also of his newfound devotion.

He was no longer so cavalier about the policeman's daughter, who was teaching music at East Whittier Elementary. His letters from Duke took their renewed romance and eventual marriage for granted. "Nothing mushy" is how she would coolly describe his correspondence. "He always kept himself in check." But he addressed her in intimate and passionate little salutations—terms of endearment "that would be of interest to psychologists," she said later—and Ola remembered them all as genuine "love letters."

On the June night he returned to the boulevard, he called her happily to say he was home at last and driving over. Meekly, Ola told him Gail Jobe was already there in her living room, and she and Jobe were seeing each other. Nixon recoiled in hurt and anger. They quarreled with the old bitterness. "Richard was furious. With that temper of his, he went through the roof," one of their mutual friends from college said, recalling the clash. "If I never see you again," Nixon lashed out at her, "it will be too soon."

Still, he went to the Welch house early the next day and carried on as if nothing had happened. In person as in his letters, he seemed to assume they would be married as a matter of course. He told her at length about Maggs's fearsome course. "Torts, that's something you cook," Ola replied in characteristic lightness. And he admonished her soberly, "You're going to have to learn something about law terms now." More than once, she remembered, he asked her to marry him, and promptly ignored the awkward vagueness of her response. For her part, Ola said nothing to Nixon about her deepening relationship with the other young man. "Well, she was dating Gail Jobe," a friend would say later, "and still keeping Richard on the string."

He returned to Duke in September 1935 with feelings visibly more mixed than his jaunty confidence a year before. Frank drove Rubin and some other students back with them, and Hannah remembered them impatiently calling Richard to breakfast the morning they left. "When I looked for him," she said, "I found him with Edward, who was asleep in his bed." He was sitting silently and tenderly beside his five-year-old brother. He was pensive and phlegmatic on the journey. On the long drive Frank regaled the older boys with political sermons on the Depression and New Deal, and his recent enthusiasm for Franklin Roosevelt, while his son remained withdrawn and obviously distracted.

Over the first months of the new term, Dick faithfully sent letters to Ola each week. "He still wrote until the middle of his second year as if we would get married." she recalled. Meanwhile, Ola accepted Gail Jobe's proposal. Before Christmas 1935, she wrote Nixon to break off at last their fitful romance. Once again, he was pained, indignant, unbelieving. For a time, he even continued to write her despite her letter. "I know he was very upset about the breakup," said a friend of Ola's who saw one of his final pleas. Then when she did not answer, he wrote a last plaintive note, and it was over.

Afterward, their friends were generally surprised and puzzled. "It ended abruptly. We never figured out why," Dick Thomson said. Few knew how starkly Nixon had lost her to another man. Only Ola's closest friends, who were aware of the many letters, sensed the depth of his feeling and of the rejection. "We were surprised that they didn't get married. And along came Gail Jobe and took her right away," Jewell Triggs would say, adding uncertainly, "By that time, maybe Dick didn't care anymore." Rumors and pretense covered the wound. Nixon himself gave Edith Nunes, who knew them both well, an explanation so implausible she was too embarrassed to confide it even decades later.

Nixon himself never admitted the seriousness of their involvement, nor confided his anguish. Rubin and other friends at Duke heard him talk about his family, the grocery, Whittier. They knew nothing of the girl to whom he wrote love letters once a week for more for a year and a half at law school. Ola and Gail married a few months later in 1936. "We just drifted apart," she told interviewers politely when asked about her romance with a future President. "He went off to Duke and, well, we just grew apart." Privately, she was more blunt. "Jobe was so much fun," she said later. "Nixon wasn't." She saw the hurt in his last letters, yet remained ever unsure of his true emotions. "I really don't know," she said wistfully in reply to a question about how he was affected by the breakup. "Who knows about him?" She recalled their dates and quarrels, his controlled but ardent letters, his proposals and assumptions of marriage, many of the small details of their years together. Yet there was something Ola Florence could not remember: whether Richard Nixon had ever said, "I love you."

"WHATEVER I . . . MAY DO IN THE FUTURE"

Academically, Duke Law had assembled an impressive young faculty in the 1930s, many of them products of the most venerable and prestigious Ivy League law schools. They were men who moved easily along the established paths that linked universities, corporate boardrooms, and the upper reaches of the federal bureaucracy, their politics less a matter of party or ideology than the common cachet of their background, contacts, or professional distinction. Especially the younger teachers embodied the growing prominence of lawyers in American business and the enlarged government of the New Deal.

The formidable Maggs, an ardent New Dealer trained at Berkeley's

Boalt Hall and Harvard, taught constitutional law as well as torts, and later worked in the Roosevelt administrations. More conservative than Maggs, David Cavers from Harvard and Lon Fuller from Stanford would go on from Durham to distinguished careers at Harvard Law, Cavers by way of a series of jobs as counsel to government agencies. Charles Lowndes, yet another Harvard Law graduate, was already by the mid-1930s a nationally known lecturer. After a similarly prodigal start at Yale Law and a respected New York firm, Kenneth Rush was a Duke assistant professor at only twenty-six, and in 1937 joined Union Carbide where he eventually became its chief executive. Cavers, Fuller, and Rush were all to play roles in Richard Nixon's subsequent career, the last an ambassador and undersecretary of state in the Nixon administration. Presiding over this precocious faculty was a suitably avuncular dean, Claude Horack, a kindly Iowan in his late fifties who had trained at Harvard at the turn of the century. Horack found his own ambition in the discreet promotion of Duke Law and its alumni and would be yet another Durham figure instrumental in Nixon's progress beyond the campus.

Together they taught the traditional law curriculum, laced with the politics, psychology, and social realism then beginning to leaven the orthodoxy of American legal education. "The intestinal theory of jurisprudence," as William Perdue, one of Nixon's classmates and closest friends, remembered one of the occasional irreverences of the younger professors, is "the importance of what a judge had for breakfast." Nixon remembered in particular Fuller's senior elective on jurisprudence, a survey of legal philosophy and history he later described as "an essential course for any law student who is planning to enter public life." At the time he seemed to relish most an extracurricular clinic that drew him beyond Duke's Gothic halls and lustrous faculty. The opposite of the law school legal aid program, which defended local indigents, the clinic placed students with the Durham County district attorney to learn prosecution practices and investigative methods firsthand. Evening interviews of witnesses and victims often took him late at night "into the jungles of the Durham outskirts . . . the rougher sections," as one observer described it, where the assignments required "a sturdy backbone and a strong stomach." The encounters with poor whites of textile mill neighborhoods and the still poorer blacks of Durham's shantytown were a sudden, stark revelation of another part of the world. Over the winter and spring of 1935–36 he devoted much of his scant free time to the clinic, winning from the Durham district attorney a formal commendation for his "excellent work" in prosecutorial briefs and painstaking investigations.

Back on the campus he worked equally hard, yet remained largely aloof from the personal contacts with faculty that were one of Duke's special strengths. There were twelve professors to less than ninety students, ready access to instructors in their offices, and tea with the administration and faculty every afternoon at four in the school's lounge. Most classes had a rare intimacy and the school a general "informality," as Richard Kiefer recalled, "that made the atmosphere friendly and easygoing." Through his first two years at Duke, however, Nixon scarcely knew the gifted young law school professors outside the classroom. "I am looking forward to my third and last year in the law school with a great deal of anticipation," he wrote in his final application for a scholarship in June 1936, "and I hope that it will be one in which I may learn to know the members of the faculty personally as well as professionally."

Near the close of the spring term Cavers singled him out as one of a handful of top students to write for Duke's respected school journal, *Law and Contemporary Problems*. Despite that distinction, despite his high class rank, he faced the same self-doubts, ending his junior year examinations as tense as ever. Earlier he had been offered a vacation job cleaning and polishing old volumes in the law library, ostensibly, as he told his parents, allowing him to research his journal article, but also a face-saving way to avoid going home at the moment Ola was to marry Gail Jobe. That steamy summer he fell in with Perdue, who sold Bibles in the pious countryside around Durham, and with another classmate who worked at the library, Frederick Albrink. All three felt the mounting strain and suspense the first week of June as they awaited announcement of the year's grades. One of those nights Nixon and Albrink worked late, and when Perdue picked them up to go to supper they walked past the darkened dean's office. "Well, the grades must be there now," Albrink remembered one of them saying. Someone rattled the locked door and then noticed the transom had been left open from the hot day. Alone on the silent, darkened floor, they quickly decided to break into the office, and Nixon and Albrink boosted the slight, wiry Perdue up and over the open transom. Perdue then opened the door and all three hurried through desks and file cabinets until they found the grades in a drawer. They found their own grades and rank, glanced at others' marks as well, then placed the cards back in the drawer and left. "We found the files with the grades and looked at them," Albrink admitted eventually, "didn't take any, didn't change any . . . this was at night, there was nobody in the building."

"We would not have looked upon it as horrendous," David Cavers was to say decades later when asked about the incident. Yet at the moment it would undoubtedly have appeared more serious. "Seemed kind of silly to me . . . there would have been some kind of punishment," said Ed Rubin, who graduated that June. Albrink later described the episode in some detail, though neither Perdue nor Nixon ever discussed it openly. "I simply don't remember the incident," Perdue would say without denying it, adding self-consciously, "I have a legal training." Had they been caught, the furtive little campus burglary would certainly have cost Nixon. The price might well have been the goodwill and profuse character references he was to receive later from Dean Horack, to whom he always appeared the most upright student and alumnus, and perhaps as well some crucial career patronage from Cavers five years later.

In the dean's office he discovered what he feared, that his average had dropped to 74.2, a low B, and his class rank to sixth. Nonetheless, only days later, on June 12, an unsuspecting Horack cheerfully informed him by letter to the law library that "your grades are sufficiently high so that you are eligible for a scholarship for the coming year covering your tuition and matriculation fees." The hoisting of Perdue through the transom was in its way a telling mark of the taut, pressured young man Dick Nixon had become and was becoming at twenty-three. It silhouetted the fragile sense of self that lay near the surface of his tenacious discipline, an unease that drove him at Duke and elsewhere both to genuine, reputable achievement and sometimes, in ways small and large, to a fugitive, self-defeating recklessness.

He broke the summer at the July Fourth weekend, going home with Richard Kiefer to Catonsville outside Baltimore. It was his first visit to the area, and Kiefer remembered how "his eyes widened as we drove through Washington." They saw the Senators and Yankees play at the old Griffith Stadium, where Nixon held onto his friend's belt as they muscled their way into the bleachers in the largest crowd yet to see a baseball game in the Capital. Under what Kiefer thought an "unmerciful" sun and with raucous fans overflowing onto the field up to the foul lines, they watched a California rookie named Joe DiMaggio hit a homer and lead the Yankees to a sweep of a doubleheader. Afterward, they drove back to pick up Kiefer's brother at a plant on the Baltimore waterfront, where the raw language of the ethnic dockworkers leaving their shift seemed a visible shock to the boy from Whittier. "Apparently," Kiefer observed, "he had never been exposed to those kinds of workers in that kind of atmosphere." The game, the longshoremen—it was his first real taste of the thronging, diverse world of the Atlantic seaboard.

The second year in Durham he had lived less severely, renting a small house with three divinity students, one of whom had a wife who cooked and washed for them all. Now for his last year he moved in with Perdue, Albrink, and Lyman Brownfield in a one-room clapboard farmhouse in the Duke Forest. For only $12.50 rent each for the year, he was again in bleak, almost primitive living conditions, with an outdoor privy, neither running water nor electricity, only an aged, unstokable sheet-metal laundry stove to ward off the Piedmont winter chill. They slept in two brass beds. Nixon got up in the predawn dark to go to his library job, often dressed with his teeth chattering so the other three could enjoy the fleeting warmth of the balled-up newspaper burning in the stove, and went off to shave and shower at the Duke gymnasium. "We outvoted him on the stove," Brownfield would say. But the mile-long dusty footpath led to the campus through a verdant corridor of wildflowers and songbirds, and they were among more than thirty students who lived in rustic forest cabins and used the school amenities, bearing common privations with a kind of *esprit*. "May it be that some of them have an eye on a political career and consider this the next best thing to being born in a log cabin?" the *Christian Science Monitor* queried, taking note of the forest dwellers at Duke. They named their house "Whippoorwill Manor," after another student bungalow nearby and the plentiful birds calling mournfully through the forest. "We had a great time there," wrote Nixon in his memoirs, recalling the place with obvious affection.

He became an editor of the school bar association journal, and his article for Cavers, "Changing Rules of Liability in Automobile Accident Litigation," was published that autumn. It was a survey of the evolving standards for defining a driver's negligence, in which he noted in some detail the requirement to stop before crossing railroad or trolley tracks, the sort of mishap that had cost Frank Nixon his job with Pacific Electric long ago. More interesting was a fall term paper in Legal Ethics, "The Lawyer Versus the Public," on automobile accident litigation. "Admitting . . . that this paper may make painful reading for the professor," he announced in a preface, "the writer believes he has obtained from its composition that which was intended, a certain amount of original intellectual excercize [*sic*] in the realms of ethical problems." In a meticulous holograph he deplored the seamy underside of the legal racket in auto accidents—insurance adjusters, "lead men," "runners," ambulance chasers, the whole cast of suspect characters preying on accident victims with fakery, perjury, and worse in what he called "this rich plum of legal business." The scandal was evident in the disreputable sociology of those involved. The lead men, he wrote disdainfully, "come from the following classes of people: politicians, police, hospital orderlies, nurses, ambulance drivers, telephone operators, newspaper reporters and doctors." Altogether, it was a system in which "the influential client gains at the expense of the poor and probably more needful one," and "the term . . . shyster has become synonymous in the minds of many people with that of lawyer." Since "the lawyer, ideally, is a public servant," he thought the only solution a strict prohibition on solicitation and, more important, "providing for the poor free legal service by competent members of the bar." In November 1936, he argued passionately much the same evidence of inequity, much the same case for free legal services for the poor, that Richard Nixon as President of the United States would heatedly deny and reject thirty-five years later.

Among the faculty he now came to be noticed as one of the better, relatively visible seniors, invited to professors' homes for supper and for the social contact he missed or self-consciously shunned the first two years. Cavers remembered him favorably but colorlessly as "one of the more active and able students." In 1962 Nixon startled his old teacher at a California reunion by recalling the small white onions Mrs. Cavers had served beside the turkey at a Thanksgiving dinner in Durham in 1936. He revealed clearly enough to some of his instructors that churning Nixon interior that so drove his work and so embedded the little white onions in memories of acceptance. Watching him in student bar activities, Lon Fuller thought him competent, "though not terribly imaginative or profound," as the scholar would remark three decades later. "And he was what today we'd call uptight," Fuller went on. "There was the suggestion of an intellectual inferiority complex."

With his peers at Duke that frailty was much less evident the final year, though never completely concealed. Nicknames were the fad of the moment. The Whippoorwill Manor foursome included "Brownie" Brownfield; the pudgy, easygoing "On-the-Brink" Albrink; and "Boop-Boop" or "Pooh-Pooh" Perdue, the intense, slender young Georgian who outranked them all academically and who was Dick's bedmate and closest friend. Nixon soon became "Gloomy Gus." Perdue thought him "somewhat limited in humor," yet the name attached less from any melancholy than from Nixon's dour practicality and what they all saw as a penchant for puncturing youthful pretentions. "This . . . came from a cartoon character who was always throwing the cold light of day on someone's rosy dreams, making comical situations," Brownfield explained. "Since the gloomy part did not really fit, the nickname soon shortened down to just 'Gus.' " They rode to dinner in Brownfield's ramshackle 1926 Packard, a jalopy they labeled typically "Corpus Juris," and Nixon joined easily in what became a revolving and ritual razzing of one of the passengers. He was "thoroughly at home in the horseplay," one of them remembered, "both as subject and tormentor just like anyone else." With Albrink he played awkward but energetic handball on university courts, exchanging raucous jokes and the mild student profanity of the place and time. "None of us [were] overly obscene . . . we said things like 'Get the lead out of your butt,' " the housemate recalled.

Still, there was always a quality of the solitary, of apartness, in the social occasions others remembered. Though he never attended the monthly beer party most law students frequented at a nearby Durham hotel, he stopped by the student union from time to time for a game of Ping-Pong or to play the piano, his music sometimes drawing a small crowd of listeners before he shyly left without lingering to talk or make friends. At Duke football games, Nixon became something of a local stadium character in the mid-thirties, yelling so much and so loudly that "some students used to sit near him at the games," as Brownfield remembered, "simply because of the kick they got out of his uninhibited . . . enjoyment." He was often too hoarse to talk the evening after Duke played. Yet in all the furious fan spirit, carried to the point of campus celebrity, and no doubt to some ridicule even amid the rah-rah college standards of the moment, he usually came and went from football games alone.

He never dated at Duke. Kiefer judged him unusually "stiff and stilted when talking to girls," while "informal and relaxed" with men. But few law students had time or money for girls, most of whom lived four or five miles away on the undergraduate campus. Rubin thought them all "sort of monastic." Men so outnumbered the available opposite sex at Duke that couples' tickets to dances customarily carried a "stag bid," which allowed lone males to attend and cut in freely, though few could recall Dick Nixon ever coming to the dances. Albrink reflected afterward that Nixon might have gone occasionally to hear the orchestras of Johnny Long or Les Brown, two Duke undergraduates who went on to big-name bands of the era, "but he never stayed longer than ten or fifteen minutes before he'd be back at his books." Still smarting from Ola's rejection and with none of the campus pressures to date that he had felt at Whittier, he retreated altogether from social life in his early twenties and spoke of his social isolation at Duke only once, blaming it on the old false pretense of poverty. "There were a few girls I liked and would have enjoyed dating," he said later, "but I didn't have the money."

Albrink watched him faithfully attend Quaker meetings in nearby Raleigh and thought him "shot full of rectitude. Some of us might fudge on the hours we worked at the library. Nix never would. He was a copybook kind of guy without being obnoxious about it. I mean he was industrious, honest, reverent, all of that." At the same time, Ethel Farley, one of the few women in the class, "disliked his 'holier than thou' attitude. He was not unmoral, just amoral, and had no particular ethical system, no strong convictions . . . he was there to learn skills and advance himself." "He was a man of such high ambition . . . with such intensity," said another classmate, "that . . . he would and could do whatever was necessary to attain the goal that he had set for himself." Bradley Morrah, who, like Brownfield, often drove them to boardinghouses for meals, "always saw him as slightly paranoid for some reason. . . . In those days he was odd, something of an oddball." To one fellow student, Nixon seemed "basically aloof, very sure of himself, and very careful to keep people from getting too close to him." To another he was "fearfully" studious, hunched over his book in the library, unsmiling, wearing "a very solemn expression" that "gave the man an unpleasing mien."

One hot spring day in 1937 he was working for Fuller in a small, close office, and came out angrily to demand that Ethel Farley and others playing table tennis in the nearby bar association recreation room quiet down and close their door. Incensed, disliking him to begin with, they refused and told him to shut his own door. He retreated sullenly. They "could feel his rage," reflected one observer, but not "his ineffable loneliness." It was, of course, the same Richard Nixon who tenderly lifted Fred Cady up the law school steps or dressed shivering in the chill dark mornings to save the stove kindling for his roommates. He left in his wake at Duke the same shifting mixture of admiration, hostility, and puzzlement that was to be the response to his career and personality, the chemistry of his public constituency, to the end.

Politically, he was outspoken among his closer friends in Durham, less plain to others. In Whippoorwill Manor bull sessions, Albrink was the lone young Democrat defending Franklin Roosevelt, Nixon and Brownfield the avowed Republicans, Perdue a cynical southerner and devil's advocate toward both parties. They remembered Nixon attacking the New Deal on grounds of individual initiative and responsibility, an old-fashioned social Darwinism he had so often heard his father expound. "Social Security is fine," he told Brownfield more than once, "but we need a certain amount of insecurity, too." It was the familiar ethic of hard work and self-sufficiency. Outside the forest cabin, his opinions were never passionate, almost perfunctory. His real politics remained his career. "I had always regarded Dick Nixon as a New Deal supporter," said a Duke classmate surprised at his emergence a decade later as a Republican congressman. At the senior beer bust in May 1937, he climbed a picnic table after a few drinks and delivered a clever little parody of a lecture on Social Security that he mockingly entitled "Insecurity." Brownfield looked on as Dick "had everyone in the proverbial stitches." They begged him to repeat the performance, and though he obviously savored the laughter and applause at the moment, he shyly refused.

Like many law students and faculty at the time, Nixon was indignantly opposed to FDR's abortive plan to "pack" the Supreme Court. But he was also a "great admirer," said a friend, of Justices Harlan Stone and Benjamin

Cardozo, the onetime conservatives who became leaders of the emerging liberal wing of the Court in the thirties. Ironically, it was Cardozo who authored in 1937 the historic majority opinion upholding the Social Security Act. Friends remembered Nixon revering as well the legendary liberal and crusading Justice Louis Brandeis. American Bar Association opposition to Brandeis's confirmation on the Court had been "unfair and a mistake," he told other students. It was something, one of his housemates observed, Dick "felt very strongly" about.

It was the festering issue of race that seemed to ignite the sharpest exchanges between Duke students, and there, too, Nixon seemed the ardent liberal. "In common with the balance of his classmates from the North and West," one of them said of him, "he was shocked and disturbed at the prevalent North Carolina treatment of the Negro population as an inferior group." The literal signs of the South's institutional bigotry were everywhere, in public segregation and in periodic outbursts of violence and lynching aggravated by the Depression. In the arguments provoked among Duke students Nixon seemed to the southerners one of their harshest critics. "He looked upon the issue of the treatment of the Negro as a moral issue and condemned it very strongly as such," said one Tennesseean, "but did not realize the problems that confronted the people of the South in regard to the Negro." Nixon was "unbending and unyielding in his opinions and moral convictions," recalled another southern law student, who thought the stubbornness on the race question made him in the class of 1937 "the man least likely to succeed in politics." Some of the most heated clashes were with his close friend Perdue, who admonished him at least to concede calling the Civil War the "War Between the States."

Nixon himself would later acknowledge "some intense discussions of the race issue" at Duke and that, "while I could not agree with many of my southern classmates on this subject, I learned in these years to understand and respect them for their patriotism, their pride, and their enormous interest in national issues." In his memoirs he added, "After my years at Duke I felt strongly that it was time to bring the South back into the Union." But that was written long after the fact, by an ex-President who had revolutionized party politics in the American South by a naked and brilliant calculus of issues and electoral votes that had little to do with arguments beneath Durham's Gothic spires in the mid-1930s.

In the spring of 1936, Nixon had been asked by Leon Rice, one of the student leaders in the class ahead, to be a candidate for the presidency of the law school bar association for the following academic year. "I wouldn't have a chance," he first told Rice. The opposition looked unbeatable: Hale

McGown, a popular young midwesterner who was in turn engaged to one of the equally well-liked young women in the class. Yet Rice persisted, and Nixon ran on a ticket with his crippled friend Fred Cady as secretary. In a quiet April election with more than a hundred students voting, they defeated McGown handily, adding still another political triumph for the young Richard Nixon.

When it was over, Brownfield and others thought it had clearly been "Nixon's first experience in politics," that "there was no real campaign or preparation for the election," and that while the student body had not "liked him better" than McGown, "the factor which swung the election to Nixon was genuine respect for his scholarship." So self-effacing and uncharacteristic seemed the candidate, even after his unexpected victory, that his Duke friends and classmates saw no hint of his future passion and profession. "He was the last person in the class," said a student who watched the 1936 campus election, "one would have picked to become a political headline."

At Duke, much as at Whittier High and College, the depth of his ambition and, even more important, the inner political mechanism of his success, remained largely hidden from his distracted, far more casual peers. In what was at Durham the third major student election of his twenty-three years, there was already emerging the patterned duality of two campaigns—the election and candidate visible to the constituency, marked on their memory, and the race and campaigner within, what had made it work and what by the nature of the game, of the pretense, was never openly revealed. In fact, once tapped by Rice, Nixon and Cady ran hard, discreetly promising job-conscious law students that the bar associaton would concentrate on employment opportunities. He would, he told them, attend to those tasks other students, even elected leaders, usually spurned, and he would above all organize and manage. "The Duke bar association officers got very good experience in managing the group," he wrote his successor a year later about the lessons of his tenure. "I don't think you can ever get too much of that." And behind the hard work, planning and promises, he once again won office that spring on the strength of an obscure but decisive factional battle. Rice had promised him the substantial support of the Iredell law fraternity against the more venerable Phi Delta Phi backing McGown. In miniature it was more than a little reminiscent of the Orthogonian revolt against the Franklins, a raw little playing out in the election of submerged tensions and social rivalries that Nixon understood if less politic onlookers did not.

The victory had one immediate tangible spoil, the use of the bar association office on campus where he could store clothes or shaving gear for his daily recourse from Whippoorwill Manor. It also brought, with the investiture banquet, yet another caricature of the winner, emphasizing that most prominent Milhous feature that would later be the cartoonist's staple. "Our New Prexy," read the caption, " 'Nose' All." "He was popular in the class," Brownfield reflected, "but I would describe it as a sort of lonesome kind of popularity."

Before Christmas 1936 he wrote Almira Milhous a characteristic letter.

> Dear Grandmother,
>
> . . . I should like to be sending you a gift which would really express my love for you but it will probably be several years before I reach such a high financial level if ever.
>
> You will never know how much I've appreciated your remembrances at Christmas, at Easter, on birthdays— and on days that have no special significance at all. More than them, however, I believe that I appreciate the fact that I have been a member of a family with such an illustrious person at its head. Sometimes in our spare moments, some of us indulge in reminiscing sessions here at school, and the boys are amazed at the remarkable person I describe as my Quaker grandmother. I myself share this respect . . .
>
> Your Loving Grandson,
> Richard Milhous Nixon

As he paid his respects to the matriarchy once more, he prepared to escape Whittier even more dramatically. Over the Christmas holiday he was to join Perdue and Harlan Leathers, another graduating senior, on a trip to New York, seeking a job with one of the large Manhattan law firms that were the professional mecca of the era. They went without formal introductions or invitations in a still-depressed economy, and the trip was in many ways quixotic even for high-ranking students in the new, small school at Durham. "Bigger offices in New York stuck pretty much by the Yale, Harvard, Columbia graduates," recalled Ed Rubin, who had watched similar quests the year before. "I can remember the trials and tribulations we had just to get past the reception room. It was then almost impossible for Duke students to get jobs in New York."

They spent a cold Christmas week in the city, staying at the Sloan House YMCA. Before they left, the three saw *Tobacco Road*, along with some other Broadway plays, and took in a performance from seats Nixon recalled as "the upper reaches" of the Metropolitan Opera. But he had little enthusiasm for the big city. "Nixon was not charmed by New York," Perdue said of the trip. "He had a West Coast prejudice." They approached most of the prestigious firms, Dick aiming in particular at Donovan, Leisure, Newton and Lombard, and the renowned Sullivan and Cromwell, where John Foster Dulles was then a young managing partner and where the hopeful applicant from Whittier was so impressed that long afterward he could recollect vividly the "thick, luxurious carpets and the fine oak paneling." That December day he was all but ignored in the plush office. In one of those strange twists of people and place that dotted his career, it was nearly twelve years before Richard Nixon would return to see a member of Sullivan and Cromwell, then as a powerful young congressman meeting without delay Foster Dulles and his brother Allen in a Manhattan hotel room for a historic secret conversation on the Hiss case.

Over the first weeks of 1937, Perdue, with his top standing in the class, was offered a promising corporate law position, and Leathers, who ranked well below Dick, was hired by the coveted Milbank, Tweed, Hope and Webb. Aside from a *pro forma*, obviously noncommittal letter from Donovan, Leisure, however, there was nothing for Nixon, and not even a lingering prospect. In his memoirs he passed quickly over the painful rejection, never mentioning the jobs won by Perdue and Leathers, though in campaigning in 1960 he would refer poignantly to Bill Perdue as "a real success" for having risen up the corporate ladder. By the time the "iffy" response from Donovan arrived, Nixon evasively wrote, "I was no longer so keen on the idea of starting out in that cold and expensive city." At the moment, he was bitterly defeated and caught unprepared. Expecting to be hired in the East, he had neglected to maintain his California residency and was now ineligible for the state bar examination the following autumn, closing off even the prospect of returning home to a law practice. Anxiously Nixon implored Horack to salvage the situation, and the kindly dean on January 8 wrote a chatty, personal letter to an old friend at Stanford Law "to remedy this slip" and intercede on the bar exam. "One of our very best students," Horack called Nixon, ". . . a man to whom I can give the very highest personal recommendations . . . a student of fine ability." The plea got Nixon added to the fall examination list, the result of a letter that might have been very different, if written at all, had Horack known of the summer night violation of his office six months before.

Meanwhile, Nixon talked with the dean briefly about a government job in Washington, Horack offering to write a contact at the Justice Department but Nixon reluctant to court another rejection. On February 11, President Nixon chaired a student bar meeting that heard J. Edgar Hoover's administrative assistant recruit for the FBI, and he was soon eagerly applying to be an agent. Once again, though he personally advised Nixon to "settle down" and establish a private practice before going into government, Horack wrote an effulgent reference. Hoover had earlier asked the dean to suggest "any exceptional young man who has an interest" in the FBI. Horack now responded, "I have such a man in mind who is to graduate in June . . . one of the finest young men both in character and ability that I have ever had in my classes . . . who can do an exceptionally good piece of research when called on to do so." Lon Fuller was less sanguine about the FBI but found Nixon serious in applying. "He came in one day asking advice . . . said he thought he might go back to Whittier and practice law. I sort of said ho-hum about that. I thought he could do better than that," Fuller recalled. "He mentioned the FBI and I said I thought he was too good a man for that, too." Nixon had replied "he didn't know why, but he was attracted to it."

His finals went well, and he indulged in a last small celebration of the three years of restless toil, "the only time that I ever remember seeing him actually let down his hair," a friend said. They tapped a keg of beer in an open lot near the school and played an impromptu softball game. "I still remember seeing him try to catch a flyball out on the field with a glass of beer in his hand," one of them recounted. His family, including eighty-eight-year-old Almira, had decided to come to Durham for his graduation. The day they arrived on campus, the law school announced Nixon third overall in his class, his 80.49 average behind only Perdue and Brownfield, and qualified for the national law honor society, the Order of the Coif. But there was no last-minute job offer, no other reward, and he crowded into the family sedan with his parents, brothers, and wizened grandmother for the long drive back to California. On their return, they stopped briefly to visit Almira's maternal relatives in West Branch, Iowa, where a family snapshot caught them all standing together on a narrow, shady, small-town street, Richard unsmiling and half hidden behind his mother.

It had been a tempering, testing end to his education, and never, least of all at its climax, the escape and recognition he had contemplated so confidently that summer before law school. "I remember that I worked harder and learned more in those three years than in any three years of my life," he would say a quarter century later. In both the opening onto the world and the disappointment at the close, he seemed to sense a decisive influence. "And I always remember," he said in 1960, "that whatever I have done in the past, or may do in the future, Duke University is responsible one way or another."

7

Return to Whittier—
Law and Politics, 1937–41

"I BELIEVE . . . I'VE CONVINCED MYSELF THAT IT IS RIGHT"

He came back home, to his old room above the garage, in an unseasonably hot basin summer of 1937. There was a momentary lift as the Whittier papers printed the promotional photography and press releases distributed to hometowns by a publicity committee he had encouraged in the student bar association, listing Nixon's impressive law school honors. "When I got home," he wrote a Durham friend, "practically everybody I met had seen the pictures in the paper. . . . They mean a great deal to the graduates." But with no ready way out of the place he had hoped to transcend, he soon became all the more sour about the apparent defeat, sinking for weeks into what the family remembered as a petulant, stubborn pout.

Even before she crossed the country for his graduation, Hannah Nixon had quietly, insistently intervened to retrieve the situation, at least in her own terms. Although since the New York trip Richard pointedly refused to make any inquiry about local jobs, she had nonetheless called on Thomas W. Bewley, an old Milhous family friend and junior partner in one of Whittier's two resident law offices, about hiring her son. "In a sense things had already been set for him," Paul Smith would remember, "because his mother had already gone to Bewley and importuned on her son's behalf that he be taken into his firm." Bewley, too, was a Whittier graduate, and he had promptly gone over to Smith at the college to ask, as the professor recalled, if it would be "a mistake" to give young Nixon a job. "I think that would not be a mistake," Smith replied in the same dour Quaker tone.

Now Bewley was telephoning the boulevard grocery to arrange an interview and offer. And Richard Nixon, twenty-four, at once proud and dismayed, was sitting sullenly in the hot dormer, refusing day after day to return Bewley's calls, while Hannah stood by quietly. It was an artifice and evasion that would go on, with a somewhat perplexed Bewley leaving repeated messages, for more than four weeks.

At the end of June, Nixon saw Duke instructer Lon Fuller, who was spending the summer in the area. Fuller urged him both to take the California bar, then only two months away, and to accept a place with a local firm, which Dick evidently told him had been tendered, though he had not yet responded to Bewley. "Mr. Fuller thought I might as well make a stab at it in September anyway, since I have little else to do and then if I fail it I can take it again in March," he wrote Horack's secretary on July 3, not mentioning the Bewley prospect among the "little else to do." "Tell Dean Horack . . . ," he warned, "that the 1st Duke graduate to take the Calif. Bar has a darn good chance to fail it the 1st time he takes it!" Still not having returned Bewley's calls, he drove into Los Angeles on July 17 for an examination and oral interview with the FBI. When at the same time Bill Perdue stopped by the grocery during a trip to California, Dick "talked as if he had been offered a job with the FBI," the roommate recounted, although the lengthy and uncertain application process with the Bureau was hardly complete. Nixon said nothing to Perdue about the job with Bewley.

The issue of the Whittier firm finally came to a head late in July, forced by the rebuke of a young first cousin embarrassed at Nixon's procrastination and rudeness. Lucille Harrison thought Richard "worn out and tired" after all the work through law school and "a little bit uppity when he came home from Duke." But ignoring Tom Bewley reflected on Lucille's own family and the larger Milhous clan, and she went to the grocery where "I had it out with him," she recalled. "Well, Dick, I don't care whether you go into it or even see him," Lucille scolded, "but you're not putting me on the spot by not answering the call, and you can at least go call." Chastened yet still avoiding the overt act, "he finally did [call] after a couple of weeks of waiting around," she remembered. "He didn't want to go into a law office here in Whittier—he wanted something better."

Early in August he wrote Horack confiding again his misgivings about the bar exam. In the cram course he had heard "some stories about other men from Eastern schools who attempted to begin studing [sic] the first of July and failed the bar in September!" He added tentatively in closing, "As you may know—I received a very good offer from a local firm on reaching home. I believe I'll probably be there once I get by the bar. But I'll let you know more about that when the big event is over." The dean replied with typical encouragement. "Dear Nixon," he wrote back August 10 in the clubbish address of the law school, "Don't worry about the bar exams for they will have to flunk all of them if they don't let you by." Meanwhile, he began a characteristically intense regimen of study for the test, attending the accelerated cram course and fleeing the store and small house for long periods of concentration, often in a spare room at the Milhous home, sometimes in a small conference room Tom Bewley had offered him in the Wingert and Bewley suite up the hill in downtown Whittier.

He took the three-day examination early in September, one of over eight hundred would-be lawyers in California, and then lapsed into weeks of apprehensive silence before writing Horack his impressions. Nixon's indecision about joining Bewley still seemed plain enough at the end of September that Horack even wrote him about a temporary academic job in Florida, while gently inquiring how the test had gone. Nixon dutifully replied on October 6, 1937: "After several false beginnings I'm finally getting a letter off to you." He was still waiting to hear if he passed the "very hard but very fair" California exam. "Now in re my employment prospects . . . I received an offer to go into one of the two good firms here in Whittier . . . on a percentage basis. They have a very good practice, mainly probate—which is of course remunerative and respectable. I believe I'll go in with them right at present.

"I would like to spend a couple of years with some government de-partment—before settling down," Nixon admitted, "but I believe it will be best to settle down and get to work—and build up a business—if that can be done." He told the dean about the FBI examination in July, and that he had no word from the Bureau. "They have been investigating my character since that time! However unless my present prospects fall through, I shall not accept the job even if it is offered to me." As it was, the Bureau was to turn him down—"lacking in aggressiveness," said the recruitment appraisal—though they would not inform him until later that year. At the close of the letter, he asked Horack's advice—"whether you believe this is the best thing to do"—about taking the Bewley job. "I believe," Nixon added sadly, "that I've convinced myself that it is right."

The tension was palpable in the grocery and house through October—what Nixon called "an unnerving experience for me and my family"—as they awaited the mailed results of the bar exam. Rumor had it that a thin envelope signaled success, a thick one, with applications for the next test, meant flunking, and they nervously checked the mailbox on the boulevard each day. It did not arrive until the end of the month, Hannah coming back in tears holding a bulging letter from the examiners. Nixon took the thick envelope and quickly closed himself in the bathroom to open it. "I did not want her to see my distress," he said later. As it was, the extra papers were instructions for new members of the bar; he had passed the examination, which more than half the applicants failed. Nixon burst back into the kitchen to announce his triumph to more mother's tears.

On November 9, 1937, Richard Nixon was sworn in before the state supreme court in San Francisco and celebrated afterward in a champagne toast with Marshall Clough, the old friend visiting from Prescott. For all his aversion, the hometown job arranged by Hannah with Tom Bewley was sealed. In the end, in the press of the bar exam and the nervous aftermath, there had simply been no alternative outside, and he had not even tried larger firms in Los Angeles. "I shall be with the firm of Wingert and Bewley, Bank of America Bldg., Whittier," he finally informed Dean Horack that November. The same note carried a small omen of his first major professional blunder as well. "They already have assigned a couple of motions to me—to be made before the L.A. Superior Court just as soon as I'm sworn in," he wrote, one of the cases to embroil his new firm in a costly malpractice charge and to haunt him decades later. "So you see they're breaking me in fast."

Whittier, the winter of 1938: "A wealthy residential city in a citrus, avocado, and walnut district," a Federal Writers' Project guide depicted it in passing, the place where Richard Nixon began his law career with such hesitation. A half century after its founding, it was more than ever the stiff, puckered-up small town, lines of class and convention encrusted on the Puente Hills like silt deposits of some ancient flood. In the 400–600 blocks north of Philadelphia Street and east of Greenleaf, a few dozen families looked down from the social as well as geographic high ground, set apart by their maids, graceful homes, and economic power as blatantly as anywhere in the basin. "Oh, there were class differences there. What we would call upper middle class lived really as upper middle class in the sociological distance," recalled Judith Wingert, the daughter of Tom Bewley's senior partner and a member of the clearly defined social elite in the late thirties. "There was a clique. You repeatedly went to parties with the same people . . . to the same country club and the same bridge clubs." And that society, Wingert's daughter remembered, was "terribly gossipy . . . terribly petty."

The mark of the town was still its willful, pious isolation. A few miles from Hollywood, Whittier's movie theaters at the end of the 1930s remained closed on Sundays. As Richard Nixon began his law practice, developers were already on the way to subdividing the great citrus empire, slowly but relentlessly devouring the fragrant, green hinterland of the town, clearing the paths for extravagant growth—and profit—that would pass by Whittier, along with the freeways it deliberately repelled. City fathers first unctuously rejected Works Progress Administration public employment for the area jobless on the grounds of a "Bolshevik" taint to the government relief. Later they came to see the virtue in their own sewer socialism, as it were, and adopted one WPA project to build spacious new storm drains, a system that would carry the basin's troublesome wild rains nicely away from the fashionable neighborhoods to a squatters' lowland out of town.

In June 1936, the summer Richard Nixon stayed in Durham, Mexican pickers with a handful of Anglo union organizers finally struck the citrus groves in neighboring Orange County, a desperate response to conditions of near slavery that drew down savage reprisal from local growers and the police, courts and press they controlled. "That pickers were banding together to make any demand," the *Los Angeles Times* wrote forty years later, ". . . smacked of unionism, which smacked of collectivism, which smacked of communism." As a result, the bloody "citrus riots," as the uniformly pro-grower local newspapers called them at the time, became a veritable "civil war." Small-town sheriffs' deputies broke out Thompson submachine guns to deal with unarmed laborers seeking a few more cents a day. Brutal suppression of the strike was soon buried away in the booster history of the region. But part of the horror had been roving bands of local vigilante night riders, wading into strike meetings swinging pick handles and throwing tear-gas bombs, attacking quiet, defenseless Mexican settlements of women and children. Among the desolated communities was Whittier's Jimtown.

The firm of Wingert and Bewley sat perched over it all, on the top floor of Whittier's tallest structure, a solid, gray, six-story, scroll-corniced building at the southeast corner where the Greenleaf and Philadelphia boundary lines met. On the site where the father of Lou Henry Hoover once had his pioneer bank, their law office was among other professionals above what was now the Bank of America. Thomas W. Bewley, whom Hannah Nixon had "importuned" to hire her son, was then thirty-five, an earnest, long-nosed young lawyer of dark hair behind round-rimmed glasses that lent him for the moment a clerical look. Born in Cincinnati, he had emigrated to the basin with his Quaker family after his grandfather, a close friend and business associate of Franklin Milhous in Indiana, lost both the Bewley grocery and lumberyard to a catastrophic fire. Bewley graduated from Whittier College in 1926, finished USC Law School three years later, and ran immediately but unsuccessfully for justice of the peace on a platform that cryptically claimed "six years' practical experience," though he was fresh out of school. He then worked briefly for O'Melveny and Meyers, a politically active Los Angeles firm, before joining Wingert in 1933, where he promptly became Whittier city attorney. A lawyer of average ability, he seemed given to the folksy, small-town manner of his origins, faithfully attending the uptown First Friends Church and marrying the daughter of a local butcher. Beneath, he was inveterately political, conservative, tough, ambitious. "We are a cold people, I guess," he would say of his frontier Quaker characteristics. "We're very warm to each other but we are too self-sufficient."

In some contrast, his partner Jeff Wingert was already sixty-eight the winter Nixon joined them, an Episcopalian with an agile sense of humor who built a comfortable estate from oil speculation and land investments. By 1938, Bewley's net worth was recorded at $5,000–$10,000, Wingert's at between $30,000 and $50,000. Rigorously honest and hard-working, Wingert had earlier dissolved another partnership for the slightest appearance of impropriety. He was also notably unmercenary and forgiving in collecting or even charging fees to clients of modest means, making him, his daughter remembered, a warmly "humanitarian . . . very much loved man." Like Bewley, he served for years as Whittier's municipal attorney. Along with most of the town's professionals, he was also a Republican disdainful of the New Deal, albeit more gently than his proud, snobbish second wife, "Jud," who hid her own rural midwestern origins, looked down on acquisitive young Tom Bewley, and once fired her Whittier maid on discovering that the woman had voted for Roosevelt.

Their work was principally probate and estates, along with retainers to small petroleum companies, Superior and Dome, and independent local oil wildcatters. The firm took on few divorce or accident actions and routinely referred elsewhere any criminal matter. It was a "respectable" enough practice, as Richard had justified it to Horack, and in a sense well beyond what he may have imagined when he took the offer. More than their rivals, their probate and estate specialty left Wingert and Bewley in a sense Whittier's society lawyers. As it was, they practiced in an era when attorneys and access to the law were far more a privilege of the well-to-do, what Judith Wingert would remember as "a luxury" in Whittier. "Practically everybody knew everybody at the upper stratum of the society," she recalled. "Most of those people had my father or, later on, Tom Bewley draw up their wills." Their clients were a veritable *Who's Who* of the recently wealthy and influential of the town. Among them were the stolid Aubrey Wardman, his fortune founded in the local telephone exchange and multiplied by oil and real estate; the Stoody family, whose construction company built the expensive Puente hillside homes; John Riley, with a booming fluid pump industry; the Leffingwell Rancho on its vast holdings south of the Nixon grocery; the Citrus Water Company, another local economic force; and others.

In the inevitable web of small-town probate and money, their legal work with inheritances and property bound them as well to the local banks and bankers, to men like Buey Allen, a discreet power in the basin's growing financial world, and particularly to the Bank of America five floors below, where a onetime teller-become-president was perhaps to be Tom Bewley's closest friend and business link, an even more seriously political and Republican Quaker named Herman Perry. They were all names—a few to be known, many more unknown—that would be vital in Richard Nixon's political rise. And they were all there, waiting, in the files of the obscure, two-man law firm he so reluctantly joined that autumn.

Nixon first came to the sixth-floor office that summer in a freshly pressed blue serge suit and waited "several minutes" to see Tom Bewley, remembered Evlyn Dorn, the firm's Canadian-born secretary who thought him "a really serious, intense person," though with an unmistakable air of pride and independence. He "gave the impression," as Dorn watched him that day, "that . . . he was there to see whether he wanted to work with *us*." Finally meeting the touted young man after weeks of unreturned phone calls, Bewley was duly "impressed," he remembered, "with his mature good looks, action and thinking." They talked for less than a half hour. Nixon was willing to do the court and general errand work both partners found onerous. Bewley offered him on the spot $250 a month. "I was satisfied at knowing the family. He was the type of fellow I would like to have in the office," Bewley said later, neglecting to mention he had also double-checked beforehand with Paul Smith. "He wanted to do trial work," the lawyer recalled, "and we needed somebody badly, so we just made an arrangement."

He returned in November 1937 for his first day of work in the same blue serge. Dorn remembered him making his office in what had been the small conference room off the suite, where he had studied for the bar, and in that sharply creased suit busying himself cleaning the dusty law books, even varnishing the shelves, of the firm's library. There were a few motions and filings to attend, but he now discovered that the extra work weighing on Wingert and Bewley was less than full-time for a third lawyer. Whatever the actual caseload, they all soon marveled at his characteristic intensity and dedication. Bewley later boasted of his young associate's quick and facile work, though when a trial was pending Evlyn Dorn and her friends often came out of the second show at a downtown Whittier movie near midnight and looked up to see the lights burning in Nixon's sixth-floor office. "He would sleep on the couch in the office some nights," she once reminisced. He also commonly sent Dorn out for a favorite lunch of a pineapple malt and a hamburger or Mexican food, if he remembered to eat at all. Bewley thought their diligent new lawyer, unlike their colleagues, never went out to lunch "just for fun."

Shoulders hunched, lost in concentration, he walked past them much as he had moved so resolutely across the nearby high school and college campuses. Often he was first in the office, and instantly absorbed. "I used to come into the office in the morning and work around my desk for fifteen or twenty minutes," Dorn recalled, "before he looked up and said, 'Oh, good morning, Evlyn.' " Eventually, he composed draft legal briefs for both partners, and Dorn found him an easy and articulate writer, if also "never quite satisfied . . . a perfectionist." As he began to dictate some of the drafts, she was astonished by his capacity to pick up the thread of an interrupted passage, to remember precisely what he had dictated, even to read shorthand upside down, pointing to the exact place among the symbols on her pad where he wanted to add or make a change. "He was the kind of boss that you wanted to do your very best for," Dorn said, remembering their growing respect for him. Watching it all as a curious, apt teenager, Judith Wingert saw in the fledgling attorney his zeal and long hours, and yet a relative ease. "He didn't seem to be a steamroller in those days," she said. "He was more relaxed."

On May 31, 1938, he wrote Dean Horack the last of his long, chatty postgraduate letters, enclosing with some embarrassment three pages of research he had owed for nearly a year on his NYA job. In atonement for the tardiness and admittedly "meager findings" of the work, Nixon added some observations on the California bar examination and an offer to help with law school recruitment. He had joined the Los Angeles County Bar Association to get "a cheaper rate" on lectures "on practical phases of the law" for new members, he told Horack, but then missed most of the sessions because of the flu. "I can honestly say without throwing any of the well-known applesauce that I believe we've got the best darn law school in the country right at Duke," he wrote the dean in closing. Read later, it was a poignantly ironic letter, in a sense one of the clear lines of demarcation in maturity and experience. Less than a month afterward, Nixon was to blunder carelessly into the most costly professional error of his infant career, snared by one of those "practical phases of the law" he apparently missed at Duke as well as in the bar lectures. The sequel soon took him into a harsher world than he still inhabited that May, in the dutiful student's rather cloying, innocent letter to his old academic patron.

The case had begun in the autumn of 1937 when a Los Angeles woman named Marie Schee retained her parents' former lawyer, Tom Bewley, in a suit to recover a $2,000 unpaid loan to Schee's uncle and aunt, Otto and Jennevieve Steuer. On November 15, six days after his swearing-in and his first Monday on the job, Nixon had been sent by Bewley to appear in the Los Angeles Municipal Court at a hearing for summary judgment on the suit, one of the "motions" he had proudly mentioned to Horack at the time. Without contest, the court granted Nixon's motion, awarding Schee her money by way of an attachment on the Steuers' house, but on agreement between Nixon and the Steuer attorney also allowing a stay or postponement of execution. Over the next few months, the matter then wound its way through failed efforts at settlement or partial repayment and toward a forced sale of the Steuers' home. Tom Bewley continued to handle in the main what was his case to begin with, including conversations with Schee and letters to the Steuer attorney. Meanwhile, at various points in the process—December 1937, January and April 1938—Richard Nixon routinely appeared in Municipal Court or signed documents on behalf of Wingert and Bewley in the case, in precisely the sort of trivial procedural detail he was largely hired to do.

The Steuer house duly came up for sale by the court marshal on June 29, 1938. The day before, Tom Bewley was ill and not in the sixth-floor office in Whittier, nor did Bewley apparently talk to his new young associate about the case before Nixon left on the twenty-ninth to go to the execution sale. "While I had no particular instructions from Mr. Bewley on the date of sale, it was part of my duty to attend to such sale," Nixon testified later, "and it was always my understanding that we were to press . . . such sale and not to grant any further continuances." He would also testify that he never talked personally with Bewley's client, Marie Schee. But he had, it turned out, naïvely asked the Steuers' lawyer at one point about the execution, saying "Maybe you can be of a little assistance to me when this comes up for sale." And the opposing lawyer had told him to bid for the property all Bewley's client was owed.

What followed might have been a classroom exercise in the law of property. Turning up alone with the marshal at the sale, Nixon should have checked to determine if there were any other liens or mortgages on the house affecting its value. Failing that, he could still bid a nominal sum for the property that would protect Schee against any such unknown claims, allowing her a "deficiency judgment" from the sale and thus leaving the Steuers still liable for the debt while Marie Schee took a deed to the house, whatever the other claims on it. He did neither. Instead, he followed the corridor advice of the Steuer attorney and purchased the house simply for the full amount owed Schee, in effect paying the marshal with the previous court judgment against the Steuers. It was an error that set off nearly five years of suits and countersuits hinging on his own "misconduct" and the "malpractice" of the firm.

There were, in fact, trusts held on the Steuer house by others, who soon began foreclosure proceedings to secure their interest. Schee's proceeds, the whole purpose of the initial suit and sale, were now in jeopardy, and Tom Bewley moved to remedy Nixon's mistake. Later that summer, Bewley advised Schee's parents and his old clients Charles and Emilie Force, who evidently had the money necessary, to buy out the other claimants and then force foreclosure themselves in order to resell the property and retrieve both their costs and their daughter's money. On Bewley's counsel, they did just that, in what was now becoming a rather convoluted real-estate maneuver. This time Bewley himself attended the sale late in December 1938, having advised the Forces to bid, as Nixon should have back in June, only a nominal sum. But what would have been prudent and professional in June was an even worse blunder in December. Another buyer came to the sale, bid more than the Forces though still less than $3,000, and thereby wiped out Schee's repayment while taking the property.

"Enraged," as one account described them, the Forces and Schee promptly turned on Wingert and Bewley and sued them for malpractice, arguing in their complaint that the firm had "carelessly, negligently, incompetently and unskillfully" advised them on the foreclosure sale. Their suit centered on Bewley's bungled gambit with the Forces on the second trusts and sale. But it traced, of course, to Richard Nixon's basic misstep, and beyond that to Bewley's failure to make sure the new young lawyer, however impressive in manner, actually knew what he was doing. Their fault obvious, Bewley within days quietly settled the malpractice suit out of court by paying the Forces and Schee $4,800 in March 1939, the amount of their various costs and stakes and, at the moment, a heavy penalty from the resources of the small firm.

The case was to drag on in various forms until the end of 1942, the Steuers moving for satisfaction of judgment after sale of their house to end Marie Schee's tangled claim on them; Schee contesting that, losing, appealing, and losing again. In a final action, still trying to exploit Nixon's original botchery and unappeased by the malpractice settlement, Schee sued to undo the first marshal's sale, and lost once again both in Los Angeles and on appeal. In those lawsuits, Nixon personally was called to defend himself by affidavit or to testify under hostile cross-examination by Schee's new attorney. There were accusations of a "spurious" letter by Bewley to cover up the bungling and even exposure of a perjured affidavit by the Steuers in support of Nixon's defense in the later cases. Each time, Nixon's own initial blunder was rehearsed, along with his occupation as "outside man," painted demeaningly as an "occasional" runner for an obscure suburban firm. Each time, his work was put on trial with overtones of the seedy.

Though Schee was defeated on the two appeals, and his own lack of skill or authority in the original case ruled beside the point by the higher court, Richard Nixon's "alleged misconduct" would be inscribed in the California appellate records summarizing the later cases. It was all uncomfortably reminiscent of some of the sharp practice he had denounced not so long before in his Duke legal ethics paper. The cases were also a bitter reminder—in Bewley's subsequent malfeasance as much as his own—of the tenor and quality of the Whittier career, of its distance from the carpeted suites of Sullivan and Cromwell.

For his part, Tom Bewley would acknowledge his own larger responsibility in the Schee debacle. "If it was anybody who caused the mistake it was me . . . he got caught in the backwash, I guess," he would say of Nixon and the sales. "I always felt he was unjustly criticized in that case." But the older lawyer remembered, too, his young assistant's own reaction at the time. "He was terribly upset about this case . . . and he was more upset not because he did anything but because I said, well, we've made a mistake, and we'll have to pay for it."

More than for any mastery of the substance or subtleties of the law, Nixon the young attorney would be remembered in Whittier for his style and technique, for the interchangeable methodology of the courtroom and politics, for the old, familiar methods of the debate platform. "As to his courtroom psychology," Bewley recalled, "he could present his case so butter wouldn't melt in his mouth, or he could take hold of a cantankerous witness and shake him like a dog." His less sophisticated partner also saw Dick's studied awareness of appearance, of audience, of oratory and theater. "He was particularly conscious of his clothing. When he tried a lawsuit, he had the right stance, and he used the right voice, which was low, but which he built up gradually with dramatic force." Bewley was even more struck by Nixon's preparation and quickness of study. "He always seemed to be way ahead of the witness and could anticipate what answers a witness would make," the partner would tell one early interviewer. Bewley thought "he could reduce an argument to its essentials. Where I'd take four pages he'd take two." Accompanying the two senior men to Los Angeles for a fraud case involving oilfield equipment, Nixon impressed them both by cleverly producing a stopwatch and carefully noting the questioning and summaries by the opposing lawyers. "When the trial ended," Bewley said later, "he knew more about it than I did—and I was representing the defendant."

Over the first year, Nixon seemed to develop a special interest in taxation as well as the firm's main practice in estates. And Bewley, increasingly taken with his associate despite the early Schee blunder, confidently steered clients to him. "Go see Dick Nixon," a Whittier city official remembered Tom Bewley telling local merchants and others more and more in 1938–39. Still, the older man had a clear sense that the intensity and cool efficiency were not for everyone. "I'd handle the divorces and the old ladies. Dick didn't have the bedside manner for that. He appealed to the up-and-coming businessmen, men like himself."

The few divorce cases that filtered through were awkward. "I remember when I'd just started law practice, I had a divorce case to handle, and this good looking woman, beautiful really, began talking to me about her problem of sexual incompatibility with her husband," Nixon once confided. ". . . I turned fifteen colors of the rainbow. I suppose I came from a family too unmodern, really. Any kind of personal confession is embarrassing to me personally . . . any letting down my hair, I find that embarrassing." A friend and fellow lawyer found him particularly "tense and morose" after one office session with an embittered couple. Nixon seemed personally distraught at his failure to effect a reconciliation. It was not only his shy propriety. Wives seeking a divorce could provoke an angry, volatile reaction. Later, when the relative purity of Nixon's speech, his lack of profanity even in private, was part of the political image, Tom Bewley admitted that there were particular times that Dick Nixon "lost his temper" and "let off steam" in cursing. "He became extremely irritated when people presented their cases and then, at the deposition, told him a different story. He regarded such dishonesty as unforgivable," the partner recalled. "Women complainers, and naggers who had only petty grievances but wanted to inflict punishment on their husbands, also annoyed him."

Wiping out the Schee episode and others, Bewley would say of Nixon's practice, "I don't remember that he ever lost a case," but the reality was that there were precious few cases to begin with. "I think you can count on the fingers of one hand the cases Nixon tried here in Whittier," recorded Merton Wray, by now a fellow attorney. "As a matter of fact, neither one of us tried very many cases in those days," echoed Wallace Black, who began his practice in the area three years before Nixon and also handled mostly probate. "There wasn't too much litigation and it wasn't worth it because you couldn't collect even after you got a judgment."

Richard Nixon would spend more than four years with Wingert and Bewley, and afterward claim proudly to have been a practicing attorney before he entered politics, the only one among modern Presidents of the United States. At the same time, in his memoirs and reminiscences he glided more swiftly and vaguely over those years than any other period in his adult life, never mentioning specific trials or clients, or even the flavor of the time and work. In professional legal terms, in light of the expectations he had at Duke and the attorneys he encountered later in politics, it was not only that Wingert and Bewley were a mundane small-town firm of uneven competence; it was, in truth, not much of a law practice by any standard.

By the close of 1939, a little more than two years after he joined them, Wingert and Bewley invited him above the line to become a full partner, and he accepted without pause. Status was some consolation for the reality of the practice. "Now for the first time I was no longer Frank and Hannah Nixon's son," he wrote about the promotion. "I was Mr. Nixon, the new partner in Wingert and Bewley." At twenty-seven, his emancipation was not quite so complete. While Hannah's intercession to get him the job was known only to Bewley, Paul Smith, and a handful of Milhous relatives, he continued to live at home, and even to work part-time for the store. Dr. I. N. Kraushaar remembered Dick making deliveries while already a lawyer in 1938, bringing groceries to a home in the heights where Kraushaar was on a house call and having to telephone his father and return for another trip when the customer objected to the cut of meat. Richard reacted to the episode, the physician noted, in his usual "serious" and polite manner. But on a proud young man, sensitive to his enforced return to the old place and life, so conscious of his standing as "son" or "Mr. Nixon," the effect was only hidden.

To Tom Bewley, meanwhile, in a relationship Bewley would describe as notably free of small talk, he had begun to tell stories about Frank Nixon's punishment of his sons, including the dunking in the Anaheim ditch back in Yorba Linda. "Dick laughed about it," Bewley recalled, though Nixon told his new employer about more than one incident. "Yeah, we got the strap" is how Dick would commonly end the stories. "I think . . . sometimes he felt he should apologize for his father," Bewley said later.

Soon after he joined the firm, Hannah invited Evlyn Dorn and another part-time secretary down to the Nixon house for dinner, a gesture of warmth and support for her son's situation like so many in the past. Evlyn, for that matter, even went with Don Nixon for a time. But the relations in the uptown office did not always extend down the boulevard, across Whittier's cordons of caste and class. The Bewleys and Wingerts did not come to the dinner. The Nixons, Judith Wingert remembered emphatically three decades later, were "lower middle class" in Whittier, their grocery someplace where "you stopped on your way back from the golf course." During their son's partnership with Wingert and Bewley, Frank and Hannah moved onto the heights northeast of the college, into one of the Stoody Spanish-style houses on Worsham Drive gracious enough for its own sprinkler system and for Milhous nieces to hold Palmer Society teas there in the living room in the early 1940s. But somehow not even their hard-won Depression success in the grocery quite conveyed them back across the threshold Hannah had passed in marrying her trolley conductor more than thirty years before.

It was part of the promise of the law, of Richard's professional respectability, that he crossed over the barrier occasionally. The Wingerts made their own gesture in 1938 when he first went to work, inviting him to Santa Anita, his first day at a horse race, and then dinner afterward at Olvera Street, the old Mexican quarter of stalls and restaurants preserved as a tourist attraction in downtown Los Angeles. Nixon was visibly thrilled and pleased. "But you know," thought the watchful Wingert daughter, "it seemed to be a very different sort of day for him." Still, there were limits. When Duke played Southern California in the Rose Bowl on New Year's Day, 1939, Dick Nixon implored Dean Horack and pulled alumni strings to get tickets, which he then proudly presented to the Wingerts. Ever the passionate football fan, he got a ticket for himself as well. Yet he would not presume on his own initiative to sit with the senior partner and his family and went to the game separately.

Amid the businessmen Tom Bewley guided to their offices, Richard Nixon was soon drawn into the ever-present boom ethic that survived even the Depression and Whittier's relative stolidity. When a bumper crop of oranges brought a costly surplus in 1938, local growers were lured again by the old, recurring dream to reinvent the national market for southern California's plenty, now to overcome the surplus in whole fruit by freezing the juice of the oranges. The technology seemed at hand. Large-scale commercial freezing of foods had begun a decade before, while the superior freshness, taste, and color of frozen food over canned products promised a growing mass market. And far more than they imagined in Whittier in 1938, far more than an outlet for surplus yields, the stakes were vast. Within twenty years, three-quarters of the nation's oranges would go to frozen juice, creating enormous wealth.

Tom Bewley remembered how one of their clients was the wholesaler and agent for "a number of growers," and some of them had come to the sixth floor to talk the firm's eager young lawyer into being the front man. Nixon was instantly excited at the prospect, and typically ready to throw himself into the work. "They convinced Dick that they could all make a fortune in the enterprise." After "some discussion," as Bewley recalled, they christened their new company Citra-Frost and made Dick Nixon both counsel and president. There was going to be all the more profit, Bewley recalled, "because of the expected saving in labor by operating on a do-it-yourself basis . . . the keynote of the company was economy." There was also, it turned out, going to be limited financial risk for the growers and wholesalers who stood to profit most. Nixon would have to put in some of his own money and find other local investors for most of the $10,000 capital they thought necessary.

Over the next several weeks, he hurried after hours and on weekends both to enlist the investors and to get the process started. The money came readily, much of it in large sums from a few Whittier businessmen, but portions, too, in hundred-dollar increments from the sparse savings of teachers and clerks, and nearly all of it as an investment in Richard Nixon and his reputation for intelligence and hard work as well as in the concept. At the outset he also won encouraging business support, a contract with Owl Drug for experimental containers, and two large shipping companies pledging to distribute nationally all the frozen juice Citra-Frost could preserve. Yet their do-it-yourself method soon proved a false economy, and the $10,000 went quickly. From the start, Citra-Frost would have a clumsy, shoestring quality that belied its potential.

Their nemesis was the chemistry. They were freezing the whole orange juice instead of the concentrate that was the secret of the process, and the error in the basic concept led in turn to a series of failures in packaging that further obscured the answer. Obsessed with finding the right container, they never seemed to grasp the importance of the contents. Month after month, in mounting frustration, they tried cans, glass jars, paper cartons, primitive cellophane bags. Bewley, who helped out himself and even committed some of the firm's money, described how his associate "used to rush out" after office hours to the little plant in nearby Pico Rivera where they brought excess oranges and where Dick Nixon in shirtsleeves tirelessly poured juice into the various containers and tried to freeze it effectively. Proud and hopeful, he brought extra cartons of the squeezed juice to friends at local service clubs, showing them "how good it was," one of them recalled.

With each failure, the money dwindling, Dick became more desperate. Evlyn Dorn thought Nixon worked at the plant "late every night after work" for months on end. In Bewley's memory, "He worked like a dog. He was out there cutting oranges and squeezing oranges day and night after he'd do the work here. And he just couldn't realize that they wouldn't make a success of that." After a year and a half, in a last gamble of capital and method, they froze the juice in small plastic bags and loaded a full refrigerated boxcar. With the car still on the siding, the bags soon exploded, leaving the interior in what Evlyn Dorn remembered as a "sticky mess," and Citra-Frost in bankruptcy.

It was an expensive lesson. The growers and wholesalers had not been willing to augment the company's meager capital, and soon resumed making their own profits when the market for whole fruit revived. Intent on the "fortune" to be made, none of them had apparently done any research or asked informed advice about the freezing and expansion of the water in plain orange juice. "He was more upset about the orange juice thing," Bewley said later of Dick, than about the embarrassing Schee case. He was also broke. Nixon lost in the scheme all his own savings from the first year in practice, though the losses—and bitterness—were even greater among the people who had trusted him to make them wealthy. Nearly forty years afterward, Bewley's law firm still carried on its books some of the costs extended in the venture. Added to Richard Nixon's share of responsibility for the out-of-court settlement in the Schee case, their new young attorney had in that sense cost the firm thousands in his first two years.

After World War II, Nixon would try to return from his own pocket $100 lost in Citra-Frost by an old Whittier schoolteacher. She proudly refused it, telling him it had been a legitimate speculation. Asked later about the venture, other stockholders in Whittier simply laughed it off. But not all were so resigned. "A few disappointed investors blamed Nixon for the failure," Earl Mazo wrote in 1959, "and still vote accordingly." Another observer thought many who had given him money "did not hide their disappointment." As usual, Tom Bewley could be more blunt. "You'll find people here," he would say decades later after the little plastic bags exploded, "who hate his guts because of that."

Over the eighteen months, Hannah Nixon watched her son's feverish dedication to Citra-Frost and to what it represented, much as she would later watch Donald grab at grandiose business success with similarly abortive results. Yet the sheer mercenary quality of it was too raw—like the investors who felt cheated—for the later confection of the Nixon political biography. Citra-Frost was to be passed over swiftly as a youthful fling, and the burning motivation in Nixon eventually denied altogether. "Public service has always appealed to me more than making money," he himself would say. His mother expunged even more completely the long nights her son spent squeezing oranges in search of wealth. "Work for Richard . . . has not been connected with making money," Hannah was to write. "I have never heard him express a desire to be a financial success."

In the wake of the Citra-Frost collapse, in mid-August 1939, he opened an office of the firm in La Habra, a settlement of four thousand southeast of Whittier. His "branch" was in the rear of an abandoned hardware store, now an unpartitioned real-estate office in a one-story building along La Habra's lone business street. "This tiny little place," a Milhous cousin who went to help him clean up and move in recalled it. He filled the spot with a homemade desk he built himself out of scraps in the Nixon garage, giving it small side shelves for his law books and six decorative false drawer fronts. He had considered taking space down the alley in the office of a young local dentist, Harold Stone, but chose the back of the old store instead, for fear the frightened cries of Stone's child patients might unnerve would-be clients.

Watching the move, Merton Wray thought Wingert and Bewley were scrambling to make more money in lean times, the new La Habra office "a means on their part to take advantage of Nixon's family connections east of town." There were only two other lawyers in or near the little town, and the press release announcing the new office described Nixon as a "young man well-known to many La Habrans, being a member of a family of that name long residents of the Lowell district." He was now in the Whittier office in the early morning and late in the afternoon, spending the interim in La Habra and infrequently taking Evlyn Dorn along as the practice warranted. From his drawerless desk he incorporated the La Habra Riding Club, secured a state charter for the Chamber of Commerce, did some work for the local Kiwanis, eventually became attorney for the Hacienda Country Club, a retainer that gave him golfing privileges at the exclusive course. But for the next two and one-half years, the La Habra office was to be a restless tedium.

Townspeople remembered the young man sitting alone at the back of Ben Roberts' Real Estate and Insurance. "He stayed out there for days on end waiting for business," as Wallace Black saw him. Celebrated at the time in *Ripley's Believe-It-or-Not*, La Habra claimed the distinction of having even more churches per capita than Whittier. In truth, it was a languid backwater that only underscored his failure at Citra-Frost and the defeat of his return home after Duke. The *La Habra Star* reported as news the Sunday dinners one neighbor had with another a block away. On "slow days"—"as they often were," one witness recorded—Nixon wandered across Central to Caplinger's Pharmacy for long coffee breaks with Stone and other locals. As with the firm's Whittier clients, however, there would be in the coffee and aimlessness a political connection for the future. Stone, who became his friend and dentist, was married to the daughter of a wealthy building and loan executive, Albert Carden, who in 1946 would become the first of many, and perhaps the most crucial, of Richard Nixon's campaign finance chairmen.

Nixon found his escape in civic clubs. As an attorney about town, he was expected to be a member of such organizations, but he now took them up with an energy and seriousness that made the clubs less a business or social device than the prelude to politics. In La Habra he immediately joined the Kiwanis and Chamber of Commerce and further afield the University Club, the Whittier College and Duke Alumni clubs, as well as Los Angeles and local bar associations. Of them all, the most active was Whittier's 20–30 Club of young businessmen. They met for Tuesday night dinner at the William Penn Hotel, donated "Safety Sally" school-crossing mannequins, sponsored a Scout troop, and started a YMCA club for Mexican children in Jimtown. Nixon "used to pound out the piano" for their lusty singing after dinner, as one member recalled. He also invited the 20–30 board to meet in his parents' presentable new home on Worsham Drive, and soon, as he did in most clubs, became president. On the whole it was the innocent male heartiness and conservative business ethic of small-town professionals and merchants on the way up, but the clubs also bred their own miniature politics.

Philip Blew, a Whittier College acquaintance, remembered Dick coming up to him and two other members after one boring 20–30 meeting, suggesting they get together to figure out how to improve programs. "Dick's starting comment," Blew recalled, "was that we should constitute a self-appointed committee and not bring the program chairman into our confidence until we had all our plans laid out." Blew invited them to his room with a bottle of whiskey, and they happily drank into the late hours, Nixon to the point that one of them had to drive him home. "We got him on the back porch . . . took off his shoes and put them into his hands," Blew described, "and instructed him to tip-toe into bed and not let his father hear him, because we knew that if his father found Dick drunk he would raise hell with him." The next day their small cabal to reform club programs was forgotten.

Twenty-Thirty provided an initiation, too, in more worldly political methods. Late in 1939, not long after the night in Blew's room, Nixon was in San Francisco at the 20–30 annual convention, busy as the campaign manager of a California candidate for the club's national presidency. Wallace Black remembered how hard he worked and planned for that election, how he got "some kind of a deal" on brandy and champagne to serve as "French 75's" at the candidate's hospitality party for convention voters, and how Dick brazenly walked through the front lobby of San Francisco's sedate Hotel Whitcamp with cases of liquor despite the management's pleas to take it up the freight elevator. Along with the "refreshments," he waged "a regular campaign like you'd have at any convention," Black remembered. "They tried to 'buttonhole' delegates and get votes . . . make some trades along the line or some deals. If some area wanted the next convention, you might make a deal . . . if they would give their votes to your candidate."

Nixon's 20–30 candidate lost in 1939, in a sense his first and last defeat at a national convention. The national club politics worked a visible excitement in him. As on college glee club trips, he talked of dreams he never disclosed at home. Black, who saw him then and thought him "always interested in politics," would be among the least surprised at his later career. "On occasion," he recalled of Dick's zealous club politicking, "he would confide that someday he'd be President of the United States."

"FOR ONE OFFICE OR ANOTHER"

Through the winter of 1939–40, Nixon launched himself back home into a flurry of political activity, the converse of the long, vacant days in La Habra. Only a relatively recent member in most of his organizations, he worked deliberately to offer himself for nomination and then to win office by much the same strategy he employed in school, arriving early and leaving late, volunteering for the tasks other young businessmen were too busy or casual to attend. He swiftly collected offices like trophies—leading the Whittier and Duke Alumni as well as 20–30, and served on the Kiwanis and La Habra Chamber boards. Afterward, friends from Whittier could look back at the decade of the 1930s, from high school to young adulthood, and count that they had "voted for Nixon," as one of them recalled, "for one office or another, either thirteen or fourteen times." Yet, remarkably, like classmates who elected him at Duke, most of those who voted for him again and again somehow did not see the seed of public political ambition, did not recognize what Wallace Black and a handful of others saw closer. So that when he returned to Whittier years later after the war to run for Congress, he genuinely seemed to many to have both the requisite experience in leadership and a decorous indifference, a kind of citizen innocence in politics that matched their own.

Nixon had begun to help Bewley late in 1938 as an assistant city attorney for Whittier. At the beginning of 1940 he now devoted much more energy to the firm's time-consuming and generally unremunerative work for the town, drafting ordinances and offering to deal with demanding city councilmen or to act as sometime municipal prosecutor in trials Bewley gladly avoided. The work gave him a minor yet visible platform. When citizens complained about a small café across from the Bank of America defying Whittier's prohibition by serving beer, he promptly posted part of the town's tiny police force outside the café, by their presence threatening customers with arrest for any show of public drunkenness and eventually driving the business to Los Angeles. An opposing attorney, Merton Wray, watched, too, as Nixon researched an elaborate legal presentation on the city's governmental authority in prosecuting an old carpenter who ran a part-time business out of his Whittier garage and whose power tools offended some of his neighbors. The man had been given a license by the city, but the political pressure was overriding, and the deputy city attorney found justification to close him down. "Well, Nixon worked out quite an argument on that doctrine . . . that defeated me," Wray remembered.

In La Habra, meanwhile, Nixon quietly moved to become city attorney in his own right for the small suburb, enlisting his friends from Kiwanis and the Chamber of Commerce, and lobbying members of the city council to replace Harold McCabe, the longtime town lawyer who was a Republican as well. "He worked on Jap Burch a lot," said McCabe, remembering Nixon's efforts with a local Ford dealer and councilman. On the receiving end of the aggressive, buttonholing politics, McCabe thought the new young challenger for his job "rather tense" and obviously ambitious. "Oh, there was no question about that," he would say of Dick's political striving. "I mean you could see it; it was apparent." But the La Habra council refused to discharge McCabe, and Nixon and his backers angrily saw the incident in terms of small-town collusion, even corruption. "We tried to get him the job of city attorney here in La Habra, and these guys wouldn't even talk to us because they had a political setup with the one attorney they had," Harold Stone explained afterward. "All their dealings were with this fellow, the protections and the rest of it that went on in back of the scenes, you see."

What "protections" or "the rest" went on "in back of the scenes" in church-filled La Habra in 1939–40, Nixon and his supporters never revealed, nor, for that matter, was it clear what he might have done as city attorney to change the "setup," which involved the same local businessmen Nixon courted in the service clubs and much the same favoritism and accommodations he and Bewley enjoyed at Whittier City Hall. At any rate, he pulled back from the La Habra defeat to pursue more openly what had been the real goal of his maneuvering and self-promotion in the two municipal legal positions—a seat in the California State Assembly.

By early 1940 it had been rumored for some time that Gerald Kepple, a successful rival attorney to Wingert and Bewley in Whittier and a Republican Quaker who had held the Assembly seat for four years in the conservative district, would forgo the coming race. In February Nixon began a hurried series of speeches to local clubs and small audiences that held much of the Republican rank-and-file in the area. His standard topic was "Nine Young Men," a parody of Franklin Roosevelt's epithet on the "nine old men" challenging the New Deal on the U.S. Supreme Court. Borrowed in part from the discussions he had heard at Duke, it was a vigorous attack on FDR's Court-packing plan and other policies that left his listeners in no doubt about Nixon's Republican loyalties. For weeks he crisscrossed the large, sparsely settled old Assembly district in a Chevrolet coupé, speaking wherever he could arrange an invitation, and paying his own mounting expenses. "I remember driving back with him from one speaking engagement," Stone reminisced. "He talked of having to give up the speeches because he couldn't afford the time or the money for the gasoline they were taking." By April Kepple had not yet announced his plans, and Nixon continued the trips across the bumpy rural roads to deliver his set speech, ending with long drives home in the darkness alone. Through the soft, citrus-scented spring nights of Orange County just before the war, Richard Nixon was beginning to travel what would be over the next thirty-four years literally millions of campaign miles.

His polished, sometimes academic recital about packing the Supreme Court was strangely divorced from the smoldering issues of his legislative district on the edge of World War II. If Whittier and the small-town society of 20–30 and the Bank of America building were, as usual, insulated from the ferment in the rest of the basin, their assemblyman was not. Decades later, Kepple looked back heatedly on the unemployment and unrest, and what seemed—as the Mexican pickers seemed to the orange growers in the 1936 riots—a dangerous labor radicalism. "Well, we were nearly broke," he would say of the state, "and talk about communist demonstrations— they picketed my home and I had to have my kids taken to school by sheriffs!" The poisonous labor-management battles from Hollywood to the citrus orchards and farm fields, the vicious reaction against Upton Sinclair's reformist campaign for governor in the mid-1930s, the gathering dependence of the state on military industry—all this and more lay beyond Whittier Boulevard in a political reality Nixon eagerly approached that winter but never entered.

Abruptly, the chance was gone. Later that spring, Kepple chose to run once more, and there was no question that the seat was his, that as a popular incumbent he would again be given ample Republican support and money to return to Sacramento. Nixon dejectedly stopped the contrived speeches, the abortive bid almost too eager from the start. He had talked discreetly with influential Republicans in the district they dominated, men like Herman Perry, who knew Nixon as what Wallace Black called "the fair-haired boy among the Quakers here," men who controlled money and workers and whose anointing was essential. They had generally encouraged his interest in politics. But while he had never been so bold as to declare his candidacy publicly, he had gone on to make the repeated speeches all over the countryside, virtually to challenge Kepple and preempt their choice, though Perry and the others were obviously waiting quietly on Kepple's decision before they would make any commitment to a replacement. And he had done it almost alone, confiding his plans to J. W. Burch and Tom

Bewley but few others. "He expressed one time that maybe he'd like to go to the State Assembly" is how Burch remembered their coy conversation at a time Dick was speaking to any group that would have him. Again, there was a subtle advantage later in the impetuous, half-hidden run. Gerald Kepple himself did not learn about his hungry would-be successor in 1940. Six years later, having become a powerful Republican elder, Kepple would be a strong supporter of modest, self-effacing Dick Nixon for Congress.

"I thought he had an aptitude there," Bewley said of his junior partner and his awkward false start in serious politics. "We gave him all the help we could, not as much as we should have probably." At best the support of the office was lukewarm. As Dick complained to Dr. Stone, there was not even gas money. Judith Wingert would remember her father remarking how much "speechmaking" Nixon was doing in those months, yet she recalled, too, an acerbic comment from Jeff Wingert, after the State Assembly campaign collapsed, that "Dick was a better politician than he was a lawyer."

When he looked back himself on his first, thwarted effort in local politics, the long night drives about the Assembly district were an embarrassment, like Citra-Frost a failure to be excised. "They talked about running me for the Assembly," he once said to Stewart Alsop in passing but without further elaboration. "As for the question you raise about my political interests and activities, pre-1945, I would sum them up this way," he wrote an inquiring publicist in 1961. "Interests—a bit above average for a fledgling lawyer, but certainly no conscious plans for a political career, activities . . . almost none." In his memoirs he mentioned not at all his avid political occupations of 1939–40: the 20–30 convention, the jockeying at the Whittier and La Habra city halls, the zeal to succeed Kepple.

For her part, Hannah Nixon never talked about the first political failure. Later, she could not recall any club Richard had joined in those years except "the Whittier little theater group." It was an ironic selection of memory. In a way, the little theater was more important. There, two years before, he had met a beautiful young woman, and fallen boyishly, desperately in love.

8

Patricia Ryan, 1912–40

ot long after Wingert and Bewley hired their new lawyer, Wallace Black ran into him in the elevator of the Bank of America building. The Community Players had called Black about taking a small part in a Whittier little theater production, but he was too busy and now urged Dick Nixon to play the role. Nixon "wasn't very enthusiastic" at first. Black persisted. "Well, if you get up there and make like a good lawyer, it might bring you some business." At that Dick took the part. He obviously enjoyed returning to the stage, and promptly decided to audition for another role in the next Community Players project, *The Dark Tower*, by George S. Kaufman and Alexander Woollcott. It was February 1938.

Elizabeth Cloes, a local schoolteacher, already had the lead in the play and knew they were having difficulty casting from the usual Whittier amateurs *The Dark Tower*'s Daphne, a "tall, dark, sullen beauty of twenty," as the playwrights saw her, "wearing a dress of great chic and an air of permanent resentment." Cloes was taking night-school shorthand at Whittier High and thought her instructor in that class fit the part well. Almost twenty-six, Patricia Ryan was a striking young woman, a slender five feet five with high cheekbones and flashing brown eyes, her long hair a golden red. She was new that year at Whittier Union, and she brought youth, stylish clothes, and an unmistakably modern air of cool if proper independence and worldliness that set her apart instantly from the rest of the more dowdy faculty. Still, she seemed pleasant and approachable, and Cloes invited her to dinner at the Hoover Hotel, convincing her to come along afterward to a tryout. Miss Ryan had a "quiet vivaciousness about her,"

Cloes thought, although there was something of the rest of Daphne's role as well, a wistfulness behind her beauty, a deeper seething in the dark expressive eyes.

They went to the audition in the Sunday school hall of St. Mathias Episcopal, one of the town's graceful tile-roofed churches near the college. As Patricia Ryan studied the script, Richard Nixon was reading for the part of Barry Jones, a "faintly collegiate, eager, blushing youth." When she then walked up to read, he was enthralled. "I found I could not take my eyes away from her," he remembered. "For me it was a case of love at first sight." He knew Elizabeth from the grocery, and he used the acquaintance to hover about the two women, "attentive all evening long," Cloes remembered. He drove them home that first night, the three sitting in the front seat with Elizabeth in the middle. "I'd like to have a date with you," he finally said to Patricia just before he let her off. "Oh, I'm too busy," she replied coolly. He laughed and drove away.

For the next rehearsal he picked them both up and afterward drove them home again, saying nothing about a date. As they were coming out the third night and he was once more taking them home, Elizabeth anxiously whispered to her friend, "Pat, you sit next to him. He doesn't want to sit next to me. He wants to sit next to you." But the pretty teacher was still aloof. "I don't want to sit next to him," she said emphatically. Then, as they stopped at a traffic light, Nixon leaned across Elizabeth Cloes and asked, "When are you going to give me that date?" Patricia laughed. "Don't laugh," he said quickly, pointing a finger at her. "Someday I'm going to marry you." She had laughed even louder at that, and then looked at him intently, "to see if he was teasing," as she related. But he seemed serious. "I met this guy tonight," she said to a friend as she came back to her apartment, "who says he is going to marry me." Afterward, Nixon himself was surprised at his words. "I wonder whether it was a sixth sense," he would say, "that prompted me to make such an impetuous statement."

She had grown up in Artesia, only nine miles south of downtown Whittier, yet in a sense far away. It was a flat, dusty, Santa Ana-swept place of less than five hundred, marginal land of the basin dotted with the hardscrabble holdings of poor whites, along with Portuguese, Mexican, and Japanese farmers growing sugar beets and alfalfa. Artesia's roads went unpaved, and cars were rare late into the 1920s. They had no streetlights until she graduated from high school, and not yet a movie theater even then. "We were culturally deprived," said Marcia Elliot, who grew up there at the same time, "the whole bunch of us."

The Ryans scratched out a thousand-dollar-a-year living on ten fitfully irrigated acres a mile outside town. Like so many basin sites, Artesia was an ironic misnomer. Their well ran furiously through the night when daytime pumping in the countryside drew off too much pressure to raise the meager, ebbing groundwater. Her father trucked the small crops of cabbage and cauliflower, pimiento peppers, beets, corn, and tomatoes eighteen miles into Los Angeles in a rickety trailer behind a Model T. Their home was a one-story, white frame bungalow, standing beside a lone bushy palm tree in the sun and the dust. For years they had no plumbing or electricity. The family of six overflowed the two-bedroom house, and she lived her childhood sharing with her older half-sister a tiny, curtained-off anteroom with space only for a bed and dresser. Her earliest memories would be of riding away from Artesia on the Pacific Electric, or of how she raced her older brothers to get into the big bed to sleep next to their mother—and always lost.

She was born not Patricia but Thelma Catherine on March 16, 1912, in a mining shack in the rough frontier copper town of Ely, Nevada, the last of three children of a miner and German immigrant widow with a boy and girl as well from a first marriage. When she was a year old they abandoned Ely, and migrated by train to southern California, finding a little "ranch" they could afford in Artesia.

Already forty-six when Thelma was born, Will Ryan was a tall, thin, mustachioed Irishman who had left his Connecticut family at nineteen to become a whaler, and then what one account called a "luckless speculator," prospecting from mining camp to mining camp, strike to strike, the American West to Alaska, the Philippines and Borneo, acquiring an unquenchable wanderlust, a store of tales to excite his children, but little else. He was a timekeeper in an Ely mine when his wife persuaded him to settle down on an arid farm in California. Suddenly stranded in a cabbage field, Will Ryan would never be reconciled to losing the rock-edged freedom of his youth. In defiance, he proudly held onto his prospector's felt Stetson among the straw hats of his Artesia neighbors, some worthless oil stock certificates, and a fierce heedlessness to pain. When a farm horse kicked him in the face, he refused chloroform as the doctor took thirteen stitches to close the gash around his nose. "Just sew it up, dammit," he had yelled, returning to his plow after the surgery. He took his reprisal, too, in whiskey, and in thundering fights with his wife that left the children cringing, especially his small, doll-like daughter, whom he dotingly nicknamed "Babe," his "St. Patrick's Babe in the morning," as he called her the day after her birth. "I detest temper. I detest scenes . . . I saw it with my father," Babe would say a lifetime later. "And so to avoid scenes or unhappiness, I suppose I accommodated to others."

The other figure of those frightening scenes, Kate Halberstadt Ryan, was born in Hesse in central Germany and immigrated to the United States at ten. She was twenty-seven when she married Ryan in the Black Hills of South Dakota, thirteen years younger than he, but already widowed with two small children after her first husband, a mining engineer from a well-to-do family, died a hero's death trying to rescue victims in a flash flood. She quickly bore two sons by Will Ryan, Bill and Tom, before Thelma, and soon aged from petite dark-haired beauty into plump, round-faced middle age. Her second marriage was uneasy at best. "You are the happiness of my life," she would say mournfully to Thelma, who sensed her dismay. Mrs. Ryan was to be remembered in Artesia for her hard work as a farm wife, her delicious cinnamon rolls, and a practiced capacity to placate or evade her volatile husband. When her family in Germany faced starvation after World War I, she furtively saved egg money from the sparse household budget and mailed it secretly to Hesse. "She lived in fear," her granddaughter wrote, "that Will, who was adamantly anti-German, would discover what she was doing." Beyond the bungalow, the Halberstadt ancestry became a family secret in any case in the xenophobia that engulfed the basin in 1917–18. Although she spoke English with a decided accent, she made her children swear never to admit that their mother was German. It was a half century before they learned her maiden name. And when Thelma was grown and married to a famous politician, and Kate Ryan long dead, the daughter would say that Kate Ryan had been born in Elgin, Illinois.

Thelma's mother was raised a Lutheran and later studied Christian Science. Her father was a fallen-away Catholic, a teasing, sardonic man with a straight-faced sense of humor in his storytelling. "He said on Sundays he was a Seventh-Day Adventist, because on Sundays he had to work," Louise Raine, one of Thelma's girlhood friends, recalled. He and his wife were also Democrats. Will Ryan—like Frank Nixon and others in the basin who felt somehow excluded or cheated—vocally supported Robert La Follette's third-party populist campaign for the Presidency in 1924. Yet the children went to local churches only sporadically, and political topics were seldom discussed at home, neither religion nor politics significant in a family life consumed by an unremitting struggle for subsistence.

They all labored in the fields, Thelma tagging along as a very small child, soon working at whatever she could manage, though there were limits to what a girl might do. Louise Raine recalled how they "used to beg to go" to the teeming market in Los Angeles when the crops were trucked in Sunday nights, "and our fathers wouldn't let us." Thelma did ride in a buggy with her father into Artesia with its handful of stores, where she waited silently, hopefully for an occasional ice cream cone if Will came back with extra pennies after shopping, and where she endured, too, a kind of torture. Ryan and his drinking friends in town would tease the pretty little girl on the buggy seat that her father was auctioning her off like a slave, that they were bidding prices for her. "My mother, sitting very straight, her red cape spread around like a fan, her eyes straight ahead," as a daughter told the story etched in Thelma's memory, "never revealed even to her father that she was terrified he would sell her."

The Ryans were "quite strict" with their children, remembered Myrtle Raine, Louise's sister in the neighboring family. Neither parent seemed outgoing or especially affectionate physically. The family recalled scenes long afterward that caught the reticence and reserve. Given a new pair of shoes by her father, little Thelma stood stiffly and in some awe, until her half-sister tugged her arm and whispered that she should go kiss him to acknowledge the gift.

She was a bright student, skipping second grade in Artesia's small red brick schoolhouse, where she was in classes with Mexican, Portuguese, and Japanese children, and where she gained recognition for her speaking recitals, including a small oration on La Follette suggested by Will Ryan. Along with the work, the father's angry outbursts, the feelings held in, there was also very much a bucolic quality about her Artesia childhood—hide-and-seek at dusk, a nearby haunted house, bareback rides on the plow horses, small dress-up plays Thelma wrote and staged with friends in a "secret" shed beneath a water tank. "We had a path from her place to ours that we'd run across all the time," Louise Raine remembered. "I can still see that path running across; came out their back door and out our back door." The Ryans' small house held little furniture. Thelma had almost no toys, a doll but no bike like her older brothers. She grew up in the early years "more of a tomboy," Myrtle Raine would say, remembering them wearing jeans that scandalized old ladies in the town. The girls worked alongside the rest and like the brothers sneaked melons from the patch and rolled cigarettes to smoke in the cornfield beyond sight of the house. "They were poor even by Artesia standards," one California historian noted, though farm life blurred such distinctions for a child. "It was very primitive, but no one else we knew had any better," Thelma once reflected.

Their lives began to change tragically in the summer of 1925. Neva Bender, Thelma's half-sister, left home in angry resentment at the relative advantages given her brother, Matthew Bender, who had been sent soon after their father's death to live with his wealthy grandparents in Los Angeles. The contrast with the Benders, whom Thelma visited with Kate on trips to see Matthew, and who lived so near and comfortably while the Ryans struggled, would long be a hidden family wound. While Neva remained a part of Thelma's life, Matthew would be absent almost entirely. Now the half-sister's embittered going left thirteen-year-old Thelma with a family about to disintegrate. That summer Kate Ryan was already ill with what would later be diagnosed as both kidney disease and cancer of the liver. The mother typically concealed her suffering for a time, though the Raine sisters visited the house to find her lying down more and more during the day, and increasingly irritable. "You kids get out, get out, get out!" Myrtle remembered her shouting.

That autumn Thelma hurried home after school, hiding the reason herself from friends, and soon took over all the meals and housework as her mother became bedridden. At harvest she cooked such large quantities of food for temporary hands that her own appetite was dulled. Her brothers helped in part, lowering the kitchen window shade, like Richard Nixon in Yorba Linda, to keep neighbors from seeing them wipe dishes. But in a pattern that would go on for years, the domestic work fell almost wholly on the younger girl, who took on with it still more her sinking mother's stoicism. "I may be dying"—Thelma long afterward interpreted her mother's attitude—"but I certainly would never say anything about it." In November, with no hospital nearby, Kate went to board with a local doctor, where she was medicated to ease the pain. Thelma visited each night to clean her, change her nightgown, and spoon-feed her. On a chill January morning in 1926, Will Ryan told his children before school that their mother had died during the night.

They held services in a small funeral parlor in nearby Norwalk, and buried Kate Ryan in Whittier, the nearest large cemetery, only yards up a gentle hill from where Arthur Nixon had been interred five months before. Thelma had wept privately at home, but came out after the services smiling bravely, walking right over to a group of her friends standing uneasily to the side. "Didn't she look beautiful?" she asked them. The next day, a classmate at school recorded in her diary, Thelma "looked very sad around the eyes. We asked her to play tennis with us." She was always, thought one of her friends at the funeral, "a tremendously disciplined person."

Through the high school years that followed her mother's death, she was bound to an oppressive regimen of hard work and poverty. She cooked, did household chores, helped farm, ran a roadside stand for their unsold produce—all with little help from a father or older brothers who were unwilling to work beyond the fields. "Her brother was always giving her heck because there would be a wrinkle in his shirt," said Louise Raine, who watched Thelma iron late into the night. "He didn't allow any wrinkles." Meanwhile, she excelled at Excelsior High School, making the honor society, debate team, and student government, playing in school dramas, though never in sports because she had to be home soon after classes to do the housework. She was now "a cherubic child with dark sparkling eyes," as a classmate saw her, "with cheeks like apricots" and a deepening, throaty voice. In high school she weighed a shapely 132 pounds, thirty pounds more than her size as a famous adult. To girlfriends she became "Buddy," her outward manner not unlike her role in the senior play that drew rave reviews in the school annual: "Penelope Lapham, in all her girlish moods, gay and serious, was charmingly portrayed by Thelma Ryan."

As in her farm childhood, there were moments of play and abandon amid the drudgery—surfboarding at the beach, shopping trips into Los Angeles, escapades with a brother's car. Yet the severity at home took its toll. To her humiliation she might fall asleep in class. Usually fastidious, she sometimes appeared unkempt, "not always able to keep herself perfectly groomed," as her daughter gently wrote later. On the one day a week Excelsior did not require socially leveling blue-and-white middies, a day of catty rivalry and new outfits, Thelma's poverty was too plain. "When I think of her, I think especially of one dress . . . I can still see her in it. She didn't have a lot of clothes," Marcia Elliot recalled. "But Thelma never talked about it," she added. "She never complained."

Pretty, intelligent, popular, Thelma Ryan nonetheless had few dates. She seemed at once shy, yet poised and remote, while potential boyfriends were wary, too, of her possessive brothers. "The boys would say, 'Well, I'm afraid to ask her for a date,' " remembered Mary Bell. George Gortikov, another student, believed her brothers were "very protective of their sister, and all the fellows just shied away." At the same time, Gordon McHatton, her opposite in the school play and a friend of Bill's and Tom's, thought her simply "aloof."

Some girlfriends saw, too, the emergence in the slaving, self-sacrificing girl of what Myrtle Raine called "a mind of her own." "You stubborn Irishman!" they heard Will Ryan yell at her in frustration. Beneath the cherub's cheeks was a cutting temper that did not subside quickly. "She wouldn't get right over it," Myrtle remembered. "When she got provoked she was provoked for a little while." Submissive at home, she could be quietly aggressive at school. Student council president while Thelma was secretary, Gortikov saw her "very, very strong personality" in action. "I know we'd be having meetings, and I was supposed to be conducting them but it ended up that she was taking over." Gortikov was impressed, too, that she made a point in the small, relatively poor school of three hundred to go "around with the right crowd." One student thought her "very ambitious," another that her "ideal and . . . dream would be to be, for instance, a congresswoman or something to do with politics."

Beside her annual photo with the class of 1929, Thelma "Buddy" Ryan listed, perhaps whimsically, "Intention: To run a boardinghouse." To Louise Raine she confided that "she wanted to have a big ranch, a cattle ranch." Whatever her goals, she left behind an admiring faculty. "Your sunny smile and twinkling eyes have long been a source of much conjecture on my part," one teacher wrote her in special tribute. "I've often wondered if you've learned the real secret of living—and now I believe you have." The admiration came in part from watching her carry on after her mother's death. Few knew her senior year she was enduring the same trial again.

The summer of 1928 his sons had finally persuaded Will Ryan to have a persistent cough diagnosed, and the county sputum test had come back positive for tuberculosis. Thelma promptly took over and nursed him through her final school terms and on into the following year, sterilizing dishes and bedclothes much as Hannah Nixon had in Prescott, caring for the house and her brothers as well, and after graduation postponing her own plans to go on with school. Like other families of consumptives, she grasped at fad cures. When one Artesia doctor recommended lamb stew, Thelma cooked it so often, her daughter revealed later, that she could never again stand to eat lamb herself. Toward the end, Will Ryan agreed to enter a Catholic sanatorium in Monrovia. Dying, he came back at seventy-four to the spurned religion of his Irish childhood. He was buried beside his wife in May 1930, leaving his three children the hardscrabble farm and his worthless oil shares.

With his death, she formally changed her name, dropping the namesake Catherine her mother had chosen, and becoming instead Thelma Patricia Ryan—ever after the Patricia or Pat of fortune-seeking Will Ryan's St. Patrick's baby.

"I thought everything started with an education," she recalled once, looking back on these years. In the fall of 1930 she enrolled as Patricia Ryan in Fullerton Junior College, a school of some three hundred students a few miles to the east, near the Fullerton High School campus it resembled. Her brothers, meanwhile, had begun working their way through the University of Southern California. In a deliberate effort to hold the remnant of the family together, she continued to cook and keep house for them, though she also declared the beginning of her independence from the old role, refusing to make dinner if either brother had not done his share of work that day. At that, the farm soon proved more than they could do or afford, and they rented the land to a Japanese farmer. She went to work as a scrubwoman in an Artesia bank, mopping out the office and lobby at dawn each morning before returning home to catch a ride to school. It was an exhausting, sometimes humiliating routine. A half century afterward she still felt a "sharp stab," as she told her family, remembering the day she had been sweeping dirt out the front door of the bank, and a car full of college classmates passed by laughing and ridiculing her.

At junior college, Patricia joined the Nightwalkers, a drama club of "some heartbreaks trying to become movie stars," one member recalled. Making her own clothes, she dressed "remarkably well," thought one observer. There were still few dates, however, still an air of the unapproachable about her. She had "a lot of poise. She carried herself with dignity, and yet she was fun," said Robert McCormick, one of the rare students to take her out. "I eventually mustered enough courage to ask her to one of the school dances." At the same time, she was largely indifferent to classes and had grown to loathe her old home. "It must be lonesome," she would write a brother away on a temporary job, "but Artesia is unbearable—so there you are." When Ryan relatives the next summer gave her a chance to visit them in Connecticut, chauffeuring an elderly couple from California in their Packard, she instantly seized the escape. "The wife, who was not well, sat bundled up in the backseat. Her husband sat beside me up front," she wrote, describing the drive across country. "And for three thousand miles he made a clicking sound with his teeth. Flat tires, mud, rain—I could take them all, but that day-long sound of clicking stays with me yet."

Her Irish aunts and cousins in the East gave her an opening on the world, suddenly free of the drudgery and death she had known in California since she was thirteen. For the next two years, she spent weekends in Connecticut with one aunt and her middle-class, Republican family, while working full-time in New York City with another Ryan aunt, a seventy-year-old nun who headed X-ray and the pharmacy at the Sisters of Charity Seton Hospital for tuberculosis. Living on the top floor of the nuns' residence next to the hospital, she did secretarial work, was an X-ray laboratory assistant and general aide. Soon she had become "The White Sister," adored and sought-after by the patients, many of them, like her mother and father, terminal. "Sometimes I feel that I should like to spend my life just working for the afflicted unfortunates—helping them to be more happy," she wrote Bill Ryan back in Artesia.

For one period she worked intensively with tuberculars in their teens and twenties. "My six months there were perhaps the most haunting of my life," she admitted. Like Harold Nixon on horseback rides or flings with the girls, the younger patients would sneak away from the hospital to go sledding in a fresh city snow. And she went along. "It gave them a lift to have someone who was well with them, not looking after them, not avoiding them," she explained. As in the months caring for her father, she had no fear of the disease, saying later, "And it almost seemed that they believed they might contract health from me."

She assumed increasing responsibility at the hospital and began to live something of the life of the career woman in the big city. Scarcely two years after her classmates had taunted her as she swept out an Artesia bank, Patricia Ryan was sightseeing in New England, visiting Washington for a tour of the White House, representing Seton at national hospital conferences with physicians and other professionals. Her letters would record her passage into a more mature young woman with an obvious new confidence and sophistication. "Last night [New York Governor] Al Smith, Mrs. and President Roosevelt, etc. attended the formal dinner and the latter gave the main speech of the evening," she wrote her brothers on Waldorf-Astoria stationery about one gathering she attended in October 1933. "Perhaps you heard it on the radio as it was broadcast."

At twenty-two Patricia was "a real beauty," one of her cousins recalled. "Everywhere she went people stared at her, she was so pretty." Young doctors "rushed her for dates," as one account put it, along with other suitors, their expensive cars and entertainments casually mentioned in her letters home. In her new cosmopolitan social life, she learned both to smoke and to drink. "But Pat was very discriminating," a cousin said of the men and the nights out. "She didn't want to waste her time." At least one beau was serious, Seton's medical chief-of-staff, a good looking, thirty-five-year-old Ireland-born physician named Francis Vincent Duke. The motherly aunt in habit, Sister Thomas Anna, discreetly encouraged the romance between the respectable Catholic doctor and the lovely daughter of her prodigal Ryan brother. Yet when Duke was on the verge of proposing, Patricia resolutely drew back, accepting more dates from other men. "Seems as though everyone I know is married and already has a family," she wrote in another letter to Artesia. "I'm glad I'm not in their boots—especially in this 'Depression' weather." But she began as well to chafe at the hovering presence of the Sisters as she saw her frequent male visitors in the nunnery parlor. *"They restrict you so here!"* she underscored in one note to a brother.

For all the New York opportunity, in part because of it, she would be ready when Tom Ryan wrote her in the spring of 1934—the spring Richard Nixon was graduating from Whittier College—offering to help her resume school at Southern California. "Am so thrilled and excited that my heart just won't act sanely," she replied. "Life is fleeting . . . I want to finish my college education." Without saying good-bye to Francis Duke, she caught a bus that summer back across the country, stopping at Niagara Falls to see the sight, standing among the traditional crowd of honeymooners placidly, proudly alone.

She moved into a small Los Angeles apartment with the two brothers and enrolled at USC with a $270-a-year scholarship plus a heavy schedule of campus work to pay her costs. Once again, though they now shared the cooking, the men relied on her to do all the housework, washing and ironing, while she carried a full load of college courses. A classmate and neighbor at USC found her quiet and attentive to others, mending her brothers' clothes, typing their term papers late at night beyond her own work. Kay Nordquist thought Pat Ryan's hair "the most beautiful . . . I had ever seen," her face and body losing its high school fullness for sharp, angular lines, "but the feeling around her . . . all womanly softness and serenity and inner strength." At the university, she was now the slightly older, poised young woman—working indefatigably an hour here, an hour there, from the cafeteria to the library to a faculty research project, but no longer somehow inferior to the careless coeds around her. USC's Shakespearean scholar Frank Baxter was moved by "how tired her face was in repose. There seemed to have been plenty of reason for it." She was nonetheless "a good student, alert and interested," he remembered, and the professor saw clearly what Pat sensed in herself. "She stood out from the empty-headed, overdressed little sorority girls of that era like a good piece of literature on a shelf of cheap paperbacks."

In her absence Francis Duke at Seton was "moping around all the time," an aunt wrote Patricia. But she made no effort to renew the relationship, and while there were again at USC numerous dates and offers, she kept the distance and freedom that were now her habit. "We were anxious to bring some boys around, but we couldn't think of any 'right' boys for Pat," a friend recorded typically. After one date, a young admirer sent her a wistful note about the pleasant yet impenetrable hedge surrounding her seductive beauty. "I was just struck with the thought that I knew so damn little about you after being at your feet a whole lovely evening," he wrote. "There was so much beneath the surface," observed a girlfriend, "and so few had the opportunity to find it."

She had won a screen test contest in Manhattan and passed it up, but back in California she now flirted with a movie career and her old love of drama. With a pretty college friend she signed on at RKO and MGM as an extra at a coveted $6.50 a day, eventually speaking a single line that was later cut from *Becky Sharp* in 1935. It was a glamorous world in contrast to Seton Hospital or USC. "I really eyed him," she said later about a studio set crush during 1936 on leading man Robert Taylor in *Small Town Girl*. Despite more chances she would be put off by the sheer uncertainty of the career and most of all by Hollywood's demeaning sexism and the demands of the casting couch. "That life is too rough, and unless you are featured the pay is low," she wrote about acting; "one of the reasons why girls are tempted to accept presents and attentions [is] sheer necessity." There were also her brothers still guarding a vestal image. When she rebuffed a director on the set of *Becky Sharp* and he appeared drunk one night at their apartment, Bill and Tom characteristically slammed the door in his face.

The far more telling job came at Christmas vacation, 1935, at Bullock's, the fashionable Los Angeles department store on Wilshire Boulevard. Standing on a crowded streetcar to and from work and still keeping house, she was salesgirl, model, and gift consultant more than ten footsore hours a day. Bullock's clientele suddenly brought to the surface deeper social feelings usually muted beneath the beauty and quiet self-sufficiency. Patricia candidly wrote her Connecticut aunt:

> The moneyed class come in and ask us to do their shopping—or give them suggestions. We go to any department of the store with them—showing our suggested gifts—or else they sit in luxurious chairs while we go all over the store and gather things for them to choose from. . . . The manager of our department is always telling or describing how I drape the lovely velvet robes, etc., around me, grin at the fat, rich customers and PFF! They buy. But this is true—and I sell more than any of the other girls. Saturday I sold over $200.00—including a lovely velvet pajama and hostess gown to one gentleman.

In the cool, grinning young woman—polished and in part left cynical by her experience—it was a flaring, implacable sense of a have-not among the haves, of the festering *Day of the Locust* social resentment so many of her class felt in southern California. And it would remain. At Bullock's she decided to abandon the merchandising major she had planned for a time at USC. She turned instead to her minor in education, to a teaching career. As she left her job at the store, she also took a first small political step. Approached by the League of Women Voters in a registration drive, Patricia Ryan duly registered to vote in California not as a Democrat, like her dead parents, but as an Independent.

She graduated from USC with honors in June 1937, awarded a B.A. with credentials to teach commercial subjects in secondary school. Along with fulsome faculty recommendations, her photograph in the university's job placement office showed a sober, thin-lipped young woman with neat, pincurled hair pulled conservatively back from her forehead, dressed for the part in a dark suit with a pert bow tie at her neck. The same hot summer Dick Nixon avoided Tom Bewley's calls and crammed for the bar exam, she cast about for one of the region's scarce teaching positions. On a Saturday late in June she was called to interview at Whittier Union. "She was the cutest thing I'd ever seen," remembered Marion Budlong, who was in the office that day. "She wore a little white hat and looked so perky." Even new Whittier teachers were customarily recruited among older women, but the superintendent was her former principal at Excelsior, and she impressed the Quaker school board hiring committee, among them Oscar Marshburn, Olive's husband, with her modesty and bearing beyond her years. They gave her the job at $150 a month. At the end of the summer, she left her brothers for a rooming house, and destiny, in Whittier.

Miss Ryan taught typing, bookkeeping, stenography, and business principles, the standard secretarial courses for eager young women like herself who were preparing to take their place in the growing clerkdom of the century. The first day at Whittier she saw the reality behind the still-dazed business optimism of the school and town. Her classroom was poorly equipped with "vintage Underwoods and Royals," one student remembered them, the run-down casualties of hard times never quite acknowledged. "The depression years," said Jean Lippiatt, who took typing from her that year, "had hurt the tax-paying farmers and orange growers more than they were willing to admit." She also quickly discovered what she recalled mildly later as the town's "unwritten codes." After the relative freedom of New York and Los Angeles, she was beginning her career in a community where teachers were not to smoke in public, nor even dress too casually, much less be seen near the local bar Richard Nixon as assistant city attorney was soon to drive out of town. "Never talk about anybody in Whittier—they're all related to one another in some way or another," a colleague knowingly advised her early in the term. High school politics and pecking order were still more treacherous. "You take a woman as young and beautiful as Pat Ryan was then and put her in with a faculty of older women," a friend would say afterward of the jealousies, "and you've got certain trouble."

She met Whittier much as she dealt with "the moneyed class" at Bullock's, with hard work, outward charm, and the expected, calculated, politic deference, concealing her contempt. At school or PTA occasions, the new Miss Ryan was careful not to upstage older faculty women. "When they were out in front of the audience, Pat would be serving the coffee, or out in the kitchen doing the dishes," said a fellow teacher. To her students, as one of them described her, "she was the first young teacher we had encountered." In the classroom she was crisp, cool, quietly and uniquely glamorous in fashionable clothes and lavender perfume. Her discipline was mute and effective. "Tardy students were warned by a direct look which hurt more than any lecture she could have given," said one pupil. But she also relished the rapport her relative youth gave her. Wearing bobby sox and school sweater, she advised the pep club, coached plays, staged rallies and skits, rounding up the smallest boys in the school, then dressing them in a rival team's uniforms for Whittier's largest football players to mow down in a mock battle in an assembly on the lawn—all to the roaring glee of the student body. At Whittier she played one of the familiar roles in American high school faculties, the teacher of nonsubstantive subjects who rehearses the cheerleaders, joins the chants and gestures of the pep section in unison, enters in a sense back into the adolescent world around her.

At the same time, her empathy and compassion were plain for those she saw as stricken, shadows of her own Excelsior years. Stopping one freckled, overweight girl to stay after school for a chat, she advised her to lose weight, think of the freckles as wholesome, and put on her own sunny face toward outside cruelty. "Smile and be pleasant" was Miss Ryan's advice about taunting boys, the grateful girl remembered. "Soon they'll be smiling back." When Mexican students missed repeated classes during picking season, she conscientiously tried to reach parents and encourage their return before making the mandatory report on truancy, a unique act of sensibility for the moment and place. At the same time, she could not see behind the little city's pretense of tolerance to the deeper reality and meaning of Jimtown. "Whittier," her daughter could write later about Pat's perception of the era, "was notably free of ethnic and racial prejudice." At one point the school paper asked her to record what she thought of Whittier Union as a newcomer. The response combined the obligatory tact and boosterism with her own gritty ethic of resilience and effort.

> Individuality, enthusiasm and pep! These are some of the fine traits in Whittier High School students which first impressed me. It is very stimulating and refreshing to see students "in action," for the same enthusiasm is employed regardless of whether the task be difficult or a pleasurable one. . . . Thus to you I say: never lose your enthusiasm—merely direct it—and that same enthusiasm will take you "where you want to go."
>
> Miss Ryan

After school, the social life of the pretty, worldly teacher was a titillating puzzle to her Whittier students, who periodically spied on her to no avail. She moved from rooming house to apartment to another apartment near the school, sometimes sharing quarters with another teacher; Marion Budlong, who became chummy when they both worked at night school in 1937–38, remembered their long girlish walks in the rain and cozy evenings of hot chocolate. One night they wandered east into the "best residential section," Budlong recalled, and Pat, pretending the wide, manicured sidewalk was a theater, solemnly taught her how to "properly enter and leave a stage." They rode in Budlong's open convertible through the orchards out the boulevard and spent much time together, though Marion like others always felt the limits of her intimacy. "Pat was never one to disclose her inner feelings, nor did she talk about her sentiments and ambitions," Budlong said. "She had an aloof friendliness."

Invariably, Pat was gone on weekends, fleeing the stifling town to stay with Neva, now married and living in Los Angeles. There her dates picked her up and then dropped her off, and she led an active social life with former boyfriends from USC and elsewhere. Her escape became a matter of pugnacious pride and independence. "I never spent a weekend in Whittier," she boasted nearly fifty years later, "the entire time I taught there."

"NOTHING SO FINE EVER HAPPENED TO HIM"

Their two characters in *The Dark Tower* became offstage lovers, her sultry Daphne on the rebound as the abandoned mistress of the male lead, shocking the audience by categorizing men alternately as "pansies" or "sons of bitches." In one scene, while Nixon as the callow Barry plays, she was to lean over the piano and sing "Stormy Weather." But Pat obstinately refused to do the song. "She was hard to work with," remembered Hortense Behrens, one of the regulars of the little theater. "If anybody ever had a mind of her own, she did." At first she had said she would not sing at rehearsal but would manage opening night. "Now don't you worry any more about that," Dick Nixon had assured the nervous director. "I've talked to her, and she promised that she will . . . the night of the performance." With the curtain about to rise, however, Pat balked entirely. "She had long red hair, you know," Behrens said, recalling them backstage. "She'd toss her head and say, 'No, I'm not going to do it.' She's so stubborn." While she only half-spoke, half-hummed the words of the song, the *East Whittier Review* thought she played convincingly "a role which called for temperament—and did she have it? Plenty! She did some fine acting as she wheeled in and out of the room, always in a semi-rage." Through it all, Nixon was utterly enamored.

He called Oscar Marshburn to find out her birthday from the school records and surprised her with flowers that March. He had also urged his parents to come to the opening of *The Dark Tower*, "insisted" as Hannah remembered it. "We didn't suspect Richard of any motive other than his wanting us to see him," the mother would say later. "But he also wanted us to see Pat, in whom he was becoming interested." At the time, he immediately asked them after the performance what they thought of the young woman in the sensuous, profane role. "I told him," Hannah said archly, that "she did her part nicely."

Following the play, Pat finally consented to go out with Nixon to a 20–30 Club ladies' night, an occasion on which he was so nervous, he admitted later, that he seemed "funny." Soon afterward she agreed as well to meet the elder Nixons for an evening of strawberry shortcake, concerned from Dick's excited description of her hit as Daphne—including his mother's faint praise—that she had been in fact too convincing in the torrid role and offended the Quaker parents of this enthusiastic new suitor. It was a quiet, uneventful visit, and Pat went away satisfied she had repaired her image. "Not until much time had elapsed," her daughter recorded, "did she realize that she was somewhat of an enigma to Dick's parents." Hannah Nixon, meanwhile, quietly ignored and later denied her son's sudden and ardent infatuation with the new typing teacher. "Writers like to say that Richard fell in love with Pat at first sight. That wasn't so," his mother pronounced in 1960. "They met, they liked each other, and when they got to know each other, they fell in love." It was a description of the courtship belied by every love letter her son wrote, everything he did in his cloying, un-daunted, often unrequited pursuit of Patricia Ryan over the next two years.

That spring of 1938 Nixon asked her repeatedly for dates. Turned down always on weekends and often during the week, he began showing up at her rooms unannounced in the evening to take her on drives or walks through the hillside blocks around the college. Pat thought him "a bit unusual," as she told a friend soon after their meeting, and continued to put him off. When she tactfully excused her own indifference by remarking lightly that she was a vagabond or gypsy, Nixon wrote her affectionate little notes addressed to "Miss Vagabond" or "My Irish Gypsy." When she pointedly arranged a date for him with her roommate, he agreed readily to go, and through the evening talked only about Pat. "He chased her but she was a little rat," said one of her friends who watched it unfold. The notes were soon interspersed with his own romantic poetry, verse she later described as having a "mysteriously wild beauty." Within weeks of their meeting, he even composed a song for her. It was one of the two com-positions, along with "Rustle of Spring," which he had learned at Lindsay, that he still knew by heart more than thirty years later—and picked out on the White House grand piano the night he moved in.

She eventually bolted her door from the inside against his weeknight visits and did not answer his knocking, though he knew obviously she was at home. Undeterred, he went off to write notes and returned the same night to slip them under the locked door. "Miss Pat," read one:

I took *the* walk tonight and it was swell because you were
there all the time . . . the wind blowing thru the tops of
the palms making that strangely restless rustling, a train
whistle sounded just as I got to the bridge. The Dip-
per . . . was pouring down on you all the good things
I've wished looking up at it in the past. . . .
Yes, I know I'm crazy, and that this is old stuff and
that I don't take hints, but you see, Miss Pat, I like you!

After much persistence, he won the privilege of driving her to Neva's
Los Angeles apartment for her Friday-night exodus from Whittier, and then
picking her up there Sunday evenings, usually after she had been brought
back from a date with another man. If she were late or out with a boyfriend
unexpectedly, he methodically killed time in the city, going to a movie,
walking aimlessly, sitting in hotel lobbies reading.

The young lawyer so abjectly hanging on those evenings in Los Angeles
was commonly thought in Whittier one of the town's more eligible catches.
"He was considered a darling bachelor," Pat would say later. "All the
mothers were getting in the act and asking him to dinner." To Judith
Wingert, whose own mother judged him "an attractive young man," Dick
Nixon was "the sort that would appeal to the matronly woman" scouting
a match for her daughter. "You know, he was a good, clean-cut, good-
looking young man, and bright." Yet the lonely hours in hotel lobbies, his
humiliating persistence in the face of bolted doors and other men, more
nearly reflected his social life than the matrons' image. Hortense Behrens
recalled a double date with Dick the winter before he knew Pat, how
she had arranged for an attractive friend to go with him and the dull evening the two couples had at Los Serranos Country Club. "It couldn't have
been *me* that was that bad," she remembered thinking after dancing with
Nixon.

Whatever the Whittier mothers believed or Pat liked to think later,
there were few dinner invitations and fewer actual dates. Before he met
Patricia Ryan, as after, there was no evidence he saw anyone else with any
interest. For all the late nights at the law office or the Citra-Frost plant,
for all the men's clubs and politics, there were still empty Saturday nights
and Sunday mornings. When he returned from Durham, Mildred Mendenhall asked him to teach the college-age Sunday school class at East
Whittier Friends, and he quickly agreed, preparing the classes carefully
and becoming "a very provocative teacher," as she recalled, with "hot and
heavy" theological discussions. The Sundays that ended in Los Angeles,
waiting fawningly for Pat to return from another date, had begun with fire
and brimstone and evangelical ardor on Whittier Boulevard.

She grew ever more uneasy at his attachment, and one night late that spring, when he dropped by once again without calling, opened the door literally to confront the issue and throw him out. Now rebuffed too openly, he finally reacted with an angry, petulant show of unconcern, a milder version of how he had responded to Ola. But within days he had written another plaintive note, almost as a farewell:

> Please forgive me for acting like a sorehead when you gently ushered me out the other night. You must have thought I was trying to put on the attitude that I didn't really give a darn—i.e., school boy bluff! . . . May I say now what I should have said then: I appreciated immeasurably those little rides and chats with you. I hope that you survived them without too much mental worry over the problem "what shall I do to get rid of him before he falls." (and that isn't said in a sarcastic way either)— and may I tell you now what I really thought of you? You see I too live in a world of make believe—especially in this love business. And sometimes I fear I don't know when I'm serious and when not! But I can honestly say that Patricia is one fine girl, that I like her immensely, and that though she isn't going to give me a chance to propose to her for fear of hurting me! and though she insulted my ego just a bit by not being quite frank at times, I still remember her as combining the best traits of the Irish and the square-heads—
>
> Yours,
Dick

Moved, she relented, agreeing to see him again and to allow the weekend chauffeuring into Los Angeles, though with an explicit understanding that there would be, as she later told her daughter, "no declarations of love or proposals of marriage." At the end of the school year, he gave her a first gift, a desk clock, which he worried in the accompanying note was "kind of . . . masculine," but which had reminded him of "that vagabond within you that makes you want to go far places and see great things." The clock was to tell her to take care of herself "because there are so many people who think so much of Miss Pat," and that she would "always be young— inside." He had been telling her she was destined to realize her wanderlust and achieve "great things" herself, and he closed with still more adoring praise. "Despite your refusal to let me be much more than an acquaintance, by all that I hold sacred, Patricia, I say that you are a great lady—and now I think you know what I mean by that."

Her note of thanks was casual, friendly, terse, ignoring his extravagant words. "I like it ever so much! Its new name is Sir Ric," she wrote, adding of the name, ". . . sort of needed your assistance so you be thinking of a better one if not approved. . . . See you soon."

That summer Dick was absorbed in Citra-Frost, and they saw less of each other. When she went to Michigan in July to buy a new car and drove back to Whittier, she broke off contact for several weeks. Unable to find her new apartment, he frantically wrote her at the high school in September 1938: "I bet you're mad with me for pestering you with a letter sent to school. But after all since you don't tell me where you are what else can I do?" He wanted "so very much to see you again—after class, before breakfast, Sunday or any time you might be able to stand me!" For the first time he referred openly to her furtive social life away from Whittier and promised the same discretion with his own dates, if that would help. In any case, "things" had happened—Citra-Frost and the prospect of fame and fortune—and he was sure she would no longer find him dull. "And of course," he concluded, "it would have to be secret— you're protecting that reputation you know! It's been years since July and things have happened and I swear you'll not be bored if you give me a chance."

Finding her apartment, he was now more measured about dropping by, but talked her roommate into letting him in to leave endearing little gifts while Pat was gone—in October a jack-o'-lantern he and eight-year-old Eddie had carved, in December a miniature decorated Christmas tree. For his twenty-sixth birthday the following January she finally responded with her own gift, a clock similar to "Sir Ric." Nixon was ecstatic. On one of Wingert and Bewley's promissory note forms he wrote out a pledge to Patricia Ryan of "four billion dollars," payable "when I'm fifty, or before if you'll let me."

In part because her own dates in Los Angeles were now fewer, in part because she simply eased her aversion and reluctance, their relationship opened noticeably in the spring of 1939. They began to go to nightclubs in Los Angeles or elsewhere in the basin and to double-date with Pat's roommates or friends. Evlyn Dorn went ice-skating with them, remembering Pat as a "marvelous skater" from her New York years, while Dick, on the ice the first time, lurched and fell again and again but kept trying. There were walks on the beach, sometimes with little Eddie, a thin, quiet child his parents watched nervously after the deaths of Arthur and Harold and whom Richard encouraged to exercise, and often with the Nixons' affectionate red Irish setter, King. Pat was fond and engaging with the small brother, and became lovingly attached to the dog. In June 1939, he sentimentally gave her a paperweight statue of an Irish setter, oxidized from silver to red to match King's fur. Over the same weeks, he also confided in her about his own family and childhood, his brothers' deaths and Frank's "hot temper," as she recalled his description. But she said almost nothing in return about her own past. Not until years later would he learn that Will Ryan, like Harold, had died of tuberculosis. "You with the strangely sad but lovely smile," he wrote in an early love letter, sensing her suffering long before he knew its history. Her life, her daughter wrote, "inadvertently . . . was becoming more and more entwined with Richard Nixon's."

That summer, too, Pat Ryan spent time with Frank and Hannah Nixon. With the father, his reputation preceding him, she was light and teasing. Privately she thought Frank Nixon a coarse man, "blustery and inarticulate," as she afterward characterized him to one of his granddaughters. "Richard's father wasn't a saint," Jessamyn West would say to her later in banter. "If he was, he was a saint with a short temper," Pat shot back in seriousness. "But for all his temper [he] never said a cross word to me."

The more formidable problem was with the one truly reputed saint in the family, the prayerful, dedicated woman who quietly worked her way with both father and son. In the summer of 1939 Pat often gave up her vacation mornings to rise at 5:00 A.M. and help Hannah Nixon bake her renowned pies for the grocery, now as many as fifty a day. " 'I can just as well come down in the early morning and help you get the pies ready,' " Hannah remembered her saying. "This seemed unusual for a busy girl," she said later of Pat's gesture. "It touched me." Yet the mother was in no doubt about the schoolteacher's motives at the time or what she was "busy" doing. All too aware of the budding relationship between Richard and Pat, she remained blind to its remarkable one-sidedness. "Hannah was convinced," a close friend revealed afterward, "Pat was chasing Dick." The predawn baking sessions were characteristically cheerful for both women, and just as typically formed no bond. The two of them, Pat once reflected, were "completely different . . . you know, she really wasn't a modern person." But it was both their similarities and contrasts that would separate them, always at a polite if unmistakable distance. After the summer of helping with his mother's pies, no one would ever remember Pat competing with a pie of her own for Dick or the family. She invariably made cakes and biscuits instead.

Part of Hannah's view of the young woman in her son's life would be mirrored in the larger Milhous family's reactions to her, which were first formed that summer as well. "Pat was a rather rugged individualist herself, she had come up the hard way," remembered Sheldon Beeson, a cousin who thought her circumstances explained much of Dick's infatuation. "I mean, if she had been a rich little gal who had been indulged by her parents, why, I don't think Dick would have been attracted to her. . . . I guess she just about fit the mold." Dorothy Robertson, who worked at Whittier High and married Sheldon in 1939, thought Pat Ryan was "very attractive, very attractive, very humble!" Yet there was no doubt that this non-Quaker teacher of business skills was more worldly than local girls. "She just gave the impression of being independent and knowing her way around," Robertson would say. Hearing the family gossip, Edith Timberlake remembered one common portrayal of Richard's new and striking girlfriend. "Back then," Edith said, "they thought she was ambitious. I heard that statement or 'accusation' of her character . . . that she was ambitious for him, for his advancement."

Ambition was real enough in the romance. "He was handsome in a strong way," Pat recalled of her increasing attraction to the man she at first avoided. "He had a wonderful quality in his voice which I have never found in another man." But she sensed, too, in fuller measure the craving that others in the law firm and family noticed only in part—what she would remember as Richard Nixon's "drive—he was going places and he always saw the possibilities. He believed that life could be good, and that problems—well, if you could not solve them, you could make things a little better."

Beyond the family, they tried to conceal their courtship from the prying town. When Pat and two of her friends drove to British Columbia to sightsee at the close of summer, she mailed chatty, innocuous postcards along the way signed "Lots of luck, Pat," and from Vancouver a scenic view with the whimsical message "Love from Mother." Nonetheless, Whittier buzzed. "You know, people talked about it," Judith Wingert recalled. "Some people felt that he should have been going with a girl from, you know, a better family. Whittier was very much like this. Somebody from Whittier and a better family, one that didn't work." And in the town gossip, like the family's, Dick Nixon's own slavishness in their early relationship was forever buried. "I think he was shy," Wingert recalled, "and in those days they used to say that she was the one that went after him."

She continued to hold her ban on his talk of marriage, setting formal periods of three or more months. Yet with their more frequent dates and the contacts with the family, he began to suggest secret trips together away from Whittier and even an elopement to Arizona. At a moment when everyone else thought him the pursued bachelor, he was more than ever the constant, smitten suitor, sending the following list to her a month before his 20–30 national convention:

Would like to take you to

> Bowl
> *Daughters Courageous*
> Sonja Henie's latest
> *Beau Geste*
> *On Borrowed Time*

also to

> Tahoe
> S.F. (convention August 29)
> Yuma(?!)
> mountains . . .

And to take you to dance and to dinner like Sunday. And to write to you—and to learn things with you and to be with you more.

She refused to elope or again even to discuss marrying, and he persisted later that autumn in another vein: "Seriously, little one, let's go to Arizona (and if you don't want to go for the purpose just suggested, we could still have fun!)" When she then rebuked him for even hinting at anything illicit, Nixon wrote her unabashedly, "You have the finest ideals of anyone I have ever known."

In February 1940, on the verge of his hurried grasp for the State Assembly seat, and four years after his final breakup with Ola Welch, he wrote Pat to commemorate the second anniversary of their meeting at *The Dark Tower*. Did she remember the "funny guy" who took her out two years before? "Well, you know that though he still may be funny—he's changed since then. But . . . he gets the same thrill when you say you'll go someplace with him." Forbidden or no, he ended with a declaration of his love and a tender Quaker address:

> And when the winds blow and the rains fall and the sun
> shines through the clouds, as it is now, he still resolves
> as he did then, that nothing so fine ever happened to
> him or anyone else as falling in love with Thee—my
> dearest heart.

> Love,
> Dick

On a March evening he drove her in her Oldsmobile to Dana Point, a rocky promontory overlooking one of their favorite beaches and near a small,

225

quaint development called San Clemente halfway between Los Angeles and San Diego. There in the dying light of an ocean sunset he proposed, and she finally accepted—though with misgivings to the end. "Even as she consented," her daughter wrote, "she was not sure she wanted to marry. She was twenty-eight years old and had been independent for a long time."

He was typically thrilled at her answer and insisted they rush back to Whittier to tell his parents. Dick took her into their bedroom in the Worsham Drive house where they had already gone to sleep, and Frank Nixon awoke to the news with loud excitement while Hannah said little. Their reaction "broke the romantic spell of the evening," as Pat retold the story, and she came away feeling the Nixons were "undecided" about the engagement. Her own relatives were hardly more approving. Tom, who knew Dick Nixon and shared a love of football, warmly congratulated her. When she told Bill in Artesia a month afterward, however, the older brother was silent for several moments and tears came to his eyes, still possessive of a sister nearing thirty. As for Neva, who had watched the beaux come and go at her Los Angeles apartment, the half-sister asked caustically, "What are you marrying *him* for? He's too quiet." Pat confided the proposal to Marion Budlong and other close friends, and Nixon would announce it proudly to the Bewleys and Wingerts one night at a small private party. But there was no public notice and almost no one else knew. "Dick never came in and said, 'Oh, I'm going to marry this girl,' " Evlyn Dorn remembered.

By April, the Assembly race gone, he decided to buy a ring and plunged into the task with the usual energy, asking a jeweler in 20–30 for advice, shopping in several stores, keeping Donald up all night on a business trip discussing the merits of stones and settings. "A man only buys a ring once in a lifetime," Don would remember him saying gravely, "and that should be a ring his wife would always be proud to wear." As it was, the ring was to be their first real clash of wills, his first act of dominance in the relationship, and in a sense a portent. While Pat wanted a simple wide gold band, he insisted on diamonds, and picked out the rings he preferred at a Los Angeles jeweler, paying more than $300. On May 1 the engagement and wedding rings were both ready, and he arranged to meet Pat at the Worsham house at lunchtime to make the presentation. When he did not appear, she went back to school in some irritation. A delivery boy from the Nixon grocery then found her in her classroom grading papers later in the afternoon, and shyly set on her desk a small May basket with the rings on a bed of straw. Disappointed, Pat pushed the basket aside and ignored it until another teacher came into the room, noticed the basket, "squealed with excitement," as both of them recalled, and put the engagement ring on Pat's finger. "Look, you're going to put on that ring and right now," her colleague said, and hurried to tell other teachers.

The rings and her lingering unhappiness brought from Nixon yet another lavish love letter, written in the same tone and language of others in the courtship, but in many ways, too, the first of what would be many such atonements and redresses in their marriage. In the spring of 1940, it was she who had a "destiny" to realize, he who would "return the benefit." "Dearest Heart," he wrote her:

> From the first days I knew you, you were destined to be a great lady—You have always had that extra something which takes people out of the mediocre class. And now, dear heart, I want to work with you towards the destiny you are bound to fulfill.
>
> As I have told you many times—living together will make us both grow—and by reason of it we shall realize our dreams. You are a great inspiration to me, and though you don't believe it yet, I someday shall return some of the benefit you have conferred on me.
>
> It is our job to go forth together and accomplish great ends and we shall do it too.
>
> And, dear one, through the years, whatever happens I shall always be with you—loving you more every hour and attempting to let you feel that love in your heart and life.

They planned the wedding for a Friday afternoon, June 21, 1940, at the popular Mission Inn in Riverside, the ornate Spanish-style tourist hotel at the edge of the desert where Dick had gone to college conferences, and where they had driven for dinner during the courtship. It would be a small ceremony, only a few of their family and friends. She could not, she told him, ask her brothers to bear the cost of a large wedding, or let the Nixons pay. For years, as a result, the size and privacy of the ceremony miffed Milhous relatives. Edith Timberlake remembered Hannah and Frank pulling up that day unannounced in her driveway in Riverside and telling her, to her astonishment, "You're going to Richard's wedding." Almira was in the backseat in her red velvet dress. Hannah held on her lap the wedding cake she had baked at the store, a little veiled bride and groom in white tails atop the crown. "They had said only just special friends would be there," Edith recalled, and she dashed off with them to the hotel without her husband. When they arrived there were only Pat's brothers and half-sister, Don and Eddie, and a few young friends, less than two dozen guests in all. "One would quite expect them to go for a fancy wedding with gifts," thought Dorothy Beeson and other relatives. "They had run off and got married, as they would say in Whittier," Judith Wingert said afterward.

The Quaker service was read by William Mendenhall, who had replaced Dexter as president of Whittier College, and held in what the inn called its Presidential Suite. They had chosen it, Pat would say later, not for any political symbolism but simply because it was the smallest and least costly to rent for the afternoon. Afterward, there was a brief reception in a nearby gallery, an organist playing their favorite popular music.

They left from the inn in her Oldsmobile with Don and others trying to follow them honking, driving southeast on the same highway he had taken to Prescott, but now toward Phoenix, the Texas border, and Mexico. "We just went," Pat said. They had packed cans from the Nixon grocery in the car trunk to save money on meals, and found when they stopped that friends back at the inn had taken off the labels, leaving them to open by chance cans of pineapple or peaches or spaghetti for breakfast or lunch. They toured the sights around Mexico City until the money they had budgeted ran out, nearly $200, most of it Pat's after his purchase of the rings. Almost broke, they drove back to California without stopping overnight in a hotel.

Near home they took a small detour. The mother of Mary Bell, one of Pat's old friends from Fullerton Junior College, was touring the majestic new Boulder Dam when she noticed a familiar face in the crowd of sightseers. "Pat!" she yelled. "What are you doing here?" The young bride answered excitedly, "We're on our honeymoon!" She seemed happier than they could ever remember her.

9

Marriage and War, 1940–44

"YOU'LL ALWAYS HAVE TO LOVE ME LOTS"

is life took a new direction that June Friday at the Mission Inn. He had wed a woman of matching resolve, of comparable if not larger ambition, of perhaps greater strength, and he had won her in a supplicant's courtship that gave her substance all the more force in their early relationship.

Their first apartment was in Long Beach, nearly twenty miles southwest of Whittier and a busy drive from the entanglements and strictures of the Puente Hills. Their jobs and his politics remained centered in Whittier, however, and under the pressures of family as well as time they soon returned. Within months they moved twice again, to a small apartment over a garage in La Habra, eventually to one of Frank Nixon's properties where they lived rent-free across from the East Whittier School, drawn back in a sense as Hannah and Frank had come back themselves long before to the big house on the boulevard.

Together, Dick and Pat Nixon now made some $4,800 a year, an ample income for a young couple in 1940, and it afforded them an active social life while they saved money as well for the travel they both relished. They soon settled into the small private rituals of a new marriage. Sunday mornings were set aside for leisurely breakfasts of biscuits and jam on the same ceremonial little dishes every week, followed by long drives and walks on the beach, often to their favorite shoreline near San Clemente. There were also nights in the gallery of the Los Angeles Light Opera and sometimes at the famous Coconut Grove nightclub. Back home on weekdays, Dick chauffeured her Whittier cheerleaders to high school football and basketball games, one of the male students remembering how "Miss Ryan . . . broke my heart" by introducing their driver as her new husband.

They socialized with "a young crowd," Pat remembered, "mostly my friends from college. . . . We liked to do active things." Good-naturedly but with little prowess, Nixon went along with them dancing and ice-skating. In small gatherings at someone's apartment he could be the hit of the party. "I will never forget one night when we did *Beauty and the Beast*," Pat once recalled, describing a living room skit. "Dick was the Beast . . . we had loads of laughs." Of the other couples, they were closest to Helene and Jack Drown. She was a pert, blond vocational guidance counselor who was Pat's assistant with the Whittier pep squad, he a bulky ex-football player going to USC Law School. It was to be a lifelong friendship, the younger, less assertive Drowns fiercely loyal personally and politically, and the Nixons dominant from the beginning. When the Drowns moved nearby into a shabbily furnished apartment, Pat Nixon with motherly dispatch took Helene in tow to Sears, Roebuck and slipcovered their couch in a bright cretonne she chose and refitted herself. "We would go out to dinner," Jack Drown once related, "and Dick would take over the menu, and order for everyone."

In their first months of marriage there was little contact with the larger Milhous clan. Muriel Kelly, who lived with Hannah and Frank during this period while attending the college, recalls the "very warm . . . very friendly family get-togethers" on Worsham Drive when the newlyweds came for Sunday dinners. In March 1941, Pat organized a party for her mother-in-law's fifty-sixth birthday and gave her a pearl necklace Hannah remembered fondly two decades later. Yet marriage not only took Richard out of his parents' house but reduced substantially the time he spent with them and other relatives, in a sense with the old Whittier in general. No longer passing somber, vacant weekends absorbed in church and Sunday school, Nixon was experiencing a kind of weaning that went on despite their living in Whittier. When the Milhouses held a family reunion at Laguna Beach in September 1941, nearly three years after Richard began to date her, it was the first time many of them had met Pat Nixon. "I thought Pat was so beautiful then that I couldn't keep my eyes off of her," said Clara Jane Lemke, who had been dating Donald and was about to marry him. "I'd never seen her. Well, [I'd] heard of them before." She was not alone. Of more than a dozen Milhous aunts and cousins asked later about their memories of Dick's early marriage, none saw them socially beyond chance meetings at the elder Nixons', and they were never invited to the young couple's apartment.

They had spoken only "casually" in 1941, Pat would remember, about Dick running again for the California Assembly. And he had told her, too, that "one of the reasons he went back to Whittier after law school was . . . to return to his hometown in order to get into politics." Whatever the face-saving explanations of husband to wife, there was nothing vague about Nixon's continued political positioning the first year of their marriage.

The summer and fall after their honeymoon, he gave a number of local speeches on behalf of Wendell Willkie, the Republican Presidential nominee. The 1940 campaign offered him a first distant link with national politics and forces in the Republican Party that would be quietly momentous in his own later candidacies. From his graduate school ties to Wisconsin, Paul Smith knew Glenn Frank, the dynamic publicist and former president of the University of Wisconsin who was a close friend of Herbert Hoover and chairman of the platform committee at the 1940 Republican convention. Before Frank died in an auto accident that autumn, Nixon would receive material to attack both the foreign and domestic policies of Franklin Roosevelt, much of it cast in harsher tones than Willkie himself was using. The contrast between the candidate and platform orthodoxy was a symbol of the backroom, frequently vicious politics in the struggle between the conservative old guard, who controlled the party machinery, and the eastern moderates with their attractive candidates, money, and influential press. That historic Republican schism often left local candidates and ambitious campaigners like Dick Nixon well to the right of the national ticket, and often more successful. As Willkie and his relatively mild opposition to FDR went down to defeat in 1940, it was a passing lesson Nixon never forgot.

He found, meanwhile, backroom politics of his own closer to home. In 1939, already president of the alumni association, Nixon had been quietly elected a full trustee of Whittier College, at the time a small yet notable honor. At twenty-six, and barely five years after his own graduation, he was the youngest member of the traditionally venerable board. In the flurry of the abortive Assembly bid and his courtship, he had been at the outset a quiet, almost meek trustee, but that was soon to change in the winter of 1940–41.

Since replacing Walter Dexter as Whittier's president in 1934, William Mendenhall had appeased conservative trustees by slowing the reforms Dexter once sanctioned. Through shrewd land acquisition, he even managed to clear the school's early Depression debt of over $400,000. Like most of his predecessors, however, he had also eventually run afoul of the highly political board and alumni, among them Tom Bewley and his wealthy clients and college benefactors like Aubrey Wardman. At this point, with large donors threatening to withdraw support unless Mendenhall were replaced, Richard Nixon came forward eagerly but discreetly as a candidate for the college presidency, maneuvering to replace the man who had married him only a few months before.

Richard Gardner, a young professor at Whittier who later researched a first, unpublished Nixon biography, would tell the story of how that winter, to the surprise of his audience, Dick suddenly seized the opportunity to talk to a crowd of college alumni for some forty-five minutes when a basketball game was delayed at Wardman gym. Ostensibly, he kept the fans "entertained" as they restlessly waited for the game to start, yet he had talked to them not on just any subject but pointedly about the importance of dynamic leadership at the college. Less openly, he lobbied both Wardman and Judge Frank Swain, a prominent college booster, and quietly went to Smith and other teachers to instigate an effort within the staff to promote his selection. "It was a serious move," as one source described that internal orchestration, "backed up by a number of younger faculty members." "Nixon would have become [college] president," Albert Upton believed afterward, "if the war had not intervened."

In the event, the trustees did not muster sufficient opposition to push out Mendenhall until the end of 1943; by then Dick Nixon was in the South Pacific. But the later casual references to his near-presidency of Whittier College, part of the résumé of recognized talent and unsolicited hometown honors, once again omitted the avid politicking behind the scenes, and thus the real point of the story. If Richard Nixon did not succeed Mendenhall in Founders Hall in 1941, as he had not supplanted Gerald Kepple in Sacramento a year earlier, in neither case was it for want of trying.

Over the same period, across the valley in La Habra, he held open the prospect of both an Assembly race in 1942 and the La Habra city attorney's sinecure. Keeping his engagement and wedding largely secret in Whittier, Nixon had gone out of his way to tell his La Habra city council patron, J. W. Burch, who remembered the young couple coming to tell him, paying court as it were, some two months before the wedding date, even before Pat was to tell her brother Bill. For the next several months, Richard Nixon was regularly in the news of the small town, often on the front page of the *La Habra Star*. In May 1940 he was earnestly telling a group of citizens that "there was no reasonable chance" to mount a legal challenge to local Union Oil drilling rights. On the eve of his wedding, June 12, he was awarding tenderfoot Boy Scout badges for the Kiwanians. That October, he headed the welcoming committee for La Habra's Pioneer Fiesta and in November went on a tour of civic clubs showing rare books and manuscripts of a local collector. He ran for and won in May 1941 the presidency of the Association of Northern Orange County Cities, representing nine communities, most of them in Kepple's Assembly district. In August he was featured speaker at the San Clemente Kiwanis. And so it went. By the winter of 1941, with the incumbent's retirement this time already clear, the *Whittier News* had begun to write openly about local Republican poli-

ticians "grooming him [Nixon] for Assemblyman Gerald Kepple's place."
How much Pat Nixon understood the depth or method of her new husband's political quests in the months surrounding their wedding was never clear. In 1959 she would say of the prewar years that "there was no talk of politics or anything of that type," yet remembering with her daughter a quarter century later that there had indeed been some discussion of an Assembly campaign. Even for a young woman politically naïve, the repeated speeches and appearances, the incessant jockeying from Whittier to La Habra were marks of unmistakable public aspiration beyond a mere law practice. And seen as vibrant idealism, as Patricia Nixon long saw it, her husband's ambition continued to be part of their romance. For his twenty-eighth birthday, she would give him admiringly a ceramic knight on a charger.

Whatever his political positioning, they had decided by the spring of 1941 to leave Whittier. Nixon talked for a time with Jack Drown about opening a law firm in Los Angeles, and they confided in the Drowns and other friends their plans to move. It was Pat who took the first decisive step by declining in May to renew her teaching contract for the next year at Whittier Union. Nixon clearly wanted out as well. Evlyn Dorn remembered him driving her home one night that spring and talking in the car for almost two hours, pouring out his hopes for a future elsewhere. "I don't think Richard Nixon wanted to practice law in Whittier. . . . He wasn't interested in staying in Whittier," she recounted. "He wanted to practice law in a big city."

In June 1941 the Nixons drove to New Orleans to embark on a two-week Caribbean cruise on the United Fruit Company's *Ulua*; the trip was a first-anniversary gift to each other and the prize of their saving over the past year. On the open ocean it was a dreary journey, with Dick seasick "for almost the entire trip," as he recalled it, lying in a cabin near the engines with the odor of the fuel amplifying his nausea. Nearer ports he was able to join shipboard parties, and Pat recorded in her trip diary a night when the men on board dressed in drag: "Dick as a Grecian lady, draped costume—sheet, turban, brooch, bosom, etc." On docking at Panama she drew a vivid picture of Colon's garish strip across from the Canal Zone: "It is often called the most immoral spot in the world—very easy to believe after an evening observing. Narrow, noisy hot streets loaded with bars, clip joints, cabarets, 'women'—a horrid existence! The place was crowded with handsome American soldiers—nothing to do and with so few Americans with whom to associate." At Havana, however, their reaction was more favorable, and Nixon took time ashore to inquire how an American attorney could set up a law practice in the Cuban capital. On their return he even talked to Evlyn Dorn about practicing in Cuba, though nothing more seemed to come of it.

The outside world of war and turmoil intruded at mid-passage on the *Ulua*. On the evening of June 22, 1941, their elderly black steward told them the ship's wireless had just picked up reports that Germany had invaded the Soviet Union in a vast new widening of the European war already twenty-two months old. The news stirred in Nixon one of the periodic reflections he seems to have had on international affairs or foreign policy before 1945. As he recalled his reaction to the great events of the thirties in his memoirs, he had not been "particularly disturbed" when FDR gave diplomatic recognition to the Soviets in 1933. Watching the Spanish Civil War in the mid-1930s, "a concerted press campaign against Franco—who was always described as a fascist rebel—led me to side with the loyalists, whose communist orientation was seldom mentioned in the newspapers." Later he had listened on the radio in Whittier to Neville Chamberlain's "peace in our time" statement after the Munich Agreement in 1938. "How excited I was . . . I was as close to being a pacifist as anybody could be in those times," he once reminisced. "I thought at that time that Chamberlain was the greatest man alive, and when I read Churchill's all-out criticism of Chamberlain, I thought Churchill was a mad-man." At the signing of the Nazi-Soviet Non-Aggression Pact in 1939, he was "strongly against Stalin, not because he was a communist but because he was allied with Hitler, whom I despised."

"We both hoped this would lead to a Russian victory and Hitler's downfall," he remembered of that June evening on the *Ulua*. "I despised Hitler, and despite my disenchantment with Stalin over the Hitler-Stalin pact, had no particular anti-Soviet or anticommunist feelings." Married and anxious to restart his career, he also plainly dreaded for personal reasons America becoming embroiled in the war. "I had so little in those days that the prospect of going into the service was almost unbearable," he would say in some candor, "and I felt that the United States staying out of any kind of conflict was worth paying any price whatsoever."

Driving back to California, Pat registered her final diary entry July 10, noting in the West, "What wonderful coolness!" after the Caribbean heat. Then on reaching the outskirts of the basin: "Always the letdown feeling at the end of a trip—just a gypsy at heart!" It was to be, Nixon wrote later, "our last vacation for several years."

She stayed home in the autumn, and they were still looking for prospects when that October Nixon received a letter from David Ginsberg, general counsel of the newly formed Office of Price Administration in Washington. Created by Executive Order in August 1941, the OPA was then part of

Washington's frantic effort on the eve of war to stabilize consumer prices and stem the threat of inflation. The prospect of a new welter of federal regulations and enforcement procedures produced an instant need—"desperate," one official remembered the autumn of 1941—for attorneys to staff the agency.

In the customary Washington connections, the lines had gone out not only to other New Deal bureaucracies, but also to the faculties whose professors glided back and forth between academia and government. From Duke, David Cavers was to be an assistant general counsel of the OPA, and he had recruited both Harlan Leathers and Ed Rubin from his Durham classes. Asked by Ginsberg for more names, he mentioned Richard Nixon from the class of '37, whom he thought still practicing with a small firm in California. The probable starting salary was $3,200, just a little more than he made with Wingert and Bewley if far less than their joint income before Pat quit her job. "But money was not a major consideration," Julie Eisenhower wrote of her parents' decision. "My mother believed they would be limited staying in Whittier, and at her urging, my father told Ginsberg he was available."

A month later, the job still up in the air, they took the train to Lansing, Michigan, to buy a new Oldsmobile, planning to stop on the way back to see the USC–Notre Dame football game at South Bend. The Southern Cal team was entraining as well from Union Station in Los Angeles as Don and Eddie dropped them off, and Pat noted girlishly in another travel diary the student sendoff: "What spirit and fun!" On the train, a telegram came from Thomas Emerson, one of Ginsberg's assistants, scheduling an interview in San Francisco, and after picking up their car and seeing the game, they drove there directly, dodging a snowstorm in Indiana, "a snowy fairyland," Pat noted. Emerson, who now had a letter of recommendation from Douglas Maggs at Duke as well as from Cavers, was impressed. "He seemed to be a clear case of what we needed," he remembered, recalling the "nice-looking boy" from Los Angeles. "I thought him intelligent and articulate and gave him a job on the spot."

Back in Whittier, they prepared for the move to Washington. On a sunny basin Sunday in early December they drove by Neva's apartment on the way to a matinee movie in Los Angeles. Her husband mentioned there were radio bulletins of some attack on Hawaii, but Dick dismissed it as "just one more of the frequent scare stories we had all been hearing." They went on to the film and walked out into the late-afternoon light to find a newsboy hawking a newspaper headlined JAPS BOMB PEARL HARBOR! "We're at war, mister," he said as Nixon bought a paper.

His going was softened at the law firm by the fact of war. Jeff Wingert, who regretted the decision, nonetheless saw the Washington job as Dick's "duty," his daughter Judith recalled, and the senior partner would plan on Nixon's return to the firm after the war, an understanding at the time Nixon did nothing to dispute. To some the move seemed a matter of personal necessity in any case, for Wingert and Bewley could not have sustained their third lawyer much longer. "It was a matter of economics" is how Wallace Black saw the OPA position. "He could get a salary." Pearl Harbor also eased some of the tension caused on Worsham Drive by their departure, and not least by Pat's role in it. As an alternative to the military, the OPA seemed to Hannah Nixon the lesser sacrifice of her son. "My mother was secretly relieved by this decision," he wrote. "Although it would take me far from Whittier again, she probably thought . . . I would stay working in the government rather than compromise our Quaker principles by deciding to fight in the armed services."

Later, the OPA job would become in his political mythology a Quaker's patriotic marching off to wartime Washington, and the history behind it obscured altogether—the urge to escape Whittier that began with Pat's abandoned school contract in May 1941, the search for jobs as far afield as Havana, the old school connections at the agency, the hiring a month before Pearl Harbor. "Our greatest hopes," Pat would remark about leaving Whittier that winter, "were to get some job with the government, where we could contribute to the winning of the war."

"TRYING TO PREVENT PEOPLE FROM GETTING AWAY WITH MURDER"

They spelled each other driving across the country for five sometimes harrowing days, slowed to a crawl through the Appalachians in Tennessee and on into Virginia's Blue Ridge by raging ice- and snow-storms that seemed to follow them. Early Friday afternoon, January 9, 1942—Pat noting the exact time on his twenty-ninth birthday—they arrived with some relief in Washington, Nixon driving directly to be sworn in at the long wooden, barracks-like buildings thrown up for the OPA and other burgeoning wartime agencies along Independence Avenue southwest of the White House. "Heard that it was impossible to find apartments in war-exploded and war-torn Washington," Pat jotted in a shorthand diary. But when they left the swearing-in that afternoon to hunt for housing, they headed by chance across the Potomac to the still partially unfinished Beverly Park apartments near Four-Mile Run in Alexandria and immediately found a landlord from California who rented them a unit despite a waiting list and arranged for them to buy used furniture at the same moment. "A miracle!" Pat exulted in her diary as they moved in that evening. "Dick's birthday was a lucky day for us."

The following Saturday morning they met Pat's cousin from Connecticut, Jo Rockwell, who was then working for the secretary of state, and together toured the usual Washington sights, monuments, and famous buildings Nixon had seen only in passing when he had first come through the city with Richard Kiefer on their summer trip in 1936. Now he was an absorbed tourist. Rockwell long remembered him "straining his neck" as he inched the Oldsmobile up East Executive Avenue past the White House.

Back at the OPA offices Monday morning, Nixon faced the less majestic, bureaucratic reality of Washington a month after Pearl Harbor, what one historian called "walking into utter chaos" as the flailing infant agency with its guidelines, regulations, and field offices tried to grasp the enormous problems of national price control and rationing. As if to match the task, it was an extraordinary gathering of officials, several of them young men, like Richard Nixon, unknown at the time and destined for distinguished careers far beyond the OPA. The agency's colorful director was Leon Henderson, "a public servant," as Robert Sherwood called him, "of exceptional ability, courage, and imperviousness," who was also given to dancing the rhumba in party hats in local nightclubs, a habit that led to inevitable newspaper photographs of the director bumping to a Latin rhythm, and made him and his agency all the more suspect and controversial among Republicans who most opposed the OPA. With Henderson was a less flamboyant but gifted group of deputies. There was Ginsberg, who would become a prominent Washington attorney; Joseph Rauh, afterward a noted civil rights lawyer and Democratic Party activist; John Kenneth Galbraith, later a Harvard economics professor, influential author, and Presidential adviser; Rupert Emerson, to be yet another author and Harvard professor of government; Merle Fainsod, who became an eminent scholar on the Soviet Union at Harvard; and Thomas Emerson, who had hired Nixon and would go on to a prestigious career on the Yale Law faculty.

In the echelons beneath, most of its members as destined for anonymity as some of the section heads were for distinction, Nixon was among some 177 associate, assistant, and junior attorneys. According to an oft-repeated story, a government employment form asked him "the lowest salary you would accept," indicating $2,800 as the minimum, and Richard Nixon had duly filled in $2,800. Thomas Emerson had the impression after the San Francisco interview that Nixon made $12,000 a year in his California law practice, a princely sum for the time. Another OPA official thought his salary in Whittier had been "between $5,000 and $6,000 a year." "He told me afterward," Jacob Beuscher, one of his superiors, was quoted as saying about Nixon's sacrifice in pay, "that he reasoned that the boys who would be hitting the beaches would be compensated at a substantially lower rate." In fact, the minimum salary for an OPA lawyer, a P-1, was $2,000, and Richard Nixon had applied and entered as a P-3 at $3,200—though at the same time both Harlan Leathers and Ed Rubin, his peers at Duke with more prestigious practices in the meantime, were both P-5's earning $4,600. At any rate, the discrepancy in salary was felt sharply in the Independence Avenue barracks. "I found that others with lesser academic records and not as much legal experience had come in as P-4's, a step higher, and some even as P-5's, at $4,600 a year," he wrote in his memoirs, still smarting from the sting and aiming at his lower-ranking Duke friends forty years later.

He was assigned first to a beleaguered "interpretations unit," from a desk out in an open bay answering letters or other inquiries and reviewing regulations in the crucial tire-rationing program. Rubber presented the first great commodity crisis of the war. Ninety-eight percent of the U.S. supply was imported from the Far East, and most of that was now about to be cut off by Japanese attacks in Southeast Asia. At the outbreak of the war, there were scarcely a half million tons of crude rubber in the country and less than 100,000 on the high seas with any chance of arriving—this in a nation that in prewar years had consumed at least 13,000 tons a month for truck tires alone, more than was now left after military allotments for all civilian uses. "The shortage of rubber is critical," read a secret memorandum to Henderson two days after Pearl Harbor from a young California economist named Arthur P. Burns. "Unless effective action is taken quickly to halt retail sales, we may lose almost all our retail inventories within a week without assurance that the products so sold will reach the points of greatest need." At the looming prospect of a disastrous run on stores, FDR had issued an executive order banning ordinary tire sales, and the OPA was promptly charged to enforce the restriction and allot emergency rations according to directives.

It was by those standards important work, if often tediously clerical. Congress had abdicated on the politically thorny issues of shortages and inflation and was already positioning to attack Roosevelt in the 1942 election. "There was even more than the usual bickering and backbiting between departments and agencies," Sherwood wrote of the Capital the winter and spring of 1942. "In the battle of Washington, as on most of the real fighting fronts, this was the lowest point of the war." Yet morale at the OPA remained high, and it was not unusual for staff, including Nixon, in the crowded wooden buildings to work late into the night or on Saturdays. "What really made it mean something," he would say, "was that we felt that we were part of a bigger cause."

There was no time or provision for orientation, and he was thrust into a line position Leathers had held, handling telephone calls and interviews, reading and sorting the welter of wires and correspondence about the new regulations from a baffled, sometimes angry public and Congress, dictating answers, preparing still more of the ubiquitous interpretations and regulations. The promptness and accuracy of replies was no abstract efficiency. OPA responsiveness was a key to both enforcement and public confidence in the unpopular program. It was on-the-job training of the most basic kind, the young lawyers expected to comb the regulations on their own initiative, and reduced to asking advice of fellow attorneys with scarcely days' or weeks' more experience themselves. From the first week, however, Richard Nixon seemed to thrive in the hectic pace and multiplying clerkdom. He was to be, the documentary record would show and other OPA officials testified, an uncommonly apt bureaucrat, conscientious, energetic, inventive—and, like almost anyone with ability in the wartime maelstrom of government, able to move rapidly up the ladder, though not without some classic bureaucratic obstacles and lessons along the way.

During his second week, "the flood of mail coming into the office reached a new height," as an OPA memo recorded it, and his own weekly "Report of Work Done" recorded crisply his week Monday through Saturday:

A. Sorted all incoming mail as to forms and classified balance.
B. Prepared new form letter—8.
C. Handled 116 interviews and telephone calls.
D. Dictated and prepared 255 wires and letters in answer to rationing correspondence.
E. Worked with Newman and Van Sickle on additional form letters which will cut down number of dictated replies.
F. Spoke to field liaison men on January 23 on general aspects of rationing interpretation in preparation for Chicago meeting. Gray, Parks, Walsh and Nash in attendance.

By February 7 he proudly reported that the "flood of inquiries" had been stemmed and the section's long-standing arrears in correspondence wiped out. "Wires are being answered the day they are received. There is no backlog of letters," he wrote grateful superiors. "Letters are being answered two days after receipt." On February 14, a month after he had arrived, R. M. Nixon was being recommended by his immediate boss to "head up" the interpretation unit, a position slated for a senior attorney at $4,600 a year.

Neither promotion nor raise came so soon, but a week later he made his mark further with an unsolicited proposal for organizing the section's ever-burdensome correspondence. In a detailed three-and-one-half-page memo, accompanied by a meticulous hand-drawn and hand-lettered diagram, he constructed a complex system for routing, answering, clearing, even sealing and stamping the torrent of mail. It was the sort of tedious task he had always undertaken and done so well from college to men's clubs. And he cast his proposal in the best of bureaucratic motives, not only to rationalize an essential function but to free officials for more important duties—"that the members of the legal staff be relieved," Nixon wrote, "from giving personal attention to routine matters in order that they may devote the bulk of their time to preparation of interpretations which require serious attention." For the most part Nixon's scheme was adopted, though its ingenious and eager author remained for the moment still buried as a veritable clerk. Outgoing letters, instructed a February 26 memo on clearance, were to be routed for substantive checking "first to Mr. Leathers and, second, to Mr. Nixon. Mr. Nixon will see that the letter is mailed."

Then, suddenly, in March 1942, there was more quick shuffling of personnel at the agency, and Nixon was "designated informally," as one memo recorded, to be both "acting coordinator of Interpretations" and "acting Chief of Interpretations sub-branch of the Rubber Branch." By mid-month he had set up the "legal mail desk" for tire rationing and devised and drawn again by hand an even more complicated, exquisite flow chart for handling mail in the adjacent auto-rationing legal unit. A supervisor's hand-written notes at a meeting sketched the new man's obvious ability and widening responsibilities:

> Review: of tough problems each field.
> Digest: gasoline, typewriters and bicycles.
> Supervise: overall studies.
> Revise: tire regulation.
> Proposal: Auto Manual.

By late April and early May, barely four months in Washington, he was preparing OPA weekly bulletins on significant tire-rationing interpretations, conducting staff meetings, and, having become the OPA expert on handling correspondence, drawing up yet a third, fourth, and fifth Nixon schema for routing mail in the gasoline legal branch, sugar legal branch, and administrative section. His new authority and assertiveness inevitably met bureaucratic resistance and self-justification. When one of his April "progress reports" noted "a fair number" of interpretations had to be returned to the originating branches for "correction," he was called on the carpet before a superior by one of the accused branches, armed with documentation showing only one such interpretation "questioned by their unit during that period."

Jacob Beuscher, Nixon's supervisor during most of his months at the OPA, thought him "a splendid right-hand and left-hand for me. Bright, anxious to assume responsibility and with a great capacity for work and accomplishment, he showed constant concern for the plight of the ordinary rationing board member and tried hard to clarify rationing complexities." Thomas Harris, an assistant general counsel, would similarly report him "diligent and hard-working, a real plugger." "I'm sure I gave him an excellent efficiency report," Harris said later. Still, the justified praise of superiors was reflected only once in formal promotion apart from putative titles in the organization. By the summer of 1942, he was a P-4 making $600 more a year, and there he remained.

It was all an intense education in the petty yet sometimes fateful politics of bureaucracy. But he continued to flourish as a kind of model employee. In May he was "farmed out" to the Baltimore field office for a week, as a report described it, assigned to instruct the floundering local OPA staff, and returning to make a dutiful report—"highly instructive to members of the unit," said another report up the line, ". . . [on] the kind of help . . . Field Offices would like to get from Washington." By June, carefully noting fifteen and one-half hours overtime beyond the wartime forty-four-hour norm, Nixon had become acting chief of the entire Rationing Coordination Unit. The archives would show him on June 27 penciling a thoughtful editing of bureaucratic prose and redundancy in the weekly report drafted for his signature and sent on to the General Counsel's office. Early in June he was again assigned to troubleshoot problems in gasoline rationing in Boston. His week-long absence left "a considerable burden of work . . . upon other members of the unit," one memo reported.

Before going to New England, he had prepared yet another painstaking study, this one on the convoluted problems of passenger-car eligibility provisions under the various auto, tire, and gasoline regulations. While Nixon was in Boston, his study received much "favorable comment," according to OPA documents, and one ranking official was "so impressed" that he moved to put the paper and its author on the agenda of one of the Deputy Administrators. When he returned, however, his own superiors and colleagues had deftly headed off his potential audition before senior officialdom and quietly diverted the rather too impressive study to a lower-level group of section chiefs who would duly obscure its authorship and claim its insights. Once more it was time-honored bureaucratic cannibalism, still another example of the practices and forces that seemed certain to limit his rise at the OPA, however zealous or competent his performance. By the time he learned of the maneuver and lost opportunity, Nixon had already decided to abandon his brief but avid career at the Office of Price Administration.

When they first arrived in Washington, Nixon had asked Horack for a recommendation in joining the city's University Club, and the form had come back promptly from Durham with the dean's characteristic warmth— "A grand person." Yet afterward there would be a sense among his OPA colleagues that Dick Nixon had never quite fit in socially at the agency, that he had been "uncomfortable," as Harris once related, "among the liberals, the Eastern law school graduates, the Jews he rubbed shoulders with on the job . . . he lacked sophistication and the big-city graces." William Messing, an OPA lawyer who accompanied him on the Boston trip, met Pat and found her "very friendly and talkative," while her husband was "terribly ill-at-ease." At the same time, J. Paull Marshall, sitting next to him, saw Nixon as friendly and compatible for similar ideological reasons. "Most of the OPA lawyers were left-wingers and it was natural that Dick and I should develop an affinity for each other," Marshall said later. "We both believed in the capitalistic system . . . the other lawyers were using rationing and price control as a means of controlling profits." But most of the personal reflection on Nixon at the OPA would come long after the fact, when the man and his politics made such judgments suspect on both sides. At the time, he had been a quiet, hard-working official whose social life over the few months was simply with his wife outside the office, whatever his unease or resentments on Independence Avenue. They had transferred their domestic routine from Whittier to Alexandria and taken only one short vacation trip during his busy early months, an April drive to Charleston, South Carolina. Stopping off to show Pat the Duke campus, he found Horack's office closed and shyly did not even telephone the dean's home.

For most of the early, blossom-filled Washington spring, they were absorbed in the question of joining the service. In a Washington full of men in uniform, wrote Edwin Hoyt, Nixon had become "very self-conscious." His OPA friend J. Paull Marshall was also involved with the Navy League and quietly encouraged him to join the navy soon after they met. But there were other considerations as well. "Nixon must have picked up the D.C. message very quickly, that any man who wanted to go into politics must have a war record," thought Thomas Emerson. It was "accepted dogma in Washington." "Those with political ambitions," Milton Viorst wrote about young officials in those months, "regarded military service as an absolute necessity." Moreover, in the spring of 1942 there was an increasing draft of childless men of Nixon's age, putting a premium on enlistment as an officer.

It was an "agonizing" decision, he once said. Back home, Tom Bewley was planning to volunteer for noncombatant service with the Friends much as Oscar Marshburn had done in World War I. "His Quaker family were troubled," Nixon's daughter wrote about the moment. But the choice was always more practical than theological, especially against the diluted, selective pacifism of his evangelical wing of Quakerism. "When the war began," he said thirty years later, "I could have been a conscientious objector, of course, very easily." But at the same time he confessed, "the idea of being a conscientious objector never crossed my mind." In the end, Pat was again the decisive influence. "He had his wife's complete support," their daughter observed. "Her acquiescence was important." Pat herself would say later, "I would have felt mighty uncomfortable if Dick hadn't done his part." On April 23, 1942, two weeks after their trip to Charleston and just after his sole promotion at the OPA, Nixon wrote Horack that "I have decided to volunteer for service." He had learned the navy needed lawyers to "handle administrative duties on aircraft carriers and at naval airports in foreign countries," and he asked the dean, once again, for a recommendation, this time to the office of Naval Officer Procurement on his "character, qualities of leadership, intellectual ability, and of course patriotism."

He left the OPA for the navy in mid-August 1942. In his political career, at odds with governmental regulation and New Deal bureaucracies, even one in which he had been so apt and so excelled, his time at the OPA became a kind of morality play—the idealistic young attorney disillusioned by economic controls and craven bureaucrats, "obsessed with their own power," as he wrote in his memoirs, "[who] seemed to delight in kicking people around, particularly those in the private sector." He repeatedly told the story of going to one of his bosses, David Lloyd, later an adviser to President Harry Truman, who said to him, "Build a little staff. Request two or three people to assist you, and then we can raise you to a P-5." And Nixon replied, according to the story, "But I don't need a staff," to which Lloyd shot back, "Then you won't get a promotion." He had seen, too, at the OPA "the terrible paperwork . . . the mediocrity of so many civil servants," he once said. These were "people angling for something and anxious not to miss the bandwagon . . . some of the remnants of the old, violent New Deal crowd." On other occasions, though, he would be more generous and grateful about the job he had taken at Pat's urging and that lifted them out of Whittier. "Working for the OPA before [sic] the war was a great experience for me," Nixon acknowledged in 1959.

The truth was that the much-maligned agency under Leon Henderson with his New Deal staff and publicized rhumba would be one of the genuine Washington successes of World War II, warding off the worst of profiteering and inflation and notably free of corruption itself in work that offered ample opportunity for it. The OPA had come into existence, and performed its historic service, against the dark side of exploitation and selfishness that lay just beneath the patriotic surface of the American economy. "We learned . . . in OPA Americans are just not that docile or law-abiding," Thomas Harris would say. And the conscientious young Whittier attorney, so devoted and good at his job as to alarm his jealous superiors, seemed to sense that reality as well, however impolitic it later became. "But I certainly worked hard, on tire rationing for example," he reminisced once, "trying to prevent people from getting away with murder."

During his OPA trip to Boston in July, he took Pat on one last idyll before the service, a long weekend at Cape Porpoise near Kennebunkport on the rocky Maine coast. Because tourism was a casualty of the gas rationing he was helping enforce, they were almost alone in a small, shuttered hotel. There were a few days of walks along the shore and through blueberry patches, lobster dinners for a dollar, quiet evenings in the cozy old inn, and then it was over. "We were so happy there," Pat would tell her daughter more than forty years later. They bought a small souvenir painting of a lobsterman's boat, and she would hang it in her bedroom throughout the war and afterward.

Wallace Black was already attending the naval officer candidate school at Quonset Point, Rhode Island, where Nixon had been assigned, and Dick wrote his old Whittier friend that summer about what to expect. "I told him some of the things to be prepared for. It was a pretty rough course," Black said, "as far as the amount of reading and studying we had to do." He left from Washington's Union Station on August 17, "that lonely ride up to Providence—every mile reminding me of the time you and I had taken it together," he wrote to Pat later. The first week in the navy he thought "the longest I've ever known—what with shots—marching—studying, etc," adding, "I thought of you so much." He found the two-month school in the late summer heat an ordeal. Beyond a brief course in naval courts—"You know, for a lawyer that was duck soup," he would say—the physical training and naval science academics were difficult, particularly navigation. "The chiefs run the navy," he said later about the hard-boiled instructors who disciplined their overnight civilian sailors at Quonset. "Believe me, those navy chiefs—they put you in your place and that is good for anybody." He learned to stand at attention. "My wife said that I had never stood straighter," he joked later. "I did not graduate with distinction from Quonset," he once admitted to a naval audience but recalled his fellow officer candidates as "quite a class." Among them he met a young lawyer from New York named William Pierce Rogers, whom he would know only casually at Quonset but who was later to be a major figure over the whole sweep of his political life.

His preoccupation during the first separation of their marriage was his beautiful wife back in Washington. Having volunteered for the Red Cross during their first few months in the Capital, she had joined the OPA herself as an assistant business analyst at $2,600 a year and started work five days after he left for Quonset. Now from his humid Rhode Island barracks he was writing her in passionate yearning. "I may not say much when I'm with you—*but all of me loves all of you all the time*," he told her early in the course. She wrote back in the middle of the night after a telephone call, "It's two o'clock but I just had to write to you to say *how very much I love you!* It was clear all over again when talking to you on the phone." Reporting on a romantic movie she had seen, she noted, using his intimate nickname, "I missed Plum's hand very much."

In the midst of the course, they spent a two-day leave together in New York, and he returned to Quonset on a lonely train ride, peering at his reflection in the railroad car window, and struck with his good fortune. "This weekend was wonderful . . . thought how very lucky I was to have you," he wrote back at the base. "I certainly am not the Romeo type and you are so beautiful."

He requested "ships and stations" and was astonished to open his orders on graduation and find a posting to Ottumwa Naval Air Station, in October 1942, "a runway," as he recalled, "that stopped abruptly in the middle of a cornfield" in southeastern Iowa. Pat left her OPA job and moved with him that autumn to the farm town. At the new training base he was an administrative aide, opening mail, assigning typing, "little more than a receptionist," as one local account described his position. Others at the base thought him "conscientious," as Thelma Metcalf, navy nurse, remembered, yet reserved and seldom at the officers' club. "He wasn't the party type," said Metcalf. Jerry Wood, who occasionally patrolled the base with him in a Jeep, thought Nixon "just as common as they come—a good Joe—a little on the meek side."

Ottumwa was altogether a deadening backwater for them, their dismay and pride hardly concealed after the heady months in Washington and the East. For fifty-five dollars a month they rented a small apartment on the top floor of a three-story brick building on a hillside overlooking the city and the Des Moines River curling through it. To their neighbors they seemed distant and unfriendly. "The only way I knew him was breezing in and out with his head in the air," said one. "They gave us the impression that he was all navy," remembered Julia Burns, who lived on the first floor. Her husband would complain that Nixon parked his Oldsmobile outside the apartment garage, blocking other tenants. Pat, meanwhile, went to work as a teller in an Ottumwa bank, where fellow employees thought her "a little bit glamorous," as one put it later; "I mean the difference between California and Iowa." Her Ottumwa friends, like Geneva Johnson, remembered that "she colored her hair. That was years before we did that," and that Pat thought her eighty-five-dollar-a-month bank salary in Ottumwa "scandalously low." "She was always scolding me to get out and go places," Johnson said, "see people and do things." Mrs. Nixon "didn't care much for those coffee socials with navy wives," one officer from the base recalled. Pat Nixon was "a little disdainful," Geneva remembered, of the local Ottumwa girls who frequented dances at the air station.

When Nixon saw that winter an announcement for applications for sea duty by men twenty-nine to thirty, he put in his papers immediately, and orders came through in the spring to disembark from San Francisco for the South Pacific. They left Iowa after seven chafing months.

They dropped the car off in Whittier and took the train together from Union Station in Los Angeles to a wrenching farewell from family and friends early in May 1943. The Bewleys came, along with Evlyn Dorn, some friends, Don and his wife, Eddie and his parents. They all had breakfast at the station's Harvey House, "a painful meal, full of sad silences," Dick remembered. "Now you take good care of your mother," he said at one point to thirteen-year-old Eddie. He would be "relieved," Nixon wrote, when the train was announced and the emotional scene over. As the car jolted out of the station, he turned to look back, and saw a picture expressive of the two people whose vastly different personalities had so shaped his life. Hannah Nixon was silent and impassive. "My mother held her sorrow in," he remembered. Frank Nixon was beginning to sob.

"NICK COULD SWAP ANYTHING"

They roomed in a small hotel in San Francisco as he waited to be shipped out, he reporting each morning to do calisthenics at Alameda naval air station, she deciding to wait for him alone in San Francisco rather than return to Whittier and finding a job as a correspondence clerk with the Office of Civilian Defense. At the end of the month the orders suddenly came. They said an emotional farewell, and he sailed May 31 on the *President Monroe*. Hardly on board, he wrote her a first letter, as he would write faithfully each day for the next thirteen and one-half months.

The voyage began with a typical wartime scene, nine officers crowded into a small cabin on the passenger-liner-turned-troopship. One of them, James Udall, was seasick most of the voyage, though Nixon, unlike his experience on the *Ulua*, apparently escaped it. "Every day," Udall recounted, "Nixon brought me crackers and soup." But there were also regular poker games aboard the *Monroe*, and Udall remembered as well Nixon's impressive performance at the table, "as good a poker player as, if not better than, anyone we had ever seen," he called him later. "He played a quiet game, but wasn't afraid of taking chances. He wasn't afraid of running a bluff."

His orders were for Espiritu Santo in the New Hebrides, an allied base where his first assignment was as a naval passenger officer for one of the marines' South Pacific Air Transport Command units, known as SCAT. Supervising and directing the movement of military passengers to and from the front, they were part of the southern anchor of Douglas MacArthur's island-hopping through the Treasury and Solomon archipelago that had begun with the Japanese retreat from Guadalcanal that February. In 1943–44 it was a strange, half-lit theater of the war, the military actions now bloody frontal assaults and flashing sea battles, now feints and phantom landings and fitful, sporadic forays. The fighting took place against a setting at once ominous and majestic. Jungles of emerald lushness rose suddenly off the beaches toward wild, sweeping mountain peaks and smoking volcanoes. During the day the heat was often unbearable, and darkness crept in around seven in the evening, an indigo night giving way to a murky false twilight at dawn and a tropical rain falling in great gray sheets.

The climax of the drive, the larger tactical goal of the campaign, was to encircle and reduce the formidable Japanese fortress of Rabaul to the north, the hinge of Tokyo's conquest in this region of the Pacific. In the war of attack and attrition, the more famous land action would be Bougainville in the autumn of 1943, though for the men involved, the months would have other names less known but still bloody—Rendova and Munda, Empress Augusta Bay, Kula Gulf, the Tokyo Express, and the infamous Slot. On an August night in 1943, not far up the chain from where Richard Nixon was stationed, the Japanese supply train of warships made their high-speed run once more through Blackett Strait, and waiting in the darkness were American torpedo boats, one of them PT-109 commanded by a young navy lieutenant junior grade named John F. Kennedy.

Nixon would be only on the edge of the action, following the point of the American advance northward on a series of small supply and transport air strips just to the rear of the shifting island lines. In the autumn he was for the most part at Nouméa, New Caledonia, but by September he had served briefly on Guadalcanal and Villa Lavella. And in the loading and unloading of the C-47s that came through his bases, there were returnees and seriously wounded as well as munitions and supplies. Again and again he would witness the cycle described by a naval historian watching the transit: "Going, they are young and in the best of health. Returning, they are old and beaten shells that once were men."

His letters home to Pat mirrored the alternation between tension and tedium with the ineffable loneliness and nostalgia of war. "Please say it always," he admonished her about telling him "I love you," "because I always look for that first . . . you are the only one for me, it's been that way from the first." From Nouméa he described Jeep rides into the verdant, scenic mountains, enclosing small cuttings of exotic plants. "You rode along with me all the way . . . I think of you when I see beautiful things." She wrote her own daily letters in return, often addressed "Dear Plum." "Always write the day on your letters so I can picture it," she told him, and thereafter they meticulously dated the texts and numbered the envelopes. Nixon worried about her room, a potential roommate, her sacrifices. "Get good dinners, see lots of shows, buy nice clothes, have your hair fixed—and anything else you want or need," he advised her, to "make up for me here," adding, "It will make me feel swell to think of you having some enjoyment." In another poignant letter from a man who had gone off by himself as a little boy and who spent most of his life in the tumult and demands of politics, he wrote: "I'm antisocial I guess, but except for you—I'd rather be by myself as a steady diet rather than with most any of the people I know. I like to do what I want, when I want. Only where you are concerned do I feel otherwise—Dear One!"

By the end of summer he was audibly eager to go up the line nearer the battle, as in Washington bored and perhaps self-conscious at his relative inaction. The "damn central office" always seemed to keep him where he was, he complained to Pat, "but I certainly wanted to get out and spend some time in a less civilized place where I would feel that I was doing more." He added in what must have unsettled her, "I'm working on an angle. . . . Keep your fingers crossed and wish hard." Meanwhile, he wrote his parents, and sent long chatty letters to old friends in La Habra as well as the Whittier law office. "You must learn to read easily and rapidly," he wrote Eddie, offering ten savings stamps for every one hundred pages read, "but you must be able to pick out the important points."

To Dean Horack on September 4, 1943, Nixon wrote, "My work is about as far removed from law as is anarchy but at least I'm picking up some practical information about aviation." He was concerned about becoming rusty as a lawyer, "the problem we shall face when we get back to work . . . After two to four years away from the law we will need a refresher course . . . It is amazing how much we have forgotten already and in another year it will be still worse." He urged Horack to encourage such classes. "With the hue and cry already being raised for government aid and control in the field of postwar job finding, I believe that professional associations might well set the pace in establishing a policy of 'Taking care of their own.' " "I often think of the law school," he closed, "and always with most pleasant memories."

His anxiety about postwar retraining grew out of long hours passed between shifts and flights in almost omnivorous reading and note-taking. "Reading everything out here," Nixon wrote his wife that autumn, including, as navy friends noted later, a daily study of "an old illustrated Bible" he had brought with him from Whittier. He purred at Pat's gift of five-dollar pajamas ("probably the most expensive I'll ever wear!") and at letters with lipstick on them ("made me feel very lonesome—what a waste"). But it would be her packages of books he relished most. "Seemed like Christmas to open them" is how he responded to two boxes in October 1943. "I have always wanted to read Karl Marx in order to be familiar with it. De Maupassant writes the best short stories the world has ever read. Van Loon's *Geography* will be an education—a review of past learning and a preparation for our trips. . . . I'll bring them back as part of our collection." He sent her some of his notes from the reading, one a notation from *Reader's Digest* on a subject of obvious mutual concern: "No danger in first baby after thirty . . . more intelligent if older parents (only because of environment). Nursing better than bottles."

Among the notes he kept with him were random reflections from the popular magazines of the time. He was clearly preoccupied with political issues and, not least, matters of career and success. From *W. D. Kiplinger's Magazine*, he noted a report on a predicted postwar trend to conservatism and private enterprise in the U.S., with a public craving for housing and consumer products. In *Liberty* he annotated a Maurice Hindus article on German atrocities in the Soviet Union, observing that "Russians hate Germans *as such*." About congressional politics he scribbled at one point "Summer of Texas on bureaucracy—favors return of power and independence to state governments. The facility with which a bureaucrat legislates encourages a multiplicity of laws."

At thirty, feeling increasingly out of touch with his own profession and stuck in an unheroic rear area of the war, Nixon also carefully recorded the comparatively prodigious records of other men—William Fulbright, an Arkansas University president at thirty-four; a Georgian who became state attorney general at thirty-six; Ben Hecht, who was a foreign correspondent at twenty-six and a well-known author at thirty; and, with ironic portent, a future adversary, Governor Earl Warren of California, district attorney at thirty-four, now Governor. On the published axioms of a former Washington budget director, he listed the rules for advance in a governmental bureaucracy:

1. Be trained for job.
2. Have passion for anonymity.
3. A good and merciless judge of men willing to sacrifice personal prestige, loyalties, and friendships to the success of the job.
4. Stick to the administrative job and leave policy to the politicians.

Amid this he sprinkled epigrams of the famous: Ben Hecht's "Fame is a sort of mummy case in which the creative talents of yesterday lie in state and glitter in mania." Bernard Baruch's "A speculator is one who observes the future and acts before it occurs." From Tennyson, "The most virtuous hearts have a touch of hell's own fire in them." A credo from U. S. Grant, "Time comes in battle when both leaders decide they are defeated. He wins the battle who goes on fighting." And one unattributed: "There's a kind of love for permanence. There's another kind that's just champagne bubbles and moonlight. It isn't meant to last but it can be something to have and look back on all your life." Frequently, he copied from magazines their patriotic lists of "what I am fighting for," noting "Emphasis on simple things . . . privilege of choosing friends . . . creeds, radio programs, etc. vote." Among his memorabilia would be a *Saturday Evening Post* advertisement, a full page listing virtues from Santa Claus to Tom Sawyer to *Gone with the Wind*, the Constitution, the Gettysburg Address—all entitled "Thank God I Am an American."

In the fall he had asked his marine commandant, Carl Fleps, to be named to head the SCAT contingent for the next advance, and at mid-December he was finally moved forward to Bougainville, though by then the island had been largely taken. To his parents he wrote reassuringly, "The only things that really bothered me were lack of sleep and the centipedes." Japanese snipers were near his airstrip, however, and bombers from Rabaul staged harassing raids on the little bases. Within days of his arrival, just before Christmas 1943, there was a heavy attack. "When it was over," he wrote later, "we counted thirty-five shell holes within a hundred feet of the air raid bunker six of us shared. Our tent had been completely destroyed."

In the midst of evacuations and forward shipments on Bougainville, he wanted to send his wife a Christmas gift and could finally report in January 1944 his triumph, some stuffed animals from New Zealand like those Pat had in her apartment in Whittier. "One of the enlisted men who had gone to Auckland," he wrote her, "remembered my request and brought back two very cute koala bears. These are very much like your two raccoons." A month later, he wrote her about another arrival, the young Minnesota Republican governor Harold Stassen, then a naval lieutenant commander and already mentioned as a postwar Presidential candidate. "I met him and furnished him transportation to his destination," Nixon proudly wrote his wife. "He is only thirty-five—a big, good-looking Swede—and I was very impressed by his quiet poise." Seeing Stassen prompted him to think of his own homecoming with Pat, an event they had both already pictured.

He promised her an uncharacteristic display of affection before the world. "Whether it's the lobby of the Grand Central or the Saint Francis bar— I'm going to walk right up to you and kiss you—but good! Will you mind such a public demonstration?"

In March 1944 he moved forward once more to Green Island, again a relatively pacified area now garrisoned by troops mostly from New Zealand. He had hoped to be part of the long-awaited invasion of Rabaul, but Japan's "Gibraltar" was now to be bypassed, cut off, and left to wither as the war moved on to the north. There were occasional bombing raids on Green but less action than at Bougainville. "The only real danger," said Lester Noble, one of Nixon's navy friends, "was the possibility of a banyan tree falling on you during a storm." Yet there were emergencies at the airstrip and indelible reminders of the war raging on ahead of them. Soon after the navy's Seabees carved out the Green Island strip, a crippled army air force B-29 from a raid over Rabaul came in for a crash landing. They all cheered as the bomber slid down on its belly apparently intact, then "watched in horror," he recalled, as it skidded into a bulldozer near the runway and burst into a ball of flames against the dusk. "The carnage was terrible," Nixon wrote afterward. He had helped clear the bodies after the explosion. "I can still see the wedding ring on the charred hand of one of the crewmen when I carried his body from the twisted wreckage."

On Green, like Bougainville, there were periodic waves of emergency supply missions, planes crowding the runway, their armaments or supplies to be unloaded, reloaded, transferred with few tools but dramatic urgency. Although he was the officer in command of work crews, Nixon often joined his unit in the feverish work, "peeled off his shirt and sweated through the hard physical labor right along with the rest of the men," as one of them, Edward McCaffrey, remembered a typical scene. Usually made up of a dozen enlisted men in addition to radio operators, aircraft technicians, and base service personnel, the units he commanded were the classic, almost Hollywood-cast cross section of the navy, young men from New York slums and the Midwest, one from a wealthy family in the South, a Mexican, an Indian, an Italian, and the inevitable Texan, J. "Tex" Massingill. Nixon was continually impressed with their variety and contrasts in writing home about his experiences and in talking about them long afterward. Lucille Parsons and other relatives thought Dick changed and broadened by both his labor and his exposure to the men in the South Pacific. "He really had a hard row to hoe. He learned how to get along with people . . . boys from all over the country to work with," Lucille recalled. "He said he never knew what it was like to be associated with people brought up in all these different ways. . . . When he came back from that he was really much more humble; I mean he saw how the other half lived. . . . I think his service in the navy really, well, made him more aware of what goes on around him than he had been."

"The war, I think, was the real catalyst," he would write in a letter explaining later his political career, "in that it brought me face-to-face with a world of problems and issues of literally earth-shaking importance and thus forced on me a reassessment of the responsibilities of a citizen of the world."

With his own men and other officers he won at both Bougainville and Green a warm, ungrudging popularity. Bare-chested, in a pith helmet his men remembered as a trademark, he joined in the manly society of the small airstrip, including the legendary navy profanity. "He could and did hold his own with the sailors and marines who passed through the base," one observer concluded. As at Duke, they all had nicknames, and his would be "Nick" Nixon, the sobriquet he disliked at Whittier College and now accepted cheerfully. On Bougainville he had begun to scrounge provisions for the exhausted fighter and bomber pilots passing through the strip, serving them precious hamburgers and Australian beer in what they christened "Nick's Hamburger Stand" or "Nick's Snack Shack." Now he did the same on Green, wheedling supplies from other outfits. "Some of the stuff was, shall we say, 'liberated,' " McCaffrey said, "but Nick could swap anything. Just a small trade would set in motion a series of bigger trades that not only had his men well-housed, but kept the hamburger stand operating. If you ever saw Henry Fonda in *Mr. Roberts*, you have a pretty good idea of what Nick was like." The weary pilots never forgot him. "It meant so much," an air force fighter pilot named Chandler Worley said later, "just a few minutes' relaxation, good sandwiches, and the coldest pineapple juice in the islands."

Beyond "Nick's" and the profanity and shared work there was also poker, and his cool, consistent winning continued after the voyage over on the *Monroe*. Five-card stud became his preferred game. "I doubt that Nick ever lost a cent at poker," Lester Wroble said after watching him night after night. "He had a passion for analysis; he always played it cautious—close to the belt, and there was never a time when he didn't know exactly what he was doing. He thought everything out beforehand and never took chances." The sittings took on their own ceremony in the island boredom—"the etiquette surrounding them was taken very seriously," Nixon wrote—and he once gave up a chance to go to a small dinner with the visiting Charles Lindbergh because he had agreed beforehand to host a poker party for other officers.

He remembered proudly once drawing a royal flush in diamonds with an ace in the hole. James Udall, his cabin mate on the *Monroe* now assigned to Green, watched Nixon in some awe as he bluffed a lieutenant commander out of $1,500 with only a pair of deuces. Pots were seldom so large, but his winnings were steady. At the end of June, he would write Pat that he had won a thousand dollars at poker, though his total take was probably more. Some of the money seems to have gone to pay off old debts back at the law office. Evlyn Dorn would remember Nixon writing them during the war about "some business matters that Pat didn't know about [and] he instructed that she not be told."

The poker games became part of the nightly ritual that included letters home. In April he finally received a long-requested photo of Pat—a studio picture from San Francisco showing a beautiful woman with fine, filmy hair aglow in the photographer's light. "Today was a wonderful day," he wrote, noting the gift. "It's wonderful to see you again and even a picture brings you so very near to me."

They had begun to discuss their postwar plans. She was still in San Francisco, working first at Civilian Defense, then for a few months at the Committee for Congested Production Areas, and since March 1944 as a price economist with the district office of the OPA. ("Your job is far more important than mine was at OPA," he had written her at the time.) Now, though ready to stay in San Francisco, she was insistent that they not return to Whittier. "Do you still like San Francisco as well or better than L.A. or D.C.? Should we live there afterwards?" he asked that spring. And after another exchange of letters in April, he wrote, "So you are inclined to stay in California instead of trying Washington or something in the East?" She told him in irritation about running into a former Whittier student in San Francisco after she had "one beer after work last evening . . . sure she whiffed it, but of course, nothing was said." He responded about Whittier: "Too many restrictions, etc. A little freedom is far more important than security, don't you agree?"

By the beginning of the summer, he had his orders to return home, and she wrote him a last, extraordinary letter, a kind of epitaph on the old independence she had regained and clearly enjoyed in his absence. It was in its way a warning and foreboding.

> I will have to admit that I am pretty self-reliant and if I didn't love you I would feel very differently. In fact, these many months you have been away have been full of interest, and had I not missed you so much and had I been footloose, could have been extremely happy. So, Sweet, You'll always have to love me lots and never let me change my feelings for you which has [sic] been so wonderful all these years. . . . Will you love me when I'm shriveled and ridiculous looking?

Nixon's last night on Green his men "borrowed all the liquid they could find," as a friend remembered it, "and gave him a big party. All of them were strong for him, and hated to see him go." He would leave with two battle stars and a commendation for his "meritorious and efficient performance as officer-in-charge" of the SCAT units on Bougainville and Green. Nixon had "displayed sound judgment and initiative," read the citation, praising in well-worn naval prose his "able leadership, tireless efforts, and devotion to duty." Privately, his marine commander, Carl Fleps, had given him "outstanding" efficiency marks. "He was that kind of officer," Fleps would say later of the rating.

He flew on to Guadalcanal and then northeastward toward Pearl Harbor. On a refueling stop at Midway Island, he got out in the middle of the night to stretch his legs and wandered into one of Midway's cemeteries, "row after row" of white crosses, as he recalled, "beginning at the edge of the runway and stretching out into the darkness on that tiny island so far from home." He would long remember standing there in the warm Pacific night. "I was overcome with the ultimate futility of war," he wrote, "and the terrible reality of the loss that lies behind it."

But for now he was excitedly on the way home. His ship from Hawaii docked at San Diego July 17, 1944. He had wired Pat, and she flew down to meet him. Nixon was at the airport gate when she got off the plane. She ran toward him, she told her daughter later, and, as he had promised, he swept her up in a joyous, uninhibited embrace.

III

CONGRESS AND
THE HISS CASE

10

Running for Congress,
July 1944–June 1946

On a balmy spring evening in wartime Washington, the moist heat of the afternoon still hovered over tree-lined streets and sidewalks of Capitol Hill.

A few days before, a Pasadena attorney named John Packard brought to his congressman and old friend, Jerry Voorhis, the shocking details of a government contract secretly concluded some months earlier. Under the contract terms, Standard Oil would be allowed to exploit for private profit the vast U.S. Navy petroleum reserve at Elk Hills in central California. The stakes were enormous. Not far from the Beeson ranch at Lindsay, part of the Teapot Dome scandal young Richard Nixon read about so indignantly twenty years before, Elk Hills was thought to be the richest oilfield in the world outside Arabia, its public land long coveted by huge oil companies. The contract gave Standard Oil five years of exclusive free drilling, with $20 million in immediate profit and the potential for billions more in the economic boom expected to follow the war. The corporation, one observer wrote later, "had succeeded where the robber barons of Teapot Dome had failed."

But now, late on this Friday evening, May 21, 1943, Congressman Voorhis suddenly walked onto the floor of the House of Representatives and revealed the terms of the contract in a bold, irate speech. Under the glare of congressional inquiry, the shady deal was soon canceled. "VOORHIS HERO IN NAVAL OIL LEASE EXPOSÉ," headlined the *Washington Post*, praising the California congressman for his "militant honesty" in bringing the "major scandal" to light. Even his conservative colleague, Georgia's irascible Carl Vinson, thought Jerry Voorhis had performed "the greatest kind of service."

With that brief flurry, however, the episode promptly disappeared from public view, soon forgotten altogether amid the larger tumult of the war.

Yet the moment went beyond a fleeting case of profiteering and the conscientious politician who uncovered it. In terms of the base elements of American politics—money and power—the event would be crucial in the 1946 congressional election still three years and three thousand miles away in southern California's twelfth district. In both symbol and substance, a warm May evening in Washington in 1943 marked the beginning of Richard Nixon's political career.

"I AM AFRAID NO MORE"

Horace Jeremiah Voorhis was then in his early forties, a pale, handsome young exception amid the ruddy coarseness of the U.S. Congress of the Depression and war years. The son of an executive for Nash Motors with some lucrative oil investments of his own, he had grown up in a well-to-do devoutly Episcopal and Republican home in the Midwest. He was educated at Hotchkiss and went on to graduate Phi Beta Kappa from Yale in 1923. But it was religion far more than wealth or class that shaped his life, and he was imbued early and lastingly with the sense of personal sacrifice, service, and egalitarianism of the social gospel. A half century later, he remembered vividly the day J. Stitt Wilson, the evangelist and socialist mayor of Berkeley, came to Yale to preach "the gospel of Christian involvement," how Wilson had engaged them at the close with a stern, quiet passion: "Now, I want everybody to stand up with his eyes open and look me in the eye, and we're going to recite the Lord's Prayer."

After college, while much of the rest of his generation and class graduated into the hedonism and boom of the twenties, Voorhis gently spurned his wealth, worked for a time as a thirty-nine-cent-an-hour factory laborer, toured German slums for the YMCA, briefly ran an Episcopal orphanage in Wyoming, married a social worker. At the end of the decade, he and his father devoted most of the family fortune to found the Voorhis School for Boys, a small tile-roofed compound for homeless young men near San Dimas, California, in the Pomona valley some twelve miles northeast of Whittier. There he earned a master's degree at the new Claremont Graduate School nearby, lectured on other campuses on American history and economics, and taught, coached, even nightly tucked in his orphans. With the worsening Depression, Voorhis was first a registered socialist, then a New Deal Democrat increasingly caught up in the basin's fervent reform politics. He helped organize cooperatives among small ranchers and farmers and walked local picket lines, all with the abiding conviction that the stricken

American system might still reflect the Christian ideal. "We could produce plenty for all but we don't do it . . . we will do it only when all producing wealth is owned publicly," he wrote in one of his first published articles in the bleak fall of 1933, adding in a characteristic blur of piety and politics, "Incidentally, we would then be living in the Kingdom of God."

Voorhis was spurred to political candidacy by EPIC, the End Poverty in California movement of Upton Sinclair's heady but vain gubernatorial campaign in 1934. He first ran and lost beside Sinclair that year in a race for the State Assembly but then emerged in 1936 to win the congressional seat in the still harshly depressed twelfth district, beating a wealthy Republican lawyer whom one reporter would describe as a "smug reactionary." His opponent had characterized their contest as "Americanism vs. Socialism," and from the beginning Voorhis faced the now ludicrous, now vicious Red-baiting that was even then the staple of local Republican campaigns. In fact, he was always a forceful opponent of the small but aggressive communist faction maneuvering at the edge of California politics. Ten years later, the morning after his crushing defeat in one of the worst smear campaigns the basin had ever seen, an old friend would write to Jerry Voorhis in bitterly ironic memory of a local convention in 1935: "I remember how you stood in the center aisle and pled with the delegates not to team up with the communists."

Rumpled, reflective, smoking a pipe in professorial mien, Voorhis worked eighteen-hour days in Congress that set him clearly apart from the customary Capitol Hill languor. His earnestness awed admirers and disarmed even cranky opponents. "Driven by conscience, he had a compulsion to master every subject that came before the House, and having mastered it, he spoke his mind," said his colleague, Paul Douglas, who watched him often in his office, with books and documents piled high, former students of the Voorhis School working on the staff. Capital reporters called him "Kid Atlas" for his eager, often impolitic shouldering of issues. But in periodic polls they repeatedly voted him among the "most serious men in Congress," the "hardest working," "first in integrity," the most consistent in "putting national issues above local ones."

When the Roosevelt administration sought a decent but resolute Democrat at the end of the 1930s to sit on the notoriously bigoted and witch-hunting House Committee on Un-American Activities, someone who could be "counted upon," as *Time* put it, "to temper rightist blasts for leftist lambs," they chose Voorhis. On HUAC he waged a rear-guard effort against the committee's habitual excesses while proving in his own right a skilled inquisitor of the communists, whom he temperamentally and philosophically loathed, even sponsoring and passing in 1940 a bill requiring registration of political groups tied to a foreign power, a stricture aimed directly at the Communist Party's allegiance to the Soviet Union as well as at the fascist German-American Bund. That legislation would be another sharp irony in light of what followed. After a decade in Congress—and despite his key role in much other legislation—the antisubversive Voorhis Act would be the only major law to bear his name. In the process, Voorhis witnessed at first hand the politics of smear and fear that made the then still isolated, disreputable committee an ugly prototype of the era to come, a moment for which he would be strangely unprepared when the venom was turned on him. When he left the committee in 1943 he had satisfied neither right nor left. "Wobbly as usual," complained committee scourge Harold Ickes, while columnist Drew Pearson thought Voorhis "so kindly and altrustic that he often defeats his own purpose." His "only real weakness," Walter Goodman, a historian of the committee, concluded afterward, "was that of a rational, fair-minded, and courteous man thrown into the company of men who were irrational, unfair, discourteous and who had the power to satisfy their rudest passions. He was like a graduate student in sociology trying to talk sense to the drunkards in a skid-row bar." In the end, it would be an epitaph on Jerry Voorhis in American politics, the image of the student reasoning with skid row.

His pet issues concerned the financial system and the curbing of monopoly, an outgrowth of both his academic interest and populist strains in the basin, the old quest of the disappointed migrants for some quick adjustment in the landscape of money and class. Voorhis wrote three books on fiscal and currency reform. But the volumes, like most of his speeches, seemed esoteric, his analysis of the abuses and solutions at the murky heart of financial power too complicated for voters or congressional colleagues. His rare "deep thinking," thought the *Washington Star News*, of one book, "bids fair to lift him to the front rank among the nation's able young statesmen." At home in the little citrus settlements and insular towns of his district, it was different: "You tell people this," Voorhis would remember of his often rambling speeches," and they just do not believe it and even congressmen didn't believe it."

Still, he would win reelection by vigor and sheer likableness if not conversion to his cause, making more than a hundred speeches a month in some of the early runs, thriftily saving a fourth of his $10,000 salary to finance the simple campaigns, taking advantage of his incumbency and a troop of mediocre opponents. The twelfth's congressman would always be far more liberal than most of his district yet able to maintain a kind of acceptance by default. By the mid-1940s he had become a thoughtful, hard-working anomaly in both Washington and California, a representative enjoying much respect and little practical influence in the corridors of Congress. Jerry Voorhis was a politician with impassioned causes and no passionate enemies—until Elk Hills.

With the exposure of the oil scandal, the congressman from San Dimas would become a more visible, formidable figure, both in silhouette and substance. It was not alone the passing sensation of his May speech, the shift from polite books to blowing the whistle on a billon-dollar deal. Slowly but unmistakably, he struck out at powerful interests, Elk Hills seeming to give his attacks a new boldness as well as authority. Beyond Standard Oil's exploitation of the reserve, he opposed the whole petroleum industry and especially the California giants on questions of federal ownership of offshore oil and the oil depletion allowance. He then fought the exemption of the great insurance companies from antitrust regulation, challenged hoary corporate privileges in patent reform, antagonized the real-estate industry with plans for ambitious postwar public housing programs. At odds with the public utilities, Voorhis advocated an expansion of public power, backed tax-deduction reform violently opposed by both advertising agencies and newspaper publishers, and openly shunned government contracts in his own district that he thought wasteful. Meanwhile, he continued to support motion picture artists and workers in their bitter struggles with the Hollywood studios, and at one point even proposed to the horror of the liquor industry a temporary diversion of grain from production of alcohol to humanitarian relief in the famines following World War II.

After Elk Hills he returned with fresh fervor to his old economic targets, denouncing California's huge Bank of America for gobbling up small banks, warning of "the cancerous superstructure of monopolies and cartels" waiting to exploit the postwar period. Enlisting the powerful Wright Patman of the House Banking Committee, he engineered a reform requiring the Federal Reserve to turn over most of its earnings to the government, interest on government bonds once quietly held by member banks that would now save taxpayers billions. While often only the voice of a lone congressman, it was all stark, reckless politics. And occasionally, as in the Elk Hills speech or the Federal Reserve reform with Patman, it reached a raw nerve, an inner ganglion of economic and political arrangements Congress seldom acknowledged, much less altered. The Federal Reserve measure, one of his supporters would recall, "really brought the wrath" of the bankers and others. By the summer of 1945, Voorhis was no longer so tame.

As the war drew to an end, Paul Douglas and other liberals thought Jerry Voorhis a "political saint," his courage in making powerful adversaries matched by modesty. In Capitol Hill's sea of ego, the young idealist even publicly disavowed the traditional prefix "Hon." before his name as a waste of paper in the *Congressional Record*. Yet Voorhis, too, like the subtle arrangements and connections he delighted in exposing, was never altogether quite what he appeared on the surface. Beneath the unpretentious earnestness was a blithe confidence, a quiet vanity and puffery. Mixed with courage was a casualness, often fecklessness toward the politics at home that made his crusades possible. Deep within the thoughtful reformer was an almost mystic streak of self-doubt and absorption. "I cannot explain it," he had written in a personal diary at the outbreak of the war. "But I do know that I am afraid no more because I am filled with fear and that I despair no more because I am so filled with despair." The inner man, as well as the inner politics of his congressional record, would play a major role in his ultimate defeat, and thus in the making of Richard Nixon.

Reunited with his wife in mid-July 1944, Richard Nixon took three weeks of leave in Whittier. It was to be his last interlude at home before he returned as a full-fledged politician intent on a campaign. Family and friends remembered him as warm, relaxed, plainly nostalgic about the place he and Pat had privately agreed to avoid in any postwar plans. Trim and tan in his naval uniform, he visited the Wildermuths for an evening of piano playing, took red roses to a bedridden great aunt, spoke at an East Whittier Friends social supper, while quietly donating to the church and even giving a generous money gift to an old Sunday school friend in the hospital—all without his wife, who had returned to her OPA job in San Francisco. He also seemed proud and brashly uninhibited after his worldly months in the South Pacific. At a luncheon of more than thirty relatives and old acquaintances from Whittier and Yorba Linda, a civilian Milhous cousin was holding forth on military and political issues when Dick shocked everyone with his profane reproach. "Then all of a sudden, without real- izing what he was saying," as James Stewart recalled Nixon's reaction, "he leaned across the table and slapped down the old fellow in a language that we used only when the going was really tough. This stopped the conver- sation abruptly. The guests were amazed." Dick Heffern, his old friend from the Fullerton High orchestra, heard Nixon talk to a Kiwanis Club meeting about his war experiences and thought him far different from the shy youngster he had once driven to concerts. "Here he had blossomed into an extrovert, speaking about . . . the future," Heffern would say. "He was just completely changed."

In August he was assigned to the Alameda Naval Air Station near San Francisco, and the day before leaving Whittier wrote to a friend still on Green Island, registering the wartime flux in southern California that would be so important to his election two years later. "Things on this side are pretty messed up," he observed. "There are lines for absolutely everything— movies—restaurants—hotels etc. . . . If you are assigned to the West Coast—don't have families come out until you find a place to live—the housing shortage is terrible." At Alameda he was a base administrative officer, "chief janitor," as he would remember the job. "Lieutenant Nixon, has my desk been dusted this morning?" his commanding officer asked in a note Nixon angrily took home to his wife, who thought the incident "hilariously funny," as she later told her daughter, and saved the tightly folded note for the next forty years. But the posting was brief and did nothing to dampen his evident enthusiasm. FBI agent Robert King and his wife, Gretchen, who had known Pat in San Francisco, remembered the young officer late in 1944 as "an idealistic dreamer" who talked over dinner about grand questions of "the future of America and the world . . . about some new order which would make wars impossible."

In January 1945 Nixon was transferrred across the country to a navy legal unit negotiating the conclusion of war contracts with private corporations, first at Philadelphia, then for four months in New York City, where they lived in small apartments, buying what Pat remembered as "cheap seats at the Met." They were in a Philadelphia restaurant in April when they heard of FDR's death, and in Manhattan weeks later, after VE-Day, when Nixon looked down from his twentieth-floor office window on Church Street and watched the tumultuous tickertape parade for General Dwight Eisenhower. "I could see him standing in the back of his car with both arms raised high over his head," he recalled of the moment he first saw the man who was to be such a force in his political future.

That summer Pat learned she was pregnant, and they were transferred once again; this time to Middle River, Maryland, a naval post on Chesapeake Bay just east of Baltimore where Nixon, promoted to lieutenant commander, worked on terminating contracts for the Martin Mars flying boats and other projects. The war now over and his discharge only a matter of time, they were still uncertain about where they would settle or what he would do, though the taste of the large cities seemed to seal the decision not to return to Whittier. James Cobey, a young naval lawyer who worked with him at Middle River and knew them socially, thought them "the dullest couple we ever met in the navy . . . very conservative, very conventional, but on the way up—happy and optimistic."

"I'm eligible to get out now but have agreed to stay until January 1— to clear up a few terminations . . . I've had enough," Nixon wrote James Stewart in October 1945. Almost as an afterthought, he added that he was soon going back to California to talk to "a group" looking for a candidate for Congress. "I don't know if it will pan out," he casually closed the letter to his navy friend. "If it doesn't I believe I'll take a crack at business in the East."

The summer and fall of 1945, through the winter of 1946, began an extraordinary juncture in American political history. The writer James Agee, like Nixon seeing Eisenhower, looked down on the victory parades from a New York skyscraper, on what he saw as the "great and small homecomings," and wrote that September in one of his memorable letters to Father James Flye: "It is lovely. And God, what most of the homecomers, and those they come home to, are in for."

Agee's premonition caught the underlying paradox of the peace. In the wake of confetti and tickertape came all the pent-up frustration of the war effort and a resurgence of social and economic tensions never far beneath the surface of national unity over the preceding four years. Weary, impatient, the nation turned its wrath toward widespread shortages, and on the vestiges of wartime government controls believed to aggravate the scarcity. Above all, there was labor unrest. Whereas industrial amity was one of the war's myths, there had been since Pearl Harbor over 14,000 strikes of nearly seven million workers nationwide, far more than in any comparable period of the nation's history. Now the old, angry Depression-era battles of labor and management raged on more than ever into the postwar months, unions increasingly blamed for consumer hardships as the economy lurched back from its wartime boom, and the business opposition to workers' demands and economic reform grew ever more powerful.

To those strains was added a deepening sense of insecurity, confusion, and disillusionment with the world at large. If peace at home seemed tardy, abroad it soon appeared lost altogether. Through the months following the atomic explosions over Hiroshima and Nagasaki, the Bomb, with its palpable prospect of Apocalypse, was only beginning its cycles of alarm and numbness in America's political consciousness. But national apprehension was clear enough, "something momentous," as the *New York Herald Tribune* editorialized that autumn, "almost unfathomable." In an existence transformed by the Bomb, the collapse of the wartime coalition with Russia would seem all the more ominous. Fearful in its relative weakness, belligerent in its new strength, the Soviet Union in 1945–46 drew apart to claim its own spoils in Europe and Asia, while the West in matching fear and belligerence retreated to the old ideological enmity and strategic containment that had been its resort since the Russian revolution. The effect of the new Cold War on American politics was enormous from the beginning. "The knowledge of victory," said *Time* in an early postwar issue, "was as charged with sorrow and doubt as with joy and gratitude."

Inevitably, the domestic strife, the shadows of stalemate and danger in international affairs, took a political toll on the ruling Democrats, symbolized by Roosevelt's jaunty, seemingly crude and inept successor, Harry Truman. From coast to coast, recorded one journalist, the country appeared "under a pall of disgust with the Truman administration." Beyond the visible lines of pickets and shoppers, the economy was in fact sustaining the basic recovery brought by the war. The physical reconversion of industry to a peacetime basis would be practically completed by the end of 1945. During the next year farm income, business profits, and industrial production would all reach new peaks, while unemployment was little more than 3 percent and the long-dreaded postwar inflation still moderate. Meanwhile administration policy stiffened toward the Soviet threat. Pentagon officials promptly drafted secret plans for atomic war gruesomely code-named Broiler and Sizzle. Still, the relative prosperity at home and the gathering ferocity of foreign policy did not appease local resentments at meat or housing shortages or fear of the Russians. By the spring of 1946, the President's popularity had plummeted in the Gallup Poll from 87 percent to 32 percent. The wife of Senate Republican leader Robert Taft reduced the national mood to a quip. "To err," she said, "is Truman."

Yet there was now something more on the American political landscape, a force that would come to dominate the country's postwar history long after the other issues of 1945–46 had disappeared. It was symbolized by a Republican Party campaign pamphlet of the time, showing the Democratic donkey wearing a turban emblazoned with the hammer and sickle of the Soviet flag. The Democrats were "so divided between communism and Americanism," pronounced Senator Taft with rather less levity than his wife, that they were "dominated by a policy of appeasing the Russians abroad and of fostering communism at home."

Like the outbreak of a dormant plague, the post-Hiroshima Red Scare repeated the hysteria and hyperbole of the interval after the First World War, though with far more virulence and breadth. As in the earlier wave, the motives of the accusers and inquisitors would be mixed—a genuine ideological fear and repugnance of communism, sheer ignorance or xenophobia, and, not least, political opportunism. "Years of languishing out of power, helplessly watching the river of legislation enacted by the most important reform administration in American history," two historians wrote of the period, "had reduced the Republican Party to fury and desperation."

The venom would run well beyond political professionals to florid, influential spokesmen of industry and religion. "The problems of the United States can be captiously summed up in two words," announced Charles Wilson of General Motors. "Russia abroad and labor at home." Father John Cronin, a Catholic publicist who was to play a largely hidden but decisively significant role in Richard Nixon's career, spoke for much of the Church hierarchy when he wrote powerful business and government patrons in the spring of 1946, "There are reasons to believe that Soviet armies may be on the march in but a few weeks. . . . Within the nation, the communist fifth column is functioning smoothly, especially within the ranks of government." The rhetoric licensed its anxious listeners everywhere to wander over the edge of political sanity. "The Reds have a lot to do with our current, very serious labor situation," Chamber of Commerce leader John J. Sullivan declared during the wave of postwar strikes in the winter of 1945–46. "We will have to set up some firing squads in every good-sized city and town in the country and . . . liquidate the Reds and Pink Benedict Arnolds."

The deliberate drumroll of fear and suspicion continued until it enveloped the political life of the nation, the Democrats themselves vying in vigilance and bellicosity. No single impulse so shaped American foreign policy and domestic politics, and the public discourse underlying both, for a generation. None would be so vital in Richard Nixon's rise from an obscure young lawyer and navy veteran waiting for discharge in Middle River, Maryland, to the threshhold of Presidential power in little more than a decade. Yet later, when Nixon had ridden the crest of the wave, had become in many ways the most successful and respectable beneficiary of the angry, troubled force, it would be forgotten that much of the force was already there, part of the remarkable setting in which he began his climb in the fall of 1945. And still later, when the moment and its exploitation had become an embarrassment, it would be simpler to believe that it had never really been so important at all.

"SALABLE MERCHANDISE"

Those national currents found particular expression, often exaggeration, in California, in the volatile political landscape that was the more immediate setting for Richard Nixon's political start.

The war had ended with vivid symbolism in California politics. On the August morning the atom bomb was dropped on Hiroshima, seventy-nine-year-old Senator Hiram Johnson lay dying in his hospital bed. Johnson was the towering political force in California, a colorful renegade progressive whom one historian would aptly call "a bloc of one" in the U.S. Senate, and whose bellowing isolationism now seem extinguished, body and soul, with the instant of nuclear fission over a Japanese city. He had left California, however, a more enduring legacy than just his florid style. Thirty-five years before, his governorship in Sacramento had been a model of progressive reform, enacting a direct primary, civil service regulations, women's suffrage, initiative, referendum, and recall. It was a lethal blow to the old political machines with their rotten patronage and bequeathed to California in many respects one of the most democratic and effective state governments in the nation. But swept away in the debris were also the discipline and organizational cohesion of both the Republican and Dem-

ocratic parties, and Hiram Johnson's hopeful reforms were to have an unexpected sequel.

As the traditional party structures collapsed, the old graft and control
simply seeped into new channels. Intended as tools of popular participation
in government, the new and exploitable levers of petition politics allowed
well-financed special interest groups and other disciplined factions—those
with the price of a public relations firm, the quarter-a-signature for petitions,
the budget for advertising—to seize the legislative agenda or punish a foe.
The press and other purveyors of image would come to replace the old
party bosses as the brokers of the new power. Throughout the state, but
most of all in the rootless, heaving migration of the Los Angeles basin,
politics passed from program or conviction to manipulation of the shifting
crowd. What emerged was California's then still unique political feudalism
and fealty, campaigns and regimes formed around personalities, with issues,
ideology, and party accountability increasingly blurred.

The archetypes of that ironic Thermidor to progressive reform were a
husband-and-wife team little known outside California but by the 1940s
legendary among the state's politicians. Clem Whittaker was a tall, thin
asthmatic, the shrewd son of a Baptist preacher and a free-lance political
reporter in Sacramento in the 1920s, Leone Baxter the crisp, equally clever
manager of a small-town Chamber of Commerce in northern California.
Together, married literally and politically in their own firm, Whittaker and
Baxter would manage, instigate, and manipulate scores of referenda and
campaigns, winning all but a handful and becoming in themselves the
equivalent of a powerful, dependable political machine. Their stern formula, as Theodore White would describe it, was to "twitch an unin-
formed electorate by its nerve ends," to reach and engage the average,
usually uncommitted California voter with a few simplified issues framed
in an emotional appeal.

Above all, they believed, the swaying of the distracted, partyless public
dictated attack on some enemy clear or vague, a fear the crowd could
somehow share. They would exploit the politics of resentment at a moment
and in a place where resentments came quickly and ran deep. Causes and
candidates might vary, though the clients of Whittaker and Baxter, reflecting the partners' own temper, were almost without exception conservative
Republicans. The essence in any case lay less in substance than in method.
And by the mid-1940s, that juncture of Hiroshima with the death of Hiram
Johnson, the unwitting godfather of the new politics of imagery, their
approach had inspired imitators at every level of California politics. "For
a million-dollar fee," a wheezing Clem Whittaker would boast, "I could
make tuberculosis popular."

The political habits cultivated in that approach to government could be raw and often vicious. California was largely a Republican preserve for the first four decades of the century. Democrats got less than a third of the votes for governor and even less for Presidential candidates. They were outnumbered ten to one in the State Assembly, sent not a single state senator to Sacramento for much of the twenties, and did not even contest primaries in half of the state's congressional districts. Then, suddenly and radically, the old order seemed in danger of changing with the great migrations of the Depression. John Steinbeck's Joads and other refugees from the Dust Bowl poured into the state with traditional Democratic sympathies as well as their discontent. By the early thirties there were over 350,000 unemployed in Los Angeles County, and 20 percent of the population subsisted on monthly welfare payments of $6.20 per family. The first test was Upton Sinclair's run for governor in 1934, the muckraking utopian socialist winning the Democratic nomination at the head of his EPIC movement, "this vast, inchoate coalition," one writer called it, "of Roosevelt liberals, Single Taxers, Socialists, Communists, Syndicalists, vegetarians, old-age pensioners, Wobblies, populists, goldbugs, and calendar reformers." It was vintage Californian. So, too, was the political reaction.

Sinclair was scorned and attacked on all sides. George Creel, the titular Democratic leader, saw no choice "between the epilepsy of Sinclair and the catalepsy" of Republicans, and thought visiting the EPIC stronghold in the basin "like plunging into darkest Africa without gun bearers." For their part, California communists labeled Sinclair a "faker and forthcoming fascist." But the more potent response came from business interests threatened by Sinclair's pledge to raise corporate taxes and welfare payments, and particularly from Hollywood studios angered by an earlier Sinclair exposé on the film industry as well as his proposed economic reforms. Vigilante teams beat up EPIC organizers in rural areas. The *Los Angeles Times* and other Republican newspapers published invented "news photos" with hired actors showing tramps streaming into the state to live off EPIC, denouncing Sinclair as a "dangerous Bolshevik beast" out to "Russianize" California. Hollywood similarly contrived and widely distributed "newsreel" footage depicting Republican supporters as respectable and Sinclair backers as dirty, unshaven, poorly educated, and often speaking in East European accents, some of the "news" spliced from an old Warner Brothers movie *Wild Boys of the Road*.

Partly orchestrated by Whittaker and Baxter, the campaign crushed Sinclair in a state where Democratic registration was nonetheless becoming a clear majority. Afterward, young EPIC supporters like Jerry Voorhis had wept in dismay at the defeat. Their opponents were less sentimental. When young Fredric March complained at a cocktail party to movie mogul Irving Thalberg about the savagery and fraud, Thalberg had replied, "Nothing is unfair in politics."

The Democrats rallied briefly in 1938 to elect their first governor of the century, and then four years later promptly fell back into relative eclipse precisely as their registration advantage grew to nearly a million voters in the wartime boom. The paradox, like most of California politics for more than a decade, resided in the shadow cast by the remarkable Republican first elected governor in 1942—Earl Warren.

With twinkling blue eyes and an easy warmth in his massively handsome face, Warren was in some ways an authentic genius of the new California method, a politician without visible politics, a candidate running above mere candidacy. He was the son of a Norwegian railway repairman in Los Angeles, and as a small child worked as a callboy for the roundhouses, waking the exhausted men in their grim dormitories to resume the morning shift, watching strikes broken by police charging on horseback. His political chance came after struggling through college and law school at Berkeley and service in World War I, when he went to work in the district attorney's office in Oakland in Alameda County, where the ruling belief, said one historian, was "in the Republican Party, the open shop, and God, not necessarily, but usually, in that order." First as assistant, then as DA himself, eventually attorney general and then governor, Warren rose as the protégé of "Silk Hat" Joe Knowland, publisher of the *Oakland Tribune* and one of the old Republican bosses anathema to Hiram Johnson. The loyalty and debt to his patron would always be there. Even in the Governor's Mansion, it was said, the Warrens borrowed their silver from the Knowlands.

Yet as governor, at fifty-one, Warren soon fixed on a fierce nonpartisanship. His instinctive moderation became a principle of policy as he steadily fostered the social legislation, highways and state institutions, the bipartisan expertise and professionalism in the Sacramento bureaucracy to preside over the state's vast wartime growth. He grew increasingly scrupulous about the influence of party or money on government. "You could support him, but you couldn't buy him," one of his backers, Stanley Barnes, recalled, remembering the governor indignantly rejecting a request for a favor from a wealthy oil executive. "I am not interested in politial machines," Warren would say in 1946. "No man should be permitted to be both governor and political boss."

At once the most popular executive in the state's history and the least responsive to party or patronage, he was a maddening enigma to Republican partisans. "One leg astride the Republican elephant and the other clinging affectionately to the Democratic donkey," a GOP leader ridiculed him. While Warren stood serenely aloof in his own political dominance, Democrats still held sixteen of California's twenty-five congressional seats. Perhaps worst of all, the governor had become plainly loath to join the ritual Red-baiting reborn with a vengeance amid postwar tensions and ambitions, to denounce the "leftists, pinkoes and outright communists" the *Los Angeles Times* defined collectively as Democrats. By the summer of 1945, Warren governed with many of his own Republicans in sullen, smoldering revolt at his policies and politics. The insurgency was to break into the open full-blown a few years later with historic consequences for California and the nation, but for the moment, the rebels had nowhere to go. "They feared the Democrats more than they feared him," one reporter wrote of the frustrated Republicans.

Discontent was all the more bitter because the party lacked even the traditional petty patronage in Sacramento. In a characteristic incident, Warren was approached early in his first gubernatorial term by a young Republican lawyer from Los Angeles named Murray Chotiner, who had campaigned for him and who now wanted state jobs for party workers and a favor on an extradition case. Warren had thrown him out of the office. "After that, I told people that if they wanted something from Warren," Chotiner would say, "they'd better not ask me to get it for them." Then, as later, Earl Warren would be above it all in a way and with a strength few of his peers understood, to the end that incongruous rarity of American politics in either party, an independent man.

Warren's disdain for party campaign organization as for party government made the GOP in 1945–46 what one leader called "a monstrous patchwork quilt," a loose collection of local groups organized around congressional district races or other parochial contests. The unique small machines of postwar California politics, fired by a twin bitterness toward Warren and the New Deal, they practiced the volatile campaign methods of Whittaker and Baxter by their own lights and left the stamp of both purpose and technique indelibly on a generation of candidates. One of them would now succeed beyond any imagination, producing out of the intraparty and partisan strife not only a rival and nemesis of Earl Warren but a future President of the United States.

Lyle Otterman, who had gone to work at the local Bank of America after Whittier College, was at his desk early one morning in September 1945 when the bank manager, Herman Perry, came in and startled him with a question about an old college classmate: "What would you think of Dick Nixon running against Jerry Voorhis?" Otterman thought Voorhis "a pretty smooth operator," whereas the last Republican candidate "bored you to death." "Well, I think it's an excellent idea. He can at least talk. That's something you haven't been able to find anybody to do yet," Otterman had replied to the powerful older man, adding to Perry's obvious delight, "If Nixon really gets wound up, he will probably run Voorhis off the platform." That same day, Otterman and others remembered, Perry had talked with Harold Lutz at the bank, with editor Rex Kennedy at the *Whittier Daily News*, with Aubrey Wardman and other wealthy Republican contributors. He then called Don Nixon at the grocery to get Dick's address in Maryland and quickly sent off a momentous letter. "I am writing you this short note to ask if you would like to be a candidate for Congress on the Republican ticket in 1946. Jerry Voorhis expects to run—registration is about fifty-fifty. The Republicans are gaining. Please airmail me your reply if you are interested." Perry added a P.S. "Are you a registered voter in California?"

The Nixons spent two days talking excitedly after receiving the letter, discussing "the heady idea of serving in Washington, " as Pat would recall their mood, though worrying about whether they would have to spend any of their $10,000 war savings in the campaign. He remembered clearly, if she did not, the lack of even gas money for his abortive assembly run in the spring of 1940. There were also misgivings about returning, after all, to the provincial small towns of the basin they had deliberately fled in 1940 and decided again to avoid after the war. Still, the chance was irresistible. Around midnight on October 1, 1945, Nixon telephoned Perry from Middle River, saying he was "honored" by the letter and "excited" at the prospect of running. Discreetly but unmistakably, he told the banker that money was a primary condition.

"If you fellows out there think you can put on a campaign, I'd like to come out," he said at the outset. At that, Perry had pulled back—"poured some cold water on my enthusiasm," Nixon rememberd. The banker cautioned that the nomination was "not his to offer," that he had written on behalf of the twelfth district group of Republicans searching for a candidate, and there were other contenders. If Nixon were serious, however, he could be flown out for an appearance before the group. Near the end of the conversation Perry asked again, as in the letter, about Nixon's registration, and wrote afterward that Dick had replied "he guessed he was a Republican because of the fact that he had voted for Tom Dewey in the South Pacific." It was to be the basis of an oft-repeated myth that Perrry and his associates did not even know Richard Nixon's politics, though the 1940 Assembly bid and other maneuvers before the war had left no doubt.

The morning after their talk, Nixon sent Perry a letter to confirm his interest. "I feel very strongly that Jerry Voorhis can be beaten, and I'd welcome the opportunity to take a crack at him," he wrote with characteristic ardor and no little prophecy. "An aggressive, vigorous campaign on a platform of practical liberalism should be the antidote the people have been looking for to take the place of Voorhis's particular brand of New Deal idealism." He added that "my brief experience in Washington with

271

the bureaucrats and my three and a half years in the navy have given me a pretty good idea of what a mess things are in Washington."

The call and letter, the ever-eager ambition behind them, thrust Nixon into the tangled Republican politics of California's twelfth district. It was true enough that the nomination as a congressional candidate could not simply be conferred by Herman Perry, though the Quaker bank manager represented a powerful Whittier faction in a larger party gathering whose avowed purpose was indeed to handpick a challenger to Voorhis. The search had begun in the frustration after the 1944 election. They seemed to have a chance that year in the wake of Elk Hills. There was party unity, ample money—everything but a candidate. "A stodgy reactionary with a colorless personality," one observer called Roy McLaughlin, the South Pasadena oilman chosen in 1944 by the party central committee. While clearly sympathetic to business, the hapless McLaughlin even showed a dismaying penchant for making appeals to labor in front of the district's more affluent audiences. "He did everything he could to discourage anybody that had over fifteen cents in the bank," Roy Day, one of the Central Committee, would say afterward. That same symbolic summer of 1945—while Jerry Voorhis was home working the district, "sunk in a morass of speeches, meetings and promises to do this and that," as he wearily wrote his Washington secretary—Day had decided to act. He followed an old party plan for a "fact-finding" organization and assembled on his own initiative local GOP activists and contributors from each of the three Assembly districts. They were roughly apportioned in ratio to Republican votes in 1944, and nearly half of them came from the lush, wealthy suburbs at the western end of the twelfth. An advertising salesman with an eye for labels, Day named them grandly the Committee of 100.

They saw themselves in retrospect as a unique grass-roots political body, "just a rump," as one of them would mockingly describe the party organization's disdain for them. Only when the Los Angeles County leaders "bitched so much about it," Day remembered, did they include members of the county committee. "I don't necessarily want the presidents of the bank or the building and loan or all the big shots up and down the main street," Day described his purpose. "That's been the trouble with our party. What I want is people that have a following." With that, the committee was to democratize the old selection process, what Day caustically saw as "two or three bigwigs [who] meet in a locked-up room someplace and pick a candidate." Yet their underlying purpose was to avoid an open primary campaign with its divisiveness and cost and to substitute their own judgment and politics for the old party organization and methods. They would preempt the nomination by giving their choice in the bargain a formidable, well-oiled campaign supported by most of the twelfth's Republican stalwarts. "We will endorse ONE candidate," Roy Day wrote one prospect, "set up a finance committee, public relations committee, campaign organization, and unite our efforts to elect." In the event, they escaped neither the "big shots" nor the "locked-up room."

Day placed stories about the search in local newspapers, and through August and September, 1945, they met in various towns around the twelfth to hear would-be candidates. It had been a disappointing train. One articulate prospect had once been registered as a socialist, and when they discovered by chance his secret, as Day remembered it, "we sure crucified him in a hurry." The rest were unimpressive, people simply "looking for a job," recalled Frank Jorgensen, a San Marino insurance executive who after the fifth meeting had been ready to disband. "My God, if this is all we can get to run for Congress, let's not waste our time," he told them. Anxiously they asked Stanley Barnes, a former football star at Berkeley and prominent young GOP attorney, but Barnes had turned them down, like many Republicans skeptical at defeating a "well-entrenched" Voorhis. "Nobody wanted to run," Barnes said later. "They asked a lot of other people to run, but they wouldn't do it." Watching periodic press reports of committee meetings, Jack Long, Voorhis's local campaign manager, wrote the congressman reassuringly on October 6, 1945, about "the effort to find someone to beat you in 1946. None of them appear dangerous," he concluded.

Then in mid-October there was a brief flurry of activity around the nomination. On the eleventh, quoting "Republican leaders" in the district and county, the *Los Angeles Times* and other papers suddenly proposed General George S. Patton, the truculent, brilliant hero of the war in Europe who had just been relieved of his command by Eisenhower for insubordination and whose U.S residence was one of the sprawling estates of San Marino. " 'Old Blood and Guts' against blue-blooded, wealthy, left-wing Rep. H. Jerry Voorhis . . . a political ten-strike if it could be done," thought the *Times*. Twenty-four hours later the boomlet was dead with a characteristically blunt statement from Patton at his German headquarters that he would "keep completely out of politics."

While Patton swiftly came and went, there was another, more serious proto-candidacy. Day himself had put forward the name of Walter Dexter, the fifty-two-year-old former president of Whittier College who had become Warren's state superintendent of public instruction. Tempted, torn between his prestigious appointment and the uncertainty of a political race, Dexter had talked with Day by telephone and wired him October 8 that "I am not certain that I should not become a candidate in the twelfth district." Five days later, in the wake of Patton's rejection, Day wrote back an imploring letter. "This district wants to go Republican, but it wants a candidate we can be really FOR and not just register a protest vote against Jerry Voorhis." Dexter, the dignified minister and educator, was "worthy of a really all-out effort," and Voorhis would "appear to be a schoolboy on the platform against you." Day urged him "to very seriously consider this matter from all angles" and promised to postpone the next Committee of 100 meeting until November 2, giving Dexter time to meet them and make a decision during a trip to Los Angeles planned for October 25. "I know, Walter, that very powerful interests want to sit down and talk this over with you or go to bat for you," Day concluded his appeal, "if you will make a definite decision to go into the race."

Over the next week, Dexter vacillated. At one point he asked Day if the "very powerful interests" mentioned in the October 13 letter might "guarantee" an equivalent job and salary of $10,500 yearly if he gave up his state position and lost the election. The committee's first serious prospect, Dexter's potential candidacy also opened the first factional schism among the searchers, the opposition ironically including Perry and some of the Whittier Quaker conservatives still galled by Dexter's liberalizing presidency at the college a decade before. "There were some who did not warm up to the idea," the Los Angeles Times reported under a headline "Dexter Boomed as GOP Hope." Yet the cheerful academic had the support of both the Times and the decisive San Marino group within the committee. Day's letter had been tantamount to an offer of the endorsement and, with it, the primary nomination. Then, four days before he was due to come to Los Angeles, the selection his for the asking, Dexter collapsed and died of a heart attack in Sacramento. "If Walter Dexter had lived and had decided to accept the offer," A. Kenneth Spencer, a committee leader, would say afterward, "we wouldn't have looked further." For the first time, though not the last, the sudden death of a rival was to be decisive in Richard Nixon's career.

On October 23, the same day Dexter's obituary appeared in the Whittier News, the paper's political column noted that "Lieu. [sic] Commander Dick Nixon was seriously being considered" for the congressional nomination. It was the first public reference to Nixon's candidacy, which Herman Perry had been quietly promoting as a foil to Dexter since the midnight call from Middle River. Even before Nixon's response to his letter, Perry had picked up a startled Don Fantz, a local appliance dealer who knew Dick in 20–30, took him along to a September 29 dinner of the Committee, and asked Fantz to give an impromptu testimonial to Nixon. On October 3 Perry had written each member of the committee on Bank of America stationery "to advise that some of the people in the Whittier area are interested in suggesting the name of Lt. [sic] Richard Nixon, USNR." The young man "served his country as an attorney for the OPA at the request of Duke

University," as Perry quaintly, less than accurately described the Washington interval, and "he resigned his position when war was declared." He also, the banker added, "comes from good Quaker stock . . . is a very aggressive individual . . . [and] was an orator and debator [*sic*] in high school and college."

Meanwhile, unaware of Perry's lobbying, Dexter himself had also mentioned Nixon to Day—"spoke very highly of him," Day recorded. In understatement, Dexter told the Republican leader that Nixon "had evidenced . . . some interest in political endeavor." By mid-October, the choice had narrowed to Dexter with Nixon an unknown if promising second. "If he does not decide to run, which of course is a big question mark, I am sure he would back Nixon," Day wrote Perry on October 12 about his conversations with Walter Dexter. "Frankly, these are the only two I found much talk for at the present time. . . . Not as head of the committee, but off the record, I would suggest that you try very hard to get Lt. Comdr. Nixon out here on November 2." Dexter's sudden passing now left a single serious prospect for the already postponed meeting.

Within days, Frank Jorgensen and others of the San Marino group drove to Whittier to check on Perry's candidate for themselves. There they talked with Tom Bewley, and even went by the grocery, "the small crossroads store," as Jorgensen remembered it, where Hannah Nixon once again quietly promoted her son and made a lasting impression. "She looked to me like a strong woman . . . she knew what she was doing." With Jorgensen's accession, Perry now wired Nixon to get a flight from Baltimore to arrive in Los Angeles October 31, for which the committee would reimburse him, as well as provide his return ticket.

Hurrying to get on a plane in the still scarce, crowded flights of the postwar autumn, Nixon asked an executive of one of the companies whose contract terminations he had negotiated, Engineering and Research Corporation of Riverdale, Maryland, to use its air travel card and accompanying preference to buy the seat. Nixon in turn would pay back ERCO a week later. In a sense, the ticket arrangement was his first act as a congressional candidate and at the time seemingly a trivial expedient. Of its kind it was also an omen. The credit card purchase was technically legal yet had the appearance of a favor from a company doing government business in which he was involved. It was one of those incidents on the gray margin of propriety, and sometimes beyond, that would plague his political life to the end.

For the moment, however, he was flying back to California to a nomination, and destiny, that was now his virtually by default, though the inner politics of the committee remained hidden from view. "Day is still without a candidate," Long reassured Jerry Voorhis again during October, adding on the thirtieth, as Richard Nixon flew westward with the committee factions prepared to approve him, "They are already commencing to fight among themselves."

Primed by Day, local newspapers throughout the district announced on their front pages the November 2 meeting, invited "any man or woman who has any desire to become a candidate for Congress," but noting in particular that naval officer Nixon "is flying here from Baltimore, Maryland, especially for the occasion." He was welcomed home as a conquering hero. On Thursday evening, November 1, Herman Perry arranged a testimonial for Nixon at Whittier's Dinner Bell Ranch. A curb-to-curb banner strung over one of Whittier's main streets announced "RICHARD NIXON IS RETURNING TO WHITTIER." Puzzled and amused, Philip Blew saw the banner and wondered what money or "claque" was behind the publicity for his old friend from 20–30. At the banquet, along with more than forty friends and relatives, were Day, the local assemblyman, and various Republican Party officials, giving the whole affair an air of official sanction. Returning veterans "don't want a dole, nor do they want governmental employment or bread lines," Nixon told them after a glowing introduction from Harry Schuyler, their old neighbor on Santa Gertrudes. "They want a fair chance at the American way of life." Beaming, Roy Day moved around the room after the dinner was over, telling the milling guests, "This man is salable merchandise."

By far the most important gathering of his visit, however, took place in private the next day, hours before he was to appear in front of the larger committee. With Nixon already obviously known and backed by Perry and the Whittier faction, Day had suggested that the candidate meet discreetly with the San Marino group apart from the formal evening session and audition speeches. At noon on Friday they came together in a small private dining room of the fashionable University Club in Los Angeles. The eight men Richard Nixon faced at lunch that day were all to be significant to the political emergence at hand, and some were crucial in his life and career for years to come.

Roy Day, besides Nixon the only nonmember of the club, was then forty-six. Balding, round-faced, with a thickening frame, he was the son of a Pomona orange rancher. After dropping out of high school, he had pitched semi-pro baseball, drifted through jobs for United Fruit in Costa Rica, and ended up back in the basin as an ad salesman for a Pomona newspaper. With the zeal, affability, and simplicity of a small-town booster, Day entered Republican politics in 1944, managing the Assembly race of a local laundryman. He emerged with a set of campaign nostrums as well as a fearsome taste for political competition. "I've never gone on the basis of just playing to win. I like to win and I play hard to win," he once described his attitude. "You have to carry the fight all the way, never get on the defensive. Nice guys and sissies don't win elections." Named to the GOP county committee from the twelfth, Day had soon become what one associate called a "Republican wheelhorse," in many ways the epitome of the citizen volunteer, relishing the process and battle more than cause or issue. He was now at the University Club because of his initiative in organizing the Committee of 100. But his role in the campaign, notable at first, would swiftly recede. The others were of a different class and cachet.

Frank Jorgensen was the informal leader of the San Marino group. Tall, heavyset, shrewd, and hard-working, he was a forty-three-year-old insurance executive on the way to becoming a vice president of Metropolitan Life. He brought to the table a nearly morbid distrust of Roosevelt and the New Deal. Having once registered as a Progressive to vote for a friend, Jorgensen kept the registration for a time, saying only half in jest, "If they shoot all the Republicans in the country, at least we Progressives may be able to live." Like other GOP businessmen and political activists, he had also clashed early with Earl Warren, going to Sacramento for a postelection favor in the 1940s and promptly being turned down in an angry, profane exchange with the governor. "What's wrong with that?" he had yelled at Warren. "We work our ass off for you during election time." Now rising rapidly in the booming corporate world of Los Angeles, successful as an organizer in community politics, he thought the old Republicans in the twelfth "far from energetic" but Voorhis far from unbeatable. "Why," he impatiently asked an early committee meeting, "are we having a congressman who had been a socialist, and now a Democrat in the Roosevelt image, representing *us*?" With Jorgenson then and now were two others from San Marino of similar age and background: Boyd Gibbons, the heir of a large Los Angeles Ford dealership, and Rockwell Nelson, another successful insurance broker. For all of them, the "*us*" meant the affluence and growing business interests of their park-like suburb on the edge of the city.

Next to them sat a fourth man from San Marino who embodied even more vividly their common goals. Earl Adams was "a blueblood of bluebloods," a Republican politician remembered him. His gray hair combed back over an aristocratic handsomeness, the offspring of a road-building fortune who had gone to Stanford and Harvard and on to the senior partnership of a distinguished Los Angeles law firm, Adams was fifty-four when he met Richard Nixon. Like the other three—and like yet another of the group in the private dining room, fifty-three-year-old Roy Crocker, a savings-and-loan executive from exclusive South Pasadena—Adams symbolized that nexus of corporations, law firms, and financial institutions that would preside over the postwar boom in the basin. They were all men of new wealth and power whose homes and politics in the once quiet twelfth district were now about to transform a Congressional campaign and more.

At the table was another man from San Marino, although present less as part of the faction in the district than as an intermediary with the authority and finance of the southern California GOP organization, and in a sense, too, as a concession to Earl Warren. He was McIntyre Faries, a lawyer and party stalwart in his late fifties, a veteran of past Presidential and gubernatorial campaigns who was one of the few members of the Committee of 100 and the only man at the Friday luncheon avowedly loyal to the Republican governor of California. Yet it was the eighth man at the University Club who seemed even more the outsider. Willard J. "Swede" Larson, who lived quietly on the Puente hillside in Whittier and owned a ranch on the outskirts of the basin, was a taciturn, weathered figure in his sixties whose presence with the younger suburban lawyers and corporate executives seemed incongruous—until Jorgensen accounted for it. Larson, he would explain tersely, carried the political proxy for Standard Oil.

Nixon came to lunch, as he appeared at dinner the night before, in his officer's dress uniform. To his consternation, Pat had given away his civilian suits to relatives while he was in the South Pacific. But here the navy blue added to the favorable impression. Above all, he struck the executives and lawyers as practical, without illusions about the essential means of politics. As in the call to Herman Perry, his first question at the University Club was whether they would have the money, the support for a campaign. "Can you fellows . . . ?" Jorgensen remembered him asking earnestly, leaving the rest politely unspoken. But in reply they "talked with him very bluntly and very frankly." Though Day, Faries, Perry, and others were experienced in campaigns, the San Marino men were relative newcomers. "Well, we don't know a hell of a lot about this thing, but we'll work our tails off," Jorgensen told him. They were businessmen who knew how to sell, and they would have advertising people with them. "A political campaign was nothing more than selling a product," Jorgensen said, describing their simple application of the Whitaker and Baxter rule. "You got a candidate. That's your product. How're you going to sell it? . . . We knew that."

They could not say how much money would be needed and none had yet been raised, Jorgensen went on. But finance was not a problem. In addition to San Marino support, there would be money elsewhere in the twelfth. Despite a formal prohibition against party contributions to any one candidate in the primary, they would use their contacts, like Mac Faries, to get GOP central committee money. Then there were Swede Larson's friends at Standard Oil, as well as other companies, industries, financial institutions. In the end, the money would be there simply because the incumbent was such an anathema. "We knew," Faries said, "we had to get rid of Jerry Voorhis."

The others spoke little, and Nixon had sat in silence for a moment when Jorgensen finished. "Well," he said finally, "I'm in your hands. If you say for me to run, I'll run." Thirty years later, Frank Jorgensen remembered the sense of satisfaction around the table. "We liked what we heard from this young fellow."

After the University Club, Nixon's evening audition before the larger committee was an anticlimax. The event would be depicted as "a triumph of private citizens and amateur politicians," though the group who now gathered at the William Penn was never a caucus of ordinary voters or even average Republicans, and their ties, like those of the men at the University Club, went far beyond the district.

Apart from the San Marino "fatcats," as one historian called the delegates from the western precincts of the twelfth, the power in the committee resided in the portly sixty-one-year-old frame of the man who was now sponsoring Dick Nixon. "Uncle Herman," they called Perry. Son of a Quaker minister, he had come to Whittier from Indiana as a young cashier in 1906, met Franklin Milhous, known Hannah and Frank before they were married, and went to their wedding. He was also, for the Nixons in the grocery as for much of Whittier, their banker, looking through rimless glasses down a large bulbous nose with the peculiar power of the small-town loan officer. "How much do you need, you darn fool? I know you wouldn't call me without you wanted money," a customer remembered him twanging playfully in his midwestern accent. The credit was usually there. Jorgensen thought him "a true, shrewd banker" who at first held a man at "arm's length" but "came around" to warm friendship. As the bank and town grew, as Perry came to be one of the city fathers and a vice president of the new statewide conglomerate of the Bank of America, he loomed increasingly prominent in the local GOP, discreetly but inevitably mixing business and politics. "You just didn't turn him down because of your connections with the bank," Harry Schuyler remembered. Wallace Newman thought him "a real bell sheep" in marshaling political money and organization. By the early 1940s he had come to be known as the district's "Mr. Republican," and however avuncular the banking, the politics had a hard edge of fear and frustration. Like many in the financial world, he despised Voorhis for the congressman's monetary theories and reforms and thought the Democratic administration "a charnel house of iniquity," as one observer described his views. Perry was "determined," as he recorded his purpose in 1945–46, "to put an end to the socialist trend of the New Deal insofar as the twelfth district of California was concerned." He saw the danger everywhere. "Since the dawn of the New Deal, the socialistic trend and the communistic era," he once wrote, even the eastern wing of his own Quaker church was "tinctured basically with communism and socialism or whatever you may call it."

In the Committee of 100, Herman Perry was hardly alone in those views and background. Of the eighty-one original members enlisted by Day from three assembly districts, thirty-four were from the wealthy suburbs in the western part of the district, twenty-four from the predominantly rural communities of the San Gabriel valley, twenty-three from the southern precincts surrounding Whittier. Harold Lutz from the Bank of America, Louis Sawyer of Whittier National Trust, Arthur Kruse from Alhambra Savings and Loan, and other figures from business and finance dominated the contingents. In the San Marino group sat John T. Garland, a favorite brother-in-law of *Los Angeles Times* publisher Norman Chandler and part of the enormous Otis-Chandler fortune. Even the committee's fourteen women were for the most part well-to-do, conservative matrons, including the wife of the vice president of Southern California Edison. Nor, for that matter, were they political novices. Most were middle-aged or older. United by the same scorn if not hatred for Voorhis, all but a handful had participated or contributed in past congressional campaigns. "It wasn't a Bolshevik, young group at all," Roy Day would say later, indignant at the popular mythology that there had been independents or even Democrats in the organization that launched Richard Nixon.

Nixon's opposition that night before the committee was nominal, mostly older men of lesser credentials whom Day and the factions had dismissed in advance or simply inserted for political appearances. Among them was Benedict, a retired army officer and bureaucrat, an unknown volunteer from Whittier named George Roth, and Sam Gist, a Pomona furniture dealer. "To give bodies to the effort," as Day wrote later, he had also enlisted Assemblyman Erwin Geddes, the former laundryman from Pomona whose candidacy even a local Republican paper thought "a big horse laugh" on the basis of his Sacramento record. But Geddes was "working with me hand in glove," recalled Day, in case his votes were needed for Nixon. The one younger prospect, a navy lieutenant and former mayor of South Pasadena, Andrew Porter, had been judged insufficiently aggressive and advised to pull out. "I fail to see in him the dash and fire necessary to knock over Voorhis," Day had written about Porter weeks earlier. The nearest competitor was Judge Harry Hunt of San Gabriel, who "has shown no sign of wanting to really get into this race," Day judged early in October, and whose "strategy to wait and play 'hard to get' has already backfired with the committee." At the William Penn, Judge Hunt spoke impressively about bureaucratic reform but put off his audience with a specific disavowal of campaign attacks on Voorhis. "He rather deplored the tendency to find fault with the opponents," reported the *Whittier Daily News*, "and declared that the people are more interested in what will happen during the next two years than what has already gone over the dam."

Nixon was the last audition, "an electrifying personality," one committee listener remembered. Thanking them for the opportunity to appear, he spoke for less than ten minutes on what he called "the two definite opinions" on the American system. "One advocated by the New Deal is government control regulating our lives. The other calls for individual freedom and all that initiative can produce," he said. "I hold with the latter viewpoint." Veterans—"and I have talked to many of them in the foxholes," he said, embellishing his military service—"will not be satisified with a dole or a government handout. They want a respectable job in private industry . . . or the opportunity to start their own business." His conclusion, in pointed contrast to Hunt's relative nonpartisanship, brought by far the loudest applause of the evening: "If the choice of this committee comes to me I will be prepared to put on an aggressive and vigorous campaign on a platform of practical liberalism and with your help I feel very strongly that the present incumbent can be defeated. Anyway I would welcome the opportunity to have a part in returning this great district to the Republican Party."

With that, the committee adjourned until its final vote on November 28. Nixon was to spend part of Saturday with Day meeting Pomona committee members privately, and then, with a ticket arranged by Boyd Gibbons through corporate contacts at American Airlines, take a tortuous eighteen-hour flight back to Baltimore to await the selection. They were all impressed, even the most seasoned and cynical. Murray Chotiner, hired by Day to write a press release on the event, had sat listening carefully in the back of the hotel banquet room. His son Kenneth remembered him coming home that night in genuine "enthusiasm" after hearing for the first time the man in whose life he would play such a historic role.

While the vote was foreordained, Perry and the San Marino group left nothing to chance over the ensuing weeks, a mark of the campaign to come. "A lot of work had been done for Dick Nixon," Jorgensen remembered of the interval. "The enthusiasm of Whittier's rump committee swamped the effort of the party regulars," the *Daily News* delicately reported of Perry's maneuvers behind the scenes to force Judge Hunt's withdrawal. "I feel very safe in telling you that it looks like a landslide for you," Day wrote Nixon in Middle River on November 12. Hunt "will probably drop out" before the vote, and "the Pomona delegation will nominate Gist as per schedule then move to make the vote unanimous for you immediately." Day also promised that Perry, Lutz, and others were working on finance. "Frankly Dick, we feel we have SOMETHING AND SOMEBODY to

sell to this district now and are going to do our very best to close the deal,"
he wrote exuberantly, adding a note of discretion: "It goes without saying
that this letter is strictly off the record, as I am still chairman of a committee." Three days later, Day sent the committee formal notice of the
balloting November 28, "your obligation and privilege . . . expressing
freely your own as well as the ideas of your constituents."

Around the district there were only faint hints and isolated criticism of
the closed politics of the committee. An Arcadia paper thought "the apparent attempts . . . to dictate the Republican candidate to the Republican
voters in next year's election is a step backward in our political methods,"
while the *Monrovia Journal* noted "Republicans are making it easy for Jerry
by practically 'handpicking' a candidate." The small liberal *Independent
Review* in Los Angeles noted Nixon's audition as Republicans "continue
to run around in circles" for a candidate. "Although the Standard Oil
Company and other allied interests are moving and will continue to move
heaven and earth to defeat Congressman Voorhis," the paper observed,
"we see no reason to feel uneasy about the ultimate outcome." On the
day Richard Nixon arrived back in Baltimore, Jack Long wrote Voorhis
once again in his habitual optimism, "You will have to hand it to the
Republican committee for working hard to defeat you. I will be greatly
surprised if they don't wind up in a fight."

On a foggy evening at the Alhambra YMCA, the Committee of 100
voted with the predictable results, Geddes and Hunt both withdrawing,
Nixon duly nominated by former assemblyman Gerald Kepple and receiving fifty-three of the seventy-seven votes. On Day's cue the Pomona delegates moved to make the choice unanimous. "Nixon is considered a natural
as a candidate," reported the *Los Angeles Times* in the first installment of
the paper's crucial backing of the young politician, noting he was "from a
family well-known in Orange and Los Angeles counties as pioneers." The
Times also thought his endorsement was "expected to produce one of the
liveliest campaigns in the state . . . [and] Republicans are confident they
have the man who will take Democrat Voorhis' measure." Shouting into
the phone on a crackling long-distance line, Day told Nixon at 2:00 A.M.
Middle River time, "Dick, the nomination's yours!" After the call the
Nixons were both "too excited to go back to sleep," Pat remembered, and
they "talked until dawn."

His victory scarcely a surprise, Nixon was already at work with typical
resolve. "I am going to see [House minority leader] Joe Martin and [Cal-
ifornia Republican congressman] John Phillips and try to get what dope I
can on Mr. Voorhis's record. His 'conservative' reputation must be blasted,"

he wrote Day December 4 in a private note accompanying his formal letter of acceptance. "But my main efforts are being directed toward building up a positive, progressive group of speeches which tell what we want to do, not what the Democrats have failed to do." The campaign would have to "bring in the liberal fringe Republicans," he believed. "We need every Republican and a few Democrats to win . . . I am really hopped up over this deal, and I believe we can win!" As he wrote, their Middle River apartment was crowded with books, magazines, and newspapers that Nixon "pored over" each night, as he told it later. He had already written Martin for help, would talk with several Republican congressmen in nearby Washington, and went to the Republican Campaign Committee, where he got tabulations of his opponent's House votes. "I was confident that I knew Voorhis's record as well as he did himself," he recorded. "As it turned out, I knew it even better."

From the beginning, he ambitiously reached out beyond the local party groups who had endorsed him and beyond their old guard conservatism to which he had appealed easily enough. The same day he wrote Roy Day, Nixon prompted a fellow officer in the Middle River post, Joseph Parker, to contact Harold Stassen, whom Parker had once supported in prewar Minnesota politics. "There is another young officer in our office who is deeply interested in the Republican Party and its liberal future," Parker told the popular Minnesota governor and Presidential contender, reminding Stassen that Nixon once met him on Bougainville. "We are both convinced that the future success of the party is contingent upon a liberal movement within it. . . . Dick particularly is interested in getting your views on matters which will confront him during his battle with Vorhees [*sic*]." Nixon could meet Stassen in New York that month, Parker suggested, or "possibly you might be in California in 1946 where you can meet Dick again." It was the obscure, small beginning of a political balancing act between the warring wings of the Republican Party—a matter of conviction as well as expedience and opportunity—that Richard Nixon was to practice with an almost instinctive brilliance throughout his career. Unanswered for the moment, the Parker letter was to bring rewards in the coming campaign well beyond Stassen's advice.

Meanwhile, more naïvely but with the same enthusiasm for his new task, Nixon tried as well to enlist his old OPA superior, Wisconsin law professor Jacob Beuscher, as a campaign manager. "I'm not as conservative as Senator Taft and not as wild as Wayne Morse," Beuscher remembered him saying. But the former boss gently turned him down, thinking of himself "as a professor . . . the poorest choice for the job he was anxious to confer upon me."

During the last week in December his formal acceptance letter ran in various district papers. In that first statement of so many over the next twenty-eight years, Nixon called for "a practical, realistic foreign policy which will have as its primary purpose the avoidance of all future wars," spurning "old-world diplomacy with its secret personal commitments." In domestic affairs, "economic dictatorship by irresponsible government agencies must never be allowed to become an accepted principle of our American system." He would present "a progressive and constructive program . . . as opposed to class hatred and economic warfare."

In the flux of the time, the war an immense social and political divide from the past, Nixon came back home as a fresh new voice and face for many who saw that publicity at the end of 1945. Few realized then or even afterward what old friends and acquaintances in Whittier understood of the man and the path he was taking—how much his opening campaign rhetoric echoed high school oratory or how much his selection reflected the instilled values of people and place. "Dick was just a kind of natural choice for a political office," Wallace Black thought of the endorsement. "He was a political animal . . . a kind of fair-haired boy . . . a pretty logical choice." Nor were they surprised at his backers and his deference toward them. "Traditionally, bankers and businessmen keep watchful approving eyes on such as Richard Nixon," Loverne Morris, the knowing society editor at the *Whittier Daily News*, would say. "He was taught to have ample respect for bankers and industrialists."

What would be whispered, or somehow obscured in later biography and political history, was an open secret in the small offices along Philadelphia or Greenleaf. Jerry Voorhis had tampered too much with the system, Merton Wray recalled, "so the bankers decided to try to get rid of him," and Dick was there with "that same ability" to sense a situation. Many of them worked and voted for him in the race ahead, though there were some who viewed the "natural choice" in a darker light. "I could see who the Republican committee were," remembered his college debating partner Osmyn Stout, "and I knew he had sold his soul."

Watching it all unfold in the press clips, Jerry Voorhis recalled only vaguely but uneasily that he had once met his new challenger, when Laura Scudder, the founder of the potato chip company, introduced him by chance years ago, before the war, to Frank and Dick Nixon at a home in North Whittier Heights. It had been a trivial episode save for what Voorhis felt as a puzzling personal animus long before they were political opponents. "I remember how he looked at me," he would say afterward. "I wished Laura Scudder had never taken me down there, I mean, it was the coldest reception I've ever had from anybody."

The Nixons returned to Whittier early in January after his discharge, moving in with Frank and Hannah in the Worsham Drive heights, Pat nearly eight months pregnant. In an arrangement between Perry and Tom Bewley, he ostensibly went back to the old law office, now to be Bewley, Knoop and Nixon after Jeff Wingert's death. But while supported by a salary from the firm, he practiced almost no law and plunged full-time into the campaign.

Along with the committee endorsement, the ever-active Roy Day seemed to come automatically as campaign manager, though Nixon quietly chafed at the inheritance. As he had tried to recruit Beuscher, soon after returning he also asked Wallace Black to manage his run, and settled for Day only when Black declined as well. At that, he soon turned to the more sophisticated Jorgensen to "ramrod" the campaign, as the insurance executive described his role, "to see that the money is there and to see that it's spent correctly . . . to pick up all the odds and ends." As part of Day's postselection organizing, Nixon began to lunch each Saturday in Alhambra with a group that included Arthur Kruse, the building-and-loan manager, as campaign treasurer, Roy Crocker as finance chairman, Perry, Day, Joregensen, and random others. There he listened attentively, "discussed the events of the previous week and made plans for the next," as Crocker recalled, and took page after page of notes on a yellow legal pad. Day and others claimed later to have "managed" the run. But from the outset there was no doubt who ultimately held all the lines and details. "Mr. Nixon always had full control of his campaign," Jorgensen would say emphatically. So complete was his attention to detail, so insistent the control, a campaign aide noted, that the candidate himself even decided the precise telephone poles and other locations "where campaign posters should be placed to the best advantage." Harold Walker, the minister at East Whittier Friends who would go along to deliver invocations at campaign rallies and speeches, saw the same command; Dick Nixon standing in the print shop as his political pamphlets came off the press, making certain every word and layout was exact.

As at the University Club, the candidate was preoccupied, too, with campaign money. Jorgensen remembered that at the start "we'd run fairly close," and he insisted that "no expenditure be made by anyone, including the candidate, until at least three of the committee had signed on." But over the first few months Crocker himself "put up several hundred dollars every month to meet expenses," as he revealed later. Although most of the finance would come later for the general election, contributions soon flowed even in the primary. Jorgensen raised $5,000 in one San Marino mailing. From Whittier, Herman Perry brought not only fresh money but large amounts from a wealthy anonymous Republican donor, a former banker, who had first tried to unseat Voorhis in 1944 and whose unused balance Perry simply kept for the next race. "The money came in regularly to use as I saw fit," Perry once boasted about his secret contributor. The same source now pledged to Nixon, as one account described it, "the money that would be needed."

They looked on a twelfth congressional district that mapped vividly the contours of change and explosive growth in the basin. The lone Pasadena Freeway cut for a few miles across one corner. But the district was still visibly apart from Los Angeles, the bloated city with its wartime migration of five thousand a week, now-permanent smog, and boomtime burlesque houses that within days of Hiroshima featured "Atom Bomb Dancers." In 1946 the twelfth was still the most agricultural constituency in and around Los Angeles County. The more than 300,000, largely middle-class population spread over nearly four hundred square miles and thirty-two small communities, geographically the largest congressional district in the basin. It remained a landscape of stucco, tile-roofed towns, of citrus rows overlooked by snowcapped peaks. And like the browning orange trees poisoned by auto pollution, or the great groves about to be interred by developers, it was slowly disappearing forever.

The district began in the east among the quiet settlements strung out beneath the San Gabriels at the northern rim of the basin. Claremont with its vineyards, shaded campuses, and midwestern Victorian homes gave way to the tiny citrus towns of La Verne, Glendora, and San Dimas; farther west, Monrovia, Duarte, and Arcadia nestled in the foothills, their groves surrounded by poultry and rabbit farms and small truck gardens. In its own rich valley to the south lay the business and residential center of Pomona, with apple and peach orchards and boasting the largest county fair in the nation. Across the valley floor lay the old fiftieth Assembly district, more white-walled and red-tiled homes in Covina and West Covina, sitting among thousands of acres of groves and the second largest citrus shipping point in the United States. El Monte, a larger town of 36,000, was nearby with its walnuts, still more oranges, and one of the basin's famous lion farms. And still farther south, through brown hills, past scattered small ranches in the shadow of ancient live oaks and ragged eucalyptus, the district took in the slopes and valleys of Whittier and La Habra.

Without the citrus trees, it could have been a congressional district in Ohio or Kansas, neat small settlements and towns separated by open stretches with both large holdings and small farms of ten to fifteen acres. Although district registration favored the Democrats 49 percent to 46 percent, this was more than ever middle America, basically conservative, sharing the national postwar restiveness over shortages in consumer goods, housing, jobs, opportunities for veterans. In a 1941 gerrymander the Republican legislature in Sacramento had sliced away the twelfth's old working-class areas in the south that had once gone for Voorhis by five to one— "nibbled at the Democratic flats," as one politician put it. Now there was almost no industry in the district, little union influence, and no political expression that could be called radical. In the spring of 1946, the congressional district where Richard Nixon challenged Jerry Voorhis would list on its voter rolls exactly one registered communist.

Yet the twelfth was not only the citrus foothills and flatland. In the western reaches of the district, the San Gabriel Valley wound toward the ocean; the highways through the rolling Monterey hills ran past still more of the old California of isolated gas stations, real-estate offices, and roadside stands. And then, suddenly, the twelfth entered a different social and economic topography. On the bedroom boundary with Los Angeles were the larger, richer communities of San Gabriel and Alhambra already engulfed in the boom. Beyond was South Pasadena, "one immense flower garden," as a contemporary travel guide described it, "noted for the number of wealthy families which dwell within and round about." A little farther was what the tourist books called "the park-like suburb" of San Marino, its "numerous attractive bungalows and palatial mansions" on land bequeathed by magnate Henry Huntington. Next to San Marino, as one writer put it, even affluent South Pasadena seemed "petty bourgeois."

Here the political sociology was stark. "I used to leave San Marino strictly alone," Voorhis would say of his campaigns. "Got just as many votes by staying out as I would if I'd gone in." It was not only that the western gold coast was conservative or even reactionary and representative of the downtown financial and corporate interests whose executives lived there in such numbers. The area was also, recorded one resident, "a stronghold of bitter-end bigotry," with racial covenants barring nonwhites and sometimes even Jews from city-owned as well as private property. Guarding the purity of it all were powerful local segregationist groups such as South Pasadenans, Incorporated, in which Roy Crocker was a longtime leader.

Their initial strategy was to concentrate on the eastern two-thirds of the district, and Nixon set off on the familiar service club circuit he had traveled in part in the spring of 1940. The early speeches were deliberately general, though with a partisan edge. He would not waste time, he told the *Alhambra Post-Advocate* in early January, "on any of today's hot problems that might be cool in June." Later that month he began a series of talks to Rotary and Kiwanis describing the "typical melting-pot crew" he had commanded in the South Pacific, their comradery, and how much his friends and other veterans were now suffering from conditions caused by "the Washington bureaucrats." On February 5 he told a press conference arranged by Day that he planned "a constructive campaign," and "we're not going to straddle the issues." But in speeches at the same time in Whittier and Pomona, he continued to attack "government controls" and stress that he was free of any dictation by "boys in the backroom."

A Lincoln's Birthday dinner on February 12 officially launched the campaign with a crowd of four hundred at a Pomona women's clubhouse, the largest gathering of its kind in the memory of local Republicans. Beneath a spotlighted portrait of Lincoln, with Nixon's parents and brothers proudly in the audience and the "Strolling Troubadours" singing patriotic songs before and after, he told them "the Republican Party must again take a stand for freedom." The Democrats, he said somberly, had "led us far on the road to socialism and communism" with their economic controls administered "by crackpot leaders." But "we cannot win solely on criticism of the present administration," he went on, and "Republicans live on both sides of the tracks . . . a party representative not of big business or of big labor but of the whole people." He would make "no commitments," he emphasized once more, to "any individual or group." Carried away again with his articulate candidate and the unprecedented crowd, Roy Day had introduced Nixon with a grandiosity they all had reason to remember. "The man I now present to you," he told them in a campaign less than two months old, "could very well go all the way to the Presidency of the United States."

"He didn't need much help with his speeches," Day remembered of the polished talks. Nixon outlined them carefully beforehand on his ubiquitous yellow pads. Still, the backers took him in hand in other ways. When the naval uniform could no longer be properly worn, and might be a liability with audiences of enlisted men, they found Nixon a gray pin-striped suit that had just come in to a Pomona department store owned by a supporter. With more difficulty, they also located a pair of size-eleven civilian shoes. Day coached him to overcome his shyness in turning his face from women, or conversely, to avoid the loud neckties he usually chose. "Dick, these women are going to remember the tie you wore, and they won't know a word you said," he admonished. "You have to look these people in the face or they won't think you're telling the truth."

Crocker thought Nixon in many ways "completely unsophisticated when he ran the first campaign." Yet he was, as ever, the constant student. When Day persuaded him to take a break in campaigning that spring and see a baseball game, he bought newspapers on their way in and sat in the stands reading and marking them. "His strongest point," as Day witnessed, often came in the coffee hours, small gatherings set up in homes around the district where he and Pat together and sometimes separately met the voters. Nixon "would ask people what they would like to have from government and then he'd reason with them," the manager remembered. He seldom made specific promises but skillfully, sometimes subtly won over his audience. Day once invited to his home forty girls from Scripps College, where Voorhis as a former Claremont teacher was generally very popular. The young women had challenged Dick, "and rather than make a direct contradiction," Day told a story with his mixed metaphors, "he would lead them around to right field, center field, and second base, into the pitcher's box, until he had won them over in his corner."

Pat Nixon had not heard the first public prediction of her husband's Presidency at the Lincoln Day kickoff. Nine days later, with Dick at a campaign meeting, she gave birth to a seven-pound baby girl, eventually named Patricia after days of indecision, and whom Nixon in a speech soon afterward pronounced "the only boss I recognize." "She will grow up in the finest state of the union, in the greatest country on earth," he told a Pomona group, "and when the time comes she will register and vote Republican."

The birth brought, too, another small omen for the congressional race. His office routinely scanning birth announcements and sending new parents in the district a government pamphlet entitled *Baby Care*, Jerry Voorhis scribbled in the copy for the Nixons, "Congratulations! I look forward to meeting you in public." Nixon answered promptly if innocuously, recalling their introduction by Laura Scudder. Then in April Voorhis wrote back almost casually on a subject that would make American political history.

> Yes, I have heard one or two rumors that you were a candidate for Congress from the twelfth district. I am sure that under the circumstances the campaign will be a clean, open above board one, and I am hoping after I am able to get home . . . that we can arrange to have some joint meetings where both of us can speak. They could either be in the form of formal debates or occasions where both of us would make addresses, whichever you might prefer.

The incumbent's offer to debate a relatively unknown challenger was part of the inner Voorhis hubris. "He had two sitting ducks in the two campaigns before that," said Day, remembering the ease with which Voorhis had embarrassed his opponents on public platforms in past races. This time, both Day and Nixon believed, it would be very different. For the moment, they did nothing about the invitation, and later there would be another opening to draw the congressman into a debate. But the April note suggested how confidently Voorhis still viewed his opposition.

They went on living in a back bedroom at the elder Nixons' until the baby was born, though when the candidate reregistered as a California voter that March it was from the old East Whittier Boulevard address for the sake of appearances. In April they moved to a small brick-trimmed, Spanish-style stucco house in a modest neighborhood between the boulevard and the college, a place "Uncle Herman got them," as Jorgensen remembered it, "pretty thinly furnished" and rented from a local barber. Another adviser called it "that lousy cottage," permeated by the stench and screech of minks being raised for extra income by the neighbors next door. Day and Jorgensen found him there, with a grassless front yard, diapers hanging out back, only a crib and couch in the bare living room amid stacks of the *Congressional Quarterly* and newspapers and what Day remembered as the always "ample foolscap paper" for Nixon's notes.

Pat soon gave herself to the campaign with her own remarkable energy and determination, sitting up in her Whittier hospital bed to do research for her husband within hours of their daughter's birth. With Evlyn Dorn from the Bewley office and her old friend Marion Budlong from Whittier Union, she began to staff the Whittier campaign headquarters, which they had furnished from the Nixons' garage and borrowed office equipment. She also faithfully attended coffees and took detailed notes on what she remembered as "six or seven talks a day" by Dick, issuing "thoughtful and sometimes quite persistent critiques of my performances," as he later recalled. About the first candidacy was an air of sacrifice and *élan*. "In the early days Pat was very anxious for Dick to do what he wanted to do," Dorn remembered, "and it was a very exciting life, to be in the center of things."

Yet there was also, in the mean little bungalow with the reeking, scream-ing minks next door, and not least in her initiation into politics, a gathering resentment and hardness. Day remembered the catty gossip among San Marino matrons about Pat Nixon's nail polish being too dark and about her taut shy manner. "She was nervous, uptight and tense," he told one author about her encounters with the sort of people she had despised as a young salesgirl at Bullock's. Once again, as she had been forced to do as a new high school teacher, she ruefully gave up smoking in public and worked painfully at developing brief, unexceptionable remarks for her own audi-ences. Early that spring she was elated when apparent passersby came into the headquarters asking for large quantities of Nixon pamphlets but then furious and embarrassed when advisers warned Nixon—and her husband in turn reproached her—that the opposition was probably taking the material to destroy it. Soon afterward, someone had broken into the office and stolen a stock of the pamphlets, and she was all the more disillusioned. More than a quarter century later, when troubling questions were asked about a break-in at national Democratic offices at Washington's Watergate apartments, Pat Nixon would say bitterly to her daughter, "No one cared when it happened to us in '46!"

The primary campaign was a harsh baptism on all sides. John Henry Hoepple, the Democratic congressman Voorhis replaced in 1936 and who meanwhile had served a prison sentence for bribery, secretly called Nixon not long before the March 20 filing deadline. As the ex-congressman later confessed the story, he was offering the Republican "my services." Nixon then "came over to see me and asked me what I wanted." Hoepple put his price at "$400 or $500" plus the candidate's promise of a civil service appointment, apparently for help in the general election, or a filing against Voorhis in the Democratic primary. "Nixon said he would have to take it up with Day," as Hoepple described it. "He did and Day told him he would have to take it up with the committee." But when the Nixon advisers then turned down the deal, Hoepple promptly filed as a Prohibition candidate "as a threat," though the whole shady maneuver seemed to benefit the Republicans in any case. "It means we have him just where we want him. He will throw the slush," Day told a friend after Hoepple's third-party entry, knowing the derelict former congressman despised Voorhis even more than the GOP. Meanwhile, the episode preoccupied Voorhis, who followed events through an informant close to Hoepple and whose own camp had evidence that Roy Day even arranged to pay the Hoepple filing fee. "The Republicans will pay him several hundred dollars and then he will peddle all the dirt in the campaign so Nixon will not have to engage in any mudslinging," Voorhis remarked to Long on March 28. There seemed a premonition on both sides, as Voorhis wrote again April 3, that the campaign to come would be "mean and continuous," though hardly limited to a third party.

Even with Hoepple's nuisance value, however, Nixon at the end of March was doing little more than continuing his rounds of the civic clubs, repeating an increasingly worn speech. By April the campaign and candidate visibly flagged. It was the moment of another obscure beginning with a historic sequel. On April 11, the campaign's hired press aide wrote Nixon sternly that "we do not have enough 'meat' in behalf of your campaign," and that the candidacy itself was at stake. The warning letter came from the public relations consultant Day had hired first to do publicity for the

Committee of 100 and then, for $580, to do similar work in the primary, that unabashedly partisan lawyer Earl Warren had once thrown out of the governor's office—Murray Chotiner.

Chotiner was then thirty-seven, a short, pudgy man with thinning hair and clock-face cufflinks that were his trademark, already a scarred and scarring veteran of California politics. "I learned a lot . . . from Murray," Day would say in a comment typical of political professionals, adding just as typically, "I don't completely respect a lot of the ways he operated." Chotiner was the son of a cigar maker in Pittsburgh who had migrated to the basin to run a chain of movie theaters and soon abandoned the family with some cruelty, leaving Murray and a brother to support an embittered, difficult mother. After a year as an undergraduate he had gone to the old Southwestern College of Law in Los Angeles and finished at twenty, the youngest graduate in the school's history. He had gone on to be a kind of prodigy as well in Republican politics, working in the Hoover campaign in 1932, running unsuccessfully for the Assembly in 1938, enlisting in Warren's race for governor in 1942, ever active in party groups and intrigue in the off years as well. But his obvious ambition and a rancorous, ruthless partisanship took their toll. "He made it very clear, too, that he didn't want Murray Chotiner to have anything to do with the campaign," Thomas Cunningham, a Warren intimate, said of the governor's own 1946 run, "because he'd had some experience, evidently, with Chotiner—in other campaigns, and he told me that . . . Chotiner was to have nothing to do with it!" M. F. Small, another Warren aide, would echo Cunningham: "Warren grew to have a great contempt for Chotiner."

All the while, Chotiner had been a lawyer in Los Angeles. Yet even from a respectable office in the Fox Wilshire Building in Beverly Hills, there seemed for many an inescapable distaste as well for his individual practice—money made off bail bonds, clients who were well-connected bookmakers and gamblers. In the 1940s he had opened his political public relations firm and hired out to local Republican groups like the Committee of 100. In the process, he was an orthodox disciple of Whittaker and Baxter, a perfect political publicist, thought one observer, for a "land of visions going sour," his anticommunism the old basin mix of fear, conviction, and demagoguery. With matching cynicism, he saw the electorate as distracted and simplistic. In 1946 he was able to work only part-time on the Nixon campaign because he was also helping to manage William Knowland's reelection to the Senate. For that run he had coined the slogan "WE WILL NOT SURRENDER," a motto in which he managed, characteristically, to convey that the Democratic opponent, Will Rogers, Jr., contemplated doing just that. Chotiner was, above all, a sad paradox of the political culture— a gifted hack with both scorn and sneaking respect in his party, shrewd and street-wise without intellect, moralistic without ethical anchor, fiercely partisan but, thus far, without a genuine political patron.

To retrieve the sputtering campaign, Chotiner now recommended that Richard Nixon launch the first frontal attack on Voorhis, and on an issue calculated to fire the local press as well as listless Republicans. Crocker was chosen as the spokesman to keep Nixon at some distance from the onslaught. The statement ran the week of April 22, 1946, in many papers the Nixon campaign's first front-page story. "ENDORSEMENT OF VOORHIS BY PAC ATTACKED," headlined the *Whittier News*. "Now that the Political Action Committee has publicly endorsed the candidacy of Jerry Voorhis . . . one of the real issues of the campaign is out in the open," Crocker was quoted as saying. "The PAC will leave no stone unturned to place in the halls of Congress men who will do its bidding regardless of . . . the people they are supposed to represent." Made up entirely of Crocker's release without journalistic context or comment, the stories ended solemnly with the statement's closing query: "There can be no mistake . . . shall it be the people represented by Nixon, or the PAC by Voorhis?"

The PAC: behind those initials was the most charged issue of Richard Nixon's first campaign. The giant CIO had formed its Political Action Committee to back the reelection of Franklin Roosevelt in 1944. Under the aggressive leadership of union leader Sidney Hillman, the body had soon become synonymous with the political power and bossisim of big labor, as well as a symbol of left-wing influence in the union. Voorhis had received CIO-PAC support in 1944 and for the backing had been promptly if lamely attacked by the Republicans. In the interim, however, the union became both more controversial and less pleased with Representative Voorhis. On April 1, 1946, while otherwise endorsing every other major Democratic candidate in the state, the CIO executive board in California had voted expressly to refuse a PAC endorsement or financial support for Jerry Voorhis on grounds of his stiffening stands on labor unrest and policy toward the Soviet Union. "I frankly hoped I wouldn't get it," Voorhis wrote Long five days later, adding, "I believe the communists are in substantial control of CIO, and between you and me I think that is why I didn't get the endorsement."

At the same time, however, there was yet another PAC of different provenance and, especially for Jerry Voorhis and Richard Nixon, a fatefully different set of endorsements. The National Citizens Political Action Committee, or NCPAC, was a nonunion counterpart of the CIO body, sharing on its letterhead some but by no means a majority of CIO-PAC officers and board members. With notably less communist influence, its national political agenda called in the first instance for public power, elimination of the poll tax, antilynching laws and other civil rights and domestic welfare measures, and conciliatory diplomacy toward the U.S.S.R. What one historian called "a mixed bag," the southern California chapter of the NCPAC in 1946 was composed of fellow-travelers, communists, and staunchly anti-communist liberals, many of the latter—like Hollywood actors Melvyn Douglas and Ronald Reagan—to join the next year the avowedly anti-Soviet Americans for Democratic Action. Now, early this same April, "fighting the communists every inch of the way," as one participant described it, the liberals had barely pushed through a southern California NCPAC endorsement of Jerry Voorhis. A political informant promptly leaked to Murray Chotiner an internal NCPAC memo on the action, and it was *that* endorsement that now provoked the Crocker attack—with the pointed and significant omission, of course, of precisely which PAC and what endorsement were actually involved.

It was the sort of political espionage and tactic in which Chotiner the bail lawyer-become-strategist delighted and to which Richard Nixon the politician was ever more drawn after this first heady taste in the spring of 1946, developing, as one aide put it, an "intensely competitive feeling in this intelligence field." So good were Chotiner's sources, in fact, that the Nixon campaign learned of the NCPAC endorsement of Voorhis more than a month before Voorhis himself. Beside a press clip of Crocker's statement sent him in Washington, the puzzled congressman could only jot, "I never sought nor did I receive any such endorsement." When he finally got formal notice from the NCPAC May 17, Voorhis wrote letters to the Los Angeles directors of both the CIO and National Citizens PACs, politely restating his concern about "the communists getting hold of some organizations," as well as over "how firm an attitide the U.S. takes" toward the Soviets. But he did not at the same time explicitly repudiate the NCPAC backing. Nor, more crucially, did the congressman answer publicly the deliberate blurring of the two different PACs in Crocker's statement. Whether even then, as early as April or May, Voorhis might have somehow caught up with the accusation—and politicians on both sides later doubted it—the lasting significance of the attack had not yet dawned on the Democrats. Meanwhile, the salvo and its prominent publicity plainly rejuvenated Richard Nixon and his laggard campaign.

The challenger now returned to the speaking circuit with new zest, and overnight it seemed to many a different race. "He carried the group by storm. He is dangerous," a worried Democratic postmaster wrote Voorhis after hearing Nixon at a Lions Club dinner May 1. "You will have the fight of your life to beat him. . . . I am getting nervous about the situation, Jerry, and not without reason." Two days later, with Jorgensen and Nelson proudly on the stage, Nixon addressed a mass meeting in San Marino. He spoke, recorded one listener, "with the agile perfection of an accomplished public speaker, attorney, and debater." Before an enthusiastic partisan audience, he also sounded eloquently most of the themes of the mounting campaign, an extraordinary mix of liberal and conservative views that would mark his early and prodigal career in the Congress and Senate.

The Truman administration had "failed utterly," its measures like "so many phony patent medicines." Decrying the prospect of "another WPA," Nixon would "cut loose the industrial giant," let free enterprise bring full employment, allow private builders to "abolish some ten million slum homes and replace them with decent housing," ask the medical doctors to "work out a medical care plan for the nation." Internationally, he told them, there would be "one world or none," and isolationism was dead. He warmly praised the United Nations and admonished his audience that "we should work with it." Yet "we should clean house" at what he called to great laughter and applause "Confusion Castle" at the State Department, where diplomats should be "our best trained men," and not political hacks or contributors. Altogether, it was, with a remarkable consistency his critics would rarely recognize, a vision and agenda Richard Nixon maintained across the next twenty-three years, into the first spring of his own Presidency.

But what mattered more that night in San Marino, what engaged his affluent audience, was the equally characteristic attack on his opponent. Voorhis's money theories were "ridiculous," he said, and the congressman could only "introduce bill after bill" and "beat his breast" while accomplishing nothing. Worst of all, he noted that "the PAC of the CIO" had endorsed Jerry Voorhis for reelection in 1946, an "open attack" on Dick Nixon by big labor when he wanted only "industrial peace" and "democratically run" unions. When it was over, the crowd stood and cheered.

Accompanying that speech and others like it went an outpouring of Nixon press handouts prepared by Chotiner along with his young assistant and one of his future wives, Ruth Arnold, who now spent even more time on the twelfth district race. "I think Nixon must have at least two writers on his publicity committee as the papers are being flooded with his campaign news releases," Long reported to Voorhis, though in fact it was the experienced and facile Chotiner who turned out most of the writing with routine Nixon approval. For a time, Voorhis and his men doubted that the new offensive, as Long put it, was "getting any too good response." Then in mid-May, only three weeks after Crocker's statement, major district papers began editorial attacks against the congressman, and on the PAC issue in particular, that were to continue with mounting ferocity throughout the race.

On May 18 the *Alhambra Post-Advocate* deplored the "radical PAC endorsements," including Voorhis without distinguishing the PACs. On May 24 the *South Pasadena Review* announced its backing of Nixon in both the June primary and general elections. "Voorhis is endorsed by CIO-PAC, his record is one of theoretical experimentation," said the editorial, and besides, the congressman had been "born with a silver spoon in his mouth." From Nixon's diligent research of the *Congressional Record* and voting lists—now passed along by Chotiner and Associates to a publisher's office in South Pasadena—the editorial went on to condemn apparent contradictions in Voorhis's positions, including his opposition to HUAC. "Nixon," the paper concluded, "worked with his hands, fought his way upward the hard way, is progressive but realistic, has . . . plain everyday horse sense," and "would go to Congress unpledged to any organization or pressure group."

It was only the beginning of the extraordinary, nearly unanimous support Nixon would receive from the district's newspapers, and the result in large measure of an ardent, concerted courtship of the press by the candidate and his backers. Chotiner and the others understood keenly the sociology and economics of the small basin papers. The conservative Los Angeles press, the *Times* of the Chandlers, and the Hearst *Examiner* were read widely. Yet their editorial positions might also be suspect because of the very wealth, power, and notoriety of the publishers, while smaller local papers were read even more, and generally trusted to be more independent. The Republicans had quietly taken a survey in one of the district towns and found that one in ten people saw the city dailies, but almost everyone picked up the local weeklies thrown free onto their porch. Even more important, the small papers themselves were largely Republican in ownership and outlook, and whatever their politics at the moment, editorials could be written to order for those who bought the requisite advertising. "I made it my business of trying to get editorials in the little throwaway papers . . . financed, practically, by the back page [ad] which would be taken by some big market. And if someone got hold of the market owner . . . or we bought an ad for $300 or something like that, we could get often an editorial," remembered McIntyre Faries. "Then these people would read the editorial and then they'd say, 'Well, this little newspaper has no axe to grind. . . . It is our little paper.' So . . . we went to these little papers. And we did that . . . in the Nixon campaign."

If some editorials were discreetly for sale, the boundary between journalism and the campaign soon disappeared altogether in the more partisan papers. At the *Alhambra Post-Advocate*, covering the largest city in the twelfth and much of the western quarter, Nixon was taken to meet publisher Alden Waite, a deep-dyed conservative and former executive in the Copley newspaper chain, and his equally anti-Voorhis assistant and ad director,

Barton Heiligers. Impressed with Nixon, Waite began to write editorials conceived by Chotiner, while Heiligers prepared advertising mats, scheduled stories, and processed both news copy and photographs for the campaign, not simply for the *Post-Advocate* but for several other district papers as well. "This newspaper became the clearinghouse for the publicity and advertising for his first campaign," Heiligers would admit years later. As part of their service, the *Post-Advocate* also assigned to the campaign a dour young USC graduate and Presbyterian elder named Herbert Klein. Ostensibly a working news reporter, Klein would be remembered by both Day and Jorgensen for his extraprofessional contribution to the campaign. "Herb helped us—let's put it that way—on publicity and writing," Jorgensen recalled.

Accustomed to a conservative press in the twelfth, to the petty slights and editorial preference for the GOP, the Voorhis camp was still not prepared for how effectively Nixon and his men would exploit that weapon in 1946, and for what now began to unfold. At mid-April, before Chotiner's decisive intervention and the PAC statement, the congressman's district office could still cheerfully if inaccurately report to Voorhis that "for the past three months . . . you have received more publicity in twelfth district papers than has Nixon." By the end of the month, however, Voorhis releases were going almost unpublished, while Long worried about the new postwar owners of small papers who were turning out to be Republican. "I am afraid," he wrote Voorhis in major understatement, "some of them are going to be difficult." When concerned Voorhis backers went to the *South Pasadena Review* later that May to protest the charge of the CIO-PAC endorsement, asking to see evidence, the angry editor first claimed to have proof, then admitted he had never seen a document and argued that Voorhis had been "endorsed by inference." In any case, the editorial would not be retracted. It was a scene repeated again and again in small papers over the ensuing weeks, and the protesters soon gave up.

By May, Voorhis was being frozen out of even paid advertising, the purchases Faries saw as so persuasive with the local press and which the Nixon campaign had now all but preempted. While publishers regularly ran Nixon releases—"free readers," Long ruefully called them—publishers in Pomona and elsewhere informed Voorhis his paid ads would be limited to small single-column five-inch displays. "Reason given was on account of paper shortage," Long informed Voorhis with sarcasm and irony; "must have space for regular customers." Characteristically, the meek, brooding Voorhis would not publicly protest or even reveal the blatant discrimination then or subsequently in the campaign—unlike his young opponent's vigorous reaction when he perceived media bias turned on him.

The Republicans' understanding of the little papers, Chotiner's canniness, the new publishers and renewed GOP aggressiveness, the fresh, well-stoked volatility of the PAC issue, certainly the original Nixon money from Perry and Crocker and San Marino—all created a different setting for politics and the press in the district. But in some ways the most decisive asset was the Republican candidate himself. From the moment of his selection, Richard Nixon had been sensitive to the importance of publicity and image, feeding Day tidbits about his meeting with Joe Martin or other newsworthy actions even before he returned to California. He had been schooled, of course, not only by Day the ad salesman or Chotiner but by his own experience at Whittier College, Duke, the dusty La Habra city hall before the war—though onlookers and reporters almost never knew that essential history and always thought him far more the earnest young Trilby to his Svengali advisers. He was astute and artful with the papers. Never at ease particularly with the working reporters, Nixon intently bored in on the owner and advertising manager, the men who made the real political decisions on coverage and endorsements, presenting the same serious, well-spoken, well-pressed appearance that won the bankers and businessmen, if only because he understood so clearly that they were, for the most part, journalists second and businessmen first. "In 1946 when young Richard Nixon passed the desk of this reporter on his way to see her editor," Loverne Morris wrote about a typical Nixon visit to the *Whittier Daily News*, "he looked neither right nor left and never smiled or stopped to chat with the office force."

His most important publishing conquest came that spring, however, outside the small twelfth district papers, and with consequences for his political career far beyond this campaign. Early in May Nixon made the Republican candidate's obligatory pilgrimage to downtown Los Angeles. His destination was the imposing building on West First Street with massive buttress piers, its polished black and pink granite base rising grandly to a great clock of red and blue neon, all of it defiantly crowned by the unmistakable bronze eagle that had survived the old union dynamiting of 1910: the *Los Angeles Times*. A rival paper called it "the greatest power of darkness" in the West, and the hyperbole was understandable. On the pirated Chandler fortune of a half billion, the paper had emerged from the war still the dominant force in the basin media, handily fending off the competition of the Hearst *Examiner* and *Herald*. Its politics, as ever, were virulently partisan and reactionary. "He published a paper devoid of fairness and justice," one journalist wrote of Norman Chandler, Harry's handsome and courtly but weak and obviously shallow heir. "He did not know better and he did not intend to know better." In any case, the hold of the *Times* on the Republican Party in southern California was awesome, an authority to anoint and to elect candidates and with a glad willingness to destroy enemies.

The pilgrimage to the *Times* began, and for all practical purposes ended, in the deceptively modest office of the paper's political editor, Kyle Dulaney Palmer. Palmer was then fifty-four, at the height of his singular power. A thick, short man with wiry curly hair gone gray, he was dapper and charming, a little like the racetrack tout he had once been, with no outward hint of his real role. "A delightfully ingratiating manner," one chronicler of the *Times* wrote of him, "and beneath it a ruthlessly cynical nature." After an apprenticeship in the *Times*'s Washington bureau, where he became what one writer called "Harry Chandler's ambassador" to the ruling Republican administrations of the 1920s, Palmer returned to Los Angeles in 1934 to work not only for the paper but also for a local racetrack and for Louis B. Mayer and other Hollywood moguls in the Motion Picture Industry Association, helping orchestrate the fraudulent, vitriolic campaign of fake newsreels and doctored photos against Upton Sinclair. Soon after, he became the *Times*'s full-fledged political editor, and wrote his own carefully read column under the pseudonym "The Watchman." Palmer would be given free rein by the fey Norman Chandler, whom he contented in turn with morsels of unprintable political gossip and private access to politicians. For the son, as for the father, he reflected perfectly the traditional politics of the newspaper, a man of the past with a simple old guard, Hooveresque view of the nation at home and a casual ignorance of the world abroad, carrying comfortably into the great *Times* Building the twin bigotry of his Tennessee origins toward labor unions and nonwhites.

It was Kyle Palmer who carried, too, the vast political dispensation of the *Times* and of the Chandler financial empire at large. It would be Palmer who endorsed or attacked, discovered or buried candidates, divined or dried up the money, smilingly advised politicians what to say, how to vote or when to retire, "dealt in intrigue hour after hour," as a *Times* history recorded his extraeditorial function over a quarter century. Not all politicians, it was true, paid the ritual obeisance. Though the two men were friends, Earl Warren bridled typically at Palmer's urging him to exploit the refurbished Red Scare in 1946, and at other pressure from the *Times*. Warren was "a fine public servant and a poor politician," Palmer wrote tartly about the man who never lost a California election in four statewide races. It made Palmer and the *Times*, like dissident Republicans elsewhere in the state, all the more eager for new, more agreeable men in the party.

In California politics they came to call Palmer the "Little Governor" or "Mister Republican," though ambitious men of both parties made the same trek to his office Richard Nixon took in May 1946, "just going by to kiss his ring," Pat Brown, a young Democrat in the 1940s, once said grimly. Yet even men who gladly used his power and respected his command, Republicans like Faries or Jorgensen, kept their personal distance and spoke of him when he was gone with a kind of detachment. About Kyle Palmer, as about Murray Chotiner, for all the backroom power and money, there hung something of the lowlife, of the twilight basin world they both prowled beyond politics, of large debts and seedy clients and a weakness for sharp practices, something unmistakably disreputable.

Once again, though, what mattered far more at the moment for Richard Nixon was simply Palmer's acceptance, even favor. And he now won both by his obvious attractiveness, that and the *Times*'s long-standing abhorrence of Voorhis, which had deepened still more in the wake of Elk Hills. "A serious, determined, somewhat gawky young fellow who was out on a sort of a giant-killer operation," Kyle Palmer remembered of their first meeting in his office. The race against a "very popular and well-entrenched" Voorhis seemed a "forlorn hope," he thought, "particularly when it was being made by a youngster who seemed to have none of the attributes of a rabble-rouser who can go out and project himself before a crowd." Yet Nixon struck a chord with the older man, much as he appealed to the other men at the University Club. "It was almost a fatherly relationship," one reporter would describe the bond begun in May 1946 between Kyle Palmer and Dick Nixon, twenty years his junior. After his visit, Palmer decided not merely to back him, which the *Times* would have done with any plausible GOP challenger in the twelfth, but to go further and check on GOP sources in South Pasadena and San Marino, who then reported their mounting enthusiasm for the early May speeches and the PAC offensive. "It wasn't too long after he settled down," Palmer would say of that interval and the feeling he shared, "that we began to realize we had an extraordinary man on our hands."

Until then, the *Times* had given him only token coverage, a Palmer story and photo on the committee selection but barely three small pieces on early campaign appearances between February and May. In quick succession Palmer now inserted in his column two notable endorsements. "So bright appear Republican chances in the twelfth district, where incumbent Democrat Jerry Voorhis has plowed under the opposition term afer term," he wrote May 17, "that supporters of Republican Richard M. Nixon believe their man is a winner. . . . He is an aggressive campaigner and has aroused considerable enthusiasm among party elements heretofore somewhat discouraged by the Voorhis technique." Two days later, The Watchman headlined a Nixon attack on OPA "bungling and lopsided regulations," and concluded, "Nixon is about the best candidate the Republicans have dug up in years . . . but unless they get out and hustle for him, push doorbells, talk him up and get the votes out, they might as well put up a bale of hay—for Hon. Voorhis is a very good campaigner, a likable chap—but a New Dealer, straight up and inside out."

In the meantime, Palmer called Nixon back down to West First Street for a second visit. Encouraged by the *Times*'s praise, the candidate was now all the more poised, and Palmer took him up the old turreted publisher's suite, beneath the eagle, to meet Norman Chandler. "His forthrightness, and the way he spoke, made a deep impression upon me," Chandler stiffly recalled Nixon's twenty-minute visit. "This young fellow makes sense . . . looks like a comer . . . has a lot of fight and fire. Let's support him," the publisher instructed Kyle Palmer, though the meeting with the young politician was in truth one of Palmer's ceremonial sops to Chandler, the *Times*'s backing already decided and announced days before in The Watchman's columns.

The imprimatur of the *Times* soon meant more than admiring and exclusive publicity. The Chandler colossus of land and investment was at the center, after all, of that community of political and economic interest shared by the large banks, insurance companies, and corporations clustered downtown within view of the bronze eagle—the *de facto* treasury of the GOP. Palmer's influence now helped free the financial support the Nixon campaign had been trying to coax from the GOP Central Committee. "Some members of the Central Committee argued that this was against party rules and illegal, since it gave a hand-picked candidate an unfair advantage over other candidates who were trying to play the game strictly according to the rules and who were relying upon the primary to decide the nomination," remembered William Roper, then a Nixon backer and witness to the intraparty maneuvers. "In the end, a way was found to circumvent the rules and Nixon . . . got the money he needed."

Contributions swiftly loosed by the *Times* were reflected in the preprimary promotional spending of the campaign. If Pat Nixon ruminated later about early campaign folders wasted on Democratic plants or stolen in the night, by the mid-May push Day had a new mass supply to cover each precinct in the twelfth, "without fail . . . mailed FIRST CLASS," an internal campaign memo ordered in an operation requiring several volunteers to address the envelopes. Fifty thousand postcards were to be signed and sent out by better-known community leaders and businessmen urging friends to vote for Nixon. While some Voorhis ads were limited to five column inches, Day was budgeting over the last weeks before the June 4 primary "weekly papers with three ads of forty inches each," as a campaign "newsgram" instructed. Ever sensitive to the internal economics and business relationships of the small papers, Day and Nixon advised local coordinators that there was that spring some shortage of newsprint and thus rationing of ad space, although hardly of the magnitude the publishers used as a pretext to truncate Voorhis's ads. They should avoid for the moment any embarrassment of advertising riches. "Large ads will be frowned on,"

Day warned the flush campaign organization; "do not commit the error of trying to run half- or full-page space." In the crucial weeks of May, Nixon and Day were also expanding the organization and targeting beyond the primary. Precinct by precinct a "Women's Division" was established to utilize a decisive grass-roots factor in any local campaign, while community organizers were told to cultivate contacts "with good church connections. It is imperative that we crack into Voorhis's church following and Nixon can do it," read a planning memorandum.

The campaign folders blanketing the district showed on the cover a youthful Nixon calling for "full production," "opportunity not regimentation," "representation for all," and "a sound progressive program." Inside, the candidate's brief biography made the most of his local background. "Born and raised on a southern California ranch . . . has a working knowledge of farm problems . . . a service station operator . . . a fruit grader in a packing house . . . [who] knows . . . the problems of the working man. . . . As a lawyer he advised business firms on problems of finance and management. . . . He knows what it means to sleep in a foxhole—exist on K rations—'sweat out' an air raid . . . attorney for the government . . . displayed extraordinary talent in simplifying complicated war regulations." It was a subtle, ethically ominous sequence of distortions and omissions: the "farmer" and "fruit grader" at age eight or nine, the "finance and management" of the bankrupt Citra-Frost, the exaggeration of his war service, the small half-truth that the talented government attorney worked so zealously on mail for the hated OPA. But only a few friends or relatives would have caught the discrepancies.

Four-column, eight-inch ads, with the portrait of an even younger, post-law school candidate, ran throughout the district under the motto "THERE'S NOTHING WRONG WITH THE COUNTRY THAT A GOOD ELECTION WON'T CURE!" Under each, town by town, was a list of local supporters. They must be "careful to diversify names to cover men and women from every walk of life," Day instructed, adding with unintended irony, given the larger provenance of the Nixon campaign: "Remember, the bootblack on the curb carries as much weight with a ballot as a bank president." Almost plaintively, his unknown Republican primary opponent, William Kinnett, ran in a few papers his own open letters to voters, denouncing not only the "Voorhis gang" but "the labor-loving Republican politicians who spend thousands to 'cash in' on the navy record of Commander Nixon. Considering the backing that these men have, do you expect any help from them?" Kinnett concluded forlornly in small type, "Resist the advertising and paid workers of the politicians."

Nixon ended the primary with attacks on Voorhis that hinted of what was to come. "On Tuesday the people . . . will vote for me as a supporter of free enterprise, individual initiative, and a sound progressive program," he told a Memorial Day gathering, "or for the continuance of the totalitarian ideologies of the New Deal administration." In an election eve statement, he struck the same theme. "I have no personal quarrel with my opponent," he said of Voorhis. "This is not a campaign between two men, but it is one between two divergent fundamental political beliefs." The incumbent congressman was for "bureaucratic control and domination . . . a planned economy by domineering bureaucrats," and "how the Communists must be chuckling with glee at that one!" He concluded that "the day of reckoning has arrived." Voters could choose Nixon or Voorhis, "who has supported by his votes the foreign ideologies of the New Deal administration."

In the June 4 primary, with only 38 percent of the eligible voters in the district going to the polls, Nixon won the Republican nomination handily by 24,397 to 12,125 for the cross-filing Voorhis, but he lost on the Democratic ticket by five to one and trailed Voorhis in total votes for both parties 56 percent to 44 percent. Elsewhere in California it was a GOP sweep, Warren winning the election outright by capturing the nomination in both party primaries, and eleven of twenty-three congressional races were also decided by double primary victories, many of them by Republicans.

After the full vote was reported late on the fifth, Kyle Palmer had called Nixon to congratulate him on the victory and, more important, the evident improvement in the GOP showing overall in the twelfth compared to 1944. Armed with Palmer's optimism, Nixon then wrote Day in longhand on a yellow legal pad a confident assessment of the campaign, in part to rally their own staff who expected for all the money and organization a better showing. He was sending personal letters to all the workers, he told Day, since the form the manager had suggested "might not be too well received." It would take time and Pat would type them, but "I feel they deserve it." One of Day's own letters "in a 'breezy' style to all hands" should also be sent. "As you and I know too many people were disappointed only because they don't know the significance of the trend since 1944. I think you could point out that here I was, a candidate unknown in the District in January—against a man ten years in Congress; that we used none of our big guns—purposely (suggesting we really are holding back some stuff—as we are)."

Voorhis had polled 60 percent of the total primary vote in 1944 and only 53.5 percent in 1946—"which is really something," Nixon continued, citing slightly incorrect figures. "Keen political observers . . . thought we ran a darned fine race, that this was the best Republican primary showing in years, etc. Frankly Roy—I really believe that's true and it's time some of the rest of the people began to realize it too. What we need is a win complex and we'll take him in November." Day should tell the campaign workers he has "sent the candidate for a much needed rest and that they will hear from him shortly." It was worth mentioning, too, Nixon added, "that we had no machine politics (all volunteers and much new blood) and were opposed by a PAC-backed candidate." He ended by telling Day to announce plans for a three-man interim campaign committee—Swede Larson, Crocker, and Day as chairman—to "keep the wolves away" in the intraparty maneuvering. In a typical footnote, Nixon told him to send the morale-lifting letter as well to "our friendly editors" who "would be interested in the statistics."

He and Pat soon left for a vacation in British Columbia, pausing to sign a sworn statement of election receipts and expenditures according to California law. His first campaign spending report recorded $590 personal receipts and expenditures, of which $555 was "contributed by the candidate," along with $5,988 received and $5,590 disbursed by the campaign treasurer, Arthur Kruse. It was by any measure only a fraction of the money that had actually come in and been spent. As the financial report was filed, Day with usual efficiency wrote and had published in most district papers the letter recommended by Nixon and addressed to campaign workers, "over three hundred of you." "From this point on," it promised, "you will see a fighting two-fisted candidate by the name of Nixon tearing into the weaknesses of the incumbent New Dealer with telling effect."

Back in Washington, Voorhis worked through the summer heat, thrashing about in congressional issues with little or no publicity in the district. "Voorhis, a top-notch campaigner, cut deeply into Republican registration to swell his total. Story is he had twenty-five paid women out punching doorbells for ten days before election," Kyle Palmer wrote Republican leaders in a confidential report on the primary. "Nixon is an excellent Republican candidate . . . [but] will need real help to win an uphill fight in November." The memo was actually designed to provoke still more GOP money for Nixon. In fact, the Voorhis campaign, with its candidate not even in the district, had no paid staff and expenditures of little more than a thousand dollars, in part because the newspapers had arbitrarily limited has advertising to only $615 over several months. A spring precinct organizational scheme in the campaign proved abortive, and in the weeks around the primary, watching Nixon's apparent "fast pace," Voorhis and Long still worried mainly about Voorhis's dour campaign photograph ("like a guy who had been involved in the attempt to break out of Alcatraz," the congressman complained) and clucked over general voter apathy. "To catch the attention of these greedy-minded people," Long warned Voorhis, "one must show them some personal material gain."

Driving home across the country at last that August, Voorhis was forced to stop in Ogden, Utah, for a painful hemorrhoidectomy. The spinal anesthesia left him nauseated and exhausted in an Ogden hotel for two weeks and weakened by a chronic headache into early September. "I can't say I was exactly ready for the 'fray,' " he wrote about the beginning of the general campaign that autumn. "But the 'fray' was certainly ready for me."

11

First Victory,
June–November 1946

"SOMETIMES YOU HAVE TO DO THIS TO BE A CANDIDATE"

Despite Kyle Palmer's sanguine reading of the primary returns and the rousing letter to Day, Nixon soon went through his own characteristic moment of funk and discouragement following the primary. Pat remembered him days after the vote, walking the floor of their empty Whittier headquarters. Like the workers he was trying to rally to a "win complex," he was let down. The Voorhis combined margin might be less than 1944 but still larger than he had anticipated, Dick told her, and they seemed hopelessly far behind, whatever their optimistic backers were saying. Like others before her—and as she would do so often and decisively in larger crises to come—his wife praised and braced him, telling him the real contest was only beginning. He would return from their vacation in the cool Canadian Rockies rested and outwardly confident. Yet the inner doubt remained. And the sense of a looming Voorhis lead to be torn down, of running weakly, almost desperately behind, was an underlying force in much of what followed.

Reflecting Palmer's view, trailing respectably but within striking distance, the San Marino group now moved to put the campaign on a more serious footing. The lingering aura of boosterism about the original selection and Committee of 100 was now to disappear altogether in the general election. Not long after his last "breezy" letter to the staff, the pugnacious but relatively awkward Day was thanked for his sacrifice and encouraged to return to selling newspaper ads in Pomona, replaced by Harrison McCall from South Pasadena. In his fifties, McCall was a successful engineer with a passion for politics and his own structural and concrete testing laboratory in Los Angeles, a business at the heart of the real-estate and financial boom. He spoke with a high, thin voice the others would imitate to their amusement. But Jorgensen typically thought him "a wise man, and he knew the district well. He was smooth." Equally important, he believed, "Harrison worked very hard . . . [and] he had a good rapport with the newspapers and reporters." They paid McCall a token $500 compared to the $1,500 given Day for the primary, and paid an average of over $700 each for the three Republican assemblymen in the twelfth district to campaign actively for Nixon during September and October. And Crocker brought into the campaign offices salaried stenographer-secretaries to replace the early volunteers. With Chotiner increasingly involved in Knowland's Senate campaign, they also hired for publicity William Arnold, the bland, diligent son of a political editor at the old *Herald-Express* and a GOP loyalist who had previous experience in gubernatorial campaigns.

Chotiner's apparent removal was a Pyrrhic victory for Pat Nixon, in a first skirmish of what would become over the next few years a lost civil war between the politician's wife and his staff. Having been in some ways the dominant partner in their more than eight years of courtship and marriage, having agreed to return to a place and society she fairly despised in order to escape eventually to Washington, having persevered in the campaign in spite of her innate shyness and disillusion, she was by the summer of 1946 almost openly jealous of her husband's deepening relationship with, and dependence on, Murray Chotiner. Archly, she noted that some of Chotiner's press releases were late, and complained to Dick. After the crucial April advice on "more meat" and the campaign's resurgence with the attack on the PAC, however, it was too late. "Politics was a harsh, even hurtful battle, a man's world, and he had difficulty thinking of women making political strategy and decisions," as their daughter gingerly described the episode. "When she voiced her disapproval, my father decided Chotiner's hard-line, street-smart political advice was more important to him than his wife's objections. So the subject of Murray Chotiner became a nonsubject." Even working most of the time for Knowland, Chotiner would remain in 1946 very much a presence in the Nixon camp, Ruth Arnold still transmitting releases and Chotiner himself, as Crocker remembered Nixon's insistence, "called in to help on the strategy."

The general campaign began, as always, with money. In part Kyle Palmer's influence, in part a shared shrewdness about the primary votes and the state of the two campaigns, the contributors now came in their numbers to a Republican who seemed capable of unseating the feared

Voorhis. Their list only began with Herman Perry's hometown donors—Aubrey Wardman, the Stoodys, John Riley, Albert Carden, and others—what Judith Wingert called the Puente Hills "wealthy people . . . and the oil interests." Under the name of "Whittier Republican Club for Nixon," they provided over $3,500 recorded contributions and even more individually or in unrecorded direct payments for advertising and rallies. The local finance was clearly formidable in a congressional district where Voorhis had never budgeted more than $2,000, and where the incumbent's total contributions in 1946 would be less than Nixon now received from Whittier alone. Yet it was also only a fraction of Richard Nixon's overall support.

Envoys from the larger oil companies soon became familiar faces in the campaign. In addition to Larson's representation of Standard Oil, it had begun with Rodney Rood of San Marino and Richfield Oil who contacted Day during the primary. "He was one I worked very closely with," the manager acknowledged later, adding coyly, "They were friendly" when asked about Richfield's actual contribution. From Superior Oil and various independents came Harold Morton, who played a similar if separate brokering role with the Warren and Knowland campaigns. In 1944, as several sources later revealed, Union, Standard, and other petroleum giants had tried openly to hire publicity writers for the hapless Republican campaign, promising "a big war chest" and making available, by one published account, some $50,000 in the vain attempt to defeat Voorhis. Now, like Herman Perry's anonymous banking associate, the oil companies and their "friendly" agents provided what was needed without ceilings. "Apparently unlimited sums of money . . . were sluiced into that congressional district," one Washington reporter would note afterward of the 1946 oil investment in the twelfth.

As early as February, Nixon's fellow Republican at the OPA, J. Paull Marshall, now on the staff of the GOP National Committee, had written the candidate about the vice president of Signal Oil, Harry March, a figure known in California politics as "the man with the black bag." "I have had a good talk with Harry March about you," Marshall told Nixon, and the executive oil executive "has suggested to me that I tell you to arrange an appointment to see him. I think he can do a lot for you if you get him interested." Signal, Marshall added, was "vitally interested in the tidelands oil executive "has suggested to me that I tell you to arrange an appointment to see him. I think he can do a lot for you if you get him interested." Signal, Marshall added, was "vitally interested in the tidelands oil question," and March "might well be interested in your opinion on the subject." When Signal's contribution to the Nixon 1946 campaign was first revealed some years later—once again only the existence of a substantial donation while the exact amount remained unknown—it was forgotten how directly such money for Richard Nixon settled old, bitter scores for the industry. Not long before Signal's contact with the candidate through Marshall, Harry March had led a contingent of oil and gas lobbyists fighting through the summer and fall of 1945 to pass the tidelands bill giving petroleum corporations offshore oil, only to see the bill vetoed by Harry Truman. "Principal pleader" against the concession, a California oil industry magazine noted angrily in September 1945, had been "Rep. Jerry Voorhis (D.-San Dimas)."

From the outset, Richard Nixon was plainly conscious of a line between propriety and taint in such political contributions, even in an era of virtually no legal accountability. Roy Day told the story of a railroad industry lobbyist who had come up to him during the primary and pressed five hundred-dollar bills into the manager's hand. "When I gave the money to Dick, he looked me straight in the eye for about twenty seconds—as if he were thinking hard about something," Day recalled. Then Nixon had said, "Roy, I want you to give the money back. . . . If they want to give to my campaign, they know where my treasurer is. I won't take it this way." Yet the campaign treasurer's reports to Sacramento were notoriously incomplete. And the candidate knew of these discrepancies, just as he knew, in careful, commanding detail, about other minutiae of the race. If he did not keep the bills Day handed him, he could reason, if the stream of cash did not appear in the books, it was all somehow not a political contribution. Most of the lavish 1946 financing was never acknowledged. Richard Nixon's furtive, mincing attitude toward political money, the gradual atrophy of ethics that ended so painfully thirty years later, began in the first campaign.

The financial support that poured in after the primary was not only significant to the campaign at hand but also to Nixon's future. An example of the substantial money he would always receive from the established party organization, and another portion of the financing Kyle Palmer helped arrange, the campaign in August secretly got more than $12,000 from the Los Angeles County Committee, funds drawn from local and GOP National Committee allocations and neatly recorded in a confidential budget circulated among party leaders. The organizational money was only part of Palmer's entrée into the larger Republican financial wellspring in southern California. Among the unreported Nixon contributors in 1946 was the acknowledged doyen of GOP fund-raisers—"The man who made up the minds for the businessmen for forty years," as Faries described him—a quiet, fifty-four-year-old lawyer and insurance magnate named Asa Call. Of a prominent old basin family, Call had gone from USC Law into a brief practice and then into insurance. A last-moment legislative bailout of his struggling Pacific Mutual Company, the result of muscular pressure on both governor and legislature from his friend Harry Chandler and others, made Call by the late 1930s something of a political legend among California insiders. Now the dour "Ace," along with Kyle Palmer, made telephone calls that could make political careers. "Over the phone, in an hour or an hour and a half," he would boast, "we could always raise enough money to run a campaign. . . .We had this list and would phone them." Call's list for Nixon in 1946 included the candidate's first contacts with Hollywood money, with Mendel Silverberg, Frank Freeman, and other money men Jorgensen remembered; and beyond them, the giant Louis B. Mayer, the film industry's redoubtable reactionary whose donation was there to settle old scores with politicians like Voorhis who had backed actors and other movie employees in studio labor disputes of the 1930s.

There were other notable names. One hundred dollars came from a young Los Angeles lawyer named Dana Smith, who would become the executor of a notorious Nixon political fund a few years later. Outside the twelfth district, there was Walter Hass, the wealthy businessman from northern California, symbolizing Richard Nixon's growing attractiveness to anti-Warren conservative Republicans throughout the state. His first congressional campaign was also the beginning of the interlocking corporate support that reached beyond executive suites to the middle managers, a foretaste of later corporate largesse and political action committees. As one example, Gladding McBean & Company was a Glendale manufacturing firm with eleven plants throughout the West and a board that included William Crocker of the Crocker Bank, Colbert Coldwell of the real-estate empire, Herman Phleger, a San Francisco lawyer who was later CIA legal counsel, the ubiquitous Asa Call, and a Standard Oil director. Then a young financial vice president, William F. Ackerman remembered a company management retreat at Ojai near Santa Barbara in the spring of 1946. "The fellows have lined up a young man fresh out of the navy. Smart as all get out. . . . If he makes it, they think he has what it takes to go all the way," Ackerman's journal recorded the company president telling them in "his always booming, resonant voice" about the twelfth district race. "We're going to help. We're going to ante up a hundred dollars . . . just pass word along that everyone here is to give a hundred." Ackerman and other younger executives were shocked by what was then a levy of "nearly a week's pay." But the corporate chief had insisted. "Send it to my office in cash—gotta get at least five thousand . . . gotta get rid of that pinko Voorhis."

Still more hidden were the funds that came from the most powerful forces in the National Republican Party, again for reasons that transcended the district's small farms, packinghouses, or fashionable suburbs. That summer, former President Herbert Hoover—at seventy-two still the "Chief," still the venerated and powerful leader of the GOP old guard— came to California for a rest before the autumn campaign. According to two Hoover intimates who later attested to the story, the former President had asked his son, Herbert, Jr., a Pasadena oilman, if Jerry Voorhis could possibly be removed from Congress. "Well, there's a young attorney named

Nixon who looks as though he has a lot on the ball," his son replied, and Hoover requested that the candidate come to see him. Nixon went, and pleaded poverty, telling the old statesman he had no money, that the war had interrupted his career, and the race against Voorhis was now "at the expense of his law practive," as John D. M. Hamilton, a former GOP national chairman, remembered the talk.

The two Hoovers then responded that they "would see to it that it [the campaign] did not cost him a cent," that they would ensure that "money was raised." As for Nixon's law practice, Hamilton recounted, the "Chief" also pledged that "through his relationship with several large corporations he would assure Mr. Nixon that, win or lose, Mr. Hoover would see that he [Nixon] got sufficient marginal corporate business to make it worth his while." Whether the former President was somehow aware of the candidate beforehand because Nixon had served on the Whittier College board with Mrs. Hoover, how much the Quaker ties between the two men influenced the backing, would never be clear. Hoover was commonly interested in promoting bright, suitably conservative young men in the GOP. Beneath the Hoover help in any case was a history of ancient wounds and long memories, the old man's legendary battles with Hiram Johnson and later discontent with the too-liberal Earl Warren, and not least Hoover's proprietary political interest and power in California. "How much do you need for that?" Mac Faries remembered Hoover agents asking in elections. And when the sum was given, any sum, there came the common answer: "You've got it right now." It was the first of a largely behind-the-scenes patronage of Richard Nixon by Herbert Hoover and the party he represented, a patronage all the way to the Vice Presidency. More immediately, however, the promised money was raised for the 1946 race, and Earl Adams, the patrician attorney of the San Marino group, in due course did offer Nixon a seat in his prestigious Los Angeles firm should he lose to Voorhis.

While the Hoovers were adding their own backing to the campaign and offering to cushion a loss, support for Nixon was coming as well from yet another quarter of the Republican Party, this time in an even more unlikely setting—the St. Paul back porch of the son of a Democratic Supreme Court Justice. The intriguing fund-raiser traced back to Nixon's original contact with Harold Stassen in December 1945. "Possessed of vaguely liberal ideas . . . [a] husky moon-faced man whose youthful vigor struck a responsive chord among many young Republicans," as one historian described Stassen, the thirty-nine-year-old Minnesota governor had come out of the navy positioning himself for the 1948 GOP Presidential nomination. Though there had been no answer to his December approach, Nixon wrote Stassen again on May 20, 1946, about a Pasadena dinner where the Presidential contender was scheduled to appear. Reminding Stassen again that they had once met on Bougainville, Nixon sent him clippings and flyers on his candidacy and wrote earnestly, "I have been very interested in following your campaign to liberalize the Republican Party because I feel strongly that the party must adopt a constructive program in order to merit the support of the voters. . . . As you no dout [*sic*] know, there is a great deal of enthusiastic support for your program among Republicans in southern California." He was coming to the Pasadena speech, Nixon proffered, and "would greatly appreciate the opportunity to talk with you briefly."

They met at the end of May. Stassen had written Nixon congratulations after his June primary victory. And by mid-summer the Minnesotan was asking one of his own backers, Pierce Butler, Jr., the son of a Supreme Court Justice from South Carolina and then a St. Paul attorney and a Democrat, to raise money for the young GOP candidate in California's twelfth. "Pierce, can you help this Nixon kid I know?" Butler's son remembered the request. "What Stassen was fishing for," he added, "was a slice of the huge California Republican delegation in 1948." There on the Butler back porch, Nixon's own ideological affinity for Stassen came together with Stassen's courtship of California supporters, and a Democratic lawyer solemnly collected contributions for Richard M. Nixon, a candidate who would be receiving similar donations from Stassen's avowed enemies in the old guard. Later, to counter Stassen support, New York congressman Leonard Hall would send Nixon his own contribution on behalf of another Stassen rival in 1948, Thomas Dewey.

From the beginning, Nixon benefited uniquely from such convoluted inner politics of the Republican Party. By skill, opportunism, and sometimes default, by using and being used with some genius, he would be a virtual GOP coalition of one, uniting party factions, otherwise mortal enemies, who often ended up with nothing else in common save their help in secretly advancing the rise of the young Californian.

Money flowed into the Nixon campaign against a nationwide billowing of political demonology that summer of 1946. GOP national chairman B. Carroll Reece announced in June that the general election would be between "communism and Republicanism," and that "the policy-making force of the Democratic Party" was "now committed to the Soviet Union." In Wisconsin, a senatorial candidate named Joseph R. McCarthy fabricated a newspaper reference to his opponent as a Communist Party sympathizer and branded him as "being used by the communist-controlled PAC." From the prestigious Manhattan law firm where Nixon failed to get a job nine years before, John Foster Dulles wrote for *Time* that summer a frightening if somewhat mythical two-part article on war-torn Russia's design for world conquest. Gratefully, *Time*'s conservative publisher, Henry Luce, sent Dulles a rave review. "I can think of no articles in my experience in journalism which so definitely accomplished a job . . . your article(s) ended all doubts as to the inescapable reality of the Russian-communist problem."

Back in the twelfth the great clash of ideologies was taking a more mundane, practical form. On June 20, Crocker wrote Nixon regarding the search for "strategically located" billboards in the district, and about a "$1,500 to $1,800" opinion survey "to determine along what lines the campaign should be handled" by Lockwood-Shackelford Co., a prominent California advertising agency they were employing for the general election. A week before, in a major *Times* column entitled "How to Win the Battle with Bureaucracy," Kyle Palmer had advised voters to elect "Richard M. Nixon for a brand of Americanism in our national political affairs which is unmixed by any other ideology, which sees clearly, thinks straight and deals squarely." Nixon, Palmer concluded after faint praise of Voorhis's sincerity, "is a good man in his own right and, moreover, he will give Voorhis a real battle . . . he can win."

Fresh from his Canadian vacation, Nixon formally began the campaign "kickoff" dinner at Eaton's Restaurant in Arcadia, an evening eagerly financed, as Stanley Barnes told the story, by the owner of one of the basin's large rock and quarry companies who was "mad as hell" at Jerry Voorhis for not getting his son into West Point or Annapolis. Barnes chaired the meeting with the first words of the formal campaign, an attack on Voorhis for "his CIO record . . . his utter lack of doing anything constructive . . . introducing over 120 bills and only one being passed." "I have no personal criticism of my opponent as a man," Nixon began his own speech, going on to charge that Voorhis was endorsed "by the PAC" and allied with "the left-wing group . . . which has taken over the Democratic Party in California."

Veterans of both campaigns remembered the swelter of that August 1946 in the basin, temperatures hovering near one hundred degrees for weeks without relief even at night. "So hot," wrote one Nixon volunteer, "the sky clanged with it." The searing days resounded, too, with the steady, slowly gathering din of Red-baiting. In mid-August, the *Times* noted the Nixon campaign "getting under way with speed," and quoted McCall: "We are not so interested in the fact that the incumbent, Jerry Voorhis, is formerly a registered socialist as we are in the fact that he has the national PAC endorsement in this election." On August 22, the Copley-owned *Monrovia News-Post* denounced the "former socialist warmly supported by the CIO" whose elections in the twelfth were "a mystery to those who do not understand just what a clever politician can do to win the votes of those who do not agree with his radical theories." At the same moment, the *Alhambra Post-Advocate* published similar anti-Voorhis editorials and circulated them on behalf of the Nixon campaign to other district papers. Obligingly, the *Whittier News* would run one of them in toto as a straight news story.

When one editor objected to such practices, proposing that his paper adopt a "neutral" stance for most of the campaign with columns offered to both Nixon and Voorhis, he was swiftly fired by the publisher and even evicted from his house. Meanwhile, at his Whittier kickoff rally on August 29, Nixon told a cheering crowd, "I want you to know that I am your candidate primarily because there are no special strings attached to me. I have no support from any special interest or pressure group. I welcome the opposition of the PAC, with its communist principles and its huge slush fund." In Whittier, too, Evlyn Dorn remembered the "red paint thrown in front of Democratic headquarters." From Alhambra, Whittier, and other offices, the Nixon campaign began to distribute "thousands" of thimbles, as Jorgensen recalled them, carrying McCall's clever message: "Nixon for Congress—Put the Needle in the PAC." By the end of August a concerned supporter was writing the still bedridden Voorhis, "Many people not acquainted with your real views have the remarkable impression either that you are a wild-eyed radical or that you are a 'stooge' of the CIO-PAC."

Without the CIO-PAC endorsement or its "slush fund," having to pay for advertising piece by piece by giving Long a personal check, Voorhis angrily responded on September 11 with an ad and news release of his own. "It is a matter of record published in newspapers throughout the state that the CIO Political Action Committee does not endorse my reelection." There was "grave suspicion," Voorhis admitted, that CIO leadership in California was "inordinately influenced by the Communist Party," but that was precisely why they had not endorsed him—"for the one effective enemy of the communist . . . is the earnest progressive . . . [who] can prove that the problems of the people can be solved by democratic constitutional means . . . [and] make totalitarian propaganda . . . hopeless and foolish." Yet the statement was run by most papers beneath or beside a rebuttal by Harrison McCall, the Nixon campaign having been given by the editors advance copies of the Voorhis release. Under headlines like the *Pomona Progress Bulletin*'s "NIXONITES OFFER PROOF PAC BACKING VOORHIS," McCall thought Voorhis's defense "only to be expected" and that "some of our statements seem to have been distorted" by the congressman. "Since the inference has been made that we have lied . . . and since the endorsement remains a fact," McCall went on, "we will offer the proof at the proper time." That "time" would come only days later at one of the more obscure and consequential debates in American political history.

"I HAD MADE MY POINT"

Following his casual note on the baby-care book, Voorhis became increasingly impatient to debate the challenger. His restiveness grew from the advantages Nixon was scoring from a controlled, unanswerable distance in advertising and partisan rallies, still more from the congressman's sureness about his own platform strength. Voorhis had never been the conventional incumbent wary of campaign debates for the opportunity they gave the challenger. Hardly a charismatic speaker, he was still comfortable and practiced before his respectful constituent audiences and had easily defeated the train of numbing Republican candidates since 1938. There was so little GOP preparation or enthusiasm for joint appearances in 1944 that Voorhis himself had to go around introducing his unheralded, almost unapplauded opponent.

"It seems to me highly desirable to arrange some joint meetings or debates with Nixon after I get home," he wrote Long during the May media attacks, even attaching a draft letter to Nixon that proposed "a series" of debates and conceded the Republicans control over the format. So confident were Voorhis aides that when Long wrote back June 11, it was not to caution but to worry that a debate proposal might appear unfair advantage, "that with your age and experience the general public might not take kindly to your challenging a boy like Nixon." Long added that since "Nixon was a champion debater during his college years" and there were "Whittier people [who] think pretty highly of his ability," maybe debates could be quietly arranged by playing to that Republican vanity, without any unseemly Voorhis challenge. Voorhis agreed "it would not be wise for me to come out and openly challenge Nixon" but told his manager to put out feelers for a Whittier meeting "or anywhere else it can be arranged." By late August the two sides had finally negotiated a joint appearance for September 20, under the auspices of the Whittier Ex-Servicemen's Association at the town's Patriotic Hall. The sole subject would be veterans' issues—a Voorhis strong point, he thought—and the congressman seemed assured of a favorable audience from his own veterans' support organizations.

Before the Whittier meeting was announced, however, the debate schedule took an ironic and unexpected twist. Late that summer, the Independent Voters of South Pasadena, a small activist group of New Deal Democrats and liberal Republicans in the otherwise conservative suburb, was trying to draw the inept but entrenched local GOP assemblyman into debate with his Democratic challenger. To flush their quarry, the organization grandly announced a September 13, 1946, "Town Meeting" on "Main Issues of the 1946 Campaign," inviting senatorial and congressional contestants along with the Assembly candidates who were the real objects of the match. Casually, cautiously, the Senate opponents answered the invitation by designating proxies, Chotiner for Knowland, Congressman Chet Holifield for Democrat Will Rogers, Jr. "I suppose so," Voorhis would sigh later when someone suggested he should have sent his own proxy, "but I just couldn't bring myself to refuse." Although the forum would be beyond his control and in overwhelmingly Republican territory, the invitation under the auspices of many of his own liberal supporters all but trapped Voorhis into acceptance. To add to the irony, the targeted Republican assemblyman refused to show up in any case. The only candidate debate at South Pasadena the night of September 13 would be between Jerry Voorhis and Richard Nixon.

The South Pasadena invitation came to a Nixon camp already divided on the question of debates. McCall and others were "reluctant and uncertain" about the Whittier meeting, as one source described them, and now all the more so about the new meeting given its liberal sponsors. Yet Nixon was "enthusiastic from the beginning," one of them remembered, and called back to the campaign discussions Roy Day, who had shared his confidence. When Crocker then added Chotiner to a key meeting, and Chotiner argued that a refusal would be humiliating, that the debate offered a rare opportunity to wound Voorhis, the decision was sealed. Still, McCall "had some qualms," as he admitted later, and in his caution imposed two conditions that would prove important. They would not agree even to announce the Whittier debate or any subsequent matches until after the September 13 meeting, and, more telling, Nixon would accept South Pasadena only if he could speak last and arrive, on the pretext of other appearances, dramatically late for the debate. Certain their champion Voorhis would come in any event, the Independent Voters group not only blithely accepted the Nixon terms but neglected to tell Voorhis of the challenger's conditions.

Between Labor Day and the debate, Nixon prepared meticulously. With Evlyn Dorn he slipped into Voorhis speeches before larger groups, sitting unrecognized in the back of the hall, studying his adversary while the legal secretary took down everything in shorthand. Back at the little bungalow or at Dorn's kitchen table, he met Day and others and sketched out the lines of the coming debate. "He said he was going to say this, and he'd say that," Day recalled the late-night sessions. "Then he would analyze and write what he thought Voorhis would say in reply to him. This was, I felt, where the man was very smart." For three days before the meeting, Nixon interrupted his campaign for what he called "concentrated preparation" on issues and tactics.

For his part, Voorhis asked one local supporter in passing what he should talk about at the meeting. The friend shrewdly suggested he take up U.S.-Soviet relations and labor legislation, both designed to show Voorhis's firmness on foreign policy and "the independence of your thinking" on labor issues, both aimed at countering the PAC question. But when the incumbent walked into the debate, it was after tiring days of campaigning and with a jumble of issues in mind. "I wanted to get across the importance of our continuing effort to give our agriculture a decent chance in the country, to improve social legislation, to improve the Social Security Act, to reform the monetary system and get rid of our debt money system," Voorhis would recall, "to expand the school lunch program . . . to provide as much relief as we could for a distressed world." It was all an eerie reversal of another, more famous debate fourteen years later, when the challenger was coolly, studiously rested and prepared, when the weary, heedless, overconfident and refracted front-runner was Richard Nixon, when the prize at stake was not a congressional seat but the Presidency of the United States.

Friday, September 13, was a warm, clear evening. Nearly a thousand people overflowed the auditorium of the South Pasadena–San Marino Junior High, "a huge success," one of the sponsors remembered it. "No recalled event in South Pasadena history seemed to equal this one in excitement." The crowd was boisterous, and, as the Voorhis supporters discovered only years afterward, carefully arrayed. "We always had a few persons seated throughout the audience to ask questions which Dick had formulated beforehand," Day revealed later. But beyond planted questions, the campaign had also "diamonded" the hall, concentrated pockets of Nixon backers sent to clusters of seats front, back, and to each side, ringing the crowd. At the door, spectators were given a two-page handout entitled "FACTS ABOUT JERRY VOORHIS," including "Mr. Voorhis was a registered Socialist until 1934 . . . is endorsed by THE NATIONAL POLITICAL ACTION COMMITTEE . . . votes straight down the line for the SO-CIALIZATION OF OUR COUNTRY . . . is a representative of the favored few." The "facts," the handout explained at the end, were "released" by the "Pasadena Unit of Pro America," an ultraconservative, nativist group who had been canvassed by Day and Jorgensen for the original Committee of 100 and were now active Nixon supporters.

With everyone assembled except Nixon, the forum began with Representative Holifield talking uninspiringly about Rogers. He was followed by Murray Chotiner for Senator Knowland, reaching with a flourish into his briefcase for "documents" to refute the Democrat and launching what one eyewitness called "an all-out tirade against Rogers and the 'left-wingers.'" Jerry Voorhis then rose and spoke in a rambling way for the allotted fifteen minutes, discussing postwar planning, the relations between executive and legislative branches, full employment, and foreign policy, "the kind of earnest political speech," said one California politician, "people had come to expect from Voorhis, who was always more professor than politician."

As the congressman droned on, Richard Nixon entered the auditorium backstage and waited until Voorhis was through. He then walked briskly into the lights, shook hands quickly with Voorhis, and with his introduction by the moderator, stood to speak amid what one witness remembered as "thunderous" applause, overwhelming the response to anyone else. With "short, pithy simplifications that sounded practical and sensible," as Paul Bullock, Jr., the timekeeper, described his speech, Nixon deplored consumer shortages and the controls of Washington bureaucracy, and found a ready villain in controversial West Coast union leader Harry Bridges, who only days before had threatened a longshoremen's strike. "The time is at hand in this country," he told them, "when no labor leader or no management leader should have the power to deny the American people any of the necessities of life." With that, "Nixon scored a hit," as the *Los Angeles Times* reported the still louder applause and cheering.

In the three-minute question periods that followed, Nixon supporters were on their feet first, asking Voorhis about his socialist registration in the early 1930s and about his "peculiar ideas about money," to which the congressman gave a typically ponderous reply. Then, in a climactic moment in the campaign and in the political lives of two men, one of the Democrats in the audience with his own Voorhis-planted question sharply asked Nixon why he was making "false charges" that Jerry Voorhis was endorsed by the CIO-PAC. As if on cue, Nixon reached in his coat pocket and slowly took out a mimeographed copy of "Bulletin No. 9," dated March 27, 1946, of the Los Angeles chapter of the National Citizens Political Action Committee. It was the memo carrying the hard-won NCPAC endorsement of Voorhis and supplied Chotiner by his informant five months before. "In long strides," as one account saw him, Nixon dramatically walked toward Voorhis, asking him to read his endorsement for himself. "Voorhis was so wrought that he forgot himself and came halfway across the stage to look at it," Jorgensen remembered the scene, "then suddenly stopped, realizing that he had made a mistake, and turned around and went back to his seat. Then we knew we had pricked his hide."

At once confused and visibly undone at the flourished "proof" of an endorsement that did not exist, Voorhis now tried to read the memo amid a mounting wave of booing and hooting from the Nixon crowd. There was silence for a moment when Voorhis "mumbled," as Bullock remembered him, that this was a "different organization." To that Nixon methodically took back the bulletin and read what purported to be a list of names of people serving on both the CIO- and NCPAC boards, including the now-deceased if still infamous Sidney Hillman. "It's the same thing, virtually, when they have the same directors," said Nixon, looking out at the audience. The boos and hoots were now so tumultuous that even Kyle Palmer was taken aback, writing afterward that the uproar was "out of character for a South Pasadena audience, regardless of which side it came from." Never before so ridiculed in public, Voorhis was most affected by the laughter that swept the crowd along with the jeers. "I mean, they'd boo and laugh at my remarks, and this disturbed me," he remembered painfully. Nixon wrote proudly of the moment: "I could tell by the audience reaction that I had made my point."

When the moderator restored order, the questions continued with Voorhis all the more shaken and verbose—"fuzzy or incomplete or uncertain," as Bullock described his responses. In contrast, Richard Nixon was crisp and articulate. Late in the program, a hulking, drunken John Hoepple barged down an aisle to demand equal time as the Prohibition candidate and asked Voorhis to "explain" his contribution a decade earlier to an alleged communist front in the Spanish Civil War. With campaign ads devoted to attacking "Jew-inspired" legislation and the employment of "Negroes, Japs, Jews, and other inferior races," Hoepple now drew indulgent laughter and applause with his question.

When it was over, Voorhis and his backers left the auditorium still numb to the magnitude of Nixon's triumph. Some, recorded Bullock, thought the challenger "transparently political, self-serving, superficial and, sometimes, downright corny." It was hardly the last time opponents would underestimate a Nixon performance. Watching them react angrily to the deliberate mingling of the two PAC endorsements, Jorgensen thought the Democrats "a little hysterical about it." Only the more worldly Congressman Holifield sensed the political result. "How did it go?" Voorhis asked him hopefully as they walked out. "Jerry," his colleague said softly, "he cut you to pieces."

Around Nixon there was obvious jubilation. The first debate was a "resounding success," his wife recalled long afterward. Not everyone among his backers was so enthusiastic or so innocent about the techniques that had been applied. "He'd use some debating tactic that we'd learned in our debating team to please the crowd," reflected his old admirer and college debate partner Osmyn Stout, who was in the audience that night in South Pasadena. "He gave these half-truths, innuendos, and built up the crowd and then by inference pointed out that Jerry Voorhis represented that type of thinking. . . . I thought to myself, What are you doing, Dick, what are you doing to yourself?" When the press of supporters around the candidate thinned, Stout went up to Nixon and asked him in sadness and anger, "Why are you doing this?" Dick answered casually, ebulliently, "Sometimes you have to do this to be a candidate. I'm gonna win." Stout only shook his head. "You'll never make it," he said as he turned away.

The challenger and his allied press followed up the victory aggressively. Nixon was "applauded enthusiastically for his vigorous statement(s)," the *Alhambra Post Advocate* reported typically in a front-page story the next morning, mentioning only Voorhis's presence and none of his statements. Three days after the debate, Nixon would tell a Pomona crowd: "There are those walking in high official places in our country who would destroy our constitutional principles through the socialization of American free institutions. These are people who front for un-American elements, wittingly or otherwise. . . . Today the American people are faced with the choice between . . . the radical PAC and its adherents, who would deprive the people of liberty . . . [and] the other who would return the government to the people . . . the philosophy for which I will fight with all my power in Congress." The same day, Voorhis went on the radio to praise the Truman administration's growing belligerence toward the Russians. "Voorhis is working hard to get from under the leftist taint in his support," Kyle Palmer observed. "Nixon and his supporters will quote the record regardless of formal endorsements or lack of them."

Over the next few days, Nixon ran throughout the district a stinging, carefully drafted ad. Headlined "THE TRUTH COMES OUT! VOORHIS ADMITS PAC ENDORSEMENT," it noted that the congressman had "inferred that his opponents . . . falsely claimed that he had the PAC endorsement. WELL, LET'S TAKE A LOOK AT THE RECORD." The ad then quoted the National Citizens chapter bulletin and went on to say that "the present Congressman HAS CONSISTENTLY VOTED THE PAC LINE IN CONGRESS." Of forty bills backed by the committee, the ad concluded, "Voorhis voted against the PAC only four times!" On September 19, the *Monrovia News-Post* worried about Nixon himself being smeared and exhorted Republicans to fight back. "Just what they will say about Richard Nixon, the young veteran with a good, clean record, who is seeking Jerry's seat in Congress, remains to be seen. But we may be certain that the CIO-PAC crowd will find some dirt to throw. . . . The most interesting development . . . is whether the Republicans are going to take this sort of a whispering doorbell ringing campaign sitting down."

Instead of slanderous strangers at the door, what came the same day was Voorhis's telegram to the NCPAC in both New York and Los Angeles to "hereby request that whatever qualified endorsement the Citizens PAC may have given me be withdrawn." The incumbent couched his renunciation in terms of differences with the NCPAC on foreign policy. Yet under the circumstances in the twelfth—the virulent distortion, confusion, and sheer ignorance surrounding the groups and initials—his wire would seem to many a half-guilty shedding of sinister backing he never had. To the end, as Chotiner had calculated, the PACs were hopelessly entangled. In a typical front-page story, carrying verbatim the Voorhis telegram to the National Citizens Political Action Committee, the *Monrovia News-Post* began obliviously, "Congressman H. Jerry Voorhis . . . whose endorsement by the Political Action Committee of the CIO has drawn the fire of his Republican opponent . . . today revealed he has demanded withdrawal of all endorsements given his candidacy by the PAC."

On Friday evening, September 20, the two candidates met again as originally scheduled in Whittier, in what might have been a very different opening debate. Before some two hundred veterans Voorhis was noticeably more terse and poised, advocating special allocation of building materials to veterans' housing and talking about the gains to taxpayers of federal ownership of the Federal Reserve system. In rebuttal, Nixon argued for "the removal of all restrictions" on builders in the housing crisis, and chided Voorhis for his "failure to support the House Un-American Committee."

But when Nixon again flourished and read the NCPAC endorsement, Voorhis calmly pointed to his request for its withdrawal and told the audience, "A man cannot be held responsible for the action of any group . . . against him or for him." The meeting, reported the Pomona paper, "was marked by a complete lack of the hooting and booing which occurred . . . in South Pasadena." Voorhis "bearded the lion . . . in its den . . . when he got more than a fifty-fifty break with opponent Richard Nixon," said the *Whittier Reporter*, the incumbent's lone supporting paper in the district, noting that "in reply to repeated sniping that he was endorsed by PAC, Voorhis . . . strongly denounced the smear campaign indulged in by opposition factions."

When the *Whittier Reporter* also wrote that the Republican "advocated complete lack of government control of housing," Nixon shot back indignantly in a letter to the editor on the "misrepresentation," which the paper then substantiated with quotations not only from the debate but Nixon campaign releases. Like Voorhis's draw or even victory at the Whittier debate, the dispute with the *Reporter* was the only incident of its kind in the race, the sole media criticism of Nixon's candidacy, and thus his only complaint about coverage in the entire campaign.

Now eager for more debates, McCall wrote Voorhis on September 25 proposing as many as eight additional meetings. The offer came after another interval of hesitation in the Nixon camp. Even with the victory in South Pasadena, Nixon himself "had some reservations," as he recalled, not because of Voorhis but rather for the cost to the campaign schedule of the two or three days of preparation for each debate. Once more, Murray Chotiner was decisive. "Dick, you're running behind," he had told him despite the afterglow of the first debate. "And when you're behind, you don't play it safe; you must run a high-risk campaign." Nixon had stopped to think and then nodded in agreement. "Good," Chotiner smiled. "I've already arranged for an announcement challenging Voorhis to more debates."

On the defensive, his grasp in doubt, Voorhis accepted the proposal five days later, "even more anxious than Mr. Nixon to have the people . . . hear the issues," as his release put it. As the campaign entered its closing month, however, it was already clear to the men on the inside that not all the battle was being fought in ads or on platforms. Supporters were telling Voorhis that the contest below the surface was growing still harsher and more strident, that Richard Nixon in private meetings, away from the press, was saying that the congressman was "at the very least subject to communistic influences." At the Congregational Church in Whittier, as in other churches or small gatherings, Voorhis would come to speak and notice "those same guys in the front row in a Sunday school class" who had booed and laughed at him in South Pasadena, what he came to call "Nixon's claque" that followed him from speech to speech. "Can't be nice in debates," Voorhis scribbled in a note about Nixon at the beginning of October, "and still hit below the belt all over the place in every other way." Yet for Richard Nixon's reeling opponent, with only a few weeks left in the race, the worst was yet to come.

The Nixon campaign had no poll to chart how much they had cut into Voorhis's primary margin, and Chotiner's tactic of running scared only fed the candidate's own deeper, instinctive anxiety. After the first two debates, there was a sense both of momentum and of fighting for his infant political life, and the mix of strength and desperation drove Richard Nixon to lash out all the more. He always thought himself "lagging behind in the vote-getting," Bill Arnold recalled of the final weeks in the 1946 campaign, so he "attacked his opponent constantly in an effort to catch up." They would push every advantage, counter every Voorhis move. And the partisan combativeness that would be his trademark soon embroiled Richard Nixon, now as later, in a costly hidden clash within his own party as well as in dubious battle with Democrats.

At the end of September, Nixon formally appealed to Harold Stassen to come to the district on his behalf. But the invitation did not reckon with Earl Warren's own ambitions. "Beginning to make known his availability for the Presidency two years hence," as Bill Arnold remembered the signals from Sacramento, Warren aides had told the Republican National Committee that "the governor does not desire out-of-state speakers in the California campaign," meaning Stassen or other Presidential rivals. Stassen himself would not violate party protocol without Warren's express permission, and Gerald Kepple appealed to the governor directly on September 30 to agree to Stassen campaigning in the twelfth, where "the race . . . is now said to be very close." Kepple's approach brought no response. Nixon then asked Kyle Palmer to intervene, not understanding that Warren was perhaps the only major California politician genuinely free of the *Times*'s writ. The answer came back through Palmer, a firm, unyielding rejection. "Right then," Arnold recorded, "a slow burn was kindled in Richard Nixon," who believed "he needed all the help he could get."

The feud with Warren worsened only days later when a Voorhis campaign brochure appeared with excerpts from numerous testimonial letters, among them one from Governor Warren in "appreciation of your splendid cooperation in assisting in the enactment of legislation enabling our disability insurance program to become effective this year." It was a *pro forma* letter of the sort Warren commonly sent to congressmen or senators of both parties on passing bills backed by the state. But in the heat of the campaign and the rebuff of Stassen, the letter took on the character of a provocation.

On October 10, Arnold wrote Warren on Nixon campaign stationery charging that the Voorhis brochure violated the governor's standard refusal to endorse congressional candidates. Nixon supporters were asking, "Should not the governor publicly disavow his letter to Voorhis as a statement of endorsement?" Arnold's complaint was peremptorily sent by registered mail with return receipt requested, for which he soon apologized in a hand-written note to Warren. ("One of our somewhat over-zealous Nixon enthusiasts here in the office was responsible . . . my letter was not intended in that spirit.") Meanwhile, Nixon himself also enlisted Ross Marshall, another friendly newspaperman of the *Los Angeles Herald-Express*, to pressure Warren. Marshall had called the governor, as Warren's office recorded, to say "most of the papers in the [twelfth] district are now in line for an attack on Voorhis," and it would be useful to "issue some type of denial of support of Voorhis during the closing days of the campaign." Once again, Warren refused to budge. "Mr. Voorhis was particularly vigilant in the matter," the governor's press secretary coolly wrote back to Arnold about the letter on the legislation, and others in both parties got the same appreciation. "Within a very short time, the Nixon burn was to become a real blaze," Arnold said of the candidate's reaction.

Hidden from public view, it was the opening round in a historic antagonism between Richard Nixon and Earl Warren. For Nixon, the governor was the fine opportunist, flicking aside younger men for his own Presidential ambition or expedient coalition with the Democrats. In Sacramento, the distaste for Nixon was there from the start, and it rose less from status or rivalry than from a judgment of character and political method. "He was far different from other Republican candidates, among them Richard Nixon," as a Warren biographer described the governor's own 1946 race. "He did not attack without proof or documentation. His opponents were not, willy-nilly, communists because they were his opponents." M. F. "Pop" Small, Warren's longtime aide, remembered how much the governor "disliked the type of campaign that unseated Congressman Jerry Voorhis." Another lifelong Warren intimate, Walter Jones, editor-in-chief of the McClatchy newspapers, looked back to 1946 and recalled, "He never did have a high regard, so far as I know, of Nixon. I can't remember when he supported Nixon. . . . I can't recall Earl Warren ever having said anything nice about Richard Nixon."

"YOU KNOW WHAT GOES ON UNDERNEATH"

"I have never seen such enthusiastic support of people getting out and working," Gerald Kepple described the grass-roots movement for Nixon that autumn in the twelfth. Zan Thompson remembered how she "walked precincts for Nixon . . . scared by big dogs and narrow streets." It was the beginning of nearly forty years of belief and hope in him, of absorption with the man and the controversies. "A whole generation of us have spent our lives working for or against Dick Nixon," Thompson reflected. From that first October, there were old names out of his past: Talbert Moorhead and Roy Newsom and Coach Newman leading a Whittier College alumni fund-raising drive under the motto "Put him there, Poets." Or the family, Lucille Parsons and Clara Jane Nixon and others, pounding on doors, passing out literature, standing on a busy street corner with a Nixon sign and hearing insults from passing cars. And always the slender, striking young redhead near the candidate taking shorthand notes on his speeches. "She constantly looked at him in almost frozen attention," one writer portrayed Pat Nixon in the final, sometimes frantic weeks of the campaign, a political wife at "a relentless vigil whenever he appears on a platform."

What they all now witnessed in varying degrees, what they were all a part of in different ways, would be one of the most intense and concerted closing campaigns in modern American politics. His insistence in the debates on arriving late or leaving early because of a heavy speaking schedule was only in part posturing. Richard Nixon was everywhere in the twelfth those last weeks. In two typical October days, he packed into a single evening audiences from Arcadia, Azusa, and Temple City, ending at the Knights of Pythias in Monrovia, then the next day a Pomona women's tea, the Wise Men's Club at a Covina café, and later successive speeches in San Dimas, all punctuated by coffees, the stroking visits to newspaper publishers, the now almost daily strategy sessions with Jorgensen, McCall, Crocker, Arnold, Chotiner.

There would be no end to the Red Scare. "PRO-RUSSIAN VOTES ALLEGED," headlined the *Monrovia-News Post* in what appeared a straight news report. "Campaign statements of Jerry Voorhis . . . that he is not pro-Russian were placed in serious doubt today by a check of the official *Congressional Record* by the Republican National Committee," the article began, charging Voorhis with six "pro-Russian" votes, which turned out to be support of wartime Lend-Lease and his old opposition to HUAC. "There is one point which I should like to make very clear," Nixon told an El Monte group in a phrase that would be his own indelible cliché as a politician. "I do not question the motives of my opponent on voting the PAC line in Congress." On October 8, in an editorial carried as a news story, the *Alhambra Post-Advocate* wondered again "just why Jerry got the CIO Political Action Committee endorsement. . . . Jerry is not a communist but not many members of the House have voted against more measures the communists vigorously oppose than he. It takes a smart politician to get the support of the CIO [PAC] . . . and appeal to voters at home as a conservative."

A few days later, the CIO opened a small campaign office in Monterey Park in the southeastern edge of the district to aid local candidates (though still not Voorhis, whom they had never endorsed). Chotiner's intelligence picked up the event, and the candidate swiftly seized it. "The communist-dominated PAC has opened campaign offices right here in our district," he would say in an oft-repeated speech. "This organization has endorsed my opponent, Jerry Voorhis. . . . I want to warn that they have a huge slush fund to spend freely. They will flood the district with paid workers to spread their doctrines . . . to seek the defeat of those who stand for the preservation of the American way of life." An accompanying Nixon ad trumpeted the *"TRUTH* About the PAC Endorsement," telling voters that Nixon at the South Pasadena debate had confronted Voorhis with "a photostatic copy of his endorsement by the communist-dominated PAC." With omens of the future, the ad concluded: "Among the extreme left-wingers with whom Voorhis kept company in voting the PAC line are Helen Gahagan Douglas, Vito Marcantonio. . . . A vote for NIXON is a vote AGAINST—the PAC, its communistic principles and its gigantic slush fund."

As Voorhis worked feverishly to emphasize his disavowal of the NCPAC and the falsity of a CIO endorsement in any case, the Nixon ads quickly grew more damning, moving from the issue of endorsement to matters of record and loyalty. "DON'T BE FOOLED AGAIN" read large newspaper displays in mid-October:

> FIVE TIMES Jerry Voorhis had the support of radical groups because he was at the time a registered Socialist and always supports the radical viewpoint . . . ON ALL ISSUES INVOLVING RUSSIA, the CIO Political Action Committee looks after the interests of Russia against the interests of America; and whenever a bill is introduced . . . that would interfere with the Russian or Communistic (subversive) program in this country, the CIO gets busy and uses its millions . . . It is NOT JUST A COINCIDENCE THAT 43 ITEMS OUT OF 46 JERRY VOORHIS HAS VOTED WITH THE CIO-PAC . . . while he has been carrying the Democratic colors in recent years for his political purposes. REMEMBER, Voorhis is a former registered Socialist and his voting record in Congress is more Socialistic and Communistic than Democratic.

As Richard Nixon discovered the dread CIO storefront office in Monterey Park, FBI director J. Edgar Hoover was in San Francisco to warn the American Legion that "at least 100,000 communists are at large in the country," Bolsheviks to be found in "some newspapers, magazines, books, radio and screen . . . some churches, schools, colleges, even fraternal orders." As the Nixon attacks on a "pro-Russian" Voorhis mounted the first week of October, the U.S. Chamber of Commerce released 400,000 copies of its long-heralded report "Communist Infiltration in the United States." Ghost-written by Father John Cronin and emphasizing communist subversion of the unions, copies went to every Catholic bishop in the country and to 80,000 Protestant clergymen, including several in the twelfth district. Nor was Nixon ever alone in the basin's politics of fear and treason, to which the national climate was often only a mild accompaniment. The Southern California Republican Women would distribute a mass "Bulletin" in October explaining the 1946 election, once more, as "Americanism or communism." Next door, in the thirteenth district, a former legislator named Norris Poulson was successfully vilifying "Red sympathizer" Congressman Ned Healy with expensive scarlet-colored ads showing an artist's flames licking around the heading "HEALY'S RECORD," a campaign in which one of Poulson's zealous aides was an ambitious twenty-one-year-old ex-marine and Occidental College student named Robert Finch.

What came to distinguish the Nixon campaign was the sheer breadth of the political and personal attack on Voorhis in the closing weeks, not alone the drumfire on communism or the PAC but the demolition of the rest of his record. If the incumbent had been dangerously busy voting with the CIO and the Russians, he was at the same time derelict and ineffectual. "Out of a mass of 132 bills introduced by my opponent in the last four years, only one has become law," Nixon told a crowd on October 10, "and that one was one that transferred the activities affecting domestic rabbits from one federal department to another." The line about the rabbits, delivered away from the numerous rabbit breeders in the twelfth who had backed the Voorhis legislation, drew laughter and applause, and he soon made it a staple in speeches and ads. Yet it was his genius as a campaigner to weave all the strands together.

He had been in Washington, had seen why government caused their problems, Nixon told an American Legion post October 18. "The OPA is shot through with extreme left-wingers . . . boring from within, striving . . . to bring about the socialization of America's basic institutions." Communists were "gaining positions of importance in virtually every federal department and bureau," part of a plan "calculated to gradually give the American people a communist form of government." Spoken many times that autumn, it was a remarkable act of expedience and cynicism for a young lawyer whose former Duke classmates and professors were among those "boring within," who himself had worked so energetically and risen so rapidly at the OPA only four years before, who only months earlier had asked his former OPA boss to manage his campaign.

At their third debate at Big Bridges Hall at the Claremont colleges, the Voorhis supporters were ready, packing the auditorium themselves and countering the handouts at the entrance with bullhorns. But Voorhis himself was again weak, "awful tired," as he admitted later, and by now intimidated by the booing he nervously anticipated. They discussed controlling strikes in public industries, and Nixon scored noticeably with a detailed program that Voorhis lackadaisically recognized only too late as "almost word for word a bill that I had introduced." Afterward, Nixon went up to his opponent in the wings, in private, and "bawled the hell out of me," as Voorhis remembered, for referring to him as Lieutenant Commander Nixon. "You're trying to represent me as an officer because you think the enlisted men won't like that," Nixon told him. Nixon was furious about the incident, Arnold recorded, and began in front of the American Legion or other veterans' audiences to point up that Voorhis had not served in the war. They debated again at Monrovia High School on October 23, and before another overflow crowd of twelve hundred, Nixon attacked him tellingly, bringing down the house with the line, "One had to be a rabbit to get effective representation in this congressional district."

The distraught congressman stayed up all night after the Monrovia debate, poring over voting lists Nixon had cited. He and his staff would discover not 132 or forty or forty-six votes, as Nixon variously claimed, but because of duplications only twenty-seven separate roll calls. The "subversive" "pro-Russian" issues were the school lunch program, soil conservation, foreign relief, opposition to higher oil prices, abolition of the poll tax, a loan to Britain, two veterans' housing bills, and a vote against exempting insurance companies from antitrust regulation. Only at the end of the race did Voorhis produce a small pamphlet explaining the "controversial" votes, reaching, as his advisers calculated, "probably five percent of the people who heard or read the charge against me."

The campaign was fought out over the final weeks in the relatively silent, secret battlegrounds of politics, in advertising budgets and quiet arrangements, in special alliances with special interests, and in whispered persuasion. Nixon's vast advantage in money and the newspapers' comparative lockout of Voorhis were charted vividly in the amount of publicity for the two candidates. The challenger would have nearly 70 percent more advertising than the incumbent, more than two and one-half times the news stories, some thirty-eight favorable editorials to two for the incumbent. The Republicans commanded an ad budget more than twice the Democrats'. And while Voorhis advertised less, his cost per ad was nearly 50 percent more than Nixon's in the same papers. Political billboard advertising was almost unknown in the twelfth. Voorhis had never used it. But now, Frank Jorgensen remembered, "the companies" had "donated" the huge signs to defeat the congressman. "God, you work over the statements that go on these billboards by the hour," Jorgensen recalled. "You fight it and you work it—your advertising people . . . we always used the red-white-and-blue motif on his billboards as much as we could—American American, American, American." They would have them, "all over the place," recalled one observer.

Tom Dixon, a Los Angeles announcer and musician, recalled how an advertising agency had called to hire him to introduce and sign off Richard Nixon for radio spots. "I won't do it unless you pay me double scale," he told them. But money was apparently no object. "And they didn't even bother to call Nixon and said that's fine. I was struck." The announcer was impressed, too, by the preparation that went into the little broadcasts: "I've never in my life seen anyone work as hard as Nixon," Dixon remembered. The candidate would know instinctively how to use the medium with short, simple formulations, and did extensive broadcasting.

Still further beneath the surface, there coursed threats and incentives. Through October, small businessmen received a letter from the "League for Good Government," a local organ of the liquor industry with the motto "PROHIBITION IS NOT COMING BACK" and warning saloon and cocktail lounge owners that Jerry Voorhis's bill to apportion grain to international relief "would help put us out of business," while "Richard M. Nixon . . . is not out fighting our business. If elected he can be expected to be safe and conservative." Bartenders were told to "give this full publicity to your customers." It was an ironic alliance for the Quaker boy from Yorba Linda and Whittier but politically formidable. "Jerry, if they ever tie you in with a dry situation," a friend had advised Voorhis earlier, "you're liable to be surprised at how many wets you are acquainted with." The word soon passed from bars to grocery stores, where Republican volunteers placed signs in the window reading "NO MEAT. IF YOU DON'T LIKE IT, SEE YOUR CONGRESSMAN." Citrus growers were told Voorhis had voted to "increase the ceiling price on Florida oranges but not on California oranges." Merchants were informed by local bankers that support or store window advertising for Voorhis could cost them their credit lines. In San Dimas, the employees later revealed, the Bank of America ordered its clerks to help the Nixon campaign as part of their jobs.

In Alhambra, residents were told that if they answered their telephone "Nixon for Congress," they could come to Republican headquarters to pick out a free electric toaster or fan, scarce small appliances that crowded the Nixon headquarters window downtown. "I would call my friends that were good Democrats and . . . they would . . . say 'Nixon for Congress' instead of saying hello. And people were doing that all over," remembered a voter. In El Monte, where residents with Voorhis's help were fighting construction of the Whittier Narrows Dam, a project favored by large real-estate interests, Nixon promised "conclusive action in Congress against construction of the Whittier Narrows Dam." In Whittier, where residents would benefit from the project, the candidate quietly told backers he favored the dam and would arrange a "solution" in Congress. And everywhere, Nixon pledged "reduced federal expenditures and lower tax rates."

Meanwhile, as Nixon joined the Monrovia NAACP, stories were circulated that the congressman's father had been active in the Ku Klux Klan, that the elder Voorhis had "hoarded scarce commodities" during his wartime tenure on a local ration board, that the Democratic incumbent had arranged a profitable government contract for a local citrus grower, and that the Voorhis family had profited handsomely from the donation of their school to the state of California. The smears and sidewalk strategies climaxed late in October with a mimeographed sheet widely distributed in the district's Catholic and Protestant areas. Entitled "A Local Jewish Political Plot Exposed," it warned that "the Jews" were supporting Voorhis, "THEIR SPOKESMAN" who protected "the subversive Jews and communists . . . in the interests of International Jewry," and who "solidly voted the PAC-CIO program . . . to destroy Christian America and our form of government." The flyer concluded: "If you would oppose the International Jew you OWE IT TO YOURSELF to vote for real genuine Americans such as Richard M. Nixon." The sheet even took a swipe in passing at a congresswoman, "Helen Douglas of the fourteenth district, whose husband (a Jew) changed his name [and] . . . is another Redish [*sic*] all over candidate." Carrying no indication of origin or sponsor, its general circulation known by leaders in both camps, the viciously anti-Semitic propaganda—like the other widely circulated rumors and threats—was never to be repudiated or denounced by the Nixon campaign.

In a desperate effort, Voorhis took out a major ad in the last week of October headed "DECEPTION OF THE VOTER HAS NO PLACE IN AMERICAN POLITICS." To Nixon's repeated charge of failure to pass bills and the stinging joke about rabbits, he listed several "legislative accomplishments," from the school lunch program to disability insurance to the antisubversive Voorhis Act. Everywhere, the incumbent was on the defensive, at one point so starkly that his campaign prepared a handout on "Jerry Voorhis's opposition to communism" prepared in the form of a defendant's legal brief, with Exhibits A through H. "They hold all the cards," Voorhis wrote dejectedly in private notes. "[They are] playing upon every national selfish impulse," he told one small group of supporters late in October. "In the open they claim a clean campaign. You know what goes on underneath."

At their final debate in the San Gabriel civic auditorium October 28, more than 1,500 people spilled out onto the lawn where they heard the candidates over loudspeakers in what one paper called a "free-for-all." Voorhis made a customary opening speech on inflation, cartels, monopoly, the need for increased Social Security, and higher pensions. Nixon countered, wrote one reporter, "accusing his opponent of sponsoring partial or complete socialization in many fields of industry [and] declared flatly that he . . . would not condone such steps in Washington." He would abolish OPA rent controls, Nixon told the largely middle-class crowd, and end government housing projects in favor of private builders. He supported the administration's new tough stance toward the Soviets and abhorred any concession to the Russians as following "a foreign line." His conclusion was dramatic. He described a "new forgotten man walking the streets," a composite of the veteran and housewife looking for a home or for consumer necessities, the "person on a pension trying to keep up with the rising cost of living . . . the white-collar worker who has not had a raise. . . . Americans have had enough, and they have come to the conclusion that they are going to do something." The ovation was booming.

In the audience, Roy Day saw Voorhis "slumped in his chair; he was whipped." The press accounts recreated the contrast of victor and vanquished. "He pauses, breathes heavily, scans the audience with tired eyes, adjusts his glasses nervously with both hands and then strikes the podium with an open hand," the *San Gabriel Sun* wrote of Voorhis. "His vigorous Republican opponent, Richard Nixon, brought to the regional scene the political conflicts that weigh heavily on the national mind." The *Sun* portrayed the challenger as the "hard-slugging opponent of the conservative viewpoint." After the debate, the crowd had mobbed Nixon aides for literature, leaving the Voorhis workers almost deserted.

There remained only the last hurried days of the race, Nixon making several speeches from morning to night amid a final, extraordinary volley in the press. The week of October 29, 1946, the *Post-Advocate* ran as an editorial, and the *Monrovia News-Post* reprinted as a news story, a remarkable piece entitled "How Jerry and Vito Voted." A vivid preview of the notorious "Pink Sheet" Nixon would use against Helen Douglas exactly four years later in a race for the U.S. Senate, the hybrid editorial-article argued that Voorhis had "lined up" with Vito Marcantonio, the lone American Labor Party congressman from New York "who toed the Communist Party line. . . . How did Jerry get away with his support of the Communist Party line? . . . Many of his former supporters are now beginning to see the light." On October 30, under a headline "MOSCOW GIVES KISS OF DEATH," the *News-Post* reported a Moscow Radio commentary in support of "progressives" in the coming election, which in turn the paper interpreted as endorsement of the CIO-PAC and thus of Jerry Voorhis.

On November 1, the local AFL executive secretary denounced the attacks on Voorhis as "the most sinister fraud in history," but Democratic Party leaders were otherwise cowed and silent. Voorhis backers now began to heckle Nixon with bullhorns, a practice, Day recorded, that "upset" him visibly. Voorhis himself finally lashed out at what he called "a lot of oil company money" in the Nixon campaign. The counterattacks struck a nerve and provoked swift reprisal. On November 1–2, the War Veterans' Non-Partisan Voters League took out quarter-page ads accusing Voorhis of "rabble-rousing, slanderous attacks on his war-veteran opponent." "Who is he to make scurrilous statements about an honest, clean, forthright young

American who fought in defense of his country in the stinking mud and jungle of the Solomons?" The congressman was uttering "sly innuendos," said the group, stressing "There is not a nickel of oil company money in the Nixon campaign." As if in echo, the *Los Angeles Times* ran a story listing Nixon's campaign contributions at a mere $370, Voorhis's at $1,000. The day the Veteran's League ad first appeared, most district papers ran as a news story a Chotiner-written statement by former GOP Lieutenant Governor Burton Fitts, condemning Voorhis for "consistently voting the Moscow PAC–Henry Wallace line in Congress" and noting "the insolence of Moscow in telling the American voter to elect PAC candidates, such as Mr. Voorhis." Fitts had been scheduled to make an address on radio, but the local station thought the speech so libelous that air time was refused at the last moment and the abbreviated statement issued instead.

That last weekend of November 2–3, residents throughout the twelfth district began to receive systematic phone calls. "This is a friend of yours but I can't tell you my name," a voice would say. "I just wanted you to know that Jerry Voorhis is a communist." Or the caller would simply ask, "Did you know that Jerry Voorhis was a communist?" and hang up. The calls came through the weekend and on to election day in "considerable numbers," as recipients later told the story, and blanketed the Alhambra area. Of the households telephoned, several were Democrats, among them a mother of a Voorhis aide and one Pomona woman who later filed an affidavit about the incident.

Paid nine dollars a day, sworn to secrecy, the callers, too, eventually told the story. Margaret Maylor answered a Nixon campaign ad for workers, and walked into the back of the Alhambra headquarters where "they had a whole boiler room with phones going all the time," as she described the scene to her family. "Well, don't you think we should say something else?" she asked the campaign workers overseeing the telephoning. "Oh, no," they had answered, and she worked for two days for them making the anonymous calls. Another young woman hired for a day remembered being "assigned to a room filled with people using the telephones, systematically calling everyone in the district." In Whittier, Merton Wray, like many others, knew of the smear, though he attributed it to Nixon's backers. "So much of it was *sub rosa*," he would reflect. "There were telephone calls and things like that by overzealous partisans."

Reports of the calls filtered gradually into the Voorhis camp, and even then they would not understand fully what was happening. That last week Voorhis went by the Covina Rotary Club "because I always had a good reception there through the years," but "this time it was cold as ice. . . . and even people that had been my friends, I was pretty sure weren't then. . . . I felt like there was an impenetrable wall up against me."

A political crescendo built in the last hours before the election. On November 2, as the anonymous calls went out from Alhambra, the Catholic Archdiocese of Los Angeles took nearly a full-page ad in the *Los Angeles Herald*, showing Francis Cardinal Spellman beside his warning: "Every communist is a potential enemy of the United States and only the bat-blind can fail to be aware of the communist invasion of our country." In Sunday morning's *Los Angeles Times*, Kyle Palmer gave his final endorsement of Nixon—"no reactionary in his thinking but . . . distinctly not a leftist or 'parlor pink' "—and delivered a last blow to Voorhis: "Once a registered socialist, and that streak in him will not rub out." In many precincts of the twelfth, Voorhis workers would complain, the *Times* endorsement was found clipped and taped inside the voting booths. On Monday, Los Angeles papers carried front-page boxes: "VOTE AGAINST NEW DEAL COMMUNISM. VOTE REPUBLICAN. VOTE AMERICAN!"

On his final campaign radio broadcast that night, Nixon repeated the familiar themes but devoted much of the time to what he called Voorhis's "last-minute . . . scurrilous attacks." In final rallies in Whittier and elsewhere, Hollywood stars appeared to endorse his election, and Nixon exhorted workers to fight off the Democrats' dirty tactics. Overnight, telephone poles and trees outside every polling place in the twelfth were covered with placards reading "Elect Richard M. Nixon *Your Congressman*," as if the challenger were already incumbent. When Voorhis supporters protested the placards to the South Pasadena election board as violations of the state code, they were turned aside.

Election night was foggy as Nixon had dinner with Pat and Roy Day at Day's favorite restaurant on La Cienega Boulevard in the Valley. When they drove away from the restaurant at eight-thirty, they turned on the car radio to hear the first returns. "Only a few hundred were recorded," he noted later, "but I was leading Voorhis by a small margin." The hand-counted ballots came in with painful slowness. Some early tallies had Voorhis leading slightly, and the Nixons' mood was almost black. Then, a little after 9:00 P.M., still relatively early, the tide shifted. Nixon pulled ahead, the lead building steadily toward the landslide it would become.

It was a crushing, stunning victory in which Richard Nixon reversed the primary results, winning 57 percent to 43 percent among the 114,321 voters. He carried every community but three and won even in the incumbent's San Dimas 491–401. Across the hills, driving through the murky darkness to visit workers, Voorhis heard on his radio the count change and then quickly go beyond reach. Alone with his wife, he remembered Kipling: "If you can . . . watch the things you gave your life to, broken, and stoop to build 'em up with worn-out tools."

In Whittier they were soon celebrating, and Nixon began to telephone to the friendly papers what was the first of so many victory statements. "The people want a new approach to their problems. . . . I believe it essential that we now get about the business of solving these problems with utter disregard of partisan politics and with an entirely practical and progressive approach," he said, adding, "I think today my greatest satisfaction over the results of this election is not for myself but for my wife and my parents. Their happiness over this success is the best reward of all." But his own feelings were deep. "Nothing," he wrote long afterward, "could equal the excitement and jubilation of winning the first campaign." Later in the evening, Kyle Palmer called to invite them down for a victory statement and celebration at the *Times* Building. With Hannah and an ebullient Frank, Don and his wife, Clara Jane, and Pat, he met Palmer in the lobby and they went up to the Chandlers' executive suite beneath the eagle. "Now, what would you like to drink?" Dorothy Chandler had asked them, and they all wanted milk. But when she walked back to the kitchen to tell the maid, Nixon had followed her and said quietly, "Could you get me a double bourbon? I don't want Mother and Father to see me take a drink."

Outside, in the basin and around the state, across the nation, he was part of a postwar Republican avalanche that seemed to open a new era in American politics. For the first time since 1928 the GOP won both houses of Congress, and Republicans now took a majority of congressional seats from California alongside the victorious Knowland and Warren. The *Los Angeles Herald* exultantly called the Democratic debacle "a mandate for Americanism." In Manhattan, Herbert Hoover predicted the election would have a "profound effect" on the world.

When he and Pat left the *Times* late that night, they dropped off his parents and brother, and went to their friends the Drowns, who had planned a special celebration. In the predawn hours they greeted the Nixons with an expensive bottle of sherry. It was not for tonight, they explained. This was only the beginning. Someday they would all "crack it over the mantel of the White House."

Like a distant but decisive battle, the outcome launching one career and shattering another, the 1946 campaign in California's twelfth district soon took on its own mythology. Only six years separated that triumphant night with the Chandlers and the Drowns from the evening Nixon was elected Vice President of the United States, and the texture and character of his first campaign by then had become, albeit only vaguely, an issue itself, hovering in the background of other races. Then, too, the protagonists added for their own reasons their own selective versions to the larger myth—until, long afterward, even when it no longer seemed to matter, neither could quite distinguish fact from fiction.

Yet this first campaign was so seminal and so important, the political year from the autumn of 1945 to the 1946 election such a watershed in the life of Richard Nixon, that its history was never simply a political weapon or defense of the moment, somehow academic. What was thought to be understood about his political beginning—and particularly what remained in obscurity—shaped in surprisingly large measure subsequent public and private images of the man by both supporters and opponents, and thus influenced much of what followed to the end. Not least, Nixon's personal sense of what he had lived through, how he chose even in candor and in private to see and not to see his own political origins, would be a significant, sometimes fateful strain in his career.

Nixon "turned a California grass-roots campaign (dubbed 'hopeless' by wheelhorse Republicans) into a triumph over high-powered, high-minded Democratic incumbent Jerry Voorhis," reported *Time* magazine after the election, adding in utter seriousness that the young winner had "politely avoided personal attacks." The legends multiplied, source fed on source. In myriad newspapers, magazines, and books the Committee of 100 became typical small businessmen and civic leaders chafing at the New Deal, even in some accounts Independents and Democrats, rather than the people, and interests, they were. The Nixon campaign came down from those postwar months in the soft tint of a citizen crusade, a candidacy from the "grass-roots" as *Time* put the half-truth, evoking images of the small contributions and volunteers, which were there, but missing altogether the other reality—the University Club, Elk Hills, the corporate levies, the vastly larger forces arrayed against Voorhis. So, too, the controversial Murray Chotiner was now in, now out of the picture, his genuine and decisive role obscured along with the events and trends he determined, reinforcing the fiction that it had been indeed a campaign of gifted amateurs.

The afterglow enveloped Voorhis personally. "I can well appreciate the esteem in which you hold Mr. Voorhis, and although we disagreed on some of the basic issues," Nixon wrote to a businessman who had inquired nine years later about the campaign, "I always had the highest respect for his integrity and for his dedication to the public service during the time he was a member of the Congress." To Stewart Alsop in 1958 he remarked almost effusively that "there was scarcely ever a man with higher ideals than Jerry Voorhis, or better motivated than Jerry Voorhis," although he also called him one of the "Don Quixotes," men who "couldn't get anything done" in Congress. Even in private, Nixon seemed to fault him only for tactics. "In 1946," he once admonished a staff meeting about the perils of campaign debates, "a damn fool incumbent named Jerry Voorhis debated a young unknown lawyer and it cost him the election."

Voorhis himself, a friend recounted, "left politics broken and discouraged," moving to Chicago to become executive secretary of the Cooperative League. He later described his 1946 defeat as an "opportunity" for religious growth: "Jesus cannot 'heal the brokenhearted' until their hearts are broken by some circumstance or revelation." But his own memoir written in the months following the race, *Confessions of a Congressman*, contained few revelations about the circumstances of the campaign, though his files bristled with evidence, often from those who experienced at firsthand the whispering, the anonymous calls, and other smears. "Oh what a dirty campaign was put up by Standard Oil, etc. against Jerry," a prominent clergyman wrote a friend that November. He had been "done in oil," a supporter told the defeated reformer. "Those on the other side who seek to tear down another's reputation by lies and trickery are evil, and . . . will destroy themselves," another constituent had written typically about the mudslinging.

In a draft of his book, Voorhis wrote methodically, "There was a lot of material . . . I had in documentary form for weeks which would have shown how the Nixon campaign was a creature of big eastern financial interests . . . how the Bank of America, the big private utilities, the major oil companies were resolved . . . to beat me. I never used it." Nor did he use that explosive passage in the final version of *Confessions*. Numbed, plainly afraid of more reprisals about his record at a moment in the late 1940s of mounting anticommunist hysteria and witchhunts, retreating in any case to a natural religious forbearance, Voorhis refused for more than a decade to comment on his increasingly prominent 1946 adversary. In a 1981 interview, the aging ex-congressman recalled indignantly that neither the CIO nor NCPAC had endorsed him—forgetting once again, as he had that September night in South Pasadena, the fateful letter he received from the National Citizens group in May 1946, weeks after Murray Chotiner knew of the endorsement. Voorhis would remember, too, how the Nixon camp proposed the debates, though it had been the incumbent in his quiet hubris who pressed Jack Long that summer to get their troublesome young foe "on a platform."

As Voorhis in his penitent silence was transformed from dangerous radical to idealistic if naïve congressman, communism and the omnipresent, omnipotent PAC of 1946 were similarly adjusted. After the first debate, the winner remembered in his memoirs, "The PAC became a peripheral but heated issue in the campaign," and "communism was not the central issue." Nixon "recalls that in 1946 he said little or nothing about communism," according to an official statement made by his office in 1959.

"He based his campaign on a thorough study of the Voorhis record, and there was nothing in that record to suggest that communism was an issue at that time." It was as if three-quarters of the ads and speeches, most of the editorials, the crucially planned Crocker and Fitts statements, the torrid last week of the campaign had all never happened. Incredibly, one friendly biographer would suggest of the last-minute anonymous calls that "it is possible that some or all of the calls were designed to hurt Nixon as well as Voorhis by making him appear guilty of vicious tactics."

Like the voters of the twelfth at the time, the subsequent imagery of the campaign was bedeviled by those confusing PACs. Even by 1968, only days after his election as President, Richard Nixon reminisced in a London *Observer* interview about the 1946 race and told them blandly, "My opponent had had the endorsement of the Political Action Committee of the . . . CIO." It was a seemingly small historic falsity they believed, or perpetuated, to the end. "Voorhis had the endorsement of the Political Action Committee of the Congress of Industrial Organizations," his daughter wrote in a biography of Pat Nixon forty years after the original lie.

Of all the censoring of 1946, perhaps the most complete would also be the most intriguing: the money. By almost every published account afterward, the Nixons themselves spent thousands of their own savings on the campaign, at one point selling that first civilian suit he was given to pay for costs, at another Pat spending her legacy from Will Ryan's ranch. Official reports filed at the time with Congress recorded only $370 in contributions to Nixon. In the more detailed affidavits and statements filed in Sacramento, the Nixon campaign listed $17,774 for both the primary and general elections, against $1,928 for Voorhis. Three decades later, Nixon backers would finally admit that the actual tallied contributions had been between $24,000 and $32,000. But the records were long ago burned, they confessed, and even then the listed money was only a small fraction of what actually went into the campaign.

12

The House, 1947–48

"A COMPLETELY POLITICAL MAN"

The Nixons left for Washington, and what would be nearly three decades of political life, basking in gleeful small-town celebration and a heady sense of destiny.

Hundreds of congratulatory letters and telegrams poured into the campaign headquarters. There were gala victory dinners in Whittier, Alhambra, Pomona, Covina, and El Monte, and, fittingly, discreet small supper parties in South Pasadena and San Marino. Exultant at what they had managed, Herman Perry assembled a group of young businessmen and professionals to support the new congressman with interim contributions and local promotion. Like the Drowns and their election-night sherry, the old banker saw no limit to the career they were launching from the orange-grove obscurity of the twelfth district. The grandiosity of it all grew out of a rare mix of motives and moment—the ebullience of postwar California staking a claim to national power and parity with the long dominant East; a strong, aggressive representative at last for the old and new money of the twelfth, for Uncle Herman and his bank clients as well as the San Marino group; and not least Nixon as a promising alternative in party and state to the rule of Earl Warren. "I'm telling you fellows," Don Fantz remembered Perry saying earnestly to the special gathering of backers he put together just after the election, "one of these days you fellows right here will be guests in the White House. I won't be—I won't be here when the time comes, but you fellows right here will be guests of Dick Nixon's in the White House some day."

Publicly, Richard Nixon was the modest, grateful, almost coy victor. "Have to start getting acquainted with our pride and joy," he said, invoking eight-month-old Tricia when reporters asked about his future plans. In private he indulged in the huge ambitions being voiced even before he took a freshman seat in Congress. "On occasion he would confide that someday he would be President," Wallace Black remembered of the days before Nixon's departure for Washington that autumn.

So large was the pretense and pride, so euphoric the triumph over Voorhis, that Richard Nixon's ultimate success seemed to some only a question of tactics. Black and Tom Bewley went to see him off, and Black remarked getting back in the car that they had just put on the road "a future President of the United States." "Oh, I hope so," Bewley had answered, though personally they were both "very disappointed" that Dick had run for Congress rather than the Sacramento legislature, where they believed he could go on to governor and thus have "a much better shot" at the White House than through the draining controversies of Congress or the Senate. "We knew he had ambitions to be President," Black reflected, "and I think most of us would rather have seen him take another route."

Away from the applause and elation, their going was more prosaic. They left the baby to be brought out later by his parents. Frank Nixon meticulously packed their new 1946 Ford, only to have his handiwork undone when Dick and Pat crossed over into Mexico for a brief vacation en route. On their return U.S. Customs made them unpack completely, Nixon the would-be President never telling the officers he was a congressman-elect, which would no doubt have saved them the search.

They arrived in Washington early in December 1946 for an orientation meeting of the new House Republicans and checked into the gracious old Mayflower Hotel while looking for a home. A *Washington Post* reporter found them there for the first time later in the month, a handsomely photogenic young couple with "time . . . growing desperately short" and their election "luck . . . gone into a tailspin" as they searched vainly for a home in the Capital's notorious housing shortage. Dick's proud parents were coming for the congressional swearing-in January 2, bringing little Tricia with them, Mr. Nixon explained, and there was "no proper place" for babies at the Mayflower. Still without prospects, they spent their first Washington Christmas driving to Gettysburg to visit his great-grandfather's Civil War gravesite, and returned for a drab late supper at the Mayflower. After Tricia's arrival and some negotiation, the hotel allowed them a crib in their room, though they would be there until March.

In what was still very much a parochial, southern city, it was not uncommon for market- and class-conscious Washington landlords to turn away on grounds of income even the new $15,000-a-year congressmen, and some representatives sheepishly concealed their occupation in applying for rentals. Eventually the Nixons leased for eighty dollars a month a modest two-bedroom, two-story garden apartment in Park Fairfax, a raw new development on the Virginia side of the Potomac less than a half hour from Capitol Hill. Yet money was never a major concern. If not wealthy like some of Nixon's congressional colleagues, they were comfortably middle class in postwar Washington. They had come to Congress with their wartime $10,000 in government bonds, another $3,000 in savings, $14,000 in life insurance, a new car, no campaign debts, and prospects of random support from their backers at home—all the product of his amply financed run and the considerable ambitions he embodied and shared.

While the Nixons looked anxiously for housing, Jerry Voorhis was closing down his congressional office. With some difficulty and often repeated attempts—"the right words never seemed to come," he confessed—the defeated incumbent sent Nixon in December a letter of characteristic idealism and forbearance. In it Voorhis recalled "most poignantly" his own hopeful arrival in Congress a decade before, the "long hours of very hard and frequently thankless work," the overriding importance of the "vigor and effectiveness" of the national legislature. He was wishing his rival well and would be "glad to be of any help that you believe I can render" before the new session. His hurt and dismay subdued but still too fresh, Voorhis added, "I have refrained, for reasons which I am sure you will understand, from making any references in this letter to the circumstances of the campaign recently conducted in our district. It would only have spoiled the letter."

Two weeks passed as the envelope wound its way from Whittier and back to the Mayflower. Then, without a reply, Voorhis returned from lunch one day in late December to find Richard Nixon standing in his anteroom amid the packing boxes. They smiled, shook hands, and went into Voorhis's bare office to talk for more than an hour. Their conversation was "guarded" and general, as Voorhis related it. At the close Nixon asked for the congressman's district mailing list, an extraordinary request among politicians even under far more benign circumstances, and Voorhis gently if plainly turned him down. "We . . . parted, I hope and believe, as personal friends," the older man later said of the scene. Nixon would be "a fairly conservative" congressman, Voorhis wrote in his 1947 memoirs, adding generously, "but I believe he will be a good one."

There was that winter one last, less-graceful sequel to the contest between these extraordinary men. Not long after the meeting in Voorhis's office, a mutual California acquaintance introduced Nixon to Stanley Long, the former Voorhis aide, who proceeded unabashedly to take the new congressman to task for the Red smears and the devastating "rabbit" attack on the Voorhis legislative record. That night, Nixon would reply much as he responded to Osmyn Stout chiding him for his sophistry in the campaign debates. "Of course, I knew Jerry Voorhis wasn't a communist," he said. "You know I knew better than that; I know the processes of the legislature and the Congress better than that," he added about the famous "rabbits." "But it's a good political campaign fire to use." Long was simply naïve to dwell on these political means. "I had to win," he told the aide. "That's the thing you don't understand. The important thing is to win."

He was now one of the historic Eightieth Congress, the spoil of the GOP sweep in 1946 and a long-awaited instrument of conservative reckoning after fourteen years under the New Deal and a fitful half century of social change and economic reform. "The United States is now a Republican country!" GOP senator Styles Bridges exulted in the restoration, and his words sounded the mood of the winners if not the reality of the nation. "They had come roaring into the Capitol filled with spleen and plannings," one observer recalled them. "Over the whole session hung the air of wrathful counter-revolution." The agenda of the new GOP majority formed out of the hot breath of their campaign rhetoric that summer and fall. "They were determined," said a biographer of one member, "to rid the government of communists, perverts, and New Dealers, get tough with Joe Stalin, crack down on labor unions, and dismantle the Office of Price Administration." Behind the bluster, the legislative politics were expedient and traditional. A governing coalition between the entrenched Southern Democrats and the new conservative Republicans would let the GOP settle old economic scores while holding at bay civil rights.

Nixon hired as all-purpose aide Bill Arnold, the Alhambra press man for the general campaign, who now, with two female secretaries, made up his entire congressional staff. Their first priority was committee assignments, a biennial scramble all the more competitive with a 1946 congressional reorganization act and the advent of the new Republican chairmen and their majorities. Looking back at the district, still rustic for the moment, Arnold urged him to try for Agriculture. Nixon swiftly dismissed the idea, and first aspired to the much coveted and prestigious Judiciary Committee, until older colleagues convinced him that as a freshman he would have little chance. Eventually he applied for and won a seat on Education and Labor, a committee at the heart of the coming assault on union power. The far more crucial assignment, however, was arranged in secret, beyond even the usual clubby, influence-lathered channels of House preferment.

That old pariah, the House Committee on Un-American Activities, was now a permanent panel of the House and loomed with fresh importance. It was usually the vehicle of florid southern racists and demagogues neither easily controlled nor taken seriously by the two parties. But in the postwar Red Scare HUAC obviously offered coveted publicity for new members. It was also in 1946 one of the spoils, and risks, of the new Republican leadership on Capitol Hill. For the first time since the Committee's creation, the GOP could channel and exploit it to larger national purposes under a Republican chairman and majority—and at the same time temper HUAC's habitual abuses, which would now also be blamed more directly on the GOP.

Unlike his predecessors, the new Republican Speaker, Joe Martin of Massachusetts, pledged at the outset of the Eightieth to cooperate fully with the Committee "to remove the Red menace from America," and the jockeying became intense for three available GOP seats, "a choice assignment," as Martin himself said later. Only three days after the election, Herman Perry had written Martin about shepherding southern California's new representative. "Mr. Nixon of necessity will need to make friends among those who will be able to give him an honest picture on all political issues," Perry told the Speaker. "I trust that you will personally take an interest in him, as he has a promising future and considerable drive and ability." The letter was much the same personal and regional brashness Perry vouchsafed more nakedly with the local backers, and Joe Martin's response was at first perfunctory: "You can rest assured that I want to see that he gets every opportunity here . . . so that his reelection will come as a matter of course." But then, as the HUAC appointment drew nearer, the Speaker was quietly but forcefully lobbied in person by a delegation of party and financial figures flown from California specifically for the purpose.

At the time, Martin kept the visit secret and off his official schedule, in part because the whole episode involved his own unseemly dictation of Committee selection to one of the new and more irascible GOP chairmen, J. Parnell Thomas of New Jersey. But the weight of the influence was decisive. The Californians had gone directly to the point of the Republican strategy to make the renegade panel publicly and constitutionally presentable. "It was a headline committee, so to speak. We wanted a lawyer. Some people from the coast came to us with a high recommendation of Nixon's legal talents," Martin would say later, though it was Nixon's clear quest for the seat and the special lobby that gave him the assignment over several other attorneys in the new House. Soon after the California deputation left, Martin called Thomas to say Nixon was the choice of party leaders. At the same moment, he informed the freshman of his selection. "We need a young lawyer on that committee to smarten it up," the Speaker told Nixon. Watching it all, Arnold thought the HUAC seat "politically dangerous" but noted later that Nixon had actively sought it anyway with "characteristic prescience."

Afterward, the new member from Whittier disavowed any desire, much less backers' pressure, for the committee assignment. He "accepted with considerable reluctance . . . because of the dubious reputation of the committee," Nixon claimed in his memoirs. He repeatedly told the story of anguishing over the choice with fellow representatives. But the real scene in the office with Arnold, the glee at Martin's call, was very different. The appointment made him the only California congressman to sit on two major House committees. "Such a plum could only mean that powerful influence had been exerted on his behalf," observed one Washington reporter, though the private political levy on Martin remained hidden. In truth, Nixon's first genuine act of congressional politics had been an exercise in concerted and powerful patronage. Owed tellingly to his California supporters, the achievement was also the precondition of the larger success of his congressional career. As for Joe Martin, the crusty New Englander and Capitol Hill veteran was under no illusions about the demure young congressman and HUAC. "No one went on a committee of that kind," he stated later about Nixon's secretly brokered assignment, "who did not wish very much to be a member."

The day after his swearing-in, a reporter turned to him in the Republican cloakroom and asked if he had any "pet project" in legislation. Capitol reporters saw Richard Nixon purse his lips, smile "ingratiatingly," as one of them wrote, and reply in a soft voice, "No, nothing in particular. I was elected to smash the labor bosses and my one principle is to accept no dictation from the CIO-PAC." The hollow echo of campaign rhetoric was soon belied by his shrewd politics and conspicuous intelligence. At the bottom of Labor Committee seniority, Nixon was within weeks commanding headlines and had slipped into the forefront of the supporters of the historic Taft-Hartley legislation to weaken the unions.

Early in February, in a small stroke of genius, he went to Scranton, Pennsylvania, to talk personally with union members in mines and factories. His resulting "grass-roots poll" and informal "report" pointed to rank-and-file concerns with union democracy, finance, and violence, targets of the emerging GOP bill, and gave him national publicity from *The New York Times* to the *San Francisco Chronicle*. He was soon avidly involved in committee drafting of Taft-Hartley, so intimately in the later stages that congressional aides, if not their jealous employers, thought Richard Nixon "a principal architect" of the ultimate legislation.

When the controversial bill came to the floor in mid-April, fought bitterly by organized labor and the Democratic minority, Nixon was at the side of sponsor Fred Hartley for an eloquent interjection in the heated debate.

Union decisions would not be made, he told the House, "in the sumptuous quarters of a labor baron in the Carlton Hotel; not in some smoke-filled room . . . where labor leaders get together and, by the stroke of a pen, decide the fate of millions of workers." Comparing their act to the Magna Carta, but mixing his metaphorical heroes and villains, he pictured King John at Runnymede and told respectfully silenced colleagues that Taft-Hartley was a veritable "bill of rights" curbing the "barons of union labor." When they passed the measure the next day by 308–107, Nixon stood for the majority's "exultant shouts" that filled the House chamber. Later that July he entered in the *Congressional Record* his own tightly argued defense of the act, "The Truth About the New Labor Law." The statement immediately became a staple for GOP congressmen defending their vote, with thousands of reprints sent around the country. It was a sequence of authentic precocity in the seniority-bound Congress and a record seldom if ever equaled again by a House freshman.

Taft-Hartley was to be the major legislation of the Eightieth Congress and the crucial labor law of a generation. Outlawing the closed shop, prohibiting secondary boycotts and sympathy strikes, curbing union political contributions, and setting the eighty-day "cooling-off" period for strikes in crucial industries, the new act marked the effective end of labor's rise to power in the New Deal. It would bring a gradual but vast turnabout in the struggle for economic power and set in motion the eventual political decline of American trade unionism, a momentous process that Richard Nixon would aid and benefit from over the next quarter century. Little of that was visible in the spring of 1947, but he had begun in office by taking an important part in a historic conservative triumph. It was an early and extraordinary fulfillment of his promises in San Marino and Whittier and Alhambra to change the direction of the nation. If that much was later obscured in accounts of his Washington origins, it was because Taft-Hartley, for all its importance, was only the beginning.

The labor panel provided his prodigy's debut in legislative history, though it was HUAC—the notorious body that came to be called simply "the Committee"—that was to be the center of his congressional career and the fount of his remarkable rise. On February 18, 1947, the day after he presented his Scranton antiunion report, Nixon rose to deliver his maiden speech in the House. Not the customary statesmanly address on policy, legislation, or cause, it was a solemn prosecutor's brief for a Contempt of Congress citation against Gerhart Eisler, an old target of the Committee who had clashed fiercely with the panel at its opening hearing two weeks before. He called the German Eisler "an arrogant, defiant enemy" and "principal character" in "a foreign-directed conspiracy whose aim and purpose was to undermine and destroy the government of the United States." In his comings and goings since the 1930s, Eisler had been given transit and then tourist visas by the Immigration and Naturalization Service, and Nixon indignantly argued that "an investigation should be made of the procedures and personnel responsible for granting such privileges to dangerous aliens of this type."

Going beyond his allotted ten minutes with a list of Eisler's crimes as a communist agent, Nixon closed with a passage that could have fit verbatim into his 1929 *Los Angeles Times* oration on the perils of liberty. "It is essential as members of this House that we defend vigilantly the fundamental rights of freedom of speech and freedom of the press. But we must bear in mind that the rights of free speech and free men do not carry with them the right to advocate the destruction of the very government which protects the freedom of an individual to express his views."

The citation was voted and Eisler convicted, his sentence a year in federal prison. *Newsweek* lauded the freshman's speech as "deeply impressive," given "in calm and measured tones and with an intense sincerity, but . . . a quality of steel behind the voice." As his attack on Eisler demonstrated, he was in many ways at home from the beginning in the inquisitional ethos of the Committee. Barely a month after being sworn in, he wrote an Alhambra supporter that "the State Department seems to be loaded with people . . . who can't be labeled as commies but who seem to have very friendly leanings in that direction." Yet his maiden speech was also an initiation in another sense, in the layers of reality and politics buried beneath the Washington surface.

Gerhart Eisler had indeed been a colorful, no doubt dedicated Comintern agent at the Lenin Institute in Moscow, in China during the thirties, and by means of passport fraud and petty intrigue in the United States during the war. But beyond that, Nixon's urging of criminal sanctions, as one Committee historian gently noted later, "took some liberties with the facts." The record showed that Eisler had not actually refused to answer questions, the statutory grounds for contempt, but insisted on the right to make an opening statement, which the Committee testily denied. Nixon's first HUAC hearing had ended in a shouting match with Eisler being taken away by Immigration officers who already had him in custody for various violations. Nor was there hard evidence for the sweeping revolutionary conspiracy Nixon attributed to the witness, including a vague, incendiary charge of some tie to an atomic spy ring recently uncovered in Canada.

Beneath the impressive speech and the Committee's "breaking" of the "Eisler Case" was a tangled bureaucratic and political skein, in which both the stormy hearing and the substance of Richard Nixon's maiden address on the House floor had been fashioned by HUAC chief investigator Robert Stripling, using secret FBI reports specifically leaked for the purpose both directly to HUAC and by way of two favored newspaper reporters. In time-honored tradition, as the FBI's own documents would show long afterward, the Bureau was using the Committee and the Eisler sensation to outmaneuver its parent Justice Department in an old bureaucratic battle, and even, in Nixon's prompted call for an investigation of Eisler's visa history, to settle similar intramural scores with the INS. Eventually Gerhart Eisler jumped bail while appealing his conviction, fled on a Polish ship, and retired to East Germany, not as the mastermind of Soviet intelligence in America but as a loyal courier rewarded with a minor academic position. Nothing, it turned out, was quite what it first seemed in Richard Nixon's much-praised maiden speech.

"SOME GOOD INFORMATION ABOUT THE COMMUNISTS"

GOP efforts to restock the Committee in the Eightieth Congress, either to exploit it or to avoid embarrassment, had in effect begun and ended with Dick Nixon. HUAC veterans and ranking backers in both parties dug in after Martin's pressured placement of the young Californian. For Nixon the result left the body at once an extraordinary political opportunity and a potential embarrassment. While easily eclipsed in competence and publicity, the rest of the Committee were not so easily civilized or shed as a matter of political repute. His eventual national prominence on the panel traced largely to who and what they were—"uncouth, undignified, ungrammatical," as one of their star witnesses described only part of their public image. But he would suffer, too, inevitably and ironically, from a kind of guilt by association with his fellow members, a process in which HUAC commonly delighted.

In the chair sat J. Parnell Thomas, born John Patrick Feeney, a plump fifty-two-year-old bond salesman and former small-town New Jersey mayor who had been on HUAC since its inception and whom one legal historian would call without exaggeration "narrow-minded, petty, emotional, vindictive and blindly partisan." "Seldom has an important congressional agency been so handicapped by the vulgarity of its leader," Robert Carr would write in a respected study of the Committee. "Thomas conducted hearings as though he were a cheap comedian or participant in a street-corner political harangue." Next in seniority was Karl Mundt, forty-seven, self-styled Republican "country boy from South Dakota" with degrees from Carleton and Columbia. His false modesty a mockery, the rotund, bald Mundt remained ever the self-righteous, half-educated provincial, a clever investigator who seemed to relish the sheer hunt for subversives. He was even more concerned about personal publicity than the choleric Thomas and brought to HUAC, concluded an observer, little more than "a series of strong prejudices and a bitter sense of partisanship." At forty-five, John McDowell, a Pennsylvania newspaper owner educated at a southern military academy, was another new GOP member along with Nixon. Like other students of HUAC, Carr judged him a man "of deep prejudices and narrow horizons . . . a complete nonentity . . . of exceedingly limited ability." His narrow hawklike face and frozen small grin lent McDowell a bug-eyed, slightly crazed look as he randomly interrupted Committee questioning, "unable," wrote one obsesrver, "to remain silent, to play the quiet role men of mediocre talents have wisely selected for themselves."

On the Democratic side, the lone new man was F. Edward Hebert, a shrewd forty-six-year-old New Orleans city editor and legacy of the Huey Long machine, who seemed about to leaven the Committee with an instinctive sense of fairness and impatience with its chronic smears and publicity-mongering. But then, bow tie taut around his bull neck, Hebert would soon succumb to his own implacable obscurantism, an obsession with college campuses as inherently treasonous. "I am from Tulane," he would drawl again and again to any witness happening to mention higher education, "and to my chagrin there are more communists who infest that place than Americans." Hebert appeared scholarly, however, beside the ranking Democrat, "Lightnin' " John Rankin of Mississippi.

An embarrassment even to his most benighted southern colleagues, Rankin was a short, slight, gray-haired lawyer of sixty-six, a vicious anti-Semite and racial bigot who once blamed World War II reverses in Italy on the presence of black soldiers at the front. Given at hearings to pawing through a scurrilous volume called *Who's Who in American Jewry* to see if witnesses were hiding their incriminating ancestry, he also delicately separated the Ukrainians from the hated U.S.S.R. because, as he explained, they were after all "the white people of Russia." With similar reasoning, he pronounced the U.S. Communist Party "75 percent Jew," urged that the Anti-Defamation League be declared a subversive organization, and defined Marxism in handy amalgam as "nothing but . . . abject slavery dominated by a racial minority." "I am not clear about the racial minority," one recanting communist offered meekly. "I am," Rankin concluded. Fortifying Rankin was a rural Georgian lawyer, sixty-two-year-old Democrat John Wood, who had been an active member of the Ku Klux Klan, though Wood and the remaining members of HUAC played almost no role during Nixon's tenure. They were, altogether, a singular group, "the worst collection of people," thought the usually phlegmatic George Reedy, who covered them regularly in the late 1940s for United Press, "that have ever been assembled in the entire history of American politics."

The mentality of the Committee, and especially its putative role—the investigation of subversives and spies, of alien forces and movements assumed to be criminal and conspiratorial by their very nature—made HUAC more than ordinary congressional committees peculiarly dependent on its staff. The staff in turn reflected the predictable sociology of this political *audo-da-fé*, a roster of zealots, turncoats, gumshoes, men eager to track down and extinguish heresy, often in penitence for their own and free of qualms about the panel's mission or methods. In their narrowness of view and authoritarianism—and like Chairman Thomas, aka Feeney, railing at the communists' use of aliases—they were the mirror image of some of those they hunted. Not surprisingly, the core of the HUAC staff were those kindred spirits of the Cold War, ex-communists and ex-FBI agents. The committee clung to such people, as Walter Goodman said of one of them, "like ladies to the interior decorator who is able to dignify their tastes and bolster their pretensions . . . for his delusions . . . his simplifications and, most especially, for his supply of names."

The chief investigator, as the staff director was called in 1947–48, was Robert Stripling, a Texan then in his mid-thirties who had dropped out of college fifteen years before and come to Washington when then–HUAC chairman Martin Dies gave him a patronage job as a clerk folding House documents. Eventually, he succeeded to the top of the staff, as Carr's history put it, "with no recognizably relevant talents or experience whatsoever," save that he was "a dedicated and fanatical man." Beyond some Washington night-school law courses, Stripling was essentially uneducated for his crucial position as *de facto* counsel. A tall, thin figure with dark circles under piercing blue eyes, he could be an ominous physical presence at hearings. The *St. Louis Post-Dispatch* saw him during the Eightieth Congress with "slicked-down black hair, a sallow, drawn face and a habit of constantly pursing his lips together, as if continually revolting at something." Yet the object of his distaste was often the self-serving and incompetence of the Committee as well as the sins of subversives. For all his limits Stripling was nonetheless a cunning, dogged interrogator and, on occasion (with historic consequences for Richard Nixon), the cold, tough detective he resembled with almost cartoon apery.

Under Stripling worked Louis Russell, a former minor league baseball player, accountant, and ten-year FBI veteran. He "used the word 'liberal' as though it were synonymous with 'radical,' " remembered one writer who knew Russell, "and made it clear that he did not like either type of person." HUAC's official liaison with the FBI, and covertly the Bureau's informer on the Committee, he even bore a pug-nosed likeness to J. Edgar Hoover, and was noted in particular for his diatribes against "well-known liberals who have acquired wealth by inheritance or marriage." Russell commanded two staff investigators, William Wheeler and Donald Appell, younger figures of wholesome square faces, wavy hair, and wide lapels, carrying, like their boss, the mien and outlook of plainclothesmen.

It was a third ranking aide, however, who was in some ways even more important than either Stripling or Russell. Then fifty-six, a quiet, fidgety man who under the name "Bert Miller" had once been a devout communist and even business manager of the *Daily Worker*, Benjamin Mandel was nominally the Committee's research director. Reporters thought him "something of the zealot and dogmatist," devoted to HUAC with the same conviction he once had for the Communist Party. The Committee publications he authored were rich in information while unrefined and badly organized, full of "so many obvious errors and grossly unfair attacks," said one conservative historian, that the authentic revelations of sedition were usually lost. Yet Mandel's real junction was always hidden. The Committee's *Hintermann*, as one British scholar aptly described him, he was HUAC's instigator and "inside man" who directed their furtive two-way traffic in informers and documents, now ushering and prompting key witnesses before the microphones, now leaking secret Committee files to useful outsiders, and more than once performing a crucial service for Richard Nixon.

None of them would fare well in the larger history of the era. The "grubby men and women who served as . . . informers, investigators and counselors," E. J. Kahn called them, "operating sometimes with the merciless savagery of rabbit-clubbers, sometimes with the subtlety of the Chinese water torturer." Yet they were all—as cohorts, voices with whispered advice, legmen—to play a significant part in Richard Nixon's career during those first two eventful years in Washington. There was also something more: in his dependence upon them, his crucial interaction with them, Nixon entered and employed, as few politicians ever do, a shadowy world of operators and fixers, a world as marginally but distinguishably apart from conventional politics as the seamy Los Angeles private eyes of the 1930s and 1940s stood apart from the upstairs, smoky, glass-doored law offices that sometimes employed them. He would strike the alliance and bargain from the beginning—and it was there, an underlying curse of Watergate, at the bitter end.

For Nixon's rise, the Committee was always at the same time more than the sum of its colorful parts. If its manners were coarse, the anticommunist wave billowing beneath them in the Eightieth Congress rose from relatively more respectable forces. Religious and ideological conservatives, old-fashioned chauvinists, courthouse southerners, northern industry, a widening stratum of the bureaucratic, corporate, and professional elite of postwar American society—all found a common fear of the foreign Red bogey blending with a common front against trade union power and reform, generally against the Democratic regime. Held at a sometimes malodorous distance, HUAC would do, as it were, some of the political dirty work of that formidable alliance of business, church, and state.

Nixon was exposed to the backstage power almost immediately on taking his congressional seat. The catalyst was far from the twelfth district of California. In February 1947, as part of the crescendo for Taft-Hartley, the Labor Committee held hearings on the highly publicized strike at the Allis-Chalmers Company in Wisconsin. As a result, the labor committee's most ardent member in the hearings was the freshman congressman from Milwaukee's fifth district, Charles Joseph Kersten. Kersten was then forty-five, a courtly lawyer educated at Marquette and a former assistant district attorney who was a devout Catholic and equally devoted to exposing what he saw as "communist-instigated" labor unrest. "Put Kersten in Congress and keep communism out" read the slogan of his Red-baiting 1946 campaign. Before the hearings, Kersten had been briefed by his contacts on the reputed communist role in the 1941 Allis-Chalmers strike, and Nixon was visibly impressed by Kersten's knowing questions and apparently intimate understanding of the issue.

Days later, standing in the lobby of the Mayflower where the Nixons still lived and where he and Kersten had attended a political dinner, Nixon asked Kersten for help in getting "some good information about the communists," as Kersten remembered it. It was the beginning of a personal and political friendship suffused with their mutual anticommunist zeal. Now, in the Mayflower lobby, Kersten promised to introduce Nixon to his own discreet advisers and experts, Monsignor Fulton J. Sheen and a scholarly, sandy-haired young priest named John Cronin.

They soon met with Sheen, about to become director of the Pontifical Society for the Propagation of the Faith and later in the 1950s something of a celebrity as a handsome, dark-eyed bishop delivering homilies on his own network television program. In 1947 he seemed to epitomize the antisubversive postwar crusade of the American Catholic Church, where, as one scholar remarked of government security inquiries, "Fordham men were [to be] clearing (or not clearing) Harvard men." Sheen accordingly advised Francis Cardinal Spellman on the cardinal's periodic imprecations against liberalism, and railed in his own lectures against public universities with their "colossal wastage of taxes to professors who would destroy America by teaching Russian Bolshevism." Those sentiments he conveyed vividly to the young Quaker representative who came round with Kersten for a long evening that February and who went away with an autographed copy of Sheen's book on communism. Still, it was Father John Cronin who was to be far more important, the man "who really taught him," Kersten would say of Dick Nixon.

The two newly elected congressmen saw Cronin repeatedly in February and March, coming the first time for only a twenty-minute appointment and staying two hours. Nixon was obviously taken with the thirty-nine-year-old priest. Cronin was a Ph.D. from Catholic University and had gone in the mid-1930s to teach at a seminary in Baltimore, where he wrote his own economics textbook, authored several pamphlets on social problems, and, most important, became active in the Catholic trade union movement. Although neither acknowledged it, he and Nixon were even likely to have met five years earlier when Cronin had been on Baltimore's wartime Rationing Board, and efficient Richard Nixon was sent down the parkway from OPA headquarters to help the Baltimore Board iron out problems in the spring of 1942. In 1946, Cronin came to Washington as an assistant director of the National Catholic Welfare Conference. Yet behind his pink, boyish face, the academic's rimless glasses and gentle manner, the priest had a hidden résumé.

Cronin was an adviser to Catholic unionists and a labor arbitrator in Baltimore during the war when he first heard complaints about strong-arm tactics and packed elections by communist union organizers on the city docks. Outraged, he had begun to write about the problem to his church superiors, and at the same time to inform the FBI, which soon fastened on the sympathetic priest as a productive source. Cronin's seminary office was thought a neutral meeting place of warring labor factions, the mild cleric-arbitrator trusted by communists and militants as well. At one point the FBI had wired the room—"a little," said one scholar who learned of the taping long afterward, "like bugging the confessional."

Cronin's secret role did not end as mere informer. From the beginning he asked in return for FBI information on communist infiltration. They had leaked him some intelligence, and he incorporated the raw material in his intra-Church reports, winning him a reputation within the clergy as an expert on communism. Then, as the war ended, as the FBI found its new mission in the anticommunist surge, J. Edgar Hoover had struck an implicit alliance with the Church and used Cronin in particular as a conduit to the Catholic hierarchy. The leaks to the priest became a stream of some of the Bureau's most sensitive investigative files on the internal security threat, calculated to educate properly the leadership of America's most populous and political denomination. Cronin's authority, his seemingly miraculous grasp of inside knowledge about the new alien danger, was renowned as well among Catholic laymen, particularly politicians like Kersten. By those convoluted politics, Richard Nixon came to be tutored in his first weeks in Washington not simply by a well-informed academic but by a veritable government operative with access to what would be some of Washington's most titillating and politically explosive secrets.

When Nixon and Kersten saw Cronin that winter of 1947, the priest had just completed more than a year of powerfully influential publishing on the strength of his covert relationship with the FBI. In October 1945 Cronin circulated confidentially among the American bishops and other Catholic leaders *The Problem of American Communism in 1945: Facts and Recommendations*, some 150 pages drawn largely from FBI views and informers' reports. The "most reliable figures available indicate that as high as 64 percent of Communist [Party] membership is Jewish, 14 percent Negro and 22 percent from other groups," Cronin wrote in an echo of Rankin. The report deplored "the liberal dupe or fellow traveler" as the key to much communist success and dramatically named names ("because of the accuracy of the [FBI] sources, it is often possible to name definitely as Communists individuals who would publicly deny their affiliation"). Cronin accused as "pro-Soviet" or worse prominent figures such as Assistant Secretary of War John J. McCloy, *New York Herald Tribune* Washington Bureau Chief Bert Andrews, and poet Archibald MacLeish among "about four hundred" others. To verify it all, he invited the bishops to check with their own informants, leading some of them to clear the report with the FBI, who not surprisingly confirmed Cronin's accuracy.

In a March 1946 speech to a communion breakfast in Washington, long before Senator Joseph McCarthy and others made such charges, Cronin had claimed "130 communists" held key U.S. government positions and that a probe of the State Department "would shake the country." The report to the bishops led directly as well to Cronin's authorship of the alarming September 1946 Chamber of Commerce pamphlet on communist subversion, published so widely and decisively on the eve of the election. Meanwhile, in February 1946, the FBI had instituted a still-wider covert "educational" campaign to leak helpful anticommunist information to selected outlets. As Richard Nixon began his term in the Eightieth Congress in January 1947, Cronin was ghostwriting yet another Chamber pamphlet on *Communists Within the Government* and the process had come full circle, the FBI citing the Chamber publications—which their own informer-priest had written from their files—as independent substantiation of their congressional budget requests.

All of this was, as customary, concealed from public view, though there lay in Cronin's well-sponsored writing the seed of vast notoriety and of national fame for Richard Nixon. Cronin had the new congressman study and imbibe not only the report to the bishops and the Chamber pamphlets but also his rarified files, much of them the classified FBI material. "I told them about certain communists in atomic espionage rings and in the State Department," he remembered proudly of his long talks with representatives. As in his written reports, Cronin named names and discussed with Nixon "the apparent indifference" of the Truman administration to the evidence of treason in its midst. By early 1947, the priest's sources inside government had gone well beyond the FBI. He was also being supplied confidential information by HUAC's own Ben Mandel, and not least by a zealous State Department security officer named Ray Murphy, a hale Irishman who like so many others in the chain had "great difficulty," as his superior later testified, "in distinguishing between a communist and a liberal." Murphy would sometimes provide Cronin, and via the priest Congressman Nixon, material not even the FBI had yet developed.

Cronin was also an intimate contact with the emerging China Lobby and its network of conservative journalists. Six months before he began briefing Richard Nixon, Cronin brought together Mandel and a group of ex-FBI men with Alfred Kohlberg, a millionaire textile importer and owner of Chinese sweatshops, who was planning a major lobbying effort to shore up U.S. support of the tottering Chiang Kai-shek regime in China. Later, Cronin, Mandel, and Kohlberg would meet to organize an anticommunist magazine, called *Plain Talk*, at the Connecticut home of Isaac Don Levine, a right-wing newspaperman whom Kohlberg hired as his editor along with a young assistant, future Nixon biographer Ralph de Toledano. Again, they were each to be significant in Richard Nixon's career now and later, and they were all present, as it were, at the beginning, Father Cronin the discreet hub of the wheel.

What was more, as Cronin told Nixon in some detail that February, there buzzed from the FBI files, from Mandel and Murphy, from Levine, eventually from Kohlberg via the others, an intriguing though still little-known pair of names. Nixon would secretly learn them, and much of their dramatic connection traced in Cronin's classified files, eighteen months before he encountered the people themselves—a year and a half before the moment he acknowledged hearing of them. He would know about them before he and his wife and baby had even found a place to live in Washington.

One was a former communist whose story of conspiracy and subversive cells in the government Cronin thought impressive and "unimpeachable," a man now going by the half-adopted name of Whittaker Chambers. The other was one of those whom Chambers repeatedly implicated, a prominent, well-connected diplomatic aide of the New Deal years, an urbane young liberal lawyer from Baltimore named Alger Hiss.

Father Cronin's instruction, the initiation into his arcane world of secret security files and fertile conspiracies, formed the backdrop to Nixon's first Washington spring, what some reporters came to call the "ides of March" of the postwar era. Between his February maiden speech on Eisler's contempt and the passage of Taft-Hartley in April was a period of mounting bipartisan chauvinism. The President would have to "scare hell out of the American people," GOP senator Arthur Vandenberg said of the administration's peacetime proposal for major military aid, in this case to a dubious Greek regime fighting communists in an ambiguous civil war. But Truman was to do just that on March 12, winning the appropriation from Nixon and others in Congress by a speech depicting the Greek conflict as part of a life-and-death worldwide struggle between freedom and tyranny. The Cold War deepened with every new international act of Soviet belligerence and tightening control of Eastern Europe. But the wave of domestic fear had a momentum of its own.

J. Edgar Hoover came before HUAC that March, wrote one reporter, "like the archbishop paying a call on a group of lay brothers." He quoted Lenin, identified communism as "a condition akin to a disease that spreads like an epidemic," told the congressmen there were more communists per capita in the U.S. than in Russia at the time of the Bolshevik revolution, and recommended "unrelenting prosecution" of subversives. "Is there any one area in which the communists are more dangerous and more deeply entrenched than any other?" Nixon respectfully asked him. Hoover cited radio, college campuses, and, above all perhaps, motion pictures. He pointedly praised HUAC's already "excellent job in focusing attention on activities of communists in the government."

It was the first time the two men had met. As the director walked out of the hearing in triumph, his old friend Bradshaw Mintener inquired about the young man asking the final questions. "That's the new congressman from California," Hoover told him. Mintener had bristled and said, "Oh, he's the one that did what he did to my Yale classmate . . . Jerry Voorhis, whom during the campaign he called a communist, and so forth." And Hoover had answered, "I know all about that, but so far as law enforcement is concerned, he looks to me as though he's going to be a good man for us."

Spurred by the general climate and by Hoover's encouragement, HUAC promptly turned to an old hunting ground: Hollywood. The result was to be a spectacle of pounding gavel and theatrics on all sides as the panel confronted a group of militant and defiant screenwriters, the famous Hollywood Ten, in what one of their number expressively called "the time of the toad." Nixon took little part in the Committee's preparatory investigations in California that spring and summer. Still, his enthusiasm was evident. Planned fall hearings would "throw the fear of God into Hollywood," he told reporters at one point the following summer. "It will be sensational," he promised in a July 30 interview. "We intend to name names and to produce witnesses who will testify they have seen some persons prominent in Hollywood at communist meetings and who will report what they said." It was to be "a case of preventative medicine . . . to prevent communists in the event of another depression from stirring up the people."

Fittingly, the public Hollywood hearings premiered in late October to banks of floodlights, newsreel cameras, and capacity crowds in the old House caucus room, mostly women, gawking and sighing at Robert Taylor, Gary Cooper, Robert Montgomery. Nixon was not a member of the subcommittee presiding over the gala, but he pointedly sat in and joined the questioning with force and consequence. Memories of Depression Whittier and its outlying migrant camps far behind, he worried about the pernicious effects of *The Grapes of Wrath* being shown abroad. Of both Eric Johnston, head of the Motion Picture Producers Association, and then mogul Jack Warner, he asked how many "anticommunist" films the studios had produced. Johnston confessed he could think of none. Warner sheepishly said he was working on one.

One of the cooperative witnesses that autumn was the president of the Screen Actors Guild, an actor with a flagging career and already, in secret, a prolific FBI informer, captioned "T-10" in the documents, Ronald Reagan. It was the casual beginning, congressman and witness, of a mutually supportive forty-year relationship between the two future Presidents.

Nixon engaged Warner in rambling exchanges about the importance of promoting "Americanism" and of Hollywood fighting communists just like the Nazis. He carefully left the shouting matches with the accused writers to Thomas and Stripling. Like a hackneyed plot, the inquisition played out for the Ten in an ordeal of contempt, jail, and professional ruin. As he had for Eisler, Congressman Nixon gave a persuasive floor speech to win their contempt citations from the House.

Cowed by the Committee, afraid of the impact of the controversy on box-office receipts, settling old scores in any case, movie executives met in secret a month after the hearings to institute a blacklist that would reach well beyond the Ten. An insidious and incalculable intimidation and self-censorship began to blanket the industry. To Nixon's insistent prodding about anticommunist pictures, and in spite of poor box office, the nervous studios proceeded to grind out over the next few years more than fifty movies on themes of communist or Russian villainy. For now, anti-Red films were "the hottest," noted *Variety* after the hearings, and by 1948 social "message" scripts on racial injustice or other suspect subjects were being dropped "like hot coals." The blacklist and artistic-political chill persisted with few exceptions for nearly two decades.

❖❖❖

He took an office in Suite 528, what they called "the attic" in the back of the House Office Building, farther than the older members wanted to walk and where freshmen could have more spacious quarters. A photographer came by from the Republican National Committee to snap the new congressman one evening soon after his swearing-in, and found Nixon there alone, working on the phone at a small desk amid bare walls, a box of envelopes partly spilled on the thin dark carpet, a pencil sharpener still in its box atop steno pads. Entering Congress he was overcome with the "same lost feeling" he had on entering the navy at Newport, Nixon told a writer. The emptiness soon disappeared in a characteristic and restless regimen of work.

Arnold remembered him waiting "until the last possible moment" before leaving for the airport or Union Station, for fear he would waste time "having to sit around and wait at a terminal." They were delayed once crossing the Potomac to National Airport because the Fourteenth Street drawbridge was up, and when the congressman missed the plane, the next one leaving in only an hour, Nixon had anxiously insisted they return to the office for the extra minutes of work. Arnold and the two secretaries worked along with him "such long hours," Dorothy Cox, one of the women, recalled, though Nixon never directly asked them to stay overtime. They would see him as a kindly if driven young politician, gently calling the women aside to point out mistakes in correspondence. Pat soon joined them to help with the backlog of constituent mail and came in from time to time to draft letters and type. "We were like a family," Cox warmly remembered of those first months, the small staff with an "*esprit de corps* . . . pulling for the boss because he gave us the feeling he was going places."

Impatient with the newcomers' powerlessness and isolation, Nixon helped organize the Chowder and Marching Society, a group of fifteen junior House Republicans. They caucused informally every Wednesday to share gossip, shards of intelligence, and views on legislation, pooling knowledge that might have come to most of them otherwise only as hearsay or in belated press accounts. Among the early members were future senators and GOP leaders: Kenneth Keating from New York; Norris Cotton of New Hampshire; Kentucky's Thruston Morton; and eventually another future President, young Gerald Ford from Grand Rapids, who came to share a car pool with Richard Nixon and Bill Arnold from their neighboring Virginia apartments. The society was for the most part "a friendly group of Capitol Hill jocks and imbibers," one reporter called them, with striking resemblance to the Whittier College Orthogonians in their haleness, lack of scholastic gifts, and the manly banding together against exclusion and tradition. And again, the sober, intense Dick Nixon emerged as their leader, husbanding their collective influence in committees and on the floor, slowly making himself as a back-corridor freshman "the center," a Washington journalist noted, "of a small power nexus."

Nixon was one of them, yet, as always, apart. He gave advice, guided Ford and others, but had no mentor in the group. He also campaigned for some of them for years afterward, forgot or turned on others, and derived few lasting political relationships among them, save with the stolid Ford. His closest friend was a thirty-six-year-old fellow freshman from Santa Monica, Donald Jackson, who had run against PAC "socialism" and who later succeeded to Nixon's seat on HUAC. But none of them were intimates.

He was attracted to a freshman Democrat who was his counterpart at the bottom of seniority on the other side of the Education and Labor Committee and whose own office was nearby in the "attic." In the spring of 1947 a McKeesport, Pennsylvania, civic group invited the two of them to discuss Taft-Hartley pro and con, and an audience of 150 at the Penn-McKee Hotel heard the first debate between Richard Nixon and twenty-nine-year-old John F. Kennedy. Nixon was bombarded with angry questions from union men and the local paper thought him less photographic than his Irish opponent with the charming grin, though he was credited with winning the debate. On the *Capitol Limited* back to Washington, they sat up late in their Pullman talking about foreign affairs, the topic that interested them both far more than domestic issues.

The train ride began a strange, mixed relationship between these historic opponents and future Presidents, men who together dominated a generation in American politics and in their different ways led the media revolution in government. They were never "close friends," Nixon would write, "too different in background, outlook, and temperament." While Nixon the young congressman was writing earnest arguments that spring about Taft-Hartley, Jack Kennedy was penning a rake's note to the Plaza Hotel to retrieve his silver cocktail shaker left behind in a weekend party. In his wealth, his tortured womanizing under the dark shadow of his imperious father, Kennedy inhabited a different world. Yet he would be there in half-expedient, half-admiring cordiality for Richard Nixon, passing along Joseph Kennedy's furtive campaign contributions, sending a warm personal note of congratulations on Dick's advance through the ranks. Only later would Kennedy caustically dismiss the Californian for his personal frailty and lack of political character. Meanwhile, Nixon, like other politicians, would stand somewhat aghast and in awe of the ultimate success of a Jack

Kennedy they knew to be so promiscuous, so much less substantial than the public image. Richard Nixon would envy, admire, fear, try to emulate at once the best and worst of his onetime McKeesport debating foe, and a tangled history emerged less from their contrast and clash than from what, in the end, they had in common.

Unlike the well-traveled Kennedy and others, the congressman from Whittier and his pretty, fine-boned wife suffered an enduring awkwardness from the beginning in the political society of the Capital. She was no more at home in the bridge lessons or cookbook publishing of the Congressional Wives Club than he in the extracurricular drinking bouts of Chowder and Marching, though both went through the motions for appearances. For all their own relative sophistication back home—the worldly couple who fled Whittier for the big cities—there were sharp reminders of polish and station. Invited to a dinner party that winter by patrician Christian Herter of Massachusetts, Nixon wore his best blue business suit and she bought a new cocktail dress, only to discover to their embarrassment at the door that they had misread the invitation and the rest of the guests were in black tie or formal gown. Over a following quarter century they would become practiced, adept, at one point archly pretentious about form and formality, and almost never genuinely at ease in the drawing-room Washington society of their era.

George Reedy remembered being asked by Arnold to come back to the "attic" with Douglas Cornell of the Associated Press and others to have a drink with the representative in his office and get to know him. It was a familiar little amenity of the time for congressmen and Capitol Hill reporters, and he and the rest had found Nixon there with the two bottles of bourbon and one Scotch dictated by protocol. Nixon had met them in shirtsleeves, called them by first names, made the politician's all-purpose jokes. Yet it was also a stiff, surreal little scene, the liquor and glasses and ice on a small table with a tablecloth, and beside it Pat Nixon, "standing there," as Reedy saw her, "with her very tight-lipped smile," giving in her reserve a first reaction of "terrible coldness." There was something of the same about Nixon despite his hearty manner. It was "a feeling," Reedy remembered thinking afterward, "that we weren't talking to a human being, but a doll wound up and pulling a string."

Nonetheless, his press relations and publicity were remarkable for a freshman, and a result of some simple luck as well as Nixon's abilities. A wire-service photographer thought them both so handsome and wholesome that they symbolized the new, younger, postwar Congress, and the result was a nationally syndicated picture—much used in later campaigns—showing Pat and Dick on bicycles gazing off like advertising models amid cherry blossoms in front of the Jefferson Monument at the Tidal Basin, the kind of imagery most of his peers passionately coveted and never received. Ollie Atkins of the *Saturday Evening Post*, later to be their White House photographer, was similarly taken with the young representative moving briskly about the Capitol, usually giving instructions to Arnold, who was at his side. Atkins photographed them exchanging documents on the stairway or parting on the Capitol portico late in the evening, all to similarly flattering effect.

If personally graceless at drinks and jokes, Nixon understood almost reflexively the needs and vulnerability of the Washington press, and handled them as a matter of business no less deftly than he and his campaign had primed the newspapers of the twelfth district. When he and Kersten decided to tour East European embassies early in 1948, systematically interviewing each ambassador on the then-burning issue of Soviet control and takeover in their respective countries, he carefully took along the AP's Cornell as ostensible aide and note-taker, giving the newsman a valuable scoop. Then, to cover bases, he quietly passed Cornell's notes to rival columnist Joseph Alsop. He appreciated no less the easy comradery in the politician's common cause against muckrakers. When Drew Pearson criticized a group of legislators in July 1947, Nixon sent a half-serious, half-jovial note of "congratulations" to the seventeen, including Senator Joe McCarthy. "Now that you have been attacked by that arch character assassin and truth distorter," he told them, "I am confident that your rating . . . will be even higher than in the past." For his part, Pearson had scarcely noted Nixon himself, but promptly got a leaked copy of the circular.

Already under occasional press attack in cartoon or editorial along with the rest of HUAC, Nixon privately sought out critical reporters, and confided his own distaste with his garish colleagues, along with leaks of Committee plans or gossip. Among his contacts was Bert Andrews, the forty-six-year-old Washington bureau chief of the *New York Herald-Tribune*, who despised the Committee and who won a Pulitzer Prize in 1947 for stories on abuses in State Department security investigations. Andrews had risen to the *Herald-Tribune* from a workaday career as brusque, facile rewrite man on the old *Sacramento Star* and *San Diego Sun*. He came out of a career and California conservatism congenial to a good, simple story, to red-blooded anticommunism without HUAC's crude buffoonery, and Nixon shrewdly sensed their common ground at the start. To Andrews and others he was the new conscience, the responsible seat on HUAC, the hunter who made the hunt respectable, and, not least, their source. To some extent he would have enjoyed good publicity in any case by his contrast to the rest of the

Committee. But his courtship of the press made it fulsome. And when the spotlight later played round to HUAC full glare, there would be not only one presentable member but a national hero.

Reflected in the early and effective coopting of the press was a fundamental truth of his arrival in Washington. Richard Nixon was quite simply more intelligent, more purposeful, by any odds harder-working than most of his congressional peers, most of the patronage-ridden staffs, and most of the reporters who covered them in the postwar era. Other politicians and journalists came and went on the scene. Some who were there grew in ways he did not. But the first months of the Eightieth Congress planted an arrogance, a private disdain for the Hill's political peerage, and, most of all, a habit of having his way with the press that affected his judgment and acts for years, in some respects into the White House over two decades later.

Outwardly deferential toward the rest of the House and particularly the senior men, he could be publicly unctuous about their customs and his own purity. When a former campaign worker in the twelfth promised a group of local petitioners he would use what one account called his "influence" with the congressman, Nixon huffily wired district papers to deny not only the "influence" but even the slightest local patronage. He had "no representative, no fixer," as other congressmen did, he said caustically, though such local offices were as often for legitimate constituent services as for spoils. To reporters from a national magazine he boasted that, unlike his colleagues, he turned down "all invitations from the lobby brigade." He would do no more than have lunch with special interest representatives, and then insisted on picking up the check, "an eccentricity," wrote the reporter, that "takes a $500 yearly bite out of his salary."

It was the sort of vocal hypocrisy few of his fellow politicians forgot, watching the troop of California backers to and from Nixon's attic office, and the meticulous care of his district interests. Judith Wingert, now in college at Penn after the death of both her parents, came down to ask his help on a legal problem with Jeff Wingert's estate, and Nixon proudly showed her the signatures in his office guest book. She saw now plainly "the drive . . . the ambition" she had not noted years before in the Bank of America building. "I don't think there's ever been any question but that Dick Nixon wanted to be President of the United States," she said of her impression on that visit. There was also no doubt, she thought, that "he sided with the companies," that he was operating "on political expediency." In the visitors' book she read familiar names of southern California oilmen and bankers, old Wingert and Bewley clients, and Whittier contributors like Buey Allen. "He was very proud," she would remember, "of the people that would come and sign that book."

❧❧❧

The New York Times called his legislative record "obscure" beyond his prominence with HUAC. That, too, was a result in part of his press relations. As the emerging star and source on the Committee, the rest of his politics, those beyond the headlines, would not seem to matter. That he was the liberal, the moderate on the Committee, or the articulate leaker among the "jocks and imbibers" of Chowder and Marching, gave a glow of moderation to the entire image. Reporters would somehow remember his record as clearly mixed, a kind of Republican golden mean that was the invention of both candidate and an astigmatic press. The political man seemed as distant as the personal. "I got to know him very well," George Reedy said afterward, "and yet I never had the faintest idea of what the man was like."

In fact, his roll calls were remarkably consistent, and the sweeping reversal of the Voorhis votes he had promised campaign rallies back in the district. Nixon voted against maintaining funds for soil conservation and school lunch programs, purchasing loans for tenant farmers, reclamation appropriations, and increasing or extending Social Security. He stood in opposition to the OPA, rent control, tax cuts for lower-income groups. He helped to defeat new funds for rural electrification, low-rent public housing, aid to education, and public power projects. He was in favor of tax reductions for the higher brackets, price-setting and exemptions from antitrust for certain industries, higher railroad freight rates, and exemption of the rail companies from antitrust. Nixon votes with a GOP majority were hedged about with the strictures of the conservative agenda. He supported abolition of the poll tax but in a bill far short of civil rights goals. His support for foreign aid excluded any governments thought under Russian influence. To the delight of business, the antiinflation measure pressed by Nixon and most other Republicans was only voluntary. He also voted for the admission of thousands of displaced persons, but the general immigration legislation carried the old, racist repugnance toward immigrants of southern and eastern European origins.

In his first session in Congress, Nixon voted with the Republicans more than nine out of ten times on what were regarded even loosely as party line votes. His support was over 90 percent as well for what were tallied as generally bipartisan issues, but those were for the most part the increasing Cold War foreign policy measures of a growing GOP-Democratic coalition. His votes joined the old guard assault on the New Deal. The roll calls followed as well the small mimeographed questionnaires he sent frequently throughout the twelfth, a "poll" that inevitably reflected the more activist conservative elements in his constituency and which he carefully used as a guide in the early domestic legislation.

Beyond Taft-Hartley and anticommunist measures stemming from HUAC, he sponsored or actively cosponsored little substantive legislation, making "no conspicuous effort," noted one reporter. The principal piece was a tidelands oil bill on the old model of his petroleum industry backers, the law Voorhis had so long fought, giving the states (and thus the companies) sovereignty over offshore fields and the right to use their domain for other purposes of private exploitation as well as oil drilling. Otherwise, he proposed minor, conservative amendments to the Social Security and Servicemen's Readjustment acts and an anti-Soviet resolution calling for changes in the United Nations charter.

California was the conspicuous exception to his orthodox cutting of federal programs, although he proudly disavowed the usual pork barrel tendencies. "Nixon's record of nonachievement for special interests in his own area would make many a machine politician blush for shame," wrote an admiring *Saturday Evening Post* after the Eightieth. Yet in an August 1947 circular letter to his California colleagues, he had been complaining bluntly about the booming state's lack of appropriate federal largesse. "It is unthinkable," he wrote them, "that the federal government would continue to spend the taxpayer's money in regions where the population has remained static without reappraising tremendously increased needs in California and elsewhere in the West." He managed it all—the plain partisanship, the often reactionary positions, the liberal-moderate, almost nonpolitical imagery—with a virtuosity even close witnesses saw only later. They recognized in Nixon then what he had been in Congress from the beginning, the phenomenon one of them would call "a completely political man."

"TRUE AND BRUTAL FACE"

The patronage that flowed from his spreading reputation was crucial in his personal development as well as political advance. In June 1947, in the wake of his role in Taft-Hartley and first appearances with HUAC, he learned he had been chosen for the House Select Committee on Foreign Aid, created in response to Secretary of State George Marshall's announcement that spring of the proposed Marshall Plan for Europe. The most important of congressional select bodies in foreign affairs during the first postwar decade, it would be known as the Herter Committee, after its aristocratic fifty-two-year-old leader from Boston who was handpicked by the eastern internationalist leaders of the GOP for his diplomatic experience and enlightened record, and who in turn brokered with Joe Martin and congressional conservatives a careful cross-section of panel members. Of the eleven Republicans and eight Democrats, half were urban, half rural, and all, as *The New York Times* noted Herter's stipulation, "from the ranks of the hard and serious workers of the House," men like Francis Case of South Dakota, Texan George Mahon, and Francis Walter from Pennsylvania. But Richard Nixon was the youngest, and the lone congressman from the Far West.

That July he went to the White House with three other GOP representatives as part of Harry Truman's personal lobbying effort on bipartisan foreign policy and aid. Nixon methodically jotted notes on the meeting after returning to the Hill and recorded Truman's modest decoration of the Oval Office, a "big pleasant room" he had seen earlier only as a tourist. The President had confided the difficulty of his decision to drop the atomic bomb, described the Presidency jovially as "the greatest show on earth," extolled bipartisanship ("some of my best friends never agree with me politically"), and gave them a small lecture of geopolitics around the Oval Office globe. "The Russians are like us, they look and act like us, they are fine people," Nixon remembered him telling them. "They can have whatever they want just so [long as] they don't try to impose their system on others." Leaving, Nixon registered the virtues of the President he was to be attacking bitterly little more than a year later—"his hominess, his democratic attitude, and his sincerity." He also noted, in another of so many small ironic gestures by a future Chief Executive who taped his own White House, that the Oval Office contained "no gadgets."

The select committee was scheduled to tour war-torn Western Europe that autumn. "This will be no junket. It will be no cross-Atlantic cocktail party . . . no sideshow excursions nor sight-seeing tours by individual members at public expense," Nixon announced with characteristic piety on the eve of the Herter trip. He embarked on the luxurious *Queen Mary* in late August to some family fanfare. His parents came to see him off in New York. They all went to see the Broadway musical *Oklahoma!* Nixon tenderly remembering his father, now almost wholly deaf, accidentally leaving his hearing aid in the hotel room in the rush but sitting cheerfully through the performance he could not hear rather than bothering the rest of them.

He also left with a last-minute somber warning letter from a formidable group of his district supporters, including Perry and the old-guard money. He would be "subjected first to a skillful orientation program by the State Department and later, to no less skillfully prepared European propaganda," and it was their "hope and belief" he could remain "level-headed." In the same insistent tone of sponsors, they reminded Nixon that the 1948 election, his as well as the Presidential race, was at hand, and the only "fundamental cure" was to "rid ourselves of all the hangover philosophies of the New Deal." But victory could be won only if Republican congressmen "are wise enough to refuse to be drawn into support of a dangerously unworkable and profoundly inflationary foreign policy and . . . that the Democrats do not succeed in so dividing our party by bipartisan internationalism that there is no longer any way to tell who is a Republican." Of its kind it was the first, though hardly the last, of blunt reminders of his patronage and position.

The select committee docked at Southampton on September 2, and stepped off into a Europe, Nixon recorded, "tottering on the brink of starvation and chaos." The journey was a dramatic catapult in his career. A year after debating Jerry Voorhis in musty high school auditoriums in an obscure Los Angeles suburb, he was now taking tea with Prime Minister Clement Atlee at 10 Downing Street, discussing international economics and the balance of power, or standing in the ruins of Hitler's Reichschancellory, implored by hungry German children trying to sell Nazi medals as souvenirs.

They soon broke into subcommittees, Nixon going south to Italy, Greece, and Trieste. To the discomfort of his Foreign Service escorts, he brashly sought out communist labor leader Giuseppe Di Vittorio in Rome and asked polemical questions about the right to strike in the U.S.S.R. and Italian communist criticism of Soviet policy. In an office suitably draped in red, the communist responded coolly with predictable answers about Russian freedom, American capitalism. At the congressman's invitation, Di Vittorio "proceeded to give our foreign policy a going-over," Nixon's notes recorded, "which would make Henry Wallace look like a piker." He thought the Italian's line "almost identical" to that of other European communists and wrote in his journal, "this indicates definitely then that the communists throughout the world owe their loyalty not to the countries in which they live but to Russia."

Flying into a Greek mountain town not far from the front of the civil war, they were shocked to be shown by government authorities a young girl whose left breast had been cut off by communist guerrillas. They arrived in disputed, divided Trieste on the Italian-Yugoslav frontier as the temporary UN mandate was beginning. Unpacking in the hotel, Nixon watched communists—"young, vigorous, full of fight"—march by to the "Internationale." With another congressman and an interpreter, he hurried into the chaotic streets where he saw the bloody corpse of an Italian boy decapitated by a grenade. "I was sure," he noted, "that what was happening in Trieste would soon be reenacted throughout Western Europe unless America helped to restore stability and prosperity." In the Balkans he had seen communism's "true and brutal face," he wrote later.

From London, Berlin, Rome, and Athens, he wrote his wife frequent letters, ignoring most of the suffering and political judgments that filled his working notes and apologizing that Pat had been forced to stay behind and that they had missed a vacation during the congressional recess. To his parents he wrote a similarly chatty, boyish account. "It was a thrill to visit the places I had always heard of," he told them. "Dad would have loved Mars Hill where Paul made his speech 'Ye men of Athens.' Mother would enjoy being here, seeing what she studied in her Greek course." Junket or no, there had been sight-seeing excursions after all. He returned in mid-October with small mementos from every stop, ornate lace placemats his wife thought an extravagance, and what he called "a truckload" of select committee notes and papers.

Most of its own skeptics converted, the Herter mission promptly ran into the acrid jealousy of the House Foreign Affairs Committee and saw its own ambitious legislative proposals languish. Nonetheless, the firsthand reports and the lobbying of individual members like Nixon were decisive in the debate on Marshall Plan aid, an impact, one historian judged, "unique in American legislative history." For the showdown vote in December 1947, Nixon was scarcely alone among conservatives. Republicans on the floor voted 171–61 for the aid, the select committee itself 14–3.

The interval had been an education in both foreign affairs and House politics, a historic last stand of GOP isolationism, and not least another source of valuable future contacts. Among the Herter Committee consultants, Nixon met and impressed a former OSS officer named Allen Dulles, who was to be an invaluable entrée into the upper reaches of the GOP and the world of covert intelligence as well. There was also a young select committee secretary who thought the congressman's travel vouchers a model of neatness and honesty and who would later devote the rest of her career to being his personal secretary, Rose Mary Woods.

The more important and fixed consequences, however, lay in the "lessons" he carefully listed from the trip—that the communist leaders were "very intelligent and very tough men"; how much the "power of nationalism" remained in Europe exploited by both right and left; that "European communism was rolling in Soviet money . . . well financed from Moscow"; and the observation that "many in the [European] leadership classes had simply capitulated to communism," when "the only thing the communists would respect—and deal with seriously—was power." At Trieste he scribbled down in pencil a hurried note for the future: "One basic rule with Russians—never bluff unless you are prepared to carry through, because they will test you every time." With amazingly little change over the next twenty years, those were the truisms, the mix of statesmanship and mythology, he would take into his own Presidency—including the rationale for lavish CIA secret subsidies to Italian political parties to offset "Soviet money" and a view of how America's own "leadership classes" had "capitulated" to public protests in the 1960s. Over the Nixon

White House two decades later would hover the bleak ghosts of Rome and Athens, Berlin and Trieste in that hungry, violent European autumn of 1947.

"I see no reason to spend the government's money to bring me back right after I arrive out there," Nixon had written his former campaign manager, Harrison McCall, who had urged him to make a quick trip home to allay conservative opposition just before the Herter mission. On his return, the *Los Angeles Times* had provided the usual laudatory coverage, quoting his dire warnings of the Soviet threat and viewing the hard-working trip of "our own Dick Nixon" as "a good cure for the skeptics who talk sourly about congressional 'junkets' and 'joy rides.' " But his weather-vane mimeo polls in the district now showed widespread criticism of the foreign aid program, and he hurriedly moved to mend the fences. From the attic he peppered friendly district papers with columns describing graphically his findings and the case for the Marshall Plan.

At the end of October he flew home to make some fifty whirlwind speeches to justify his support of the aid, Arnold and many of the 1946 staff pressed into emergency service on a schedule resembling the hectic last days of an election campaign. Typically, Nixon appeased old conservative prejudices by ridiculing effete and suspect U.S. diplomats ("a lot of them just aren't trained for their jobs") or acknowledging the weakness or decadence of the Europeans but then evoking a fierce anticommunism and the specter of another world war ("America faces her greatest danger after she has won a war"). He went back to the district yet again for a flurry of speeches after the mid-December congressional vote on European recovery. When he finally returned to Washington that Christmas, the tide of opinion had been turned.

In the small, usually obscure arenas of House constituent politics, it was still another remarkable episode. Richard Nixon was a congressman voting his convictions—along with the advice of influential Washington advisers like Cronin and Andrews and the powerful eastern wing of the GOP—and then not simply ignoring or braving the opposition at home but working feverishly to win it over. "The whole experience ended up enhancing my popularity," he wrote of his exceptional courage and industry. He owed the triumph in part to resources few congressmen commanded so readily, to support and money from some of those represented in the partisan warning letter he received before going to Europe. The backing made possible five transcontinental flights and district tours during the Eightieth Congress, three more than afforded by his official allowance, and the vital margin for his election victory the following year as well as for the

Marshall Plan crusade. As in the 1946 race, money was ever the lubricant for his considerable skill and energy.

W. T. and Molly Mason Jones, professors at the Claremont colleges, remembered Dick Nixon that autumn at a large party in Pomona he attended without Pat after a day of speeches. They played charades in teams and Nixon joined in. He pantomimed and barked out his guesses with obvious intensity, trying so hard that at one point he broke into a sweat. But he seemed strangely inept, rigid, going through the motions of the game with his mind somewhere else. The Pomona evening was a kind of metaphor for his home life the first years in Washington. Mrs. Clifford Moore, the Nixons' domestic and babysitter for the next decade, remembered them at Park Fairfax in a fixed routine. After a quiet breakfast, invariably with fresh orange juice and the newspaper, the meticulously dressed congressman went off to the Capitol, to return in the evening with the same briskness and distraction. "He'd give you a quick smile and it's over," Mrs. Moore would say, "and he'd go into his study." After a drink and dinners of what Moore thought "just plain, regular food," he played with the baby for "fifteen or twenty minutes," and then retreated again to read in his study, while Pat "spent most of her time reading or sewing in her bedroom." It was a quiet, almost artificially placid home. "They would always solve their problems without arguments," Mrs. Moore related. "I've never seen them unhappy or dissatisfied."

The young congressman and his wife danced occasionally at the Shoreham Hotel in Washington, and later in 1947 spent weekends visiting Hannah and Frank Nixon, who had left Whittier for a farm near Menges Mills in York County, Pennsylvania, a short drive from the Capital. In their sixties the elder Nixons had made the cross-country move to the working farm to satisfy a nostalgic impulse in both to return to the rural life of their childhood, but also, as one observer said, "to promote a real closeness with Richard and Pat and their baby daughter."

The move reflected the relatively comfortable financial circumstances of the entire family. The store they left to Don was becoming a thriving $40,000-a-year business. In addition to the $6,000 Pennsylvania farm, the parents purchased a $7,500 three-bedroom home in Lakeland, Florida, and sent young Eddie to Duke. Beyond the rented Park Fairfax apartment, Dick and Pat bought a new $15,000 ranch-style home in South Whittier, adjacent to the Candlewood Country Club fairway. Soon after his election to Congress, Richard Nixon had even joined a group of investors about to buy the graceful old Hacienda Country Club in La Habra, though the deal had fallen through at the last moment. Outwardly, from the quiet, well-ordered home to the modest but far-flung real estate, it all seemed a serene portrait.

Beneath, Pat Nixon quietly seethed. She was not the unsophisticated, small-town housewife too timid to venture out without her husband, she told an interviewer later. "I had already traveled a lot and lived in many of the large cities of this country," she said, adding of the San Francisco interval she had relished, "I had supported myself for two years and had fun doing it." It was the plaint of a strong, independent woman now suddenly caught in a Washington marriage with a man increasingly absorbed in his public career. The balance and texture of the relationship had swiftly changed. She "began to despair that the camaraderie and carefree times of her early married years were a thing of the past," her daughter later wrote of her feelings.

Precious free time away from politics or the insatiable demands of the Congress her husband tended to give to his nearby parents, who were now both in frail health. "Mother always had scorned complainers" is how Julie would bluntly record Pat Nixon's disdain for the in-laws who had descended on them just as they had worked so hard to escape Whittier. Now pregnant with their second child, she was genuinely torn, her sense of neglect and self-pity mixed with a respect, almost reverence for what she saw as her husband's political idealism and mission—his "capacity to do great things," as she often put it. She finally poured out her discontent at the end of 1947. Nixon, she confided later, was "stunned." Rather than talk it through, he wrote her, characteristically, a long love letter, on the model of so many he had sent from the beginning, promising his "abiding love" and "to spend more time at home."

"FELLOW DEMOCRATS"

Nineteen forty-eight, the year of his reelection, began with a winter and spring shrouded in a war scare. In February a *coup d'état* in Czechoslovakia enveloped Eastern Europe's only remaining democracy in the Iron Curtain, and tension on the divided continent built toward the Berlin Blockade that would descend in June. Against that backdrop of fear and bleakness, Nixon framed his campaign strategy, a now subtle, now bald mix of Cold War, anticommunist jingoism and strictly local politics in California's twelfth district.

Staying with Don during the December 1947 visit, he met with McCall, Jorgensen, and others to prepare for the race. As usual, the candidate worried about having enough money. He was certain many of the powerful contributors they had in 1946 would now be absorbed in the national election, and they would have to be aggressive. "I feel there will be so much emphasis upon the Presidential race," Nixon wrote McCall anxiously before the meeting, "that the congressional candidates will be completely left out unless they go out and put on their own campaign." As at the University Club two years earlier, however, Jorgensen and the other backers were relatively unconcerned about finances. The money would be there again, even if largely from local assessments.

The advisers were more alarmed about the troublesome issues—the foreign aid hostility he was still quelling, the continuing blockage of the Whittier Narrows Dam—and the lack of punch in his self-generated congressional publicity, the unread newspaper columns on back pages or radio programs shunted by the stations to slack hours. Some district Republicans were saying "flatly," McCall would relate, "they did not think he could win the nomination in a primary election." What followed was typical of Nixon campaigns. Preparing for the coming battle, supporters like John Riley and even Tom Bewley had begun the rituals of small-town politics, going out that winter to visible vacant spots on the brown Whittier hillsides to make big "N's" with whitewashed rocks, advertising their man like a high school football team. But along with the initials and door-to-door canvasses were the Jorgensens and McCalls, men who understood the less visible ways and means of local elections. And it was their shrewdness, given force by the money they knew was available, that was to be decisive in 1948.

Their twin strategies were at once to exploit the incumbency around the communist issue, and yet to cut off Jerry Voorhis, or any other potentially strong opposition among either Democrats or Republicans, by running the same Richard Nixon virtually as a consensus, nonpartisan candidate. They reckoned with the old shifting, boomtime sociology of the basin, the area now in the most convulsive growth in its history and the population of the twelfth on the way to doubling. It was a well-proven axiom in California politics that new, relatively unsettled voters tended to elect the familiar face and name of the incumbent, with his party affiliation or real politics discreetly blurred. Public shallowness made the state's cross-filing a virtual incumbents' preservation act. In 1946, eleven sitting congressmen had won in the primary from their nonpartisan position atop the ballots of both parties.

Now, they decided, Dick should go for the preemptive primary win. The Nixon newsletter was to be changed from the original "Under the Capitol Dome" to a more nonpartisan, almost journalistic "Washington Report." Conservative district newspapers, always fearing a Voorhis comeback, would be warned about the importance of the congressman's nonpartisan identification. From late 1947, Nixon was to be front-page news as the twelfth's vigorous young man in Washington, but to all appearances a man without a party. Moreover, the campaign itself would deliberately court Democratic endorsements and votes. It was a small *tour de force* in candidate imagery that made the soon-forgotten race of 1948 a prototype of later, more notable campaigns in 1962 and 1968.

From the beginning, the campaign blended effectively his Washington, national assets with local organizations and appeal. In January 1948, soon after his thirty-fifth birthday, he was named one of the country's "outstanding young men" by the National Junior Chamber of Commerce. He had been formally nominated by the Pomona Junior Chamber at the instigation of Roy Day and other backers, but Father Cronin and his patrons in the national Chamber were instrumental in the final selection, which cited Nixon pointedly as "probably the best-informed man in Congress on communist activities." The award made front-page headlines for two days across the twelfth, the *Whittier News* blaring "Nation Pays High Tribute to Rep. Nixon," with no indication of the "Rep.'s" political party.

Little more than a week later, Day and other fund-raisers canvassed contributors. "Many reputable national leaders of our party have named Richard M. Nixon as an outstanding new member of Congress," Day wrote one well-to-do Pomona businessman. And though no opposition was in sight, the letter went on ominously: "It is a matter of common knowledge that radical labor leaders, members of the communist party, and communist-front organizations are going all out to 'get' Nixon. They *have* the money and will *spend* it. We want to be ready to meet them on any battleground they may choose." At the recent strategy meeting with the congressman, Day confided, supporters had decided on "the advisability of raising ample funds immediately to cover any eventuality arising in the coming campaign," and because of "the strong possibility that Nixon can be reelected in the primary." Of more than $20,000 initially targeted, the "share" of Pomona and the forty-ninth district was now $5,000, and the need was "urgent." Once again, Arthur Kruse of Alhambra Savings and Loan was campaign treasurer, and Day, Jorgensen, McCall, and others were the finance committee overseeing contributions and spending, though Nixon in Washington maintained his usual close control. Jorgensen remembered Bill Arnold coming back to the district from time to time, approving their newspaper ads "but . . . never . . . a heavyweight." It was Richard Nixon who decided the details as well as the strategy, including the wording of Day's fund-raising letters. "We'd always consult him, of course," Jorgensen recalled of 1948. "We'd design stuff and send it along to him, get his approval of it, surely. He was a pretty wise politician, you know."

The fund-raising began that February to news of the communist coup in Prague and what was in the twelfth an almost equally heralded congressional resolution introduced by Nixon and Kersten in the wake of the Czech events, recommending military aid to any central European nations requesting it. Their measure called for "solemn warnings to the conspiracy in the Politburo that any further steps of aggression, internal or external, will be actively resisted by every means at our disposal." The contributions swiftly poured in and made an immediate impact on his radio campaign. Now using paid time rather than public service announcements, the Nixon recordings from Washington were broadcast on local stations in early evening prime time, announced beforehand, like any network program, by newspaper ads bearing the congressman's photograph without mention of party. The candidate was also at pains to link the "internal" and "external" threat. Headlined as "NIXON BLASTS TOTALITARIAN CANDIDATES," a February 7 statement attacked Henry Wallace and the emerging Progressive movement as virtual accomplices of Moscow.

Meanwhile, the opposition floundered. "Political activity . . . on the Democratic side is as dormant and uninspired as I have ever seen it," an old supporter wrote Jerry Voorhis in his Chicago coop job that February. "The Democrats . . . exhibit complete lack of enthusiasm for all the potential candidates at every level." A small delegation tried to coax Voorhis into a comeback race, but he quickly declined. They then approached "other well-known Democrats," one of them remembered, with the same results.

The Democratic search committee finally turned to one of their own, and he consented, "out of desperation," as the candidate himself remembered. He was Stephen Zetterberg, a thirty-one-year-old attorney, Coast Guard veteran, and former senatorial aide in Washington who had worked briefly for Voorhis while studying for the California bar in the fall of 1946. Over the past year he had been on the edge of Democratic politics as he began a law practice in Pomona. With a pregnant wife and three children, he was without campaign funds or even promises of the requisite support when he finally announced his candidacy April 12, with barely six weeks remaining until the primary. To make matters still worse, as Voorhis gently warned him, the name Zetterberg, though Swedish, would likely "sound" Jewish to many in the district and awaken some of the vicious anti-Semitism evident in 1946. After that crushing defeat, Voorhis had come by Zetterberg's law office and forlornly left him a file of speeches and a small metal box of cards listing names of past Voorhis workers, many of them old-timers and even Republicans who had since gone over to Nixon. The little box, Zetterberg would remember, was all that was left of the mythical Democratic-radical machine.

As Voorhis drew back and Zetterberg slowly became a candidate by default, Nixon's publicity mounted everywhere in the twelfth, commonly with front-page stories identifying him politically only as "the congressman." When he fell carrying Tricia down icy steps at Park Fairfax in mid-February, holding the baby up unhurt but painfully fracturing his left elbow, widespread stories of the accident and convalescence added to his celebrity. He was getting "fantastic news coverage," as Zetterberg saw it from a distance, "even with pictures of him in the hospital." By early March, the representative was impatiently back at work and even more in local headlines, attacking Attorney General Tom Clark for his laxity on "Reds" in government.

McCall now announced formally that Nixon would be cross-filing in the June primary. Despite the early whispering of the conservatives, he was unopposed in the GOP contest, as well as on the Democratic ballot facing Zetterberg, who refused to cross-file on principle. Moreover, it was to be a three-way race, further splintering the Democratic vote. Margaret Porter, a longtime liberal activist, was running apart from them in her own primary and then in the general election on the Independent Progressive Party slate that the Wallace forces were fielding on the left throughout the state. Rarely, even for California, had partisan lines been more blurred and confusing, or, in terms of the great Cold War issues facing the nation, more significant. But in press coverage that was now typical, McCall's notice of his cross-filing ran prominently in local papers without indication of which party Congressman Nixon had represented to begin with or exactly what crossover he was making. Only the *Los Angeles Times* in a small back-page item listed him among other filers for the primary as "Richard M. Nixon (R.) Incumbent."

His cross-filing was swiftly followed by the triumphant announcement of a bold Nixon initiative in local affairs, a small masterstroke in twelfth district politics that at once eliminated a nagging old problem while producing new headlines and, more important, new supporters and contributions. "WHITTIER NARROWS DAM CONTROVERSY SETTLED WITH VICTORY FOR EL MONTE," the *Times* headlined on March 18. Behind the newsprint was a classic little story of land, money, and power, and a "victory" the *Times* and other accounts did not fully explain.

For fifteen years, with Voorhis's constant support, the residents of El Monte had fought the $40 million Whittier Narrows project, a proposed dam astride the Rio Hondo River that would provide flood control for Whittier downstream while its reservoir inundated and sacrificed hundreds of homes and community facilities upstream in El Monte. Over the lengthening duration of the controversy, the dam acquired powerful champions, including the U.S. Army Corps of Engineers and real-estate interests eager to develop the flood plain. The politics were punishing. Under the developers' spur, state and Los Angeles County officials joined the lobby for the dam, at one point refusing to improve roads in the El Monte area unless residents dropped their opposition. Even so, the small town held on, their local congressman's opposition crucial in the protocol and pork barrel of dam-building politics in Washington and the developers unable to dislodge Voorhis—until 1946.

Confidentially promising in the campaign to satisfy both sides, Nixon continued publicly to oppose the dam as late as the beginning of 1948. "NIXON SILENCE DOOMS WHITTIER NARROWS DAM," announced a January 24 account of his opposition to the plan before the House Appropriations Committee. To the beleaguered El Monteans, the battle seemed won for another year. But Jorgensen and McCall had warned him privately in the December strategy meeting that the Whittier Narrows issue could be crucial both in their cross-filing strategy and in fund-raising. As if to underscore the point, Nixon was lobbied that winter by Ed Pauley, a onetime Democratic National Committeeman from California and now a representative of both oil and real-estate interests. "I called on him, and pointed out that it would be a mistake if he were to think of this project strictly from the interest of his district," Pauley remembered of their meeting. "He listened seriously and agreed with my reasoning."

Nixon now quietly negotiated a fresh project proposal with the Corps of Engineers, while reaching back into the district to coopt the support of the Reverend Dan Cleveland, president of the Anti–Whittier Narrows Dam Association of the San Gabriel Valley, El Monte's own citizen lobby. In the "compromise" announced in mid-March, the "new" dam was only a mile and a quarter downstream from the old proposed site. Cleveland's own Church of the Barn and the Texaco oil refinery were spared, while both community facilities and five hundred homes would be swallowed up in the new reservoir, scarcely fifty fewer than the latest Corps proposal Richard Nixon had flatly rejected two months before. But as the dam went forward, developers readied plans for the suddenly valuable land downstream, the Reverend Cleveland, a Democrat, endorsed Congressman Nixon for reelection, and Pauley-inspired contributions, many from wealthy and powerful Democrats, would come to Nixon both in 1948 and 1950. Of its kind the deal was a footnote to the 1946 race. El Monte had been one of the few communities to go for Jerry Voorhis.

There was one apt sequel, almost unnoticed. In basin politics, some water projects would always bear more scrutiny than others. Three weeks after news of Whittier Narrows, the *Los Angeles Times* featured Congressman Nixon's indignant search for profiteers in Arizona's request for its legal share of the Colorado River irrigation, water flowing along the border of the two states but then going almost exclusively to southern California. "I intend to find out just how much land speculators are behind the scheme,"

Nixon told the paper. "Some startling reports have reached me and I propose to find out if they are true."

The strategy of the nonpartisan incumbent dictated that Nixon remain in Washington, taking no note of opposition in the district and making the most of House politics for the campaign. Two episodes, both centered on HUAC, brought him the sort of continuing national attention they hoped for that winter and spring, though not without a price beyond the moment.

The first was the Condon case, one of the Committee's more celebrated and abortive security tempests. Dr. Edward Condon was then director of the National Bureau of Standards in the Commerce Deparment, a forty-six-year-old scientist of some eminence who had worked on the Manhattan Project. He was an outspoken liberal, with friends and memberships on the left, a wife of Czech descent, and, perhaps worst of all, the admiration and patronage of Henry Wallace, but nonetheless no authentic blot on his security record. Recuperating from gastrointestinal hemorrhages at Walter Reed Hospital, HUAC Chairman Thomas had called in reporters March 1 to issue, in striped pajamas, an impromptu Committee report calling Condon "one of the weakest links in our atomic security." Behind the baseless charge was Thomas's own dyspepsia in general with nuclear experts, like Condon, who had recently succeeded in having the Atomic Energy Commission placed under civilian rather than military control, and not least the Committee's echo of similar generic distrust of "liberal" scientists in Hoover's FBI. In his "report," Thomas even quoted selectively from a purloined FBI letter in Condon's security file, noting the scientist had been in contact "with an individual . . . alleged to have engaged in espionage activities with the Russians." HUAC left out of its dramatic press release, however, the next and determining sentence in the letter: "There is no evidence to show that contacts between this individual and Dr. Condon were related to this individual's espionage activities."

The episode was the Committee at its atavistic worst. In the custom of Martin Dies, they jovially dismissed Condon's pleas to testify in his own defense and publicly indicted the man's career and loyalty on shreds of misinformation. When Thomas and Rankin demanded the original FBI letter and Condon's complete file, Harry Truman angrily countered by ordering executive departments to refuse congressional requests for security records and to refer all subpoenas to the White House. The clash of constitutional prerogatives around Dr. Condon and his supposedly juicy file soon became irresistible campaign fodder, and Nixon joined in the fray in full cry. On March 5, he wired Commerce Secretary Averell Harriman to release the FBI letter, leaking to the *Los Angeles Times* his lengthy, polemical telegram before it arrived on Harriman's desk. Six days later, he warned that Congress might take "drastic action" if Harriman continued to hold the letter, telling the *Washington Times-Herald* "the Condon case brings down the iron curtain between Congress and information in the hands of bureaucrats to which Congress is entitled." Later, as Thomas and the others blustered even louder, Nixon would take the position that he was thinking only of "Condon's best interests."

But then a storm of press and public outrage broke over the committee, particularly from the academic and scientific communities, and Nixon quickly and apologetically wrote one of the leading critics, his old Duke patron and professor Douglas Maggs. "I was not a member of that subcommittee [releasing the report]. In fact, I read the committee's report for the first time in the newspapers on March 1," he offered. Maggs would be "glad to know" he had moved to have Condon heard "at the earliest possible date." Within HUAC, Nixon had "consistently opposed" issuing such reports before public testimony by the accused and was working on "a set of general rules of procedure" to avoid the old abuses. Nixon went on: "I want to assure you that my own position in this case is completely neutral and that [if] I, on the basis of all the evidence, become convinced that Dr. Condon has been unjustly charged as a result of the committee report, I shall publicly so state my conviction and do everything that I can to see that the injustice to Dr. Condon is remedied."

A personal *mea culpa* for his benighted colleagues, the Maggs letter was sent to other academics as well, an anxious, belated effort to separate him from the backfiring controversy. Privately, he later agreed with Bert Andrews that the treatment of Condon was "shameful," and he did not even allude to the case in his memoirs. Yet he continued in the politics of Capitol Hill and his own reelection to side with HUAC on the issue of Truman surrendering the file. It was a florid tolling of the same themes of full disclosure and executive privilege in which he would reverse roles as President a quarter century later. At one point in the Condon affair, he scribbled a personal note that would be altogether ironic when his own administration refused to release information: "When Cong. can't get info from Exec. dept./info which is bandied about to press/then high time Congress did something about it."

To Nixon's urging that it was a question of solemn prerogative, the House voted in April and again in May to order the surrender of the FBI letter on Condon, and then to compel executive departments to give over files demanded by Congress. But the Senate had no stomach for the certain Truman veto and constitutional confrontation awaiting such legislation and let it die untouched. By summer the Atomic Energy Commission cleared Condon anew. There the case rested for the moment, the gossip about the scientist having been for Nixon and the HUAC, wrote one reporter, "as tempting . . . as the key to the local arsenal would be to delinquent teenagers."

He had gained still more California headlines from the uproar. But the passing publicity was at a lasting and significant cost. Unlike the Hollywood hearings, where he had escaped relatively untarnished by the rest of HUAC, his part in the Condon case identified him for many with the worst of the Committee—as one of those politicians, Walter Goodman wrote, "who would walk where ambition led." In particular, the affair left a first legacy of distrust and suspicion in academic and scientific circles that would thicken into near-professional anathema, despite his solicitous gestures like the long letter to Maggs. It would be a political liability for Richard Nixon for years to come and soon a touchstone for his own wounded resentment and alienation vis-à-vis an intellectual world that might have been a much greater ally and resource for him.

His second major Washington activity that spring was a mixed asset as well. In February he had been named to head a HUAC subcommittee for hearings into "proposed legislation to curb or control the Communist Party of the United States." Their witnesses ran the gamut from the Daughters of the American Revolution to the attorney general to the American Civil Liberties Union. The hearings produced the perennial HUAC bill to outlaw the Communist Party, and now, too—on J. Edgar Hoover's advice that simple outlawing might be counterproductive—a bill to "register" the party and its front groups. The legislation would require the attorney general to name the suspect organizations and made it a crime to seek to establish "a totalitarian dictatorship," which was the real purpose, said the bill, of the communists in any case.

Mundt, now running for the Senate in South Dakota, maneuvered to have the legislation named for himself when it came to the House floor. But the Hill press, watching Nixon's effective steerage of the bill through the subcommittee, soon rechristened it Mundt-Nixon. Richard Nixon had planned and conducted the hearings with "dignity and intelligence," wrote one critic of the measure. "Bill to Tie Reds' Hands," the *Los Angeles Times* would call it in its own idiom with exclusive credit to Nixon. At the same time, across the country, the bill also drew powerful opposition, the *Christian Science Monitor* deploring it as a "political proscription which could be turned by any party in power against any minority."

In the mid-May floor debate, Nixon managed the legislation with skill and recognized fairness. "It will once and for all spike many of the loose charges about organizations being communist fronts," he argued at one point for the bill's relative moderation, and at another juncture even joked with liberal opponents that the law would not, after all, affect groups advocating either public housing or public power. Mundt-Nixon passed the House 319–58, one more Hill triumph for the freshman, though a reflection too, wrote one observer, of "a year when the nation was busily looking for ways to deport, dismiss, blacklist and jail its Communists."

Clearly an assault on civil liberties, Mundt-Nixon's requirement of registration by what it defined *a priori* as a conspiracy amounted to banishment of a political party and idea, and harbored in its veiled language chaotic confusion. One Republican leader would announce his support of the measure *because* it outlawed the communists, another because it just as certainly did *not*. Despite the parliamentary triumph in the subcommittee and on the House floor, Nixon's attic office was under an avalanche of mail opposing the legislation. During the final debate, he would even ask the FBI to investigate "forgeries" in what he charged was an orchestrated press campaign to influence congressmen. At that, the controversial bill ran into a formidable coalition of GOP moderates and conservatives in the Senate, where it was summarily scuttled by majority leader Robert Taft, with the quiet outside support of another quarter of Republican power, Earl Warren.

Mundt-Nixon also drew him into the 1948 race for the GOP Presidential nomination, with still another exposure to some of the more covert, serpentine politics of the moment. On May 17, on the eve of the House vote, Thomas E. Dewey met Harold Stassen in a climactic radio debate in the crucial Oregon primary. Their topic was outlawing the Communist Party; Stassen was in favor, Dewey opposed, the latter calling a legal ban "nothing but the method of Hitler and Stalin . . . an attempt to beat down ideas with a club . . . a surrender of everything we believe in." Advising Stassen for that debate were his chief aide, Warren Burger, Senator Joe McCarthy, and Nebraska publisher Fred Seaton, all future Nixon supporters and allies. Nixon now sent them and Stassen, whom he backed for the nomination, a terse and thoughtful defense of the bill for the Minnesotan to marshal in the debate.

Outwardly, it was a familiar GOP confrontation, a younger but more conservative, midwestern Stassen versus the eastern, moderate wing of the party, Dewey. Yet the hidden politics, which Nixon learned to some surprise both before and after the debate, were not so straightforward. Discreetly behind Dewey was an array of conservative Taft forces seeking to block Stassen's emergence on the right. Privately backing the New York governor as well was that other Republican Presidential prospect seemingly above the old ideological division, Earl Warren, whose conservative opponents in his own California GOP were generously financing Stassen. The 1948 nomination fight was a brief but vivid glimpse of the whirlpool factionalism of the Republicans—in which personality, parochial advantage, old private and provincial quarrels often mattered more than any doctrinal purity—and one Richard Nixon never forgot.

Moreover, beneath those maneuvers was an even deeper layer. Former FBI assistant director William Sullivan, one of Father Cronin's contacts, remembered that "there was such a rush" to get secret FBI material to Governor Dewey for the debate—material Sullivan and many agents worked "for days" to cull from the supposedly confidential files—that it was "sent in a private plane." The FBI that vigilantly pursued other federal employees for violations of the Hatch Act prohibiting partisan political activity—the FBI that supported Mundt-Nixon and its young Californian author in Washington—now acted as covert campaign staff to Tom Dewey. It was all in aid of J. Edgar Hoover's expectation, as he confided to Sullivan and other aides, of gaining the attorney generalship or even a Supreme Court seat in a Dewey administration. For similar reasons of prospective bureaucratic rewards, Dewey would also receive the secret campaign support of another, newer federal bureaucracy, the recently established Central Intelligence Agency.

In the nationally broadcast debate from Portland, Stassen argued stridently for outlawing the communists, though neglecting to use Nixon's own persuasive summary of the legislation. In rebuttal, reading a statement from the bill's cosponsor Karl Mundt (provided in a self-serving political maneuver by the conservative Mundt), Tom Dewey managed to argue that the bill would not, in fact, outlaw the Communist Party and that Stassen had thus "surrendered" the point by backing Mundt-Nixon. The twisting semantics and backroom alliances tipped the scales. Dewey was widely thought to have "won" the debate, finishing Stassen's candidacy with an Oregon primary victory and going on to win the nomination against Truman.

Besides an education in the contortions of Presidential campaign politics, the incident had one further consequence for Nixon. In large part from his loyal help to Stassen, money from the California Stassen men punctually came to his own 1948 primary campaign in the twelfth, contributions, of course, from the same forces Earl Warren was defying. The 1948 alliance with Stassen thus deepened still more Nixon's earlier schism with the governor in Sacramento and the ever-growing tendency of California's anti-Warren, right-wing Republicans to see the young congressman from Whittier as their putative champion.

On the evening of May 17, as Stassen and Dewey prepared for their debate in Oregon, Nixon returned to his attic office in Washington from the day's floor fight and wrote Roy Day confidentially but irritably about the final primary push in the district. Two days before he had spoken by three-way long-distance hookup with Herman Perry, Tom Bewley, and Assemblyman Tom Erwin. All three urged him to return for at least one swift trip to the district before the election, a rally in El Monte on May 22 in support of the Mundt-Nixon bill. He was loath to leave Washington amid the ongoing debate but finally relented, insisting on flying both ways in the new, faster DC-6 aircraft, to be gone only the weekend without missing any floor action.

"Frankly," he grumbled to Day, "I was placed in the position that if I did not go out and we lost the primaries by a few votes, I would probably be blamed by all hands. . . . Of course, if I do come and we lose anyway, they will all have forgotten what was said at this time." His press releases, he assured Day, would stress the quick trip and diligence to House duties, and especially the endorsement that week of his bill by prominent Republicans, among them John Foster Dulles, Dewey's principal foreign policy adviser. They should arrange for the American Legion to come out in strength for the El Monte rally, and hope for a publicized confrontation with opponents of the bill. "I would guess that it might well be picketed by the communists from Los Angeles," Nixon wrote of the rally, "which, of course, would make great news in the district." He thought Steve Zetterberg "in rather a poor spot" opposing the bill, a rare reference to his rival, whom he never named in public. Critics of the legislation, like the CIO, he told Day, "took the commie line hook, line, and sinker."

As it was, Mundt-Nixon passed the House May 19. His hurried trip would be only excess insurance in an already overwhelmingly well-financed, well-coordinated reelection campaign. At the beginning of May, thanks to McCall and Jorgensen, "prominent Democrats" had endorsed the congressman in front-page, bold-headline articles throughout the district. Nixon earned "bipartisan support," went a typical "news story" some days later, "because of his untiring efforts to protect the people of his district regardless of party." There followed a mass mailing of postcards addressed to registered Democrats, from lists the campaign quietly obtained from official rolls as well as spirited from Democratic Party records, expedients that became necessary when Voorhis had refused to turn over to his successor the former representative's mailing list.

"Fellow Democrats," the postcard announced, "you are assured of able and progressive representation" with "Congressman Richard M. Nixon. He gets things done!" It was signed "Democrats for Nixon, J. R. Blue, Chairman." Afterward, there were questions about whether Mr. Blue was a Democrat or even existed, and Jorgensen would hedge. "I can't remember," he would say when asked exactly who these "Democrats" were. "Sometimes it's paper," he said of the bipartisan endorsements, "but most of the time it's headed up by [real] people." Out in the booming new suburbs and even in the older settlements, the postcards had impact. Walking the precincts alone, Zetterberg found numerous voters who were convinced that Congressman Nixon was the Democratic candidate and flourished the postcard to prove it.

Kyle Palmer joined the press acclamation on May 18, announcing Nixon's coming visit and calling hihm "one of the ablest and most fearless of the younger generation in Congress." "He will stand up and fight for what he believes to be right, and he swings from the floor . . . living up to his campaign promises," Palmer concluded the *Times* endorsement, again without mentioning the incumbent's party. Meanwhile, local papers ran their prescribed editorials on the virtues of Mundt-Nixon, usually entitled "Russia Won't Like Richard Nixon." There was great danger, said the *Azusa Herald*, in the "Communist Party (yes, it is active in Azusa too!)"

He arrived in Los Angeles at midday on May 22, twelve hours late after a harrowing flight during which his airliner put down in Amarillo because of a fire scare. His men were waiting at the airport with a chartered private plane to whisk him to El Monte, first for a meeting at the civic auditorium, and then to the rally of seven hundred at the high school, where they found the opposition pickets he had hoped for, in this case CIO volunteers. "In his characteristic forthright manner," the *Times* news story described Nixon using the literature passed out by the pickets, "the young congressman and World War II serviceman held up the pamphlet, read various points in it, and declared that they were utterly false and that the bill did not do what the pamphlet said it would do." In an emotional moment the press did not report, Richard Nixon had begun the meeting by describing not the false fire alarm but a terrible storm his plane had flown through: "There was lightning and thunder and he was not sure they were going to get through at times," one in the audience retold the story. "And he said there were probably people present in the audience and outside picketing him . . . that would have wished that he would have died and that his plane would have come down, but he did make it through and he was there, despite this." The crowd had responded in prolonged applause and cheers.

Before departing for Washington the next evening, he met to exhort primary campaign workers, held press conferences to extoll Mundt-Nixon, and, in a quaint, old-fashioned gesture of the Capitol Hill pols he looked down on, even promised local postal workers a federal pay raise. He also left behind an office poll to be published by district papers, showing "73 percent" of the district in favor of Mundt-Nixon. Only deep in some accounts was it clear that the actual figures were 9,500 in favor of the bill out of some 100,000 questionnaires sent out and a little more than 13,000 responses.

Four days before the primary, the twelfth was blanketed with advertising addressed to "Fellow Democrats," calling Dick Nixon "a fearless champion of Democratic principles." With little money, Zetterberg ran small, half-inch ads, often dwarfed incongruously beside the Nixon spreads. Ostensible news photographs of Nixon, with no indication that they were paid political advertising, ran widely in local papers with the caption "Your Congressman . . . has proved that he deserves your vote . . . regardless of party affiliation."

On election eve, they called in the dues from Whittier Narrows and put El Monte's Reverend Cleveland on prime-time radio. "I'm a Southern Democrat . . . and I am going to vote for our good congressman Richard Nixon tomorrow," he announced. "Now there may be some Republicans listening to me. If there are . . . you also can vote for Richard Nixon. He will be on your ballot also." The minister went on to talk darkly about "people with strange ideologies" and "stranger" names. "Take God into the polls and vote for Nixon," he told them, "in order to avoid people of questionable philosophy." Listening on his car radio, Zetterberg knew the Red-baiting, anti-Semitic slur was scarcely aimed at third-party candidate Margaret Porter. Going into the same station for his own last-minute radio appeal, the Democrat met the preacher coming out. "Oh, you're Steve Zetterberg," Cleveland explained heartily. "I've made my deal with Nixon in [the] primary, but I would like to talk with you as soon as the primary is over."

There would be no postprimary for Zetterberg's candidacy. The next day, Nixon was in effect reelected by winning the Democratic primary 21,411 to 16,808, with Porter running a distant third. Zetterberg registered only $660 in campaign contributions and later admitted to spending more than $2,000 in six weeks. Nixon legally recorded less than $13,000 given to Kruse, while estimates of the cost of his advertising and radio time alone came to some $35,000. Even so, the victory was not that impressive. More than half the California congressional incumbents gained reelection by cross-filing in the 1948 primary. Both Republicans and Democrats in Los Angeles and adjacent counties won on the other ticket by larger proportions than the well-publicized representative from the twelfth.

For Nixon and for the nation, however, the significance was simply that he had won, that he could comfortably ignore the general election and concentrate on events in Washington that hot summer to come in 1948, when a witness named Whittaker Chambers came before the Committee.

In June Nixon attended the GOP National Convention in Philadelphia, though not as a member of the official California delegation, where he had wrangled Roy Day a seat but avoided one himself. "Something less than an ardent Earl Warren supporter," Arnold recalled Nixon's politicking at Philadelphia. "He devoted himself in talks with delegates, in hotel lobbies and elevators to a Stassen buildup." Dewey easily won the nomination, however, and gave Earl Warren the Vice-Presidential spot as Richard Nixon looked on from the gallery like an ordinary spectator. With press credentials from the *Pomona Progress-Bulletin*, his assistant Arnold "absurdly enough had a better vantage point . . . than did 'the boss.' "

After the ritual California newspaper photographs—one in the *Monrovia News-Post* showing Nixon and Day awkwardly flanking a smiling Earl Warren and his ally Senator Knowland—the congressman returned to Washington at the end of June and to his wife in her final month of pregnancy. They drove to the hospital late in the evening of one of the hottest Independence Days in the history of Washington, and before dawn the next morning Pat gave birth to another baby girl they immediately named Julie.

His wife then came home to find Hannah Nixon fatigued and ill herself from babysitting Tricia, and the new mother, against doctor's orders, began an exhausting routine of care for newborn, child, and mother-in-law in the sweltering Washington July. Anxious, still trying to atone for the grievances she had hurled at him months before, Dick promised her a long-postponed vacation in the fall and booked tickets for a Caribbean cruise in November.

Meanwhile, however, there were loose ends of the expiring Eightieth Congress. A grand jury in New York had produced none of the Soviet espionage indictments expected of it, and there were those who hoped the Committee on Un-American Activities might somehow revive the issue.

13

The Case I, August 1948

"CONCEALED ENEMY"

arly in the summer of 1948, a plain-faced man in a neat dark suit and well-brushed fedora circumspectly made his rounds on Capitol Hill. He was FBI Assistant Director Louis Nichols, and his covert mission was to leak ostensibly confidential FBI counterintelligence files to friendly congressional committees. Ironically, aptly, what Nichols carried in his briefcase—official secrets unofficially dispensed for bureaucratic and political advantage—set in motion the great spy scandal of the century, and ultimately hurtled Richard Nixon into national prominence.

For more than a year, a federal grand jury for the Southern District of New York had been sitting in the cavernous Foley Square courthouse in Manhattan, listening to the charges of FBI informers and to the denials of numerous government officials, past and present, whom the informers accused of communist subversion. The grand jury was to be the culmination of a two-year FBI investigation into Soviet espionage. Yet after hundreds of hours of testimony there was no documentary evidence of the allegations and scant corroboration among the government witnesses, most of them contrite ex-communists. "Somewhat squeezed oranges," Attorney General Tom Clark disdainfully called the cases.

As the jury failed to return the expected indictments, however, J. Edgar Hoover and his men had blamed the Justice Department and the Truman White House. The director moved at once to vindicate the FBI, put political pressure on the laggard Democrats, and not least to preserve his own stock in an election year, to make "the public," as Nichols himself wrote in a secret memo, "understand and realize the difference between the FBI and the attorney general." So it was that Nichols—known in the Bureau as "Hoover's ghost," his chief lobbyist and public relations agent—was dispatched to carry top-secret files to Senator Homer Ferguson, an ambitious Red-baiting Michigan Republican whose Senate Investigations Subcommittee could be counted on to hold showy public hearings on the FBI charges. "He was getting reports before I got them," Attorney General Clark would grumble about Ferguson's "direct pipeline" to the FBI. At the same time, Nichols was also to walk over to the House side of the Capitol, to encourage the ever-ready Committee on Un-American Activities to stage some of the same helpful testimony.

The briefcase full of classified files rescued Richard Nixon and the rest of HUAC from an embarrassing hiatus as Harry Truman combatively called the Eightieth Congress back into a special August session before the 1948 election. Roundly condemned for the Condon fiasco and other episodes—for what *The New York Times* called "more than a year of baseless rumor-mongering"—the Committee was faced with reopening some already worn inquiry, a further wringing of the Eisler affair or even one of Congressman Rankin's rancid old favorites, "Communist infiltration of Negro organizations." Hoover's bureaucratic flanking attack on Clark and Truman suddenly gave them a fresh agenda. The Committee would gladly grab Clark's "squeezed oranges." "I feel we are now free to proceed with the taking of open testimony from various witnesses who were subjects of the grand jury investigation," a still-ailing Parnell Thomas wrote Mundt privately on July 26 after the leaks from the FBI. The new hearings, the chairman was assured by high-level sources, would expose "certain espionage activities against the government of the United States."

Code-named the "Gregory" case, the leaked FBI files featured as star witness Elizabeth Terrill Bentley, and she appeared before HUAC on a sultry Saturday morning the last day of July. A Vassar graduate who became a communist courier, now disenchanted with the movement, dubbed by the press with some exaggeration as the "Beautiful Blond Spy Queen" or a "Nutmeg Mata Hari," Bentley told the congressmen much the same story she had walked in off the street to confess to the FBI in 1945. Smitten with her fatherly Soviet spymaster, for some years she ran secrets from a ring of communist agents and sympathizers in and around the U.S. government. After her lover died late in the war she grew disillusioned. "The international communist movement, I realized, was in the hands of the wrong people," she confessed to HUAC, still prone to the wide-eyed schoolgirl credulity that had made her messenger and mistress. For HUAC's part, Congressman McDowell chivalrously praised the witness for her "courage to walk through the valley of the shadow of publicity."

In her recollections Bentley implicated more than thirty conspirators, most prominently Assistant Secretary of the Treasury Harry Dexter White; Commerce Department aide William Remington; and the head of an alleged Washington cell and the FBI case namesake, a low-level government economist named Nathan Gregory Silvermaster. Still, she had never met personally many of the accused, including White. As before the grand jury, her testimony was in large part hearsay and wholly undocumented. The Bentley hearing made headlines only at the cost of more criticism of HUAC's penchant for unsubstantiated charges. "If it were corroborated," one reporter wrote of Bentley's story of treachery, "the House committee would very soon take on the glory of the Minutemen; and if it were disproved, the Committee would go down as a discredited band of vigilantes." But before the weekend was out, Stripling remembered, the Committee was suffering in many newspapers "a tremendous campaign of vilification." To make matters still worse, Ferguson's Senate subcommittee was insisting on jurisdictional rights to pursue Bentley's most promising suspect, William Remington. At the same moment, GOP campaign leaders were pressuring the Republicans on HUAC to continue their inquiry, "to keep the heat on Truman," as Parnell Thomas remembered the telephone calls that weekend.

Almost desperately in need of a sequel to Bentley, the Committee staff now turned to a name and story already familiar in HUAC files and, more important, in Father John Cronin's educational briefings of Richard Nixon. When the FBI learned that the informer would not be called before the flagging Manhattan grand jury in any case, the Bureau, knowing his testimony, quietly urged his HUAC appearance through Frederick Woltman, a friendly journalist who in turn suggested the name to both Stripling and Mundt. Anxious to blunt the critics, Stripling had immediately issued a subpoena on August 2 for testimony the next day, typically announcing the news to HUAC's favorite Hearst reporters even before the summons reached the witness himself at his office high over Rockefeller Plaza in New York, where he was now a senior editor at *Time* magazine. That evening and the following morning, as the Committee hoped, both the press and an ABC radio documentary on communist subversion advertised HUAC's imminent new exposé on "Soviet espionage."

Richard Nixon himself met the hastily called witness in Stripling's office only minutes before the August 3 hearing. A journalist from *Time*'s Washington bureau had accompanied the editor. "He's ready," said the reporter, nodding toward a pudgy, awkwardly shy man of forty-seven, with narrow, darting eyes that "preferred," said someone who knew him, "to consult the floor rather than the interlocutor's face." Nixon thought him "one of the most disheveled looking persons I had ever seen, everything about him . . . wrinkled and unpressed." Stripling introduced the figure as Whittaker Chambers.

About to be the most famous witness in Committee annals, perhaps of the entire Congress, briefly but dramatically a pivotal figure in Richard Nixon's life, Chambers brought that morning to Stripling's office a bizarre and tangled history. He was born Jay Vivian Chambers into a tormented family—a capricious, bisexually philandering father who soon left him with a mother permanently embittered and neurotic, a demented grandmother who wandered about their ramshackle Long Island house throwing open windows and raving that they were all trying to gas her, and a beloved but equally troubled younger brother, who in alcoholic agony soon committed suicide. Seeming to rue his own survival, Chambers was a gifted, precocious young man, ever the misfit, and by college making a bohemian virtue of it.

Lionel Trilling, a fellow student at Columbia in the 1920s, remembered his thick, squat physique and, above all, the rotting teeth that would later play their part in the case. His appearance seemed "calculated to negate youth and all its graces," especially the mouth, thought Trilling, "a devastation of empty sockets and blackened stumps . . . the perfect insigne of Chambers's moral authority . . . [which] annihilated the hygienic American present—only a serf could have such a mouth, or some student in a visored cap who sat in his Moscow garret and thought of nothing else save the moment when he would toss the fatal canister into the barouche of the Grand Duke."

In chronic personal despair and a brooding conviction of the West's irreversible decay, Chambers drifted deep into American communism, first openly, then as an underground agent of alternating aliases, bravado, and furtiveness. He would find his visored cap and canister in a melancholy self-dramatization, the moody, brilliant college poet, the ever-unfulfilled talent, diverted by history to revolutionary courier, and later, reaction's martyr. All the while, as the rumpled clothes and fugitive eyes announced rather too well, he became an irrepressible, skillful poseur and player of roles. More instinctively, Chambers was the lowlife, prowling for homosexual forays with vulnerable boys while living his other parts as family man and secret agent.

When he abandoned Marx and Stalin in 1937–38, he found religion, eventually Hicksite evangelical Quakerism. But he would retain the common core of both faiths, a stiffening, mystical sanctimony and an abiding sense of self-sacrifice. From a sordid life of invention and deception, he would now come to fame on the strength of his credibility. Whittaker

Chambers wanted everyone to understand, an observer noted later, that "he harbored the conscience of Raskolnikov and the mission of Jesus Christ."

"EITHER HISTORY, HYPOTHESIS, OR DEDUCTION"

Standing in Stripling's office that August morning, he seemed a reluctant witness. HUAC staff investigators led by Mandel had interviewed him in March 1948, and Chambers, expecting as an FBI informer to be called before the Manhattan grand jury, had then begged off from public testimony. "I am more apathetic about involving others," he had written a friend soon after his defection a decade before. "It is good, at every ultimate moment (I learned this at my brother's death), to have harmed no one needlessly and [that] takes more strength than the easy violent will ever know." Ever after, Chambers claimed the same anguishing hesitation in informing on his old colleagues. In fact, he was to tell the story again and again, the emphasis and version shifting with the moment and audience. Only months after his break with the communists, while still nervously in hiding from some feared Soviet reprisal, he had confided part of his experience to friends, and even tried to sell a magazine article on underground methods through reporter Isaac Don Levine. Fearing prosecution for espionage himself, he at first refused to talk to U.S. authorities without a promise of immunity. Then, days after the Nazi-Soviet Non-Aggression Pact of August 1939, he went at Levine's instigation to see Assistant Secretary of State Adolf Berle, a member of Roosevelt's original "Brain Trust" and then the President's ranking adviser on internal security.

On a cool Saturday evening at the beginning of that September that saw the outbreak of World War II, the three men sat out on lawn chairs and later in the book-lined study at Berle's old estate nestled in the hills of far northwest Washington. Chambers recited in some detail, and Berle took down on ten pages of foolscap, a description of the communist network in various government agencies as Chambers had purportedly known it in the late 1930s. There were unmistakable allusions to spying, moving Berle to make notations about "aerial bomb sight detectors," "plans for two super-battleships—secured in 1937," and a classified cable from the U.S. Embassy in the Soviet Union that "immediately went back to Moscow . . . such came from Washington." Listening with fascination and excitement to a fuller, more incriminating account than he had heard before from the informer, Levine would remember that Chambers told Berle explicitly that "certain State Department officials were taking files out of the department to be copied or photographed and forwarded to Russia."

At the end of the list of subversives—Berle's diary entry that night noted he had "slowly manipulated" the visitor to divulge as much as possible—Chambers added the names of two mid-level State Department aides missing from his earlier confessions: first, "Donald Hiss . . . brought along by brother," and then, as Berle recorded,

> *Alger Hiss*
> Ass't to Sayre—CP—1937
> Member of the Underground Com.—Active
> Baltimore boys
> Wife—Priscilla Hiss—Socialist—
> Early days of new Deal

Typing up his notes later that night with the heading "Underground Espionage Agent," Berle went on to do somewhat perfunctory checking on "the two Hiss boys," as he testified later, and got equally perfunctory if reassuring endorsements from their prominent superiors and patrons. Still later, Berle also mentioned Chambers's accusations to President Roosevelt over a White House croquet game. But FDR insouciantly waved aside the whole tale as one more witchhunt to discredit the New Deal, and between croquet shots he snapped angrily at his security adviser. Berle could tell his informer, said the President with unusual vulgarity, "to go fuck himself."

Chambers, meanwhile, having come out of hiding and gone to work for *Time*, awaited a full-blown federal investigation with some portent. His revelations, he boasted to another ex-communist, were "on the President's desk." When nothing soon came of the approach to Berle, however, he continued to repeat or broker his story in various quarters, now with the added and ominous overtone of an official cover-up. "By then I was certain," he wrote later, "that the administration was more interested in suppressing my story than in discovering the facts." Later in 1939 and again in 1940, Levine went to the notorious HUAC proffering Chambers's testimony. Stripling, then a junior assistant, seemed indifferent, though Martin Dies was always ready for an exposé. The splenetic chairman immediately called a press conference to promise sensational spy stories, solicited a hefty magazine advance for an article on the scandal, and then mindlessly dropped the article and Chambers to move on to the next headline. Despite that brush with HUAC, however, Chambers by 1941 was quietly in touch with the Committee's own resident defector, Ben Mandel, whom he had known as a fellow communist and who had even issued Chambers his party card in the 1920s. Mandel was to help leak his old comrade's accusations to Washington journalist William Allen, though after furtive meetings and histrionics on both sides, Allen failed to publish anything, yet another effort to no avail.

At the same time, another former communist who had heard of Chambers's exploits gave his name to the FBI as a onetime Russian agent, triggering late in 1941 an incipient espionage investigation, including FBI interception of Chambers's mail. When the FBI eventually did interview him for the first time in May 1942, the Bureau was not aware of the 1939 testimony to Adolf Berle, though Chambers clearly assumed they knew the details and that his spy story was at long last being heeded. While he mentioned Alger Hiss and other names given Berle, his prolix account was now rambling and diffuse, almost shoptalk among intelligence operatives. The two FBI agents, straining to keep up, came away with no express charges of espionage or copied documents. "Most of his information," the initial FBI report concluded, with vast irony in light of its sequels, "is either history, hypothesis, or deduction."

Even after the FBI requested and received Berle's more explicit and alarming notes in 1943—notes he had casually filed away after his cursory check and Presidential rebuff—the four-year-old allegations of espionage went unpursued. By the Bureau, as by Berle, it was a train of distraction and ineptitude—"a rotten lousy bumbling operation," one Truman aide called it afterward. And those first failures would inflame the whole affair when it exploded later, driving the FBI to dubious zeal in atonement for its earlier lapses, feeding the suspicion that bureaucratic carelessness was a sinister cover-up, making the putative crime all the more real and politically momentous. Still, for the moment, Whittaker Chambers, his promoters, and the story persisted. During the 1940s, Levine, Mandel, and others carried his recital of communists in government to other State Department officials, to respected GOP senator Warren Austin, to anticommunist labor leader David Dubinsky, even to gossip columnist Walter Winchell, a favorite FBI conduit. Some of those in turn anxiously repeated the charges to Roosevelt, who dismissed them as airily as he had Berle.

Then, as World War II was ending, the old accusation swiftly took on fresh impetus. In the interim, Alger Hiss had risen rapidly in the State Department and become the most conspicuous government official of those initially named by Chambers. Specializing in the emerging issues of postwar international organization, Hiss was a key aide to FDR at the historic Yalta Conference of the U.S., Britain, and the Soviet Union in February 1945, organized and chaired as temporary secretary-general the founding session of the United Nations at San Francisco that April, and by July became director of the State Department's Office for Multilateral Affairs. Armed with the new celebrity of at least one name among the alleged conspirators, J. Edgar Hoover began early in 1945 sending summaries of the Chambers file to the State Department security office, where Ray Murphy, urged on by his close friend Mandel, now interviewed Chambers himself in March 1945. Murphy's own three-page memorandum on the meeting, essentially repeating the old allegations once more without specific reference to espionage, was in due course leaked to Father Cronin, various conservative reporters, and to Mandel, finally filtering back in the circuit to the FBI.

In May 1945, after Hiss's return from San Francisco, where he was seen in a widely published news photo shaking hands with a smiling Harry Truman, the FBI interviewed Chambers again, this time for some eight hours. The agents' twenty-two-page report gave enlarging personal detail, including Chambers's account of a last visit to the Hiss home at the end of 1938, trying in vain to talk them into joining him in breaking with communism. Hiss had bid him farewell, Chambers told the FBI, "with tears streaming down his face," unable to defect because of "his loyalty to his friends and principles," and in large part because of the "fanatical loyalty to the Communist Party" of his strong wife, Priscilla.

The internal security process quickened in the fall of 1945 when a Russian Embassy defector in Canada, Igor Gouzenko, told the FBI that he once listened to a Russian officer exult that the Soviets had a spy who was "an aide" to the American secretary of state, though Gouzenko never learned the operative's name. A few weeks later, as part of her own confession to the FBI, Elizabeth Bentley recalled that she, too, had once heard indirectly about a communist in the State Department, someone she remembered as "Eugene Hiss." And when Bentley also named a ranking Treasury official, Harry Dexter White, the FBI had suddenly been given two "security risks" high in the Truman administration.

Accordingly, in the winter of 1945–46, Hoover began both to lobby for the removal of Hiss and White and to circulate among the White House, Justice and State Departments regular secret reports on "Soviet Espionage in the United States," documents that ominously blended the Chambers accusation against Hiss with the scanty Gouzenko and Bentley allusions and characterized them all as "accurate." What had been "history, hypothesis, or deduction" four years earlier was now transformed. "The reports kept getting bigger and bigger," remembered Stephen Spingarn, a White House security aide. They were also variously leaked to Father John Cronin.

In December 1945, the FBI began what would be a twenty-two-month wiretap on Alger Hiss's home phone, later adding intensive physical surveillance. Neither would produce evidence of wrongdoing. But only days after the FBI instituted its covert anticommunist "educational" campaign early in 1946, Hoover approached Secretary of State James Byrnes about easing Hiss out of government. It was to be a process of FBI leaks to friendly congressmen, who might then pressure the suspect's resignation without the necessity of formal charges. An open hearing, Hoover warned, would only "compromise" the Bureau's sources and investigation. When Hiss did not then immediately depart, the director arranged to have Walter Winchell broadcast that the "leanings" of State Department aides "have passed from national scandal to national danger," while "the question of the loyalty and integrity of one high American officer has been called to the attention of the President."

Under a cloud of rumors, Alger Hiss was to leave government in January 1947, becoming president of the venerable and prestigious Carnegie Endowment for International Peace just when Richard Nixon started in the Eightieth Congress. Nonetheless, the accusations continued, sometimes with more detail and drama than any of the widely circulating FBI leaks. Taking up his own notes from the old Berle interview as well as ongoing contacts with Cronin and Mandel, Isaac Don Levine published an outright charge of treason in the December 1947 issue of Kohlberg's new anticommunist *Plain Talk*. "Certain high and trusted officials in the State Department, including one who had played a leading role at Yalta and in organizing the United Nations," Levine wrote with everything but Hiss's name, "delivered confidential papers to communist agents who microfilmed them for dispatch to Moscow." Finally, in mid-July 1948, only two weeks before the Bentley and Chambers testimony to HUAC, a Hearst reporter, testifying to a Washington State legislative committee, had read from a leaked FBI report repeating verbatim Chambers's old charges against the Hiss brothers and others.

"An open secret among government officials and newsmen," Whittaker Chambers would call his recollections well before he answered the HUAC subpoena. Gradually, ineluctably, the once-depreciated Chambers story had been revived and joined to the swift bureaucratic and political currents of the postwar moment.

For Richard Nixon, the significance of that murky genealogy was how much he already knew of the story well before Chambers's HUAC appearance—and what he did not know.

Old Committee files were dotted with references to Chambers from his "open" party past through the mid-thirties, and the FBI supplied through Nichols a synopsis of his allegations, to the point that Stripling would even have on hand August 3 the government personnel records of many of those Chambers was to name in his initial testimony. But Nixon also possessed— as the rest of HUAC did not—the remarkable tutelage from John Cronin. The early Chambers interviews with the FBI as well as Levine's eyewitness version of the Berle meeting were plainly woven into the priest's report to the bishops, which named Hiss four separate times and which, of course, Nixon had first studied several months earlier. Drawing on his latticework of official and private sources, Cronin had featured prominently Chambers's charges, and an explicit threat of exposure in light of Hiss's new prominence. Whittaker Chambers, Nixon would read in Cronin's report, was no longer so "apathetic about involving others."

> In the State Department, the most influential communist has been Alger Hiss. The writer has seen an affadavit [Murphy's memo] by an editor of a nationally known general magazine stating this editor was in one of the primary communist cells to infiltrate the early New Deal . . . and that among his companions [was] Alger Hiss. . . . It is reliably stated that this editor plans to release such a statement if Alger Hiss becomes permanent secretary of the United Nations organization.

Father Cronin had also passed along to Nixon secret FBI summaries on "Soviet Espionage," including a November 27, 1945, installment on which Nixon would draw so prodigiously that it became known sarcastically inside the FBI as the "Nixon memo." When HUAC questioned Attorney General Tom Clark in hearings on the Mundt-Nixon bill in February 1948, the freshman congressman appeared to know clearly the thrust of both the Bentley and Chambers stories—long before either testified in public. On that occasion, however, he had as always carefully guarded his advantage, concealing the gushing FBI leaks from the Democrat Clark as he concealed the Cronin connection from the rest of the Committee.

Then, on the eve of the Chambers testimony, Nixon had received yet another windfall of official secrets from inside the Executive Branch, a discreet accompaniment to the GOP pressure on Thomas to continue the inquiry beyond Bentley. The old Office of Strategic Services, now the newly formed Central Intelligence Agency, saw Republican candidate Dewey as a future patron and champion and was eager to promote the spy probe as an election-year embarrassment to Truman. Then, too, Elizabeth Bentley's charges had implicated, among others, senior OSS officers, and the new CIA was anxious in any case to divert some of the security opprobrium to the rival State Department, in this case to Alger Hiss. For their own bureaucratic reasons, then, the CIA encouraged the late summer HUAC hearings much as Hoover's FBI had quietly helped the New York governor in the Oregon primary debate the previous May. In the process, they had singled out Nixon as the lone responsible Republican on the

Committee and supplied him with their own investigative files on the Chambers-Hiss allegations, reports that largely paralleled the FBI leaks and offered no new evidence, yet by their very existence reinforced the charge.

Finally, added to all the impressive secret documents and perhaps equally important, there was Father Cronin's own expert assurance. He had "told Mr. Nixon," the priest remembered from their early meetings before the August 1948 hearings, "that Mr. Hiss was in fact a communist and that, therefore, Mr. Chambers's story probably had some credulity [*sic*]." With all his authoritative prior knowledge, "Nixon was playing with a stacked deck in the Hiss case," Cronin would say later of his famous pupil.

Yet no less important to the events about to erupt was what also had been lost in all that well-aided premonition. The portentous FBI and CIA summaries and extracts filtered through Cronin or others conveyed little or nothing of the nagging ambiguities and inconsistencies that had already begun to litter Chambers's tale of high treason. Obscure in all the leaks and inspired journalism was how much the basic accusation wound twistingly back through the maze to a single source. If Father Cronin, Levine, Mandel, Murphy, J. Edgar Hoover, Walter Winchell, and sundry other reporters and Washington figures "knew" Alger Hiss was a communist, it was because Whittaker Chambers had told them. In the end, as at the beginning, the case would come down to the clashing truths, and lies, of two men. Now it burst into the open mainly because Richard Nixon chose so deliberately and famously to believe one of them. It was a career-making act he owed in part to hard work and shrewd instinct, to temperament, political calculus, and courage, but in ample measure as well to the hidden force, and limits, of Father Cronin's "stacked deck."

The committee began at mid-morning in executive session, a precaution lest Chambers's unrehearsed testimony somehow backfire. Mundt was in the chair, flanked by fellow Republicans McDowell and Nixon; Democrats Rankin, Hebert, and Petersen; and Stripling with his dour investigators Russell, Wheeler, and Appell, though not Mandel, whose long and intimate ties to Chambers were still unknown to all but Nixon.

Dingy shirt collar curled up over his wrinkled suitcoat, the witness was sworn in and read in a low monotone a prepared statement: "Almost exactly nine years ago . . . I went to Washington and reported to the authorities what I knew about the infiltration of the United States government by communists," he began, without enumerating the checkered history of his subsequent confessions. As Committee members yawned, he then droned through a description of his intellectual seduction by Marxism-Leninism, his repudiation and break, his sleepless hiding for a year afterward with "revolver within easy reach," and then, finally, "the apparatus." At the mention of names, HUAC sprang awake. "Hell, why is this in executive session? This should be in the open," one of the southerners drawled. Summoning reporters who were waiting in the corridors for the usual leaks after a secret hearing, they quickly adjourned for public proceedings to the much larger Ways and Means Committee chamber, which Stripling had knowingly reserved beforehand for the eventuality.

The public address system was not working, and Mundt reminded the mumbling witness to speak louder as he began his statement once more for the reporters and a handful of spectators. The second time, for a larger audience, Chambers delivered it with evident feeling and effect. "I know that I am leaving the winning side for the losing side, but it is better to die on the losing side than to live under communism," he quoted himself telling his wife at the time of his defection. His congressional appearance and the publicity had "darkened, and will no doubt continue to darken, my effort to integrate myself into the community of free men," he said in closing. "But that is a small price to pay if my testimony helps to make Americans recognize at last that they are at grips with a secret, sinister, and enormously powerful force whose tireless purpose is their enslavement." At that his voice broke, and the echoing room was suspended in silence for several seconds. Richard Nixon was visibly impressed. "This one incident," he told a reporter afterward, "convinced me he was not putting on an act."

Moments before his dramatic finish, Chambers had already sent the reporters scurrying to file for the evening papers. The Washington "underground" he depicted was founded by Harold Ware, dashing, Soviet-educated son of the Communist Party's legendary "Mother Bloor," and included Nathan Witt, a former lawyer for the National Labor Relations Board; John Abt, another ex-New Deal bureaucrat; and Lee Pressman, a government attorney who later became general counsel for the CIO. All three were lower-level officials and known leftists long since gone from federal service. Bentley had earlier mentioned both Witt and Abt. It was the added name Chambers now gave, replete with notable attainments, that provided reporters the headlines. They were all in the conspiracy together, he swore, "as was Alger Hiss, who, as a member of the State Department, later organized the conferences at Dumbarton Oaks, San Francisco, and the United States' side of the Yalta Conference." There was a moment's pause as Chambers looked up and reporters scribbled. Then he continued, "The purpose of this group at that time was not primarily espionage. Its original purpose was the communist infiltration of the American government. But espionage was certainly one of its eventual objectives. Let no one be suprised. . . . Disloyalty is a matter of principle with every member of the Communist Party."

Following the statement, Stripling led the witness through a prepared line of questions eliciting more names of former officials and "cell leaders"—Victor Perlo, Charles Kramer (alias Krivitsky), Henry Collins, Donald Hiss—and the HUAC staff was ready for the record with the personnel files of the Hiss brothers, Abt, and Pressman. All the names were familiar to Nixon from Cronin's files, though he later wrote baldly in *Six Crises*, "This was the first time I had ever heard of either Alger or Donald Hiss." Directing "the whole business," Chambers said, was a shadowy Comintern figure named J. Peters, who had prudently decided that promising young men headed for "power and influence" in government should eventually be detached from the larger group and operate only through liaison with Chambers. Among those elect "clearly was Alger Hiss." Chambers described his risky last visit to the Hiss home at the end of 1938 to "break him away from the party," added tautly that "Mrs. Hiss is also a member of the Communist Party," and told of the tearful parting of the two men. "He cried?" Stripling asked in surprise. "Yes, he did," the witness replied evenly. "I was very fond of Mr. Hiss." Nixon, who had by now read the story in various forms, said nothing.

His testimony turned for a time to Harry Dexter White, whom Chambers identified as "a fellow traveler" if not "a registered member" of the party. "In other words, White was being used as an unwitting dupe?" offered Hebert. "I would scarcely say 'unwitting,' " Chambers shot back. Mundt and Rankin then waxed on the atheistic horrors of communism and its equivalence to fascism, Mundt adding on behalf of his China Lobby supporters the suspicion that Alger Hiss was running in the State Department "one of those communist cells which endeavored to influence our Chinese [*sic*] policy and bring about the condemnation of Chiang Kai-shek." When Chambers identified Hiss's current job as "head of the Carnegie Foundation for World Peace," the acting chairman saw the bitter irony at once. "Certainly there is no hope for world peace under the leadership of men like Alger Hiss," said Mundt. Rankin allowed that he was not surprised Carnegie was located in New York City; you could not get away with this sort of thing in Mississippi.

Amid all this, as usual, Nixon's own questioning of the witness seemed relatively crisp and incisive, though sliding by in the humid August morning was an omission of some magnitude. Ever mindful of his own added liability, not only as repentant Marxist but onetime foreign agent, Chambers had skirted subtly the question of actual espionage, "not primarily" the group's purpose "but . . . certainly one of its eventual objectives." "I should perhaps make the point," he said at one juncture about Hiss and White, the "elite" rising men, "that these people were specifically not wanted to act as sources of information . . . their position in the government would be of very much more service to the Communist Party." It seemed almost to absolve them of spying. Nixon questioned Chambers closely about his first approach to Berle "nine years ago," intent on whom Chambers had named. The witness was "fairly sure" he had reported the same group to Berle. Then, when Nixon seemed about to ask exactly what Chambers told Berle about the operation, pointing toward the stolen secrets he had described in 1939, a refracted Representative McDowell interrupted: Was this "the A. A. Berle who became an ambassador?" McDowell demanded, about to pounce. And Chambers had come quickly to Berle's defense, insisting the New York liberal lawyer was "an anticommunist." Nixon did not pursue the Berle interview, and the moment was lost.

Over the next four months, Nixon and HUAC would fail to draw from their star witness the truly sensational heart of his story, only led to it in the end by others. But for now the names, particularly Alger Hiss's, seemed enough. Mundt excused Chambers, extolling his "courage and good patriotism." He had been, Rankin added, "a splendid witness." Outside, in the sticky heat of the Capitol Hill afternoon, the early editions were already drawing their own conclusions. "TIME EDITOR," thundered a typical headline, "CHARGES CARNEGIE ENDOWMENT HEAD WAS SOVIET AGENT."

"THE FINEST OF YOUNG AMERICANS"

A reporter had telephoned Alger Hiss about the charges the night before Chambers testified, and after more calls the afternoon of the third, Hiss wired the Committee, asking to appear in his own defense the morning of August 5. It was scarcely the first time he had confronted the old accusations, though never before with such notoriety. When Secretary of State Byrnes told him about the swirling FBI and congressional stories in 1946, Hiss had gone promptly to Bureau headquarters to deny any disloyalty. After he became president of the Carnegie Endowment in 1947, Alfred Kohlberg and then–Minnesota congressman Walter Judd had raised similarly vague charges with the chairman of the Endowment board of trustees, John Foster Dulles, but Hiss had assured Dulles there was nothing to the allegations. There followed in 1947 FBI interviews of both Alger and Priscilla Hiss, more rumors and gossip, and early in 1948 even a brief appearance before the Manhattan grand jury with still another reassurance to Dulles. Each time, the questions wound back in some way to the enduring Chambers allegations. Each time, Hiss's categorical denials seemed to dispose of the matter.

"No lark more blithe than he," his high school yearbook lauded Alger Hiss. The career that followed seemed to fulfill the prophecy. Handsome and charming, admired for both his wit and seriousness, he had gone from Johns Hopkins to Harvard Law, where he was a protégé of Felix Frankfurter, then to a coveted Supreme Court clerkship with Justice Oliver Wendell Holmes. "I know of no one who as a young man more completely exemplified the finest of young Americans," a friend at the time wrote typically. After a brief law practice with patrician firms in Boston and New York, he was invited to Washington at the outset of the New Deal to work on the legal staff of the Agricultural Adjustment Administration, Roosevelt's dynamic agency for rural reform. From there Hiss had gone on to act as counsel for a celebrated Senate committee investigating the munitions industry, then for a brief stint under the solicitor general, and in 1936 to the State Department, where he rose over the next decade from staff aide to the assistant secretary for economic affairs to his eventual prominence at international conferences at the close of the war.

"A New Dealer who was simultaneously in the Washington *Social Register*," one observer said of Alger's easily worn prestige. Like his tailored suits with the fresh white handkerchiefs in the breast pockets, his sponsors and associates seemed impeccable—Felix Frankfurter, Dean Acheson, Woodrow Wilson's son-in-law Francis Sayre, Adlai Stevenson, a powerful roll of Democratic Washington, and even, eventually, John Foster Dulles and the more conservative Republican Carnegie trustees. That summer Hiss was forty-seven, with his foreign policy credentials and contacts one of a handful of men in line for still higher office in some subsequent Democratic administration. His less talented, less well-connected State Department successor when he left for Carnegie, a cautious bureaucrat named Dean Rusk, was to be President John Kennedy's secretary of state a dozen years later. Then it would be largely forgotten that Alger Hiss, had he survived the still vague, single-source stigmata in his postwar security file, might just as well have had that cabinet post instead of Rusk. HUAC would have before it not only one of the bright young men of the New Deal, a figure widely seen as a symbol of the liberal regime, but also one of its heirs apparent.

Yet behind the Hiss composure and polish was another reality. He had been raised in Baltimore in shabby gentility, left with a stern, loveless mother after his father walked upstairs one day and slit his own throat in a ghastly bloodbath. His sister later killed herself, and a favorite brother committed virtual suicide in his twenties after a reckless binge of dissipation. Alger had emerged outwardly mild and gentle, stoic, unseeing, tightly controlled, a life divided between public propriety, even honors, and a shrouded, private squalor.

"DO NOT TAKE THIS FATAL STEP," his mother had telegraphed him before his wedding. Priscilla Hiss was a modern woman of her era, educated at Bryn

Mawr, bohemian, restless, dipping into eastern orthodox Quakerism, psy-choanalysis, socialist politics. His courtship, like Richard Nixon's, had been cloying. Alger had ridden back and forth with her on trains and ferries, trying to persuade this attractive, sophisticated girl not to marry a rival, Thayer Hobson. Then, when she spurned Hiss, and when Hobson soon left her with a small child after a stormy marriage, Alger was there to help her through an abortion, and to marry her, becoming an attentive father to her son. Afterward, she was in many ways the dominant of the two, "a rather self-assertive woman, who had no intention of letting Alger 'steal the show,' " remembered William Marbury, Hiss's friend and attor-ney. "It almost seemed as if she resented the attention which his friends paid to him. Like Anthony Trollope's Mrs. Proudie, she would interrupt him when he was asked for his opinion and answer for him."

The House Caucus Room, the Capitol's largest hearing chamber, was packed with spectators and press the morning of the fifth when Hiss arrived with Marbury. A man with a reputation, and future, to protect, Hiss had received discreet advice on his testimony from Undersecretary of State Dean Acheson and others. He had recoiled indignantly at Foster Dulles's suggestion that he could confess some youthful 1930s flirtation with radi-calism, now plead older and wiser, and be done with it. As Hiss sat waiting to testify, Stripling came over to ask if he had a prepared statement to submit, and the witness reached inside what Stripling remembered as "his neat coat" and touched his heart. "What I have to say will come from here," he whispered. Privately he was contemptuous of HUAC. "I had no respect for Mundt, for Thomas, Rankin (I thought he was evil), for most of the others," he said later. "Of course, I didn't realize then what shits they were," he admitted afterward to his son. "And then I just couldn't believe that anyone wouldn't love me, once I was there."

The crowd, and Washington opinion, seemed to fortify his confidence. That morning a Herblock cartoon in the *Post* had shown an innocent man in an arena being attacked by a vicious tiger labeled "Smear Statements," watched gleefully from the stands by the fat faces of Thomas and Mundt, and a death's-head Rankin. Hiss was familiar with the caricatures, except for a younger, dark-haired jowly figure peeking around their shoulder, the congressman from Whittier.

Hiss began his testimony with a brief written declaration "to deny unqualifiedly various statements about me . . . by one Whittaker Cham-bers." He had never been a communist or sympathizer and did not know any of his friends to be. Hiss knew some of those named by Chambers but only innocently as old acquaintances or as fellow officials. He had never heard of Whittaker Chambers until the FBI mentioned the name among others in a 1947 interview. "So far as I know, I have never laid eyes on him," he said firmly of his accuser, "and I should like to have the opportunity to do so."

Stripling asked the witness to recount his career, and only moments into the testimony Nixon interrupted forcefully, asking who had recommended that Hiss come to Washington. "Is it necessary? There are so many witnesses who use names rather loosely before your committee," the witness said, rebuking the congressman. They sparred, and Nixon, instantly on edge, insisted. "I would like a direct answer to the question." Hiss grudgingly named Justice Felix Frankfurter and two more minor officials. Stripling then routinely resumed his questions about Hiss's résumé, though reporters noticed how Nixon's face had visibly reddened during this first fleeting exchange. "He was rather insolent to me," Nixon told a journalist afterward. "Frankly, I didn't like it."

Nettled himself, Hiss clipped off his record, which was "impressive," thought Nixon, "to everyone in the room." Mundt was soon perplexed at the sheer force of the Hiss denials. "I want to say for the committee that it is extremely puzzling that a man who is a senior editor of *Time* . . . should come before this committee and discuss the communist apparatus working in Washington, which he says is transmitting secrets to the Russian government." The reference to espionage, more specific than any Chambers had given in open testimony, passed by unnoticed as Hiss replied of Chambers that he had "no possible understanding of what could have motivated him." As an aside, Rankin observed *Time*'s past "smear attacks" against HUAC and that he would not be surprised "at anything that comes out of anybody connected with it." Stripling asked again if Hiss had ever seen Whittaker Chambers.

"The name means asolutely nothing to me, Mr. Stripling."

Given a wire service photo of Chambers taken two days before, Hiss replied, "If this is Mr. Chambers, he is not particularly unusual looking. He looks like a lot of people. I might even mistake him for the chairman of this committee." The audience broke into laughter. Hiss turned to acknowledge them with a smile, and the chunky Mundt answered self-consciously, "I hope you are wrong in that." Hiss went on to say that he "would not want to take an oath" without seeing the man in the flesh.

"Is he here today?" he asked.

"Not to my knowledge," answered the chairman.

"I hoped he would be."

All the while, Mundt and the others smiled, grimaced, raised an eyebrow in the banter, though Richard Nixon "never smiled," noted a reporter, "and never took his eyes off Hiss's face." Studying the witness now like a theater critic, now with the intensity he had focused on opposing attorneys or jurors in the first trials with Wingert and Bewley, Nixon thought the testimony "a virtuoso performance." Afterward, his impressions of class and contest were pungent. Hiss, he noted, studied the photo of Chambers "with an elaborate air of concentration." The witness had insultingly turned his back on the Committee, "tilting his head in a courtly bow and smiling graciously" when he compared Chambers to poor Mundt, and his "friends from . . . the Washington social community . . . broke into a titter of delighted laughter." Quietly seething, Nixon quickly scanned his notes, seized on Hiss's careful wording "by the name of Whittaker Chambers," and motioned for Mandel, who was standing nearby. He remembered Chambers's party aliases from the FBI reports and asked the aide to call Chambers to see if Hiss might have known him under another name.

But all this was hidden at the moment. The session soon ended in what British journalist Alistair Cooke saw as "a moment of rare innocence." Stripling and Mundt seemed ready to concede a case of mistaken identity by Chambers and wanted the informer recalled. Nixon amiably suggested "in justice to both witnesses" a private meeting of the two men to avoid a further "useless appearance" by Chambers. Even more glazed than usual, McDowell suddenly asked Hiss almost apologetically if "you feel you have had a free and fair and proper hearing this morning?" With a characteristic nod and smile, Hiss thought he was "treated with great consideration," albeit he deplored the "great public press display . . . of completely unfounded charges against me."

Nixon made a last gesture, asking if the witness did not agree that the government should make "every effort" to root out subversives. Every effort, said Hiss, "compatible with the protection of the reputations of innocent persons." Mundt tried his own tack: would Hiss ("if you were in charge") hire a communist anywhere in government, even "as a charwoman?" Hiss played again with words but ended, "I would not." Once more a reporter saw the exchange and Hiss's obvious advantage "sit sourly on Mr. Nixon's stomach." Still watching intently, Nixon thought him at once "much too careful a witness" and "a little too mouthy."

By now it was over. Mundt thanked Hiss for "forthright statements." Rankin even stepped down from the Committee dais to shake hands with the witness, having to work his way through a crowd of reporters and wellwishers congratulating Hiss. "He had the day completely," Nixon ruefully wrote afterward. Only as they were rising to leave did Mandel finally return to Nixon with some consolation a reply from Chambers about other names. He had known the informer, Mandel said, not as Whittaker Chambers but as a comrade called "Carl."

At the same moment, hundreds of miles away in a Vermont village where the Hisses took a summer place, Priscilla uttered yet another name in the puzzle. She had finally seen the New York papers trumpeting the charges against her husband and a photo of Chambers that reminded her of someone. "I remember a dreadful man," she had said to a friend, "named Crosley or something like that."

"WHETHER OR NOT THE TWO MEN KNEW EACH OTHER"

As Nixon had left the hearing following Chambers's testimony two days before, a young woman stopped him. "Don't you know that Whittaker Chambers is an incurable drunkard?" she had said quickly, then walked off before he could say anything. Now, in the wake of the apparent Hiss vindication, doubts about the credibility of Chambers and his accusations loomed large, HUAC looking foolishly, wantonly duped by some seedy turncoat. Mary Spargo, a former aide to the panel and now a sympathetic *Washington Post* reporter, pulled Nixon aside in the Capitol corridor outside the caucus room. "How is the Committee going to dig itself out of this hole?" she chided him. "This case is going to kill the Committee unless you can prove Chambers's story." He was still smarting from Spargo's words when he walked minutes later into the House restaurant for lunch and found more angry dismay among Capitol reporters, who descended on him, their ready source and the "reasonable" man on the Committee. He remembered Ed Lahey, a conservative journalist for the *Chicago Daily News*, "literally shaking with anger" as he spoke: "The Committee on Un-American activities stands convicted, guilty of calumny in putting Chambers on the stand without first checking the truth of his testimony."

Nixon was eating lunch disconsolately when word reached the dining room and quickly spread that President Truman had forcefully condemned the Committee at his morning press conference. The Bentley and Chambers information had long since been known to the FBI, Truman said in a slap at Hoover as well, and had been presented to a grand jury that found it "insufficient to justify indictment." Public hearings now were "serving no useful purpose" while "doing irreparable harm" to reputations and federal morale. Truman reiterated his refusal to disclose to "a congressional committee" any employee loyalty files, and added a famous gibe. "They are using these hearings as a red herring," he said caustically of HUAC, "to keep them from doing what they ought to do." Meanwhile, across the city in a private club, Hiss, Marbury, and other friends were at their own luncheon, celebrating the triumph.

That afternoon, HUAC filed gloomily back into executive session, "in a virtual state of shock," as Nixon recalled the hour. "We've been had.

We're ruined," wailed Mundt, who was running for the Senate in South Dakota and banking heavily on the hearings. Scornfully, the threatened politicians blamed the Committee staff, personified by Stripling and Mandel, for the failure somehow to warn them or further check Chambers's allegations before the rushed hearings and lurid headlines for which they were all so eager only hours before. Mundt thought "it was quite apparent the Committee had been taken in by Chambers," and unless HUAC could develop some "collateral issue" that would take them "off the spot, take the minds of the public off the Hiss case, the Committee would suffer a great deal of damage."

Hebert voiced the wish that had taken hold of most of them during the morning session. "Let's wash our hands of the whole mess," said the Louisianan, and then suggested as a face-saving device that they vote to turn over the Chambers and Hiss testimony to Attorney General Clark and "ask him to determine who was lying." Mundt was ready to entertain a formal motion, and even Stripling, usually the skeptic and pursuer, seemed resigned to cutting their losses. Like the sudden death of Walter Dexter or the spring of 1946 when Nixon's fledgling campaign began to flag before Chotiner's Red-baiting barrage or the point in their first debate as Jerry Voorhis challenged his attack on the PAC endorsement, it was one of those fleeting, decisive moments in Richard Nixon's political career when events might have taken a very different turn.

Now Nixon suddenly spoke up to save the inquiry. He began by playing on the Committee's already bruised pride and political vulnerability. To shunt the case to Justice would only confirm their disgrace, "a public confession that we were incompetent and even reckless in our procedures," he argued. "We would never be able to begin another investigation without having someone say, 'Why do you amateurs insist on getting into these cases? Why don't you leave the job where it belongs—to the experts in the Department of Justice?'" Nixon would later tell Bert Andrews that he was "hopping mad" himself that so little staff work had been done for the first two hearings, allowing Hiss to rebut Chambers without factual challenge. But here in the executive session he shrewdly defended the HUAC staff, whose support he needed then and later, and at the same time prodded the Republicans and Rankin with the partisan suspicion they all shared—the specter of an administration cover-up.

Chambers had told his story to the government before, Nixon reminded them, but "no action had ever been taken to check the credibility of his charges." They must know the case would be dropped if they handed it back to Justice. Now that they had opened the matter in public, whatever the controversy, they had "a responsibility . . . to see it through." Encouraged in his own instinctive combativeness, Stripling chimed in that, after all, "a *prima facie* perjury was somewhere involved." They had to carry on "if only for that reason."

Nixon then went to his own suspicions of Hiss's testimony, the careful, qualified answers about not knowing anyone "by the name of Whittaker Chambers." Hiss had put on a "show," was "too sensitive" when questioned about his patrons, too "smooth" a witness. They might never establish whether Hiss was a communist—one man's word against another's. "But we should be able to establish by corroborative testimony whether or not the two men knew each other," he told them. "If Hiss were lying about not knowing Chambers, then he also might be lying about whether or not he was a communist." It was a historic syllogism: Chambers the subversive. Chambers knew Hiss. Hiss the subversive.

Suddenly it was plain, and seemingly within their grasp. Stripling added ominously that he, too, was "vaguely dissatisfied with some of Hiss's answers." More telling, the chief investigator had heard "a calculated whispering campaign" against Chambers, rumors that he was an alcoholic, had been in a mental hospital, suffered from paranoia. Nixon remembered the woman in the corridor. It was the sort of slander, Stripling pointed out, that the communists typically spread to discredit a legitimate witness.

Just before the closed afternoon meeting, Mandel had suggested to Nixon "a simple procedure," as Chambers later described it, and Nixon now proposed it as an alternative. A subcommittee could question Chambers in secret to prove details of his personal relationship with Hiss, his knowledge of the man, and then question Hiss on the same points to compare the answers. Mundt and Hebert bruited again their pessimism but soon relented. They voted to establish a subcommittee—Nixon as chairman with McDowell and Hebert—to see Chambers *in camera* as soon as possible.

Elated, Nixon returned to the attic office to reflect on his victory in the Committee, though also to brood on the risks. "I had put myself, a freshman congressman, in the position of defending the reputation of the Un-American Activities Committee," he wrote of that afternoon. "I was opposing the President of the United States and the majority of press corps opinion, which is so important to the career of anyone in elective office." As he called for the transcript of Chambers's testimony and began to pore over it, he evidently felt his own political liability tied to HUAC as never before. "No one was more aware than I that the Committee's past record had been vulnerable to attack," he remembered, noting that "even some of the Committee's own members were mounting an all-out attack on alleged 'sloppy' procedures." The none-too-cryptic reference was to Hebert, the canny Democrat who resented Nixon's past publicity. Now, sharing the latest press acceptance of Hiss and cynicism toward Chambers, Hebert was bidding to become the favored "source" on HUAC, lumping Nixon with the unsavory rest. The folly or effectiveness of the Committee may have had little impact on his seat in the twelfth district, but HUAC's national prominence, and the powerful forces increasingly behind its scenes, obviously bore on any larger ambition. His plea to pursue the case was an act of political calculation, for California as for Capitol Hill.

It was also, even more privately, a decision based on his strategic foreknowledge of the Chambers charges from Cronin and the leaked official files. What had gone unsaid in the crucial executive session was as vital as his arguments, his sense of Chambers's persistent and gradually expanding testimony to the FBI about Hiss, and not least the prospect of still more information from Cronin or other official sources in the unfolding inquiry. From the beginning, beyond politics or covert intelligence, there was also his thinly concealed distaste for Alger Hiss, the personality and symbol. The clash and hostility heating his first red-faced exchange were to remain. "Nixon had his hat set for Hiss. It was a personal thing," Stripling said later. "He was no more concerned about whether Hiss was [a communist] than a billy goat." In any event, the prey was formidable, the stakes large. There was a palpable sense after the opening testimony that Congressman Nixon was stepping personally and politically into a major confrontation and opportunity. Stripling would say to him somberly as they began, "You're in the big leagues now."

As Nixon studied the Chambers transcript, his adversary practiced his own politics. After the celebration lunch, Hiss wrote an ingratiating letter to John Foster Dulles to soothe the Republican board chairman and his nervous trustees. "I am quite conscious . . . of a very definite sense of relief." Hiss told him of his success, enclosing a copy of his opening denial before the Committee. For his part, Dulles noted the seeming victory yet remained cautious when another trustee suggested an open vote of confidence for the wrongly accused Hiss. Dulles's brother, Allen, knew the young representative Nixon on HUAC, an able and serious man, and both the Dulleses were advisers to GOP Presidential candidate Tom Dewey. "It seems to be better," concluded the chairman, putting off the endorsement of Hiss, "to defer decision until after the present hearings have been concluded."

Nixon worked late that night over the testimony and awoke August 6 to still more misgivings. Both radio and newspapers blared the Hiss domination of HUAC and the administration counterattack. "TRUMAN CALLS SPY INQUIRIES A REPUBLICAN RED HERRING," headlined the sedate *New York Times* across three columns. The *Washington Post* deplored the "branding" by the Committee and "the entry of our society into the twilight zone between government by law and government by lawlessness." A Justice Department press conference announced dramatically that a three-year, half-million-dollar investigation into the Bentley and Chambers charges "failed to turn up evidence that would justify prosecution of the communist espionage now unfolding before congressional committees." He was not "prepared," Nixon wrote later, for such "fury and vehemence," though even more disturbed at the corridor reaction of House colleagues.

The Republicans he encountered the next day, like the journalists in the dining room after the hearing, were clearly persuaded by Hiss's denials. After several unsettling comments, Nixon anxiously approached the respected Christian Herter, a discreet supporter of the Committee yet with high-level friends and contacts in the State Department. Herter told him the "consensus" at State was that Hiss was innocent. "I'm afraid the Committee has been taken in by Chambers," Herter admonished. Nixon assured him he was not choosing sides. "If Chambers is lying, he should be exposed. If Hiss is lying, he should be exposed," he argued, and in either event HUAC now had a solemn "obligation" to find out. Repelled by the circus but carefully politic, Herter could only agree. It was the artful position Nixon took throughout the case with the crucial, ever-self-protective figures of the eastern establishment—most notably the Dulles brothers—who found HUAC's inquisitions at once farcical and menacing, aggravating and politically useful. Heading off Herter, Richard Nixon forestalled any serious House revolt against HUAC in those tenuous hours after the Hiss testimony and won for himself invaluable time.

He now began a stream of calls to Father Cronin, who in turn quickly set up a secret channel of information with one of the FBI agents with whom the priest had worked on waterfront intelligence, Ed Hummer. "He could have got in serious trouble for what he did," Cronin recalled of Hummer. "But Ed would call me every day, and tell me what they had turned up; and I told Dick, who then knew just where to look for things, and what he could find." No FBI files survive on the Hummer calls to Cronin. Whatever risks the priest thought his FBI friend was running, it was clear afterward that leaks were duly authorized at the top of the Bureau. Assistant Director William Sullivan among others knew of them. At any rate, the Hummer-Cronin-Nixon traffic was to become brisk. The congressman gave the priest his direct office number, and Cronin, as he later acknowledged, "phoned Nixon's private line frequently between August and December, 1948, supplying those FBI tidbits."

They arranged to question Chambers in New York the following morning, Saturday, August 7, and took the train up Friday night with "little optimism," as Stripling saw them forlornly, "in our little subcommittee." They need not have been so glum. A new publicity counteroffensive was already starting. The FBI had that day begun to telephone newspaper columnists critical of HUAC, warning them, as one official memo put it, with "personal and confidential information" about the validity of the Chambers allegations. Before the congressmen left Washington's Union Station, Nixon had given the *New York Herald Tribune* the first of what would be dozens of tailored stories over the ensuing weeks and months. The "House spy-hunters," reported the paper, "left Washington today for a clandestine rendezvous with a mysterious witness billed as able to 'crack wide open' current espionage investigations." As for the witness himself, Mandel had told him in advance that they were going to be testing, as Chambers described it, "my factual, intimate knowledge of Alger Hiss, his household and habits." He would be ready. Friday night in New York Nixon again worked into the predawn hours on a list of questions—still stung by the Hiss appearance and "determined," as he wrote, "never to go into another hearing of the Committee . . . without being at least as well prepared as the witnesses themselves."

Chambers found them the next morning in a stale, wood-paneled room of the deserted Foley Square courthouse, "shuffling around nervously" and "overtly polite under an air of fret." He noted that "Ben Mandel hovered around me with disquieting solicitude." Then, facing him close across a counsel table, the ever-present aides drawn up behind them, the subcommittee, mostly Nixon, began firing prepared questions. Reporters recalling the transcript were struck later at what one called the skillful "workmanlike curiosity" of Richard Nixon, the printed record clipping along almost entirely in single-line dialogue.

Chambers testified that he was known by Hiss and the others only as "Carl," an underground alias. He reiterated that the Ware group was "in no wise an intellectual study group" but rather "to infiltrate the government." In the late 1930s the Hisses had one son, "Timmie" Hobson, about ten, "a slightly effeminate child," Chambers added. Hiss nicknamed his wife "Dilly" or "Pross." She called him "Hilly." Chambers said he stayed overnight at the Hiss home "from time to time" and "as long as a week," making it a free "informal headquarters" on "the communist pattern." They had a maid, a cook, a "very nondescript" library, furniture they had "pulled together," a cocker spaniel boarded at a kennel on Wisconsin Avenue while they vacationed on Maryland's Eastern Shore. "Hiss is a man of great simplicity and a great gentleness and sweetness of character, and they lived with extreme simplicity," Chambers told them.

Mandel broke in to ask if the Hisses had any hobbies. Yes, said Chambers, they were "bird observers" and once "to their excitement" had seen a prothonotary warbler. "A very rare specimen?" McDowell, himself an amateur ornithologist, perked up, and Chambers said he had never seen one though "I am also fond of birds." Nixon then resumed his list. "Did they have a car?" Chambers described as old Ford, "black . . . and very dilapidated" with windshield wipers that turned by hand, and then a new 1936 Plymouth. Mandel interrupted again with a pointed question: "What did he do with the old car?" Chambers revealed that Hiss had "insisted" on giving it away through a communist car lot for "some poor organizer in the West," adding that the transaction was "against all the rules of underground organization . . . and I think this investigation has proved how right the Communists are in such matters. . . . I should think the records of that transfer would be traceable."

Nixon pressed on. The witness could not recall the Hiss silver pattern or china. They did not drink with Chambers. Hiss was "five feet eight or nine" and walked with "a slight mince." Mandel once again interjected that "a picture of Hiss shows his hand cupped to his ear." And Chambers replied, "He is deaf in one ear." Priscilla Hiss was "a short, highly nervous little woman" with a habit of "flushing red when she is excited or angry, fiery red. . . . She came from a Quaker family." Chambers also knew Donald Hiss, whose wife, unlike Priscilla, was "not a communist, and as a result everybody was worried about her." The informer described the general location of a succession of four houses where Alger and Priscilla had lived in the 1930s and wanted to point out that "my relationship with Alger Hiss quickly transcended our formal relationship. We became close friends." Near the end, Nixon suddenly asked him if he would submit to a lie-detector test.

"Yes, if necessary."

"You are that confident?"

"I am telling the truth."

They ended, said Stripling, "dazzled by detail." In a private memo on the session, Nixon noted it was "quite apparent from his detailed answers . . . that either he knew Hiss or that he had made a very thorough study of Hiss's life for the purpose of being able to testify against him." At the same time, he was impressed that "some of the answers had the personal ring of truth about them, beyond the bare facts themselves." Looking at the very minutiae of the testimony, settings and events more than a decade old, Hebert and others on HUAC would still have their doubts. The memories were too good, they worried. To that Nixon argued that Chambers was of course "of extraordinary intelligence" and that as an agent "he had to train himself to carry vast quantities of information in his head," an assumption that traced to Richard Nixon's own preconception of a secret operative rather than any evidence of Chambers's actual work.

Nevertheless, he rode back on the train to Washington that Saturday evening with nagging doubts. "Could Chambers . . . have concocted the whole story for purposes of destroying Hiss," he recorded, "for some motive we do not know?" He was still troubled by the contrast between the two men. Chambers the furtive communist, Hiss with his lustrous record and, to fit the myth or so Nixon thought, "a fine family." Then and later, especially to highlight the apparent paradox of the scandal, he would see them both largely as their public caricatures.

In fact, Chambers's testimony of the seventh was an intricate mixture of fact, fiction, and titillating digression. The transcript of the executive session with rapid-fire questions and answers covered less than a third of the more than two and one-half hours of the hearing. Chambers had been allowed to go off the record to tell them at length the story of his approach to Berle through Isaac Don Levine and some of the subsequent FBI and Murphy interviews. That detour, consuming the bulk of the morning, added no material facts to the question of his actual acquaintance with Hiss. Of the other intimate recollections, some were to be wholly, unaccountably at odds. Hiss was an erect six feet, a man four inches taller than Chambers described him, and neither deaf in one ear nor with a "mince" in his walk. Priscilla had never been called "Dilly" by Alger or friends and was raised a Presbyterian, coming to Quakerism only much later and never a member of a Meeting. They had never hired a maid and cook at the same time. The Hiss library and furniture had distinctive features an observant, literate man like Chambers might well have noted. He also had small but vivid details wrong about their drinking habits, Timmie, the places they lived.

Yet those discrepancies were now dismissed or ignored. Whatever the pretense of an objective search for the truth, whatever the ostensible role of Hebert and McDowell on the special subcommittee, the investigation now clearly belonged to Richard Nixon and the HUAC staff, and their purpose from the beginning, their personal and political vindication, was to confirm Chambers's account, not to weigh its ambiguities. On the ride back Nixon and Stripling made a list of the items to be checked by Mandel's research staff and the investigators over the coming week. They arrived at Union Station that night to see *Washington Post* editorials that caught their purpose with raw intensity. "In effect," said the paper, "the committee is usurping the function of a grand jury." The sensational public charges and denials of the last week had brought an "absurd, and indeed shameful impasse," an "inescapable" question of "perjury" that could be fairly settled only in court. "As things stand," the *Post* concluded, "it is the Committee which is subject to the most serious indictment of all."

❖❖❖

Nixon entered now on a week of frenetic activity, the period from August 9 through 15 in some ways the most important of his early career. Stripling sent the HUAC staff through Washington to comb the lease records of Hiss's Georgetown apartments and houses, the files of the Wisconsin Avenue kennel, the transaction documents on the old Ford. They could "get no assistance whatever from the intelligence agencies of the government due to the President's freeze order," Nixon complained later with some hyprocrisy. In fact, the secret calls to Cronin continued almost daily, with Hummer offering advice on methods if not material already discovered by the FBI. Meanwhile, as Stripling recalled, HUAC's witness chair was "seldom cool." Keeping it warm was a train of the accused, most of them named by Bentley and to whom Nixon reacted with unconcealed belligerence as the week wore on. On Monday the ninth he listened to Victor Perlo's denials and attack on "headline spy sensations" and sharply warned Perlo that he was opening himself to a perjury indictment. When Abraham George Silverman, described by Bentley as the go-between with Treasury's Harry White, expressed his "deep shock" and took the Fifth Amendment, Nixon was acid: "It is pretty clear, I think, that you are not using the defense of the Fifth Amendment because you are innocent."

White himself appeared on Friday the thirteenth. While at Treasury he had been one of the authors of the vengeful Morgenthau Plan to reduce postwar Germany to a peasant economy, but also a creator of the World Bank, and later a director of the International Monetary Fund. Balding, with short gray hair, a small mustache, large eyes fixed behind rimless glasses, White was a gifted, eloquent man who admittedly knew and championed some of the accused during their federal service yet staunchly denied Bentley's story and lectured HUAC on the absence of cross-examination and other rights of the courtroom. White was recovering from a heart attack, and at one point in the testimony Chairman Thomas—"with his ineffable bad taste," as one writer described it—remarked snidely on White's "condition," and revealed the witness's private note to the Committee beforehand asking for periodic rests during the hearing. The former Treasury official had replied gallantly to win the applause of the gallery. Again, HUAC seemed put in its place.

But congressman Nixon was unabashed. He had seen from Cronin, as the rest of the Committee had not, Chambers's added charges against White in the later FBI and Murphy interrogations, charges that matched Bentley's impressively. When White now referred to HUAC's "star chamber proceedings," Nixon retorted that star chambers, after all, afforded no right of self-defense and reached summary judgment; the Committee would go on to study White's case most carefully. For the only time in the session Harry White drew back, seeming to sense the cold authority and menace of the rejoinder.

Nixon's increasingly combative tone in the hearings was resonant of his own private prosecution of the case, and it would be the events behind the public scenes that made the week historic. He read and reread Chambers's testimony of the seventh as soon as it became available that Monday. Still uncertain and restive, he tried to locate the informer by telephone, found him at his farm at Westminster, Maryland, and set off from the Capitol early the afternoon of the ninth to see him alone, leaving the office almost furtively "to avoid publicity." He made the two-hour drive through backroads of the green Maryland countryside to convince himself, as he told Bert Andrews, that Chambers was testifying "about a man he really knew."

They sat talking for more than two hours in rickety rocking chairs on the porch of the small farmhouse. Laconic, given to lengthy pauses in his answers, Chambers puffed on a pipe and lent the impression of a reflective, meek, passionately private man approaching his notorious confrontation with a deep reluctance yet fatalism. He introduced the congressman to his wife, Esther, a dark-complected, plain woman even more shy and taciturn than her husband. Both of them were worried, he told Nixon, about the embarrassment to their children from the affair. Again, Chambers spoke almost affectionately of Alger Hiss, and this time of Priscilla as well. "He said he thought they were both in the communist movement for the highest motives," Nixon would relate to Andrews. Chambers added few new details to his earlier description. But there were memorable bits of intimacy. Priscilla was "very sensitive about being teased," the informer recalled, and Chambers "used to like to tease her for just that very reason."

Nixon told him "bluntly," as he recalled, that members of the Committee and others disbelieved his story and suspected he had told it out of some unknown personal animus—a voicing as well of Nixon's own inner qualms. "I could not have a motive which would involve destroying my own career," Chambers answered. He had risked his reputation and *Time* editorship out of a duty to warn the country of the communist conspiracy, not "simply as a clash of personalities." Usually gazing off to the rolling countryside as he talked, he now turned dramatically to Nixon and said, "This is what you must get the country to realize." At the moment, Chambers not only remained at his job with *Time* but would have the substantial political and financial backing of publisher Henry Luce for months to come. Yet it was the air of weary sacrifice, if not the fact, that struck his younger visitor on the porch. "The answer," Nixon noted afterward about the vital matter of motive, "seemed logical to me."

Trying again to spur him, Nixon told Chambers that the Justice Department had already requested a transcript of the August 7 Foley Square testimony, and it would probably leak to Hiss, bringing more questions and attacks. Drawing on the pipe, rocking slowly, Chambers seemed impassive. Then, as he finally rose to leave, Nixon mentioned almost casually that he was a Quaker. Chambers brightened and told him his own family attended the local Friends Meeting. Of course Priscilla was a Quaker, too, he added, and at that he snapped his fingers. "Here's something I should have recalled before," he exclaimed. "Mrs. Hiss generally used the plain language when she was talking to Alger in the home."

Nixon went away deeply impressed. "I knew from personal experience that my mother never used the plain speech in public but did use it in talking with her sisters and her mother in the privacy of our home," he recorded. Someone who simply heard Priscilla Hiss talk in her own house might have told Chambers about her habit, he realized. But that afternoon, as Nixon remembered Chambers's story, "the way he told me about it . . . gave me an intuitive feeling that he was speaking from firsthand rather than secondhand knowledge." He drove back to Washington at twilight with new confidence. "On that day," he confided later, "I became certain that Chambers actually had known Hiss."

Back in Washington, amid the political furor and still unanswered questions, the doubts soon returned. On Tuesday morning he suddenly reached out beyond the HUAC and its staff for reassurance and help. Quietly bypassing the protocol of going through Thomas as chairman, Nixon called directly Senator Homer Ferguson, whose own subcommittee was beginning its probe of Bentley and Remington with less fanfare than hoped. The congressman asked if someone on the Senate investigative staff might read and judge the credibility of Chambers's secret testimony from New York, and Ferguson, an avid Dewey backer eager to see both scandals develop, promptly sent over his young staff counsel, Bill Rogers.

William Pierce Rogers was also thirty-five that summer, barely six months younger than Nixon. They had entered the navy together at the Quonset officer candidate school in 1942 but knew each other there only in passing, and they were still no more than nodding acquaintances. Rogers came from a small town in upstate New York. The son of a successful insurance agent and bank director, he had lost his mother at thirteen. When the Depression took the family savings, he was forced to work his way through Colgate and then Cornell Law, where he finished fifth in a class of ninety the same year Nixon graduated from Duke. Handsome and genial, Rogers soon went to New York City to volunteer for the staff of crusading district attorney Tom Dewey, offering to take a job for nothing. "If I work for you, then everybody will know me," he explained his willing sacrifice to Dewey. "I'll never have to prove I'm able or honest, because people know you only hire able and honest people." It was the sort of flattery and guileless charm Bill Rogers dispensed easily along with his broad grin, though also a remark of ironic portent.

Rogers was hired by Dewey, made a competent if unremarkable record as an assistant prosecuter, and eventually went on to a series of high offices, never having to prove much more than he first predicted. After the navy he returned briefly to the DA's office and then in 1947 on Dewey's patronage had gone to Ferguson's subcommittee, looking into war profiteering and now, with the same discreet instigation by the FBI, communist espionage. As counsel, Rogers performed his assignment well enough, and gave the Dewey campaign ready access to the subcommittee's political tinder. Yet then, as later, there was something inescapably bland and shallow about the affable, loyal Republican lawyer. He would please his political patrons by "being superb on the little niceties that don't matter," said one observer. From behind the smile and reassuring good looks emerged no conviction or intellect unsettling to superiors. "He's a master," one associate would describe him from the late 1940s through a long and prominent career, "of the lily pad operation."

They met in Nixon's private office. Rogers read the transcript of the Foley Square session, and in his confident, almost offhand way pronounced it dependable. "I don't think there is any doubt about it," he told the congressman. "No one could make up a story in that detail and have it false without getting caught at it." Nixon had paused for a moment and then seemed to revert to his uncertainty without hearing the confirmation. That was the point, he told Rogers. If Chambers were lying, they would catch him and apologize to Hiss. "On the other hand," he came back, "if Chambers is telling the truth, this is a serious matter." Rogers went away with what he called a "moral impression" of his contemporary intent on "doing the right thing, the fair thing." He also sensed clearly the indecision and tenuousness others had seen at Duke, in Whittier, and in the 1946 campaign. "He is basically not a confident man. Not cocky, doesn't think that his ideas are necessarily right to begin with," he would say later. But here on the unfathomable credibility of Whittaker Chambers, as for much to come, Bill Rogers supplied part of that needed assurance. It was the start of a long, significant, sometimes simple, sometimes tortuous relationship between the two men, the brooding and uncertain Nixon ever more dependent on his attractive, easygoing friend, turning to him at moments of crisis and needed companionship, and in the end inflicting a strange but historic punishment.

Rogers's reading of the testimony triggered the next decisive episode of the week, plunging Richard Nixon headlong into the Republican Party and establishment politics that had begun to swirl about the case. After seeing the Senate aide, Nixon called his colleague and friend Charlie Kersten for the same purpose. At dinner together that Tuesday night, Kersten read the transcript and concluded Chambers was convincing, still another certification. Nixon returned from their meeting, however, to take a disturbing message. The influential Carnegie Endowment trustees—including John Foster Dulles, the GOP's shadow secretary of state—were readying a public endorsement of Alger Hiss while Hiss backers had already begun direct congressional lobbying, both acts aimed at the wavering majority of HUAC.

The next morning Nixon found Kersten in the Caucus Room after a labor committee meeting and worriedly told him about the warning. "A big gun was being mounted to further blast the Committee," Kersten remembered, and "Dulles [had] let it be known to Nixon of the impending Carnegie salvo." Kersten urged him on the spot to see Dulles immediately with the secret August 7 testimony, using the Chambers details and familiarity with Hiss to give pause to any Carnegie intervention on behalf of its accused president. Emboldened again, Nixon quickly went off to telephone Dulles at the Dewey campaign headquarters at the Roosevelt Hotel in Manhattan and returned minutes later to say the adviser and Carnegie chairman agreed to meet that evening. He asked if Kersten would come with him for moral support, and the Milwaukee lawyer agreed. They would go up on an afternoon train, Nixon apprehensive that, whatever the drawbacks for Truman and the Democrats, the Dulles patronage of Alger Hiss now made the whole affair a potential embarrassment as well to the Republican Presidential candidate. "I was aware that the Dewey campaign organization," he recorded, "would undoubtedly be grateful if I decided to go along with the rest of the Committee and let the case pass into a preelection limbo."

What awaited them at Dewey headquarters was not quite what it seemed. William Rogers had promptly alerted Dewey's campaign manager, Herbert Brownell, Jr., to the August 7 testimony, and Brownell in turn warned Dulles. As it was, Dulles himself was still resisting any overt Carnegie support for Hiss and beginning in characteristic caution and self-interest to edge away from the man he had helped hire with lavish endorsement a year and a half before. Moreover, added to the public furor of the Chambers charges, the Dewey campaign received that week a further caution from still another source.

The weekend after Hiss's appearance, while Nixon and his still-skeptical subcommittee of Hebert and McDowell mulled over the latest Chambers testimony with such mixed feeling, a State Department officer named John Peurifoy had paid a nervous middle-of-the-night visit to his friend, Congressman Karl Mundt. "I'm torn between loyalty and duty," Peurifoy told Mundt. He owed "all I am . . . in this town" to Dean Acheson; he did not want to do his patrons a disservice. "And still, I'm a good American," Mundt remembered him anguishing. "And I know that what you are saying about Alger Hiss is true, because I have access to security files in the State Department." Peurifoy, who was an assistant secretary of state for administration, then showed Mundt the dossier, and they "spent two or three hours" going over it. Convinced afresh of Hiss's guilt, Mundt rejoined the HUAC hearings that week with fresh fervor—though, like his colleague Dick Nixon with some of the same purloined files via Father Cronin, Mundt did not share his encouraging inside information with the rest of the Committee. He did, however, warn Dewey manager Brownell, to whom he had been regularly leaking HUAC material.

Dewey must "not commit himself in any way which might prove tremendously embarrassing," Mundt would write Brownell, in the event "this tangled web of evidence should take a surprising and nation-rocking turn." What may have been most "surprising" to the Dewey advisers at the moment was Peurifoy's dramatic nighttime turn. Only months before, John Peurifoy had assured Foster Dulles of Hiss's innocence when the Carnegie chairman checked on one of the early periodic complaints by Kohlberg and others. Dulles had written in a Carnegie memo recording his call to the State Department aide in March 1948: "Peurifoy indicated that while he thought Hiss might be mentioned in some of the FBI files, he himself was absolutely satisfied as to the complete loyalty of Hiss, and that he knew of no evidence of any kind which cast any doubt on the matter." It was, altogether and typically, an example of the craven, *sauve qui peut* mentality that now seized many in government as well as those awaiting the Dewey regime, and which served to benefit Richard Nixon, HUAC, and the Republicans. Lost in the gentlemanly scramble was the awkward fact that Peurifoy's midnight files in August were essentially the same he had found without "doubt" in March and that the sole source of them all was Whittaker Chambers.

Dulles meanwhile had learned as well from Hiss—earnestly politicking himself within the Endowment and without—that friendly congressmen would be lobbying Hebert, Rankin, and others on Hiss's behalf. It was that tidbit, coupled with the call from Rogers about Chambers's secret testimony, that prompted the warning to Nixon. No "big gun" was being loaded at the Endowment, but Dulles and the Dewey camp were more concerned than ever to ally themselves with the serious young congressman who was leading the HUAC hunt and if possible to flush out his own knowledge and intentions. Nixon's anxious train ride to New York the afternoon of August 11, secret transcript in hand for Dulles to read for himself, was the result.

Nixon and Kersten now entered this murky labyrinth of personal and political motive at the Roosevelt Hotel with some awe. With Dulles was his brother, Allen, the former OSS official whom Nixon knew from the Herter mission. Herter himself and C. Douglas Dillon, a Manhattan banker and another senior foreign policy adviser in the campaign, moved importantly in and out of Dulles's hotel room office during the two-hour session with the young representatives. Foster Dulles was "very polite," Kersten remembered, and spoke vaguely, disingenuously, about some "expected Carnegie organization public support of Hiss." Nixon handed over the Foley Square transcript, which the brothers proceeded to read carefully. Nixon pointed out the rich personal detail of Chambers's recollections, including the story of the prothonotary warbler, which the brothers found somehow amusing. Talking to senior figures of the party and establishment, men whose law firm had not considered him little more than a decade before, he was careful, deferential, yet now, on this, the insider.

In silence Foster paced the floor in front of the suite's fireplace for several minutes. "There's no question about it. It's almost impossible to believe," he finally spoke, "but Chambers knows Hiss." Nixon asked if "I was justified in going ahead with the investigation." And Dulles replied instantly, formally, "In view of the facts Chambers has testified to, you'd be derelict in your duty as a congressman if you did not see the case through to a conclusion."

He walked out of the Roosevelt with Kersten into the hot New York night confident that he had undermined Hiss's home support, and with what he saw as express approval from Republican leadership to pursue the case. Later he would write of Dulles's "political courage and integrity" in bidding him continue. Amid all the intrigue, what Nixon knew and did not know, the men upstairs had scant other choice. As in so much of Richard Nixon's dealings with senior figures in the GOP and especially the formidable eastern establishment, there would be the lingering question of who had used whom. For Alger Hiss, the Nixon trip to the Roosevelt had one immediate consequence. Two days later, Hiss was to call his board chairman and ostensible adviser, asking if he should not take the initiative and simply see Chambers face to face. But Dulles advised, "strongly," as Hiss noted, that it would be "improper" now that HUAC had "assumed jurisdiction" of the inquiry. Representative Nixon, it was understood, would duly arrange a confrontation.

The two congressmen spent the night in Manhattan, and the following morning paid another important call. Nixon grasped the chance in the city to meet as well Isaac Don Levine, whom both Cronin and Mandel had recommended as a shrewd anticommunist reporter and collaborator with Chambers. Receiving them in his editor's office at *Plain Talk*, Levine quickly recounted how the informer had tried to tell his story in the late 1930s. As Kersten watched in some amazement, Levine brought out the original notes he had excitedly scribbled on Hay Adams Hotel stationery after returning from Chambers's confession to Adolf Berle that September night in 1939. Some of the notations, Kersten remembered, "were on the back of an old envelope." It was confirmation of the incident to which Chambers had alluded only in passing in his first testimony, though Nixon had also seen references in the secret FBI reports. In Levine's jotted list Nixon recognized most of the names, including "Alger Hiss" and "Mr. White," along with two others from the State Department set to appear, "Duggan" and, spelled phonetically, "Wadley."

Back in the attic office later on the twelfth, Nixon continued his restless canvass for bolstering allies, calling over now his shrewdest choice, the *Herald Tribune*'s Bert Andrews. It was not only that he had carefully cultivated both the journalist and his Republican paper. Andrews's prizewinning book critical of government loyalty procedures and of HUAC in general gave him special credibility. "If you became convinced that Chambers was telling the truth," Nixon once wrote Andrews about the reason he telephoned him that afternoon, "no one could level a charge of bias against you." Yet there was also a hidden bonus and irony in the calculation. Andrews had won an earlier prize in 1945 for a series of articles on the Yalta accords in which he clashed bitterly with Alger Hiss. The stories disclosed Roosevelt's secret agreement to give the Soviets two extra votes in the new UN General Assembly, a concession later and mistakenly blamed on Hiss's influence at Yalta. At the time, Hiss had upbraided Andrews for printing a leak officials thought damaging to the prospects for the UN, and the relationship between the two men, once cordial, ended angrily. If a past critic of HUAC, Bert Andrews would also come to the case with his own private and abiding dislike for one of the protagonists.

They "sparred around for a bit," Andrews remembered of the first minutes in Nixon's office. The congressman was still unsure how much he could tell the reporter without uncontrolled publicity, and Andrews assured him, in the old Washington transaction of press and politician, he could say anything "on an off-the-record basis." "I would, of course, want to be free to use the information if it became possible to use it without injuring the investigation" is how Andrews later described the familiar bargain: cooperation in return for an exclusive. Nixon agreed. He gave Andrews a copy of the secret August 7 testimony, and they arranged to go together to the Westminster farm that Sunday, where the reporter could privately size up Chambers.

On the Friday HUAC questioned Harry Dexter White, the Committee also subpoenaed Alger Hiss for a further hearing the following Monday, and Nixon—unable to wait for or rely alone on the date with Andrews Sunday—restlessly drove out to the Chambers farm again on Saturday morning. This time he took along Stripling, like Andrews for his supposed "sixth sense" about the veracity of their informer. The three men met and talked for some time, punctuated by Chambers's pregnant pauses and rationed revelations. Stripling came away still convinced that Chambers knew Hiss but also shrewdly conscious that the witness was evasive even in his apparent precision. "He's holding something back," the aide remarked to Nixon on their return drive. "He's trying to protect somebody." Bob Stripling would accept the testimony, pursue Hiss, adopt Whittaker Chambers as HUAC's confessor, yet in his inherent cynicism never doubt the basic artifice in it all. "Chambers is a peculiar individual," he would later advise the FBI; "he sits and lights his pipe, he is cold and calculating, and he knows exactly what he will do three weeks hence."

On Sunday with Bert Andrews, Nixon went back to the Maryland countryside yet again. Chambers remembered the sight of the two of them as they "sauntered down the lawn slope to the farmhouse," and Andrews's "listless handshake" and "skeptical manner." Nixon had introduced the reporter, saying frankly he was "personally anxious to get his opinion of what he thinks of you." He told Chambers, "I'd advise you to trust him, but I warn you that he'll want to ask you some blunt questions." Chambers had eyed the stranger warily, recalled his book critical of loyalty inquiries, wondered why he was now helping Nixon. Annoyed, Andrews told him he was simply against "railroading," and "the chances are you will be indicted for perjury just because [Hiss's] story will be believed over yours." At that Chambers had nodded. "To me," Andrews went on, "this is a great news story, either way it goes." The informer then fell into another prolonged silence, "thirty or forty seconds," Andrews remembered, an interval so empty "that people . . . sometimes wondered whether he had gone into a trance." Finally, Chambers agreed to be questioned.

Andrews "grilled him," as Nixon recalled, asking in quick succession about rumors of alcoholism and insanity. Nixon then brought out photographs of the Hiss residences with addresses marked on the back, holding them against his chest to hide the notation as Chambers gave the correct location for each. Was there anything more, they asked, about the Hiss hobby of bird-watching? "Chambers went into one of his 'trances,' " Andrews noted, and then wordlessly left the room, returning with two books on ornithology that he claimed Alger Hiss had given him. He seemed to answer "all questions," thought Andrews, "but volunteer nothing." At the same time, the reporter was impressed as the two Chambers children moved in and out of the room sharing an obvious warmth and affection with their father. "I did not believe it possible that a man who loved his children in that way would endanger them for any evil reason," Andrews told Chambers later when the two had become friends.

Before Nixon and Andrews left that Sunday, Chambers summoned another, still more intimate detail. He recalled getting up early one hot morning while staying with the Hisses in Georgetown and finding the door to their bedroom left open for a night breeze. "Hiss had his arm under Mrs. Hiss's neck," he told his two enthralled visitors, "and both were sleeping soundly."

They drove back to Washington talking excitedly about the case, Nixon elated that Andrews seemed persuaded of Chambers's credibility. "Your old man's got a helluva story," he said proudly to Andrews's son Peter as they came into the reporter's apartment and closeted themselves in an air-conditioned study to talk "for several hours." If Hiss could somehow be caught, of course, it was the congressman who had the "story" as well, and a great political trophy. But inside the cool study Andrews lectured him sternly on the "careless methods and insufficient staff work," the "smeared witnesses" and unsustained questioning that had "time and again" stymied and discredited HUAC. Hiss would "get off," even with Chambers's testimony, Andrews warned, if the Committee performed as usual. As always, Nixon agreed knowingly about his crude colleagues.

Andrews now launched into a rapid-fire plan to protect the political legitimacy of the inquiry and to push the private investigation. Of course, there should be a confrontation between Hiss and Chambers, but in secret to minimize potential embarrassment to Nixon and the Committee. And if Chambers turned out to have mistaken the accused for somebody else, "an unqualified apology could be made to Hiss." How about the Ford he had read about in the executive session testimony and the different houses where Hiss lived? Nixon said the investigators had not traced them all yet. Andrews shot back with a street reporter's checklist: What did public records say? Was the Ford sold, traded in? Who owned it now? Did Hiss have another car at the time? What about dates, utility bills? Nixon smiled. "Go ahead and laugh. But I'll bet it can be done," the reporter told him. "You've made up your mind, haven't you?" Nixon said, laughing. Andrews answered that he was "positive" Chambers and Hiss knew each other. "No one could invent all the little items Chambers has told. . . . It just doesn't make sense." From this point on, Bill Arnold would remember, Bert Andrews was virtually a member of the staff, no longer merely a reporter but "acting as an adviser to Dick." Andrews now told Nixon that he should press Hiss at the hearing the next day, that a confrontation should come soon, that the HUAC staff should be "ordered to explore every rathole."

That night, back in Park Fairfax, Nixon telephoned Louis Nichols of the FBI to ask if the Bureau, as Nichols's memo put it, "could develop fingerprints on slick paper which were twelve years old," a reference to the bird books Chambers had shown them. After hurriedly checking with the FBI laboratory, Nichols told the congressman that the chances were "remote." And as a matter of their mutual interest, Nichols went on to tell him "that furthermore if we did do this for them [HUAC] and there were no fingerprints, it would appear his case might be weakened." It was the first of what Nichols recorded as "numerous calls" from Nixon as the congressman avidly followed Andrews's advice and explored every "rathole."

It had been an extraordinary week of uncertainty, doggedness and brashness, impressive reassurance—the three visits to Chambers, Rogers, Kersten, the Dulles brothers, Levine, the further hearings, the hard-eyed Stripling and Andrews convinced in person by the informer. In seven days he had enlisted formidable allies, the *Herald Tribune*, the Dewey campaign. "It was during this period," he would write about the week in a private memo afterward, "that I finally reached a definite conclusion that Hiss was not telling the truth on the issue of whether or not he knew Chambers." The advisers and advice decisively strengthened his hand. Nixon hardly formed his "definite conclusion" alone, though in his own subsequent accounts and others the men who spurred and channeled him that week, particularly Andrews, would shrink in importance. During this interval he might have stepped back, as the others on the Committee did, waiting as usual for something more to turn up from an informer or the FBI filling their vacuum. He might simply have prepared to apologize to Alger Hiss for the usual spectacle of unsustained charges. But in the end, despite his unsureness and precarious, mercurial judgment, Richard Nixon had kept at it with his habitual intensity and application, subduing his own inner weakness and misgiving as much as actually advancing the inquiry. The political courage and perseverance were exceptional.

And now the campaign continued. As he made the weekend journeys to Westminster, Nixon was also quietly giving tactical leaks to the Associated Press and several Washington and New York papers, telling them on background, as an anonymous HUAC source, that the Committee was "unable to find a flaw" in Chambers's story and that diligent Congressman Nixon had visited Chambers at his farm searching for "additional backing" for the informer's story. At the same time, he gave Andrews the go-ahead to run stories based on the secret Chambers testimony from August 7. Having promised the *Herald Tribune* an exclusive, Nixon was already slipping parts of the transcript to other reporters. Meanwhile, the FBI planted with captive national columnists like David Lawrence columns favorable to the Bureau and HUAC, and deploring, as Lawrence did that weekend, the failure of the New York grand jury "to assure convictions." Nixon's own leaks were a broadening tributary into the torrent of national publicity. That weekend *Life* magazine appeared with a major spread on Hiss and Chambers, the crime and cover-up taken for granted in the headline: "THEY INDICATE GOVERNMENT WAS SLOW TO ACT AGAINST COMMUNIST NETWORK."

Watching all this, Bert Andrews the veteran newsman was all the more impressed with the sum of Nixon's eventful week as he slowly learned of it. The young, respectful, shrewd politician was, as Andrews had thought from their beginnings in 1947, apart from and above the rest. Like other patrons and sponsors back in California, the hardened reporter now saw his own power and ambition in Dick Nixon. "Bob," Andrews would say to his *Herald Tribune* colleague Robert Donovan, as the case unfolded, "I can make that fellow President of the United States."

Events now moved swiftly in a series of Committee hearings. The proceedings were supposedly still closed, but in fact leaked instantly by Nixon to Andrews and others in the press, transforming the secret testimony into an August of continual black headlines. In that furtive war of private inquisition and public exposure, Nixon soon found an unexpected ally—Alger Hiss himself.

They reconvened with Hiss on Monday, August 16, brushing aside the accused's mounting apprehension at the secret testimony and stories already given to the papers. "This is an executive session," Thomas said in assuring him of confidentiality, "and that speaks for itself." Nixon now led and dominated the questioning with no pause for the usual seniority. He asked Hiss "to bear with me" as they went back over some of the perplexing contradictions. Either he or Chambers had testified falsely, and one of them "must, if possible, answer for that testimony." Hiss denied again he had been a part of any underground, or even known any "Carl." When Nixon showed him photos of Chambers, he thought the man "not completely unfamiliar," though he wanted to see him in person.

But this was someone who allegedly "stayed overnight in your home on several occasions," Nixon persisted. Hiss still would not say and asked yet again for "an opportunity to see the individual." They would arrange that, Nixon told him, though not before they eliminated any questions of mistaken identity and obtained under oath some "clear conflict on certain points of testimony." Passing unchallenged by Hiss, it was a remarkably candid explanation of how much HUAC was guarding itself *in camera* lest Chambers still had the wrong man entirely and how much the hearings were plain entrapment. But Hiss went on, confident, combative. "Yes, sir," he replied sarcastically, there were indeed conflicts.

They had a brief exchange about the prospective testimony of Hiss's stepson, Timothy Hobson, who was alienated from the Hisses and under psychiatric care, having been discharged from the navy for homosexuality, though neither man mentioned the latter fact. Solicitous, Nixon assured him no embarrassment would come to the young man. At that Hiss shifted indignantly to his own public humiliation. "I have been angered and hurt," he said of all the leaks and the committee's apparent acceptance of Chambers's credibility over his own. "I have seen newspaper accounts, Mr. Nixon, that you spent the weekend . . . at Mr. Chambers's farm in New Jersey."

"That is quite incorrect."

"It is incorrect?" said Hiss.

"Yes, sir, I can say, as you did a moment ago, that I have never spent the night with Mr. Chambers."

Once more, it all passed—the fine deceit in not "spending the weekend" or "the night" in "New Jersey," the snide misstatement of Hiss's refusal to identify Chambers as someone who stayed "overnight" at his house. Nixon's remark was a first surfacing of the reflexive speculation already whispered among the Committee staff and Washington reporters. There must be something perverse, ugly, queer linking these two men from different worlds, something even beyond a conspiracy where gentlemen could have kept to their own. After hearing about Whittaker Chambers talk in his odd mystical way of personal habits and bedroom doors, the coarse men of HUAC and the press room had begun to believe he was Alger Hiss's dark indiscretion in more ways than one.

But here Hiss was intent on the use of Chambers's stories to test or trip him, in which his own testimony would aid the accuser. Whatever he said now could be used against him. It was Nixon's turn to be indignant. He resented the "very serious implications" that their goal was "to get information with which we can coach Mr. Chambers so that he can more or less build a web around you." Stripling interjected that they all had "a very open mind," and showed the witness another photo of Chambers. Hiss still could not identify him. At that moment, the hearing began slowly to take a momentous turn.

"I have written a name on this pad in front of me," Hiss suddenly offered, "of a person whom I knew in 1933 and 1934, who not only spent some time in my house but sublet my apartment." He added quickly, however, "I do not recognize the photographs as possibly being this man." This was a name who might account for some of the stories in the press.

Nixon asked where Hiss was living at the time, and again Hiss was worried his reply might somehow only arm Chambers. The surface civility disappeared, never to return. "Questions will be asked . . . and I want the witness to answer," Thomas barked. Again the reasonable, conciliatory man on the dais, Nixon told Hiss he should grant them "good faith." They were there to "test the credibility of Mr. Chambers, and you are the man to do it." Hiss, unappeased, came back angrily that they had known beforehand what Chambers would say about him. But Stripling assured him that they had not known in advance of the accusation. And now Richard Nixon, who knew far more of the long history than even Stripling, was again silent.

This clash over the stage management of the hearings opened the floor to Hebert, who honestly did not know of all the FBI files and Chambers before the affair began, and whose bull neck was now rigid at Hiss's seeming diversion. "Whichever of you is lying is the greatest actor that America has ever produced," the southerner told Hiss. "Up to a few moments ago you have been very open, very cooperative. Now you have hedged." Hebert asked earnestly about the informer, "What motive would he have to pitch a $25,000 position as the respected senior editor of *Time* magazine out the window?" And Hiss again invoked his station and status. Did Chambers's confessed past as communist and traitor have no bearing on his credibility?

"No," drawled Hebert. "Because, Mr. Hiss, I recognize the fact that maybe my background is a little different from yours, but I do know police methods and I know crime a great deal. And you show me a good police force and I will show you the stool pigeon. . . . Some of the greatest saints in history were pretty bad before they were saints." Exposed in part by Hiss himself, in part by the subterfuge of Nixon and Stripling, it was the gulf between the New Orleans night court or parish politics and Harvard and Georgetown. The encounter cost Alger Hiss his only potential defender on the Committee. Hebert's wisdom on stool pigeons and saints would be one of the passages leaked verbatim following the hearing and "accepted in vast sections of the press and public," said a reporter covering the case, "as the gospel truth."

Once more Nixon broke the tension from Hebert's rebuke to inquire about household servants who might test Chambers's story. Strangely, no one had yet asked what name Hiss had written on his pad several minutes before. Nixon then suggested a brief recess for Hiss to call Priscilla in Vermont to arrange for her testimony. When the witness soon returned, Nixon assured him there was "no hurry" about Mrs. Hiss testifying, and Hiss replied, "That is kind of you." Alger Hiss then announced, "The name of the man I brought in—and he may have no relation to this whole nightmare—is a man named George Crosley."

Crosley was a free-lance writer, he told them, covering the Senate committee investigating the munitions industry, and Hiss as committee counsel had met him in the course of their work. The writer had a wife and baby and needed a place to live for the summer in Washington. The Hisses sublet them an apartment they happened to be vacating early anyway and allowed the writer and his family to stay "several nights" at the new Hiss home before Crosley's furniture arrived. Nixon abruptly broke into the story to ask about Crosley's wife. "She was a rather strikingly dark person, very strikingly dark," Hiss answered. Nixon later recorded his barely concealed excitement. "I was the only member of the Committee who had seen Mrs. Chambers and I knew she was dark and strikingly so." Hiss's sudden introduction of Crosley "left no question in my mind whatever" that the two men knew each other.

At the moment in the hearing, however, he had gone on for good measure, asking Hiss another, aparently incongruous question. It revealed in fleeting passage, though no one seemed to notice at the time, how much the congressman really knew about the history, one of the details unearthed from Mandel and Levine out of a past no one else on the dais yet knew. What interested him was the distinguishing mark of Whittaker Chambers in the 1930s even more than the dark complexion of his wife. On the intriguing subject of Crosley the free-lance writer Richard Nixon now asked Alger Hiss crisply:

"How about his teeth?"

And Hiss answered obligingly again, "Very bad teeth. That is one of the things I particularly want to see Chambers about. This man had very bad teeth, did not take care of his teeth."

Stripling then asked his own question prompted by Chambers's Foley Square testimony and Mandel's purposeful query about a car. "What kind of automobile did that fellow have?" No kind, said Hiss. Chambers had taken Hiss's old, abandoned Model A Ford. "I threw it in." Hiss remembered vaguely giving Crosley the old jalopy along with the apartment, all for the rent on the sublease. He could not remember the formal transfer, though there had been a certificate of title.

Nixon and Stripling now drew him into gathering detail, much of it matching the Chambers account. Yes, his wife called him "Hilly," and he called her "Prossy." Despite his earlier reluctance to supply Chambers with personal facts, Hiss now even volunteered about Crosley matters not yet raised by Chambers and so not questioned by the Committee. Crosley had not paid his rent but had once made a token payment in kind. "He brought a rug over which he said some wealthy patron had given him. I have still got the damned thing." Later, the memory of the carpet would seem a gratuitous self-incrimination. Eventually asked about it himself, Whittaker Chambers would explain that it was not a rent payment at all but a gift from Soviet intelligence. The offering was part of the poisonous dynamic between HUAC and their complex prey. Now strangely vague and unremembering, now given to vivid memory—the rug, the old Ford "dark blue with a sassy little trunk on the back"—Alger Hiss seemed to wrap it all in what one of his defenders called "a compulsive need for exactitude," making his equivocations all the more cautious and equivocal and his realized memories all the more stark. "The lawyer in Alger Hiss was very strong," wrote one scholarly observer. "Yet this was the very quality," added another student of the case, "that impressed the Committee, especially Nixon, that Hiss was a master spy and a consummate actor."

On the afternoon of the sixteenth, however, the scripting and intrigue would belong to HUAC. Amid the personal details, Nixon asked to be excused while he went out briefly to consult other members on another matter, leaving the otherwise quiet McDowell alone with Hiss. Just before the break Nixon had been questioning Hiss about hobbies, and the witness had mentioned ornithology. "I think anybody who knows me would know that."

McDowell now talked lightly with Hiss while the others were gone. Then, as Nixon was returning with staff aide Appell—the hearing back on the record—McDowell asked casually:

"Did you ever see a prothonotary warbler?"

"I have," said Hiss brightly, "right here on the Potomac. Do you know that place?"

"What is that?" asked McDowell, and Richard Nixon joined the play, turning toward McDowell. "Have *you* ever seen one?"

"Did you see it in the same place?" asked Hiss, almost in comradeship, adding for their information, "They come back and nest in those swamps. Beautiful yellow head, a gorgeous bird."

The official transcript would give no trace of the icy, satisfied silence that now fell over the Committee. The small bird from the swampy Potomac woodlands was to be more dramatic confirmation of Whittaker Chambers. In its widening coverage of the case, much of it supplied by helpful calls from Congressman Nixon, *Time* was to publish schemata of the communist conspiracy alongside a portrait of the prothonotary warbler.

Before it was over, Nixon wondered if Hiss "would be willing to take a lie-detector test" since "Mr. Chambers . . . said he would." Hiss did not know what experience Nixon had with the test in his own law practice, a none-too-subtle reminder once more of their respective stations. But Hiss had consulted prominent attorneys and had little confidence in the mechanism that "registers more emotion than anything else." Clearly annoyed, Nixon pressed. Hiss said he would "consult further." The answer on the test, Nixon noted afterward, was "one further factor" in determining the guilt of the witness.

Stripling closed the hearing with still more questions about Hiss's associations, alleged members of the Ware group he admitted to be acquaintances yet who were "known" communists. Hiss continued to deny coolly any knowledge of their guilty politics, and at one point the exasperated Stripling exploded. "Furthermore, I read a lot of government files from time to time—and I don't say this disparagingly—but I have seen your name for years in government files as a person suspected of communist activity." Once more, it was a revelation of the long, FBI-larded background of the inquiry, an admission of what Hiss had earlier charged about their prior knowledge of Chambers. Stunned, the witness simply stared at Stripling, silent.

There remained the schedule for the crucial confrontation between Hiss and Chambers, and Thomas set the date for more than a week later, August 25. Nixon warned that "if you have a public session, it is a show," and Stripling worried it might be "ballyhooed into a circus." Hiss told them bitterly, "As far as consideration to me after what has been done to my feelings and reputation, I think it would be like sinking the Swiss navy. No public show could embarrass me now. I am asking to see this man." Thomas assured him there would be no leaks from this session, not from HUAC. "Every person in this room with the exception of yourself has stood up and raised his right hand and taken an oath that he will not divulge one single word of testimony given here this afternoon." Hebert echoed, "We have sworn ourselves to secrecy." There would be "absolutely no publicity," said Stripling. "We don't want it here," Nixon concluded emphatically. They adjourned to the twenty-fifth.

Within minutes that evening, Nixon was on the phone to Chambers, asking if he had actually taken Hiss's apartment and if Hiss had seen Mrs. Chambers, that she could have been the same "strikingly dark" woman. "When Chambers answered yes to both these questions I terminated the conversation," he recorded in a memo, "because I knew that the case had been broken and now it was simply a case of getting the two together for the purpose of establishing that Hiss knew Chambers." But the notation in his later diary of the event never conveyed the passion—and expedience—of what followed. Alone with Stripling in the HUAC private office adjacent to the hearing room, Nixon pounded the table and shouted, "That goddamned Hiss! He's a lying son of a bitch!"

He now began his usual restive vigil over the day's testimony, waiting impatiently for a battery of secretaries to transcribe it page by page, then going through it exhaustively, now with Stripling, now by himself. Meanwhile, there were the inevitable leaks of tidbits and generalities from secret Hiss testimony. In the wake of complaints by Hiss about the press, and the Committee's chorus of assurances, there were also precautions. The news that Hiss had been asked to take a lie-detector test and balked, along with other fragments of the hearing, would go not to Andrews directly but to the *Herald Tribune*'s Carl Levin, via a third party, a former FBI agent. Later in the case, Nixon would use both Bob King, Pat's old San Francisco friend now gone from the Bureau, and former FBI agent Patrick Coyne as crucial intermediaries, particularly with the FBI itself.

He and Stripling spent "several hours" that evening studying the testimony. When the weary Texan finally went home at midnight, Nixon was still tenaciously at the transcript, his pursuit of Hiss swiftly becoming obsessive as he closed in. Through the night he was intermittently on the phone with Andrews for advice and exultant exchanges about the testimony. Andrews told him they should not wait for the Hiss-Chambers confrontation but stage it, as Nixon noted, "at the earliest possible date before Hiss could build up his story." Both of them believed Chambers and Crosley the same man, and that Hiss—if not Chambers—would be capable of constructing an elaborate fiction to mislead the Committee. They must "flush him," as Nixon wrote later, "before he had time to fill in more details of his deception."

Sometime during the night they apparently learned as well from Andrews's newspaper that Harry Dexter White had died suddenly of a heart attack, only three days after his own HUAC testimony and the caustic comment by Thomas about his coronary condition. It was a potential public relations disaster—the image of a respected high official hounded to death by the committee, "a victim of tyranny," as one columnist later called him. The news sealed the necessity for an immediate meeting of Hiss and Chambers, with the hoped-for sensation of their confirmed relationship drowning out the new wave of criticism over White's death. Nixon reached a groggy Stripling at 2:00 A.M. and told him to arrange the confrontation that afternoon, August 17, in New York. Stripling said he had "reached the same conclusion." They decided on an executive session in Manhattan's Commodore Hotel.

"I IMAGINED MYSELF IN HIS PLACE"

Whittaker Chambers had meanwhile fallen into one of his periodic funks after Nixon's series of visits, "listless and undecided," he wrote in his memoir *Witness*. "My first sense of purpose had crumbled under the impact of the public spectacle that had developed and the human wretchedness that my testimony had caused." He stayed in Westminster that Monday and "forced myself" to go back to work at *Time* in New York on Tuesday. Yet at the Baltimore railroad station he had "felt a curious need to go and see the Committee . . . the only people left in the world with whom I could communicate," and eventually took a train instead to Washington. Near noon he was entering a back door to the House Office Building "to avoid lurking newsmen" when he ran into an astonished Mandel, Appell, and Stripling, who had been frantically trying to locate him. Stripling fixed him, Chambers recalled, "with a somewhat birdlike stare," and said somberly to his colleagues, "I believe he must be psychic." They hustled him back to Union Station and onto a train for New York. Appell showed him in grave silence the morning headline telling of White's sudden death.

At Penn Station in Manhattan they waited until the car emptied before spiriting their witness out a back stairway of the station, Appell to take him by foot and taxi on a roundabout trip to the alley ramp of the Commodore, and Chambers quietly noted every detail of the melodramatic maneuvers. Appell, Chambers, and another HUAC bodyguard then waited in the bedroom of Suite 1400 while in the adjacent sitting room Nixon and McDowell, bustling with Mandel, Russell, Wheeler, and Stripling, all prepared the scene. The Committee would sit with its back to the windows overlooking the noise and traffic of Forty-second Street, Hiss facing them in a chair near the door, and to the side and slightly behind, a sofa, "where," as Nixon once proudly re-created the careful setting, "Mr. Chambers was to sit."

Late that afternoon McDowell called Hiss a few blocks away at the Carnegie Endowment and asked if he could drop by the Commodore at five-thirty, telling him Nixon and "one other" were there. As they waited, Nixon noticed that the ordinary hotel room had at least "one feature . . . in keeping with the high drama of the Hiss-Chambers case." On the wall were Audubon prints.

Warily, Hiss brought along a friend, Charles Dollard of another Carnegie foundation, and the two of them now walked into Room 1400 to find the two congressmen and small crowd of aides, all soon to be joined by Parnell Thomas. The meaning was clear, and to their mixed amusement and contempt, Hiss pointedly asked if someone could call the Harvard Club. He would have to cancel his six o'clock date; this was obviously going to last longer than the ten or fifteen minutes he had been led to believe.

"I do not for a moment want to miss the opportunity of seeing Mr. Chambers," Hiss began. But he also wanted the record to show that he had just learned of Harry White's fatal heart attack, "which came as a great shock," and he did not feel "in the best possible mood for testimony." The Committee said nothing. Hiss then went on in rising indignation about the press accounts of his closed testimony the day before, the lie-detector request, plans for Priscilla's appearance, and "other bits of my testimony which could only have come from the Committee." But Richard Nixon assured him that the *Tribune* story certainly came from "sources outside the Committee and outside the Committee staff." Hiss could ask the reporter if he didn't believe a congressman.

"I, too, was greatly disturbed when I read the morning paper," McDowell offered in obvious sincerity. "I have no idea how this story got out." He had guarded himself carefully, said the Pennsylvania representative, eyes widening. He had talked to no one "except my wife in Pittsburgh." But if he "should discover" the leak came from the HUAC staff, McDowell would see that they were fired. He did not mention his fellow members. "I join you," he told the witness, "in feeling rather rotten about the whole thing." It was the Committee's last moment of empathy for Alger Hiss.

Nixon now motioned Russell to bring in Chambers, who came through the bedroom door and took a seat on the sofa beside his old friend Mandel. Nixon and the others watched as Alger Hiss, his tormentor at last entering the same room, stared blankly straight ahead, out the windows, not turning to look at Whittaker Chambers.

Nixon asked them to stand and face each other. "I ask you now if you have ever known that man before," is how he put the long-awaited question. Hiss asked if the other man could "say something." With Nixon's permission Chambers, plainly nervous, spoke in a high-pitched, strained voice.

"My name is Whittaker Chambers."

Hiss walked toward him and said to him directly, "Would you mind opening your mouth wider?"

Chambers repeated his name "almost through closed lips," Hiss remembered, and again Hiss asked him to open his mouth, turning to Nixon to remind him of the bad teeth—"You know what I am referring to, Mr. Nixon."

Nixon watched Hiss reach out and motion with his thumb and finger for Chambers to open wide, Hiss's hand a few inches from his mouth. "I wondered," Nixon recalled the moment, "whether Chambers was tempted to bite his finger."

Was his voice lower before, Hiss asked as Chambers gave his employment. Then:

"I think he is George Crosley, but I would like to hear him talk a little longer. Are you George Crosley?"

"Not to my knowledge. You are Alger Hiss, I believe."

"I certainly am."

"That was my recollection."

Only a year and a half later, on the stand at a second trial, would Whittaker Chambers testify that he had "never been able to remember" among more than a dozen aliases quite which name he had adopted while living in Hiss's apartment. One of those names, a pseudonym he had used along the way to author pornographic poetry, was George Crosley.

Nixon interrupted. There was "some repartee . . . between these two people" and Chambers should be sworn. "That is a good idea," Hiss said sarcastically, breaking in on Nixon, and after McDowell administered the oath, Nixon flared. "Mr. Hiss, may I say something. I suggested that he be sworn, and when I say something like that I want no interruptions from you." Losing his own temper, Hiss hurled back his permanent grievance on the leaks. "Mr. Nixon, in view of what happened yesterday, I think there is no occasion for you to use that tone of voice in speaking to me, and I hope the record will show what I have just said." "The record," Nixon replied ominously, "shows everything that is being said here today."

Chambers was asked to read randomly from a copy of *Newsweek*, and Hiss thought his voice "sounds a little less resonant than that I recall of the man I knew as George Crosley."

Nixon then asked if Chambers had dental work done since the 1930s. Chambers explained "some extractions and a plate," but Hiss wanted to know the name of the dentist, "to find out . . . if what he has just said is true." Chambers acknowledged his teeth had been "in very bad shape."

Nixon "could hardly keep a straight face," as he wrote later, but soon thought the "comedy had gone far enough." He turned to the accused: "Mr. Hiss, do you really feel that you would have to have the dentist tell you just what he did to the teeth before you could tell anything about this man?" Denying Hiss's request to question Chambers himself, he went back over the testimony of the sixteenth, the apartment, car, rug.

Could Hiss not at last identify Crosley? Stripling interjected. But Hiss only asked if he could put further questions. "Do I have Mr. Nixon's permission?" Hiss asked acidly, and Nixon answered yes, provided Chambers could also question Hiss.

"Did you ever go under the name of George Crosley?"

And again a lie. "Not to my knowledge."

Had he sublet the apartment? No. Had he not brought his wife and baby to live there?

"I most certainly did," Chambers replied, and Hiss asked him to "reconcile your negative answers."

"Very easily, Alger. I was a communist and you were a communist."

Chambers had never actually paid rent or subleased, he would later explain. It was a simple accommodation among comrades. "This oracular statement," Hiss wrote later, "revived my earlier sense of fantasy or dream."

Nixon now turned to ask Chambers about the apartment, but Hiss suddenly interrupted.

"Mr. Chairman, I don't need to ask Whittaker Chambers any more questions. I am now perfectly prepared to identify this man as George Crosley."

Stripling quickly asked him to produce three others who knew Crosley on the old Senate munitions committee, and Nixon reminded him that Chambers had again identified him, here face-to-face, as a communist. Hiss was now furious, reckless. He would ever after claim that Chambers was the onetime casual acquaintance he had described, now become for some inscrutable reason a character assassin. "I would like to say that to come here and discover that the ass under the lion's skin is Crosley, I don't know why your committee didn't pursue this careful method of interrogation at an earlier date before all the publicity."

"Well, now, Mr. Hiss, you positively identify—" McDowell began and Hiss broke in bitterly: "If he had lost both eyes and taken his nose off, I would be sure."

McDowell got from Chambers the same "positive identification," and at that point Hiss rose out of his chair and walked toward Chambers, "shaking his fist," as Nixon saw him, while "his voice quavered with anger."

"I would like to invite Mr. Whittaker Chambers to make these same statements out of the presence of this committee without their being privileged for suit of libel. I challenge you to do it, and I hope you will do it damned quickly."

Russell took hold of Hiss's arm to restrain him. "Hiss recoiled as if he had been pricked with a hot needle," thought Nixon.

"I am not going to touch him," he said shrilly to Russell. "You are touching me."

McDowell called a brief recess, returning to acrimonious argument from Hiss about Chambers responding to his libel challenge. Hiss again denied every accusation. "You must have formed some sort of affection for this man," McDowell put to Hiss in puzzlement, "to go through all the things that you did to try to [have him] occupy your home, take over your lease, and give him an automobile." But both men persisted in their stories.

In parting anger and sarcasm, Hiss said his wife was on her way from Vermont for testimony the next morning and asked if HUAC intended to publicize these proceedings. Flustered, knowing the leaks that would happen anyway, McDowell could only plead, "I don't know. I don't know." Nixon promised Hiss an answer "in five minutes" but never gave one. The small spectacle ended at 7:15 P.M. with Thomas saying vacantly, "That is all. Thank you very much."

"I don't reciprocate."

"Italicize that in the record," Thomas said to the stenographer.

"I wish you would," said Alger Hiss.

It had all ended, wrote one reporter later, "in a naked and desperate scramble for reputation." Looking on, Hiss's friend Dollard thought, as he later described in a memorandum, "Alger behaved very badly, was very irritable . . . both McDowell and Nixon were trying to be fair." Afterward, Nixon himself remembered in strange somberness "a sense of shock and sadness that a man like Hiss could have fallen so low. I imagined myself in his place . . . not a pleasant picture to see a whole brilliant career destroyed before your eyes."

At the moment, however, the mood was different than the considered memories. When the door had closed behind Hiss and Dollard, the Committee and its informer stood looking at each other for a moment. Then Stripling broke the silence with a parody of his own Texas drawl. "Hi-ya, Mistah Crawz-li?" he said to Chambers. They all laughed.

"The Committee would be vindicated and I personally would receive credit for the part I had played," Nixon recorded of the triumph at the Commodore. As it was, the vindication and credit were not left to chance. Forewarned by the nocturnal calls from Nixon, Bert Andrews had gathered Jack Lotto, an International News Service investigative reporter noted for his enterprise, and another journalist, and slipped into the Commodore hallway outside Room 1400. When Hiss and Dollard had then gone inside, the three reporters attached a hearing aid to the door, "turned up the volume," Lotto revealed, "and tuned in on it play-by-play." The first sensational news stories of the confrontation were on the New York streets that night not long after Hiss and Dollard left the hotel.

Going without dinner in order to ensure making the morning dailies, Nixon spent the rest of the evening telephoning the press. He no longer bothered to speak on background, and the next day the wire services and major newspapers led, as *The New York Times* wrote, with "details which were given by telephone tonight by Representative Nixon." He would stay over alone to question Priscilla Hiss the next morning, and Nixon asked Appell to remain with him in his room. After hours of calling other newsmen, he had then placed a call to Bert Andrews and Appell fell asleep. When the aide awoke he found Nixon still talking to Andrews. Looking at his watch in surprise, Appell "realized" as he said later, "that the call had already lasted for over three hours."

Meanwhile, Whittaker Chambers had what he would describe later as an inspirational dinner with his employer, Henry Luce, who compared the informer to the man in the New Testament born blind and restored to sight by Jesus Christ. Not far away, Alger Hiss picked up Priscilla at Grand Central, dined, and returned home to find his telephone jangling with reporters who had already talked to Congressman Nixon. Between calls, he telephoned Foster Dulles, who again counseled caution and respect vis-à-vis the Committee. Desperate, Hiss called his own midnight press conference. Looking haggard and tense, he told reporters, "I do not believe in communism." But his denial would be buried beneath the Nixon headlines and "details" the following day.

The next morning Nixon as a subcommittee of one in executive session took testimony from Scripps-Howard reporter Nelson Frank, another former leftist turned anticommunist who knew Chambers in the 1930s, and who swore that he had recognized him from current photos "as soon as I looked at the face." Later came Isaac Don Levine to repeat for the record much of what he had privately told Kersten and Nixon a week before. He also thought Chambers easily recognizable from the agent of the thirties and a "crystal honest person, dependable, sound, patriotic, intelligent, without malice toward anyone, with a high sense of justice and fair play." It was more icing on the cake, and the testimony promptly leaked to the Hearst papers, some HUAC members reading the August 19 story before they saw the confidential transcript.

But it was in between Frank's and Levine's that the most interesting interview took place, a bare ten minutes with Appell out of the room and Nixon alone with the stenographer and Alger and Priscilla Hiss. He was "tired," Nixon confessed later, and thought that "Mrs. Hiss's testimony was not too important . . . that the battle was won, that I could afford to relax," though he added, too, "Undoubtedly I subconsciously reacted to the fact that she was a woman."

When he asked Priscilla to take the oath, she wondered—"demurely," he thought—if she might "affirm" rather than "swear." "Subtly, she was reminding me of our common Quaker background," he recalled, though there would be no evidence that either of the Hisses knew Nixon's religion at this point. To his questions about George Crosley, she had only misty impressions: "It all seems very long ago and vague."

Crosley she recalled as a "small person, very smiling person—a little too smiley, perhaps," and in the end a "sponger." She went on in a personal vein, "I don't know whether you have ever had guests, unwelcome guests, guests that weren't guests, you know." But Richard Nixon, the assiduous prosecuter of her husband, did not quite know, and with that the questioning stopped. He thought her "nervous and frightened" and told her gently he appreciated her coming.

"I am glad it has been so quiet, because that was really what I had a strong distaste for," she replied. "I would like to thank you for our just being together."

He was not so accommodating that even this small session did not leak to the press. The following week *The New York Times* would report Priscilla's questioning as "another step in the efforts of Mr. Nixon . . . to pierce the disparity and contradictions" in the case. But he sensed his first major failure in the hunt and attributed it to a "crisis" syndrome of psychic letdown and flawed judgment in the wake of battle. "I should have remembered that Chambers had described her as, if anything, a more fanatical communist than Hiss," he wrote of what he had once read in the FBI files. "I could have made a devastating record had I also remembered that even a woman who happens to be a Quaker and then turns to communism must be a communist first and a Quaker second."

What he lost, however, was no mere chance to uncover another subversive, but a fugitive opportunity to start toward the cryptic heart of the Chambers-Hiss relationship. Priscilla Hiss, strong and intricate behind the demure surface, was scarcely a bystander in her husband's life, and Alger's relationship with Whittaker Chambers, as with almost anyone else, was almost certainly triangular. But then that would have meant a patient, painstaking search for the truth of the unfolding human tragedy, and not the political expedience and sensation the case had long since become.

If the week before the Hiss testimony and Commodore confrontation had been for Nixon a period of covert, ingenious positioning, the week after now became a time of national celebrity and further triumph, all pointing toward HUAC's announced public confrontation of the two protagonists August 25. Back in Washington amid the headlines later on the eighteenth, he received and promptly flourished Hiss's formal written refusal to take a lie-detector test. That day, too, at the Carnegie Endowment, Foster Dulles made a first request of Alger Hiss for his resignation, the beginning of the abandonment by the establishment Nixon had hoped to achieve with his flying mission to the Roosevelt. On the other side, Nixon quietly shored up the ever-moody, ever-anguishing Chambers. Thinking "I could not go through another public hearing," the informer came by to see him in the attic office later that week to ask if the twenty-fifth might be called off. Patiently, Nixon told him the session would save him from imminent indictment.

"It is for your own sake that the Committee is holding a public hearing. The Department of Justice is all set to move in on you in order to save Hiss," Chambers remembered him arguing. "They're planning to indict you at once. The only way to head them off is to let the public judge for itself which one of you is telling the truth. This is your only chance."

Nixon had then added: "If there is anything else that you have not told us about Hiss, now is the time to tell us. Think hard about it. If there is anything else, for your own sake, tell us now." Chambers's refusal or inability to supply "anything else" in response to Nixon's request in August would have historic consequences, and perhaps determine the outcome of the Presidential election of 1948. But for now it was enough for the congressman that he had persuaded the informer to appear at the Committee show August 25. He had certainly succeeded in frightening him. He "liked and trusted" Nixon, Chambers remembered, and on leaving his office reflected that "my choice lay between procuring my own safety and the agony of others." He felt, he wrote, like "a very small creature, skirting the shadows of encircling powers that would not hestitate to crush me impersonally as a steamroller crushes a bug."

As for genuine concern about a Justice Department indictment, secret Nichols memoranda on Nixon's "numerous calls" to the FBI that week would show no trace of the congressman inquiring about a federal indictment of Chambers or trying to head one off. As Cronin or myriad other sources may well have told him, none was yet in the making.

With Chambers kept in line, on the twentieth Nixon held another one-man hearing with Abt, Pressman, and Witt. He heard them refuse to answer "incriminating" questions, then went out afterward to denounce Harry Truman for "willfully obstructing an investigation which is absolutely essential to the security of each and every person in this country." On the twenty-first he gave an extensive briefing to *The New York Times* on the evolution of the case. On the twenty-fourth he heard ex-Communist Louis Budenz testify vaguely of having heard Hiss's name, and then the more enigmatic testimony from an owner and employee of the Washington car lot, where Hiss's old Ford had apparently been disposed of in a questionable transaction involving a former communist—though whether by Chambers or Hiss it was never clear.

Toward the August 25 public confrontation, Nixon now worked, as one observer saw him, like "a man possessed, a prizefighter peaking for a title bout." By his own account he spent "as much as eighteen to twenty hours a day" at the office, and drove the HUAC staff, which he had now in effect taken over, "at an even harder pace," pressing them on Andrews's persistent advice to seek out the District of Columbia records on Hiss's cars and rental leases. "I was 'mean' to live with at home and with my friends," Nixon recalled, "quick-tempered with the members of my staff . . . lost interest in eating . . . [and] getting to sleep became more and more difficult." Their daughter would later record Pat Nixon's own memory of the period, that her husband had "immersed himself in the case with an absorption that was almost frightening."

Bert Andrews came by the attic on the twenty-fourth and was shocked at the young congressman's haggard appearance. "You look like hell,"

Andrews told him, advising him to go home and take a sleeping pill. It was more sound guidance. He took the pill, "slept for twelve hours," he remembered, "and woke up the next morning physically refreshed, ready for the most important test I had had up to that time."

Nearly a thousand people jammed the caucus room on the twenty-fifth, while Capital police wrestled outside with another three hundred in what one reporter called "a day of infernal heat." Alistair Cooke of the *Manchester Guardian*, like other Europeans a little amazed and appalled at the whole inquisitional process, vividly caught the scene inside in the glare and swelter of that yet new accompaniment to politics, television lights:

> The cameras buzzed and roamed like speculative flies
> over the dripping audience; catching open-mouthed cit-
> izens in moments of unsuspected prurience or vanity;
> demonstrating to countless households, up and down the
> eastern seaboard, television's peculiar and terrifying gift
> for casting an intensely private eye on scenes of utmost
> publicity; elbowing along the Committee table and tak-
> ing long, revealing glances at the darkly handsome Mr.
> Nixon, the unmoving bald head of Mr. Parnell Thomas,
> and the skeptical shruggings, ash-flicking, and nose-rub-
> bings of Mr. Karl Mundt, who came to the point of saying
> out loud that at first he had been charmed by Hiss but
> now was inclined to share his wife's view that he had
> been taken in by the man's "sauvity."

The Committee was now more than ever tribunal, a body never again so powerful or freshly reputable and Alger Hiss more than ever the cautious lawyer on trial, maddeningly constrained to speak a straight declarative sentence. No less than 198 times, by HUAC's avid count, Hiss would qualify his answers by some phrase like "according to my best recollection."

They stood again, facing each other for the crowd. Hiss knew Chambers as George Crosley but in the intervening week had found no one else from the old Senate who remembered the free-lance writer.

Cooke saw Nixon "the most watchful of all committeemen . . . straining at the leash" on the subject of the old Ford. Had Hiss given Crosley/Chambers a car? "I gave Crosley, according to my best recollection—" Hiss began. And Richard Nixon, who as a young man proudly husbanded his own Fords, who advised his little brother Eddie to charge for rides, was disbelieving, almost folksy in his skepticism: "Well, now,

just a moment on that point. I don't want to interrupt you on that 'to the best of my recollection' but you certainly can testify 'yes' or 'no' as to whether you gave Crosley a car. How many cars have you given away in your life, Mr. Hiss?" Laughter swept the room.

For more than an hour, Nixon pressed the discrepancies surrounding the car, meticulously laying "the basis," thought one legal historian, for a perjury charge. HUAC investigators had found the title signed over by Alger Hiss to a Cherner Motor Company and from there to a former communist. They confronted Hiss with a photostat of the title, but he still could not, would not, be certain.

"Could you be sure if you saw the original document?" asked Mundt.

"I could be sur-er," Hiss said almost lightly. There was laughter again.

"Well," added Thomas, "if that were the original would it look any more like your signature?" And more laughter and titters.

At one juncture Nixon pointed out that if he had let Chambers or anyone else use the car for a time while he retained the title, Hiss would be liable for the car. Certainly a lawyer "who stood extremely high in his class at Harvard Law School" would know that. "I certainly did not realize it," Hiss answered, opening again the chasm between his world and accident cases in the offices of Wingert and Bewley.

"I have no present recollection of the disposition of the Ford," Hiss finally concluded. Hebert slumped back in his chair: "You are a remarkable and agile young man, Mr. Hiss."

Hiss would dismiss the Ford and the leases, the swarm of dates and details as "housekeeping" matters a busy man might naturally forget. "The important charges are not questions of leases, but questions of whether I was a communist." But Richard Nixon, at the climax of the hunt as at the beginning, insisted on the primal, certifying question of the two men and their relationship. "The issue in this hearing today is whether or not Mr. Hiss or Mr. Chambers has committed perjury before this committee." It was by the apparent "housekeeping details," he told them, that HUAC could begin to measure "truth or falsity."

And there was always George Crosley. "You have made much of the point of bad teeth," Nixon taunted him at one point, recalling his Commodore performance. "My question may sound facetious, but I am just wondering: didn't you ever see Crosley with his mouth closed?" Still more laughter and afterward an underlying murmur in the crowd.

They were feeling "disgust" on the dais, Nixon would tell Andrews afterward, and clearly sensed it as well in the perspiring but enthralled audience, much less the invisible televison world beyond.

At the end—"his reputation . . . now thoroughly destroyed," as one of his biographers noted—Alger Hiss could only plead a personal tragedy, his victimization in some enigmatic psychological accident, which none of them believed or perhaps even understood.

"My action in being kind to Crosley years ago," he told them, "was one of humaneness, which surely some members of the Committee have experienced. You do a favor for a man, he comes for another, he gets a third favor from you. When you finally realize he is an inveterate repeater, you get rid of him. If your loss is only time and money, you are lucky. You may find yourself calumniated in a degree depending on whether the man is unbalanced or worse."

Whittaker Chambers now took the stand to rehearse his record and accusations. In stark contrast to Hiss, he was calm, unequivocal, and questioned by the Committee only gently and briefly.

Alger Hiss had been "the closest friend I ever had in the Communist Party," he told a hushed room.

Nixon asked him about all the rumors and gossip about his motives.

"I do not hate Mr. Hiss," Chambers said in melancholy and drama. "We are close friends, but we are caught in a tragedy of history. Mr. Hiss represents the concealed enemy against which we are all fighting and I am fighting. I have testified against him with remorse and pity, but in a moment of history in which this nation now stands, so help me God, I could not do otherwise."

It ended nine and a half hours after it began, with well-wishers and photographers crowding around both Chambers and Nixon. Like Jerry Voorhis after his debates with his aggressive challenger two years before, Alger Hiss left the caucus room almost alone.

After nearly a month of mounting tension and sometimes frenzy, his triumph of the twenty-fifth was to be mixed and in some ways short-lived. Watching Alger Hiss "grilled . . . mercilessly for six hours" and Whittaker Chambers questioned for "only an hour and forty minutes without anything resembling a comparably exhaustive inquiry into details of his past," the *Washington Post* remained unconvinced. "Its approach has been too biased," the paper said of its old nemesis HUAC, "its investigation too cursory to warrant any faith in its findings. And there are far too many ends left loose."

By the twenty-eighth, Nixon and Mundt had hurried through the Committee an "interim report," highlighting the "evasive testimony" of Hiss and the contrasting record of Chambers, "for the most part forthright and emphatic in his answers." But that, too, failed to impress papers like *The New York Times*, which concluded that "the Committee has not proceeded in a manner that commended confidence . . . [and] it is not clear that it is getting at the real spies, or the really dangerous ones." Richard Nixon, it seemed, had been able to command headlines with a flood of leaked testimony, but not in the end to capture as well the editorial respectability or complete "vindication" he had expected.

Inside the Truman White House, at the same moment, HUAC's probe earned more grudging respect. Two days after the public confrontation, Presidential aide George Elsey secretly won approval from Truman to have the Justice Department take over the Hiss-Chambers case to determine who had lied—"whether the perjurer be Hiss or Chambers." Truman would have little choice but to take legal note of what he had dismissed sneeringly only weeks earlier. Richard Nixon had clearly won the round. The President also worried at the close of August about J. Edgar Hoover and how he might exploit the case now, having inspired the congressional furor to begin with. "The trouble," a White House aide noted Truman's chronic irritation with the FBI, "was that Hoover was concerned with his own future."

Meanwhile, two more developments suddenly propelled the case forward. A Baltimore paper broke the story on the twenty-seventh that Hiss and Chambers, albeit at different times, had bought the same old farm near Westminster. Nixon telephoned Chambers immediately for an executive session about the farm. Chambers brought along his little boy to Washington, and Nixon, obviously "somewhat upset" by the new development, as Chambers recalled him, had introduced the boy to newsmen outside the HUAC hearing room with the words: "This is Mr. Hiss's young son."

Inside the hearing room, Stripling, too, was disturbed at the new information. "You answer questions readily enough," he told Chambers, "but I notice that you never volunteer information." The investigator would always feel, as he had told Nixon earlier, that this odd man was holding out on them.

That same night, Chambers went on *Meet the Press*, a nationally syndicated radio program, and the panel of newsmen promptly challenged him to make the public statement Hiss had sought at the Commodore. "Alger Hiss was a communist and may still be one," he told them, noting later to himself that with those words "I crossed the bridge." Unlike HUAC, the interviewers were unsparing and dubious. As Chambers left the studio to walk up Connecticut Avenue, a messenger ran up to him with a note to call Congressman Nixon's personal number. "It was a damned outrage," Nixon told him about the program. But Chambers himself sounded resigned to criticism and even a libel suit.

With Congress adjourning, the case was suddenly suspended in a kind of limbo. The Democrats were ready to "soft-pedal that red herring," Bert

Andrews reported, while the Dewey forces had ordered transcripts of all the HUAC hearings and "are having them analyzed." On August 29, despite the still-widespread editorial criticism, a Gallup Poll found eight in ten Americans believed HUAC "should continue with its spy investigations," though with reelections to win and no more witnesses, the Committee was now on its way home.

Richard Nixon would soon return to California a hero from the case, now a figure of national reputation—and controversy—ready to use his assured reelection to campaign for other Republicans, and even for the Presidential ticket, telling cheering audiences how he had pursued Alger Hiss.

Yet behind the fame and retold glory he still seemed to vacillate, seized with moments of remorse and uncertainty amid the congratulations. Before he left for Whittier, Nixon went again to talk to Levine, who saw him as "a troubled man in those days" despite the success. He probed the writer once more about the mystical Whittaker Chambers, on whom he had staked so much, on whom his new prominence rested.

"Are you convinced from your knowledge of Chambers and of the whole case," Nixon could still ask Levine that September, "that he is telling the truth?"

14

The Case II, September–December, 1948

"I THINK THIS IS WHAT YOU'RE LOOKING FOR"

Bert Andrews left Washington that September to cover the Dewey Presidential campaign, but before going he thoughtfully arranged for Dick and Pat Nixon to spend a long Labor Day weekend at a seaside resort near Washington on the Delaware shore. On their return, Nixon sent him a letter of warm appreciation for the "wonderful vacation down at Ocean City thanks to your efforts." Their room was "the best . . . they had in the hotel" and "we both had a chance to relax completely and enjoyed ourselves tremendously," the congressman wrote his influential friend. "The weather was perfect, except for the fact that we tried to take two weeks of sun in about three days with the usual results."

But the fulsome September 7 letter, marked "PERSONAL & CONFIDENTIAL," was business as well. Nixon wanted Andrews to know that HUAC investigators were still working on the Hiss-Chambers case through the election period. He enclosed for the reporter "a blind copy" of a letter Nixon had written that same day to John Foster Dulles, summarizing "my reactions" to the case and suggesting how the HUAC hearings might be exploited in the GOP campaign. The copy was "solely for your own information," he wrote the reporter, though adding a gentle warning Andrews might well pass on to the Dewey camp: "I certainly hope that Dulles for his own sake and Dewey's as well, will be able to announce in the near future that Hiss has left the endowment [*sic*]." He was also sending along "some random notes which I have made" on the inquiry "in the event you decide to do a piece on the whole case." Nixon wanted "to express my appreciation again for the many hours of thought and the good words of advice and counsel which you gave me during the last hectic three weeks."

The promise of further investigation, the warning, the notes for another planted article, the leaked copy of the "personal and confidential" letter to Dulles—now available to Dewey aides through Andrews should Foster for any reason neglect to pass it on—were all part of the ceaseless politics he practiced on the eve of his own departure for California. If still unsettled about Chambers, still seeking privately from Levine some ultimate assurance, Richard Nixon would go on with Andrews, Dulles, and others, and especially in public, as the convinced prosecutor.

He had tried to go again to the GOP campaign headquarters at the Roosevelt in person, but was not able to schedule a meeting before his departure for California. To Dulles he now wrote a revealing seven-page reflection on the case, actually two separate letters, one offering campaign and policy recommendations for Dewey, the second marked "PERSONAL" and carefully setting out his conclusions about Alger Hiss. He began the campaign advice with a morsel of secret information gleaned from Cronin. Dewey should not let Truman get away with the "red herring" tag. Under government surveillance Elizabeth Bentley had at one point received from a Soviet embassy official $2,000 and "the FBI now has it," corroborating her own espionage if not the names of her coconspirators. "There is no doubt whatever," Nixon assured Dulles, claiming justifiably "we have been in close touch with the FBI throughout the proceedings." There was, after all, much Presidential campaign fodder in the HUAC hearings. He suggested Dewey propose suspending the Fifth Amendment privilege in cases involving national security or government employees. It would have destroyed a fundamental Constitutional right, though the congressman was intent on the political benefit—"some restrictions on the defense in such cases would certainly meet with popular approval at this time," he assured Dulles.

Most of all, he advised, the Republicans should be aggressive. He had urged Dulles before that Dewey advocate "strengthening the espionage laws." On that, "the record of the administration is completely vulnerable and should be attacked without question during the campaign." HUAC had tried to draw out Truman, to no avail. "In any event," he repeated, "the administration is completely vulnerable and should be attacked." They should also be "attacked" for the failure to prosecute and deport alien communists. It was an echo of the racist nativism that mixed so easily with anticommunism in southern California if not the rest of the country. "I realize that there would be some difficulty in making a political issue out of this because of the danger of alienating certain minority groups,"

441

Nixon conceded, "but I think that it can be handled tactfully enough and that it will make a very powerful issue."

Harry Truman was telling them to forget red herrings and get on with the domestic agenda. But it was the President who should be called upon "to forget politics and to cooperate with the Congress in getting the communists out of government," Nixon continued, obviously warming to his subject: "Another point which should be stressed during the campaign is the ease with which communists and their sympathizers were able to get on the federal payroll . . . that under the New Deal communist affiliation was probably the best recommendation possible for a person who wanted to get ahead in government." HUAC so far "has only scratched the surface" of subversion, and Dewey should promise "relentless and vigorous prosecution and investigation under an administration which is not afraid of the political consequences of finding disloyal persons on the government payroll." In early September 1948, before the stunning conclusion of the Hiss-Chambers case, before the rise of Senator Joseph McCarthy or the further worsening of the international climate with the U.S.S.R., it was a remarkable foreshadowing of the future campaigns Richard Nixon would run, and with the popular acclaim and success he now held out to Tom Dewey.

Yet it was the companion letter to Dulles that was even more extraordinary, a disarming, straightforward, in some ways brilliant appeal to the establishment elder to scuttle Alger Hiss. He had "attempted to approach this case as objectively as possible," as he told Dulles at the Roosevelt a month before. "In fact," he added, "I would say that if at the beginning I had any prejudice one way or the other, it was more likely that I favored Hiss rather than Chambers, due to the fact that I have close friends in Washington who are also very friendly with Donald and Alger Hiss." The passage was a small if notable dissimulation about his own private and public life. Unless one stretched to count Christian Herter, a respectful congressional colleague but hardly an intimate, there were no such "close friends" of both Hiss and his hunter, though the claim served at once to shore up Richard Nixon's credibility as well as his social standing. At any rate, after "devoting many hours to studying the testimony and all aspects of the case," Nixon's judgment was restrained.

> I have come to the conclusion that, at the very least,
> Hiss deliberately misled the committee in several im-
> portant respects during his appearances before it.
> Whether he was guilty of technical perjury or whether it
> has been established definitely that he was a member of
> the Communist Party are issues which still may be open
> for debate, but there is no longer any doubt in my mind

that for reasons only he can give, he was trying to keep
the committee from learning the truth in regard to his
relationship with Chambers.

He went on to describe Hiss's relationship with George Crosley, how
HUAC learned that "on at least one occasion he and 'Crosley' road [sic] to
New York together from Washington in an automobile," that they "jointly
became interested in a broken-down Maryland farmhouse near Westminster." Yet Alger Hiss had not recognized the photographs of Whittaker
Chambers, photographs "shown to numbers of disinterested people" who
had no doubt it was Chambers. He did not explain to Dulles that the
"disinterested people" were all ex-communists or those, like Levine,
scarcely neutral in the controversy. He briefly described Hiss at the Commodore: "one of the most unconvincing acts that I have ever seen put on
by a supposedly intelligent man." Then there was the old Ford, more
confirmation of Chambers while Hiss had been "vague and evasive."

What had been plain also in the HUAC hearings, Nixon shrewdly told
Dulles, was that Alger Hiss apparently did not disclose to Foster Dulles
and the other Carnegie trustees when he was being hired the full story of
his past encounters with the FBI and the doubts raised about his loyalty.
The Committee had "the definite impression that he [Hiss] had not been
forthright with the Foundation [sic] at the time that he was being considered
for the position." It was a crucial fillip to signal that the jumpy Carnegie
trustees could be largely off the hook with HUAC and, even more important, with Nixon's formidable press allies.

"It is, of course, quite possible that I may be subconsciously prejudiced
against Hiss," Nixon continued, "but I certainly would not want to allow
that prejudice to influence you in any manner at all in your consideration
of this case." And further in the letter: "I know that you will make whatever
discount you consider necessary for personal bias which is bound to enter
into a matter of this type when one has worked on it as long and hard as
I have during the past few weeks." Nor did he want "to give the impression
that I hold a brief for Chambers either personally or otherwise. All I know
is that his story to date has proved correct." But the point for Dulles and
his Endowment colleagues was clear. Richard Nixon was telling them to
fire Alger Hiss, who "most certainly has not conducted himself, in my
opinion, in a manner which befits holding the position that he holds at the
present time."

He ended on another personal note. "I might add for whatever it is
worth that I can see why Mr. Hiss is so well liked by those that know him.
He makes a most favorable impression and I will frankly tell you that I
have seldom regretted so deeply the necessity of having to carry through

with a case as in this one." In this second "personal" letter, he was no longer the political zealot of the first letter, but now a reluctant pursuer, drawn on by the inescapable evidence and public duty to trace down a man he liked, a man with whom he shared friends.

Dulles replied with an uncharacteristic effusiveness. He thanked Nixon for his "very useful and sound suggestions" on the campaign, and was having them "immediately sent to Albany for the governor's personal perusal." Then, in his own separate, second letter marked "PERSONAL," he wrote Nixon in Whittier: "I am deeply indebted to you for setting out so carefully your conclusion with reference to Hiss." The congressman could appreciate that "it was a difficult situation for the trustees." Dulles was "very glad" they understood that Carnegie had been misled in hiring Hiss.

Promptly circulated by Dulles to most of the Carnegie Board (though concealed from Hiss and his staunchest supporters), Nixon's letter further cut the establishment ground from under Alger Hiss just as the headlines waned. Alger had refused to resign at Dulles's suggestion after the Commodore, and assembled for the Board chairman his own barrage of supportive letters from a score of notables. He now hung on tenuously to his Endowment presidency and its veneer of patronage as cautious trustees waited to see if the scandal would somehow abate. Already on August 20, Dulles had begun writing for Dewey manager Herb Brownell, and the protective, sanitized "files," a series of exculpatory memos explaining Dulles's personal distance from the accused ("I had no intimate association with him . . .") and his vigilance whenever allegations had come up in the past.

For the moment, the Endowment trustees would hold off firing Hiss and thereby all but concurring in his guilt, even with Congressman Nixon's earnest, persuasive letter. One new board member in particular was skeptical and repelled at the inquiry thus far. "You will understand that I have no means of knowing anything at all about the specific facts of this particular case," he wrote an Endowment officer later that September, "but it does strike me as curious, rather as incomprehensible, that there can be any recognized or legal procedure whereby the reputation of a man can be almost destroyed merely on the basis of another's startling accusations." He had signed the letter in his unmistakable script: Dwight D. Eisenhower.

"HE ESCAPED INTERMENT"

Nixon flew to Los Angeles the day after writing Andrews and Dulles and without pause took up the advice he had given Dewey. In a campaign that took him throughout California on behalf of GOP candidates, he began in Whittier, regaling a hometown audience on the case, telling them darkly the public would not learn "half the truth" about Russian espionage until they had a Republican administration not "afraid of skeletons in the closet." For two weeks he traveled up and down the state. On September 22 he was in San Francisco for a press conference dramatically staged next door to an appearance by prominent American communist Elizabeth Gurley Flynn, who denounced Mundt-Nixon as a "form of lynch law." Nixon followed with the much-delivered line about "skeletons in the closet," and urged Truman to "put the national interest above politics and cooperate with Congress to get them [communists] off the payroll." The President, he told reporters, was taking "the line followed by the *Daily Worker*," though the *San Francisco Examiner* also noted of the "serious-minded young congressman" that "he lauded the FBI." He was en route back to Washington, he told them, for "important new developments" in the spy case which he could not discuss—"that's as far as I can go."

His dramatic shuttle back to the Capital proved to have nothing to do with Hiss and Chambers and was only in part on HUAC business. Ostensibly, he was there to cosign and announce a lengthy Committee report on atomic espionage. But the inconclusive report allowed Nixon to attack President Truman once again for preventing J. Edgar Hoover from testifying before HUAC, and the story put the California representative on the front page of *The New York Times* along with both Presidential candidates.

Privately, Nixon returned to the attic office fuming at what he came to see as the first of a series of smears aimed at his role in the Hiss-Chambers case. It came with a September 20 Drew Pearson column charging that the "real estate lobby" was exploiting various public figures at industry-staged celebrations of the Constitution, and that Congressman Nixon, who spoke to a realtors' group in Alhambra September 17, "went so far as to give the real estate lobby permission to write a statement for him—with no strings attached." It was all designed, said Pearson, to make voters forget the lobby "pulled wires against public housing and slum clearance." Seeing the column in the *Los Angeles Daily News*, Nixon was furious. He wired Bill Arnold at length to "investigate immediately" with both the realty lobby and Pearson's office to determine the source. "INTEND TO TAKE NECESSARY STEPS TO OBTAIN PUBLIC RETRACTION BY HIM AND BY *LOS ANGELES DAILY NEWS* AND *WASHINGTON POST*." Nixon angrily telegraphed his aide about his arrival two days later. "GIVE THIS INVESTIGATION PRIORITY OVER ALL OTHER OFFICE BUSINESS SO THAT WE CAN GET IT [*sic*] COMPLETE TRUTH OF MATTER."

A sheepish Arnold soon admitted that while the Nixons were at Ocean City he had cleared a blurb written by the lobby and published over Nixon's name in the realtors' national publicity. As for the rest, Nixon had indeed spoken to the real-estate group in Alhambra—among his most powerful local supporters, after all—and Pearson and his assistant, Jack Anderson, would never reveal their source in any case. "I am afraid that we might let you in for further unfair treatment in the Pearson column if we were to demand a retraction," Arnold warned. There the matter rested, although Nixon continued to fume.

By itself it was a trivial incident, scarcely a political pinprick amid the celebrity he had begun to enjoy. But it was the beginning of what Nixon would describe later as "an utterly unprincipled and vicious smear campaign" that he attributed to his pursuit of Alger Hiss. The incident was the inception, too, of an acrid, quarter-century running battle with Drew Pearson, and later Jack Anderson, in which Nixon was increasingly incensed—whatever the validity or falsity of the story—and ever more impatient to turn up the guilty "source." Pearson's column was yet another early warning that Richard Nixon, who could enthusiastically advise a Dewey to "attack" and dish it out himself, had some difficulty in taking it.

Aside from the spurt of front-page publicity over the HUAC report, the brief return to Washington was a worrisome interlude. Nixon learned that the FBI's Louis Nichols had come by the office more than once in his absence to complain about Nixon's public boasting over the August hearings. In vain Arnold had tried to smooth it over with Hoover's man. On the evening of September 28, Nixon placatingly called Nichols at home, and the official recorded their conversation in a secret memo the next morning. Had the Bureau seen the recent press clips from San Francisco showing how much "Nixon praised the FBI"? the congressman asked. He was going on a campaign speaking tour "for the next month, and . . . in each speech he contemplated pointing out how the FBI has been on the job."

Nixon went on "that he appreciated the difficult position we had found ourselves in and he wanted us to know that . . . he had nothing but admiration for the Bureau." But Nichols was not appeased. He and his fellow agents had seen "a gratuitous crack" reported from Nixon somewhere "about the Committee having done more in three days than the FBI had done in eight years." That was hardly accurate, and Nichols chided him. "As a matter of fact, I had stayed up until after midnight one night trying to find some basis whereby we could be of assistance to him . . . and I thought his crack was most uncalled for." Nixon agreed "thoroughly," but "the unfortunate part was that he was not quoted correctly." He had meant to attack their common adversary, the attorney general, and simply to contrast the committee's progress on the case with the Justice Department's.

"Nixon again apologized," Nichols noted. He asked the agent to make certain the director knew of his call, adding that the FBI "could rest assured that if there was any way he could help he would do so," and "that any comments he had made . . . were a matter of strategy." Beneath that passage in Nichols's report, FBI deputy director Clyde Tolson would jot "(strategy to get a headline for Nixon)!" "I was favorably impressed with Nixon's attitude," Nichols concluded. His superiors were less sanguine. "Nixon plays both sides against the middle," wrote Tolson at the bottom of the memo, J. Edgar Hoover adding below, "I agree. H."

The episode was one more mark of the Byzantine politics in which Nixon was now entwined. He must "attack" the government, take the plaudits of the crowd for "breaking" the case, yet not offend the acute public relations sensibilities of Hoover and his men who had their own quiet war with the administration, and whose covert leaks and support were so instrumental in the whole affair. Much as he courted Dulles while pursuing Hiss to Dulles's potential embarrassment, it was a politician's "middle," against which, as Tolson observed, Richard Nixon struggled to play both ends.

Meanwhile, as Nixon was scolded by both Drew Pearson and the FBI, the case itself moved on inexorably. Only a week after Chambers's accusations on *Meet the Press*, the public pressure mounted for Hiss to make good his angry threat of a libel action. "Well, Alger, where's that suit?" asked the conservative *New York Daily News*, while even the *Washington Post* thought "each day of delay [in filing] . . . does incalculable damage to his reputation." Urgings came as well from Hiss's establishment supporters, though there the advice was mixed. Figures like Harvard president James Conant pressed privately for him to sue, fearing that if he did not, as one of Hiss's lawyers reported Conant's view, "a flood of similar charges against political and academic figures would soon follow." At the same time, Foster Dulles predictably opposed any litigation with further publicity before the election, while other Carnegie Endowment trustees and Hiss backers, including his own attorneys, "advised him to go slow," as one of them recalled. By the end of September, however, Hiss had concluded that a public vindication was the only choice, both personally and professionally, "that if he failed to sue Chambers his reputation would be so irretrievably destroyed," as an associate put it, "that the Endowment would have to dispense with his services anyhow."

At the last moment before the filing William Marbury, an old friend and one of his lawyers in the suit, would interview both Alger and Priscilla at length. He warned, as Marbury remembered, "that if there were any skeletons in the closet of either one of them, they would certainly be discovered if suit were filed, and they both assured me there was no cause for worry on that count." Alger eventually went off to the office, leaving

Marbury alone with Priscilla, and in another hour of talk she supported their story without change, flatly denying any communist connections. Yet the attorney was troubled and found her "somewhat mystifying," as he recalled long afterward. "I got the impression that she felt in some way she was responsible for the troubles which had come to Alger."

The libel suit for $50,000 was filed on September 27, 1948. Offers of help, contributions to a legal fund, advice on strategy and tactics, rumors about Whittaker Chambers, including the gossip about homosexuality and insanity, poured into the Hiss camp. His lawyers prepared to expose the accuser's squalid past and destroy his dubious credibility in a series of probing depositions. To all this, Chambers himself reacted characteristically, with alternating despair and laconic menace. "I do not think Mr. Hiss will sue me for slander or libel," he had said on *Meet the Press*. At the same time, he signed over the Westminster farm entirely to Esther in a forlorn effort to make himself "judgment-proof." Now he responded to the litigation almost with bravado. "I welcome Mr. Hiss's daring suit. I do not minimize the audacity or the ferocity of the forces which work through him. But I do not believe that Mr. Hiss or anybody else can use the means of justice to defeat the ends of justice." Enraged, Hiss raised the damages to $75,000.

Richard Nixon returned to California early in October to begin a steady round of campaign speeches and to start a nine-state tour on behalf of the Dewey-Warren ticket. To the old service clubs in the twelfth district, to air force base audiences, to the statewide Chamber of Commerce he rehearsed the sequence of the August hearings, concluding with a sober, deep-voiced appeal to combat the "Communist Menace," as local papers now capitalized the specter. He advocated "a program of education in which the American people are told the truth about communism and the truth about our own system of government." As usual, his coverage was lavish. When he traveled outside the district or state, the *Whittier News* and other papers carried almost daily "progress reports" on the campaign, including Nixon's own observations on races and politics in other regions, virtual news dispatches in which he could be surprisingly candid and almost nonpartisan. From Minnesota he would telephone the *News* about a "promising" Democratic senatorial candidate who seemed a "likely winner," an energetic local politician named Hubert Humphrey.

His campaign trail continued to intersect curiously with the serpentine politics of the case. In part on Andrews's recommendation, he had been invited by the *Herald Tribune* to participate in the paper's prestigious forum in mid-October, asked to speak on "loyalty in government service" along with a list of older distinguished guests. "The *Herald Tribune* wants to have the honor of making you known to the country as an able human being," Helen Reid had written him, telling him in equal flattery afterward, "Your part on the panel was a very high spot and the verdict of many was that you carried away the laurels." Nixon had outlined to them his own proposed "Code" for HUAC hearings, guaranteeing any witness the right of a full defense, character witnesses, questions of his accuser, and freedom from television coverage, "an unreasonable burden," he thought.

The day before the congressman impressed the influential forum audience, Alger Hiss and one of his lawyers were meeting at the Harvard Club with one of Bert Andrews's fellow reporters on the *Herald Tribune* who was now quietly cooperating with the Hiss libel suit. "Andrews was on friendly terms with Mr. Nixon," the journalist told them according to the lawyer's memo of the meeting, and "Mr. Nixon had political ambitions and would do anything that Bert Andrews asked him to do." Whatever Andrews's past role in the case, the reporter explained, the paper was now seeking information on Chambers's mental health and Andrews could "suggest" the embarrassing findings to Nixon to warn off HUAC. "Nixon would have no objection to anything which might damage the reputation of the Committee if it enhanced the political future of Mr. Nixon," he said in describing the paper's and Bert Andrews's inner cynicism about the congressman they were publicly honoring at the same moment. Nothing would come of the search by reporters or Hiss investigators for some damning information on psychiatric problems or even asylum commitment in Whittaker Chambers's past. But the small Harvard Club intrigue revealed once more the layered politics of the affair, in which not all of Richard Nixon's hidden detractors were imaginary.

He went on to campaign for the national ticket elsewhere in New York, Illinois, Ohio, Minnesota, Missouri, the first modest version of what would be six national tours on behalf of other GOP candidates when his own election was not at stake, one of the monumental records of party loyalty in the century and a major asset in his own abiding popularity in the Republican rank and file. Returning to the basin for the last week of the race, Nixon made a point to go into the fourteenth congressional district to campaign, albeit in vain, against popular incumbent Democrat Helen Gahagan Douglas, a vocal opponent of HUAC and recognized future rival. "Everywhere I have been the Democrats seem to have given up hope on President Truman," he cheerfully told the *Whittier News*.

In private, however, he was exasperated about the GOP debacle he saw taking shape. On his return from one tour he met Arnold in Whittier, tossed his hat on a chair, and did not even stop to say hello. "We're losing this thing—we're throwing it away," the aide remembered him warning.

"I didn't find any Republican enthusiasm anywhere, and I was in some pretty conservative places. The party leaders and workers are rolling in complacency; they think it's in the bag. Well, it isn't, and I'm going to tell . . . Joe Martin and Charlie Halleck that it isn't, and they had better do something about it." Arnold also heard him mutter caustically afterward, "Earl Warren might as well be sitting on his butt in Sacramento for all the help he's given us." Later, embittered Warren supporters would accuse Nixon of virtually ignoring Dewey's running mate in his national appearances, and Nixon would say with a smile, "Those people in the Middle West would have thought I was unduly biased if I had built up a fellow Californian too much."

But it was the top of the ticket that was squandering the election, surrendering the initiative to an indomitable, pugnacious Truman, beset on the left by Henry Wallace's Progressives and in the South by Strom Thurmond's Dixiecrats as well as the GOP favorite. "No one gave Harry S Truman a chance except Harry S Truman," *Newsweek* said of 1948. Back in Albany in September, Dewey had brushed aside Nixon's advice to attack on the subversive issue, both as a matter of temperament and the backfire of the issue in 1944. "He wasn't going around looking under beds," a campaign aide would say. Dewey told supporters in one strategy session that he would take the issue of communists at home and abroad and "fleck it lightly." Meanwhile, the men from the Hotel Roosevelt prepared to take power. Foster Dulles, in Paris as part of a bipartisan UN mission, confidentially cabled Dewey the future President that he would do nothing at the UN "which might face you with the necessity of going to war to vindicate Security Council decision(s)." On the stump, Truman relisted what he called the "new GOP—Grand Old Platitudes." "Herbert Hoover once ran on the slogan " 'Two cars in every garage,' " the President reminded a typical East Coast urban audience. "The Republican candidate this year is running on the slogan 'Two families in every garage.' "

On election night Nixon paused in the twelfth to acknowledge his own victory. Foreordained, it was still impressive. He polled 141,887 to the Progressives' 19,664, his total more than double his 1946 vote and some 25,000 greater than the combined totals with Voorhis two years earlier. He drove with Pat and Bill Arnold from Whittier to GOP headquarters in downtown Los Angeles, where there was deepening gloom as workers listened to national returns. Arnold watched Nixon's dark "skepticism" as party leaders adopted the night's cliché of conservative radio commentators—"Wait 'til the farm vote comes in." By midnight on the coast, Harry Truman's victory seemed astonishing. The President would win a plurality of more than two million in the popular vote, carrying Los Angeles County and with it California. In the result, Nixon's own earlier victory in the primary loomed all the larger. "He escaped interment . . . last June," one

California magazine wrote of the representative from the twelfth, "well ahead of the surging pro-Truman tide."

In Truman's wake came renewed Democratic majorities in both the House and Senate, the fearsome CIO Political Action Committee seeing the election of the vast majority of congressional candidates it endorsed and supported. Afterward, the upset would be attributed to several factors— the Republican complacency Nixon clearly saw, Dewey's own relative aloofness and lack of personal appeal beside Truman the feisty country boy, and not least a popular reaction against the rightward lurch of the eightieth Congress, particularly in the urban centers and farm states providing the President's margin. "No searching analysis of voter motivation is necessary," wrote one historian, "to prove that Truman's supporters reaffirmed their loyalty to the New Deal." Few observers thought Dewey's exploitation of the communist issue would have made a significant difference. Truman's foreign policy was staunchly anti-Russian, and the Progressives on his left placed the President all the more in the middle of the political spectrum.

Yet Richard Nixon was never so sure that the unfinished inquisition against Hiss, his own unheeded advice to "attack," had not been crucial. "Probably because of the uncertain status of the Hiss-Chambers case, Dewey felt it was not proper to give too much prominence to the issue of communist infiltration," he wrote later, almost petulantly, about the election. "I found great interest in my audiences when I discussed the Bentley charges and our investigation of the Hiss case. But what I said, of course, received no more than local attention in the areas in which I spoke."

Dewey's disaster clear, they left the Los Angeles headquarters with the Drowns and went by for the late show at the Coconut Grove. Hildegarde the chanteuse was on stage, and she called up Nixon after Jack Drown told her that "a great congressman" was at one of the tables. Before the nightclub audience he used a line that would be part of a famous television speech only four years later, when Richard Nixon was on the national ticket himself. "I realize, folks, that most of you are Democrats having fun. I almost wish I were one of you," he deadpanned. "It just happens that I love Democrats. I even married one." A pause and then another small falsehood for effect: "I'd like to introduce my beautiful wife, Patricia Ryan, who was born on St. Patrick's Day, and who was a Democrat when I married her." The Coconut Grove resounded with applause and cheers.

"CERTAIN AREAS . . . BETTER LEFT UNEXPLORED"

They came back to a Washington where the political landscape was suddenly altered. Charlie Kersten had gone down to defeat in his blue-collar Milwaukee district. McDowell and others on HUAC were part of the GOP casualties. As if to compound the disgrace, two days after his own reelection Parnell Thomas was before a federal grand jury on charges of repeated payroll kickbacks, soon to be indicted and convicted. To no avail but much irony and the amusement of his victims, the chairman of the House Un-American Activities Committee no sooner took the stand himself than he claimed the Fifth Amendment. Even the redoubtable Stripling prepared to leave after the end of the year, forsaking the hunt for subversives for the more lucrative oil business back in Texas.

Unlike the dispirited Republicans, Harry Truman returned to the Capital the week after the election to a hero's welcome, more than a half million people lining the way from Union Station to the White House, as fire trucks formed triumphal arches with their ladders, bands played, and confetti rained on the smiling winner. The President would soon begin to refer to HUAC as that "defunct" committee. Down Pennsylvania Avenue in the Justice Department, Tom Clark prepared for the new Democratic congressional leadership a draft resolution to amend House rules and "terminate" HUAC. "Dewey's defeat and our loss of both houses of Congress," Nixon wrote glumly of his own predicament, "turned me overnight into a junior member of the minority party, a 'comer' with no place to go."

Out in Westminster, Whittaker Chambers had listened to the first returns put the Democrats ahead, told his wife tersely, "I think President Truman has won," and then gone to bed and "slept soundly." But he awoke to the old fearful air of persecution. "I took it for granted that the election results automatically meant that some way would be found to punish me for having tried to expose Alger Hiss," he wrote of the morning after, adding about his friends on the HUAC staff or at *Time*, "Scarcely anybody I knew supposed anything else."

It had been an eventful autumn for Chambers. Even after the filing of the libel suit, Chambers mused with Levine and others that Hiss would pull back, "postpone the action, on one pretext or another, until people lost interest," as Levine remembered the attitude of his friend, "who had no stomach for battle." Meanwhile, the informer denied under oath that the case involved actual espionage. Did he know of U.S. officials "furnishing information to any unauthorized sources?" he was asked after finally being called to the Manhattan grand jury on October 14.

"I can't say that I have specific knowledge of the transfer of information," Chambers answered.

Later in the session a juror asked again if he could give "one name of anybody . . . positively guilty of espionage against the United States?"

"Let me think a moment and I will try to answer that. I don't think so, but I would like to have an opportunity to answer you tomorrow more definitely. Let me think it over overnight."

And the next morning the sequel: "I do not believe I do know such a name."

The day Chambers testified, *The New York Times* had reported a Justice Department determination that evidence "so far available is deemed insufficient" for a perjury prosecution of either Hiss or Chambers for their testimony before HUAC. Justice would take "no action," said the *Times*, "unless new facts became available." Yet at the same moment, like a ghost in the rafters, Isaac Don Levine was telling a very different story, publishing in *Plain Talk* that October a detailed account of Whittaker Chambers telling his story "under a magnificent old tree" at Adolf Berle's estate in September 1939. "We learned that the business of filching from State Department and other secret government files had been well organized by the communist apparatus," Levine wrote, "that most of the important papers would be microfilmed and replaced before they had been missed, and that the material would be delivered to Soviet couriers, operating under aliases, for transmission to Russia." The article would go largely unnoticed in the preoccupation with the election and its aftermath.

Meanwhile, Alger Hiss and his attorneys plunged forward. They would not pursue the question of Chambers's putative homosexuality, Hiss afraid that the subject would expose his own stepson, Tim Hobson, to some retaliation. But their strategy was to impugn the character and background of the informer with any other means, and the attorneys set a series of depositions in Marbury's Baltimore office beginning November 4, two days after the election. The ground seemed fertile to establish some strange, perverse motive, perhaps obsession, in Chambers's acts. At one point a Hiss attorney, like Nixon and his cohorts, took the initiative of driving to Westminster, and asked a diffident Chambers to show him something Alger Hiss had given him in their alleged friendship. At the challenge Chambers turned on his heel, went straight to the farmhouse basement, and quickly returned. "With some ceremony," as his visitor described it, he then carefully unfolded for the lawyer a small, tattered piece of cloth. It was once part of the upholstery fabric of an old wing chair belonging to Alger, Chambers explained. He had cut it out, had it dry-cleaned, and kept it as a memento for thirteen years. The attorney went back to his client and described the scene. "My hair stood up," he told Hiss, who explained to friends later that the lawyer, after all, "had never heard of fetishes."

At the first deposition Chambers appeared with his own prestigious attorneys, assisted by a counsel for *Time*. But they could not prevent Marbury from excavating the witness's pungent history. Chambers had, he admitted, been forced to withdraw from Columbia, written pornographic poetry, stolen a roomful of books from the New York Public Library, made false affidavits and applications, lived in a New Orleans house next to a whore named "One-eyed Annie," and on and on. The next day, Marbury probed the relationship with Hiss. Angry and frustrated, Chambers felt in the deposition questioning, as he wrote later, "a tone of carefully modulated evil playing over me," the interrogation like "three boys in the schoolyard of my childhood, who had wet on a lollipop and then offered it to a fourth boy. Only now the lollipop was being offered to me." The accuser suddenly widened his charges. Hiss had "occasionally" given the communists "bits of information," he told them.

"You mean he handed you a document?" asked Marbury.

"I frequently read State Department documents in Mr. Hiss's house."

"Well, now, what kind of documents?" Marbury went on. And Chambers explained that "Mr. Hiss very often brought a briefcase with documents home, and I used to read those that were interesting." Most of them, accounts of trade agreements or reports from Vienna, "were not very interesting," Chambers continued, and "I would not say that I ever obtained any documents from him . . . I never transmitted a State Department document from Mr. Hiss to the Communist Party."

Both sides would see the brief incident as a warning to the other. At the close, Hiss's lawyers repeated their earlier demand for Chambers to produce any "letters or other communications" from Alger Hiss to prove his libelous statements. If he did have anything, Chambers's own attorney advised him, he "had better get it." But the witness thought the other side should be careful, too, that his reply about documents should have told them "that there were certain areas . . . better left unexplored." The depositions were adjourned for a week and a half, with the prospect of more hostile questioning ahead.

It was in this interval that Nixon came to see Whittaker Chambers again, stopping by Westminster with Pat and the girls on the way to visit Hannah and Frank at Menges Farm to the north. "He was in a mood of deep depression," Nixon remembered. With Truman's reelection, the informer was worried that the grand jury would now be allowed to lapse and that HUAC, even if it survived, would find "its powers . . . greatly weakened." At the same time, Nixon thought him relatively unconcerned about losing his *Time* position, or "everything he owned" if Hiss won the libel suit. Nor did the informer tell him about the embarrassment and pressure of the initial depositions, "how successfully," Chambers noted later, "the Hiss forces had turned the tables with the libel suit." Chambers would mention "in passing," Nixon recalled, that he was soon to resume the libel depositions, but the schedule seemed unimportant.

Whittaker Chambers tried to rally his old advocate to some action, though the congressman seemed resigned and now powerless. "There was nothing at all I could do about the election results," Nixon wrote almost apologetically of the visit. "My mind at that time turned to some purely personal matters." He had promised Pat once more the oft-postponed vacation and brought home tickets for a ten-day Carribbean cruise on the S.S. *Panama*, due to embark from New York November 17. "This time," he had assured his neglected wife, "absolutely nothing is going to interfere with our vacation."

Before they left the farm that day, however, Chambers would remember Nixon giving vent to his rancor. "I have a vivid picture of him, in the blackest hour of the Hiss case," Chambers wrote, "standing by the barn and saying in his quietly savage way (he is the kindest of men): 'If the American people understood the real character of Alger Hiss, they would boil him in oil.' " The wistful virulence was not enough. When the Nixons had gone, Chambers remained in the depths, virtually abandoned. "Some of my great friends had already taken refuge in aloofness," he thought. Now "I was sundered from the nation . . . I felt incredibly alone," he recalled, adding, "Richard Nixon was busy with his own affairs."

On November 12 a wildcat strike in the New York docks postponed indefinitely the sailing of the *Panama*, and Nixon settled into a comparatively quiet routine of congressional housekeeping to prepare for the next session. Two days later, Chambers sent a telegram to his wife's nephew in Brooklyn: ARRIVING AROUND ONE. PLEASE HAVE MY THINGS READY. WHIT. On the quiet autumn Sunday, following some of the old furtive precautions of his underground past, he wound his way to the one relative's house, then another, where, as they both testified later, the nephew pulled from an abandoned dumbwaiter shaft a bulky, cobweb-covered envelope Chambers had given him to hide more than a decade before. Left alone, Chambers swiftly examined the contents of the package, and then he closed it. "Good God," he muttered as the nephew came back into the room. "I did not know that this still existed."

On November 16 the libel depositions resumed, now with Esther Chambers. Tense, already fatigued from predawn farm chores, she described her own "friendship" with Priscilla Hiss but was visibly strained by Marbury's questioning. She returned the next day with her husband to complete her deposition and soon had burst into tears and cried for several minutes during an account of the family's poverty following Whittaker's defection. After lunch, Chambers himself was to be deposed again. But before the questions could begin, the witness produced "with a flourish," as it seemed to Marbury, a pile of documents.

"I was particularly anxious, for reasons of friendship, and because Mr.

Hiss is one of the most brilliant young men in the country, not to do injury more than necessary to Mr. Hiss," Chambers began a statement. But in looking for papers "put by" and thought destroyed, he had discovered these documents, which "reveal a kind of activity, the revelation of which is somewhat different from anything I have testified about before." He had gone through "turmoil," Chambers said, about whether to present the papers in evidence, but his lawyers advised that "I practically had no other choice." Later, Chambers would write that while Esther testified the day before, he had been in "agony," dissuaded from suicide only by "a sense of the weight of God's purpose laid upon me." He would also claim afterward—sharing his wrath with Congressman Nixon—that he had been provoked to reveal the documents by the harsh questioning of Esther by Hiss's lawyers. Yet he had gone for the envelope two days before she was deposed, had already shown the papers to his attorneys, already held the fateful package under his arm that morning as he waited in Marbury's outer office while his wife wept inside.

As the Chambers attorneys marked and numbered each exhibit and a photostatic copy, one of them read for identification a few words at the beginning and end of each set of papers, words that would soon figuratively resound in Richard Nixon's rise—"Paris: To the Secretary of State, Strictly Confidential . . . signed Bullitt; Rome: To the Secretary of State, I learn in strictest confidence . . . signed Phillips; Vienna, To the Secretary of State . . ." The litany continued numbingly. Stunned, William Marbury stared at the table, recognized among the pile of mostly typed documents some small notes in Alger Hiss's handwriting, and realized, as he wrote later, "the devastating effect." Bill Marbury had gone on a "fishing expedition," one of his Baltimore friends would quip in a Maryland twang, "and, by God, he caught the whole damn sea bottom."

Chambers then launched into a description of the espionage arrangement with the Soviets, an account he would repeat often with varying detail. The Russians wanted intelligence and the American party was ready to oblige, both for proletarian loyalty and needed subsidies. In the late summer or early fall of 1937 he and Hiss had gone to a Brooklyn movie. They waited on a lobby bench on the mezzanine and soon met coming out of the darkened theater a short, stocky, red-haired man named Boris Bykov, a Russian colonel in finely tailored suits who was the *rezident*, chief of Soviet intelligence in the United States. Conversing in German with Chambers translating, the skittish Bykov led them on a winding route by foot and subway to a Chinatown restaurant, where he asked Alger Hiss to procure documents, and Hiss agreed.

"What?" exclaimed Marbury, voicing the incredulity of a generation.

"Mr. Hiss agreed," Chambers said again, now in full command.

Bykov had wanted Donald Hiss to do it, too, Chambers went on, but Alger was not certain his brother was "sufficiently developed yet" and Donald never did hand over papers. As it was, Alger brought home to Georgetown "a fairly consistent flow of such material as we have before us here." Priscilla typed most of them. "It became a function for her," Chambers explained, "and helped to solve the problem of Mrs. Hiss's longing for activity, that is, communist activity." Sometimes there was no chance to type copies; hence the short handwritten notes by Alger. "Would you like to ask questions at that point?" Chambers gloated. Marbury floundered through some perfunctory testimony on Chambers's motives and then adjourned, ending what a Hiss biographer would call "that appalling day in November." In his apparent shock, the lawyer took photostatic copies of the documents but did not question where or how Chambers had retrieved them. He did not ask if there were more.

An investigator for the Chambers attorneys came to their office after the deposition and found "almost total confusion" as they examined closely their client's revelation. Across Baltimore at Marbury's office the impact was all the greater. Chambers had handed over sixty-five single-spaced typed pages containing word-for-word copies or summaries of State Department cables and other documents, along with one War Department memorandum and the four small notes in Alger Hiss's handwriting. Ranging over a period from January to April 1938, the documents dealt with military, diplomatic, and political developments in the prewar crisis. Covering both Europe and the Far East, the formulation of U.S. policy as well as intelligence and analysis on the intentions of other powers, much of the material had been designated in the originals as "CONFIDENTIAL" or "STRICTLY CONFIDENTIAL," among the higher security classifications of the time. The originals would show, too, that the author of the summaries had sometimes selected and precisely excerpted from a longer text only those items of military significance. Moreover, and in a sense most disturbing to some of Hiss's attorneys, the typed summaries resembled in format and even language the small notes penciled by Alger Hiss. "*March 3* Johnson U.S. chargé at London cabled that . . . ," read a typical note. The typed summaries took a parallel form: "*Feb. 14* Gilbert, U.S. chargé at Berlin, cabled . . ." or "*Feb. 17*, Phillips cabled from Rome that Ciano . . ."

Shown the documents, Hiss confirmed that at least three of the small notes seemed to be in his handwriting, chits he may have made routinely for his own use or to brief his superior, Francis Sayre, and then thrown away. He had never seen the typewritten papers, he told Marbury, though the subject matter was typical of material crossing his desk in the late 1930s. Hiss could not imagine how Whittaker Chambers came to have all this. In that case, Marbury told him, "he could have nothing to lose by turning the papers over to the Department of Justice." Hiss agreed, and Marbury on November 19 handed over photostatic copies to a Justice Department aide. Still ostensibly secret but known by several people, the sensational documents—or at least knowledge of their existence—would now begin to wind back toward Richard Nixon.

Four days after receiving the documents, Justice asked the FBI to take up a fresh investigation of Whittaker Chambers. After the informer's flat denial of espionage to the grand jury in October, Justice "now wants to institute perjury charges against Chambers," as an FBI report put it. "Interesting," noted Hoover at the bottom, "but I wonder why they don't move against Hiss also." Meanwhile, the Bureau was obtaining photostats of the papers, while learning from Chambers's attorneys something of the story about Colonel Bykov and the cache of secrets hidden in a Brooklyn dumbwaiter as insurance against retaliation when Chambers defected. Their client, the lawyers told the FBI, had hestitated retrieving his "life preserver," and still had "a sincere affection" for Alger Hiss.

William Marbury would scarcely agree. Despite Hiss's adamant denials, the lawyer was certain his client would be prosecuted. At lunch on November 28 with both Alger and Priscilla, he warned them an indictment of Alger seemed "quite likely" and he might even be convicted. "Priscilla looked stunned," Marbury recalled—"went into a panic," her husband himself described it later—though Alger was confident "truth would prevail" in an orderly judicial process. Marbury told them to locate old papers typed on whatever typewriter they used at home in 1938, "since this would be the best possible way," he thought, "of establishing that Chambers was lying."

The dock strike over, the *Panama* was due to sail from New York Thursday afternoon December 2, and Nixon planned to spend his last two days in the office handling correspondence. The morning of December 1, Justice Department officials met secretly to go over the case, and asked the FBI to question Chambers about "any other documents that he might have which are governmental in character." The request percolated through the bureaucracy, and agents made plans to see the informer two days later. But by then, all of them—the vacationing congressman, the Bureau, Justice, and the two protagonists—would be overtaken by a bizarre series of events. It began, as usual, with leaks.

That same morning of the first, the *Washington Post*'s Jerry Klutz, in his much-read column, "The Federal Diary," broke the uneasy silence that had fallen over the libel suit. "Since Alger Hiss sued Whittaker Chambers for libel, attorneys for both men have been taking depositions," Klutz reported. He then added without further elaboration or attribution, "Some very startling information on who is a liar is reported to have been uncovered." In its own early edition that day, however, the *Washington Daily News* carried a United Press story that contradicted the Klutz item. "The Justice Department investigation of the Hiss-Chambers affair is about to die for lack of evidence, it was disclosed today," the dispatch began. "Unless something new turned up soon, officials said, there would be little use going to a grand jury with the information obtained so far."

Whether the UP story was intended as some bromide, or whether—more likely in the politics of press and government—both articles were intended to flush the Baltimore documents, would never be clear. In either event, the effect was swift. Seeing the articles as more proof that HUAC was "going down the drain," as he put it, Stripling anxiously called Nixon. After some discussion, Nixon in turn telephoned Bert Andrews, who thought the UP item "a deliberate leak" from Justice and agreed to sound out the stories.

Andrews assigned his *Herald Tribune* assistant to query Justice, where an official commented nervously, "I can't answer any questions about the Hiss-Chambers case. Number one—this is too hot. Number two—I just can't say anything about it." At a desk nearby, Andrews himself methodically called a list of potential sources. The Baltimore libel judge, Alger Hiss, and Chambers's attorney all blandly refused any statement. William Marbury had called Justice himself about the UP story and been told to "pay no attention to it," that an "announcement" was imminent, heightening his fears the government would go after Hiss as well as Chambers. Now Marbury was snappish when Andrews called him and asked if the libel depositions and evidence were still with the Baltimore court. "The answer to that is no," the Hiss lawyer had barked back. And finally Chambers, Buddha-like but portentous in tone, had added to Andrews's suspicion with his own *pro forma* refusal to comment. "Andrews at once drew the proper journalistic inference that if nobody would talk about what had happened in the libel suit," the informer wrote afterward, "something had happened."

Meanwhile, Nixon and Stripling were being supplied far more than broad hints about the new "startling information." Nicholas Vazzana was a young attorney in private practice who had been hired as an investigator for the *Time* magazine lawyer assigned to aid Chambers, and had rummaged through the HUAC files and met Stripling as part of his job. Most important, Vazzana was there in the office of Chambers's lawyers just after the November 17 deposition when they all excitedly examined the Baltimore documents. Now on the same Wednesday morning, Vazzana had seen the United Press report and was alarmed and frustrated at the seeming Justice cover-up, as he told the story later. Though under the same injunction as the other attorneys not to discuss the case, he went to Stripling's office to revive somehow the drooping HUAC. Vazzana's historic appearance that day on Capitol Hill would be another of the affair's small, enduring mysteries. "I just didn't want to see the case die," he would say, insisting he went to Stripling on his own initiative. Others saw his presence as part of a deliberate scheme by Chambers and *Time*. "Through a lawyer named Vazzano [*sic*]," Marbury would write in a solemn law review history of the libel suit, "he [Chambers] dropped a hint . . . that he had some valuable information."

Seeing Stripling, Vazzana was less than subtle. The HUAC staff chief thought "he seemed unusually pleased with himself," and asked why. "Can't talk or I might be held in contempt of court," Vazzana replied. Stripling took the almost burlesque cue—"Something," he wrote later, "prompted me to keep him around the premises"—and hurried Vazzana off to "say hello" to Nixon, hoping the congressman could elicit the information.

They sat in the attic office, and after awkward small talk Stripling mentioned that Vazzana was privy to some interesting new facts. Nixon was naturally eager to know whatever he could tell them. "I can't discuss it with either of you," the investigator began. "But I suppose I can tell you it has something to do with the Hiss-Chambers libel suit and it concerns documents." He and Nixon were not able, Stripling recalled, "to maintain our poker faces when he mentioned 'documents.' " Then, for over two hours, as Nixon and Stripling showered him with questions, Vazzana gradually revealed much of the story of the November 17 deposition and the dramatic disclosure of sixty-five pages from secret documents alongside memos in Hiss's handwriting. "I am under an admonition from the Justice Department not to reveal their actual contents," he said of the documents. But there was no question of apparent espionage.

When he had finished, Richard Nixon was obviously agitated. "Do you think I should still go on vacation?" he anxiously asked Vazzana. "That's your decision, Mr. Nixon," the lawyer told the ruffled politician, "not mine."

Afterward, Nixon went off to lunch with Stripling at Ted Lewis's Restaurant near the Capitol, visibly "nervous and highly irritable," as the HUAC aide described him at the moment. It was all clearly a Chambers plant to give them a chance to "break" the case once and for all, Stripling thought, and they had to move fast. They should drive to Westminster and see Chambers immediately. But Richard Nixon, who had restlessly gone to the farm three times in one August week, who had called or summoned Whittaker Chambers at so many turns, was now sullen and inert. Brooding over the election and his seemingly stalled rise, dismayed that after all his courtship Chambers had not given the documents to him, not least torn between ambition and the vacation that had come to mean much to his marriage, he was trapped, and furious. "I'm so goddamned sick and tired of this case I don't want to hear any more about it," he exploded at Stripling. "And I'm going to Panama. And the hell with it, and you, and the whole damned business."

Stripling tried to tell him again the documents would break open the whole affair, and the credit would be his alone. Mundt was still basking in his Senate victory in South Dakota, McDowell defeated, Thomas about to stand trial. But at that Nixon "cussed me out real good," Stripling remembered, and the staff man sat there—like so many other aides after him—silently listening to the harangue, waiting for the storm to pass and the old calculation to return. "Hell, I'm not going to Westminster. I'm going to Panama," he told Stripling, "and you can do what you damn want to, but I'm through with it." They strode back to the House Office Building in tense silence.

Nixon returned to his office only to find Bert Andrews, who now recounted the sum of his phone calls with an enthusiasm that wrenched the congressman all the more. "I think Chambers produced something important at the Baltimore hearing. I have a hunch that he may have another ace in the hole," the reporter told him. "Why don't you try to find out?" Now with a peer and influential outsider, Nixon was no longer abusive, though still irritable and petulant, "with the rueful air of a man who has a thousand things to do before leaving on a trip," thought Andrews. Finally, he agreed to see Chambers, and Andrews left. Not long afterward, Stripling called for one last request. "Goddamn it," Nixon shouted into the phone, "if it'll shut your mouth, I'll go." Later, when Nixon recorded his own version of the eventful day, all of the pulsing reality—Andrews's calls and visit, Vazzana's vital intelligence, Stripling's urging, especially his own rancor—had disappeared. "Playing a long hunch," he wrote in *Six Crises*, "I suggested to Stripling that we drive to Westminster at once and talk to Chambers."

They found Chambers in a farmer's dirty overalls, the old house smelling "of another generation," Stripling recalled. "A stuffed raven stared at us from a wall. An old German Bible lay opened on the table." They spoke briefly about the election, "the way men talk," one of them said, "when they are trying to avoid a topic." Stripling then pulled out a crumpled copy of the *Washington Post* column, and when Chambers had read it, Nixon handed him a clip of the other UP story. Chambers gazed out the window in prolonged silence, saying finally, "That is what I have been afraid of."

"I know why you're here," he said suddenly, turning to Stripling.

Nixon stepped in impatiently. "You don't have to go into details. Just answer this: did you drop a bombshell in Baltimore not long ago?" Chambers replied with a thin smile, "Yes, I did," and told them he had produced "some new evidence . . . documentary evidence" in depositions two weeks earlier. It was "so important" the lawyers had turned it over to the Justice Department, which had forbidden them to discuss the case. "So I can't tell you what was in the documents. I will only say that they were a real bombshell," he said, adding again, smiling, "But the first one was nothing compared to the second."

Nixon asked if Justice had the only copy of the documents. "No, I wouldn't be that foolish," Chambers replied. There were photostatic copies, and "another bombshell if they try to suppress this one."

"I'm here for that second one," Nixon said solemnly.

Chambers only shook his head, though "not in an unfriendly manner," Stripling remembered. "You keep that second bombshell, don't give it to anybody except the Committee," Nixon told him. All the while, as Chambers noted, Stripling "never took his eyes off mine," measuring every reaction.

Chambers then began to speak quietly, almost confessionally, about his motives in bringing the new evidence. "You will understand this," he said, looking at Nixon, the fellow Quaker.

"When I testified before the Committee last August I wanted to expose the communist conspiracy, but I did not want to destroy the humans involved. I sat for a whole day in meditation . . .

"But after my testimony they spread stories that I was insane and that I was a pervert.

"Then they called in my wife and were very tough with her. It made me angry. I know as a Quaker I must never act in anger. So I sat another day, and I came to the conclusion that the only thing to do was to tell everything I knew, to spare no one. . . . We've got to know what we're confronted with in this country."

Nixon and Stripling were mute before the testimony, and then as they rose to go, Chambers returned to a more worldly matter. "Do you know of any very good photographic technicians?" he asked Stripling.

"Sure, we've got one on our staff."

"But the man I want must be very, very good."

"He's good."

"I'll let you know," Chambers said softly, and they left in the darkness.

"Well, what do you think he's got?" Nixon asked the aide as they drove away. "He doesn't know what he has," Stripling answered, "but whatever he has, it'll blow the dome off the Capitol. Certainly you're not going to Panama now?"

"I don't think he's got a damned thing," Nixon said sarcastically. "I'm going right ahead with my plans." He would note later that "under the circumstances I wondered whether I shouldn't postpone my vacation" and then added in candor, "But I didn't have the heart to tell Pat the bad news."

The tension easing during the two-hour drive back to Washington, he told Stripling obliquely about the "predicament" with his wife and promised he could fly back from Panama if it proved necessary. They left each other at Stripling's Committee office, apparently nothing more to be done until Nixon sailed back from the Canal Zone nearly three weeks later.

From his attic office about 10:00 P.M. Nixon now telephoned Bert Andrews and asked him to come over right away. Andrews agreed and took a taxi. But just before or after calling Andrews—and whether alone or with Stripling would never be clear—Richard Nixon placed an extraordinary call to the FBI.

Reaching Louis Nichols at home, he told him "on a strictly personal and highly confidential basis," as the agent recorded it, that he was going to Panama, would be at the Tivoli Hotel, planned to return on December 15, and three days later would resume hearings on the Hiss-Chambers case. He "understood," Nixon said, "that the Department of Justice told the FBI that there was no violation involved and that consequently no further action was to be undertaken by the FBI." But now Nixon knew that "Chambers recently let go and turned in some highly incriminating documentary evidence typed by Mrs. Hiss, turned over by Hiss to Chambers, and by Chambers ultimately to the Russians." He knew, too, if the FBI did not, that Justice had these documents. Further, "Chambers did not tell the FBI everything he knew and as a matter of fact still has other documents and material that substantiate and vindicate his position which have up to this time not become publicly known."

He was going to subpoena "these documents" at the December 18 hearings, Nixon told Nichols, and this "strictly personal and highly confidential [call] was merely to apprise the Bureau so that the FBI would not be caught off base." He was handling all this, Nixon emphasized, "so that there will be no criticism to [sic] the FBI." "He particularly urged," Nichols noted, "that we do nothing about the information which he has just furnished as he [Nixon] feels the statute of limitations has run out." They must "not tell the attorney general," the congressman told him, since Clark would only try to block the Committee. Significantly, Nichols's report added, "He [Nixon] also asked that the Bureau not look for the documents themselves."

Under the circumstances his call to Nichols was audacious, even fool-hardy. No longer the annoyed skeptic he had been through the day with Stripling, he was now currying Hoover "so the FBI would not be caught off base," instructing them to mislead or ignore the attorney general, asking the government's criminal investigative agency "not to look" for espionage evidence Nixon himself intended to exploit publicly a few weeks later. But in yet another decisive small twist in the case, Louis Nichols now ended his report with a recommendation, in effect, to honor the congress-man's remarkable request. "It looks like the only thing we could do would possibly be to inquire . . . if . . . [Justice] has any documentary evidence without revealing the reason for our inquiry or our source," he wrote. "Do so & let me know the result," Hoover penned at the bottom of the memo. Though expressly warned of Chambers's further evidence, the FBI would hold back, giving Richard Nixon a historic opportunity.

One more intervention rescued him that night from his own folly and hesitation. Soon after the call to Nichols, Bert Andrews arrived at the attic, and Nixon poured out the story of the trip to Westminster, though not the crucial inside details supplied by Vazzana that morning. "You were too nice to Chambers," Andrews chided. "Did you just ask for anything he had? Or did you slap a subpoena on him?" Nixon meekly admitted he "hadn't really thought of a subpoena." Once again tutor and goad, Andrews was insistent. "Look, before you leave town get hold of Bob Stripling. Tell him to serve a blanket subpoena on Chambers to produce *anything* and *everything* he still has in his possession. He couldn't possibly be held in contempt for giving you documents if he has any that haven't been sub-poenaed by the court."

Andrews left soon after midnight and Nixon remained an hour or so, brooding about the day. "I could not understand why Chambers would have withheld any important information from the committee," he wrote, recording his lingering sense of personal betrayal by the unpredictable figure who had become so central in his career. But he was also worried, as always, that the new evidence Vazzana described might somehow prove bogus, that the official hiatus and silence since November was not cover-up or common bureaucratic delay but some trap set by the administration. "I could not help thinking there was some good reason the Justice Department was acting this way," he wrote later. Eventually, he subdued the pique and suspicion and decided on an immediate subpoena. Stripling could indeed, as they had discussed, summon him back dramatically for the results. "I spent much of that night trying to decide whether to issue a subpoena for the rest of Chambers's material" is how he told the story afterward, omitting the Andrews and Nichols conversations. By the time he left the House Office Building between one and two o'clock in the morning he was once more exuberant at the prospect of a new resurgence and celebrity in the case.

Working through the night to provide offices for the new members the next day, the House doorkeeper, William "Fishbait" Miller, met Nixon coming down the darkened corridor. The congressman was "in high spirits" and "on needles to get away," Miller later said of the incident, "but . . . so delighted with something that he had to share it." Nixon had cheerfully asked him, "You are working very late—or early—aren't you?" Miller told him about the new office assignments. "What about you, Mr. Nixon, are you just ending your day or beginning your day?" He thought the usually serious young congressman looked "very elated and keyed up, as if he were dancing on wires. Even his eyes were dancing." And Nixon had answered, "I'm going to get on a steamship and you will be reading about it. I'm going out to sea and they are going to send for me. You'll understand when I get back, Fishbait."

As he watched Nixon hurry down the corridor, Miller mused on his phenomenal importance as a freshman in the House. "Thank you very much, Mr. Nixon. Have a good trip," he called after him.

"What the hell is he talking about?" the doorkeeper had muttered to himself as Nixon disappeared. "I realized that I had been in on the beginning of something most peculiar," Miller wrote in his memoirs, "but I didn't know what at the time."

"THE GREATEST TREASON CONSPIRACY IN THIS NATION'S HISTORY"

Before dawn Nixon telephoned Stripling, asking to meet him at the HUAC office at 7:15 A.M. to allow the Nixons to make an 8:00 A.M. train for New York. But the aide was caught in traffic and arrived too late. Waiting for Stripling was a note from the congressman parroting Andrews the night before: "It is highly important you serve subpoenas [sic] on Chambers for everything he has. I mean *everything*." Having decided to act on his own whatever Nixon did, Stripling was already preparing a comprehensive *subpoena duces tecum*, to be signed by House Speaker Joe Martin, when Nixon telephoned from Union Station a few blocks away to check on the action. He was calling, he told him, just to make sure Stripling had gotten the note. Within the hour, Nixon had called once again, this time en route by the train's radio telephone. Nervously, he wanted to make sure no one else on the Committee broke the new material. "Get what you can from him and sit tight," he said, trying to rein in Stripling, adding, "I'll be back the day after Christmas," a week later than he had secretly assured Nichols and the FBI he would reopen hearings.

With obvious anguish and reluctance, like a star being taken from the game, Richard Nixon shouted orders and encouragement over his shoulder as events receded from his control, or so it seemed. Later, Levine and others, not least the HUAC staff, thought he had become strangely passive, or cynically fled the scene to let Stripling bear the onus if Chambers proved at last a fraud. But if HUAC, already threatened with extinction by Truman's victory, was now to be betrayed by its preeminent witness, Nixon's voyage to Panama was unlikely to save him from the humiliation. What all the explanations before and after did not reckon with, however, was the most decisive factor of all—his personal life. It was one of the few—and last—instances of Nixon allowing family concerns to override political considerations. In the end, as he testily explained to Stripling, for better or worse he had to make this vacation for his wife.

As always, Nixon was hardly alone in either calculation or turmoil. At the hour his train clacked toward New York, Bert Andrews was acting on the midnight meeting with Nixon to cable John Foster Dulles in Paris: "NEW INFORMATION MAKES ME STRONGLY BELIEVE YOU SHOULD PERSONALLY GET OFF HOOK ON OUR ENDOWMENT FRIEND." An alarmed Dulles could or would do little from afar without first quietly lobbying his Carnegie colleagues. But the wire from a mutual friend and press contact would come as a further confidence and warning from young Dick Nixon and counted as another shrewd political gesture.

The night before in Westminster, Chambers had mentioned he was coming to Washington to testify on an unrelated matter before a State Department loyalty board. Stripling now telephoned him to stop by the HUAC offices, just catching the informer, his overcoat already on, as he stood uncertainly in the farmhouse kitchen. Chambers was pondering the next act in his drama, always knowing well ahead what he would do, as Stripling told the FBI.

He had indeed preserved a second "bombshell." Beyond the Baltimore documents he had held back from everyone, hidden in his bedroom, two strips of developed microfilm, plus three small cans containing rolls of yet undeveloped film, and a single typewritten note. On Thanksgiving weekend, a week after producing the other documents, he had flourished the microfilm before friends in New York, calling it "the clinching evidence," and telling them, "This will vindicate me." Then he seemed exhilarated and almost playful, remembered one of his friends, "like a kid planning something mischievous." By the morning of December 2, Chambers had all but decided to give the rolls to HUAC to counter the administration cover-up or retaliation he saw in the wake of the Baltimore documents. "I concluded," he later wrote of his suspicions, "that there were powerful forces within the government to whom such information . . . was extremely unwelcome . . . [and] this was why . . . the House Committee . . . had at last to force the indispensable disclosure."

Now clearly anticipating some Committee action, worried, too, as he wrote, that Hiss "investigators" might "ransack" the house, he hung up from Stripling and decided on a more picturesque hiding place for his remaining secrets. He cut off the top of a pumpkin, scooped out the pulp and seeds, wrapped the microfilm in waxed paper, and placed it inside, putting the top back on and carrying the pumpkin to the edge of his patch. "The whole art of concealment," he proudly explained afterward, "lay in its complete naturalness and its complete unexpectedness."

Early that afternoon, as Dick and Pat were boarding the S.S. *Panama*, Chambers stopped by HUAC, and Stripling, reaching out to shake hands like a practiced process server, held the subpoena half hidden and pressed it into Chambers's pudgy palm. He was to deliver "all paper, documents and other matter" concerning any of the people or events mentioned in the recent hearings. Stripling remembered him, like most subjects of a summons, looking back "oddly for a moment," then shrugging and breathing a sigh. "All right, I'll turn the information over to you. It's at my home."

As an earnest of what he already intended, the informer handed Stripling the small typewritten note he had withheld along with the film. Dated "3/4/38" it read: "Karl—If you have given up playing around with my girlfriend, she wishes you would take your stuff out of her closet, so she can use it for her clothes instead of yours! [signed] H." Whether the relic of some extramarital affair or, as Chambers vaguely claimed, a cryptic reference to moving a spy's photographic equipment from some apartment, the "H" apparently never denoted Hiss, and the note figured no more in the case. But now Chambers told Stripling gravely he should "attempt to locate the typewriter from which this note was typed," and the mysterious tidbit whetted HUAC staff appetites all the more. They waited what Stripling felt "an eternity" until Chambers completed his testimony elsewhere and returned to Capitol Hill around five-thirty. Then Donald Appell and William Wheeler drove him to Baltimore, where he picked up his own car, and the investigators and Chambers drove in tandem to Westminster.

There remained one more preliminary. Learning from Stripling that the subpoena was served and the delivery in process, Andrews limbered up for the breaking story. Late that Thursday the reporter sent a radiogram to Nixon aboard the *Panama*, repeating now for the record what they both already knew twenty-four hours earlier, but giving Nixon a chance to husband the exposé and make "news" even from shipboard off the Atlantic coast. The message would provide, too, the beginning of the justification Nixon would need as well with his wife. Andrews radioed:

INFORMATION HERE IS THAT HISS-CHAMBERS CASE HAS PRO-
DUCED NEW BOMBSHELL. CHAMBERS HAS BEEN QUESTIONED
IN LIBEL SUIT BROUGHT BY HISS. INDICATIONS ARE THAT
CHAMBERS HAD PRODUCED NEW EVIDENCE. ALL CONCERNED
ARE SILENT. HOWEVER, JUSTICE DEPARTMENT PRACTICALLY
CONFIRMS INDICATIONS, SAYING CASE TOO HOT FOR COM-
MENT. INFERENCE IS NEW INFORMATION IN JUSTICE DEPART-
MENT HANDS. MAY LEAD TO REOPENING OF NEW YORK GRAND
JURY'S INQUIRY AND MORE INTENSIVE PERJURY INQUIRY
HERE. IN VIEW YOUR COMMITTEE'S ROLE, CAN YOU TELL ME
WHETHER COMMITTEE WILL REOPEN ITS INVESTIGATION.
ALSO WHO WILL BE CALLED AND WHEN. ANY OTHER DETAILS
APPRECIATED. PLEASE RUSH ANSWER COLLECT.

Chambers and the aides drove slowly to Westminster. He had told them on the trip to Baltimore that the prize was hidden microfilm. At the farm, the informer struck out first into the inky darkness toward the patch, but soon turned around, muttering, "I can't see." He walked back to the farmhouse kitchen, reassuring Esther about the extra headlights in the driveway and with Appell and Wheeler watchfully trailing him. Chambers then switched on some dim yard lights and led the two investigators into the shadowy patch. He picked up one pumpkin, dropped it, then another. Lifting off the severed top, he reached in and brought out the rolls of developed film and the small wrapped cylinders. He turned to Appell. "I think this is what you're looking for." In the cold, still Maryland countryside it was, as Alistair Cooke wrote later, "the final bathos to the Committee's gift for melodrama."

The two square-jawed aides were aghast at the scene. "What is this, Dick Tracy?" one of them said. "I don't think this one is any good," Chambers told them about one of the little tubes whose cap was damaged. "I think the film inside has been light struck." They asked, still puzzled, "Is that all?" According to his own account and Stripling's, Chambers nodded, "That is all," and they walked out of the patch. But before the two investigators hurriedly left, Chambers also gave them photostats of the Baltimore documents, including a memorandum written on yellow foolscap by Harry Dexter White. On their return Appell and Wheeler parked briefly at the first well-lighted stop in Westminster, a place called the American Café, where they marked the small cylinders for identification. It was nearly midnight when they reached the outskirts of the city, and Appell cautiously took the film and photostats home overnight, carefully hiding them, as he later told the FBI, in the handkerchief drawer of his bureau.

Whittaker Chambers watched them go and professed afterward a weary indifference to the show he had staged. "I tossed away the top," he wrote casually of his famous pumpkin. But top and pumpkin were neatly together when a news photographer appeared some time later after the discovery was a national sensation. Like Appell and Wheeler, the newsmen from the city never noted that Westminster and Carroll County, Maryland, had experienced killing frosts almost continually since mid-October. More than four inches of cold rain and snow had softened and rotted the season's pumpkins left on the vine, making it impossible to hollow them out. Like so much else in the case, the hiding place for what became known as the Pumpkin Papers was artful but hardly "natural."

Friday morning, December 3, Richard Nixon was settling into shipboard routine on the *Panama* when Andrews's wireless arrived. Joining in the subterfuge he radioed back: "HAVE ADVISED STRIPLING TO INVESTIGATE AND ADVISE ME REGARDING NEW HEARINGS. WILL REOPEN HEARINGS IF NECESSARY TO PREVENT JUSTICE DEPARTMENT COVER-UP. WILL ADVISE DATE, WITNESSES, ETC., UPON HEARING FROM STRIPLING."

Back at the Capitol, Stripling was meeting Appell and Wheeler, and after trying in vain to read the 35mm microfilm merely by holding it to the light, he sent the assistants off to bring back an enlarger. Still unable to read anything in the daylight-filled HUAC chamber, they crowded into a tiny windowless men's room nearby, locked the door, placed the enlarger atop a sink, plugged it in and turned out the lights. Stripling unrolled the developed film and never forgot the words that leapt out from the stamped and numbered official cable: "DEPARTMENT OF STATE/STRICTLY CONFIDENTIAL."

Stripling now dispatched Wheeler to secure blowups of the developed film, and Appell to have the unexposed rolls processed by a trusted photographer they knew at the Veterans Administration. As the HUAC staff worked feverishly over their find, Justice announced blandly that "new evidence" would be placed before the New York grand jury—a reference to the Baltimore documents. Anticipating a great furor with the news of the Pumpkin Papers as well, Stripling now called Andrews to the Committee office, and the two fired off successive radiograms to Nixon. From what Stripling had already seen of the microfilm documents, HUAC would soon be locked in a political and press battle with the administration, and under mounting pressure to give up the evidence to the FBI. The Nixons were dining at the captain's table on the *Panama* with two other congressmen Friday evening when the purser brought in Stripling's message: "SEC-

OND BOMBSHELL OBTAINED BY SUBPOENA 1 A.M. FRIDAY. CASE CLINCHED. IN-
FORMATION AMAZING. HEAT IS ON FROM PRESS AND OTHER PLACES. IMMEDIATE
ACTION APPEARS NECESSARY. CAN YOU POSSIBLY GET BACK?"

Nixon read the wireless aloud to the curious table. Smiling gamely but
in obvious diappointment, Pat "threw up her hands," as he remembered,
and said to the company, "Here we go again."

When Stripling had briefed Andrews on the apparent gravity of the
microfilm as well as the copies of the Baltimore documents, the reporter
drafted his own characteristic message to the *Panama*, which Nixon received
hours later.

> DOCUMENTS INCREDIBLY HOT. LINK TO HISS SEEMS CERTAIN.
> LINK TO OTHERS INEVITABLE. RESULTS SHOULD RESTORE
> FAITH IN NEED FOR COMMITTEE IF NOT SOME MEMBERS. NEW
> YORK JURY MEETS WEDNESDAY. COULD YOU ARRIVE TUESDAY
> AND GET A DAY'S JUMP ON GRAND JURY. IF NOT, HOLD HEAR-
> ING EARLY WEDNESDAY. MY LIBERAL FRIENDS DON'T LOVE
> ME NO MORE. NOR YOU. BUT FACTS ARE FACTS AND THESE
> ARE DYNAMITE. HISS'S WRITING IDENTIFIED ON THREE DOC-
> UMENTS. NOT PROOF HE GAVE THEM TO CHAMBERS BUT
> HIGHLY SIGNIFICANT. STRIPLING SAYS CAN PROVE WHO GAVE
> THEM TO CHAMBERS. LOVE TO PAT. [SIGNED] VACATION-
> SPOILER ANDREWS.

Only when Appell and Wheeler returned to the offices after 6:00 P.M.
Friday did Stripling and the others see the full dimension of their haul.
They brought back photos of fifty-eight pages of State Department memoranda and cables from Chambers's previously developed strips and sev-
enty-eight pages of assorted Navy Department documents from the
unprocessed rolls, one of which, as the informer warned, was light-struck
and blank. That evening Stripling proudly called in a commercial photographer to take their portrait grouped about the rolls of microfilm and copies
arrayed on a table, Stripling himself unrolling some film, all peering intently, like hunters around a rare carcass.

Later that night of December 3, the FBI finally interviewed Whittaker
Chambers in Baltimore, a day too late for the microfilm but now beginning
to piece together the rest of his story. The "bulk" of the documents,
Chambers told them, had been turned over either by Alger Hiss or another
official at State, Henry Julian Wadleigh, the name Levine had heard at
Berle's and spelled only phonetically. Interviewed by agents the next day,
Alger Hiss again denied passing any of the documents and spent much of
the session explaining Chambers's "psychopathic personality," maintaining

as he would for the next four decades that a man so disturbed might have "real affection and admiration for another person and still engage in actions to hurt that same person." There was no "possibility" he or Priscilla had typed the Baltimore documents, Hiss insisted, and he did not know the whereabouts of the old typewriter they had in the mid-thirties and disposed of after 1938.

While the agents listened to Chambers and Hiss, HUAC readied its grand announcement of the Pumpkin Papers. Of the members, only Rankin would be there for the December 4 press conference, looking even in his habitual animus a bit overwhelmed by the tiny frames of celluloid with their foreign place names, HUAC now gone beyond its old frothy malevolence and fantasy treason. With Andrews's help by telephone, Mundt issued from South Dakota a suitably florid statement "as chairman of the subcommittee handling this matter." The films "have been the object of a ten-year search by agents of the United States government," he said, inventing history, and "are of such startling and significant importance and reveal such a vast network of communist espionage within the State Department that they far exceed anything yet brought before the Committee." The story would make national headlines for days, complete with photographs of the posed pumpkin. With some irony, only the man whose leaked files and bureaucratic scheming had set it all in motion six months before now seemed confused. His zealous Bureau suddenly scooped and embarrassed again by Nixon, Stripling, Andrews, and the rest of the bizarre train, J. Edgar Hoover could only glower mutely through his scribbled comments at the bottom of FBI reports. "What are the facts?" he asked that Saturday. "Here again I heard nothing of this for several days. I should have been advised *at once*. H."

In response to the messages from Stripling and Andrews, Nixon radioed back that "he wanted arrangements made for him to leave the ship," as Andrews recorded it. Stripling—overnight the staff chief not of a dying committee but of a congressional force to be reckoned with again—pulled strings through the military liaison with Congress, and orders to pluck the congressman from the *Panama* were flashed to the seventh district Coast Guard commandant in Miami. Before dawn Sunday morning, a Coast Guard PBM amphibious aircraft took off from St. Petersburg for a more than four-hour flight to the rendezvous, a point called Hole in the Wall in the lee of Acklins Island in the Bahamas, some four hundred miles southeast of Miami and near the course of the *Panama* on the windward passage to the Canal Zone. The Coast Guard confirmation of the pickup reached the cruise ship scarcely an hour before the PBM was to land, and Nixon dressed hurriedly, taking only a light gabardine topcoat. He would leave his bitterly disappointed wife to fly home from the next port of call, "hardly able to believe that their chance . . . had been thwarted," as her feelings were later described. A little after eleven o'clock a *Panama* lifeboat transferred Nixon to the PBM in a calm sea, and he eagerly sat in the copilot's seat most of the way back to Florida. Meanwhile, Stripling and Arnold had arranged for the press to be on hand for the arrival on the mainland, and the rush added to the scene of urgency. When photographers caught the crusading young congressman emerging from the PBM to a waiting crash boat, a wirephoto on front pages across the nation, he was wearing a business suit and dark shoes but still the stark white socks of a Caribbean tourist.

To the reporters waiting in the crash boat at the Dinner Key air station at Miami, Nixon provided a floating press conference, giving them lead quotes even before they docked. "It is no longer just one man's word against another's," he told them, though he had hardly described the issue that tenuously at the end of August or in election speeches. He was going back for "by far the most important [hearing] the Committee on Un-American Activities has conducted." The moral of the inquiry would at last be clear. "It will prove to the American people once and for all that where you have a communist you have an espionage agent."

At the same time, when one of the reporters asked specifically for a comment on the Pumpkin Papers, he seemed taken aback. "What is this, a joke?" he said, and listened with unease to the exotic story of the nighttime scene in the pumpkin patch which the radiograms had not included. Having landed at the air station as the heroic spy catcher charging back to the Capital, photographed and quoted by the national press like an arriving President, Richard Nixon now took the tedious flight up to Washington with some of the same old misgivings. The pumpkins seemed too theatrical, even for Whittaker Chambers. "Now I wondered," he wrote, "if we really might have a crazy man on our hands."

Stripling picked him up at the airport late Sunday night and briefed him excitedly during the short drive to Capitol Hill about the pumpkin patch and the contents of the papers, including Stripling's own trip that afternoon to the Maryland estate of former undersecretary of state Sumner Welles, who told the aide about the code-breaking implications of the documents. "If any agent of a foreign power saw these," Stripling quoted Welles as saying, "he could have broken our code [*sic*]." In fact, cryptography was the least significant intelligence yielded by any of the documents. Some of the cables were sent in "Gray" code, a U.S. cipher in use since World War I and long ago generally broken, while other State Department codes of the late 1930s, albeit of higher classification and relatively more complicated, were by then already generally compromised as well. "No U.S. diplomatic code at the time would have given the average European cryptanalyst any difficulty," historian David Kahn would say later of the prewar period, "and everybody [in government] was perfectly well aware the codes were insecure."

Less than an hour after seeing the documents that night—"after one quick look," Andrews called it—Nixon would tell the anxious press that it was all "conclusive proof of the greatest treason conspiracy in this nation's history . . . proof that cannot be denied [and] . . . puncturing the myth of the 'red herring' President Truman created." The evidence was "shocking," he told them. In oblique reference to broken codes, he said he would call State Department officials to appraise the microfilm, "which gives you an impression how damnably important these documents are." He described the microfilm to reporters as "hundreds" of secret papers making a pile "more than three feet tall." Inside the locked, guarded Committee room, unseen by journalists, the photographed documents stacked up to little more than an inch.

Soon after his arrival, Nixon learned through the Cronin-Hummer channel that Justice was moving to indict Chambers, and he also included in his late-night remarks to the press a defense of the informer, the first of so much maneuvering over the coming week to stave off the indictment of one man while publicly prosecuting the other. He was deeply concerned, Nixon added to his description of the microfilm, at the "apparent lack of interest by the Department of Justice in getting at the crux of the case. It seems to be trying frantically to find a method which will place the blame for possession of these documents on Mr. Chambers." Once more, the fact was that the embarrassed government was now beginning to target Alger Hiss as well. A Justice official had told Chambers's attorney two days before that Chambers was no longer the only object of investigation and the department would "let the chips fall where they may." Yet the administration's own early flippancy and cynicism over the spectacle of the pumpkin was the complement to Nixon's hyperbole. Asked about the microfilm as he was leaving a White House meeting that weekend, Attorney General Clark had quipped, "I'm filing all my important papers in pumpkins these days." A quarter century later, after serving on the Supreme Court, Tom Clark would still dismiss the "whole pumpkin affair" as "a concoction of Nixon and Chambers."

Whatever the artifice of the disclosure, the documents themselves were not all so easily ignored. Sending the press away with still more sensation, Nixon went back into the HUAC chamber and began an avid reading of the material with Stripling. He saw the exhausted aide leave in the early morning hours to go home for some sleep but himself worked through until dawn. "He was flabbergasted by the information," Stripling wrote of his reaction, though some of the material on the two microfilm rolls developed by the Committee was mundane. Among Chambers's dramatic cache were instructions for painting fire extinguishers and ordinary manual data available in Washington libraries. Other navy information, dealing with airplane fuel, radios, instruments, and engine parts, was more plausible espionage but marginal at best. Later, Nixon would privately show Hiss attorneys at their request the navy documents, though both HUAC and the government prudently kept the actual contents of two rolls secret for decades to come, adding to the mystery and avoiding the question of their triviality. Nonetheless, the State Department documents on the two strips of developed film were of a different magnitude.

Many of the fifty-eight prints dealt with economic relations between the U.S. and Nazi Germany on the eve of World War II in Europe, including a reciprocal trade agreement proposed by the State Department that would have been of transparent interest to the Soviet Union at the time, and a sensitive controversial issue in U.S. policy at home and abroad. In addition, the film showed ten pages comprising three telegrams, two from posts in China and one from Paris in January 1938. All dealt with the current Sino-Japanese war on subjects of military and diplomatic interest to the U.S.S.R., all bore the receipt stamp of the office of Assistant Secretary Francis Sayre, all were neatly initialed as having been seen by Sayre's aide, Alger Hiss.

As Nixon read and reread the documents through the night, the case had drawn even tighter around his prey, though neither the congressman nor the government yet knew how tightly. Earlier that day, while Richard Nixon was flying home in alternating glee and doubt, William Marbury received an alarming call from an associate in New York. At their own initiative, the Hiss camp had hired document experts, and Alger and Priscilla had produced some old letters typed by Priscilla in the early 1930s to compare with the copied dispatches disclosed by Chambers. The experts now concluded, reported Marbury's associate, that both the letters and the espionage documents were written, probably by the same typist, on the same typewriter, the old Hiss Woodstock.

The next morning, not visibly haggard from his nightlong vigil over the documents, Nixon met what *The New York Times* called "a record assembly of reporters" and released a copy of Chambers's November 17 deposition, which Stripling had subpoenaed from Chambers's attorney. Along with the story of Hiss and Colonel Bykov, Nixon also alluded to Committee "exhibits" determined to be in Hiss's handwriting, the copies of the penciled notes Chambers had given to Wheeler and Appell along with the film and other Baltimore documents. Could such notes be a routine work product somehow removed from State by someone else? one reporter asked. "I have read the record carefully," the congressman pronounced, "and it is apparent that the forms and content of these documents were obviously not intended to simply be a part of the State Department records."

The horde of journalists was then let into the HUAC hearing room to see at last for themselves the actual microfilm from the pumpkin. It was a crush of popping flashbulbs and whirring newsreel cameras that sent pictures of Nixon and Stripling, and often Nixon alone, once again all over the nation. Repeated from a dozen angles, the shot was basically the same, what would become one of the emblems of the era. America saw an intense Richard Nixon posed with a small magnifying glass while Stripling held the film or simply Nixon holding up the sinister roll himself, peering into the black celluloid, seeming to read intently what he could not possibly see, though in a message clear to everyone.

"What's the emulsion figure on these films?" one of the cameramen asked them casually as the first tattoo of photographs died away. They looked puzzled, and the photographer explained that the manufacturer's code on the film would designate the year the roll was made. The film appeared to be Kodak, he told them. They could check with the company to verify the authenticity of the strips. Both suddenly unnerved by this latest loose end, Nixon and Stripling remained for a few more pictures and then left HUAC for the congressman's attic office, trailed by Bert Andrews and Chambers's investigator Nick Vazzana, who had reappeared at the HUAC rooms to witness the spectacular sequel to what he had set in motion five days before.

As they gathered around Nixon's desk, Stripling telephoned the local Eastman Kodak office and officially requested that a Kodak official, Keith B. Lewis, come immediately to Capitol Hill. Lewis arrived promptly, examined the film, and called his corporate headquarters in Rochester, New York. He waited on the line for a time while someone checked and the others in the office talked among themselves, then put down the phone and turned to them as they fell silent. "This film," he said matter-of-factly, "was manufactured in 1945."

There was a moment of mute shock as they all stared at one another. Then Nixon broke into fury and despair. "Oh, my God, this is the end of my political career," the fledgling congressman cried. "My whole career is ruined!"

As the Kodak official meekly left the office, Nixon turned toward Vazzana, shouting, "Well, you got us into this! This is your fault. What are you going to do about it?"

"Well, it's not my fault, I didn't know there was any microfilm there," Vazzana said in defending himself. "It's your problem, not mine." But Nixon persisted that the young lawyer must "do something," and his angry outburst soon grew "abusive," at least as Vazzana himself remembered it.

"Get hold of Chambers! You'd better get hold of Chambers," Nixon shouted. Vazzana telephoned Harold Medina, the *Time* attorney in New York, and was surprised to discover that Whittaker Chambers was in Medina's Wall Street office on another matter at the same moment. Stripling started to talk to the informer, but was by now sputtering in anger himself, though at the informer rather than Vazzana. "I was too mad at him to trust myself on the phone," Stripling remembered, and they handed the receiver to the fuming Nixon while Stripling picked up an extension to listen. Stripling would remember the near-hysterical congressman "controlling his voice well" as he began to speak to Chambers, but in the same room Bert Andrews thought it "the harshest tone I had ever heard him use."

"Am I correct in understanding that these papers were put on microfilm in 1938?"

"Yes," Chambers answered softly.

"Well, we have just had a report from Eastman Kodak Company that film of the type you turned over to us was not made by the company until after 1945."

There was a pause. "Impossible," Chambers breathed almost in a whisper.

"What *is* this? What do you have to say?" Nixon's voice rose, and hung there for several seconds. He thought Chambers might have hung up until the voice came back in anguish.

"I can't understand it. God must be against me."

"You'd better have a better answer than that! The subcommittee's coming to New York tonight and we want to see you at the Commodore Hotel at nine o'clock and you'd better be there." Nixon slammed down the phone. He remembered afterward, "I took out on him all the fury and frustration that had built up within me."

In Medina's office, Chambers put up the receiver slowly, and wandered out into the Wall Street crowds. "I had felt," he wrote later, "that Richard Nixon was one of the few friends who really understood what was going on." Dazed and muttering to himself, "God is against me," the informer began to plan suicide.

Back in the attic, Nixon faced his own self-immolation. Slumping, he "wearily suggested we call off the press conference," Stripling remembered. But the HUAC aide insisted they own up. "No, damn it, we won't. We'll go down and face the music. We'll tell them that we were sold a bill of goods . . . that we were all wet," Stripling told him. "This would be the biggest crow-eating performance in the history of Capitol Hill," Nixon thought. He buzzed his secretary and told her to tell the press gallery there would be a press conference in the office in five minutes.

Reporters were already filing into the outer office and Stripling and

Nixon were about to meet them when Lewis suddenly called back. "I checked with Rochester after I got back to the office, and it seems we have made a little mistake," he told Stripling. "Those films you showed me were made in 1937." Stripling dropped the phone, let out a Texas rebel yell, leapt onto the couch, then grabbed an astonished Nixon and danced him awkwardly around the room as he shouted the good news. His career unruined after all, Nixon stood quietly for a moment and uttered an epitaph on his own prolonged agony in the case as well as the latest episode. "Poor Chambers," he said. "Nobody ever believes him at first."

Nixon asked Dorothy Cox to call Chambers back. "I wanted to tell him of the new report and express my regrets for what I had said earlier," he wrote later. But the informer had gone, and they could only relay the message to Medina. As for the waiting reporters, they would have another press conference anyway, Nixon announcing that the dates of manufacture of the film coincided with Chambers's larger story. It showed, Andrews remembered him coolly telling the press, how thoroughly the Committee was "checking into every aspect of the case."

"A POLITICAL BABE IN THE WOODS"

They dashed from the Capitol to Union Station to make the late-afternoon train for New York and to begin a period of savage political infighting with the Justice Department to exploit the headline politics of the scandal. Stripling had scheduled an executive session that night at the Commodore to hear Chambers testify on both the microfilm and the Baltimore documents. But even before they left, ranking Justice Department officials had come by the Committee for a stormy two-hour meeting, demanding that HUAC refrain from taking testimony from witnesses, like Chambers, who would appear before the grand jury, and forgo, too, releasing any of the secret documents bearing on the investigation. In the private session Nixon had been unyielding and acid about the sluggish government response to the Baltimore documents. An assistant attorney general explained that a "full field investigation" by the FBI was under way, and Nixon shot back, "What took them so long?" When the officials left in a huff, the congressman had gone indignantly to the press and made his own demand, with added irony for the future. The White House and its Justice Department could no longer be trusted to deal with their own cover-up, he told the reporters on background. The case now called for the appointment of a special attorney general, a "special prosecutor."

On their arrival at Penn Station Monday evening, Nixon and the HUAC entourage were met by a U.S. attorney trying again to head off their questioning of Chambers and even to take custody of the microfilm. There was a heated argument on the platform that moved eventually to the Commodore, "marked by considerable table-thumping and raised voices," reported *The New York Times*. "The air was so blue with shouts of meddling and bad faith," according to one account, that Stripling threw open a window onto a Manhattan street and yelled at the officials, "We might as well let them hear all about it!" Eventually, they reached a compromise, Nixon for HUAC agreeing to give Justice copies of the full-size photographs taken from the microfilm, Justice acquiescing in Chambers's Committee testimony though he was still under grand jury subpoena. The question of further HUAC leaks, inevitable in any event, was left moot.

Meanwhile, the object of the jockeying moved eerily in and out of the scene. Whittaker Chambers had telephoned Medina later that afternoon and learned of the mistake on the film but remained inconsolable—"All that pointless pain continued to roll me under in a drowning wave," he wrote. He wandered the West Side of Manhattan, bought two large tins of cyanide insecticide at a seed store, and deposited the poison at a Penn Station locker, narrowly missing HUAC and the U.S. attorney. He was walking toward the Commodore's main entrance when Appell pulled him into a taxi and spirited him to the back ramp to avoid the swarm of newsmen in the lobby. "You mistrusted me for a time today," Chambers said petulantly to Stripling as he sat down to testify. He repeated the story he had told Marbury and later the FBI, adding now espionage contacts in the Aberdeen Proving Ground, the Bureau of Standards, and the navy, and an account of the Bukhara rugs given by Bykov to Hiss, Harry Dexter White, and Julian Wadleigh. He had no more documents, he assured them, but Stripling was understandably leery. "Look me in the eye," the scowling Texan said repeatedly to the witness. "Are you *sure* you have nothing else to show us?"

After testifying, Chambers would go to his mother's old home on Long Island, write a note saying "my testimony against Alger Hiss was the truth," and try to asphyxiate himself with the toxic fumes of the insecticide. He awoke retching and to the scolding of his mother. "The world hates a quitter," she told him. But he would remain bruised by the Nixon phone call and the poisonous politics he had finally uncapped, ambitions at once his weapon and curse. "We were now on another plane, crisscrossed and violated by the tracks of worldly interests and their passions," he wrote afterward.

The Committee returned to Washington December 7 for a series of hearings, Nixon resuming with finesse both the public and covert battle with the administration. After hearing Chambers at the Commodore, he had called a midnight press conference among the reporters crowding the lobby, and told them, "We have learned from unimpeachable sources that the Justice Department now plans to indict Chambers for perjury. . . . If Chambers is indicted first, Hiss and the others will go free because the witness against them will have been discredited as a perjurer." Later on the seventh, HUAC heard Mundt's nervous State Department informer, John Peurifoy, call the documents proof of "systematic and surreptitious looting." The next day they took testimony on the issue of code-breaking from the former chief of State's cryptographic office, retired after forty-two years and in the entire government the man perhaps least able to acknowledge that America's prewar diplomatic codes were breached in any case. On the eighth, too, Isaac Don Levine returned to repeat the story of their 1939 approach to Berle and to defend Chambers's previous perjury before the grand jury as a reluctance to implicate further former comrades. Nixon read into the record Chambers's own emotional explanation from the Commodore executive session, and yet again, in statements from the dais and in the now-inevitable press conference afterward, attacked Justice for plans to indict the informer "before any of the other people involved in this conspiracy."

Over the same period, he continued the old convoluted politics with the FBI. When Bureau agents called at HUAC seeking copies of the Pumpkin Papers, Nixon adamantly refused, saying copies had already been given to the U.S. attorney in New York. Afterward, HUAC's Louis Russell had pulled aside one of the agents and "confidentially advised . . . ," as the report read, "his opinion that Congressman Nixon was out to embarrass the Bureau . . . in connection with this matter." Yet that same evening Nixon saw former FBI agents Patrick Coyne and Bob King, casually showed them the secret documents, and confided that HUAC was "very anxious" to get "specimens" of the Hiss typewriter. In a conversation he was no doubt certain Coyne and King would pass back to their former employer, Nixon told them, as Coyne indeed reported, that he "is extremely mad at the attorney general . . . for not having more vigorously prosecuted this whole matter, but . . . had nothing but praise for the director and the Bureau." Nixon added that "he had worked very close [sic] with the Bureau and with Mr. Nichols during the past year on this matter." It was a notable little example of the uneasy marriage of convenience between policemen and politicians that had spawned so much history since Nichols made his rounds that past July. Predictably, a secret memo on the conversation was waiting the next day on the desk of Hoover, who scribbled aptly at the bottom, "This fellow Nixon blows hot & cold. H."

There would be no boundary to the maneuvering. On December 9 King informed the FBI that Nixon was "considering approaching President Truman" in some confidential manner to spur the investigation. A few days later Nixon quietly went to Undersecretary of State Robert A. Lovett, showed him the documents HUAC was otherwise guarding so jealously from the State Department and others in the administration, and "briefed" the official, as an FBI report described it, "with the request that Mr. Lovett bring the true facts of the case to the attention of the President." Impressed with the young congressman's secret diplomacy behind partisan lines, and with the earnestness of his argument for Hiss's prosecution, Lovett promised to lobby Truman. At the same moment, Nixon continued what *The New York Times* called "the heated rivalry" between HUAC and federal prosecutors. As Justice pressed for the microfilm, Nixon now promised early release, now drew back. Within hours of the private meeting with Lovett, he was holding his fourth major press conference in six days, pressuring Truman and Clark to "tighten the espionage law." The genuineness of the documents and of Chambers's latest confession, he assured reporters, were "not open to any possible doubts."

It was an electric surge of celebrity and power that made his covert dickering with a President, the defiance of Justice, the furtive, teasing collusion with the FBI, almost natural. As Richard Nixon navigated grandly through Washington in the days after his recall at sea, hundreds of letters of support piled up in his office. Truman defiantly referred again to the famous "red herring" December 9, but now editorial backing for HUAC, still tenuous after the August hearings, was national and bipartisan. "The situation," conceded the *Washington Post*, "has completely changed with the seizure of the microfilms." In a view typical of papers nationwide, the *Washington Evening Star* thought recent events "something more than a feather in the cap of the House Committee." "By this time," Nixon wrote in one of those many passages that would haunt his own White House, "not even the immense power of a President who has just won reelection could stop the march of truth."

Everywhere the symbol of the Committee's vigilance and success was Congressman Nixon. For most of December 1948, his photograph and name were rarely absent from front pages throughout the country. He had become a national hero and a favorite of the media. Even the Washington correspondents' irreverent Gridiron Club was revising its Christmas skit, a private burlesque for the Capital establishment, to feature crusading Dick Nixon and the Pumpkin Papers.

While Nixon stood before the flashbulbs or quietly manipulated the government, Alger Hiss and Whittaker Chambers, along with a cast of supporting witnesses, were trooping in and out of the New York grand jury room, Hiss now summoned to appear every day as the panel entered its final deliberations. Chambers resigned from *Time* that week, nudged by magazine executives nervous at the still more sensational controversy but with a generous settlement from Henry Luce that supported him for years. "No one can share with me this indispensable ordeal," the informer said in a lachrymose resignation statement. *Time* portrayed its erstwhile senior editor to and fro at the Foley Square Courthouse, "as unprepossessing as a baker—a calm, pudgy little man who kept an old pipe in the pocket of his untidy blue serge suit . . . a brilliant intellectual." Regardless of the din of publicity and the accumulation of documents, however, Alger Hiss continued to deny earnestly any espionage, and the case seemed to rest in the end on Chambers's admittedly shifting story. By Friday, December 10, with the grand jury due to expire on December 15, the foreman secretly told Justice prosecutors, as Bert Andrews later reported the events, that "there would be no indictment against Hiss as matters stood." Further pursuit, if any, would apparently have to await a later grand jury and, more significant, a passing of the roiling political moment.

Nixon had maneuvered both in public and private for a chance to testify himself before the grand jury, though not at the cost of formally surrendering the microfilm, which had been the Justice Department's price of admission in the backstage negotiations. Now, with indictment of Hiss about to be lost despite the public furor, the familiar combination of luck, leaks, and Nixon's initiative would once more alter events. On Saturday the eleventh the *Herald Tribune* ran in its city edition a detailed story by Bert Andrews on the initial mix-up on the manufacturing date of the Kodak microfilm. Censoring Nixon's personal panic, the article reported accurately Kodak's own confusion, and prosecutors in New York now picked up the story for one more stab at the HUAC microfilm. "NEW YORK HERALD TRIBUNE," began a Justice Department telegram to Nixon, "TODAY REPORTS CONFLICT OF STATEMENTS TO YOUR COMMITTEE AS TO MANUFACTURE OF SAID FILMS. IT IS CRUCIAL THAT TRUE FACTS AS TO THIS AND CONTENTS OF FILMS BE DETERMINED AT ONCE BY GRAND JURY."

Aware from his own informants of the impasse in the grand jury, Nixon seized the telegram himself for his own trip to Foley Square on Monday, December 13. Andrews saw him before he left, neatly dressed, "a shiny new calfskin briefcase in his hand." On the eve of his going there was a small showdown in the Committee, an assertion of the political authority he had long since claimed. Nixon had come by Stripling's office, encountered Rankin there as well, and told them he was going before the grand jury with the film after all. "Rankin nearly had a fit," as Stripling later told the FBI. But the freshman congressman coolly insisted he could stave off both the court and the Justice Department, took the film "on his own responsibility," and with Appell and Wheeler in tow as escorts struck off for New York, now as in the past a veritable committee of one. With Wheeler carrying the film and Nixon's new briefcase as a decoy, they were delayed by a train wreck en route and arrived at the courthouse only late in the afternoon.

Before the jury and impatient prosecutors, Nixon was audacious and brilliant. He politely refused to leave or surrender the actual microfilm, though they could examine it in his presence. When the jury then voted to subpoena him, he was taken before a federal judge under the implicit threat of contempt. "He did not want to be abhorrent," read an FBI account of Nixon's response to the judge in chambers, "but would have to take it [microfilm] back to the Committee and then it would be turned over to the FBI." It was a matter of constitutional prerogative, he argued, and the exhibits of the Committee were the property of the House of Representatives until released by the House, a solemn authority one lone congressman obviously did not have. Prodded by the court to avoid a larger clash of power, the prosecutors agreed to a compromise in which Nixon would turn over the film to the FBI for examination the next day and it would in course be returned to HUAC.

He would return triumphantly to Washington with the microfilm. But even more important, he had made his own impressive case before the grand jury, managing to recount the conclusions of the HUAC prosecution. Microfilm in hand, carrying the authority of several months of highly publicized congressional investigation, he was a formidable figure before the panel, and along with Hiss and Chambers a recognized celebrity. Outside the jury room, he even used the waiting throng of reporters to issue an unveiled political warning to the officials and jurors a few feet away inside. "The indictment of Chambers for perjury without anybody else would constitute a whitewash," he announced.

Hours before, the jury had seemed unwilling to act, Hiss's indictment stymied. One of the Justice prosecutors had confided to a Hiss lawyer earlier in the day that Chambers was clearly "unstable and abnormal." Though no one save Chambers's mother knew yet of the informer's attempted suicide, the Justice official now told Hiss attorneys that he "expected for several days to pick up the paper . . . and read that Mr. Chambers has jumped out of the window." The next morning, following Nixon's dramatic appearance, the same official would call Hoover's office in Washington with an altogether different view. "They were making very real progress," read the Bureau memo of the call, "and were going to end up with an indictment."

On December 14, the Committee held a final hearing in its Pumpkin Papers series, and Nixon gave his fifth crowded Capitol Hill press conference in eight days. The film, he said, "has furnished the link of evidence which we needed to establish that Soviet espionage, conducted in cooperation with members of the Communist Party in America, has been amazingly successful." An indictment of Chambers, he warned yet again, would "give the greatest encouragement to the communist conspiracy in this country." At the same time, before the grand jury, the FBI was adding another and decisive "link." For days, more than 250 agents in forty-five field offices, and thirty in Washington alone, had searched for specimens of Hiss letters or other documents from the late 1930s. Now Ramos Feehan, a Bureau documents expert, testified before the grand jury that two specimens discovered, including an application for one of Timmie's schools, had been typed on the same typewriter as the Baltimore documents. On that same day, in the corridor outside the hearing room, Hiss was quietly threatened by prosecutors with a coindictment of Priscilla if he did not confess. But he stuck to his story "in an amazing manner," reported one Justice official.

The next and final day of the grand jury, Alger Hiss was summoned a last time, asked if he had passed documents to Chambers, and, if not, to explain how the Baltimore documents were typed on his typewriter. "Until the day I die, I shall wonder how Whittaker Chambers got into my house to use my typewriter" is how Nixon recorded his testimony from "reports [that] leaked out" from the ostensibly secret proceedings. Nixon added from his informant's account of the moment: "A ripple of laughter went through the jury room."

On the afternoon of December 15, 1948, the grand jury announced the indictment of Alger Hiss alone. Richard Nixon was sitting nervously in his office when a secretary brought in the press ticker. "I had a great sense of relief," he remembered. Calling an immediate press conference, he told them in a prepared statement, "The indictment of Alger Hiss vindicates the many long months of work done by our Committee despite criticism from all sources from the President down. The indictment establishes beyond doubt the justification for committees of Congress investigating in this field."

In New York the weary grand jurors disbanded and would tell their story only years later. The vote to indict had been one more than a majority. "Hiss's indictment was a close vote," one of them would say afterward. "I was never convinced that Hiss was guilty of the crime we indicted him for. Chambers perjured himself many times, but the final decision of the jury was 'He's our witness, we are not going to indict him.' It was a politically inspired matter."

In the euphoria that followed, there was a fleeting but tarnishing reminder of the old HUAC. On December 20, ten days after being questioned by the FBI, a former State Department official and Hiss friend named Lawrence Duggan fell from the sixteenth floor of a midtown Manhattan building. Isaac Don Levine had named Duggan in his latest testimony to the Committee. Now eager to exploit more headlines, Mundt called together Nixon and Stripling within hours of the death, combed the files for Levine's reference, and told reporters at a midnight press conference that Duggan's name figured in the Hiss case. Asked what others the Committee believed to be involved, Mundt replied jauntily, "We'll name them as they jump out of windows."

The crudity provoked an immediate furor in the press and Congress, giving bent to the accumulated frustration with the Committee's vast new prominence, even among HUAC's own neglected rump. Hebert denounced the release of Duggan's name as "a blunder, a breach of confidence and a violation of agreed on procedure." Rankin, in newfound fastidiousness, thought it "atrocious." Taken aback by the mounting criticism, Nixon himself swiftly retreated, telling a television audience that he thought Duggan was "clear of espionage" and joining Mundt in a remarkable statement of veritable apology, in which the two congressmen admitted their press conference merited "honest criticism" and they regretted the "misunderstandings" and "misinterpretations." Yet even their new, chastened sobriety was ironic. Duggan had been named as a communist contact and sometime agent by other witnesses, and his apparent suicide left another of the several mysteries of the larger case. Along with Harry White's, Duggan's death would be one of five connected to the Hiss-Chambers affair, including the unexplained fall in a Justice Department stairwell of an official who had notarized the transfer of Alger Hiss's old Ford.

Even before the Duggan episode, Nixon had taken a tone of public modesty about HUAC's controversial past. "I'll admit the Committee has made mistakes and deserves criticism," he told Bert Andrews when the reporter interviewed him formally on ABC radio December 18. The handling of the Condon matter, he said, had been "unfair." But about the Hiss case he would have no apology. On December 31 he proudly released the final HUAC reports on the affair that he had largely supervised. The Eightieth Congress had been "the most active and productive period in the history" of the Committee, HUAC proclaimed, describing the Hiss case as "the most startling disclosures . . . which should rock our national complacence to its foundations." Meticulously, Nixon personally underlined the salient passages for John Foster Dulles and sent them off. Just before the indictment, the Carnegie trustees had voted Hiss a three-month leave with pay, and Dulles would now move to oust him completely.

Back in the Capital, it was politics as usual. Soon after the holidays, HUAC's Russell called Louis Nichols late one night to relay an important message to J. Edgar Hoover from Congressman Nixon. "Nixon . . . had heard that there was a rumor being circulated that Nixon was after the director and the Bureau," read one of Nichols's ubiquitous memos. There was "no truth to this," the congressman wanted to assure them. "He is on the side of the Bureau and the director," Nichols recorded, "and if we ever want proof we should ask him for it."

Of Nixon's own bright future in the wake of the triumph, there seemed no doubt. "A scholarly but unstuffy man of assiduous work habits, with a reputation for thoroughness and integrity," *Fortnight*, a California news magazine, described him in a cover story at year's end. There was even talk of the "young lawyer from Whittier" running for the Senate, reported the magazine, though, of course, Richard Nixon was still "a political babe in the woods after little more than two years in public life."

15

The Case III, 1949

t would be called the "year of shocks." The events of 1949, wrote historian Eric Goldman, "loosed within American life a vast impatience, a turbulent bitterness, a rancor akin to revolt."

Inaugural Day dawned for Harry Truman that January with crystalline clear skies, a calliope at the head of the seven-and-one-half-mile parade whistling out into the crisp Washington noon the strains of "I'm Just Wild About Harry." Then, almost suddenly, the tooting and triumph died away. Within months the economy sank into a postwar recession. China fell to the communists. The Soviet Union exploded its own atomic bomb. More completely each day the fear and fury of anticommunist hysteria seemed to envelop the nation, and the bright air of Inauguration was soon leaden with suspicion and frightened conformity. A patriot, said one college president, mourning the extinction of dissent, was someone "who tells all his secrets without being asked, believes we should go to war with Russia, holds no political view without prior consultation with his employer, does not ask for increases in salary or wages, and is in favor of peace, universal military training, brotherhood, and baseball." It was in many ways the certifying, ratifying year of the Cold War. And month after month, a continuing drama seemed to encompass and epitomize it all: the trials of Alger Hiss.

No single episode, not even the spectacle of pin-striped treason in the New Deal, would account for America's descent into what one British historian called aptly "The Great Fear." Yet now, as in the summer and winter before, no other event so fixed the politics and popular mania. As

486

symbol if not substance, the case in the courtroom marked the boundaries of a national passage. In the weeks before the appearance of the Pumpkin Papers and Alger Hiss's indictment in December 1948, Harry Truman had been a grinning, confident victor. Ten days after the final verdict, in January 1950, beleaguered at home and abroad, a weakened President was announcing the decision to build the hydrogen bomb, "to see to it," as he told the press somewhat tremulously, "that our country is able to defend itself against any aggressor."

In the months before the case came to trial, Richard Nixon became a relatively discreet if famous onlooker, for a moment almost magnanimous toward Alger Hiss while relishing his political victory and sparing no opportunity to attack the administration. Though HUAC had briefly surrendered the Pumpkin Papers microfilm to the FBI lab as part of Nixon's mid-December deal before the grand jury, the FBI was requesting another examination early in January 1949, and Nixon and Stripling, still husbanding their prerogative and prized possession, again held back. "Same old runaround from this outfit," Hoover scribbled on a secret report of the maneuverings. At the same moment, however, Nixon was offering one of Hiss's attorneys, Edward McLean, "full access" to the microfilm, and confiding to the defense lawyer what HUAC had never announced to the press—that of the three previously undeveloped rolls, one was blank and the other two bore Bureau of Standards or navy documents with "no State Department papers," as McLean's memo recorded their conversation. The day after the concession to McLean, Nixon was at a scholarly conference at Dartmouth College, making news by attacking the attorney general's recent proposal to legalize wiretapping in serious espionage cases. The Truman administration plan was "far too drastic," he told the applauding professors and students, and should be "thoroughly debated in Congress and the press before action is taken."

As always, such politics distinguished him from his less adept HUAC colleagues. When the *Washington Post* editorialized that January on the new HUAC in the Democratically controlled Eighty-first Congress—a committee "expected to have a much higher regard for the rights of citizens and a better understanding of the investigative function of Congress"—the liberal paper endorsed the reassignment of only one member of its old nemesis: "We hope that Representative Nixon will be returned to the Committee because of his extensive knowledge of the spying activities explored in the past."

Privately, he was less statesmanlike. FBI reports showed Father Cronin passing to an eager Nixon as well as to the Bureau juicy tidbits of gossip from inside the Hiss defense. In the wake of the Pumpkin Papers triumph, the microfilm itself became a kind of talisman to be displayed to visitors or simply possessed. Stripling would describe to the FBI that March how Congressman Nixon might call for the film from the HUAC safe for no apparent reason and keep it in his attic office all day long, requiring a Committee secretary to retrieve it late in the evening.

Meanwhile, the old furtive battle of leaks and threats continued. As the trial neared, Chambers confessed to the FBI his once obsessive homosexuality and tortured history of promiscuity, a series of encounters, as he wrote in a statement, in "fleabag" hotels in Manhattan and Washington or in "parks and other parts of town where these people were likely to be found." He was making the confession, he told the agents, because "Alger Hiss's defense obviously intends to press the charge that I have had homosexual relations with certain individuals." But amid the agonized admission, he stoutly denied any liaison with his victim. He had never mixed secret business and secret pleasure, never been tempted. "At no time did I have such relations or even the thought of such relations with Hiss or with anybody else in the Communist Party or connected with communist work of any kind." Soon afterward, Chambers's admission leaked to reporters, who then approached HUAC with the story. But Nixon eventually dissuaded them from publishing the sensational revelation on the grounds it was a political ploy by Tom Clark to cripple the prosecution. Dick and others on the Committee were "incensed, angry and quite agitated over this matter," Louis Russell promptly informed Hoover—though the congressmen and their own favored newsmen had frequently talked and joked in private about the long-standing rumor of some sexual "perversion" in the case. But now Nixon felt "the Department of Justice is going out of its way to discredit and embarrass the Committee," Russell reported, and that "the attorney general should and could be impeached for this action."

For his part, Whittaker Chambers continued over the winter and spring of 1949 his own selective leaks of information and FBI testimony designed to discredit Alger Hiss, usually through the agency of his old HUAC advocates. "Chambers still sees Congressman Nixon and . . . Nixon talks to Mundt," an FBI report in April noted, tracing the provenance of one story revealing secret pretrial interviews. To shore up their witness, the FBI now took Chambers through rehearsal after rehearsal of his story, including sessions in which the informer could question a onetime Hiss maid on details of the Georgetown households Chambers was supposed to know, allowing him to alter his own recollection to fit the servant's. At the same time, FBI agents interviewing Timothy Hobson pointedly mentioned some of Hobson's homosexual friends, leaving no doubt, as Hiss had feared, that the government prosecutors would retaliate in public against the psychologically fragile young stepson if the defense raised the sexual issue with Chambers.

Lusts and secrets aside, Chambers by the eve of trial had added even to his own characteristic sense of grandiosity and self-righteousness. "Surely every man is but a hair's breadth from Christ and the devil, and only the final revealings will show to whom each of us belong," a Pennsylvania Quaker had written Chambers, Nixon, and the Hisses in January, appealing to all the fellow Christians for an end of the affair in the spirit of their common faith. "It is for this that I cry aloud: Friends, stand still in the Lord, judge not." Only Chambers answered. "I must lay bare the sin of the world and the century," he wrote back. "Perfidy and terror are the works of the age which has resolved to live without God—therefore, the confession that I have to make is a confession of perfidy and terror."

"IMMUTABLE WITNESSES"

For twenty-seven humid days in June and July, 1949, the New York trial was the nation's chief drama. In the courtroom it was once again Chambers versus Hiss, and now Thomas Murphy, the hulking, handsome government prosecutor against Lloyd Paul Stryker, short, chunky, Hiss's flamboyant and florid defense lawyer with close-cropped white hair and a penchant for biblical anathema. Chambers, he told the jury, was a "furtive, deceptive man . . . a confirmed liar . . . a blasphemer . . . a communist conspirator and a thug . . . a moral leper." Stryker thought somebody ought to have preceded this rumpled witness into court, shouting, as in the ancient alarm, "Unclean, unclean!" It was, like so much of the case, vivid theater. But here, too, much of the play, particularly Richard Nixon's stage management, was largely invisible to the audience.

With Mandel providing the extracurricular staff work, Nixon assembled HUAC files on the defense witnesses, and along with Mundt quietly canvassed for derogatory information, including a dossier on federal Judge Samuel H. Kaufman, the Truman-appointed jurist presiding over the trial. "Our mutual friend, Ben, has told me that you have available some interesting information," Mundt wrote Isaac Don Levine on June 10, looking for something discrediting about the Hiss team psychiatrist, Dr. Carl Binger, and also "on what manner of man this fellow Judge Kaufmann [sic] is." When they then quickly concluded during the opening week of the proceedings that Judge Kaufman was biased in favor of Hiss, they prevailed on Nevada's GOP senator Pat McCarran to convey to the bench a naked warning of political reprisal. "McCarran told Judge Kaufman that he hoped it would not be necessary," Louis Nichols reported to his FBI superiors, "for the Senate Judiciary Committee to make inquiry as to how the judge functions in the Hiss-Chambers case."

From the earliest stages of the trial, Richard Nixon would be avidly involved in encouraging, even coaching the prosecution. His go-between was Victor Lasky, a conservative reporter for the Scripps-Howard *New York World-Telegram* who was close to Thomas Murphy as well. "As you probably realize Dick has a heck of a lot at stake in the outcome," the journalist wrote Murphy. "Anyway, I got a couple of things which he thought you should [*sic*] like to know, based on his many dealings with our boy, Alger, in the House committee." Soon after the prosecution began its argument, there followed from Lasky another "Dear Tom" letter on Nixon's behalf to the assistant U.S. attorney. "Rep. Richard Nixon, with whom I spoke over the weekend, asked me to relay (unofficially) his appreciation for the 'excellent' job you are doing at the trial," Lasky wrote. "He also asked me to tell Donegan that despite previous 'misunderstandings,' Nixon wished Donegan well and luck in the case," the reporter went on, smoothing over the congressman's past clashes with Justice and adding insistently in handwriting to the typed sentence "(would you please tell Donegan?)."

Lasky transmitted to the prosecutors as well Nixon's own "Memorandum on Hiss Testimony Before Committee," a nine-page, single-spaced document "which has never been released," and which enumerated lines of questioning over some twenty separate issues, from the car and farm to matters of the hand-written notes, Yalta, and even Hiss's habits and manner as a witness. As a legal or strategic guide, the Nixon memo was unsophisticated and largely irrelevant, lingering over details of the HUAC hearings that the case had already transcended and sprinkled with the nostrums of Dick Nixon's small-town law practice—"I would be pretty sure the jury would feel . . . I think reading this testimony to the jury would be most effective . . . I think it would be necessary to put on somewhat of an act." Yet the offering was nothing if not earnest and typically detailed, with the congressman, like the prosecutors, in no doubt of the defendant's guilt. "Just another example," Nixon explained one point, "of how Hiss becomes the artful dodger when faced with a question that might embarrass him."

As the trial entered its last two weeks with the outcome still uncertain, Nixon moved again secretly to spur the government. Julian Wadleigh had testified about turning over State Department documents to Chambers in 1936–38, though he would neither implicate Alger Hiss nor rule out that some if not many of the stolen documents might have come from Wadleigh himself. On June 28, Nixon called the FBI's Louis Nichols in some urgency to say that Wadleigh "probably knows more about the case than he has so far indicated" and "may be willing to talk more." Wadleigh was an "idealist" who hoped Hiss "would come clean under pressure," Nixon told the

FBI. He thought Wadleigh now has "a guilt complex" from the prospect that "Hiss will probably get off . . . because Wadleigh did not come clean." There was "information in [Wadleigh's] neighborhood pertaining to this," he assured Nichols. An FBI agent should tell Wadleigh the trial is "not going too well," and "if Wadleigh could be gotten into the right mood, bearing in mind the guilt complex . . . he might come through." Nothing new resulted from his proposal—clearly the result of the young congressman grasping at some of the plentiful wisps of gossip surrounding the trial— though both J. Edgar Hoover and the prosecutors promptly ordered a reinterview of Wadleigh. But the episode was another example of Nixon's impatience and anxiety on the sidelines.

Once more, as Murphy was cross-examining Hiss late in the trial, Nixon sought to bolster what he saw as the laggard prosecution. In late June he wrote Lasky to pass along to Murphy for his summation eleven questions to highlight inconsistencies in Hiss's congressional as well as trial testimony over the past several months. Nixon urged that "all these contradictions . . . should be set forth in short questions with yes or no answers so that the jury and the press can get the full benefit of them." Again, too, his prompting centered on the Hiss-Crosley relationship, which had been far more significant to HUAC than to the ongoing trial. Nervously, he asked Lasky to "call me at noon today collect and let me know what developments have been." He was planning "to come up to New York tomorrow night," Nixon told him. In a hand-written "P.S." penned in large script, he struck a note of near desperation about the prosecution's ebbing moment.

> 5 pm
> I just had a long tel. conversation with a
> newsman covering the case in New York who is
> not pro either H or C. He insists that Murphy
> *must keep* H on stand at least two more days.
> He says H is looking worse as time goes on & at
> all costs to keep going over & over the testimony
> so that they can see him thoroughly.

At that, the Nixon letter via Lasky would not be the last in the almost constant exhorting and advice to the prosecution by the small coalition of men who had quietly propelled the case along from the beginning. The congressman's letter was still fresh in his hands when Tom Murphy was visited the night before his final statement by the ubiquitous Isaac Don Levine, who—like Lasky, Nixon, Mundt, and Mandel—was proffering political and legal tactics to win the conviction they all saw as so crucial.

Late in the evening of July 7, the jury returned to Kaufman's court hopelessly hung, four of the twelve refusing to agree to Hiss's conviction. Fury at the defeat was instant. Jurors reported to have voted for acquittal received anonymous threats by phone and letter. With apparent leaks from the prosecution, Lasky and other reporters printed portions of the confidential transcripts of deliberations in the judge's chambers, showing Kaufman's rulings against the government. An enraged Nixon alongside a handful of House colleagues publicly denounced the judge and demanded an investigation of his "fitness to serve on the bench." Kaufman's "prejudice for the defense and against the prosecution was so obvious that the jury's eight to four vote for conviction frankly came as a surprise to me . . . when the full facts of the conduct of this trial are laid before the nation, the people will be shocked," Nixon told the press following the deadlock, although privately in his letters and FBI calls he had clearly thought the trial winnable.

In a formal statement he accused the court of political bias. "I think the entire Truman administration was extremely anxious that nothing bad happen to Mr. Hiss," he lashed out at the President, while treading a careful line in calling for a special prosecutor to augment Murphy. The assistant U.S. attorney he had secretly coached "did a great job against great odds," he added. "I mean no disparagement of him when I say that it might be wise—considering the importance of the case—to appoint a special prosecutor to work with him. I think Mr. Murphy might welcome such assistance." In the ensuing congressional controversy, defenders of the administration soon deplored his attacks on the bench as "reckless and irresponsible," as one Democratic senator put it, and new HUAC chairman John Wood rebuked Nixon at an unusually stormy public session, calling forth from the representative from Whittier one of the more memorable and ironic plaints of the whole affair. "A handful of administration apologists, who find themselves unable to defend Judge Kaufman's conduct . . . on the facts," Richard Nixon said solemnly, "are attempting to turn the case into a political issue which it is not."

Behind the public furor, the reaction and maneuvering were even more forceful. Within days of the hung jury, Nixon was again calling the FBI to inform, now on Hubert James, the foreman of the jury who was known to have urged acquittal and whom the Bureau had already investigated during the trial for alleged pro-Hiss or liberal sympathies. Murphy had moved in chambers that James be excused, but Kaufman had rejected the notion in one of the secret proceedings later publicized. James was said to have "played an active part" in a Henry Wallace rally during the 1948 election, while his wife "is a member of the 'left-wing' group of the League of Women Voters," Nixon told an agent sent round after his call. If James had any "preconceived idea of Hiss's innocence," the foreman "should be prosecuted."

Meanwhile, other partisans were moving to undercut the Hiss defense from within. As the government prepared over the summer to retry the case, Isaac Don Levine met discreetly with defense attorney Lloyd Stryker and Allen Dulles at the home of Archibald Roosevelt, Theodore's youngest son and, like Dulles, later a ranking official in the CIA. Their purpose was to undercut Stryker's evident commitment to his client, and Levine would describe the lawyer as "visibly shaken by my review and by my answers to the questions posed by him and Mr. Dulles." As it was, Alger Hiss as a matter of style would replace the theatrical, old-fashioned Stryker before the second trial with a more sedate if less effective counsel. But Stryker had been willing to continue, and the Levine-Dulles subversion might have had a withering effect on the defense. Similarly, supporters of Chambers and Nixon privately wrote Supreme Court Justice Felix Frankfurter, who had appeared as one of many prominent character witnesses for the defendant, warning the Justice ominously, as one of them told him, that "it would be unwise to go out on a limb for Hiss." Whatever the effect of such threats, Frankfurter and other notables would not testify at the subsequent trial.

In the interval before the second prosecution began in mid-November 1949, there was a sea change in both the larger and more immediate setting. Over the summer and autumn the trial would be framed against the testing of the Soviet atomic bomb, the ratification of the North Atlantic Alliance, the retreat of Chiang Kai-shek's defeated remnants to Formosa amid bitter charges of betrayal and treason hurled at the administration by Washington's China Lobby. Inside the Foley Square courtroom the climate turned as well. In the judicial rotation, the much-maligned Kaufman was now succeeded by Henry W. Goddard, an appointee of Warren Harding with judicial prowess to match. The new judge would nap regularly on the bench during testimony and promptly corrrected Kaufman's imputed prejudice by seating Alice Roosevelt Longworth and other fans of the prosecution in special places facing the jury. For that matter, there would be no reason for Nixon and his associates to impugn the second trial jury, whose forelady was a member of the church where Goddard was vestryman and later professed that she thought him virtually deified. Another woman on the jury was the wife of a Foley Square bailiff who owed his job to the federal authorities. Three more had relatives employed by the FBI. When the Bureau cautiously told Murphy of the compromising relationships only days into the second trial, the prosecutor requested "that it be kept quiet," and concealed the manifold taint from Goddard as well as from the defense.

The first trial had revolved about the testimony and personality of Chambers. The centerpiece of the second was to be the Baltimore documents and most crucially the old Hiss Woodstock typewriter, for which both sides had searched diligently following the indictment and which the

Hiss team had apparently found and then introduced at the first proceeding, a machine with the serial number N230099. Impounded by the court between the trials, the Woodstock was to be what a later generation, in another political scandal, would call the "smoking gun" of the affair. Drawn up to the full six feet four inches of his 240-pound frame, his walrus mustache waxed in the manner of an Edwardian guards officer, prosecutor Thomas Murphy would pose for photographers beside the fateful machine and documents, one of which, he told the jury, "is secret to such an extent that we are going to have the judge not to permit you to see it." In less tangled syntax, he would call them solemnly "the immutable witnesses."

The other, equally essential link in the government's evidence was the so-called Hiss Standards, two letters and two other papers admittedly typed on the original Woodstock and voluntarily given the FBI by the Hisses themselves, the latest dated seven months before the earliest Baltimore documents. It had been the FBI's identification of the Hiss Standards with the Baltimore documents that was crucial in Hiss's indictment. Thinking the typewriter itself would exonerate Hiss, the defense enlisted typewriting experts in the spring of 1949 only to find to its shock and consternation that their own authorities judged both the Baltimore documents and Hiss Standards to have been typed on N230099, one of the consultants even identifying Priscilla Hiss personally as the typist.

At almost the same time, a secret report from J. Edgar Hoover in May 1949 also concluded that N230099 "has been identified by the FBI laboratory as being the machine which was used to type documents . . . known as the Baltimore documents," though legally the Bureau had not yet had a chance to examine the actual Woodstock discovered by the defense and would not be allowed legitimate access to the machine until a special agent took specimens from the court-impounded typewriter five months later. With those apparently categorical findings, however, the "immutable witnesses" entered a legal and evidentiary labyrinth that would make the final trial of Alger Hiss not only a political spectacle but one of the judicial travesties of the century.

Embarrassed by the defense's discovery of the Woodstock that spring, the FBI had immediately launched a sweeping investigation into the origin of the typewriter. They had already learned in their earlier search the machine's general history: it had belonged to Priscilla's father in his Fansler-Martin Insurance Agency, was purchased as the sole machine of the business at the inception of the partnership in 1927, was never traded in for another machine, and had been taken by Fansler to pass along to his daughter when the agency disbanded in 1930. The Bureau had even found the Woodstock salesman who sold the typewriter to Fansler-Martin in 1927 and who subsequently resigned from the Woodstock company in December

1927. Business records and repeated FBI interviews with Fansler's surviving partner, an agency secretary, and the typewriter salesman himself all confirmed the sequence.

Yet now, with the appearance of the defense Woodstock, the scurrying agents made one more, somewhat startling discovery. Woodstock factory records showed that typewriters manufactured in 1927 bore serial numbers between 159300 and 177100. According to a secret FBI report, "serial number 230099 was placed on a machine between March 1929 . . . and August 1930." And though the agents would find no direct record of the specific sale to Fansler-Martin, they did track down, as their report put it, "sale of a machine with serial number 230098, one digit lower than the machine in question . . . in Philadelphia, Pennsylvania, on September 21, 1932." The defense's Woodstock—the typewriter identified on all sides as the necessary incriminating link between the documents, the Hisses, and historic espionage—had been manufactured two to three years *after* the purchase of the actual, original Fansler-Martin typewriter. And a companion machine had been sold more than *two years* after the partnership dissolved. The machine sitting there in the courtroom, the FBI knew all too clearly that spring of 1949, was the wrong typewriter.

Almost desperately, pathetically, J. Edgar Hoover ordered his agents on May 25, 1949, to interview the Woodstock salesman once again "to obtain an explanation as to how he could sell a machine which was manufactured in 1929 to the Fansler-Martin partnership in 1927." When the salesman, like the other witnesses, stood by his story, the Bureau simply ascribed the fateful contradiction to his "unreliability," even investigating his possible theft of a machine from Woodstock, though company records showed "no inventory shortages prior to 1933," as a Bureau report concluded. Meanwhile, according to an FBI report of June 9, 1949, "typewriter specimens . . . from Fansler-Martin," including the agency's business correspondence with Northwestern Mutual Life, "have been definitely found nonidentical with the Chambers documents." Evidently the Baltimore documents had not been typed on Priscilla's hand-me-down Woodstock after all. But in its own secret investigative files, the Bureau again explained away the crucial discrepancy, in this case by what a report called "normal use and wear" of the typewriter.

Through it all, the FBI would continue to swear by its tainted evidence, and the prosecution would increasingly exploit it, while conflicting facts were kept secret from the court and defense as well as higher levels of the Justice Department and the public at large. Required under federal rules to have either two witnesses to perjury or confirming documentation for a single accuser, Murphy rested his case largely on the Woodstock. "We will corroborate Mr. Chambers's testimony by the typewriter," he told the first trial jury. The hand-written notes or microfilmed dispatches might have somehow been stolen by another source, including the self-confessed Wadleigh. But the typewriter would pin the crime to the Hisses.

At the first trial, FBI typewriting expert Ramos C. Feehan testified, as he had before the grand jury, that the Hiss Standards and Baltimore documents were produced on the same machine, although Feehan and Murphy were careful not to identify Woodstock N230099 as the culprit, and Feehan went unchallenged by a technically cowed and uncertain defense. Then, between trials—despite the knowledge that N230099 could hardly have been the right machine—the FBI lab made one of several specific findings that the specimens taken from the impounded N230099 and the Baltimore documents were typed by the same typewriter. "The typewriter with Serial #N230099, which was used to type the specimens . . . was the typewriter that was used to type the evidence," concluded an October 27 secret report. "These specimens," repeated a typical subsequent memo, "were later compared by the laboratory with the documents presented by Whittaker Chambers and were found to have been prepared on the same typewriter."

At the second trial, Feehan and the prosecution again skirted a sworn verification of the typewriter and again went largely unchallenged by the defense. Yet Feehan's identification of the Hiss Standards with the Baltimore documents would now be all the more absolute, the prosecution's authority in court seeming to grow in proportion to the caprice of the evidence it held *in camera*. In Feehan's careful dissimulation and at two other crucial points, the United States government effectively suborned perjury on the fraudulent Woodstock. "No identity with E. UUU [the defense typewriter 230099] was attempted or needed," the prosecution falsely represented to the court in reply to a later Hiss petition for a new trial, though the FBI files were swarming with such attempted and much-needed "identity." At another juncture, a sworn FBI affidavit before the federal court claimed that "the Federal Bureau of Investigation has never had any informaton as to the existence of any other Hiss Woodstock machine other than trial exhibit UUU," while, once again, secret Bureau files contained a fat history of that "other" machine.

But it was Murphy himself who most epitomized the brazenness of the deception. "If you think that any bit of evidence in this case, any bit, material or immaterial, was manufactured, conceived or suborned by the FBI, acquit this man," he pronounced to the jury in his summation. "The FBI ought to be told by you that they can't tamper with witnesses and evidence." Examining the FBI files decades later, even historians of the affair who believed Alger Hiss in some measure guilty would be shocked

Sarah Wadsworth
Nixon, "my Sally Ann,"
around 1878. *Whittier
College.*

Samuel Brady Nixon.
Whittier College.

Almira and Franklin Milhous shortly after their marriage. *Whittier College.*

BELOW: The Milhouses in front of their new Whittier home on the boulevard. Hannah is at left. *Whittier College.*

ABOVE: Richard's birth-
place in Yorba Linda.
The Anaheim Ditch ran
by a few yards away on
the right. *Courtesy Department of Special Collections,
USC Libraries.*

Hannah and Frank at
their wedding, June 1908.
Whittier College.

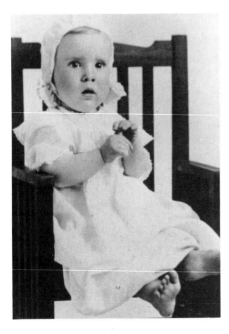

Richard Milhous Nixon.
Whittier College.

BELOW: Family portrait in Yorba
Linda: Harold at left, Don on
Hannah's knee, a pensive Rich-
ard at right. *Whittier College.*

(Left to right) Harold, Richard, Arthur, Don, and canine friend, around the time of the move to East Whittier. *Whittier College.*

BELOW: Nixon's service station in the early 1920s, before the grocery was added. *Whittier College.*

ABOVE: Whittier Union's athletic managers, 1929–30, Nixon at the upper left. He threw himself into the activity after losing the election for student body president. *Whittier College*.

Ola Florence Welch and her suitor. *Whittier College*.

High school graduation
portrait, Whittier Union, 1930.
Whittier College.

Hannah and her boys
on a family outing.
Whittier College.

An irrepressible Harold Nixon with his horse in Prescott. *Whittier College.*

BELOW: Harold Nixon convalescing in Prescott, around 1929. "I don't think he would stay in bed . . . for anybody." *Whittier College.*

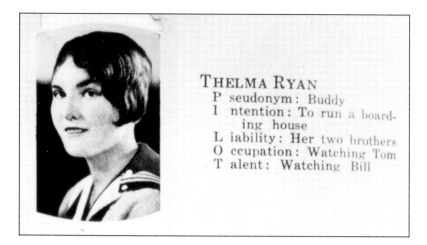

THELMA RYAN

P seudonym: Buddy
I ntention: To run a boarding house
L iability: Her two brothers
O ccupation: Watching Tom
T alent: Watching Bill

Thelma Catherine "Buddy" Ryan, class of 1929, Excelsior High School.
Courtesy Department of Special Collections, USC Libraries.

The interior of the grocery in the 1940s. Behind the clerk is the small belfry office where Richard studied and kept the books.
Whittier College.

Duke Law honor society, 1937. In the first row, just below Nixon, is Lyman Brownfield, fourth from right, and at the far right is William Perdue. Frederick Albrink is at the far right of the second row. *Whittier College.*

"Nick" Nixon in the South Pacific, 1944: Poker winnings, love letters, and dreamy, anxious formulas for success. *Whittier College.*

The studio portrait Richard received on Green Island, April 1944. A few weeks later, Pat wrote him, "You'll always have to love me lots." *Whittier College.*

Dick and Pat (at left) on an outing with friends before the war. Don is sitting beside them. *Whittier College.*

Pat and friends around the time of her wedding. *Whittier College.*

FACING PAGE, BOTTOM: Congressman Voorhis, left, at work with Chairman Martin Dies on the prewar House Un-American Committee. His loathing of communists and antisubversive legislation would turn to bitter irony in the 1946 race. *Courtesy Department of Special Collections, USC Libraries.*

Nixon returning to his Whittier law office after the war (1946). *George M. Lacks*, Life Magazine, *© 1953 Time Inc.*

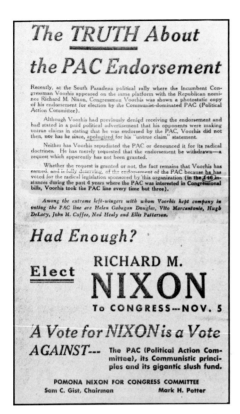

The twisted "truth" about the PAC and Jerry Voorhis. Even after the first debate and public acknowledgment of the two separate organizations, the Nixon campaign and the press stuck to the smear.

BELOW: The congressional candidate and his wife campaigning in the spring of 1946. *Whittier Daily News.*

Richard and Pat early in the 1946 race, with Senator and Mrs. William Knowland at left. *UCLA Special Collections.*

Tricia and her father, February 1946. "The only boss I recognize." *Wide World Photos.*

With Whittaker Chambers (left) and Robert Stripling, posing over one of the many headlines they made in the summer of 1948. *Wide World Photos.*

With Stripling, reading the Pumpkin Papers for the benefit of the photographers. *Courtesy Department of Special Collections, USC Libraries.*

The dramatic return to Miami from the *Panama,* Sunday, December 5, 1948. *Courtesy Department of Special Collections, USC Libraries.*

BELOW: With HUAC colleagues and the press after his return from the Caribbean: (left to right) Nixon, Karl Mundt, F. Edward Hebert, and John McDowell, looking on in characteristic distraction. Taking notes at the right is reporter George Reedy of United Press. *Courtesy Department of Special Collections, USC Libraries.*

Equipped with HUAC aide William Wheeler, formal blue suit, and a new briefcase, Congressman Nixon brings the coveted microfilm to Foley Square, December 13, 1948; he's about to make his historic intervention with the Hiss grand jury. *Wide World Photos.*

BELOW: Spyhunters: F. Edward Hebert, Richard Nixon, and Robert Stripling on the steps of the Foley Square Courthouse after the secret questioning of Chambers on personal details, Saturday, August 7, 1948. *Wide World Photos.*

FACING PAGE, TOP: Raising money for the 1950 race: (left to right, back row) Tom Pike, Charles Thomas, Bernie Brennan. California congressman Donald Jackson is seated at Nixon's left. *UCLA Special Collections.*

FACING PAGE, BOTTOM: Campaigning in the spring of 1950 atop the woody wagon, at a small town along the central coast. *Wide World Photos.*

Helen Douglas in 1950: (LEFT) in Washington in January as she confidently fought off Downey's challenge; (BELOW) after voting in the June primary. *Courtesy Department of Special Collections, USC Libraries.*

FACING PAGE: The infamous "Pink sheet." Only a careful study of the record revealed the fraud. *Helen Gahagan Douglas Collection, University of Oklahoma.*

DOUGLAS-MARCANTONIO VOTING RECORD

Many persons have requested a comparison of the voting records of Congresswoman Helen Douglas and the notorious Communist party-liner, Congressman Vito Marcantonio of New York.

Mrs. Douglas and Marcantonio have been members of Congress together since January 1, 1945. During that period, Mrs. Douglas voted the same as Marcantonio **354** times. While it should not be expected that a member of the House of Representatives should always vote in opposition to Marcantonio, it is significant to note, not only the great number of times which Mrs. Douglas voted in agreement with him, but also the issues on which almost without exception they always saw eye to eye, to-wit: Un-American Activities and Internal Security.

Here is the Record!

VOTES AGAINST COMMITTEE ON UN-AMERICAN ACTIVITIES

Both Douglas and Marcantonio voted against establishing the Committee on Un-American Activities. 1/3/45. Bill passed.

Both voted on three separate occasions against contempt proceedings against persons and organizations which refused to reveal records or answer whether they were Communists. 4/16/46, 6/26/46, 11/24/47. Bills passed.

Both voted on four separate occasions against allowing funds for investigation by the Un-American Activities Committee. 5/17/46, 3/9/48, 2/9/49, 3/23/50. (The last vote was 348 to 12.) All bills passed.

COMMUNIST-LINE FOREIGN POLICY VOTES

Both voted against Greek-Turkish Aid Bill. 5/9/47. (It has been established that without this aid Greece and Turkey would long since have gone behind the Iron Curtain.) Bill passed.

Both voted on two occasions against free press amendment to UNRRA appropriation bill, providing that no funds should be furnished any country which refused to allow free access to the news of activities of the UNRRA by press and radio representatives of the United States. 11/1/45, 6/28/46. Bills passed. (This would in effect have denied American relief funds to Communist dominated countries.)

Both voted against refusing Foreign Relief to Soviet-dominated countries UNLESS supervised by Americans. 4/30/47. Bill passed 324 to 75.

VOTE AGAINST NATIONAL DEFENSE

Both voted against the Selective Service Act of 1948. 6/18/48. Bill passed.

VOTES AGAINST LOYALTY AND SECURITY LEGISLATION

Both voted on two separate occasions against bills requiring loyalty checks for Federal employees. 7/15/47, 6/29/49. Bills passed.

Both voted against the Subversive Activities Control Act of 1948, requiring registration with the Attorney General of Communist party members and communist controlled organizations. Bill passed, 319 to 58. 5/19/48. AND AFTER KOREA both again voted against it. Bill passed 8/29/50, 354 to 20.

AFTER KOREA, on July 12, 1950, Marcantonio and Douglas and 12 others voted against the Security Bill, to permit the heads of key National Defense departments, such as the Atomic Energy Commission, to discharge government workers found to be poor security risks! Bill passed, 327 to 14.

VOTE AGAINST CALIFORNIA

Both recorded against confirming title to Tidelands in California and the other states affected. 4/30/48. Bill passed 257-29.

VOTES AGAINST CONGRESSIONAL INVESTIGATION OF COMMUNIST AND OTHER ILLEGAL ACTIVITIES

Both voted against investigating the "whitewash" of the AMERASIA case. 4/18/46. Bill passed.

Both voted against investigating why the Soviet Union was buying as many as 60,000 United States patents at one time. 3/4/47. Bill passed.

Both voted against continuing investigation of numerous instances of illegal actions by OPA and the War Labor Board. 1/18/45. Bill passed.

Both voted on two occasions against allowing Congress to have access to government records necessary to the conduct of investigations by Senate and House Committees. 4/22/48, 5/13/48. Bills passed.

ON ALL OF THE ABOVE VOTES which have occurred since Congressman Nixon took office on January 1, 1947, HE has voted exactly opposite to the Douglas-Marcantonio Axis!

After studying the voting comparison between Mrs. Douglas and Marcantonio, is it any wonder that the Communist line newspaper, the Daily People's World, in its lead editorial on January 31, 1950, labeled Congressman Nixon as "The Man To Beat" in this Senate race and that the Communist newspaper, the New York Daily Worker, in the issue of July 28, 1947, selected Mrs. Douglas along with Marcantonio as "One of the Heroes of the 80th Congress."

REMEMBER! The United States Senate votes on ratifying international treaties and confirming presidential appointments. Would California send Marcantonio to the United States Senate?

NIXON FOR U. S. SENATOR CAMPAIGN COMMITTEE

NORTHERN CALIFORNIA	CENTRAL CALIFORNIA	SOUTHERN CALIFORNIA
John Walton Dinkelspiel, Chairman	B. M. Heblick, Chairman	Bernard Brennan, Chairman
1151 Market Street	820 Van Ness Avenue	117 W. 9th St., Los Angeles
San Francisco—UNderhill 3-1416	Fresno—Phone 44116	TRinity 0661

Douglas on general election night in November. *Courtesy Department of Special Collections, USC Libraries.*

Election night. The new senator exults. *Wide World Photos.*

Senator Nixon and Representative Gerald R. Ford pose for a picture in Nixon's office after a talk on January 23, 1951. *Wide World Photos.*

Reading a stack of angry telegrams critical of President Truman's firing of General MacArthur, April 11, 1951. *Wide World Photos.*

ABOVE: Dana Smith preparing the accounting on the Fund. *UCLA Special Collections.*

With Senator William Knowland in the California seats on the floor of the Convention just before the 1952 Presidential balloting. Later that afternoon, when asked to introduce Nixon's name as Vice-Presidential nominee, Knowland would ask bitterly, "I have to nominate that dirty son of a bitch?" *Wide World Photos.*

Victory in Chicago. The happy couple bask in the cheers as Speaker of the House Joe Martin looks on. *Wide World Photos*.

Holding Tricia during their triumphal homecoming to Whittier, July 28, 1952. *Wide World Photos*.

Richard Nixon and his parents in 1952. *UCLA Special Collections.*

The Nixon House in Spring Valley, 1952. The Democrats attacked it as "an elaborate home" made possible by the Fund, and even Ike had enduring questions unanswered by the Checkers speech. *Courtesy Department of Special Collections, USC Libraries.*

With Rose Mary Woods and the congratulatory wires and letters after his Vice-Presidential nomination. *Wide World Photos.*

July 5, 1952, aboard the *GOP*, posing with a somber Earl Warren the morning after "the great train robbery." *Wide World Photos.*

Answering the heckler at Marysville, September 19, 1952. *Wide World Photos.*

Richard and Pat on the set of Checkers. *Courtesy Department of Special Collections, USC Libraries.*

At the attacking climax of Checkers, asking the Democrats—and Eisenhower—to make the same accounting. *Wide World Photos.*

At Wheeling, Nixon breaks down on Knowland's shoulder.

Western Union lines were jammed all over America after Nixon's "Checkers" speech. Pictured here are rows of busy operators in Los Angeles. *UCLA Special Collections.*

At the door of the plane with Eisenhower in Wheeling. *Courtesy Department of Special Collections, USC Libraries.*

BELOW: July 11, 1952: the demonstration after Knowland had placed his name in the nomination. At left is Murray Chotiner, less than seven years after he had first heard the impressive young Naval officer speak before the Committee of 100. *Wide World Photos.*

Audition at the Waldorf, May 8, 1952. (Left to right) William Pfeifer, New York State Committee Chairman and key fund-raiser, Senator Nixon, and an elated Tom Dewey, who later that evening proffered Nixon the Vice-Presidential nomination under Dwight Eisenhower. *Wide World Photos.*

With Ike and Mamie at the Convention podium. *Wide World Photos.*

ABOVE: On the beach in Florida after the 1952 election. *Wide World Photos.*

Inauguration, January 1953: (left to right) Herbert Hoover, Richard Nixon, Dwight Eisenhower, and Harry Truman. *Wide World Photos.*

by the government's misconduct. "Murphy's words," concluded one team of scholars, "convey a horrifying cynicism."

The second trial thrashed about in much the same ambiguity that had haunted the case from the beginning. Goddard allowed, as Kaufman had not, the testimony of another communist-become-informer, Hede Messing, who claimed to have met Hiss once as a fellow agent. But the social encounter, even as related by the repentant witness, was vague and enigmatic. The title to the old Ford remained, as Stripling conceded, "a mystery," confirming neither protagonist. When the government sought to tie a $400 Hiss bank withdrawal to another loan to Chambers and to the latter's purchase of a car just before his defection, the evidence would be mired in suspicious irregularities in the records of the automobile sale. Julian Wadleigh again testified that he was a source for Chambers in State, that he had not known Hiss as a fellow conspirator, that he did not or could not hand over all the documents in question. But it would be clear, too, as Wadleigh's own superior said later, that there were "virtually no security arrangements in the Department at the time . . . [and] it would have been the easiest thing for Wadleigh to have taken . . . any number of papers from my desk or from others' desks."

Even prompted and rehearsed by the FBI, Whittaker Chambers continued to be a mystically uneven witness, lethally certain about some details, utterly unaccountable in others. Under cross-examination in the second trial, he was suddenly unable to recall that there were only two small bedrooms in the Hisses' Thirtieth Street house where he had sworn to HUAC to have slept often, where he had supposedly watched Alger and Priscilla entwined in bed, as he told Bert Andrews and Richard Nixon that Sunday afternoon in August 1948, one of the alluring early details of his story. Yet beside his accuser, Alger Hiss struck the same old self-defeating aloofness and arrogance. A well of contradiction, he was the defendant who somehow thought himself above reproach and thus even above thorough legal preparation, whose very mannerisms offended jurors who were so plainly of a different caste and class. Hiss was at once to be credited as the meticulous master spy and impostor, while trafficking in stolen documents neatly checked off with his initials, copied in his own handwriting, or typed on his wife's old lurching, telltale Woodstock.

The puzzle composed and dissolved in quicksilver forms as the typewriter sat by in its own mute perjury. Richard Nixon tried anxiously to telephone Lasky in the last weeks of the second trial. On New Year's Day 1950, the reporter wrote back confidently from his own vantage point close to the prosecution: "Alger will NEVER be acquitted . . . and he stands a good chance of being convicted. . . . He did batter down several collateral issues . . . BUT . . . he still hasn't been able to crack the basic story—

the typewriter and the typed documents," Lasky assured him. Ben Mandel had spent a day at the trial, surveying the event he had done so much to initiate, and Lasky thought they were all optimisitc. "In short, Dick, I'm not worried a bit."

Even so, the congressman fretted. As Murphy effectively blunted the late testimony of defense psychiatrist Carl Binger on Chambers's mania—a skillful cross-examination that Alistair Cooke called "the first public trial run of the common man's resistance to psychiatry"—Nixon again gave the FBI a helpful tidbit to discredit the opposition. "Ben Mandel has told him," Nichols wrote of Nixon's call January 11, 1950, ". . . about an incident wherein Dr. Binger . . . was brought before the Massachusetts State [sic] Medical Association on unethical charges growing out of a book that he [Binger] published." Even Father Cronin joined the effort by calling his old FBI handlers with gossip that Dr. Binger possessed a "slight" communist record.

As it was, the doctor's politics were moot. "They were typed on that machine," Murphy said, pointing to the documents and then to the Woodstock in his summation, adding, "Our man said it was," though Feehan had made that judgment only in secret. "It is the contention of the government that this is the typewriter upon which the Baltimore exhibits . . . were typed," said Judge Goddard, compounding the error in his charge to the jury.

Early on the afternoon of January 21, 1950, after less than twenty-four hours of deliberation, Mrs. Ada Condell, the rotund forelady from the Bronx, spoke the historic words in a low, shaking voice: "guilty on the first count and guilty on the second."

There were to be many sequels, but two seemed especially apt. Later, at a St. Patrick's Day parade, Thomas Murphy, the victorious prosecutor, would sound an echo of the forces of class, religion, and newfound nativism that had long before fed the current that crested with the conviction of Alger Hiss. "I can't even recall one Irish name among the many thousands called upon [sic] before the House Committee on Un-American Activities," Murphy told the cheering crowd.

As for the typewriter, it was not only that technical expertise was still too primitive in 1949 to make the identification of typewriter and typed papers that chilled the defense and armed the prosecution, but that the FBI's technical competence was a particular sham. William Sullivan, a former FBI assistant director and one of the recipients of Father Cronin's intelligence, would reveal in his memoirs three decades later how much the vaunted Bureau lab, weakly staffed and managed, was a bureaucratic joke within the agency, how much field agents compensated for technical incapacity and the upper levels covered up the failure. "The FBI laboratory is in fact a real-life counterpart of the busy workroom of the Wizard of Ox—all illusion," Sullivan wrote of the kind of evidence that largely convicted Alger Hiss.

Years after the verdict, Hiss would call Sullivan in retirement, asking the former ranking official about persistent rumors that Richard Nixon somehow conspired with the Bureau to manufacture a fake machine. "I know we were giving Richard Nixon . . . every possible assistance," Sullivan remembered. At the same time, he would have to tell Hiss that there was no Woodstock ingeniously made in the lab, albeit not for want of zeal. "Had Nixon asked the FBI to manufacture evidence to prove his case against Hiss, Hoover would have been only too glad to oblige," Sullivan believed from his intimate perspective on the case. But "even if we had wanted to, we simply would not have been capable of it."

Reporters found Richard Nixon the Saturday afternoon of the verdict, posing with the *Washington Evening Star*'s banner headline "HISS GUILTY . . . ," wearing the satisfied mien of the successful spy hunter and the dark-browed seriousness of Hannah Milhous's now-famous son. "I consider this verdict a vindication of the congressional methods of investigation when they are accompanied by adequate staff work and fair procedure," he told the press. That night he went on radio to be interviewed by Bert Andrews and promised further exposure of an administration cover-up. "I have information . . . which will show that this conspiracy would have come to light long since had there not been a definite, determined and deliberate effort on the part of certain high officials in two administrations to keep the public from knowing the facts," he answered Andrews's prearranged question about the background of the case. The congratulatory mail began that weekend. "The conviction of Alger Hiss was due to your patience and persistence alone," Herbert Hoover now wrote him, clearly pleased with the young congressman he had quietly financed four years before. "At last the stream of treason that existed in our government has been exposed in a fashion that all may believe." Two days after the verdict, at one of the largest press conferences ever held on Capitol Hill, the second-term representative from Whittier repeated the same charge, describing what he called the Red "Master Plot" to subvert America and managing, thought one writer, "to crow over Hiss's conviction."

The media furor produced, too, the seemingly inevitable personal clash with the administration. Hours after Nixon's press conference, reporters asked Secretary of State Dean Acheson about the conviction of his former State Department associate and friend. "I should like to make it clear to you that whatever the outcome of any appeal . . . I do not intend to turn my back on Alger Hiss," Acheson told them in some defiance, referring the mostly puzzled correspondents to Matthew 25:36—"Naked, and ye clothed me: I was sick, and ye visited me: I was in prison, and ye came unto me." It was, wrote one historian, "as courageous and as genuinely Christian an attitude as American politics has ever produced," and at the same moment "a tremendous and totally unnecessary gift" to the opposition. Nixon promptly labeled the secretary's allusion to the Last Judgment as "disgusting" and took the opportunity to cast the conviction still wider. "Traitors in the high councils of our own government," he said in a none-too-veiled reference to Acheson and others as well as Hiss, "have made sure that the deck is stacked on the Soviet side of the diplomatic tables."

With elaborate heralding, asking for a special order to address the Congress, he went to the floor of the House on January 26, 1950, to deliver his own dramatic summation, a four-hour speech he entitled "The Hiss Case—A Lesson for the American People." The speech would come a day after Alger Hiss was sentenced by Goddard to two concurrent five-year terms.

Of its kind, it was remarkable congressional oratory, given in triumph to a crowded, attentive chamber with many of those colleagues who had once doubted him, who had urged him to pull back after Hiss's first testimony in early August 1948. A recapitulation of the case as it unfolded before HUAC, the speech would be reprinted and distributed about the nation by the hundreds of thousands, Richard Nixon's first public reflection on his own meteoric career. It was also a first exercise in the discreet censoring of history. In an account filled with names, the accusers and accused, many of the most important actors would be missing. He would briefly credit Stripling and Mandel, who "did particularly effective work in suggesting penetrating questions to be put to the witnesses." But nowhere visible were the truly pivotal figures and moments—Bert Andrews, the Dulles brothers at the Roosevelt, Nick Vazzana and his leak about the Baltimore documents, Louis Nichols and his FBI colleagues, and not least the gentle, sandy-haired Baltimore priest and informer named John Cronin.

The Committee had known from the beginning (though he did not explain how) that Chambers "had made charges many years ago . . . concerning communist activities among federal employees." But as the confrontation developed between Hiss and Chambers, HUAC found it "particularly difficult because we could get no assistance whatever from the intelligence agencies of the government." He ran through the chronology of August and December 1948, and the discovery of the Pumpkin Papers, stressing how "amazingly effective" the spy ring had been, how "injurious to the national security" the cables and memos and the presumed code-breaking. Even with the documents, however, it had still been largely

Chambers versus Hiss, and Julian Wadleigh proved a necessary witness. "Mr. Wadleigh's admission was important primarily because it had the effect of taking the case out of the realm of fantasy," Nixon told the House in an extraordinary passage, "and provided solid corroborative evidence to back the Chambers story." It was a small mark of how tenuously he had always held the Chambers testimony, as if the whole hunt had indeed been "fantasy" before Wadleigh's emergence so late in the sequence, as if the State Department clerk were not a veritable alternative or stand-in for Hiss as the source of documents.

Yet few if any on the floor or in the galleries knew the nuances of the case, and he held them fast, flourishing halfway through the speech the text of Harry Dexter White's hand-written memo Chambers had surrendered to Appell and Wheeler more than a year before along with the microfilm and photostats of the Baltimore documents. White was now dead, Wadleigh beyond the statute of limitations, Hiss punishable only indirectly by a perjury charge, he said with a heavy air of regret. The country would be cheated of the penalty for such treason. Their conspiracy had been "so well entrenched and so well defended by apologists in high places that it was not discovered and apprehended until it was too late to prosecute those who were involved in it for the crimes they had committed."

"No blame can attach to the FBI for failure to expose the facts of this case," he was careful to add of his ever-sensitive allies in the Bureau. "First, above all," Nixon would list among the "lessons" of the affair, "we must give complete and unqualified support to the FBI and J. Edgar Hoover." If anyone were ever "successful in obtaining an investigation of the FBI and access to its records, a fatal blow will have been struck against the protective security forces of this Nation," he said at one point of the files that would have showed the tainted evidence on the Woodstock, as well as his own secret role and the relentless political corruptions of the FBI. "I am sure that the members of the House will join with me in resisting such an attack and in supporting the finest police organization which exists in a free nation today." The chamber responded with ardent applause.

He closed with sweeping proposals to toughen the espionage laws and loyalty checks, for "an extensive educational program" about communism, and with appeals for "whole-hearted support" of HUAC, "the most unpleasant and thankless assignment in the Congress," he called it, but without which "the Hiss conspiracy might never have been exposed." Near the end was another passage of almost eerie portent for his own Presidency as he spoke of Truman's purported cover-up. "It is customary practice for any administration, be it Republican or Democrat, to resist the disclosure of facts which might be embarrassing to that administration in an election," he said that January morning in 1950. "This is a statement of fact, though, of course, I do not mean to justify that practice, regardless of the nature of the skeleton in the political closet."

The peroration came with a sophistry of numbers and a ringing call to arms. Five years ago, when Alger Hiss was arranging postwar conferences, he told them, the "Soviet orbit" was only 180 million and "the odds were nine to one in our favor." Now 800 million lived "under the domination of Soviet totalitarianism" and "the odds are five to three against us." That had been the real cost of the Hiss case and the cover-up. "We owe a solemn duty . . . to expose this sinister conspiracy for what it is," he said in a rising voice, "to roll back the Red tide." He left the floor to a standing ovation, members reaching out to shake his hand, thronging him in the cloakroom outside.

"THE GREAT LESSON TO BE LEARNED"

Over the following week, Truman announced the building of the hydrogen bomb. J. Edgar Hoover proudly if chillingly revealed the arrest for Soviet espionage of Klaus Fuchs, a British scientist assigned to the Manhattan Project at Los Alamos during the war. And Albert Einstein warned that a new generation of nuclear weapons might extinguish all life on the planet. From front-page reports of the Hiss trial, public discussion in New York turned to the prospect of mass graves in Central Park following a Russian attack.

Across the nation, Republicans prepared their ritual Lincoln Day speeches to exploit the greatest Red Scare of all, and in Washington the GOP Campaign Committee scheduled a hard-drinking Wisconsin senator to make some obligatory appearances in the hinterland. There would be stopovers in Las Vegas and Reno, where the senator could also indulge his appetite for gambling, but the tour would begin more or less obscurely, with Joseph McCarthy addressing the Ohio County Women's Republican Club in Wheeling, West Virginia.

Earlier in January, before the Hiss conviction, McCarthy had gone to dinner with some advisers at the Colony Restaurant in Washington, casting about for an issue that would win him prominence and support for his reelection fight two years later. They had talked about the St. Lawrence Seaway or a new pension plan. But Father Edmund Walsh, a friend of John Cronin's and a prominent Catholic educator at Georgetown University, had urged the issue of communist infiltration, and the senator liked the idea instantly. Still, McCarthy was not sure how much he should emphasize the theme; for a time the ladies in Wheeling thought he would speak about aid to the elderly or housing. Then came the Hiss verdict and Dick Nixon's triumphal speech to the House. McCarthy asked Ed Nellor of the *Washington Times-Herald* and other conservative reporters close to HUAC and the case to help write the speech, and he delivered it in Wheeling on the evening of February 9.

What McCarthy said then and later would reflect the man and his singular temper, but in many respects the provenance was clear. "The great lesson to be learned is that we are not just dealing with espionage agents who get thirty pieces of silver to obtain the blueprints of a new weapon . . . [but] a far more sinister type of activity because it permits the enemy to guide and shape our policy," Richard Nixon had told the Congress two weeks before. "One thing to remember," McCarthy now admonished the Ohio County women, "is that we are not dealing with spies who get thirty pieces of silver to steal the blueprint of a new weapon. We are dealing with a far more sinister type of activity because it permits the enemy to guide and shape our policy." Typically, McCarthy would go on to improve on Nixon's bloated figures. There were now eighty billion "under the absolute domination of Soviet Russia," the Wisconsin senator said preposterously in Wheeling, while "on our side, the figure has shrunk to about 500,000." Then, near the end, local newsmen remembered the most shocking line, the ultimate extrapolation of Alger Hiss: "I have here in my hand a list of 205—a list of names that were known to the Secretary of State as being members of the Communist Party and who nevertheless are still working and shaping policy in the State Department."

At first there was little coverage of the Wheeling speech, and McCarthy himself could never even find the rough notes from which he had spoken, including the plagiarized passages from Congressman Nixon. But the next day he made much the same speech in Salt Lake City about "fifty-seven card-carrying members of the Communist Party" in the State Department, and the day after that the same talk in Reno. Soon the footnotes did not matter. By the end of his tour the senator would be making national headlines, and by the end of March he would be overwhelmed with contributions, awards for Americanism, and, more important, the awe and obeisance of GOP leaders. "Tell me, Senator, just how long ago did you discover Communism?" a reporter's wife asked caustically at a party that spring. "Why," Joe McCarthy said, smiling, "about two and a half months ago."

As McCarthyism entered the language, christening an era as well as a political method, HUAC flourished. Days after Wheeling the Mundt-Nixon bill was revised, and eventually, under the patronage and name of Senator

McCarran and with added restrictions, was passed over Harry Truman's veto. In the Eighty-first Congress, the Committee had been granted $200,000 without debate, and it promptly grew into a small empire, a staff of seventy-five swelling beyond the old rooms, six hundred file cabinets holding HUAC's peculiar currency and treasure, more than a million names. The FBI viewed with mixed feelings the resurgent power of its old ally and rival. "This is an intolerable situation," Hoover wrote angrily across yet another report, in March 1950, on the Committee revealing Bureau sources. "HUAC in seeking headlines is wrecking our measures for internal security. H."

Yet HUAC's most prominent member remained a public and private champion of the FBI. When FBI abuses aborted the espionage prosecution of Justice Department aide Judith Coplon, when an agent perjured himself in the Coplon trial and wiretaps were found to have violated Coplon's privileged conversations with her attorney, Richard Nixon nonetheless stood by the Bureau. When the National Lawyers Guild, a left-wing group Hoover called "shyster and subversive," investigated the FBI, it was Richard Nixon who warned Hoover in advance of the probe and who later quietly intervened with the press to dilute coverage of the Guild findings. As part of its burgeoning files, HUAC at Nixon's urging would keep dossiers on "activities against the FBI," including reports on Hoover's formidable bureaucratic rival, the Central Intelligence Agency.

For its part, the Bureau reacted to the nettlesome problems of the Hiss typewriter or the Coplon wiretaps by burrowing still deeper into official secrecy. There would be far more than J. Edgar Hoover's old "DO NOT FILE" file, a cache of records on political figures and unsavory Bureau interventions. In 1949–50 agents were given a new classification code named "June Mail" to cover all information acquired through "sources illegal in nature" or from "extremely sensitive sources" such as key political figures. Discreetly censoring even their own secret reports, agents were to attach to memoranda a special "administrative" page for all "facts and information which are considered of a nature not expedient to disseminate or would cause embarrassment to the Bureau, if distributed," allowing the FBI to evade even court-ordered disclosures.

Afterward, when the mania of the era had run its course, the actual yield of such extreme measures would be remarkably small, save in terms of the bureaucratic and political power of the FBI itself. By any standard, there had been no massive "infiltration" of the federal government by communists, though party members were clearly scattered about agencies in the vast expansion of the bureaucracy that came with the New Deal. Most prevalent in Agriculture, congressional committees, and the National Labor Relations Board, they "were not primarily organized for espionage," concluded one conservative scholar, but for "the promotion of left tendencies in the development of the public policies of the respective agencies," and even then generally thwarted. Of the half million civil servants in Washington alone in the 1930s, not even the ever-prolific Whittaker Chambers could implicate directly or indirectly more than "about seventy-five" people sympathetic in some way with communism. In the wake of the Hiss trials, some 2.5 million government employees would be checked for loyalty. Following numerous hearings, only 270 were fired, of whom sixty-nine were later reinstated. The FBI, even in its vast post-Hiss power, could establish not one case of espionage among the dismissed.

Watching it all from the Texas hills as the patron saint of Un-American Activities, the choleric Martin Dies thought young Richard Nixon "the only congressman ever to profit by anticommunist activity," so hugely did the Californian now eclipse his sometime colleagues on HUAC. Mundt went on to a dull, dead-end career in the Senate, clinging to a final term despite physical incapacity. Hebert gave only slightly more notable service as a chairman of the House Armed Services Committee, while Rankin and the rest slid into merciful obscurity.

Nixon's own appraisal of his considerable benefits from the case was always Pyrrhic, amounting to a theme of persecution. "The Hiss case proved beyond any reasonable doubt the existence of Soviet-directed communist subversion at the highest levels of American government," he wrote, still convinced, thirty years afterward. And in the very "overwhelming evidence of his guilt," he believed the legion of liberals and Hiss partisans "turned their anger and frustration toward me," as if Richard Nixon were somehow responsible for the deception. "While there is no doubt that my reputation from the Hiss case launched me," he concluded in his memoirs, "it also turned me from a relatively popular young congressman, enjoying a good but limited press, into one of the most controversial figures in Washington, bitterly opposed by the most respected and influential liberal journalists and opinion leaders of the time."

Over the next dozen years there appeared no limit to the "utterly unprincipled and vicious smear campaign" he saw unleashed by his exposure of high treason. Almost every attack or criticism by the press or oppositing politicians could be traced to his unforgivable victory over Alger Hiss. "Bigamy, forgery, drunkenness, insanity, thievery, anti-Semitism, perjury, the whole gamut of misconduct in public office, ranging from unethical to downright criminal activities—all these were among the charges that were hurled against me, some publicly and others through whispering campaigns which were even more difficult to counteract," he wrote in *Six Crises*.

No "lesson" of the case, no personal or political conviction, no explanation or justification of history, then and afterward, would be more fixed in the man—or, for that matter, in the woman who saw the episode widen still further the slowly growing gulf in their marriage. "One thing I want to make clear to you," Pat Nixon would passionately tell her daughter exactly three decades after that historic Washington summer of 1948. "The reason people have gone after Daddy is that no one could control him— not the press, not the lobbyists, not the politicians. He did what he felt was right, and from the time this became apparent in the Hiss case, he was a target." "Vindictiveness of some of the Hiss supporters," Julie Eisenhower wrote of her mother, "caused an irreparable crack in her idealistic view of politics." For both the Nixons—a bond of agreed martyrdom—the case was ever afterward to be a kind of revelation of political reprisal as well as triumph, and so, too, a rationalization of Richard Nixon's politics and methods not only in 1948–49 but to the end of his career.

In fact, Nixon's performance in the case had been both more and less impressive than his public reputation among either admirers or critics. His sense of timing, the enlistment and use of powerful allies, the studious preparation and shrewd questioning, his sheer instinct for the evidence and witnesses were all formidable, at times brilliant. Yet he had also been given prior and secret advantages far more than even his closest collaborators imagined. His victory had been won with considerable help against a sluggish bureaucracy and politically complacent administration. At critical moments, despite his covert aid, he had responded not with the calm strength and well-honed resolve he would depict in his own renditions of the story but with sometimes quavering uncertainty, self-righteousness and panic, fear and near despair.

So, too, the rewards were private as well as public. "The Committee had helped to make him," wrote Walter Goodman, "but he, more than any other member, had been responsible for giving the Committee its great year." His monuments would be the resurrection of HUAC from the swift death Harry Truman had planned for it after the 1948 election and in a larger sense the resurgence of the Red Scare in American politics, with McCarthyism and all that implied. His genius, and luck, was that others, principally Joe McCarthy himself, would come to personify far more the excesses of the era and movement. Nixon would emerge from the case much as he began it, seen among his peers as the relative moderate, his moderation both fact and fiction but rendering the Red-baiting cause more respectable, an accommodating, largely uncritical press making him a national figure and his politics a national craze.

More quietly, in 1949, still president of Columbia University and no longer so skeptical a witness to the Hiss case, Dwight Eisenhower told a friend he was "anxious" to be briefed confidentially on the new communist internal security threat. The friend had called Alfred Kohlberg, who promptly suggested both Louis Budenz, the well-traveled informer, and Richard Nixon. Eisenhower preferred the congressman, and he was secretly "called in," as Kohlberg's wife remembered the arrangement. The general and the precocious politician had hit it off, Nixon afterward writing one of many "Dear Alfred" letters to thank the powerful lobbyist for the discreet introduction to Eisenhower more than a year before their first acknowledged meeting. The case, and his secret allies, had given Richard Nixon a vital first entrée, aptly secret, to the next President of the United States and the man who would shape his political future.

Still, the enemies were real as well as imagined. They arose far less out of revenge for Alger Hiss—in the end, the defendant would have very few genuine champions in the press or establishment, let alone among practicing politicians—than in an often visceral revulsion at the Nixon method and manner. The powerful Democratic Speaker of the House, Texan Sam Rayburn, nearly forty years in Congress, now saw in the newly famous congressman from Whittier a calculation, an unctuousness and am- bition unusual even by the feral standards of Texas politics. Like other Democrats, liberal and conservative, Rayburn watched intently the cease- less exploitation of the case, and the cowing of witnesses that followed in HUAC's flowing tide. The story would travel swiftly in the congressional cloakrooms about Dick Nixon once coming down from the Committee dais and berating, shouting, they said, at some trembling, small-fry left-winger, a little tailor from Baltimore. Rayburn and many of his colleagues never forgot that story and others like it. "That ugly man with the Chinkapin eyes," the Speaker would say of Nixon. "He has the cruelest face of any man I ever met."

Resentment and fear of his astounding success certainly drove the op- position as well, but the politics of the case were frequently so blatant that even the supporters and silent patrons were moved to acknowledge the congressman's extraordinary habits. "That Nixon as a politician in those days had his weaknesses," Isaac Don Levine wrote of what seemed his strengths, "that he was out to build his popular image with the customary tools of politics, aggrandizing credit to himself at every opportunity, was the expected thing." Levine saw, too, the rich historical irony of a politician exploiting so grandly the forces that terrified his countrymen, the con- gressman from Whittier in a sense nurtured by that old frightening impulse that splashed "IWW" on the wall of the Yorba Linda packinghouse. "I came to realize," Levine reflected, "that the spectacular rise of Richard Nixon sprang from the subsoil of the Russian Revolution which was reshaping the whole world." And in 1949–50 it was a growth that had only just begun.

But neither enemies nor friends could easily plumb the depths of cynicism engendered in Richard Nixon by the case that made him famous. It was always more than the assumption of hostility and reprisal. The deeper meaning went to the marrow of the political process, to discovered truths about how Washington worked. "I shall always be grateful that . . . I had the requisite energy and drive to cope with it" is how Nixon ended his description of the affair, his "first" crisis in *Six Crises*. It was the sort of gloss that prompted Bob Stripling to burst out in an interview years later, "*Six Crises* is pure bullshit!" What they had witnessed together was scarcely limited to "energy" or "coping." The case was heady schooling in the manipulation of the press and legal system, in the frailty and caprice of congressional colleagues, in the craven ambition and ready cannibalism of the establishment, in the easy disregard of secrecy and procedure on all sides, in the significance of covert action and alliances and the utter politicization of every governmental act.

The lessons he felt and learned beneath the public surface came through in private conversations more than twenty years later when he confronted what he thought a similar "crisis" in his own Presidency. "I went through all this in the Hiss case and we won that," Nixon would tell an aide. The battle then, too, could be "won in the press" if [we] "mobilize our friends" and "leak stuff out." They would once more "need Hoover's cooperation" and the target could be "tried in the papers" and effectively defeated "before a committee." In a political career of nearly three decades, from an obscure congressional candidate in the old twelfth district to international statesman, no other episode or experience would so mark Richard Nixon, so inspire such pride or sense of success, burn so deeply its cynical, scarring moral.

His appeals exhausted, Alger Hiss surrendered himself to federal marshals on March 22, 1951, at the Foley Square courthouse where so much had unfolded. It was scarcely six years since he had been chosen as the first temporary secretary general of the United Nations, two and one-half years after Whittaker Chambers met Congressman Nixon and his subcommittee in a stale room in the same building for that historic Saturday morning session on personal details. The Supreme Court had denied a writ of *certiorari* in the case when Justices Frankfurter and Reed, both character witnesses for Hiss, recused themselves. Now the famous prisoner sat staring impassively in the back of the penitentiary van, wearing a natty tweed overcoat, herringbone suit, and collar pin, handcuffed to an unknown black convict who fearfully hid his face from the photographers.

"The conviction of Alger Hiss was a triumph of due process," wrote liberal reporter Richard Rovere, and critic Irving Howe, echoing a wide stratum of the political intelligentsia at the time, thought the traitor caught by a "principled anticommunism." In the savage triviality of literary politics, factions voted Hiss guilty in grim ignorance of the real case, pinned their reputations to the verdict, and resisted untoward history as a personal affront. A motion for a new trial failed during Hiss's imprisonment in Lewisburg Penitentiary, and he served out forty-four months of the five-year sentence. Only much later did the release of thousands of government documents under the Freedom of Information Act show what Hiss lawyers documented as several improprieties and "repeated intrusions" by the prosecution into the defense camp, including FBI cooption of a shadowy defense investigator, and the scandalous discrepancies in the history of Woodstock N230099. Armed with the documents, Hiss would file in 1978 a petition for writ of error *coram nobis*, seeking to have the conviction set aside because "the prosecution withheld and concealed evidence which was exculpatory . . . [and] misrepresented material facts . . . to the court and jury."

The case ended characteristically. In the final legal word, Judge Richard Owen of the Southern District of New York dismissed the *coram nobis* petition in 1982 in a lengthy opinion containing by one careful analysis over a hundred factual mistakes and which a longtime student of the case called "inexcusably careless, error-ridden, and irresponsible." Owen, like the perplexed FBI before him, swiftly passed over and off the "highly contradictory and far from conclusive" history of the Woodstock and found it natural "that the prosecution did not wish to venture upon this sea of confusion with the jury." Anyway, argued the judge, "Felix [*sic*] Feehan," the FBI typewriting expert, had corroborated Chambers, and the Hisses' Woodstock, whatever its origins, "had concededly typed both the Baltimore documents and the Hiss 'Standards.' " The opinion thus ignored at once not only the corruption of the evidence and trial but the very heart of Ramos Feehan's historic evasion. The authority who blithely identified the false Woodstock with the documents could obviously no more accurately identify the documents themselves. Through it all, only politics proved immutable. Judge Owen, it turned out, would come to the case as a staunch Republican Quaker, appointed to the bench in 1974 by then-President Richard Nixon.

The vilified judge from the first trial, Samuel Kaufman, once captured the two elusive protagonists in an apt epitaph. Whittaker Chambers, he remarked to a friend, had told "more than the truth" and Alger Hiss "less." Ever afterward, Hiss remained the sophisticated idealist as startled victim.

Decades later he could still not understand how a jury "could believe that creep after seeing the two of us," just as he could not quite fathom the Committee's motives, a matter that puzzled few other intelligent observers. "You know, a congressional hearing, familiar territory to me," he said to his son and biographer. "It was a shock to discover that they were saying one thing and doing another. They were really on a witch hunt." But then, he would add long after his defeat, "[The Committee] wasn't very bright, wasn't very alert, and didn't think the way I did."

Like an elegant, unperturbed cat suddenly caught under a great net, he batted at this web and that, never escaping or even sensing the envelopment. He went to jail for a crime not constitutionally proven, in a protracted political show trial from Congress to courtroom that gave his insistence of innocence, his cause, a force far beyond its intrinsic substance, another case that refused to die because the political poison and injustice were always too palpable, even when still carefully concealed in FBI files. Yet it was also the paradox of Alger Hiss's posterity, as of his early encounters with Nixon and HUAC, that what David Riesman called his "special elements (special guilts, special arrogances, special impatiences)" drove on and justified no less his prosecutors and accusers. Having long danced about the question of homosexuality and issued contradictory statements about their historic triangle in Georgetown, he said of Chambers and Priscilla in 1975, "He never made a pass at me, but he had a hostility to the point of jealousy about my wife and a calm, almost paternal attitude toward me which is unexplainable in any other way."

George Crosley, one more free-lancer looking for a story, the man who sublet an apartment, who took a car in the bargain, who was strangely absent yet present with a "calm, almost paternal attitude"; about the attachment to this seedy, pudgy man with the rotten teeth, Alger Hiss could never tell the whole truth. Nor was he honest about the early ties to the Ware group, the heady romantic adjunct of the idealism that so long fired his defense. Party member or no, spy or no, in the end his lies would never justify the matching political and legal deceptions of the United States government. Worse still, he lent them credence and disguise.

A few saw the vast disproportion between personal scandal and the national political crisis it unleashed, whatever the furtive transactions between the debonair State Department clerk and the lowlife communist courier. "And they even took an old tired-out ass-end-of-history picture involving Alger Hiss and made a national sensation out of it," said Stephen Spingarn, the White House aide on internal security in 1948–49. It was one of the many ironies, thought Spingarn, who saw the larger product of the Bureau, that J. Edgar Hoover and the FBI generally "did a piss-poor job on counterespionage," that the nation would never be able to gauge the real toll of Soviet intelligence while its hopelessly political and publicity-conscious federal police lined up a handful of romantics and misfits from the Depression era.

It was harsh irony as well, as Spingarn and others observed, that in the process America's guardians became a mirror image of their dreaded adversaries, the legendary Colonel Bykovs, self-righteous and hypocritical, the end justifying the means. In the wake of the Hiss case, the FBI would grow into an unprecedented and in many ways unbridled American secret police, staging its own forays into domestic politics much as the CIA conducted its own foreign policy. By the early 1950s, however, those abuses were only beginning, wholly invisible, and their political triumph was nearly complete. If Alger Hiss became the symbol of a New Deal generation to his enemies, he was by conviction and lockup in Lewisburg even more emblematic to liberals, who came to see themselves and their idealism in the same guilty lineage of naïveté if not treason. Typical of the new Cold War vogue and bellicosity overtaking both liberalism and the Democrats, party figures like Arthur Schlesinger, Jr., corresponded chattily with Karl Mundt during the case, speaking "the language of McCarthy," thought Carey McWilliams, "with a Harvard accent."

As for Whittaker Chambers, his martyrdom was typically more mysterious, and mixed. "His ego cried for a mythological halo which he sought to create around his own image," concluded his onetime promoter, Isaac Don Levine. Next to the secret and public testimony, his most affecting weapon would be *Witness*, his prolix 1952 autobiography. In it, he resolved the nagging complexities of the case and of history on the model of his semiliterate FBI interrogators: by the simple equation of liberals and subversives. "When I took up my little sling and aimed at communism, I also hit something else," he wrote. "What I hit was the forces of that great socialist revolution, which, in the name of liberalism, spasmodically, incompletely, somewhat formlessly, but always in the same direction, has been inching its ice cap over the nation for two decades." It was a formulation at the end that echoed the forgotten behind-the-scenes beginnings with Father Cronin and the Chamber of Commerce. It also found more dainty expression, not surprisingly, in *Six Crises*. "At a less rigorous level," Nixon wrote of the case,

> somewhere in a vague area that goes by such names as "positivism" or "pragmatism" or "ethical neutralism"—Hiss was clearly the symbol of a considerable number of perfectly loyal citizens whose theaters of operation are the nation's mass media and universities, its scholarly foundations, and its government bureaucracies.

This group likes to throw the cloak of liberalism around all it beliefs. . . . They are not communists; they are not even remotely disloyal. . . . But they are of a mind-set as doctrinaire as those on the extreme right, which makes them singularly vulnerable to the communist popular front appeal under the banner of social justice. In the time of the Hiss case they were "patsies" for the communist line.

In the years after the trials, the Nixons, sometimes with Hannah and Frank, occasionally visited the Westminster farm, the adults sitting stiffly around the dining room table or in the warm kitchen, watching the children playing outside. "To them, he is always 'Nixie,' the kind and the good, about whom they will tolerate no nonsense," Chambers wrote of his own son and daughter and the visiting politician. There were also a few social meetings at the Nixons' home in Washington. Father Cronin and Nixon himself composed suitably laudatory reviews of *Witness*, with Chambers adding polite editorial suggestions for Nixon's 1952 essay in the *Saturday Review*, pages they thought "enemy territory." In his review, nonetheless, Nixon would acknowledge that many thought Whittaker Chambers "a fat repulsive little creature."

The book charted the informer's spiritual conversion as well as political epiphany, though some were not so sure. "In the midst of this complex religious struggle Chambers makes an unsuccessful attempt at 'self-execution,' " wrote one prominent Quaker reviewer. "This all leaves one feeling that religious assurance is yet to come to this troubled spirit, and that the race with catastrophe is not over."

As it was, Whittaker Chambers's loyalties and alliance were to be as protean for Richard Nixon as for Alger Hiss and earlier comrades. While he continued for a time to correspond politely, even warmly, with the rapidly rising young Californian, Chambers characteristically nursed his cyclical disenchantment. "I hand my mantle to him," he had once told the *Baltimore Sun* about Senator Joe McCarthy. By the mid-1950s, however, not even his former Republican champions were sufficiently zealous, and he soon predicted their downfall as well.

"I do not think that Dwight [Eisenhower] and Richard [Nixon] and Joseph [McCarthy] will be out of the way by next April," he acidly wrote a friend in the autumn of 1954. "I do incline to think that I did not make clear my attitude about the first two members of the triad. . . . I chiefly say: 'Give them a little more rope.' "

IV

SENATE RACE

16

Maneuvers,
November 1948–December 1949

"WHEN YOUR STAR IS UP"

While Richard Nixon became a celebrated figure in the nation's politics of counterrevolution, the California he left behind was swept with revolutionary change. The upheaval came not with sinister enemy agents or ideology but in the old familiar shape of the boom. And at the end of the 1940s, it was a boom like no other.

For a moment it seemed that the vast migrations of the Depression and war might somehow melt away from the basin and the rest of the state. Soon after the Japanese surrender and the end of gas rationing, Los Angeles papers counted with nativist glee the exodus at an old Colorado River border crossing into Arizona of over four hundred cars in one day laden with the battered furniture and bedsprings, the rope-tied suitcases and trunks, the assorted small children, dogs, and goats that marked the Okies and Arkies heading home. "What a relief!" one writer wrote of "the quiet jubilation" of Californians well rid of the refugees. Then, within weeks, the tide rushed back in. Over one typical postwar month, the border patrol tallied 130,000 people entering the state along a narrow desert highway, "their noses and radiators," as one observer described them, "pointed toward the promised land."

Not just another wave of migrants, this time it was a historic shift of weight on the North American continent. During much of the mid-1940s, enough people came to California to make up a new city of 40,000 every few weeks, more immigrants by 1947 than the total population of Los Angeles County before the war. The basin itself exploded at the rate of

515

16,000 newcomers a month, Los Angeles nearly doubling to more than two million and suddenly the third largest metropolis in the country. By the 1950 census, the nation had grown by 15 percent, California by an astounding 55 percent, making it second only to New York. There were now four million new Californians, as if the combined inhabitants of Nebraska, South Carolina, and New Hampshire had all moved in during the decade. "World history records no other purely voluntary migration of such size," Governor Warren's office pronounced. It was a gain "so large," one study registered, "as to represent a substantial redistribution of the population of the United States."

The influx was largely young adults in their twenties and thirties, many of them veterans who had passed through during the war and now returned to stay. Most came from states west of the Mississippi, and on the whole they were both younger and marginally better educated than prewar residents or earlier migrants. But the postwar boom brought as well hundreds of thousands of unskilled workers, a new pilgrimage of poor blacks that gave Los Angeles the third largest black ghetto outside the South, and the inevitable troop of the elderly, the ailing, the retired, more than a quarter of them already dependent on some form of public assistance. In their multitudes they clustered about the cities. By the late forties nearly 80 percent of the state population lived in major metropolitan areas, 42 percent in Los Angeles alone. With two-thirds of the remaining "rural" population concentrated in small cities and towns, the new California would also be among the most highly urban and suburban states in the union, as always that remarkable mixture of the frontier and the familiar, past and future.

Alternately alarmed and exultant at the unparalleled growth, the state's government and business leaders pretended for a time that it was all one more cycle in the historical pattern, pointing proudly to more than a million and a half new jobs, and to what Earl Warren's office in Sacramento called with little exaggeration "gigantic" development, production, and profits. Even apart from desert and mountains, it was said, California's population density was still relatively low. The very size of the Los Angeles basin, some eleven hundred square miles and America's largest urban land area, seemed to cushion the explosion. "People simply fill up the vacant spaces," recorded one witness.

The illusion of easy absorption was to be short-lived. In 1948 there were suddenly 100,000 more children in school than the year before, a half million more telephones needed, sewers overflowing to the point of a public health disaster. Though Warren's farsighted planning and progressive programs for state services had been extraordinary, averting the worst, prisons and asylums, hospitals and highways were soon overwhelmed. "California," wrote one journalist, telling the other set of boomtime distinctions at the end of 1949, "has the highest unemployment rate . . . the highest rate of exhaustion of natural resources of any state in America . . . unparalleled shortages of housing, power, fuel, water and land." Before the decade ended, the state was already blinking at the ominous brownouts of an overtaxed and ebbing supply of electricity. And settled oppressively over the basin, a murky effluence of growth, was what an official report called a "low, gray pall of exhaust, incinerator, and factory fumes," the soon legendary smog of Los Angeles that made the region's once miraculous balance of sea and land breezes a modern curse. To many it would be an ever-present emblem of the corruption of paradise.

As usual, however, the flush of wealth, the sheer vitality of the boom, the proud singularity of the place, were all infectious. "Still the pacesetter, falling all over itself, stumbling pell-mell to greatness without knowing the way," one social critic wrote in 1949. More than ever there was a sense of national prologue, that what the rest of the country someday would be, California was now becoming. "The nation needs to understand this tawny tiger by the Western Sea, and to understand this tiger all rules must be laid to one side," thought Carey McWilliams at the height of the boom. "California is no ordinary state; it is an anomaly, a freak, the great exception." So too, he might have added, were its peculiar contours of power and politics.

"THE FIRST THING YOU NOTICE . . . ARE THE SHOES"

Like the successive migrations before it, the postwar boom in California would be superimposed on the old economic and social structure of the state and for years left the rudiments of that power untouched. Meanwhile, the burst of growth and prosperity would have a side far darker than crowded institutions or snarled roads. Outside the bursting cities and suburbs, much of the wealth and influence in California still traced to its huge agricultural empire, symbolized by the majestic Central Valley, the rich plains of the Sacramento and San Joaquin rivers that stretched five hundred miles long and a hundred miles wide between the Sierra Nevada and the Coastal Range. "A great air-conditioned, outdoor hothouse," as one writer called it, the Valley grew nearly a billion dollars in crops by the late forties, by itself more productive than most farm states in the nation and still only a fraction of California's total agricultural income. Yet now, no less than during the depths of the Depression, it was an empire erected on human misery.

From the highways, looking out on the thriving fields, the human reality of California farm labor seemed almost invisible. You could travel the length of the valley at high season, remarked one observer, without being aware that a "phantom army" was somewhere camped nearby. "But once you know that this curious 'hidden' world exists," he went on, "you are forever conscious of it." Robert Ellis, an editor of *Ebony* magazine, found them one crimson dawn:

> Out of the shacks they come; from tents, old railroad cars, shanties, lean-tos, trailers, wooden cottages and cabins. Out of their shelters they come; by the thousands, the tens of thousands, ragged-dressed children, ragged-dressed grandfathers, Mexican, Whites, Negroes, Okies, Arkies, Texans, pioneer Califorians, ex-GIs, ex-union men, ex-nonunion men—maybe 200,000 people in all.
>
> Bandanna-wrapped, stern-faced women sweep the dust from dirt floors, light up a pot of beans or peas; kids shout for milk; fathers take old pails and move down to the public wells for water.
>
> No jobs: no farm work, no city work. Two hundred thousand people beached, struggling to breathe.

When the jobs were there, in the fields from four-thirty in the morning until sundown, the farm workers earned at most six or seven dollars a day in back-breaking labor and were victimized not only by the work and housing but also by a flourishing underworld of lotteries, gambling, cock-fights, and portable prostitutes hauled from settlement to settlement in trailers. Though the prewar migrant work force had been as much as half white, the new boom landscape at the end of the 1940s took on more than ever the pall of racism. Most of the laborers were Mexicans, both legal and illegal, and outside Bakersfield, in the infamous Cottonwood settlement, some 10,000 blacks lived nine and ten to a room in shacks without windows or plumbing.

The children became the paradigms of the culture. "The first thing you notice at Firebaugh School are the shoes," wrote a Fresno journalist visiting a migrant camp in 1948. "Eight-year-olds walking around . . . with their father's work shoes. High shoes, low shoes, button shoes, but not children's shoes." In the midst of the nation's richest cropland, the same children routinely went without breakfast and lunch and many without food for twenty-four hours at a stretch. By Christmas 1949, before the Valley's flourishing cotton harvest was half picked, another reporter found that twenty-eight migrant babies had died from starvation, bowel infections, and gastroenteritis in Fresno and Kern counties, where billboards proudly advertised "A Billion Dollars in Sunshine." Over the ensuing three months another eleven infants were found to have starved to death, fatalities officially blamed on the "indifference" of parents. "Hunger, sickness, and misery is in the San Joaquin," reported one Valley editor, while *The New York Times* recorded "a new cycle of destitution among farm workers." Yet press and public attentions were fitful and meager. The farm workers constituted "American DP's," the displaced persons of postwar prosperity, wrote Roscoe Fleming for *Frontier* magazine. "So, now it's back to *The Grapes of Wrath*." Describing conditions no better than the worst of the early thirties, Flemming's dispatch would be dated January 1, 1950.

Up and down the profitable trunk of the state stretched the offroad hovels of the hidden army, in what one visitor from the East called "the largest continuous line of rural slums in all the Americas." The Latin comparison was apt enough. Though the Central Valley was dotted with smaller yeoman farms, the dominant economic and political forces in the region—and in many respects in the entire state—were the great California latifundia, vast private plantations and corporate farms covering thousands of acres. Around them spun the intricate financial web of pricing, processing, and distribution, of land and capital costs that made even the relatively small farmer dependent on the cheap labor of unorganized migrants. "Many phases of California will not bear public scrutiny," wrote Carey McWilliams after a period as the ranking state official dealing with farm labor, "such as certain phony marketing agreements, the lush subsidies, the wanton destruction . . . of tons of food, the rigging of market prices and so forth."

Typical of the giants was the huge Di Giorgio Farms, including a twenty-thousand-acre plantation in Kern County, twenty-seven other properties around the state, and a spreading conglomerate of packinghouses, lumber mills, box companies, wineries. "Di Giorgio is to farming what Tiffany's is to jewelry," boasted the *San Francisco Chronicle*. But the labor unrest and politics surrounding the quality produce were not always so estimable. A strike over union recognition in the late forties was savagely broken, the chairman of a workers' committee murdered in a rain of bullets as vigilantes of unknown provenance stormed an organizational meeting.

Feeling the need of organization themselves, the growers had formed the Associated Farmers of California in the mid-thirties, pledged to "vigorous and curative action" in quelling labor unrest and representing, said one observer, "the police power of California agriculture." Associated Farmers variously blacklisted workers, ran a statewide intelligence service and its own security force, periodically summoned the state legislature's Committee on Un-American Activities to brand complainers as subversive. The power of the owners only began, however, with formidable lobbying in Washington and Sacramento or its hired enforcers in the fields. For the ultimate strength of the system was in the pervasive connections between farming and the other economic giants of the state. Among the landlords of the Valley were not only the Di Giorgios and others like them but also Southern Pacific, Standard Oil, and the Bank of America.

"In California," rued one critic in 1948, "industry and agriculture are one." Land and water, electric power and oil, above all capital and finance—the elemental forces of boom wealth and development in both city and countryside were bound together here by 1950 as perhaps nowhere else in America, the portent of a national economy of conglomerates and of interlocking directorates yet to come for the rest of the country. In the profits and power of large-scale corporate agriculture lay the eventual doom of the Valley's small farmers. Then, too, the big growers and their government allies hastened no less the gathering invasion of the cheap, manageable "Alambristas," the illegal wetback migrant laborers from Mexico, in place of the "braceros," or legal workers, with their awkward red tape, contracts, and negotiated wages. It was once again California as a foreshadowing of two great, still unseen social and economic developments in the United States at large—the strangling death of the family farm and the flood of Mexican immigration—that were to become crises for the entire country four decades later.

The public policy decisions that would shape that future for the state and nation were fought out in issues and for stakes few yet understood.

At the end of 1949 the first canal flowed into Fresno from the heralded Central Valley Project, a $2 billion, seventy-five-year-old federal scheme for integrated stream control, widespread new irrigation and major power generation, all vital to the economy of the region and state. At once seen as indispensable yet dubious, the project had long been fraught with controversy, centering on a turn-of-the-century reclamation law that ostensibly restricted coveted public-financed irrigation to farms of no more than 160 acres per individual owner. The 160-acre limitation began as a deliberate effort in the Progressive era to curb land monopoly and absentee ownership of large tracts in the vast western expanse watered at taxpayer expense. By the 1940s the statute rested on modern sociological findings as well as the original Jeffersonian idealism. A recent scholarly study of the Valley under federal auspices had documented graphically that the giant corporate farms with their shantytown migrant labor represented social "impermanence and alienation," while small farms and more equally distributed income fostered "social cohesion . . . stability and community."

Yet now the reclamation water was to be channeled to a Central Valley where a handful of land barons and corporations held more than half the irrigatable acres, a very caricature of the feudal land pattern the law was supposed to thwart. Predictably, the large growers fought the old limitation bitterly in order to tap into the free public irrigation. The project was "trying . . . to force communism upon the people of the San Joaquin," charged local congressman Alfred Elliott in 1947, arguing that the 160-acre limitation would only encourage land ownership by "undesirables." "Remember the Japanese and the trouble we had with them," he warned, adding wartime enemies to the postwar Red bogey. Meanwhile, the Di Giorgio combine sounded a similar patriotic alarm by full-page ads taken in major papers around the country. The statutory requirement eventually to sell off excess irrigated lands, said the company, amounted to a Russian-like "confiscation" of private property.

With matching fervor and arguments, the same array of California interests opposed the development of public electrical power with its lower rates in competition with corporate utilities and especially federal jurisdiction over the oil-rich tidelands off the coast. The potential of the underwater petroleum was believed by 1949 to be colossal—estimates of over twenty billion barrels, an energy equivalent of the agribusiness wealth of the Central Valley. Despite Presidential vetoes and federal court defeats, oilmen fought ceaselessly to shift tidelands ownership from Washington to the more congenial precincts of the Sacramento Assembly. "From the standpoint of your own personal contacts and friendships and all it's more satisfactory . . . to deal with state officials in the oil situation," said Roy Crocker, echoing his financial clients on the virtual carte blanche enjoyed by oilmen with local regulations. It was "a stand based on the simple truth," said one California journalist more bluntly, "that a state legislature is far easier and cheaper to buy than the federal government."

As it was, the oil lobbyists themselves could be brazen in their purpose. California magnate Edwin Pauley, an old Truman friend, was said to have lobbied the still-bewildered new President on the tidelands issue even as Franklin Roosevelt's funeral train wound its way to Hyde Park for the burial. He could "raise $300,000 from oilmen," Pauley openly boasted, for any Democrat who helped return the tidelands to the states. There was at least "one kind word for federal regulation," Superior Oil's William Keck was reported to have told associates. "Under federal regulation so much money would not have to be spent on local officials."

California politics at every level reflected the impact and agenda of those forces commanding food, fuel, and money, though the enduring realities were sometimes obscure in the tumult of the postwar boom. "Amorphous and unpredictable," the *New Republic* in December 1949 called the "new political empire [that] has sprung up in California . . . six million established residents . . . notoriously independent . . . four million new residents . . . without settled political allegiances." Yet for the fundamental questions of power and economics in the state, the partisan whims of an expanding postwar electorate did not seem to matter all that much in the late forties. On questions of land and labor in the Central Valley or corporate sovereignty over the tidelands, Californians would find politicians and their powerful backers largely the same, whether Republican or Democrat.

The growers and oilmen and the financial world behind them had found their most vocal political champion of the era not among the GOP, but in the state's ranking Democrat, the sixty-five-year-old senior U.S. senator named Sheridan Downey. The senator's career was in many ways symbolic—some said a parody—of the evolution of the Democratic Party in California from Depression to postwar prosperity. Rising in the old "thirty-dollars-every-Thursday," share-the-wealth politics of the basin, Downey stood for lieutenant governor as Upton Sinclair's EPIC running mate in 1934 and four years later was elected to the U.S. Senate with the backing of both the highly mobilized retirement groups and organized labor. In Washington, "a slight, grayish, strikingly handsome man," as one magazine saw him, he had introduced the obligatory pension plans cherished by his constituency of jaded retirees, advocated a postwar United Nations and international control of atomic energy, and supported veterans' benefits and federal pay raises.

By his reelection in 1944, however, Downey's politics shifted visibly. He ardently backed state control of the tidelands and became a virtual spokesman for the motion picture industry. The one-time EPIC senator, it also turned out, had been an irrigation lawyer with what one inquiry called "substantial" holdings of his own in the Central Valley, and he soon turned to a continuous, often venomous attack on the 160-acre limitation. What the State Department later supplied for Joe McCarthy, the Department of the Interior provided for Sheridan Downey. His battle in hearings and on the Senate floor was epitomized by a book, ghostwritten for him and privately published in 1947 under the title *They Would Rule the Valley*, the ominous "They" being reclamation officials "planning and plotting the destruction of a free economy to institute totalitarian rule over the Central Valley." "Downey had a real phobia about thinking there was a bunch of communists in the Bureau of Reclamation," said his friend and backer Oliver Carter, who at one point watched Sheridan filibuster against Interior appropriations simply to prevent salary payments to officials he disliked most. To liberals, meanwhile, the senator "was elected by the little people of California," as *Frontier* magazine put it by the beginning of 1950, "but promptly went over to the side of the corporate landowners and the Pacific Gas and Electric Co."

Whatever Downey's personal mania with Bolsheviks lurking behind irrigation laws, his turn to the right responded as well to formidable forces in the state Democratic Party. In southern California in particular, much of the Democrats' leadership had lately migrated from the American South with a traditional conservatism that distinguished sharply, as Downey did, between the white union members or pensioners of Los Angeles and the black or brown laborers of Fresno and Bakersfield. Though often eclipsed by the younger Bill Knowland, though still comparatively little known in some corners of the state, Sheridan Downey played shrewdly the pressure group and factional politics commonly transcending party in California, including the continued support of both labor unions and large corporations. The canny old politician understood clearly enough that the personal machines of California Democracy were as easily greased as any other by the vast money of oil and agribusiness.

The senator "could expect reelection . . . against a Republican," concluded the *New Republic* as Democrats looked ahead to his campaign for the third term in 1950 despite wafting rumors of ill health. In addition to Central Valley acreage and powerful patrons, the distinguished, wavy-haired Democrat was said to have acquired a painful ulcer. It was possible, too, that Downey might face some challenge from the left in his own party. But even then it was assumed that in California's wild crossover voting Republicans as well as conservative Democrats "will swarm to the Democratic primary booths to vote for Downey," as the *New Republic* predicted—unless, that is, they could all do as well or better with a Republican.

"WE'RE GOING TO GO"

"I have just finished reading *They Would Rule the Valley*," a fellow member of the California delegation wrote Senator Downey warmly on January 20, 1948, "and I want to take this opportunity to congratulate you upon rendering a real service to the people of California and of the entire country by setting forth in such graphic manner the facts concerning the Central Valley controversy." The admiring reader was Representative Richard Nixon, who before the year was out would begin planning in his own "graphic manner" to take away the senator's seat.

Watching him that dreary election night in Los Angeles in 1948, as the Democrats decisively won back the Congress alongside Truman's stunning victory, his aide Bill Arnold thought the grasp for the Senate had taken hold of Nixon almost from the moment of the GOP debacle, noticeably before the Pumpkin Papers and Alger Hiss's indictment and trials. There was obviously in Nixon an impatience and ambition straining at the creeping levitation of House preferment, though also a kind of desperation and fatalism in the reach. "He was perfectly willing to risk defeat in the Senate rather than to remain in the House as long as a Democrat . . . was in the White House and the Democrats had gained their control of Congress," said Arnold, remembering the young congressman confiding his plan and then dismissing the assistant's misgivings. "The House offered too slow a road to leadership, and [I] went for broke," Nixon later told a friend privately. He "would either become a senator or return to Whittier and practice law."

In Washington the Nixons had become friends with George MacKinnen, a GOP congressman from Minnesota, and his wife, Betty, and MacKinnen's own unexpected defeat in 1948 left as well an intimate sense of the precariousness of House seats, almost a premonition that they would be coming after him soon. Nixon "was well aware of the shifts in the mood of the voters every two years," his daughter later recorded that acutely felt vulnerability. He "did not want to be retired involuntarily like George MacKinnen." Still, the twelfth was plainly a safe seat by any standard, as safe or safer than the Senate from California, and Bill Arnold saw behind his restiveness a much larger purpose than the added status or longer term or potential Republican control of the upper chamber. The incumbencies of Knowland and Warren barred any other effective rise in California for another six years, and the congressman even in the fall of 1948 seemed fixed on Downey's Senate seat as the best, most available means to his ultimate goal. "It is my firm belief that, early in the going, Nixon had a secret ambition to seek the Presidency," Arnold wrote in his memoir. The Senate would be simply one of the "steps in the direction of the original ambition."

In February 1949 the Nixon staff began a new, wider polling of opinion in the twelfth district, as many as 150,000 questionnaires on domestic issues of potential use against Downey, including Taft-Hartley or price control measures in which the senator had supported the Truman administration, but clearly avoiding statewide topics like the tidelands or acreage limitation where the two men were indistinguishable. If Downey were generally thought well entrenched, the numbers from the 1944 race were mildly encouraging. The Democrat had won by 52 percent to 48 percent against Frederick Houser, the colorless, ultraconservative Alhambra lawyer who lost to Voorhis in the twelfth in 1936 and subsequently became lieutenant governor under Warren. Even in a lackluster race, Houser ran more than 300,000 votes better than the national Republican ticket and was swamped only by FDR's surprisingly heavy California margin of nearly a half million over Tom Dewey—a coattail the Democrats would certainly not enjoy in 1950. In a confidential GOP "Analysis" of the 1944 Senate figures widely circulated among state party leaders, including Nixon, it was concluded that the Republicans might well "overcome" Downey's 150,000 edge.

Despite that calculus, however, Nixon found scarce enthusiasm and even opposition when he first broached the Senate run with old supporters early in 1949. "I guess I must have probably irritated him," Gerald Kepple said, remembering their talk and Dick's obvious pique and disappointment. "I told him I didn't think that it was smart because we were going to lose a congressman and we wouldn't get a senator. . . . I didn't think that he could beat Senator Downey." Kepple was typical of the initial skepticism in the district. "All my friends, almost all, urged me not to run," Nixon once recalled of those weeks. "Downey . . . looked almost impossible to beat."

To some it seemed that even the family was trying to ease him away from further politics, despite the sensation and triumph of the Hiss case. Harold Stone, his old friend and dentist from La Habra, remembered a dinner that winter at Laura Scudder's Los Angeles home with Dick and Pat, the elder Nixons, and Frank's expansive brother Ernest, now a prominent agronomist and owner of a string of prosperous potato farms in Pennsylvania. The uncle was offering Richard the management of the farms if he chose to leave Congress. "He'd be independently wealthy," Stone recalled Ernest saying. To Uncle Ernest's apparent surprise, Nixon had replied flatly, almost irritably that he would "stay in politics." In the earliest weeks of positioning for the Senate it was only his wife who appeared unquestioningly in favor of the race, a woman still fiercely committed to her husband's integrity, gifts, and destiny, and all the more ambitious for him in spite of the strains of the first congressional term. "In the midst of the negative voices, he had one vitally important backer who believed he could and should win, Pat Nixon," wrote their daughter long afterward. Ironically, it would be the last campaign in which she filled such a vacuum and the last she would wholly approve.

Together, they reckoned on the asset so palpable to them in Washington if yet less palpable in the small towns of the twelfth—his astonishing celebrity in "the case." "I recognized the worth of the nationwide publicity that the Hiss case had given me—publicity on a scale that most congressmen only dream of achieving," he wrote of the moment. During the first months of 1949, his exploits as a spy catcher would be told and retold every Thursday evening over the Pasadena and Pomona radio stations that now carried his "reports" from the Capitol throughout southern California.

In April he was again back in the basin to appear before large gatherings of crucial constituencies, including a speech to the eight hundred members of the Merchants and Manufacturers Association on the antilabor legislation in the Eighty-first Congress. The strategic target of the trip, carefully arranged with Harrison McCall and other party backers, was a passionately partisan address before a thousand Republicans in the Biltmore Bowl, followed by a closed meeting that night with the Los Angeles County Central Committee. They should "quit this Pollyannaish whistling in the dark about a 'close election' last November," he told them. The Truman administration had now "swung far to the left," and "the Capital is full of power-drunk, arrogant bureaucrats who are determined to ride roughshod over those who would oppose them in the interests of the people." Washington was "rubber-stamping" liberalism "even more than in the palmiest days of the New Deal," and unless the GOP won key races like California's in 1950, "both the Republican Party and its principles will be smashed."

It was a stern, hectoring lecture in the shadow of a stunning defeat, capped by a six-point program in which the Whittier congressman, at the outset of only his second term in the House, brashly prescribed both a national and a statewide agenda for his party—"cut the large government down to size . . . check the abuses of both management and labor . . . positive action in the field of civil rights [where] there has been too much lip service . . . resist socialization of free American institutions . . . take a clear, aggressive stand against communist infiltration . . . place national security above partisanship in foreign policy." Once more, he seemed to reignite his career by a combination of ringing oratory and quiet politics. Following the Biltmore and Central Committee, he quickly made the rounds in the district, from small house meetings in San Marino to another rally of five hundred in Pomona. By the end of April 1949, he emerged with discreet backing for a Senate run from Mac Faries and Roy Crocker as well as the ever-ready Roy Day, and, more important, the first promises of money from the southern California fortunes surrounding Asa Call.

Once again, too, his ambition found fertile ground in the tortured inner politics of California Republicanism. He returned home that spring to a party in which the old seething insurrection against Earl Warren had burst into the open amid the shock of the Dewey-Warren debacle. In December 1948, some 125 prominent basin conservatives, including John Barcome, the former county chairman, formed themselves into a rump group called "Partisan Republicans," denouncing their governor publicly as "wishy-washy and namby-pamby." The revolt raged more than ever at Earl Warren's dogged moderation and refusal of governmental favors, now thought somehow to have doomed the national ticket as well as slighted the GOP faithful. "Sacramento hotels are filled with determined-looking individuals who are working both openly and secretly to accomplish the governor's administrative eclipse and his political demise," wrote Kyle Palmer, jauntily describing the mood of intraparty vengeance. Making a political "gift" list for a *Los Angeles Times* column on Christmas 1948, Palmer would select for Earl Warren "Attar of Partisanship," adding almost contemptuously in dialect, "Just squirt a leetle on, Governor." To Faries and others like him, powerful Republicans wavering between old friendship for Warren and the erupting rebellion, Palmer acidly offered "just the thing . . . a box of starch." In the year ahead, they would all find the wanted gifts—the acrid odor of partisan battle, the stiffening resolve of a new champion—in Richard Milhous Nixon.

Early in the soundings, Nixon had called Frank Jorgensen, who like most of the others advised him at first to stay in the House, to which "this district will send you back again and again and again." At the same time, the well-connected executive mentioned the rumor already begun to be heard, that Sheridan Downey was sick and might not run again. "Only talk," Jorgensen had said to discount it, but the gossip plainly spurred Nixon on. When Jorgensen called back a few days later to say he had "found some people interested" in Nixon's Senate candidacy, Dick pushed him to set up one of the first private meetings with the Los Angeles money men, and then, on the model of his historic luncheon at the University Club three and a half years earlier, a crucial foray into northern California.

Jorgensen contacted an old business friend, Albert Mattei, then president of the Honolulu Oil Company and a longtime financier in GOP politics in the north. Mattei, like Jorgensen and the San Marino group of the twelfth district, arranged for the two of them to meet some of the most influential "bankers and businessmen" of San Francisco, as Jorgensen remembered them, at the exclusive Pacific Union Club in the city. At first it was all formal and muted, in the manner of the more stylish, sophisticated city, and they ate lunch to small talk. Then with smoke and dessert the older Mattei had leaned back and asked Jorgensen, "All right, kid, what's on your mind?"

"I'd like to introduce you to the next senator from the state of California," Jorgensen answered, almost "facetiously," he thought. But the men at the table seemed utterly serious. "I allow how that is a pretty good idea," Mattei had said quickly, and the others echoed him. Their money and favor would be with Nixon with almost no questions asked. It was an impressive show of how far the young congressman's reputation had traveled in the headlines from Washington. Afterward, Mattei steered them to more potential backers in the city's financial district.

Later, on the way back on the *Lark*, the overnight train to Los Angeles, Jorgensen and Nixon stripped to their shorts on the warm, muggy spring evening and sat talking at length in their compartment. The money would be there but the problems were still formidable—Downey's intentions, other Democratic contenders, and potential Republican rivals still uncertain. Finally, Nixon fell silent, in "deep study," Jorgensen remembered.

As the adviser wearily climbed into the upper bunk, he turned and said, "Well, you've made up your mind, haven't you?"

"Yes," Nixon said. "We're going to go."

At that Jorgensen came awake, and back down the ladder. "Who the hell's going to run your campaign?" he asked.

"Why, you fellows in the district."

"Dick, we're amateurs at this business. . . . We could run one for you in the district, but when you talk about the state we've got a real problem on our hands."

But Nixon was adamant and insisted they find someone with wider experience they could oversee. Jorgensen suggested as chairman Bernard Brennan, a Los Angeles lawyer who had been active in earlier Warren campaigns. Still, Brennan could not perform the detailed, day-to-day management, and Jorgensen did not have the time to do more, as he told Dick, than "act as ramrod and keep it glued together." Finally, the insurance man had come up with the right name. "Why not Murray Chotiner?" he asked. "A pretty agile individual . . . good political sense."

"All right," Nixon readily agreed as the train clacked down the coast through the warm night. "You make your deal with him."

His campaign surfaced on May 20, 1949, well before any rival's, with the formation of California Volunteers for Good Government, a group of young and middle-aged lawyers and businessmen aptly drawn from anti-Warren, often pro-Stassen elements of the party and who were now supporting his Senate candidacy, said the *Los Angeles Times* for appearances, "without the authorization of Rep. Nixon." Among them, typically, were David Saunders, a basin lawyer who had been statewide chairman for Harold Stassen in 1948; Thomas Pike from San Marino, with his own oil drilling company; and Pasadena attorney Dana Smith, who would later handle campaign finances and more. The emergence now met what one observer called "open hostility" to the run from some of the old supporters in the twelfth, chiefly Herman Perry, and Nixon moved promptly to mollify or at least pay deference to the men who had launched his career, yet whom he now easily moved beyond in the reach for statewide money and the old Stassen network. In late May he asked Tom Bewley to bring together privately in the old law office the core of the 1946 campaign, including Harrison McCall, Day, and Jorgensen, as well as Perry.

An hour before, preparing the scene, he met Roy Day in an out-of-the-way little restaurant "somewhere west of Whittier," Day remembered, and told him about the northern as well as southern support and the thickening rumors of Downey's retirement. "He had some inkling that Sheridan Downey was going to drop out," Day said of their quiet talk over coffee. There was no longer any question about running for the Senate, and he asked Day to preempt Herman Perry's objections in the meeting. Bewley would fan out their chairs in front of the congressman, and Roy should position himself to make all the arguments for the Senate candidacy, to urge Dick Nixon to do what he had already decided. "So, my job . . . [was] to sit on the end of the semicircle facing him," Day recounted. "When he got ready to talk to us he looked around, knowing damn well who he was going to call first . . . me."

Minutes later in Bewley's office, Day would play his assigned role, give "the sales pitch," as he said. "When I got through they didn't have anything left to talk about," he said later, laughing. But despite Dick's contrivance, despite support from Jorgensen and McCall similarly prearranged, Herman Perry had reacted with indignation, then un-Quakerly wrath, "really upset about it," as Day told the story. "You're going to crucify this young man if you send him out and run him," he told them, pleading with an earnest but silent Nixon not to "sacrifice" himself. When Roy Day persisted, the banker stood up, pointed a finger, and said angrily, "Mr. Day, you obviously do not have the best interests of this community at heart. You're nothing but a politician." His face and bald head quickly flushed, Day shot back, "I'm not about to ask a young man to sacrifice himself because of our petty fears. . . . When your star is up, that's when you have to move."

Not that old man Perry truly doubted Nixon could win a Senate race, Day would say afterward. "No, he just wanted to keep Dick in Congress. You know, his buddy from Whittier." In the stormy, half-scripted exchange atop the old Bank of America building was a symbolic passage in Richard Nixon's career. The question was far less his promotion—for which Perry and others in the twelfth long held their own extravagant hopes—than the cession of influence and control. He was leaping onto the statewide and national stage with an array of backers, issues, ambitions far beyond the small-town power of the district. It was a parting—in some sense a discarding—of his original political sponsors that was implicit, inevitable from the University Club onward, there in the deeper breach between San Marino and Whittier, the new basin and the old. They left the sixth floor "on a note of uncertainty," as one account put it, after an "emotional and inconclusive get together." But Herman Perry had clearly lost, been passed by. "If we had all come out against him—told him not to—I don't think he would have run," Roy Day thought afterward. Most of them had gone along despite misgivings, some with a resignation that Richard Nixon and larger forces beyond them all had already made the decision.

During the summer of 1949, while his Washington allies quietly maneuvered between the Hiss trials, Nixon skillfully spun the case in and out of his fledgling, still undeclared California campaign. In the span of a few weeks he would make headlines with a major speech before national editors in Salt Lake City on the continuing necessity of HUAC, speak throughout California as an ostensible noncandidate on official Committee tours, mail everywhere pamphlets, press releases, and reprints that lauded his role in the spy scandal. It was one of those speeches, a formal address followed by lively questions and answers at the USC Law School, that impressed and effectively recruited a graduating law student named Patrick Hillings, who was about to move from campus politics to the presidency of the Los Angeles County Young Republicans.

Twenty-seven, a veteran, a local boy educated in El Monte and Los Angeles, Hillings was a steely, square-jawed conservative—he had first contacted the congressman asking for HUAC dossiers on rival student groups at USC—and characteristic of the younger men Nixon now began to attract as a matter of substance and deliberate promotion. It was the beginning of a small Nixon "machine" outside both the older group in the twelfth and even the Stassen supporters he inherited, a new echelon of postwar Republicans who would be his men. "Nixon became in those days the champion of this younger group," Hillings recalled of the deliberate appeal to him and his peers in 1949–50, "and as a result, we were able to build around him a very active political organization which later went on to form the nucleus of his campaign group in California."

He had asked Hillings immediately to begin, like Jorgensen, discreet canvassing about a Senate candidacy, and his private correspondence with both conveyed his mood and calculation through that summer. To the younger man and newcomer, he was chatty and avuncular yet circumspect, offering advice on starting a law practice, cautioning that Hillings and his zealous friends should not smear the United World Federalists ("most certainly not a communist-front organization"), justifying at length his attacks on Judge Kaufman in the first Hiss trial. He had approached Bill Knowland asking support for a Senate bid, Nixon wrote Hillings on June 8, 1949, but Knowland was cagey and would back him only "if he comes to the conclusion that I would have the best chance to win." By July 20, in the wake of the controversy over Judge Kaufman, he was reining in Hillings's zealous promotion: "As far as the Senate race is concerned, I think it is just as well to let it roll along at the present time without saying to [sic] much about me individually. I am inclined to think that things will shake down by the end of next month and that in the meantime a lot of quiet groundwork can be done which will mean a great deal to us."

Three weeks later, Nixon was writing Frank Jorgensen in a much more personal, self-justifying tone, rebutting again the argument about losing his "safe seat." He had "built up quite a file of people who have written me pro and con on the Senate matter," and despite all the cautioning, "I have virtually reached the conclusion that although it is admittedly a long shot, it presents such an unusual opportunity that the risk is worth taking, provided, of course, that we do not have too determined an opposition in the primary." In any case he was impatient, and 1950, he believed, would be a watershed election. After barely a term and a half in Congress and in spite of his extraordinary success and prominence in the Hiss case, he now thought the seat in the House of Representatives hardly worth having. "Unless the Republicans do make substantial gains in both the House and Senate in 1950, which necessarily would mean a Republican trend," he wrote Jorgensen forlornly,

> I seriously doubt if we can ever work our way back into power. Actually, in my mind, I do not see any great gain in remaining a member of the House even from a relatively good district if it means that we would be simply a vocal but ineffective minority.
>
> On the other hand, if the trend is on, the chance for winning the Senate seat in California will be good. If the trend is not on, rewinning the House seat might prove to be a rather empty victory.

It was in many ways definitive of the man and his fundamental political views then and later. He would have scant patience or respect for the Constitutional role of the legislative opposition, the rich but leisurely give-and-take of the congressional process in which, in truth, the minority Republicans of the 1940s often prevailed in a *de facto* coalition with Southern Democrats, a regime that was the enduring reality of Capitol Hill for a generation regardless of electoral tides. Least of all was there a sense of simply serving or representing his conservative district as he had so often promised the twelfth in 1946 and again in 1948. Out of Washington's oppressive August heat, he had sent Jorgensen an unusually candid testament to an all-or-nothing appetite for larger power and to his already growing frustration with ordinary democratic politics.

"I came around because I was a friend and he wanted me to do it," Frank Jorgensen would say of his own response to Nixon's audible anxiety and pretense. Though Hillings and others were told to "let it roll," it was Jorgensen who now did the "quiet groundwork." In late summer 1949 he personally courted key Republicans in the strongholds of San Diego and Orange County and secretly approached prominent newspaper publishers.

They took no chances with the press. Roy Crocker remembered Kyle Palmer "a little cool" at the first talk, months earlier, about Nixon challenging Sheridan Downey. But Jorgensen found no hesitation by summer. The *Times* and rival Hearst papers would be wholly behind Nixon, a winner, a comer, and not least a counterweight to Earl Warren. "There wasn't any question about it," Jorgensen said later, "that Kyle was with us." Afterward, Palmer himself bragged that he had called Dick Nixon late in 1949 to suggest a Senate campaign to begin with, that the *Times*'s patronage and the accompanying money suddenly prompted the young congressman to a race he had not considered. Whether the columnist's vanity or Jorgensen's diplomacy at the moment, Palmer and the *Times*, like others that summer and autumn of 1949, would fall into place as one more alliance for a battle already long planned.

Over lunch at the Los Angeles Athletic Club, Jorgensen also moved to recruit as statewide chairman Bernard Brennan. Then forty-seven, Brennan was the stuff of small-town basin lawyers, not unlike Tom Bewley or Jeff Wingert. He had gone to law school with Chotiner's partner and older brother, was a city attorney for Glendale after graduation, then had launched into a more lucrative private practice in downtown Los Angeles and become increasingly active in GOP politics, a southern California manager for the Dewey Presidential campaigns in 1944 and 1948 and in the interim a coordinator for Earl Warren in 1946. "I know the governor is deeply grateful for all your hard work and loyalty," a Warren aide had written him after that victory in the primary. Yet Brennan, like so many other conservatives, was soon alienated by the governor's independent style and policies. Now he accepted the Nixon campaign chairmanship from Jorgensen without hesitation and without salary, and he welcomed Murray Chotiner as campaign manager. "I don't think we could find a better man," Brennan told Jorgensen, though hiring Chotiner would not be so simple or quite so congenial.

They invited Murray to lunch, again at the Athletic Club, and Chotiner agreed quickly enough to manage the run. Then they asked about pay. "I knew [him] quite well by that time, knew how to deal with him," Jorgensen related. "All right," the bluff insurance salesman asked him. "Now, how much money is it going to cost?" At that point Chotiner "got his negotiating hat on and gave me a price," Jorgensen remembered. He wanted $25,000 for the primary, $35,000 for the general. Jorgensen countered, "Murray, you're talking through your hat." Finally, after some bickering they had settled on $12,500 for the primary, and the fee for the general to be negotiated when the nomination was won.

They had bought, they understood, a willful, abrasive man as well as a gifted political strategist. "I knew that Murray was very impatient with people who didn't have the IQ that he had," Frank Jorgensen would say. "He had the habit of a man like that of tramping on them. He'd move ahead. He'd just leave wreckage behind him, but he'd get the job done." So now, at the beginning, in the early fall of 1949, Jorgensen and Brennan "outlined our organizational plan" to him, told Chotiner exactly what they and the backers and candidate expected him to do. "If you do not follow the plan, just pick up your hat and go home. Do we understand this?" Jorgensen said characteristically, and Murray had answered, "I understand it." Chotiner "did a magnificent job for us in that campaign and never caused a bit of trouble," Jorgensen remembered a quarter century later. By then, ironically, history had made Murray Chotiner not merely skillful executor but evil genius of what turned out to be perhaps the most notorious, controversial campaign in American political history—and the crucial little bargain at the Athletic Club was long forgotten.

That September, too, they made the first estimates of the cost of the race, Nixon himself calculating $100,000. To begin to pay for Chotiner and others as well as for an opening swing around the state, Asa Call and Brennan secretly canvassed a select group of twenty men for $1,000 each, "our Committee of Twenty," as one witness called it, covert contributors who would never appear on the official financial reports. At the same time, initial pledges in the north and south reached $30,000, and added to that the hidden Committee of Twenty would thus take the campaign halfway to its quota even before the race had formally begun.

"The thousand dollars was put up by each of the twenty men," said Mac Faries, recalling some of his friends who thought Nixon's victory assured with so much money. Yet from the first calls in the autumn and winter of 1949, Bernie Brennan also promised the hidden donors a good deal more than just Sheridan Downey's seat. "This man is running for senator" was how Faries made one pitch to a contributor. "[But] we think and have thought since the start that he was Presidential material and we expect to make him President. He could be President."

In mid-September Nixon began a carefully ordered drive that would climax in a formal announcement. On the fourteenth, Hillings arranged a virtual draft from the Los Angeles County Young Republicans, and days later the *Los Angeles Times* similarly headlined the congressman's warning to the local American Legion about the communist "peril" from "infiltration, political intrigue, or the overthrow of existing government." At the end of the month he flew into Los Angeles with Pat and the baby girls, landing to some fanfare, met by a *Times* reporter as well as Don and Clara Jane. The congressman then rushed off importantly to address the Beverly

Hills Republican Women and within hours was back at the airport to fly to Tulare in the Central Valley, where another audience would urge him to run for the Senate. Everywhere he was solemnly modest about the honor and responsibility of a race, telling one group of promoters from the Los Angeles Central Committee, as an aide remembered, "I have to pray about it." Murray Chotiner would discuss the tactics of spontaneity and reluctance in a later GOP strategy meeting: "It is really simple to let the people select their candidate. All you have to do is to get a number of people talking, 'Now if we can only get so and so to run for the office.' "

Ostensibly, Nixon came home for a three-week tour of the state in order to arrive at a "final" decision on the race, though in fact it was to fend off still vague but forming opposition within the party. "Take it from me, Nixon has made up his mind to run," an anonymous supporter leaked to the *Times* September 30, hinting that he had been persuaded by promises of heavy backing in the north. But the same day the paper reported Frederick Houser ready to run again as well on the basis of San Francisco money. "Must be 'The City' boys are very tired of Sen. Downey," concluded Chester Hanson, one of Palmer's political writers. The jockeying produced its lighter moments. Not long afer Nixon's return, Jorgensen was asked to bring him along for a conference with yet another rival, Los Angeles County Supervisor Raymond Darby, who had been the first Republican in 1949 to announce for the Senate. The two men sat in the office of a Darby supporter at the Merchants and Manufacturers Association, where they were treated alternately to staged telephone calls announcing extravagant contributions for the supervisor and to Darby's own bluster: "Dick, you're a nice fellow but you can't win. . . . I'll just smother you." Nixon was silent behind his dark eyebrows, glancing occasionally at Jorgensen, who grinned broadly and finally announced, "Thank you very much. . . . We're still running for the United States Senate." As they left the building afterward, Dick Nixon was still laughing out on the street, much amused at the crudity of the effort.

Now publicly coy, now privately fierce, his campaign went forward amid the swirling crosscurrents in California politics. While he and Jorgensen laughed at the Darby ploy, the campaign carefully circulated to state newspapers the texts of a Fulton Lewis broadcast on the California Senate race in which the commentator reported "extensive backstage efforts under way to get both [Darby and Houser] . . . to withdraw." Lewis portrayed Nixon as "a young, tough, toe-to-toe slugging veteran campaigner who made a brilliant record in the navy during the war, and since has made a brilliant record in the House . . . undoubtedly the most brilliant record . . . by any young congressman in a great many years." If Nixon "agrees to run" after all the urging, said the popular conservative radio commentator in early October 1949, "it ought to be one of the great tests of voter sentiment in the entire election campaign picture next year." Meanwhile, anti-Warren conservatives launched a brief, abortive gubernatorial boomlet on behalf of incumbent lieutenant governor Goodwin Knight, while still another Republican faction urged the Senate candidacy on Earl Warren. But the governor promptly announced, "I will not be interested" and thus signaled both the end of Knight's back-door bid and Warren's own run for an unprecedented third term in Sacramento—all further aligning GOP rebels behind Nixon.

On October 7—a day on which he was still telling the press that reports of his candidacy were "absolutely untrue"—Nixon wrote a "confidential" letter to Perry and other skeptics, ending even the private pretense of indecision. "After considering all the factors involved, I have definitely decided to file for the Republican nomination for United States Senator in 1950," he told them. The formal announcement would come on November 3 after the tour of the state and still more orchestrated endorsements, drafts, and public demurring.

A crowd of over five hundred—"most . . . from the upper middle class, most of them . . . past forty," wrote one witness—gathered that evening in the old Ebell Club House in Pomona where he had made local political history four years before. Now, in much the same scene, the "citizens band" of the American Legion played patriotic strains, a Catholic priest said grace, and a pair of Girl Scouts led the pledge of allegiance. They arranged for Herman Perry to arrive late, the crowd standing and cheering after Roy Day introduced him as "the man who made Mr. Nixon." The disgruntled old banker had beamed. "This suggested that his original friends are still with him, pitching," wrote a local columnist, not missing at least part of their purpose.

One editor in the crowd thought Pat Nixon stylishly dressed in a black velvet suit with matching hat, and, in rapt attention to her husband, "far and away the happiest lady in that room . . . quite an asset to Mr. Nixon." The candidate himself suffered a scratchy throat from this statewide tour and had to tailor the speech to a live radio broadcast on a statewide hookup but was still in impressive form. "The Democratic Party," he told them, "has been captured and is completely controlled by a group of ruthless, cynical seekers after power who have committed that party to politics and principles which are completely foreign to those of its founders . . . phony doctrines and ideologies which are now being foisted upon the American people." The GOP could not win by "pussyfooting" on the choice between freedom and "state socialism." He then went on in the most widely quoted sentences of the evening: "They can call it planned economy, the Fair Deal, or social welfare. It's still the same old socialist baloney any way you slice it."

It would be a carefully crafted speech, drawing sharp partisan lines while appealing to conservative Democrats, saying almost nothing about his own record, the Hiss case, specific California issues or conditions. Eloquent of the surroundings, there was at least one familiar echo from the past. "The opposition will be well financed," he warned. "A huge slush fund is even now being wrung from the hands of workers for the purpose of opposing any candidate who will not take his orders from a clique of labor lobbyists in Washington." There was "only one way we can win," he said, bringing them to the climax. "We must put on a fighting, rocking, socking campaign."

They opened the campaign headquarters adjacent to Jorgensen's Metropolitan Life office in the Garland Building at Ninth and Spring in Los Angeles, in space given them by the owner, Jack Garland, Norman Chandler's brother-in-law who had been among the original Committee of 100. Before they were through, the operation would consume the entire second floor. But for now Nixon received callers in Jorgensen's comfortable suite, the insurance man shooing them to a back office when Metropolitan Life clients came in, lest Democratic customers be offended.

On the announcement of his chairmanship November 16, Brennan proudly called the candidate "virile, young . . . aggressive, fearless, honest, eminently qualified," though a week later he was secretly warning campaign workers about Nixon's age and regional hostility toward the basin's great and raucous city. "Avoid referring to Nixon as a young Republican," he wrote in a "confidential memorandum" dated November 23, 1949.

> Avoid overemphasizing his youth. Emphasize his aggressive, hard-hitting, fighting ability, his new look in government, his interest in all the people, his new approach to campaigning, etc. Along with it emphasize that with his new look he has the required maturity, dignity and insight. Emphasize at all times that Richard Nixon is from Whittier in the Pomona Valley. . . . There will be great kindred feeling for a Whittier man, but resentment against Los Angeles.

Above all, he advised them, they were to hold off attacking directly other candidates until the general election.

By the time of Nixon's formal announcement, his own Republican nomination seemed manageable enough. But the Democratic field had been complicated by the entry of a formidable challenger to Downey in the primary, an extraordinary and talented woman, already a celebrity beyond politics. "Mr. Nixon can defeat Senator Downey," thought a typical publisher who saw the rousing Ebell Club announcement. Yet "only the Republican party, every bloomin' one of them working all the while" would have a chance against the woman. It was a feeling widely held among Nixon backers as they watched the developing primary clash on the other side— except for Chotiner and the congressman himself, who seemed to relish the prospect of a run against her, who thought her politics perfectly suited for the campaign they contemplated. "Actually," Murray Chotiner would say with a smile about the Democratic primary fight, "we wanted her to win."

17

Primaries, January–June 1950

he was Helen Mary Gahagan, born in 1900 the daughter of an exuberant Scotch-Irish clan of successful men and equally strong women. Her father was a noted engineer whose dredging company helped carve out New York's Idlewild and La Guardia airports, Jones Beach, the Holland Tunnel, and other great public works. Respectably Republican and Episcopalian, the Gahagans were a family "of some means," as she remembered her childhood in a large townhouse on Brooklyn's fashionable old Park Slope.

After private girls' schools and two years at Barnard, Helen had grown into a gifted, iron-willed, statuesquely beautiful young woman, and she stubbornly defied family decorum, especially her imposing papa, to go into the theater, where she became an almost overnight success. From Broadway she went on to study voice, singing to acclaim in opera houses throughout Europe, and eventually returned to acting in motion pictures. When the Nixons were settling into the gas station on Santa Gertrudes and Richard was pedaling his bike to grade school, she was already an accomplished actress and singer before the footlights of two continents. Not long after her debut, critic Heywood Broun listed her among the ten most beautiful women in America, and another critic had added lavishly, "Helen *is* the ten most beautiful women."

In 1931 she married one of her Broadway leading men, Melvyn Douglas, and began a succession of experiences that would eventually draw her from the stage into politics. Driving across the country to Hollywood with her new husband, she was plunged suddenly into the horde of Depression migrants, "thousands of them," she once remembered of the roadside scene, "living in boxcars and in caves dug out of the sides of the hills." It was the end of her inherited Republicanism. There followed a honeymoon trip around the world with similarly vivid impressions of Japanese militarism and, later in the 1930s, a concert tour of Europe, which she indignantly cut short after a still more searing brush with Nazis and anti-Semitism. Back in southern California in the summer of 1938, just home from the hospital with a second child, she was resting in her bedroom one Saturday afternoon while some Hollywood friends used their patio for a small fundraiser. "Helen, for heaven's sake, come outside and listen to what is being said," her cousin had exclaimed as she burst into the room. "They say there are migrant children in California who have pellagra!" Shocked, disbelieving, she had gone to the patio, been deeply moved by what she heard, and in a sense never looked back.

One of Hollywood's most glamorous and political couples, both Helen and Melvyn became involved in the movie colony's several antifascist fronts at the end of the 1930s. Both joined the John Steinbeck Committee to aid farm workers, and Helen soon became devoted in particular to the cause, organizing charity Christmas parties for migrant children, visiting the ditch bank hovels and squalid farm camps of Kern County. To some who knew them, Melvyn Douglas seemed in many ways the more intellectual, at first the more activist in his support of liberal causes against the studio moguls— "the strongest thing that Helen had," said an old mutual friend. But it was she who soon emerged into organized politics. Friendly with Franklin and especially Eleanor Roosevelt, the Douglases even occasional overnight guests at the White House, she first served on Presidential advisory committees for the WPA and then the National Youth Administration. By 1940 she was elected Democratic national committeewoman from California and a delegate to the national party convention; a year later rose to vice-chairman of the party central committee in California; and by 1944, again at FDR's urging, became a candidate for Congress.

It was all on the pattern of her meteoric rise in the theater and propelled by much the same vibrant energy, commitment, versatility, and charisma, albeit no less by powerful patronage and her earlier celebrity. In politics she would appear at once freshly idealistic and artless, yet also aggressive, astute, determined to make her role as a woman and for the political process at large far more than the customary frill and passivity many expected. "Helen has really been in the smoke-filled rooms, and that's the first time that's happened with any woman," one Democrat remembered her at the 1944 national convention. Yet it was all at a price, tolled in the bitter resentment of the traditional and more conservative women she quickly superseded in the California party, in the enemies she took along from her husband's old industrial and political battles in Hollywood, in the hostility she aroused as an assertive female in politics as well as for her incendiary causes. From the beginning, though, she seemed impervious, her courage sometimes amounting to bravado and as easily worn as her stage success. "Personally, I've never been afraid of anything," she told one interviewer typically, "at least I can't think of anything right now."

She was attacked darkly for "reported leftist support" as early as the 1940 run for committeewoman, and in the 1944 congressional race branded as "a political gypsy"—twin charges of subversion and carpetbagging never to disappear from her California opposition. Guided by devoted liberal amateurs, backed by the *Los Angeles Daily News*, she won the House seat impressively in the basin's fourteenth. It was a patchwork, largely Democratic district embracing the ethnic, financial, and industrial heart of the old city between Sunset Boulevard and the southern boundary of Los Angeles. Figueroa Street was a stark borderline between a small "silk stocking" enclave of sprawling estates and private parks on one side and, on the other, blue-collar neighborhoods, skid row, the largest black ghetto west of Chicago, and what one politician called "a set of slums that would put Port Said to shame." "I just love the Negro people," Helen Douglas would innocently exclaim to one early rally at a black church, only to be chastened and politically educated by what she felt was the "cold silence" at her condescension. In Washington she soon became more adept in her commitment to racial equality, hiring one of Capitol Hill's first black aides, desegregating the House cafeteria, nominating minority students to West Point, publicizing the heroism of black troops in World War II.

Albert Cahn, a distinguished physicist and congressional adviser on nuclear issues, remembered a moment in the mid-1940s when he went to the Hill to testify with Bernard Baruch, and Clare Boothe Luce, the glamorous Republican counterpart of Helen Douglas, rushed down from a committee dais to kiss Baruch with some display. When the scientist asked Baruch after the hearing why the congresswoman had never kissed Cahn before testifying, Baruch had replied with a smile, "You don't have a million dollars."

There were no similar jokes or judgments about the gentlewoman from California. Hard-working, poised, serious, she became chairman of the Democratic freshmen and an unabashed New Deal liberal at a moment when the old ardor was fading elsewhere in Congress. Stubbornly she fought Taft-Hartley, maneuvered to force discharge of public housing legislation, coauthored the McMahon-Douglas bill on civilian control of atomic energy. To dramatize inflation and price decontrol, the disparity between soaring corporate profits and common wages, she strode dramatically onto the floor of the House with a wire shopping basket on her arm, full of ordinary groceries with prices that had doubled in the postwar months.

With a cosmopolitan temper and background, she relished international politics and quickly became one of the ranking and influential Democrats on the House Foreign Affairs Committee. Despite her lack of seniority, Douglas would be an alternate U.S. delegate to the UN General Assembly in 1946 and a prominent champion of the Marshall Plan, the Bretton Woods Agreements, Israeli and Philippine independence, and economic aid to prewar South Korea. She came to Congress after 1945 on the uneasy, sometimes invisible threshold of fateful issues that would shape America's relations with the rest of the world for the next half century—the character, limits, and expedients of the emerging rivalry with the Soviet Union. Douglas would vote readily for a buildup of military manpower and air force bomber groups, twice for extensions of the peacetime draft, and for major arms aid to Western Europe. "The Soviet Union . . . has deliberately created an atmosphere of fear and danger," she wrote in August 1949. Yet she saw too clearly the Faustian bargain of Cold War foreign policy, "that we were willing to support any government," she said later, "even if it was indifferent to the needs of the people, if they were against communism."

In the late 1940s Washington was taking the first steps down a long road—allying with tyranny to fight tyranny, enlisting evil as a means to good. It began with weapons and money for oppressive but anti-Soviet regimes in Athens and Ankara and led off decades later into the mists of Vietnam and Central America. Helen Douglas instinctively bridled at the start. "She agonized over it," an aide said of her decision to vote against Truman's Greek-Turkish aid that swept Capitol Hill with fresh chauvinism. She advocated use of the UN to curb Soviet aggressiveness rather than the old imperial, bilateral alliances and encirclement, and was disturbed even more by the absence of safeguards or remedies against the misuse of U.S. aid. "We propose to extend aid to Greece and I heartily approve of that. We must be very sure this aid will produce democratic and sound economic results," she told the House in 1947, warning prophetically of "the incompetence, corruption and oppression which exists in the present . . . government."

Privately she clashed with Dean Acheson in the State Department as well as with the majority of Democrats and Republicans, and her questioning independence of the Truman administration on foreign policy would be notorious, sometimes an object of derision in the House. When she and a handful of others—Republican Jacob Javits of New York, the conservative Arthur Vandenberg of Michigan—tried in 1947 to control the flow of weapons, making the aid conditional on amnesty for political prisoners or UN-supervised elections, they were shouted down and overwhelmingly defeated. "Across the floor of the House," she remembered of her futile effort to rally votes, "I often caught the new congressman Richard Nixon watching me, obviously delighted."

Her positions on domestic issues were equally at odds with Nixon's and some thought recklessly challenging of powerful forces in California and her own state Democratic Party. The early devotion to migrant labor expanded in Congress into a passion for the Central Valley Project and the beleaguered 160-acre limitation, alien issues to her bungalow-and-tenement constituency in Los Angeles. With similar conviction she fought the oil companies on surrender of the tidelands, advocated public power over private utilities, incurred the wrath of the lumber industry with a reforestation and controlled-cutting law for the redwoods, even at one point proposed a congressional inquiry into one of the sacred patrons of the postwar boom, the real-estate lobby.

But it was her vocal opposition to HUAC that was perhaps most conspicuous. She was one of the seventeen lonely representatives opposing the contempt citations against the Hollywood Ten. And though she supported several of the Committee's contempt motions, including Richard Nixon's for Gerhart Eisler, her votes were selective, case by case, "a sort of court of appeal in the House," as she described her insistence on a full airing of HUAC accusations from what she saw as their "bearpit sessions." She never lost her own unconcealed contempt of the Committee's methods and mission. "Persuasive poison," she called it in an early speech.

At the end of March 1946, against the rising roar of Red-baiting in the basin and throughout the nation, Helen Gahagan Douglas had risen in the House to deliver what she called "My Democratic Credo." She began almost matter-of-factly with words that later haunted her: "Mr. Speaker, I think we all know that communism is no real threat to the democratic institutions of this country. But the irresponsible way the term 'communism' is used to falsely label the things the majority of us believe in can be very dangerous." She went on to extol free enterprise and democracy and to deplore the Soviets, rooted in "the cruelest, most barbaric autocracy in world history . . . [and] communism has no place in our society." But it was also a fervent plea against monopoly and socioeconomic injustice and the mounting hysteria. "The fear of communism in this country is not rational," she said. "And that irrational fear of communism is being deliberately used in many quarters to blind us to our real problems. . . . I am nauseated and sick to death of the vicious and deliberate way the word communist has been forged as a weapon and used against those who organize and raise their voices in defense of democratic ideals."

In her defiance of the tide she was usually irrepressible. During one floor fight HUAC's John Rankin had again and again spoken scornfully of Douglas and other liberals as "these leftists, these communists. . . ." And she had leapt to her feet, demanding to know "if the gentleman from Mississippi is addressing *me?*" Rankin refused to acknowledge her, and the House was in a storm until Speaker Sam Rayburn was summoned. Lyndon

Johnson, relishing her courage and the parliamentary clash, came in to whisper to Rayburn, "Are you going to let the man from Mississippi run the House of Representatives?" Scowling, Rayburn had then forced a humiliated Rankin to reply, "I am not addressing the gentlewoman from California." Yet such triumphs were few and fleeting. No speeches or duels exorcised the stigma. The lower corridor of the old House Office Building where she had her suite beside a few other liberals would be known caustically on Capitol Hill as "Red Gulch."

The Washington press corps had rated Jerry Voorhis and Helen Douglas first and second respectively as the most outstanding Western representatives of the Seventy-ninth Congress, and she continued to gather honors, one of the "twelve smartest women in the world" listed in the *Book of Knowledge,* among *Pageant* magazine's "twenty most influential women in America." At home, as for Voorhis in the twelfth, the awards and respect of her Washington peers seemed less impressive. She won reelection handily in 1946 without ever returning from the UN General Assembly. But two years later GOP billboards covered the district, black voters were threatened with prosecution if not "properly registered," and conservative Democrats called her "our little glamorpuss . . . plotting to give the atomic bomb secret to Russia," one of Washington's "Russia Firsties . . . little playmates in the mire of communism." A stream of anti-Semitic propaganda referred to her as "Congresswoman Douglas-Hesselberg," the latter her husband's name before he changed it for the theater as a young man. "You can't elect this woman that sleeps with a Jew," ran one common refrain. "I know for a fact that I lose out on lots of roles in this town because my wife's a Democratic congresswoman," Melvyn Douglas told a Hollywood reporter at the time. It was all, as one political observer called it, "the dirtiest campaign [in California] since 1934." Still, she won decisively.

On the eve of that 1948 election, her manager, Ed Lybeck, toted up Helen Douglas's obvious liabilities in a confidential memo. She was "the wrong sex politically" for the place and era. She was alternately seen as "a traitor to her class," as a "communist," as a "social fascist" (by the communists), as a "nigger lover," as anti-Catholic for her criticism of the Franco dictatorship in Spain. Her supporters were mostly poor, her enemies generally rich, from oil to agribusiness. "She sometimes reminds you of a cripple carrying a couple of trunks trying to beat out a bunt," Lybeck wrote, adding the paradox so familiar to those who knew her, "I have never met a more completely satisfactory candidate."

At nearly fifty, she remained a strikingly handsome woman, five feet seven inches tall and large-boned while trim and graceful, with sparkling blue eyes, a compelling smile, her hair turning from black to auburn in the light. Carefully conservative in dress and makeup, she would be the first to resent that her beauty and sheer vitality carried influence beyond the seriousness of her work or causes. Yet by 1949 her personal presence was inseparable from the political. "The feeling of warming one's hands at a glowing fire," a friend and supporter said, describing the aura of her personality for both men and women. Like her future rival from Whittier, she would know well how to wait for a dramatic entry. The charm held audiences otherwise lost by her penchant for long, self-indulgent stump speeches. "A beautiful person," Democratic campaign committee aide Kenneth Harding said later, "[who] . . . got by without making people mad."

The charm exerted its gravity, too, on her fiercely loyal staff, aides who had shopped for the items in her famous grocery basket speech as they shopped for her clothes and whose awe and adoration would be at once strength and weakness. If, like Jerry Voorhis, she was out of step with most of the Congress, if she had made enemies of powerful interests and faced a postwar electorate no longer so fired as she by the causes of the 1930s, she labored against no inner angst or self-doubt. Politic or principled, calculating or uncompromised, Helen Gahagan Douglas was not given to losing.

She returned during the GOP-dominated Eightieth Congress to give a second "market basket speech," only to find the chamber all but empty. When a slum-clearance provision was eliminated from a housing bill, when Speaker Joe Martin refused to recognize her after a dozen attempts to be heard, she had gone back to "Red Gulch" and quietly wept. She was "frustrated, furious, and heartsick," she wrote afterward, at the liberal impotence in Congress. Like Richard Nixon—at much the same moment with precisely opposite estimates of the political present and future—she visibly chafed at her role. Her impatience came to rest almost inevitably on Sheridan Downey and what she saw not only as the senator's larger cooption but particularly his "vicious tactics" in attacking the 160-acre limitation and the Bureau of Reclamation.

Along with Nixon and the Republicans, she had heard rumors that Downey would not run again. She also thought it "well-known" after the 1948 election that Richard Nixon "had his eye on a seat in the Senate in 1950." Early in 1949 she went to various Democrats in the California congressional delegation urging them to make the race. "Somebody has to do it, won't you do it?" an aide remembered her imploring. Ironically, it might well have been Jerry Voorhis whose seniority and ambition would have moved him to run at such urging, had he survived in 1946. But no one responded, and there seemed only the prospect of a conservative southern California successor even if Downey did bow out. "There are no halfway houses vacant," Lybeck reminded her in June 1949. Either she ran for the Senate herself or else loyally accepted Downey or some like-minded replacement.

Douglas was absorbed with the Red-baiting fights on the Hill for the first half of 1949, but that summer she returned once again to the Central Valley. Touring the migrant camps with photographer Dorothea Lange and her husband, Berkeley scholar Paul Taylor, the car piled with notebooks and studies, they were impressed anew with the plight of the workers, the importance of the project irrigation for small farms, and her decision was sealed. Lybeck was apprehensive but resigned. "I'd rather lose you in a hell-bending race for the United States Senate than lose you just because you got bored," he wrote her. Above all, she needed money. "Now you can win . . . you'll be rather a long shot . . . but for Christ's sake don't commit suicide with no dough," her manager pleaded. "Maybe you can't crucify mankind upon a cross of gold, but you can sure as hell crucify a statewide candidate on a cross of no-gold."

Seeing the party split coming, ranking California Democrats met secretly in mid-September 1949. Liberals tried to ease Downey into a federal judgeship, but the senator was unmoved while still undecided on the race. At the last moment, her old adversaries in the party discreetly bid for crucial concessions. Bill Malone, one of the more powerful Democratic bosses from the early 1940s, would call Douglas to offer her a clear field in 1952 against Knowland if only she would hold off now. "That's not the issue, going to the Senate," she responded angrily with a small speech on the significance of the 160-acre limitation. Then Les Claypool, political columnist of the *Los Angeles Daily News*, her sole media support, had tried in vain to persuade her to change her position on the tidelands.

At the same time, "Black Jack" Elliott, a venerable party power and fellow oilman of Ed Pauley, invited her to a private supper with many of the state's leading publishers, an audience she could never otherwise command. "Helen, there isn't anything you want politically that you can't have. *Anything*," Elliot told her, if only she would reconsider her view on the tidelands. After dinner, she rose amid the cigar smoke to deliver a ten-minute lecture on the perils of Standard Oil and the virtues of federal control. Elliott and his guests left mutely furious. "My sense of security was solid," she would say about her course. On October 5, 1949, Helen Douglas announced her Senate candidacy against Sheridan Downey and the anticipated Republican, Richard Nixon—"just going," said one onlooker, "hell-bent for election."

"Her entry brightened my prospects considerably," Nixon wrote of the Douglas candidacy, reckoning, like the divided Democrats themselves, on a piercing brawl for the nomination. "If Downey won the primary, he would be weakened by her attacks; if Mrs. Douglas won, she would be easier to beat than Downey." The prospect spurred on his campaign's already thorough preparation for the eventual battle. As in 1946, it had begun with money and the quiet marshaling of backers and by the time of Helen Douglas's announcement had moved on to the equally crucial cultivation of the press. Between mid-October and mid-December 1949, Murray Chotiner began painstaking calls on editors and publishers. The first approaches were only a "survey" of local views and issues—"do not try to sell him your candidate," Chotiner would later instruct Republican tacticians on these opening rites with the media. But the personal calls were accompanied by letters asking for advertising information—implicitly holding out the prospect of election year revenues to the small papers especially—and still later by the careful personal attentions of the candidate.

Of sixty-two papers canvassed from San Diego north through the basin and desert and partway up the coast and Central Valley, altogether more than a fourth of all the state's publications, thirty-five were already strongly favorable or well inclined toward Nixon and many of the remainder friendly if undecided. In almost verbatim summaries of hour-long sessions, Chotiner meticulously set down local passions and peeves, the perceptions of Downey and Douglas, of Earl Warren and party politics, and exactly what the newspapers knew, and did not know, about Richard Nixon.

With the same care, they began to organize the distinct southern and northern wings of the campaign. In Los Angeles Brennan would be "the boss man," as one of them called him, though Frank Jorgensen was again the self-styled "ramrod," seeing himself as "the invisible man" controlling the flow of money by a committee composed of the oil driller Thomas Pike, business executive Elwood Robinson, and Dana Smith. Once more they enlisted Herb Klein, still ostensibly a news reporter in Alhambra and later San Diego, to handle publicity and to help write the campaign's own canned editorials. Jack Drown and Ray Arbuthnot, a propertied rancher from the eastern basin, worked early as advance men; and Chotiner and Nixon made a point of formally hiring leaders of the Young Republicans whose initial support was so visible, among them Walter Forward, a young GOP activist from San Diego, and Joseph Holt III, a twenty-five-year-old ex-marine and now insurance agent who was state president of the YRs. "He's hand-carrying him around everywhere," Keith McCormac, then another young party stalwart, would say about Holt and the others introducing Dick Nixon to audiences of veterans and younger people.

In the feudal factionalism of California politics, they were very much on their own. Congressman Nixon had gone proudly to Sacramento at the beginning to tell Earl Warren personally that they should run separate campaigns, and the governor, cool and correct, readily agreed to what he always did anyway. "Warren wasn't having anything to do with him, that's for sure," said McCormac, recalling the early moments of the 1950 race. But the traditional separation from the larger party and other candidates—sharpened by the old enmity with Warren and now by the generational gap of the new men Nixon made his own—left them all the more a candidate and campaign apart, defining their own issues and methods, their own isolated and precarious sense of loyalty. In any case, the men in the south, old and new, would share hard edges of ambition and conservatism, a sharpness that was the hallmark of their booming region, of their place on the outskirts of the GOP, and ultimately of their solitary candidate.

In the north, it was subtly but significantly different. In San Francisco, old Stassen supporters had put Nixon in touch with John Walton Dinkelspiel, a forty-five-year-old attorney, municipal judge, and former navy associate of Stassen himself. Dinkelspiel then organized "Northern California Citizens for Nixon" in late October, drawing together men like Dwight Merriman, a well-known real-estate developer; Robert Hornby, a utility executive; and others of similar age and background. "I trust you realize that I am a high-grade neophyte as to political campaigns," one of them wrote, and though some were casual Stassen backers in 1948, the description fit most of them. Dinkelspiel drew up a modest budget of $34,050 for the primary and wired Harvey Hancock, a retired public relations man for Pan American Airways, to come on as the paid "pro" handling the press and other management. Hancock was to coordinate activities with Murray Chotiner, the "overall planner of the campaign," as Dinkelspiel saw him.

The northerners seemed to defer politely to the hierarchy. "We hope to be of further service to you in whatever way you or Mr. Brennan may determine best," Dinkelspiel had written Nixon in November 1949. Yet when the campaign actually began, they soon had reason to balk. "I have your letter of February 16, suggesting certain billboard slogans," Dinkelspiel wrote Chotiner bluntly that winter. "You asked my opinion, so I will give you my frank reaction. I think 'New Leadership for America's Future' is excellent. *I do not care for the others.* Sincerely." Dinkelspiel remembered that over the ensuing months there were "many instances . . . [in which] we did not agree with what Mr. Chotiner had planned."

It was the reflection of a northern California where the partisanship was less harsh, the division between Richard Nixon and Earl Warren and other politicians less stark, the Nixon men less parochial and punishing. When it was over and the partisan and personal bitterness lingered so long, John Dinkelspiel would draw a pointed distinction about his province of the 1950 campaign. "They're all people of the highest integrity that we had in northern California," he would insist. "I know of no one that we had that had any questionable reputation of integrity."

At the end of January, Nixon eliminated the last potential challenges to his own nomination. Accomplished partly in secret, it was a small political *tour de force* combining effective use of his national celebrity, careful politicking, and, not least, Kyle Palmer's imperial intervention with the dispensations of the *Los Angeles Times*.

A loose confederation of GOP activists from throughout the state, the California Republican Assembly had emerged since the 1930s to fill part of the peculiar void created by weak parties and cross-filing. By 1950 the assembly's endorsement was thought crucial for statewide candidates. At the least, the organization's mid-winter caucus the weekend of January 28–29, 1950, at windswept Pebble Beach on the Monterey peninsula, appeared the last chance for Nixon's Republican rivals to halt his initial money and momentum.

The principal threat lay less with Darby than with fifty-five-year-old Frederick Houser, then a superior court judge. Patrician son of a state supreme court justice, a Harvard lawyer and state assemblyman, Houser was a three-time loser for Congress in the twelfth before winning the lieutenant governorship in Warren's first term and then running his respectable race against Downey in 1944. He remained a colorless, square-jawed GOP perennial albeit with the assets of wealth and two decades of political visibility. Ironically, his familiar name had also become in 1950 perhaps his largest liability, popularly indistinguishable from Fred N. Howser, a notoriously corrupt incumbent attorney general on the way to losing reelection in the GOP primary. As the assembly meeting drew near, however, Judge Houser personally lobbied the group's Senate endorsement committee with some effect, while Nixon was bound to Washington for the dramatic climax of the second trial of Alger Hiss and for the congressman's long-planned, triumphal floor speech on the case.

By the scheduling of his major House speech for Thursday, January 26, it was clear Nixon could not rush back to the Monterey coast without sacrificing much national publicity in the Washington aftermath, and with Brennan and Chotiner the candidate decided on bold tactics, including what was then a still extraordinary technical expedient. Bill Arnold called Dinkelspiel in San Francisco, told him Nixon had to stay in Washington for the weekend, and asked the lawyer to carry to Pebble Beach a special tape recording of Nixon addressing the CRA selection committee. Meanwhile, they planned, the House speech would make headlines for Nixon the day before the assembly meeting. The headlines did materialize all over California and Dinkelspiel took the tape, only to discover on Saturday that nonetheless an assembly subcommittee had already voted six to three to endorse Houser, with the full committee likely to follow suit the next day.

Then, Sunday morning, the delegates at their scenic coastal lodge awakened to quite another part of the Nixon thrust, in specially delivered copies of the *Los Angeles Times* an extraordinary editorial entitled "Nixon for U.S. Senator," a glowing endorsement at least four months early even for the primary. "There is nothing unusual about a citizen's ambition to become a candidate for public office," the editorial began, "but occasionally there is something unusual about the candidate himself." It went on to damn Downey faintly as "kindly, industrious, courageous, and ineffective," and Helen Douglas not so faintly for a "doctrine of class hatred and social antagonism." Yet Richard Nixon "has steadily risen in the esteem of his colleagues and in the confidence of his constituents . . . attracted national notice . . . expresses the ideals and aspirations of a generation."

That afternoon Dinkelspiel played the tape for the full committee— the first such recording he had ever heard, Nixon's voice rising and falling from the whirling spools. "The tape was very effective," he recalled. The assembly committee voted by one man to endorse Richard Nixon as the Republican nominee for United States senator. "It was very important . . . the most prestigious nonofficial Republican convention," Dinkelspiel said later of the assembly and their small *coup* by tape and tailored editorial. The endorsement would give the campaign then and afterward the valuable aura of what the San Francisco lawyer and so many others like him saw as a moderate, "middle-of-the-road Republicanism."

Jorgensen and then Kyle Palmer supplied the sequels that sealed the victory. Still emboldened by his near endorsement at Pebble Beach, Frederic Houser lingered at the edge of the race, and the bullish Jorgensen took a small deputation of prestigious Nixon backers to confront the judge openly. It was a discreet but threatening session. They warned the judge curtly of Nixon's superiority in money and national prestige, of the power of the younger voters rallying to the congressman, of the personal consequences of an acrid primary fight and party split, particularly if Downey or Douglas then won. "Fred Houser thought he wanted to [run], but we had a talk with Fred," Jorgensen would relate dryly. "And after we had some conversation, he decided not to run for senator."

As for Raymond Darby, the bluffing Los Angeles supervisor, he, too, would be treated to a quiet conversation. As Bernie Brennan later confided the story, Palmer went to Darby saying the *Times* could only support Nixon but promising the paper's powerful endorsement for Darby if he now ran instead for lieutenant governor. Incumbent lieutenant governor Goodwin

Knight, Palmer told him, "would not run for any office . . . unless he had the support of the [*Times*] coalition," and Darby would emerge unopposed on Earl Warren's virtually unbeatable ticket that fall. In the event, Darby accepted, "quietly shoved out of the race to leave Nixon more running room," said one witness. And the *Times* and Palmer technically "kept their promises," as Brennan would say. But while Darby got the paper's formal editorial endorsement, the jovial Goodie Knight ran anyway, and—like Nixon a cat's paw of the anti-Warren money and power—was given lavish front-page coverage by the *Times* throughout the spring. "As an unwanted candidate," one reporter wrote, Ray Darby would receive in the bargain "a terrific trouncing" by Knight in the primary.

"They . . . talked to some prominent Republicans . . . and got their advice," Roy Crocker later wrote of the Houser and Darby episodes, obscure little classics of California's internecine politics. "They all reluctantly backed off." The clearing of rivals left Nixon with only fringe opponents on the GOP primary ballot, though they, too, were vintage Californian. There was Dr. Ulysses Grant Bixby Meyers, a "consulting psychologist" for a lonely hearts agency, and Albert Levitt, running, judged one news account, "on a straight anti-Vatican platform."

Reporters found Richard Nixon somber and almost dolefully serious that winter despite his Pebble Beach triumph. "Black brows drawn in the troubled frown he often wears" is how Mary Ellen Leary saw him through a series of speeches a month after his thirty-seventh birthday, warning the GOP "in his grave, deliberate fashion that it must stand for a 'better life' if it wants to fight the modern slavery of the master state." Small basin papers thought his first stump speech "Republican through and through." In his early appearances he could be harshly partisan, charging in one typical address that "defensive" Democratic foreign policies "would lead inevitably to war." With that Palmer extolled him again in a long February column: "In no bellicose or challenging mood . . . neither show off nor a blusterer . . . a remarkable figure in contemporary political and public life. He is young enough to be bold and wise enough to be prudent, and his perceptive qualities are exceptional . . . an old head on young shoulders." A week later, Gerald L. K. Smith opened a California rally of his Christian Crusade with his own hearty endorsement of the new candidate. "The man who uncovered Alger Hiss is in California to do the same house-cleaning here," he told them. "Help Richard Nixon get rid of the Jew-Communists."

Yet the early campaign was plainly mixed, in search of a unifying theme among a broader state constituency with regional issues and a clear three to two Democratic majority in registration. While denouncing the Truman administration's "socialism" and state "slavery," he readily joined liberal Democrats that March to propose the distribution of some $2 billion in surplus federal food for school lunches and the needy. While deploring extravagant public works, he canceled campaign speeches with a flourish in mid-March to fly back to Washington to "fight any move," said the *Los Angeles Herald Express*, to divert to Arizona part of the state's federally supplied water from the Colorado River. If strident about the Democrats and their prospective "war" for some audiences, he was carefully moderate with others. Before the annual banquet of the Republican Assembly in San Francisco in late March, he criticized Truman's diplomacy but called benignly for a "bipartisan" conference with the White House, formally including figures such as Warren, Stassen, Dewey, John Foster Dulles, and "General Dwight Eisenhower" among the President's "top foreign-policy advisers." Days earlier, he had dodged questions about Senator McCarthy's latest charges by suggesting a similar "impartial, nonpolitical commission" to investigate the State Department, and he was now discreetly absent from a HUAC floor debate when the Democratic chairman, Georgia's John Wood, grandly announced to a stunned House that the Committee was assembling "a subversive [*sic*] blacklist" of more than one million names.

The ambivalence and caution traced in large part to the confused, often stormy circumstances in the race for the Democratic nomination between Douglas and Downey. "Nixon . . . appeared to be up against a stone wall," thought Arnold, without a clear sense of his opponent or the political ground to be staked out. Downey was now reported withdrawing, now pugnaciously taking up Douglas's heated challenge. In a Chotiner strategy that drew force from precisely planned attacks or evasions, Nixon was plainly at a loss. "We are still trying to figure out what it's all about," Dinkelspiel had written Nixon early in March in response to anxious questions reverberating from the candidate about Downey's intentions and the prospects in the Democratic race.

By the end of the month the congressman's own initial velocity seemed spent, as they faced with uncertain tactics an intensive eight-week tour of the state, beginning in the Central Valley. Would he merely echo Sheridan Downey by dismissing Douglas and the agricultural, power, and oil issues or try again to attack the amorphous common-party identity of the conservative senator and liberal congresswoman, risking loss of Democratic voters spread vaguely along the spectrum? Then, the last weekend before he was to start the trip, the answer came. In yet another frequent pattern in his career, Richard Nixon would be rescued and revived in the spring of 1950 by the angry jostling and divisions of his Democratic opponents.

"MONEY . . . *VIOLENTLY* SPENT"

For a few weeks after announcing, Helen Douglas had refrained from even mentioning Downey's name, but her genuine contempt and habitual passion soon poured into the open. "Why don't you erect a dam at the top of Mount Shasta reading "For Exclusive Use of Pacific Gas & Electric and Associated Farmers?" she exhorted a meeting of Democratic women in Redondo in mid-November 1949. In the great Washington clashes for water and power and food, she told them, "Our senior senator simply wasn't there."

Meanwhile, California Democratic leaders flew back to Washington to implore the vacillating Downey to run. "They didn't want Nixon; they were very much afraid of Nixon. They knew Nixon and they didn't trust him," remembered State Chairman Oliver Carter, one of the group who liked Helen Douglas personally but believed her no match for the young challenger from Whittier. "I just figured in a head-to-head fight with her, statewide, he'd beat her. . . . It would be a very nasty campaign." Along with Bill Malone and Representative Clair Engle, Carter found Downey "quite hostile" to his female challenger. "He wasn't concerned about having to beat Nixon in the general election," the chairman recalled, though an early private poll for Downey actually showed Nixon defeating him by a narrow margin. Still, the senator seemed reluctant to join a primary fight and in fact suffered from a severe ulcer, driven to bed in wrenching pain the morning after the party men had met with him.

Then, early in December, under pressure and goading, Sheridan Downey had "exploded political dynamite," as one contemporary account put it, addressing a Los Angeles party dinner with a ringing declaration of candidacy, a strong defense of his positions, and attacks on Douglas as "not factually informed." His apparent emergence in earnest now gave impetus and shape to the intraparty backlash building against Helen Douglas. "Oil money came in here on railroad gondolas. They would shovel it off," Democratic fund-raiser Alvin Meyers recalled of the contributions to Downey. Her stands on the tidelands and agribusiness, he remembered, "resulted in money being not only lost, but spent against her—*violently* spent." With Downey openly declared, Democratic conservatives moved as well to extinguish Douglas contributions from traditional backers, provoking her in late February to an extraordinary public charge that state leaders of her own party were conspiring to "shut off money" for her Senate bid.

During January and February the candidates traded harsh blows by radio and press, with Downey attacking her opposition to Greek-Turkish aid and other votes as "extremist." By early March, however, the senator seemed again to falter. Once more Carter and the leaders met anxiously, once more the incumbent wavered—his indecision, said a San Diego reporter, throwing "a sack of sand into the already grinding, sputtering, and generally malfunctioning state Democratic political machine."

But while Douglas flayed "our part-time senator" and vowed to stay in the race "to the end," the attacks against her continued all the more bitterly by proxy. Women's clubs and her former rival for national committeewoman were marshaled for public repudiations. In a *Times* column headlined "To Be or Not to Be," Kyle Palmer waxed indignant on the plight of Sheridan Downey, "a gentle and simple man [who] . . . has worked hard and faithfully—if ineffectively," versus "sharp-tongued, rabble-rousing Rep. Helen Gahagan Douglas . . . a scolding woman . . . not at all averse to campaign brawling." When in late March Douglas voted against the latest appropriations for HUAC, a familiar ghost made a reappearance. In prominent stories, both the *Herald-Express* and *Times* reported the denunciation of Douglas by an obscure group called the California Democratic Women's League, charging her with votes "indicative of left-wing sympathies" and association with "left-wing obstructionists," most notably the infamous Vito Marcantonio. "Democrats should wake up," the papers quoted Mrs. Paxton Lytle in the March 28 story as saying, "and see where she is trying to lead us."

At ten o'clock that same night in Washington, Sheridan Downey called *Los Angeles Daily News* correspondent Frank Rogers and asked the reporter to draft his withdrawal and retirement statement for release the next day. "You write it," Downey told him. The senator was checking into Bethesda Naval Hospital for his ulcer, not even caring to see or hear the announcement before it was put out to press. Rogers later thought him convinced that "he could not beat Nixon, and he just didn't want to hassle it." But the statement blamed ill health and excoriated Helen Gahagan Douglas, saying Downey was not up to "waging a personal and militant campaign against the vicious and unethical propaganda" of his woman challenger.

Angrily responding in kind, Douglas called his claim of physical incapacity "a cheap gimmick" and in the parting blow turned a scornful but fitful adversary into a grim enemy. When it was over, as Douglas herself ruefully recorded afterward, Sheridan Downey had not simply stood aside to nurse his ulcer as he seemed ready to do that night he called Frank Rogers, but instead "missed no opportunity to attack me."

Richard Nixon greeted Downey's exit and the Democratic bloodletting with private glee and some public confusion. Wishing the senator "a complete and speedy recovery," he announced to the *Times*, "I have never regarded the senatorial race as a personal matter, and I shall strictly adhere to that policy." Over the past weeks he had quietly told reporters that he hoped the senator would win the nomination, that he believed Helen

Douglas would be the tougher opponent in November—a calculated tactic in courting Downey Democrats while marshaling for the race both he and Chotiner actually wanted with the liberal. Now, in the same background briefings that last week in March, he quickly welcomed the latest turn, "trying to interpret Downey's retirement," the *San Diego Union* reported, "as a big boost for Nixon."

Not even his newly adopted campaign optimism, however, could gauge what now suddenly happened at the same moment behind closed doors on the Democratic side. Downey's departure would leave Douglas bruised from their sporadic fighting. Moreover, the attacks and split were to continue still more savagely. The same night Sheridan Downey withdrew, the California Democratic forces abhorring Helen Douglas had already found a surrogate to enter the race in his stead. A little after noon the next day, Downey's retirement statement still hot on the wire, the new candidate wired the senator with characteristic flourish: "If my entrance into the race can relieve your anxiety and help you concentrate on getting well you may be sure I will make as strong a campaign as possible."

He was Elias Manchester Boddy—some suspected just plain Chester Boddy beneath his pretensions, but in any case a classic California genus. Voice and lungs weakened by a gas attack in the Argonne, Boddy had come to the basin for his health in the early 1920s, carrying fifty-five dollars and a reputation for peddling the *Encyclopaedia Britannica*, "a crack book-salesman," said one observer, "with an inclination toward metaphysical speculation." The combination was all too apt for the time and place. He was soon a well-known promoter of local books and magazines, including a stint under Harry Chandler at the Times-Mirror Publishing Company. When basin businessmen then took over Cornelius Vanderbilt, Jr.'s bankrupt *Daily News*, they hired the florid salesman as publisher. By what one writer called "consummate bluffing and financial finesse," Boddy proceeded to keep the paper alive or sometimes even thriving as a visible if minor rival to the *Times* and other giants. Only later did it become known that the "finesse" included a crucial loan from Southern California Edison, $2 million in support from oil companies, and a secret annual subsidy of $250,000 from the Hearst chain on an option to buy the paper.

Outwardly the tabloid was the Democratic foil of the Chandlers, generally backing the New Deal and given to publicizing the social and political fads of the basin, which in turn boosted circulation. On closer examination Boddy never crossed his hidden investors. The paper abruptly reversed its position on municipal water and power after the Edison loan while Boddy himself in a much-read column coyly refused to endorse Upton Sinclair in

1934, devoting his last articles before the historic election to a series on Plutarch's *Lives*. Mentioned for the Democratic senatorial nomination in 1946 against Knowland, the publisher had rejected it unctuously—"I do not believe it is possible for a man to be true . . . as a journalist . . . in politics." Since then Boddy had turned more and more to cultivating his camellias on what one reporter called a 168-acre "princely estate" in La Cañada, where his postwar views grew openly conservative and chauvinistic and his *Daily News* columns dwelt on Proust and Plato. "Unpredictable, erratic and . . . tangential," as one fellow journalist called him, the former encyclopedia salesman seemed destined for an eccentric retirement.

Now at fifty-nine, with silver hair, handsome lined face, and the mustache of a British gentleman whose manners he affected, Manchester Boddy was to be the Senate candidate of the powerful Democratic right in California and another colorful, fortuitous figure in Richard Nixon's rise. State chairman Oliver Carter thought him "a lion tamer . . . no more a politician than you could shake a stick at." Nonetheless, he was instantly endorsed by party leaders and backed by Ed Pauley and Black Jack Elliott. Boddy had favored the 160-acre limitation briefly in the mid-1940s and consistently praised Helen Douglas, "my only big-circulation champion . . . a personal friend," she remembered. For a time the Douglas campaign would be able to use effectively Boddy's recent praise of her as "one of California's great women." But his sudden candidacy and betrayal at the end of March 1950 "puzzled even my most ardent supporters," Helen Douglas recorded afterward, and was "a crippling blow," particularly because of the loss of the *Daily News*.

Worse still, Boddy took up in stride the Red-baiting that had been building in March. "There is indisputable evidence," he said in a campaign inaugural delivered hours after Downey's withdrawal, "of a statewide conspiracy on the part of this small subversive clique of red-hots to capture, through stealth and cunning, the nerve centers of our Democratic Party." Shaken, Douglas again responded caustically. "It's the same tired plot with a new leading man," she would quip to one reporter.

At a Bay Area CIO meeting on March 30, she lashed out not at Boddy but at the ultimate beneficiary of the salesman's dramatic last-minute entry, charging Richard Nixon with "nice unadulterated fascism" in his earlier campaigns for the House. "The whole GOP campaign this year will consist of crying 'communism,' " she warned them. Nixon was "a demagogue who will try to win by fear and hysteria." Those who heard her that weekend thought Helen Douglas forceful and determined yet her tone already somehow desperate and flailing. It was a small luncheon in any case, and her impassioned prediction went unreported beyond the CIO paper itself, a portent of what was to come.

❖❖❖

In a wood-paneled Mercury station wagon donated by an Alhambra dealer and packed with sound equipment and files, Richard and Pat Nixon set off on a statewide tour at the beginning of April. Fittingly they began on a Monday morning in Maricopa in Kern County. In a routine repeated again and again, they parked the wagon at the corner of the small-town crossroads, played music over the loudspeaker to attract a crowd, and distributed to the first gatherers ten large placards with instructions on how to use them. While he stood in the street or on the tailgate to give his speech, Pat passed out a new supply of thimbles like those they had used so effectively in 1946, and there were fifteen to twenty minutes after every speech for questions and answers. Then, at the candidate's signal, the townsfolk with the placards held them up, spelling in sequence I LIKE NIXON, and the rest of the crowd, delighted at the little show, cheered and clapped.

It was less what one reporter called the "commodious" woody wagon, the music, or the curbside performance that now fired the campaign and more the new clarity of thrust that came with Downey's departure and the Boddy-Douglas civil war on the other side. In the rich farm towns between the mountains he could now praise the retiring Democratic senator as a martyr to his cause, charging in Downey's echo that Bureau of Reclamation "politicians" were trying to "socialize the water supply in the Central Valley." The acreage limitation, he told them, was "a phony issue . . . to divide the people of the Valley through a campaign of hatred and misrepresentation . . . to set the small farmer against the large." The theme was repeated in town after town, and in Fresno he struck out against "extremists" who were "carrying on the controversy over private versus public power." Democratic policies amounted to "absolute controls over the farmer," he warned. The regulations "would require an army of snoopers many times larger and more vicious than the OPA."

They wound north into the bay area, and in Berkeley, a Douglas supporter heard Richard Nixon speak on April 13, 1950, in front of the university's famous Sather Gate. "To the great surprise of most of us," the student, a debate captain, wrote Helen Douglas,

> He gave a magnificent speech. He is one of the cleverest speakers I have ever heard. . . . The questions on the Mundt-Nixon bill . . . and the problems of international communism were just what he was waiting for. Indeed, he was so skillful—and, I might add, cagey—that those who came indifferent were sold, and even many of those

who came to heckle went away with doubts. . . . If he
is only a fraction as effective as he was here you have a
formidable opponent on your hands.

He would make twenty-one major addresses in twenty-one days by one
count, and his headquarters claimed over thirty-nine street-corner speeches
and two radio interviews per day during the first two weeks of the tour.
While he moved through the remote rural towns, back in the basin the
campaign was carefully orchestrated to keep the congressman in the headlines, if sometimes straining the definition of news. On April 11, the *Times*
featured a Kyle Palmer story simply quoting "Long Beach civic leader"
Jack Drown on Richard Nixon's defense of states' rights in the tidelands,
Drown characterizing Helen Douglas's record as "voting against California." The dispatch bore all the earmarks of being written in full by Chotiner,
and neglected to mention that Drown was a Nixon campaign operative.

Like such press plants, his talks were in part set pieces, in part tailored
to the widely ranging local issues and audiences. "Nixon always had something that he'd dug up about the various towns . . . we were going into,"
remembered Roy Day. The candidate navigated cautiously the often
treacherous differences between California's cities and countryside, north
and south. At the posh St. Francis Hotel in San Francisco he tactfully
backed away from the controversy over Senator McCarthy. "Only the Communist Party is profiting" from McCarthy's charges, he told a more liberal,
moderate audience. He had "no opinion concerning the validity" of the
accusations. If the claims were untrue, the Wisconsin senator should be
"forced to pay the political penalty for making false charges." A few days
earlier he admonished a similar gathering against "wild unsubstantiated
charges of disloyalty" and "indiscriminate name-calling in the field of anticommunist activities."

Nonetheless, the old issue was never long subdued. The same day he
deplored "unsubstantiated charges," he called in another statement for the
deportation of radical union leader Harry Bridges. Over the next few days,
he proposed a full trade embargo on Russia, raised the specter of an imminent Soviet attack on the West Coast and a suggested Easter prayer
dealing with the "threat to the peace and security of the world" posed by
the "godless would-be 'supermen' of the Kremlin." Wherever he went, he
was always being asked about communism and the Hiss case, Nixon told
Dinkelspiel. "There's no use trying to talk about anything else, because
it's all the people want to hear about."

Outside the more sophisticated bay area, and particularly in the basin,
the tone soon became bellicose. The young congressman was the "Number-
One Target of California Communists," the *Herald Express* said, quoting

Nixon headquarters, and the paper promptly ran the complete text of the January 26 House speech on what it called "Alger Hiss and a crew of communist traitors gnawing into the heart of America." "It is my earnest conviction that Russia would wage war against us today if she thought she could whip us," Nixon told an agitated audience April 19 in San Luis Obispo. He would repeat much the same dire message—adding on occasion that Russia and other communist nations should be expelled from the UN— before business clubs, meetings at Masonic Temples, dinners of the Native Sons of the Golden West, up and down the southern coast and through Orange County.

At the Biltmore in Los Angeles he urged that the United States take "the offensive in the cold war" and capped the triumphal swing through the south with a rally of two thousand organized by Jack Drown at the Long Beach Auditorium. A handful of union activists picketed the gathering, later to be reported as simply "the commies." To the delight of the large crowd, the loudspeaker of the Nixon station wagon blared out at the handful of demonstrators a popular tune, "If I Knew You Were Comin' I'd've Baked a Cake." Inside, his supporters cheered raucously almost every line. "This was one of the greatest thrills of my political career," Nixon told a reporter afterward.

As usual, he was not alone in such politics and took both example and legitimacy from the accompanying national trend. "I know he is no communist," John Foster Dulles conceded in his 1950 New York senatorial race against Herbert Lehman, "but I also know that the communists are in his corner." In Mosinee, Wisconsin, the townsfolk staged that spring a mock "communist coup" in which there were "firing squads," "nationalized" businesses, and photos of the "arrests" featured in newspapers in California and around the country. On May 2, 1950, a Nixon friend and fellow freshman congressman from the Eightieth, George Smathers, decisively defeated incumbent senator Claude Pepper in Florida's Democratic primary, and the political moral of their contest reverberated across the nation.

Reportedly spending at least $1 million, Smathers called his Fair Deal opponent the "Red Pepper," an "apologist for Stalin" ("He likes Joe and Joe likes him"), and an "associate of fellow travelers" in "the spiraling spider web of the Red network." While his backers put out a pamphlet entitled "The Red Record of Senator Claude Pepper," Smathers regaled rural Florida with Pepper's subversive sympathies for blacks and expressed shock that the senator's sister had gone off to the big city to become a known "thespian," or that Claude Pepper actually practiced "celibacy" before his marriage. Like other southern moderates in 1950, Pepper would go down to defeat for his putative "socialism" and relative racial tolerance, but it was the Red-baiting that was most resonant in the press and congressional corridors. "Nixon Jubilant," the *Herald Express* headlined, reporting his reaction to the Smathers victory. "I am confident that the people of California, like those in Florida, also will register their disapproval at the polls this year," he told the paper. He would admit later that he "carefully studied" the Florida primary and eventually "adapted what he could to his own campaign."

As in the Voorhis race, his first direct attacks against Helen Douglas in the primary would come chiefly from the friendly press and surrogates. Her "chosen associates are to be found in fellow-traveling circles in Hollywood and on the extreme left . . . and they know how consistently she has given aid and comfort to American traitors and conspirators," said a Santa Monica paper in mid-May. "She was subsequently an ally of Communist Party-liner Vito Marcantonio in Congress . . . [and] the communists and fellow travelers who picket Nixon . . . will be found cheering and working for Mrs. Douglas." Anonymous letters to the *Times* at the same time joked about the "Marc and Gahagan team," while the *Santa Ana Register*, one of the papers first wooed by Chotiner months earlier, wrote that "Mrs. Douglas has traveled the 'pink fringe' sufficiently long that whether she actually believes in the communist form of government is unimportant."

On May 13 a large ad in the *Los Angeles Times*, sponsored by an obscure "wage earners' committee," called for the defeat of Helen Gahagan Douglas, "labor boss candidate for U.S. senator," with the caption "Florida won a battle for freedom . . . George Smathers campaigned for individual liberty . . . and his victory was a triumph for free Americans over labor bossism." And in yet another echo of 1946, Carl Greenberg of the *Herald Examiner* reported, in what was ostensibly a news dispatch, that the former "actress and housewife" had been "untrained for the hard job of a representative," had a "poor" attendance record in Congress, and failed to pass any of the "only sixty-nine general bills and resolutions" she had introduced.

Nixon himself appeared above such attacks during the final weeks of the primary, conveying an "almost casual approach to the voter," thought the Marysville paper after his last drive through the north, adding in rare if mild reservation, "not the type of man to stir great emotions in the breast of anyone." By plane, train, and the familiar woody wagon, he moved again back and forth through the Valley and the sparsely populated counties north of Sacramento and San Francisco, in several speeches each day warning against "socialism," seldom mentioning either of his opponents by name. While more union hecklers stood outside on Fisherman's Wharf with signs—"San Francisco does not want you, Mr. Nixon"—he gave a rousing speech to backers at Joe DiMaggio's Restaurant on the subject of "fellow travelers and communist sympathizers" in the State Department and climaxed his bay area campaign in a torchlight parade up Market Street with actor Edward Arnold and other Hollywood celebrities.

Only once in the primaries did he confront Douglas directly, at a mutual appearance at San Francisco's Commonwealth Club, and then not with a political assault so much as a ridiculing prank. First to speak, Nixon flourished a telegram and read out an endorsement of his candidacy signed "Eleanor Roosevelt." At the look of utter dismay on Helen Douglas's face the largely Republican audience roared with laughter, and Nixon went on to give an effective, well-applauded speech, Douglas coming after him visibly undone and almost stammering. "I was bewildered . . . in shock," she remembered. "And it seemed to put me in a ridiculous position." Only after the luncheon did the Douglas camp discover the wire came not from Mrs. Franklin D. Roosevelt but from an obscure Eleanor P. Roosevelt, a widow on Theodore's Republican side of the famous family.

Congressman Nixon was fully expected, said the *Times*, to "sweep the Republican primary and show up remarkably well in the Democratic totals." With less than three weeks to go, Kyle Palmer turned to the race on the other ticket, where Boddy trailed Douglas. The publisher's campaign "thus far has been a colorless affair, too much dignity, abstraction and statesmanship," thought the columnist. "He might still defeat the lady if he tried—in a political sense, of course—to slap her around a bit."

As it was, the Democrats hardly needed Palmer's advice on how to beat up a woman.

"DOING OUR JOB FOR US"

"I was scarcely aware that Richard Nixon was holding back," Helen Douglas recorded during the last weeks of the 1950 primary. "I was too busy defending myself from Democrats."

While her own staff worried about her health in what one aide called an "impossible pace," she crisscrossed the state, often perched in the tiny bubble cabin of a three-seat helicopter that made somewhat harrowing landings in shopping centers or on narrow rural roads. Like an adult trying to explain to children that ghosts need not frighten them, she told a small crowd in San Marino, "The danger of communists taking over here is utter nonsense." And to another in Monrovia: "One communist walking through Monrovia would not turn the whole town communistic." In early May she called Smathers' victory "the dirtiest campaign in these United States" and repeated a standard line: "I'm a Roosevelt Democrat. . . . We know every Democrat will be called a communist. But those who scream 'communism' and then vote against a civil rights program, housing, and social welfare . . . are sowing the seeds of communism."

Yet she struggled in vain that spring against a widespread and apparently well-organized whispering campaign about her character, her subversive acts and friends. Douglas wrote for advice a close House colleague and conservative Democrat, the stoic John McCormack of Massachusetts, who had heard himself some of the rumors from California friends. But the veteran of Boston's roughhouse races could only write back resignedly in a private note May 9: "The unfortunate thing about politics is the small, mean, and sometimes filthy stories that the friends of friends of an opponent circulate. . . . It is most unfortunate that there are so many evil-minded persons in the world, particularly in a campaign."

Unreconciled as always, she stood outside a Convair plant in San Diego, barred by management from setting foot on the property, and lashed out in a speech to five hundred factory workers at the men she thought ultimately behind the hysteria in both parties. "I have utter scorn for such pipsqueaks as Nixon and McCarthy . . . trying to get us so afraid of communism that we'll be afraid to turn out the lights at night, and will run to Papa Taft for protection." Privately with her staff, Douglas would more than once refer to Richard Nixon as "that pipsqueak," and again in public as a "peewee who is trying to scare people into voting for him." The epithets obviously stung. In his memoirs nearly three decades later, Nixon would quote them as proof of her "viciously personal" attacks and of his own comparative forbearance. At the time he was furious.

The two of them once spoke the same day to different audiences in a northern railroad town, and Bill Arnold came back from monitoring Douglas's speech to report to Nixon her "unflattering" remarks. "Did she say that? Why, I'll castrate her!" he replied to the aide. When Arnold reminded him that such retaliation was "impossible" for a woman, Nixon had shot back peevishly, "I don't care, I'll do it anyway." Watching his candidate's continuing rage back at headquarters, Chotiner's dictum was stern. "You can't get into a name-calling contest with a woman. The cost in votes would be prohibitive," one source remembered him insisting, and then adding what they could all see: "Let the Democrats continue to chew each other up—they're doing our job for us."

Her slurs against Nixon were largely lost amid the mounting clamor within the Democratic primary. "A very haphazard, spur-of-the-moment organization" is how Frank Rogers, now a Boddy aide, saw the publisher's impromptu campaign after Downey's withdrawal. But the money soon flowed, and by mid-May the assaults on Douglas were well coordinated and almost daily. Mrs. Mattison Boyd Jones and Mrs. Paxten Lytle charged that Douglas "has too often teamed up with the notorious extreme radical,

Vito Marcantonio," and a former American Legion commander soon followed the women with the same denunciation and headlines.

The day the Legion attack was widely published, Douglas tried to give a scheduled speech outside University Library at USC, only to be showered with seltzer and hay by initiates of the Skull and Dagger Society and then loudly booed as she took off her soaked coat to continue the speech. Reported by wire services, the incident drew embarrassed apologies from USC students and administrators and exposed no visible political ties between either the Nixon or Boddy campaigns and the young society initiates in their tuxedo jackets, top hats, and shorts—though Manchester Boddy appeared on campus three days later to polite applause when he accused the congresswoman of "communist sympathies." Nixon supporters at the school formally condemned the incident in the *Daily Trojan* and implicitly denied any responsibility. At the same time, the campaign headquarters in the Garland Building seemed to know of the event and other attacks like it almost instantly. "Nixon knew everything that was going on," radio announcer Tom Dixon remembered of their impressive intelligence network. "If someone threw paint on Helen Douglas he knew about it."

Beyond the dousing and anathemas, Douglas also encountered by late May what one visiting correspondent called "a virtual newspaper blackout" in southern California, moving even a former superior court judge to question publicly the apparent "suppression of news." In Boddy's *Daily News* and elsewhere, she took out small-print ads to defend her voting record and 98 percent attendance at roll calls, to announce campaign schedules printed routinely for Boddy and Nixon but not for her, to reassure those "so distressed for the past few days by the kind of things that have been said."

But the last week in May her paid publicity was no match for reports of Sheridan Downey's condemnation over statewide radio. Her record, said the senator, "shows little hard work, no important influence on legislation, and almost nothing by way of solid accomplishment. . . . Mrs. Douglas in my estimation does not have the fundamental ability and qualifications to be a United States senator." Even a Sacramento paper friendly to Douglas judged the Downey broadcast "political dynamite," and his words along with the earlier Red-baiting would be quoted in a flurry of Boddy newspaper ads and radio spots over the final days.

The *Chicago Sun-Times* reported "considerable dough" pouring into the Boddy campaign from "powerful private oil interests," and Boddy's own backers boasted in Washington that $200,000 would be spent to defeat Douglas in the last two weeks of the race, though neither item was carried by the California press. What did appear were full-page ads citing still again her failure to pass legislation, the identity with Marcantonio, and her vote against Greek-Turkish aid. On the eve of the primary voting, Downey charged that she had given "comfort to Soviet tyranny," a veritable definition of treason. And even in a rasping and failing voice, Boddy returned to his original theme of "red-hots" ready to take over the party.

Despite it all, by the final week she still held an evident lead over Boddy in most areas of the state. "I despise these little men who would stampede us into hysteria," she told a CIO convention June 4, ending to a standing ovation and shouts for more. The old fire remained. Yet reporters watched, too, the frantic schedule, the pressure of the press blackout, and the steady battering all take a visible toll over only a few months. "Helen . . . is still a beauty," thought a Hollywood writer, "but hard campaigning has deepened the lines of character in her face and she no longer has the appearance of a movie star."

Following Chotiner's tactic, Nixon impatiently stood apart from the bitter Democratic battle for most of May, then moved aggressively in the last week before the primary to exploit his advantage. In a final instruction to GOP workers, Brennan told them "the eyes of the nation are on this senatorial election," and Dick Nixon needed "an overwhelming complimentary vote from all of the Republicans." There seemed no doubt of his popularity, even adulation among the party faithful, some of whom were moved to borrow from the New Testament. "Mr. Nixon," the *Times* quoted his women's group as saying, "will show the truth, the light and the way to the peoples of the world."

But it was the dissident, divided Democrats he courted most openly in the late primary drive, advocating both public and private development to "keep pace" with the population boom, arguing for higher pensions beyond Social Security. "Democrats for Nixon" were organized under the names of J. Bert Easley, a former New Deal housing official; Rollin McNitt, Jr., the son of a well-known Roosevelt activist in the state; and others, including, buried in the list, Uncle Hugh Nixon, whose politics and World War I enlistment had once scandalized the Milhouses. As in 1948, the appeal climaxed with the mass mailing of a carefully composed flyer, once more entitled "As One Democrat to Another." Under impressive national press blurbs, Nixon was shown bare-chested with pith helmet in front of his tent on Green Island, emerging from the Coast Guard flying boat on the way back to the Pumpkin Papers, working a child's puppet to the delight of his pretty wife and photogenic little girls. "The Man Who 'Broke' the Hiss-Chambers Espionage Case," said the brochure, "stands firmly for a strong America." Nowhere was there any word of his party affiliation.

The mailing drew an immediate response from the Boddy camp if not

Douglas. Earlier in May, Boddy had criticized Nixon mildly for his relative youth, provoking an indignant defense from Kyle Palmer and a cutting personal attack on the fifty-nine-year-old publisher. "If we send [to the Senate] a man who is approaching the sere and yellow age," the *Herald-Express* quoted an anonymous "Nixon spokesman" at the time as saying, "he won't last long enough to get sufficient seniority to do us any good." Later, Nixon himself had taken a swipe at Boddy's obviously well-financed campaign, telling a Sacramento press conference, "I don't think money can buy an election in the state." Nevertheless, Boddy was at first reluctant to attack Nixon as well as Douglas. "Frank, you know, I've never even met Nixon," he told Frank Rogers, who urged him to take on the Republican. Then the two men were introduced in a San Francisco hotel lobby during the campaign, and Rogers saw Boddy's attitude change over the spring. "He despised the man's politics and personal ethics even then," the aide remembered.

Now Boddy's campaign lashed back at the flyer. "This die-hard reactionary comes before the people . . . and tries to tell them he rates a large Democratic vote," announced Bill Malone. In the *Daily News* and other papers there appeared a full-page ad on election eve headed "WARNING TO ALL DEMOCRATS." A large cartoon showed Richard Nixon in a pin-striped suit coming out of a "GOP" barn, trying to feed the Democratic donkey a pitchfork of hay captioned "Campaign Trickery." "What manner of candidate is this who will use the United States mails in an attempt to delude Democrats into believing he is one of them?" asked the ad. In one passage, a copywriter's effort at rhyme coined a political byname for a generation. "Look," it said, "at Tricky Dick."

In final press briefings, Nixon headquarters would reply only with statistics from the candidate's herculean effort—fifty counties visited, 15,000 miles driven in the woody wagon, more than six hundred talks, 65,000 thimbles passed out. To the *Chicago Tribune* Nixon had already accounted for last-moment attacks. "The commies really don't like it," he told reporter Seymour Korman, "when I smash into Truman for his attempted cover-up of the Hiss case . . . but the more the commies yell, the surer I am that I'm waging an honest American campaign."

He was the first to vote in his Whittier precinct the morning of the June 6 primary, and the family and campaign staff gathered that evening at the Garland Building headquarters to hear the returns by radio. By ten o'clock they could trace the silhouette of an impressive victory. He had won the GOP nomination with a resounding 70 percent. And while Helen Gahagan Douglas despite the smears had defeated Manchester Boddy by over 350,000 votes, Nixon took more than 22 percent of the Democratic total, nearly 320,000 voters and only 5 percent less than Boddy. Of nearly two and one-half million ballots cast statewide, he had beaten Douglas by 42 to 35 percent, with Boddy's conservative anti-Douglas votes likely to belong to Nixon in the general.

"An analysis of the primary vote yesterday clearly indicates we are on our way to victory in November," he announced in a midnight statement. About the coming race he was confident and already combative. "I welcome Mrs. Douglas as an opponent. . . . It won't be a campaign of personalities but of issues," he told the wire services. She would have to tell where she stood on the issues, he added, "or I'll do it for her."

Across the city that night, the Douglas campaign was elated as well. "We were just riding high. We thought there's just no way she could lose. People really understood," Helen Lustig remembered. "We blinded ourselves to a lot of things." In the glow of victory there was a sense that the worst was behind them, that Manchester Boddy's defeat might somehow discredit his tactics.

As Douglas and her aides vacationed or prepared to return to the Capitol for a summer session of Congress, only a press-clipping clerk in Los Angeles read the portents. "Here is a clear choice between an American progressive and a siren in a 'beautiful' red dress," the *Herald-Express* said of the Nixon-Douglas contest. "Manchester Boddy was a sacrifice to the pinko lady of the hustings." And from Washington, Drew Pearson noted a curious item two days after the primary. A news picture service had received a request from an anonymous source in California for photos of Douglas, "any picture," said Pearson, "linking Congresswoman Helen Douglas with Paul Robeson, Henry Wallace, Claude Pepper, or Moscow."

18

General Election, June–December 1950

he weekend after the primary, the candidate and his men gathered in secret at a San Ysidro ranch just outside Santa Barbara. Their ostensible purpose was to bring together the regional wings of the campaign to discuss organization and finance. But the meeting became decisive, too, for strategy and tactics and was a telling moment in the race.

For most of three days he talked and planned intently with Brennan and Chotiner, John Dinkelspiel and Harvey Hancock from the north, Jorgensen, Roy Crocker, Gerald Kepple, and the advance men Ray Arbuthnot and Jack Drown. Typically, it was Jorgensen who voiced bluntly the special character of the race. "Now we have a woman . . . in opposition," he began. "I've learned enough in politics to know that the average woman in politics reasons with her emotions rather than her head." Despite his periodic rage at Douglas's rhetoric in the primary, Nixon was concerned that he not appear too blatant, too bullying in exploiting her weaknesses, "always ready to explain that he had to be very circumspect 'in running against a woman,' " Arnold remembered of his self-consciousness, almost apology about tone and technique. "I knew that I must not appear ungallant in my criticism of Mrs. Douglas," Nixon wrote in his memoirs. Yet at San Ysidro they agreed from the outset on a precisely scheduled, carefully worded campaign of needling and pressure. They would obtain the Douglas itinerary, and "several advance men" would move ahead of her in what Jorgensen called "stop and drop," especially up the Valley from Bakersfield. "We worked the hell out of him. But he was ahead of [her]," Frank remembered. "Two, three, four days—whatever you could work out. He'd stop and drop something for Mrs. Douglas to answer." And "our suspicions were right," Jorgensen would add afterward. The "emotional" woman seemed to spend much of her campaign answering Dick.

They decided to take a poll, not to match the two rivals—"don't waste the money to see whether your candidate is ahead," Chotiner would say—but to "begin to find out the things which you can talk about." The campaign theme was to be "a strong America," though it was obvious before any polling that the candidate would concentrate on his favorite issue. "Nixon . . . was very high on this communist thing," Jorgensen remembered. "It was his time—a time that he fit into the picture, no question about it." Some of them, Chotiner recalled, thought the Red-baiting "overworked" after Boddy's defeat, that Nixon should now "talk about labor and agriculture in the state of California." Now they determined to exploit even those tactical misgivings within the campaign and give them a sinister cast. "I have been advised not to talk about communism, but I'm going to tell the people of California the truth," Nixon would say to audience after audience, as if he had been ominously warned off. "If your candidate should get up in front of a meeting and say, 'I have been told that I must not talk about this subject, but I am going to tell the people of our state just exactly what is going on,' " Chotiner would explain the device later, "you will be amazed at what happens."

"A perfectionist," Chotiner said of Richard Nixon then and later in the Senate run, "a general who demanded absolute precision and carefully planned coordination in every move. . . . Nixon wanted to do everything himself." Still, Chotiner thought that sort of control "simply not possible in the slugging matches of political campaigns . . . the heat of battle . . . in which quick, tough decisions have to be made." The two had clashed during the early weeks and would again. "Dick, you can be either the candidate or the manager. But you can't be both," Chotiner remembered scolding. "A candidate's job is to make speeches and reach the voters. You go out and do that, and let us make the other mistakes."

But at the ranch above Santa Barbara there was no question that Richard Nixon was in charge, that he knew as much or more than his advisers. "Nixon would listen" to all the advice of experienced men, Kepple recalled, "but he would come back with ideas that indicated that he had done a lot of homework before." Once again the candidate would be in command of the slightest campaign details, the disparate lines large and small, public and covert, that fanned out from the headquarters. There were always some matters, Chotiner told later writers, "it's better for the candidate not to know in so many words." Yet Richard Nixon was not that kind of figurehead. "He knew," remembered Richard St. Johns, a young aide who traveled with him frequently in 1950. "He considered a good politician always involved. It was not like him not to know."

At San Ysidro that weekend they also plotted the heightening contacts with crucial constituencies, the media and advertising campaign, and the role of auxiliary groups. Roy Crocker was to preside over the mobilization of the large landowners and great Central Valley interests—in part because he had some agricultural education, a ranch of his own, and numerous friends in that select world, in part, too, because as a Los Angeles financial executive he epitomized the nexus of money and property that was California agribusiness. They also planned "considerable newspaper advertising," Dinkelspiel recalled, and reckoned once more, as in 1946 and 1948, that if the papers "know they're going to get enough . . . political advertising that's paid for," in Crocker's words, "they'll kind of lean your way." It would be the yield, too, from Chotiner's patient canvass the previous autumn. Kenneth Chotiner, Murray's son, remembered the "cases and cases" of liquor that had gone to newspaper publishers and political writers at Christmas and the warmly cultivated relations all over the state. Not least, beyond the newspapers, they decided to buy "a great deal of radio," as Dinkelspiel noted and to make the first substantial investment in crude television spots for the still small Los Angeles market.

In addition to papers and broadcasting there would also be billboards, hundreds of them, quarter, half, and full sizes, usually red, white, and blue, on the theme of Richard Nixon "On Guard for America." Those signs might be "the worst designed . . . you can imagine, from an artist's viewpoint," Murray Chotiner would joke, but there was the simple, stark message of man and office. And it was everywhere, the coverage beginning in April for the primary and building in the autumn to over fourteen hundred boards statewide, even sprouting into Tijuana, Mexico, "to catch the weekend tourist trade," as one source described them. By late summer, "ELECT CONGRESSMAN RICHARD NIXON U.S. SENATOR" stared at drivers and pedestrians at almost every major intersection in Los Angeles, sometimes from all four corners. At the ranch they sowed what Helen Douglas would later see to her dismay as California become "a garden of Richard Nixon billboards."

On the last day at San Ysidro, they talked of people and of the money to pay for it all. "Flying Squadrons," zealous groups of volunteers, sometimes deliberately all male or all female, sometimes mixed, would be recruited and sent out to heckle Douglas, "planted there just to embarrass the candidate," Crocker explained afterward, or to saturate busy downtown streets handing out Nixon literature. Like the billboards, the Flying Squadrons were to be everywhere—except, that is, in the north, where the courtly Dinkelspiel simply omitted them much as he had tersely refused some of Chotiner's florid advertising copy. At the same time, throughout the state were the myriad committees Jorgensen set up with such relish. "Committee, committee, committee, committee," he would boast, "for beauticians . . . for aviation, for garbage collectors, a committee for masseurs . . . hell, I had committees from knife-sharpeners down." They planned the auxiliaries not only to heckle, or to mobilize money and votes, but in particular to penetrate Douglas's Democratic strongholds, including Hollywood labor unions, where the campaign would pay labor men to form the committees and groups that knifed into the heart of her support. Finally, they would leave the ranch that Sunday evening, June 11, with an architecture of the most wide-ranging and lavish funding in the history of California politics, contributions both in and out of state that would go far beyond the impressive money already given Richard Nixon simply to win his uncontested senatorial nomination.

"ALWAYS ASKING FOR MONEY"

After the session at San Ysidro, Nixon stopped to deliver the commencement address at Fullerton High before returning to Washington. Warning the graduates on the lovely old campus that they faced a great crisis—"whether the American system of government can be maintained"—he joked lamely about the "political implications" of his experience a quarter century earlier in the school orchestra. "I was playing a violin and not [like Harry Truman] a piano," he told them with only a few chuckles in the audience. He then took a flight back to the Capital long enough to attack the administration on the closing of a veterans' hospital at Van Nuys and flew out again to the basin to address a state convention of the Veterans of Foreign Wars in Santa Monica. It was Saturday, June 24, 1950.

He left Washington as part of a larger exodus of politicians and officials from the hazy, humid stillness of an early summer weekend. That morning Harry Truman was flying a similar westward course home to Independence, Missouri, for a brief vacation. Secretary of State Dean Acheson was at his graceful Harewood Farm near Sandy Spring, Maryland, now guarded night and day because of threats inspired by Senator McCarthy's mounting attacks and accusations. The weekend news was eloquent, too, of the time. A federal judge had just denied the final arguments of three of the Hollywood Ten in their trial for contempt of HUAC. At Berkeley, the regents of the University of California had voted unanimously to fire 157 faculty and staff for refusing to sign an oath that they did not belong to the Communist Party. Earl Warren openly opposed the oath, while Nixon had straddled the slowly seething issue in the primary. No loyalty oath would deter a "real communist," but it would be "a tragedy if large numbers of teachers left" over the controversy. "I hope the faculty members will sign the oath under protest," he had told a radio audience, "and then try to get the question worked out by negotiation or through the courts."

Now, as both Harry Truman and Richard Nixon flew across the nation in the hot afternoon, the gravity of the old disputes and positions shifted invisibly beneath them. On the other side of the world, in a cold predawn rain, a murderous artillery barrage suddenly burst over the thinly defended South Korean lines along the thirty-eighth parallel. As Congressman Richard Nixon was preparing to speak to the VFW near the pier in Santa Monica, the first alarmed cables from U.S. Ambassador John Muccio in Seoul were clattering into the State Department decoding machines.

The war in Korea: within hours, U.S. armed forces were to be committed to the defense of the south "in a seemingly routine manner," as one historian recorded Harry Truman's decisions, and "turning back . . . thereafter was practically out of the question." Seeing the invasion by North Korea as a direct, orchestrated Soviet challenge to U.S. interests and prestige—the fall of South Korea having "calculably grave . . . repercussions" everywhere, as the U.S. Embassy in Moscow cabled Washington that weekend—both the administration and their right-wing critics forgot their earlier depreciation of Korea's strategic importance. Forgotten, too, was how much the chauvinistic, feudal oligarchy in South Korea resembled the brutal Communist Party zealots of the north. Only long afterward would U.S. intelligence learn or begin to measure the Byzantine nationalist politics within the Soviet camp, politics that left Moscow with much less actual control or instigation in client governments like North Korea than presumed or feared in the simple demonology of the postwar years. But none of that would matter now. No subtleties of international communism would be recognized or pondered by either Republicans or Democrats as the sudden fighting in northeast Asia seemed to give awful reality to the worst evocation of the Red peril. Without the outbreak of war that summer, some other political posterity for the country—even for the 1950 Senate race in California—might have been possible. With it, the sequels seemed inevitable.

"It happens that I am a Quaker; all my training has been against displays of strength and recourse to arms," Nixon told one audience after the outbreak. "But I have learned through hard experience that, where you are confronted with a ruthless, dictatorial force that will stop at nothing to destroy you, it is necessary to defend yourself by building your own strength." In the days after the invasion he warned darkly that HUAC files forecast a communist "reign of terror if we ever cross swords with Russia." American subversives had been "given a virtual blueprint for revolution," including, as wire services and the *Los Angeles Times* reported with some alarm, "instructions on how to contaminate food supplies, wreck trains, seize arsenals and cities, dismantle rifles and small artillery, sabotage defense plants, and deprive major industrial cities of lights, power, and gas." Calling Truman's commitment to the war of U.S. troops, ships, and planes "business as usual," he urged "complete military and economic mobilization to block Red domination of the world," the establishment of a "world police force" with or without UN approval, and a "no strike" pledge by American labor. His opponent's foreign policy, he told American Legionnaires without mentioning Helen Douglas by name, "would be a stab in the back to Americans who are fighting and dying in Korea." His words were both echo and example for the national stridor. J. Edgar Hoover tallied again his old "potential fifth column," announcing 540,000 subversives at large, exactly 6,977 of whom were said to be "underground" on the West Coast.

Helen Douglas watched a veritable "panic" in those summer weeks, "most acute," she recorded, "in California, which saw itself closest to the outbreak." Her aides remembered the sense of political siege in a race in which they still hoped to define the issues. "And we were very fearful about her having to go on the defensive," Helen Lustig would recall. By reflex and urging, anxious to preempt the coming assault, Douglas soon summoned her own earlier support of Korean aid. "This is the only foothold we have in northeastern Asia. Is it worth the game or not?" she had asked in a January 1950 floor debate over the assistance. "It seems very emphatically that it is."

In the same maneuvering, Richard Nixon had joined other House conservatives in a 192–191 vote to kill a $60 million aid authorization for South Korea, on the grounds that the bill did not include arms and money as well for Formosa, as the China Lobby had urged. Weeks later, Nixon voted for Korean aid when money for Chiang's regime was included in the package. But Douglas now seized on the first vote, adding that Nixon himself had been allied against foreign aid with the infamous Vito Marcantonio. Before an oil workers' convention in Long Beach, a few weeks after the start of the Korean fighting, she called McCarthy "a political madman who insulted America's intelligence," deplored "Nixon's whining . . . alibing [*sic*] and distorting" in explaining his Korean aid votes, and asked California editors to "check the facts . . . before printing the campaign drivel emanating from my opponent's headquarters."

Once more, she struck out in a personalized attack while Nixon remained more sweeping and subtle, and the very effort to turn the issue of toughness and loyalty—to grant the legitimacy of the anticommunist discourse even ironically—seemed to backfire. "She made news just as the man who bit the dog made news," Kyle Palmer typically greeted the tactic at the end of July. "Her sudden zeal to smite the Reds hip and thigh was . . . a tribute to her ability to recognize a fact when she meets one head-on. Her somewhat ridiculous linking of Nixon with her old legislative pal and collaborator, Marcantonio . . . smacked more of the comedienne." Later, Murray Chotiner thought her summer attacks the true watershed in the race. "Well," he would tell Republican audiences, "she was defeated the minute she tried to do it, because she could not sell the people of California that she would be a better fighter against communism than Dick Nixon. She made the fatal mistake of attacking our strength instead of sticking to . . . our weaknesses."

The Korean War came as a kind of fearsome vindication of Richard Nixon's Senate candidacy, and his campaign thrived in the political climate billowing out of that fateful June weekend in 1950. But another, even more immediate effect of the war on his fortunes remained hidden, at least for the moment. Within the campaign, the fighting in the Far East spurred and enlarged the major financial backing that would determine much of the race and his future beyond the election. With each new defeat reported that summer from the UN "police action," with the beleaguered U.S. Army reeling back to a last bare foothold at the tip of South Korea, the contributions to Nixon were to build, until the money and the power it represented grew beyond even what they had planned so ambitiously at the San Ysidro ranch.

The core of his money, then and later, was from the old and new wealth of the California boom. Some already prominent, more of them still relatively unknown yet increasingly powerful, his backers were now a roll call of the state's corporate and financial elite: Robert Di Giorgio, thirty-nine-year-old nephew of old Joe Di Giorgio, the pioneer of the farming empire, and now from his San Francisco office the executive vice president and heir-apparent of the corporation as well as the future director of Pacific Telephone and Telegraph, the Bank of America, Union Oil, and other giants; Dean Witter, then sixty-three, the founder of the brokerage house; "Dad" Bechtel's fifty-year-old son, Stephen, heir to the Six Companies that built Boulder Dam, the succeeding Bechtel Corporation, and a small host of directorates from Morgan Guaranty Trust to the Southern Pacific; Howard Fieldstead Ahmanson, at forty-four already presiding over an expanding empire of savings and loan and insurance holdings in the basin and elsewhere and whose worth would multiply by the millions; Thirty-four-year-old Walter Haas, Jr., the grandson of Mrs. Sigmund Stern and soon to be president of Levi Strauss & Co. as well as Di Giorgio's colleague on the giant utility and bank boards; Henry Salvatori, forty-two, a handsome, chain-smoking Italian immigrant who was quietly cultivating a fortune in oil exploration and an ideological passion for anticommunism; Justin Whitlock Dart, then forty-three and president of Rexall Drug and Chemical on the way to his own corporate empire; and Charles Ducommun, thirty-seven, Stanford- and Harvard-educated heir to a flourishing Los Angeles steel and metals corporation, a realty company, and still more utility and banking directorates.

From much the same provenance came Richard Rheem, whose Rheem California Land Company erected a fortune in investments and oil development; John Krehbiel, a forty-five-year-old insurance broker and managing agent with Aetna; Charles Thomas, who had rescued Foreman & Clark clothiers from the Depression and built a business and civic power in Los Angeles; C. Arnholt Smith, a fifty-one-year-old millionaire banker and manufacturer from San Diego with fleets of taxis and tuna boats along with a drive for influencing local politicians; and, not least, two basin car dealers—Henry Kearns, who would expand his San Gabriel Valley Motors into insurance and land development; and Harry Francis Haldeman, owner of another very successful Los Angeles auto franchise, who accounted not only for substantial campaign support in 1950 and afterward but also for an ambitious son who would become Richard Nixon's chief of staff in the White House.

Most of the money of individual donors would come from the south or from statewide interests, though in San Francisco Dinkelspiel and his more muted organization tapped men like corporate executive Arthur Dolan; investment banker W. W. Crocker and Alvin Derre of the Crocker Bank; industrialist J. D. Zellerbach; Colbert Coldwell of the real estate and investment fortune; the owner and publisher of the *San Francisco Chronicle*, George Cameron; Judge Orla St. Clair; and occasional "anonymous" contributors for as much as $2,500 in repeated donations. A handful on the overall list—Thomas, Dolan, Derre—were GOP activists then or later. A few were relatively closer to the candidate and campaign—Krehbiel, Ducommun, and especially Arnholt Smith, whom Pat Nixon would remember long afterward as "one of our first supporters." They and hundreds like them were solicited in successive waves beginning in late July 1950, the Nixon men canvassing the prestigious streets and suites of Los Angeles and San Francisco at intervals of only days and nonetheless finding frequent repeat contributors.

Most of Nixon's supporters, who saw him as a defender or advocate of their views and vested interests, not only opposed or feared Helen Gahagan Douglas but also deplored Earl Warren. "The sources that had refused to help Warren were all available to Nixon," a Warren biographer wrote of

1950 political finances in California. Yet it was the genius of his fund-raising and intraparty appeal that Richard Nixon also cut deeply into Warren's loyal support. Mac Faries remembered a private dinner given by Bernie Brennan to thank major contributors to Nixon, among them the original Committee of Twenty with their crucial thousand-dollar donations early in the race. There were awkward encounters. "Some of those . . . were people who had supported Warren pretty strongly and they were surprised to see each other there," Faries told the story.

The California backing, as a matter of both personal contacts and the wider common interests of class or business, led as well to major contributions outside the state. "There was a tremendous drive for money in Texas for Nixon," Alvin Meyers remembered; "oil money and oil rallied it." The contributors included multimillionaire H. L. Hunt and Houston's Hugh Roy Cullen, who along with Texan Clint Murchison were drawn to Nixon for his national reputation as a conservative and spy hunter as well as his support on the tidelands and oil issues in general. Some Texas magnates, it was said, were even given to providing favorites like Karl Mundt and Joe McCarthy stock market tips involving their own corporations— "sure things," as reporter Ed Nellor described the inside information.

At the same time, oil support came, too, by way of the industry's California Democrats. Ed Pauley remembered Congressman Nixon, Chotiner, and another aide all coming to his Los Angeles office unannounced the day after the primary. Nixon was "diplomatic" and "sought my advice as to how to proceed," the oilman would say later. "I said I couldn't possibly advise him on Republican Party policy but assured him that my discouraging my friends from voting for Helen Douglas was about as much help as he could expect." At that, as Pauley recalled Nixon, "His eyes lit up. Apparently my attitude was what was on his mind when he came to see me." Privately, the approach to Pauley brought far more than discouragement of Douglas voters. "They raised a lot of money," Meyers would say of Pauley and Black Jack Elliott. "The oil money that came into the state from outside . . . came through that little group."

Again, as in 1946, there was Mendel Silberberg as the liaison for large Hollywood money, led by Louis B. Mayer, who was "always helping," Jorgensen would remember, "the king of the roost." If Jerry Voorhis had been a target of the moguls' political money for his support of actors, writers, and studio workers in labor disputes, the contributions now flowed against Helen Douglas in part because of Melvyn's industry feuds a decade or more before. Old scores in Hollywood also accounted in some measure for one of the more discreet contributions to the Nixon campaign that summer. Soon after the primary, Congressman John Kennedy had come to the attic office in Washington. Finding Nixon gone to California, he then asked to see Bill Arnold and handed the surprised aide a thousand-dollar check from Joseph P. Kennedy, who had fought his own studio wars with industry liberals. "My father wanted to help out," Nixon later quoted the son as saying. He obviously could not openly endorse a Republican, Jack Kennedy told Arnold, "but it isn't going to break my heart if you can turn the Senate's loss into Hollywood's gain." Arnold, as he later recounted, had "routinely" sent the check on to the campaign headquarters in the Garland Building, where it, like so many others, was never officially reported or copied, an expedient they would have cause to regret when John Kennedy became an opponent himself a decade later.

So flush did the campaign become that Nixon was soon able to dispense his own contributions in turn to Republican candidates for Congress or state attorney general, nearly $10,000 in such gifts recorded in the north alone during that summer and fall of 1950, a first powerful senatorial patronage months before the election. One young staff aide remembered Justin Dart almost casually handing out hundred-dollar bills for incidental purposes. "Money didn't seem to be important," thought Mac St. Johns, if only because it was so plentiful.

Still, his campaign pressed unrelentingly for its share of general GOP money, seemingly as much out of pride and prerogative as genuine need, another mark of the Nixon faction's bristling independence and parvenu status in the party. "Nixon's enthusiasts were always asking for money," Faries remembered, regardless of the wealth in their coffers. Their requests in 1950 were for as much as $40,000. Trying to help several candidacies, the GOP Central Committee could at first apportion only $15,000 to the Senate race, and Faries remembered Dick Nixon himself as "never critical . . . big enough to understand this kind of spreading things around." Yet the candidate's men, with their more naked ambitions and pretense, were slighted and bitter. "Some of his enthusiasts would be mad, see," Faries said later about the party money, "because they saw Nixon going on up to be President."

Ironically, such insistence on party allotments as virtual entitlement would embroil Richard Nixon in the first small campaign finance scandal of his career, an early exposure of the shady passing and repassing of political money that was to haunt him to the end. The trail began with Owen Brewster, then a sixty-two-year-old GOP senator from Maine, a direct descendant from the Mayflower whose reactionary politics were a staple on Capitol Hill. Asked if he would at last support the Democratic administration following Pearl Harbor, Brewster had replied tartly, "If I am compelled to a choice between Roosevelt and Hitler, I choose Roosevelt." Drew Pearson called Brewster "the kept senator of Pan American Airways" for his notorious ties to the airline, and in the late 1940s the senator had been accused of what one sworn witness called outright "blackmail" in offering to quash a congressional inquiry of another airline in return for its corporate merger with Pan Am. Now Brewster was chairman of the Republican Senate Campaign Committee, which dispensed funds to GOP candidates around the nation. And that May Dick Nixon had importuned him for a $5,000 contribution—"besieged me," as Brewster later testified about the calls from Milton Young of South Dakota as well as Nixon.

Committee rules strictly prohibited contributions in primaries, favoring one Republican over another. "We have taken a very firm vote that we not do that kind of thing to advance money," Brewster told a later inquiry. But the pressure had been considerable, and the senator with his wife's cosignature had borrowed from a Washington bank $5,000 each for Nixon and Young. To hide the payments further, Brewster then used as a go-between "a man who had a capacity," as he said later, "to keep his mouth shut." The middleman turned out to be Henry "the Dutchman" Grunewald, described by *Time* as "an influence peddler," by another writer as "gambler-lobbyist-fixer-fugitive," and who was soon to be indicted on thirty counts involving tax fraud and other political corruption. In early May 1950 Grunewald quietly advanced $5,000 to the Nixon campaign. The money was then repaid in August when an official Senate Campaign Committee contribution was given to Nixon.

When the transaction was publicly revealed in the spring of 1952 during a congressional probe of Grunewald's taxes, there would be passing embarrassment to Nixon, because of both Brewster's breach of GOP campaign finance practices and the employment of a notorious middleman. Then Nixon would stoutly deny that he even knew Henry Grunewald was the go-between, though in May 1950 the money had come directly from "the Dutchman" in one of the largest single contributions received in the race. It "can hardly be doubted," one student of the campaign later concluded, that the candidate knew the source. Even more intriguing, however, were the connections that remained hidden. Before his death, Grunewald would confess to Drew Pearson that he had given similar secret payments of $5,000 in cash to Tom Dewey and Herbert Brownell in New York, that he had helped arrange a job for Dewey protégé and Nixon friend Bill Rogers on an investigative subcommittee under Brewster, and that he later had a falling out with his political friends over an alleged indiscretion by Rogers with Grunewald's daughter.

It was a fleeting glimpse of seedy bagmen and Washington favors, an underworld of money and influence Richard Nixon had begun to touch just as he had encountered on HUAC the shadowy backstage reality of the anticommunist impulse. When his 1950 Senate campaign reported its finances in Sacramento after the primary and general election, the Brewster-Grunewald "advance," like so much else, never appeared. Though he listed some $1,250 in a Senate Campaign Committee contribution in the last weeks before the election, neither the remainder of the $5,000 nor the August repayment to "the Dutchman" were ever legally recorded.

Nixon was back and forth between Washington and California in the tense atmosphere of the midsummer after the outbreak of war, and he would pause during the politics and fund-raising for an episode that held another portent of the future. As in 1946, he was again quietly receiving financial and political help from Herbert Hoover, including contributions from the Hoover sons, Allen and Herbert, Jr., as well as from other wealthy patrons of the old guard. In July, the former President invited him to the annual retreat at the exclusive Bohemian Grove, a rustic, sylvan men-only resort in the majestic redwoods outside San Francisco. There, at lunch at Hoover's "Cave Man Camp"—"about two places from the bottom," as Nixon remembered his place at the long table—he heard the featured speaker, another invited guest, Dwight Eisenhower.

Then president of Columbia University, Eisenhower was already widely mentioned as a potential GOP Presidential nominee in 1952, though he continued to disavow any political ambition. Nixon himself in a postprimary press conference had listed the general among the contenders, along with Warren, Stassen, Taft, and Dewey. Hoover obviously stood behind Taft and the GOP right, and Eisenhower was now "deferential to Hoover but not obsequious," as Nixon recorded his manner and remarks "in enemy territory." The war hero spoke without notes—"not a polished speech," Nixon thought—and was applauded by the conservative businessmen only when he endorsed the loyalty oath at Berkeley.

After the talk Eisenhower was politely ushered out, and Nixon went back with the others for a postmortem around a campfire in the Grove's inky afternoon shadows. "Eisenhower's personality and personal mystique had deeply impressed the skeptical and critical Cave Man audience," he recorded afterward. "But the feeling was that he had a long way to go before he would have the experience, the depth, and the understanding to be President." It was another remarkable glimpse at how much the young congressman was already at home with the old Hoover wing of the GOP, how much he already stood apart from Dwight Eisenhower in patronage and politics, a reality often forgotten in the historic relationship that was soon to unfold between the two men.

As the Nixon campaign harvested its abundant money, the Douglas forces struggled for support. Her backers sent out mailings in New York and Washington, held parties for wealthy eastern liberals, but the national donations could not compensate for the lack of contributions back in California. Paul Ziffren, a young Democratic lawyer trying to raise funds in Los Angeles that summer, remembered having to resort to the affluent clients in his own tax practice, people who gave because "they had a strong personal attachment to me," he would say. President Truman had even approached Sheridan Downey to seek party unity after the primary, and the still-embittered senator refused any reconciliation with Douglas. By late summer it was clear that powerful Democrats had not only deserted her candidacy but also chilled other donors, especially the petroleum interests in the South and West. "There is no question," Alvin Meyers said later, "that the very oil people who showered down for Nixon were for Democrats in other situations and in other states." "The oil people . . . had in mind what should be done with her," Ziffren's wife recalled, remembering their cold reception among the traditional donors, and "oil . . . controlled the Democratic party."

Helen Douglas returned to the Capital that August amid other omens. In the basin, Los Angeles County supervisors unanimously enacted emergency ordinances requiring registration of "all communists." Meanwhile, *Life* magazine reported Nixon ahead as a result of the Korean War. In a national column widely used by the Republicans, *Newsweek*'s Raymond Moley attacked her "so-called liberalism . . . positions contrary to any rational dealing with communist activities."

On entering the House chamber she went to pay her respects to Speaker Sam Rayburn, and the solemn Texan congratulated her on the primary victory but admonished her gravely. "Now, don't make any mistake," he said. "Take that young man out in the finals." Darting a glance at Nixon already in his seat on the floor, Rayburn added softly, "His is the most devious face of all those who have served in Congress in all the years I've been here."

Before them was the McCarran-Wood bill, a slightly revised version of the original Mundt-Nixon legislation, which had now carried the Senate in the climate of national fear. Passage in the House seemed inevitable, and the issue the latest test of loyalty and resolve in the new wave of anticommunism. The night before the vote, a local Washington television station even carried a Defense Department film on "communist infiltration" that prominently featured Congressman Richard Nixon. As the roll call neared in Washington, Lybeck and others were in the Democratic campaign headquarters in the Alexandria Hotel in Los Angeles when the phone rang. It was Helen Douglas calling from the House cloakroom. The vote was coming up, she told them.

"You know what I'm going to do."

"Yes, Helen, we know," Lybeck had replied wearily.

"Okay, just wanted to tell you because you know what this might mean."

In the moments before the tally, a tense silence began to fall over the House, and Douglas remembered Nixon across the chamber "laughing and talking" with GOP friends. One by one, her Democratic colleagues from California and elsewhere came by her seat to whisper their advice to go along with the bill. "This . . . is going to pass overwhelmingly. Your vote won't matter. Anyway, Truman will veto it," one of them urged. "You won't be able to get around the state fast enough to explain," Chet Holifield had told her softly over her shoulder. "He'll beat your brains in." She listened and said nothing as the clerk moved through the roll.

"Douglas of California."

"No."

She was one of twenty. In a later statement she told the House, "I will not be stampeded by hysteria nor will I waver for political expediency." Afterward, Douglas went to the House dining room for lunch with John McCormack and others. As she approached the table, they all rose. "How does it feel to be a dead statesman, Helen," one of them asked, "instead of a live politician?" She replied jauntily, "Just fine."

Celebrating their victory, Republicans that day paid special tribute to Richard Nixon on the floor of the House. Led by California's Donald Jackson, a dozen GOP congressmen trooped to the microphone to extol Nixon's "untiring service" to the anticommunist cause and predict his election to the Senate. After lunch, Helen Douglas walked back into the chamber during the testimonials, "smiled at Nixon," as a UP reporter noted, and sat down pensively. She remembered it as a strange moment of relief in the midst of apparent damage and defeat. "I believed," Douglas wrote afterward, "the worst was over."

"BUT IT IS NOT A SMEAR, IF YOU PLEASE"

The morning after the House vote, Nixon headquarters in Los Angeles released a lengthy attack by Bernie Brennan on Douglas's "soft attitude toward communism." Brennan did not mention the McCarran-Wood bill in a statement plainly drafted before the passage, but the timing was clear. "During five years in Congress, Helen Douglas has voted 353 times exactly as has Vito Marcantonio, the notorious Communist Party–line congressman from New York." He went on to recite her votes on Greece and Turkey, HUAC, contempt citations, and other Cold War measures. Why did the *Daily Worker* call her a "hero"? Why did they prefer her to Richard Nixon? "The communists have the answer," he said, hinting darkly at secret ties.

"How can Helen Douglas, capable actress that she is, take up so strange a role as a foe of communism . . . when she has so deservedly earned the title of 'the pink lady'?" Brennan concluded. "Perhaps she has just heard of the chameleon that changes color to suit conditions, or perhaps Helen Douglas has decided pink isn't becoming anymore, or at least while we are in a bloody war with communists."

The term "pink lady" was no more novel than the comparison with Marcantonio. Manchester Boddy and the Hearst press had called her "pink" or "pinko" as early as April. But the Brennan statement was now to take on a force and circulation far broader. Published by the *Los Angeles Times* the same morning it was released, a major story the paper called with no apparent pun "a red-hot broadside fired into the Douglas camp," it was distributed and reported nearly verbatim throughout California. That same evening, Nixon himself spoke on a statewide radio broadcast on "the Korean situation," calling for the resignation of Dean Acheson and "all-out mobilization immediately." Within days, a further Nixon release with similar blanket coverage reminded readers of the Douglas-Marcantonio votes (now "354 times exactly"), her roll call against McCarran-Wood, and the radio attack on Acheson.

Later that week, however, appeared the most conspicuous product of the campaign, an accompaniment to Brennan's "pink lady" but soon a popular symbol in itself. On the pattern of 1946, Nixon had ordered them to do a detailed survey of the Douglas record for embarrassing votes. In mid-June, between San Ysidro and the outbreak of the Korean War, they had released a simple mimeographed two-page listing of what were called her "Votes Against Un-American Activities Committee . . . Foreign Policy . . . Internal Security . . . National Defense." By the beginning of September, in the wake of Brennan's assault and McCarran-Wood, they decided to publish much the same record in a striking and ingenious new format. Entitled "Douglas-Marcantonio Voting Record," it began: "Many persons have requested a comparison of the voting records of Congresswoman Helen Douglas and the notorious Communist Party–liner, Congressman Vito Marcantonio of New York." The two had voted together "354 times" since 1945, and "while it should not be expected that a member of the House . . . should always vote in opposition to Marcantonio, it is significant to note not only the great number of times which Mrs. Douglas voted in agreement with him, but also the issues."

Under a bold "HERE IS THE RECORD!" they listed her votes with Marcantonio in shocking categories: "Communist Line Foreign Policy Votes," "Against Loyalty and Security . . . ," "Against Congressional Investigation of Communist and Other Illegal Activities," and even included the tidelands under the rubric "Against California." Except for McCarran-Wood and the oil votes, it was the same record listed in June and summarized by Brennan, though now adding "ON ALL OF THE ABOVE VOTES, which have accrued since Congressman Nixon took office on January 1, 1947, HE has voted exactly opposite to the Douglas-Marcantonio Axis!"

Approving the final copy at the print shop, they had asked to see samples of colored paper. "And in the stock we found a piece of paper that had a pinkish tinge to it," Chotiner said later, "and for some reason or other it just seemed to appeal to us for the moment." Printed on eight-and-one-half-by-fourteen stock, it would soon be known all over California as the Pink Sheet.

Only a careful analysis of House votes would have revealed the reality. Of seventy-six major roll calls during the Pink Sheet period, Douglas and Marcantonio voted together fifty-three times as part of either a majority of the Democratic Representatives or of an overall House majority, including Republicans. On the remaining issues, most dealt with public housing, rent and price controls, and liberal domestic measures. Beyond her lonely, qualified vote against Greek-Turkish aid, the sole internal security votes they shared apart from the majority were on Mundt-Nixon and its clone, McCarran-Wood, where Douglas, notably, was in the company of both Democrats and Republicans as well as Marcantonio. It would always be a bittersweet irony that Vito Marcantonio's votes against the Cold War were as easily matched with GOP isolationism as his domestic radicalism with the New and Fair Deals, that on foreign or defense questions ultraconservatives like Robert Taft or Kenneth Wherry could be counted voting with the Harlem congressman almost uniformly, as Joseph and Stewart Alsop wrote in a column that summer of 1950. But then Taft and Wherry were not being Red-baited, and almost nothing of the reality of congressional politics or records would be known or reported in California this autumn. The Pink Sheet and its ominous "Axis" would be widely accepted on its face.

It was a document "that my campaign committee issued" and had been "inspired" by Boddy's earlier attacks, Nixon said afterward of the Pink Sheet, as if somehow Marcantonio had not been summoned earlier in 1946 and 1950, the June record or Brennan statements had not been released, and they had not deliberately chosen the paper. "Whatever interpretation was later placed on these facts, no one was ever able to challenge their accuracy," he wrote of the flyer in his memoirs. "All we added was the mordant comment of the color of the paper." Then and later, his men took much the same view. "It was her record rather than herself which was the object of disapproval," wrote Arnold. "No lies—these are facts we got out of the *Congressional Record*," Jorgensen would insist. "But we put it on pink paper. People drew their own conclusion. . . . Oh, there's been a lot rougher politics than I'd ever use!" Murray Chotiner later cited the sheet as an example of the influence of "color" on a political campaign. "But it is not a smear, if you please," he would instruct Republican audiences, "if you point out the record of your opponent." At that, however, Nixon apparently shrank from going further with the smear. When later in the campaign he found yet another anti-Douglas flyer being set in bright red letters, he ordered Arnold to have the rest of the run done in blue. "In other words," the aide recorded, "he bent over backwards to prevent criticism of him for using unfair tactics."

Nonetheless, after a first printing of 50,000, the Pink Sheet was soon reordered in a half-million copies and handed out on street corners, in clubs, factories, businesses, and neighborhoods all over the state—"more requests and demands for this literature than any other," Chotiner proudly recalled. Not everyone in the campaign was so enthusiastic. Once more Dinkelspiel balked at using it in the north, though some copies were distributed there. "Well, I didn't feel then, and I don't feel, that it's necessarily a proper approach," he told an interviewer a quarter century later. Herb Klein, who was to spend much of the later campaign in Washington on a newspaper assignment, watched the sheet emerge, and "was glad," as he wrote later, "I had no part in the idea." Both Douglas and Nixon were "reckless in their charges," he thought, despite his continuing loyalty to Nixon and his recruitment of friends from the Junior Chamber of Commerce to the campaign. But the Douglas-Marcantonio comparison was "unfair" whatever its provenance or provocation. "The Pink Sheet," Klein would conclude in his memoirs, "was a smearing distortion."

"Throughout the campaign I kept her pinned to her extremist record," Nixon later wrote about the use of the Pink Sheet. Helen Douglas would try in vain to counter with lengthy comparisons of her voting record with Nixon's. But the defense, like Voorhis's four years earlier, was tedious and confusing. "The electorate can be frightened more easily than it can be comforted," concluded Byron Lindsley, who watched the uneven battle unfold as chairman of her San Diego campaign. For its part, the Nixon camp was carefully selective as well about the congressman's past votes. "We never put out the complete voting record of our candidate . . . in spite of the demands from people within our organization," Chotiner admitted later. "We only put out the record in general terms on issues such as: 'Voted for reduction of taxes . . . Voted for military preparedness' . . ."

The Pink Sheet and its accompaniments were soon reflected in a spate of end-of-summer newspaper attacks. The *Long Beach Independent* thought Douglas "not even loyal to the state . . . a sincere 'pink.' " "California voters should know that if they vote for Helen Douglas," editorialized the *San Diego Union*, "they are voting aid and comfort to communism." Early in September, Hearst columnist George Rothwell Brown produced a major series on California's U.S. Senate race, centering on the revelation that "Helen Gahagan Douglas has generally been found voting in the House of Representatives with Vito Marcantonio." Reading the columns approvingly in Washington and continuing to court Brown himself, Nixon wrote Edmond Coblentz of the *San Francisco Call-Bulletin* on September 5, thanking the prominent newspaperman effusively for a small party given for wealthy backers in the bay area and also for instigating the Brown series, "pointing up the real issues of the campaign."

Among the Democrats, Eleanor Roosevelt saw at once the force of the Pink Sheet and repeatedly urged her California protégé to "set the record straight," as Helen wrote later. But Douglas remembered herself "always off-balance, working so hard and fast to cover the state" that she did not respond. Only after the race was over did she reflect on what might have been—an immediate statewide radio rebuttal, some ringing statement about "the deliberate lie." Yet at the crucial moment, like Jerry Voorhis, she would not quite fathom what was happening. "I failed to take his attacks seriously enough. I wasn't nearly shocked enough when I saw the Pink Sheet," Helen Douglas would say. "I just thought it was ridiculous, absolutely absurd."

Douglas formally began her final campaign in a radio speech just after Labor Day, again calling Nixon so reactionary that Taft was a "flaming liberal" by comparison. "Upon our winning depends the future course of the world," she said grandly, albeit with more prophecy than anyone imagined. The speech brought her the last major publicity for weeks. In any case, it was soon overwhelmed by a fresh chorus of replies. The head of a Nixon women's committee blamed Douglas for the "bitter bloody war in Korea," calling her congressional record "most pleasing to the Kremlin." "We do not say that she is a communist," former Boddy supporters now endorsing Nixon were quoted as saying by the *Los Angeles Times*, "but she could not have followed the Communist Party line more closely had she been." With the usual allusions to gender as well as no substance, Kyle Palmer dismissed her in a September 10 column as "a gifted mimic . . . an emotional artist . . . a superficial student of weighty matters, a demagogue . . . a veritable political butterfly, flitting from flower to flower . . . while others—Nixon among the foremost—have pulled up the weeds, sprayed the plant lice, squashed the snails, killed the worms, and tilled the soil." To underscore the contrast, and Douglas's feminine frailty, he added of her opponent: "Make no mistake about Dick Nixon. . . . There is nothing superficial about his makeup and no emotional instability whatsoever."

"And when you start the campaign, start it with a bang," Chotiner later advised GOP strategists. Richard Nixon launched his own final drive of 1950 on September 18 with a statewide radio hookup and a highly publicized sweep by private plane from breakfast in San Diego to lunch at the Biltmore in Los Angeles, then the afternoon in Fresno and evening in San Francisco. It was all dramatic new barnstorming, the portent of a campaign style that would envelop American politics, the rush from city to city, region to region, the hurried press conferences, the seemingly natural, necessary shrinkage of issues to a few simple slogans and themes.

Listening to the broadcast, Helen Douglas remembered his voice "calm and reassuring." Nixon pointedly praised Sheridan Downey, who had "fearlessly taken a strong stand against communist aggression at home and abroad," and then quickly came to the point. "At the outset of this campaign, I am confronted with an unusual situation. My opponent is a woman," he began. He had been advised to "raise no questions as to her qualifications," that "to criticize a woman might cost the election." But he had "weighed this problem carefully" and decided the people were "entitled" to know her positions as well as his. "I want to make my position crystal clear," Richard Nixon said solemnly. "There will be no name-calling, no smears, no misrepresentations in this campaign. We do not need to indulge in such tactics."

He would then go on immediately to explain how "the record of my opponent disqualifies her," how she had once said, "Communism is no real threat." Her votes against HUAC revealed what she meant. "If she had had her way, the communist conspiracy in the United States would never have been exposed, and Alger Hiss instead of being a convicted perjurer would still be influencing the foreign policy of the United States. . . . If she had had her way our troops in Korea would have been even less well prepared than they are." Then this passage much reported:

> I want to point out one very significant thing about all
> of the votes I have mentioned. These were not party
> line votes. My opponent did not vote as a Democrat.
> She did not vote as a Republican. . . . It just so happens
> that my opponent is a member of a small clique which
> joins the notorious communist Party-liner Vito Marcan-
> tonio of New York, in voting time after time against
> measures that are for the security of this country.

Interrupted frequently by applause, he went on to discuss his own "firsthand experience" with the communist conspiracy and to urge "all-out mobilization" and "complete victory" in Korea. "I believe we should not stop at the thirty-eighth parallel unless a complete military capitulation is inflicted upon the North Koreans," he emphasized. Briefly, near the close of the speech, he referred in one sentence to "domestic questions." "I am squarely opposed to costly, nationalization projects," he said, "which are designed to step up the program of regimentation of the people." Repeated at every stop that day, the keynote speech would say nothing about California issues.

The next day Nixon was back in the basin before still more applauding and cheering crowds along a familiar path—breakfast with the Elks in Alhambra, then San Gabriel, Rosemead, Temple City, Arcadia, Monrovia, El Monte, a television appearance with movie actress Irene Dunne, and dinner once more at Pomona's Ebell Club. He was scheduled to appear with Douglas before the Los Angeles Business and Professional Women's Club on September 20 to discuss "The Trend of Communism in the United States." But at the last moment Douglas had backed out in order to stay in Washington to support Truman's veto of McCarran-Wood. Appearing in her stead was the lackluster Democratic gubernatorial candidate, James Roosevelt. The occasion became another Nixon triumph. "Mrs. Douglas should speak for herself so that every person in California may know just . . . why she has followed the Communist Party line so many times," he said in a statement before the debate. Newspapers reported "gales of laughter" from an audience of five hundred in the Biltmore Ballroom when organizers announced Helen Douglas "delayed by congressional duties" and "wild applause" for Richard Nixon. At the end of his formal speech— a powerful "denunciation of communism," as journalists described it and a vivid contrast to Roosevelt's—the ovation went on so long that he was forced to stand and motion for quiet to allow the meeting to conclude with a question period. "James Roosevelt," the *Examiner*'s Carl Greenberg reported typically, "last night publicly allied himself with Congressman Vito Marcantonio, who votes the Communist Party line." With the same tone, the *Times* editorialized on the "Douglas-Roosevelt-Marcantonio Axis."

At the end of September came the event that had been implicit in Helen Douglas's candidacy and Nixon's own strategy from the outset—the major defection of prominent Democrats. In a release that made front-page news in Los Angeles and throughout the state, sixty-four "of California's best-known and most influential Democrats," as they styled themselves, endorsed Richard M. Nixon and his "sturdy Americanism." "She has voted consistently with Vito Marcantonio," said the statement. "Belated flag-waving cannot erase this damning record, nor can the tawdry pretense of 'liberalism' excuse it." The group was led by George Creel, Woodrow Wilson's propagandist during World War I as well as Upton Sinclair's Democratic rival in the 1930s. The seventy-four-year-old onetime Progressive had backed Helen Douglas when she began in politics a decade before. Like many California Democrats, Creel now gravitated to Nixon out of resentment at the attacks on Downey, a growing Cold War chauvinism, and not least a presumption that the old Progressive battles had somehow been won. "No longer do powerful and unscrupulous aggregations of capital, sitting behind the screens, pull strings that make a whole country dance to their fiddling," he wrote at the height of the boom.

"We didn't have to recruit him," Jorgensen would say sarcastically about old George Creel, who over the ensuing years privately adopted Nixon as a kind of Republican protégé. Still, they paid the prominent Democrat $16,000 and directed openly and covertly through "Democrats for Nixon" much the same intraparty sabotage worked in the primary. "The Malone organization here is doing nothing for Helen," Creel proudly wrote a friend that autumn from San Francisco, "and Sheridan Downey is on the ground, doing everything in his power for Nixon, but very secretly." In Whittier Janet Goeske, a close friend of Hannah Nixon, would remember her surprise at discreet letters from the incumbent Democratic senator urging his former supporters to vote for the Republican candidate. With Creel on the public list were only a handful of politically significant names—lawyer John Irwin, once briefly touted as Downey's successor; Kathleen Norris, the author; an American Legion commander and former officeholders. But key figures like Downey, Pauley, and Elliott remained behind the scenes. Ostensibly neutral, Manchester Boddy would quietly tell fellow publishers in Oakland at the end of September that he, too, was backing Dick Nixon.

"We never let the committee think it was running the campaign . . . that they were above and beyond the pale of the regular organization," Chotiner said later of the renegade Democrats. On the other side, Carey McWilliams thought them "a set of political has-beens . . . [who] have made a political living by coming out . . . with noisy endorsements of Republican candidates." Yet publicly as privately their role was significant. "I do not regard my candidacy or the principles upon which it is based in any narrow sense of partisanship," Nixon said, welcoming their support in yet another well-publicized story. He used the theme widely to lift the anticommunist crusade, the Red-baiting, securely above party or domestic issues.

"TRUE IN MAY—EQUALLY TRUE IN NOVEMBER," headlined a "California Democrats for Nixon" ad throughout the state, quoting Downey's "aid and comfort to Soviet tyranny," and Boddy's "red-hots." Later in October there was yet another mass mailing to "Fellow Democrats" using Downey's list and others. "Is Helen Douglas a Democrat?" the brochure asked. "THE RECORD SAYS NO!" Reciting the Pink Sheet litany, the Downey anathema, and attacks on Nixon by the *Daily Worker*, it asked, "How will a real Democrat vote in this election? . . . Our troops in Korea [are] not thinking about partisan politics." Unlike Nixon's primary mailing to Democrats attacked by Boddy, the general election flyer went largely unchallenged by the harried Douglas campaign. It would be years later before she confronted the transparent meaning of asking if Helen Douglas were a Democrat. "What was I supposed to be," she caustically asked a questioning reporter in 1956, "a Republican?"

Douglas had learned of the defections and Downey's underground opposition days before the Creel announcement and in evident desperation wired old supporters to come to dinner September 26. "I have run into a frightening crisis. I need your help, your advice, your support." But she emerged from that evening, as she recorded, still "fully determined to wage my own campaign and ignore the tactics of my opponent . . . sticking to my record all the time with Gahagan stubbornness." She would grimly call him Tricky Dick and publicly deplore the "irrational fears" and "whispered calumny." Yet she felt "ashamed and debased," as she described it afterward, to answer the charges more specifically. To the end she would be half-consious, half-contemptuous of the smears, anxiously and angrily striking out while never fully confronting them. "Don't say I sent it," she wrote a friend, enclosing a Nixon ad, as if her very awareness would be an embarrassment. It all "made me feel," she later described her sense of dismay and helplessness, as if "I was standing in the path of tanks."

Inside, the Nixon Senate campaign was only in part the juggernaut it seemed to opponents. Behind the elaborate planning and coordinated attacks was a rich, shifting, often troubled mixture of Nixon the politician and man, of the people he gathered and allowed about him, of outside forces using his candidacy for their own purposes. And in that, far more vividly than the 1946 run against Voorhis, his organization of 1950 was in many ways a foreshadowing of other Nixon campaigns—and of a Nixon government—to come.

They remembered Bernie Brennan as the "quiet boss" as the campaign machinery moved into still higher gear that summer and early fall, "such a gentleman and such a nice person," one staff aide called him, though there was no real question about his underlying fervor, how much he relished his public assaults on "the pink lady." "It was hard for me to align him with the skulduggery that went on," recalled Tom Dixon, once more the contract radio announcer. "But he had to be a part of it." It would always be easier to ascribe the ruthlessness of the campaign to a more abrasive, less polished Murray Chotiner, whom they saw as "the noisy boss," ever impatient with staff and volunteers. Chotiner would be a laughing, joking man over drinks outside the headquarters. But Dixon and many others believed him "the true genius of in-fighting . . . pulling every mean string he could."

"I don't think Murray had any political principles other than winning," an old adversary would recall, though again there was no doubt of his convictions about Helen Douglas and those like her. "I think he truly believed she was evil . . . really an evil person," his son Kenneth remembered. "He would equate a liberal or a Democrat with a communist." It was clear, too, by September how much he fired and then drove the organization, what Jorgensen called "his thinking, his facility to execute, to get the campaign rolling, on the move." And if Chotiner remained the hired manager, bound by Jorgensen's original order at their Athletic Club lunch to "follow the plan," he worked in easy tandem and mutual admiration with the candidate himself. "He always considered Nixon a genius," said Jack Chotiner, Murray's brother and former law partner. Watching them together at the headquarters or on the telephone while Nixon was traveling, another aide thought Chotiner "the only man Dick ever really listened to." At the same time, it was that dominance and intimacy of the shrewd, pudgy, unsavory lawyer—Murray Chotiner's virulent methods found a home with Richard Nixon—that as much as any other factor deepened the isolation of the Senate campaign from GOP moderates around Earl Warren, drawing Nixon all the more into a sense and reality of running alone, apart from even party loyalties and allegiances. "Murray Chotiner was an extraordinarily astute details man," remembered Victor Hansen, Warren's southern California chairman in 1950. "I've said everything when I say that. We wouldn't have any part of him in our campaign."

Beneath Brennan and Chotiner, the staff labored at a fixed, stiffening distance from the thirty-seven-year-old congressman. Bill Arnold and Dorothy Cox came from the Capitol Hill office with somewhat more ease and familiarity, though the relatively bland, cautious Arnold was again as peripheral to the important decision-making as in 1948. Others felt much the same barrier, "always this relationship of a hired person," one of them said afterward. "It was impossible to get close," remembered Mac St. Johns, who traveled with the candidate and his wife and performed a myriad of other duties. Tom Dixon, who spent perhaps even more time with Richard Nixon, introducing radio shows and warming up rallies, thought it a curious "caste system." The formality and reserve only reinforced the conformity. After the weekend at San Ysidro ranch, it was not a campaign in which second thoughts were voiced in the ranks about the Red-baiting strategy or the sheer vitriol of the public and private attacks on Douglas. In the north, Dinkelspiel merely continued quietly to ignore or to mute what he could. Other prominent figures at the edge of the campaign—those whose comparative independence might have given them a voice—tended to be if anything more zealous than the candidate or his manager.

Mac Faries would call them the "coattail riders," assorted advisers, agents, and envoys, the famous and near-famous and obscure who crowded around the Nixon campaign that autumn. Some came in the inquisitional ardor unleashed by the Hiss case, some to capture a new United States senator, some out of old California enmities for Helen Douglas or Earl Warren or both, some for patronage of a rising young politician of heady national promise. Almost all of them urged him on in the tactics and intensity born of the Chotiner-Nixon union, lending what happened that autumn of 1950 the legitimacy and authority carried by their power and reputations. In charge of Los Angeles volunteers, H. Allen Smith was an assemblyman and ex-FBI agent who was convinced, as he told the *Los Angeles Times*, that the country could no longer "temporize" with communists. Actors Richard Arlen and George Murphy made frequent appearances for Nixon and could be far more strident, Murphy dwelling caustically on Helen Douglas's acting, on "how bad an actress she was," remembered Georgia Sherwood, then Dixon's wife, who accompanied them on some tours. "George Murphy was part of it . . . a filthy campaign."

Beyond the constant, often extravagant coverage of the *Los Angeles Times*, Kyle Palmer was more than ever the discreet adviser and patron, reviewing or writing speeches, adding his own barbs against Douglas and then incorporating Nixon passages into his columns. "Nixon was always coming over to Kyle's for advice," one of Palmer's friends remembered. Now added to the *Times* was the same kind of backroom help from California's other press behemoth. Almost on his deathbed, William Randolph Hearst had quietly assigned Nixon forty-nine-year-old John Clements, officially the public relations director of the Hearst Corporation but in fact the overseer of the publisher's lavishly financed "Communist Program." With files from informers, defectors, and other sources "as good as the FBI," as one Nixon campaign aide described them, the Hearst office under Clements would provide research information to Nixon, McCarthy, and other politicians. They routinely planted articles and editorials throughout the newspaper chain and beyond, acted as gatherer and dispenser of political intelligence, and even as intermediary with large contributors—all of which were now performed for the 1950 Senate campaign in California. As for Clements personally, a wealthy man who owned his own string of New Jersey newspapers and was later editor of the ultraconservative *American Mercury* magazine, it was a matter of gender as well as national peril. "He couldn't stand ladies," Richard St. Johns remembered. "And he couldn't stand Helen Gahagan Douglas."

They would have no shortage of such public relations help as Chotiner sprayed throughout the California press an almost daily stream of releases, statements, articles, editorial attacks, and endorsements. During the closing weeks, one writer even found publicists on loan from the National Association of Manufacturers, men said to have participated as well in the Smathers primary fight against Pepper and similar races. But in some ways the most intriguing aid remained secret well after the election. Early in October, Nixon met in Los Angeles at the Ambassador Hotel with David Charney and Leo Casey of a New York public relations firm named Allied Syndicates Inc. A former publicist for the New York World's Fair as well as for the GOP and the Willkie Presidential campaign, Casey had been called by Charney to Los Angeles on an urgent overnight flight and was to chair an "Independent Voters Committee for Nixon," with special efforts to mobilize the black vote and to play up the congressman's role in the investigation and conviction of Alger Hiss. As Leo Casey told the story afterward, his full-time services in California during the last month of the race were supposed to be goodwill for Allied Syndicates, for which the Nixon campaign would "open some doors" in West Coast business, as his boss Charney explained at the time. Only later did Casey learn, as an associate in the firm told him, "You were working for the China account." Allied Syndicates, it turned out, had been retained at $60,000 a year by the Bank of China as part of the burgeoning China Lobby to prevent Washington's recognition of the new People's Republic in Peking and the consequent freezing of $300 million of Nationalist bank assets in the United States.

During the campaign, Casey was "firmly pushed aside by Chotiner when he tried to inject himself into the private councils," as one witness described it. He spent much of October "doing nothing in his suite at the Beverly Hills Hotel." After the election, however, the publicist had been praised for his work by Allied Syndicate superiors and told to go to Washington and "deliver Nixon to the Major," Chinese military attaché Louis Kung, a favorite nephew of Madam Chiang Kai-shek. Shocked at the whole episode, Casey resigned from the company and subsequently warned Nixon himself, who politely thanked him for the information. When Casey later told his story to a reporter in 1952, Charney admitted the Bank of China retainer and Leo Casey's role in the Senate race but denied any China Lobby connection. Casey had been paid, he said, by the Nixon campaign. For their parts, both the Chinese and Richard Nixon refused comment. Yet at the time, in October 1950, in the wake of Nixon's Ambassador Hotel meeting with Charney and Casey, the politics had been understood. Within days, Richard Nixon had made a special statewide broadcast deploring the "American failure to aid free China" and pledging his own support in the

U.S. Senate for the Chiang Kai-shek regime, a promise he was to keep without stint. At the time, too, Leo Casey and his "Independent Voters" were kept circumspectly in the background. Their substantial expenditures, Casey's salary, and the Beverly Hills Hotel bill never appeared in the campaign's legal spending reports.

Finally, lacing through the publishers and lobbyists, zealots and celebrities, was a group of extraordinary women. Republican women, Nixon once remarked to Tom Dixon, were the "great haters," and his campaigns would always seem to draw examples for the stereotype. One of them, whose husband ran a prosperous basin business and who thought Earl Warren an outright "socialist," led the formal women's organization, denouncing Helen Douglas with evident venom, setting a small legion of like-minded matrons on street corners and at telephones to spread the same message. Others, without titles or formal roles, were still more significant. Among them was Hedda Hopper, the nationally famous Hollywood gossip columnist; Ida Koverman, a native Californian, once a secretary to Herbert Hoover and now the powerful political aide and liaison for Louis B. Mayer; and Grace Stormer, yet another political figure from the corporate halls of Hollywood. In a familiar irony they were—like the woman they so passionately opposed on the other side—sophisticated, well connected, independent. It was Hedda Hopper who acted as go-between for the Ambassador Hotel meeting of Nixon and the China Lobby. Grace Stormer was the first to link his campaign with legal firms and privately disaffected Democratic union leaders of the entertainment industry, relationships with increasingly powerful forces in southern California and the nation that would be crucial in his future. Personally, said a friend, Ida Koverman "couldn't stand Nixon," found him a young boor. But the hardened veteran of studio political wars was the loyal operative of Louis Mayer and the Metro-Goldwyn-Mayer empire, and by money and contacts she efficiently promoted the Red-baiting that was the moguls' obsession more than her own.

The leader of the group, however, and by far the more intimate and important in Richard Nixon's rise, was perhaps the most colorful of all—Adela Rogers St. Johns. The daughter of one of the basin's celebrated criminal attorneys, she was advertised as "the world's greatest girl reporter" while a feature writer for Hearst's old *Los Angeles Herald* in the 1930s. She had covered some of the great stories of the era, from the Lindbergh kidnapping to the Roosevelt White House, writing as well nearly a score of novels and screenplays, and cultivating along the way a hard-drinking, caustic, irrepressible brilliance. Nominally a Democrat, her politics were an exotic mix of metaphysics, newsroom gossip, and shrewd insight. Her first husband had owned a ranch near Whittier where young Richard Nixon sometimes delivered groceries, and when oilman Henry Salvatori introduced Adela formally to Nixon in 1950 it was an instant adoption—the wiry, leathery-faced writer of fifty-six and the fresh young politician to be tutored.

She would take up her patronage with typical energy and assertiveness, touring dozens of house parties with novelist Kathleen Norris, enlisting her sons Mac and Dick in the campaign, writing a glowing story on the Nixon family as well as copy for ads, including part of the Pink Sheet. It was Adela St. Johns who introduced Nixon to Hearst's John Clements and also to a young business contributor of far-flung interests named Howard Hughes. When she once argued that they should tone down for public sensibilities the Red-baiting in a proposed ad, campaign reporter Ralph de Toledano watched while Murray Chotiner "mollified her and got her out of the room," and the ad later "appeared as originally planned." Years afterward, Nixon himself would introduce her with the line, "Mrs. St. Johns is the first person to tell me I would be President." And she had replied, predictably, that she told that to all the young congressmen. "He was furious," she said. Yet she endured and was taken seriously more often than not. Richard Nixon would find her salty enthusiasm and advice on public relations fascinating, a guide and reassurance like no other as he moved onto the larger stage.

Now, as in later races, there would be uneasy questions about how much the campaign reflected both the staff and the various patrons, how much the candidate had lost control of his own run. "What created Nixon was the group around him," Tom Dixon would say after attending the advertising strategy conferences. "He was not the boss in this group." So, too, Adela St. Johns thought the candidate could not have been aware of blatant racism in the Los Angeles headquarters. On October 5, she related with alarm to Dorothy Cox the remark by Gordon Smedley of Chotiner's staff that the campaign was "not particularly interested" in the black voters of Los Angeles. "You know what we do with them where I come from," Smedley had reportedly told a local political figure. "Put 'em in a truck and dump 'em in the river." There were others similarly "incensed over the attitude of the L.A. headquarters," Cox reported to Nixon four days later, and Mrs. St. Johns "wanted to get word to you . . . she didn't feel you knew what was going on, etc." Later in the race, Adela witnessed for herself the candidate's own ambivalence about the black vote. Walking with him one night into a gym in Oakland, they unexpectedly found a black audience waiting for his appearance. "He saw it and cursed like a pirate," she remembered, though after composing himself had gone on to make "a very good speech."

Just as Jorgensen and others of the inner circle in 1950 had seen Richard

Nixon in command of planning and tactics from the beginning, those with him on the road watched a campaign more and more reflective of the candidate's personality. Georgia Sherwood remembered long delays at night rallies in which her husband tried to hold the restless crowds. "We were simply told that he'd had a tantrum," she said of Nixon, "and he was taking it out on the party higher-ups by refusing to appear." As the race wore on through October, Nixon became plainly more reluctant to stop in the big cities, where the setting could not be controlled, where Douglas supporters or union pickets might heckle him. "L.A. and San Francisco scared shit out of him," Dick St. Johns remembered. "He was comfortable in the crossroads, the one-signal towns, the Whittiers. Those were his folks."

The tensions were in some ways most visible in the evolving campaign of Pat Nixon. Babysitters and friends remembered her at their house on Honeysuckle Lane in Whittier sewing draperies and slipcovers, and how she "gratefully" accepted extra travel suits and dresses knitted by some local women. Then came the grueling twelve-hour days of the station wagon tours, passing out thimbles, listening to speeches, anxiously phoning home "several times" a day, her daughter recounted, to check on her children, who were staying with Hannah and Frank or other relatives and friends. She carefully rolled her hair between towns and kept a record of clothes worn at various stops to avoid duplications. Her face, recorded Dorothy Cox, "would look so tired in repose. And I knew that she was probably more tired than even she looked." A campaign handout invited voters to "Meet Mrs. Pat Nixon . . . well-informed, intelligent and thoughtful young woman, seriously interested in national affairs and problems of government . . . a good housekeeper and devoted mother . . . missing her little girls."

By October, behind the façade, she had grown wearily, in some ways bitterly, disillusioned. "My mother in particular, recoiled from the shrillness of Helen Douglas's personal characterizations of my father . . . 'pip-squeak' . . . 'peewee' . . . 'tricky Dick,' " wrote Julie Eisenhower. But another biographer believed Pat Nixon no less affected by the "assaults on Mrs. Douglas as the 'pink lady' and the 'anti-Semitism' of Gerald L. K. Smith." "Pat heard them all," reported Lester David. In the same vein, historian Fawn Brodie would write, "The effect of the 1950 campaign on Pat Nixon, as she watched her husband destroy the actress-politician—a role not altogether unrelated to her own—can only be guessed at."

The Dixons remembered a painful scene that autumn when the four of them were at a small radio station in northern California and Nixon was rehearsing a familiar speech. Just before air time he had looked up at his wife sitting nearby and peremptorily motioned her to leave, "like he was telling a dog to go outside," remembered a shocked Georgia Sherwood.

"You know I don't want ever to be interrupted when I'm working," Nixon had said as she left. Afterward, embarrassed, Pat had told the Dixons, "You know Richard doesn't like to have me in there. I don't know why but I make him nervous. He's such a great man." Days later in Fresno, Mac St. Johns saw much the same scene reenacted. His wife had come in to tell him it was time to leave, and Nixon shot back testily, "I'll go when I'm damned well ready."

"I'd never heard any wife cut off in public so curtly without a rejoinder, not even a dirty look," Tom Dixon recalled. "I felt sorry for her. She was gracious and honorable but weak with him. His ego had to be toadied to." Despite that clash and other petty slights, Sherwood heard Pat Nixon talk about nothing else save her husband and daughters. "She was very mad for him then," she thought, and had "subjected herself to him to the point where she had almost no personality." Still, some were convinced that Pat Nixon found her moments. "She could be waspy and stung him a lot," Richard St. Johns remembered scolding moments at home or headquarters. And if Mrs. Nixon was the exhausted martyr in public, repelled by the savage politics, the staff saw evidence, too, that she felt the opposition attacks even more than the candidate himself—and sometimes egged him on. "How can you let them do that?" they remembered her taunting. "He'd say something and then change it the next morning," Dick St. Johns recalled. "There's the old political adage that you don't argue with the head sharing a pillow."

Eventually the friction between candidate and wife spread to the staff as well. Her resentment and aloofness toward some of his aides, especially Chotiner, the old rival from 1946, became apparent. By the end of the campaign, Chotiner's moves had insulated Nixon from what they saw as her needling interference. "Murray got her to go away," recalled Dick St. Johns. Another aide thought at least one fact clear about the prospective senator. "His wife," he remembered, "hated politics."

In early October a poll by Mervin Field, the first test of strength since the primary and the historic events of the summer, showed him well ahead of Helen Douglas, 39 percent to 27 percent. Nixon was likely to command a clear majority of the 34 percent undecided, as well as a two-to-one margin among former Boddy voters and over a third of all registered Democrats. The figures indicated a 57 percent–43 percent final victory. Yet "the race is still very close," Field wrote in the *San Francisco Chronicle*, citing the potential "vote-switching . . . [that] can make a considerable change in the picture" and the volatility and closeness of the Truman-Dewey contest in the state only two years earlier. The specter of 1948 produced in Nixon if not his organization the combined anxiety and ferocity that was becoming his political hallmark. Once again, as in 1946, he ran the final leg of the race as if he were desperately behind.

Outwardly, he set what the admiring press called a "man-killing pace." Mary Ellen Leary of the *San Francisco News* followed him—"a thinned-down, tired-looking Richard Nixon"—through a typical thirty-six hours in the north that October.

> Then he talked to a Republican women's group, met a second one for coffee, called at his campaign headquarters . . . Chinese food in Chinatown, pork chops and steaming mugs of coffee in the Mother Lode . . . roast chicken in the plush hotels . . . through the rain to Parkmerced and the wind slaps the banner . . . and snarls the name NIXON. . . . At the Empire mine shaft at 6:45 A.M. meeting 150 miners before they went to work. . . . The speech there: advocacy of a free market for newly mined gold. . . . Then into Nevada City for an 8 o'clock breakfast. . . . You've been up since 5:00. It has been raining ever since, too. But just as cheering as the coffee: the handclasp of . . . a Democrat. Into the shops at Grass Valley, and a cobbler says, "So you're the fellow Helen Douglas says does everything wrong." . . . After luncheon, women whisper an assurance, "I'll pray for you." Two said: "We hope to vote for you for President someday."
>
> *That* doesn't keep you awake on the plane ride to San Francisco. Neither does the storm . . . forced down at Concord. . . . There's a major radio talk tonight, skim the text again. . . .

Late each night he talked with Chotiner and Brennan, rehearsing the day past and talking through the next. Concerned at his frantic schedule and mounting sensitivity to hecklers, they pulled Roy Day from his Pomona paper to travel with Nixon over the last three weeks, the crusty printer to be a mix of bodyguard and sympathetic ear. "I'd case the crowd and . . . see if we got the right people in the front rows, so there wouldn't be hecklers up there to upset him or get on the radio or the loudspeakers," Day said. On one flight north, a young correspondent from *Life* magazine, otherwise pro-Nixon, had probed too deeply and angered the candidate. "He was really upset with her because she was getting awfully sticky with her questions," Day remembered. Dick had told him after the flight, "I think if there was any way of doing it, I'd have thrown her off the plane." And it would be Roy Day who more than any other single person beyond Richard Nixon himself heard the relentless drumbeat of those last weeks. He never called her a communist, Roy Day would insist, but in the next breath the old retainer would add that "Nixon said that she was the wife of Melvyn Douglas, who was listed as a communist sympathizer," explaining that her voting record was the same as Marcantonio's. "That's what Nixon said," Day would recall of the unveiled attacks. "He said that up and down the state."

With Day the ever-loyal minion, the staff skillfully stage-managed the only direct confrontations with Douglas herself over the closing days of the race. She had cautiously spurned formal debates after the debacle with Jimmy Roosevelt, inviting some public criticism but avoiding what had happened to Jerry Voorhis. Then Douglas agreed to a joint appearance in Beverly Hills, only to arrive late and be greeted by laughter and derision. Seated behind her, Nixon had made "a big show," as Arnold remembered, of looking at his watch when she entered from the wings, and then, unseen by Douglas, "crossing and recrossing his knees in gestures of impatience" during her remarks. The audience hooted. After that she was all the more loath to meet him anywhere, and reluctantly agreed to another Beverly Hills gathering only when Nixon headquarters told the League of Women Voters that he could not make it because of a previous commitment across the basin.

It was all a ruse, as Day proudly told the tale later. They had deliberately planted the story of the schedule conflict with Douglas headquarters, then rushed out of the other meeting early to a room in the Beverly Hills Hotel, where Nixon and Day waited nervously while Chotiner "was over casing Douglas's talk," as Roy said afterward. Richard Nixon had loitered by the magazine rack in the lobby to avoid being recognized while Day registered for the room. "We ought to get the word, we ought to get the word, Roy. It's time," he kept saying as he paced the floor of the room. When Chotiner called, they "tore down," Day remembered. Nixon strode into the hall just as Helen Douglas had started to take questions from the audience. There was an immediate uproar from Republican supporters, and Douglas could not go on speaking, "drowned out," said one witness, "by foot stomping and handclapping." Once again angry and defeated, she finally left the auditorium. "That is where Nixon tore her to shreds," Day said, recalling the speech that followed.

"I DON'T THINK HE'LL EVER BE ANYTHING BUT WHAT HE ALWAYS WAS"

They fought out the remaining battles at a distance, often with surrogates but in mounting savagery.

Early in October, Senator Joe McCarthy came to San Diego, warmly "plugging Nixon's candidacy," as one editorial described it, and leaving behind some memorable passages. "Ask the basket cases if they agree that Acheson is an 'outstanding American.' . . . The chips are down . . . between the American people and the administration Commicrat Party of betrayal." Two days after McCarthy's speeches, the *Los Angeles Times* published a matching cartoon showing a large hammer and sickle, the blade labeled "Douglas Vote Against Un-American Activities Comm." and the caption advising voters "Let Your Conscience Be Your Guide." At the same time, Nixon himself maintained his usual careful public distance from the senator and his rhetoric. While word of the McCarthy endorsement and assault spread swiftly, the California press, including the wire services, effectively buried his visit to the state, the United Press sending out a story only when queried by subscribing papers that had heard the political rumors. Similarly questioned, Brennan would admit McCarthy had "made complimentary remarks" about Dick Nixon but insisted the visit was not "for" the candidate. The tactic both magnified McCarthy's brief foray and censored his extremism for the general public. Hearing the ricocheting reports, Helen Douglas thought the Wisconsin senator "going up and down the state campaigning for Nixon," a charge pro-Nixon reporters easily ridiculed.

Meanwhile, there would be ample publicity for what Nixon called his opponent's "foreign legion," a troop of prominent Democrats who came to support the Douglas run with plainly uneven results. Harry Truman's personal ties to Ed Pauley and the California oil Democrats, along with an early preference for Sheridan Downey, had only deepened the party split and left the administration at best ambivalent about the Douglas candidacy. In May the White House had leaked that the President believed both Douglas and the patrician Jimmy Roosevelt political "liabilities." As late as mid-September Truman was complaining privately to an aide that Helen Douglas was a "nuisance." At the end of that month, Truman warily and with further demoralizing effect announced he was abandoning earlier plans for substantial 1950 campaigning in California. In the President's stead would come several lesser figures, including Vice President Alben Barkley and Attorney General Howard McGrath, most of them visibly indifferent to Roosevelt and adding to the Senate race only another GOP target.

While Richard Nixon denounced outside "interference" and local newspapers reported "an invasion . . . by eastern 'furriners,' " Alvin Meyers watched Barkley sit in his hotel room "drinking bourbon and branch" and later talk to a small gathering where "he didn't produce a vote." In a press conference at the Biltmore, McGrath condemned HUAC and the "maligning propaganda" against Douglas, but in the process handed Nixon still another opportunity to rehearse the Hiss case. "Alger Hiss would have been prosecuted in any event by the Department of Justice," McGrath told reporters almost as an aside. Listening was Ralph de Toledano of *Newsweek*, Isaac Don Levine's former assistant and lately coauthor with Victor Lasky of *Seeds of Treason*, an early account of the case reflecting both HUAC and FBI versions of the affair. "Speaking as a newspaperman" with "no desire to inject himself into a political fight," as the *Los Angeles Times* reported, de Toledano promptly issued his own lengthy statement on the case, crediting Nixon and the Committee and accusing the attorney general of "setting the record on its ear."

Truman himself would stop over briefly in San Francisco as the McGrath controversy erupted. But Douglas and other party candidates sat well apart at a Presidential appearance that was notably nonpartisan. Despite the virulence of Republican attacks on the administration as well as on Helen Douglas, the national Democratic leadership would defer to its traditional California constituency and money and largely look away from the Red-baiting that was so soon to be turned full upon them. Among the desultory outside help, Douglas supporters remembered later only one committed politician, young Hubert Humphrey from Minnesota, who went up and down the San Joaquin Valley talking to farmers and migrants. At the same moment another young Democrat of promise came and went without comment on the roiling politics. The week Joe McCarthy spoke of "Commicrats," Congressman John F. Kennedy visited California for several days, watching in cautious silence.

While the public campaign raged, the other, *sub rosa* politics reached their nadir in the final three weeks of the race. "The vilest of graffiti directed against . . . Douglas appeared on fences, walls, and in public washrooms from border to border," recorded one witness. In neighborhood meetings, women were told by Nixon campaign workers earnestly—"in a homey fashion," as an observer remembered—"that Mrs. Douglas admitted she was a communist, or was an hysterical, neurotic woman, or that her private life was not all that it should be." Before all-male civic clubs, with reporters absent or safely coopted, Congressman Nixon drew laughter with a favorite line that the lady was "pink right down to her underwear," or implying with raised eyebrows and stage grimaces some sexual liaison between Helen Douglas and Harry Truman. Charles Hogan, a UN Secretariat official, spent part of that autumn in Carmel, south of San Francisco, and was "absolutely shocked," as he said later, at what appeared to be a lavishly financed "whispering campaign" against both Melvyn and Helen Douglas in the fashionable little town, a coordinated effort evidently duplicated throughout the state.

Seemingly everywhere, too, was the foamy backwash of anti-Semitism. Over the summer, Gerald L. K. Smith and Wesley Swift had stepped up their "crusades." Referring to "my friend Richard Nixon," warning ironically against "the movie Jews" backing Douglas, Smith had told audience after audience, "You Californians can do one thing very soon to further the ideals of Christian nationalism and that is not to send to the Senate the wife of a Jew." When Douglas repeatedly demanded to know if the slurs represented GOP campaign policy—"considerable prompting," one witness called her questions—Nixon had issued from Washington on August 31 a formal repudiation of Smith, albeit with its own edge. "I want to make it clear that I do not want that support and that I repudiate it. . . . I am ONE candidate who can state that I have never sought nor accepted the support of either a fascist or a communist organization." Yet in contrast to almost every other election-year release from the attic office, the statement was consigned in most California papers to a small story interred on the back pages. The anti-Semitic attacks continued. Smith thus addressed election-eve rallies on the advertised theme of "Helen Gahagan Douglas, Alger Hiss's pet." Hate literature flooded smaller communities like Santa Ana. Phone banks were organized to call with the question, "Did you know that Helen Gahagan Douglas is married to a man whose real name is Hesselberg?" Nixon postcards were sent to Democratic Party offices addressed to "Helen Hesselberg Douglas" and asking voters to "protect your future" by voting for Congressman Nixon, signed "Uncle Sam."

So sweeping and vitriolic became the efforts that Nixon was tainted regardless of the formal repudiation. Watching the campaign in San Francisco, where wealthy Jewish contributors were among Nixon backers, John Dinkelspiel worried about the backlash of what he would call later "an underlying accusation against Nixon for being anti-Semitic." They prompted the Anti-Defamation League of B'nai B'rith to issue its own statement exonerating Dick Nixon personally of anti-Semitism. Still, the slurs and suspicions persisted. "We attempted to counter them as best we could," Dinkelspiel would say. "It's a very difficult problem to solve."

"It was the most race-baiting thing I believe I've ever heard," battle-hardened Oliver Carter, Downey's onetime patron, remembered. "Just made me sick at my stomach." Feeling a "mudslide" of gossip and bigotry, what she called "word-of-mouth vilification," Douglas was at first reluctant to reply to the racism or to enlist her celebrity husband, whose play touring the nation that autumn was often picketed, patrons warned against "the communist inside." Finally, to the desperate pleading of her staff, Melvyn Douglas put out a personal statement on October 18. "I am not now, nor have I ever been, a communist or a fellow traveler," he said in an outraged, humiliating explanation of his liberal period in Hollywood. "Anyone who calls me a communist or fellow traveler is either a fool or a deliberate liar . . . he resorts to whispered insinuations. He is a political disease." Now straining, his wife followed with her own four-page résumé of their political activities together, from their wedding to Congress, trying to show that "Melvyn and I both deeply believe in our democratic form of government." Typically, the California press largely ignored both statements.

The Douglas campaign flailed back at the calumny, though the actual authors of the graffiti, the whispers, the smirking asides, were usually far removed, and the underlings or the relatively innocent were caught in the fire, only deepening the rancor on all sides. Coach Newman and his wife remembered how enraged Douglas workers had turned over a GOP campaign car—for no apparent reason, thought the Whittier couple. "WOMEN FOR NIXON" ribbons across their breasts, GOP volunteers were stationed at every corner of downtown Los Angeles to hand out Red-baiting flyers with some cutting remark about the "pink lady." When one of them in front of a department store unknowingly approached Evie Chavoor, Douglas's longtime personal aide, Chavoor "slapped her," as she told the story afterward, "and then . . . ran like hell." In their bitterness and frustration, like Jerry Voorhis and his men before them, the Douglas camp became impatient and resentful toward a seemingly gullible, indifferent public. "If we could just shake it into them," Helen Lustig remembered feeling.

On the stump, their candidate's own biting rhetoric now mocked Nixon for voting with Vito Marcantonio, now mirrored the Red smear with sinister images of fascism. "The temporary success of the Republican Party in 1946, with its backwash of young men in dark shirts, was short-lived," Douglas told one gathering. Her ads admonished the public: "DON'T BE CONFUSED," "EXPOSE THE 'BIG LIE' FOR YOURSELF!" and, much as Voorhis had attempted four years earlier with a similar ad, "THOU SHALT NOT BEAR FALSE WITNESS." But once again the print was small, the explanation far more complicated than the original charge, the focus on foreign policy or internal security issues that were the Republican strengths. For his part, Nixon denounced the use of biblical commandments as "sacrilegious," and a spokesman called righteously that "the dark shirt he wore" was as a hero "fighting the fascist dictators." "When Douglas advisers went on the attack, it was worse than useless," thought Frank Mankiewicz, an Assembly candidate; "it was counterproductive." In a candidacy now utterly on the defensive, countercharging and vying in strident patriotism, the effect also was the comparative obscurity of the genuine issues in California. Only rarely in that final month of the 1950 senatorial election did the old causes break through the crust of fear and recrimination, causes that had drawn Douglas to the race: water and power, the tidelands, the migrant misery.

Beneath its raw public surface, the Douglas campaign struggled against both the insidious intraparty defections and its own refracted efforts. Although private Democratic polls in early October showed the race still reasonably close, still potentially winnable by Helen Douglas, the campaign seemed haunted at every turn. As Paul Ziffren later confessed, they literally could not even buy support from traditional backers. In return for an endorsement, the *Los Angeles Daily News* had asked them to pay off what were claimed to be Manchester Boddy's "campaign deficits." Yet even when Ziffren raised the money and handed over the veritable bribe, the *News* editorial support was "curiously left-handed," as one writer described it, readers of the *News* "at liberty to infer that they could, if they wished, vote for Mrs. Douglas with reasonable assurance that she would not commit treason." Meanwhile, the remaining loyal Democrats seemed to ignore old contributors and neglected ward or district organizations. "A fantastically inept campaign," Carey McWilliams reported to the *Nation*. "In Los Angeles, the CIO may be supporting the candidates it has endorsed, but if it is, then new and secret methods are being used, for on the surface one would never know the CIO existed."

In part it was because the Douglas campaign lacked any real grass-roots structure beyond the unions, in part because of a diffuse campaign strategy that spread the candidate and the money too thinly, too indiscriminately among the great urban areas and the sparsely populated rural counties. Behind the flawed schedule was what Alvin Meyers called the "tugging and pulling and hauling" of a zealous, competitive, idealistic staff and an equally willful, sometimes defiantly oblivious Helen Douglas. "Our campaign was like a calm center, with all that hysteria going on around us," she wrote, "while we plugged away . . . unable to touch it." Yet they were feeling no less the effects of Richard Nixon's formidable politics across class and party lines, the courting of organized labor with chauvinist and ethnic appeals, the quiet cooption of the Hollywood and other unions that made his 1950 Senate campaign a prototype of later runs for the Presidency in 1968 and especially in 1972. It was true, Myers and others would say later, that much of Helen Douglas's money came from the labor movement, but in the end "they didn't vote for her."

Then, too, there were the furtive defections from famous supporters. Ronald Reagan was formally listed among a Hollywood group endorsing Helen Douglas. But one night during the autumn his girlfriend and future wife, Nancy Davis, had taken him to a Nixon rally led by actress Zasu

Pitts. "The pink lady who would allow the communists to take over our land and our homes as well," Pitts called her in a particularly venomous speech, and Reagan, already a secret FBI informant, came away converted. Not long afterward, Ron and Nancy had held a quiet fund-raiser for Richard Nixon. "I'm trying to help a senator [*sic*] get elected and we're giving a party for him tomorrow night," actor Robert Cummings remembered of a strange middle-of-the-night call from Reagan. Thirty years later, Helen Douglas writing her memoirs on her deathbed and Ronald Reagan about to be elected president, she was still unaware of the betrayal. "Several people, Ronald Reagan among them," she recorded, "worked hard for me."

"You sense it; you feel it; it comes to you," is how Frank Jorgensen remembered the Nixon momentum in those last weeks. Day after day skywriters at fifty dollars an hour chugged out a puffy white NIXON against the still, deep blue of the coastal clearness. The ubiquitous streetcorner ladies handed out a seeming inexhaustible supply of flyers and pamphlets, "tens of thousands" by one calculation. Joe Holt and a squad of eager young Republicans followed Helen Douglas to every speech, every rally, handing out the Pink Sheet. And when the garment workers printed a counter handbill on the Nixon record, "We got ahold of most of the sheets," as Roy Day recalled, "and threw them out in the Pacific Ocean." In Marysville and other remote towns of the north, Douglas supporters found in shock and dismay repeated newspaper ads listing the latest local casualties from the Korean War, next to the Pink Sheet tally of the "Douglas-Marcantonio axis." "What are we fighting for in Korea," said one caption, "when we have this representing us in the United States Congress?"

The casualty lists were only a small, relatively obscure front of his broader advertising offensive. "Meet Richard Nixon" was a skillful, professional facsimile of a spread in *Life* magazine—"one of the best pieces that we had was a takeoff on *Life*," Chotiner would say; it was "practically nothing but pictures, if you please." Less memorable was an outsized cartoon showing Helen Douglas holding the communist *People's World*, wooed by a deranged Henry Wallace under a night sky whose moon was Stalin and stars were small hammers and sickles, or simply Helen Douglas's face superimposed on a cartoon figure submerged in a huge toilet, hand on the flusher and saying, "Good-bye, Cruel World!" In still more variations of the Pink Sheet, she was described as an "extreme left-winger who has consistently fought to prevent exposure and control of communists," her voting record labeled simply as "Douglas-Marcantonio." Nixon's radio and television ads echoed the themes, sometimes even more shrilly:

Fight the Red fear with a fearless man—Dick Nixon.

Old Glory Forever—Red Glory Never.

*If you want to work for Uncle Sam instead of slave
for Uncle Joe, vote for Dick Nixon.*

Don't be left, be right, with Nixon.

Don't vote the Red ticket, vote the Red, White, and Blue ticket.

Be an American, Vote for Nixon.

In late October, along with the ads and circulars, came a stream of letters to the editor in various regions of the state, often so thoroughly prearranged that the text was accompanied by photos and capsule biographies of the writers. Thus Mrs. Ruth Peters, secretary of the local Chamber of Commerce, typically wrote *The Hemet News*: "As for Helen Douglas I consider her a traitor for defending communists in our government, communists who have been ruthlessly murdering our helpless boys . . . [and] her campaign for the U.S. Senate [is] a personal threat to my security." Hearing a similar commentary on a Los Angeles radio station, the Douglases' twelve-year-old daughter was in near hysteria as she greeted her mother one night: "Mummy, Mummy . . . they are saying terrible things about you!" Soon after the letters began to appear, Douglas's car was pelted with stones and her dress splattered with red ink at one appearance. Now frightened, her aides insisted she travel with bodyguards through the closing days of the race. In Visalia, in the heart of the Central Valley, she gave an impassioned speech, and a migrant worker came up to her afterward with tears in his eyes. "They haven't made you afraid, they haven't made you afraid," he repeated, and she was mute with emotion. Elsewhere in the Valley, vigilantes coerced farmers known to be Democratic supporters. And, as in the small towns of the twelfth district four years earlier, local businessmen—including one prominent vintner—were threatened with the loss of vital bank loans if they backed Douglas. "You wondered, is this a democratic election," Helen Douglas said to an interviewer years afterward, "or are we in a war, an undeclared war?"

Nowhere was the battle more concerted or furtive than for the state's Catholics, three-fourths of them registered Democrats. California politicians paid their ritual obeisance to the Church hierarchy, even the proud Earl Warren calling formally at the archbishop's residence in Los Angeles. Early that fall, Douglas brought in Jiggs Donahue, a Truman Democrat and prominent Catholic layman from Washington, to campaign among the Church constituency. At the same time, she had pointedly refused to support for a federal judgeship a Catholic who was both the archbishop's candidate and a crony of Ed Pauley. But such factional politics, and old grievances against Douglas for her opposition to Franco's clerical fascism, only gave a sharper edge to the larger Catholic patronage of the era's Red-baiting, and the Democratic efforts to salvage the vote were no match for what was promptly mobilized for Richard Nixon.

From Archbishop J. Francis McIntyre a letter went out to all parish priests in the Archdiocese of Los Angeles, ordering that their sermons for every Sunday of October 1950 be devoted to "the evils of communism" and "the fact that communists have infiltrated the [sic] high governmental positions." Priests were to endorse no specific candidate, mention no names at the altar, but the archbishop privately made his wishes known, and the sermons admonished that "the woman running for high public office should not be elected." Other priests in the state simply counseled their congregations "not to vote for anyone," as one witness recalled it, "whose name had been mentioned with communism's." Despite the pretext of nonpartisanship, priests in some heavily labor areas preached openly against Douglas the Sunday before the election. In San Diego the diocesan lawyers headed Democrats for Nixon, and church bulletin boards featured large sample ballots marked for Nixon. Pink Sheets were often distributed to congregations as they left Mass. Yet when Douglas supporters attempted to counter by stationing their own backers on church steps, distributing a rebuttal pamphlet called "A Message to Catholics from Catholics," the tactic drew formal denunciations of Douglas from the pulpit. In matching venom here, as elsewhere, the Douglas supporters even tried to portray Pat Nixon as a "fallen-away Catholic," though the smear did scarcely more than further harden and anger the Nixon camp. Meanwhile, Catholic laymen active for Douglas were privately reprimanded by McIntyre, and Protestant churches as well took up the anticommunist fervor echoing from the Catholic naves. "California is not France, and Archbishop McIntyre is not Richelieu," one of the Douglas Catholics wrote a monsignor afterward. But by then the votes had been cast and the parallels become all too real.

While the clerical politics, like so much of the contest, went on in the shadows, a handful of journalists outside the state reported the California race with alarm and dismay. "Nixon does not say that Mrs. Douglas is a communist, but the innuendo is left there," commentator Elmer Davis broadcast on October 30, "and traveling correspondents report that the open campaign against her is being supplemented by an intense and vicious whispering campaign." The *Milwaukee Journal* likened the 1950 Red-baiting to the demagoguery of Huey Long: "He had the ability to steal reason and judgment from the minds of men, leaving them furnished with nothing but prejudice and emotion, mostly hate." In a column ten days before the election, despite the decades exploring the cynical underside of American politics, Drew Pearson thought the contest unique. "There is nothing too vicious for the opposition to say about Mrs. Douglas," he wrote, in a race where "the big ranches, the utilities and oilmen have combined to urge one of the most skillful and cutthroat campaigns against her I have ever witnessed." The Pink Sheet he judged "one of the most skillful pieces of propaganda I have seen." The columnist also saw details and latent connections others did not seem to glimpse. "The one-hundred-sixty-acre limitation . . . public power . . . and tidelands oil," he concluded, "are the real issues in the California campaign—not communism." But the Pearson dispatch was variously refused, censored, or instantly rebutted by California newspapers, and the columnist himself editorially condemned. "I stuck my neck out for Congresswoman Helen Gahagan Douglas," Pearson noted in his diary two days before the vote.

Of some 250 daily and weekly papers in the state, Douglas advisers calculated at the beginning no more than thirty-eight potential endorsements. But by the final week only a handful of those had materialized, her backing essentially reduced to small rural journals and the fringe independents of Los Angeles and San Francisco. Ruth Finney of the Scripps-Howard *San Francisco News* wrote detailed articles in early October contrasting the Nixon and Douglas congressional records, the only journalism of its kind in California in twelve intense months of the senatorial race and the sole documented exception to the Pink Sheet and its companions. But even Finney's reporting, like Helen Douglas's hurried rebuttals, contained discrepancies and ambiguities Nixon alertly seized upon in a half-page letter to the editor October 27, in effect the last word on the only authentic press discussion of issues and positions. In any event, the *News*—on which Douglas counted heavily—had already endorsed Richard Nixon. "He is no witch hunter," they concluded. "From the outset of his first campaign he made it clear he would be his own boss, and he has been ever since."

Days later, the respected *San Francisco Chronicle* added its own backing in a similarly admiring view of the Nixon campaign. "We don't go along with those who attempt to smear Mrs. Douglas as a fellow-traveling 'Red,' " wrote editor Paul C. Smith. But while "some of his views do not coincide with our own," Congressman Nixon had shown "concise, uncluttered reasoning" and "he has avoided the illiberal excesses of the McCarthys." Aptly enough, the *Chronicle* reflected the Nixon campaign itself in the north. Dinkelspiel and the wealthy contributors distastefully spurned or ignored the smears while selectively seeing the best and most thoughtful in their young candidate. Once more it would be Richard Nixon's genius and luck—

in California as in Washington—to have it both ways. Campaign excesses went unheeded or excused by those who saw or wanted to see another promise. The same zeal and venom made him the candidate of the California reaction that would eventually find his views suspect. Yet for now the press campaign begun months before by Chotiner ended in stunning victory. On the eve of the 1950 election, Richard Nixon would have the parroting support, editorial endorsement, almost exclusive coverage of more than 240 California newspapers, an acclamation in which criticism of any stripe was virtually unknown, and the blackout of Helen Douglas begun in the primary all but complete.

As in 1946, the final days of the campaign brought together every strain. "RIGHT NOW NIXON IS LOSING . . . Not Enough Money," warned a mid-October appeal to "independent voters" from Nixon fund-raisers at Warner Brothers Studios, though the secret letter acknowledged over $90,000 already given the campaign in GOP allocations, far more than ever openly admitted. Richard Nixon was in fact both well financed and well ahead, but the carefully targeted plea cut further into potential last-minute contributors to Douglas, many of them Democrats and "independents" tempted to hedge their bets. Meanwhile, the candidate began what he called the final "offensive," vowing to "take off the gloves," as he told a radio audience October 23. "I have deliberately disregarded the tactics being used by my opponent," he announced, at once charging Douglas with "glaring misstatements" while justifying his own attacks. "If there is a smear involved, let it be remembered that the record ITSELF is doing the smearing," the *Los Angeles Times* reported him as saying. Two days later, in a column widely reprinted and distributed en masse by the Nixon campaign, Raymond Moley again evoked the sinister Vito Marcantonio. Disposing of Barnard, Harlem, Helen Douglas, and subversives in one stroke, Moley noted that Nixon's opponent "got a somewhat sketchy college education not too far from Marcantonio's district." In quick succession, local Republican pollsters predicted a certain but narrow Nixon victory, and George Creel drew more headlines with the Nixon Democrats' closing attack on Douglas and "the Red fronts with which she was associated."

The day Creel spoke, the *Los Angeles Examiner* featured an admiring biography of the candidate under the headline "NIXON LIFE STORY LIKE FILM SCENARIO." His background was "so average American," wrote Carl Greenberg, "that, unless you found it out for yourself, it would smack of a campaign manager's imagination." There was the Whittier store, church, college, courtship, then the war and Congress (with the 1946 campaign omitted), the unsought seat and heroism on HUAC, and a concluding tribute from Hannah Nixon: "I don't think he'll ever be anything but what he always was—a stickler for honesty and doing the right thing." On Monday, October 30, the last Field poll showed Nixon ahead commandingly, 49 percent to 39 percent, with 12 percent undecided. But as if they were ten points behind, the campaign dispatched scores of workers to ride trolleys and buses to leave Nixon handouts on the seats or to walk the streets thrusting flyers under windshield wipers or on car seats all over Los Angeles and San Francisco. They had bought 10,000 extra copies of the *Saturday Evening Post*'s "How to Pick a Congressman" with its mythology of the Committee of 100 and the 1946 campaign and distributed the eighteen-month-old magazine methodically among barber shops, beauty parlors, and doctors' offices, "anyplace where a person has to wait," Chotiner instructed. Helicopters dropped sheets including familiar slogans—"EVERY COMMUNIST WHO GOES TO THE POLLS WILL VOTE AGAINST NIXON AND FOR MRS. DOUGLAS. WHICH WAY WILL YOU VOTE?" Thousands of postcards went out with the message, "VOTE FOR HELEN FOR SENATOR. WE ARE WITH HER 100%." Sent to white suburbs and small towns, the cards were signed "Communist League of Negro Women."

A week before the election, headlines blared Brennan's charge that "the Douglas campaign has hit an all-time low" in "falsifying" the Nixon record, while in the same issue the *Times* pronounced Helen Douglas "the darling of the Hollywood parlor pinks and Reds." In that editorial, the *Times* identified Douglas as "the glamorous actress . . . who, though not a communist, voted the Communist Party line in Congress innumerable times." In thousands of papers in the early edition, the text omitted the "not," a mistake for which the paper offered an "explanation" two days later. Meanwhile, Nixon headquarters appealed earnestly for still more recruits to its women's "Flying Squadron," the roving bands of volunteers sent out to distribute literature or heckle at Douglas meetings. Later that final week, they mass-mailed to Sheridan Downey's list and others one more Nixon pamphlet to "Fellow Democrats." And in still another repetition of 1946, ads and handbills all over the state announced "PRIZES GALORE!!! Electric Clocks, Silex Coffee Makers with Heating Units—General Electric Automatic Toasters—Silver Salt and Pepper Shakers, Sugar and Creamer Sets, Candy and Butter Dishes, etc. etc." if the winner answered the phone "Vote for Nixon." On November 1 Nixon revived once more Sheridan Downey's primary indictment that Helen Douglas "gave comfort to the Soviet tyranny." It was all part of a concerted, fully publicized series of headquarters statements and press conferences over the last week to counter what were termed the Douglas "smear," "propaganda," or "complaints of smears," though the *Times* and other papers routinely carried Richard Nixon's charges or refutations in a strange isolation with no reporting even now of the fugitive Douglas remarks that ostensibly provoked them.

His campaign in the basin was to reach its "rousing climax," as Kyle Palmer's column advertised, in a "giant rally" at the Hollywood American Legion Stadium Thursday night, November 2. Actor Dick Powell would be master of ceremonies with Dennis Morgan singing and speeches by Adela St. Johns, Hedda Hopper, and Coach Newman as well as the candidate. Following a torchlight parade, he spoke to a roaring crowd, accusing Douglas of "the big lie" and reminding them of the 354 votes with Marcantonio. Powell read a polished dramatization of the Hiss case, part of a radio show they were beaming throughout the state, a "cloak-and-dagger . . . production," said one observer, in which "the apprehension and perjury conviction of Alger Hiss was presented to appear as important as the North Atlantic pact or even victory in Korea." Then, the stadium still hushed, Powell's visibly pregnant wife, actress June Allyson, closed with what Nixon remembered as a "short and moving speech" about the future, her unborn child, the importance of defeating Helen Douglas.

It was all capped the next day by a full-page cartoon and large-print editorial in Hearst's *Los Angeles Examiner*. His back against a stone wall labeled "National Security," Uncle Sam behind the safety of the wall smilingly ploughing a field, a handsome, muscular Congressman Richard Nixon stood with shirtsleeves rolled up, a shotgun labeled "Military Preparedness" in one hand, a net called "Communist Control" in the other. Perspiring rodents—labeled "Spy," "Conspirator," "Appeaser," "Soviet Sympathizer"—fled him in terror. The editorial, entitled "A Shocking Contrast," attacked Douglas's record. The cartoon was captioned simply "ROUGH ON RATS."

There remained two predictable sequels to be played out the last weekend. Through the summer and fall, the Nixon forces had maneuvered ceaselessly to get the endorsement of Earl Warren, the governor so many Nixon backers despised yet still an immensely popular politician whose bipartisan appeal might have an influence on the dissident Democrats they were courting. Nixon had gone again to Sacramento after the primary to suggest they now "coordinate their campaigns," but Warren gently refused, reminding the congressman of his own argument against a "package ticket." "No, Dick," said the governor, smiling, "I prefer your original argument of separate campaigns." Kyle Palmer had then tried to bring them together over a private dinner with Norman and Buff Chandler at the editor's Los Angeles home—Nixon standing in front of the fireplace, as Tom Cunningham remembered, telling war stories of his 1946 campaign or the hunt for communists, trying to charm and entreat the man whose power he at once challenged and needed. "There was tremendous pressure for Warren to come out . . . for Nixon," an assistant recalled. But Warren was adamant in his usual independence. When an aide asked after the dinner if he were going to help the congressman after all, he snapped angrily, "Oh, let Nixon take care of himself."

It was not only, Warren's friends would say, that Nixon's partisanship threatened in the long run the fragile GOP-Democratic coalition the governor had nurtured in California, not only that there were so many virulently anti-Warren people in the Nixon camp. It was also a matter of style and substance in the anticommunist craze. Earl Warren, as Bill Arnold noted caustically, would never praise the handling of the Hiss case, even in private, and would never use the Red scare in his gubernatorial campaign against Jimmy Roosevelt, though both Roosevelt and the Democratic candidate for attorney general, Pat Brown, competed in chauvinism on the subject. "He felt the attacks on her patriotism," a Warren biographer wrote, "were grotesquely unfair." Still, they tried to force his hand, Joe Holt and his Young Republicans at every Douglas appearance not merely heckling or passing out Pink Sheets but pressing Helen Douglas to endorse Jimmy Roosevelt or attack Warren in hopes of provoking the governor. As late as October 28, Warren was still resisting, still formally disavowing any endorsement in other races. Then, in San Diego the final weekend, an exhausted Douglas, her eyes glistening with emotion, had finally shot back at the hecklers, "I hope and pray [Jimmy Roosevelt] will be the next governor, and he will be if Democrats vote the Democratic ticket." Elated at the breakthrough, Chotiner had taken the call from Holt and hurriedly arranged to get a copy of the Douglas remarks to Bill Mailliard on the Warren campaign plane, who then showed it to the governor. Trapped, knowing he would be besieged by the press and Nixon backers at his own speeches, Warren released a statement from Sacramento on November 4: "I have no intention of being coy about this situation. As always I have kept my campaign independent from other campaigns. The . . . reports from San Diego that Mrs. Douglas has said she hopes and prays Mr. Roosevelt will be the next governor of California does [sic] not change my position. In view of her statement, however, I might ask her how she expects I will vote when I mark my ballot for U.S. senator next Tuesday."

In Los Angeles, Brennan called his own press conference to celebrate the triumph and claim the endorsement Warren had not quite given. "It is a pretty good bet that Richard Nixon will mark his ballot for Governor Earl Warren," he joked with reporters. But back in the statehouse, Warren himself was privately more bitter than ever. It was all a "scurrilous attack on Helen Gahagan Douglas," Pop Small recorded. The Nixon campaign was "not content with defeating an opponent," Warren told his longtime press aide, "he wants to destroy."

As Douglas was giving her teary reply in San Diego and the long-sought statement was being wrung from Warren, the Nixon phone banks were humming in another election-eve torrent of anonymous calls. "Oh, Mrs. Smith—or Jane or whatever," one witness said in describing the familiar line from 1946, "did you know that Helen Douglas is a communist?" Then the inevitable click as the caller hung up. What had been only the twelfth district four years earlier was now a massive operation covering almost all of southern California, though notably sparse in the north. Afterward, it would seem they "were just going down telephone books," as one Douglas aide remembered, "calling everybody." Hearing the smear himself, one Hollywood producer was so enraged that he commissioned a survey of households receiving the calls but was then reluctant to release the findings. More than two decades after the event still another producer, a friend who had received a call as well, gave the results to the University of California, showing over 500,000 calls throughout California. Even then, the Douglas aides had suspected the worst. "We knew it was going to happen because some of us knew what happened to Jerry Voorhis," Byron Lindsley would say. But, like Voorhis, they were powerless to stop it.

"The mood of the crowd had become dangerously ugly," Helen Douglas remembered. "I was almost too tired sometimes to drag myself out of the car and up the steps to the podium." She knew it was "hopeless," she would say later, but as always "I was determined not to quit." Four days before the vote Harry Truman finally spoke out against the press blackout: "Most California newspapers are either boycotting or misrepresenting the views of Rep. Helen Gahagan Douglas," he told White House reporters. It was, Douglas backers thought, far too little too late, and, aptly, Truman's remarks went unreported in much of the state. Furious, beaten, she lashed out at the opponent she now commonly called "Tricky Dick." "Shame! Shame! Shame!" she cried out to a San Diego audience, sunglasses covering her eyes dark with exhaustion. "They are trying to get you scared in this campaign. . . . I despise communism, Nazism, and Nixonism. . . . As for me, I would rather be right than senator."

On Monday morning November 6, election eve, Californians, like the rest of the country, awakened to ominous headlines from the war in Korea. "M'ARTHUR IN THREAT TO STRIKE AT REDS IN CHINA," bannered the *Los Angeles Times*. "Fresh Communist Troops Pouring into Korea Battle." It was the beginning of the Chinese intervention in the war. Plunging across the thirty-eighth parallel after their flanking invasion at Inchon, marching up the narrow valleys of North Korea to stand over the Yalu River and peer into China, the U.S. forces were about to be hurled back to the old postwar Korean boundary in one of the bloodiest retreats in modern history. But most of that would come later in November and December. For now it was only clear that uncertainty, danger, and more war lay ahead. The effect was to deepen all the more the anticommunist fear and fervor, though in California's senate race the issue was already settled.

That night the Nixons made the first of what would be so many family televison appearances, Tricia and Julie squirming next to their nervous mother when the camera turned to them during the candidate's final thirty-minute appeal. Afterward, he dropped them off and went out with Roy Day, Chotiner, Adela St. Johns, and her son Mac, who took him to the south Los Angeles home of black football star and Nixon supporter Kenny Washington, where they drank beer, and Nixon played the piano with a kind of fierce abandon. "Dick had a terrible time relaxing," Mac St. Johns remembered.

Early the next morning he voted in East Whittier with the ritual smiles for photographers but soon fell into a dark melancholy. He insisted they picnic on the beach, but the day was cloudy and raw and they spent the afternoon in a deserted movie near Long Beach. Driving home, they passed Douglas sound trucks broadcasting "Thumbs Down for Nixon," and he arrived at Honeysuckle Lane almost despondent. "He was sure we had been defeated." But as they gathered after dinner at the Garland Building, the magnitude of his victory was never in doubt. Far more than any poll had forecast, he defeated Helen Douglas by nearly 700,000 votes, a crushing 59 percent to 40 percent, and the largest plurality received by any senatorial candidate in the nation. Though Warren's landslide over Jimmy Roosevelt was even greater—more than a million-vote margin and sweeping all fifty-eight counties—the Nixon strength statewide was formidable. He had run well ahead of the GOP congressional slate and won tens of thousands of Democratic votes in every region, including the heavily unionized areas and the farmers of the Central Valley. It turned out that not even the handful of California communists could bring themselves to support the woman who was so widely thought to be their champion or dupe. "The attitude toward Helen Gahagan Douglas was that she was only the lesser of two evils," one of them would say afterward, "that there was no difference between them." The triumphant senator-elect and his wife soon left the celebrating headquarters and made the rounds of victory parties throughout the basin. "Dick was so exuberant," Pat re-membered, "that wherever he found a piano he played 'Happy Days Are Here Again.'"

Not far away in downtown Los Angeles, Helen Douglas found her own headquarters "a desolate scene," the workers in what seemed "brutal shock" at the sheer depth of the defeat. She went from person to person, and a local photographer caught her trying to comfort young volunteers in scowls and tears. "HELEN GAHAGAN DOUGLAS CONSOLES HER STAFF," read the caption. Outwardly, she seemed composed, resigned, though some were not sure. "I think inside she was deeply hurt," said Charles Hogan. The next morning she would hurry off to San Francisco to thank and encourage her staff there, and the strength had almost given way. A black skycap had come up to take her baggage from the car with tears streaming down his face. "Oh, Mrs. Douglas," he said. "Oh, Mrs. Douglas, what have we done to you?"

A week after the election, in a telephone interview from Whittier, Nixon would explain to *U.S. News & World Report* that the major issue of the race, and the reason for his victory, had been the administration's Far Eastern policy. "I pointed out that, had it not been for the fall of China, the Korean War would not have happened," he told the magazine, though in fact his specific attacks on the "loss" of China by a State Department "clique" had been only one thrust in the larger assault, and come relatively late in the campaign. Internal security and government spending were other, lesser questions, he added, saying nothing about local California issues. The losers saw the results in more cynical, rudimentary terms. "You carried six Assembly districts, all of which are either predominantly colored, Jewish, or Mexican," Ruth Lybeck wrote Douglas about their debacle in the basin. "The new homeowners, who for the first time in their lives have something to call their own and think they got it by their own efforts, looked into their new TV screens, were convinced by what the Republicans had to say, and went out and voted themselves back into mother-in-law's apartment." Others, who saw the inner reality of the politics and practices, were even more certain about cause and effect. "I think it hurt, yes," an elderly Roy Crocker would say a quarter century later, admitting the massive smear of the telephone calls. "It hurt Helen Gahagan Douglas, yes." Rollin McNitt, who supported Boddy and then, like so many Democratic leaders, stood aside in the general, was equally sure. "Frankly," he told an interviewer years later, "it was the 'Pink Sheet' that the Nixon people put out that defeated her . . . it was just enough."

Whatever the provenance of his victory, once and future backers pronounced it auspicious. "Your victory was the greatest good that can come to our country," wired Herbert Hoover in uncharacteristic effusiveness. From other wings of the GOP came similar praise, Dewey's manager Herbert Brownell calling it a "brilliant campaign," Allen Dulles writing from Sullivan and Cromwell that "we are all gratified," and Harold Stassen expecting "splendid leadership in the Senate as in the House." At Harvard, three days after the vote, Congressman John Kennedy told a group of students that he was "personally very happy that Helen Gahagan Douglas had just been defeated . . . by Richard Nixon," as one instructor recorded his remarks, and on November 14 Kennedy wrote a friend privately, "I was glad to . . . see Nixon win by a big vote."

Of its kind, Nixon's victory was one of a series nationwide. In Maryland, McCarthy aides and right-wing reporters assembled and distributed half a million copes of a faked photo showing Democratic incumbent senator Millard Tydings, a vocal McCarthy foe, in apparently intimate conversation with Communist Party leader Earl Browder. A congressional inquiry would later attribute Tydings's loss to a "despicable back-street type of campaigning," but his trouncing was matched in Utah and Washington, where both Democrats were similarly smeared. A Republican victory would be "a housecleaning of his sympathizers and party-liners," Everett Dirksen said of Joe Stalin, and went on to win the Senate race in Illinois. When it was over, the GOP had added five Senate and twenty-eight House seats, only slightly better than the average midterm gain, and the overall impact of the Red-baiting was by no means clear. Yet it was the great smear campaigns that loomed larger than life for press and politicians whether Democratic or Republican. "Both groups," wrote a historian of the vote, "interpreted the election as a mandate for McCarthy and guided their actions according to their heightened perception of his political potency." Election night, the old HUAC source and champion reporter Ed Nellor had hosted a drunken victory party at his home in the Virginia suburbs of Washington, inviting among others Karl Mundt, McCarthy, and Dick Nixon, who was already beginning his own celebration across the country. Late in the night the septic tank backed up, and Nellor roared with laughter as McCarthy and the others gleefully waded barefoot in the muck. "The symbolism," wrote a McCarthy biographer, "somehow escaped him."

On November 20, while the Nixons were vacationing in Palm Springs, Sheridan Downey announced his retirement in ten days, clearing the way for the new senator's early appointment by the governor and an advantage in seniority. Nixon received formal notice of the move in a call from Earl Warren when he returned to Honeysuckle Lane that night, but the deal was already struck. In Sacramento to confer with Warren two days later, the Republican senator-elect publicly pledged his support for two of Downey's Democratic friends lately nominated by Truman to the federal bench: Oliver Carter, who had opposed Douglas from the beginning; and William

Byrne, the Catholic layman whose oil-drenched politics had moved Helen Douglas to defy both the White House and the archbishop on his appointment.

On December 4, 1950, some two years after his initial decision to run, Richard Nixon took the Senate oath in the old, small Capitol chamber once used by the Supreme Court, the Senate floor itself being remodeled between sessions. He was, duly noted the *Los Angeles Times*, a kind of prodigy, the first GOP senator from southern California in generations, and now, a month short of his thirty-eighth birthday, the second youngest man in the upper body of the Congress. Only Huey Long's son from Louisiana, Russell, would be younger. The hall was packed with Republican congressmen and senators sensing his growing power. And crowding the doorway, straining to catch a glimpse of the ceremony, were familiar and symbolic figures from the California forces launching him—Gerald Kepple from the Committee of 100 and the original backers; Herbert Hoover, Jr., representing his father and the GOP old guard as well as oil and the postwar suburban power of Pasadena and San Marino; Murray Chotiner and his faithful assistant, Ruth Arnold, the interior architects of both 1946 and 1950. Not least, there was an envoy from the new power and money of the Senate campaign, an obscure ex-California assemblyman and Republican Party official named Frank Waters, who had just been hired as personal and corporate lawyer for industrialist Howard Hughes and who would be the go-between some years later in a fateful loan from Hughes to the Nixon family. Pat and the girls remained in Whittier.

There was one more small, apt, and ironic coda to the eddying politics of it all, though it was hardly visible amid the smiles and back-slapping of the ceremony that day. Having announced he would return to private law practice, Sheridan Downey instead became a $40,000-a-year oil lobbyist for the city of Long Beach and the combine of petroleum companies leasing its multi-billion-dollar oil properties. As a former senator with floor privileges, Downey became a powerful force behind the scenes, authoring, as one writer recorded, "many stirring statements by Senator Nixon . . . and others in the battle against creeping socialism." Among the achievements of the former Democratic senator, it was said, would be a strong plank in the next GOP platform favoring states' rights in the tidelands.

Yet then, with the election of a Republican President two years later, Downey was summarily fired, and the new Vice President of the United States would be the young man from California whose career Downey and so many other Democrats had helped advance so crucially into the Senate in 1949–50. "The big corporations and other fellows who put up the money," an aide of Downey would say bitterly as they left Washington, "don't feel they need us anymore."

❖❖❖

Even more than the 1946 campaign, his run for the Senate became a spectral presence in Richard Nixon's subsequent political career, a hoary ghost repeatedly exorcised but echoing in ironic allusions and sequels across the next quarter century, yet another memory that would not recede despite the tidying of reality on both sides.

At its climax and in the immediate aftermath, the race brought Nixon the harshest personal criticism yet seen in national publications. In the *New Republic*, Carey McWilliams deplored his "brazen demagoguery" and called him "a dapper little man with an astonishing capacity for petty malice . . . a distinctly third-rate Tom Dewey." Having received angry and accusatory calls himself after speaking for Douglas, author Harry Flannery wrote in *Commonweal* about Nixon's "Red Smear—applied thick and constant." "They did the smearing," he said of both the California press and the Nixon campaign, "and did it in such a lurid fashion that the people were roundly frightened about voting for Mrs. Douglas." Nearer home, the *Los Angeles Daily News*, despite its calculated dispassion during the general election, afterward deplored the campaign as "the dirtiest in state history," a distinction previously held by the similar rout of Upton Sinclair.

In December and January, the Institute for Journalistic Studies at Stanford did a survey of the campaign coverage over the last ten weeks by twelve California newspapers, measuring nearly half the daily and Sunday circulation in the state. The academic findings were eloquent of the hostility and effective blackout that enveloped Helen Douglas: circulation of the ten pro-Nixon papers outnumbered the two pro-Douglas by nine to one, with no Douglas support at all in Sunday editions; decidedly "favorable" stories about Nixon made up over 60 percent of his coverage in most papers, and attacks on Douglas were nearly 70 percent of the "news" about her run. At that, the study reflected only a fraction of the larger suppression and distortion, and none of the inner arrangements. On the eve of the election, both Drew Pearson and the UCLA student *Bruin* had reported a typical offer of a thousand dollars in campaign advertising to one small-town editor in return for a Nixon endorsement. But that story, too, had been among the casualties of the coverage.

If the press history was eventually recorded in part, the money, its magnitude and various sources, remained obscure as always. The first accounts were part of the campaign itself. Nixon contributions had been only $4,209, the *Herald-Examiner* reported in the last week of the contest, while Douglas had taken in $42,757 and spent only $17,365. The *Times* repeated the Douglas figure in a contemporary story, listing union and personal contributors to the Democratic "war chest" while ignoring Nixon's finances altogether. In Washington after the election, Nixon officially reported $2,020 in expenses. Weeks afterward, to the state of California, Nixon would officially list $5,805 in contributions and $2,495 out of his own pocket, and the required list of donors carried only a fraction of the smallest gifts. Ever punctilious, the northern campaign on the same day reported contributions to various Nixon committees and subcommittees of more than $245,000, including some of the most prominent names in California banking, agribusiness, and the corporate world. Yet there would be no similar legal accounting of the far larger financing in the south. Meanwhile, Helen Douglas reported $156,172 and Earl Warren $324,000, both campaigns conspicuously less well financed than the new senator's.

Only years later would the shards of their extraordinary backing turn up, like random relics in an archaeological dig. Chotiner would later admit to an inquiring young scholar that their billboards alone had cost "around $50,000," while Jorgensen later put the statewide figure at $125,000. A single direct mailing to California's registered Democrats and Republicans cost approximately $350,000, another study showed, and the Nixon campaign had done at least two of them officially and almost certainly several other mailings to targeted portions of both groups. Television and radio time had been similarly lavish, Tom Dixon remembering the sophisticated and costly "two-way loops" they used for his radio shows throughout the north and the Central Valley. One wealthy contributor later boasted to Douglas's brother, Walter Gahagan, that over $350,000 had been spent on field workers, the house parties, the street brigades, the small army of advocates, and often whisperers, all over the state. So it went. As early as 1951, one source placed the total campaign at $1.6 million, calling it a "conservative estimate." A former editor of the *Daily News*, Ernest Brashear, still later counted billboard and other comparative costs and reckoned the total "at least $1 million and possibly twice that amount." Whatever the precise figure, it was clear in the end—as in 1946—that Richard Nixon's election and further rise had been richly financed, mostly in secret.

As for the victors, there was no eventual acknowledgment of the money and almost no second thoughts about what had happened. "We gave the poor woman a rough time," the bearish Jorgensen said long afterward. "She just was in water over her head . . . unfortunately didn't have people around her who could be a hell of a lot of help for her." To *The New York Times* Murray Chotiner insisted, "We never accused her of being a communist, or of sympathizing with the communists, or of being in league with them." As he would tell Republican strategists, "But it is not a smear, if you please, if you point out the record of your opponent." As usual, Roy Day was artless by comparison. "This reminded me," he once privately told Nixon, commending him for a belligerent press conference in a later race, "of the guy who kicked hell out of Voorhis, a few commies, Helen G., and some others."

Biographers swiftly and discreetly interred the campaign. "Chotiner and his associates" only "gathered" the Boddy attacks, wrote Earl Mazo, and "added an embellishment here and a nuance there." Bela Kornitzer repeated Chotiner's assurance: "We only stated the facts." "Nixon's original intention of playing down the communist issue and battling it out on other questions of policy had been taken from his hands," explained Ralph de Toledano, "first by the advantage thrust at him by the Democrats during the primary war, second, by the sudden popular outburst of anticommunism and third, by the tactics Murray Chotiner devised." By 1960, Stewart Alsop could conclude that "Mrs. Douglas started the game" of smears, and more than a decade later columnist Roscoe Drummond could refer to the " 'sneaky, tricky ruthless campaign' waged against Mrs. Douglas by her Democratic opponent" and "Nixon's pallid version of the same thing."

Nixon himself took up the refrain. "I don't have to tell you what the atmosphere was like," he explained to a British journalist eighteen years later. "I had been presented with a great deal of ammunition by Mrs. Douglas's fellow Democrats earlier in the year, and I did not hesitate to use some of it." Helen Gahagan Douglas and the Senate race appeared nowhere in *Six Crises*. At one juncture in 1958, in an off-the-record conversation with British publisher David Astor, he was asked how the rumored methods of the Senate campaign could be reconciled with his apparently far more moderate politics of the moment, a "new" Nixon readying to run for the Presidency. He had paused for several seconds of tense silence and then told Astor simply, "I'm sorry about that episode. I was a very young man." But the comment was no sooner leaked than denied: "There is no basis in fact for this statement," said his office in May 1958, and he privately circulated to supporters and friendly reporters, including biographers, a lengthy justification of the campaign against Douglas as well as of the Voorhis race. Its tone was resonant of the original:

The impression that she was pro-communist is both due to and justified by her own record.

Even the choice of the color pink [for the Pink Sheet] was reasonable in that the work "pinko" generally connoted one soft on communism which was, indeed, Nixon's conclusions [sic] *as to Mrs. Douglas.*

Although Nixon did not call her names, she was party to a whispering campaign that he was anti-Semitic and Jim Crow.

Nixon is a birthright Quaker and constitutionally incapable of bigotry.

The amount . . . filed for Nixon campaign expenditures . . . has never been questioned by anyone and must, therefore, be accepted as true and honest.

According to his memoirs, the "commies" who picketed him in 1950 had softened only slightly into "tightly organized bands sent out from local left-wing labor and political organizations . . . to disrupt my speeches by a continuous counterpoint of critical questions and derisive observations." Similarly, Manchester Boddy was "a lifelong Democrat who despised Mrs. Douglas's left-wing leanings," swiftly erasing their friendship and the *Daily News*'s warm nurturing and support of her career before March 1950. "Although I constantly questioned her wisdom and judgment in light of such a record, I never questioned her patriotism," he wrote. Her campaign had been one of "stridency, ineptness, and self-righteousness," and "anyone who takes the trouble to go back through the newspapers and other sources of the period . . . will find that things happened as I have described them here." It would be his first and last published word on the race—six and one-half pages out of nearly eleven hundred, with no untoward trace of Joe Holt's hecklers or the Flying Squadrons, the Korean War casualty ads, the postcards and racial slurs, the press monopoly, the patrons, the sexual allusions and "aid and comfort" insinuations of treason, the calls and prizes, and so much more.

It was the watchword and comfort of the losers that Helen Douglas "got through unscathed," as one aide said later. "Nixon had his victory but I had mine," Douglas wrote in her own memoirs after a detailed chapter on the race. "He hadn't touched me. I didn't carry Richard Nixon with me, thank God." Like much of her campaign itself, it was a brave front though political illusion. A gifted woman of rare experience in both foreign policy and domestic affairs, she would be after the autumn of 1950 a discreetly banished outcast in her party, a succession of Democratic Presidents shying away from an appointment that would have been natural in any other circumstance. Asked about naming her an assistant secretary of the interior, a post she knew so well and had long defended in Congress, Truman would tell an aide, "We may be taking on too many fights . . . let me think about it." Of the response on the other side there was little doubt. Having branded her so thoroughly, Republicans could scarcely countenance her return to public life. When Mac Faries anxiously wrote Senator Richard Nixon in January 1951 about a "rumor" of Douglas's appointment to the UN mission, Nixon had privately promised that "such an appointment would cause considerable controversy should it come to the Senate." When a 1953 slander trial in Los Angeles revived the old charges of "Red discussions" at the Douglas home in the 1940s, when Helen furiously contemplated her own formal denial and libel suit, friends had advised her fearfully against any statement that would allow her to be hauled before HUAC where "two crackpots . . . swear you attended communist meetings . . . and then you will be prosecuted for perjury," as one group of supporters wrote her about the implicit danger of jail. "And don't forget Nixon." Subdued by the threat, she had not challenged the testimony. "He killed me politically," Helen Douglas finally admitted in an interview a quarter century after the campaign.

Remarkably like Jerry Voorhis, she repeatedly vowed a forbearing silence about her destruction. "I wanted to forget it," she once wrote. But the genuine wrath soon spilled out. "A truly vicious one," she called Nixon's campaign in a 1952 letter. "They used the same techniques then that were used in Florida, North Carolina, and Maryland. . . . People were paid to deliberately spread lies." Nor did she hesitate in subsequent campaign years, as her old foe became a national figure. to denounce his "innuendo and distortion." The personal rancor ran still deeper. At the mention of Richard Nixon's name, their friends would note, Helen Douglas fell uncharacteristically tense, and Melvyn often simply left the room. "And thank God we won't have to listen to the Kewanis [sic] Club fellow for the next four years," she wrote after the 1960 Presidential election. "I have come to the conclusion that he is without intellectual stature." At the same time, again like Voorhis, she revised her own history of the event. "I did not particularly want to go to the Senate," she wrote an admirer in 1959. To an academic inquiry in 1962, she wrote blithely, "the campaign policy was one of 'no attack towards Nixon.' I determined this policy and used it in all my campaigns. . . . The personal attacks [by Nixon] caused annoyance rather than hardship."

Despite the reactions and rationalizations of the two antagonists, despite the flawed and piecemeal history, the 1950 campaign seemed to take on national legend. Old passions burned a decade afterward and a continent away. At Boston's Jordan Hall in October 1960—speaking, ironically, on behalf of the same John Kennedy who supported her opponent—Helen Douglas would be splattered with rotten eggs much as she was once showered with hay and seltzer at USC. But it was Richard Nixon, many thought, who seemed to pay an even higher price. "His enemies, like Abou ben Adhem's tribe, increased tenfold, and with them grew the myths of Nixon's 'reprehensible conduct' during that campaign of 1950," wrote an admiring biographer. The race left a legacy of bitterness and worse, in California, a remnant not merely of defeated political opponents but the authentic irreconcilable enemies, the permanent opposition he imagined and feared elsewhere. "I've never gotten over my hatred of him, really," Juanita Terry

Barber, a young Douglas aide, would say in 1976, and her words would echo again and again through the ranks of those who experienced the 1950 race. Even in Washington, though welcomed and lauded by the surging McCarthy forces, Nixon would encounter for the first time after 1950 the cutting personal affronts he had never known at the height of earlier HUAC controversies. Invited to Joseph Alsop's fashionable Georgetown soirée one Sunday shortly after the election, he was visibly ill at ease among the mixed Democratic and Republican guests. Averell Harriman, who had spoken for Douglas in Los Angeles a few weeks before and heard the smears firsthand, came in at one point, noticed Nixon, and in flamboyant disdain walked out of the party, saying loudly, "I will not break bread with that man."

Even sharper than the Hiss case—and all the more added to it—it was the 1950 campaign that fixed a singular doubt and resentment about the extraordinary young politician from California. Seemingly without peer in the GOP, he was also singularly disturbing, in the emerging shadow of questions about technique, integrity, character. And for those who watched 1950 haunt later races, who knew the reality of the contest, there was an equally pungent irony. The desperate, destroying campaign against Jerry Voorhis by an unknown challenger might have been understandable. Against Helen Douglas in the political moment of 1950, most of it had been wantonly needless. It was also the last election Richard Nixon would win in his own right for the next eighteen years.

Beyond the candidates and their fate, history in a larger sense would mock the great causes of 1950. It was not the greedy Republican landowners who undid Helen Douglas's cherished 160-acre limitation in the Central Valley but rather a Democratic Bureau of Reclamation that soon found a way around the controversy to protect and preserve its own bureaucratic position. If a corporation had ten or even a hundred shareholders, it would be entitled to federal irrigation for 160 acres per shareholder, the bureau soon ruled. And an owner could legally deed out 320-acre parcels to various married relatives and children. It might not be "spiritual compliance," the bureau chief would tell Congress, "but technical compliance was good enough." Neither Sheridan Downey nor Helen Douglas, it turned out, had quite understood what or who really ruled the Valley.

Finally, as for the equally legendary Vito Marcantonio, the ghost in the rafters of the California race, he, too, had gone down to defeat in 1950, ousted from his seat by an extraordinary coalition of Democrats and Republicans. Richard Nixon ever afterward relished telling his aides about his own friendly rivalry, even respect for the vilified fellow congressman— "sincere," as one Nixon biographer described his estimate, "not merely a political opportunist." Once during the 1950 race, as Nixon would relate a favorite story, he and Marcantonio had been caught together on a traffic island crossing the street near the Capitol, and the New Yorker had whispered to him, "I hope you beat that bitch out there in California." Like the overflowing septic tank at McCarthy's party, the irony seemed to escape him—that this was the attitude toward Douglas of the people she was supposed so traitorously to champion.

Marcantonio died four years later, not a communist after all, a biographer concluded, but a genuine "American radical, one of the last surviving members of a species fast becoming extinct . . . a bigot in favor of human rights, introducing ideas which might one day become part of the American mainstream."

V

RUNNING MATE

19

The Senate, 1951–52

"A FEW FRIENDS . . . OF CONSIDERABLE VALUE"

n a cold Washington evening, scarcely a week after his swearing-in as the new junior senator from California, Richard Nixon was attending a holiday party in the second-floor ballroom of the Capital's posh Sulgrave Club on Massachusetts Avenue. It was December 12, 1950, destined to be a memorable night in Washington social history.

Among the other celebrities were two protagonists fresh from the fall campaign, columnist Drew Pearson and the increasingly controversial Wisconsin senator, Joseph McCarthy. Once an ingratiating source for Pearson as for other journalists, McCarthy had come under increasing criticism by the columnist after the Wheeling speech and now saw his Red-baiting ricochet in Pearson's attacks on the senator's own tax dodges and "quickie divorces." While McCarthy deplored "homosexuals" in the State Department, Pearson even turned up what was said to be an authentic "sexual pervert" on the senator's personal staff. He had not decided, McCarthy told friends a few days before, "whether to kill Pearson or just to maim him."

A prankish Washington hostess seated them at the same table that night at the Sulgrave. After bourbon, the main course, and an exchange of insults, Joe McCarthy lunged across to grab and gouge Pearson at the back of the neck, yelling, "You come out, we'll settle this." Innocently sitting between them, Congressman Charles Bennett rose to stop the assault. But the Florida politician, partially crippled by childhood polio, was upended in the scuffle and fell helplessly and heavily to the ballroom floor. As McCarthy turned to pick up the crumpled Bennett, an obviously shaken Pearson quickly walked away. The incident seemed over.

But then the other guests, including Nixon, watched with fascination as McCarthy strode out after Pearson, catching the older, smaller man in the cloakroom. "Well, Drew," the senator said, clapping him roughly on the back, "a pleasant evening, wasn't it?" The journalist nervously thrust into his jacket for the coat check. "Don't you reach into your pocket like that," McCarthy said dramatically, grabbing Pearson's arms, kneeing him twice in the groin. (An old Indian once told him that "if you kneed a guy hard enough, blood would come out of his eyes," the senator would say later, and in the Pearson fight "I would have found out if that was true.") Now, as the columnist bent over in pain, he gasped, "When are they going to put you in the booby hatch?" At that McCarthy slapped him back and forth, "movie-villain fashion," said one account. He was slapping Pearson again, full palm, knocking him to the floor, when Senator Nixon came into the cloakroom.

"That one was for you, Dick," McCarthy said. "Let a Quaker stop this fight," Nixon announced loudly, and then more softly to the attacker, trying to pull him away, "Let's go, Joe." Like a triumphant fighter dancing the ring, McCarthy refused to leave. "I won't turn my back on the son of a bitch," he said excitedly. "He's got to go first."

Afterward, when Pearson had hobbled away, Nixon walked McCarthy out of the Sulgrave. They spent a half hour trying to find the parking place Joe was seemingly too drunk or agitated to remember. Joe would not forget later the same night, however, to call friendly reporters with a vivid description of his exploit. He had just kicked old Drew Pearson "in the nuts," he boasted, and lifted him "three feet in the air." For his part, somber and discreet, Richard Nixon declined public comment on the incident, except to observe that "such foolishness should not be bandied about in times like these." Retelling the story in private, he marveled that he had never seen anyone slapped so hard. "If I hadn't pulled McCarthy away," Nixon would say, "he might have killed Pearson."

Three days after the Sulgrave, McCarthy went to the Senate floor to denounce Pearson as "the voice of international communism," a "Moscow-directed character assassin," a "twisted perverted mentality." McCarthy then advocated a patriotic boycott of the Adam Hat Company for sponsoring Pearson's radio show, and the manufacturer presently announced its withdrawal. To many, the senator's power seemed all the more fierce and formidable—though congressional colleagues knew, too, that McCarthy had learned of the advertiser's cancellation well before the fight and denunciation and that Joe had walked out of the Senate chamber after the speech blithely wearing his own Adam hat, a gift from Pearson himself in happier days when they were mutually useful source and reporter.

Back in the basin, reading the national publicity about the event and Nixon's intervention, Herman Perry wrote his protégé mockingly about a "letter of censure" the Whittier Lions Club had "almost" sent their new young senator for stepping in to save Drew Pearson, the despised liberal who had not only smeared McCarthy but criticized Dick Nixon and defended Helen Douglas. "They definitely feel," Perry underlined in a December 14 note, "that you should not have shown your Quaker training in stopping the fight!"

The Sulgrave episode seemed to capture at once the venom and hypocrisy, the rawness and volatility that was Washington and American politics that bitter partisan winter of 1950. Nixon entered the Senate and the national stage with growing prominence when the forces that had propelled him so far so fast since a similarly seething winter of 1945—a mood of fear and resentment, a GOP in angry and impatient opposition—were in many ways at their zenith. In Korea, this first winter of the war turned into savage defeat as MacArthur's army, expecting Christmas victory parades in Tokyo, reeled back from the Chinese counterattack along the Yalu. While Dick Nixon and the others dined at the Sulgrave, twenty thousand marines and GIs were trudging the last miles of a terrible frozen gauntlet back from the Chosen Reservoir. They would have their Christmas Eve Dunkirk at the fired port of Hungnam, withdrawing to a fixed front in central Korea where the war would hemorrhage casualties for two more years. To the familiar targets of foreign policy and internal subversion the Truman regime soon added a string of political and bureaucratic corruption small and large, what journalist Robert Donovan called an "aura of scandal" that deepened the rancor of charge and countercharge on all sides. Like McCarthy stomping after Pearson into the club cloakroom, there was throughout Washington a grim sense of scores to be settled, blood to be drawn.

Freshman Richard Nixon once more caught the crest of that tide. The ensuing months in 1951 were in a sense a continuation of his Senate campaign, echoing in questions of loyalty at home and toughness abroad, joined by rising indignation at corrupt practices in politics and government. As in earlier stages of his career, he would exploit those forces, even lead the surge, while appearing the relative moderate. Joe McCarthy, concluded one historian of the time, "dramatized intolerance, lent it crude, villainous features, personalized it, stole it away from the low-profiled bureaucrats." In the cloakroom fight or on the Senate floor and elsewhere, McCarthy and others provided the uglier face of the period's partisanship. Like the vulgar, heavy-handed men of HUAC a few years before, they lent Richard Nixon, who practiced much the same politics, a far more respectable image—the

Quaker who stopped the fight, despite the half-mocking, half-serious dismay of the Whittier Lions.

In crucial assignments for the new Eighty-second Congress, he benefited directly from Joe McCarthy's growing power and patronage, became a "tacit ally," thought one reporter, when McCarthy named him in late January 1951 to the permanent investigations subcommittee of the powerful Senate Committee on Executive Expenditures. It was not only that the subcommittee would be, rather like HUAC, a valuable forum for political attacks and headlines in the unfolding scandals. In the appointment Nixon unseated Republican Margaret Chase Smith of Maine, whose "Declaration of Conscience" had been the sole Senate protest against McCarthy's methods in the 1950 campaign. The Democrats might be complacent about communism, she had said in a famous speech, but the GOP should not "ride to political victory on the four horsemen of . . . fear, ignorance, bigotry, and smear." An obvious retaliation against Smith and a reward for Nixon, her ouster was largely greeted in the Senate by what Justice William O. Douglas called "the Black Silence," a leaden atmosphere of intimidation on both sides of the aisle.

Nixon seized the moment not in the first instance in the Senate but in an intensive round of national appearances, twelve formal addresses in January and February alone. Through 1951 he would make some forty-nine speeches covering twenty-two states, taking him back and forth across the entire nation three times and on more than a dozen regional swings. His audiences ranged from the Women's National Republican Club to local party groups to national corporate meetings and business association conventions. Only three of the dates were in California, including a Whittier College Fiftieth Anniversary Dinner in March 1951 at the Ambassador Hotel, where he attracted national publicity in any case by inviting John Foster Dulles to share the honors at the event established decades before by Walter Dexter.

He would later explain his sudden national scheduling as being "caught up" in what he saw as the Republicans' "almost desperate determination not to fail again" after the 1948 debacle. "The Republican National Committee decided to use the young Senator from the second most populous state for fund-raising," wrote Julie Eisenhower. Yet relatively few of the occasions were arranged by the RNC, and only a handful could be construed as fund-raisers. Nixon's own fees for 1951 were over $6,600, derived from sixteen speeches with honoraria as well as a paid lecture tour.

He confided his purpose more candidly in a letter to Herman Perry after only two months in the Senate, describing proudly the crowds he had already drawn—2,100 outside Philadelphia, 750 in Louisville, 600 in Grand Rapids, over 1,000 in St. Paul. He was speaking so widely, he told his old patron, "bearing in mind the fact that a few friends in other states may prove to be of considerable value in the future."

Though many of the talks were the old recitation of the Hiss case, he also spoke out more than ever on the larger, Presidential issues of foreign policy. Before the GOP National Women's Club he proposed that U.S. military and economic aid be conditioned on recipient nations joining the war in Korea "against Red China." Over a CBS network broadcast he argued that the European allies should "bear their proportional share of the burden of rearming" in what he termed a new worldwide "battle . . . for the minds, the hearts, and the souls of men." To yet another statewide radio audience in California he argued for U.S. troops and military assistance for Europe to develop a "will to resist" communist aggression.

In a favorite theme he set out "a four-point program for avoiding a third world war and bring[ing] peace and security in our time": military might, a strong economy, "effective internal security," and winning the "ideological struggle." The U.S. "should quit talking about containment and defense and go on the offensive in the ideological struggle," he told one cheering Nebraska crowd. "We must never write off the people behind the Iron Curtain." The speeches were typically featured in the California press as well as in local coverage and occasionally in national accounts. As early as mid-February 1951, the *Los Angeles Times* reported "a definite 'Nixon trend' " among "Republican women voters throughout the country," though the paper did not explain for exactly what purpose. He was, said a local representative of the National Federation of Republican Women, "the man of the hour."

Typically tart, unimpressed by her pupil's adoption of the Cold War rhetorical vogue, Adela St. Johns wrote him scathingly on March 26.

> In my experience, the words "ideology" and "ideological" convey no real meaning to the everyday American, including me. Your recent speeches haven't amounted to much anyhow, but they have brought less light to hearer or reader because of the use of these confused and confusing words. If you have anything to say, and yourself understand what it is, honest thought will enable you to put it with that true simplicity which touches every mind . . . and I tell you one man, one man, who would speak truth simply could be the leader we wait for so pathetically, so hopefully. . . . Don't let the emptiness of meaningless words rub off on you. . . . It is a major

> disappointment to find you resorting to such gup and
> believe me when I say many of us have suffered severely
> from the pompous quotes.

The caustic criticism caught him up short. Within days he was warning the GOP Central Committee in Los Angeles against vague rhetoric and "repeating the error of overconfidence evident in 1948." A few weeks later he would caution Boston Young Republicans about language and appeals that did not reach the majority of the voters. "I say we Republicans have been talking to please ourselves for the past twenty years," Nixon told them, "and have found out that there aren't enough of us to win."

Soon after Adela's stern advice, he found a less abstract issue in an event perhaps inevitable since the outbreak of the Korean War: Truman's dismissal of Douglas MacArthur. The immediate cause was the general's all-too-public scorn for the White House and the Pentagon restrictions on the bombing of Manchuria and the "unleashing" of Chiang Kai-shek. Beneath, the issue went far deeper to matters of larger postwar policy, Presidential power, and personal rancor. A climax of lapse and folly on both sides, the recall on April 11, 1950, was one of those acts by which eras are marked. It was the beginning of the deliberate limit and containment of the postwar, postcolonial conflicts gnawing at the boundaries of the U.S.-Soviet rivalry in the nuclear age. But the sequel, too, was a profound frustration and poison in American politics at the unwon but costly little wars of the peripheral struggle, from Korea to Vietnam. In the basin there was scant debate about geopolitics or Constitutional command. They hanged Harry Truman in effigy in San Gabriel. Flags flew at half-mast as the Los Angeles City Council adjourned "in sorrowful contemplation of the political assassination of General MacArthur."

Claiming to have received "more than five hundred telegrams" protesting the firing—"uninspired telegrams," he felt constrained to add—Nixon hurried to the floor to join a colloquy with other outraged GOP senators. "If any group in this nation is happy today over the action of the President," he said in a widely quoted passage, "the Communists and the stooges for the communists are happy, because the President has given them exactly what they have been after—General MacArthur's scalp." Less reported in the heated remarks were his charges of virtual treason by the administration and his explicit advocacy of a wider war. "As a direct result, I may say, of . . . action on the part of our State Department and our government, China did go communist . . . we must bring the war to a conclusion with a military and diplomatic victory . . . [and] that means bombing China across the Yalu River." At one point in the colloquy, he answered a Democratic challenge with the seeming dilemma, the conundrum of ends and means, that was to haunt his own policy in another limited war in the Orient two decades later. "Asia may not be the place to defeat communism in a war, but Asia is a place where we can lose to communism without a war," he told the crowded chamber, "and it is a place where we can lose to communism with a war—either way."

The episode was laced with such small, unseen portents. As a gesture if not a serious policy, he introduced a resolution to restore MacArthur's command regardless of Truman's authority, an attempted usurpation of Presidential power similar to some Nixon would himself face at removal of a mutinous subordinate twenty-two years later, albeit then not a general but a special prosecutor. At Duke in early May 1951, he repeated his "program" for ending the war "with victory, not appeasement," showing his earlier bellicose reaction to MacArthur's recall no mere impulsiveness in the Senate colloquy. He would "establish air reconnaissance" over China, he told a law school group, "remove restrictions on Chinese Nationalists on Formosa," and cede U.S. field commanders "authority to bomb" Manchuria. Again, it was a kind of foreshadowing of his own later war policy—unleashing an Asian client army while attempting to bomb the enemy into submission.

As MacArthur came home to a triumphal reception, tickertape parades, and a dramatic farewell to Congress, Nixon was still denouncing "one of the most vicious smear campaigns in history . . . now ready to be sprung" by the White House. From personal conviction as well as in response to his California constituency, his ardent defense of the controversial general put him temporarily at odds with much of the leadership of the GOP, including the 1948 ticket. Both Tom Dewey and Earl Warren saw MacArthur as a strutting figure of dubious policies and, more ominously, as a potential right-wing claimant for the 1952 Republican Presidential nomination. When the MacArthur furor receded, however, it was Nixon's increasingly strident attack on the Presidency and executive power that remained to mock his own future. Charging a White House "smear" of MacArthur by a leak of "secret" papers, he insisted that no administration could use "national security" to cover its blunders or political acts. "The new test for classifying documents now seems to be not whether the publication . . . would affect the security of the nation," he said in an attack that again produced favorable headlines, "but whether it would affect the political security of the administration." More than twenty years later, the same attack would be turned on the Presidency of. Richard Nixon, in which critics thought "national security" had become the ultimate mask and pretext for partisan politics.

Before he moved so rapidly and so assertively into a national speech circuit and into international issues that winter and spring of 1951, even before his swearing-in and the Sulgrave incident, Nixon had begun to gather fateful and extraordinary financial backing. A postelection political subsidy from private interests, mostly in the basin, it would underwrite not only his nearly continuous promotion in California as an incumbent U.S. senator but also his concerted bid for national prominence.

Less than a week after the election, Herman Perry had sent a "confidential" note to Room 607 in the Bank of America Building, Nixon's Whittier office in Tom Bewley's old suite, reminding the victor to thank a list of local businessmen, and professionals—including John Riley and executives of an oil company as well as of the great Murphy Ranch. Their campaign donations would not, as Perry put it discreetly, "show up on the surface in a material way." At the same moment, the 1950 finance chairman in the south, Dana Smith, had already begun to telephone many of their largest and wealthiest contributors in the race—men whose names were similarly invisible "on the surface" of the legal records—to solicit entirely new money to meet the considerable expenses anticipated for the senator-elect. The first donation arrived on November 15, 1950, only eight days after the defeat of Helen Douglas. Smith promptly opened an account in the First Trust and Savings of Pasadena, where he himself banked, in the same building housing his own law firm. It was the small, quiet beginning of what would come to be known in American political history as simply the Fund.

In concept and purpose, the money was to be much the same as the interim contributions and ongoing campaign finance provided for Richard Nixon from the moment he first won elective office. It had all begun in the late autumn of 1946 after the victory over Voorhis, with Herman Perry organizing donations from bank clients and businessmen, telling them grandly that someday they would be "guests in the White House." Drawn from Aubrey Wardman, the San Marino money and other old backers in the twelfth, that early support had been relatively modest, a few hundred dollars here, a few hundred there. Nonetheless, it was clearly valuable in Nixon's many extra trips home, the constant publicity and promotion, the off-year campaigning that had distinguished his congressional career since the spring of 1947. The crucial defense of his Marshall Plan vote and Herter Committee internationalism, the decisive early maneuvering for the 1948 primary victory, the long, painstaking prelude to his Senate run—all that and more had been financed by the discreet flow of money.

Like so much else, the early interim contributions were largely unrecorded, never publicized or listed in congressional or state campaign spending reports, acknowledged or alluded to only in Nixon's private correspondence with Perry or Roy Day. At the same time, there were those who knew about the subsidy beyond the small group of local donors. "I mean, we all knew the fund was there . . . a fund for him when he went to Congress," remembered Keith McCormac, the Bakersfield conservative only at the edge of early campaigns. While in the House, Nixon himself mentioned the support almost casually to Republican National Committee publicity man Robert Humphreys, "on several occasions," Humphreys later recalled. Prominent southern California executives also knew of the donations through the usual network of business and Republican politics in the basin. When the subsequent senatorial version of the subsidy became a national controversy, however, when Richard Nixon seemed so visibly shocked and embittered at the furor, there was little understanding of that history outside California. Few knew how much or how long the young politician had been accustomed to the private money and the impunity from public exposure or question, how much the support had made him one of the most active and well-financed congressmen in the nation, despite his lack of personal wealth.

Immediately after the 1950 election, as Nixon once told a reporter, Bernie Brennan and Murray Chotiner had proposed a "year-round campaign" for the next six years. Donors remembered that Brennan in particular "suggested" expense money for the Senate. But the name on the trust account, the central figure then and later, was Dana Smith, the fifty-two-year-old lawyer from San Marino and Pasadena who had first contributed to Nixon in 1946 and presided over the lavish flow of southern California contributions in 1950. Bald, large-featured, eyes slightly protruding behind round wire-rimmed glasses, Smith was heir to an Oregon lumber fortune, educated at Cornell, a well-to-do suburban attorney and director of the family's Smith & Sons Investment Company with tastefully decorated offices in San Marino. "An American Gothic character" is how one observer saw Dana Smith, "as ingenuous in politics as he is shrewd in business."

In retrospect the epigram seemed at least half wrong, if not reversed. Whatever his other gifts in a world of inherited wealth and genteel law and investments, Smith by the end of 1950 was a skilled political fund-raiser, understood the "arrangements to finance public figures," as one reporter described him, "knew what to do on their behalf." In his memoirs Nixon would eventually remember that it was Smith more than any of the others who proposed the special contributions. Whatever the relative credit or blame at that postelection meeting, there was never any question that the money would be needed, should be sought, or that the wealthy, well-connected Pasadena lawyer would oversee the payments. "He [Nixon] and

Bernie asked me to look after the fund," Smith wrote a prospective donor some months later, "so I am handling it through a trust account subject to review by Bernie and a couple of other stalwarts of Dick's campaign." From the beginning, with Dana Smith himself rather than Brennan or Chotiner, there was a sense that the support was to be far more significant than occasional bills picked up or Herman Perry's extra airline tickets.

The money was to be a major supplement to a senator's $12,500 salary plus the more than $75,000 officially provided for personal tax-free expenses, telephone, telegrams, and stationery, one round-trip air fare to the home state per session, and office staff—the last because of California's size one of the largest payroll accounts on Capitol Hill. They would use the added cash, as Smith wrote one potential contributor, for:

> Transportation and hotel expenses to cover trips to California more frequently than his mileage allowance permits. Payment of airmail and long-distance phone charges above his allowances. . . . Preparation of material . . . to send out to the people . . . who have supported him. . . . Defraying expenses of his Christmas cards to the people who worked in his campaign or contributed financially. . . . Paying for getting out material for radio broadcasts and television programs. . . . [and] various other similar items . . .

"We want you to start campaigning right now for 1956, and we think that the way to do it is to have available the funds to make speeches, make trips to California and so forth," Nixon later wrote of the motives of his aides and backers. "So it was worked out . . . simply a campaign fund." But their purpose was never merely his reelection. Smith and the others, including many of the largest donors, saw their dynamic new junior senator not only as an effective legislator and politician representing their interests in Washington but as a unique spokesman and advocate of the boom status quo. More than a lawmaker, as Smith would describe him, Nixon was to be above all a "salesman." "A group of us here," he wrote a 1950 contributor from Bakersfield, "after the dust of battle had settled and we found that Dick was safely elected, began to realize that electing him was only part of what we really wanted to accomplish. We not only wanted a good man in the Senate from this state, but we wanted him to continue to sell effectively to the people of California the economic and political systems which we all believe in." Implicit in the finance was the enduring paradox of Nixon the rising national figure, Nixon the representative from the twelfth and now the senator from California, especially southern California.

"He had advanced so quickly that his supporters felt it might be difficult for him to keep his feet on the ground," recorded a foreign journalist who later interviewed many of the contributors. "They decided that [the Fund was] the best way to keep him anchored to his constituency."

Like the earlier subsidies, the Fund was never strictly secret, though certainly not public. As Smith explained it to donors, the money seemed hedged about with scrupulous conditions, "so that any possible criticisms of it would be completely disarmed," he told one questioner. Yet the very precautions revealed how much they were aware of the latent embarrassment and controversy. Contributions were to be limited to "people who have supported Dick from the start" and "a maximum of $500," Smith told supporters, "so that it does not provide any way for people who are 'second-guessers' to make any claim on the senator's particular interest . . . [and] it can never be charged that anyone is contributing so much as to think he is entitled to special favors." Of his own role, he added: "Nobody is drawing any salary or other compensation out of this, so you can count on it that the money will be effectively used where it will do all of us, including Dick, the most good." There were assurances then and later that the donors would remain anonymous. "The names . . . were not to be furnished at any time by Dana Smith to Richard Nixon . . . so that contributors couldn't claim favoritism," Earl Adams remembered. Yet the usually meticulous Smith omitted that restriction in the actual fund-raising. "We would be delighted to have you join us in this program," he wrote in a typical letter to donors, "and Dick will of course be very appreciative of your continuing interest."

On December 28, 1950, Smith drew up in his own careful longhand a draft budget for 1951 totaling $21,000, including $7,500 for radio advertising and $5,700 for mailings, of which almost half would be for 20,000 Christmas cards to be sent to Senate campaign workers and contributors. They raised money steadily in the basin through the winter and spring, and at the end of June, Brennan, Chotiner, and Smith traveled south to San Diego, then north through Riverside, Fresno, and San Francisco asking for donations of between $100 and $500 among key Nixon supporters. "They were seeking contributions for it all the time," McCormac remembered. When the June swing produced only a single contribution, Smith followed with another series of letters in August, September, and October, "in hopes," as he wrote Ben Hoblick in Fresno, "that you can do the necessary stirring around and send in a few checks."

Long afterward, in an effort to show the openness and breadth of the Fund, Nixon would write that Dana Smith had sent first "a few hundred," then "several thousand" letters in those mailings. But the supposedly complete records of the Fund later turned over to investigating lawyers and accountants contained only two modest files of such correspondence and only a small fraction of the letters claimed. Whatever the reach of their appeal, the results at the time were at once impressive and disappointing. By October 30, 1951, they had raised over $16,000, of which Nixon had already spent nearly $12,000. Yet all but a few hundred dollars had come from Los Angeles County, and Smith faced the prospect of going back to many of the same contributors for the 1952 money. By its first anniversary, the Fund was scarcely a statewide campaign chest but the creature of seventy-six powerful backers, what *The New York Times* would call "an abbreviated *Who's Who* of wealthy and influential southern California business figures." It would be those patrons and their interests, more than any of Dana Smith's cautious limits and disavowals, that gave the Fund its essential character.

They were a distinctive group. Of the seventy-six, only two were from outside the basin, and those accounted for only $125 of the total. More than twenty were from San Marino and Pasadena, the continuing weight of his original backing. Some were familiar and important faces from the 1946 and 1950 races—Earl Adams, Jack Garland, Jack Drown, and Harold Lutz, the lone name from Whittier; Herbert Hoover, Jr.; the Stassen campaign lawyer, David Saunders; the fathers of past and future aides, J. Frank Holt and Henry Haldeman; Henry Kerns, the San Gabriel auto dealer who lent them the "woody" station wagon; and a few who had played more public roles, giving and raising money against Helen Douglas, oilmen Henry Salvatori and Thomas Pike, Charles Ducommun of the metals and realty fortune, Elwood Robinson from Los Angeles advertising, and others.

But in checks or cash from $100 to $1,000, most of the money came from figures still invisible in the unrecorded or unregistered contributions of the congressional or Senate races. "Only . . . people who have supported Dick from the start," Smith had stipulated. His orderly tallies of the Fund would now reveal, ironically, not only those subsidizing the new senator but also a silhouette of the hidden finance of past campaigns.

More than a fifth of the donations came from major oil interests, some with sizable government contracts. In addition to Pike, with his drilling company, and Hoover, president of United Geophysical and a director of Union Oil, there was Earl Gilmore, with his own land and petroleum combine; William Hubbard, president of Anselma and Realitos Oil; Mortimer Kline, a former counsel to the Federal Petroleum Administration in World War II and now a prominent Los Angeles lawyer specializing in corporate oil; Earl Jorgensen, presiding over Jorgensen Oil as well as a director of Northrop and Transamerica Corporations; Edward R. Valentine of Fullerton Oil; Tyler Woodward, chief of Southern California Petroleum Coporation; Leland Whittier of Belridge Oil; R. R. Bush, a Pasadena oilman; Rodney S. Burkee of Lane-Wells and Petro-Tech oil equipment companies; Frank Seaver, whose Hydril and Doheny Stone Drill Companies were similarly important in the industry; and William O. Anderson, yet another prominent California oil explorer and producer.

In much the same pattern, one-fourth of the money went to Smith's account from wealthy men in basin manufacturing, merchandising, and other large interests. Thomas Arden was a maker of thermometers and thermostats; William Coberly, the president of California Cotton Oil; Harold McClellan, the founder of Old Colony Paint; Kenneth Norris of Norris Thermidor; P. G. Winnett of Bullock's department store; Rudolph Wig from Douglas Aircraft and his own engineering company; and a trio of prominent dairy executives: Thorkeld Knudsen, Alford Ghormley of Carnation, and J. W. McKenzie, together accounting for much of the milk production in the vast market of metropolitan Los Angeles and throughout the state.

The oilmen and manufacturers were connected well beyond their corporations through the interwoven directorates of local and national business. But it was to be the old intricate latticework of boom real estate and finance that dominated the contributions, providing nearly 40 percent of the total. His backers wound in and about the new golden empire erected on land and banking and investments. W. Herbert Allen, a longtime supporter, ran Title Insurance and Trust Company; Fred Bixby had founded Fire and Marine Insurance and came to own much of Long Beach; J. Benton Van Nuys conducted the Van Nuys building and real-estate barony; Walker Smith, Dana's brother, presided over Red River Lumber and Shasta Forests; Hulet P. Smith ran Arcadia Mortgage; Robert E. Hunter was director of Citizens National Trust and Pacific Finance; Charles Goethe owned a legendary string of California ranches; John Marble combined beef cattle ranches and a mortgage company; George and Louis Rowan were leaders in Los Angeles and Pasadena real estate; Joseph Crail was president of Coast Federal Savings and Loan; John Bacon was in San Marino real estate; R. L. Easton was a well-to-do San Marino stockbroker; and so it went.

Largely in their fifties and sixties in 1950–51, a handful younger and a few retired, they represented vividly the billowing wealth and influence of the postwar basin. Most would remain discreet powers in the business and political world of the region for years to come, some in continuing and direct patronage of Richard Nixon. Across their differences of background, professions, and special interests, they would contribute now, as in the 1950 race, with a common distaste and alarm at the Democrats and even Earl Warren and a common devotion to "the economic and political systems which we all believe in," as Dana Smith put it, arrangements after all, by which they had accumulated their fortunes and which they now funded

Richard Nixon to preserve and "sell." Above all, they shared the singular political and cultural marks of their place in California's own sharply demarcated social, economic, and political system. The young politician from Whittier would be, at long last, *their* senator. Not a single contribution to the Fund, to Richard Nixon's "ongoing campaign," would come from the more liberal, cosmopolitan world of San Francisco and the north.

He spent the money quickly, most of it over 1951. Nearly $3,000 went for airlines or hotels and some for the largely empty-handed trips by Brennan and Chotiner to raise more subsidies. Eighteen hundred dollars bought radio recordings, and another $771 was paid for newspaper ads during the first year in the Senate, including publicity photographs of both Dick and Pat. Over $5,500 covered the cost of engraved address plates and Christmas cards, 16,000 of them for 1950, 25,000 for 1951. In all, $12,876 would be disbursed directly by Smith for various expenses in both Washington and California and another $5,102 to Nixon himself in reimbursement for still more Senate office expenses. There were speech reprints, recordings, stationery and postage, telephone and telegraph beyond allowance, salaries for added staff, freight for the thousands of Christmas cards, and taxi fares for staff working overtime. Even at that, Herman Perry solicited ten more Whittier donors for hundreds of dollars in stamps for the Christmas 1951 mailing, items that would never appear in Dana Smith's accounting.

By the beginning of 1952, the Pasadena account was nearly depleted, and Smith had tried in vain through Alvin Derre and Arthur Dolan in San Francisco to get $5,000 from the United Republican Finance organization for northern California. The northerners continued to put them off, and between November 1951 and the summer of 1952, Smith, Brennan, and Chotiner could raise only $2,200, much of that from repeat contributions. He was "tremendously indebted to our special group for what they have done to make our programs possible in the past," Nixon wrote Smith, "but I don't feel that they should continue to bear this burden indefinitely." Smith tried again to no avail to elicit party support for the subsidies. In a June letter of thinly veiled anger, Nixon wrote his Fund executor about the perennially sore question of GOP organization money: "I think the time has now come for us to have a showdown with Republican Finance on obtaining assistance for our program. . . . I feel very strongly on this matter, and frankly, I intend to condition my future cooperation with Republican Finance on whether they support our program."

Nixon proposed they ask for $10,000 a year from southern California, only $5,000 from the north. But on June 11 by return mail Smith wrote back confidentially and almost forlornly. They would need at least $20,000 "as your reelection year begins to come closer," and as it was, the northern GOP had been vaguely promising then evading a $5,000 contribution for several months—"it is apparently more convenient for them to forget about it." Plainly loath to return to their original wealthy donors, spurned by the north and by the party in general in a campaign year when Nixon was still four and one-half years from his own reelection, that summer of 1952 they were watching Dana Smith's once impressive trust dwindle away.

Ironically, as the Fund was about to become most famous, most important politically, it was virtually bankrupt. It would be ironic, too, that it had made possible in part what it was designed to mitigate—that by that same summer, Richard Nixon had become a national figure playing for interests and stakes far beyond southern California. The subsidies spent so swiftly in 1951–52 for California had simply freed other resources for that national effort.

He had not even paid off the last engraving bill, Smith wrote the senator on the eve of the 1952 Republican Convention in Chicago. He was counting on $500 someone had promised Bernie Brennan. "If that comes in promptly, I could clean up the . . . bill and still have a little in the bank to take care of your convention expenses and so forth," Smith added. "After the convention I might have a little more time to scare up enough money here and there to see us through the summer."

The Fund was a discreet added appropriation for a Senate office Nixon conducted with an ever-anxious, sometimes obsessively fussy intensity. At breakfast by 7:00 A.M., often the first to arrive at the three-room suite in number 341 of the Old Senate Office Building, he presided over a staff of twelve that was deliberately weighted toward the clerical processing of heavy constituent correspondence and the constant round of his personal promotion. With Bill Arnold, still the administrative assistant and press officer, were only two other substantive aides: James P. Gleasen, a lawyer dealing with price controls and other legal matters, and John J. Irwin, the conservative Democratic attorney from the basin who had been instrumental in the 1950 race. Nixon had recruited Irwin as both GOP minority counsel for the investigations subcommittee and as a personal aide assigned to California defense contracts, water, and reclamation problems and other state subjects. Unlike most other Senate staffs, the trio was largely absorbed in correspondence and constituent services to the virtual exclusion of more substantive duties, save for Irwin's part-time liaison with the subcommittee. They were not expected or wanted to draft bills or analyze policy.

From the first weeks, Nixon had kept to himself almost entirely the crucial legislative and political work, a pattern of independence and relegation he had followed in the House. "The primary function of an administrative staff is to take care of the problems of constituents," an office memo declared on March 30, 1951, "so that the senator does not have to be bothered and can thereby devote the time necessary to legislation." Throughout his brief apprenticeship in the House and Senate—for that matter, throughout his political and administrative career across twenty-two years prior to his Presidency—he would have almost no experience managing a genuinely professional staff, in delegating, apportioning, entrusting substantive responsibility. Nor in that preparation, except for Irwin and an occasional few others, would he take on aides of abilities generally comparable to his own.

Below the three men, Nixon hired nine secretaries and stenographers who variously typed and performed the lesser tasks. Among them was Dorothy Cox from the House attic office; Pat's longtime friend at Whittier Union, Marion Budlong; and, beginning in late February 1951, a thirty-two-year-old secretary from the Herter Committee named Rose Mary Woods. Red-headed, a small plain woman from a devout Irish Catholic family in Ohio, Woods came to Washington to work with her sister in the Office of Censorship during the war, stayed on to work in the House, and with a crisp efficiency now moved almost naturally from one side of Capitol Hill to the other. Rather resembling her new employer, she was both controlled and volatile, a mix, she would say, of "my mother's cool head" and "my father's temper." It was the beginning of an intimate, fierce, sometimes tortured but lifelong loyalty to Richard Nixon. Like so many others of her vocation and temperament, Rose Woods was to be the proverbial office wife, the ubiquitous lower-case "rmw" of his dictation and personal letters and memos for nearly a quarter century.

"A special twentieth-century breed, those ladies who guard the boss's door and fend off the telephone calls and read his mail," one observer wrote of them, devoting their spinsterly existence to politicians, "women largely without private lives because the real world is right there in the vortex spinning around the great man . . . without husbands because the job takes most of their time and energies . . . with small fiefdoms of their own encompassing subsecretaries . . . the messenger service . . . selfless, happily job-enslaved, eager to be useful, they are the vestal virgins in the temples of business and politics, the Indispensables." Inevitably, Rose Mary Woods's emerging role brought her into close contact with Pat Nixon, who as in the House periodically helped out when the office faced unusual burdens. Yet unlike Murray Chotiner, the only working relationship of comparable intimacy, Rose Woods was accepted by Pat with a kind of mutual respect, and the shared sorority of two working-class professional women dedicated each in their own way to Richard Nixon. They were "careful never to cross each other or to second-guess a decision," Pat Nixon told her daugher more than three decades later.

From the outset he would be complimented for his "very efficient staff," as California lieutenant governor Goodwin Knight told him in March 1951, though there was also the predictable impatience, particularly from old supporters in the twelfth who felt neglected in the move to the Senate. "They complain that the same prompt and courteous response from your office is not in evidence now," Herman Perry wrote him barely four months after the swearing-in. To this and other random disgruntlement, Nixon responded by harrying the staff on to a further forced pace, mainly on constituent correspondence, and with a kind of bureaucratic absorption and fastidiousness reminiscent of the eager clerk he had been a decade before at the OPA. "For the past two weeks I have been making a careful spot check of the outgoing mail," he told Irwin, Arnold, and Gleasen by memo in late March 1951, and was "quite concerned about the quality."

The senator followed with his own scheme for the distribution and handling of the letters among the men, and the next night dictated to Dorothy Cox again his own "pet phrases" for answering inquiries—instead of "I am *confident* remedial action will be forthcoming," which "gives the constituent too much hope," they should write, "I am *hopeful*. . . ." One man should be "in the office at all times" to greet visitors, especially businessmen and others who may be "sensitive when they are told the senator is not in" and must not "feel they are getting the brush-off." As for the seemingly unavoidable "crackpots," Nixon realized "it wasn't a pleasant task," but they had "to take the bad with the good." Besides, occasionally a crackpot had "something to offer." He admonished them "to bear in mind the case of Whittaker Chambers, whom everyone thought was a crackpot!"

Above all, there was the endless mail. The piles of unanswered letters, the lure of some procedural escape or all-efficient scheme, nagged at him in the United States Senate as it had in the old temporary buildings of the OPA in the spring of 1942. When he heard complaints about the mail during a trip to Los Angeles in April 1951—letters never acknowledged or, worse, responses received later than those from Knowland's office—he seethed. "Under no circumstances," he wrote the male aides, were they to delegate their mail assignments, and "until further notice, I want all mail dictated by any of you, no matter how routine, sent in to me for signature." They were to report all mail two weeks or older, keep all unanswered letters in baskets on top of their desks, and eventually work late one night a week and Saturdays until one o'clock. "I cannot emphasize too strongly that I am counting on the administrative people . . . to assume responsiblity and to take care of such problems," he wrote April 4, 1951, "so that I do not have to take action myself."

At the same time, they were to be scrupulous in their own propriety, segregate sensitive political matters, and be ever mindful of the Nixon image. "The general rule is never to accept any gift from an individual who has a matter pending in the office," he told them all in another of the stream of interoffice memos before Christmas 1951, and, "when a gift is offered I want you to bring the matter to my attention." As for his own benefits, financial contributions and otherwise, they were to turn every offer or name over to Marion Budlong, who would prepare "supporter cards," a vital task for which she would be relieved (unlike the men and their other duties) of some of the endless correspondence. Moreover, they were all to be alert to any opportunity to advance his cause. When replying to inquiries about legislation on liquor advertising in March 1952, for example, they should add a casual "P.S." which the boss had clipped from the *Monterey Peninsula Herald*: "You don't see our junior senator, Richard Nixon, on the cocktail tours of Washington, where many important people like to be seen."

By June 1952, Irwin was announcing his resignation to return to a California law practice, but Nixon made no apparent move to replace him, though deeply absorbed in politics and GOP policy with no other aide able to fill the role. His final thoughts for his Senate office before leaving for the Republican National Convention in the summer of 1952 would be the mail backlog and Saturday work schedules. Afterward, it would seem almost amazing to reporters and colleagues that he had risen so rapidly through the House and Senate with so little substantive involvement by his staff, that there were no key aides—save Rose Woods and a few of the secretaries—who would go on with him to the next level of his remarkable career. Only later still was it clear how much the strangely truncated, letter-laden Senate office reflected the deeper priorities of his brief tenure, how much politics and personal maneuver overshadowed all else, making the twelve harried men and women almost incidental beyond keeping up with the mail.

"These goddamned chiselers who use T," White House press aide Roger Tubby wrote in his diary that spring of 1951. "He should get rid of them as fast as they are forced into the light." The objects of Tubby's anger and frustration were a train of Democratic cronies and politicians whose corruption continued to poison the administration, from ingratiating gifts of deep freezes and mink coats to outright kickbacks, tax fraud, lax prosecution of influential Democrats, and blatant favoritism and political influence in major federal loan programs. Yet through most of 1951, as in an earlier wave of scandal, the beleaguered "T" of Tubby's lament, a defiant, too loyal, often morally and politically oblivious Harry Truman, did little to stem the tide. "There have been only two or three Presidents . . . as roundly abused and misrepresented . . . as I," he indignantly wrote former aide Clark Clifford. Once again, as in the Hiss case, Truman's reflexive fury and contempt at the partisan attack blinded him to the depth of the genuine problem. And once again, the snappish defensiveness and inertia in the Oval Office opened a way to Richard Nixon. It was still another moment of irony. "Truman stood in the eye of a hurricane of scandals that swirled around him while he did nothing," Nixon said of the period. The next time such charges would be hurled at a chief executive, it was twenty-two years later and the Presidency was his own.

In the summer of 1951, Nixon introduced in swift succession legislation designed to highlight the running scandals, a bill to suspend the statute of limitations on all offenses involving performance of federal jobs, including members of Congress, and another measure to arm grand juries with their own special counsel and investigators to probe government officials, with jury immunity from dismissal by federal judges. In October he denounced Truman's new security "gag order," a White House effort to check leaks on both foreign policy and internal corruption. There had already been deplorable evidence, he said, of "classifying information as involving the national security with virtually little or no justification" while "generally speaking the public interest is best served by allowing as much information as possible to reach the people." In the widely publicized statement he added, "If we grant such tremendous power to the Administrative Branch of the government we may find ourselves heading rapidly toward a . . . dictatorship." By December Nixon was calling for the replacement of Attorney General J. Howard McGrath by J. Edgar Hoover, the latter to head a "clean-up squad."

In many ways his most celebrated attack on the larger issue of corruption came that autumn. Republicans had been gleeful when Democratic National Chairman William Boyle was implicated in a loan scandal, but "the cigar then blew up," as one reporter put it, when Guy Gabrielson, the GOP National Chairman, was exposed in an almost matching offense. As other politicians drew back, Nixon grandly urged the resignation of both chairmen. "The basic issue," he said in an October 15 statement sent to newspaper editors throughout the nation and even echoed by the liberal Americans for Democratic Action, "is whether a high official of the National Committee of either major political party should be in a position where he can profit financially from the influence which he may be able to exert with government agencies." The call caused "consternation" in both parties, a congressional archive recorded solemnly, while winning headlines across the country. He would go on to pursue the issue in the investigations subcommittee, draw Vice President Barkley into the charge, and advocate a special bipartisan congressional committee to conduct a "complete and thorough . . . house cleaning," as he told a Kansas audience.

Obscured in the commotion was a first glimpse of the inner politics of the Presidential campaign still seemingly months away. To strike at Gabrielson was not only to appear above partisanship in a national story but also to rid the National Committee of a creature of Robert Taft and an avowed conservative who clearly preferred the more affable Bill Knowland among California's senators for any future national office or prominence. "He saw Gabrielson," a onetime Nixon backer, William Roper, would say, "as a lion in the way." At the moment, though, such motives and calculations seemed remote, and the young senator's evenhanded concern for public virtue a rare exception in Washington's seamy mores. "He emerged," one journalist wrote of Richard Nixon's first eighteen months in the U.S. Senate, "as a champion of integrity in public life."

He crusaded against the administration's corrupt practices while continuing to sound the old themes of subversion, albeit in modulated tones that plainly set him at a safe distance from McCarthy. In Washington or elsewhere, it was as if he were campaigning again for the Senate in northern California, a careful shifting balance between dire warnings and moderate remedies. "Anyone who thinks communism in this country is just an idea is crazy as hell," he was reported in an oft-quoted climax to many lectures and speeches on the Hiss case. Yet he also endorsed Truman's proposal for a distinguished commission on internal security and individual rights. The position won still more favorable publicity without giving ground on the issue. "Being a man of the world, Nixon hardly expects politicians to stop behaving like politicans. Whenever there is a Red probe on Capitol Hill, there is the probability of political haymaking," columnist Holmes Alexander wrote after a lengthy interview with the thoughtful new senator in April 1951, yielding a major article headlined "Nixon Strongly Favors Individual Rights."

Still caustic, often savage in criticism of Dean Acheson and the regime's foreign policy over the ensuing months, Nixon went on to flay the opposition on its "soft" policies and "betrayals." He would summon the communist menace along with McCarthy and others in voting to override Truman's veto of the McCarran-Walter Immigration Act, legislation which narrowed citizenship requirements and reaffirmed the hoary Red Scare and racist quotas of 1924. At the same time, before Massachusetts Republicans in November 1951, he warned no less earnestly that "indiscriminate name-calling and professional Red-baiting can hurt our cause more than it can help it." Having advocated in that Boston address a GOP internal security program that was "fair, sane, intelligent, and effective," he was at pains with newsmen afterward to explain he was merely "stating a principle," and "did not have Senator McCarthy or anybody else in particular in mind." His politics soon veered backward. In April 1952 Senator Nixon went to the floor to laud producer and industrialist Howard Hughes for firing a screenwriter, Paul Jerrico, for his refusal on principle to tell HUAC his political affiliation. What Hughes had done to the writer, Nixon told the Senate, "deserves the attention and approval of every man and woman who believes the forces of subversion must be wiped out."

"A MAN WHO HASN'T A SINGLE CRONY"

So industrious was his speaking schedule around the country, so well aimed and publicized his forays on the national issues of corruption and communism, that Nixon in the Senate seemed once more, as in the House, somehow above petty parochial politics. "He has taken," complained *Frontier*, the liberal western monthly, "only a perfunctory interest in . . . [California's] immediate and local problems." Beyond his politician's ultrasensitivity to constituent carping about the mail, it was true, he led no California crusade, assumed no readily identifiable color of place from the vast and powerful state that had sent him to the Senate. He might have been, judging by his press clippings—the self-reinforcing record from which such vague portraits were usually confected— a senator in the Eighty-second Congress from any of a dozen large states. It was a measure of Nixon's remarkable national reach and attention in 1951–52 that a few months later, when he became truly famous, his name and at least an impression of his record or positions would be known to millions, while many of them had no idea what state he represented. Yet hidden in the national imagery was an equal diligence toward the inner politics of his home base, a concern for "local problems" that verged on the venal, and attention to California interests, especially those of his own Fund contributors, that was much more than perfunctory.

That diligence began, as always, with the media. While the Washington office churned out releases and radio recordings—much of the publicity purchased by the Fund—Chotiner and Nixon himself maintained the old contacts, in constant exchange with their sizable journalistic claque to burnish the junior senator's style and impact. When a *San Diego Evening Tribune* editorial board interviewed both Knowland and Nixon late in 1951, Herb Klein at the paper promptly wrote Bill Arnold in Washington of the newsroom reviews: "Two or three of those attending commented that Knowland now talks a little too formally . . . sort of like making a speech. They thought Dick has retained an ability to talk in a relaxed manner, more informally." When Governor Warren in October 1951 designated a California Newspaper Week, Chotiner quickly provided Nixon with a congratulatory letter to every editor in the state, praising their "high journalistic standards." "Nowhere in the land," read the letter, "is the principle of a strong, free independent press better exemplified than in California." Such ministrations were seldom *pro forma*. Only a few months before, when the shady Brewster-Grunewald contribution to the Nixon Senate campaign was exposed in congressional testimony and made front-page headlines in Washington, the revelation was scarcely visible from the basin to San Francisco. "California newspapers either suppressed the news story or gave it but slight publicity," one reporter wrote later, creating a barrier around the senator that *Frontier* called drolly the "Paper Curtain."

There were the irresistible and obligatory political opportunities in local issues. The ever-admiring *Los Angeles Times* reported Senator Nixon pleading that some of the excess steel released by Defense authorities in 1951 go for building badly needed California schools. With the same California chauvinism, he sparred intermittently with the Bureau of Reclamation or Arizona in the ongoing water wars between and within the western states. But he showed no serious or sustained interest in most of the underlying issues of the boom that had shaped the sociology, framed the debate, and channeled the money of the Senate race. Used, and used up as public notoriety receded and the problems remained, the campaign fodder was swept aside. It was eloquent of the issues and politics, of the landscape of his California power. The passionate struggles that consumed Sheridan Downey and Helen Douglas, and to some extent the winning candidate himself, only two years before—irrigation and land holdings, the "socialization of the Valley," the sanctity of public or private electricity—were all but invisible in the Senate office of Richard Nixon from 1951 through the summer of 1952.

His attention to constituents and old patrons was customarily more quiet, if no less telling. After Herman Perry, now retired from Bank of America to become a business consultant and realtor, asked for help in smoothing federal financing for a vast new headquarters and warehouse in La Habra for Alpha Beta supermarkets, Nixon intervened forcefully with the Federal Reserve. Already blanketing southern California and about to become a regional giant, a model of the corporate groceries Frank Nixon once despised, Alpha Beta was soon constructing its complex with a crucial banking variance. "This we attribute directly to your interest in the matter," the corporate secretary wrote Nixon in December 1951, wishing him "continued usefulness in Washington during the New Year and for many more to come." Some services were more public. In September he went to the Senate chamber to extol film producer Edmund Grainger for his latest RKO technicolor hit, *Flying Leathernecks*, starring John Wayne in what Nixon called in a speech written by studio press agents "a splendid combination of documented . . . history and an original story portraying the immortal achievements of our Marine Corps air arm." Like Alpha Beta,

RKO's publicity director wrote him appreciatively: "You are regarded as a staunch friend of the film industry and have many friends here." Lavishly promoted by the marines and the Pentagon, the film was showy propaganda for large military budgets and RKO's 1951 version of *Patriotism and the Spirit of America*. Moreover, among the "many friends" was again the studio's chief investor, Howard Hughes.

Not all requests from supporters were so easily accommodated. When pipeline contractors urged him to block a new welfare fund for basin plumbers and steamfitters, Nixon quickly wrote back that "practical and political considerations prompt me to be a little cautious." He would only make a "recommendation" to federal authorities, and "misunderstanding . . . is bound to arise when my action becomes known to the members of the trades in California." He was less hesitant in the summer of 1951 when Paul Smith, the new president of Whittier College, proposed a Richard M. Nixon Chair for the small institution. In letters to Smith and Perry, he admitted "giving considerable thought" to the flattering, rather remarkable idea, an endowed professorship in the name of a thirty-eight-year-old politican in Congress less than five years. He worried that "other educators would frown upon the idea," and "I think it would be unwise to give anyone the impression that we are trying to build up my name, or for that matter to exploit it, in behalf of the college. If I had a more generally accepted national reputation, I think the situation would be different." But then the chair might lead to "good sound teaching," unlike other colleges that received "heavy" private endowments "and whose professors then proceed to disparage and discredit the system which made possible their salaries." At any rate they could count on "substantial donors" for the chair from "our campaign," Nixon told them in July 1951, naming specifically not Whittier or California money but his powerful southwestern oil backers, Hugh Roy Cullen from Texas and C. A. Owen from Tulsa, who "might welcome the opportunity to assist such a program."

One of Paul Smith's characteristic enthusiasms, eventually to languish and be forgotten when the namesake was far more famous, the Nixon Chair with its out-of-state oil endowment was bound to have been a political embarrassment sooner or later. His vain endorsement of the proposal that first summer in the Senate was an obvious lapse from his otherwise careful politics. Still, there was soon another, involving again his sedate Quaker hometown and one more early example of the tainted money and influence that had begun to collect about his career.

In August 1951, Tom Bewley was retained by the Manhattan lawyers for Western Tube Corporation, a new entity planning to build a plant in Whittier to manufacture seamless tubing for oil wells. The potential profits were considerable, though under Korean War controls the company required a federal Certificate of Necessity as well as government finance. Bewley agreed to represent the company on a contingency basis and became its corporate secretary reasonably expecting large fees when the plant was established. Herman Perry was elected vice president and a director. What made Western Tube noteworthy was not its boom prospects or well-connected local boosters, however, but the other director and *de facto* owner, Nicolae Malaxa. One of the shadowy, truly remarkable scoundrels of the era, he was a charming, wealthy, Rumanian businessman who had supported the Nazis, become a partner of Hermann Goering's brother, and was implicated in the Holocaust, all in the Balkans during World War II. Then by similar bribery and protean politics he became a favorite and profitable capitalist under the successor communist regime in Bucharest before moving to the United States in 1946. It was a chronicle of political and business debauchery with few parallels, much of it vividly traced in Malaxa's immigration file, in which captured secret Nazi documents referred to him as "the financial mainstay" of the Rumanian fascist Iron Guard. The grisly record had effectively blocked his postwar attempt to gain American citizenship.

Scarcely a month after Bewley had been retained, he and Malaxa's New York lawyer visited Nixon's Senate office, where Arnold "did a swell job," as Bewley cryptically wrote him afterward. By September 14, 1951, Nixon had drafted for cosignature with Knowland a formal appeal to the Defense Production Administration seeking approval of the Certificate of Necessity for Western Tube—"a plant important, strategically and economically," the letter said, "both for California and the entire United States." At the same time the company sought, and Nixon also supported, immigration for Malaxa on a "first-preference quota," on grounds that he was "personally indispensable in [the] building of this essential plant, and that his presence was immediately required on the scene at Whittier." In the tangled sequel, the certificate was granted, including a substantial tax write-off, and Malaxa was eventually given permanent-resident status. Nonetheless, the Western Tube Whittier plant was never built. The scheme simply faded away, no longer so "important strategically and economically," particularly after Malaxa's record and the Nixon connection were exposed by Drew Pearson in 1952. In a colloquy on the House floor as late as 1962, congressmen would charge that the whole Western Tube enterprise had been an elaborate fraud to ease Malaxa's immigration, if not to realize a quick profit through political connections.

As the Malaxa episode continued periodically to embarrass him over the ensuing decade—a thickening folder in an office file entitled "Smears and Special Cases"—Nixon would claim that his advocacy of Western Tube and the Rumanian rogue had been innocent and incidental, despite Bewley and Perry sitting so pointedly on the board of Western Tube. It seemed one more essential California business, he argued. He did not share in Bewley's legal fees. No favors had been asked or given. Yet the taint was in many ways indelible. When Malaxa's lawyers had sought out Whittier and Tom Bewley, one attorney and town among so many in California, the firm was still clearly listed as Bewley, Knoop and Nixon—California's crusading young senator still conspicuous on the letterhead. Western Tube's Whittier address would be 607 Bank of America Building, only months before the senator-elect's own office where Herman Perry had written him on delicate matters of campaign finance and backers. Finally, as Bewley himself admitted in a memorandum to Rose Woods years after the events, the onetime partner had personally introduced Nixon to Malaxa early in the process. On his first trip to Washington for Western Tube, Tom Bewley had even asked "Arnold or one of the girls," as he recalled, "for any information that might be available about Malaxa" and sat reading the incriminating file in Dick Nixon's Senate office. In a calculus of personal gain and local power, they had all wantonly joined company with a figure Richard Nixon would have publicly excoriated, had Nicolae Malaxa turned up in the closet of the opposition.

The Malaxa case was only one of several acts of agency in which Nixon quickly, sometimes dramatically, responded to California patrons. The more important episodes involved contributors to the Fund, though links between his public acts and those private interests remained hidden simply because the Fund itself remained discreetly tucked away in Dana Smith's books and the narrow world of California political money. Afterward, he would claim that his special senatorial backers understood clearly that the Fund entitled them to no special access or favors. But the actual solicitations from Smith and others had carried no explicit restrictions on contacts or lobbying. By the summer of 1952, he was confronted with a number of pressures, large and small, from the men who were privately financing him.

The train began with Smith himself when his family's Red River Lumber Company in March 1951 filed in the U.S. Court of Claims for a disputed tax refund of $500,000–$600,000. Two months after the filing Smith had gone to the Senate office, where John Irwin called the Justice Department and personally escorted the curator of the Fund for a thirty-minute talk with an attorney in the tax division, leading, as Smith acknowledged later, to "some progress" in the case and an eventual settlement. But the help did not end there. Smith later sought senatorial intercession as well in a personal matter of some embarrassment. In April 1952, visiting Cuba with his wife, the dour lawyer had been lured into a classic tourist come-on at

Havana's San Souci nightclub and lost more than $4,200 at Cubolo, a suspect dice game. Back in Pasadena Smith angrily stopped payment on his First Savings and Trust check for the losses, and the casino threatened litigation to collect in California. He then wrote for the help of the U.S. Embassy in Havana, with a cover letter from Senator Nixon saying Smith was "a highly respected member of his community," and Nixon "would appreciate anything the embassy might be able to do." In the eventual lawsuit, Dana Smith was upheld with evidence that U.S. and Cuban authorities both considered the Cubolo debts uncollectible.

In his first spring in the Senate, Nixon had also quietly introduced without remarks S–1029, a bill that would allow private interests to take out oil leases on military property, including Tyler Woodward and William Anderson, two basin oilmen and Fund contributors who had been trying in vain since 1949 to lease exploration sites on the reservation of Camp Roberts, California, along the central coast near Hearst's San Simeon. Destined to die in committee, the deliberately obscure leasing bill was in its own way an evocation of another time and another politician, Jerry Voorhis and the contract he had discovered on the naval reserve at Elk Hills during a Washington spring only eight years earlier. The legislation came, too, alongside major Nixon votes in support of southern California oil and the petroleum industry in general—against cutting the 27.5 percent oil depletion allowance, in favor of a transportation charge and pricing act wanted by the major petroleum companies, in favor of state ownership of the tidelands, voting down an amendment devoting federal income from the offshore leases to improve schools.

Divisions were rare among the backers, and he was seldom forced to a choice among their views or vested interests. One of the dairymen on Smith's rolls urged the lifting of the quota on Danish blue cheese, arguing like the State Department that the relatively small imports would help strengthen Europe against communism. But Carnation's Alford Ghormley and others were adamant to maintain the quota, and Nixon voted to restrict all cheese and dairy trade with the NATO countries, an act generally at odds with his other positions in favor of aid to Western Europe. Similarly, he would reflect the views of his banking supporters in the basin by voting against a withholding tax on dividends and corporate bond interest and in favor of an amendment allowing mutual savings institutions or building-and-loan associations to exempt up to 10 percent of their reserves from taxation. There were matching roll calls on issues of concern to the real-estate and development forces who led the Fund donations—votes to cut public housing from 50,000 to 5,000 units, to shorten rent controls by four months, to remove rent control from federal supervision, and perhaps most notable, a June 1952 effort to block 10,000 public housing units in Los

Angeles. Enlisting Knowland, he fought vocally but in vain the already established $13 million federal contract, echoing the well-financed anti-housing campaign in the basin under the Committee Against Socialist Housing, aptly called CASH and led by a savings and loan president and one of the Fund's early donors, Joseph Crail.

Smith's gambling peccadillo aside, and except for the oil leasing concession and the abortive attack on Los Angeles public housing, by the summer of 1952 Nixon could point to an impressive and consistent representation of his patrons' interests, maintaining and extending crucial financial arrangements in which government alternately subsidized or countenanced their gathering profits in the boom. He would have cast the same votes without the Fund, his supporters later claimed. But that did not account for dropping in the hopper a tailored special-interest bill like the Camp Roberts oil leasing or the extracurricular zeal of his work on other oil votes and the legally futile fight against public housing.

It was also true, as Nixon passionately argued later, that the Fund did not go simply or directly to some personal enrichment or merely onto the Senate payroll, where the more than $18,000 might have paid for three or four added stenographers and typists to divide the correspondence. In their general promotion of their "salesman," as Dana Smith called him, the basin contributors had reckoned on higher stakes and invested in something beyond a senator's goodwill or greater congressional office efficiency, something more tangible in 1951 and the early months of 1952 than the hugely promising but still unrealized national potential of Richard Nixon. They had purchased the security of their own growing control over the California colossus of the 1950s. When his Senate votes and favors were tallied, it would be clear that the Fund was never so much about a senator's income as about the continued wealth of his patrons, about the gift Dick Nixon could and would give back in return for the subsidies: power.

As in the House, his critics would see a puzzling lack of conventional pattern in his Senate votes, "the flexibility that suggests an almost total indifference to policy," wrote Richard Rovere. In fact, his record overall, like his faithfulness to the Fund donors, was again remarkably of a kind. He would be no more active legislatively as a senator than as a representative, cosponsoring some thirty bills, introducing thirty private relief acts and only thirteen measures of his own, none of them memorable. He voted to reduce funds for soil conservation, flood control, and highways; against supplemental plants for the Tennessee Valley Authority, as part of a near-total rejection of public power projects; against price ceilings on scarce agricultural products; in favor of price-control increases to reflect "necessary and unavoidable" costs; for abolition of the Depression-era Reconstruction Finance Corporation; in favor of more money to check "wetback" migration. He supported Alaskan and Hawaiian statehood and opposed the poll tax, though he was also one of three senators on the Labor and Public Welfare Committee voting to keep the major civil rights legislation of the Eighty-second Congress "bottled up in committee," as one writer recorded it.

In foreign affairs, he stood with only a small handful of Republicans against cuts in economic aid and was a supporter of NATO, of emergency relief to Yugoslavia, and of the pivotal commitment of U.S. troops to European defense. Yet he would also cosponsor the controversial Bricker Amendment sharply limiting the Executive's Constitutional treaty power, oppose further ground troops for Europe without mandatory Presidential consultation with Congress, limit the money spent for nonstrategic humanitarian aid under Point Four, and vote in effect to cripple reciprocal trade agreements. Characteristically, he cosponsored a bill for an unconditional grant of wheat to ward off mass starvation in India, then retreated to make the shipments half loan, and finally voted without comment or question for famine relief with credits dependent on an Indian agreement to provide the U.S. with strategic materials, an utter reversal of the intent of the original legislation he had introduced.

It was the annals of an orthodox, often deeply conservative Republican senator whose qualified internationalism—a natural corollary, after all, of his domestic anticommunism—set him apart from the GOP right more in appearance than in reality. His occasional and publicized defiance of the party majority on foreign aid, against an already vestigial delaying action by the Taft wing, masked an otherwise comfortable partisanship. Only slightly less than in the previous Congress, Richard Nixon voted in straight party unity with the conservative-dominated Capitol Hill GOP 70 percent of the time in the Eighty-second Congress and supported nearly 90 percent of measures with broad bipartisan backing. One survey of the sessions judged his domestic votes if not his international stands a sign of "remarkably tightfisted illiberality."

But then back in California, there were always elements of his own constituency, like the Senate opponents to foreign aid, who lent the record a semblance of liberalism. Watching the Labor Committee, Keith McCormac was appalled by Nixon's time-honored practice of voting out bills that might mollify his own union supporters from the 1950 race and then relying on right-wing Republicans and Southern Democrats on the Senate floor or even the House to kill the unwanted measures. "Look, Murray, listen, what's this guy doing back there?" McCormac remembered asking Chotiner in mid-May 1951. "Why, Keith, we never counted Nixon as a *conservative*," Chotiner told him. And McCormac had answered bitterly, "Well, you sure suckered us."

The Nixons' personal fortunes prospered along with the political. Soon after the beginning of the term, they bought a new $41,000 house at Forty-eighth and Tilden in Spring Valley, a fashionable area of Northwest Washington. In May 1951 they sold the Honeysuckle Lane home in Whittier for a profit of $4,000. With that money and the sale of their war bonds—paying what Nixon described to Herman Perry as "a very substantial down payment" of $20,600 and $145 mortgage installments—they moved into the newly built two-story residence in July. For the seven rooms, including a third bedroom for the inevitable sojourns of Frank and Hannah, Pat Nixon hired an interior decorator and indulged her own tastes for the first time. Following an adage learned long ago as a Bullock's salesgirl, she mirrored a living room wall for a sense of expansiveness and chose for the rest what one visiting reporter described later as a "bright California look with its cheerful aqua walls, peacock blue draperies and a touch of spring green in furniture covering." In the master bedroom a Washington artist was commissioned to paint what Julie would remember sprouting on the wall behind her parents' blue-quilt-covered bed as "a graceful, free-floating tree in shades of green and blue." The new house also came with a less airy backdrop, one of Spring Valley's restrictive covenants barring resale, rental, or any other conveyance to "any person of the Semitic race, blood or origin." The deed carefully defined "Semites" as embracing "Armenians, Jews, Hebrews, Persians, and Syrians," though an added agreement between buyer and developer did not exclude "partial occupancy of the premises by domestic servants," origins notwithstanding.

By March 1952 they had purchased for Frank and Hannah another Whittier house on Anaconda off the Boulevard, the parents' California residence in addition to Menges Farm and a Florida house. On top of his $12,500 Senate salary, their 1951 tax return would show over $7,000 additional income, most of it from the speeches. As usual there was a new car, now a 1950 Oldsmobile from the Whittier dealership of college classmate Clint Harris. By June 1952 William Rogers, now in a prestigious private law practice in Washington, was writing his friend Dick Nixon about submitting the young senator's application to Kenwood Country Club, another exclusive, all-white presence in the affluent Maryland suburbs of the Capital. "I am sure you will have word very soon," Rogers assured him, obtaining a guest card for Nixon in the meantime before they both left for the Republican National Convention.

After barely eighteen months in the Senate, they lived a comfortable, upper-middle-class existence in Washington, free to spend the margins of the extra speech honoraria as well as the $12,500 Senate salary, money that without the Fund would have been almost certainly eaten away by the expenses of his restless politicking in California and elsewhere. In terms of personal finance, the subsidies from Dana Smith's Pasadena account both absorbed ongoing political costs and provided as it were a kind of job security and career insurance. In the controversy that broke later over the Fund, Nixon was said to have even admitted to a friendly Washington reporter that without the subsidies he would not have been able to buy his new home in Washington. Acknowledged or not, like the law office sinecure and the little stucco cottage in 1945–46, like the interim donations of 1947–48, like the ample, eventually lavish financing of his House and Senate campaigns, the Fund made possible a politics of affluence without personal wealth or sacrifice, made possible the down payments, property, and pretense otherwise well beyond their means.

Outwardly, it seemed idyllic, the popular and outspoken young Californian, his wife decorating their new white brick home, tending two young daughters while active in the Senate Ladies, wearing their Red Cross nursing caps and rolling bandages every Tuesday. The tensions were not far from the surface. *Frontier* reported Nixon at mid-1952 a humorless, grinding politican "almost hermitlike in his association with others . . . not a man who seeks out personalities and cultivates them either for his own aggrandizement or education . . . a man who hasn't a single crony in the Senate or House," and with no "time-filling pastimes . . . no hobbies." While partisan, the description reflected much of what his closest associates had seen as well.

Soon after moving into the new house and only a few months in the Senate, Nixon developed what his daughter later described as "severe back and neck pains." After trying several physicians and being told the problem was extreme tension, he sought out Arnold Hutschnecker, a Manhattan internist specializing in psychosomatic medicine and author of *The Will to Live*, a popular small volume on motivation and psychic health that former Senator Sheridan Downey, still ulcer-ridden and now Long Beach's oil lobbyist, had presented to Nixon when it was published earlier that year. By his own description, Dr. Hutschnecker would deal with "the emotional conditions" of his patients—"the misery, tension, the unhappiness." Of his book Nixon would later say casually, "I liked it and looked the doctor up." Beginning now at the outset of his Senate term, the visits to Hutschnecker's Park Avenue office were to continue with frequency for four years, ending only under the threat of public exposure and political embarrassment.

Tense and solitary, he also began at this same juncture other personal relationships of future moment. As GOP aide Bryce Harlow told the story afterward, George Smathers, the Florida congressman and later senator following the scurrilous 1950 race against Claude Pepper, had once seen Nixon at a Republican stag party on the Hill. Dick looked stiff and forlorn amid the comradery, much as his old Yorba Linda playmates had once seen him sitting in disconsolate loneliness at a Fullerton High football banquet. Known around the Capitol as "The Collector," a gregarious, handsome charmer with his own considerable network of interests in Florida, Smathers had "taken on" Dick, urging him relentlessly to take an impulsive vacation in Florida. Nixon did go, alone, in December 1951, met at the train by Dick Danner, whom Smathers had introduced to him in Washington in 1947, a former FBI agent, city manager of Miami, and campaign aide of Smathers, now running his own Ford dealership in Vero Beach.

"Dick is on the verge of a physical breakdown. We're all concerned about him," Smathers had telephoned Danner from Washington that December, and Danner remembered Nixon looking like a "northern hick" getting off the train in winter clothes. After three days in Vero Beach at the Driftwood Hotel, they had visited a Miami osteopath, and Danner called an old Florida friend, Charles "Bebe" Rebozo, to arrange a cruise. "Bebe, get your boat and meet us at the doctor's office," Danner remembered ordering. The three men went out around Miami Bay, and the senator obviously liked the dark, taciturn Rebozo, the beginning of yet another historic friendship. "I remember all too well how you met 'the congressman' [sic] . . . dressed in a heavy winter suit in the middle of the Miami heat," a friend later wrote Danner. "You took him to buy clothes, and held his hand during his most difficult days. I also know . . . how much influence Bebe can have on that ex-congressman."

On his return, Nixon wrote Danner effusively in January 1952: "Words cannot express my deep appreciation for all the many courtesies that you and members of your organization extended to me during my visit to Florida." He would "report to George," Nixon added, "how very well you handle visiting firemen. . . . I still hope, incidentally, that we can eventually set up that party out at the Yacht Club!" The visit yielded, too, a local clipping from the Vero Beach paper, which Smathers passed to his colleague, showing "U.S. Senator Bob Nixon" outside the Driftwood, casually, atypically dressed in sport jacket and open-collared shirt. "See you were traveling under an assumed name down there," Smathers wrote him playfully.

For the Florida senator, it was one more acquisition in a group of friends and Miami Beach vacationers he would squire for exclusive retreats and stag parties and which would include not only some of his most powerful

Senate colleagues but also three consecutive future Presidents: John Kennedy, Lyndon Johnson—and Richard Nixon. For Bebe Rebozo it was the beginning of an extraordinary relationship that would take him from obscure if enterprising Miami businessman at the end of 1951 to honored guest at the next Presidential inaugural a year later, and eventually to White House confidant. In the hurried trip was the first small seed of a controversial Florida connection that was to both enrich and haunt Richard Nixon in the years ahead.

Yet at the moment all that remained hidden, to unfold as a result of the remarkable events of 1952. Not even the shrewd, cultivating Smathers could have guessed that the "hick" senator they consoled and entertained in Vero Beach, and sent back to Washington so impressed and grateful, would suddenly emerge over the next few months by dint of singular effort and design as one of the most prominent figures in American politics—and remain so for a generation.

20

Positioning,
May 1951–June 1952

y the summer of 1951, there was
no question of Richard Nixon's larger ambition, only of the channel it
would take. Already uneasy and impatient with the pace and power of the
Senate yet emboldened at the reception given his speech tours and Washington statements, he sent Chotiner around California at the end of June.
The circuit was not only to accompany Smith and Brennan on replenishing
the Fund but also to take advance political soundings, "to acquaint the
key fellows in Dick's campaign with his plans," as Chotiner wrote one of
them, "and to exchange ideas on how Dick can render even greater service
to the people of California."

As usual, the revolt against Earl Warren roiled within the state GOP.
They should "put the governor on the spot" for endorsements of 1952
Republican candidates, Herman Perry typically wrote Nixon at the time.
Otherwise, their titular leader "does not have any honorable reason to
expect support from members of the party." Chotiner's talks in Fresno,
San Diego, and elsewhere were carefully circumspect. But with Warren as
despised as ever by the right and thought unwilling to run for a fourth term
in any case, some of the Nixon men came away that summer with the sense
that the thirty-eight-year-old senator was ready even now to go after the
statehouse next, one more expected threshold, one more race in a permanent campaign toward ultimate office. "I honestly believe Dick . . . had
his ambitions set on being elected governor in 1954," one of them would
say later, "and then making his run for the national ticket about 1960." But
that more modest, still ambitious timetable did not reckon with the historic
opportunities already opening before him in the 1952 Presidential election,

nor with his own extraordinary exploitation of the unfolding politics, his irrepressible calculus and drive.

Young and fresh, hard-working and politically gifted, on the wave of California's new national power, he was seen as a postwar internationalist yet domestic conservative, and a seemingly moderate leader of the anti-communist purge. Richard Nixon came to the Senate in many ways a logical choice as the Republican Vice-Presidential nominee, a complement to the older men of other views, other regions and forces, who were striving for the Presidential nomination. The same summer Chotiner made his reconnaissance in California—nearly a year to the week before the GOP convention and long before his name was publicly mentioned for the office— a remarkable secret gathering of powerful men of both wings of the party, men representing both leading Republican contenders for the White House, would in effect hand-pick Senator Richard Nixon for the Vice Presidency. Other rites of selection and passage, private and public, would follow, until it seemed in looking back that his emergence and nomination were natural, effortless, ineluctable.

Yet the GOP Presidential or Vice-Presidential choice in 1952 was by no means preordained or settled even by the eve of the convention. There was a third man in the race for President as well as another formidable Vice-Presidential contender, both from California, either of whom could have blocked his rise, and changed the history of postwar politics. How Richard Nixon threaded his way among all these rivals and factions, preserving both his anointment and his options in California and on the national stage, was one of the great, largely unseen prodigies of political positioning—a brilliant, audacious, sometimes reckless maneuver that would affect his life for better and for worse long into the future.

The Republican Presidential field began with Dewey's vindicated rival after the disaster of 1948, Senator Robert Alphonso Taft. Now sixty-two, the son of a President and Chief Justice, he was the heir apparent and early favorite to restore the GOP nomination, and probably the White House, to the old guard. "The Tafts were Ohio, American, aristocracy, and the Taft boys went to Yale," as one writer summed up his provenance. "They were men of intellect and property and respected both." It would be Bob Taft's tragedy that the respect was not returned by many of his own kind. Henry Cabot Lodge, Jr., a fellow senator of similarly famous lineage, saw him with the mixed regard and condescension typical of the more moderate, largely eastern wing of the GOP. "An extremely likable and honorable man," Lodge conceded, "but whose views seemed to be wrong for the times."

The views in question were never so simple as either his rivals or right-wing votaries pretended. Beneath the antiunion strictures of Taft-Hartley and the loathing of big government was an abiding social conscience that struggled to find creative new programs for decent housing or health care. The other side of his cautionary isolationism was a shrewd suspicion of self-defeating entanglement with foreign tyranny and a rare sense of the base Soviet weakness, of U.S. bullying and provocation in the infant Cold War. And through it all ran a stolid adherence to principle, leaving him to stand on the Senate floor—misunderstood, vilified, nearly alone—condemning the grimly popular Nuremberg Trials as a travesty of *ex post facto* law and prosecution. After Taft's failed bids for the nomination in 1940 and 1948, one hardened reporter concluded there was not "a fiber of demagoguery in him . . . a rare combination of ability, courage, courtesy, and integrity seldom encountered in politics or anywhere else for that matter."

Yet the dignity and rectitude of Taft the statesman could become a lethal aloofness and indifference in the Presidential candidate. Looking out owlishly through rimless glasses, speaking in a flat midwestern timbre, he commanded no personal charisma and remained, despite a life in elective politics, painfully brusque, impulsive, and irascible, often oblivious to perquisite and pride in a profession in which each eclipsed substance. He was a gentle, private man, coming home early from political meetings in 1951–52 to read to his wife, Martha, lately crippled by a stroke, tenderly pushing her along in a wheelchair to state dinners and then cutting up her food and feeding her. It was the very lack of a comparable sensibility in politics—sometimes as much his manner as his positions—that clouded Taft's long-expected inheritance of the GOP nomination. He had offended Earl Warren sorely by neglecting to meet the Vice-Presidential campaign train coming through Cincinnati in 1948, and he bore Tom Dewey's perpetual contempt. "How in the world can I placate Mr. Dewey?" Taft implored his advisers in 1951. It was a question without answer, the toll of too many old clashes, real or imagined, and another precondition of Richard Nixon's rise.

Nixon himself saw Taft on the verge of the campaign as "very proud and very shy . . . shy and stiff." Like much of official Washington, he witnessed and recounted the affecting scenes of the GOP leader gently feeding a paralyzed wife, though he was ultimately more impressed by the Taft political disability. He would "never forget" seeing Bob Taft on the campaign trail in New England, he wrote later, rigidly refusing in front of a television camera to give some little girl his autograph, and yet stopping to explain to her—"with devastating reasonableness," Nixon thought—how hand-shaking took less time from a busy schedule than signing his name. Taft's "abrasive personality," he concluded, "would be a serious disadvantage in a Presidential campaign."

He had decided, too, that "Mr. Republican," as the senator was respectfully known, mistook the central issue of their era. At a McKinley Day Dinner in Ohio in 1950, Nixon had spoken about "the threat of communism at home and abroad," and Taft followed with an admonition about the still "greater" peril of socialism in America. "What concerned me was his failure to recognize that many socialists were dedicated anti-communists," Nixon said later, remembering that speech with a scruple that would have surprised many of his California foes. "The major threat we faced was not socialism, but communist subversion supported by the international communist movement, and Taft's failure to understand this distinction raised questions in my mind about his grasp of the whole international situation."

At the time, when the front-runner quietly sought his backing early in the race, he did not openly refuse. Taft's envoy was Tom Shroyer, an author of Taft-Hartley who knew Nixon both from the House and as staff director of the Labor and Public Welfare Committee in the Senate. They would talk several times, the young senator respectful if a bit reserved. "I thought he was quite sympathetic in our first conferences during the latter part of 1951," Shroyer remembered. "Nixon liked Taft, but he did seem to have a few doubts about Taft's chances to win." As the courtship went on, Nixon appeared to soften even his private estimate of the candidate. "I don't say Taft can't win," he said to friends in a remark later leaked to a Washington reporter, "but I do say I am not sure he can win."

It was a distinction without meaning in his own larger calculus. From the beginning it would be clear that Bob Taft was not merely a stuffy campaigner of questionable views but also far closer and more compatible with California's other senator, who was widely expected to wield the West's new power in a Taft regime and even be its Vice President. "His most ardent supporter," Nixon tersely noted, "was Bill Knowland, my senior colleague." Now, as Nixon talked sympathetically to Tom Shroyer in 1951, he was already about the delicate secret process of joining Taft's principal rival, all the while mollifying and temporizing with a conservative constituency that was at once his strength and nemesis—and doing everything he safely could to thwart both Taft and Knowland.

The man who barred Taft's easy succession to the nomination and who provided Richard Nixon his historic alternative, was the nation's lingering hero of World War II, Dwight David Eisenhower. A year younger than Taft, he seemed all that the old guard leader was not—virile, magnetic, a soldier of easy charm, above political ambition. An admiring columnist later catalogued the wholesome personal aura that drew so many to this ruddy, bald, reassuring figure with penetrating blue eyes. "His manner is genial . . . his smile is attractively pensive, his frequent grin is infectious, his laughter ready and hearty," Arthur Krock wrote of him. "He fairly radiates goodness, simple faith, and the honest, industrious background of his heritage." It was typical of the public imagery. It was also the genuine but beguiling outer face of a far more sophisticated, calculating leader than most imagined, in truth one of the masterful politicians of the century.

He was raised the third of six boys in a tiny white farmhouse near the railroad tracks in Abilene, a small frontier town left behind at the windswept center of the Kansas prairie. Like Frank Nixon, his first political memory was of William McKinley, six-year-old Ike carrying his coal-oil torch in a fiery, smoky parade against Bryan and the Democrats in 1896. And like Richard in Yorba Linda, he heard the locomotive whistles in the country stillness and dreamed of becoming a conductor, of getting out. After an ordinary start at West Point and missing a combat command in World War I, he seemed relegated to a series of unrewarding staff assignments. "He was obscure, unknown, and unremarkable," one biographer observed of his career in the torpor of the interwar army. Then, suddenly, he was rescued from oblivion by Pearl Harbor and a summons to assist the chief of staff.

Under George Marshall's astute patronage the rest became familiar history—"P. D. Eisenhauer," as a White House usher recorded his first visit to the West Wing in 1942, rising from lieutenant colonel to four-star general in less than two years, Supreme Commander of the Western Allies, postwar chief of staff, president of Columbia University, and in 1950 back to the command of a fledgling NATO. When it was over, the Presidency itself would seem only another step, "like a continuation of all I've been doing since July, '41," he entered in his diary after the first day in the Oval Office, "—even before that." In fact, even the staff exiles of the twenties and thirties had provided their preparation—"study and self-discipline over many a superficially empty year," as one historian put it—and not least an impressive schooling in the military-industrial nexus that would loom so large in postwar America. (In one of the curious, small intersecting paths of Richard Nixon's world, Eisenhower in the early thirties had served on the U.S. War Policies Commission, an inquiry into munitions production and procurement that led to the Nye Committee and in turn to Alger Hiss's consequential lunches with a snaggletoothed writer named Chambers.)

Eisenhower's was, above all, a political education, if not in party mores or elective campaigns then in the art and artifice of leadership and in the habits of government, from the crucial middle levels of bureaucracy to the prickly interplay among heads of state and general staffs. That the politics were learned in and of the army made the lesson, and the practitioner, no less formidable. The likable Ike—his ease casually mistaken for a certain shallowness—was relentlessly serious, intelligent, a gifted operator now open and earnest, now ingratiatingly indirect and cunning. "A man who shaped events with such subtlety that he left others thinking they were the architects of those events," explained a correspondent who watched him navigate so shrewdly the Grand Alliance. "And he was satisfied to leave it that way." With the acquired and instinctive skills went, too, a self-assurance, a sense of emotional security and intellectual conviction, a pride and ambition all so tested and embedded that he came to wear them, like his officer's bearing, effortlessly, almost invisibly, regardless of the outer appearance.

Democrats, including California's James Roosevelt and Helen Douglas, had courted him before the 1948 campaign, knowing little more of his real political views than anyone else. He thought their party "a mixture of extremes on the right, extremes on the left, with political chicanery and expedience shot through the whole business." Like Taft, he came to call the New Deal "socialistic," though, wholly unlike his rival, saw himself as a "militant liberal," beyond ideology or crass partisanship. "There is no difference between the two great parties," he wrote on New Year's Day 1950, at a moment when Richard Nixon was beginning in such partisan earnest his run against Helen Douglas. "I belong to neither." Yet his imminent Republicanism and Presidential candidacy—both appearing the inspiration of citizen impulse—were hardly spontaneous. Ike the political adept as nonpolitical would be nurtured and brought to that natural "continuation of all I've been doing" by a remarkable group of wealthy and powerful businessmen, a kind of political cartel cornering the market for their popular general. His heralded citizen campaign would be born of one of the most accomplished and remorseless machines in American political history.

"If the American people want me, they know where to find me," he once snapped at reporters besieging him during a NATO tour. His postwar career was one of constant disavowal of any interest in the Presidency, and constant preparation for the run, an omen of what one student of his private papers would call "America's most covert President." He quietly despised the more primitive reactionary tycoons of the GOP—including some who backed Richard Nixon—and a few of those who had listened skeptically to his speech that summer of 1950 by the lake at Bohemian Grove. "There is a tiny splinter group," he once wrote his brother Edgar about those who wanted to abolish Social Security or labor laws. "Among them are H. L. Hunt . . . a few Texas oil millionaires, and an occasional politician or businessman from other areas . . . and they are stupid."

Yet he harbored a ready affinity for more modern men of finance and corporate power. Eisenhower's own financial circumstances were comfortable enough with the pension and perquisites of a five-star general: "in 1949 . . . a very grand $18,761 in base pay," as one historian described it, along with money for quarters, a $5,000 "personal allowance" and free medical care, all in perpetuity regardless of other employment or income. But the men of industrial or banking fortunes commanded truly vast and decisive resources and a politics seemingly more subtle and elevated than the jostling of government and the army. "They impressed him," wrote biographer Blanche Wiesen Cook, "with their erudition, their easy use of power . . . the efficiency of their style . . . their selfless attitude toward public events." As he eagerly wrote a friend about his first invitation to Bohemian Grove with its society of the commercially rich and famous, "I am truly anxious to go."

He both sought and accepted their inseparable personal and political enlistment. Beginning in earnest after Dewey's defeat in 1948, his correspondence and calendar brimmed with an elite group. At the core were men like William Robinson, vice president of the *New York Herald Tribune* and president of Coca-Cola; Henry Luce; Clifford Roberts, president of Reynolds & Company; Philip Ried, chairman of General Electric; W. Alton Jones of Cities Service Oil; Texas oil magnate Sid Richardson, and others. They alternately stocked him with steaks and smoked turkey, investment tips and stock holdings, outlets for writing or even greater publicity, a clipping service and intelligence bureau, and, above all, political advice and more influential corporate contacts. All but anonymous, a financier with reach throughout American business, New York investment banker Edward Bermingham arranged a series of stag parties for Ike, where the companies of the "invitees," concluded one observer, "read like excerpts from lists of *Fortune*'s annual 500"—Pullman, Montgomery Ward, International Harvester, Quaker Oats, Sears, Roebuck, the Santa Fe Railroad, Maytag, Swift meat packing. Behind, still more discreet than Bermingham, were Winthrop Aldrich of Chase National Bank, Thomas Parkinson of Equitable Life Assurance, and Thomas Watson of International Business Machines, figures who secured Eisenhower his civilian interlude in the presidency of Columbia University and who among them dispensed the great political proxies of the nation's vast industrial and banking dynasties, Rockefeller, Mellon, and Morgan.

The general's shadow promoters were to be historically important not only in sculpting his views—increasingly conservative and orthodox in domestic affairs alongside a Russophobic internationalism—but also to reinforce the conviction he carried into the ring: Dwight David Eisenhower would emerge as a genuinely consensual nominee and leader, the first since George Washington, at once in the midst yet above politics. "You might have the spectacle of someone being named by common consent rather than by the voice and manipulations of politicians," he confidentially wrote an old army colleague after the war, adding pointedly, "so-called drafts . . . have been carefully nurtured, with the full even though undercover support of the 'victim.' " No idle pretense, it would be fundamental to how Eisenhower saw himself and others.

Ultimately, no other factor would more easily draw him to Richard Nixon or more sharply set them apart. He would be the great soldier nicely balanced on the ticket by the young politician, the leader above politics who also, as a matter of root and character and calling, was above his partisan deputy. Yet Eisenhower was disconcerted by traits in others that mirrored his own, notably ambition and maneuver. In Nixon he would see some measure of himself. Both came well promoted by powerful patronage, by hard work, loyalty, intellect, yet with a fierce vestige of independence. Ike sensed early that common tempering and strength, and, when the time and necessity came, moved to preempt the contest.

His crypto-candidacy had begun with a quiet and characteristic act of hubris. About to leave for the NATO command, he told aides he was summoning Taft to his Pentagon office, and if the senator were wholly in support of the Alliance, Eisenhower would declare himself "forever, and beyond any question, out of the political scene." With his own matching sense of gravity, Taft demurred. "He repeated his refusal to make the point clear, and so finally we parted," Eisenhower wrote in his diary, "and, of course, I did not go through the part of my plan that would have depended upon his affirmative reply." The general left for Europe at the beginning of 1951, to return seventeen months later as a candidate for the GOP nomination.

"I COULDN'T THINK OF A BETTER PROSPECT THAN NIXON"

Nixon had seen him five times before, in a sense across the gamut of the two men and their evolving roles. He had been an obscure officer looking down on the triumphant general in a Manhattan tickertape victory parade, again a watching bystander when Ike marched as a celebrity in General John Pershing's funeral cortege in 1948, closer still when the general briefed Nixon and other congressmen on European affairs. Then came his own secret, personal visit to Eisenhower in the Hiss case arranged by Alfred Kohlberg in 1949 and, in the summer of 1950, at Bohemian Grove watching Ike's auditioning speech before he took the NATO command. In the spring of 1951 Nixon was invited to attend a World Health Conference in Geneva, and he seized the chance to see Eisenhower again in another private meeting. He filed a formal request through channels but also asked backstage help from Frank Carlson, a Kansas senator openly promoting Eisenhower's candidacy. Nixon would interrupt his Geneva schedule "any day the week May 14–20 inclusive," read the official cable request, "at his [the Supreme Commander's] convenience."

They met in Paris on the morning of May 18, 1951, against the backdrop of political paradox. Nixon was fresh from a speech to the Ohio Bar Association extolling Douglas MacArthur's "personal victory" over Truman despite the recall. For his part, Eisenhower was privately dismayed at the still surging popularity of MacArthur and his Taft allies—an angry coalition of isolationists and chauvinists in which Nixon had been, after all, an outspoken participant. In contrast to his visitor, and on the stern advice of his somewhat unnerved backers, the general was trying diligently not to be drawn into the political turbulence back home, to "maintain silence," as Ike promised one of them, "in every language known to man."

Not for the last time they slid past the apparent contradictions in their politics and style. If Eisenhower was now in any measure aware of Nixon's part in the MacArthur outcry or of the war policies advocated by the senator, his current exhange of briefings and correspondence with the shadow backers, usually studded with such details, did not reveal it. Nor would he and many of his men know, then or even later, the inner substance and reality of the young Republican's campaigns and political derivation in California. Again, from the beginning, it was part of Nixon's gravity with the general and the special politics of his emergence that he occupied a relative blind spot in Eisenhower's sophistication and experience. It seems to have been enough that May morning in Paris that Carlson had identified the West Coast senator as a supporter of NATO and that Eisenhower knew him casually from earlier meetings. The Supreme Commander was glad to lobby for continuing votes as well as to court in the process another GOP politician.

Erect and vital and "impeccably tailored," as Nixon remembered him in his trademark "Eisenhower jacket," he now rose from his desk to greet the senator and motioned him to a large sofa at the end of the office for a more informal talk. He spoke "optimistically," Nixon thought, about Western European rearmament and recovery and the success of his mission. "What we need over here and what we need in the states is more optimism in order to combat the defeatist attitude that too many people seem to have," Eisenhower told him. More important, he also echoed Nixon's themes of economic and ideological warfare, their shared adoption of the emerging Cold War consensus of the early 1950s—that the U.S. must not only build a military preponderance at home and abroad but also wage an unprecedented struggle of money and politics against the Soviet threat. "Being strong militarily just isn't enough in the kind of battle we are fighting now," Nixon recorded Eisenhower as saying in their sofa talk. The observation particularly "impressed me," he wrote long afterward in his memoirs, "because, then as now, it was unusual to hear a military man emphasize the importance of nonmilitary strength." In the small passing exchange was a seed of a new era in American foreign policy, when the international penetration of U.S. business and commerce, Washington's psychological warfare, and covert intelligence intervention by the United States would reach a zenith and when the general and senator now discussing the "battle" in abstract would preside over it all.

In addition to their agreement on the Cold War, Eisenhower had one other significant sense of the senator. "He carefully steered away from American politics," Nixon noted, "but it was clear he had done his homework." Ike mentioned that he had read *Seeds of Treason* by de Toledano and Lasky and was struck by the authors' admiring portrait of Nixon in the Hiss case. "The thing that most impressed me was that you not only got Hiss, but you got him fairly," Eisenhower said. It was yet another precept of his unfolding ideology and politics. The Carnegie Endowment trustee once sympathetic to Alger Hiss had come to see communism as a menace at home and abroad even beyond his habitual repugnance at the Russians. Yet Eisenhower would always proudly distinguish himself from the Red-baiting craze of the era by a fine disdain for demagogic rhetoric and practices. And he would carry to the end the fixed assumption that Richard Nixon shared this as well. "The feature that especially appealed to me was the reputation that Congressman Nixon had achieved for fairness in the investigating process," Eisenhower wrote later. "Not once had he overstepped the limits prescribed by the American sense of fair play or American rules applying to such investigations. He did not persecute or defame. This I greatly admired."

The senator himself was impressed in Paris "not [by] the substance of Eisenhower's conversation so much as his manner," and thought it "easy" to see the general's skills in foreign policy and as leader of an alliance. He felt "in the presence of a genuine statesman," Eisenhower "by far the most qualified of the potential Presidential candidates." He wrote afterward: "I came away convinced that he should be the next President. I also decided that if he ran for the nomination I would do everything I could to help him get it." But there was something else in the charming, impeccable soldier that the shrewd younger man saw, too: the flicker of the inner stoniness and ultimate distance that was to shape their relationship as much as any policy or mentality. "A warm smile and icy blue eyes," Nixon wrote more candidly after the general was gone. "Beneath his captivating personal appearance was a lot of finely tempered hard steel . . . exceptional warmth but . . . always a reserve, even an aloofness." He thought Eisenhower imbued with "a very definite sense of dignity . . . not the kind of man who appreciated undue familiarity."

While in Paris, Nixon also met with Washington's patrician ambassador, David K. E. Bruce; with one of Eisenhower's closest friends and advisers, General Alfred Gruenther; and with American union leaders as well, including Victor Reuther, assigned to the U.S. mission to mobilize European labor against communist infiltration. Back on the floor of the Senate, he was cautiously discreet about the visit. "I had a very interesting experience . . . when I sat in the office of General Eisenhower in Paris. I was impressed . . . with the excellent job he is doing against monumental odds. . . . He pointed out to me that one of the greatest tasks which he has at the present time is to convince our allies abroad of the necessity of putting first things first." To the *Los Angeles Times* Nixon was far more fulsome, saying he was "much encouraged" by the general's achievements, including a "lessening of political influence" by communists in forthcoming French and Italian elections and a new "will to resist" among Europeans. At the same time he left to Arnold the more delicate task of commenting on the general's Presidential plans. "Nixon also received the impression that Eisenhower would accept a U.S. offer to run for President in 1952," the *Times* reported, quoting "an aide," "although the senator was unable to determine whether the Supreme Commander would plump for the Republicans or the Democrats."

Four days after his return from Paris, Nixon was telling a meeting of GOP leaders in West Virginia that 1952 would be "the last chance for power for the Republican party." The election could be won only by "a constructive program" that emphasized "winning the ideological war with communism" and methods "on a scale far greater than any we have ever contemplated before." In Paris, meanwhile, Eisenhower was complaining to one of his backers about the train of visiting " 'big shots' who came to tell him what his duty was," not something the respectful Senator Nixon had done. It was always unclear at precisely what moment the thought of their ticket first dawned, at least with the general. When a steel company lobbyist and Republican fund-raiser visited Eisenhower around the same time in 1951, Ike confided a list of possible running mates, though his own candidacy was still months from its own careful consummation. "They're no good," the lobbyist had said of the list. "General, you have to carry California. So the only man, of course, is Nixon."

On the weekend of June 23–24, 1951, Nixon was one of a small group of GOP senators and congressmen invited to a secret meeting at the Clarksboro, New Jersey, estate of Amos Peasley, a wealthy Mormon who had been a backer of Harold Stassen in 1948. Instigated by the Eisenhower camp, the purpose of the gathering was to launch Stassen himself as "a stalking horse" against Taft in the early Republican primaries the following winter. It was to be "the delaying action for Eisenhower," remembered Bernard Shanley, the Newark lawyer and GOP national committeeman assigned to oversee the task.

At the center of the Eisenhower strategy, Tom Dewey took a typically unsentimental view of Stassen's role—"useful as a counterirritant," he thought his old rival and the GOP's unredeemed prodigal son, "even though nobody else in our group trusts him." As it was, they made Stassen sign a formal statement of principle at Clarksboro to be tucked away in Shanley's safe and stipulating "that Stassen would not be a candidate vs. Eisenhower for the Republican nomination" and "that if Eisenhower became an active candidate Stassen intended to support him." Along with Nixon were Joe McCarthy, Walter Judd of Minnesota, Stassen manager Warren Burger, and others from the 1948 campaign, a strange group secretly forming around a phantom candidacy. Yet there would be no doubt, etched in the veritable contract signed by the mercurial Stassen, that Richard Nixon was, from the Clarksboro weekend, part of a concerted effort to make Dwight Eisenhower the next President.

Four days after Clarksboro, Nixon made in effect a first speech of the veiled campaign, a keynote address by radio from Washington to a Young Republican national convention in Boston. "We have lost 600 million people to the communists in six years," he said, repeating the familiar arithmetic of the postwar crisis. They must put on a "fighting, rocking, socking campaign . . . cut all nondefense expenditures right down to the bone . . . recognize the existence of the fifth column in this country." Above all, Republicans ought to spend less time fighting one another and "more time fighting the enemy." They must choose a candidate "who can best sell our program to most people."

A more decisive sequel came three weeks later, once again at Bohemian Grove. Ellis Slater, a liquor industry executive and one of Eisenhower's longtime and closest friends among his business patrons, attended the midsummer "Hijinks" of the Grove. "A strange blend of boyish pantheism, tribal self-congratulation, artistic dalliance, and amateur pageantry," one writer said of the annual ceremony. Another witness called it more simply an adult "jamboree, saturated with sunshine, whiskey, and tycoons." In the private forest north of San Francisco Taft had already made a ritual speech earlier in 1951, and Slater noted with satisfaction the cool reception in late July to a similar address by General Albert Wedemeyer promoting Taft.

Soon after his arrival Slater went to "Cave Man," the camp of Herbert

Hoover, where he found "the Chief," as Hoover was known throughout the Grove, along with Clarence Buddington Kelland, the author of Richard Nixon's favorite boyhood books and now an influential GOP conservative from Arizona. Kelland had written in 1950 the "Declaration of Principles," an official party credo that had reduced the essential American issues to "liberty versus socialism" and condemned social and economic legislation since the New Deal so harshly and categorically as to provoke the outright public rejection of Dewey and other moderates. After "two or three drinks," as the visitor noted in his diary, they asked Slater to make the case for Eisenhower's nomination. "Even though Taft was a great man, and the foremost Republican, I did not believe the Republicans could even elect a dogcatcher," he later recorded. "It was imperative that the Republican candidate be able to swing a high percentage of the independent voters as well as the dissident Democrats." It was the primary and ultimate Eisenhower argument and now countered by Hoover and Kelland as "a defeatist attitude." But Slater, known for the "Slats" and "Ike" intimacy of his relationship with Eisenhower, made an impact and, equally important, was accepted among the powerful patrons of the Grove as an Eisenhower confidant and envoy, representative of the general's own views.

After a week in the forest camps, a group of twenty, including major figures from California business, adjourned to San Francisco for a private luncheon with Slater on Saturday, July 28, 1951. The scene was the "club-house" of the parent Bohemian Club, a stately six-story building near the city's financial district. They met off the main reading room, which "looks like it was developed," wrote a visitor, "from one of the traditional clubmen cartoons in *The New Yorker* . . . little statues on pedestals and tables, high vaulted ceilings, a plush Oriental rug." When Slater had again expounded on the general's decisive popularity, "the conversation got around to a discussion of a possible running mate for Eisenhower." As he wrote that night, "Knowland and Nixon were apparently on the minds of the Californians." Slater had instantly satisfied their regional ambition and given an unequivocal choice. The Hiss case was the edge over Knowland.

> I went on to say I couldn't think of a better prospect than Nixon and I remember giving these reasons: He was young and would therefore attract the youth vote; he had military experience; he would probably carry California (without which a candidate might not be elected); he was experienced in both the House and the Senate; but, most of all, if it had not been for Nixon, Hiss would not have been in jail, and since communism was bound to be a major issue in the campaign coming up in '52, Nixon

would attract all of the anticommunist vote which would
be substantial enough to win the election.

This time Slater recorded not even *pro forma* dissent from the Hoover
old guard. On Sunday he was on a plane back to New York and four days
afterward lunching and golfing with Dwight Eisenhower on the outskirts
of Paris, where he carefully briefed the general on his talks at the Bohemian
Grove and Club. A year before the GOP convention, the meeting had in
effect certified Richard Nixon at once as a conservative nominee for Vice
President acceptable to Eisenhower and as the Eisenhower selection from
among the choices of both the old guard and California power. There had
been no doubt about the gravity of the secret exchanges. "They would
have to be quite careful," Slater entered in his diary what he had told
Hoover and Kelland and the others from the beginning, "because I would
be reporting their conversations back to Eisenhower."

Still, by the autumn of 1951 Taft remained well ahead in early polls of
likely convention delegates. He was solidly in control of both the National
Committee and convention offices, while the Eisenhower campaign, its
candidate still loftily demurring in Paris, seemed problematical. In October
Pennsylvania senator James Duff pried from the general a private admission
of his Republicanism and willingness to accept a draft ("No man who is
an American can refuse nomination to the highest office in the land"). But
it was Duff's old rival and Taft's unappeasable nemesis, Thomas Dewey,
who now took over the backstage direction of the candidacy, and with it
Richard Nixon's future as well. From secret meetings in Dewey's old
headquarters in the Roosevelt Hotel, they settled on Henry Cabot Lodge
as campaign manager with the new Eisenhower headquarters nearby in
Manhattan at the Commodore. "And don't forget," Dewey reminded them
after an early meeting, "let's get a hell of a lot of money." With John Hay
Whitney and other backers as well as Dewey's own considerable New York
financial network, they would raise some $4 million over the ensuing
months, making it then, even before the presence of a formally declared
candidate, the richest prenomination campaign in American political history.

So, too, there were prominent, well-placed men among the small initial
advisory group drawn up around Lodge: General Lucius Clay, perhaps
Eisenhower's closest adviser from the war years; Senators Harry Darby and
Frank Carlson of Kansas; former California executive and Marshall Plan
administrator Paul Hoffman; and Dewey's campaign manager from 1944
and 1948, Herbert Brownell, the New York lawyer whose "gentle, reason-

able manner, and studious appearance," thought Lodge, "concealed tremendous energy and . . . formidable ability." Yet the inner rivalries and weaknesses of the circle taxed even Dewey's imposing machinery. Clay, an old army engineer and supposedly the coordinator and diplomat, charged by Ike "to keep everybody feeling good," operated from what one of them saw as "deep-set dark eyes and devastating frankness." In their numbers they soon saw Lodge, the Boston Brahmin, as a "lightweight" of unjustified pretense and authority, "doing his best," one banker remarked acidly, "with the tools he possesses." Lodge made Brownell "squirm," wrote Clay, who shared the sensation.

The ebullient Hoffman from Pasadena entered "like a hurricane," Clay cautioned Ike, and "likes to be the bridegroom at each wedding, the corpse at every funeral." As for Harold Stassen, their "stalking horse" who privately pledged himself "1000 percent," Clay thought him an "enigma," and like Dewey noted that "no one, I repeat no one . . . trusts him fully," a judgment that turned out to be prescient. They were also compelled to shield the frailty of their legendary semi-candidate. When a pro-Taft journalist seemed close to obtaining a copy of General George Patton's diary—with vivid and documented passages on Eisenhower's wartime infatuation with his British chauffeur, Kay Summersby—Senator Lodge moved swiftly to secure a suitable political appointment for the lawyer of General Patton's widow, and the embarrassing diary entries remained hidden.

By the end of 1951, however, Dewey was drawing a coy Eisenhower toward candidacy and the campaign into uneasy coherence. By then, too, a historic alliance with Richard Nixon was already being forged. On the eve of Eisenhower's long-awaited declaration, an enthusiast had tried heavy-handedly to coerce the governor of California into supporting the general, and Dewey quickly sent one of his trusted aides to California "to soothe Earl Warren's bruised feelings." There was far more than sensibility and protocol behind Dewey's concern. The looming struggle between Taft and Eisenhower, and the potential for deadlock, gave all the more impetus to Warren's own dark-horse, third-man candidacy for the Republican nomination. They would not challenge Warren's proud command of the California delegation as a favorite son, though the state must be denied to Taft and the convention votes pulled to Eisenhower if and when they were needed. To tolerate or even seem to endorse Warren's candidacy while effectively subverting it, to block Taft in California without openly alienating the state's volatile and wealthy right wing—all that would be the subtle and demanding politics before them. And for the task they would have the decisive covert help of the general's running-mate-in-waiting.

Richard Nixon was to be a " 'fifth column' assigned to undermine Warren's position within his own delegation," remembered Bill Pfeiffer, an intimate in the early strategy sessions at the Roosevelt and Dewey's New York State GOP chairman. Nixon was not only to balance the unruly California forces but to maintain his own original credibility and acceptance with the old guard that was his vital cachet as a prospective running mate at Bohemian Grove. The senator's liaison for the mission was to be Maxwell Rabb, Lodge's former Senate aide now ensconced at the Commodore. Nixon's public statements and speeches were to be monitored by Ab Herman, Dewey's man on the Republican National Committee; as early as October 1951, Herman began to appear on Nixon's distribution list along with the usual favored journalists. Nor was there any dispute about the reward, already broached by Ellis Slater at the Bohemian Club. "Long before anyone had given serious thought to Nixon as a Vice-Presidential possibility on an Eisenhower ticket," Herb Klein acknowledged afterward, "Chotiner had discussed the question with Governor Thomas Dewey and Herbert Brownell."

The political battle lines behind which Richard Nixon would operate were formed early and sharply in California.

With characteristic independence, Earl Warren had refused to criticize Truman in the firing of MacArthur and "broke all ten of the Republican commandments," noted one journalist, by even praising Dean Acheson at the 1951 signing of the Japanese Peace Treaty in San Francisco. At the same time, Warren went out of his way to denounce both McCarthyism and the emerging GOP southern strategy, calling the rampant Red-baiting "not the American way of doing things" and dismissing Karl Mundt's alliance with the racist Democrats as a "disgraceful thing," violating "every civil rights principle the Republican Party has stood for since the days of Lincoln." As if to complete the cycle there was even a swipe at Richard Nixon and the current senatorial craze with Truman scandals, which required, the governor would say, a "powerful floodlight of . . . aroused public opinion," not "the measly flashlight of an occasional investigation."

In the early autumn of 1951, Warren had returned from a trip to the East knowing that powerful forces in the internationalist and business wings of the party were committed to Eisenhower. The preference was not only a result of the general's popularity or Tom Dewey's distaste for his old running mate—"years of rivalry . . . many moments of pique," as one reporter saw it—but genuine alarm at Warren's progressive bent on issues such as utilities and public power, regulation of corporate practices, health insurance, and civil rights. "They wanted a man in the White House who would not turn many leaves forward," wrote Leo Katcher, who as a West Coast correspondent watched the rejection. Nonetheless, Warren had decided on the fight, a bid for the Presidency to cap his career, at least to stop Taft and perhaps give him weight with a new Republican administration. Later, his many critics would charge Earl Warren with a rotten bargain for Eisenhower patronage as early as that trip of autumn 1951, though there would be no documentation of any real deal on either side—and then and later much evidence of an almost fatalistic, bitter seriousness in his run. "He knew what the odds were . . . was too good a politician not to know," said his old friend Edward Shattuck, "but he felt he could beat them—and he never gave up."

The visible odds in California soon took shape in the perennial heaving rebellion of the right and plans to run another slate in the 1952 primary to deny Earl Warren the state delegation. With Knowland bound to Warren by old family loyalties, the pro-Taft forces had quietly turned first to their seemingly natural leader and counterpoint to the governor, Dick Nixon. Chotiner met with a deputation of the conservatives on June 29, 1951, in Fresno to gauge their strength and intentions, "a meeting called where Nixon was supposedly going to tell us what he was going to do for us," one of them described it. "Nixon, we felt, would go along with us," Keith McCormac remembered them believing after the Fresno meetings.

For a time, Nixon even appeared to be edging toward a public break with the governor and possible leadership of an insurgent delegation. Many Republicans feared that Warren as a Presidential candidate "would follow his usual tactics in California and try to go it on an every-man-for-himself program," Nixon told the *San Francisco Call Bulletin* in early August. He evoked his own deep resentment from past races. "They want a candidate who will go all-out for the party, sink or swim." But then Chotiner and Nixon both held back. When the rightists came into the open with an anti-Warren gesture—a resolution at a Young Republican convention in early October opposing "nomination of any Presidential candidate who has a reputation of having given ground to creeping socialism"—Holt, Hillings, and other Nixon men swiftly combined with moderates to defeat it. It was to be typical of the skillful Nixon tactics—privately sympathetic and publicly ambiguous, careful to stop short of any overt schism with Warren.

Days after the YR convention, a group of the conservatives met in secret at San Francisco's Palace Hotel, a first step toward fielding their own delegate slate. Promptly leaked to the *Chronicle* and McClatchy papers, the move hastened Warren's own timetable and in a sense flushed the junior senator. On November 7, Nixon was enlisted with Knowland, five GOP congressmen, and a number of state officeholders and party officials in an open telegram to Warren. The cable extolled the governor's "high sense of integrity and public duty . . . your extraordinary accomplishments—an exceptional . . . respect and confidence of the people of your own state," and went on to "urge that you declare your intention to seek the Republican nomination for President." Part of Warren's orchestrated announcement, a matter of Nixon signing words drafted in the governor's office, the telegram was a bitter pill in Senate suite 341. Bill Arnold remembered how much, even in 1951, Nixon still blamed Warren not only for the California slights but also, wrongly, for muffling the Red-baiting in the 1948 race and thus for the Republican defeat. But he had no choice if he were to avoid a break, Dewey's shrewd dictum.

Still, when Warren formally declared his candidacy on November 14, Nixon was subdued and "somewhat cautious," as the *Los Angeles Times* noted. There were many "good men" mentioned for the GOP nomination and "certainly Earl Warren is one of them." The next day at a press conference back in the basin at the Ambassador, he was far more considered. During a recent speaking tour he had found Warren with "surprisingly large support at the grass roots." After front-runners Taft and Eisenhower, the governor was "the strongest dark horse," and, if nominated, Warren should "win handily" over Truman or any other Democrat. People felt the governor "completely honest" and "electable by virtue of his warmth, his personality, and his family." And then a careful rebuke: "But actually the country does not know too much of where he stands . . . he lacks strength among the people who nominate outside of California. This may be partly because of his reputation for liberalism—which certainly would help him if he is nominated—and partly because the Republicans want a fighting drive. They want someone who will hit and hit hard on major issues."

As for Eisenhower, the senator thought "he has hurt himself some . . . has been playing it a little too coy and people are beginning to lose some of their enthusiasm. . . . I feel he will have to make his move . . . but there's no doubt as to whether he would be a vote-getter."

The weekend following Warren's declaration, the GOP State Central Committee met in San Diego, expecting a formal endorsement of the governor. But anti-Warren forces were able to hold off any action, another sign of the primary struggle to come. Angrily, McCormac and Lloyd Wright, a Los Angeles lawyer and Taftite, cornered Nixon in the old U.S. Grant Hotel in San Diego and "put the heat" on him, one of them remembered. Nixon had been telling Wright and other rebels he would be in their delegation. Then came the obsequious wire to Warren. "And he was evasive," as McCormac told the story, "and said that he had to do it and that sort of thing, for the unity of the party and that kind of garbage." They pressured him again to break with Warren, not to join the governor's slate. Even then, Nixon assured them. "Why are you guys so upset?" he had said. "Well, don't worry, if I'm on this [Warren] delegation I'll be for Taft."

For Warren, the sequel to his announcement was anguishing. Almost immediately he was forced into the hospital with what was officially explained as an emergency appendectomy but was in fact major surgery for abdominal cancer. As his physicians predicted, his recovery would be complete. But the actual illness soon leaked to anti-Warren doctors in the American Medical Association, and Taft backers promptly spread word the governor was dying of a malignancy. A special "hate sheet" was circulated in California with the same report. "You don't have to be concerned about Warren. I know the doctors who operated on him," Herbert Hoover told a dinner of ranking Republicans that autumn. "They opened him up, took a look, and sewed him up again." So personal were the attacks that they soon enveloped the Warren family as well. "I took a strong dislike to a dog named Fala, and I'm afraid I might take a strong dislike to teddy bears or honey bears or what have you," one of the rebels said to cheerful applause at one meeting. "Honey Bear" was the well-known family name for the governor's daughter, Nina, still crippled from a recent attack of polio.

The insurgents were a roll call of the right-wing forces behind Nixon in 1950 and earlier. On the executive board of their "Independent Republican Delegation Committee" sat C. Arnholt Smith, the San Diego banker and developer who had financed much of the race against Douglas in the south. Others included Jack D'Aule; John Barcome, the former Los Angeles County chairman instrumental in 1946; actor Adolphe Menjou; Genevieve Blaisdell; oilman William Keck; and State Senator Jack Tenney of the Sacramento Legislature's own Un-American Activities Committee. When it was clear Nixon would not lead their rival delegation, they had tried in vain to get Herbert Hoover, General MacArthur, even former House Speaker Joe Martin, whose agreement to reversion of the tidelands had endeared him to California oil.

The choice finally fixed on a less famous but ideologically certified congressman from Bakersfield, Thomas Werdel, whose politics would be aptly summarized in his run in 1956 as a Vice-Presidential candidate alongside T. Coleman Andrews in the segregationist States' Rights Party. Financed by Louis B. Mayer, the Associated Farmers, and similar forces, they represented the accumulated enemies of Earl Warren's singular governorship, "every special interest to which he has refused to bow," observed the *Daily News*, "every unhappy politician who didn't get what he wanted, and all the right-wingers of California." They were almost unanimously for Taft, though many would have preferred the imperious MacArthur, and they could interest neither in campaigning for them against Warren. The other GOP contender they despised in the old animus of West versus East. "When you mentioned Eisenhower," McCormac recorded, "you might as well have talked about Joe Stalin. . . . They formulated . . . that Eisenhower was a product of the international bankers, per se."

It was now Richard Nixon's political genius that he maneuvered to secure his flank with the right-wing rebels despite his nominal backing of Warren, and even to use his influence to undercut Taft as well as the governor. In the weeks following Warren's announcement, Nixon would manage to convince not only the insurgents that he was secretly for Taft, but even Knowland, whose own genuine preference for Taft and Vice-Presidential ambition were not far beneath the surface of his tribal loyalty to Earl Warren. "Warren didn't understand that Nixon was also working with Taft forces," one of the insurgents would say. In the same vein, McCormac remembered, "Nixon was conveying to Knowland that he was for Taft. And then he was conveying to the other people he was for Ike. . . . But he [Knowland] didn't grasp the situation as to what Nixon was going to do to him. See, he believed that Nixon was an honorable man."

Meanwhile, Dick's own men helpfully moved in and about the Werdel forces, Pat Hillings being privy to the insurgents' tactics and finance and reporting promptly to Nixon. Grass-roots organizations of the Werdel delegation campaign were penetrated by Nixon campaign people at the town and county levels. In Whittier, typically, Aubrey Wardman and Herman Perry oversaw funding of the rebels, while Harold Lutz, Talbert Moorhead, and others were active in the organization. Only later did Keith McCormac and others see how pervasive the Nixon infiltration had been, how easily Bill Keck or Jack D'Aule could have reported back to Chotiner or Nixon on the weekly strategy sessions in Keck's office. There were so many of the senator's loyalists and potential informers in the camp of the rival delegation that, as one of them would say, "Nixon was in the position that he couldn't lose either way."

So also, as Taft told his supporters in California, the Ohio senator now "had assurances from Nixon . . . that Nixon would be for Taft," as a member of the Werdel group remembered. In December 1951 Taft vacillated fatefully about campaigning more aggressively in California. In the end, he would decide to hold back, believing Knowland's secret assurances of future support in the state—themselves based in part on Nixon's confidences to Knowland—and in some measure on Nixon's own private pledges. In vain McCormac and a handful of other conservatives tried to educate the front-runner in the twists and savagery of California politics. "But we still couldn't . . . we couldn't get Taft over to the idea that Nixon was going to cut his throat," one said afterward. "He believed, because Nixon had told him all along, that Nixon would be for Taft . . . so, actually, California was where Taft lost out."

It was by any odds a complex, convoluted game, played out in shifting twilight loyalties. By the end of the year Richard Nixon had seduced and infiltrated the anti-Warren rebels, yet so properly remained publicly loyal and self-effacing toward the governor that his own conservative patrons fretted at the apparent debasement. "Hardly a day goes by but what I come across one of our enthusiastic supporters with whom I have to argue and reason relative to your present posture," Herman Perry wrote, chiding him about his public support for Warren, adding in a plaintive postscript, *"You must not take* a modest position." Nixon reported back reassuringly on December 12 on yet another gambit: "I had an hour with MacArthur and another hour with Hoover when I was in New York on Friday. As you can imagine, the conversations were extremely interesting."

At the same time, though Nixon did not vouchsafe it to Perry or others at home, Harold Stassen had returned from a visit to Eisenhower in Paris, concluding that the general might not run after all, and that his own "stalking horse" candidacy might be more serious than he had contracted for at Clarksboro. In a December meeting in the Senate office, he first approached Nixon about the Vice Presidency in return for Stassen support in the California delegation. To complete the tangled skein, that same December Dana Smith would become fully active as the main fund-raiser for Eisenhower in southern California and arrange a secret meeting between Nixon and Paul Hoffman of the general's inner circle.

Few saw or even sensed the intricate machinations and balancing. J. A. Smith and Keith McCormac of the Werdel campaign could not judge by year's end which men to trust in their own inner group. Yet the Nixon compromise of their faction was still so effective that they were all but alone in the certainty that the senator with his furtive oaths and compacts was playing some double or triple game in the struggle against Earl Warren. "We decided that Nixon was welching," McCormac remembered, and that "we'd better go about our rat-killing in some other manner."

"BOY! FROM NOW ON PLAY IT CLOSE TO YOUR VEST"

Richard Nixon began 1952, the pivotal year of his political life, in the treacherous undercurrents of Republican politics. Not knowing of Stassen's rekindled ambition or the dangling of the Vice Presidency before the California senator, Stassen manager Bernard Shanley wrote Nixon on January 10 a "very confidential" letter about heartening private poll results in their supposedly "stalking horse" campaign for Eisenhower. "Harold leads Taft at almost exactly a sixty-forty basis," Shanley reported cheerfully from the Wisconsin primary, valuable intelligence on the softness of Taft support if not Stassen's strength. Nixon now continued the intensive schedule of national speeches, more than thirty in the first four months of 1952. Again in Boston in January he called for a "fighting campaign" and a "new policy to meet . . . issues," an implicit rebuke of Taft's conservatism. Before a Manufacturers Association gathering in Philadelphia a month later, he appealed for party unity and deplored the sharpening Taft attacks against Eisenhower. It was a kind of epitaph on what the Democrats had done in the California Senate race of 1950. "If we don't quit fighting each other we will find that all of our top candidates are softened up to the point that any one of them . . . will be a pushover."

At the same time, as always, he and his men were alarmed at any question about his pose. When a Los Angeles paper referred even in passing to rumors that Nixon was sympathetic to Eisenhower, Perry nervously tried to run down the leak with Dana Smith and the Eisenhower campaign in southern California and worried in the same breath that Nixon not appear too pro-Warren either. "Personally, I have taken no one into my confidence except Tom [Bewley]," he wrote Dick January 16. "I think it is all the more important that you take a strong position and exert your influence [vis-à-vis Warren] without tipping your hand." As if on cue, Nixon followed with a speaking tour of California in February. He gave another mild endorsement of Warren in Fresno, in San Francisco exhorted Eisenhower to join the race, and in a Lincoln Day address in Los Angeles charged the GOP to "convince the nation they are worthy to govern and that illegal or unethical practices will not be tolerated." Back in Washington, he deplored the rumors that Earl Warren had entered the race as part of some "hope" for a cabinet or Supreme Court post but admitted off the record that he "had only reluctantly joined the state GOP group which urged Warren to declare his candidacy." In any case, he told the *Times* and other papers February 21, there were no ulterior motives or secret allegiances in his support of the governor. "It is my understanding, and I am sure that Earl Warren will confirm this, that none of the Warren delegates will be pledged to any other candidate as their second choice."

By the end of March, with Eisenhower still at his Paris headquarters hanging back from the race, Nixon supporters worried anew that the strategy—and the Vice Presidency—might be fading. "I am convinced if Eisenhower is not the Republican candidate, it could easily be MacArthur for President and Bob Taft for Vice President," one of them wrote him. Herman Perry added March 26, "I would also suggest that you play your cards very close to your vest because Taft might not accept the second spot."

The advice still fresh, the senator left for Hawaii in early April to speak at a GOP fund-raiser and for a long-promised vacation with his wife. He even invited along the Drowns as a surprise for Pat, and the two couples spent ten days at Honolulu's Surfrider Hotel, taking hula lessons and nighttime swims. "It was the last carefree vacation I ever had," Pat Nixon would wistfully tell her daughter.

But the politics that made her lament were never really absent. "That'll be Ike's and the GOP's big test," he told the $100-a-plate dinner in Honolulu, confiding that the "general's boosters in Washington are confident Ike will return from Europe . . . in June." He "favors" Warren, he told the island's press. The governor of California might hold "one hundred votes and the balance of power" at the convention. Until then Warren's position was to "smile sweetly at both sides." He also talked more intimately about his own visit to Eisenhower a year before. "Ike," the *Hilo Tribune Herald* reported of his impression, "had been bitten badly by the Presidential bug" and seemed certain to run. On his return to the mainland in mid-April, Nixon was still urging Eisenhower on, telling the *Los Angeles Times* the general should "change his mind" and come home. "He owes it to his party to state his views before the nominations are made." In Sacramento at another fund-raiser he told Republicans their Presidential nominee would need "the support of Democrats by the millions," an obvious Eisenhower strength. Warren, he conceded in a news conference afterward, had "tremendous appeal" to Democrats but was "suspect among Republican leaders in the midwestern and eastern states."

Watching his old candidate thread his way and almost cheerlead an Eisenhower return, Roy Crocker thought it clear that Nixon now supported the general, whatever his public pretense to be a Warren loyalist. By the close of April, however, the senator may have had his own doubts. "I believe Warren and MacArthur are the strongest dark horses at the moment," he wrote Roy Day almost disconsolately on April 22. It was a judgment that gave all the more urgency to his efforts to subvert Earl Warren, stave off yet preserve his constituency on the right, and promote Dwight Eisenhower, all in the few crucial months left before the Chicago convention.

Nixon's interlude of uncertainty that spring reflected the deeper drift in the Eisenhower campaign. In February 1952, Clay privately pressed the general to return, and the business boosters put on a showy if vapid rally in Madison Square Garden. Thirty thousand streamed in after the boxing matches late on a cold winter night to hear political speeches and watch a woman tennis professional bat balls into the audience. Shown films of the crowd's devotion at their residence outside Paris, Ike and his wife, Mamie, had been deeply moved, to the point of "a sniffle once or twice," a witness reported. Yet even the flowing eastern money momentarily ran thin when Ike still did not return in the last crucial days before the New Hampshire primary. Clay was forced to raise emergency funds among Texas oilmen, a resort that further mortgaged the campaign and its future. Despite absentee victories in New Hampshire and an impressively staged Minnesota write-in ("Certainly, it was not gremlins who wrote his name on all those ballots," Dewey would quip), despite beating Taft by nearly 400,000 votes in a half-dozen primaries, the general seemed mired in his majestic wait for consensus.

His politician's patience exhausted, Tom Dewey eventually fired off a hand-written note to Paris, predicting that without Eisenhower the GOP might turn to Douglas MacArthur. It was the ultimate goad. "The best clerk who ever served under me," MacArthur once said of Ike, while the latter thought MacArthur himself something of a temperamental, theatrical fraud who "likes his bootlickers." Clay had even told him after the recall in 1951 that MacArthur remained "what you and I have always thought, which makes him most vindictive." The specter of his old army superior and adversary finally stirred Eisenhower to commitment. While Nixon was still in Hawaii that April, Ike privately prepared to relinquish his command and join the race at last. In a sense, the same right-wing MacArthur potential Nixon and his men had anxiously reckoned earlier in March now revived both the stalled Eisenhower draft and Richard Nixon's own prospects.

Meanwhile, in California Nixon exerted to make the most of his uneasy public presence in the Warren camp. Once more his advisers peppered him with urgings about his prerogatives and chances for tactical advantage. Brennan, Perry, and Kyle Palmer jointly deplored "the way they have pushed Dick around" for support against the insurgents, though the governor's admirers regarded the junior senator, as one of them said later, "certainly no better than neutral." If Warren's slate won the primary, Perry insisted, "it will be on account of your presence in the delegation. Don't let Murray or Bernie *kid you about this fact. It is not to* [sic] *late to drive a bargain*. You must not let them take that delegation away from you."

Along with the other Warren delegates, Nixon would sign on March 22 the legal pledge of loyalty required by the California Election Code: "I, Richard Nixon personally prefer Earl Warren as nominee of my political party for President . . . and hereby declare I shall, to the best of my judgment and ability, support Earl Warren." Before signing, however, he privately assured his men that there was no real alternative "in view of the fact that the Warren delegation was pretty sure to win," and that he had "insisted that we have people . . . not . . . particularly pro-Warren either as delegates or alternates." Perry at one point replied grandly and ruefully that Dick Nixon might even have been considered as a Presidential contender himself, "if you had not been tied down to Warren's coattails." By then, however, Nixon had already begun a more subtle and far-reaching tactic to "drive a bargain" of the kind Perry would ultimately approve if never fully appreciate.

At the first discussions of a Warren slate, the junior senator had tersely declined to be a delegate, knowing his absence would be conspicuous in the Warren ranks. Knowland was sent to implore him to join. After several conversations the price became clear. "It took considerable arm-twisting to get him to agree, and, when he did agree," a California reporter wrote later, "it was with the understanding that he would have a say in helping to make up the delegation." As he had promised his skeptical advisers, Nixon would be able to select at least twenty-three of the seventy delegates. "It was to give Nixon a place on our delegation . . . and to have him satisfied with his place," Warren himself later explained. In early spring it was a seemingly obscure agreement to appease a wavering, status-conscious politician. In the summer heat of Chicago, it was to be a fateful surrender.

His leverage over selection of the delegation traced to Warren's struggles as a dark horse and the mounting force and bitterness of the California insurgency with which Nixon was still quietly colluding. While Eisenhower continued to hesitate, Warren had decided to campaign actively for the May Wisconsin primary against both Taft and Stassen, though the burden in Sacramento left only weekends for flying trips to Milwaukee or the Dells. It was a more liberal Republican constituency. But even there, Warren was dogged by the immense Eisenhower popularity waiting impatiently to be released. "Would it help Eisenhower more if we voted for Stassen or for you?" a man in Beloit asked him. And Earl Warren, sixty-one, white-haired, seeing himself as a front for no force or man, drew up his bearlike frame and answered, "I am immodest enough to say I think any Wisconsin voter would serve his best interests if he voted for me."

He flew back to California to face attacks from the right of mounting ferocity. The slate fielded behind Congressman Werdel, openly studded with Nixon backers from 1950, was now financed by a million dollars raised mainly from oil and agribusiness and in the din of a doomsday, dead-end rhetoric. "We want to give a chance for all who want to vote against this atheistic, materialistic, socialistic program now in force," Werdel said typically at a Los Angeles rally. "This is their chance to do something about it, and if they don't do it, then God help us!"

Repelled by the personal as well as public assaults on Warren, backing his Presidential candidacy in any case in unabashed California chauvinism, even the *Times* rallied to the governor. "Despite honest disagreement," Kyle Palmer would write, "[the paper] reiterates its unreserved confidence in the governor's integrity, his exceptional administrative ability and . . .

his general qualifications for the Presidency of the United States." For similar reasons, a group of establishment conservatives—and Nixon backers as well—had come together under Preston Hotchkis at the California Club to raise the relatively modest $90,000 the Warren slate budgeted for the south, figures like Asa Call and Norman Chandler, Willard Keith and Neil Petrie. But even these moneyed elders of the southern GOP would then be personally rejected and vilified by the Werdel campaign, showing the depth of the right-wing animus, much of it outside the basin in the Valley and farther south to San Diego, centers, too, of Nixon strength. "I don't think I've ever been in a campaign," Hotchkis would say, "where every member of the [finance] committee took so much abuse."

Watching the venomous civil war from his special vantage point—wanting Earl Warren weakened and undermined, though not to the point of actual defeat by what would be Taft or MacArthur delegates—Nixon publicly appealed for party unity. "We are in imminent danger of throwing this election away by engaging in bitter recrimination and counterrecrimination between factions," he wrote out in laborious, somewhat jerky longhand, apparently on a plane back to the state early that spring. "I urge that all our contestants . . . before it is too late . . . give each this assurance: I am out to beat you and win our party's nomination, but if I fail, brother, I am with you all the way to November. For the sake of our country, our state, and our party, one of us is needed in Washington to help put an end to communism, crime, and corruption." At the same time, Jack D'Aule, from the 1950 Senate campaign and now instrumental in the Werdel group, was quietly dickering with Herman Perry for at least *sub rosa* support. "I am of the opinion that we in Whittier should not carry on an aggressive campaign against the Knowland-Nixon-Warren group . . . due to our personal respect for Dick," Perry wrote D'Aule May 2 with a copy air-mailed to Nixon. "However . . . if the elections were today and the voters of Whittier decided the winner, the Werdel group, I am sure, would be the chosen delegates." Their double game would continue throughout the primary.

"If you have to make a talk in California before [the primary] 6/3/52 (and God forbid)," Perry wrote him about the treacherous politics at the beginning of May, "don't mention the name of Warren." Nixon quickly assured him that "I do not intend to make any more speeches in California until after the primary." And then added: "Incidentally, I am going to speak before the New York State Republican Convention [*sic*] at the Waldorf Thursday night." The Manhattan speech was anything but incidental in his own calculations, a crucial part of more preconvention positioning with the Eisenhower camp while he cautiously turned away from the vicious delegation fight in California.

He met Paul Hoffman yet again that spring to assess the race on the coast. But it was another friend and patron whose lobbying reinforced his earlier enlistment as the Eisenhower "fifth column" in return for the Vice Presidency. Bert Andrews of the *Herald Tribune* now made his reappearance and continued to promote Nixon with both Hoffman and Dewey, selling him, said one of Andrews's fellow journalists, as "an up-and-coming young senator who could give a boost to foreign aid and who would be effective in stirring up anticommunist ammunition." When Dewey asked Nixon to address the New York State GOP's annual $100-a-plate dinner, it was in the wake of a carefully engineered Eisenhower victory in the New York primary in April and a purge of almost all but Dewey loyalists in the state delegation. The speech was a further audition before powerful New Yorkers who would be at the core of Eisenhower strength and strategy at the Chicago convention only two months later. Although it was familiar campaign rhetoric of the kind he had delivered often, Nixon put aside all other Senate and political work for an entire week of preparation, composing and memorizing outline after outline to fit the speech into the half-hour live radio broadcast Dewey had purchased. "I knew I faced a major test before a highly sophisticated audience," he wrote afterward.

At the Waldorf-Astoria that night, old Dewey rivals and potential Taft supporters found themselves seated well back in the hall behind pillars. Dewey and New York senator Irving Ives spoke briefly and then turned to the young Californian, who was "keyed up for the occasion," as he recalled it. His much-rehearsed performance was delivered without text or notes. They had to put on a "fighting" campaign at this fateful juncture for the party. Their candidate would have to stand firmly on principles yet attract "millions of Democratic and independent voters," a careful formulation for both right and center which he had honed well in California. He now delivered it all flawlessly with obvious energy and zest in contrast to the more subdued Dewey and Ives, ending exactly at twenty-nine minutes, letting the thunderous standing ovation impressively fill the last long minute of the radio broadcast. Ives, a GOP liberal, and conservative congressman John Taber both congratulated Dewey at the same moment Nixon took in the applause at the podium, a kind of symbolic and simultaneous approval of the two wings of the GOP.

When the speaker sat down at last at the head table after the triumph, Dewey with some ceremony pulled the cigarette from his trademark cigarette holder, stamped it out in an ashtray, reached for Nixon's hand, and even put his other arm around him. "That was a terrific speech. Make me a promise. Don't get fat, don't lose your zeal. And you can be President some day." Nixon felt "somewhat embarrassed by the generosity," though he thought the usually understated Dewey "simply indulging in the usual gesture of trying to say something nice to a fellow political practitioner after a major effort." "It was not the first time," he noted as well, "that someone had suggested that I might be Presidential timber."

Only afterward did he conclude that Tom Dewey was not prone to that sort of "political puffing," at least about the Presidency. Later that May evening they had come directly to the political point of the moment. Invited up to Dewey's twenty-fourth-floor suite at the Roosevelt, he met Brownell and longtime Dewey operative Russell Sprague, both charter members of the first secret draft-Eisenhower sessions held with Clay and others at the same hotel. They talked for an hour and a half before Nixon caught his train back to Washington. With little pause, Dewey held out the Vice Presidency, the first face-to-face offer since the nomination had been discussed by Brownell, Chotiner, and others months before. Nixon replied that he would be "greatly honored," as Dewey recounted, and they had sent him off to his train with the arrangement understood, still weeks before Dwight Eisenhower returned to the United States to enter the race.

"A fine speaker," Dewey would say of Nixon, with "a very fine voting record in both the House and Senate, good, intelligent, middle of the road, and at this time it was important to get a senator who knew the world was round." His youth and naval service were important, too, and "most of all," as Dewey remembered their judgment, "he was an extraordinarily intelligent man, fine balance and character." Yet it was also clear that they were always relying on the enthusiastic reports of others, like Andrews, more than their own probe of the Nixon record and politics in California. "Everybody whose opinion I respected said he was an absolute star," Dewey would explain. "So I pretty much made up my mind that this was the fellow."

Dewey's approach put Nixon all the more under what one observer called "a subtle constraint, obliging him to engage in some deft footwork." Whether more or less subtle, his secret ties to the Eisenhower campaign grew broader and stronger through May 1952, and thus the stakes in his California gambit still higher. Two days after the historic chat at the Roosevelt, Brownell pulled him aside at a Gridiron Club dinner in Washington to repeat that he and Dewey had both settled on Nixon as "the best running mate." The senator and Ike were to be the ideal "team," Brownell remembered. "The President, who was experienced on the world scene, running with a young, aggressive fellow who knew the domestic issues and agreed with the President's policies." But the soft-spoken and deliberate New York lawyer had also made clear again the essential bargain—"That

Vice-Presidential lightning could strike," as one Washington correspondent later recounted the episode, "in return for . . . support within the California delegation."

There followed still another private meeting with the inner circle, this time at Washington's Mayflower Hotel and for most of the afternoon with General Clay and one of Dewey's fund-raisers, Harold Talbott, along with Brownell and others. Decades later, Nixon would account for the Mayflower session as a "wide-ranging discussion of foreign and domestic policy" and the advisers' attempt "to get to know me better and to size me up." But it was an unlikely group and moment for such an abstract exercise on the "issues," or even an added audition. Clay's presence, and especially Talbott's, bespoke the paramount subject of present and future campaign financing from California and elsewhere, including potential mutual backers among the great petroleum fortunes of the Southwest. Like the Nixon Senate run of 1950, like Clay's last-minute foray to fund Eisenhower for New Hampshire in February, the GOP Presidential and Vice-Presidential campaigns to come in 1952 were to be generously financed by H. L. Hunt and other prominent oilmen, connections that may well have been coordinated and furthered at the Mayflower.

Before the end of May, Senator Nixon had become not simply one more name for the Vice Presidency whispered about Washington or the hustings, the campaign's time-honored bait to attract disparate ambitions and support. He was, from the Roosevelt and Mayflower, a part of secret and strategic deliberations at which his would-be rivals could only guess. With unfailing instinct for improving his position still further, even for the intramural politics of the eventual regime that was taking shape in the Eisenhower candidacy, he boldly wrote John Foster Dulles in mid-May, enclosing highlights of his Waldorf-Astoria speech. Dulles remained an influential force in the GOP eastern establishment, albeit not a member of the Dewey-Clay inner group. The May letter made sure Dulles understood the senator's rising stock with the other powers in the campaign. It came, too, as part of a continuing Nixon correspondence that periodically and none too subtly reminded the shadow secretary of state of their mutual history in the Hiss case, and of the potential political embarrassment to Dulles in the early Carnegie Endowment ties to Hiss. Nixon would vouch for Dulles with the right if the occasion arose, his letters suggested, and Dulles was well advised to support the senator's ambitions in turn.

Meanwhile, Nixon continued his national speeches, repeating much of the New York address in Detroit on May 17, saying he was pledged to Warren yet unmistakably making the argument for Eisenhower's broad bipartisan appeal. Afterward, on the Senate floor, Henry Cabot Lodge huddled at his desk with the third proffer of the month of the Vice-Presidential nomination under Ike. They would need someone to "hold the line for the general," and "Nixon responded with natural warmth to the notion of being Vice President." This time Lodge told Eisenhower directly about the offer, though there is no evidence to suggest that Dewey, Brownell, or Clay had been so explicit with the general about their own talks with Nixon.

At any rate, Eisenhower at the time blandly approved his manager's approach, was "entirely favorable" by one account. It was characteristic of the campaign that its hesitant hero still in Paris left much of its strategy and tactics, including the politics of selecting a running mate, to his distant political machine. "And the first thing I knew about a . . . Presidential nominee . . . having a great influence on the Vice-Presidential selection was, I think, about the moment I was nominated," Dwight Eisenhower would ruminate some years later. "I said I would not do it [make the selection]. I don't know enough about the things that had been going on in the United States."

"A MORAL OUTRAGE WAS REQUIRED"

While Eisenhower's advisers commissioned Nixon, and even as the general packed for home, the campaign continued to sputter. A Gallup poll at the beginning of May showed Eisenhower leading Taft four to one among independent voters, a decisive margin for the general election and confirmation of Nixon's own argument. Nonetheless, Dewey and his men read with foreboding the less-heralded signs of Taft's tightening grip on the GOP regulars, the party machinery, and thus the nomination. The danger was charted in successive delegate counts that defied the popular vote or independents. By the day Nixon spoke at the Waldorf, Taft led 385 to 282, with 604 needed to nominate. Later in May press estimates gave the Ohio senator a continuing lead of 462 to 389, with potential Taft votes climbing well over five hundred. They must somehow reverse the relentless, largely hidden momentum of delegate politics. "A moral outrage was required," Richard Norton Smith wrote in his brilliant biography of Dewey. They would find it, with rich irony, in Texas.

On May 27, at the Texas State Convention at Mineral Wells, the Taft regulars maneuvered ruthlessly to shut out an influx of Eisenhower backers emerging from an unprecedented attendance at precinct caucuses weeks before. Many of the excluded newcomers were Democrats or independents, obliged to sign a Republican loyalty oath yet assured, too, by their Eisenhower organizers that they could "vote Republican one day, Democratic the next." Both their convention votes and local party control threatened, the Taft forces simply elected their own slate to Chicago, and the Eisenhower camp bolted to put forward a rival delegation.

The result was a small but historic episode of blunder, hypocrisy, and political exploitation. The crusty regulars vilified the Eisenhower supporters as "left-wingers, Reds, New Dealers." Yet the insurgents, led by Dallas oilman Jack Porter, were largely conservative Democrats and Republicans embittered by Truman's stands on racial justice and tidelands oil. "From a civil rights point of view," wrote one liberal reporter, "the Texas Taft delegates might even be preferred to the Eisenhower." At any rate, Brownell and Lodge moved quickly to denounce the Texas "steal" and Taft "dishonesty," the thwarting of "the very basis of free government." They knew well enough the seamy, expedient character of their own Texas support, the deliberate extraparty packing of wealthy Democrats and racists. The leader of the Taft forces they now denounced, Henry Zweifel, had served as Tom Dewey's 1948 campaign manager in Texas. "There was an element of phoniness running through the *cause célèbre*," observed *The Reporter* magazine. "Southern Republicanism has been the skeleton in the GOP closet since well before the turn of the century."

In the days following the Texas imbroglio, Lodge publicly and privately rejected all attempts to compromise this and similar delegation disputes, and Brownell began to marshal a corps of lawyers—among them William Rogers—to mount the major convention struggle over credentials that would turn the tide for Eisenhower. Manhattan advertising firms were mobilized along with the rest of the campaign to sell the issue as democracy and justice versus dictatorship and exclusion. They debated the right name for their challenge amendment to gain the seating of the Eisenhower delegates, and a young Pennsylvania congressman named Hugh Scott would brightly ask, "What about 'fair play'? After all, who could be against fair play?"

Still, they needed the pivotal votes of the favorite-son delegations both to seat their disputed slates and to create the final momentum toward nomination. "Some way had to be found . . . to join with Eisenhower on something," Lodge wrote of the states not yet committed to either Ike or Taft. "That way turned out to be the 'fair play' amendment." Mineral Wells had satisfied one condition of the Eisenhower-Nixon victory. California would provide the other.

The tactic of "fair play" made it not only desirable but imperative that Earl Warren's slate win the California primary and that the result be a delegation that would vote for the climactic Eisenhower amendment when the showdown came. Armed with repeated new assurances and charges from the campaign command, Nixon turned his attention homeward at the end of May and to a primary eve tumult and enmity between Warren and the insurgents unprecedented even in California.

The orders had gone out to the state from the Commodore to back Warren more openly as soon as the Texas maneuvers had been decided. Even before the expected lockout and revolt at Mineral Wells, the southern and northern "Volunteers for Eisenhower," led by Dana Smith, had called simultaneously for a vote for Warren in the June 3 primary, on the announced promise that "at the proper time members of the Warren delegation will give support to General Eisenhower." Yet the Werdel onslaught continued with relentless hostility and ample money evident from billboards to broadcasts. The same day the Eisenhower camp in effect endorsed the governor, novelist and ardent Nixon supporter Kathleen Norris denounced Warren in a statewide radio speech for "those New Deal–Fair Deal–Double Deal policies we hope to eliminate in November."

Battered as never before in public and private, Warren lashed back. "Should it appear that I cannot win the nomination, my delegates shall be released to vote for any candidate of their choice," he told backers in Oakland. But he was a serious, independent candidate for President with "no alliance" to the others, giving lie to "the widespread reports that 'a vote for Warren is a vote for Eisenhower.' " And now in that role he faced "a coalition of hate, backed by enormous sums of money." His right-wing opponents were "scurrilous," "venomous," guilty of "chicanery" and "duplicity," he said in another speech of extraordinary anger and emotion. Erupting was the wrath of all the years of pressure and partisan backroom lobbying that Earl Warren so despised, for which he had thrown Murray Chotiner and others out of the governor's office and for which he was now despised in return. "Never has there been such lavish use of campaign funds in a primary . . . the combined hate and opposition of unworthy seekers of special privilege, of improper immunities, and of unmerited political favors or personal preferment. . . . They have become public enemies to a large and alarming extent."

"The heat is on," Perry wrote Nixon special delivery the weekend of Mineral Wells. He sternly advised him in the acrid California atmosphere not to "make any special statement on behalf of [the] Gov. (the great White Father)." But McCormac saw the junior senator "a little frantic" about the potential Werdel strength, and hurrying to "do something to cut down on that vote." He was right. In a "personal and confidential" note to Perry, Nixon anxiously attached an endorsement he planned for election eve, trying to the end to straddle his conflicting interests. "I think you will agree that the enclosed statement is for the Warren delegation and not for

Warren himself," he wrote. "I don't see how anybody in the Werdel delegation could object to this—particularly since I am a member of the Warren delegation and naturally would be expected to desire the support of the voters."

The statement—issued from the Washington office but quickly picked up and rereleased by Warren headquarters—was a small masterpiece of ambiguity. While indignantly denying that Warren's slate was captive, he managed to hold out the role as kingmaker and at least the implication of an eventual Eisenhower vote in Chicago. "I believe that anyone who knows me and my political career realized I would not have gone on the Warren delegation as a rubber stamp for the governor or any other man, and that is true . . . of the other members of our delegation." With Taft and Eisenhower apparently deadlocked at "slightly over five hundred delegates" each, California "is in a position to name the Republican nominee for President . . . [and] with its seventy votes . . . holds the key to the situation." He was careful to bow to the right. "I know personally Tom Werdel and many of the members of his delegation, and I want to make it clear that I have a great regard and respect for them and the views that they have, but I honestly believe that the Warren delegation is better qualified to represent California." Then the virtual presumption of Warren's failure and promise of support for Eisenhower: "Once Gov. Warren releases the delegation we shall be free to look over the field and select the man best qualified . . . the very strongest possible nominee."

"One would expect a loyal delegate," observed one close reader of the crucial paragraph, "to use the word 'if.' "

His statement pleased the professionals on neither side, "came as close to writing off Warren as it could without actually doing so," thought a pro-Warren journalist, while angering some of the Werdel ranks as well. "I sometimes wonder if the hard work that was done for you . . . to defeat Jerry Voorhis was worth the effort that was put forth," one of the rebels wrote him after hearing "your glowing terms of [sic] Earl Warren." In any case unsure of the public impact at the eleventh hour, his supporters pulled out every stop. A last-moment calling, whispering campaign was launched against some of the insurgent delegates or backers, particularly Los Angeles's growing community of East European émigrés, who were accused of bigotry or worse against Jews. "The Eisenhower forces tended, and the Nixon forces rather tended," McCormac remembered bitterly, "to treat us like we were anti-Semitic."

On June 3, the Warren slate won a comfortable victory of almost two to one statewide, though there were signs too of the power Nixon had both feared and placated on the right. Werdel swept Orange County and the south. Warren's strength was significantly weaker than 1950 in key regions, a loosening at last of his remarkable grip on the California electorate. In the aftermath, Nixon men credited their dodging senator and themselves with much of the governor's victory. Nixon thus extolled Harvey Hancock for "the great job you did for Warren in northern California," adding that if Hancock "hadn't piled up the votes up north . . . the final result would have looked pretty bad." Others thought that "without your support in the final stages . . . Earl Warren would have been left at home." Perry even sent him a hasty longhand note the day after the primary, reporting a "little gossip" that Dick was now to get 30 percent of the Eisenhower campaign funds in California, apparently as a reward.

To Herman and others he wrote back that he was "in substantial agreement" about his own contribution. The Werdel insurgency "may have a salutary effect in that it will convince the top party people that they can't run roughshod over the opposition," and "I think you will agree now that it is much better to be on the inside of the delegation with some power to affect its action rather than on the outside looking in." Of the money, he added: "That rumor about me getting a cut out of the Eisenhower campaign funds is about the best one I have ever heard yet. I could use the money but, unfortunately, no one has offered me such a deal!"

In fact, the problem was not so much the Eisenhower camp's ingratitude or money as a sudden and unexpected by-product of the bitter primary. Along with the convention slate, Bill Knowland had won an impressive reelection by capturing both the GOP and Democratic nominations. "Earl Warren has dim prospects as a compromise candidate in a situation that seems more and more to be a straight Ike-Taft contest," observed *Time*. "California's more promising figure now is Knowland, who has the bark and grain of Vice-Presidential timber." Columnist Doris Fleeson thought Knowland offered "a likely prospect for both Senator Taft and General Eisenhower."

Then forty-four, a man of thick handsomeness, Bill Knowland "could play the part of a Roman senator with no coaching at all," thought one writer. "His enormous outer self-possession may make visitors squirm and fidget . . . but . . . [he is] a man of solid, obstinate honesty." Knowland was not quite yet the "Senator from Formosa," as his critics would caustically label him later for his chauvinism toward the Far East. He had experienced his anticommunist epiphany in a dramatic visit to Chiang Kai-shek's doomed Chungking in 1949, and his domestic politics, like his foreign policy, was moving steadily rightward. Now in the wake of the primary triumph, the shadowy and ubiquitous Paul Hoffman even approached Knowland about the Vice Presidency—though with or without the sanction of Dewey and the others would never be clear. Knowland's characteristic response, as he related it later, was that "he was for Warren, that he would stay with Warren all the way." The rejection promptly turned Hoffman back toward Nixon, though Knowland's new stature remained on the eve of the convention, making his predicted selection by Taft all the more likely—and with lingering prospects in the Eisenhower camp that still threatened Richard Nixon.

In early June there was another brief flurry as twenty of his former House colleagues, including some of the Old Chowder and Marching Society, publicly proposed Nixon as convention keynoter, "a national figure," their telegram called him, with "a reputation as one of the outstanding orators of the Republican Party." It was a futile gesture, if an added fillip to his general prestige. Guy Gabrielson, the Taft national chairman and object of Nixon's earlier attack in the Senate, brusquely ignored the congressional petition and predictably named General MacArthur to deliver the keynote. As it was, Nixon supporters worried that their man might be forced into quite another speech of dubious distinction, nominating or seconding the nomination of Earl Warren. "Bill Knowland is the proper person to do this job," Nixon wrote tersely at mid-June. "I have neither the desire nor the intention of accepting such an assignment." Seeing events move quickly toward Chicago, including some hint of Hoffman's abortive approach to Knowland, Herman Perry fretted again in his fatherly manner, urging that his young protégé simply survive all the crosscurrents, whatever his national ambitions or intrigue. "I believe by proper manipulation," he wrote early in June, "you yet can come through the critical period of the convention without being harmed."

It was in part Knowland's new prominence as a rival, in part another secret meeting with Hoffman early in June, that prompted Nixon to the most risky act of his positioning. On June 11 he sent to one of his California mailing lists of 23,000 Republicans his own poll of Presidential preference. With the Fund exhausted, the mailing went under his Senate frank. A "Dear Friend" letter began with the premise that Warren's candidacy was hopeless. "As you know, Governor Warren has announced that if it should appear that he cannot obtain the nomination he will release the delegates to vote for whoever [sic] they individually feel is best qualified." Ostensibly, Senator Nixon was now asking for guidance. "Consequently, I am writing to a selected group of those who were active in my campaign for election to the Senate for the purpose of obtaining their views on this problem." Respondents were to mark their envelopes POLL for the convenience of the office staff, and "your reply will be for my information only and will be held in confidence." Below a dotted line they were asked to fill out the form:

> From my conversation with other voters and my analysis of all the factors involved, I believe that——is the strongest candidate the Republicans could nominate for President.
>
> (Signature may be withheld if desired)

Well aware of the political explosiveness, he tried to husband the results carefully. "The poll letters are to be kept absolutely confidential," he ordered Marion Budlong a week after the mailing. "I want you to do the counting and give the results to me. No one else in the office should handle these letters and I do not want you to discuss the results with anyone inside or outside the office. I want to make sure there will be no inadvertent leaks and if we have only the two of us working on it I think this can be done."

Whatever his plans, the existence of the poll and reports of a decisive Eisenhower margin over both Warren and Taft were leaking in California within twenty-four hours of his memorandum to Budlong. On June 10, Kyle Palmer wrote an extraordinary and seemingly spontaneous column in the *Times*:

> Some of the eager beavers who are so busily engaged in conjecturing how many ballots Warren will expect them to stay hitched [for] might ponder the significance of Knowland's position and attitude. When Earl Warren's status has been determined one way or the other, Bill Knowland will regard himself as a free agent. And not before. Why am I so sure? Do you know Bill Knowland? If not I can let you in on an important fact: he is an honorable man. He didn't make the pledge to support Earl Warren for President with any shabby reservations. Honorable men don't stab their friends—or enemies— in the back!

It was a solemn and stinging rebuke from his old patron on the irreducible ethic of commitment in California GOP politics, however unbridled the byplay and ambitions. Warren remembered that it was Kyle Palmer, too, who first told him of the poll, leaving the governor "infuriated," as one observer described it in apparent understatement, and his men outraged at the "stab in the back." "I told Palmer that was not consistent with the oath that all the delegates had taken to support my candidacy," Warren wrote in his memoirs. "He expressed the hope that Nixon's announcement [*sic*] would not be published, and as far as I know it was not."

In fact, they summoned Bernie Brennan, who flew urgently to Washington and walked into a Nixon office where Marion Budlong was still counting the largely pro-Eisenhower returns. "I was deeply troubled," Brennan said later, "about the way Nixon and some of his closest associates were working for Eisenhower long before we left for Chicago." While the poll was still in the mails, Brennan had watched Pat Hillings trying to persuade Warren delegates to desert to Ike on the first ballot, telling them, accurately enough, "there's no penalty in the [pledge] law." Now he carried an ultimatum from Warren and Palmer not only to suppress the poll but to stop the other subversion as well. "I warned Nixon that if this group did bolt," his old manager admitted afterward, "he would be finished as a man of honor."

The Brennan mission stayed any outright publication of the poll results, though it came too late for equally telling preliminary leaks to both eastern and California papers. Apparently chastened, Nixon told the Associated Press that it would be "improper" to name a "second choice" for the nomination "until Warren releases the delegation," adding pointedly, "if that time should come." His new discretion brought a long, almost exonerating article from Palmer on the "rumors" about the preferences of the California delegation. Eisenhower might have fifty delegates on release, yet Taft could also have as many as thirty or more. Nixon had taken a private poll, Palmer acknowledged. "But inquiry into that action elicits from the senator not only an unequivocal reaffirmation of his own promise to give Warren his full support 'as long as he feels he has a chance to win,' but an explanation that he is merely trying to pierce the fog caused by conflicting claims of Taft and Eisenhower supporters." The senator in any event "plans to keep the information confidential." Palmer advised the whole delegation to hold its counsel: "A well-kept secret might come in handy" in Chicago.

With the convention less than two weeks away, the storm over the poll seemed past in California and Warren at least mollified for the moment. At Eisenhower headquarters, however, the impact of the whole affair turned out to be well worth the cost. The campaign had seized on both Warren's primary victory and Nixon's furtive poll to spur the nationwide search for delegates and especially to reinforce the maneuvers on "fair play." California, it was said, would be coming to Chicago with strong Eisenhower support despite their first-ballot pledge to Warren. Dewey pronounced his "fifth column" a success. "Nixon maintained his aloofness with perfection," he would say years later. Lodge later believed the Vice Presidency sealed "two weeks before Chicago" by Nixon's apparent mastery of his home state. In the coming fair-play fight, the manager would say, "I couldn't think of anybody else who could keep the California delegation in line."

Due in Chicago on July 1 for a meeting of the Resolutions Committee, Nixon took the last weekend to make the keynote address at the Massachusetts state GOP convention at Worcester. He conferred privately again with Lodge and watched the renomination of his colleague for a Senate run against a formidable Democratic challenger, John Kennedy. Asked about national convention prospects, he told reporters that the Presidential race was "still wide open," and "if it becomes clear that either Eisenhower or Taft will win, we will all press for Knowland as Vice President."

He would take none of the Washington aides with him for the great events ahead, and even discouraged their attendance at the convention. "I want to make it clear that I will not need and do not plan to use the services of any member of the staff in Chicago," he instructed them in a peremptory memo.

Inevitably, still only half privy to the politics at play, Herman Perry worried. "Unless someone routs Earl Warren . . . out of the dictator's spot, California is apt to wind up without much to show for their trip to Chicago," he wrote Nixon in a letter addressed to await him at convention headquarters. Uncle Herman then scribbled an unnecessary postscript: "Boy! From now on play it close to your vest."

21

Convention, July 1952

"YOU WOULDN'T BE ANYBODY IF IT WASN'T FOR US"

umid prairie heat had enveloped
Chicago that July. Delegates, reporters, assorted camp followers of the
convention milled about in the heavy atmosphere of hotel lobbies, often
streamed out across Balbo Drive between the Blackstone and the mammoth
Conrad Hilton, or wandered up Michigan Avenue, wearing their buttons
and gaudy badges as if to ward off the swelter. Occasionally, a blast of the
city's legendary wind swept the streets, leaving walkers suddenly chill
and clammy. Most of the time, an unusual stillness hung over the lakefront.

At the International Amphitheater, three and a half miles south of the
Loop, erected upwind at the east edge of the great Chicago stockyards,
over twelve hundred delegates would swarm about the floor and the flag-
draped rostrum, busily watched over by announcers, photographers, newsreel and television cameramen on tiers above. Yet they all flailed against
the heat. Smoke drifted listlessly in the darting spotlights. High overhead
from the shadowed cavernous ceiling trailed long white banners with huge
stars, suspended motionless in the thick air. Like the delegates, the enormous pennants seemed to be waiting for something.

"The spectacle of two massive forces in collision," one writer called
the 1952 Republican Convention. The clash of Taft and Eisenhower would
be seen from the beginning as a struggle for the soul of the Grand Old
Party, a historic accounting on its past in the political wilderness and its
expected future in power. And so it was—though in ways and with ironies
no one could predict that muggy summer in Chicago. Out of the wounds
and animus of eleven days, the defeated would forge their ultimate triumph

over the party, and the victors would go on to eventual eclipse. In the cynical, expedient tactic of one camp was sown the historic "southern strategy" of the other, and a subsequent revolution in the electoral landscape of the Presidency. For that, and for the new determining force of television and image in American politics, it was to be for all parties the pivotal convention of the postwar period. Not least, it was the event that launched Richard Nixon onto the national scene, where for more than twenty years he rode easily, with masterful success and sullen failure, the forces let loose this July.

In a sense, it was also the most witnessed, the most reported political gathering yet in American history. Journalists, photographers, radio and television crews seemed everywhere. In homes, bars, furniture store windows, the public watched the first nationally televised party convention. News conferences and interviews filled the air. A blanket of releases covered the spacious press sections to the right and left of the speaker's rostrum and the platform behind. Yet when it was over—another portent of the future—the peering public, even most of the delegates in the long rows of chairs of the amphitheater floor, knew little of what had really happened. The essence of the old drama remained its secrecy and mystery, its exclusiveness—now masked as much as ever, perhaps more, by the presence and apparent authority of the news media. The nomination of a President, and the national emergence of Richard Nixon, would still take place largely beyond public view.

Ironically, it was at the behest of Earl Warren that Nixon came to Chicago for the crucial days of maneuvering just before the convention. California was due a seat on the Resolutions or Platform Committee, and at mid-June Warren and Knowland as the senior state figures and dispensers of the patronage had decided to ask the senator. "I told him that you were desirous of him taking on this assignment," Knowland wrote the governor in a "personal and confidential" letter. "He said he will be glad to serve in that capacity." They all had a mutual California interest in some of the issues before Resolutions—particularly tidelands oil and reclamation policies for the Central Valley. To ensure a platform reflective of his own views and his patrons, and for the very prestige of the committee seat, Nixon had readily seized on Warren's offer. But by far the greater value was the vantage point he was now given in the pitched battle between Taft and Eisenhower forces over the credentials of disputed delegates. It was to be another opportunity to aid the Eisenhower campaign at a decisive moment and, still more important, to appear as one of the few Californians with inside and authoritative information in the confusing whirlwind of rumors and claims that surrounded the duel for the nomination. Warren and Knowland, somewhat naïvely, reckoned on neither—nor on what more Nixon would do with the advantage.

When he arrived in Chicago July 1, Brownell and his team of lawyers had already been there for a week, poised in a suite in the Conrad Hilton to devise both testimony for the credentials hearings due to take place July 1–4 and strategy for the floor fight to follow. Brownell was also, as he admitted later, "giving more than a stray thought to a running mate for the general." Nixon was soon evident in the corridors of the Hilton in a discreet reconnaissance for both Eisenhower's and his own cultivated strength, taking "soundings," one reporter noted, "with state leaders, many of whom were indebted to him for his appearances at party pep rallies in 1951." Meanwhile, the credentials contest began typically. "There is nothing to compromise," Lodge announced from Eisenhower headquarters, adding with no conscious irony, "I can imagine nothing more undemocratic than for a small group of men meeting in secret to arrogate unto themselves the right to disenfranchise thousands of American citizens."

In a first small test July 1, the National Committee voted unanimously to seat the Taft Florida slate over eighteen disputed Eisenhower delegates. The debate was redolent of the southern factions of both camps. When an Eisenhower lawyer charged the Taftites with losing black votes, the Florida chairman replied blithely that "Negroes . . . left the Republican Party when they were paid one dollar to vote for . . . Senator Claude Pepper in the 1950 Democratic primary." As it was, the more significant vote had come earlier in the day. Well before the session opened, Lodge's men summoned radio and television teams to the hearing room, and the National Committee members entered to find themselves surrounded by klieg lights, cameras, and microphones. Angry and preempted, the committee hastily voted sixty to forty to bar any broadcast of their deliberations. The closure produced for Eisenhower the predictable and desired result, an outcry from the media that would force Taft eventually to relent and another jot in the larger imagery of fairness versus furtive villainy.

In and out of the Resolutions Committee, Nixon could only hear delayed reports, or else look on as one more spectator as the action unfolded in the credentials hearings. Once again he would benefit from turns of circumstance and personality. California's representatives on credentials were McIntyre Faries and Marjorie Benedict, Warren loyalists from the National Committee and part of the state delegation. Both now voted with the Eisenhower minority on the seating of Florida and against the bar of radio and television, reinforcing the impression of Eisenhower strength in California. "Warren told me to use my own judgment and I did on hearing each case," Faries said later. In part it was a political calculus that Taft was not significantly ahead and that a vote with Eisenhower was in the interests of the eventual convention floor standoff from which Earl Warren might emerge as the compromise. In late June and the opening days of July, the Eisenhower managers tactically obscured their real delegate strength. "It was desirable for . . . Warren . . . to think we were a little bit behind Senator Taft," Lodge acknowledged later. "Whoever is working for a deadlock tries to help the candidate who is behind."

Mac Faries was also chairman of the convention panel on radio and television and was personally affronted by the peremptory vote to close the hearings. The dignified Los Angeles lawyer took offense, too, at what he saw as the sheer seediness and presumption of the Taft people—"rowdy and boisterous," as he said afterward, "and they were not in the same social strata, as say, a lot of [our] people were in." In those last days before the convention Faries had even gone secretly to see Bob Taft. "Mac, what has happened to me?" Taft asked, and Faries told him how much his own tactics and people were hurting him. Taft said he estimated thirty-three votes in the California delegation. "You've got about nineteen," Faries replied, "all you can count on, and you're not going to get those on the first ballot." Taft seemed disconsolate, saying only, "I know." Faries had immediately reported all this back to Earl Warren, and his intelligence added still more to the sense in Sacramento that the front-runner could be stopped short of the nomination, and that in Taft's apparent passivity the Warren delegation was safe from any attempted raid, at least from one camp.

They had organized dinners all over the country. Lodge remembered their lobbying on the Texas "steal" "an immense effort . . . to make sure no delegate could escape hearing the story." Their real preconvention coup, however, had come at the end of June at the national governors' conference in Houston. There, too, the GOP governors were dined and entertained by Jack Porter and other prominent Eisenhower backers, coming away "impressed," said *The New York Times*, "by the indignation expressed by the Texas residents over . . . Mineral Wells." To offset the Taft committee victories in Chicago, Dewey and other pro-Eisenhower governors then drafted a long telegram to be sent to the convention signed by every Republican governor at the conference. It began with bland rhetoric about the GOP adhering to "the highest standards of honor, integrity, and fairness." Buried in a second page was the Eisenhower position urging "that no contested delegate may vote to determine the outcome of any contest," a change in convention rules that would emasculate early Taft support and turn the momentum. "To win in 1952," read the manifesto, "the Republican Party must make it clear to the people of the United States that it offers an inspiring and welcome alternative to the corruption, political favoritism, and lack of moral integrity which now exists in the national administration. It can do so only if the Republican nominee enters the campaign with clean hands, and no question can be raised regarding the methods employed in securing his nomination."

By a combination of outright deception and indolence and distraction among pro-Taft governors—three did not read beyond the first page before signing and one was dazzled into ready agreement by sharing the spotlight at a national press conference—they garnered the signatures of all twenty-three GOP governors at the conference. Among them was Earl Warren, "forced into a trap," as a Califronia writer saw it, because he still believed every weakening of Taft led not to Eisenhower's victory but to deadlock and his own nomination. While complaining that Taft was stealing the convention, concluded one historian, "the Eisenhower people had 'stolen' the governors' conference at Houston."

Lodge thought the "Houston Manifesto" beyond "our wildest dreams," and the effect on the convention-eve maneuvering was electric when the document was released July 2. With the press describing it as a decided "blow" to Taft, the governors' telegram eclipsed news the same day of another credentials victory over Eisenhower, this time to seat Georgia regulars and give Taft at least 493 committed delegates to Eisenhower's 412. The burst from Houston also drew the first of many responses from the outmaneuvered Taft extremists. Handbills began to appear outside convention hotels, denouncing "Ike the Kike, financed by Phooey Dewey's international bankers." At the same time, the cooption of the governors emboldened Richard Nixon as well, and in an extraordinary formal statement cleared with Eisenhower headquarters, he issued his own "warning" on the credentials hearings he had been anxiously watching.

Like the manifesto, his statement was a major event in Chicago and made front-page news in *The New York Times* and elsewhere. But it was also addressed in the first instance to the California delegation assembling the next day in Sacramento to entrain for the convention. The latest Taft victory on the Georgia delegates posed grave doubt whether the convention would be run "with complete integrity and fair play," Nixon told the press, and he was now "convinced" the disputed Eisenhower slate from Texas must be seated.

> The issue of which delegation from Texas is seated . . . is bigger than the Taft-Eisenhower contest. . . . The real issue is whether the Republican Party is to survive. It is whether the GOP is to be a closed

corporation or open to all people who want a change of administration in Washington. It is whether the voice of the people shall be heard. It is whether the selection of the Republican candidate for President is to be determined by the will of the people or by a small clique of politicians who happen to control the party machinery.

They could not run against Democratic "corruption," he said, echoing Houston, "if our own hands are not clean." He had conducted his "own investigation," the senator told a sizable group of national reporters, and had concluded that the Eisenhower Texans complied with state law. The Taft organization "should not take the law into its own hands and disenfranchise thousands of Texas voters." He then went on:

> If the Republican Party approves the Texas grab, we will be announcing to the country that we believe ruthless machine politics is wrong only when the Democrats use it. Not only is the future of the Republican Party in the South at stake. The Republican Party can't hope to win this November if it limits its membership to the minority that has not been large enough to win for national elections.

The argument and idiom clearly belonged to Dewey and Lodge, and much of the language may have been secretly drafted by Brownell's staff publicists. Yet *The New York Times* and other papers promptly reported Nixon as a "spokesman" from the "group" of favorite-son delegations and the young senator himself "thus far . . . not committed publicly in the battle between General Eisenhower and Senator Taft."

To an Associated Press reporter asking about California and the Vice Presidency after the statement, Nixon modestly commented once more that Bill Knowland would be "an outstanding candidate" as running mate for either Taft or Ike, though he was "certain" that Earl Warren would not again take second place on the ticket. But the *San Francisco Chronicle* now reported Nixon "a prime mover" in the important maneuver to change the convention rules in Eisenhower's favor, and the inevitable corridor rumors began that Nixon himself was one of the likely choices to run with the general. On the National Committee Mac Faries heard that talk as well, and he duly reported it back to Sacramento.

Still, the telltale signs and intelligence were discounted. Warren asked his old ally, California Senate president Harold Powers, to look into the story. But when "Butch" Powers checked with his own sources in Ike's camp in Chicago, Colorado governor Dan Thornton, himself a would-be Vice President jockeying for the nomination, Thornton knew nothing, "had no idea," Powers would say, that Dick Nixon was privately backing Eisenhower or even being considered as a running mate. When Warren aides talked with West Coast journalists covering the preconvention developments, the answers were the same. Speculation centered instead on Knowland. Reporters from California believed that if anyone from the "state received the nomination," as one of them told an interviewer later, "it would be the senior senator." On the eve of their departure for Chicago, despite Nixon's pro-Eisenhower statement on the "Texas grab," Warren and his aides still had no clear sense of the stakes for which Richard Nixon would be playing over the next few days.

The evening of July 2, following his much-publicized statement, Nixon met with Murray Chotiner in Chicago, and his old manager excitedly urged him to fly out to meet the California delegation train en route eastward from Sacramento. Nixon was to tell them that the tide had turned decisively toward Eisenhower, "that there wouldn't be any deadlock," as Chotiner recalled their conversation, "and if there was no deadlock, then Warren didn't have a chance." He was also to administer that dire news to Earl Warren himself. Above all, the delegates must be convinced that the "big issue," as Chotiner remembered it, "[the] fair-play resolution . . . would go in Eisenhower's favor." Given the political realities, there could be no question that California would vote for Eisenhower, for the winners, when the credentials issue came to the floor.

Nixon made the flight reservations and planned to board the special California train when it passed through Denver the night of the Fourth of July.

"YOU'D HAVE THOUGHT *HE* WAS THE CANDIDATE"

The California delegation assembling in Sacramento that week was the product not simply of Earl Warren's primary victory but of last-minute, backroom politics of accident, carelessness, and betrayal. The result for Richard Nixon was another major advance toward the Vice Presidency.

They had chosen the initial names for the delegation earlier in the spring. Warren assigned the task to a small party committee, including Knowland, Faries, and, as their concession to Nixon, Bernie Brennan. The rest of them had "misgivings" from the outset, Faries would say. But a Nixon hand in the selection was the negotiated price of his own name on the slate. "Brennan was available . . . was a semi-professional," Faries remembered. "And Brennan had the time to do it, and . . . offered to do it." They canvassed local GOP leaders for suggestions, and the methodical Brennan made a card index on all the names. At the Athens Club in Oakland, the committee sat down with the governor for a grueling eleven-hour meeting, Warren impressing them with his questions, insights, sheer knowledge about the knotty personalities and topography of California's Republican politics. They emerged with a slate that seemed balanced among the feudal factions of officeholders and regions.

Delegates were to swear to the pledge of Presidential preference for Earl Warren, with an added affidavit that they believed him the "best candidate" the party could nominate. Nonetheless, before and after the Oakland meeting, Faries had warned his old friend and leader about the Eisenhower inroads. "A lot of these people, while they'll sign up to support you, are not definitely for *you*," he told Warren in a telephone conversation. "We can't help that," the governor answered. "We want to get the best people, and if they sign up, I will trust them on their support." Faries would add later with audible bitterness that "he trusted their integrity, and it was their *integrity* to follow what they said they would do!"

Then, after the primary, a number of the initial delegates gradually began to drop out for mundane personal or business reasons. They quickly convened a "final selection committee," and Brennan now, too, helpfully became its secretary, handling the increasingly urgent details as the deadline for final designation drew near. Again Faries talked to Warren "two or three times" to warn about the potential danger in replacements. Caught up in the late June flurry that took him to the Houston conference and to a speech at the National Press Club in Washington, the governor was again trusting, almost phlegmatic. "He felt, and maybe he was a little bit like Bill [Knowland], a bit naïve," Faries said afterward, "he thought if a man gave his word in writing he would stand by it."

It would come down to fateful small power wielded by the man who sent the final names to the printer. "So Bernie Brennan went on and made a lot of last-minute substitutions," Faries recounted. "A number of names had to be shifted. Practically everyone was shifted onto . . . we'll say Eisenhower supporters." Among the new delegates or alternates placed without consulting Faries or others on the committee were Mac St. Johns, John Dinkelspiel, Harold Lloyd, Harrison McCall, Tom Bewley, Ray Arbuthnot, Walter Haas, a fresh troop of Nixon backers added to the two dozen already ceded. Of their ultimate loyalty to Dick Nixon there was no doubt. "A lot of people on the delegation wanted *him* to be President of the United States," said Roy Crocker, who was one of them. Earl Warren had read the final printed list with mounting dismay and erupted at one old name in particular. Among the alternates from Los Angeles was Murray Chotiner. Furiously, Warren called Faries, who could only sputter. "I felt very badly about it," the national committeeman admitted later, "because I hadn't put thumb screws on where I should."

At the same time, Chotiner had compounded the effect by another stroke in some ways as telling as Brennan's. In the hurried apportionment of convention assignments and logistical details before Chicago, Chotiner readily volunteered for the housekeeping chores few others wanted. And Warren's staff, longtime Sacramento loyalists with only a rudimentary sense of a modern convention campaign for the Presidency, agreed almost routinely. Consigned to Murray Chotiner were all the political decorations and banners on the train, transportation details from the handling of luggage to provision of buses and automobiles in Chicago, physical accommodations for the working press, radio and TV people aboard the train, the arrangements and staff for the delegate suites at the Knickerbocker Hotel, and even the telephones and outfitting of Warren headquarters on the fifteenth floor of the Conrad Hilton, where Chotiner arrayed the California campaign only four floors above Eisenhower's operatives. It was these logistics that brought him to Chicago in advance of the delegation and thus to the scene of the preconvention maneuvering with Nixon. The same day Nixon denounced the "Texas grab," *The New York Times* discovered the pudgy lawyer at the Hilton rooms, wearing a natty white suit with a loud silk tie and his usual clock-face cufflinks, surrounded by a thousand outsized Warren badges. Who would get the badges? a reporter asked. "Anyone who'll wear 'em," Chotiner answered jauntily.

The governor had been tempted simply to throw Chotiner off the delegation and cancel his supervision of the train and convention arrangements. At the last moment he relented to avoid a split with Nixon. Chotiner "was probably Nixon's closest political associate," Thomas Mellon said of the decision, "and in Warren's attempt to be fair, he gave his approval. He was quite a headache." Added to the debacle of the final delegate selection, the Chotiner presence left the governor and some of his men once more on edge. "We knew from [that] . . . time," said one of them, "we had to watch Nixon." They asked the ever-loyal Knowland to stay "in day-to-day touch" with Nixon to gauge his actions. Yet the monitoring in the last days before the convention—like Faries's reports from the National Committee—was fitful at best. Knowland would not know that his fellow senator was flying out of Chicago that July Fourth to board the California train.

About to leave for the convention, Earl Warren did take one last secret precaution. His private secretary called Paul H. Davis, an old friend who had been one of Eisenhower's vice presidents at Columbia University. The two men had already talked privately in May, Warren asking intently about Eisenhower's qualifications and Davis offering the governor later to "serve him in Chicago . . . if there was any special task for me," as Davis put it in a sealed memoir. Now, after much searching, the governor's secretary reached Davis in a small town in Illinois and asked him to rendezvous with Warren privately in Chicago, to check into a hotel away from the other delegates and await instructions.

The delegates gathered in the State Assembly chamber on the morning of Thursday, July 3. Frank Jorgensen remembered Sacramento "hotter than the hinges of hell," the small capitol shimmering in the dry mid-summer. Warren had summoned them for a last meeting on California soil to impose the unit rule—requiring the entire delegation to cast its votes with the majority—and to elect Bill Knowland chairman, two more measures to safeguard discipline. Standing in the well of the chamber, the governor now addressed them affectionately as "my delegation" and gave an impassioned little address on the Republican Party, speaking almost prophetically to what awaited them. "The most fundamental things in political life are being submerged by personalities," he told them. "In the last analysis, it is more important to know what the principles of the party are going to be than who the standard bearer should be." The GOP must be a "dynamic, forward-looking party" and not "turn its back on human progress in a vain search for the old days of the past." Above all, Warren would strike no bargain for the nomination. He was "without any intention of making any personal deals for personal aggrandizement or . . . to serve as a Presidential nominee-maker." It was, some realized afterward, a kind of epitaph on his governorship, and on an era in the party, the state, the nation.

They adjourned to lunch, then drifted down to their special train, christened the *GOP*, at the old Western Pacific terminal. The Pullman cars had been sitting in the torrid sun all day. Boarding, one of the delegates recalled, "was like walking into an oven." Jorgensen, Hillings, Arbuthnot, and McCall soon took down the partition between their adjoining berths to make a single large compartment, "bribed the porter," as one said, to bring a tub of ice, and stripped down to their shorts to sit and drink. Slowly the *GOP* pulled out of the hot valley and up the canyons of the Sierra Nevada, though the higher, cooler air gave little relief. Jorgensen would remember how "the cars just baked all night." Despite the heat, the governor's supporters and their accompanying families were soon in a holiday mood, "exhilarated," thought one observer. Warren himself seemed more optimistic than ever. "There wasn't anything phony about these high spirits," one delegate said. "We took our cue from the governor . . . and he was full of confidence. Not cocky, he wasn't ever that, but he gave you the feeling that he was hopeful." Many of the men put on gold shirts with "Warren" in blue block letters stitched on the back. Someone began playing the piano in the lounge car, and the suntanned Warren daughters, each wearing a bright orange baseball cap marked with a "W," danced gaily with delegates to repeated renditions of "California Here I Come."

Elsewhere, through the corridors, politics had begun to stir. Butch Powers remembered Joe Knowland—the original political patron of Earl Warren—telling everyone who would listen that his son should not take the number-two spot on the ticket, the prize many thought he would be offered by either Taft or Eisenhower. "I hope Bill don't accept that Vice Presidency," the old publisher muttered; "I hope Bill don't accept that Vice Presidency." Back in the compartments with Jorgensen and his group, and with other Nixon men, there were soon "splinter meetings and caucuses," as Bernie Brennan remembered them. Yet walking through the cars, stopping to say hello, Brennan himself felt a cold, awkward silence when he appeared in the swaying doorway. The reaction was symptomatic of the tension, the high stakes, the grim zeal that rode with them that night across the Nevada desert. It was not merely that Brennan the dour lawyer was a teetotaler in a hard-drinking crowd. He had flown back at Warren's behest to rebuke Dick Nixon on the Presidential poll and was now characteristically insisting that he must uphold his delegate's oath to back the governor. Despite Bernie Brennan's devoted work in 1950, despite his crucial service to Nixon in packing the delegation at the last moment—a maneuver that had put many of them on the train—they now froze him out. "You had to go all the way with them or you were excluded from the meetings," Brennan remembered sadly. "I had made it plain that I was going to live up to my obligations and go down the line for Warren."

They celebrated the Fourth aboard the *GOP* with small ladyfinger firecrackers and still more dancing and singing in the lounge car. For all the suddenly hushed meetings Brennan had come upon the night before, there was still an air of lightness. "You stay up all night and you drink a lot of liquor and you eat a lot of food," Jorgensen would say of that first night, "and you don't accomplish a blessed thing except to enjoy yourself." To the traveling press that day, Warren gave a relaxed, sometimes cheerful interview, still reckoning on stopping both Taft and Eisenhower, the deadlock that would open his own path to the prize. Disputed delegates should not vote "until the results of the contests are determined," and there should be a full "open door" policy in the committee sessions, he told them, implicitly siding with the Eisenhower forces while obviously refusing to endorse the general. Asked about rumblings of defection in his own delegation, Warren was solemn. "It boiled down to a question of honor," *The New York Times* reported. And the governor simply believed that "it would be dishonorable for delegates pledged . . . to leave him until he had released them."

Then, at Grand Junction, Colorado, a report reached the train that

Senator Nixon would be boarding that evening at Denver. Sitting with Warren when the news came, Butch Powers saw the governor visibly arch. "It was very much a surprise, and I could see there was quite a bit of feeling between them." Someone told Brennan that Nixon would want to talk with Warren. But when the Nixon men made no move to relay that to the governor's party, Brennan as a courtesy informed one of the secretaries in the party. At that, the response was curt: Warren would arrange no meeting but would be in his car; if the senator came by, they could talk. Spurned by both sides, Brennan lost patience with the petty gesturing and issued a minor ultimatum. "You tell Earl that as soon as Dick gets on the train, I'm going to take him back to that car and I'm going to press that button," he told the secretary. "If he wants to see Dick, he'll open the door. If he doesn't, he won't." Brennan reminded her, as he told the story, "that there were a lot of Eisenhower and Taft people on board and that there were also a lot of newspapermen."

Nixon flew to Denver that Independence Day from a preconvention battle still raging. On the third the National Committee voted to seat sixteen more challenged Taft delegates from Louisiana, Mississippi, and Missouri, giving the senator 510 votes to Eisenhower's 414, with 132 pledged to favorite sons and 151 still in dispute. The morning of the Fourth the Taft-dominated committee again overrode Eisenhower protests to split the bitterly contested Texas delegation twenty-two to sixteen. The action propelled Taft within seventy-five votes of the nomination. First told of the Taft "compromise" to split the Texas slate, Eisenhower had remarked, "Gee, that sounds good." But his managers, still banking on moral indignation, swiftly censored their candidate. Lodge denounced the split and rejected even Herbert Hoover's offer to arbitrate. "My God," Brownell had said at a meeting discussing the Taft offer, "don't you see we can't accept it? We'd lose our only issue." As for Ike's unguarded "Gee," Lodge would explain later that "it had been understood from the outset between the general and our group that our group was running the campaign."

Eisenhower headquarters now confidently claimed over 650 votes to pass a fair-play amendment on the convention floor, a strike that would wipe out Taft's southern delegates and with them his growing lead. Taft quickly countered, and courted still more right-wing votes among the favorite-son delegations, by announcing dramatically if vaguely that General Douglas MacArthur "would not reject" the Vice Presidency on a Taft ticket. As Nixon left Chicago, former House Speaker Joe Martin was predicting that the venomous fight between the two front-runners might well lead to the selection of some "third person." Martin named Earl Warren in particular along with the less likely MacArthur or Stassen. The Californian was clearly the most promising dark horse. By the close of preconvention hearings and barely forty-eight hours before the opening gavel fell, the nomination still hung uncertainly in the balance. And all this—the shifting, ambiguous aggregate of Chicago hotel corridors, hearing rooms, and campaign headquarters—Richard Nixon would know well as he waited that Friday evening for the *GOP* to pull into Denver.

He boarded the California train with his own, far more settled reality and priority. Going directly to the joint compartment of Hillings and Arbuthnot, Jorgensen and McCall, he told them excitedly, as Jorgensen recounted, that "Eisenhower was running very strong and that Taft had lost ground in the delegation fights of two or three states." It was virtually the opposite of what had happened officially over the past two days, and an analysis even more optimistic than Lodge's public posturing. Nixon talked to the four "quite some time," one of them remembered, and "he even mentioned his own possible [Vice-Presidential] candidacy." That he was on the train and speaking behind closed doors with his men soon ran through the cars already tense and uncertain about his boarding. "The little circle around Warren were incensed that he would talk to his friends before he would report to the governor," Jorgensen recalled, "and they managed to stir up considerable commotion."

Caught again between the two factions and his own sense of duty, Bernie Brennan eventually walked back to the four-man compartment and offered to escort Nixon to see Warren. Before going to the governor's car, they stopped to eat a snack in the dining car and Nixon repeated his Chicago report to Brennan, though he was now more qualified with his onetime campaign chairman. "It was his feeling Eisenhower would get the nomination," Brennan recalled. "A great deal, of course, depended on what happened about the contested delegations from the South."

They then walked back to Warren's compartment and were admitted "at once," noted Brennan, who, to his relief, thought the governor seemed "pleasant and casual." After Brennan had left, Nixon went on to give Warren what the press would call from the senator's description "a report on preconvention committee sessions." By the governor's own spare account, Nixon "paid his respects to me and said if any of his friends got out of line to let him know." His own personal loyalty was complete, Nixon had assured him. "When he got on the train at Denver," Tom Mellon remembered, "he told Warren he was supporting him one hundred percent."

What happened next was to become another part of the rich lore of their state's singular politics. One writer judged it "the precise moment when the California party began to come apart." But that overlooked nearly a decade of festering resentments. It was in truth one more sequel, now almost a climax, of a breach already long separating the men, their factions, their political practices.

The senator soon left Warren's compartment and began methodically to work the delegate cars. "I remember Nixon going up and down the train, beaming and shaking hands with everybody," said a Sacramento reporter watching the passage. "You'd have thought *he* was the candidate, not Warren." On a brief stop in the press section, he was asked about rumors of his own Vice-Presidential nomination and answered emphatically that the talk was "ridiculous." He casually told the journalists he had given Warren a general "report" on the credentials fight and without further details or interpretation soon returned to his tour of the delegation. With Hillings in tow, he now quickly organized a series of meetings crowded into the compartments and aisles of a car largely occupied by his own faction, though a majority of the Warren delegates were invited too. Ostensibly, the gatherings were for the same kind of briefing on Chicago given to the governor. But as the *GOP* slid out through the night across the prairie and brush of eastern Colorado, his message was very different.

"Warren had very little if any chance of getting the nomination," John Dinkelspiel remembered Nixon telling them. "The California delegation could effectively insure [sic] Eisenhower's victory . . . [and] if they could be counted on by the Eisenhower people, would have a very strong effect on the convention." Otherwise, Nixon warned, California would be "left at the post" as Eisenhower moved on to the nomination in any case. He also spoke movingly, as listeners later recounted, about the "Taft fraud in Texas and Georgia," and told them they would have a chance to vote early on the fair-play amendment, "moral issues regarding Texas and Georgia where Taft stole the votes." They must join the Eisenhower bandwagon with no more delay. When some delegates asked about breaking their oath to Warren, Hillings reportedly told them "that that would be all right because the law provided no penalty for that." In any case, Dinkelspiel and others remembered Nixon urging "that it should be made publicly known that the delegation would throw its strength to Eisenhower as soon as it could." As Dinkelspiel recalled, he argued "either that the delegation should not vote for Warren on the first ballot, if Warren were willing, or if he insisted that the delgation keep its pledge, that it be made known in advance that the delegation at least on the second ballot would vote for Eisenhower rather than Taft, not just sit back and not state its position." And while the senator himself did not immodestly mention the subject in those meetings, his men soon spread word of California's expected reward for the defection. "If they acted quickly and did not waste their votes," one writer reported, "the delegation could suggest Nixon as Vice President."

Stunned by his insider's description of Taft's corruption and the Eisenhower streamroller, by the apparent certainty of the general's nomination despite press reports and delegate counts, some of the Warren loyalists hurried back to the governor's compartment to ask anxiously about what should be done. Warren's own version of those calls would carry a barely constrained rage. "During the night, the Nixon delegates—but not the senator as far as I know—held caucuses and urged other delegates to vote for General Eisenhower on the first ballot," he wrote many years later. "Some of those who were importuned came to me and asked what the situation was. I told them what I had told the voters: that the delegation was not a front for anyone, and that no matter what happened it was obligated to vote for me on the first ballot at least." In private with his closest aides that night, Warren was angrier than they could ever remember him. They knew clearly enough, Tom Mellon would say, "that these people were running around virtually asking the delegates to violate their oath."

Richard Nixon's open defiance and bid for the delegation raced through the cars. "If you're on the front end of the train you have to run pretty fast before the statement gets to the back end," Jorgensen said of the scene. Seated in one of the last cars, only an alternate, Tom Bewley soon knew that his old law partner and protégé was a few cars away politicking with "the big shots" for nothing less than the leadership and direction of the state's seventy votes. "A hullabaloo," Bewley would say, "over who would run the delegation." There was an acrid sense now, too, among the Warren men of how much preparation and positioning had gone into these climactic hours, how much strength Nixon truly commanded on the GOP speeding to Chicago with its Warren shirts, banners, and baseball caps. Down the aisles to the intense late-night meetings came not only the Nixon people in their numbers but also the marginal Warren supporters swayed by the June poll or by Nixon's implicit, long-cultivated support of Dwight Eisenhower as the only sure Republican winner in November. And the senator seemed to know them all, exactly "where the Eisenhower votes were" and those "so fully committed to Warren that he couldn't make any progress with them," as Tom Mellon ruefully said later. "His work in this connection was done long before he got on the train."

It was a remarkable episode in the politics of the era. But the night was not yet over for Nixon as he finished the last of the delegate meetings and his men drifted back from further lobbying. They found themselves together with the senator in one of their compartments, and there followed an extraordinary scene. Unnoticed, Thomas Mellon and his family occupied roomettes nearby. Late that same night, the train's primitive air conditioning had gone off, and compartment doors were flung open to get some air. Mellon and another delegate, Ron Button, were about to go to sleep when they began to hear what Mellon called "this big discussion."

Mellon could make out clearly the voices of Jorgensen and Hillings, now joined by Jack Drown. Nixon had just campaigned impressively throughout the delegation for its defection. But now his closest supporters were pressing him even further to lead an open break with Earl Warren, whatever the rest of the Californians decided. "They were working on Nixon . . . to cut Warren up . . . really putting the heat on him," Mellon said. "They kept hammering Nixon to be sure that he didn't weaken his position in being for Eisenhower." Dick was arguing that they would have to be cautious, await developments and coordination with the Eisenhower camp—"no doubt," reflected Mellon, because he "had worked out something with Cabot Lodge . . . on the possibility of the Vice-Presidential spot." Still, his California men did not seem to care about his ambition, the convention tactics, or subtleties. They would settle now, in Chicago, in Earl Warren's last bid for high office, all the old accumulated scores of appointments never made, advice never heeded, a conservatism betrayed. "Hillings was pretty ruthless, Jorgensen was very ruthless about it," thought Mellon, who remembered that "the arguments were so loud through the night that their words could be overheard up and down the car."

At one point they reminded Dick Nixon just how much they and their views and their friends represented his essential constituency, his southern California money. Mellon could hear his indignant, wounded reaction.

"Well, after all, I am a United States senator," Nixon told them.

"We don't give a damn what you are," they answered brutally. "You wouldn't be anybody if it wasn't for us."

The next morning, Earl Warren gave another, less ebullient news conference calling for a convention of "fairness and openness," words that for many now took on a double meaning as the delegation struggled with the inner turmoil of the night before. Nixon's report out of Denver was said to have brought "good news" for the governor. Sought out by both the *Los Angeles Times* and *The New York Times*, the senator himself told journalists that Warren's chances were indeed "very bright in the event of a deadlock" and that the governor was regarded in Chicago as "the front-running candidate" after Ike and Taft. On all sides it was a fig leaf for the press, maintaining Warren's command and hiding the damage Nixon had inflicted.

Later that afternoon, Nixon slipped off the train at Cicero on the western outskirts of Chicago—left it "furtively," said one observer—and was met by a car that drove him the last few miles into the city ahead of the train.

Warren's own arrival in Chicago was emblematic. With a band playing the inevitable "California Here I Come," the governor disembarked at Union Station to a welcome by Bill Knowland and a cheering throng of several hundred supporters. But as Warren and his family then led the delegates and crowd in a triumphal parade through the station to waiting buses, his aides were making an appalling discovery. Arranged by Chotiner, the buses had been decorated that morning by loyal staff with "Warren for President" signs. Now, in front of Union Station, they stood there draped with huge banners proclaiming "Eisenhower for President." One Warren assistant frantically pulled off the Eisenhower banners and taped up makeshift Warren pennants just as the delegation arrived.

They rode into downtown Chicago that Saturday evening past Eisenhower sound trucks blaring the incessant message of the fair-play strategy: "Thou Shalt Not Steal." Bob Taft would appear later at the Hilton, flourishing some five hundred telegrams from delegates pledging their votes and loyalty to the end, "perhaps the most impressive display of personal strength," observed one reporter, "made by any political leader in American history." Yet the starch Ohioan thrashed awkwardly against Lodge's refusal to compromise the delegate contests on any basis and what he called the "unlimited use of propaganda" by the well-financed, carefully staged campaign of his heroic rival. Nearly mobbed when arriving the same day at another Chicago station, Ike had spoken with a breaking voice, near tears, at a candlelight ceremony for World War II dead. Behind the scenes, his campaign was less sentimental. Lodge and Dewey pressed Stassen to lobby Warren on the fair-play vote while the California governor was still unpacking. In Brownell's command suite that Saturday night, they calculated the defection of at least Nixon's faction of the California delegates after the senator's dramatic interception of the train, though they hoped as always to avoid an open rift with Warren. "Before the convention," press secretary Jim Hagerty would say, "it looked like we were going to get a third of the California delegation there. . . . But we didn't want to have an out-and-out fight with the governor himself for many reasons."

At the same hour, however, Taft himself claimed secret "assurances of twenty-five from California if Warren ever released them," as he recorded later. When indications of the prospective Taft vote in California promptly coiled back to the Eisenhower camp through its elaborate intelligence network, the worry produced a new flurry of Nixon activity. While the rest of the Californians were housed in the Knickerbocker, Nixon now took his own suite of rooms in the Stockyard Inn, "where we could gather and keep reports moving and all this liaison work," said Jorgensen. It was to be a veritable command post of his Vice-Presidential candidacy. Mac Faries remembered the frenetic activity of these "Nixon meetings" from the moment of their arrival in Chicago that Saturday evening. At one juncture they even telephoned Keith McCormac back in Bakersfield, trying to induce the Werdel backer to identify and influence the Taft votes suddenly feared in the delegation. "Nixon had one of his stooges call me, and they wanted to use my name back there," McCormac related. "They must have had some recalcitrants." The calls, the comings and goings, the restless meetings—it would all go on with Nixon and his men through the week, gatherings until two o'clock in the morning, as Faries remembered, "practically every night."

Nixon was notably absent from a first caucus of the California delegates Saturday evening at the Knickerbocker. Wearily they adjourned to reconvene Sunday night for their crucial caucus vote on fair play, which was due to be introduced on the convention floor early Monday morning. Some of them had already begun to call the episode the night before by the name it would carry for years—"the great train robbery." When hesitant aides finally informed Warren about the added incident with the buses and Eisenhower banners, "he was mad as hell," recalled Oscar Johnsen. "He thought that Nixon and Chotiner had pulled this fast one." In angry retaliation, Warren partisans moved to leak a story to California reporters that Nixon had tried, as one version went, "to entice California votes away from Warren in return for second place on the Eisenhower ticket." But the newsmen were intent on the Taft-Eisenhower struggle and largely ignored the stories.

Earl Warren would go to bed his first night in Chicago in a mood of deep dismay. "How do you account for him doing a thing like this?" he said to his old friend Victor Hansen. "I just can't understand anybody doing such a thing as that."

"IT WAS A BEAUTIFUL MANEUVER"

Outwardly, Sunday seemed a sultry lull in the battle, a sequence of churchgoers on quiet downtown streets and dutiful evening receptions. Helene Drown persuaded Pat Nixon to stand in line more than an hour to shake hands with Dwight Eisenhower at an open reception for delegates and wives. He was, after all, a celebrity. "We may never get to meet him again," Helene told her. When the two women came through, the general was unusually warm when an aide whispered in addition to her name, "the wife of *Senator* Dick Nixon." Pat thought his striking eyes "round, baby-blue and mesmerizing."

While the public ceremonies were politely acted out, the inner politics, as one writer saw them, were more and more a matter of "high drama and blunt orders." One of Taft's floor managers approached Mac Faries with the first of what would be several offers to give Knowland the Vice Presidency in return for California votes. "Why, no. I wouldn't do that . . . as long as Earl Warren is in the picture, I will support Earl Warren," Knowland had said when Faries called him in the presence of the Taft man. Afterward, as usual, Faries called Warren to report the incident, and the governor relished the loyalty. "Well, of course," he told Faries. "I knew that Bill would be that way and that is it."

Other exercises of power and fealty were hardly so civil. "This is the way I want it," said Governor John Fine, ordering the Pennsylvania contingent to vote for fair play. To hesitant New York delegates, Dewey eloquently deplored the "rape of the Republican party" in the Taft seating victories before the National Committee. But he spoke, too, the harsh language of power and patronage. Their votes on fair play would determine their own jobs and the jobs of many of their friends and constituents. "Fearing for their paychecks," said one account of the pressure, New York State employees were soon "calling wavering delegates in droves." That same evening, Winthrop Aldrich's yacht lay at anchor in Lake Michigan, with a gala "open house" for delegates under the banner of SHOE, "Supreme Headquarters Operation Eisenhower," while "fully one hundred persons," as one report counted them, acted as Aldrich "runners and liaison men." Later, Taft supporters would bitterly tell stories of key delegates pulled aside and offered "a thousand bucks a vote," as one man testified, for the fair-play showdown the next morning.

While Pat Nixon was being charmed by Eisenhower, Dewey agent Ab Herman watched her husband, as the New York committeeman said later, "obviously working California for Ike." The hours leading up to the Sunday night caucus were consumed with more lobbying, reconnaissance, and petty intrigue. Nixon carefully surveyed Warren's potential second- or third-ballot strength in other delegations for whatever the intelligence might yield in arguing for fair play. Meanwhile, they had planned to monitor Warren's own moves as closely as possible. Victor Hansen was sitting in an inner office of the Warren headquarters Chotiner had organized at the Hilton when he was startled to hear a phone ring where none was supposed to be. When he finally found and picked up the partially hidden telephone, a familiar voice said questioningly, "Who is this?"

"Vic Hansen."

"This is Dick Nixon. Is Murray there?"

"If he is, I haven't seen him," Hansen responded, adding in some puzzlement, "You mean Murray Chotiner?" And Nixon said matter-of-factly, "Yes. Will you please ask him to call me."

Surprised himself to hear Hansen apparently talking on a phantom telephone, Verne Scoggins had come into the private office and asked incredulously, "Where the hell did that phone come from?" They found no record of the installation, and Scoggins angrily had the line taken out. "Murray Chotiner had installed it so that he could relay information from Warren's headquarters to Nixon, and vice-versa," Hansen, laughing, related years later. "So the eavesdropping started pretty early." In charge of Warren's delegate search, Milton Polland saw similar undermining in the wake of the bus and telephone incidents. "His people, whether upon his direction or on their own," he would say of Nixon, "did everything to sabotage all of the work that we had [done] at the headquarters for Warren."

Knowland opened the tense caucus at the Knickerbocker on Sunday night with the half-joking, half-nervous line they would remember him using at almost every meeting of the delegation that week. There was no truth to the stories, he told them to weak titters, that "he and Warren were not speaking to Nixon." But with that, he then came quickly to the point. He was "not interested in being merely a bandwagon jumper." The fair-play amendment would prevent the sixty-eight Taft delegates previously seated by the National Committee from voting on over a hundred other contested delegates and thereby shift the balance of votes, perhaps the entire convention, to Eisenhower. He would not argue the merits of the two cases, neither of which was plainly right. What was "fair," Knowland contended, was to split their vote, preserving California's neutrality and keeping "alive" the chances for deadlock, for Earl Warren.

There was no set agenda for caucus speakers, yet no pause when Knowland had ended his remarks and stepped back. Richard Nixon moved right away to the microphone—"rushed" to it, some thought—and began a powerful speech on both the "moral issue" and the practical political consequences of their vote. Nixon had "used every bit of influence he could" before the meeting, Tom Mellon recalled. Now he appealed again to strains of idealism, pride, self-interest. To accept somehow the earlier decisions on seating was to forfeit their independence and very function. "If we were to feel that we were automatically bound to accept the decisions of our committees here, there would be no reason to come to the convention at all," he told them. "We could let the committees nominate." But most of all, the Taft delegates were wrongly chosen, a moral and political blight they would carry into the election, their first chance to win the White

714

House after twenty years of Democratic rule. "Any candidate who is nominated for the Presidency," he said, in pointed reference to Warren as well as the others, "would have a far greater difficulty winning with those contested Taft delegates than otherwise."

It was another of those milestones in Richard Nixon's rise—rather like the stage in South Pasadena where he first met Jerry Voorhis or the moment when HUAC nervously adjourned from hearing Alger Hiss and nearly abandoned the inquiry. But this hot night in the Knickerbocker, for all his preparation and effectiveness, it was his protagonist who tipped the balance. Earl Warren, they all agreed, might have imposed Knowland's split, might have dictated enough votes under the unit rule to carry them in any direction. "It was his delegation," Mellon would say despite the feared Nixon influence. Instead, the governor seemed to echo Nixon's own argument about the "morality" of the choice. "You have to go back to the state of California and face the people of California," Warren told them in a stunningly brief statement. "You vote your conscience." In a hushed count, they balloted sixty-two to eight to support fair play.

Ever afterward, Earl Warren's admirers saw it as an act of supreme integrity and selflessness. His "last chance for the Presidency," a biographer called it. "He knew how the vote was bound to go," said a delegate. "There were a lot more Ike people than Taft people in the room. But he didn't hesitate." Yet at the moment there was hardly that sense of sacrifice, nor was the appeal to "conscience" so politically disinterested. To vote against fair play would have reversed the careful positions Warren already took at Houston and in his train press conferences, the very basis of his strategy. In Chicago on Sunday night, as over the last weeks before the convention, he continued to overestimate Taft's power and misjudge the momentum given Eisenhower by the credentials victory. That much, too, was a tribute to the deliberate effort by Lodge and the others to mislead the favorite sons on Eisenhower's relative strength or the ultimate consequences of fair play.

Moreover, hidden in Warren's sanction of fair play was an added factor few yet understood, even in the California delegation. Among the contested Eisenhower states admitted under the amendment would be scores, perhaps hundreds, of prospective votes they reckoned for Earl Warren in a later ballot when the hoped-for deadlock materialized. In a fateful sense, Ike's backing in the southern contingents was also Earl Warren's. It was not in spite of the governor's ambition but because he was so serious that there was never any question where California should place its weight. "We had delegates—secondary support in many of these delegates [sic] who were going to be seated—that we did not have had the Taft people been seated," Milton Polland said later. "They were supporting this Eisenhower resolution and actually what they were doing was supporting people that they wanted to vote for Warren."

As they filed out of the caucus room, the news of their vote reverberated swiftly through the hotels and headquarters. Knowland hurriedly called together Taft and Eisenhower envoys in a last effort to stave off a floor vote the next morning. Nixon, meanwhile, triumphantly reported the caucus to the Eisenhower managers, assuring not only the seventy California votes on fair play but a probable bolt in the Presidential balloting later in the week. There would be no subtleties or explanations of Warren strategy, of second- or third-ballot plans, in the picture he and his men now drew in whispered conversations. "Nixon used that [vote]," Polland remembered, "as a means of indicating to the Eisenhower people that the Warren delegation was crumbling apart."

Sensing more starkly than Warren what was coming in a fair-play floor victory, Knowland had meetings in his suite through the night, "suspiciously upholding the Taft interest," one writer said in describing the Eisenhower camp's view of his efforts, "in his zeal for a backroom settlement." On a gray and sticky Monday morning, Taft supporters clustered outside hotels and in the amphitheater galleries, singing what seemed endless refrains of "Onward, Christian Soldiers." Early that morning, too, Connecticut governor John Lodge, Cabot's brother, found Nixon at the convention and made a point of introducing him to Eisenhower's floor manager, the crusty New Hampshire governor Sherman Adams.

Minutes before the convention opening, Cabot Lodge was asked to come to the party chairman's office behind the speaker's platform, where he found Gabrielsen, three of Taft's managers, and Bill Knowland. "Of solemn mien," as Lodge remembered him, the somewhat haggard Knowland told him about the California caucus vote for fair play—which Lodge already knew, of course, in some detail from Nixon. There was "another way" to achieve "the same result" without a divisive floor vote, Knowland went on carefully. And that result would "not be inconsistent" with the California caucus. The Taft men then proposed that the contested delegates would simply abstain on any votes until their own seats had been settled— the technical goal of fair play without the larger, ulterior purpose of a resounding floor defeat of Taft. "It was a wonderful thing for Senator Knowland to seek to arbitrate the dispute and . . . certainly the senator was due a great deal of credit . . . to work the thing out peaceably," one of them remarked.

Lodge was mute. He remembered hearing outside the little office "the muffled growlings of the huge crowd." Wary of the apparent surrender, fearful of its impact, he sparred briefly with the Taftites and then asked for time to call his colleagues. He was given fifteen minutes and finally reached Brownell, who told him immediately that this compromise, like the others, should be rejected. Lodge returned to tell the Taft men and discovered that Knowland had already anticipated the answer and gone back to the floor in defeat. It had been the last chance to stem the tide.

Equipped with fourteen electric bullhorns to offset any tampering with microphones, the Eisenhower forces now pressed on through parliamentary delays and ultimately to a roll call Monday afternoon. With Warren's California, Stassen's Minnesota, and Fine's Pennsylvania providing the margin, the fair-play coalition won 658 to 548. The Eisenhower southern delegates would be seated, the Taft lead obliterated. The larger psychological and political impact, as Dewey and his cohorts had foreseen, was crushing. "Winning the nomination for President seemed suddenly and vividly to open up before us," Lodge recorded. Jim Hagerty saw the Monday vote as the great dividing line between "two conventions . . . the credentials convention and then the regular convention." In the first, Taft had been in control; in the second, Eisenhower's victory now suddenly loomed.

Beginning with the Houston Manifesto, thought *The New York Times*, "the Eisenhower strategy group had taught their Taft counterparts a lesson in elementary politics." Yet another writer believed Taft "crassly maneuvered into being branded a vote vandal." There would always be the question of what might have happened if the old guard senator had merely instructed his doggedly loyal delegates to vote for fair play and sidestepped the opening-day defeat his foes so long arranged for him, an eventuality "with unpredictable consequences," Lodge confessed. As it was, Taft himself proved their ultimate ally. "The alternative," he wrote of the credentials vote, "was surrender on matters in which we were in the right." Like stopping to explain to the little girl in New England why he could not pause to sign an autograph, he would follow his own severe drummer to the end.

Nixon was on the floor for much of the fair-play jockeying, though the rest of his campaign went on around the drama in the hall. At one point he slipped away to the Blackstone for a secret meeting with Brownell; Talbot, the fund-raiser; and Dewey aide Russell Sprague. Still later, he would meet again with Paul Hoffman and John Lodge. While his managers were forcing the credentials vote and conferring with Nixon, Eisenhower himself was receiving Earl Warren Monday morning in a courtesy call that ran longer than most. "Neither Warren nor I am going to get involved with a lot of pinkos," the general vouched after the governor departed, "but we're not going to be dragged back by a lot of old reactionaries either."

Reporters intent on the floor drama or Eisenhower as the emerging front-runner did not notice Earl Warren's tight-jawed vexation when ushered into the meeting at the Blackstone by Murray Chotiner, apparently there in some official role for Ike. "Imagine my surprise," Warren wrote in understatement, "when the doorkeeper who admitted me to the general's suite was Murray Chotiner, one of the managers of my train." Whether Chotiner was actually functioning in the Eisenhower wing or, more likely, simply there and posturing to defy his old enemy, the remarkable operator with the flashy ties was in frequent conversation with Herb Brownell, this day as others, over California developments and Richard Nixon's fortunes.

Douglas MacArthur's keynote speech that night came as an anticlimax after the fair-play vote. The usually histrionic general was lackluster. Nonetheless, Nixon and his men were prepared. Aping Dewey's gesture for New York, whose delegation boycotted the keynoter, Nixon sent Hillings through the California seats just before the speech, telling them, "Headquarters does not want you to applaud the general—he might be a compromise candidate." Most of the delegates were obediently silent during the address. Yet some of the most ardent Nixon backers—Irene Dunne and Harold Lloyd—were also, of course, the most conservative, and cheered MacArthur in angry defiance of orders they assumed to have come from Warren. "When Governor Warren learned of what had happened he roundly denounced Hillings," noted one report of the incident. Warren now gave orders to bar Nixon or his aides from the inner rooms of his headquarters, though some of his men thought it much too late.

Meanwhile, no scolding or sanction dimmed the triumph of fair play. In his hotel suite, shunning MacArthur, Dewey quipped that he would now advise Bob Taft simply to surrender and get it over with. Back on the floor, Richard Nixon's own credit and reward for the California votes seemed certain. "I saw Dick the very first night . . . and told him things were shaping up his way, that he was going to get it," a key Lodge assistant told of whispering to the senator. In the convention din Nixon had shrugged almost casually and said nothing—a man clearly not surprised he was going to be the Vice-Presidential nominee.

"There was a gory majesty to the proceedings, a fearful courage and a sense of history being made" is how Richard Norton Smith described the scene in the aftermath of the Monday vote, as eastern power once again wrested the Republican nomination and party edifice from a bitterly thwarted old guard. Fair play had disenfranchised the contested delegates and broken Taft's hold, but there remained significant roll calls on the

seating of various southern delegations, and the maneuvering and counterattacks went on relentlessly.

On Tuesday morning, Earl Warren finally struck back with the weapon
he had reserved before coming to Chicago. He summoned Paul Davis,
Eisenhower's former vice president at Columbia and now holed up at an
out-of-the-way hotel off the lakefront. Davis recorded the extraordinary
episode but kept it long secret. He had a message to be given "orally and
confidentially" to Eisenhower, Warren told him. As Davis then listened in
some wonder, the governor explained:

> The problem is this. We have a traitor in our delegation.
> It's Nixon. He, like all the rest, took the oath that he
> would vote for me, until such time as the delegation was
> released, but he has not paid attention to his oath and
> immediately upon being elected [a delegate], started
> working for Eisenhower and has been doing so ever since.
> I have word that he is actively in touch with the Eisen-
> hower people. I wish you would tell General Eisenhower
> that we resent his people infiltrating, through Nixon, into
> our delegation, and ask him to have it stopped.

"I tell you, but you needn't tell Eisenhower at this time," Warren added
somberly, "that if he doesn't do that, we're going to take measures that
will be harmful to his candidacy."

Davis went directly to Eisenhower's personal suite at the Blackstone,
talked briefly to Frank Carlson, and was promptly admitted to "a long
session" with the general, despite "literally hundreds" waiting in the corridors to see him.

"Well, I am not at all sure that his information is correct," Eisenhower
said when Davis had delivered his message, "for my understanding is that
we are definitely letting the California delegation alone and not trying to
interfere with it in any way whatsoever." He wanted the Warren candidacy
to be "strong," Ike went on. In the event of a deadlock he hoped the
Californian got the nomination. To that he added an old and heartfelt
dread: "If anything should happen to his [Warren's] candidacy, then the
nomination might fall to MacArthur and that would be a calamity."

It was vintage Eisenhower, acknowledging—and now practicing on
Davis—their strategy to avoid a break with Warren, yet discounting, though
not denying to an old associate ("I am not at all sure"), the covert, often
unsavory Nixon agency that was the dark side of the policy. Outside in
the streets, as if in mockery, Taft loudspeakers droned out a tune called
"Poor Blind Ike."

Still, Eisenhower was plainly uneasy with the conversation. "Several times," Davis remembered, Eisenhower stopped him as he was starting to leave, saying edgily, "Just a minute," and then talking about some other matter in the campaign. At one turn, however, he felt constrained to prepare the way for the bargain already made at the Bohemian Club and elsewhere. "I think it is highly desirable that for Vice President we have a young man such as Richard Nixon," he said to Davis that Tuesday morning. "He appears to me the aggressive, able kind of fellow that we need in Republican leadership. We need more young men. He looks like the right type." Conscious of the time consumed and the general's unease, Davis at last moved toward the door to leave, and Eisenhower added a final assurance. "Now if there is any further difficulty about our interfering with the California delegation, either you tell me or ask Earl Warren to phone me and I will take such definite, positive steps that it will certainly stop."

Paul Davis immediately carried the conversation back to Warren, who seemed satisfied. But in Eisenhower headquarters or on the amphitheater floor the result was less plain. Watching intently, Drew Pearson saw Nixon's "continued undercover sniping" against both Warren and Taft. By Tuesday they had even summoned the ever-ready Roy Day from Pomona, and dispatched him on what he called "my assignment in '52," prowling delegate hotels. "Isn't it too bad that Taft is such a wonderful person, but he's just not electable? It's just a shame," Day remembered his line. "I'd shake my head from side to side and put on a forlorn look and then go on and talk to somebody else. I made the elevators . . . the restaurants . . . really covered the hotel lobbies." In suite 1102 of the Hilton, Jim Hagerty "monitored reports," as one account put it, from those "sent out to infiltrate the enemy camp." And even after the Davis-Eisenhower talk, Hagerty would remember Dick Nixon being "very active." "It began to look quite at the start of the convention," he remembered of the opening days, "that California wasn't going to . . . remain as a favorite son."

In all this skirmishing, Warren, Eisenhower, and Nixon were hardly unique. The day after his fair-play debacle, Taft was making his own half-desperate foray into California. Despite the delegation's decisive vote on fair play, Taft would secretly propose to Bill Knowland a remarkable exchange. If California's seventy votes could somehow be thrown to Taft on the first ballot, and if the Ohioan then failed to get the nomination on that roll call, Taft would switch all his delegates to Knowland. "Senator Knowland of California has received an offer from Taft which really takes him up on the mountaintop," Drew Pearson recorded in his diary. "There's no doubt that he would have swung *his* vote or as many as he could influence toward the candidacy of Senator Taft," Knowland aide Paul Manolis remembered. But once again—even if Knowland might somehow have carried a unit rule revolt to swing the delegation—the approach foundered on Knowland's enduring loyalty to Earl Warren and Warren's stony insistence on his own candidacy.

The last forty-eight hours before the Presidential and Vice-Presidential balloting would be another period of alarums and excursions, and of last-moment brokering that alternately made and unmade Richard Nixon's finely wrought run for the ticket.

Milton Polland watched Nixon on Wednesday and Thursday still avidly "selling . . . those who were on the fence," telling uncommitted delegates all over the floor that California would go to Eisenhower, that the bandwagon was irreversible. His men even planned a large reception at the Knickerbocker honoring Senator Nixon and aimed at vacillating delegates—until Mac Faries learned of the plans, demanded to know why Warren and Knowland were not being "honored" or included as well, and the aides sheepishly retreated. At that, the indefatigable Eisenhower men continued to probe for California votes through other means, Eisenhower's secret assurances to Davis and Warren notwithstanding. But when Sherman Adams approached Knowland on the floor and asked to "discuss" the situation, Knowland "hardly spoke to me," as Adams recalled. "He only scowled, shook his head violently, and turned his back to me." It was yet another gesture that seemed to reinforce Richard Nixon as Eisenhower's man—and candidate—in California.

Soon after Knowland's snub of Adams, Eisenhower paid a ritual call on the California delegation at Warren's invitation. Ostensibly, he appeared, like Taft and the favorite sons, as part of a schedule for the delegates to hear every candidate in person. But his reception by the Californians was almost tumultuous in the small caucus room. The general came, said a biographer, "with the clear knowledge that the junior senator . . . had been lined up as his running mate."

Wednesday, July 9, brought the first published reports of Nixon and the Vice Presidency. "He is being boomed as a possible running mate for Eisenhower but denies any ambition to be Vice President," wrote the *San Francisco Chronicle*. The dispatch generated far less attention, however, than a front-page story the same day in the *Chicago Daily News* signed by its publisher, John Knight, who flatly predicted and endorsed an Eisenhower-Nixon ticket. At a moment when candidates and factions were elbowing frantically for coverage in Chicago's tendentious and rabidly partisan press, the story had its own interesting provenance. An ardent Eisenhower backer, Buff Chandler of the *Los Angeles Times*, "went into a huddle" with Knight, as she told the story later, and persuaded him to publicize "my team." Lodge promptly issued a statement saying blandly there had been "no discussion of a Vice President," while *The New York Times* added weight to the statement itself by calling it a "strategic denial."

Nixon, reported the Chandlers' *Los Angeles Times*, "knew nothing of any movement for an Eisenhower-Nixon ticket." To the United Press the young senator said again in modesty, "It's the first time I ever heard of it and I expect it will be the last." He joked with journalists that he had even sent out for extra copies of the *Daily News*. "That will probably be the last time we'll see that headline, and I want to be able to show it to my grandchildren." Yet the publicity was undeniably powerful and legitimizing, and obviously intended in part as a further lure to the California delegation to follow Dick Nixon. As if to confirm his own prediction, Knight sent a *Daily News* reporter to do a feature on the wife of the putative "running mate." Pat Nixon, the paper said in the first of what would soon be countless such profiles, was "Senator Nixon's Man Friday," housewife and mother as well as her husband's one-person staff in Chicago, taking care of his correspondence and "other business chores."

On Wednesday, too, the convention cheered lustily as Joe McCarthy reminded them of Alger Hiss and of the great triumph of the politician now celebrated on the *Daily News* front page. "One communist on the faculty of one university is one communist too many," McCarthy said, delivering his rousing litany. "One communist among American advisers at Yalta was one communist too many." In its platform the 1952 GOP convention would provide what one historian called "complete sanction to the Wisconsin senator," charging that the Democrats "have shielded traitors to the nation in high places."

Yet the hotter passion was reserved, as always, for the intramural clash of ambition and region. In the Wednesday night debate over the Georgia seats, Everett Dirksen of Illinois took the podium for Taft in a calculated effort to rouse the convention against Tom Dewey and the forces he symbolized to so many. In his deep and mellow tones, the oratory of another era, Dirksen began gently by addressing his "good friends from the eastern seaboard," urging them to "search their hearts" before voting to unseat the Taft Georgians. Then, amid warming applause, he turned dramatically to the right and below the podium toward the New York standard and fixed Tom Dewey with a pointing arm and forefinger. "We followed you before and you took us down the road to defeat. And don't do this to us again." Suddenly, Dirksen's last syllable drowned out, the amphitheater filled with a rush of boos and angry cheering. For a moment, the convention seemed on the verge of chaos. Fights broke out in some contingents. Visitors leapt on chairs in the galleries to hurl their catcalls and epithets at the small dapper man with the mustache, whom Alice Roosevelt Longworth had once called sneeringly the bridegroom on the wedding cake. Cabot Lodge watched in alarm as some Taft delegates walked up the aisles near where Dewey sat and "shook their fists in his face."

The savage frustration of intraparty defeat and two decades out of power poured over Dewey. But then his own defenders were soon in the aisles as well, and the wave slowly receded. Watching on television, Earl Warren thought Dirksen had "treated Tom Dewey, the 1948 standard-bearer, as though he were a pickpocket," and was appalled. "I have always felt that the despotic manner in which the convention was run," he wrote later, "lost Senator Taft a sizable number of votes." Through it all, Dewey had sat impassively, staring back at Dirksen with a thin smile that one writer described as "a fearful rebuke to his opponents." It was the serenity of a man who had counted his votes. Before the session adjourned near 3:00 A.M., the Eisenhower slates from Georgia and Jack Porter's renegade Democrats and oilmen from Mineral Wells had been seated by resounding margins. Taft himself would look back on Georgia as "the key vote." John Dinkelspiel remembered Dick Nixon coming back to the hotel excitedly after that stormy late session, pressing weary California delegates anew that it was now only "realistic" to support Ike.

Delegates awoke Thursday morning to the stark arithmetic of the bloody credentials struggle. Eisenhower now led Taft for the first time 502–485, the sum of the shift in southern delegations and a margin that would grow during the day. An echo of the previous night's howls, a Taft broadsheet was circulated calling Dewey a "blight" and "THE MOST COLD-BLOODED, RUTHLESS, SELFISH POLITICAL BOSS IN THE UNITED STATES TODAY," a front for "the same old gang of Eastern Internationalist and Republican New Dealers." The invective would be no replacement for the lost seats. Taft now made one last grasp at California. After his scheduled visit to the delegation, he saw Warren privately and virtually begged for the votes.

"This is my last chance," Taft told him plaintively. There was a cabinet post, the attorney generalship. The California governor could have "anything I desired," Warren remembered. MacArthur wanted the Vice Presidency, it was true, but Taft "could even take care of that." Warren replied coolly that he sought no federal job and would be happy to return to California. "Well," Taft offered, "Bill Knowland can have anything he wants." Warren only stiffened. "No, Senator, we will go ahead as we promised." Victor Hansen remembered Taft leaving by the service exit to avoid questions and the crowds. Reluctant to go, he had backed out into the freight elevator and up against a large trash can, losing his balance and falling in. "Oh, my! Get me up from this," he cried to an aide. Hansen thought the small mishap "hurt his dignity," one more insult added to the final defeat rising before him.

California was to caucus a last time before the Presidential nominating speeches and balloting, and "emissaries beat a path to the door," as *The New York Times* noted. After Taft came Harold Stassen, courting Warren while Warren Burger dickered with Knowland. Together, the two delegations could be "kingmakers" for Eisenhower, the Minnesotans argued, though Stassen's irrepressible ambition still flashed nakedly, and his own men believed he had long since reneged on the Clarksboro contract. For a few minutes in Warren headquarters at the Hilton there would be the spectacle of two future Chief Justices of the United States Supreme Court palavering over convention votes and backroom combinations. But again Earl Warren drew back. "I couldn't help feeling sorry for him," Drew Pearson remembered of those fateful hours. Pearson found Knowland clearly "peeved with Senator Nixon" and the rumors of his Vice-Presidential nomination. But Earl Warren was somehow philosophic about the larger prize of the Presidency, which he sensed passing him by again. "I haven't the money and I can't go out and make the deals necessary to raise the money to stage a real campaign," the governor told Pearson in confidence. "You have to hock your soul in order to do it."

Knowland opened the caucus later at the Knickerbocker with a suddenly encouraging if vague report that "scattered delegates from various parts of the country" would vote for Warren the next day. The delegates must "stand firm and not be dismayed by rumor." He warned against "efforts to stampede" the delegation and again urged them to "approach the job prayerfully and not take action on unfounded rumor." To the delight of Warren aides, it was a thinly veiled attack on Nixon, who sat silent and expressionless in a row of leaders seated on a small platform facing the delegates. Knowland brought a cascade of applause and cheers by telling them he was not "guaranteeing" Warren's victory, though both Taft and Eisenhower would be short on the first ballot "by a considerable number of votes," and "we have the opportunity to nominate Earl Warren as President of the United States." Even if their governor judged he had no chance and released them, Knowland concluded, "California will act solely in the interest of the Republican Party and the nation, and not engage in any type of deal whatsoever."

Earl Warren now rose to more yelling and clapping. As San Francisco reporter Clint Mosher watched carefully, "The governor pointedly ignored Nixon . . . sitting beside him on the platform." Mosher wrote later, "The Warren boys suddenly realized that the Nixon-for-Vice-President boom was the real McCoy. They were enraged." After acknowledging the ovation and several in the audience, Warren just as pointedly turned to recognize Nixon. "His attempt to recover by mentioning him belatedly," thought Mosher, "only emphasized the snub." The governor then went on to voice his "tremendous pride" in the loyalty of the delegation. "Win, lose or draw or whatever happens," he told them, it would be "one of the proudest moments" of his life to have their ballots tomorrow. He turned to thank Knowland effusively. He would not trade their senior senator "for any six chairmen of other delegations."

It was the low point of Richard Nixon's convention. Twenty-four hours earlier proclaimed the running-mate apparent on a Chicago front page, buoyed still more by the Eisenhower seating victories Wednesday night, he might have been the star of this final California caucus, the true favorite son about to be anointed with the Vice Presidency. Instead, he was now facing the all-but-open contempt of both Warren and Knowland, in a chastening demonstration of the political authority both men still commanded in open battle.

Their caucus performance was masterful, in part a calculated slap at Nixon, in part sheer bravura on a night when Eisenhower by most counts crept within fifty votes of the nomination. But it was also the high-water mark of Warren's problematical strategy of deadlock. Faries and others reckoned over a hundred random votes for the governor on the second or third ballots. What was more, the shrewd Polland had gone to Dirksen after the explosive scene Wednesday night. Dirksen and his camp were "so bitter against Dewey," Polland remembered, that they had now agreed to swing to Warren against Eisenhower in a deadlocked convention. "We had that worked out fairly well," Polland would say. The five hundred Taft stalwarts plus California's seventy and the other "scattered" Warren second-ballot votes could put them over the winning 604. Warren and Stassen had agreed at least to recess and caucus after the initial balloting. It would depend entirely on stopping Eisenhower on the first roll call.

Yet for all that, a plausible vision of victory, Mac Faries still found himself late that night arguing heatedly to hold some of the California delegates. "I had to work to try to straighten some of these people out," he said later. A few hours from the presidential vote, Dick Nixon still exerted his pull on the bound delegation. Despite the upbraiding at the caucus, the senator was "supremely confident," wrote one editor, "that he would break the Warren delegation in the second ballot." It was to be a bitter struggle to the last.

Ironically, at the same moment Earl Warren was consolidating his hold on the delegation—and humbling Dick Nixon—the very importance of the California votes seemed to recede for Eisenhower. On the convention floor that Thursday, Taft and Warren would be placed in nomination to impressive demonstrations, dinned in the numbing choruses of "Onward, Christian Soldiers" and "California, Here I Come." But in the relative quiet of the inner Eisenhower suites, the delegate count for the next day neared six hundred, and the managers turned more attentively to their decision on the Vice Presidency. By one account, Brownell, Clay, and Dewey had all agreed earlier on Nixon. Brownell now took the final steps. If it was Dewey's machine that drove the convention, it was his old campaign manager who gripped the wheel. "Herbert Brownell sits constantly with Eisenhower," Pearson recorded in his diary. "Ike seems bewildered by it all [and] constantly asks: 'What do we do next, Herb?' "

Dining with Brownell alone Thursday night, an occasion scheduled specifically to discuss a running mate, the general was still unclear about the protocol of the politics. "I thought the convention had to do that," Eisenhower said when Brownell asked if he had any particular preferences. They had then discussed an earlier list of possible candidates, including Nixon, Congressmen Charles Halleck and Walter Judd, and Governors Dan Thornton of Colorado and Arthur Langlie of Washington. All were relatively young, midwestern or western, and internationalists, Eisenhower's general criteria, though he thought the California senator three years older than he was. Of these names, as Brownell and Eisenhower both related their conversation, they mainly "talked about Nixon."

Still, on the threshold of final selection, Knowland lingered as a rival. Despite the general's list and a palpable distaste for Knowland among other Eisenhower advisers, Brownell met with Chotiner on Thursday to discuss both California senators. If each represented the new power of California and the West, who would be the better campaigner? Brownell questioned. "I gave him my candid opinion," Chotiner would say, "which was that Nixon had a shade as a campaigner and also appealed more to independents and young people . . . just a shade in favor of Nixon." Brownell then asked with evident concern about Earl Warren's reaction to the selection of Nixon. They would not want to lose California in November to some intraparty bitterness. By his own account, Chotiner's reply was at best disingenuous. "I said I didn't know but that there had not been any warmth between the two." Posed the same question about Knowland's reaction, Chotiner related an almost equally misleading anecdote about the senator's wife. "You tell Dick not to think of saying anything of it, to go right ahead, and as it is awfully close not to think for a moment how Bill would feel about it," he quoted Helen Knowland as saying, though by then she was as outraged as her husband at the Nixon tactics. "Well, if Bill Knowland's wife feels that way about it," Brownell reportedly said in turn, "why that must be it."

Later that evening there were two separate scenes that caught the differing perspectives on the moment. "Concluding that my work was finished," as he wrote afterward, Paul Davis was packing to leave Chicago. He had called Earl Warren and received grateful thanks for his mission to stop Nixon. Meanwhile, Pat Nixon was returning to the hotel from a late dinner with Helene Drown to find Dick waiting for her and "anxious to talk." With the publicity of the day before, Nixon had assured her that the press was "only guessing" and dismissed the prospect of the Vice Presidency with his wife much as he did with questioning reporters. Now, in the closing hours, he moved at last to bring her along on the ambition and future he had been scheming and striving to realize for so many months. The talk of being on the ticket looked serious, he told her. "If this Vice Presidential thing is offered to me, do you think I should take it?"

As he expected, her reaction was negative. "My mother was wary and realistic," wrote Julie Eisenhower. "She resisted being swept away by the surface glamour of the idea. The . . . Senate campaign and its heated rhetoric was still a vivid memory, and she dreaded the prospect of having to leave Tricia and me, then six and four years old, for another long campaign." Another writer concluded that Pat Nixon "wanted—at this point desperately—to be left alone to raise her family in peace."

They talked into the night, and at 4:00 A.M. Nixon telephoned Chotiner to come to their room. Padding down the hall in house slippers and silk robe, Chotiner "could tell that Pat had been talking against it." None of them would describe the chemistry of this threesome in the predawn in a Chicago hotel room. But the contest was all too plain—the resentments that went back to 1946 and 1950, the clash once more of purpose, allegiance, career. Chotiner now launched into a rapid-fire argument, ostensibly addressed to the senator, who hardly needed persuasion, but of course aimed directly at Pat Nixon. He repeated much of the extraordinary monologue in an interview years later.

> Dick, you're a junior senator from California and you will always be a junior senator from California. Bill Knowland is young and he's healthy, and unless something should happen to him, you will always be second man in California. The junior senator from California doesn't amount to anything. There comes a time when you have to go up or out. Suppose you're the candidate and we lose? You're still the junior senator and haven't lost anything. If you win and are elected Vice President and at the end

of four years you become all washed up, you could open
a law office in Whittier and have all the business in town.
Any man who quits political life as Vice President as
young as you are in years certainly hasn't lost a thing.

There would be no record of Pat's response to this remarkable outpouring,
the demeaning of the Senate seat they had fought so savagely to gain, the
prospect of a Whittier law practice and the small-town, relative-strewn life
she despised. When Chotiner left near sunrise they were "still debating,"
as the aide remembered. "I guess I can make it through another campaign,"
she finally conceded, though apparently believing, too, that she had talked
him out of it. "Pat was sure she had won," wrote Lester David, "and that
he would refuse an offered bid."

As they wound down—"too excited to sleep and too weary to get in
bed," wrote their daughter—the morning newspapers were prominently
reporting Senator Richard Nixon "in the front rank of possible running
mates to General Eisenhower." From leaks by Brownell and Chotiner, *The
New York Times* reported as well the names of Halleck and Langlie, and
Knowland in the "second rank." But "for three days," said the *Times*,
"Senator Nixon's name has led the field in Vice-Presidential conversations
among inner-circle groups at the convention."

Leaving the Knickerbocker that morning, Knowland was still defiant.
"A lot of misinformation was being spread," he told reporters, and Eisenhower and Taft would be short on the first ballot.

The roll call began minutes before noon. California's seventy came soon
for Warren but with only a handful of the other expected votes. Taft took
an early lead. Then Michigan turned the tide to Eisenhower, and the margin
held. Jeers welled up again as Dewey cast New York's massive vote for
Ike. As the tally moved.on, it seemed clear Eisenhower would be only a
few votes short. An audible stir began to run through the delegates and
press.

Jim Hagerty was nervously working the floor when an excited reporter
asked him if they would get the needed votes changed from California.
And Hagerty answered sharply, "We don't want them from California."
They would not confront Warren; there would be no appearance of a deal.
The choice was Nixon.

Besieged by his own delegates to join the rolling Eisenhower bandwagon, Stassen frantically sent Warren Burger to ask Knowland once more
if California would join Minnesota in a change of vote to put Ike over, "as
a means of healing party wounds," according to one listener. Knowland

answered coldly, "We don't want any credit or any responsibility for *that* nomination."

Then, as the roll moved to an end, Knowland suddenly had second thoughts. "I've got to go and phone Earl right away to get his authority and see what to do," he blurted to Mac Faries. But he soon came back after repeated attempts and slumped in his chair. "I can't get Earl, can't find him, can't get hold of him."

The District of Columbia was now voting, four places from the close of the call, and the bulky Burger was surging forward up the aisle to get the ear of Chairman Joe Martin. Minnesota would be changing its count. The tally ended at 595–500. They lifted Minnesota's standard off the floor and waved it furiously amid rising cheers and chants from the galleries. "Here we go," Tom Dewey muttered. Thirty-five minutes after the ballot had begun, Minnesota switched nineteen votes from Stassen and nominated Dwight Eisenhower.

In the general's suite, Brownell leapt across the room to congratulate his candidate. Eisenhower then shook hands with his staff and brothers and, again teary-eyed, walked into the next room to see his wife, who was in bed with a toothache. At his own headquarters, Bob Taft was characteristically stoic. "I can take it," he said. "After all, I've had plenty of practice." Returning to his suite, he bent over and kissed his crippled wife, telling her quietly, "Well, this was always one of the alternatives." In Warren's rooms, aides wore what one reporter thought were "forced smiles," and there was no more free orange juice for visitors. Milton Polland was sitting with the governor as they quietly watched the television broadcast of the final moments. The delegate strategist would be in awe of the victory he ascribed to Nixon as well as Brownell and Dewey. "It was a beautiful maneuver," he concluded.

Afterward, there was much speculation about how California had been "left behind," about Knowland's hubris or a deliberate effort to embarrass and deny Richard Nixon. But none of that reckoned on Earl Warren's towering pride this day. His answer would have been clear even if Knowland had reached him. "And, of course, when it got that close to Eisenhower, there were importunities made on me to turn our delegation over, which would have clearly done the job for him," Warren recalled, "and I wasn't going to let it be said that I was a patsy for anybody else."

As the convention recessed for the naming of a running mate, excited delegates hurried toward the exits and someone yelled irreverently, "Last one out is the Vice President!" For many, the mood was awful. Coming upon Dewey in a hotel lobby, a Taft supporter had to be held back from hitting him. Everywhere—hallways, elevators, lobbies—Taft delegates wept openly. "For the stalwart five hundred and their allies," wrote one historian, "the loss to Eisenhower was almost too much to bear."

Eisenhower crossed the street to the Hilton to call on Taft—describing him as "a very great American"—and then fought his way back to the Blackstone, where Cyrus Sulzberger found him "in a curious mood of dazed elation." As sandwiches were served and champagne uncorked, Sulzberger noticed Eisenhower "sitting all alone on the sofa as if he were an invisible man . . . looking rather pale and stunned with his thoughts obviously far, far away, while we all drank to him as if he didn't even know he was there." After a brief lunch with his wife, the candidate began to go over his acceptance speech and met once again with Brownell about the Vice Presidency. When someone asked him what he was planning, he replied with a grin, "I've got to talk to Herb. You know, I've never been a candidate before."

It all seemed casual, foreordained. "I gathered from talking to the 'boys,' " Sulzberger wrote, noting the corporate executives who wandered in and out, "that it has already been agreed that Richard Nixon of California will be the Vice-Presidential nominee." Ellis Slater was standing with Bill Robinson, champagne glass in hand, when Eisenhower suddenly came out of the bedroom and said, "I have my man for Vice President."

"Who is that?" Slater asked.

"Nixon."

And Robinson said to the nominee, "Slats told you that last year."

The precise moment and sequence of the selection was lost in the furor after Eisenhower's triumph. Nixon may have heard it first only minutes after the balloting, even before they left the amphitheater, when Cabot Lodge pushed his way through to the California seats. "Dick, it's all decided," Mac Faries remembered overhearing Lodge say. "Eisenhower has agreed that you are going to be the Vice-Presidential choice." Lodge ticked off the considerations of balance—someone from the Congress, a Navy man and World War II veteran, "a man who can stand up and speak." Faries listened to him ask above the din, "Will you do it?" and Nixon, of course, "said he would." Nixon had then left, and Faries and a friend waited for Knowland. "This is going to be awful tough on Bill, let's get him out of here," one of them said. They took Knowland in tow, got a car, and drove aimlessly through Chicago, saying nothing about Nixon or the Vice Presidency, talking, Faries said, "about kings and cabbages, and so on." Knowland did not ask either, though he had to go back to the hotel before returning to the convention; his shirt, they noticed, was "as wet as a sheet."

At the Hilton headquarters, Brownell duly organized the ceremony of consulting the party leaders. They invited Earl Warren along with thirty or forty others "to select a Vice-Presidential candidate." But the governor of California understood what had happened all too well. "Believing that was already a *fait accompli*, I declined," he wrote tersely in his memoirs.

The rest drifted in later in the afternoon and lounged about on chairs and divans, a few women and mostly senior party men who now took off their coats and lit up cigars and cigarettes in the already stuffy air. "It reminded me," said Sherman Adams, "of a ward committee in Philadelphia discussing the selection of a candidate for alderman." Among the group, in addition to Brownell, Lodge, and Dewey, were Lucius Clay and Paul Hoffman; several senators; Arthur Summerfield, the Michigan auto dealer who was the new national chairman; Governors Fine, John Lodge, and Thornton; Roy Roberts, publisher of the *Kansas City Star* and an old Ei-senhower crony; and not least Texan Jack Porter and other southern leaders whose revolt had been at the heart of their victorious strategy.

Brownell began the meeting as chairman saying the nomination was wide open. "No deals have been made," he told them solemnly. Adams, for one, was impressed. "It was by no means obvious," he wrote later of Brownell's performance, "that the decision had already been made by Eisenhower, on the recommendation of his principal advisers." The kindly and somewhat doddering Alexander Smith of New Jersey—"a grandmother kind of senator," one of them called him—promptly gave a brief oration on "what a wonderful thing it would be" to field an Eisenhower-Taft ticket. Summerfield thought that "a fine idea." And while Dewey and Brownell remained stonily silent, it seemed for a moment almost possible. Then someone pointed out how much they would need Taft in the Senate, and Dewey's redoubtable Russell Sprague, party to so many of the compacts with Dick Nixon, remarked gravely that with Taft not even General Ei-senhower could carry New York state. Senator Carlsen chimed in that Taft himself had called before the meeting to suggest Ev Dirksen. Again there was silence. "After what Dirksen said the other night," Governor Beardsley of Iowa finally said in slow midwestern cadence, "the people of Iowa wouldn't use him to wipe their feet on." Brownell suggested they move on.

They tossed out names now almost perfunctorily from previous news-paper accounts—Thornton, Driscoll, Judd, Halleck, Knowland. Brownell ruled that anyone "sponsoring" a particular candidate could make a state-ment and then leave. "We only wanted those open to conviction to stay," he would explain. "We didn't want sponsors on the jury." After more desultory comment and a deliberate lull, Dewey looked around the faces and asked, "What about Dick Nixon?" He then gave what his biographer would call "a lucid outline of the senator's advantages, stressing age and campaigning gifts." Hoffman offered that Nixon came well recommended in his home state. "I told them that everything I had heard about Senator Nixon was good," he said later. "He was well-liked in southern California, had made a fine showing in the campaigns, and I thought he would be a great help to the ticket . . . one of the Republicans who had an enlightened view on foreign affairs."

Beyond that, neither Hoffman nor anyone else appeared to be aware of further details about the senator—the existence of the Fund, the 1950 race, or even the savage infighting with Warren over the past days and weeks, though Hagerty and others in the Eisenhower camp believed Nix-on's work in the California delegation a salient reason for his selection. In any case, when Hoffman had finished it seemed clear to them all, as one observer put it, that "the Dewey forces were prepared to make a fight for Nixon if necessary."

Brownell "called quickly for a show of hands," as one of them recalled, and every arm in the room went up. The group cheered its decision and then adjourned with a "bustle and scraping of chairs," recorded Adams, who concluded it was all "a pretty mundane affair." In less than two hours they had followed what the *St. Louis Post-Dispatch* thought "the same hap-hazard system by which the major parties traditionally select their candi-dates . . . concerned more in finding a man who could bring 'balance and votes' to the ticket than picking one for his qualifications and experience to be a 'reserve' President. . . . No attention was given to the possibility that the man they picked might someday be called on to take over the full powers and responsibilities of the Presidency."

A Dewey aide was dispatched to find Pat Nixon and instruct her to "keep a smile on her face" for the television cameras at the convention. At the same moment, with Dewey sitting casually on the edge of a desk and Sprague, Summerfield, and others milling about, Brownell telephoned both Eisenhower and Nixon. Nixon had returned to the Stockyards Inn to find his room uncooled and stifling. He had stripped down to his shorts and was lying on top of the bed covers, "trying to think cool thoughts," as he remembered. Chotiner soon burst into the room to report the latest conversation with Brownell, that they were going into the ratifying meeting of party leaders at the Hilton. Despite that news, despite Lodge's earlier assurance on the floor, Nixon remained worried that the nomination would somehow elude him at the last minute. "I knew that some of Eisenhower's more liberal advisers had preferred Earl Warren to me," he wrote afterward, "and that some of his more conservative advisers had preferred Bill Knowland or even Bob Taft."

Half asleep in the afternoon heat, he heard the phone jangle, reached for it, and heard Brownell's voice, apparently talking to Eisenhower on another receiver, and then saying to Nixon, "We picked you."

Brownell told him Eisenhower wanted to see him "right away," adding slyly, "that is, assuming you want it!" In his own account, Nixon did not even take time to shower or shave; he threw back on his wrinkled suit, feeling "hot, sleepy, and grubby." But Chotiner, who now rushed about finding a car and even an impromptu motorcycle escort, thought Nixon "calm and pensive" on the way to Eisenhower. He asked Chotiner to call Hannah and Frank in Whittier. "They're probably watching TV," he remarked.

As they sped away from the Stockyards Inn, Pat Nixon was in the same building having lunch with Helene Drown and Chotiner's wife, watching a movie on a restaurant screen. A notice—"Ike chooses Nixon"—flashed out, and she remembered being so stunned that a bite of sandwich "fell out of my mouth." She ran in the heat to the amphitheater to find the convention corridors already buzzing with her husband's nomination. "I guess I was one of the last to learn that he had accepted," she said later.

Entering Eisenhower's rooms at the Blackstone, Nixon told the crush of reporters, "I am tremendously surprised and I hope to conduct a fighting campaign with a fighting candidate." Lodge then put his arm around him and ushered him past the press, saying as they went, "He has done as much to rid this country of communists as any man I know."

Inside, Nixon found Eisenhower waiting for him at the door to his private suite. He plunged forward, saying "Congratulations, Chief" in the address they had always reserved for their last President, Herbert Hoover. But the general visibly bristled and was obviously "displeased." It was "the first hint," as Nixon told his daughter long afterward, "that beneath the engaging, disarmingly wide smile, Eisenhower was reserved and protocol-conscious." After an introduction to Mamie Eisenhower and brief small talk, the general was again "very serious and formal." Their campaign would be a "crusade" for ideals, he told Nixon. "Will you join me in such a campaign?" The younger man was "taken aback by his formality," but answered stiffly, "I would be proud and happy to."

Eisenhower was glad he was "going to be on the team." He wanted no mere figurehead Vice President but a "member of the team," able to "step into the presidency smoothly." He talked at some length about his own reluctance to run and the final pull of "duty." Throughout Nixon thought him a "beguiling mixture of personal savvy and political naïveté," though Eisenhower seemed clear enough that Nixon should "flail the Democrats" while the Presidential candidate remained "above the battle." "The hero," his new running mate concluded at the outset, "needed a point man."

He and Chotiner went directly from the Blackstone to the floor of the convention and to an evening of public triumph mixed with private rancor. Dewey had hoped to nominate him. But the wounds of the week were thought too deep, and they turned instead to Knowland as a gesture of unity both in California and with the Taftites. For those who knew the real story, it was scarcely a less painful choice. In Nixon's version, Knowland said he would be "proud and happy" to place his colleague before the convention. Standing next to Knowland on the floor when the request came, Milton Polland clearly heard Knowland's candid response. "I have to nominate that dirty son of a bitch?"

Nixon went personally to ask Ohio's John Bricker to deliver a seconding speech, but the conservative senator refused in his own resentment. "After what they have said and done to Bob Taft over the last few months, I just cannot bring myself to do it," Bricker told him, flushed with emotion. "I was taken aback by the depth of his feeling against the Eisenhower forces, and for the first time I realized how difficult and how important my role as a bridge between the party factions was going to be," Nixon wrote of the incident, though he would say nothing about the scars he had left in his own California GOP.

At the podium before the milling, reassembling convention, Knowland delivered a predictably lukewarm nomination speech. "I could tell that he would have rather had a beating than had to do that," Keith McCormac thought, watching television back in Bakersfield. "He would rather have been anywhere but there, nominating Nixon." In the seconding speeches, Governor Driscoll of New Jersey praised him more enthusiastically as a "fighting representative . . . who knows the smell of the herring and its color, too." An old member of Chowder and Marching, Congressman Ben Giull of Texas, described Nixon warmly as "capable, lovable, and fine," while Congresswoman Cecile Hardin spoke into the television cameras of Dick Nixon's "sincerity and integrity, his keen sense of right . . . his deep faith in God." "No man," Governor Frank Barrett of Wyoming told them, "did so much as Dick Nixon to put the fear of God in these men who would betray their country." Pennsylvania's Fine then moved swiftly for nomination by acclamation, and a little after 6:30 P.M. July 11, Richard Milhous Nixon became his party's nominee for Vice President of the United States.

Standing in the midst of the California delegation flanked by Chotiner, he flung his arms around his colleagues, waved exuberantly to the crowd, and looked about for Pat, who was making her way in similar excitement from the visitors' gallery. As he waited, a CBS technician thrust a headset at him, and he did television's first live convention floor interview with Walter Cronkite and Edward R. Murrow. "I am amazed, flabbergasted, weak, and speechless," Pat told reporters trailing her in the tumult. "We heard rumors, but we heard rumors about a lot of people. I wasn't prepared for this." Someone asked if she would campaign, and she answered, "We work as a team." Asked about his pretty wife coming down the aisle, Nixon paused and then said to a reporter, "She's never been on the federal payroll." When she reached the California standard, she kissed her husband in genuine joy, and then laughingly repeated the kiss for begging photographers who missed the first. As they were slowly ushered to the platform by Jack Porter and other official escorts, the convention routinely passed a resolution on the authority of the National Committee to "fill any and all vacancies which may occur . . . in the ticket," an unnoticed act that was to brook large in his life and career only a few weeks later. But for now all was lost in his remarkable success.

With the band pealing out "It's Gonna Be a Great Day," they mounted the platform, Pat kissed a reddening Joe Martin, and the roar swelled around them. Only four years before Nixon had been in the galleries of the Philadelphia convention, an obscure congressman without a seat on his state's delegation or even a pass to the floor. Now he heard "for the first time," he remembered, "the thunderous sound of several thousand people shouting themselves hoarse and stamping their feet and clapping for us." He would feel "exhilarated—almost heady." Afterward, Pat would tell friends that the ovation made her "forget the long campaign that we would have to endure."

Later, to the stirring strains of the "Field Artillery March," the Eisenhowers and Nixons appeared together, prompting another uproar. "I know something of the solemn responsibility of leading a crusade," Eisenhower said in his speech. "I accept your summons."

Nixon began his own brief acceptance with a rousing tribute to Ike: "Haven't we got a wonderful candidate for the President of the United States?" He promised to win "a victory for America" and pointedly reached out to Taft by praising him as "one of the really great senators, one of the greatest legislative leaders in the history of American life." At that the frustrated Taft delegates went "wild," he recalled, though "too wild for the taste of some of Eisenhower's liberal advisers, who felt that Taft's ovation was more enthusiastic than Eisenhower's . . . [and] that I had done this purposely in order to belittle Eisenhower and build myself up." It was not his last "run-in," he noted, "with this small but determined group."

His speech officially closed the GOP convention, and he went to a crowded midnight press conference with his old supporters—Frank Jorgensen, Harrison McCall, Roy Day, Tom Bewley, and others looking on proudly. He and Ike would make the Vice Presidency a "working job," he told the reporters. The most important campaign issue of 1952 would be "destroying the forces of communism at home and abroad." In its early edition that morning the *Los Angeles Times* would headline "NIXON RETRIEVES STATE PRESTIGE LOST BY WARREN."

His old press supporters in the basin were hardly alone. "Nixon is alert, vigorous, and serious-minded," concluded *The New York Times*. Eisenhower might have chosen someone out of political expediency. "Instead," pronounced the *Times*, "he chose Senator Nixon—without benefit of deals . . . on what we hope and expect will be a winning ticket in November."

22

Campaign Interval,
July–September 1952

"THE GREATEST MOMENT IN HISTORY"

He began his first national race in a distorted, half-lit aura of media celebrity that was to follow him into the future. Standing near the press tables at the Chicago convention when the word of Nixon's selection was confirmed, Clare Boothe Luce thought she heard "shouts of rage and disbelief" from reporters around her. But there was no similar testimony from others at the same place and moment, and much to the contrary. Her memory, like Nixon's own recollection of hostile journalism in the Hiss case, read back into history the aversion of later years. No less in the 1952 campaign as so often before, a bland, largely admiring press was an accompaniment and condition of his rise.

Within hours of his nomination, the wire services discovered the attractive little Nixon girls. "I want everybody to vote for my daddy," exclaimed Tricia in a nationwide story, and an Associated Press photo of the same prominence showed the youthful candidate holding his two daughters next to a pretty smiling wife. Pat Nixon, said a biography circulated by the National Committee, was the "same age as the senator," "attends [the] Quaker church," and worked at a discreetly unidentified "government job" while her husband was in the navy. *Time* reported her as "a lifelong Protestant" and her husband as "deeply religious," "rarely smokes or takes a drink," with "nothing McCarthyesque about . . . [his] methods." In the postconvention coverage Nixon would be invariably portrayed as a figure of youthful vigor and enthusiasm yet with mature seriousness and modesty.

The same glow soon surrounded the candidate's gray-haired parents proudly watching television in their stucco house on a quiet street in East Whittier. To a troop of reporters, Hannah soberly repeated the family story about the little boy reading about Teapot Dome and announcing, "When I get big, I'll be a lawyer they can't bribe." The mother described her own modest reaction to her son's nomination for the Vice Presidency. "It's just like a dream." She added that her husband had said, "Ike and Dick will make things snap." In his own more candid quote, Frank Nixon told the Associated Press, "I really didn't want Dick to get into this job. . . . I felt that he'd do a good job as a senator and then later he could be a candidate for President."

Other, less-publicized statements suggested the seventy-four-year-old father's fire and pride, now usually muted by physical ailments and the family's careful concern for public reaction. "Mr. Truman isn't going to like Dick's nomination," Frank confided to a *Los Angeles Times* reporter, "because he hates Dick like a rattlesnake."

Behind the public façade, the Vice-Presidential candidate moved deftly to shore up his prize with the badly bruised and riven GOP. While Pat flew back to Washington, he had stayed behind to make the rounds of Republican leaders with Eisenhower, and then to pay his own private calls, small acts of ritual and deference that were ultimately to help save his candidacy and career.

One of their first steps was to appease the party's most volatile figure, Joe McCarthy. Even absorbed in all the preconvention maneuvering in California and in his controversial private poll, Nixon had been careful to maintain the muted alliance with McCarthy. He had interrupted a crowded schedule in mid-June to deliver the keynote address at the Wisconsin state convention of the GOP in Milwaukee, where he brought three thousand delegates to their feet with an evocation of the "communist fifth column in the United States," a ringing endorsement of McCarthy's reelection, and the promise of a "fair" investigation of McCarthy's charges by a Republican administration. McCarthy, meanwhile, played his own protean politics. Preferring MacArthur and toying with Taft, he even offered secretly at one point prior to the convention to help pirate Eisenhower delegates with the help of an old friend who had double-dated with him and who also knew Dick Nixon—an ardent young Republican lawyer from Washington named John J. Sirica.

Now, in the aftermath of the convention, McCarthy was grudgingly ready to accept Eisenhower in large measure because of Richard Nixon. Like the old guard at the Bohemian Club, McCarthy and his vocal constituency saw the Vice Presidential choice as a tangible concession. "Insiders understood that Nixon's appeal involved not only geography and youth but above all the senator's close ties to Joe McCarthy and his allies," wrote Wisconsin scholar Thomas Reeves. "If the GOP had to swallow Ike . . . the presence of Nixon on the ticket would do much to appease the far right."

"While they all knew that I had been for Eisenhower, they appreciated the fact that I had not been involved in any of the preconvention attacks on Taft," Nixon claimed in his memoirs. "Also, the Taft people tended to be organization-minded and they considered me to be a good organization man because . . . I had spoken for party fund-raising and other affairs. . . . They knew I would hit hard against communism and corruption." By any measure, it was an amazingly condescending and disingenuous view of his relationship to the conservatives he had worked so doggedly to subvert and vanquish.

On the national level, as in California, the political chemistry of Richard Nixon and the right was volatile and complex. In addition to McCarthy, he and Eisenhower formally received the embittered John Bricker and other Taft supporters on Saturday, July 12, and late that night Nixon made his own respectful call on Robert Taft. They enjoyed a "general discussion," the defeated leader said afterward, and a "friendly chat" about how to elect Eisenhower. Outwardly the obeisance was paid, though Taft refused to discuss his role in the campaign and many of his followers remained irreconcilable. In private, Taft himself came away with a harsher sense of what had happened in Chicago and before, including the intrigues blanketing the California primary and its delegation. Not long after Chicago, he would describe Nixon with an air of regret as "a little man in a big hurry" possessing a "mean and vindictive streak." The young senator's personality tended to "radiate tension and conflict," the Ohioan confided to his old friend Joseph Polowsky. Taft held "a fervent hope that the new Vice Presidential nominee would never occupy the Oval Office."

Nonetheless, his grasping rather too plain after the fact, the young Nixon would remain for Taft as for McCarthy and others the sole consolation in a battle won by what Taft called wrathfully "the power of the New York financial interest." The old guard's postconvention accommodations of money and influence were fashioned accordingly to make the most of the salvage. With the appointment as national chairman of Arthur Summerfield, the Michigan Chevrolet executive with his General Motors proxy, the Eisenhower campaign would also acquire the backing of yet another of America's great dynastic fortunes, the Du Ponts, who had formerly supported Taft and now controlled the General Motors Corporation. And Summerfield, far more conservative than most of his new colleagues in the Eisenhower camp, would be above all a powerful Nixon patron in the campaign to come, with historic results. It was a politics only vaguely felt, if at all, as the Republicans decamped for home in the July heat. "Nixon is a difficult man to categorize," concluded *The Reporter* magazine, watching his postnomination pilgrimage back and forth between the wings. "Perhaps the answer is that he is simply too young and ambitious to have any irrevocable choice between old guard and new."

What onlookers seldom understood was how deliberately and brilliantly Nixon blurred those choices, pursuing a politics not of wing or doctrine so much as ceaseless self-advancement. The same Saturday he received callers with Eisenhower, paid homage to Taft, and attended Summerfield's installation as chairman, he had gone round as well to have a drink with Harold Stassen and his men, still another fiefdom in Republican feudalism. After Minnesota's decisive first-ballot switch, they were a faction of obvious favor and influence regardless of Stassen's caprice. Nixon now flattered and enlisted them and implicitly criticized his new patrons. Together they would be the forces of "realism" in the campaign, tempering the conservatives on one side and Eisenhower on the other, as Bernard Shanley recorded Nixon's approach in his diary. "Because he felt that kind of influence in the camp was needed . . . he made it perfectly clear that he wanted our help," Shanley noted, thinking the deferential and slightly conspiratorial little visit "a splendid recognition by Senator Dick that Harold Stassen had always been and would always be recognized as his mentor." When the nominee had left, they all agreed that it might have been more politic for Ike to have as a running mate "a young outstanding Taft man." But certainly Nixon would do—Harold Stassen's man at court.

There were at least some limits to such double and triple games. Nixon was never so nakedly ingratiating with his ultimate Vice Presidential patron, Tom Dewey, who in turn held the candidate and his men at a respectful distance. Having seen the Californians at work in Chicago, especially the tactics practiced on Earl Warren, Dewey's cold-eyed New Yorkers were forewarned. They would not allow the Vice-Presidential candidate to extend his ambitious reach to Manhattan or the upstate GOP. He would "castrate Murray Chotiner," one of them promised, "if he set foot in the state." Bryce Harlow, a young Eisenhower aide, remembered vividly Richard Nixon's admiring reaction to that recognition of political prowess: "He thought Dewey was about the toughest guy who ever came down the pike."

As he hurried to secure his party flanks, there remained, ironically, a relatively hidden breach he never moved to bridge, perhaps never fully sensed, or else dismissed in the euphoria of the moment. "I am happy to hear of the selection of Senator Nixon," Earl Warren had said in a formal statement the day of nomination, congratulating Eisenhower and calling the half-California ticket "a great honor to our state." Bill Knowland officially told his family's *Oakland Tribune* that Dick Nixon was "an excellent choice" for the Vice Presidency. Behind the façade, both men writhed. "If Nixon had not double-crossed Warren, the nomination could have been won for California's governor!" one of their mutual friends burst out to a Los Angeles journalist in the hours after the convention. To stories that the choice of Nixon had been made early in the week, that the junior senator's "second choice" was Eisenhower, Knowland commented with barely concealed resentment. "I was for Governor Warren, period," he would say. "I didn't have a second or third choice."

While Nixon courted the national factions, the California delegation packed to return to the coast, only to discover an added indignity—somehow the Warren campaign budget had come up short, and the governor and many of his supporters were forced to pay for part of the Chicago facilities out of their own pockets. "The bitterness of the Warren crowd toward Nixon is tremendous," noted the *Examiner*'s Clint Mosher. "Many of them would forever consider Nixon's name roughly synonymous with treachery," another writer recorded. Clustered in the lobby of the Knickerbocker that Saturday, waiting for taxis to take them to Union Station, they pointedly raised their voices "for the obvious purpose of being heard at considerable distance," as a reporter promptly noted. "I'd rather lose with Taft," one of them said in this stage conversation, "than win with Nixon." Already, some had begun to talk to the press about the discreet, interesting, special "Fund" Senator Nixon had solicited in California.

Yet it was Earl Warren, outwardly phlegmatic, who seemed in some ways the most affected. In the wake of the multiple defeats and disappointments, his longtime friendship with Knowland, "political and otherwise," as he put it later, "cooled markedly." But the full brunt of that would come later. For now, he shared their common abhorrence of the other politician in California's trio of national competitors. "He had absolutely no use for Nixon," Warren's friend Richard Rodda said of the mood following the convention. The judgment was to last. Long afterward, in the most hallowed chambers of American justice, Earl Warren's law clerks would hear him talk of 1952 and Richard Nixon "in terms," one of them said, "that would ordinarily be reserved for someone who has proved to engage in serious violations of criminal law and ethical conduct."

Days after returning to Washington, Nixon brought in Murray Chotiner as Vice-Presidential campaign manager, and Chotiner soon assembled the rest of the staff in a headquarters on the fourth floor of the Washington Hotel, aptly overlooking Pennsylvania Avenue, the Treasury, and, just beyond, the White House grounds. They were a reflection of the candidate's almost solitary work and society in Congress over the past five years, of his relative self-sufficiency, and of his reliance on old political loyalties. George McKinnen, the Minnesota congressman defeated in 1948, was now summoned from Minneapolis to act as "research director," the sole assignment of any substance in a campaign where the candidate would compose or extemporize his own speeches, hammer out his own positions. The rest were Californians. Although with no formal title, the square-jawed Hillings was to travel with the candidate, an all-purpose accompanying congressman, loyal aide-de-camp, political sounding board. As usual, Chotiner's efficient Ruth Arnold would be assistant manager. Glen Lipscomb, a conservative Los Angeles assemblyman and veteran of the 1950 race, was "executive secretary," another administrative function.

There were two important newcomers. To supplant Arnold as press secretary, they recruited thirty-nine-year-old James Bassett, a former *Los Angeles Times* reporter who had recently become political editor of the *Los Angeles Mirror*. Educated at Bowdoin, a navy veteran, a graceful writer, the thoughtful, bespectacled Bassett lent an almost academic air to the small staff of otherwise narrow background. He had first met Nixon in Whittier three years earlier when the then-congressman admired a feature article the journalist had done on Hillings, Holt, and other young Republicans. In the summer of 1952, he thought his new employer "young, eager, and somewhat naïve" but a politician who "seemed to have good counsel."

Along with Bassett came Edward Rogers, on leave as assistant manager at the Hollywood ad agency of Dancer, Fitzgerald and Sample, where he was recognized as one of the bright young men of West Coast television, still in his thirties but already an experienced producer credited with popular programs such as "The Lone Ranger," "Amos 'n' Andy," "Double or Nothing," "Beulah," and "Mystery Theatre." Rogers had met Chotiner, then Nixon, in 1950, helped with the Senate race, and would now be the campaign's full-time director for radio and television. Like Bassett, he regarded the candidate as "young and fresh," and in television terms "relatively easy material to work with," as he put it in a later interview. Mentioned only at the end of the press release announcing the campaign staff, Ted Rogers was promptly ignored by newsmen when he accompanied the candidate for a first strategy meeting with Eisenhower in late July. In many ways, his would be the most important appointment Richard Nixon had made since Roy Day had brought him Murray Chotiner in 1946.

After another conference with Summerfield, Nixon prepared to fly to Denver and meet Eisenhower at the general's fishing camp at nearby Fraser, Colorado. It was to be the first personal encounter of the two running mates beyond the crowded rites in Chicago two weeks earlier. Nixon brought along his wife, Chotiner, Pat Hillings, and Rose Woods as well as Rogers.

But the obviously informal, rustic setting of the fishing camp worried him, and before going he telephoned Cabot Lodge's aide and liaison Max Rabb. "He seemed to be troubled," Rabb remembered, "fearful that he could not keep pace with the [future] President in fishing and golf." He had never "indulged in those sports," Nixon told Rabb, and "never could come to like them," though a month before he had been eagerly applying through Bill Rogers for a golfing membership at Kenwood. The call to Rabb was the anxious, self-conscious plaint of a man suddenly thrust into a company in which he seemed disarmed, ill-at-ease, by the very setting. It was to be typical of this awkward pairing he had fought so hard to achieve.

At the airport in Denver he was in his element, telling waiting newsmen that the new Democratic nominee, Illinois governor Adlai Stevenson, was "the same old deal," and predicting a historic GOP victory in the South because the Democrats had not chosen segregationist Georgia senator Richard Russell as Stevenson's running mate. In Fraser the scene was something of what he feared. "Nattily dressed in a light gray business suit," as one reporter saw him, he arrived at the door of the cabin to whirring newsreel cameras and a laughing Eisenhower pointing at his clothes and ordering him off to change into borrowed khaki fishing gear. When a photographer handed him a trout net, Nixon exclaimed, "What is this?" There followed a casting lesson from the general. The shivering young senator was then sent to stand knee-deep in a frigid Colorado stream and later to peel potatoes with Senator Carlson while Eisenhower and his friends heartily cooked up roast beef—all photographed by press and newsreels that caught Richard Nixon's strained smile and wary flinch and duck when the general flicked back his fishing rod to demonstrate what all the rest of them seemed to know. "The general and I discussed campaign organization and strategy," he assured reporters afterward, though Ike in fact had waved aside most political talk around the table in the cabin. He at least learned how to cast, Nixon told the Associated Press as he left, adding ruefully, "But I caught no fish."

"I'VE FINALLY MADE IT"

They flew home to the basin for a triumphal "Welcome" to be staged in Whittier the evening of July 28. Chotiner had gone ahead from Denver to organize the nationally publicized gala, and the scene evoked every strain of the candidate's small-town hominess and new-won political fame. At the insistence of the national campaign, Warren, Knowland, and Lieutenant Governor Goodie Knight—bitter rivals past and future—were on hand to smile as he arrived in Los Angeles. "Welcome to California, Dick,"

Warren said as the cameras rolled again. "All the people of California are rejoicing at your success." From the airport there was a motorcade to a suite at the Ambassador and then later to old Hadley Field at Whittier College, where the largest crowd in memory was gathered. A marine color guard was poised at one end of the gridiron, at the other the Nelles reform school drill team and band. In the sea of faces were high school and college friends, old Whittier families, Paul Smith, Chief Newman, Roy Day, Frank Jorgensen, Dana Smith. "He was the boy they knew who never quit, the boy they knew who fought for what he believed and never yielded," rhapsodized the *Los Angeles Times*. "And they loved him." A Long Beach reporter watched Pat and Hannah looking on as he entered the stadium: "They stood, one thirty-four years old [*sic*] and the other sixty-seven . . . under the blazing lights in the din of music and cheers. . . . Tears glistened in their eyes and they were happy, proud, grateful tears. The mother, a plump little Quaker woman with gray hair and hazel eyes . . . Pat . . . an attractive, friendly woman with red-gold hair . . . [who] carried American Beauty roses."

He addressed the "distinguished guests on the platform behind me," and then with a grin and roar, "all of you distinguished guests in front of me." It would have been "great" even if only Governor Warren or Senator Knowland had come, he told them, but to have all of them . . . "Well, for Pat and me this is the greatest moment in history." He paused and looked out over the field full of people and then to the packed bleachers. "You know, it took me eighteen years to do it, but I've finally made it. I've got off the bench and onto the playing field." The Whittier crowd roared again. "Yes, and we'll win this time, just as Chief Newman's teams won—going away and a mile in the lead."

He then read a letter from the wife of a marine corpsman in Korea, a mother with a two-month-old baby living on eighty-five dollars a month, yet who had sent him a check for ten dollars for the campaign. "I feel confident with you and General Eisenhower in the White House," she had written, "lonely Americans like myself will be united with their loved ones now in Korea." Again an outburst of cheers and applause. "I am going to step down from here and I want every one of you to come up and I want to shake hands with you," he told them. For more than an hour he and Pat greeted the throng. It was, they all thought, a fitting tribute and beginning. "I knew it all the time," Roy Day boasted to reporters. And over and over, seemingly from "anyone in Whittier," the press repeated the proud prediction, "Watch Dick. Some day he will be President."

The Whittier welcome was to be typical of these opening weeks. In public, Nixon would set much of the tenor and cadence of the national

744

race from late July through mid-September and in the process enjoy almost utter impunity, free of criticism and counter by either the press or opposition. Behind the scenes, the start was equally impressive. The stamp of his conservative patrons was pressed on the strategy and organization of the campaign. In California he forged his ties to an even wider, more powerful group of patrons and began the first overt steps toward the long-awaited takeover of the state party from Earl Warren. "He believes in giving younger people . . . the ball," Nixon buoyantly explained his relationship to Eisenhower that summer, "and letting them run with it."

He left the euphoria of Hadley Field for an intense round of fiery speeches interspersed with quiet maneuver. To a southern California fund-raising dinner honoring the Vice-Presidential nominee, George Murphy had announced, "Party labels don't mean anything anymore. You can draw a line right down the middle. On one side are the Americans; on the other, the communists and socialists." And Dick Nixon, before many of the Werdel backers and his own 1950 supporters, responded in old familiar language with what reporters now called "the battle cry of the party": "We are going to clean out the communists in Washington, the fellow travelers, and those who give them aid and comfort." Later, in San Francisco, he again pronounced "the door wide open for Republicanism in the South" because of the Democrats' failure to nominate Senator Russell, assured a rally in Fresno that Dwight Eisenhower "doesn't belong to anybody," and told a cheering convention of Ohio Taftites in Columbus that Adlai Stevenson was the "captive candidate" of the CIO and "machine bosses."

Meanwhile, he moved to ensure his own machinery. With Summerfield and other aides, he and Chotiner flew into Denver from Columbus and hurried off to a secret strategy conference of the campaign high command at Eisenhower headquarters at the Brown Palace Hotel on July 31. Introduced by the National Committee's public relations director, Robert Humphreys, the centerpiece of the meeting was a formal "campaign plan," ostensibly to be discussed and adopted by Eisenhower and his staff. In fact, the plan had been carefully cast and solidified by Summerfield, Humphreys, and the Vice-Presidential candidate well in advance of the gathering—"complete from stem to stern," Humphreys would say later, and "Nixon and Chotiner met with us on it before locking it up and taking it to Denver."

Humphreys presented the plan on large flipboards—"advertising agency style," he wrote—and there was only desultory comment from Lodge as both Eisenhower and Nixon sat silently and the strategy was adopted without dissent or substantive question. Humphreys methodically went to the hotel boiler room the next morning, built a fire in the furnace, and burned the boards one by one, though secret condensations of the plan were kept for Eisenhower, Summerfield, and himself. At the heart of their strategy were three elements. It was necessary to reunite "the hard-core vote of twenty million Republicans . . . split asunder by the Eisenhower-Taft struggle," thereby ensuring a conservative thrust. Second, the disparate volunteers, "citizens," independents, and Democrats-for-Eisenhower, in many ways the electoral key to the campaign, would be brought politely but decisively, as Humphreys explained later, "under the control of Summerfield and the Republican National Committee." The party apparatus and congressional-senatorial establishment would remain in command. Finally, both the general and his attractive young running mate were to exploit wherever possible the incalculable new weapon of television, to use, as Humphreys put it, "informal intimate televison productions addressed directly to the individual American and his family, their problems and their hopes."

When Eisenhower remained noticeably too quiet during the whole session, Sherman Adams went up to him afterward and asked if anything were wrong. The general seemed oblivious to the operational consequences of the Humphreys-Nixon scheme, what Adams called "the behind-the-scenes maneuvering of the politicians," yet deeply offended by the apparent disregard of his real talent. "All they talked about was how they would win on my popularity," he groused to Adams. "Nobody said I had a brain in my head."

Nixon left Denver with the campaign plan apparently intact and returned to the basin for a private supper with more than three dozen new financial backers, who now gravitated to his Vice-Presidential candidacy like a sure and lucrative investment. The scene was Kyle Palmer's impressive house on Malibu Beach, the occasion a letter read ceremoniously by Palmer from Senator Taft pledging "support [for] the Republican candidate and . . . to continue my battle for the principles on which the Party should stand." Taft had added, "I know the Republicans can win with the right kind of campaign," another pull toward the conservative orthodoxy Richard Nixon was supposed to guard.

But the essential business of the evening was money. Beside the familiar figures from the Nixon financial list—Asa Call; Neil Petrie; Louis B. Mayer and his agent, Mandel Silberberg; Charlie Thomas; Justin Dart; Thomas Knudsen—there were powerful new faces. While Chotiner, Jorgensen, and Dana Smith moved through the crowd and steered the right men toward the candidate, Nixon met and courted them in their numbers: Walter Annenberg, the publisher of the *Philadelphia Inquirer* in tow to Pennsylvania governor John Fine; assorted Hollywood tycoons and executives Darryl Zanuck, Joseph Schenck, Harry Cohn, Mervyn LeRoy, Eddie Mannix, and Harry Brand; Leonard Firestone of the tire and rubber fortune; Al Gock, chairman of Bank of America; Norman and Harrison Chandler of the *Los Angeles Times*; *Mirror* publisher Virgil Pinkley; Lawrence Block, the Beverly Hills real-estate magnate; William Mullendore, representing California utilities; and more than a score of others like them. Nixon casually outlined the plan just approved at the Brown Palace—the stratagems Bob Humphreys had been at pains to incinerate after the briefing—and specifically held out a new GOP offensive and success in the American South, challenging and eventually breaking the grip of the Democrats. It was, Palmer recorded afterward, a heady evening with broad new horizons of Republican power. Nixon promised them "an all-out battle waged in every section of the country," with "every expectation of winning." Now and over the next two decades, it was to be a message and audience worth hundreds of thousands of dollars to his own and Republican campaigns.

From there he flew on to Sacramento and a meeting of the GOP State Central Committee, where his own candidate, thirty-seven-year-old assemblyman Laughlin Waters, was installed as the new state chairman, and Nixon supporters Mildred Younger, Al Derre, and Arthur Dolan took key committee positions. Fresh from his private gathering at Palmer's beach house, he again publicly attacked Stevenson as the tool of bosses and extolled Ike as the "candidate of the people." In a side trip to an American Legion convention, he also deplored the administration's restraint in Korea. U.S. troops should never be sent abroad unless "we can provide them with the military superiority to win wars."

Going from victory to victory, he continued to bask in a favorable, sometimes slavish and quietly coopted press. When Victor Lasky prepared a major article on Nixon that August for *Look* magazine, the writer dutifully submitted it in advance to Murray Chotiner lest "anything untoward" might appear and for "your office to catch any such things." It was a practice that would be followed often by other journalists for articles and even books in the years ahead. "After all, we are pretty fortunate to have it written by someone who had at least a friendly attitude," Nixon wrote Lasky appreciatively. Watching the prodigal course of his protégé across the national scene, Herman Perry back in Whittier was jubilant, already envisioning the Presidential succession he had predicted years before. "P.S.," he added in his flowery old-fashioned hand to an admiring letter in early August, "We'll see you at the White House in 1960."

Just as his conservative patrons were solicitous of his role on the ticket and future financial backing, the Eisenhower camp was eager to clean up any unwanted debris from his earlier races. When talk of anti-Semitism soon resumed from the 1950 race, the southern California campaign promoted another public exoneration from the Los Angeles Jewish Community

Council. Featured by Palmer in his Watchman column, a council statement noted that "against Sen. Nixon the insinuations of anti-Semitism have been particularly vicious" but had been deemed "utterly and totally unfounded . . . after the most assiduous inquiry." The charges persisted, however, eating into Eisenhower contributions from the Jewish community, in the East in particular. Dewey even dispatched his own liaison, Bernie Katzen, to combat among politicians and donors the unsettling mix of rumor and reality still reverberating from the attacks on Helen Douglas.

For similar reasons, Paul Hoffman wrote Nixon August 20 to urge "your making civil liberties and the rights of minorities a major theme for your public addresses. . . . Quite obviously, the smear campaign which has been directed against you will give special significance to what you have to say on . . . civil liberties." At that Nixon bristled. Hoffman's letter was relegated to a clipped answer from Chotiner, who wrote back "about your suggestion that he make a speech [sic] on the subject of individual liberties and the rights of minorities." The senator "intends to do so," Murray informed Hoffman in the campaign's last word on the subject.

A similar effort to hold at bay another unseemly ghost brought him the first small furor of the race. On August 21 Nixon gave a fulsome interview to Roy Roberts's *Kansas City Star*, talking at length about the goal of the campaign "to stencil Trumanism" on Adlai Stevenson. Korea, corruption, economic issues, and communism would be principal issues, with the saga of Alger Hiss "a major part" of his message. "The most devastating thing that can be said about the Truman record is that he has lost 600 million people to the communists," he told the *Star*. "There's one difference between the Reds and Pinks. The Pinks want to socialize America. The Reds want to socialize the world and make Moscow the world capital. Their paths are similar; they have the same bible—the teachings of Karl Marx." It was the vintage theme of the Hiss case and the 1950 race, and the same day he moved just as typically to adopt another tone for a different region and audience. To William S. White of *The New York Times*, he leaked through aides a story designed to emphasize his own distance from Joe McCarthy. White was even supplied with an illustrative quotation to show Nixon's moderation. If the Vice-Presidential candidate were speaking on the subject, even in McCarthy's Wisconsin, he would blame Truman for "causing the issue of McCarthyism to rise" but then state: "Charges, nevertheless, should not be made until one has the facts to back them up, and when charges are made that cannot be substantiated, the person making them hurts the cause for which he is fighting." For Nixon and his men it was all a familiar gambit, repeating the point-counterpoint of so many California speeches in 1949–50, evoking the Red Scare in the south and then the implicit anti-McCarthyism so resonant in San Francisco and the north.

Here, in the hands of a more independent, sophisticated press, the technique promptly backfired. White's lead drew a logical if unintended inference from the planted story and centered not on Nixon's moderation but rather on the issue of the ticket's endorsement of McCarthy in the latter's own Senate race in Wisconsin. "There will be no endorsement for Senator Joseph R. McCarthy . . . when Senator Richard M. Nixon . . . goes into Wisconsin to speak during the national campaign," he began. There were "present strong and fixed determinations" in the Nixon camp for the Vice-Presidential candidate to criticize "methods Senator Nixon deplores and considers harmful rather than helpful in the fight against subversion."

In the resulting uproar, White defended his original story, repeating his "full awareness of the sensitivity of the issue but . . . full faith in the source of his information" with "no conceivable doubt of its authenticity." Nixon and Eisenhower were besieged by reporters and both forced into more precision on the controversial subject than either had wished. The ticket supported Joe McCarthy's reelection, Nixon told a Washington press conference. "I want to make it clear that in supporting any particular candidate neither I nor General Eisenhower will endorse the views or the methods of Republican candidates which happen to be different from our own." They recognized that in both parties "there should be room for individuals who have differing views on key issues," he went on, and a Republican administration would bring a "fair, sane and effective program of investigation of all the charges . . . and removal from the government payroll of those who are a threat to national security."

In what wire services called "a somewhat confused news conference" in Denver later that day, Eisenhower enveloped the issue in what would be characteristic rhetorical fog. He would support McCarthy "as a member of the Republican organization" yet would not "give blanket endorsement to any man who does anything that I believe to be un-American in its [*sic*] methods or procedures." Reminded of McCarthy's ringing attack on his old patron, George Marshall, for "a conspiracy so immense . . . so black," Ike called Marshall "a perfect example of patriotism" and added matter-of-factly, "I have no patience with anyone who can find in his record of service to this country cause for criticism."

Scrambling to repair the damage with both right and center of the party, Nixon followed with an interview the next day with *U.S. News and World Report*. "You would never have had 'McCarthyism' " without Truman's lack of "honesty" in dealing with subversives, he offered. "The way to get rid of so-called McCarthyism is to elect a new administration which will deal with this problem honestly." Still, the genie had been released. In the Brown Palace an indignant Eisenhower asked Charlie Kersten, "What can we do about McCarthy making unproved charges?" At the same time in the basin a "Hollywood Committee for McCarthy" raised generous donations with a membership of prominent Nixon backers, including Harold Lloyd, Louis B. Mayer, Adolphe Menjou, George Murphy, and Dick Powell. In the late August episode provoked by Nixon's artless leak, there fell the foreshadowing of a historic confrontation of Eisenhower and Nixon with Senator Joe McCarthy and the forces he represented.

The tempest over McCarthy was soon gone, Nixon's favorable relations with the press apparently none the worse. Ernest Brashear of the *Los Angeles Daily News* wrote a scathing September series on the nominee in the then-liberal *New Republic*, recounting some aspects of the California campaigns and finance. "Nixon's public personality and his private personality," he concluded, "shake hands as strangers when they meet." With similar misgiving, Bert Andrews's otherwise conservative and mild-mannered colleague at the *Herald Tribune*, Robert Donovan, thought Nixon "a hard, narrow, ambitious man, cheerless and partisan to the point of repugnance." Like others, however, Donovan kept his views to himself at the time, while Brashear's criticism reached only a small partisan audience and as journalism was all but unique. The far more common rule to such exceptions was coverage of the kind represented in the interview the candidate had given the *Kansas City Star*, in which he blithely told the paper he had "no other sources of income except his salary as a senator," ignoring his more than $6,600 in speech fees in 1951 as well as the Fund. The Nixons, as the *Star* made the point, "are as familiar as most Americans are with the household budget crimp resulting from 'the twin pincers of high taxes and high prices.' "

Matching Lasky's cleared profile for *Look*, Pat Nixon was soon featured in her own little memoir in the September 6 *Saturday Evening Post* and then the October *Reader's Digest*, together reaching millions. "As told to" Joe Alex Morris, "I Say He's a Wonderful Guy!" was the young wife's fetching version of their résumé. "I married a crusader," she began in the tone the piece would never desert, "a quietly determined fellow who in six years has taken in stride all the bumps in the political road from small-town obscurity to the Republican nomination for the Vice Presidency." Like his interview with the *Star*, her recollection contained not only the expected political gloss and mythology but also the first of what would be so many, often unaccountable tailorings of reality, sometimes small in themselves yet adding up eventually to a disturbing sum. Thus their courtship became "almost three years" instead of the year and a half it had been in truth, and Dick "spent almost four years in the South Pacific" rather than the actual thirteen and one-half months of his overseas service.

"SIDESADDLE ADLAI"

Despite such lavish and flattering publicity for the Vice-Presidential nominee, the Republican press worried openly by summer's end over the apparent lethargy at the top of the ticket. Eisenhower himself, complained the *New York World Telegram and Sun* in mixed metaphor, was "running like a dry creek," and the candidate would have "to come out swinging." Both the editorial rebuke and the general's lackluster start in the race were noted gravely at the Commodore headquarters. Their opponent was at once vulnerable and impressive. A reluctant candidate himself, Adlai Stevenson carried the millstones of war and the twilight corruption of two decades of Democratic rule, yet he was also a gifted man of rising eloquence and with a bright young staff not conceding the odds. "While it was never possible for Adlai Stevenson . . . to win the 1952 campaign," wrote one of Ike's own concerned aides, "most certainly . . . it was possible for Dwight Eisenhower to lose it."

The result from Labor Day on was a noticeable new partisanship in Ike's speeches, now billed as his "two-fisted attack" on the "mess in Washington." But the spur was felt, too, in Richard Nixon's already strident rhetoric. When the Stevenson camp at the end of August alluded to "a plan" for ending the Korean War but then refused to reveal details as a matter of national security, Nixon lashed back. "If he has had such a plan he should have disclosed it to the Joint Chiefs of Staff . . . [and] if he does not have such a plan he should honestly tell the American people that he has no easy solution to the Korean War," he said in an indignant statement. "Mr. Stevenson is putting out bait for votes and working a cruel hoax on the men fighting and dying in Korea and their families and loved ones . . . if he continues to leave the impression . . . that he has some magic formula which could bring the Korean War to an end on an honorable basis." Sixteen years later, Richard Nixon would campaign for the Presidency on his own "secret plan" to end another bitter and unpopular Asian war.

Promising that "the real swinging will come in the weeks ahead," Nixon set off for an early September tour of Republican New England that was to be a shakedown for the campaign organization, though also a honing of increasingly sharp, personal attacks that would make 1952 an offshoot of his earlier races. On the Maine coast they visited a local dock only to have a live lobster nip Pat's finger and then grip the candidate's lapel until it was pried off in some alarm. Rhetoric on the swing seemed equally fierce. "If the record itself smears, let it smear," he said in Bangor. "If the dry rot of corruption and communism, which has eaten deep into our body politic during the past seven years, can only be chopped out with a hatchet, then let's call for a hatchet." A day later, he called Stevenson "a tired relic of a whole series of deals, of dubious State Department training and of leftist leaning." His job, Nixon told small but respectful Republican crowds, would be "naming names." For every scandal or spy case in Washington "there are ten which haven't yet been uncovered." The GOP would take the United States "off the cringing defensive and put it on the righteous offensive." The Truman-Acheson policies and a "wishy-washy" State Department were "coddling atheistic communism" and would condemn the nation to "ultimate national suicide." At nearly every stop was unmistakable imagery to impugn the masculinity of the urbane Stevenson, whom he now called "sidesaddle Adlai." "Like all sidesaddle riders, his feet hang well out to the left," Nixon told his audience. In the same theme he could allude to McCarthy's drumbeat of accusations about subversive homosexuals in the Foreign Service. Adlai served up "clever quips," he added, "which send the State Department cocktail set into gales of giggles."

Meanwhile, back in California, Chotiner took up another McCarthyesque variation in remarks to reporters, hinting darkly that "there has been a tremendous amount of work done on Stevenson by our research committee and before the end of this campaign we will prove he is not deserving of the high office of the Presidency nor qualified to hold that position." Between them, there emerged in the first week in September the outline of what was later to be a familiar refrain. "One can see them developing," a student of his campaign techniques wrote of the New England barnstorming, "the scandal-a-day administration, the 'four-headed monster that was Korea, communism, corruption, and control,' the boys dying in Korea while Mr. Stevenson makes jokes—and as Mr. Nixon gets the most effective phrases and themes worked out and polished, he then repeats them at each turn. By the end of the campaign, his speech has become a veritable masterpiece of planned spontaneity and deliberate loss of temper."

Yet as Nixon perfected his organization and stump speech, and Eisenhower began his own attacks, there would also be a significant and growing distinction between the general and his hard-hitting running mate. On the morning of September 12, Eisenhower breakfasted with Taft at Columbia University, seeking old-guard support in return for assurances of federal patronage for Taftites, a $60 billion ceiling on taxes, and, not least, a vague promise that the despised Tom Dewey would be nowhere near the cabinet. Their meeting was to be called "the surrender of Morningside Heights," and brought harsh criticism. But it also won the coveted Taft support—their foreign and domestic policies were separated by mere "difference of degree," the senator reassured his followers after the breakfast—and produced a new confidence and independence in the Presidential candidate.

Joining the Commodore staff at the same time, speech writer Emmet John Hughes found an apt Eisenhower ready to contrast Stevenson's humor with the grave seriousness of the issues and to deplore "communists in government" or "the experts in shady and shoddy government operations." But the general also stood clear of the personal slurs, the vague calls for taking the "offensive" or "full victory," the contradictory, demagogic exploitation of Korea as a "Democratic war" in the same breath with charges of Democratic appeasement.

"Eisenhower disdained and ignored them," Hughes wrote later of most of the themes that were becoming staples of his running mate's campaign. "It was unthinkable—and everyone near him knew it was unthinkable—that he would willfully twist a fact, distort an issue, or delude with an empty pledge." Hughes would note, too, the signal changes in people and process at this point—the relative rarity of Summerfield or even Sherman Adams at the substantive discussions of Eisenhower speeches and positions. Nor was there any role for other political figures that Hughes had expected to wield at least some influence—notably, Joe McCarthy and Richard Nixon. "Of all those absent from the intimate circle of advisers," Hughes wrote of McCarthy and Nixon that mid-September, "none were more conspicuous—or more remote." Dwight Eisenhower, who in effect had been given his Vice-Presidential nominee, who seemed resigned, almost supine, some weeks before at the Brown Palace strategy session with Humphreys's impressive flipboards, was increasingly becoming his own man.

There was, moreover, another quiet step of independence and sophistication that was to have an effect on Richard Nixon then and later. While still in Denver late that summer, Eisenhower summoned Earl Warren for a private and intense two-hour conference. The general was "somewhat concerned," Warren recorded, at reports that a diehard right-wing faction in California would conduct a write-in campaign for Douglas MacArthur in the general election and siphon off a decisive hundred thousand votes to "tip the balance." Warren had assured him the danger was slight, that "he should win handily." But Eisenhower "continued to be alarmed" and avidly courted Warren's aid against elements that included some of Dick Nixon's supporters. One more swirling little eddy in GOP politics, a distraction far out of proportion, it was the specter again of the old fearsome MacArthur ghost that Dewey had used to provoke Eisenhower earlier that spring. But the consequence was to draw Eisenhower closer to Earl Warren, to reckon the governor no less and perhaps even more than Richard Nixon a key to the ticket's success in California, and thus a further mark of Eisenhower's independence. And all this—public and private—would have a bearing on the fateful episode about to shatter the September monotony of the presidential race.

❖❖❖

"I am filled with superlatives in regard to your visit here," Christian Herter wrote Nixon after the New England swing. The note was typical of the widespread personal praise he had received by mid-September, putting into still sharper relief the occasional public criticism and his prickly sensitivities. He thanked Herter by enclosing a lone *Washington Post* editorial at odds with his recent call for a "righteous offensive" in foreign affairs and even asked the well-connected Bostonian to write a friend at the paper. "I feel, however, that the *Post* will never forgive me," Nixon added, "for the embarrassment I caused them in the Hiss case."

They headed west for the formal launching of the campaign, stopping once more in Denver for a conference with Ike on September 15. Nixon now thought the Brown Palace had taken on "the aura of a command post," swarming with aides and visiting dignitaries, and Eisenhower "accorded the respect, honor, and awe that only a President usually receives." Ike was outwardly friendly, though with "a quality of reserve which, at least subconsciously, tended to make a visitor feel like a junior officer coming in to see the commanding general." In their review of strategy, Eisenhower now made it plain he would stress "the positive aspects," as Nixon remembered their talk, while Dick continued the attack. "I was to hammer away at our opponents on the record of the Truman Administration, with particular emphasis on communist subversion because of my work in the Hiss case." Nothing was said, apparently, about the often acrid tone of Nixon's rhetoric or of potential Democratic counterattacks. Mid-September polls showed the Republican ticket leading 51 percent to 42 percent, with 7 percent undecided, and a 45 percent name recognition of Richard Nixon compared to only 32 percent for Stevenson's running mate, Alabama senator John Sparkman. Even more telling, a nationwide survey at the same moment showed 68 percent of daily newspapers in support of Eisenhower-Nixon, only 17 percent for Stevenson-Sparkman. "The road ahead," Nixon wrote on leaving Denver, "seemed full of promise and not pitfalls."

Their route back to the basin was another series of sentimental homecomings, culminating in his traditional campaign kickoff at Pomona, this time to begin a whistle-stop tour up the San Joaquin Valley and into Oregon and Washington before again heading eastward. On September 16 the Nixons stopped at Ely, Nevada, where an elderly man gave Pat a nugget from the gold mines and said he had known Will Ryan forty years before. Flying on to California, they spent the night in the Mission Inn, where they had been married, and Pat set out the next day for a neighborhood welcome in Artesia while her husband campaigned in the old twelfth.

"When I wrote to you on June 11 to ask for your opinion as to the strongest candidate the Republicans could nominate for President," a Nixon letter told supporters of the old poll and contributors' list, "I certainly never dreamed I would be writing you in September as the Vice-Presidential nominee." Now they were all to gather at the Pomona railroad station for a gala, nationally televised sendoff. Hoagy Carmichael, George Murphy, the Pied Pipers, and other celebrities were to lead the elaborately staged event. Ten cars of a specially chartered train would bring Whittier supporters twenty miles over to the station on a spur line, with Francis Anthony Nixon, "who once ran streetcars," as *The New York Times* noted, joining the Whittier train crew.

His son's train, the *Nixon Special*, had a lavish car equipped with "large beautiful beds for the candidate and his wife," according to the *Los Angeles Times*, as well as two lounge cars, a work car for the press with typewriters on long tables, and even a special crew of Southern Pacific agents and Western Union "experts" to handle the expected flow of copy for newsmen from Nixon's hard-hitting attacks on the Democrats. Not least, the Vice-Presidential nominee was to be introduced at Pomona by Earl Warren. "The requirements concerning your appearance at Pomona . . . is [*sic*] as follows," began the peremptory letter from Nixon headquarters to the governor, adding the assumption that Mrs. Warren would present Pat Nixon with a bouquet of roses and, almost as a final affront, that "you will have your own car to take you to and from Pomona."

At 7:00 P.M. in the autumn twilight on September 17, the Pomona Municipal Band began to play, and the Pledge of Allegiance was given by a Korean War veteran and son of a member of the Committee of 100. Roy Day followed with his well-practiced tale of greatness seen from the beginning. Not Mrs. Warren but Day's two daughters presented the bouquet of roses to Pat as "second-generation Committee of 100." Then, as the Pied Pipers led the audience in "Grand Old Flag" and nationwide televison and radio began their broadcasts, George Murphy, privately one of the governor's harshest opponents, introduced Earl Warren, who in turn presented the candidate. Warren was so "carried away by the excitement," as Nixon later wrote, that he concluded the introduction with the words, "I now present to you the next President of the United States."

Though suffering a slightly sore throat, the nominee was in good form. "Dead Americans are live issues," he told them. "This crusade begins tonight—right here in California." Reporters saw Senator Nixon "obviously touched by the outpouring of enthusiasm" and the crowd of some 15,000 "roused to a high pitch." He attacked the administration that had "bungled us into war" and tolerated "a dangerous fifth column." Who can best clean up the mess in Washington, who can get rid of the communists and bring peace? he asked them in a series of questions. And each time they roared the answer: "Eisenhower!"

Then, "at 8:59½ sharp," as the television scenario dictated, the train began slowly to pull out of the station, the Nixons standing at the back of the last car, the candidate intoning with outstretched arms to the station throng and the television audience, "If you believe as I believe, come along on this great crusade." Pat's "red-gold hair glistened," wrote her daughter, "a vivid contrast to the coal black of my father's." Another reporter thought "the tracks stood out under angled floodlights, creating a version of the path to glory."

Aboard, as they crept out of the station, there was the same sense of auspicious beginning. "The *Dick Nixon Special* departs from Pomona," read their official itinerary, "en route to forty-eight states to put Ike in the White House." Only a few miles away in Los Angeles, the train lurched onto a siding in the Southern Pacific Mission yards, laying over for the night before moving on to another dramatic station scene at Bakersfield the following morning.

23

Campaign in Crisis I,
September 18–21, 1952

"WE OUGHT TO PUT NIXON ON TV"

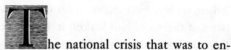he national crisis that was to engulf them down the tracks traced its origin to events of weeks before and in a larger sense to the toll of Richard Nixon's past in California politics.

An admirer of Jerry Voorhis and critic of Nixon since the 1946 race, Dan Green was editor and publisher of the *Independent Review*, a small Los Angeles weekly. Angry Warren backers had leaked to Green something of the senator's performance in Chicago as well as rumors of a private Nixon slush fund, which the editor had not been able to confirm. Yet when Green published his version of the convention maneuvers in August, another source—"a wealthy landowner and former Democrat of the San Marino area," Green would describe him—had called up to confirm not only the events in Chicago but also the existence of the Fund. In fact, he was a donor himself, having given $250 "just preceding Christmas of last year." Dana Smith had called to say how much Dick Nixon needed help. "They are so poor that they haven't a maid and we must see to it that they have a maid," the source quoted the Pasadena lawyer as saying. Then there were the senator's Christmas cards and other expenses. Smith had told them to send "anything from $100 to $500" to the First Trust Building in Pasadena.

To substantiate all this, the source had even invited Dan Green to see his canceled check with Dana Smith's endorsement as trustee. Not long after that another contributor and anonymous source told Green that the Fund totaled more than $17,000, with a check once sent to Richard Nixon for some $3,000. Like the other informant, he offered convincing detail and corroboration. As it turned out, the figures would be close enough to the actual accounts to suggest someone with intimate knowledge of either Dana Smith's private books or the Senate office records.

In the meantime, Green discovered three other journalists digging up the Fund, all of whom had picked up the rumor as part of their routine work on Nixon profiles: Leo Katcher of the *New York Post*, Ernest Brashear of the *Los Angeles Daily News*, and Richard Donovan, West Coast writer for *The Reporter*. All had developed sources for the story, including a Los Angeles County official who claimed to have been "pressured" to contribute to the Fund. Still, it was Green's canceled check and precise figures that were "clinching," as he proudly wrote later. By early September the newspapers and magazine had seemed ready for a joint release of an obviously important story. Then the *Daily News* suddenly flinched. Worried about the liberal bias of the other publications, *Daily News* general manager Robert Smith had insisted the story also be pursued by Peter Edson, a conservative Scripps-Howard columnist, and the information was discreetly shared with Edson with release planned for no sooner than September 18. Meanwhile, parts of the story had leaked to both Drew Pearson and *Newsweek*, though Pearson ignored it for the time being and the then-pro-Republican news magazine dismissed the reports as "a political stunt."

The mixture of distraction, accident, naked partiality, cravenness, and calculation was characteristic of what followed. The next ten days were to make political history, some of it played out before the nation and ultimately before the largest audience ever to hear the speech of an American politician. But much of that history, the fate and future of Richard Nixon, was shaped by the more obscure politics and sociology of the news media and by the increasingly complex and decisive interplay between the media and politicians—to which the public would be half-wondrous, half-unwitting spectators.

"BUT DICK DID JUST WHAT WE WANTED HIM TO DO"

It was on Sunday, September 14, that Richard Nixon learned that some publicity on the Fund was in the offing. When the nominee appeared that day before "Meet the Press," Peter Edson was one of the panelists, and the friendly columnist pulled him aside after the program and asked, "Senator, what is this 'fund' we hear about?" The story had been "kicking around" ever since the convention. "There is a rumor to the effect that you have a supplementary salary of $20,000 a year, contributed by a hundred California businessmen." Edson's tone made clear his own skepticism. The convention, wrote one of his conservative colleagues, had been "a scandal-monger's paradise," and the Nixon story "like a nursery rhyme in a sea of garish murder mysteries." Edson had even checked the gossip with other California journalists, including Jim Bassett, just before Bassett joined Nixon's staff, but to no avail. And yet the rumors persisted.

As Nixon and Edson now talked, telegrams and phone calls were already coming into the studio to congratulate the candidate on his performance on the program, and Nixon was relaxed, almost casual in the face of the question. What they had heard was "all wrong," he told the columnist. The stories "might be referring to a political fund . . . set up by my supporters . . . used to pay expenses." Edson could get "details" by calling Dana Smith, who "knew much more about that than Nixon did himself," as the reporter remembered their conversation. Nixon said he did not know the identity of the Fund contributors and "had made no effort to find out." He added, too, that no favors had ever been given any donors, and that his wife had never worked on the office payroll—though he did not explain to Edson how much the Fund had made possible Pat's extensive travel and campaigning with him, including publicity photos of them both. Nixon then gave him Dana Smith's telephone number in Pasadena, and they parted, the politician confident that the query had been handled. It was "such an innocent beginning," Richard Nixon wrote later, to "the most scarring personal crisis of my life."

Edson telephoned Smith the next day, saying he was calling at Dick Nixon's suggestion, and the lawyer readily explained the subsidies in the terms and justifications they had long anticipated. It was only expense money, carefully administered and with individual gifts limited to avoid the appearance of proprietary contributions. Warming to his theme, Smith even suggested to Edson that "other states" might adopt the same plan to finance senators "who had no independent incomes" and thus prevent undesirable outside "pressure." Soon after Edson's call, however, Dana Smith was also visited at his Pasadena office by Brashear, Katcher, and Donovan. All explained they were doing "profiles" of the Vice-Presidential nominee and asked specifically about the Fund—though they did not add, as Edson had been careful to say, that they had been referred by Nixon himself. Nevertheless, to the three reporters in person Smith was even more talkative.

Describing the mechanics of the money in much the same terms used with Edson, Smith went on to explain the donors' motives—not "to own a senator" but to "see that Dick," as Donovan later recounted, "was denied none of the things that a senator's station in life required." The government had been "selling centralized control" for years. The New and Fair Deals were "full of commies, men who believe in big government and those who have a backward-looking philosophy—the real reactionaries," Dana told them. "Our thinking was that we had to fight selling with selling, and for that job Dick Nixon seemed to be the best salesman against socialization available. That's his gift really—salesmanship." Later in the interview he would add, "Here we had a fine salesman for free enterprise but he didn't have enough money to do the right kind of selling job, so we got together and we've been taking care of some of these things for him."

As for California's other senator and Republican governor, Smith was equally blunt. "Knowland is almost unknown. . . . Warren has too much of the other point of view, and he never has gone out selling the free-enterprise system. But Dick did just what we wanted him to do." One of the journalists reminded Smith that his signature had been on the check repaying the controversial Brewster-Grunewald loan in 1950. Even at that the lawyer seemed unconcerned. "If I signed the check then I must have been the person who repaid it," he replied. But the money must have come from the Senate campaign, not the Fund. He named a few contributors to the Fund, and some others "who were instrumental in Dick's career." With that the interview ended.

Late Monday afternoon in Pasadena, as Nixon sat down in Denver for a strategy session with Eisenhower, there was once again the assumption that any awkward criticism had been averted. Dana Smith did not even bother to call the candidate or his office to tell them about his talks with Edson or the three unexpected reporters.

Early on the seventeenth before the televised send-off from Pomona, one of the reporters assigned to the train had told Jim Bassett that his paper was planning a story the following day about "a Nixon fund." "That's probably the Peter Edson story . . . nothing to worry about," Nixon replied when Bassett told him. But then, near midnight, the train parked on the siding in the Mission Yards, a staff man from the Los Angeles GOP headquarters came hurrying across the darkened tracks and clambered aboard. A *Los Angeles Daily News* story on the money was due to appear the next morning, he told them, and "it might cause trouble." Whether thinking this the same Edson dispatch or another manageable story, Nixon remained outwardly calm, though the midnight visit stirred the first sign of concern. He now called a 1:00 A.M. meeting in his private compartment, with men still awake and milling through the cars after the excitement of their departure ceremony.

Those who gathered would be his small command staff for the coming ordeal. They were Chotiner, Hillings, Jack Drown, acting as "train manager" in scheduling the whistle-stops, and a last-minute addition to the party, the Washington lawyer William Rogers, whom Nixon had invited along as an "adviser" for his ties to both Dewey and Brownell. In her bedroom nearby, Pat Nixon did not join them. Bassett, the press secretary, was also notably absent, as he would be from nearly all the similar sessions that followed—a mark that they viewed the controversy from the beginning less as a press matter than a political problem.

Nixon began by reviewing the rumors of a story and telling Rogers for the first time the outline of the Fund—"set up at Dana Smith's suggestion," how "scrupulously careful" they had been to "avoid any possible charges of improper collection or use," how Smith, "an impeccably honest man," acted as trustee. After a few questions about the expenses and sums involved—Nixon "remembered" something between $15,000 and $18,000 collected and disbursed—Rogers had been unconcerned. "I don't see anything to worry about," he told them. The subsidies were neither illegal nor improper and seemed better accounted for than other political funds. "If your opponents try to make something out of it, they'll never get anywhere." After they talked a bit more, Chotiner chimed in impatiently, "Hell, there's nothing to this thing; its ridiculous." And with that, Nixon himself seemed reassured. To take the matter seriously, he concluded, would only "play into the hands of those making the attacks." They would simply "ignore" whatever was published.

As the *Nixon Special* sat on its Los Angeles siding in the predawn hours of September 18, across America the Fund story was starting its own lurching passage into the press.

Peter Edson wrote his column after interviewing Smith, and routinely mailed it out to several hundred subscribing papers for publication the eighteenth. It began: "Republican Vice-Presidential candidate Richard M. Nixon has been receiving an extra expense allowance from between fifty and one-hundred well-to-do southern California political angels since he entered the U.S. Senate in 1951." There had been "rumors about his finances" since the convention, the story went on, but on being questioned Nixon had confirmed the existence of the Fund as if he had nothing to hide. Dana Smith was "the only man who knows the names of all the contributors." No favors were asked, and if any donor tried to seek advantage, he would have been "dropped from the list," according to Smith. Mrs. Nixon did not work on the senator's payroll, though the young senator had sizable expenses such as speech recordings and help with heavy correspondence. "Nixon's disclosure of the subsidy points up the plight of a young senator without a substantial private income," Edson concluded. "His alternatives are to make additional income writing magazine articles or making speeches or practicing law on the side." The columnist did not report that Nixon had done exactly that as well, increasing his Senate salary by more than 50 percent in 1951 with speeches on top of the Fund.

Edson's story was what Nixon himself would later call "fair and objective." In any case, it was all but censored. Although most of his subscribers routinely ran his columns, only three major dailies and a handful of lesser papers now ran the Fund article, most of them burying it on back pages. Confined to Edson's syndicated version, the story might have come and gone much as Nixon and his men expected. *The Reporter* account drew no attention either. Given the choice between the relatively tame Edson column and a more detailed and critical account by their man Brashear, the *Los Angeles Daily News* discreetly "suppressed its own story," as one journalist recalled, and inserted Edson deep in the back pages.

Of those to break the story, it was the *New York Post* that made the difference. A Ph.D. in psychology from Columbia, part of an accomplished, politically sophisticated family, Leo Katcher was a sometime Hollywood screenwriter and a West Coast correspondent to the *Post*, in his personal politics less a partisan liberal or detractor of Nixon than an admirer of Earl Warren, and subsequently one of the governor's biographers. In addition to the leads developed by Dan Green and the interview with Smith, Katcher had turned up his own sources among the contributors. "We've been paying his expenses for some time now," one of them said to him ominously. "I don't like the idea of this man being a heartbeat away from the Presidency." Another had told a story of the Nixon campaign getting Di Giorgio Farms money "on the sly," as Katcher related long afterward. Like most journalists of the time, he now wrote for the *Post* only a fraction of what he knew and supsected, including the existence of an entirely separate pool of money. As Dana Smith shuffled through papers while talking to them, Katcher had seen documents with lists of subscribers headed "Nixon Fund No. 2," a lead he could not confirm in time for his story. As it was, the dispatch he cabled back to New York that week in September was formidable enough.

In the *Post*'s tabloid style the article was played to shock. Headlined "SECRET RICH MEN'S TRUST FUND KEEPS NIXON IN STYLE FAR BEYOND HIS SALARY," Katcher's report opened: "The existence of a 'millionaires' club' devoted exclusively to the financial comfort of Sen. Nixon, GOP Vice-Presidential candidate, was revealed today." Nixon later called the lead with some justification "a masterpiece of distortion . . . clever example of the half-truth." When Katcher's younger brother covered the Vice-Presidential campaign later in the race, Nixon would say to him, "You did all right by me but your brother Leo is a son of a bitch." Beneath the lurid lead, however, the body of Katcher's text was accurate and relatively thorough, acknowledging both Donovan's and Brashear's suppressed work as well as Nixon's "Meet the Press" admission to Edson, an act described as "anticipating disclosure" and "to offset rumors." The story went on to quote liberally from Dana Smith on the "Nixon fund program," and, unlike Edson, to identify the donors as possessing "financial interests in such fields as banking, oil, real estate, railroads, and manufacturing."

The *Post* hit the streets in Manhattan at ten o'clock Thursday morning. Across the continent, the *Nixon Special* had moved slowly out of the basin around the San Gabriels toward the Valley, and for a time the calm continued. Although the United Press promptly reported the story in full on its wire, the usually competitive Associated Press remained silent. Throughout the nation, much of the pro-Republican media shrank back as well. "Numerous publishers and editors preferred not to believe what they had read on the UP wire," *Post* editor James Wechsler wrote later, "and were hoping the AP would never confirm it." In New York the Hearst *Journal-American* ignored the *Post* story altogether, while the Scripps-Howard *World-Telegram and Sun* eventually consigned Edson's column to a back page under the headline "MYSTERY ANGELS HELP KEEP NIXON DEBT-FREE." For several hours that morning and afternoon, despite Katcher or Edson, despite one wire service, the news of the Fund and thus its larger political reality in effect would not exist.

As the *Nixon Special* rolled north, Keith McCormac and Congressman Tom Werdel readied to meet it at the Southern Pacific depot in Bakersfield and to collect a recent debt. "I'd been lied to, double-talked and everything," McCormac remembered, thinking of primary and convention maneuvers. But the Werdel conservatives had not exposed Nixon. They were even supporting the GOP ticket despite Werdel himself facing a tough race and being ignored by Warren and the rest of the party. "I went along with you band of cutthroats. Now you come along with me," McCormac pleaded with Chotiner, and Nixon was now to embrace Werdel during his Bakersfield whistle-stop. At the 9:00 A.M. rear-platform speech, he did just that. "Who can clean up the mess in Washington?" he asked the sizable crowd, and they answered on cue "Ike can!" Then, his arm around Werdel, Nixon told them what a fine congressman the rebel had been, how much he should be supported.

Entering the observation car afterward, the cheers still ringing as the train pulled out, the senator was expansive. "Well, Keith," he said to McCormac, "when I get to Washington, why, we're going to take care of you." Unimpressed as usual, the young conservative simply handed him a copy of a small local paper, apparently one of the few to pick up the breaking United Press summary of the *Post* story. "Have you seen this?" McCormac asked. The headline read "NIXON SCANDAL FUND." Nixon suddenly slumped in a seat and stared at the page, transfixed as McCormac tried to speak to him. Soon Chotiner and Hillings came hurrying in and physically helped the stricken candidate back to his compartment. "So, when I handed him that paper he almost needed intensive care," McCormac remembered "They almost had to take him off the train."

In the little more than an hour before the next stop at Tulare, they worked feverishly to compose the candidate, "finally got him unshook," as McCormac witnessed it. The story had not yet reached the traveling press contingent, and Chotiner was still ridiculing the impact. But at Tulare the strain was evident. Whatever his assurances, Chotiner now ran to a station pay phone to call the Los Angeles headquarters, trying to set up a telephone conversation between Nixon and Eisenhower at Fresno, their next stop. When the train began to pull away while Nixon was still speaking, the candidate had to cut short his speech, concluding with "Come along and join our crusade," as some of the crowd actually followed the caboose down the tracks. Afterward Nixon furiously upbraided his old friend Jack Drown for allowing the engineer to start too soon. Bill Rogers broke the tension by pointing out the excitement of the crowd drawn after the moving car. At once Nixon seemed pleased and even laughed self-consciously.

The respite was short-lived. Some reporters who had heard of the *Post* exposé jumped aboard at Tulare, spread the word, and were now pressing for a statement. Bassett was sent out to tell them the candidate refused comment "at this time" and would not say anything until "he has an opportunity to study the statement made by attorney Dana C. Smith." At Fresno they nervously called again to locate Eisenhower, but could get no answer from Los Angeles. "Ike," McCormac concluded, "was in the weeds." Nixon now made another brief address and quickly retreated without speaking to reporters, who listened at the rear platform and then tried in vain to follow him back inside the car. Following the scramble, a worried Bassett told them that the press would be barred from the candidate's car until further notice. Three hours into the triumphant tour, the campaign was suddenly enshrouded.

As the Nixon train was nearing Fresno, Bob Humphreys in Washington had returned from lunch to find the UP wire copy on his desk at the Washington Hotel campaign offices of the National Committee. Humphreys was then forty-seven, a small, dark-complected man with sharp features and darting eyes. "He seemed made of springs," a friend wrote of his energy and versatility, from pool, golf, tennis, to classical music and little theater. But Humphreys's ultimate passion was politics. Out of a Scotch-Welch heritage in the Midwest, with only a year of college, he had risen through a seventeen-year career in reporting to a job as senior editor at *Newsweek*, then given it all up to work for the Republican National Committee after the 1948 debacle. A fair-minded journalist who deliberately hired assistants of differing views, he was nonetheless fiercely, sometimes paradoxically partisan and rigidly faithful to the GOP as an institution. Not least, he was even more militantly anticommunist, passing along leads to HUAC, quietly intoducing Dick Nixon and Bob Stripling to reporters whose coverage they could influence in the Hiss trial, abiding and abetting Joe McCarthy despite a personal loathing. That remarkable ability and loyalty, single-mindedness and zeal now all converged on the crisis enveloping the brooding young Vice-Presidential nominee a continent away, and ultimately were to save the candidacy.

Significantly, Humphreys's own understanding of the Fund had been gleaned from Nixon's occasional comments about it. "Never a secret . . . actually . . . could be considered a wholesome thing," he once described it in a letter. "The fund was several years old [in 1952] and had been subscribed to by a group of politically spirited citizens in California, none of them wealthy." That afternoon at the committee, however, he clearly sensed the political peril if not the full reality of the subsidies and swiftly called upstairs to Nixon headquarters in Washington to try to reach the Vice-Presidential candidate at his next stop. Meanwhile, he dictated a statement to be issued by Karl Mundt, denouncing the story immediately as "smear tactics" and "a filthy maneuver by left-wingers, fellow travelers, and former communists."

When the call back to Humphreys finally came through from Madera, California, at nearly 4:00 P.M. Eastern Time, it was not Nixon but Murray Chotiner, saying that they knew of the *Post* story and, less accurately, that Dick had met with the press simply to confirm the existence of the Fund. Chotiner's tone was still dismissive. Not knowing of Nixon's virtual seclusion or initial shock, Humphreys thought they were "taking it rather casually" and admonished Chotiner that the story was "going to be much bigger than we dreamed." He then read out the Mundt statement and advised that Nixon "go on the offensive with the same angle," preferably as soon as the next stop. Chotiner said he would relay the message and hurried back to the train.

Minutes after that conversation, Humphreys telephoned GOP chairman Summerfield on the Eisenhower campaign train, the *Look Ahead, Neighbor, Special*, as it chugged into Des Moines. By now, the Democrats' own national chairman, Stephen Mitchell, had called for Nixon's resignation in yet another UP item. "Senator Nixon knows that it is morally wrong," Mitchell said of the subsidies. "General Eisenhower knows that it is morally wrong. The American people know that it is morally wrong." Still, little of that news or any other about the Fund had penetrated the Eisenhower train. Bundles of the *Des Moines Register* had been thrown aboard that morning while they moved across Iowa, though the paper carried only the Edson story on page eight. Through the farm belt, meanwhile, Eisenhower drummed out the theme of an "Honest Deal" to replace Democratic kickbacks and cronyism. He would "rather not be elected President than to be elected by the help of those who have lost their sense of public morals," Ike had told the audiences. Now reading those wire reports from the Midwest, Humphreys thought the comparison with the Fund "ominous."

Others sensed no less the inevitable embarrassment in Eisenhower's own unctuous rhetoric. The headquarters staff at the Commodore saw in the same tickers a grim prospect. "It threatened to demolish, with eloquent mockery, the more righteous pretensions of a campaign that had christened itself, without excessive modesty, a 'Crusade,' " Emmet Hughes wrote of the sudden revelation of the Nixon Fund. "It invited the Democratic candidate . . . to caricature the massive display of Republican righteousness as a shabby kind of political revival meeting." With his own hard-won instinct for trouble, Tom Dewey in Albany had already fired off a telegram to campaign headquarters almost as soon as the Katcher story appeared, urging that Nixon be scheduled to come soon to New York to combat the "smear campaign."

When Humphreys now reached Summerfield, however, the inevitable reporters' questions had not begun on the train, and the committee aide extracted a crucial promise from the new chairman, who shared both his stern partisanship and an orthodox commitment to the Vice-Presidential nominee. "Nothing [should] be said from the train that was not in support of Nixon," Humphreys urged. They "had to put up a solid front." Summerfield readily agreed and for a time the wall held. Eventually asked by reporters about the wire accounts, Jim Hagerty would reply coolly, disdainfully, "We never comment on a *New York Post* story."

After his Des Moines speech that afternoon with no knowledge of the gathering storm, Eisenhower serenely took a nap. "His managers had decided not to distract him," wrote one observer. "Their man, they reckoned, was too new to rough-and-tumble politics." That night, coming into Omaha, the *Look Ahead, Neighbor* would get another bundle of papers, this time the *Omaha World Herald* with the Edson story benignly placed on the last page under the headline "Beneficiary of Trust Fund," as if Dick Nixon had received some family legacy. But then, as the general spoke in Omaha and went to bed still unbriefed, a fuller realization of the story set in. Aware not only of the newspaper and wire accounts but also of the beginning of radio and television coverage, the campaign cars hummed with speculation. Unnerved, Summerfield himself tried to reach Nixon for some "explanation." Dana Smith's helpful money had finally hit the Presidential train with a "jolt," observed a reporter who boarded in Des Moines. And while Dwight Eisenhower slept on in blissful ignorance of the event, his staff "was thrown into a turmoil."

Back on the *Nixon Special*, Chotiner quickly sat down with Rogers to prepare a formal written statement in light of Humphreys's call and to quell the mounting demands on Bassett from reporters whose numbers were still growing at each stop. Coming more than three hours after they had learned the thrust of the exposé, the single-page release was matter-of-fact and belied the mounting anxiety on both trains as well as at headquarters. At the same time, it sounded themes of self-righteousness and justification that would echo often over the next five days. Far from improper, Chotiner and Rogers wrote, the Fund was itself a kind of proof that Richard Nixon did not engage in the usual shady practices of political finance on Capitol Hill, that he was actually saving public money.

Nixon had been "informed," the statement began, of a newspaper account "of a fund collected by some of my supporters in the 1950 senatorial campaign to take care of political expenses which I believe should not be charged to the federal government." The "facts" of the money were said to be these:

> It handles postage for mail on which I do not choose to use the much-abused senatorial franking privilege. It defrays necessary travel expenses. It pays the cost of printing speeches and documents which otherwise might have been printed at the taxpayers' expense. It pays for extra clerical help needed to answer mail from my home state of California which has 11,000,000 population.
>
> As an alternative I might have resorted to the use of tax-paid facilities, [and] free government transportation, or I might have put my wife on the federal payroll as did the Democratic nominee for Vice President. I did none of these, nor have I been accepting law fees on the side while serving as a member of Congress. I prefer to play completely square with the taxpayers.

There was no accompanying identification of the donors, and Bassett refused to elaborate on the statement. For his part, Nixon continued to avoid the reporters, walking quickly through to the lounge car to meet boarding politicians along the route and then returning briskly to his compartment, where he was ostensibly "boning up on the local color," as he put it later.

They released the statement about 1:30 P.M. West Coast time, just before the Merced stop. Within minutes it was part of the first Associated Press acknowledgment of the story, wire items run after 5:00 P.M. in the East and carrying both Mitchell's call for resignation and Nixon's defense, though little of the original Katcher or Edson revelations several hours after they had been published. The delay was significant. Despite the apprehensions inside the campaigns, the news would remain effectively blanketed that night for much of the nation. Only three major evening papers would print the story, and those were confined to Edson or the early UP wire. "Editors were in no hurry to get the news into the paper," concluded one historian of the journalism in the episode. "They were even less enthusiastic about getting it onto the front page." Yet on the tracks north from Merced up the Valley, Richard Nixon imagined and brooded over just the opposite. Mitchell's statement would make "most of the front pages," he thought, while Mundt's defense about the "filthy" accusation was going to be "lost in the back pages." Sequestered in his compartment that Tuesday afternoon, he would nurse from the beginning the smoldering presumption that the "press" was now largely, almost naturally and inevitably against him. He applied afterward a familiar axiom: "An attack always makes more news than a defense."

At Stockton, then at the last stop of the day at Sacramento, Chotiner and others anxiously searched the newspapers in vain for some expression of backing from Eisenhower. At the same moment, ironically, the story was slowly spreading behind them. What so many editors had ignored or tactfully obscured elsewhere in the nation was big news that afternoon in local basin papers like the *Pasadena Star-News*, which headlined of Dana Smith, its new hometown celebrity, "PASADENAN DISCLOSES NIXON FUND DONATIONS." In a lengthy front-page article, the *Star-News* ran Nixon's refusal to comment at Fresno, Hagerty's terse ridicule of the *Post*, and a detailed rendition of the Katcher dispatch, even including a damning admission by Dana Smith that the original *Post* story "was essentially correct." Moreover, new details were being added. One contributor was quoted as saying he had been "appealed to on the ground that the Nixon family needed a larger home and couldn't at that time afford a maid." Now, too, Smith was offering names—Robert and George Rowan, John Garland, Norman Chandler, Edward Robinson, Tyler Woodward, and some who would not appear on later lists: Wallace Butler, nephew of Pierce Butler and conduit of much of the Stassen money; various public relations executives from large California businesses; and Whittier's own "Audrey [*sic*] Wardman."

However fitful or patchy the press coverage and wider public awareness, such reports traveled north by telephone on the political circuits far faster than the Nixon train, and the effects were awaiting the candidate that evening at Sacramento. At the capital station, where Earl Warren and the delegation had entrained little more than two months before for their fateful journey to Chicago, the reception crowd was still large and enthusiastic. But local politicians hung back noticeably from the usually coveted photographs with the national candidate. Picking up the aloofness, already suspecting defections, Nixon instantly turned "gloomy and angry," as one reporter described it. They were scheduled that evening to make a quick side trip by plane to Reno, Nevada, and as he was leaving for the airport a reporter confronted him with Mitchell's statement. "It's an attempt to pull a political smear," Nixon answered hotly. "Why doesn't he [Mitchell] ask Sparkman to resign because his wife is on the government payroll?"

In her own interview with the society reporter of the *Sacramento Bee*, Pat Nixon was outwardly composed. "I don't talk politics. I talk on home-making or children," she insisted, but then added, "I'm very pleased with the way the campaign is going. There were wonderful crowds all morning. It was very impressive." In private, she was already deeply upset, "blinking back the tears she seldom tolerated," as one writer portrayed her, wondering "if any political office was worth the sacrifice of a good name."

The rally in Reno that night was a mix of public fervor and hidden anguish for both of them, frequent currents in the days to come. When they returned to trainside in Sacramento near midnight, Nixon was agitated. In an impromptu statement to sleepy reporters, some of them routed from their Pullman berths, he lashed back for the first time in the terms Humphreys had written for Mundt and recommended to Chotiner. At this end of the first official day of his campaign, a day of rising rancor and uncertainty climaxed by this late-night gathering of reporters in the Sacramento yards, he returned to old familiar images and themes, and found language that remained remarkably unchanged through the crisis. It was another typical "attempted smear by the same left-wing elements which have fought me ever since I took part in the investigation that led to the conviction of Alger Hiss," he told them. "They have tried to manufacture and create an air of suspicion over a matter which is completely open and above board in every respect. If they think that by such tactics they can slow up my attack against communists and corruption, they will find out differently. I intend to continue to expose the elements which have been selling this country down the river, until the crooks and the communists and those who defend them are driven out of Washington."

Striding back to his car he seemed again confident, relieved by the counterattack, sure the apparent furor could be ignored or would somehow fade away, despite his outburst. "When I turned off the light in my state-room that night I was still convinced that because the attack was entirely partisan, it would not stand on its merits," he wrote. "I thought it would eventually run its course and be forgotten, provided I continued [*sic*] to play it down."

Much of the national press did continue to ignore or bury the Fund news Friday morning, September 19, though by now the wire services were "buzzing," as one editor recorded. On the *Look Ahead, Neighbor*, anxiety had mounted steadily. Bernard Shanley remembered being awakened in his sleeper at two o'clock that morning to find "terrible turmoil" and "grave concern" among the campaign aides. They decided finally to tell the general at an 8:00 A.M. meeting. In preparation, Summerfield hurriedly called Chotiner in Sacramento, waking him before dawn California time, to take down the complete text of Nixon's statement outside Merced, of which they had only seen wire accounts. Assembling in Eisenhower's car were Sherman Adams, Senators Carlson and Seaton, Summerfield, and two of the candidate's more personal confidants, his brother Milton and Boston investment banker Robert Cutler. Flourishing the Merced statement, Summerfield urged immediately that they issue a statement in effect "clearing" Nixon. But the others, after a night of nervous speculation, were unimpressed by the one-page release. Reporters were already asking for names of contributors, and only more details would stem the Democratic charges. Nixon's brief explanation could "not be allowed to end the matter," as one of them later leaked the arguments at the meeting to *The New York Times*. The incident had to be "treated with the utmost seriousness." At the very least, they would have to make some statement from the train.

Eisenhower had listened intently to the discussion, "the calmest person in this manufactured hurricane," thought Cutler. "But what are the facts?" he finally asked. "Let's find out the facts before I shoot my mouth off. I don't believe Dick did anything wrong." Hagerty could give some statement, but they should play for time, "wait and see." Asking Cutler for a pencil, Eisenhower then retreated to a corner of the car and quickly wrote out a private message to Nixon, crossing out and interlining as he went.

Dear Dick—Our press representatives are pressing me for a statement on quote Nixon unquote which I am obviously unable to give beyond an expression of personal confidence. In the certainty that the whole affair comprises no violation of the highest standards of conduct, a critical question becomes the speed and completeness of your presentation of facts to the public. I suggest immediate publication by you and Mr. Smith of all documentary evidence, including amounts received in full, all payments from it, the exact nature of the speeches, letters, and documents for which expenses were met out of the fund. The fact that you never received a cent in cash is of the utmost importance and should be made clear in the evidence given the public. Any delay will be interpreted, I think, as reluctance to

let the light of day into the case and will arouse additional
doubt or suspicion. Could you not consider the advisability, coincidentally with giving the documents to the
public, of inviting the Democratic Chairman of the Committee on Elections in Government to examine your complete records and to make his findings public?

Our train schedules today seemingly prevent a telephone conversation but you know I am ready to consult
with you on the matter whenever it is physically possible.

Such a readiness and announcement on your part
would, I believe, be effective in meeting this charge.

When a typist had transcribed the copy, Cutler retrieved the hand-
written original as a souvenir, "characteristic," he thought, "of Eisenhower
in a cloudy crisis." Whatever else, it was an extraordinary little document
in the history of campaign politics. In terms clear and simple, the Presidential nominee was instructing his running mate to make an "immediate"
and fully documented disclosure, even prescribing the accounting, suggesting the Democrats be invited to check the tallies, as it were, and tolling
the "additional doubt and suspicion" in anything less. For all his customary
control and composure, Ike had grasped all too well the political danger of
the Fund, for his own candidacy as for Nixon's. And while Cutler admired
the general's command, others saw different reactions that morning. The
Fund, one of them told Emmet Hughes afterward, "had staggered and
shaken" Dwight Eisenhower.

As the long telegram was dispatched to Nixon and their train started
south from Omaha through the lush farmland of the Missouri Valley, Eisenhower continued his attacks on Democratic corruption. Seaton soon
quietly dropped off at Ike's order to be in further telephone contact with
California, and Hagerty issued what was designed as a first interim statement. "I have long admired and applauded Senator Nixon's American faith
and determination to drive communist sympathizers from offices of public
trust," it began. As for the charge of "unethical practices" alleged by the
opposition, "I believe Dick Nixon to be an honest man. I am confident
that he will place all the facts before the American people fairly and
squarely." The general intended to talk with his running mate, the statement announced, "at the earliest time we can reach each other by telephone."

At the same moment back in Washington, Bob Humphreys was methodically calling Republican leaders to promote public statements for
Nixon and to check sentiment around the country. Reflecting the virtual
press blackout, he found "the Nixon story hadn't even made a small dent

on the public consciousness," as he subsequently reported to Summerfield, "and next to none on the politicians." It was the Eisenhower statement promising full disclosure that started what Humphreys would call "the real bonfire." He had worried that Nixon's original response was inadequate and too defensive. In any case, the Presidential nominee's obvious concern now suddenly legitimized the issue. It would never truly be national news, Humphreys judged—only a tempest in the New York and Washington press, on the two trains, among advisers or friends of the candidates, a few party leaders, some editorial writers. And the process was let loose not by the Democrats or the press so much as by Ike himself. "We did the . . . 'biting' on the whole story," the former journalist would say later.

Aboard the *Nixon Special* they awoke that Friday to a cool misty Sacramento dawn and to a *Bee* editorial calling Richard Nixon "the pet protégé of a special interest group of rich southern Californians . . . their subsidized front man, if not, indeed, their lobbyist." The train started north again through the rich valley above the capital, through thick rows of peach, pear, and almond trees. At Marysville, the first stop an hour away, where some of the notorious Korean casualty ads had appeared in 1950, he denounced Sheridan Downey's old enemy. It was "time we had engineers," he told the sunburned and straw-hatted crowd of farmers and ranchers, "rather than the propaganda agents in the Bureau of Reclamation."

Then, as the whistle blew and the train began to pull out from the twenty-minute stop, a voice in the crowd broke into his final sentences: "Tell them about the $16,000." Nixon reacted instantly. "Now, I heard a question over there—Hold the train! Hold the train!" he shouted. Someone from the party yelled to the engineer; the cars stopped a hundred yards down the track. "The Alger Hiss crowd," Nixon said in an aside to the press as the crowd surged forward around the caboose. Turning again to the audience, he pointed his finger at the man who yelled and, as he remembered, "let him have it."

"I heard a question over there. He said, 'Tell them about the $16,000.' And I'm going to talk about that on this score." And he went on:

> You folks know the work that I did investigating the
> communists in the United States. Ever since I have done
> that work, the communists and left-wingers have been
> fighting me with every smear that they have been able
> to do.
>
> Even when I have made—after I received the nom-
> ination for the Vice Presidency, I want you folks to

know—and I'm going to reveal it today for the first time—I was warned that if I continued to attack the communists and the crooks in this government that they would continue to smear me, and, believe me, you can expect that they will continue to do so.

They started it yesterday—you saw it in your morning papers. They tried to say that I had taken money, $16,000. What they did not point out is this: that what I was doing was saving you money, rather than charging the expenses of my office, which were in excess of the amounts which were allowed by the taxpayers and allowed under the law. Rather than taking that money, the taxpayers' money for those purposes, what did I do?

What I did was to have those expenses paid by people back at home who were interested in seeing that the information concerning what was going on in Washington was spread among the people of their state.

Let me go on and say this. What else—What would you rather have me do?

They had interrupted him often with applause, but the crowd responded especially loudly at this point, and he seemed inspired to go on, "talking rapidly and with full voice," as one journalist described the scene.

I'll tell you what some of them do. They put their wives on the payroll. That's what Sparkman did.

I don't believe in putting my wife on the payroll, and taking your money and using it for that purpose. I think most of you will agree with me on that.

And Pat Nixon has worked in my office night after night after night, and I can say this, and I say it proudly, she has never been on the government payroll since I have been in Washington, D.C.

More clapping and shouts of approval. He paused, and then resumed loudly, "Point two:

What else would you do? Do you want me to go on and do what some of those people are doing? Take fat legal fees on the side?

Perhaps you ought to know this: during the time I have been in Washington—I am proud of this—I've never taken a legal fee, although as a lawyer I could legally but not ethically have done so. And I am never going to in the future, because I think that's a violation of a trust which my office has.

Just let me say this before I leave, let me say this: they have told you, and you can be sure that the smears will continue to come and the purpose of those smears is to make me if possible relent and let up on my attack on the communists and the crooks in the present administration.

I'm going to tell you this: as far as I am concerned, they've got another guess coming, because what I intend to do is to go up and down this land, and the more they smear the more I'm going to expose the communists and the crooks and those that defend them until they throw them all out of Washington.

It was then, and would remain, a singular act of stump-speech demagoguery in an American national campaign. He had not only evoked the Red bogey where none existed, not only misrepresented the Fund as somehow a substitute for and saving of public money, but also branded his Vice-Presidential opponent and many of his congressional colleagues as blatantly unethical. It was all of a part with the pose and self-justification he had struck from his first months in Washington, the conviction that whatever he did, however he did it, was to be explained and if necessary excused by his enemies and by the grim, widely accepted image of a sweeping corruption and laxity in government and politics.

Wild applause now interrupted him several times again as the speech wound down. When he had ended, the train slowly moved out on Jack Drown's signal, the Marysville crowd waving Nixon banners and "cheering thunderously," as he remembered the scene. "I walked back into my private compartment feeling better."

At Chico, another hour north, there was a gathering of eight hundred waiting around the small station. He puzzled them for a moment by recalling one of his former classmates at Whittier College as their high school vice principal, a man who in fact worked at Marysville down the line. But he quickly recovered by bringing up what he called "the smear." They could expect the attacks "from now to election day," but he was "proud of my record," and was "not going to let up."

After the speech, they stayed in the Chico station for thirty minutes while Chotiner took calls from the Eisenhower train and Nixon talked briefly with Seaton somewhere in Nebraska. Bassett meanwhile tried valiantly to appease and hold off the insistent press. "It may be assumed that General Eisenhower was not aware of the existence of the trust fund," Bassett told them carefully in reply to a question. Before there had been "no point in bringing it to his attention, since its existence was no secret, [and] no attempt had been made to hide it." Senator Nixon did not think he was doing "anything unethical." As for the telephone calls, these were normal "liaison conversations," and, yes, the Fund had "come up." The Eisenhower aides had been told about the crowd reaction at Marysville and were "very pleased."

Asked if anyone had requested of Nixon a further explanation of the money, Bassett told them he was "sure that was not the program." In truth, of course, it was the sole subject of the tense transcontinental calls. Seaton talked first with Chotiner, telling him Eisenhower wanted to "get to the bottom of this thing." Typical of his attitude from the beginning, Chotiner had recoiled. "What more does the general require than the senator's word?" Finally getting Nixon on the line, Seaton told him of the personal message coming from Eisnhower, "penciled out" by the general himself, Seaton said, and asking for "full documentary evidence." Nixon listened stonily and soon handed the receiver back to Chotiner, who then worked out with Seaton a public reply from the running mate that Ike could read in his speech that night. "It was clear to me," Nixon remembered, "that Eisenhower was not committing himself."

The day was growing hot in the valley, and the *Nixon Special* was late. After standing in the sun for more than an hour, the crowd had thinned to only three hundred as they drew into Red Bluff. Again without waiting for a heckler, Nixon reminded them of the "smears" from "communists and crooks" and warned that unless he and Ike were elected, "boys fourteen, fifteen, and sixteen will be over in Korea fighting or in the army." At Redding, the temperature nearly one hundred degrees in the shadow of the great Shasta Dam, he spoke once more about the "frantic attempt to smear me," the "outright lie" that he had "received money from Californians"—though few of his listeners there or anywhere else in these small towns of the north had yet seen newspaper accounts of the Fund. "Do you think when I come out to California to make a political speech the taxpayers ought to pay the bill?" And the seven hundred people spread across the tracks shouted "NO!"

"I used it throughout the day," Nixon said later of the much-practiced argument justifying, blurring, skirting the Fund. Thus he explained as a "communist smear" a story that had come not from Alger Hiss or some cabal of leftists but from Earl Warren's own embittered Republicans, and he justified as taxpayer "savings" political expenses his official Senate allowance could not and would not have paid in any case. However ironic, however deceptive, it was successful. The audiences at the small stations from Marysville northward he imagined larger than those the day before. And his counterattack seemed to satisfy and convince them, to arouse even greater support. "The overwhelming majority were with me," he remembered proudly. It was a conviction of underlying popular support, of popular acceptance of his argument, that he would carry throughout the crisis and on to national vindication.

Back off the platform and once more inside the train, away from the satisfying rejoinders and boisterous crowds, they moved in a different reality and mood. Local politicians were even more visibly diffident. From calls back to the Washington Hotel office, some in the party knew what Nixon himself learned only later—that women on his headquarters staff were in tears from the flood of calls, most of them urging Nixon's ouster. There were bleak and menacing reports as well from wire copy that the California Franchise Tax Board planned to investigate Nixon's state income tax returns and even those of the donors. The inquiry would be in the hands of Republican controller Thomas Kuchel, a dour Warren man whose presence—at least for Nixon, Chotiner, and others who knew the sordid intraparty history—might well threaten a settling of old scores.

After talking with Seaton, they had telephoned Dana Smith to tell him to prepare and to release a list of donors. There was some relief when he assured them the figures were in order and that the list, as Nixon put it, would simply show "professional and business people," far from the *Post*'s "millionaires' club"—though the actual truth lay well between both descriptions. Still, Pat Hillings thought the tension in the cars that hot afternoon rapidly becoming "unbearable," the thickly forested isolation of upstate California all the more shadowed and oppressive. Both Nixons were "almost frantic for news," as their daughter wrote later, and "utterly frustrated" by the evident lack of support from that other supposedly gala campaign train, the *Look Ahead, Neighbor Special*, rocking its own troubled route from stop to stop down the bluffs of the Missouri.

"CLEAN AS A HOUND'S TOOTH"

"We have to get rid of people who regard public service as an opportunity to enrich or aggrandize themselves," the general had said at Nebraska City and other stops. At St. Joseph, Missouri, he delivered the same promise of "peace and honest government" to a crowd of eight thousand packed into the railroad yards, standing on rooftops, perched on telephone poles. As the train pulled out, however, paper boys threw on copies of the *St. Joseph News-Press*, typical of the small papers beginning to take note of the story more than twenty-four hours after it broke, which now carried a special item at the top of its front page. The *News-Press* supported Ike, said the note, but with the exposé of the Nixon fund, someone in the composing room had written a little doggerel for the Presidential candidate:

> *We have often heard the shout,*
> *We must turn the rascals out.*
> *The rate they're leading us to ruin isn't slow.*
> *But cleaning up their own backyard*
> *May be just a wee bit hard*
> *When millionaires are slipping them the dough.*

Another thousand greeted Ike and Mamie at Kansas City, but as they drove away from the majestic old Union Station, smiling and waving from a convertible, they looked out on crowds with signs reading "DONATE HERE TO HELP POOR RICHARD NIXON." "Silent pickets rebuked him," wrote a *Life* correspondent, and no answer of "communist smear . . . could still the rising political clamor." Trying to rest at his hotel, Eisenhower could hear the incessant—some now thought mocking—blare of the GOP sound truck outside: "If you're tired . . . of crooked officials, elect General Dwight D. Eisenhower."

Roy Roberts's ever-loyal *Kansas City Star* featured that evening Nixon's countercharge of smear and even Dana Smith's recommendation of the Fund for all "public-spirited citizens." At the same moment, however, an enterprising *Star* reporter was filing a late dispatch that "some advisers were telling the Republican candidate that he should ask Senator Nixon to resign as Vice-Presidential nominee." Following suit, the AP reported "Eisenhower advisers . . . sharply divided tonight as to whether Nixon should be asked to get off the Republican ticket," adding in a wire dispatch later read on the *Nixon Special*, "a few of the . . . Presidential nominee's associates . . . seem to indicate that public reaction may determine Nixon's fate."

That night in Kansas City, Eisenhower began his speech by reading the ostensible Nixon reply Chotiner had drafted over the phone with Seaton from Chico. Because of "continued misrepresentation," the senator was asking for a "complete accounting" from Dana Smith "to prevent any misunderstanding." The whole affair was "a deliberate smear attempt," Nixon's statement went on. The facts would show that the contributors asked nothing and received nothing "in any way of special favors, consideration, or treatment," and "not one red cent was spent by me for personal use." This "legitimate political fund" came from "an earnest and unselfish desire . . . to support my fight against communism and corruption."

Finished reading, Eisenhower added pointedly if disingenuously a passage he and aides had drafted and redrafted: "I have worked with and have confidence in Senator Nixon. . . . Knowing Dick Nixon as I do I believe that when the facts are known to all of us they will show what is right. Both he and I believe in a single standard of morality in public life." After the speech Hagerty told questioning reporters "the idea of dropping Nixon never was mentioned" in the day's deliberations. But the press aide notably refused to assure them that Nixon would remain on the ticket. "Everybody is waiting [sic] the report of the [Fund] trustees," he told them. It was going to be up to Nixon to account, fully and persuasively.

The reception to Ike's Kansas City speech, still another on corruption and "bossism," was polite yet noticeably restrained, the burden of the Fund already plain, or so it seemed to watching aides and reporters. The nearly ten thousand in the audience cheered rarely—once when Nixon's statement promised full disclosure. Disturbed beneath his legendary Yankee composure, Sherman Adams called Herb Brownell, and afterward, almost simultaneously from New York and Kansas City, seized with the same thought, both these phlegmatic men reached to telephone Bill Knowland, then on a speaking date in Honolulu, asking him to return to the mainland immediately to join the Eisenhower train, a Vice-Presidential replacement in the wings. As he left Hawaii, an excited Knowland told reporters the crisis "will be overcome," though he "supposed" the Democrats would capitalize on it. In his hotel suite, meanwhile, the usually relaxed and serene general tossed about in a fitful, half-sleepless night. Back on board the train at his typewriter, an AP reporter punched out the fitting lead for Friday's last dispatch: "An atmosphere of gloom prevails today on the Eisenhower train."

The *Nixon Special* was leaving its last California station as the general faced his pickets in Kansas City, and in the hours of the waning autumn afternoon, before their first stops across the line in Oregon, Richard Nixon convened another meeting of the staff. This time there was Jim Bassett as well as Chotiner, Rogers, and Hillings. Although he was "irritated," Nixon said of his own mood, "I was not in the least discouraged." In any case, Chotiner was again defiant. In the end, he told them, the attacks would only spur on a listless Eisenhower campaign. "All we've got to do is get you before enough people talking about this fund, and we will win this election in a landslide," he told his beleaguered politician. Rogers agreed that the Democrats had "overplayed" their hand, that the press exposure had come "too early" to sustain public interest and could be offset by further explanation.

Only Bassett was at odds with their self-reinforcing optimism. The train reporters were pressuring him for a formal press conference, for a definite time when Eisenhower would have his promised conversation with Nixon, for more details on the money. They had been rushing off for telephones at every stop, even knocking on the doors of nearby houses when station phones were tied up. And each time they returned with new gossip about how "serious" the story had become, if not in actual coverage at least on Ike's train. Bassett urged a press conference, but Nixon was again adamant against any contact with the press beyond the rear platform speeches. "This would only give a bigger play to a story that was already receiving more attention than it deserved," he recorded of his refusal.

It was after nine that evening when they arrived in Medford, Oregon, where Chotiner was suddenly given shocking news that was already humming on midnight wires from the East. The *New York Herald Tribune* and the *Washington Post*, both supporting Eisenhower, were publishing editorials the next morning calling for Nixon's sacrifice, the *Herald Tribune* for at least his "formal offer of withdrawal," the *Post* for outright resignation. There was no question, pronounced the New York paper, that the "financial arrangements by which the Republican Vice-Presidential nominee furthered his work were ill-advised." They could wait with Eisenhower for a full report, but Ike had to "keep the big objective in view," and Nixon should meanwhile tender his resignation. "How this offer is acted on will be determined by an appraisal of all the facts in the light of General Eisenhower's unsurpassed fairness of mind." The *Post* was less dainty. It reminded readers of Nixon's attacks on party chairmen Boyle and Gabrielsen. His departure now in light of the Fund "would provide the Republican Party an unparalleled opportunity to demonstrate the sincerity of its campaign against loose conduct and corruption in government." Ike's hoped-for housecleaning in Washington, it added, "will be gravely handicapped if his running mate exemplifies the unethical conduct that he is denouncing."

A handful of pickets were on the edge of the Medford station crowd as Chotiner learned of the editorials, and he and Rogers quickly decided to keep the bad news overnight from their already nettled and weary candidate. Trying to ignore the pickets, wearing a "forced" smile, Nixon, like Tom Dewey and other uncomfortable candidates before and after, stood by while Medford's fur-clad "Cave Men" inducted him into their booster organization in a lengthy ceremony.

The train was parked for the night on a Medford siding, and Nixon was returning to his compartment when he happened onto a reporter who had heard the news himself. "Senator, do you have any comment on the *Washington Post* and *New York Herald Tribune* editorials?"

"What editorials?"

"Both have editorials tomorrow morning saying that you should offer your resignation to General Eisenhower."

By one account, Nixon simply shook his head and said nothing. In his own version he recalled that "I felt as much of a jolt as if the train had suddenly started to move." Hurrying back to his bedroom, he ordered a porter to find Chotiner and Rogers. As he waited he felt "hit by a real blockbuster" and agonized over the implications. The *Post* might be an old enemy, critical of his campaign tactics even now amid their endorsement of the Republican ticket. But the painful blow came from the *Herald Tribune*, so influential in the eastern wing, the Reids and others he had courted so long and carefully and who had been so instrumental in his rise, not least Bert Andrews, himself on the Eisenhower train, all of them "personal friends," as he said later. Worse, the paper was clearly the organ of the chummy corporate elite behind Ike's candidacy. The editorial would not have scuttled him, he was sure, "unless it also represented the thinking of the people around Eisenhower."

Chotiner and Rogers trailed in, sheepishly admitting they had known earlier but hoped to spare him. Chotiner then showed him a wire copy of the *Herald Tribune* editorial, and he was again "struck with the enormity of the impending crisis"—or, as he put it more plainly, that "the fat was in the fire." Reading about the general's "unsurpassed fairness of mind," he thought the self-serving too blatant even for Bill Robinson and the paper's hierarchy. "That sounded," he said later of his reaction, "like the official word from Eisenhower himself." He also watched as Bill Rogers, the easterner and Dewey-Brownell protégé, was visibly "shaken" by the establishment dictum, while Murray Chotiner, the second-story Los Angeles lawyer, still wearing his loud California ties and clock-face cufflinks, was loyally "furious." "How stupid can they be?" Chotiner burst out about "those damned amateurs around Eisenhower"—most of them men who had tapped Nixon to begin with and who had spun out the intricate, sometimes treacherous staging of his nomination. If they "just had the sense they were born with," Chotiner was saying, "they would recognize that this was a purely political attack and they wouldn't pop off like this." His old manager would insist then, and again and again, "If you get off, Eisenhower will lose."

The candidate was also equally angry—"experiencing some of the same emotional reaction that Chotiner had put into words," he wrote later. He curtly told Rogers to call Dewey while Chotiner talked to Seaton the next morning. As for his own telephone conversations, he would talk to no one "except Eisenhower himself," who "alone had the authority to make a decision."

It was two o'clock that morning when Chotiner and Rogers left, and he was exhausted, thinking he had put on "a reasonably good front" but now feeling "the full weight of fatigue and depression." As at so many similar moments over the past six years, he turned to his wife. Waking her, he descibed the *Tribune* editorial and his speculations about Eisenhower's aides. Like Chotiner, she was dismayed and bellicose. "Maybe I ought to resign," he said finally, and she had flashed, "You can't think of resigning. If you do Eisenhower will lose." Then she had gone on in searing personal terms. "Look, if you get off, you will carry the scar for the rest of your life," he remembered her arguing passionately, shoring him up once again. "He can put you off the ticket if he wants . . . but if you . . . do not fight back but simply crawl away, you will destroy yourself. Your life will be marred forever and the same will be true of your family, and particularly, your daughters."

The *Herald Tribune* and *Post* were only part of a nationwide outpouring of editorial comment that Saturday morning. Their news pages having largely masked the story at its inception, and even for a second day as well, editors by Friday evening could scarcely ignore the stream of wire reports from the two Republican trains. No other news seemed made by either ticket. The Fund had become, for the moment at least, the story of the 1952 campaign. Nearly one hundred newspapers responded with editorials September 20, most of them still pro-Eisenhower though disapproving of Nixon's subsidies by a margin of almost two to one. Only a handful joined in urging his removal. But there were few strong defenders and much critical judgment throughout the nation.

His enthusiastic backer at the nomination, *The New York Times* now thought the Fund "a practice . . . not to be condoned." Acceptance of the money, said the *Chattanooga Times* in response to Nixon's own publicized arguments, "does not become ethical merely because 'leftists' disclosed the facts. Nor . . . merely because other senators use unethical means to supplement their incomes." The Republican *Denver Post* deplored "the failure of Richard Nixon to resign . . . or be asked to quit by General Eisenhower," while the Democratic *Louisville Courier-Journal* reminded its readers, "The facts as laid out by the *New York Post* are not denied." The Fund "creates the occasion for corruption whether corruption exists or not," observed the uncommitted *Milwaukee Journal*, while the *Santa Fe New Mexican* shrewdly remarked of the donors, "If Nixon at any time incurred their displeasure, the funds would be cut off. . . . 'The mess in Washington' . . . now becomes 'the mess in California.' "

Always loyal, the *San Diego Union* simply invented the provision that the Fund's "bills . . . were handled by a committee of well-known public leaders, men of good reputation." But the still-neutral *Washington Star* gave voice to what was now haunting so many on the Eisenhower train and at the Commodore: "Had the facts been known in advance, it is virtually certain that Mr. Nixon would not have received the GOP nomination." The point was echoed forcefully in Henry Luce's *Time*, otherwise so admiring of the ticket. The Fund might have been somehow understandable in the "polite anarchy" of California politics, but there were "other ways" to cover legitimate expenses and no excuse for the *de facto* secrecy of the money. "Few professional California GOPoliticos knew of the fund," *Time* concluded in its familiar argot. "Nixon erred grievously in not telling Ike— and the public—the whole story before the campaign began."

In Washington, even before he had seen the editorial reactions, Bob Humphreys awoke Saturday morning driven by the thought "that we ought to put Nixon on TV in as dramatic a way as possible." It was his "pet theory," Humphreys would say, that "when adversity hits, try to convert it into something you can capitalize on." He called Kansas City right away to reach Summerfield, who was not yet aware of the rising press storm. The chairman thought the television speech a good idea, but worried about raising the money for an unbudgeted, unplanned appearance. Could they get a commercial sponsor? Paid or free, Humphreys quickly replied, it was "more important, with so much at stake" that the decision "should be considered by the best brains in the party." He then read out to Summerfield a list he had drawn up in bed, men to be consulted on giving Nixon a national program to defend himself. They were, not surprisingly, figures of the right, of the conservative and anticommunist GOP, reckoned to back the young senator and recommend to Eisenhower a national TV appeal—Joe Martin, Karl Mundt, Charlie Halleck, Roy Roberts, John Cowles, Bob Taft, Joe McCarthy. Bob Humphreys had carefully packed the jury for his own proposal, for Nixon's chance at recovery and redemption, and his like-minded party chairman promptly agreed. A half hour later, Summerfield called back from Kansas City to give the go-ahead for the telephone polling and to add only one more name at Sherman Adams's suggestion—Bill Robinson of the *Herald Tribune*, likely to be the lone dissenting voice in granting Dick Nixon his television reprieve.

The inclusion of Robinson was a mark of Dwight Eisenhower's own gathering ambivalence in the crisis. Learning of the *Herald Tribune* editorial as his train left Kansas City for St. Louis Saturday morning, Ike angrily fired off a "personal and confidential" message to Robinson, his longtime patron and friend, rebuking the paper for its "hair-trigger" reaction. "Without a full knowledge of the facts, I am not willing to prejudge any man," he told the publisher. "I have had a sound regard for Dick Nixon, as a member of the United States Navy, as a strong congressman and senator, and as a man. I have had reason to believe in his honesty and character. As you know, I've admired him greatly." Yet the essence of Ike's complaint was less a matter of Nixon than the aspersions on his own judgment and fairness, and the *Tribune*'s implicit preemption of his decision. "Quite apart from the campaign, I could not jump to the conclusion that such a man, whom I trusted to be my running mate, was bad," the general went on, promising "if there is real money at stake [*sic*], there will be prompt and conclusive action by me. That has always been my way of acting . . . being sure not to go against the principles of fairness and justice."

It was a gray and rainy fall Saturday across central Missouri, and the weather matched the mood on the *Look Ahead, Neighbor*. Eisenhower had been "let down" by both Senator Nixon and the Presidential campaign staff, some of the latter plaintively leaked to the press corps, adding to the divisions of reproach and responsibility, power and purpose, already rapidly opening among the advisers. That weekend an Associated Press poll showed Ike not only well ahead in popular percentages but also decisively leading in electoral votes, with Adlai Stevenson still short of election even if he won all the states still rated as a toss-up. In a sense, the Fund would be the first crisis, the first major decision, of the Eisenhower Presidency, and the hidden inner currents of the affair now symbolized vividly the forces and personalities congealed around this hero as politician and eventually around his administration.

"Keep your respective chins up and do not let smears or sniping bother you," Tom Dewey had cabled the key advisers as the story spread. But the crisis offerred an irresistible opportunity for recrimination and further jockeying among men whose selection and lengthy secret squiring of Nixon had nevertheless overlooked this potential disaster. After Eisenhower's instruction to "find out the facts," Adams had telephoned Paul Hoffman in Los Angeles, asking him to begin "an immediate investigation" of the Fund "to find out if it was clean." Hoffman variously told Adams that the Fund was nothing to worry about, that he had known about it himself (though he had not mentioned it to Eisenhower or his advisers), and proceeded to blame Dana Smith for letting out the story. Smith's admission to the press was a "bad idea," Hoffman told Adams, despite the "very righteous" nature of the subsidies.

At the Commodore headquarters, meanwhile, Emmet Hughes witnessed "a mixture of emotions, ranging from a cool and somber concern to an instant and heated exasperation with the man causing all the trouble." After a "far from dispassionate" discussion, Herb Brownell polled the collected volunteers and independents and found "a considerable majority" in favor of dropping the tainted running mate forthwith, exactly as the *Herald Tribune* urged—a mounting anti-Nixon sentiment that set them, then and later, clearly at odds with the National Committee and GOP headquarters in Washington. None of the men in Manhattan seemed more perturbed now than Lucius Clay, Eisenhower's trusted fellow general who had joined in so much of the early promotion and political deployment of young Senator Nixon. In a "long discussion" on the subject, Hughes found Clay "angry and vehement," the acerbic old soldier feeling "particular responsibility and disenchantment" over their bungled choice.

Like Murray Chotiner, Bob Humphreys would be savagely disdainful of Clay and the other "amateurs" and "citizens" of the campaign, a group they saw as hostile toward Dick Nixon since the convention and whom they now blamed with some reason for the leaks of "panic" and divided counsel from both New York and the train—what Humphreys called "the building up of the story to enormous proportions." Yet it was still another irony of the episode, and a crucial turning point, that Lucius Clay now held back from pressing what might have been his own decisive view. At Jefferson City, halfway across Missouri, an obviously troubled Eisenhower ran into the station in a downpour to call his old army colleague in New York. Instead of then urging the removal most of them at the Commodore favored, however, Clay cautiously told Ike to delay a final decision until events unfolded a bit more and Brownell could meet the train and talk to the general in person in Cincinnati the following Monday. Brownell in any case would be carrying the all-but-unanimous views of the New York advisers that Nixon should go.

As it was, Lucius Clay's advice purchased precious hours for the campaign's most fateful decision and reinforced Eisenhower's own bridling at the mounting pressure, his instinctive reluctance to move ahead in this unfamiliar and dangerous political terrain. As Ike hurried back aboard in the rain at midday Saturday, Richard Nixon and the men on both coasts trying to save his candidacy and career would have a historic margin of time.

In southern Oregon that Saturday morning, Nixon felt his commodious train, the same flag-draped cars that had left Pomona so grandly three nights before, "like a prison with its inexorable schedule." At the first stop at Roseburg, the gathering of around five hundred appeared larger than expected, though with what he saw as "Democrats" and "hecklers . . . [who were] more aggressive." Two hours later they rode into Eugene and the first large hostile signs held aloft among a crowd of some two thousand. Two junior college students carried one reading "WILL THE VEEP'S SALARY BE ENOUGH, DICK?" Rogers noticed a banner waving with the message "PAT, WHAT ARE YOU GOING TO DO WITH THE BRIBE MONEY?" Still another placard was printed on both sides—on one "SH-H-H, ANYONE WHO MENTIONS $16,000 IS A COMMUNIST," and turned around "NO MINK COATS FOR NIXON—JUST COLD CASH."

He launched into the usual speech and then pointed defiantly toward the double sign. "That's right, there are no mink coats for Nixon, nothing for which the taxpayer has paid, no mink coats for Nixon and no mink coats for Pat Nixon, his wife. I'm proud of the fact that Pat Nixon wears a good Republican cloth coat, and she's going to continue to." The phrase "came to mind," he wrote afterward, not only because he wanted to turn the attack back on the "Democrats' mink coat scandal" but also "because I had long been aware that I was unable to afford a fur coat for my wife."

As the train then lurched away and Nixon was still speaking, the crowd moved angrily against the silent pickets, denouncing the students as "dirty communists" and homosexuals, flailing out to hit Charles Porter, a young Democrat and later an Oregon congressman, who held the double-sided placard. Police on the station platform tried to reach Porter in what journalists would describe as a "near-riot," though not before the protesters had been assaulted. Porter's sign was pulled down and "torn to shreds," as Nixon recorded with a sense of satisfaction. "The violence of the attacks was finally beginning to backfire," he wrote. "Those supporting me were resentful . . . not only listening to what I had to say and believing it, but also . . . willing to fight back, just as I was."

While this melee was unfolding, Bassett distributed yet another formal statement on the Fund, saying that "at my request" Dana Smith was making public that day the full list of donors to "a political fund established to permit me to carry on my fight against communism and corruption above and beyond my official duties in Washington, D.C." The handout repeated in numbered points what he had been saying at the whistle-stops—that the money was "strictly for political activities in which all public servants must take part," enabled Nixon to meet costs "without recourse to padding my federal office payroll," had never been secret or involved "one penny for my personal use," was altogether "normal, legitimate, open." The contributors were "longtime supporters of mine," the Eugene statement said, contradicting earlier assurances that Nixon had never known their identity. Did this mean the senator had no thought of withdrawing? reporters asked Bassett. "It speaks for itself," he snapped. "Draw your own conclusions."

They approached Salem, the state capital, with added tension, Nixon worrying that Oregon Republican governor Douglas McKay would snub him. McKay was a well-publicized candidate for the Eisenhower cabinet, and they had already heard rumors about the "political heat" in Oregon, how some of McKay's "friends" were urging the governor to avoid a planned motorcade. But near one o'clock the *Nixon Special* arrived to find McKay waiting with a warm welcome, and the two politicians rode together smiling in an open car through the small city, though Nixon noticed "scores of sign-carrying hecklers" along the route. At the steps of the capitol the local GOP organization had turned out a crowd of fifteen hundred for his address, including a claque of students from Willamette University, and the reception was again enthusiastic.

In the early afternoon in Salem, however, they were besieged with reports of the events breaking two or three hours ahead of them in the East. Saturday, like Friday, would be a series of periodic spasms, of public acclaim darkened by private alarms. Out from the Eisenhower train, through the press corps, there sped rumors of the general's calls and conferences, of the urgings of "this friend" and "that friend," as Nixon bitterly referred to the corporate executives and patrons he lumped with the *Herald Tribune*'s treachery. By Salem they had heard, too, of Clay's call in Jefferson City, and Nixon saw party and personal intrigue behind the issue of the Fund. "Some of those who had supported other Vice-Presidential candidates began to build up a dump-Nixon movement," he wrote, although there had never been any real competitors for the nomination, save Knowland, who had hardly enjoyed the backing of Clay or the eastern moderates. Yet when they learned now of Knowland's summons from Hawaii, it was another blow, and a plot seemed fully palpable. Nixon believed the Presidential campaign advisers were divided at best between two groups with none essentially on his side—"those who thought I should be dropped immediately and those who wanted to wait and see how public reaction developed."

His only defense seemed to come from the old guard and Red-baiting right, some of the men to whom he had shrewdly paid court after the Chicago maneuvers. The price of his own past unctuousness and partisanship, Democratic attacks were steady and often caustic, Sparkman suggesting an inquiry by the same committee Nixon had exploited to harry the Truman regime, Oklahoma's Kerr mockingly announcing "bundles-for-Nixon" containing "postage stamps and Christmas cards." In reply, Joe McCarthy charged that Adlai Stevenson was once "recommended by Alger Hiss for a top job," while GOP senator George Aiken of Vermont allowed that "many senators supplemented their official incomes." Old patrons Herbert Hoover and Joe Martin both defended the California money that Hoover in part had made posssible and whose pressure Martin had felt as early as Nixon's appointment to HUAC.

"I think the tide has finally begun to turn," Rogers said as he burst into Nixon's compartment after the speech at Salem. The lawyer was flourishing a report of a statement made by Bob Taft, who saw "no reason" why senators should not receive such subsidies. "The only possible criticism would arise if these donors wanted some legislative or other favors," Taft had said, adding in a kind of cynical candor that there was no need for such favors in Nixon's case. "Those who contributed to the fund probably agreed 100 percent with his legislative position anyway." Nixon later thought it "ironical" that Taft supported him after the wounds of the convention, though he attributed it to partisan self-interest of "an experienced politician and party man." "He was not so naïve," he wrote of Taft in the crisis, "as to think that I could be dropped from the ticket without creating a break in our ranks big enough for the Democratic campaign to drive through to victory."

Otherwise, they took scant comfort from the national reaction. One response in particular his men greeted with contempt and sly suspicion. Adlai Stevenson's first comment on the Fund had been characteristic. "Condemnation without all the evidence, a practice all too familiar to us, would be wrong," the Democratic candidate told reporters pestering him. Just as characteristically, on the *Nixon Special* they saw his forbearance and slight subtlety as fey weakness, Stevenson's usual pattern, Bill Rogers quipped, of "considering the problem very carefully before making the wrong decision." Chotiner, as Nixon recorded him, "smelled a rat" as well. He would "lay money against odds that Stevenson is afraid of something here," he told them. "I bet he has something to hide." Chotiner's skepticism may have been more than intuition. At the National Committee in Washington, Bob Humphreys had gotten from a friend in Chicago the first tip about a similar fund for Stevenson and his appointees in the Illinois governorship. By Saturday morning, Humphreys had become what he called "the focal point for passing . . . rumors on to Nixon," and in what were dozens of phone calls to Chotiner, the Stevenson fund was soon to be a major topic.

While they anxiously examined each shard of the political furor, Pat was "constantly on the phone to my mother," as Nixon described it. Hannah was at their Washington home babysitting for the girls, and the frequent calls bespoke the mounting apprehension of the wife and mother. Back in Whittier the anguish was still deeper. Joe Johnson, Frank's old friend from Yorba Linda, went by their house on Anaconda as the Fund scandal grew and found Frank sick in bed but furious with his famous son. He was "very disgusted with Dick that he would ever let himself get into that position," Johnson recalled. "There was no earthly reason for it and he was pretty near mad [at] the guy . . . no reason to take that money." Only afterward did Richard Nixon learn that Frank Nixon was nearly hysterical during the episode that seemed to doom his son's meteoric career, and even beyond throughout the general election. "I found out," he acknowledged later, "that my proud and combative father had been reduced to bouts of weeping as each new smear surfaced."

While the *Nixon Special* paused uneasily in Salem, then slowly moved up the tracks toward Portland, another two and one-half hours out of touch, the *Look Ahead, Neighbor* was responding to its own restless timetable. At every rural stop in Missouri, bags of letters and telegrams were being hauled to the train, with at least half of them calling for Nixon's removal. Hearing of the large deliveries, the press was more clamorous than ever. At mid-afternoon, Hagerty came forward to announce the fifty-fifty split in the mail, hardly a reassuring vote of public confidence, and an admission that "revealed," wrote one observer, "how close the party elders were to a decision." The train reporters even took their own poll among themselves and voted forty to two to jettison the Vice-Presidential nominee. They promptly passed the tally to Eisenhower via Hagerty, with the cynical aside that most of them expected a "whitewash."

In the general's car it was now clear that the candidate would have to talk directly to the press for the first time since the issue emerged. After some dickering it was agreed that he would meet them informally in the time-honored subterfuge of "on background" and not for attribution, though quoted as "the highest source on the campaign train" and thus unmistakable to sophisticated readers. At four that afternoon beers were poured in the press car and Eisenhower entered, as one writer remembered, to "equivocal smiles all around." Did he consider "the Nixon thing a closed incident?" With a deep, wrinkling frown that would become famous at future press conferences, Eisenhower shook his head heavily and launched into what was a strikingly candid rendition of his own inner dilemma.

"By no means," he answered. He was disturbed that Nixon was making statements about the charges without checking with him or his organization and that his own staff had not told him of the Fund until Friday morning, several hours after they heard the news. Still, he had just learned of the problem and knew Nixon "little and only briefly," but he found it "extremely hard to believe" that a young man of thirty-nine with such a future "could be guilty of wrongdoing." Then he leaned forward and told them earnestly, "I don't care if you fellows are forty to two. I am taking my time on this. Nothing's decided, contrary to your idea that this is a setup for a whitewash of Nixon. . . . Of what avail is it for us to carry on this crusade against this business of what has been going on in Washington if we, ourselves, aren't as clean as a hound's tooth?"

He was resolved to "get at the facts," Ike went on, and did not want to talk to Nixon personally until he had "all the facts." Even though he still had "confidence in Senator Nixon's honesty," the basis of his judgment would be not only whether the money was "illegal" but whether "it was in any way immoral." The report on the Fund "must be clean as a hound's tooth or else." Whatever the phrase, his ambivalence was plain. "Just what the 'or else' means," wrote James Reston, "is still doubtful in General Eisenhower's mind."

Privately, he was by now far more pessimistic about the results of a removal. "There is one thing I believe," he told Sherman Adams after the press backgrounder. "If Nixon has to go, we cannot win." Adams had tried to reassure him: "Wait and see," he said simply. Yet the evidence from the campaign's own intelligence was increasingly bleak. That afternoon, one of Clay's friends and head of a volunteer clipping service for Eisenhower had cabled Adams: "Objective survey of leading Eastern newspapers clearly shows Nixon now major liability . . . [who] will inevitably cost Ike the editorial support he now enjoys." Adams and others were struck, too, by the ominous difference in Eisenhower's crowds since Kansas City, what even Warren Francis of the *Los Angeles Times* called the "jeering attitude" at the whistle-stops at the neat small towns strung out above the Missouri River as the train wound toward St. Louis, the heartland of values and judgment that the Republicans must win to enter the White House at last.

Amid all this only the redoubtable Humphreys brought good news. The GOP leaders he had telephoned all day Saturday were almost uniformly against dumping Nixon. It was another measure of the division in the party, between East and West, liberal and conservative, citizen and regular, though Humphreys's scribbled notes on the stalwarts' private conversations showed various misgivings about the young senator. "Make it clear Dick didn't get a penny. Nail [the] bastards for trying . . . drop it," advised Joe McCarthy. "Don't let Dick get mad." Congressman Charlie Halleck wondered "how many votes will it cost us?" but was also "afraid to trust Dick . . . I can't think of a good speech he could make." Karl Mundt thought the whole affair "not good," that they should simply "take [the] McCarthy line . . . [that] 'I need money.' " Ike's friend and patron, Roy Roberts, reminded Humphreys of the *Saturday Evening Post* article by Pat Nixon celebrating the Nixons' poverty. They should "say it and keep [their] mouth shut." Say "I'm poor" and that the Democrats had jumped "on a poor man" whose wife worked. Tom Coleman told him Nixon was "immature," but they should let the Fund "pass into the background . . . [it] won't hurt a bit on November 4." Coleman "wouldn't have him [Nixon] do [a speech]—won't make an impression." Publishers John Cowles and Palmer Hoyt were "100 percent Nixon" and thought "Dick was innocent" yet also believed that the episode was a "tragic thing" and the "whole campaign in some jeopardy."

Late Saturday night Humphreys cheerfully reported to Summerfield in St. Louis that party leaders were in favor by "approximately ten to one" of putting Dick Nixon on national television to explain himself, the idea Humphreys had first hatched that morning. The sole dissenter on Humphreys's carefully crafted list had been, as expected, Bill Robinson, whom Humphreys finally reached in a golf club locker room that evening. "Bob, I wouldn't put him on TV," the powerful *Herald-Tribune* executive told him. "I'd throw him off the ticket."

As if they could hear Bill Robinson's verdict being uttered, the collective anathema of Eisenhower's corporate Republicans, the Nixons came to the close of their third day of the campaign in an air of oppression. Several reporters of the *Nixon Special* had thought the Marysville and Eugene speeches, as one of them wrote, "a reckless belligerent counteroffensive . . . [that] left a bad taste." At Salem the tone became more moderate, the candidate himself retreating to a less strident "explanation" of the Fund. "Even visiting Democrats," wrote one journalist wandering through the crowd, "seemed sympathetic to Nixon and . . . not especially outraged." By the last stop at Portland, amid fresh rumors of an Eisenhower dump and a new ferocity among the oppositon, there had begun in the press corps a sense of sympathy for the young politician as prey.

The party paraded through downtown Portland that Saturday in a dank chill at dusk to only sparse crowds and a bare scattering of applause. Then, outside his quarters at the Benson Hotel, there was suddenly a swarm of pickets blocking the entrance, some of them tossing pennies into the car, others in dark glasses with canes and tin cups and signs saying "NICKELS FOR POOR NIXON." They jostled and shoved the candidate and his wife as they tried to make their way into the hotel. Journalists in the lobby watched Nixon hurry past, "tight-lipped and gray-faced," snapping a "no comment" when asked about reports that he was about to be replaced.

Their suite was no refuge from the pressure. They found an "urgent" message to call Sherman Adams in St. Louis, and Nixon angrily told Chotiner once more that he would talk to no one but Eisenhower. "Whatever happened," he recalled indignantly, "I was not going to be fobbed off on staff aides." Also awaiting them were reports that two more pro-Eisenhower papers, the Richmond *News Leader* and *Times-Dispatch*, were now both calling for his outright resignation over what the latter termed his "clandestine arrangement" with the Fund.

In her own bedroom Pat Nixon sat disconsolate, in a kind of shock, looking "like a bruised little kitten," thought Helene Drown. "It can't be happening. How can they do this?" she muttered again and again. "It's so unfair. They know the accusations are untrue." On this chill night in a Portland Hotel it was the wounded dismay of a woman who saw their world, and so much of her own sacrifice, suddenly collapsing. In a sense, too, it was an ironic echo of other moments of pain and incredulity, of Jerry Voorhis in the closing weeks of the 1946 race, of Helen Douglas and her family pounded by attack in the fall of 1950. The Drowns felt "the oppression . . . so thick that you could cut it with a knife." They finally spirited her out of the Benson for a ride to majestic Multnomah Falls on the Columbia, where she took off her shoes and dipped her feet in the icy river. Sitting there on the bank, Pat Nixon was soon laughing, almost gay, as one of the Drowns later told the family, but "a laugh of one who wakes up momentarily from a nightmare."

When his men had completed a first round of calls, Bassett entered with more bad news, word of Ike's backgrounder some four hours earlier and what Nixon called sarcastically the general's "colorful phrase" about a hound's tooth. He thought "the implication" all too clear—"that he would have to prove himself 'clean as a hound's tooth' if he hoped to stay on the ticket." He would write afterward that "our little group was somewhat dismayed by . . . Eisenhower's attitude. I must admit that it made me feel like the little boy caught with jam on his face." In truth, they were enraged, "as furious with Eisenhower," said one observer, "as Eisenhower's managers were with Nixon."

When their outburst cooled somewhat, he ordered Rogers and Chotiner to talk to everyone they could reach around the Presidential candidate—Adams and Summerfield, Dewey and Seaton. Bassett was to find out what he could from reporters on both trains, while Hillings counted the telegrams and letters to the train or hotel and did his own check of congressional Republicans. Nixon would carry on with an evening rally arranged by the Oregon campaign committee, and they were to reconvene afterward to deliver their reports.

Grasping at every potential source, they tried desperately to gauge Eisenhower and the depth and authority of the swirling signals to quit. Yet in all the angry reaction and barked orders on their arrival in Portland, none of them mentioned yet the saving resort already taking shape a continent away, the prospect of a nationwide television speech. Of the many anxious, imploring calls his men were to place from the Benson Saturday night, none was to the man who would be in the historic hours and days ahead Richard Nixon's most powerful if obscure ally, the sleepless, ever-planning Bob Humphreys in Washington.

A throng of eighteen hundred packed the auditorium at Portland's Grant High School. Once more Nixon was lifted and vindicated by their cheers. Beneath a giant portrait of a smiling Eisenhower—the Presidential nominee who had not telephoned him for two days of deepening crisis and whom he defiantly refused to contact himself—he raised his arms in a characteristic wave and declared his "fundamental faith in the American people to make a decision if they know the facts." If he had spent any of the Fund for personal use, "I should never have accepted the nomination . . . [and] I would get off the ticket right now." Would they have the taxpayers pay for his political broadcasts or his trips? And like all the other audiences up the coast, they roared "No!"

He had been warned back in 1948 when he went after the communists that "they would get me," he told them. But he was going to keep hunting the "crooks and communists," and "all the laughing and giggling you hear from the other side isn't going to cover it up." Fully understood or not, the old allusions to conspiracy and homosexuality, the old summoning of fear and prejudice, now evoked once more shouts and ovations. And Richard Nixon stood on the high school stage in Portland, as he had stood elsewhere in 1952 and before, basking in the support and near-adoration of his public, vindicated by the people if not the establishment he privately condemned. Afterward, they flocked to the platform, jammed forward to shake his hand, and over and over told him, "Don't quit," as he proudly repeated the story. The *Los Angeles Times*'s Chester Hansen found two young Republican women outside the school who had been "concerned about the expense-fund story" and who now after hearing the explanation "gave it [the Fund] their hearty approval." Such reactions were "comforting to the Nixon campaign entourage," reported the *Times*. Nowhere, from the hot Central Valley through the neat, cloudy, small cities of Oregon, would he face an audience that did not cheer his claim of smears and savings, did not accept his distorting view of public morality and political motives, did not scorn and when the chance came even punish his opponents, did not certify the speech he would eventually make to the nation.

The fervent crowd kept them an hour longer than planned, but too soon he was back at the Benson, locked again with the ambiguous, agonizing calculus of the very different people and politics encircling Dwight Eisenhower two thousand miles away. The euphoria of the giant rally, like all the others, was short-lived. He did not want "any sugar-coated reports," he told his men. But the strong front soon disappeared, and Nixon seemed "completely shaken and despondent . . . edgy and irritable," as some of them described him later. "His campaign managers did not know what he might do," Edwin Hoyt wrote about "the worst of it" Saturday night. "It was conceivable that he could blow up." Bassett began by telling him about the forty to two press vote on the Eisenhower train and about television and radio commentary as well as newspaper columns predicting his removal from the ticket. But he was quick to add that the *Nixon Special*'s own reporters were growing more sympathetic, impressed by the crowd reactions to his stock speech and "beginning to blame Eisenhower for not making a decision one way or the other." Rogers and Chotiner brought their own intelligence that the view of Ike's "staff, friends, and advisers was just as bad" as the media's. One of the Presidential campaign aides, Chotiner told him grimly, had even begun to lobby members of the National Committee to "demand" his resignation. Nixon would find "the only relatively bright spot," as he recorded later, in Pat Hillings's report that the conservative congressional party, Republican senators and representatives, were still largely with him, urging that he "stay on the ticket and fight it out." Hillings had been able to reach only a few of them, however, and they assumed that except for Fred Seaton and random others, the Capitol Hill wing of the GOP wielded comparatively little influence on the *Look Ahead, Neighbor.*

When they had finished, he finally put the questions hanging over them since the first stunning reports at Bakersfield three long days before. Would staying "lead to Eisenhower's defeat?" Would getting off "assure his victory?" Should he "take the initiative and resign?" Typically, Bassett was more cautious, less pugnacious, and cynical about the press and Eisenhower's own eventual decision. It would depend, the aide told him, on whether he could defend himself "more adequately to the press and to the country at large." Like Humphreys back in Washington, Jim Bassett saw clearly enough that the crisis ignited and fed by the media could be dampened if not extinguished by the same means, though the burden would be on the senator himself, "whether I was able to get my story across," as Nixon put it afterward. Next, Rogers told him, "you should fight it out" unless or until Ike actually asked for his resignation. Hillings, "still young enough to have 'fire in his belly,' " thought Nixon, was even more bellicose. How could they hope to counter "the press and other opinion makers . . . so overwhelmingly against us?" Nixon asked him. And the twenty-nine-year-old congressman answered combatively if vaguely, "You don't have to win them. The best way to answer them is to beat 'em." Bassett cool but challenging, Rogers the bland lawyer stating the obvious and joining their defiance, Hillings the loyal client and zealot—in the shadings and blending of all three was the reinforcing mix of so many other decisions to come, so much other advice by men who variously soothed, appeased, spurred, nurtured, used Richard Nixon the man and politician from the Benson Hotel in 1952 to the White House two decades later.

Now, as later, there was one man in the room who seemed to voice the harsher, instinctive judgments Nixon felt himself. The role was once again Murray Chotiner's. "This is politics. The prize is the White House," he began a gritty little lecture on the underlying forces at work. Dick was only "the lightning rod" because the Democrats were afraid of attacking Ike the hero, and were it not the Fund, "they would be taking you on on something else." If he resigned or was pushed off the ticket, Chotiner went on, "Eisenhower won't have the chance of a snowball in hell . . . your friends and those who supported Taft will never forgive him, and the Democrats will beat him over the head." The story had gotten out of hand because of "the delay and indecision of the amateurs around Eisenhower." Nixon himself could overcome that. "Every time you get before an audience, you win them," Chotiner said, echoing Nixon's own thoughts. "What we have to do," he concluded, "is to get you before the biggest possible audience so that you can talk over the heads of the press to the people. The people . . . are for you but the press is killing you." In recounting Chotiner's words later, Nixon would leave unspoken the larger political implication he and Chotiner understood so well, that he must go "over the heads" of Eisenhower and his men as well as the press, that it was the *Look Ahead, Neighbor* as well as the reporters who were "killing" him.

They left his suite after 3:00 A.M., though not before Bob Humphreys intervened from Washington with a dramatic call to Chotiner. After phoning Summerfield with the loaded consensus in favor of a nationwide television speech, Humphreys had been trying all night to arrange free broadcast time, albeit with serious misgivings. "My heart wasn't in it," he told a colleague, "because I felt that we had to control the timing." Still, he had "at least a nibble" from a Pittsburgh agency that controlled a Westinghouse program that Sunday, and in the predawn hours from his home in Northwest Washington he reached Chotiner in Portland to tell him "what was going on." There followed excited conversations at the Benson, and the sudden agreement that Humphreys's national program was the answer. "Meet the Press" was another possibility, but Chotiner immediately rejected it. They must have complete control, he insisted, "without interruption by possibly unfriendly press questions."

In any case, Rogers added, Sunday was too early. "Let them shoot their wad first," he said of the Democrats, "and then give it to them." Chotiner called back Humphreys to tell him "free time was out of the picture—Nixon didn't want it." The National Committee had allotted television time to the Vice-Presidential candidate, he reminded Humphreys. They should use it for the speech. Humphreys remarked that Summerfield was reluctant to spend the resources. "If Dick is off the ticket," shot back Chotiner, ever the campaign manager, "all the printing you'll have to do over again will cost you a lot more money than a television program."

Left alone in his suite, Nixon brooded into the Oregon dawn. As he set down his thoughts years later, there was no false modesty in his view of the problem. "I believe that what I did would affect the future of my country and the cause of peace and freedom for the world." Adlai Stevenson he deplored as "all veneer and no substance." Dwight Eisenhower was plagued by "lack of experience in political warfare" and by "several equally inexperienced associates," including, apparently, some of the same men who had selected Richard Nixon as the running mate. He would have to be guided by "my own analysis of the facts and politics as I knew it to be," he recalled. "If I were to resign from the ticket it would be an admission of guilt, Eisenhower might well lose the election, and I would forever afterwards be blamed for it." He resolved to do "everything within my power to stay on the ticket—with honor." A television speech risked everything, and "the slightest mistake might spell disaster for me." Yet there seemed no other choice. The inevitable decision made, he went to bed as the sun was rising behind the Cascades and "slept better than I had since the night the train pulled out of Pomona four nights before."

Despite his dawn decision, Sunday, September 21, was to be the most anguishing day of his early political career. If Bob Humphreys in Washington and Chotiner and Nixon across the continent in Portland had together fixed on a dramatic television appeal, the decision was not yet ratified by Eisenhower or his nebulous command. Their options to deny his attempted vindication, to remove him regardless of the speech, or, perhaps worse, to let him struggle longer still in his distant limbo remained all too real. As Richard Nixon fell into an exhausted sleep at sunrise, his future—and the nation's—still hung uncertainly in the political crosscurrents of the campaign.

That Sunday morning in New York, the *Times* published in a front-page dispatch from Pasadena the list of Fund contributors released the day before by Dana Smith, calling the names "an abbreviated '*Who's Who*' of wealthy and influential southern California business figures." The *Times* emphasized, too, from Smith's accounting that the payments "totaled $18,235 rather than the amount of 'approximately $16,000' mentioned by

Senator Nixon." An accompanying front-page story and a lengthy "digest of press comment" reported national editorial disapproval of the subsidies "by a ratio of almost two to one." "Many of the editorials absolved Gen. Dwight D. Eisenhower . . . of knowledge of the fund," observed the *Times*, "and there were numerous expressions of regret that the general had been placed in an embarrassing position." The *Times*'s own editorial page gave voice to the angry regret already gripping so many of the powerful Eisenhower backers. Had the Nixon Fund been known among the general and his men at the convention, said conservative columnist Arthur Krock, it "would certainly have caused them to look elsewhere" for a Vice-Presidential candidate.

Reactions were swift and forceful. Reading the coverage, financier Bernard Baruch nervously telephoned Tex McCrary, an early supporter, who quickly passed along the call to the Eisenhower train. Baruch urged solemnly that Nixon not "deprive this nation of a great leader" and thus "retire to the ranks of the private citizen, where he can continue his life dedication, the fighting of communism." In Washington the same morning, Republican senator Wayne Morse of Oregon told a national television audience that Dick Nixon might be "personally . . . honest" but had made "a mistake in judgment" that was now "very costly to this campaign."

The shock waves once more rolled east to west. In the Eisenhower party, now at the Hotel Statler in St. Louis, the Sunday morning news was accordingly grim. In a 7:00 A.M. telegram, Clay's friend Oscar Solbert of the Eisenhower Research Service in Washington again peppered Sherman Adams and the others with starkly annotated reports on press reaction. "NO AMOUNT OF WISHFUL THINKING CAN ALTER BRUTAL FACTS THAT NIXON IS FINISHED," Solbert cabled. "EDITORS BASE THEIR VERDICT NOT ON NIXON'S SELF-JUSTIFICATION WITH WHICH THEY AGREE, BUT ON HIS SELF-EVIDENCED POOR JUDGMENT WHICH THEY FEEL AUTOMATICALLY DISQUALIFIES HIM AS POTENTIAL SUCCESSOR TO PRESIDENCY." Clay's old army friends, now self-appointed political advisers, even repeated Baruch's formula of martydom for the ousted running mate, a graceful retirement without involving the general. "IF NIXON WITHDRAWS HIMSELF," Solbert's urgent telegram went on, "HE WILL GO DOWN IN HISTORY AS GREAT HERO WHO SACRIFICED HIMSELF FOR HIS OWN HIGH PRINCIPLES AND IKES [SIC] GREAT CRUSADE . . . [BUT] PRESENT OMINOUS EDITORIAL SILENCE INDICATES NIXON REPEAT NIXON SHOULD MOVE FAST TO WITHDRAW PERSONALLY, UNEQUIVOCALLY, IRREVOCABLY, AND IMMEDIATELY." There would be no evidence of what direct effect, if any, such dire urgings of Baruch, Solbert, and many others had on Eisenhower himself, but the imprint was plain on the men around the candidate. In a hastily scrawled note that morning, Sherman Adams set down with his own underlined emphasis Solbert's cabled warning that critics of the Fund were "loaded for *bear*."

Awakening to the clamor of the crisis, Robert Cutler remembered Sunday in St. Louis as "a long day of argument and telephoning" with "as many theories about what should be done by Eisenhower and Nixon . . . as there were voices in consultation." Robert Burroughs, a former national committeeman from New Hampshire who was both an intimate of Adams's and early promoter of the general, was assigned with investment banker Ed Bermingham and others to canvass GOP and business leaders throughout the nation, a far broader survey than Humphreys's stacked poll of the conservative wing. They promptly reported to Ike and Adams the sharply demarcated reactions—eastern and southern states where "the largest number . . . feel Nixon should resign," the West Coast who thought he "should be kept on the ticket and defended," the Midwest "more open-minded" and with "a majority opinion who favor keeping Nixon." In an impassioned call to Adams and subsequent memo to the general, Burroughs had also urged that Nixon be ordered to "drop all other plans" and fly to meet Eisenhower. "Nixon should be grilled," he told Adams, "and ought to make a statement in his honor which he knows cannot be disproved as to every point in his use of the fund . . . whether or not there have been other sources of funds, where he got the money to buy his big house, and just how he used every penny."

Burroughs then went still further to implore Eisenhower to mount a major initiative on the insidious power of money in politics, "to go on record as condemning the practice of senators, representatives, and others in both parties receiving a large amount of money from groups of individuals, and from labor unions." Burroughs and the others could "tell you . . . names of prominent men in several states" who could testify to the widespread practice of such "substantial" contributions "year after year." Ike should support the legislation introduced by Wayne Morse "to mitigate these dangerous practices" and emphasize the "tremendous dangers to our whole system of government if it is possible for syndicates of men, or labor unions, to subsidize members of the Senate and House and cabinet members." Eisenhower should even favor, he urged, a form of public financing for campaign costs and greater allowances for congressional expenses, as well as public disclosure and strict accounting of all contributions.

For a fleeting moment in September 1952, provoked and then all but lost in the furor over the Fund, it was a New England conservative's earnest premonition of the pervasive corruption of American politics decades later—of the contribution scandals and fitful reforms left by Richard Nixon's own Presidency and of an era at the end of the century when political action committees and other combines, Burroughs's "syndicates" by other names, effectively purchased and dominated the United States Congress and the Presidency regardless of party.

The ultimate object of all the admonitions, Dwight Eisenhower felt himself "bombarded . . . through telephone calls, telegrams and letters," including "several of my most trusted friends . . . with urgent pleas to remove Mr. Nixon from the ticket." The other side, including one of Ike's brothers, argued that "should I hesitate for a second in condemning these trumped-up charges . . . thus showing my utter (and presumably blind) faith in my personally chosen campaign partner, our defeat was certain." Characteristically, Eisenhower saw himself as the prudent mean between two impulsive extremes. At one point Sunday he even took up Cutler's suggestion of an "impartial umpire," asking the aide to approach former Supreme Court Justice Owen Roberts to arbitrate somehow between the competing campaign factions and make his own inquiry and findings regarding the Fund. How the seventy-seven-year-old retired judge, a Hoover appointee noted for his stern rectitude, might have viewed the money and affected Richard Nixon's political fate would be another unanswered question of the episode. Although Cutler promptly recruited Justice Roberts Sunday afternoon, Sherman Adams had already sealed other arrangements for examination of the Fund, one with rather more predictable results.

From earlier conversations with Paul Hoffman to determine if the money were "clean," they had by Sunday settled on an appraisal by the Los Angeles law firm of Gibson, Dunn and Crutcher, to be accompanied by a quick audit by Price Waterhouse and Company, accountants also headquartered in southern California. It was another crucial turn. Gibson, Dunn was a venerable conservative firm from the gold coast of South Spring Street, counting among its clients the wealthy and powerful of the basin who supported the Fund, and among its partners rising young Republicans, including William French Smith, a future attorney general in the Reagan administration. Elmo Conley, the number-three man in the firm now in charge of the Fund inquiry, was a personal friend of Hoffman and other prominent GOP leaders and on a first-name basis with Adams, who noted with satisfaction that afternoon in St. Louis not only that the firm was one of the "oldest" in Los Angeles but also that "Elmo" would be handling the matter.

Amid the clashing advice and predictions of Sunday, however, the decisive impact of the selection of an auditor was not yet felt, and watching the pressure build to push Nixon from the ticket, Chairman Arthur Summerfield took still another key step. Early in the day he called Humphreys in Washington and ordered him to get the next plane from National Airport for St. Louis, to be available to offset with Eisenhower the anti-Nixon sentiment. Anxiously, Humphreys searched for a booking and finally found one on a TWA "puddle jumper" through West Virginia and Ohio though only as far as Kentucky. In Louisville, airline officials asked him to leave the plane, but he stoutly refused—"wouldn't budge," as he remembered—and the flight finally took off for St. Louis with the dauntless political aide still in his seat. From the mundane small drama of a passenger who would not be bumped in Louisville, Humphreys would be present that night in St. Louis for further vital events in the saving of Senator Nixon.

"WE BOTH KNOW WHAT YOU HAVE TO DO"

In Portland, meanwhile, it was soon what Nixon called "another long day of ordeal." The candidate was awakened not long after falling asleep by an urgent phone call from John Riley in Whittier. To his old backer Nixon sounded dejected and defeated, "hadn't heard from anybody . . . ready to give up . . . ready to throw in the sponge," as Riley described it to a mutual friend. "You're not doing anything until I come up there," Riley told him, and rushed out to collect Tom Bewley and take the next flight from Los Angeles to Portland. When the two men later walked into the suite at the Benson, Nixon seemed overcome with emotion and there was a long silence before anyone spoke. "We just flew up to tell you that all the folks back in Whittier are behind you one hundred percent," they finally said. "Dick, everything will come out all right," Bewley offered. "These accusations will boomerang and will get the campaign off the ground." Nixon looked up at his old law partner but said nothing. At that, convinced he was about to quit altogether, Riley blurted out that he should "come down to Los Angeles" and make a speech explaining himself. "You tell the truth and you'll win the people."

The Whittier emissaries soon left the room, and Nixon called his wife to go with him to the First Friends Church service in Portland, Bassett hurriedly telling reporters that the unscheduled outing was not made known because "Dick doesn't believe in political religion." When they returned after eleven that morning, Bewley, still waiting outside the suite, thought the candidate "a changed man." Nixon "grabbed" his hand, and said, "I'm not worried anymore." At the same time, another supporter, bay area lawyer Aylett Cotton, was entering the Benson through the picket line of protesters, many still wearing dark glasses and carrying tin cups and "NICKELS FOR POOR NIXON" signs. Ushered in to see his friend, Cotton was "amazed," as he said later, "by the way he controlled his temper." Still, Cotton heard "bitterness in his voice when we talked about the charges made against him." Once again in sinking spirits, Nixon told Cotton as they parted, "I sometimes wonder whether it is worth it."

Hillings now brought in the pile of telegrams and letters received by midday Sunday, including some five hundred cables urging him for the most part to "keep up the fight against the smear gang" or "carry on to victory." Among them, echoing Riley and Bewley, was a telegram signed "The Aroused Citizens of Whittier," and reading in part: "We know you are honest and forthright, we sent you to Washington to fight corruption and communists in government and to protect and represent the citizens of California. We have never regretted backing you with our resources and energies and we again reaffirm our faith in you and pledge to you our full support in your crusade against such evils. We are fighting mad." They called in the press, whose photographers found and recorded a wan, thinly smiling Nixon sitting on a hotel sofa before the pile of messages, and commenting, "It's nice to know your friends are behind you." The *Los Angeles Times* and others were quickly given excerpts of the telegrams that the *Times* ran as a story the following day, including the wire from Whittier and similar sentiments from Beverly Hills and San Marino. The display was meant to counter stories from the Presidential candidate's train, where Hagerty had said telegrams were running fifty-fifty on the issue of Nixon's removal. "Persons around General Eisenhower have got a bit 'hysterical' over the developments," wrote *The New York Times*, duly quoting "an implied feeling among some of the senator's associates."

With the press gone, Nixon began an afternoon staff meeting by telephoning Tom Dewey in Albany to say that he was innocent of all the allegations and was considering "a major speech" to put the issue to rest. The candidate apparently did not mention television or Humphreys's conversations with Chotiner on the subject of buying time. For his part, Dewey was polite and noncommittal in this first conversation of the crisis with his protégé, though privately he was wary, hanging up the phone and promptly instigating his own poll of Republican voters on the charges surrounding the Fund. In any case, the respites provided by church, visiting friends, or the almost jaunty call to Dewey were short-lived. As Hillings and the others reported on the day's adverse press and the gathering reactions, Nixon visibly sagged once again, his voice as weary as Riley had heard it that morning and "cracking with emotion" as another remembered. Jack Drown thought Dick "seemed to age a lifetime" that Sunday and watched him "sit limply in an armchair, his arms dangling over the sides" while he talked of a television speech only "halfheartedly." Eventually, Rogers suggested there might be no choice but to resign, that Eisenhower's lack of support or contact was politically lethal. There was a brief replay of the meetings the night before. Chotiner argued again that he could not quit. "Too many people believe in you. You can't let them down," Hillings told him. All the "enemies" who had been trying to "get" him would only "gloat" at his fall.

Into this uninspired dialogue now burst two more extraordinary messages. The first, sent for "personal delivery only," came from Harold Stassen in Philadelphia;

> After a thoughtful review of the entire situation Dick I have regretfully reached a conclusion which I feel that I should frankly tell to you. I consider it to be imperative for the success of the Republican campaign to clean out Washington and for your own long term future that you now send General Eisenhower a message of this nature.
>
> "I deeply regret the embarrassment which has been caused to you and to your campaign by the Dana Smith fund which has assisted in my expenses these past two years. I assure you that I have not personally profited one cent from these funds and my relationship to the committee has been honorable in every way. It is obvious to me however that the entrenched opposition will now use this situation to blunt the drive of your superb campaign to clean out the mess in Washington and will handicap the effort to bring in your urgently needed leadership for future peace for America. Above all else your Campaign must succeed for the good of America. My situation must not become a diversion for them to draw across your path. I therefore herewith extend to you my offer to withdraw as your running mate and assure you and the people of my continued devoted efforts to serve our country in the ranks and to defend America against Communist infiltration and subversion."
>
> I do not know Dick what the General would then do. If he decides to accept your offer Earl Warren should be named to step in. I am certain that for the success of the Eisenhower campaign he must have the opportunity to make a clear cut decision. Otherwise it will divert and drag from here on for him and for you and above all for the essential movement for good government in Washington. In the long run it will also strengthen you and aid your career whatever may be the immediate decision or results.
>
> With my best wishes,
>
> Harold E. Stassen

The cable from his old, original patron in Republican politics, a patronage enmeshing California money and party maneuvers far beyond the public record, had a searing effect, and the suggestion of Warren only compounded the fury. Nixon later called it "a severe blow . . . when my situation was desperate," a polite formulation of the feelings of the moment. Years later he was still bitterly incredulous. "Then there were telegrams—from Harold Stassen, for example," he said later, describing the crisis to reporter Stewart Alsop. "Have you seen Stassen's telegram? You ought to!"

As Stassen was drafting his apocalyptic advice from the president's office at the University of Pennsylvania, Hannah Nixon in Washington was composing her own telegrams. Watching the scandal unfold as she babysat for Tricia and Julie at the Tilden Street house, she was "completely shaken," as she later told Bela Kornitzer. "I watched every moment on television and I felt I could hardly carry on. . . . I was more worried about Richard's health than about his political future." Saturday evening she had sent cables to both Eisenhower and her son at the Benson, the latter opened by Hillings as it was delivered to the suite Sunday afternoon. Seeing it was personal, the congressman in some embarrassment quickly handed the wire to Nixon, who read it in front of the rest of them, while Chotiner talked long distance once more with Summerfield in St. Louis, pleading that Eisenhower issue some further statement of confidence in his running mate.

> GIRLS ARE OKAY. THIS IS TO TELL YOU WE ARE THINKING OF
> YOU AND KNOW EVERYTHING WILL BE FINE. LOVE ALWAYS,
> MOTHER

Then, as they all looked on, the Vice-Presidential candidate "broke down and cried," as Hillings related the story. On the telephone with Summerfield, Chotiner remembered being "frankly . . . more worried about Dick's state of mind than about the party." They quickly filed out, to "give him time to compose himself," one recalled. When Hillings opened the door to the suite and looked in some time later, he saw the same strangely stark figure Drown had seen earlier. "Dick was sitting in a huge leather chair, his arms stretched out, his hand dangling in that characteristic way of his. . . . I knew I was in the presence of total despair."

Slowly, cautiously they picked up the discussion, and at one point Nixon rose almost defiantly out of his virtual collapse in the armchair, pacing the room in thought and muttering to himself, "I will not crawl." Yet the blows continued to fall, felt or furtive. In the midst of their conference Bill Rogers quietly took another call from Washington, not on some new development with the Fund but from "another major figure in the Eisenhower movement," as the anonymous caller would be described, advising the ambitious Republican lawyer to leave the Nixon entourage now or "risk his own future."

Late in the darkening afternoon, Dewey brought matters to a kind of climax with his own call now from the Commodore headquarters in Manhattan. The men around Eisenhower, he told Nixon bluntly, were almost unanimously "a hanging jury" on the Fund. Though Dewey himself was not one of them and Eisenhower had made no final decision, there seemed to be a consensus among the advisers that the senator discreetly offer his resignation from the ticket. Then the New York governor and two-time Presidential candidate presented what he described as Nixon's only resort, adopting what Humphreys and the Nixon camp had already resolved, though with an added and ominous twist. "I don't think Eisenhower should make this decison. Make the American people do it." It was a powerful, probably decisive endorsement of the popular appeal they had hoped for. But Dewey went on: "At the conclusion of the program, ask people to wire their verdict in to you in Los Angeles. You will probably get over a million replies, and that will give you three or four days to think it over. At the end of that time, if it's 60 percent for you and 40 percent against . . . say you are getting out. . . . If it is 90 to 10, stay on." Then came, with equal candor, the bare political logic of the referendum: "If you stay in, it isn't blamed on Ike," Dewey said, "and if you get off it isn't blamed on Ike. All the fellows here in New York agree with me." Even the calculus of Richard Nixon's own career survival would be couched in terms of the inescapable priority of the campaign, the hard, sometimes humiliating political truth of his candidacy and would-be Vice Presidency—the overriding interest of Dwight Eisenhower.

Nixon replied that a television speech was "exactly what we had been discussing" and thanked the governor for his "suggestion." Dewey closed by advising him to "start making plans right away." The situation was "too tense," he warned, "to wait much longer." He "had great respect for Dewey's political judgment," Nixon wrote about the call afterward. But at the moment the proposal for some public response and a make-or-break count stirred immediate worries about a trap. "Some members of my staff . . . feared a concerted campaign might be put under way to 'stack' the replies against me," Nixon acknowledged later, though it was hardly clear whether the putative vote fraud was expected from the Democrats or from his own party. In the poisonous, pitiful isolation of the Benson this Sunday evening, all enemies seemed plausible.

It was now after 5:00 P.M. in Portland, and Nixon prepared to go off to a dinner at the Temple Beth Israel, an appearance originally scheduled, ironically, to meet what was thought in early September one of the few real problems of the campaign—the persisting charges of anti-Semitism from the 1950 race. Before he left there was one last call, this time from Summerfield in St. Louis. Hearing rumors rocketing in the other direction, that Nixon was depressed and potentially unstable, that the senator might stage some volatile press conference, Summerfield was calling to appeal for calm. He should "call off" for the moment any planned talk with reporters, he told Nixon, assuring him that "the great majority of the national committee" wanted him to stay on the ticket. The candidate agreed to hold no conference until further consultations. But neither the Dewey nor Summerfield calls lifted the deeper gloom and sense of dread in the suite. The sculpted rug of the hotel corridor outside was littered with room-service trays and dirty dishes as Chotiner, still in his ubiquitous silk polka-dot robe, watched Nixon leave for the synagogue. "For all we knew," the aide remembered, "it was going to be the last speech of the campaign."

The exact origin of Tom Dewey's proposal of a television speech and some appeal for public messages—a prefiguring of the ultimate event—would never be certain. Whether prompted by Nixon's earlier call to Albany mentioning a major address, by reverberations from the Humphreys and Summerfield jockeying to save the candidacy, or simply by some depth in Dewey himself, it had the signal effect of bringing the anti-Nixon New York headquarters behind the idea of a potential vindication before a nationwide audience, including the not inconsiderable issue of how the television time was to be financed. Dewey's intercession thus satisfied at least half the precondition for a saving speech. At almost the same hour, Bob Humphreys's stubborn arrival in St. Louis was to provide the other.

Delayed by his own argument with TWA over keeping his seat, Humphreys was late landing at Lambert Field, and, met by Summerfield, he discovered to his dismay that Eisenhower had already left the Statler for a private dinner party. The opinions around that table, as they soon heard, "were unanimous that Nixon should be thrown off the ticket." The "hanging jury" described by Dewey seemed real enough. Summerfield was feeling ill but took Humphreys immediately to Union Station, where they met in Sherman Adams's drawing room on the campaign train, and the national committee aide did the talking while the party chairman sat by uncomfortably.

Adams and Humphreys now "had it hot and heavy," as the latter remembered. To each proposal for handling the controversy, the stony New

Englander was "most caustic." He was "putting forth every argument I could think of that Nixon must be kept on the ticket," Humphreys later recalled in a private letter, and Sherman Adams "didn't think much of my arguments and said so." Yet Adams did not sound convinced altogether that Nixon should go, and Humphreys persisted. They were only helping the Democrats, he contended, and at one interval repeated in audible disgust a version of Murray Chotiner's point twenty-four hours before: "What do you plan to do, change every piece of literature, every billboard, every campaign poster, every sticker in the land with Nixon's name and picture, and how the hell do you think we are going to do that?" Adams, like all the others haunted by the looming logistical nightmare of the ticket change, was nonetheless unmoved, albeit "incensed," as Humphreys recalled, his reply "icy almost to the point of absolute zero centigrade."

Having "broken through the boiling point," Humphreys sat silent for what he remembered as "a full minute to get hold of myself." After the heavy pause he added a final jab. "All right, answer this one: on Friday morning the general said, 'I intend to talk with him [Nixon] at the earliest time we can reach each other.' Do you mean to tell me we can convince the American people that for the last sixty hours Dick and Ike have not been able to get together on the telephone when anyone knows that all the general has to do is pick up the phone and call him?" Humphreys paused again. "No wonder everybody thinks there is a plot to throw Nixon off the ticket."

Eisenhower's typical perch above the public fray, his enigmatic silence, was the tactic and habit that had anguished the Nixon camp from the beginning and was now provoking the running mate to reckless despair as well as proving an embarrassment to Ike. At his outburst Humphreys expected to find Sherman Adams "jumping across the table and throttling me," but instead the manager coolly picked up a phone and ordered that a call be set up between Eisenhower and Nixon when Ike returned from his supper later that night. The general would in essence leave the decision to Nixon, and the young senator would opt for a last redeeming speech, which Humphreys and now Dewey and others had settled on, shielding Eisenhower for one more step. His mission accomplished, Bob Humphreys turned to the ailing Summerfield and said quietly, "Let's get out of here." They left Adams's railroad car, and their momentous little showdown, without another word.

While his opportunity was being secured on a station siding in St. Louis, Richard Nixon was appearing in visible exasperation before the men of Portland's Beth Israel. Introduced by one of his hosts with an embarrassing enumeration of past allegations of anti-Semitism, he listened at the speakers' table with his lips pursed and his right hand wearily holding his forehead. He returned to the Benson near 10:00 P.M., almost midnight in the Midwest, with still no word of a call from Eisenhower. His men had arranged for a physician to come up to the suite to try to relieve a worsening rigidity in his neck, apparently the recurrence of the agonizing muscular tension he had suffered earlier, which had prompted his first visits to Dr. Hutschnecker. The doctor's impromptu massage had scarcely begun when the long-awaited call finally came from Ike.

"Hello, Dick. You've been taking a lot of heat the last couple of days. I imagine it's been pretty rough."

Nixon thought his voice "warm and friendly" yet also "deeply troubled."

"It hasn't been easy," he answered.

After some awkward small talk about campaigning, Nixon mentioned Dewey's call about a speech and told him, "I'm at your disposal." Eisenhower later interpreted this or a similar remark as a willingness to resign. "Though he offered to quit the ticket if I asked him to, I flatly refused," Ike wrote of the conversation tersely in his memoirs. It was, of course, the very decision, and onus, the general and his men hoped to avoid.

"This is not my decision," Eisenhower answered.

Nixon then replied—"crisply," he thought—that he was "glad" to take responsibility for any decision but Ike and the public ought to "hear my side of the story." With a sharpening edge in his voice, he warned the Presidential candidate against "some of those people around you who don't know a damn thing about it."

Evenly, Eisenhower went on that it was "difficult" to judge what was best. "I have come to the conclusion that you are the one who has to decide what to do. After all, you've got a big following in this country, and if the impression got around that you got off the ticket because I forced you off, it is going to be very bad. On the other hand, if I issue a statement now backing you up, in effect people will accuse me of condoning wrongdoing." Again it was plain whose interest was paramount.

Eisenhower paused, "as if waiting for me to fill the gap," remembered Nixon. But the younger politician simply waited in the crackling silence of the long-distance line. Ike finally added that he had just returned from dinner with "friends." By one account, "none of them knew what to do," by another they "were in disagreement as to whether . . . [Nixon] should stay on or get off." But they had all agreed the senator should have a chance to speak to the country.

"I don't want to be in the position of condemning an innocent man," Ike said. "I think you ought to go on a nationwide television program and tell them everything there is to tell, everything you can remember since the day you entered public life. Tell them about any money you have ever received." It was a moment without parallel in American politics, an unprecedented financial disclosure for a candidate at any level, much less national, and a historic order from a war hero and Presidential candidate to his beleaguered running mate.

There was another gap in the conversation as Nixon absorbed the reality.

"General," he asked almost plaintively, "do you think after the television program that an announcement could then be made one way or another?"

Eisenhower hesitated again.

"I am hoping that no announcement would be necessary at all, but maybe after the program we could tell what ought to be done."

The uneasy decorum was now shattered.

"General," Nixon answered heatedly, "I just want you to know that I don't want you to give any consideration to my personal feelings. I know how difficult this problem is for you." If he damaged the ticket, he would "get off and take the heat," but some decision must be made after the speech. "There comes a time in matters like this," Nixon instructed the former Supreme Commander, "when you've either got to shit or get off the pot. The great trouble here is the indecision."

His men in the room at the Benson were aghast. On the line across the nation, Dwight Eisenhower remained seemingly unprovoked. "We will have to wait three or four days after the television show to see what the effect of the program is," he answered, like an insistent parent.

With this the conversation swiftly ebbed into more small talk, and Eisenhower, still avuncular, ended almost lightly. "Well, Dick, go on the television show. Good luck and keep your chin up."

Putting the phone down, Nixon thought it plain that Ike would "not have objected" had he proffered a resignation from the ticket. But the general's stern avoidance of responsibility for the dump put him in an impossible situation. "I felt that his indecision or his unwillingness to come out and ask for it [a resignation] relieved me of any obligation in that regard," Nixon wrote of their talk, adding acidly, "It is one thing to offer to sign your own death warrant; it is another to be expected to draw it up yourself."

The call had come as a kind of release and as a galvanizing force at the end of a day of miserable lethargy. Briefing his men on the thrust of the conversation, Nixon told them to confirm the finance and timing of the broadcast with Summerfield and others, and then retreated alone into his bedroom to reconstruct the Eisenhower call on a yellow legal pad. Ike had "resolved the dilemma," he wrote, by putting the responsibility "on me."

Now it was up to Dick Nixon "to assume the responsibility completely and without any compromise." He added pointedly and with a new belligerence: "If I considered the broadcast a success, I would stay on the ticket. If I thought it was a failure, I would get off." Now, he concluded, "everything was up to me."

After his exercise with the pad he walked into his wife's room and told her about the call from the nominee. "The whole episode had already scarred her deeply," he noted in his memoirs. By Sunday night at the Benson, Pat Nixon, like her husband, was in considerable pain from a stiff neck, and he found her in bed but unable to sleep. As in the days before, she had been on the phone with Hannah in Washington, nervously checking on the girls. "We both know what you have to do, Dick," she said eventually when he had finished his rehearsal of the talk with Eisenhower. Once more she shored up his fitful resolve. "You have to fight it all the way to the end, no matter what happens."

For the next two hours following the Eisenhower call, his men were on the phones arranging the details of the speech. Yet again his quiet allies elsewhere were also vital. The seemingly inexhaustible Humphreys and a still queasy Summerfield worked through the night in St. Louis to raise the estimated $75,000 cost of the prime time. Leonard Hall of the GOP Congressional Campaign Committee quickly committed $25,000, part of which was National Committee money. When they could not locate Everett Dirksen of the counterpart Senate Committee, Hall and Humphreys simply "pledged" the same amount "in Everett's behalf," as Humphreys recalled, leaving an irate Dirksen but making the program possible. Similarly, Ben Dufy of Batten, Barton, Durstine and Osborn, the prestigious advertising agency for Dewey, then Eisenhower, swiftly knit up a network of more than sixty NBC television stations, some 190 CBS radio stations and virtually all of Mutual Radio's more than five hundred stations in every corner of the nation. In consultation with television adviser Ted Rogers, Nixon aides in Portland initially held out for thirty minutes on Monday night, a slot just after the popular "I Love Lucy" and near guarantee of a massive audience. But after much jostling, and Nixon's own concern that he could not be "ready" in less than twenty-four hours, they fixed on the half-hour, 9:30–10:00 P.M. Eastern Time, following the Milton Berle show Tuesday evening, a time no less choice.

The traveling press in Portland had been alerted at 11:00 P.M. to stand by at the Bensen for an announcement. Earlier, Bassett had told them the senator was preparing "a complete statement of my entire financial history," a statement accompanied by the description of the candidate as "fighting mad," and an added swipe from Nixon: "I realize that it [the financial statement] will be misrepresented, but I feel that when any question is raised about any public official he should make this information available to the public." Now at eleven-thirty Bassett appeared again in the press room with reports already coming over the wires from St. Louis about an Eisenhower-Nixon talk. The general's men had wasted no time redressing the embarrassment Humphreys had flung at Adams over the delay in contact. Bassett confirmed that they had spoken, but could "not tell you any more about the phone call." Would Nixon continue campaigning? "That is the plan now," he told them. Twenty minutes later the reporters were again asked to stand by, but more than an hour passed in anxious waiting.

After 1:00 A.M. Bassett finally returned with Nixon and several of the staff. "You all know the guest of honor," Bassett said in introducing the candidate, who stood somewhat nervously, hands in pockets, looking at the ceiling of the flower-wallpapered hotel room while the reporters began scribbling on their pads. "I've come down to announce," Nixon began, "that I am breaking off—" His words had "an electric effect on his hearers," reported Gladwin Hill of *The New York Times*, who thought it clear Nixon "paused to enjoy the startled looks." At what he heard as an "audible gasp" Nixon laughed, and he noted later that "Clint Mosher of the *San Francisco Examiner* almost jumped out of his skin."

After the taunting he went on with a statement explaining he was interrupting the trip to return to Los Angeles for the broadcast, in which he intended "to lay before the American people all the facts concerning the fund which was used for political purposes . . . and . . . my entire personal financial history from the time that I entered political life." Senator Harry Cain would be filling in for his schedule in Washington State, and then, "I shall resume the tour the day after the broadcast is made."

"That means you're staying on the ticket?"

"That means," Nixon answered quickly, "that I intend to continue the tour." He thought this "a truthful answer," he wrote later, because he intended to continue to work for Ike in any case, though "the result of this reply, which was not unexpected as far as I was concerned, was to create increasing suspense about what I would do in the TV broadcast."

Not all the reporters appreciated the sparring, and one intervened, "Let's get this straight." Bassett insisted this was "not a press conference," but the journalists clamored for an asnwer. "Give me a little time on this," Nixon said in resignation, and left the room to huddle with Bassett and Chotiner. "My answer to that question," he said in returning, "is that I have no further comment than, to continue the tour, we are going to take a chartered DC–6 to Los Angeles." He and his men then left abruptly. "Obviously," observed *Time*, "the decision was up to Ike Eisenhower, and Ike had not yet made it."

24

Campaign in Crisis II,
September 22–24, 1952

"CHECKERS"

Minutes after the sparring press conference ended in Portland, Eisenhower's train was already pulling out of St. Louis, still pursued by the scandal and the intramural Republican politics it had unleashed. A telegram from the *Herald Tribune*'s Bill Robinson caught up with the candidate early Monday morning in Owensboro, Kentucky. Responding to Ike's defensive letter of two days before, the publisher pointed to passages laudatory of the general in the paper's stinging September 20 editorial and quoted as well the somewhat softer tone of yet another editorial appearing that morning. "Senator Nixon has now provided a public accounting of the fund," said the *Herald Tribune* September 22, in response to Dana Smith's weekend release of names and a ledger of donations and expenses. "The facts bear out the expression of confidence in the senator's integrity made by General Eisenhower in Kansas City. . . . Mr. Nixon can be charged with no dishonesty of motives or conduct." But the commentary then went on: "The confirmation of Senator Nixon's integrity and of the propriety with which his backers conducted themselves does not mean that such a practice is a satisfactory one." High ethical standards, argued the paper, meant avoiding even the appearance of special influence or dishonesty. If expense allowances for senators from big states were not enough, taxpayers should be "ready and eager" to pay the bill without the risks or taint of private subsidies.

"Long after this present campaign," concluded the editorial with much prescience, "the problems raised by Senator Nixon's full and honorable accounting will have to be faced." It was an echo of Robert Burroughs's secret appeal hours earlier, a warning in virtual unison from GOP conservatives and moderates about the spreading poison of money in American politics. Moreover, Robinson's telegram included a pungent private note to Ike. "This editorial comment represents consensus opinion of what we should say at this moment," he added. "My own personal view is that Nixon's continuation on the ticket seriously blunts and dilutes the sharp edge of corruption issue and burdens you with heavy and unfair handicap. This view shared by Cliff [Roberts]."

The *Herald Tribune* dictum and Robinson's own continuing pressure came, too, with a stream of other telegrams, many from the South. Passing through Ed Bermingham and others at headquarters, they came despite—and often because of—the newly published list of the California personalities and forces behind the Vice-Presidential candidate. "Overwhelmingly against keeping Nixon," wired the Georgia Youth for Eisenhower, while the Young Republicans of Atlanta were "aghast at Nixon's actions." Southern Democrats supporting Eisenhower, the seeds of a GOP revolution in the old Confederacy, were especially harsh, sometimes with unforeseen irony. "Nixon is as expendable as a Normandy paratrooper, Nixon is Humpty Dumpty no matter what," cabled Winton "Red" Blount, a Montgomery magnate for Ike in 1952 and sixteen years later Richard Nixon's postmaster general.

Whatever the maneuvers and raw feelings behind the scenes, the crisis had by Monday morning opened wide and much too visible fissures in party ranks. While the *Herald Tribune* registered its editorial distaste, *The New York Times* reported a forty-eight-state survey indicating "a close contest" for the presidency and the fund crisis as "likely to hurt the chances of election of both General Eisenhower and Senator Nixon if the latter continue on the Republican ticket." In the same issue Gladwin Hill reported from Los Angeles that the whole scandal had begun with a leak from a "disgruntled Warren Republican." The unnamed source had been "rankling over what had happened at Chicago," and Hill's dispatch referred as well to the "cabal" formed against Earl Warren in the California GOP earlier that year—though without elaboration on either episode. In Sacramento, Earl Warren himself was magisterially "silent" on the fund, noted the *Times*, the governor declining comment "until all the evidence has been presented." Meanwhile, there were even matching reports that the young senator's former patrons in the preconvention and Chicago intrigue against Warren, notably Henry Cabot Lodge and Lucius Clay, now, too, "favored Mr. Nixon's withdrawal."

Much of this Bob Humphreys dutifully if alarmingly passed along to Murray Chotiner—"the various questions, rumors and angles . . . by newspapermen, columnists, Democrats, Republicans and what-have-you"—in a "dozen" telephone conversations that day and the next. Although Humphreys was at pains not to ask, Chotiner offered repeatedly that he "did not know what Nixon was going to do" with the planned broadcast. No sooner had Eisenhower hung up on their Sunday night call than efforts began to try to influence and control the stratagem they had settled on, and with it the young politician at the other end of the country. When the *Look Ahead, Neighbor* pulled out of St. Louis, instructions were left behind for Humphreys to fly to Los Angeles to "help produce the Nixon show." But the RNC aide argued with his usual passion that the senator "should be completely on his own. . . . Nixon must be in a position of having no outside counsel if the public was to be convinced that here was a man telling his own story in his own way," he told Summerfield and others, and then added with his own insight: "Nixon . . . [is] far better at this type of thing than any of us, including BBD&O . . . and the whole kit and kaboodle of advertising and public relations experts in our retinue." When Humphreys "flatly refused" to go to California, Summerfield and then the redoubtable Bernard Shanley were pressed to take on the mission. By Monday afternoon in St. Louis, however, Humphreys had staved off the interference—"there had been general agreement established that everybody would let Nixon alone," as he recorded—and he took a plane back to Washington, happily thinking his crucial work for Nixon completed.

Eisenhower, meanwhile, was striking a more casual pose. Appearing unexpectedly in the press car, slouching informally on a small red couch, he told traveling reporters about his call to Portland and his advice on full disclosure. "I do not want to nag . . . [or] prejudge him," he said easily. Off the record, he was "uncertain" about his own proper responsibility in deciding the case. Perhaps it should be judged by the Republican National Committee, he remarked. He was certainly against public officials taking money from secret funds (though he "wonders if the Nixon fund really was secret," reported James Reston), and he would personally publicize any such fund "to see how it looked" before taking money from it himself. In any case, as several accounts recorded his words, he felt that "Mr. Nixon is a grown man and a United States senator, and as such he is on a hot spot," and he should have "every chance" to satisfy both Eisenhower and the public. As he spoke, wired press summaries continued to pour into the train, including reports that the column inches devoted to Nixon now exceeded those for both Eisenhower and Stevenson throughout the country. On national television Drew Pearson was charging that he had received a menacing phone call from Nixon's train, threatening to brand him as a communist if he spoke against the Vice-Presidential candidate.

In Cincinnati, Herb Brownell met the train as arranged days earlier and immediately sat down with Eisenhower and Adams in the general's private car, "with the shades . . . carefully lowered," one of them recorded. In what Adams remembered as his "quiet, calm manner," Brownell did most of the talking. They should take no further step or stand until Nixon spoke, he advised them. Dewey's private poll of Republican reaction, quickly commissioned after the first call from Nixon Sunday morning, showed less than 20 percent "disturbed" by the fund. Although forty-eight hours before Brownell had been ready to carry the consensus of the New York head-quarters that Nixon must be dropped, he was now certifying the decision already made to depend on the speech. Ike could decide anew after the broadcast. Despite the other pressure, his counsel now left them without question astride what Adams called "a risky and unpopular tightrope" waiting on Nixon. It was the last moment at which the plan for the broadcast itself might have been altered, though their attempts to control the event would continue.

"I'LL NEEDLE THEM ON THIS ONE"

Nixon flew to Los Angeles that morning aboard the spacious DC–6 with ruminations of betrayal and some desperation. "I had been deserted by so many I had thought were friends but who had panicked in battle when the first shots were fired," he wrote. "I must become a positive asset. . . . I knew I had to go for broke. This broadcast . . . had to be a smash hit—one that really moved people . . . one that would inspire them. . . . I had to launch a political counterattack." From the seat pocket in front of him he took out postcards promoting the airline and scrawled notes for the speech much as he once wrote for college debates on small index cards. At one point Chotiner walked down the aisle and bent over to talk. He still thought Adlai Stevenson strangely reserved in attacking the Fund. Chotiner told him again, "I bet he has something to hide." When Nixon returned to his notes, he listed a theme from earlier speeches—the comeback about Pat's cloth coat amid the Democrats' mink coat scandals—and a note to defend the access to public office of "common people" who could not afford the expenses. He would "lay out for everyone to see my entire personal financial history." Later in the flight his wife noticed his notes on personal assets and asked plaintively, "Why do we have to tell people how little we have and how much we owe?" He had answered, "People in political life have to live in a fishbowl." But she was unappeased.

"But aren't we entitled to have at least some privacy?"

"I had no choice but to use every possible weapon to assure the success of the broadcast," he wrote afterward, and his notes on the plane included one more. He remembered the gift to his daughters of a cocker spaniel puppy named Checkers, and how Franklin Roosevelt in a bitter campaign against Dewey had accused the Republicans of attacking "poor Fala." "Using the same ploy as FDR would irritate my opponents and delight my friends," he recorded. Reminiscing later about the tactic, he once told a friend: "I got a kind of malicious pleasure out of it. I'll needle them on this one, I said to myself."

A crowd of some four hundred had begun to mill about the runway in Los Angeles an hour before their mid-afternoon arrival. On hand were Pat's brothers, Bill and Tom Ryan, as well as Representative Donald Jackson and organized supporters with signs reading "NIXON WILL FIGHT AND WIN," or "WE TRUST IN NIXON." Pat smiled and waved "in pleased appreciation," wrote a reporter, as they came together down the ramp and paused to acknowledge the cheers. But Nixon was noticeably red-eyed and made his own wave with a fierce grimace, his mouth drawn down tight and chin jutting out defiantly. They stood on the hood of a sedan parked near the clamoring crowd at the fence as Jackson introduced him as "a thoroughly honest, sincere fellow," adding suddenly, "The existence of such a supplementary fund as Senator Nixon's is not unusual." "This is the time you find out who your friends are," Nixon responded. "We won't let you down." Around them swirled ominous rumors and leaks as well as the cheers of well-wishers. The United Press quoted a member of the Nixon party at the airport as saying the senator would withdraw "within the next seven days" and that he "has been thrown to the wolves." The anonymous source added of the next scheduled campaign stop, "He will never go to Missoula." Later, at the Ambassador Hotel, where the contingent moved into a thirty-two-room wing, a Western Union operator traveling with the party mentioned to a friend that he believed Nixon would resign in the next twenty-four hours, and "within minutes," as Herb Klein recorded the incident, the prediction became another bell-ringing bulletin on the United Press wire.

While the candidate closed himself off in his suite at the Ambassador, his wife was still suffering "excruciating pain from her stiff neck," as her daughter described the moment, and the Drowns thoughtfully took Pat Nixon to their home in nearby Rolling Hills, where Helene put her old friend to bed. Bassett soon told the waiting press that there would be no advance text for the speech. Nixon was rumored meanwhile to have exploded at the torrent of advice and criticism: "I don't want to talk to anybody—nobody at all—including members of the staff." The desired effect was to heighten suspense about the event to come the next evening. "I made up my mind," Nixon admitted afterward, "that until after the broadcast, my only releases to the press would be for the purpose of building up the audience." He worked through the afternoon, scarcely touching room-service hamburgers sent up on his arrival, and ordered "round-the-clock research" by Rose Woods and another secretary, gathering financial details from both California and over the telephone from his Senate office in Washington. That evening he took an hour's swim with Bill Rogers in the Ambassador pool and returned to eat supper in his room. Unnoticed later that night, he took a walk with Rogers in the quiet back streets near the hotel, trying out themes of the speech, and getting Rogers's encouragement "to go forward with the plan."

They learned on returning what Chotiner so shrewdly expected and Humphreys first discovered from his informant in Chicago long days earlier—that Adlai Stevenson on Monday had first admitted existence of his own fund, what would turn out to be a total of $18,150 from a thousand donors, surplus campaign contributions from 1948 that Stevenson used as governor of Illinois to augment salaries of state appointees. A jubilant Chotiner came in to confirm the story. "He was hiding something," he said. "Otherwise he would have been at your throat like the rest of them." Nixon would later recount the Stevenson fund story with evident bitterness about "the blatant double standard" he thought applied by the press. But for now they took the first news with some glee and resolved to use it in the speech. Before going to bed, he excitedly pulled out his airplane jottings about poor men seeking public office, a thrust he would now use all the more forcefully against the wealthy Stevenson. After midnight Nixon called Albert Upton and Paul Smith at Whittier College to ask for "suitable Lincoln quotes" for the speech. They called back with two passages, one of which he would use. "God must have loved the common people," went the maxim, "he made so many of them."

The morning of the speech brought no relief from the pressure felt in successive waves by Eisenhower and his men. In St. Louis the liberal *Post-Dispatch* ran a powerful cartoon showing a GOP elephant as pious angel in heaven under the banner "Crusade for Purity," confronting a soiled, singed, redolent Nixon with heavy eyebrows, five-o'clock shadow, and clutching a bag of money. "Why," says the elephant in clerical pose, "where have you been, Dickey Boy?" In the same issue the paper reported Dana Smith's request for help in his tax case and John Irwin's 1951 call to the Justice Department. The story prompted a brief flurry at the White House, in which Truman was said to have ordered the attorney general to look into the fund. That story was subsequently denied by the Presidential press secretary, but anonymous Justice officials insisted that a "study" was being made on the question of criminal sanctions for Nixon's receipt of "any salary . . . from a source other than the government or a state agency." Even the fund contributors were being investigated, reported *The New York Times*. In the *Times* at least, the headlined story of a possible Justice inquiry obscured a report the same day about Stevenson's admission that his own campaign money had been used "to reduce the financial sacrifice" of Illinois state officials. Still, outside Manhattan and a handful of other papers, the partisan shading of the national press blunted even this impact. Only four other papers carried the *Post-Dispatch* story on the Smith-Irwin connection.

In vivid contrast to the reluctant and spasmodic early coverage of the Nixon fund, seven newspapers carried front page the first fragmentary reports of a "Stevenson fund" on Monday, and every major evening paper in the country ran the continuing story on Tuesday prior to Nixon's broadcast. As it was, both the initial and subsequent reports had been instigated through a leak channeled by Bob Humphreys and the Republican National Committee. Having been alerted to the existence of the Stevenson subsidies on Saturday, Humphreys had set up his own "inquiry" with Republicans in Chicago. "We busted the story on the day of the Nixon broadcast," he would say later, but added ruefully, "Nobody paid much attention to it."

On the Eisenhower train in Ohio, telegrams were now running three to one against Nixon, and the planted stories on Stevenson seemed scarce comfort. The ever-ready Oscar Solbert and his research service of Clay's old officers reported that "Stevenson has made remarkable recovery" despite revelation of his own fund and warned that Democrats were readying against Nixon "a 'new angle' on the alleged Gruenwald [*sic*] loan." Local Eisenhower-Nixon clubs were reporting "slacking efforts . . . heart gone out of crusade." That day, too, having put his own seal on the television appeal, Tom Dewey confided his inner thoughts in a letter to his mother. He thought the fund "disturbing," he told her, "but I have heard nothing to indicate that he is not an absolutely honest man who has behaved extremely well." After what an aide later described as "twenty-four hours of indecision," the patron had finally resolved to back his protégé to the dramatic end of the crisis—"albeit," wrote Dewey's biographer, "with undeniable misgivings."

The bright spot of the midday for the Presidential party would be a summary report from Paul Hoffman that the Gibson, Dunn and Price Waterhouse results were in, and the Fund found to be "absolutely clean, both legally and from the economy standpoint," as Hoffman explained. "There was no evidence," he concluded, "that there had been any expenditure that couldn't legitimately be called a campaign expense." Hoffman made his report to the train on the basis of a telephone call without actually seeing the lawyers' or accountants' findings. His friend Elmo Conley had been unable to reach him before he left his Pasadena office of the Ford Foundation that Tuesday morning. Conley had gone directly to the Nixon quarters at the Ambassador. On the eve of the broadcast, none of the Eisenhower command would have yet examined the audits, and from Hoffman's telephoned report Ike assumed—and would continue to assume—that the Fund itself was now "out of existence," though in fact Price Waterhouse had found another trust of "some $11,000" deposited by Dana Smith since the Republican convention, with over $300 of that already disbursed to Nixon's Washington office.

As Hoffman was vouchsafing the Fund, the politics of dumping Nixon continued to churn, with a worried, uncertain, still vacillating Eisenhower at the center. Following up his Monday cable in person, Bill Robinson boarded the *Look Ahead, Neighbor* in Ohio between Cincinnati and Cleveland on Tuesday morning, and the sight of the *Herald Tribune* executive being ushered directly to Ike set off alarm bells among conservatives. Congressman Charles Halleck, one of Taft's men who had joined the train earlier, watched Robinson walk past to the candidate's car, and at the first chance anxiously telephoned Art Summerfield, who had gone back to Washington. Fearing that Robinson might yet undo all they had wrought, Summerfield called Humphreys to go along with him to Cleveland to head off the danger, though the latter was reluctant to make yet another trip. For a while it seemed the chairman would go alone. But an hour later Summerfield called back to say he was "holding the plane" at National Airport until Humphreys arrived, and Humphreys rushed out the door of his office without even taking his hat, off an another hectic trip to save the candidacy of Richard Nixon.

They arrived in Cleveland as Ike's parade was ending at the Carter Hotel. After waiting only thirty minutes, Humphreys was called into Eisenhower's suite, where he found the general "half reclining" on a twin bed and a number of advisers sitting around the room. They had been "checking out the various rumors about the Nixon finances," Major General Jerry Persons told him, and they wanted to ask Humphreys to check one report from "a fairly good source."

"We have been told that the Nixons redecorated their house and retained a Georgetown decorater to do it for $10,000," Persons continued. "When the work was completed, Mrs. Nixon paid the entire amount in cash."

"I don't have to check it. I know the answer," Humphreys shot back. He then told the story of being at the Nixon home only eight days before and how he had "exchanged pleasantries" with Pat Nixon. "That is a stunning circular couch, where did you get it, Sloane's?" he asked her. And she answered, "We brought that from Whittier—it was in our house there." Then he had remarked, "Those beautiful drapes—don't tell me they didn't come from Sloane's," and again she replied, "No, the material came from Lansburgh's and I made the drapes myself." They made small talk about other furniture, and he and Dick went to work. Humphreys told the story with his reporter's eye for detail and dialogue—much as he would record later the scenes and utterings of the drama he was living through at the moment. At the end, he told them forcefully, "There is absolutely no question in my mind that this rumor is wholly false."

When he had finished, Persons and Summerfield agreed on Nixon's innocence in their own brief statement. But Sherman Adams and other key men in the suite made no comment, and the general himself, still lying on the bed, said nothing. Yet when Humphreys left moments later, there ensued one of the remarkable and more decisive steps of the whole affair. Despite Bob Humphreys's graphic description of Pat Nixon's homemade decor, despite Hoffman's assurance of a "clean" fund, Eisenhower remained beset by the billowing rumors, less now by any one story raised or denied than by the dulling weight and distraction of the whole. It was, as Bill Robinson and others ceaselessly reminded him, a "burden" he was bearing unfairly, possibly at the cost of the election. Now early evening in Cleveland, still mid-afternoon in Los Angeles and less than three hours before the speech, Eisenhower took the only clear-cut initiative of the five days since the fund crisis fitfully erupted. He asked Leonard Hall to call Dewey, who in turn was to reach Dick Nixon and convince him to resign from the ticket at the climax of his speech, regardless of his defense or the public reaction.

Like so much of the inner politics of the 1952 campaign, and of the national administrations to follow, Ike's own responsiblity for the act was to be muffled, the advice to Nixon to drop off the ticket attributed to the men around the Presidential nominee, though with suitably unmistaken authority. The prescribed resignation would give them ultimate control over a speech now taking shape utterly beyond their ken. It would also preserve for the general the option to take back his young running mate in magnanimity if the speech somehow turned the tide entirely. In a sense, Hall's call to Dewey was the exercise by Ike of Nixon's offer to be at his "disposal," though its manner and timing also made the senator his own executioner, the one duty he had refused. In command at last of the situation, or so they hoped, the general and his men left the suite at the Carter for a relaxed dinner together before the television broadcast and Eisenhower's speech afterward.

It was eighty-seven degrees in Los Angeles that Tuesday, an unseasonably close day even in the muggy warmth of basin Septembers. Richard Nixon arose early after only four hours' sleep and resumed his preparation, a rapt, ruminating inner process in which he would make successive outlines but write no text and recite no specific lines. It was the well-practiced technique of the debater, especially in rebuttal, a skillful mixture of meticulous preparation and extemporaneous delivery, and he had applied it well, often brilliantly, as in his pivotal audition speech before the New York Republicans the previous May, a speech that had ironically brought him here to the desperate seclusion of the Ambassador.

"Only when I could deliver a speech without memorizing it, and if possible without notes, did it have the spark of spontaneity so essential to a television audience," he wrote in *Six Crises*. Yet now there seemed "not enough hours in the day for me to get the ideas firmly enough in my mind." He saw himself once more, as in the Hiss case, pushed beyond a boundary of mental and physical tension. "Edgy and short-tempered . . . can't eat . . . can't sleep," he recorded. "I had experienced all these symptoms in the days since our train left Pomona." He was now utterly alone, and elevated, he thought, to a kind of "selflessness," a detachment about his fate. "The attacks from my *former* Republican friends and from press and radio commentators had taken their toll" (emphasis added). And though he did not mention the agonizing cramps and stiffness in his neck—or his wife's almost identical affliction—he thought it all to be noted and accepted, signs that he was "adequately keyed up, mentally and emotionally, for the conflict ahead," part of "going through the fire of decision . . . the necessary and even healthy symptoms incident to creative activity."

In any case, he worried fretfully about the press, now descending in numbers on Los Angeles, including what he saw as "the 'top-name' reporters from the Eisenhower train," who along with the others were besieging his aides for advance copies of Nixon's address, which would be televised at deadline for most morning papers in the East. "They are here so as to have front-row seats for the hanging," Bassett joked darkly with him that morning. But he was adamant when the staff urged him to provide some sort of advance text to aid more accurate and sympathetic coverage. "I overruled them all, " he wrote, thinking first of the drama and suspense and contemptuous, too, of the suddenly unreliable filter of reporters. "I knew that any advance notice of what I was going to say would cut down the size of my television audience. This time I was determined to tell my story directly to the people rather than to funnel it to them through a press account."

At 10:00 A.M. he got further confirmation of the Lincoln quote from Smith and Upton and then at noon welcomed Elmo Conley's legal review and audit. Essentially done on the day before from Dana Smith's correspondence files and his prepared accounting entitled "Statement of Richard

M. Nixon Expense Fund," the documents Conley delivered to the Ambassador were remarkable in their simplicity. The Price Waterhouse audit was a page-and-a-half report with Smith's own two-page balance sheet on the Fund attached. The accountants essentially confirmed Smith's arithmetic and noted various "canceled checks, approved invoices, and other supporting documents" also provided by Smith and by the senator's Washington office. It was a simple auditing test of the internal consistency of the Fund, showing that while the money defrayed clerical and travel expenses according to Nixon office memoranda—"these memoranda did not permit us to independently confirm these expenditures," they said of some $1,500—none apparently went to the senator directly. Price Waterhouse also noted that Dana Smith's files showed that "since July 21, 1952," ten days after the Vice-Presidential nomination, "some $11,000 has been deposited in the . . . trust account," which they did not examine and which Smith assured them "will be accounted for as campaign contributions." The legal opinion from Gibson, Dunn & Crutcher, in turn, was based on the Price Waterhouse findings and the same Smith files seen by the accountants.

In ten and one-half pages, the lawyers reproduced Dana Smith's first projected budget from December 1950, justifications and quotations from Fund-soliciting letters, and a repetition of the disbursements listed by the Pasadena attorney. Beyond that, they also "interviewed a number of the contributors." Not surprisingly, nothing in Smith's files or the interviews showed that donors were "promised, offered, or had any understanding with respect to or reason to expect any favor, attention, services, action, decision, vote, or assistance of any kind from Senator Nixon with respect to any proceeding, investigation, claim, charge, application, contract, hearing, question, matter, cause, or legislation." In "two instances," they noted, contributors had admitted to contacting Nixon "to request his assistance in connection with matters pending before a department or agency of the government," but in each case the senator "declined to take any action or render any assistance." They had given the money, concluded Gibson, Dunn, so that Dick Nixon could "continue effectively to sell the people of California the economic and political views which they [the donors and the senator] mutually shared."

But they saw no connection between that expectation, the contributors' considerable private interests, which Gibson, Dunn discreetly neglected to mention, and the senator's votes or actions. Thus they came to a legal conclusion that the Fund was neither salary nor bribe, was not "received . . . for the senator's attention to [sic], or service, or with the intention to have the senator's action influenced on any matter." "To the extent that we have been able to check with the contributors," the attorneys added, "any such understanding or intent appears to be expressly lacking."

Finally, in the letters and balance sheet given them by Dana Smith, there was "no evidence that Senator Nixon assisted any contributor in the prosecution of any claim," and the money "did not constitute income to the senator under the applicable federal or state income tax laws." Tyler Woodward's and William Anderson's special oil lease sought at Camp Roberts, the votes for the banking industry, the dairy issues at odds with his other stands, the crusade with Joe Crail and the developers against public housing and rent controls, Dana Smith's tax claim for Red River lumber or his gambling adventure in Havana, the constant battle for Colorado River water for the manufacturers and builders, Alpha Beta, Hollywood promotions and the Malaxa affair, the supplement that allowed him to cultivate his career so well and move to Spring Valley—in the hastily typed legal prose and citations of the September twenty-third opinion, the political and financial realities of his Senate passage remained blithely hidden, two worlds in which shadow and substance were long confused.

Reading the reports, keeping Elmo Conley on tap through the afternoon, Nixon immediately recognized the absolution by the prestigious firms and incorporated the conclusions, if not the methodology, into the early part of the speech. Hoffman had told him that an audit and "legal opinion" would not only sway a television audience, but also "have great weight . . . with Eisenhower's associates from the world of finance and business, on whose judgment," he recalled somewhat caustically, "the general placed such great reliance."

At four-thirty, as Eisenhower and his party were still dining in Cleveland, he summoned Chotiner and Rogers to discuss Dewey's proposal that the audience telegram or write their reactions to the speech. Where should the messages be sent? he asked them. They talked about directing them to Eisenhower or to Los Angeles, or conceivably to the friendly confines of the Republican National Committee, where Humphreys and Summerfield could be counted on, unlike the Eisenhower camp, to make the most of positive responses. In the process there were more bitter recriminations, and Nixon on the eve of his nationwide appearance seemed to fall into another slough of self-pity and despair. Then, scarcely an hour before he was due to leave for the studio, the extraordinary call ordered by Eisenhower burst onto their small scene.

It was one of Dewey's associates, Alger Chapman, asking for Bill Rogers, and Rogers took the call in another room of the suite. When Chapman inquired if Nixon were available, Rogers told him in some exasperation that the candidate was in the next room "crying his eyes out." At listening to Chapman repeat this news, Tom Dewey grabbed the phone without further ceremony and, by one account, "demanded" to talk with Nixon. Rogers then passed the phone to Hillings, who said the senator was "not available."

"Don't give me that business," Dewey insisted. "I've got to talk to him. It's absolutely essential."

"My orders are, Governor, he's not to talk to anybody."

"You get him right now. I'm not going to get off this phone until you do it."

With this, Hillings in his own passing of the buck went into the adjoining room and quietly told Chotiner that Dewey was on the phone. "I think I know what it is," Chotiner told him and went to the phone to try himself to shield their fragile politician.

"I'm awfully sorry," Chotiner told Dewey. "He's out someplace and I can't reach him."

"Well," said the familiar, cool voice from New York, "I'll hold the phone."

There followed a leaden interval as the two-time Presidential nominee stubbornly held the receiver and three thousand miles away Murray Chotiner calculated the costs and consequences. After what seemed long minutes, they finally brought Nixon on the line.

"Dick?"

"Yes."

"There has just been a meeting of all of Eisenhower's top advisers, and they have asked me to tell you that it is their opinion that at the conclusion of the broadcast tonight you should submit your resignation to Eisenhower. As you know, I have not shared this point of view, but it is my responsibility to pass this recommendation on to you."

There were several seconds of more dead line, and Dewey tapped the receiver. "Hello, can you hear me?"

"What does Eisenhower want me to do?" Nixon was "stunned," and he struggled to speak with "as even a voice as I could summon."

He now thought Dewey "hedged," explaining that he had not talked personally with Ike, that he "did not want to give the impression . . . that this decision had been approved by Eisenhower." But then those who asked him to call had such a "close relationship" with the general that this request surely "represented Eisenhower's view as well as their own."

"It's kind of late for them to pass on this kind of recommendation to me now," Nixon answered bitterly. "I've already prepared my remarks, and it would be very difficult for me to change them now."

He should continue with his planned defense and explanation of the fund, Dewey told him. He could make plain he had "done no wrong." But in conclusion he should tell the nation that he did not want to be "in any way a liability to the Eisenhower crusade," and thus he was "submitting his resignation" to Ike, and, Dewey added, "insisting that he accept it."

At this point there was another ominous pause, and Dewey filled the long-distance silence with what his own biographer called "an almost surreal afterthought."

"I've got another suggestion as to how you can follow this up and come out of all of it the hero rather than the goat. What you might do is announce not only that you are resigning from the ticket, but that you're resigning from the Senate as well. Then, in the special election which will have to be called for the Senate, you can run again and vindicate yourself by winning the biggest plurality in history."

More silence. Nixon remembered the idea as "mind-boggling."

"Well, what shall I tell them you are going to do?" Dewey finally pressed.

Nixon "looked like someone had smashed him," thought Hillings.

But then the old temper flared and he recovered, "Just tell them," he said slowly, "that I haven't the slightest idea what I am going to do, and if they want to find out they'd better listen to the broadcast."

"And tell them," Nixon added in his heat, "I know something about politics, too." He slammed down the receiver on the man who more than any other had elevated him to national prominence.

He remembered his men "dumbfounded" when he recounted Dewey's suggestions, though Chotiner had clearly suspected and feared the point of the call. "You certainly aren't going to do it, are you?" Chotiner blurted out.

"I just don't know. You . . . had better get out of here and give me a chance to think." He retreated into his bedroom, shaved and showered, and put on the light-gray suit, white shirt, and dark tie selected for the broadcast, all "almost in a daze," as he remembered. "Dewey's telephone call had . . . shaken my equilibrium." In the few minutes remaining he went over his outline once again, decided to speak from the rough notes, and resolved, too, that under the circumstances of his virtual dump from the ticket, he would ask the public to send their responses to the National Committee. He would cloak his motives in concern for the general's candidacy, but the political confrontation was unmistakable—"It would be the politicians rather than Eisenhower who would take the responsibility for removing me from the ticket."

Just before he was to leave, Chotiner stuck his head in the door and delivered, "bluntly," thought Nixon, his own ultimatum.

"Dick, a good campaign manager must never be seen or heard. But if you're kicked off this ticket, I'm going to break that rule, I'm going to call the biggest damn press conference that's ever been held. I'm going to have television present, and I'm going to tell everybody who called who, what was said—names and everything."

"Would you really do that?" Nixon asked almost boyishly.

"Sure I'd do it. Hell, we'd be through with politics anyway. It wouldn't make any difference then."

Murray Chotiner had been the unwavering partisan in the crisis, Nixon would say later. He had defied the revelations, defied Eisenhower's tremulous men, even resisted the idea of having to go to Los Angeles to make the television speech because "it might appear that we were thrown off stride by this maneuver of the enemy." And now the "enemy" was his own party and Presidential running mate, to be given their due in a final searing press conference of revelations and inside stories. Chotiner's threat gave him a palpable "lift." "In the whole fund matter," Nixon would repeat to friends, "Chotiner was the strongest of all—like a rock."

Pat now joined him, back from her day's rest at the Drowns's. He pocketed the five pages of notes, still scribbling at the last moments, and they slowly walked out side by side down the hotel corridor. Bassett, Rogers, and a bodyguard accompanying them, the rest of the staff came out of their rooms in silent, solemn vigil and support. "It seemed like the last mile," he wrote of the walk to the elevator.

While Nixon was enduring the eleventh-hour call from Dewey, Eisenhower was convening after dinner in Cleveland yet another meeting to discuss the crisis coming to a climax with the speech that night. Humphreys and Summerfield arrived late and found in the candidate's hotel suite a council of some twenty people, nearly everyone of consequence in the train party. The general sat archly in a straight-backed chair, facing Bill Robinson and Senator Carlson on a sofa with the rest hugging the walls, as if trying to avoid notice or question while Ike doggedly sampled opinion. Carlson was arguing tentatively for Nixon, with Robinson interrupting to point out the liabilities and then at Ike's initiative delivering his own unequivocal advice to be rid of the sullied running mate. "What do you think, Sherm?" Eisenhower asked Adams when Robinson had finished. But the New Hampshire governor sat in thick silence for several seconds before answering cautiously, "avoiding taking a position," thought Humphreys. Then Summerfield leapt in with a defense of Nixon, but the argument aroused Eisenhower's lightning wrath. Bob Humphreys long remembered the characteristic response. "The General's opening words of his one sentence were said with a glare on his face and he was biting off the words obviously in anger," he wrote, "but by the time he ended the sentence he was all smiles and conciliatory in tone."

Summerfield's was to be the lone voice for Richard Nixon. Robert Cutler offered that there "had to be a face-to-face meeting" between Ike and Nixon "before the thing could be completely settled, regardless of what the broadcast produced." None of them seemed especially to agree with

Cutler's advice, and the dauntless Summerfield even opposed it as humiliating to Nixon, but Eisenhower mutely took in the suggestion. The group adjourned to the Cleveland Public Auditorium, where they would watch the television program and Ike would later address an assembled audience. Before they left, Humphreys on his own initiative hopefully scurried to set up a television hookup and potential time for Eisenhower following the Nixon speech, on the assumption that if the address were a success, Ike might exonerate his Vice-Presidential nominee then and there in the fervor of the moment. Despite the Dewey call, despite the sentiment of the cowed gathering in the suite, they would do all they could to the last moment to salvage the ticket.

They climbed what seemed endless stairs to the manager's office perched at the crow's-nest level above the hall. There the party from the suite joined Mamie Eisenhower and a handful of what Humphreys remembered as "local bigwigs"—all assembled before a large table-model, wooden-frame televison set, topped by a metal aerial pointed toward the roof. As the broadcast was beginning, there was a commotion when a news photographer broke through into the office. He was allowed to take a quick picture of Mamie and Ike sitting together before the television set, Mamie's hand on a tuning knob as Nixon's face came on the screen. Then the photographer was ushered out, and the Eisenhowers retreated to a sofa, next to Bill Robinson, where they began to watch. One of those standing behind them, witnessing the candidate and his men fixed on the screen high above the restless crowd below, Cutler felt the issue of Richard Nixon's political future "blowing through the American sky like a giant free balloon."

There had been a breathless silence as Nixon and his small party walked out of the quiet hotel lobby and took the twenty-minute ride from the Ambassador to the NBC studio, one block from the famed intersection of Hollywood and Vine. The candidate sat in the front seat of the Cadillac limousine, nervously shuffling his notes, scratching out points on taxes now apparently irrelevant with the Gibson, Dunn opinion. A handful of cheering Young Republicans were at the studio to greet him. Among them that night, ironically, was the son of one of his supporters and a future White House chief of staff who would figure in still another dramatic television speech to the nation twenty-two years later—H. R. "Bob" Haldeman. But now the senator scarcely noticed them as he walked—"grim-faced," reported *Newsweek*—down the ramp to dressing room "B" where a makeup man would apply "beard-stick" to the troublesome shadow of his freshly shaved face. As Nixon had insisted, the 750-seat El Capitan Theatre, home of the "Colgate Comedy Hour" and "This Is Your Life," was empty. They had first planned to do the show from the main studios of NBC a few blocks away but came to the El Capitan because of its more powerful lighting. Accompanying reporters were confined to a nearby room where they would watch the speech on a set like everyone else, while a battery of stenographers transcribed his words in an improvised press room back at the Ambassador. Ted Rogers had shaped the approach with a single direction—"Keep it simple," he had told both Nixon and the production crew. Yet the dark, vacant seats of the theater and exiled journalists, the apparent vacancy of the scene, hid painstaking preparation and considerable activity.

In the still infant art of television, it was a thoroughly professional operation assembled by Rogers and the advertising agencies. Directing was John Claar, like Rogers a veteran of other network shows and currently in charge of the popular serial "Our Miss Brooks." To assist them both, the campaign had sent James Ellis of the Kudner Advertising agency and more aides from the ever-present Batten, Barton, Durstine & Osborn, who worked closely with still more NBC officials and the three main cameramen. They had all met in virtually continuing conference since Monday afternoon, consulting Nixon and his men repeatedly on the tenor of the speech. As stage setting they had chosen what Rogers called "a GI bedroom den," including a simple desk and armchair and a bookcase with wooden prop books with painted titles, one of them captioned *Roosevelt Letters*. Nixon described it later and rather casually as "a flimsy-looking, nondescript room," but the appeal to the postwar middle-class audience was clear and vital. "Many viewers were moved by the intimate drama of the Richard Nixon show," a Los Angeles reporter wrote later. "But they did not know that the spectacle was stage-managed by Hollywood soap opera experts."

Now, too, in the minutes before the broadcast, they took the star through a careful rehearsal of what were to seem natural, spontaneous gestures. The television men asked him to sit at the table, then stand next to it, then to repeat the same movements and stances again and again. As they prompted, Nixon practiced posing with one hand on the table and, in another position, with a hand informally in his pants pocket. Under similar direction he smiled, and smiled again, cracking momentarily the frozen-lipped frown he had worn since leaving his hotel room. They would have Nixon "going doggedly through the directed motions," wrote a witness "almost to the moment of curtain time." Meanwhile, Pat Nixon stood by, "nervously clasping a handkerchief," said one observer. Rogers himself had been skeptical about including the candidate's wife in the broadcast. But Nixon would have it no other way. "I want to feel she is here," he had said. In her simple knit dress, one made by Whittier supporters for the Senate race, she was now placed in the armchair, earnestly coached to strike a relaxed pose, her head with its tightly set hairdo turned slightly at an angle, her parchment-like, drawn face held in a thin smile from which the pain and stress were scarcely concealed.

There would be no other distractions. Rogers shunted Chotiner and William Rogers to a draped booth out of sight. Nixon complained briefly that he was hoarse, his throat hurt, he was nervous. Rogers assured him he would be all right. The producer then drew a chalk line around the desk and told Nixon that if he stayed within it the cameras could "get a picture and a good one." It was what Rogers called "preventive TV." He asked Nixon how he would be concluding the speech. "I don't know but you'll know when I'm finished," the politician answered. Rogers would simply have to "feel it," but he would know when it was over. "He told me he would like to be completely on his own," Rogers would say afterward.

The lights were given a final adjustment, and they left the set briefly for the dressing room. At three minutes to go, Rogers knocked on the door. Nixon suddenly turned to his wife. "I just don't think I can go through with this." And she had answered, as she had in 1946 and so many similar moments, "Of course you can." They went back to the set and watched the seconds tick off. At Rogers's suggestion, his senatorial calling card was the opening title of the program. As the director pointed to Richard Nixon, more than sixty million Americans were waiting in front of their still-novel television receivers, what would be calculated as 48.9 percent of the possible viewers. In the end, the constructed drama and suspense, even Eisenhower's anguished temporizing, had drawn a crowd beyond their wildest calculation. It was the largest witness to a political speech in world history, and long the greatest audience for a single event in the annals of American broadcasting.

"My fellow Americans," he began, sitting behind the desk, an earnest, dark-haired young man backed by the ersatz draperies and bookcase of his studio den. "I come before you tonight as a candidate for the Vice Presidency and as a man whose honesty and integrity have been questioned." Watching in Washington, Hannah Nixon "shuddered" at her son's opening words. She was "grateful," she would say later, "that Tricia and Julie were asleep."

He was on the partisan attack from the beginning. The "usual political thing" was to ignore or deny such charges, but "we've had enough of that . . . with the present administration," and he felt the best answer "to a smear" was "to tell the truth," and "I want to tell you my side of the case." They had no doubt heard the charge "that I, Senator Nixon, took $18,000 from a group of my supporters." The question was not simply whether it was illegal, but whether "morally wrong," whether the money went for his personal use, was "secretly given and secretly handled," was contributed for "special favors." Having set up the standards, he would satisfy each.

"Not one cent of the $18,000 or any other money of that type ever went to me for my personal use," he told the camera, adding in the old rationale, "every penny of it was used to pay political expenses that I did not think should be charged to the taxpayers of the United States." Nor was it "a secret fund," and as proof he cited his ready admission to Peter Edson, who already had the story. As for favors, he made a sweeping claim:

> Let me point out, and I want to make this particularly clear, that no contributor to this fund, no contributor to any of my campaigns, has ever received any consideration that he would not have received as an ordinary constituent.
>
> I just don't believe in that and I can say that never, while I have been in the Senate of the United States, as far as the people that contributed to this fund are concerned, have I made a telephone call for them to an agency or have I gone down to an agency on their behalf.

Having followed his hand-written outline meticulously, at this point he pointedly omitted a cryptic phrase he had scribbled under the section on favors to contributors—"six wrote me."

How had he spent the money? He explained the salary and allowances for senators and asked the television audience as he had asked the gatherings at the whistle-stop in California and Oregon: should the taxpayer pay for printing a political speech, for a "purely political speech," for political broadcasts? And if not, how could this be done? "I don't happen to be a rich man so I couldn't use that." He would not put his wife on the payroll, like Sparkman and others. "That's his business and I'm not critical of him," he said of his Democratic counterpart. "You will have to pass judgment on that particular point." As for his own reasons, "I have found that there are so many deserving stenographers and secretaries in Washington that needed the work," he explained, "that I just didn't feel it was right to put my wife on the payroll."

He now motioned to Pat. "My wife's sitting over here. She's a wonderful stenographer." The camera panned over but seemed hesitant to leave Nixon, including her tense, half-smiling silhouette only in the corner of the picture and then swinging back to televise for a moment the top of the desk. He spoke on. "I'm proud to say . . . Pat Nixon has never been on the government payroll."

There were other ways to finance the costs, such as a legal practice, but he spurned that, too. It was another notable point at which he departed from his carefully crafted notes. His outline here listed "speeches," an obvious reference to the potential extra earnings from honoraria. He had added, as if in explanation of his own considerable income in 1952, "except this year—when volition to help . . . down payment—very little."

By now he had lost the early tenseness and palpably warmed to the challenge. "I began to feel that surge of confidence that comes when a good speech has been well prepared," he wrote. "I began to feel instinctively the rhythm of its words and the logic of its organization . . . felt warmed by the bright lights, and I opened up and spoke freely and emotionally . . . as if only Pat were in the room and no one else were listening."

"And so," he went on, the Fund had been the "best way to handle these necessary political expenses," to convey his message "of exposing this administration, the communism in it, the corruption in it" and to "accept the aid which people in my home state of California . . . were glad to make." He repeated that "not one of them has ever asked me for a special favor." But there would be no names, no amounts, no details. Gone, too, were the solicitations or the cause of "selling" free enterprise to California. "Just about an hour ago," he continued with similar license, he had received the results of the "independent audit" that "I suggested to Governor Sherman Adams." He then read from the Gibson, Dunn & Crutcher letter: "Based on all the pertinent laws and statutes, it is our conclusion that Senator Nixon did not obtain any financial gain from the collection and disbursement of the fund by Dana Smith; that Senator Nixon did not violate any federal or state law." "Now that, my friends, is not Nixon speaking," he assured them, "but that's an independent audit which was requested because I want the American people to know all the facts and I'm not afraid of having independent people go in and check the facts, and that is exactly what they did." With a flourish he had concluded reading the legal opinion with the law firm's signature line on the letter. But the pressured stenographers in the adjoining room of the studio had confused the name of the signing attorney as "Alma H. Conway," and no one had given them the actual document. For more than a decade afterward, the egregious phonetic error remained uncorrected in publicly disseminated and widely republished versions of the speech. Elmo Conley and his special provenance of partners and clients, along with the actual scope and substance of both the Gibson, Dunn and Price Waterhouse findings, remained obscure.

By now he was some twelve minutes into his half hour, and while the style was relaxed, sometimes intimate, the arguments simple and convincing, the report of accountants and lawyers outwardly impressive, it was thus far an ordinary speech. Except for the audits, it was largely what he had told the trainside rallies the week before with favorable yet limited effect. But here, at the bottom of his second page of notes, Nixon picked up Eisenhower's instruction of full financial disclosure, and the thrust and tone took a new and decisive turn. "But then I realize," he continued,

> that there are still some who may say, and rightly so, and let me say that I recognize that some will continue to smear regardless of what the truth may be, but that there has been understandably some honest misunderstanding in this matter, and there are some that will say: "Well, maybe you were able, Senator, to fake this thing. How can we believe what you say? After all, is there a possibility that you may have feathered your own nest?"
> And so now what I am going to do—and incidentally this is unprecedented in the history of American politics—I am going at this time to give to this television and radio audience a complete financial history; everything I've earned; everything I've spent; everything I owe. And I want you to know the facts. I'll have to start early.

His hesitant notes read "I came from relatively poor family," which he spoke as "our family was one of modest circumstances and most of my early life was spent in a store out in East Whittier." He evoked "Mother and Dad" and "five boys" and "we all worked in the store." There was more working through college and "to a great extent" through law school, and then Pat. "We had a rather difficult time after we were married," he revised their history, "like so many of the young couples who may be listening to us." Then the war, with both modesty and drama: "Let me say that my service record was not a particularly unusual one, I went to the South Pacific, I guess I'm entitled to a couple of battle stars. I got a couple of letters of commendation, but I was just there when the bombs were falling." Pat had been "an economist for a government agency," and from early marriage and the war the "total of our savings" was "just a little less than $10,000," and "every cent of that, incidentally, was in government bonds." In his notes he had followed the $10,000 with another number, then scratched it out and wrote "five into campaign," in reference to the 1946 run, but then thought better of it and never voiced the claim. Here is where they started into politics, he went on, and what had he earned since then? "Well, here it is—I jotted it down, let me read the notes." He was moving swiftly now, easily on to the third page of his detailed notes with a flowing earnestness and feeling. He would say of the speech: "I probably had been preparing to do it all my life."

Beyond his congressional and senatorial salaries there was $1,600 from old estates in his Whittier law firm (though no "legal practice" or fees "after I went into politics"), "an average of approximately $1,500 a year from nonpolitical speaking engagements and lectures," Pat's interest in her father's farm of $3,000, and his own inheritance of $1,500 from Franklin Milhous. He then quickly described their eighty-dollar-a-month apartment in Park Fairfax, and the savings for a house: "What did we do with this money? What do we have to show for it? This will surprise you, because it is so little, I suppose, as standards generally go, of course, in public life."

Another inventory. He listed the house in Washington "which cost $41,000 and on which we owe $20,000," and the Whittier home "which cost $13,000" and where he repeated the mistake in his notes that "we owe $3,000" rather than the actual $10,000 mortgage. But more important: "My folks are living there at the present time." He had a little insurance though none on Pat and the girls, a "1950 Oldsmobile car," "our furniture," no stocks or bonds or business interests. As for their debts, they owed the $20,000 mortgage in Washington, the $10,000 (now correct) in Whittier, $4,500 to the Riggs Bank of Washington, another $3,500 to his parents— "and the interest on that loan . . . I pay regularly, because it's the part of the savings they made through the years they were working so hard." And, finally, a $500 loan on his life insurance. "Well, that's about it," he concluded. "That's what we have and that's what we owe. It isn't very much but Pat and I have the satisfaction that every dime we've got is honestly ours. I should say this, that Pat doesn't have a mink coat. But she does have a respectable cloth coat. And I always tell her that she'd look good in anything."

"I didn't think I could take it," Hannah said afterward of his itemized account of personal worth in front of sixty million people. "But I drew courage from my faith. That carried me through." In the draped booth at the El Capitan, Murray Chotiner let out shouts of glee as he watched the same performance. When Nixon spoke again of his wife and her coat— this time phrasing it her "respectable Republican cloth coat"—the camera once more panned in on her and what *Life*'s Robert Coughlan saw as her "unblinking, thinly smiling, fixed gaze" at her husband, a stark concentration that disconcerted many viewers. "I didn't know the camera was on me and I wanted to listen," she said later, "because I didn't know what he would say."

Now he paused imperceptibly and delivered the planned lines that would give the speech its name, make it famous, and notorious.

> One other thing I probably should tell you, because if I don't they'll probably be saying this about me, too. We did get something—a gift—after the election. A man down in Texas heard Pat on the radio mention the fact that our two youngsters would like to have a dog. And, believe it or not, the day before we left on this campaign trip we got a message from Union Station in Baltimore saying they had a package for us. We went down to get it. You know what it was.
>
> It was a little cocker spaniel dog in a crate that he sent all the way from Texas. Black-and-white-spotted. And our little girl—Tricia, the six-year-old, named it Checkers. And you know the kids love the dog and I just want to say this right now, that regardless of what they say about it, we're gonna keep it.

"It isn't easy to come before a nationwide audience and air your life as I've done," he continued. The Democrats seemed to think you had to be rich to hold public office. "I believe that it's fine that a man like Governor Stevenson who inherited a fortune from his father can run for President." But men "of modest means," men like Dick Nixon, must also be allowed in the arena. Now the Lincoln quotations. "Because, you know, remember Abraham Lincoln, you remember what he said: 'God must have loved the common people—he made so many of them.' "

He was on page four of the notes, in the last third of the program, and Ted Rogers was coming out of the director's booth, kneeling beside the camera, holding up the fingers of both hands to signal ten minutes left. The tension was now utterly gone, and he felt "in complete control of myself and of my material . . . calm and confident."

"And now I'm going to suggest some courses of conduct." He would turn the deflected attack back on his attackers, all of them. In the draped booth Chotiner smiled broadly. Stevenson should explain his own fund—"where the money went directly into their pockets"—and Sparkman, too, should account for "what outside sources of income he has had."

> I would suggest that under the circumstances both Mr. Sparkman and Mr. Stevenson should come before the American people as I have and make a complete financial statement as to their financial history. And if they don't

it will be an admission that they have something to hide. And I think that you will agree.

Because folks, remember, a man that's to be President of the United States, a man that's to be Vice President of the United States must have the confidence of all the people. And that's why I'm doing what I'm doing, and that's why I suggest that Mr. Stevenson and Mr. Sparkman, since they are under attack, should do what they are doing.

In the auditorium manager's office, high above the hall in Cleveland, the Presidential campaign party had been watching in rapt, sometimes wrenching attention. By now some of them were choked with emotion, a few even weeping softly, though at the end of the sofa one viewer had remained dry-eyed and impassive. Dwight Eisenhower held a small block of paper and methodically tapped the pad with a pencil as Nixon spoke. But then the increasingly confident, aggressive figure on the screen was attacking Stevenson and Sparkman on the issue of full disclosure, and in the attack implicitly challenging Eisenhower to do the same, the general whose shadow candidacy had been financed so long and so lavishly by private interests, whose sizable profits on his war memoirs had been shielded by a special tax dispensation accounting the royalties as capital gains rather than income. At Nixon's words "something to hide," Eisenhower jabbed his pencil into the pad, a small detonation that startled the room. "I'd always liked and admired Ike, of course, but I'd often wondered how smart he really was," one of the politicians in the room would say. "After that, I knew—Ike got what Dick was getting at right away, while the others were weeping and carrying on."

Back in the El Capitan, Richard Nixon was moving the counterattack to yet another plane. He had spent the first part of the speech at the desk, humbly, studiously enumerating his assets and liabilities, his logical, exceptionable justifications. Now he was up and moving, hand in pocket or arms gesturing, fists clenched in strength and emphasis, much as they had rehearsed him. "In spite of my explanation tonight other smears will be made; other smears have been made in the past. And the purpose of the smears, I know, is this—to silence me, to make me let up." The old, dark danger moved center stage, and he gave the watching nation a small five-minute sample of his best stump lines. "Well, they just don't know who they're dealing with." "They" have been "violently opposing me" since the Hiss case, but "I have no apologies to the American people for my part in putting Alger Hiss where he is today." And, of course, he would continue to fight. "Because, you see, I love my country. And I think my country is in danger." Six hundred million people "lost to the communists" and 117,000 U.S. casualties in Korea. Those in the State Department "that made the mistakes which caused that war and which resulted in those losses should be kicked out." The danger was too great. "In the Hiss case they got the secrets which enabled them to break the American secret State Department code. They got secrets in the atomic bomb case which enabled 'em to get the secret of the atomic bomb, five years before they could have gotten it by their own devices." For their corruption and softness on communism, Truman and Stevenson were not fit to be President. Only Eisenhower "recognizes the problem and . . . knows how to deal with it."

Ted Rogers held up three fingers for the few minutes left, and Richard Nixon was in the close, on the final, fifth page of the notes. It had been an extraordinary, brilliantly selective capsule of his career and argument, defining, even imposing the terms of his own judgment, without a trace of the realities of his past campaigns, the identity or interests of his backers, the impact of the Fund on his career and personal affluence, or—perhaps most telling—without a sense that anything essential about politics or life was missing. Now he came back to the letter from the young marine wife he had read to the Hadley Field crowd in Whittier, the wife of the corpsman in Korea with her eighty-five-dollar-a-month allowance and a donation for "great Americans like you and General Eisenhower in the White House." He looked deep into the camera lens. "Folks, it's a check for ten dollars, and it's one that I will never cash." Why couldn't they have "prosperity built on peace rather than prosperity built on war?" Eisenhower was the man "that can lead this crusade."

At last, the question of his resignation: "Let me say this: I don't believe that I ought to quit because I'm not a quitter." In the Spring Valley home, Hannah uncharacteristically shouted back at the television screen, "No, and you never have been." But as if to prove the point, he was going on. "And, incidentally, Pat's not a quitter." Again the line he had used to please the Los Angeles nightclub crowd that dreary election night in 1948, and again the camera moved toward his immobile wife. "After all, her name was Patricia Ryan and she was born on St. Patrick's Day, and you know the Irish never quit."

At this dramatic climax, his notes read, underlined, "I could insist on stay—" This, too, he shrewdly omitted, and went on with Dewey's line: "But the decision, my friends, is not mine. I would do nothing that would harm the possibilities of Dwight Eisenhower to become President of the United States. And for that reason I am submitting to the Republican National Committee tonight through this television broadcast the decision which it is theirs to make."

In Cleveland the general once more stabbed his pad with the pencil, now so hard that the lead broke off in an audible crack that again startled the hushed room. "Let them decide whether my position on the ticket will help or hurt," he went on. "And I am going to ask you to help them decide. Wire and write the Republican National Committee whether you think I should stay on or whether I should get off. And whatever their decision is, I will abide by it."

He was utterly lost now in his peroration, coming with amazing precision to the last lines of his original notes as Rogers nervously signaled ten seconds. "Regardless of what happens," he would continue this fight to "drive the crooks and the communists and those who defend them out of Washington." He was walking toward the camera, arms outstretched, in a last appeal.

> And remember, folks, Eisenhower is a great man. Believe me. He's a great man.

Ted Rogers was rising out of his crouch, the camera fading in search of a last period on which to end.

> And a vote for Eisenhower is a vote for what's good for America.

Suddenly they were off the air, and though he had apparently nodded to Rogers at the "cut" signal, Nixon was still talking, still walking right into the "head-on" camera and hitting it with his shoulder. "He was in a complete emotional daze," Ted Rogers remembered. A cameraman, tears running down his cheeks, darted forward to catch Nixon. "I'm sorry, Ted, I loused it up," he said desperately. He turned to pick up the speech notes on the desk, stacked them neatly for a moment, then hurled them to the floor in disgust and stepped back to bury his head in the stage drapes.

"YOU'RE MY BOY"

"Well, Arthur," Eisenhower said to Summerfield when the broadcast was over in Cleveland, "you sure got your money's worth." Adams thought also that he heard the general lean over to Mamie, who was visibly moved, and remark that Dick Nixon was "a completely honest man." Waiting for them in the auditorium below, the Ohio Republican audience, some 15,000 well-dressed businessmen and gray-haired ladies with corsages for the occasion, had heard Nixon's words over the public address system, and many of them were openly weeping. One of Taft's conservatives, Congressman

George Bender, moved to the microphone and shouted, "Are you in favor of Nixon?" And the tearful crowd went wild, screaming, whistling, leaping from their seats. The roar lifted toward the manager's office above, where Nixon's old nemesis, Bill Robinson, was suddenly his most enthusiastic supporter. "In thirty minutes," Humphreys recorded, "he had done a complete about-face." There was a "quick huddle," as Humphreys saw it, and most of the onlookers were ushered out of the room so that the general might hurriedly revise his speech. The tumult in the hall now formed into a rhythmic chant led by Bender, and it reverberated in the crow's-nest office: "We want Nixon, we want Nixon!" "Already," Bobby Cutler noted of the first moments after the speech, "the wind was bending the grass."

At the same moment in the El Capitan there was confusion and, for Richard Nixon at least, continuing despair. Chotiner and Bill Rogers had come hurrying out of their booth to congratulate him and found him embraced by his wife but still disconsolate that he had not told the millions where to send their wires. "I'm sorry I had to rush at the last; I didn't give the National Committee's address," he told them. "I should have timed it better." But Chotiner and the others assured him it was a success, and he soon composed himself, thanking the technicians, posing with Pat at the desk for a still news photographer. When he went back to have his beard-stick removed, the makeup man said to him proudly, "That ought to fix them. There's never been a broadcast like it before." Ted Rogers burst in to tell them, "The telephone switchboard is lit up like a Christmas tree." Still, he moped. "Pat, I was a failure," he told her when they were alone in the dressing room, to which she said, like the others, "Dick, I thought it was great."

"I couldn't do it. I wasn't any good," he mumbled. Bassett rushed in to embrace him with the same congratulations, and finally, he seemed to relent. "Let's get out of here and get a fast one. I need it," Nixon told him. Moments later, waiting reporters noticed tears in the eyes of both the candidate and his wife as they left the theater. "It was not an easy speech to make," Nixon said as they entered the limousine, Haldeman and other Young Republicans cheering in the background.

Once in the car Nixon slumped down beside his wife and stared grimly out the window—only to notice, as Bill Rogers later told the story, a great Irish setter bounding along beside the Cadillac as it slowly pulled away. He turned back to the rest of them, scowled, and said bitterly, "Well, we made a hit in the dog world, anyway." Richard Nixon, an intimate said later, was still "sick with the certainty that he had failed persuasively to vindicate himself." Nonetheless, his wife made the ride back to the hotel with a fierce delight. "Pat was particularly pleased," her husband recorded later, "that I had not stayed on the defensive but had needled Stevenson and gotten in some good licks on the campaign issues."

In Cleveland they scurried to prepare Eisenhower for his reaction and appearance before the crowd clamoring for his running mate. Earlier that day, the ubiquitous advertising men had planned carefully for the requisite spontaneity of the moment. "Tonight will make history. This will be the turning point in the campaign," Bruce Barton, the elder of BBD&O, had told his man on the scene. "The general must be expertly stage-managed, and when he speaks it must be with the understanding and the mercy and the faith of God. My suggestion is that . . . the general come out with the following memo in his own handwriting: 'I have seen many brave men perform brave duties. . . . But I do not think I have ever known a braver act than I witnessed tonight.'" Ike now duly conferred with the speechwriters and sat down near the mute television set to write out his new remarks. With the crowd still thumping beneath them, he called in Summerfield, Humphreys, and press secretary Jim Hagerty to read aloud what he had penned. "I have seen many brave men in tough situations. I have never seen anyone come through in better fashion than Senator Nixon did tonight."

Ever sensitive to their moody politician at the other end of the country, Humphreys reminded Ike that there had been "no communication to Nixon as yet." Eisenhower swiftly dictated a telegram to Hagerty, then told him to polish it. "Rewrite it and make it sound better. Hand it to me on the platform," he ordered, and moved off to address the crowd. "I have been a warrior and I like courage," he began before his scripted lines. "Tonight I saw an example of courage." Yet as the crowd applauded his every approval, he also spoke cautiously. "I do not mean to say that there will not be some who will find new items on which they will want further explanation, possibly." But there had been no doubt of Nixon's courage. Ike told the story of George Patton's controversy in World War II—"He committed an error . . . he made amends for his error"—and spoke of the gravity of Democratic corruption next to "whatever error of judgment may have been committed by Senator Nixon." Yet as his address unfolded, it was clear how decisively Eisenhower was departing from the prescribed acceptance of his running mate, how much the Nixon speech offended and challenged him, how skillfully he was now appeasing the emotional audience while pulling authority back to himself.

"I am not intending to duck any responsibility that falls upon me . . .

[as] the standard bearer of the Republican Party," he told them, saying that the chairman of the National Committee was "certain to call upon me." The final decision would be his whatever the junior senator from California had proposed. "I am not going to be swayed by the idea of what will get the most votes," he went on, ". . . by what may appear to be administrative convenience . . . in this campaign." It would depend on whether "I myself believe that this man is the kind of man that America would like for its Vice President," and it was "obvious that I have to have something more than one single presentation necessarily limited to thirty minutes." He was going to summon Nixon to see him personally. "I possibly am now guilty of being a bit egotistical. But in critical situations in service to my country I have had to depend on my judgment as to men . . . whether a man was fit to command . . . or . . . whether this man should be saved from the executioner's squad." It was a remarkable evocation of his continuing role as Supreme Commander, a powerful reaffirmation of his political life-and-death authority over Richard Nixon. And he alone would decide. "Except for asking for such divine guidance as I may be granted," Eisenhower told the now-hushed crowd, "I shall make up my mind, and that will be done as soon as I have had a chance to meet Senator Nixon face-to-face." In closing he read the text of the telegram to Nixon that Hagerty had hastily edited, squatting on the floor, and slipped in front of him at the lectern. Like the speech, its courtly prose was unmistakable.

> Your presentation was magnificent. While technically no decision rests with me, yet you and I know that the realities of the situation will require a personal pronouncement, which so far as the public is concerned will be considered decisive.
>
> In view of your comprehensive presentation my personal decision is going to be based on a personal conclusion. To complete the formulation of that personal decision I feel the need for talking to you and would be most appreciative if you could fly to see me at once. Tomorrow evening I shall be in Wheeling, West Virginia. I cannot close the telegram without saying that whatever personal admiration and affection I have for you, and they are very great, are undiminished.

As Ike spoke, the National Committee in Washington was already swamped with calls, much like Republican headquarters and newspapers and other switchboards across the nation. "Eisenhower, to the end, voiced no judgment that could be taken as a thoughtful appraisal of the merits of the matter," observed his New York speechwriter Emmet Hughes. Yet now Richard Nixon had in his own desperate defiance and public rebellion engaged the one issue on which the general would make a stand—his own prerogative and power. "He spoke to the crowd in Cleveland," wrote one of Eisenhower's biographers, "but his words were darts directed at the National Committee and at Nixon."

Amid the clash of personality and politics, life and business went on at the El Capitan. When the theater had emptied of its few historic occupants and the lights dimmed, while Eisenhower was beginning to speak, far away in Cleveland, NBC prop men came in to remove the "GI bedroom den" Ted Rogers had ordered for the evening, which had now played such a role in American history. It would be needed again soon for another network serial.

When the Nixons and their party reached the Ambassador, the lobby that had seemed silent and funereal an hour before was now thronging with supporters. Overwhelming his bodyguard, they "mobbed" the candidate, as he happily described it, clapping both Nixon and his wife on the back, grabbing their hands and shouting acclaim—"Great," "Magnificent." Upstairs the staff greeted them with the same enthusiasm, and Herb Klein of the *San Diego Union* was there to congratulate him. Still, for a few minutes, "we waited tensely for reaction," remembered Klein, who eventually took a call from a man in Florida who said the Western Union lines were jammed and he was calling instead to urge Nixon to stay on the ticket. With that, what Klein called the "deluge" would begin. Telegrams and calls poured into the suite from everywhere. Of the callers Nixon remembered in particular Hollywood mogul Darryl Zanuck, an old supporter, who told him extravagantly that the speech had been "the greatest production I have ever seen."

As the excited minutes wore into more than an hour, however, there was still no congratulatory message from Eisenhower. Hagerty's telegram, already delayed by the editing and insertion in Ike's speech, was to be all but lost in the torrent of cables descending on the Ambassador. Then at mid-evening they got the first wire bulletin of the Cleveland address. Eisenhower had "declared he could not make a personal decision until he saw me face-to-face," Nixon bitterly remembered, "that a half-hour presentation was not enough." The report was shattering. As one campaign aide now recorded the reaction, "elation turned to shock and rage." The candidate himself "exploded," wrote another observer, and Julie Eisenhower acknowledged that "my father felt despair, then anger." "What more can he possibly want from me?" Nixon asked Chotiner. "I'm not going to crawl on my hands and knees to him." In another corner of the suite Pat Nixon was echoing his words in the same indignation: "What more does that man want?"

Nixon now thought Eisenhower "completely unreasonable" and his own situation beyond endurance. "I had been prepared for a verdict. I was expecting a decisive answer," he wrote later. "I didn't believe I could take any more of the suspense and tension of the past week." Soon after reading the wire bulletin, his fury building, he silenced the still-celebrating room of staff and supporters and dramatically announced that "if the broadcast had not satisfied the general, there was nothing more I could or would do." He would, he told them, "simply resign rather than go through the stress of explaining the whole thing again." Calling Rose Woods into an adjoining room, he then hotly dictated a telegram of resignation, addressing it not to Eisenhower but to the Republican National Committee, in a last act of defiance.

As the secretary left the room, Chotiner quickly intercepted her, took the dictated wire, and tore it up. "I don't blame him for being mad," Chotiner told her. "And it would serve them right if he resigned now and Ike lost the election. But I think we ought to let things settle a bit longer before we do anything this final." He then went in yet again to soothe and bring under control the now seething, now morose candidate. A resignation was premature, Chotiner told him, but neither should he be humiliated. They should simply wait out Ike, allowing the apparent tidal wave of public support to foreclose his choice. "Chotiner . . . insisted," Nixon reported of their talk, "that I not allow myself to be put in the position of going to Eisenhower like a little boy to be taken to the woodshed, properly punished, and then restored to a place of dignity." They agreed that the general "would have to make a decision before I went to see him," and in the meantime they would resume their own campaign schedule with the planned flight that night to Missoula, Montana.

Instead of a resignation wire—and still to appease Nixon's anger—they would send Eisenhower a curt response saying they could not come to Wheeling and would not be available until the next weekend. "Will be in Washington Sunday and will be delighted to confer with you at your convenience any time thereafter," read the telegram. In Cleveland that night Sherman Adams would note the "cool reply to Eisenhower's request for a meeting," and one reporter thought other Presidential campaign aides "shocked" at the wire. "That was not independence, it was insolence," wrote an Eisenhower intimate. "Relations between the two traveling groups had plumbed their depth." By the time Nixon's testy cable had been received, however, events had already moved on decisively.

The cable had hardly gone from Los Angeles, and the decision been made to go on to Missoula, when Bob Humphreys finally got through the clogged switchboard to Chotiner in the Nixon suite. Still in the auditorium manager's office in Cleveland, Humphreys listened briefly to Chotiner describe the situation, and then asked him to hold the line. Anxiously, he turned to the rest of the men in the office—Summerfield, Persons, Senator Karl Mundt, and Congressman Les Arends. "We've got plenty of trouble in Los Angeles that only you, Arthur, can straighten out," he told them. "If you other three gentlemen won't mind . . . " He handed the phone to Summerfield.

Despite Humphreys's alarm the national chairman sounded jovial. "Well, Murray, how are things out there?"

"Not so good," Chotiner answered grimly.

"What in hell do you mean, not so good?"

"Dick just wrote out a telegram of resignation to the general."

"What! My God, Murray, you tore it up, didn't you?"

"Yes, I tore it up, but I'm not so sure how long it's going to stay torn."

"Well, Dick is flying to Wheeling to see the general, isn't he?"

"No, we're flying tonight to Missoula."

"What? My God, Murray, you've got to persuade him to come to Wheeling."

At this, Chotiner delivered the ultimatum, engaging Summerfield's and the committee's own prestige.

"Arthur, we trust you. If you can give us your personal assurance [*sic*] from the general that Dick will stay on the ticket with the general's blessing, I think I can persuade him. I know I can't otherwise." At this point, Chotiner deliberately broke off the call, saying they had to leave for the airport for Missoula. He gave the national chairman a parting warning: "Dick is not going to be placed in the position of a little boy coming somewhere to beg for forgiveness."

Nerves were now raw on both sides. Frantically, Humphreys opened a telephone line to the Los Angeles airport gate where the Vice-Presidential campaign plane would be departing, while other Eisenhower aides tried to call back the Ambassador. But when Senator Fred Seaton finally reached the suite, Chotiner refused the call. "Let the bastards wait for us this time," he told Klein and others. Then, minutes before Nixon and his party were to leave for the airport, at least one more call came through. Whether it was the private instigation of Humphreys or others around Eisenhower would never be certain, though it clearly came in reaction to what Chotiner had told Humphreys and Summerfield.

On the line was Bert Andrews, now traveling with the Eisenhower train, and Nixon relented to come to the phone to talk to his old friend and adviser. What was he planning to do? Andrews asked him after praising

the speech. "I told him bluntly," Nixon recorded, "that under no circumstances would I meet Eisenhower under the conditions he apparently had
laid down." In another extraordinary intercession of the evening, Andrews
now talked to Nixon "like a Dutch uncle," as the latter remembered, the
journalist's voice "darkened . . . in flat, measured words." There was no
indignity or risk in going to Wheeling, Andrews told him—but a real issue
of allowing Ike his due. "Richard," he began solemnly, "you don't have
to be concerned about what will happen when you meet Eisenhower."

> The broadcast decided that. Eisenhower knows it as well
> as anyone else. But you must remember who he is. He
> is the general who led the Allied armies to victory in
> Europe. He is the immensely popular candidate who is
> going to win this election. He is going to be President,
> and he is the boss of this outfit. He will make the right
> decision. But he has the right to make it in his own way,
> and you must come to Wheeling to meet with him and
> give him the opportunity to do exactly that.

Either Andrews's practiced sense of the personal politics, his shrewd hearing
of Ike's Cleveland speech, or both, it was a forceful argument, and Nixon
himself thought it had "the ring of truth and of good common sense." Yet
as the party left for the plane to Missoula, the issue was still far from
settled.

Two hundred people, cheering and waving placards, were waiting for
them at the Los Angeles airport at 11:00 P.M. Nixon clambered onto a car
to thank them and to repeat twice for the newsreels what he called his
"slogan": "We haven't begun to fight!" Inside the terminal, Humphreys
and Summerfield were again on the phone with Chotiner, who told them
the candidate, as Humphreys noted, "was on the plane and wouldn't get
off it." Humphreys, who normally penned a small, tight script, now
prompted Summerfield with a descending ladder of notes in a large, excited
scrawl:

> Art
> tell him
> to intercept
> Dick before
> he says something
> to *press*
> Ike's phone number
> Superior

1–6979
Dick should
hold at
that airport
until you
have talked
to Ike
He
must
intercept
Nixon
They're
crappin' you—

Nixon has
not left
yet
Have a wire . . .
opened up
between you
and Dick at
airport while
you get Ike
out of bed—

But Chotiner would not be moved, and the National Committee men could only secure a promise that they would talk again in a few hours in Missoula. In the middle of the night in Cleveland, it would seem that the proud, volatile Nixon might now resign after all, that the whole elaborate salvage since the crisis broke might only come apart in the end. For the moment, only they knew fully the potential for disaster. The Eisenhower train had pulled out of Cleveland at 2:00 A.M., as Nixon was arriving at the airport. "Clutching this secret to our breasts," Humphreys wrote, "Arthur and I went back to the hotel . . . and tried to get an hour of sleep before we talked to Nixon."

Emotions were no less tense in the West. Sent ahead to advance Missoula, Jack Drown had heard the speech on the radio and went out later for a walk. A passing cowboy noticed his "Nixon Staff" button. "You're with Nixon?" he said. "Here's a hundred dollars. That's the best speech I ever heard." And Drown was too choked to speak. On the plane heading for Montana, Nixon was "both elated and fretful," wrote a *Life* reporter, "taut and knotted as a half-unwound rubber band." The staff was celebrating aboard the big charter transport, and at one point he joined them, only later to break down in sobs and finally to fall asleep in a front seat. At the Missoula airport at 1:00 A.M. Mountain Time, Drown thought they had drawn out "three-quarters of the townspeople" on a bitterly cold night. But only seventy-five persons were on hand, with the mayor presenting the exhausted Nixons the key to the city.

As they stood on a dark windswept runway in Montana, the nation was responding to his speech by historic proportions. As many as four million telegrams, letters, cards, and calls came cascading into addresses from the Ambassador to the Eisenhower train, to the Senate office as well as the National Committee, even to the elder Nixons in Whittier. There were messages from throughout the forty-eight states, Alaska, Hawaii, and Puerto Rico, from Canada, Americans abroad, ships at sea. Overwhelmingly, it was favorable, by one study as much as seventy-five to one in favor of keeping him on the ticket, and full of accolades—"a deserving young man," "a big man," "a great man," "a modern-day Lincoln." They wrote and called and wired, the avalanche would show, for a variety of motives, a sense of their own political efficacy and participation, out of partisan or candidate loyalty, and even on the questions of communism, Korea, corruption, and prosperity—though one analysis of over 300,000 telegrams and letters revealed that only 7 percent made any reference to such substantive issues. Most of all, they had responded to Nixon himself. "Not so much because they had been convinced that he was innocent of the charges against him," concluded a scholar studying the messages, "but more because he had succeeded in projecting an image of himself to which they could respond. . . . As a man who shared their own feelings, thought as they thought, and valued what they valued . . . a reflection of themselves, and in their responses they seemed to say " 'We trust him; we believe in him because he is one of us.' " For a single dramatic half hour in the autumn of 1952—as for so many smaller audiences before and after—Richard Nixon had become the quintessential American politician.

In the early morning hours of September 24, *The New York Times* would report the first "flood" of telegrams running two hundred to one in Nixon's behalf, while its editorial writers praised the senator's "composure and assurance" and thought it clear Ike would retain his running mate "unless some wholly new element were introduced." Tom Dewey judged the speech "superb" (though he thought it "silly" for Ike to make a similar financial disclosure), and New York's Russell Sprague pronounced Nixon "a national hero." Headlines in the largely Republican press that morning would be lavish with bannered words such as "extraordinary," "magnificent," "eloquent." Several papers prompted readers to contact the National Committee. "CLIP THIS AND SEND IT," announced a three-column-wide sample telegram in the *New York Journal-American* that said, "After hearing Senator Nixon, I believe he is an honest man. I want a chance to vote for Eisenhower and Nixon."

"Without a trace of malice or contention," began the *Los Angeles Examiner*'s account of his remarks, which took up most of the front page and included its own address box for the National Committee. "His action had the effect of wildfire," reported Carl Greenberg. "Thousands were in tears of emotion." From Whittier alone there were some six hundred wires as citizens stood in line outside the Western Union offices, and Frank Nixon was widely quoted as saying characteristically, "It looks to me as if the Democrats have given themselves a good kick in the seat of the pants." Dana Smith's desk would be piled high with envelopes containing contributions from a penny to $250, the first of what would be more than $60,000 in small donations to pay for most of the cost of the broadcast.

Even old enemies joined the chorus, including the *Washington Post*. Having waited quietly in the wings on the Eisenhower train only to be thwarted again, Bill Knowland expressed "full confidence" in his fellow Californian. Among the torrent of telegrams was one reading "Congratulations on a superb presentation, Dick," and signed "Harold Stassen." Some still kept a cautious silence. Locked in a close race for the Senate with John Kennedy, Cabot Lodge took his phone in Boston off the hook for several hours surrounding the speech, and in Sacramento, as expected by those who knew him, Earl Warren said nothing. In any event, there were few in the press, at least at first, who seemed to question what had happened. In Pasadena Dan Green, whose investigations had started it all, wrote bitterly about the careful professional preparation at the El Capitan, the attempt to "confuse and emotionalize" the audience, and also an element few others saw or understood beyond the basin and its history— "the Aimee Semple McPherson appeal for telegrams . . . old-time revival stuff!" Across the nation, *Variety* echoed Green's review: "A slick production . . . parlaying all the schmaltz and human interest of the 'Just Plain Bill'–'Our Gal Sunday' genre of weepers."

Sitting in their pajamas at the Carter, Humphreys and Summerfield placed their anxious call to Nixon in Montana. To their surprise they reached him almost right away, still up in the predawn at Missoula's Florence Hotel. For the next half hour the two men talked to him in relays, first Summerfield, then Humphreys, reassuring, appealing, calming. At one point Humphreys the old reporter discovered enterprising Cleveland newspapermen eavesdropping at the door of the suite and ran them off down the hall. When he returned he found Nixon "evidently . . . somewhat mollified," though agreeing largely to what Chotiner had posited the night before—they would have to "get a commitment" from Eisenhower that he was staying on the ticket before he "would even consider going anywhere to meet the general." Humphreys now worked feverishly again to set up a call from Summerfield to Eisenhower as the campaign train rolled through Ohio and to arrange for Nixon's DC–6 to land that night in Wheeling.

For their fateful, certifying call, they found Eisenhower in Portsmouth, Ohio, on the river not far from Vinton County where Frank Nixon had been born. Sherman Adams thought the general had "already made that decision privately, and he was merely waiting until he and Nixon could appear together to announce it publicly." But now Adams and the Presidential candidate squeezed together into a phone booth at the Portsmouth station, Adams doing much of the talking and listening on the single receiver, and heard Summerfield's appeal to grant Nixon his commitment. Decision or no, it was another confrontation of Eisenhower, the national chairman conveying the Chotiner-Nixon threat that they would simply not heed an order without a guarantee of vindication, without in effect taking the choice again out of the general's hands. "If the ticket had been headed by a . . . professional politician," wrote Stewart Alsop, "Nixon would have been slapped down and slapped down hard." But now in the few minutes in the booth, his telegram about the evening meeting already public and Wheeling only a few miles away, Eisenhower agreed. Like all the rest that morning, he had already seen the wave of popular sympathy surging behind Nixon. "The president-to-be eyed its crest in some wonder," concluded Emmet Hughes, "and, in effect, shrugged and nodded."

Over the next fifteen minutes, Summerfield reached Nixon again to assure him the deal had been struck and "everything would be all right," arranged for Nixon's arrival at nine-thirty that night in Wheeling, and ordered the telephone poll of the National Committee members that would provide the party formality for the settlement. Still unshaven and in their pajamas, Humphreys and Summerfield sat wearily for a moment in the Carter, silently reflecting on their rescue of a Presidential ticket.

In Missoula, despite his deliverance, Nixon was still tense and restless. After the Summerfield calls he went out alone at dawn to walk the streets of the small town. At nine-thirty he was back in front of the hotel to appear before more than four thousand people crowded up and down Main Street. He spoke "unusually slowly," thought reporters, and departed from his usual repertoire. "I love my country," he said, repeating with emotion a line from the speech. In America, he went on, "a person from a humble family can run for office; for the Senate—even the Vice Presidency. And when enemies attack him, he can go on television and the radio and all he has to do is tell the truth." Politics, he told them earnestly, was "a dirty game," but that should not discourage any young people. "The thing to do," he concluded, "is go in and clean it up."

Nixon remembered the flight to Wheeling as a long "victory ride," the staff and reporters in "rollicking spirits" and singing raucous songs. At a stop in Denver he had exuberantly addressed an impromptu airport crowd, most of them passengers, with the new postspeech slogan: "We have not begun to fight." Finally, at rest, he slept the last leg of the flight east.

Meanwhile, Eisenhower was telling a West Virginia crowd that young Dick Nixon had been the victim of an "attempted smear." The general afterward led a motorcade out of Wheeling up a winding mountain road to the airport to meet his triumphant running mate. The flight was forty-five minutes late, and they waited in silence in the cool darkness. Then, as the plane landed and before Eisenhower got out of his car, reporters behind witnessed a touching scene. The general suddenly leaned over and laid his head on his wife's shoulder, pausing.

Nixon was hurrying to straighten his tie and help Pat on with her coat when Chotiner gasped, "The general's coming up the steps!" They had scarcely turned to look when Eisenhower was there, "grinning all over," Pat remembered. "You didn't have to come down here to meet me," Nixon said. And Eisenhower replied, "You're my boy." Reporters in the central compartment watched in embarrassment as Nixon threw his hands to his face and again broke into tears. For those who watched the scene closely, it was another measure of Eisenhower's innate political genius, and luck— the younger man, the winner, appearing haggard and emotionally distraught, still coming on his public summons whatever the secret assurance, the older man, as one writer described him, "looking gracious, kind, generous, as if supporting an embattled man rather than picking up strength from a victorious one." When Nixon had composed himself, they appeared now together at the door of the plane, smiling and waving to the crowd of three thousand that had gathered.

They were to take the twenty-minute ride together with Sherman Adams from the airport to Wheeling stadium. Nixon neglected protocol by getting in on the right side of the limousine, then apologized and tried nervously to change seats. But Eisenhower only put his hand on his shoulder and said easily, "Forget it, no one will know the difference with all the excitement out there." It was a murky night in Wheeling as the motorcade moved slowly back down the mountain road, and both Nixon and Adams expected Eisenhower to say something about the crisis they had just been through. But he sympathized briefly with what Nixon "had gone through in the past week," and otherwise chatted almost casually about other matters, "blithely talked about the comparative merits of whistle-stopping and rallies," Nixon recalled in amazement, "as if nothing unusual had happened."

The conversation in the trailing limousine, where Mamie rode with Pat, was momentarily more candid. Mrs. Eisenhower had been silent most of the way but nervously began to speak when they became separated in the gloom from the rest of the motorcade. The Nixon story had only hurt the campaign, she was saying. "I don't know why all this happened when we were getting along so well." Pat Nixon replied in controlled fury, "But you just don't realize what *we've* been through." Her icy tone, she told her daughter a quarter century later, "ended the conversation."

At the stadium, where six thousand more were waiting, the candidates circled the track in an open convertible, and Eisenhower spoke first. It was a lengthy speech on the diversity yet unity of the GOP, on the coalition of conservatives and moderates, and on issues from foreign policy to prosperity to civil rights. Finally, he turned toward Nixon and mentioned "my colleague . . . subject to a very unfair and vicious attack" but who had "vindicated himself" and "stands higher than ever before." He would ask the senator to speak, but before that, he wanted to read two messages, the first "a tribute." It was Hannah Nixon's telegram to Eisenhower five days before.

> Dear General:
>
> I am trusting that the absolute truth may come out concerning this attack on Richard. When it does, I am sure you will be guided aright in your decision to place implicit faith in his integrity and honesty.
>
> > Best of Wishes from one
> > who has known Richard
> > longer than anyone.
> > his mother
> > Hannah Nixon

The crowd roared, and Ike went on to read Summerfield's cable announcing that 107 members of the RNC had unanimously supported Nixon. "Let there be no doubt about it," read the telegram, "America has taken Dick Nixon to its heart." Another cheer welled up, and suddenly Nixon was before them.

To reporters who had followed him through the trials and tears of the past seventy-two hours, he now seemed "completely at his ease." He told them there had been "two times in my life when I think I have been prouder to be an American than any other time." The first he described as the moment he looked down on Ike in the World War II victory parade in Manhattan. The second had been this day, when the crisis they had experienced "made us realize that all you have got to do is to tell the people; all you have got to do in this country of ours is just to tell the people the truth and not hide anything from them."

Eisenhower might have ignored the charges against his running mate, he told them—much of what he and his men had secretly hoped Ike would do—but there had been no "cover-up" and Eisenhower had waited "until the evidence is in." "And if he will do that with me," he told them, "just think what he is going to do when he becomes President. . . . I want you to know that this is probably the greatest moment of my life."

When the speeches were over, hundreds thronged the platform to shake their hands. Among them was Bill Knowland, who told him, "That was a great speech, Dick." Again, as he remembered the moment, "I had exhausted all of my emotional reserve," and he burst into tears and buried his head on Knowland's shoulder.

But it was not to be over, even then. Following the rally Eisenhower invited both the Nixons back to his railway car, not simply to talk but to ask them specifically about the old charges Humphreys had thought laid to rest in Cleveland, the rumors about Pat's interior decorator. Angry, denying it all heatedly, barely controlled, Nixon gave him in reply a small lecture on a political campaign.

> This is just like war, General. Our opponents are losing. They mounted a massive attack against me and have taken a bad beating. It will take them a little time to regroup, but when they start fighting back, they will be desperate, and they will throw everything at us, including the kitchen sink. There will be other charges but none of them will stand up. What we must avoid at all costs is to allow any of their attacks to get off the ground. The minute they start one of these rumors, we have to knock it down just as quickly as we can.

He was not sure that Eisenhower, still treated "extremely well" by reporters and politicians, "completely grasped what I was saying" until he had been longer in politics.

Riding back to the hotel, Pat took his hand and held it wordlessly. "I knew how fiercely proud she was that we had come through," he wrote afterward, "but I also knew how much it had hurt her . . . although she would do everything she could to help me and help my career, she would hate politics and dream of the day when I would leave it behind." It would be a "long time," Pat Nixon later told friends, before she forgave Dwight Eisenhower. Nixon himself would write of the whole week-long episode as "a deep scar which was never to heal completely." He had begun the campaign feeling young and vital. "The fund crisis made me feel suddenly old and tired."

Going to the hotel in another car with an AP reporter, an exhausted Chotiner had delivered his own epitaph. "Nixon won this one," he said suddenly to the journalists. There was the clear sense of more to come.

25

Aftermath, September 1952–January 1953

"THE MOST IMPORTANT THING IN THIS LIFE"

he morning of September twenty-fifth, exactly a week after the *New York Post* broke its story on the fund, Richard Nixon left Wheeling a national celebrity. As he walked out of the McClure Hotel, a cheering crowd was waiting in the lobby, and women in the hotel beauty shop rushed out from under dryers to swarm around him, like "bobby-soxers," wrote one reporter, "after a film star." His victory now seemed complete. While he rested at the McClure that morning before resuming the campaign schedule, Summerfield sent him a formal telegram notifying him of what the chairman tactfully called "the combined decision" of Eisenhower and the National Committee. "They not only want you to remain on the ticket as the party's Vice-Presidential candidate," the wire read, "they demand it."

The candidate now refused to say more about the Fund. On a swing west and south, reporters asked for a meeting for "additional questions," but he told them brusquely, "No, no, definitely not . . . my statement [the speech] answers everything." In Oklahoma City, where members of the state press association had interviewed Sparkman on the same subject the day before, he cut off all questions from a breakfast audience of nine hundred, telling reporters that the national GOP headquarters had advised against some "mass press conference." While Nixon remained obdurate, the pressure mounted on Adlai Stevenson to explain his own fund. Stevenson himself had not deigned to watch the Nixon speech, and his closest advisers who did, as one of them wrote later, were "unimpressed." Nonetheless, the challenge issued from the El Capitan could not be ignored. After a matching period of anguish and confusion the Democratic presidential campaign would release an accounting that weekend following the dramas in Los Angeles and Wheeling, awakening grumbling reporters at four o'clock in the morning to give them a Stevenson statement and a promise of later release by both Stevenson and Sparkman of their tax returns for the past ten years.

In fact, the listed contributions and the donation of over $18,000 to supplement the salaries of Illinois officeholders represented only a very partial accounting. In books still concealed, Stevenson's fund from past campaign money and fresh solicitations totaled some $146,000, including required contributions from state employees and some unsavory disbursements, such as payment for "bowling costumes for girls," personal Christmas gifts to newspapermen, Stevenson dues to private clubs and charitable donations, and $286 to pay the orchestra playing at a dance for his sons at the Springfield Governor's Mansion in 1949. With his uncanny if shameless instinct for the opposition's kindred scandals, Murray Chotiner had promptly written a secret memo to Bob Humphreys "to point out the gaps in Stevenson's fund explanation" and suggest lines of attack on both the Democratic Presidential candidate and Senator Sparkman. Loath to reopen the subject they were so well rid of, Humphreys and his colleagues discreetly shelved the advice. Like the Nixon television speech, Adlai Stevenson's statement and eventual tax returns would be accepted as complete by most of the press and public, and the Democrat, mirroring Richard Nixon, indignantly refused to entertain further statements or press conferences on the subject.

"He never got over resenting the press's equating his fund to Nixon's," wrote Stevenson biographer John Bartlow Martin. The sentiment was richly reciprocated. "The press treated Stevenson with kid gloves," Nixon wrote of the incident. "His refusal to talk to reporters received only a mild reproach, and the obvious impropriety involved was all but ignored editorially." Yet at the end of September 1952, the sum of the Stevenson fund furor was to further vindicate Richard Nixon, and in their ironic mutual resentment, their tendentious disclosures so readily accepted, both politicians left untouched the larger common scandal of political finance.

Following Stevenson's statement and less than a week after the Nixon speech, *The New York Times* would conclude from a forty-eight-state survey that the Vice-Presidential candidate's dramatic television appearance had been a "shot in the arm" to the Eisenhower campaign and "exceedingly helpful" to other GOP candidates in general. Everywhere, reported *Times* correspondents, Nixon had infused an often sluggish run by Eisenhower. "Nixon was so utterly sincere that no one could doubt his honesty," went a typical man-in-the-street interview. "I always thought such funds were evil, but now that he has shown that they are a necessary evil . . . we should forget these funds and get down to the more important issues." Beyond the campaign itself, some thought Nixon had altered profoundly the image of the two parties, and thus the American political landscape. "Tuesday night," wrote Scripps-Howard columnist Robert Ruark,

> the nation saw a little man, squirming his way out of a dilemma, and laying bare his most private hopes, fears, and liabilities. This time the common man was a Republican, for a change. . . .Here was a guy who was hit on the head with a sudden disaster that could kill his career. Here was a boy who was suddenly laying it all out on the table for everybody to look at. . . . And Dick Nixon . . . has suddenly placed the burden of old-style Republican aloofness on the Democrats.

On Nixon and his men the effect of such early verdicts was now a kind of euphoria, even gaiety, in contrast to the morose tension of the past days. Flying into Washington on the Sunday after their historic week, Bassett had told Nixon that the traveling press and campaign party who had been with them since Pomona—some fifty altogether—should be recognized in some way, and the senator had formed "on the spot, fourteen thousand feet above sea level," what he called the "Order of the Hound's Tooth," replete with membership cards with a small sliver of ivory symbolic of the clean tooth, Checkers as mascot, and Pat Nixon as president. There was an added irony in the canine symbol playing on Eisenhower's remark. Only days after the speech, Checkers was becoming, Nixon wrote proudly, "the best-known dog in the nation since Fala," and the recipient of dog food and collars, blankets and even a kennel.

Less lightly, the address itself was being called the "Checkers speech," a label Nixon soon found offensive—"as though," he wrote, "the mention of my dog was the only thing that saved my career." Still, in this first afterglow of late September they could look back on the ordeal with a black humor. Despite the bitter memory of the last-minute call from Alger Chapman, then Tom Dewey that Tuesday evening at the Ambassador, the call that had in a sense climaxed the confrontation with Eisenhower and all but pushed Nixon from the ticket, Chotiner adopted the incident for the code name of future political espionage. His spies and informers for the next fifteen years would be cryptically, and with no small irony for those aware of the origin, "Chapman's friend."

There was far less whimsy in the Eisenhower campaign in the week of their strained reunion at Wheeling. Whatever the tonic effect on the ticket or the resurgence against Stevenson, the crisis cost the general an embarrassing loss of face in some of the press and raised an issue of indecisiveness and indirection that would remain to plague his Presidency. "As revealing as anything else in the whole episode," wrote columnist Thomas Stokes, "was the way the nominal Republican maestro, General Dwight D. Eisenhower, dallied so long over the problem of his running mate that the young man himself—the accused—had to step in and take over. And how he took over!" Walter Lippmann thought the speech and its sequel "a disturbing experience . . . with all the magnification of modern electronics, simply mob law." "What the television audience should have been given was not Senator Nixon's personal defense . . . [which] should have been made first before Eisenhower," he went on, but rather "Eisenhower's decision, backed up by a full and objective account of the facts . . . of law and of morals." The respected columnist and thinker saw in the Republican nominee "an alarming disposition to improvise his great decisions, to proceed by intuition, without careful exploration."

Eisenhower's own public reaction after Wheeling continued to be staunch and avuncular. "He is a courageous, four-square young American, with years of service ahead for his country," he said of Nixon in thousands of letters sent out in response to messages. "My personal confidence in him was never shaken; and his manly and full statement to the American people, answering the unfair attacks on his integrity, more than justified that confidence." Privately, the view was grim. Again through Solbert's research service, Clay and others emphasized to Eisenhower and Adams the public perception of Nixon's intramural victory. A September 27 press summary highlighted a *Wall Street Journal* story quoting anonymous Nixon aides telling the senator that "Ike must from this moment on negotiate" with Nixon, and the same sources "making acid comments about the way Eisenhower had dealt with their man." Solbert reported with similar portent the conservative *Chicago Tribune*'s late-September judgment that "it would hardly be an exaggeration to say that in the public mind, the Republican ticket is now Nixon and Eisenhower, rather than Eisenhower and Nixon."

If Bill Robinson and others had been moved and converted by what they saw on the television set in Cleveland, many remained cynical and caustic. Three days after the speech, Fred Seaton, Bernard Shanley, and others were having drinks when Tom Stephens remarked, "There was just one thing left out of the program."

"What was that?" someone asked.

"It was the portion," Stephens went on, "where Checkers, the Nixon dog, crawled up on Dick's lap and licked the tears off his face."

They all roared. Recording it in his diary, Shanley thought the joke "more than apropos" simply because "the program was so corny." The Checkers speech had "left its scars," wrote Peter Lyon. "The association of the two principals was lastingly tainted; neither would ever wholly trust the other again."

For Nixon, part of the wound would be his own enduring sense of the hostility of Eisenhower headquarters in New York as well as of many on the Presidential train, and thus of the core of the future White House staff. The product, as Emmet Hughes observed in considerable understatement, was "much detachment, some disparagement, and a little distrust." In the days following the crisis at least, the political and personal moral seemed plain to the senator and his men—"that the way to deal with Eisenhower," as Stewart Alsop put it, "was to be aggressive and tough as nails." But there were other, more insidious lessons as well.

The fear, evasion, and taunting of the press that had begun in some measure during his harrowing train ride up the coast now deepened into a wary, sometimes rancorous suspicion. Accustomed to praise and easy acceptance if not political complicity in the media, shielded even during the crisis and soon to return to almost uniformly uncritical coverage, Richard Nixon nonetheless nursed his disillusionment. "By the end of [the] '52 campaign," Jim Bassett would recall, "he had utterly no use for the press." Others saw the same animosity. Ted Rogers had thought Nixon before the crisis and speech a careful, even solicitous practitioner with the press, always available for small interviews and personal chats that were the manna of the relationship between politician and reporter. After the vindication and anointment at Wheeling—as he showed instantly in the curt refusal to answer more questions about the fund or even discuss political finances— he was aloof and privately contemptuous. Rogers remembered times when the campaign bus or plane was ready to leave and newsmen were late, including the core of ten or so who had been with them from the beginning and who were "members" of the "Hound's Tooth." Told they were not there, Richard Nixon would spit out, "Fuck 'em, we don't need them."

His venom seemed worst for the writing press, and it had a historic corollary, a sense of the television camera as the decisive new weapon of modern politics, the means to circumvent the press as well as his party and partisan rivals. "He had an immediate consciousness of the power of television," David Halberstam wrote, recording Rogers's observations from the Checkers watershed. "He had done it his way, with no impertinent questions and answers at the end. Suddenly television was magic . . . he could go over their heads."

There would be no doubt in the days following his triumph that the speech itself, more than the preceding crisis, had its price in at least a small segment of the national press, that his imagined new detractors were in some measure real. When the first flush of Wheeling and the massive public sympathy had subsided, editorial commentary began to question both his argument and method. "He probably convinced all but the hopelessly prejudiced that he derived no personal financial gain from the fund," wrote columnist Clifton Utley. "But he did not make any convincing case for the propriety of accepting such a fund. He failed to show any recognition of the possible abuses." In a more blunt calculation, the Democratic *St. Louis Post-Dispatch* concluded, "The result [of the Fund] was that he had more in his own pocket by virtue of the money put into his expense pocket." In successive articles through late September and early October, Gladstone Williams, the McClatchy correspondent in Washington, pointed up that none of the fund expenditures went for purposes that Senate expense accounts would pay for in any case, that Nixon was saving himself money though not the taxpayers, that by Nixon's own figures the senator's net worth was nearly $30,000, far more than most Americans and "not a bad sum to accumulate over the last five and a half years with so little principal to start with." Williams noted, too, Eisenhower's windfall of "around $600,000" as a result of his special tax ruling on the million-dollar royalties from *Crusade in Europe* and "much censure" among reporters for Nixon's refusal to discuss the Fund after the speech had raised new questions.

By mid-October, the focus of criticism had turned more personally, more directly on Nixon himself, an ironic reflection of a speech in which he had so effectively made his image and identity the compelling issue. Much of the reaction went to fundamental questions of character and even religion. "By his initial acceptance of it [the Fund] he irrevocably placed himself in the debt of men with a special axe to grind," said the liberal Catholic weekly *Commonweal*, "and only a legislator with a dull sense of political morality could ever incur such a debt." The *Christian Century* similarly deplored a deeper problem of values in "the nation which could not see instantly the morass into which the young Republican nominee had wandered and which he was trying to tell himself was not there . . . something wrong . . . a state of moral confusion and ethical relativism." "There is a mess in Washington," concluded the *Century*, "because there is a mess in us."

Inevitably, critics set the tone and purpose of the speech against the stoic integrity of Nixon's own reported faith. "He may aspire to the grace and nobility of Quakerism, but if so he has yet to comprehend the core of the faith," wrote Richard Rovere. "It would be hard to think of anything more wildly at variance with the spirit of the Society of Friends than his appeal for the pity and sympathy of his countrymen . . . on the ground that his wife didn't own a mink coat." In Whittier that October, a group called the "Whittier Citizens Committee," some of them Quakers and

Republicans, opened a headquarters on East Philadelphia Street. It was the first vocal opposition within his own community, and it was obviously virulent, as if the resentment had been long building. The committee soon began issuing statements demanding a full accounting of the finance of Nixon's past campaigns as well as of the Fund and explanations of the Brewster-Grunewald affair, his ties to Malaxa, and the role of the China Lobby, questioning the "emotional stability, honesty, and loyalty to the democratic concept of government" of this " 'hometown' boy."

Through it all, feeding Nixon's own bitterness and sense of persecution, there grew in some the seeds of an almost instinctive, inchoate revulsion at the man individually if not his party and politics, a throbbing wish to be rid of this troubling new phenomenon for reasons hardly defined yet deeply felt. "We sincerely hope we will be spared the experience of again bumping into this young man in a hurry," the moderate *Reporter* wrote October 14, 1952. "Somehow, we still cannot work up any great anger at him . . . [but] we cherish the hope that we shan't be bothered with him again—and that his widely advertised talent for salesmanship will find more rewarding outlets outside of politics."

"I HAVE NO FURTHER AMBITION"

Richard Nixon now hurtled into the last month of the campaign with a partisan zeal and harshness that was to be his mark for years to come. When Truman contended that General Eisenhower had misjudged Soviet intentions at the end of World War II, Nixon accused the President of "gutter politics at its worst" and "the most vicious smear in history." Early in October the *San Francisco News* and then *The New York Times* broke the story that the senator had used his franking privilege to mail out his infamous preconvention poll of Californians on the GOP Presidential nomination. But Nixon simply ignored the story, was "unavailable" to reporters on the subject, and replied with rising attacks on what he called the "enemies" of America. "Know your enemy for what he is," he told a New Jersey audience, "a godless, ruthless, realistic, and sinister foe that has infiltrated some of our key institutions." In New York he yelled himself hoarse at a World Series game between the Dodgers and Yankees, went by the Marble Collegiate Church for a chat with the Reverend Norman Vincent Peale, dined in private with Herb Brownell, and still found time to denounce the "shameful Yalta Agreement," promising "liberation" of Poland and other Eastern European nations from "communist slavery." Everywhere he referred darkly to Stevenson's deposition testimony on the reputation of Alger Hiss, "the arch spy of our generation." When a group of prominent attorneys, including William Donovan of the OSS and several Eisenhower supporters, publicly rebuked the attack on Stevenson, "for what any good citizen should have done under the circumstances," the candidate ignored them as well, and continued the onslaught.

Two weeks after Checkers, he was drawing teeming, enthusiastic crowds at every stop, frequently in traditional Democratic strongholds such as South Boston. The throngs seemed to spur his rhetoric. Truman was "playing cheap, dirty politics," was "AWOL" as Commander-in-Chief in campaigning for Stevenson, he told them. The Democratic nominee himself was only "Mr. Truman's stooge," without "backbone training," and "a graduate of Dean Acheson's spineless school of diplomacy which cost the free world six hundred million former allies in the past seven years of Trumanism." When Stevenson countered that the GOP with Eisenhower was trying to sell the nation an unopened "fancy khaki-colored package," Nixon replied, "I'd rather have good old American khaki than State Department pink." By mid-month the accusations had grown. "I charge that the buried record will show," he told a Utica, New York rally, "that Mr. Truman and his associates, whether through stupidity or political expedience, were primarily responsible for the unimpeded growth of the communist conspiracy within the United States . . . that Mr. Truman, Dean Acheson, and other administration officials for political reasons covered up this communist conspiracy and attempted to halt its exposure."

As in 1946 and 1950, the campaign, its rhetoric and tactics, would be thoroughly his creature. Stump speeches continued to be largely extemporaneous, and even television appearances only loosely scripted. The candidate himself would be his own intelligence and planning staff, ever on the outlook for perils and opportunities, however marginal. Thus an October 1, 1952, memorandum to Chotiner and Bassett:

> The *People's Daily World* carried a story on the China Lobby in its issue of September 25. It seems to me that this could be used in one of two ways: the first way I am suggesting only as a possibility. I doubt if it would be advisable. That would be to anticipate the attack by proclaiming that the communists have already set the line for the next attack by running this story in the communist papers and predict that it will be picked up by the left-wing press.
>
> The other way is, of course, to wait until the left-wing press does pick it up and then to point out that the line was first established by this communist paper.
>
> It is significant to note that the editors of the *People's*

Daily World are now under indictment for conspiracy to
overthrow the government by force and violence.

At the same time, as always, he could be carefully modulated for the
constituency at hand. His friend Ralph de Toledano from *Newsweek* watched
him shrewdly appeal to a predominantly Democratic industrial town in
Connecticut with talk of an "all-American team" in Washington and the
"survival of America." In Michigan and elsewhere he would be heckled
and was obviously irritated, though learning to control his temper and
deflect the attacks. "You know, folks, I always am glad to see the hecklers,"
he said typically in Kalamazoo, "because, you see, I've been heckled by
experts." Bill Henry of the *Los Angeles Times* thought Nixon "a masterful
performer" at a Manhattan television speech and impromptu rally in late
October. On the basis of little preparation and only fragmentary notes
supplied by Chotiner, he had made "a restrained, underplayed appeal to
reason" on the subject of the controversial McCarran Immigration Act
and its blatant political bars to asylum or citizenship. Afterward, he had
greeted the crowd warmly, including a few navy veterans who served with
him in the South Pacific. People might think Nixon "a rabble-rouser,"
concluded the correspondent, but he was "actually . . . soft-spoken and
restrained in manner."

Yet the same day Henry's dispatch appeared in Los Angeles, Nixon
was again flailing Stevenson with the tattered effigy of Alger Hiss: "If
Stevenson were to be taken in by Stalin as he was by Hiss, the Yalta sellout
would look like a great American diplomatic triumph by comparison." The
Democratic candidate, he said in a standard phrase, was guilty of "going
down the line for the arch traitor of our generation." Defending his testimony about Hiss's impeccable public record and image, Stevenson vainly
cited early support of the convicted man by John Foster Dulles and even
Eisenhower himself. But the Nixon charge seemed to stick and inflamed
the personal and political bitterness of the campaign on both sides.

The reality was always far more than the placid surface or even florid
rhetoric reported by the press. For a major televised speech on the Hiss
case October 13, the FBI had secretly leaked to Nixon fresh and politically
useful details from their files, including Attorney General Tom Clark's
1948 threat to "catch any son-of-a-bitch furnishing information to congressional committees" and "throw his ass out of the building." Nixon had
already aroused new Bureau admiration by saying "nothing would please
the Kremlin more" than a Stevenson victory. Now in a chilling speech—
an effort to "make the nation's flesh creep," said the *Washington Post*—he
told his gruesome story of treachery and cover-up, of Clark and Truman
trying to "fire" FBI agents for cooperating with HUAC. Just as in the

old days on the Hill, he quoted liberally from J. Edgar Hoover. As for the director himself, Hoover read with relish a detailed report of Nixon's address but was still a bit puzzled by the nuances of the case that had done so much for both his own power and the GOP Vice-Presidential candidate. "Please clear up the difference," he penned at the bottom of a long memo, "between the 'Balt[imore] papers' and the 'Pumpkin Papers.' H."

Behind the façade it was much the same shrouded world of implacable enemies and wavering friends. Following the televised speech on the case, and the same weekend Bill Henry saw Nixon seemingly so amiable and relaxed, Bob Stripling, now an Eisenhower worker in New York, visited Nixon at the Barkley Hotel. The former congressman-become-celebrity was "agitated," Stripling remembered, almost desperate about the Democratic and press attacks on him. "Strip, those sons-of-bitches are out to get me," he told his old staff investigator. "They got Mr. [J. Parnell] Thomas, they tried to get me, and they'll try to get anybody that had anything to do with the Hiss case."

The anxiety had already spilled over into furtive political surveillance of putative enemies. When a Los Angeles couple sent out savage little brochures soliciting "Bundles for Nixon!"—seeking contributions for "a full-time maid," "25,000 Christmas cards," "clothes and travel befitting the senatorial status," or other purposes—some Republican recipients were actually taken in by the parody, and the candidate was furious. Chotiner immediately asked the southern California organization to "check" the couple. The result was an October 10 report supplying the perpetrators' address, auto registration, employment history, and findings from the local police, sheriff's office, and credit files.

Back on the *Look Ahead, Neighbor*, Eisenhower knew little of the inner details of his running mate's campaign and was shielded from some of the most heated language, though occasional messages specifically quoted Stevenson-Nixon exchanges about the general himself, including the reference to "State Department pink." While far more temperate and dignified in tone, the head of the ticket was seized in October with his own dilemmas in the matter of obligatory Red-baiting. Foster Dulles and others had conspicuously praised Joe McCarthy—the senator had "aroused" the nation "to a real danger of communism," Dulles said in a Boston interview—and as Ike's campaign moved toward Wisconsin he was under increasing pressure to avoid any criticism of McCarthy, in effect endorsing his methods. Having long resisted even entering the state, Eisenhower finally prepared for a speech in Milwaukee with a specific passage defending his old army patron George C. Marshall, whom McCarthy and other Republicans had repeatedly vilified. At the last moment, however, the urgings of local Republicans and the National Committee had been too much, and Ike relented, appearing with McCarthy and excising from the already released text of the speech the vindication of Marshall. It was another mark of the force of the anticommunist politics Richard Nixon led and embodied and also of the general's own deeper vacillation and hesitance. "The event gave warning," thought Emmet Hughes, "that certain qualities of the man . . . could be wrenched in the play of politics and made to seem misshapen."

Bassett called it "the speech"—Richard Nixon's litany of the 1952 race, delivered nearly ninety times to set audiences, at some 140 whistle-stops and in more than two hundred cities and towns, mostly in the East and Midwest. There were always the lines about replacing Acheson as secretary of state, about the choice between Stevenson or Eisenhower sitting across the table from Joe Stalin, about the corruption and cover-up and effete cowardice and dubious loyalty of the Democrats. Journalists soon grew numb. "Only a few would go out to make sure nobody shot him," Bassett would say. At one point the speech became so hackneyed that the press secretary had it typed up as delivered and shown to the candidate, who was "shocked" at how "simplistic it had become . . . it was garbage."

Yet Nixon was dogged. The terms and lines changed little, and the applause continued from what Bassett and the reporters thought surprisingly "gullible" crowds, people in search of demons to blame or fear. "He was a good ogre-monger," Bassett remembered, the politician in his dour dedication either "the oldest young man or the youngest old man in Washington" in 1952. The press secretary saw, too, the apparently widening distance between husband and wife, the two Nixons sitting across the aisle from each other during flights, then as the plane circled to land coming together to "put on their Dick and Pat smiles," Nixon putting his arm around her only for photographs. She seemed to despise campaigning that October. Once she had simply disappeared while they frantically looked for her. Without telling anyone, Pat Nixon had gone shopping and to a movie, wanting a whole day to herself.

There was a last flurry of controversy and angry exchanges in the final week of the campaign. Charges of Nixon's anti-Semitism reemerged, and even Murray Chotiner was deployed in front of Jewish groups to vouch for both the Nixons as "the finest young couple that America has ever produced." At Texarkana, Texas, on October 27, speaking to an airport rally from his DC–6, Nixon launched into his old attack on Truman and Acheson and Stevenson, but suddenly with added venom. They were all, he said, "traitors to the high principles in which many of the nation's Democrats believe." Three days later, in equally incendiary terms, he accused Stevenson of having "a Ph.D. degree from Acheson's College of Cowardly

Communist Containment." He later described Dean Acheson with his mustache and finely tailored suits as "the perfect foil for my attacks on the snobbish kind of Foreign Service personality and mentality that had been taken in hook, line, and sinker by the communists," though he would also "regret the intensity of those attacks." For the equally patrician Stevenson there would be no such remorse: "He reminded me of Oscar Wilde's definition of a cynic as a man who knows the price of everything and the value of nothing." Again, their views were mutual. Nixon was the one man in public life, Adlai Stevenson told a friend, that he "really loathed."

At the end of October, the Democrats and other critics struck on several fronts. Democratic National Chairman Stephen Mitchell charged that Nixon relatives owned real estate "conservatively valued at more than a quarter of a million dollars," including a $12,000 house in Florida belonging to the elder Nixons, and Donald's drive-in restaurant, "Nixon's," in Whittier, appraised at $175,000. In an immediate, angrily scribbled response, Nixon countered that his parents' real estate "is very modest," his brother only leased the drive-in, and he had neither contributed to nor profited from either the real estate or restaurant. It was one more embittering, scarring personal attack, without apparent foundation, and yet it was another curious foreshadowing of a time when Donald's drive-in and his parents' property would be all-too-real issues, and scandals.

At the same moment, Drew Pearson published a false report that the Nixons had fraudulently filed for a veteran's exemption for Los Angeles property taxes and a somewhat more accurate account of Nixon's intervention on behalf of Dana Smith and his gambling peccadillo in Havana. The first provoked Pat Nixon's considerable wrath, and she passionately discussed a libel suit with Bill Rogers, once Pearson's friend and attorney, who ultimately dissuaded her. As it was, a threatening legal letter was drafted by another lawyer demanding a retraction from Pearson, and the incident added still more to their hatred of the powerful columnist. By telegram Nixon demanded a similar retraction of Pearson's inaccurate claim that the senator had been in Havana and Florida with Dana Smith. Protests and veiled warnings were also sent to ABC and Pearson's advertising agency and radio sponsor. State Department records would eventually confirm Nixon's letter on Smith's behalf, though only after a search of files in the Havana Embassy when it was found that the Washington copy of the letter had mysteriously disappeared, "filched," Pearson recorded, "by some Republican spies" in Foggy Bottom. Meanwhile, rumors continued to fly about more Democratic or press revelations incriminating Nixon, and the candidate grew all the more resentful. "Forgetful critics would later remember my counterattacks without recalling the lies and distortions that often bred them," he wrote in his memoirs.

He returned to the basin for a last push, scheduled to travel over four hundred miles and make fourteen speeches in southern California alone, many in towns of the old twelfth district. It was all to climax at the Hollywood Legion Stadium with another gathering of movie personalities, including Ward Bond, Hoagy Carmichael, Hedda Hopper, Mary Pickford, Jane Russell, and Adela Rogers St. Johns. Before the gala rally, however, his appearances turned ugly. When one heckler threatened to break up a meeting, the candidate reportedly lost his composure and shouted, "When we're elected, we'll take care of people like you," then motioning to Los Angeles party aides, "Okay, boys, throw him out!" At another speech in Long Beach, there was even more violence. "A gang of roughnecks in his entourage," recorded Drew Pearson in his diary, "beat up several people in his crowd carrying anti-Nixon signs."

With only three days to go, he made a dash across country to Boston and then flew back nonstop on a new Super Constellation, the first such transcontinental flight, to land at Ontario ouside Los Angeles early on the day of the balloting. He had blandly turned down Sherman Adams's invitation to be with the Eisenhowers election night, wiring that he and Pat would return to Los Angeles, "our own county." They were met by Don Nixon, Hillings, Bernie Brennan, and other old supporters, and after visiting Frank Nixon briefly, went in a motorcade to vote in his East Whittier precinct. He spent yet another election day wandering and restless. Driving with Bill Rogers down the coast to Laguna Beach, they played touch football in the sand with Camp Pendleton marines. He "would make a better Vice President," one of the marines joked, "than he would a football player."

They returned to the Ambassador later in the afternoon. Nixon tried to sleep for a time but was awakened at 6:00 P.M. by a dozen excited aides and supporters. Still early in the evening in the East, it was already a crushing victory. Eisenhower was on the way to winning by over 6.5 million votes, adding twenty-two seats in the House and a single Republican senator, giving the GOP a majority of one in the upper body.

Downstairs at the Ambassador, the site six weeks before of their special anguish, the waiting crowd went "wild," as the *Los Angeles Times* described the moment. Reporters surrounded them as they inched through the crush, taking ten minutes to go only a hundred feet. Finally, they made their way to the Gold Room where television and newsreel cameras were positioned. "We want to express our appreciation," he began. But only the last word could be heard above the roar, and he had to start again. It was as if he were the Presidential winner, not the running mate sharing glory with some superior but the hero himself, come home to savor the victory with those who had thrust him so swiftly to the power they coveted.

In Springfield, the Governor's Mansion was "deadly quiet," one witness remembered, and Stevenson eventually went to a downtown hotel to concede. "No one needs to feel sorry for me," he told tearful backers. "I've been spared a great ordeal." Across the nation, in the Commodore in Manhattan, "the modish gowns and well-tailored suits swirled around," as Eric Goldman described the Eisenhower victory party. The winner's first call had been to Herbert Hoover, "trying to identify . . . with a tradition," thought Emmet Hughes as he watched the talk, "a 'team' that was still essentially foreign to himself." Later Ike and Mamie went before a throng delirious with the final reclaiming of power after twenty years. Thousands joined Fred Waring in singing an anthem of the night: "Where, Oh, Where but in America Can You Sing True Freedom's Song?"

Reporters noticed Pat Nixon was even thinner than usual on their return to Washington and visibly exhausted. Within days they had slipped away unannounced for a Florida vacation, hosted again by George Smathers's friends, Bebe Rebozo and Dick Danner. When they had returned, a grateful Vice President–elect wrote Rebozo "how very much all of us enjoyed our Florida vacation. . . .You were just what the doctor ordered!" "We have put your name," Nixon added, "at the top of the list for inaugural ceremonies, etc."

At that, politics seemed little affected by the tightening personal ties. Within only days of the election, Smathers joined Senator William Fulbright of Arkansas in announcing that they would introduce legislation to provide that if Eisenhower should die in office, especially during the first half of a term, Richard Nixon would occupy the Presidency only until the next congressional election, when a new national vote would select a successor. Both sponsors emphasized that their proposal was not directed at their colleague Dick Nixon. But the law would clearly limit him to less than two unelected years in the White House at most, and angry Democrats rallied to the idea in the wake of the campaign.

Already there was talk as well of the controversial young Vice President being dumped by his own party from the GOP ticket in 1956. At his first major Washington press conference since the victory, he was forced to disclaim higher ambitions and discount his own prospective purge even before he had taken an oath of office. "So far as I am concerned I feel that I have accomplished my major political ambition—to throw the Democrats out and get in," he told them. "I have no further ambition except doing the best possible job I can. . . . Nobody can get me excited with any attacks or speculation as to whether I get renominated four years from now." It was all symbolic of the strife, the struggle for political survival, that lay ahead.

There was a small, strange portent, too, in the Nixons' trip to Mexico City at the end of November to attend the inauguration of the new Mexican president, Adolfo Ruiz Cortines. At a U.S. Embassy reception during the celebration, Nixon pointedly slighted the lame-duck Democratic ambassador, former New York mayor William O'Dwyer, but greeted warmly Mexican dignitaries and U.S. officialdom. Among the young embassy aides, one was particularly admiring and slipped a calling card with a note into the pocket of the Vice President–elect as he stood in the receiving line. "My wife and I want to thank you for the magnificent job you're doing for our country," said the handwriting on the back of the card. The other side announced "E. Howard Hunt, Jr., Attaché."

To fill Nixon's vacant Senate seat, Earl Warren now defiantly named California state controller Thomas Kuchel. A forty-two-year-old Warren loyalist whose office had begun its own inquiry into the Fund and its contributors in the first days of the crisis that past September, Tom Kuchel, like the rest, would be remembered, and catalogued. "Steps are being taken," Murray Chotiner privately assured a supporter in late November 1952, "to collect all the malicious falsehoods, distortions, and innuendos that were spread during the campaign."

The Milhous family clan and many of his old supporters—Herman Perry, Tom Bewley, even Jap Burch from the La Habra City Hall, and many others—would gather for the inaugural. It was to be a grand, festive celebration after all the fatigue and bitterness of the Fund crisis and campaign. Assigned to guard the family, a secret service agent remembered Pat Nixon, despite her ordeal of the past months, "full of hope and great expectancy." His parents and brothers were with them at the Spring Valley house, and he would take his oath of office on two ancient Milhous family Bibles Hannah had solemnly brought for the occasion.

There was an intimate family dinner before the inaugural balls, and at the last moment a flash of the old, distant life. "I am not going to wear those blasted tails!" Frank Nixon had yelled about the formal clothes he called "a monkey suit." Hannah had been embarrassed and stymied, and Dick finally intervened. "All right, Dad. We're getting into these clothes." Frank repeated, "I'm not getting into these clothes." But his son had insisted, "Oh, yes, you are." And the old man relented at last, muttering about the house and to relatives afterward, "They made me do it, they made me do it."

While the others were talking excitedly, Hannah gently drew her older son aside and pressed upon him a small piece of paper on which she had written out a message in her archaic, Whittier schoolgirl's hand. At this zenith of her Richard's historic rise in human affairs, his arrival at the threshold of vast power, she was moved by some premonitory sense to remind him of his past. Hannah Milhous Nixon had reached back in her faith to that other tradition of their place and moment—not to the toil or salted promise of Yorba Linda, the bright, crafty hero in Scattergood Baines, the striving, sleepless student, the halls of small-town law, or least of all the cruel and cynical necessities made of politics, but to that other world and thought of George Fox and his followers in the Yorkshire stillness, trying to grasp something more than temporal ambition, a power beyond what could be readily seen and learned in Whittier or Washington. In her note, she spoke a reassurance, and a warning, one more quiet little talk in the special bond between this mother and son.

"To Richard," it began:

> You have gone far and we are proud of you always—I
> know that you will keep your relationship with your
> maker as it should be for after all that, as you must know,
> is the most important thing in this life.
>
> With love, Mother

He did not read it until he was alone later that night. Deeply moved, he put the note in his wallet and carried it throughout his political life.

ABBREVIATIONS

AES	Adlai E. Stevenson Papers (Princeton University)
AHP	Alger Hiss Papers (Harvard Law Library)
AHS	Arizona Historical Society
APA	*Alhambra Post-Advocate*
ASU	Arizona State University Archives
BAN	Bancroft Special Collections (University of California at Berkeley)
BAN/OH	Bancroft Oral History Project (University of California at Berkeley)
BG	*Boston Globe*
CAC	*Covina Argus-Citizen*
CRA	California Republican Associates Archive (Los Angeles)
CSA	California State Archives (Sacramento)
CSU	Special Nixon Collection (California State University at Fullerton)
DDE	Dwight D. Eisenhower Presidential Library
Duke	Duke University Archives
EB/OH	Edmond Brown Oral History Project (University of California at Berkeley)
EMH	*El Monte Herald*
EW/OH	Earl Warren Oral History Project (University of California at Berkeley)
EWP	Earl Warren Gubernatorial Papers (Sacramento)
FBI	Federal Bureau of Investigation Documents (Allen Weinstein Collection, Truman Library)
FNT	*Fullerton News Tribune*
GK/OH	Goodwin Knight Oral History Project (University of California at Berkeley)
GKP	Goodwin Knight Papers (Stanford University)
HGD	Helen Gahagan Douglas Papers (University of Oklahoma, Norman)

HGD/OH	Helen Gahagan Douglas Oral History Project (University of California at Berkeley)
HH	Herbert Hoover Presidential Library
HI	Hoover Institution Archives (Stanford University)
HST	Harry S. Truman Presidential Library
JFD	John Foster Dulles Papers (Princeton University)
JFK	John F. Kennedy Presidential Library
JV/OH	H. J. Voorhis Oral Histories (Claremont Colleges)
JVP	H. J. Voorhis Papers (Claremont Colleges)
KMP	Karl Mundt Papers (Dakota State College, Madison, S.D.)
LAHE	*Los Angeles Herald Examiner*
LASP	*La Habra Star-Progress*
LAT	*Los Angeles Times*
LBP	Leslie Baird Papers (Private)
LC	Library of Congress
MNP	*Monrovia News-Post*
MU	Marquette University Special Collections
NA	National Archives (Washington, D.C.)
NYHT	*New York Herald Tribune*
NYP	*New York Post*
NYT	*New York Times*
PPB	*Pomona Progress-Bulletin*
PSN	*Pasadena Star News*
QC	*Quaker Campus* (Whittier College paper)
RDP	Roy Day Papers (University of California at Berkeley)
RN/OH	*Richard M. Nixon in the Warren Era* Oral History (University of California at Berkeley)
SB	*Sacramento Bee*
SD	State Department Archives
SDU	*San Diego Union*
SFC	*San Francisco Chronicle*
SPR	*South Pasadena Review*
SU	Stanford University Archives
SZ/OH	Steven Zetterberg Oral History (Claremont Colleges)
SZP	Steven Zetterberg Papers (Claremont Colleges)
UCLA	University of California at Los Angeles, Special Collections
UCLA/OH	University of California at Los Angeles, Oral History Projects
USC	University of Southern California Archives
UU	Fawn M. Brodie Research Collection (University of Utah, Salt Lake City)
VPA	Richard Nixon Vice Presidential Archive (National Archives, Laguna Niguel, Calif.)
WCA	Whittier College Archives
WDN	*Whittier Daily News*
WDN (I)	*Whittier Daily News*, Inaugural Edition (January 18, 1969)
WP	*Washington Post*
WS	*Washington Star*
YLHS	Yorba Linda Historical Society
YN	(Young Nixon) Richard M. Nixon Project, Oral History Program (California State University at Fullerton)

NOTES

Prologue

Page

2   "chocolate flood": Sibley, 52; a history of the Colorado on which I have drawn gratefully, along with conversations with John R. Erickson, consultant to the Colorado River Compact.

2   "Journey of the Dead": Juan Bautista De Anza, the first European to traverse what is now the Imperial Valley, quoted in Sibley, 53.

2   "I want to say to you": Powell at the Second International Irrigation Congress, Sibley, 56.

2–3   "What is the key": *Sunset*, 1900, quoted in Sibley.

3   "visible wrath of God": McWilliams, 103.

3   "grandeur": Richard Henry Dana, 1835, on "the only romantic spot in California," CSU, from his *Two Years Before the Mast*.

3–4   For the war's California campaigns, see *American Heritage* 9, no. 5 (August 1958): 8–21.

4   "Take a sprinkling": G. F. Parsons, *The Life and Adventures of James W. Marshall*, quoted in Heizer and Almquist, 201.

5   "scenes conjured up": quoted in McWilliams, 120. "I had half a million": created by novelist Theodore Van Dyke; see McWilliams, 123.

5   "a quaint, uneventful little city": "On the Brink of the Boom," *California Historical Quarterly* 52, no. 1 (Spring 1973).

6   "pleasant to note": Smythe, 105.

6   "Here in the Southwest": *American Heritage* 9, no. 5 (August 1958): 5.

6   "America in flight from herself": L. P. Jacks, quoted in McWilliams, 8.

6   "west of the West": quoted in McWilliams, 113.

6   "a theatrical green": Carey McWilliams's own observation as a young migrant in the early 1920s, ix.

7   "A wretched land": McWilliams, 208.

7–8   Owens Valley bond issue *et seq.*: the story is summarized by Halberstam, 165–67, as well as in Kahrl and several other sources in the bibliography.

9   "about to die, salute you.": quoted in McWilliams, 190.

869

9 "learned the three R's": quoted in Kahrl, 18.

9 unappeasable: two years after the Owens aqueduct opened and touched off still more expansion, the city was foraging for more water northward toward the Sierra Nevadas.

9 the Boulder precedent: in the end, though few saw it, it was more nearly Los Angeles and its brawny politics that made the great Western water system than the system making the city.

10 "Henry, it sounds a little ambitious": Sibley, 62.

10 "an extraordinary existence": Theo White, "Building the Big Dam," *Harper's* (June, 1935): 113–21. (An accomplished writer in his own generation, White is not to be confused with the later eminent political journalist, Theodore H. White.)

10 $48 million . . . largest ever offered; labor unrest: Linda J. Lear, "Boulder Dam: A Crossroads in Natural Resource Policy," *Journal of the West* 24, no. 4 (October 1985): 82–94.

10–11 "the way the Aztecs built pyramids": West, *Hide and Seek*, 30. vast growth: McWilliams, 371ff.

11 hidden price: Lear, 91–92.

11 "a sinister suggestion": quoted in McWilliams, 199. "some sort of destiny": *ibid.*, 369.

12 "enormous village" and "the folks": see especially Adamic's *My America* (1938).

12 "not the imagination to transcend": Stuart Edward White, quoted in McWilliams, 159.

12–13 "a glacial dullness"; "a vast fungus": from William Huntington Wright's *The Smart Set* (1913); see McWilliams, 157.

13 "basest and most brutal": quoted in Olmsted and Wollenberg, 4.

13 "California was willing to have . . . born inferiors": Heizer and Almquist, 200.

13 "Racism . . . as deep and pervasive": Walton Bean, "The Role of Radicalism in California Politics," *California Historical Quarterly* 51, no. 3 (Fall 1972): 220.

13 "A California politician": from Kenny's interview in *American Heritage* 20, no. 4 (June 1969): 22.

14 "Los Angeles . . . melting pot": quoted in McWilliams, 232.

14 "Incessant migration": McWilliams, 238.

15 "conspiratorial pattern": the La Follette Committee, quoted in McWilliams, 283.

15 "owned Los Angeles, in fee simple": McWilliams, 274.

15–16 "in senile dementia": McWilliams, 275. municipal election: Martin J. Schiesl, "Progressive Reform in Los Angeles under Mayor Alexander, 1909–1913," *California Historical Society Quarterly* 54, no. 1 (Spring 1975): 37–57. "main qualification": McWilliams, 241.

16 Progressives' foreign policies: Thomas G. Patterson, "California Progressives and Foreign Policy," *California Historical Society Quarterly* 47, no. 4 (December 1968): 328–42.

16 "bitter lessons of politics": Johnson quoted in NYT, October 29, 1932.

16–17 "segregation of the unfit": quoted in McWilliams, 181. "one colossal swindle after another": *ibid.*, 297. "absolutely selfish, very empty": quoted in *ibid.*, 181–82. "defeat of the American dream": *ibid.*, 311.

17 "hungry, questing crowd": quoted in McWilliams, 313. "mixed multitude": *ibid.*, 368. "typically American": Morris Markey in *ibid.*, 342.

17 "its roots and mentor": quoted in McWilliams, 370.

Chapter 1. Families, 1878–1912

26 "never yelled orders . . . I felt terrible about it": WDN(I).

27 "austere type of man"; Ezra's whipping; "wasn't . . . a tender-hearted type": YN, Timberlake, 9, 13, 14.

27 "full of love . . . ever seeing them in despair": Kornitzer, 39. "too much for our morals": YN, Timberlake, 14.

27 "tossed his songbook . . . great mane of white hair": West, *Hide and Seek*, 237.

27 "too overbearing . . . who will deny?": Jess Griffith to Jane Milhous, Joshua's twin sister, Hoyt, 138.

27 "Africa," located at the county seat, Vernon, Indiana: see Hoyt, 149, who concluded gently of local Quakers, including the Milhouses, that "not all of them could bring themselves to break the law of the land."

28 "capital to spare": Hoyt, 167. motives for the move: Faber, 23, drawing from the daughters' testimony. Jessamyn West recorded that Franklin "turned down" fertile land in Illinois and Iowa "because it was so much less beautiful than the unfertile, picturesque hills of Southern California." "On Words and Men," 2. Hoyt, 166, says he also "suffered from bronchitis in the humid air of Indiana, and . . . was greatly relieved in the drier air of the West."

28 "leave thee with my name": Arnold and Clark, 3.

28 "strong community . . . Christian influence"; "with much prayer": Arnold and Clark, 12, 13. See also James B. Moore's "The Town" (c. 1976), 15–16, a private manuscript found both in WCA and CSU.

28 water problems: Moore, 12–13.

28–29 "people of other denominations . . . we say come": Moore, 8.

29 "for Friends of like mind and spirit": religious historian Glen Dumke paraphrased in La Shana, 114.

29 "men of no conscience" and "crop of suckers": Arnold and Clark, 28, 31.

29 boom and bust: Moore, 9. lots from $100 to $2,000 and "beyond the ken of normalcy": Arnold and Clark, 30.

29 "heroes of their day": Arnold and Clark, 32. Henry's bank and other development: Moore, 21–22, Arnold and Clark, 113.

29 "All welcome" and Coxey's Army: cited in Moore, 30. Whittier College President Paul Smith told the story in the institution's fiftieth anniversary address in 1951, describing Jacob S. Coxey, who organized the protest march, as "one of the earlier California 'crackpots.' "

29 armed patrols against hungry urchins: YN, G. Ellis Triggs, 19.

29 "ideal city of dreams": Arnold and Clark, 19. Ordinance against nonwhites and "pure bigotry": YN, Nichols, 21. Restrictive covenants are discussed in several YN interviews: see especially Otterman and Randall.

29–30 accounts of elaborate Milhous move: see Faber, Schulte, and YN, Timberlake, as well as Hoyt and Kornitzer. Mattie Newsom (YN) remembered that Franklin had the five-bedroom Boulevard house "all planned" in Indiana well before the migration.

30 bustle of the clan: YN, Timberlake, 16. "astounding": Hoyt, 173. By one family count, the next generation in California yielded some fifty-two Milhous first cousins: YN, Cato and Funk, 3. "every tramp . . . always taking somebody in": Spaulding, 15.

30 "Mr. Rancher": YN, Barton, 3. "a comfortable living": YN, Agnes (Mrs. Herman) Brannon, 17. A local society writer called them a "larger family of prosperous . . . ranchers": WDN(I).

30 "main thing . . . to make an asset"; bean picking; Hannah hiring out as housemaid at five dollars a week: YN, Timberlake, 4-6, 30.

30 "liked to cook . . . our mainstay": YN, Timberlake, 21.

31 "revival fervor . . . Hands . . . laid on" and suicide: West, *Hide and Seek*, 233 ff. "Hannah encouraging me to go forward": YN, Jane Milhous Beeson, 17.

31 praying in clothes closet: Nixon, *RN*, 8. "just really her life": Jane Milhous Beeson in Schulte, 63.

31 "quite a bit of German": from a February 1960 interview by Flora Schrieber summarized and recast in the *Columbus Dispatch*, January 19, 1969.

31 "gentle . . . soft of voice" and only one "beau": YN, Timberlake, 43, 22.

31–32 Brady legend: Hoyt, 98, who speculates that Brady "may have even been a friend" of George Nixon, Sr., a direct Nixon ancestor who served in the Delaware militia.

32 The Nixon lineage is traced in Hoyt, 4–98, *Burke's Presidential Families of the United States of America*, and with rich detail in a series of private manuscripts: "Richard Nixon's Ohio Traditions" (1960) by Carl D. Sheppard, and Raymond M. Bell's "History of the Nixon, Milhous, Trimmer, and Wadsworth Families" (1954; revised edition, 1966), "From James to Richard: The Nixon Line" (1957), and "The Ancestry of Richard Milhous Nixon" (1954; revision 1966, and second edition, 1970), all at CSU and WSA.

32 volunteered to serve for another: author's correspondence with Mrs. Francis Herbert Obetz, a former aide to Ohio Governor James Rhodes who discovered George Nixon among the original roster of Company B, Seventy-third Regiment of the Ohio Volunteer Infantry. The grave of Richard Nixon's great-grandfather is near the site of Abraham Lincoln's address at Gettysburg.

32 "my Sally Ann": Abrahamsen, 4. The Wadsworths had migrated from Maryland to Ohio. See the Bell manuscripts, cited above.

32–33 early life in the Hanging Rock Iron Region: see Sheppard and Bell, manuscripts, and Hoyt, 98–99. "Untainted by aristocracy": *American Heritage* 15, no. 4 (June 1964): 11. The milestones of Samuel's life may also be traced in the files of the *Republican Tribune* of McArthur, Ohio.

33 TB exodus: Sheppard describes the "primitive cabin" and the memory of Walter Nixon, one of Frank's brothers, of Sarah's tiring, futile walks.

33 living out of a wagon: Gardner, 4.

33 "we were so poor": Sheppard, 24. "root, hog, or die": Ernest Nixon in Kornitzer, 71.

33 "she was hard and beat Frank:" the testimony is from another of her stepchildren, as quoted in Abrahamsen, 6, who concludes that Samuel's second wife, Lutheria Wyman, was "a harsh stepmother." References to the abuse are found as well in Olive and Oscar Marshburn, UU, and in Hannah Nixon's later conversations, Kornitzer, 237–238. See also Brodie, 37.

33 "poor, strange. . . . We were newcomers": Kornitzer, 71. Ernest was five years younger. "ragged . . . ready pair of fists": Nixon, *RN*, 5. Sheppard, 24, vaguely describes Vinton County memories of the Nixon children as "unusually well educated," thought to be the result of having teachers as parents.

34 "In the sweat of thy face"; "weak and lazy": Kornitzer, 71–72. "Potato King": Gardner, 7. Frank's early jobs are described by Gardner as well as Sheppard, Hoyt, and by Hannah Nixon in her memoir, "A Mother's Story."

34 "fancy dresser . . . pride . . . the armor": Abrahamsen, 7; Kornitzer, 71–72. "Republican, of course": the story is told in several family accounts, and in most detail in Hoyt, 102.

34 "cancelled by pride and prickliness": Wills, 169. "said he was quarrelsome": Kornitzer, 71.

34   job with Columbus Railway and Light: Frank began as a day laborer.

34–35   "he swore vengeance": "Nixon's Father Gets Cold Feet," *Echoes* (Ohio Historical Society), May 1974, which contains the most detailed account of the episode.

35   "so danged mad": Coughlan, 147. In Coughlan's working draft (copy in DDE), he quotes Frank Nixon's sole if slightly garbled public version of the campaign: "I was so danged mad and I asked a friend of mine if he knew any lawyer who would run . . . and get an ordinance passed."

35   "any favors you can show them": the original is photographed in Kornitzer, 73. possessions in a bundle; "nothing . . . but struggle and hardship": Sheppard, 25. In the first decade of the century, Ohio was second among states of origin for the flood of immigrants into Southern California.

36   "for each cent": Ruth Kedzie Wood, *The Tourist's California* (New York, 1914), 308. For Pacific Electric, see also McWilliams, 129 ff.

36   "lonesome . . . strayed. . . . His was love at first sight": YN, Timberlake, 22.

36   "I immediately stopped going": Gardner, 9–10; Hoyt, 171. "faster worker": Olive Milhous Marshburn in Abrahamsen, 22. "overpowering": Abrahamsen, 18.

36   family unhappiness; "she wasn't strong enough . . . leap out of the fire": YN, Timberlake, 22, 35, 43.

37   "stay at home and go to college": YN, M. Barton, 3. "stay up . . . in the night": YN, Timberlake, 22. "We wanted Hannah to go on": YN, Timberlake, 31.

37   "You sure deserve honors": *Thoughts in Verse*, 14. The poem is entitled "To Hannah and Francis," dated June 1908.

37   "Hannah is a bad girl": YN, Hadley Marshburn, 5.

37–38   "flimsy cottage": Faber, 26. "another world"; "you were ostracized . . . taboo"; "virtually kicked out": Arena interview. Much of the testimony of the cruel community reaction is recorded in the still closed Nixon Oral History Collection, Whittier College.

38   "insisted" return "down home": Faber, 26 "jolly and . . . nice"; "didn't like to join": YN, Jane Beeson, 6. "generous"; "took it out of herself": YN, Timberlake, 43.

38   "took him over . . . make over him": YN, Timberlake, 51, 56. angry spanking: Arena interview.

39   the photo: see FNT, November 23, 1968, and Schulte, 18–19.

Chapter 2. Yorba Linda, 1913–22

Page

40   "anticipations of a little one"; "timid and certainly modest": Butz, 107.

40   record cold wave: *The Register* (Orange County), November 11, 1968; see also YN, Dixon, 6, Butz, 20–21, and *Los Angeles Daily Times*, January 9, 1913.

40–41   birth: Ella Eidson's accounts are in FNT, December 31, 1968, and Schulte, 3ff. (under the name Ella Furnas). Readers should also be aware that the Shulte collection edits many of the YN interviews, with sometimes notable omissions from the original dialogue. Harold in tow: Spaulding, 28.

41   "screamer": Hoyt, 180. "decided voice": Abrahamsen, 24. "real good looking": H. Nixon.

41 "I've got another boy": YN, Corbit, 9.

41 breast-fed Russell Harrison: see YN, Parsons interview. frailty: she had already begun to suffer from the gallstone condition that would plague her the rest of her life, and she was beset by recurrent ear infections during Richard's first year. "putting up such a squall"; "a good preacher": YN, Timberlake, 40, 52–53.

41–42 posed with pumpkins: Spaulding, 30. "not lots of fun": Eidson Evans interview, UU.

42 "got along with his dad"; "never heard a cross word": YN, Burdg, 7, 4.

42 "never a crybaby . . . around his father": Brodie, 68. "wanted his way": YN, Shook, 8. "used to cry loud"; "biggest crybaby in Yorba Linda . . . dad could hear me": YN, Ryan, 7, 10.

42 "Bird": H. Nixon. "quite a talker . . . when he got big": YN, Burdg, 3.

42 "first thing . . . wanted": UU, Johns. "a fastidiousness . . . not . . . one you wanted to cuddle": Jessamyn West interview, UU.

43 "up and bawling": Eidson Evans interview, UU. "managed to get up"; hiding scar: Nixon, RN, 3. Olive Milhous Marshburn (UU) remembered Austin's reassurance of a shaken Hannah.

43 "many a start": Gardner, 19. "any other tow-headed": YN, Shook, 8ff.

43 "always sickly"; "ill a great deal": see Evans, Howard, and Johns interviews, UU. Another neighbor thought Harold "weakly" but "healthy all the time he lived in Yorba Linda." See YN, Pickering, 9, 24–25.

44 "one vast sanitorium . . . soothing death beds": McWilliams, 99–100.

44 "burning cheeks": West, Hide and Seek, 133.

44 "a horrifying earthquake": Butz, 11. The Yorba heritage is traced in Butz, 8–17 and Virgil Sharol Buck, "An Historical Study of the Yorba Linda School District," a 1967 Master's Thesis at Chapman College. Bernardo's father, who signed his bequest with an X, was a royal escort of Father Junipero Serra in the founding of California's missions.

44 "happy tranquil days": quoted in David J. Langum, "From Condemnation to Praise: Shifting Perspectives on Hispanic California," California History no. 4 (Winter 1983): 284. Robert Louis Stevenson in his 1880 essay "The Old Pacific Capital" thought the Spanish "curiously unfitted to combat Yankee craft."

45 "great black soaring buzzards": West, Hide and Seek, 236. "sun came up . . . evening breezes sprang up": West, "On Words and Men," 2.

45 Janss: the empire is described in part in LAT, May 30, 1971, and in the founder's obituary, LAT, March 6, 1972.

45 "choice ranches": the ads appeared in the Orange County Tribune, May 25, 1910. "inexhaustible . . . water"; gallons per plot: Butz, 21.

45 "loaf sugar": YN, Pickering, 14.

45–46 "like brick dust . . . stock could drink it": Schulte, 20; YN, Pickering, 2. "very nearly desert": Hoyt, 175. eighteen-inch icicles: Butz, 20.

46 "just visible at the pass": West, Hide and Seek, 22. hair white with dust: YN, Pickering, 2. vicious blow: Butz, 91

46 salted promise: The Register (Orange County), November 11, 1968, gives an account of the settlers' struggle.

46–47 "outdoor hothouse"; "gold coast": McWilliams, 208, 207. "needed capital . . . habits . . . ability": J. Eliot Coit in McWilliams, 214. As the industry grew apace after 1890, stories of success and wealth were common, and reported earnings of $1,000 to $3,000 per acre.

47 Nixon house: still standing, it and others in the area, including the Wests', are described in the California Department of Parks and Recreation Historic Resources Inventory (Sacramento). See Serial numbers 30–2621–1 and 30–2621–3. Mrs. Cecil Pickering, 13, also describes the interior in the YN interviews. livestock: Brodie, 67.

47 "full of young men"; "mighty raw": West interview, UU. "coyotes . . . thick"; "nothing except dust": YN, Pickering, 5.

48 "white Anglo": YN, H. Warner, 11.

48 "took it away": YN, Pickering, 10. "capital of the world": Butz, 30.

48–50 "a simple home": this and her ensuing quotations and impressions of the period are from Mary Elizabeth Rez, YN, who recorded that Hannah was "all worn out" after caring for Harold.

49 "nothing . . . cushioned": YN, Critchfield, 19. The house did have piano by 1916, Rez noted, though none of the boys appeared interested in it.

50 "very strict parents": Schulte, 8.

50 "too lenient": LAT, July 24, 1960. "angel unaware . . . wasn't exerting her will power": Marshburn interview, UU.

51 "let you choose any side": YN, Shook, 3. "clip a hedge": Spaulding, 93, who also calls him, 22, "forever the disrupter."

51 "not lickety-split like his dad": YN, Shook, 9.

51 "fired up . . . got over it just as fast"; "never . . . carried any grudges": YN, Corbit, 26. "boisterous geniality": West, *Hide and Seek*, 239. "Frank was . . . different": Jackson, 54A.

51 job to job; boys' chores: for the most part, Frank went on maintaining orchards for absentee owners, some of them friends of Franklin Milhous. He joined Fred Johnson during 1916–17 in a small business to haul and sell feed and fuel, while continuing to carpenter and maintain orchards. Johnson's Victorian script ledger of their sales (copy in CSU) duly carried the receipted "assistance" of Richard Milhous and Donald Francis Nixon, scarcely ages five and three.

52 "argue either one or both": YN, Corbit, 27. "head over heels": YN, Shook, 3.

52 Frank fights Janss and pool: see YN, Johnson interview. "a little radical": YN, Burdg, 8. "he might be out . . . with a banner": YN, Shook, 19. Shook thought him "more than a liberal . . . a pink tinge . . . a pink," and quotes another Yorba Linda friend, George Kellogg, calling Frank Nixon "very much of a liberal-minded fellow."

52 "just went pale and white": Coughlan, 148. "arguments stiffened"; portrait of Bryan: Kornitzer, 78. "seething with discontent": McWilliams, 288.

52 "with it": West, "Four Years—For What?," *Whittier College Bulletin*, May 1954, 17.

53 "His cheeks flamed . . . at least be ethical": West, *Hide and Seek*, 239–40.

53 "Grace, I swear": West, *Hide and Seek*, 239. "not much hugging or kissing"; "real manly"; "pincher and squeezer": West interview, UU.

53 "lost in bed"; "a Milhous in bed"; "his amorous propensities": West, *Hide and Seek*, 101, 239.

54 "considered . . . refined": YN, Critchfield, 7. "timid": YN, Gauldin, 3. "quite reserved"; "stay-at-home": Schulte, 12. errands of mercy and death-bed promise: see Marshburn interview, UU; YN, Johnson interview.

54 "She would have been there": YN, Shook, 14. See YN, Johnson interview. "balance the wheel": YN, W. Barton, 6. "Nobody could dominate Frank": YN, Shook, 4.

54 "she wanted to please": Marshburn interview, UU. "ruled . . . by love": YN, Rez, 10.

55   "crazy out there . . . overwhelmed": Arena and Rothmann interviews. "run into it more": YN, Timberlake, 22.

55   "only kept us poor": H. Nixon. "wouldn't consider them poor at all": Howard interview, UU. "above . . . middle income": YN, Shaw, 57. "modest circumstances": YN, Corbit, 12.

55   elegant china closet: see West interview, UU. YN, Critchfield, 6, 7, 22, describes Frank's "touring car," a possession her parents and others in the tract did not enjoy.

55–56   "always . . . ties . . . hats": Schulte, 27. "a little better": YN, Critchfield, 18. "always . . . money": Marshburn interview, UU. "landed gentry": West interview, UU.

56   "in a string"; adults napping: YN, Shook, 1; Critchfield, 42. "California!": West, Hide and Seek, 88.

56   "outside her status": McPherson interview, Rothmann interview. "arrogance about the Milhouses": Hoyt, 183. "To think thee's gone" "no one to answer my call": Thoughts in Verse, 19, 21.

57   "Hannah had quite a problem": McPherson interview. The Milhouses were not the only intrusion in the bungalow. Samuel Brady Nixon died in 1914, and his widow, Lutheria, later moved to Southern California, living for a time with Frank and the family, as did Frank's half-brother, Hugh, and his widowed sister, Carrie Wildermuth. Moreover, Franklin Milhous visited Yorba Linda regularly to oversee other property he owned there. Relatives were a sprawling, nearly constant presence in their lives in the years before 1920. Family tensions took on a doctrinal cast with U.S. entry into World War I. Though the pacifism of basin Quakers was long since diluted, reaction to the hostilities was mixed, with an undercurrent of pro-German sentiment as well as the wave of national chauvinism sweeping the area. Fred Johnson recalled being "ostracized" for not buying war bonds, and Harold Nixon told friends he had once been forced to kiss the American flag because of his presumed lack of patriotism as a Quaker. Whereas Oscar Marshburn, Olive's fiancé, volunteered for the Friends ambulance corps much to the approval of the Milhouses, Hugh Nixon enlisted as a doughboy with Frank's vocal enthusiasm, another symbol of the grating incompatibility of Hannah's family and her husband.

57–58   "a real live doll!" et seq.: from Richard Nixon's "My Brother, Arthur R. Nixon," handwritten in a ruled composition book and given to Bela Kornitzer by Hannah Nixon in 1959. See Kornitzer, 61–66.

58   "I want a girl": YN, Shook, 4.

58   "withdrawn"; "this will all be built up . . . awfully funny": YN, Critchfield, 23–25.

59   school scene: see YN, Barton and Ryan interviews. "freshly starched white shirt . . . joined in . . . scrubbed . . . funny thing": Mary Skidmore interview in Schulte, 78.

59   "absolutely the three R's": Schulte, 81. "Please call my son Richard": Schulte, 78.

59–60   "like a blotter": Schulte, 78. "very envious": YN, Critchfield, 3. "photographic mind": Schulte, 81. "Richard could say it": YN, Pickering, 24. George thought he had completed "thirty or forty books, maybe more," by year's end.

60   "by himself . . . solemn child"; "not to play around": Schulte, 78, 82.

60–61   "so jealous": YN, Critchfield, 4. "didn't think it was necessary": Schulte, 34. "wanted to run everything": YN, Shook, 16.

61   "No child prodigy": Hannah in LAT, September 18, 1960. "beyond . . . usual grasp . . . such a weight": Kornitzer, 45. sex education pamphlet: West interview, UU. "seemed to need me more": H. Nixon. "wanted his mother

alone": Olive Marshburn in Abrahamsen, 84. "lots to say": see YN, Iwatsuru interview.

61   "I didn't understand . . . Frank, of course": West, *Hide and Seek*, 240.

61–62   "natural ear": H. Nixon. "switch in her hand": YN, Critchfield, 6.

62   childhood play: see YN, Shaw, West, and Critchfield interviews. "haunted house": Nixon, *RN*, 3.

62   "marked you": Vera Glaser, "She Whispered Six Names into the President's Ear," Women's News Service dispatch, May 1969, CSU.

62   "idyllic": Nixon, *RN*, 3. "sweetest music": Mazo, 20.

62–63   "while Richard would . . . read": Schulte, 35. "a leader but not . . . serious": YN, Critchfield, 45.

63   "sort of took the stage": YN, Timberlake, 52. "never can recall him laughing": YN, Critchfield, 12, who remembered Richard "hooping it up when we were playing boats or . . . cars, but never that giggling fun." "very competitive . . . a game out of this": YN, Wildermuth, 2. "sensitive . . . real desire to win": YN, Sheldon Beeson, 3.

63   "my baby brother's life": Kornitzer, 64. "badly spoiled": YN, Pickering, 7.

64   "miserable . . . ditch": YN, Rez, 7. YN, Cecil Pickering, 7, tells the story of Frank backing the car into the canal.

64   "no child in his right mind . . . that forbidden stream": West, "Four Years— For What?" 16.

64   "never yelled at them . . . cross . . . you mustn't do that": YN, Pickering, 9. once whipped Harold so hard: see YN, Merle West interview as well as Marshburn interview, UU. "sure yanked them out": YN, Merle West, 9. "Frank, you'll kill them!": Jessamyn West interview, UU.

64   "temper . . . impressed me most": Nixon, *RN*, 6.

64–65   "afraid of Frank . . . thrashed": YN, Johnson interview. "awful temper": YN, Ryan, 7. "I got the strap": Bewley interview, UU. "learned early"; "ever spanked Richard": Kornitzer, 78–79. Cecil Pickering remembered Richard's surprise when he encountered discipline from another quarter. While Hannah was distracted with one of Arthur's illnesses and Pickering was caring for the other children, Richard misbehaved, and his mother told the neighbor to "spank him if he doesn't mind you." "I just gave him two swats," she said, "and his eyes were that big!"

65   "All of us . . . with minimum": see YN, Shook, 5, 6, 14. "won't buy fertilizer": YN, Pickering, 13. "didn't do anything . . . very stubborn . . . because he was Mr. Nixon": Schulte, 79, 83.

66    $45,000 offer: see YN, Smith, 5. "fairy tale stuff": West interview, UU.

66   caste economy: McWilliams, 218–26, who writes, "It would be difficult to imagine a sharper line of social cleavage than that which separates these . . . workers from . . . the managerial elite." *IWW* on packinghouse: YN, Critchfield, 30. "couldn't keep it clean": Schulte, 21. For a description of the 60,000-square-foot Yorba Linda lemon house, see Butz, 123–24.

66–67   "sixteen weeks of misery": Mazo, 21–22. "We would work": Spaulding, 44. "hard but happy": Nixon, *RN*, 4. "spotlessly clean . . . they'd look clean": YN, Critchfield, 43. "Richard was ashamed . . . difference": see YN, Corbit, 17, and Pickering interview.

67   Franklin's bequest: his brother William, even more prosperous, pledged in 1919 a $50,000 contribution to build a Whittier Hospital. See Arnold and Clark, 186–87.

67   "tired to death": West interview, UU. approach to Mundts: WDN(I). measuring traffic and deliberations: David, 51; Mazo, 21. sold at a loss: from the original $150 per acre paid by Franklin Milhous.

67 disparaging stories: see Hoyt, 182. Richard told the story of lost wealth to de Toledano (1956) and others; Hannah repeated it in "A Mother's Story." Though two early biographers, Gardner and Mazo, were essentially correct in their versions, Spaulding returned to the theme in 1972, writing that Frank Nixon had foolishly passed up a chance to be wealthy in both Yorba Linda and Sante Fe Springs.

68 "simply starved out": Schulte, 30. "liked the whole family . . . quite a loss": YN, Corbit, 27.

68 "rancher was a liar": YN, Pickering, 14.

Chapter 3. East Whittier, 1922–26

Page

69 "Brisk cities": Ernest Peixotto, *Romantic California* (New York, 1927), 256.

69 "one of the prettiest": YN, Randall, 30. "like a June bride": Schulte, 135.

70–71 Whittier in the twenties: see YN, Schuyler, Triggs, Williams, Arroues, Randall, Smith, West, Saxton, Palmer, and Dixon interviews. Earl Chapman in Schulte, 134, tells the story of the doughboy dance and community outrage.

70 "rendezvous for . . . undesirables": Arnold and Clark, 215. "just knew . . . weren't wanted": YN, Randall, 29.

70 "unwritten agreements": YN, Otterman, 33. YN, Marcelina Arroues, 5, tells of the more open "law against blacks" in neighboring Brea. racial discrimination in churches: see YN, Brannon, 12 and Cato and Funk, 14. "pecking order . . . cleavage": YN, Smith, 8–9. KKK: "Anaheim Regime: Once It Was the Klan," LAT, September 6, 1970.

71 "no particular poverty . . . little criminals": YN, Randall, 30. "fifty miles away": YN, Perry, 4.

71 moves and house on Santa Gertrudes: see YN, Saxton, Schuyler; Costello, 21, Abrahamsen, 91. The station property had been part of the original Leffingwell purchase in 1880. Lot 10, Tract 3359, it had been owned by Mr. and Mrs. W. F. Mundt and was little more than a quarter of an acre, running 270 feet southwest along Santa Gertrudes, with 114 feet of frontage on the Boulevard, the old Los Angeles and Santa Ana Road.

71–72 amid great ranches: Schulte, 153–56. Paul Smith remembered the "atmosphere of the . . . neighborhood . . . one of affluence," and the Leffingwell and Murphy giants having "a profound effect upon Richard Nixon" as examples of "foresight" and "development."

72 "out in the desert": YN, Ryan, 1. "customers lined up": Wills, 162. $2,500 in tire sales: Gardner, 23. The history of the East Whittier Friends building is traced in Arnold and Clark, 283–84.

72 "getting right to work . . . quiet . . . history and geography": YN, Burum, 3, 22–23. perfect attendance: *Kansas City Star*, October 31, 1955.

72–73 letters: reproduced, the latter in the original, in Kornitzer, 57–58. "Psychiatrists will undoubtedly have a field day," Bela Kornitzer wrote all too accurately of the "My Dear Master" letter Hannah Nixon had proudly and artlessly given him in 1959.

73–74 debates: WDN(I); Spaulding, 56. "importance of fighting hard": Mazo, 24.

74–75 Terhune and Kelland: recorded in Nixon's own handwriting in response to constituent questions about childhood reading, see VPA "Favorites" File, Series 320–253. "tapeworm . . . Down East cross": NYT, February 19, 1964 in Kelland's obituary. "He studied . . . public consciousness": from Kelland's *The Highflyers* (New York, 1918).

75   "Never a day . . . light in his eyes": Spaulding, 53, 55.

75–76   "clubhouse" and play: YN, Sutton, 5; Wildermuth, 7. not "very close": YN, Mendenhall, 7. "peacemaker . . . cut loose . . . went back a year": Wills, 171. "not a happier boy": Kornitzer, 64.

76   "our gossipy neighbors": compare Kornitzer, 61–64, and the version in *A Self Portrait* (script of a film prepared for the 1968 Republican Convention, text in Mugar Library, Boston University).

76–77   Almira's levees: YN, Sheldon Beeson, 4; Paldanius, 5. "matriarchy"; "special interest: Nixon, *RN*, 13. "real favorite": YN, Sheldon Beeson, 4. "see her especially": YN, Agnes (Mrs. Herman) Brannon, 7.

77   "five-dollar bill" and inscription: Nixon, *RN*, 13. "away by himself"; "star-gazing": Johns interview, UU. "off by himself": Mazlish, 54.

77   "small, dark, and old-fashioned": YN, I. Chapman, 18; YN, Schuyler, 4 ff., describes the considerable trade with the hands from the big ranches, limited only by the store's inventory.

77–78   "Come tomorrow . . . marvelous pies": YN, Schuyler, 5. "As soon as . . . able": Jackson, 54B. "So you'd come home . . . mostly study and work": LAT, May 10, 1969; Abrahamsen, 49.

78   "thumper": Hoyt, 188, and Gardner, 28. "He could be hard . . . give them cracks": Abrahamsen, 91. "big voice": YN, Wildermuth, 16. "tempestuous arguments": Nixon, *RN*, 6.

78   "Just don't argue": Coughlan, 148. "never find him . . . we'd hunt him": YN, Wildermuth, 6. "like two bulls": YN, West, 8. "boys . . . as big a hollerer": YN, Wildermuth, 16. "Dick talk wild": YN, West, 8 *et seq*. "Now hush . . . you make them hush": Gardner, 25. The theme of Frank Nixon's verbal abuse, and of the sons' angry retaliation, runs throughout the recollections of relatives and acquaintances in this period. See YN as well as Schulte, Coughlan, Gardner, and Brodie.

79   "slop Jake": YN, Parsons, 7. "towering angers": Wills, 166.

79   Sheriff and Sunday school: YN, Kraushaar, 5. "argued vehemently": Nixon, *RN*, 6. "I hate Standard Oil": YN, Smith, 24. "line . . . to see her": YN, Jane Beeson, 12. It was a standing family joke to "rescue" customers: see Nixon, *RN*, 6 ff.; and some patrons seemed "afraid" of the encounters: see Brodie, 44, 54. Sheldon Beeson (YN, 6) thought Frank had reversed the usual commercial rule, and "the customer was always wrong."

79   "made you feel welcome": YN, Letts, 24. "all the Nixons . . . like this": YN, Wildermuth, 23. "just Frank's way": YN, Herman Brannon, 23.

79–80   "interesting aspect": YN, William Milhous, 9. compassion and credit: see YN, Mendenhall. "they all had some food . . . wasn't . . . talked about": YN, Kraushaar, 5. Wills, 166, describes his charity given in "fierce privacy," though he also calls it "recriminative."

80   "Hannah up there?": YN, Parsons, 8. no physical affection: see YN, Herman Brannon, 24 ff. "yell at her, too": YN, Mendenhall, 13.

80   "honking the horn": YN, Paldanius. 22. leaves showers early: YN, Timberlake, 12. "grandmother . . . mad . . . Uncle Frank would be calling": YN, Lucille Harrison, Parsons, 8.

81   "avoid an argument": YN, William Milhous, 9. "My husband . . . a debater . . . tried to soothe": H. Nixon. "never complained . . . you knew she was": YN, Letts, 4.

81 "I tried not to yell": Kornitzer, 40. "immensely effective with that voice"; "And my mother had known about it": *A Self Portrait.*

82 "if he had been the disciplinarian he thought he was": YN, Wildermuth, 17.

83 "convinced": Nixon, *RN*, 9. "quite a normal boy": YN, Jane Beeson, 11. "little simple things" and progress: Schulte, 56; YN, Jane Beeson, 9; Spaulding, 45. See also YN, Sheldon Beeson.

83 "I'm going to be an honest lawyer": YN, Jane Beeson, 12. The story is also frequently told with Richard saying the same words to his mother in East Whittier, a sequel that may be accurate as well, though it fits the later political legend too easily. The timing of publicity on the Teapot Dome scandal, as well as the proximity of Elk Hills, gives credence to the Lindsay version.

83 "I learned later": Kornitzer, 65. "Even at that age": Nixon, *RN*, 9. "sort of a loner": Marshburn interview, UU.

84 "The doctors are afraid"; "how much he enjoyed it": Nixon, *RN*, 10. "wish you had another baby . . . So you would stay home": Dorn interview, UU. "I can still see Richard . . . silent and dry-eyed": H. Nixon. "not a day": Nixon, *RN*, 10.

84 "the ways of our Lord": Mazo, 25. See also Faber, 27–29. "feelings of remorse": Marshburn interview, UU. "half believed . . . divine displeasure": Nixon, *RN*, 10. Arthur's death certificate, inaccurately giving his name as "Arthur Burch [sic] Nixon" and indicating treatment from July 29 to August 10, 1925 by Dr. H. P. Wilson, including "blood and spinal fluid" tests, recorded the cause of death as "Encephalitis or tubercular meningitis." But Dr. Wilson listed the origin or contracting of the disease as "not determinable," and there would be no autopsy. In the family there were persistent rumors, even mystery, about the tragedy, with some stories that Arthur had been struck in the head with a rock. See Gardner, as well as Sanden and Marshburn interviews, UU. Floyd Wildermuth (YN, Wildermuth, 18) remembered "they would never say exactly what it was he died of."

85 "lively and gay": Gardner, 23. "stirred within Richard . . . his need to succeed": H. Nixon.

85 "outstanding member": Gardner, 37. "My plans for the future": J. Eisenhower, 85. "Footprints on the tennis court": Jackson, 54B.

85–86 "extremely religious . . . fanatic"; "following the death": YN, Letts, 16. refuses to eat at church: YN, Parsons, 11. heated testimony, "not the kind": YN, Letts, 16.

86 "basic . . . evangelical belief": YN, Burbank, 4. "just like Methodists": YN, Burum, 6. "stand up . . . set them straight"; "If God is for us": YN, Burbank, 12, 17.

86–87 "We must have a revival": YN, Smith, 5. "mostly lower-middle-class": McWilliams, 262. revivalists in general: McWilliams, 249–62, 343.

87 "both fascinated"; "never went to bed": Nixon, *RN*, 14. Frank "faithfully": YN, Jane Beeson, 17. "We joined hundreds": NYT, January 26, 1969. The original passage is from Richard Nixon's own testimonial in Reverend Billy Graham's monthly magazine, *Decision,* November, 1962. See also Mazlish, 31.

87–88 "much more of a swinger"; "headstrong, devil-may-care": Abrahamsen, 86, 89. "like a bug": YN, Palmer, 16. "too much like his father": Faber, 28.

88–89 "Hannah wasn't too happy": Marshburn interview, UU. Mr. Moody's School: Morrow interview. Relatives mistakenly thought the school "more or less Friends." See YN, Timberlake, 23. "never particularly religious": Nixon, *RN*, 12. "weren't strapped for money": Marshburn interview, UU. "needed a change": YN, Parsons, 5.

Chapter 4. Intervals—Fullerton, Prescott, Whittier Union, 1926–30

Page

90   "give back the sunshine": McWilliams, 359. "Americanization"; "foreigners": *The Pleiades, 1927* (Fullerton Union High School Yearbook). See YN, Letts, 18–22, and Schulte, 96 ff. for a further description of the community.

91   "great pains": H. Nixon. "other children didn't smell good": Jackson, 54A. grades: from the "Permanent Record of Fullerton Union High School," copy in CSU. "knew all the answers": YN, Letts, 3; Sutton, 4.

91   geometry: Coughlan, 148. "remarks and cracks": YN, Burbank, 4. Otis score: "Permanent Record," CSU.

91–92   "shy . . . not a born speaker" *et seq.*: Gardner, 38. contest record: see Gardner and *The Pleiades, 1928.* "skill as . . . superior education": Cannon.

92   "We argued all the way": Kornitzer, 52. "just the argument": YN, Letts, 2.

92   "scrappy": FNT, November 7, 1968. "He used to be the dummy": YN, Shaw, 43. "terrific beating": Schulte, 100. "right back up . . . always there . . . tried so hard": Schulte, 103.

93   "so ill at ease": YN, Critchfield, 14–15.

93   "very much at ease" *et seq.*: YN, Heffern, 11 ff.

93   "grown up . . . considered the farmers": YN, Heffern, 10. "a certain group . . . outside looking in": YN, Letts, 22.

93–94   "a loner": YN, Heffern, 6. "never . . . the nerve": Coughlan, 151. "wouldn't let me disobey"; "dislike us girls so! . . . make horrible faces": Kornitzer, 54.

94   "expensive private sanatorium": Nixon, *RN*, 11. "father refused": Nixon, *RN*, 7. "go to the grave": Costello, 21. For the early efforts to treat Harold, see also YN, Critchfield, 45, Wildermuth, 19, and Dorn interview, UU.

94   "very dangerous work . . . against . . . orders": Abrahamsen, 89.

95   "Please use cups": see "Growing Up In Prescott," *Arizona Highways*, August 1985: "Prescott, Pearl of the Pines," *Arizona Highways*, July 1935; Melissa Ruffner Weiner, *Prescott: A Pictorial History*, AHS; "At Pamsetgaaf," *The Paper* (Prescott, Arizona), July 15, 1976.

95   bags of groceries: Brandt interview; Hough interview, UU. For a description of the house and setting, see Bumpus interview, UU, with the woman who purchased it in 1930.

95   entrust store; regular trips: Brandt interview; YN, Timberlake, 36; Nixon, *RN*, 11. The old route is described in a 1935 promotional pamphlet, "Prescott and Yavapai County," ASU.

96   "sort of like leprosy": Williams interview, UU. "keep his distance": Hough interview, UU. "dark and serious": Gay interview, UU. "till the butter butts: Williams interview, UU.

96–97   "square . . . sissy": Clough interview, UU. "hard-working"; "most exclusive": Ruffner interview. "most popular": Costello, 23. "basic education": Ruffner interview.

97   "never touch alcohol"; "practicing both sides": Clough interview, UU. "a rather sad life": Brandt interview, UU.

97–98   flirtations: Brandt interview. "She was cute": Gay interview, UU. "scared me to death": Brandt interview. "what she wanted": Clough interview, UU. "pure steel": Arena interview. "He just insisted": YN, Timberlake, 25.

98 "he wasn't taking care": YN, Palmer, 9. "strong-headed": YN, Sutton, 7. "None of them": Brandt interview; Bumpus interview, UU.

99 "pains cleaning . . . produce": H. Nixon.

99 "old Dick could peel": YN, West, 5. "I never drive by": WDN, July 28, 1955. "Dick hated it": YN, Smith, 6. "He didn't want anybody to see him": YN, Parsons, 3. refuses apron: see YN, Cato and Funk, 16; Parsons, 4.

99 "pretty good"; "no outside labor": YN, West, 10–11. sold parcel: YN, Schuyler, 15.

99 "never thought . . . ourselves . . . poor": Alsop transcript.

99–100 "only ones": A Self Portrait (script of a film prepared for the 1968 Republican Convention, text in Mugar Library, Boston University). He went on to relate how his parents compensated: "My mother . . . got some bunting," and "my father went out and got some ice cream, and what a feast we had!" "more fireworks than we did": YN, Wright, 14. "didn't have to be as tight": YN, Parsons, 6.

100 "Odd . . . still like . . . those things": Mazo, 25. "always watched his diet": H. Nixon. "always bickering": YN, Sheldon Beeson, 5.

100 "very fact of separation": Nixon, RN, 11. "couldn't get along without her": YN, E. Brannon, 4. "difficult time . . . those of us who remained home": A Self Portrait.

101–2 "hit the line hard": Gardner, 44. "Many, many . . . had jobs": YN, Nichols, 7. "tired of arguing": Gardner, 47; also see Hoyt, 191. "walked right by": YN, Agnes (Mrs. Herman) Brannon, 18. "famous overnight": YN, G. Ellis Triggs, 3.

102 "never one to just goof around": YN, Sheldon Beeson, 3–4. "got to dig": Gardner, 46. "hardly keep him": Newsom interview, UU. "pound the table": YN, Palmer, 14. "ability to . . . slide round": Costello, 23. "something mean": White, 59.

102–3 "offended some . . . admired rather than liked him": WDN(I). "dogmatic, pedagogical": YN, Forrest Randall, 1.

103 "seeking to promulgate . . . pietistic interpretation"; "sore point": YN, Wray, 4–5. cheers and PTA pays: YN, Elizabeth Rees Glover, 4.

103–4 "splendid oration": WDN, April 25, 1929. "The framers": WDN, January 18, 1969 and East Whittier Review, January 19, 1969 reprinted both his 1929 and 1930 orations.

104–5 "white spot"; "Red Squad"; "Shove Tuesdays" et seq.: McWilliams, 289–313, traces the reaction. vigilantes attack and scald: Howard A. DeWitt, Images of Ethnic and Radical Violence in California Politics, 1917–1930 (San Francisco, 1975), 102. DeWitt notes the riot went on amid "raucous laughter," and the vigilantes later "took nine Wobblies to Santa Ana Canyon and beat them almost to death"; "bloodiest arena": Morrow Mayo in McWilliams, 277.

105–6 "America's Progress" et seq.: WDN, January 18, 1969.

107 The results of the competition are charted in Cardinal and White, 1930 (Whittier High School Yearbook). "His mother didn't like that": YN, Hadley Marshburn, 6.

107–8 "the political machine": Mazo, 21. See also WDN(I). Logue was "a very nice person": YN, Elizabeth Rees Glover, 9. "hotly contested . . . sandwich boards": WDN(I). campaign: see FNT, November 7, 1968, Schulte, 119, and the interview with Robert Logue, East Whittier Review, January 19, 1969.

108 "ever did have smooth going": Newsom interview, UU. "colorless . . . wonderful missionary": YN, Randall, 21. "didn't care whose feet . . . students hated him": Johns interview, UU.

108 "had something new . . . no hard feelings": WDN(I). "I suffered my first": Nixon, RN, 14.

108-9   "He took care of the details": Flynn. *Aeneid* episode: Nixon, *RN*, 14. "I'll do anything": Kornitzer, 56.

109   "so romantic": Spaulding, 61. "I just about died": Ola Welch Jobe interview, UU. "really quite handsome": Shearer. "smartest man that ever was": Morgan transcripts.

109-10   "brought her out to the best": YN, G. Ellis Triggs, 3. Prom *et seq.*: YN, Nichols, 3; David, 56-57.

110   "anything fast": Marshburn interview, UU. "a good father"; sixty dollars a month: Clough interview, UU.

110   class prophecy: *Cardinal and White, 1930* (Whittier High School Yearbook); YN, Nichols. "stay away from Brunettes": Casoni, 7.

110-11   "dreamed of going . . . east"; "enormous expense": Nixon, *RN*, 14-15. "We needed Richard": H. Nixon.

111   "above average . . . good citizen": Gardner, 49. "Richard didn't think": Dotson interview. "nothing could have dimmed": Nixon, *RN*, 15.

Chapter 5. Whittier College, 1930-34

Page

115   "cuddled up here": YN, M. Wray, 16. For descriptions of the college as it was in the early 1930s, see Gardner, 51; Wills, 152; YN, Hornaday, Triggs and Gibbs; *The Acropolis 1930-34* (Whittier College Yearbook), WCA.

115-16   two flags: YN, Smith, 22.

116   "We invite you down"; "They loved us": see YN, Hornaday. "cheated . . . and vice versa": YN, Stout.

116   "in social terms": *Whittier College Bulletin, 1933-34*, 38, WCA.

116-17   "for more rapid change": YN, Smith, 18-19. Maxwell Anderson episode: Schulte, 150. "Now things smell better" *et seq.*: Hoyt, 199. social origins of students: see YN, Tani, Edith Brannon; *Whittier College Bulletin, 1930-31*, 41-44, WCA.

117   "aristocrats of the campus": YN, Farnham, 18. "kept out the poor": Brodie, 113. "didn't think . . . democratic": YN, Hornaday, 26.

117-18   "considerable experience": QC, September 19, 1930. reception: QC, September 26, 1930. "road to hell": Morgan transcripts.

118   "only trophy": Nixon, *RN*, 19. "no athletic ability": YN, Wunder, 3. "I remember running": Nixon, *RN*, 1080. "Thanks, Wunder": YN, Wunder, 3-4.

118   "Get those crates back"; "out of scrapes": YN, Ellis Triggs, 10.

119   "didn't have invitations": YN, Murle Marshburn, 6.

119-20   "one *student*": YN, Triggs and Gibbs, 18. "push and hold . . . together": Jewell Triggs in *ibid.*, 23. "The bean boys": YN, Farnham, 18. constitution and song: Brodie, 14; Nixon, *RN*, 17.

120   "secret ritualistic stuff": YN, Burchell, 8. initiation: YN, Ellis Triggs, 12; see also YN, Otterman; Nixon's own letter to Dean Triggs, November 3, 1955, Whittier College File, VPA. "great deal of repercussion"; "all ended well . . . really going to do things": YN, Hornaday, 25.

120-21   "very tough thing": Brodie, 115. "big pigs": Gardner, 54. "ferment was ripe": YN, Wray, 6; WDN, January 18, 1969. "haves and . . . have-nots": Alsop, "The Mystery of Richard Nixon."

121   "something of an opportunist": YN, Harris, 7. "just as vicious": YN, Stout.

121   "impeachment": QC, March 20, 1931.

121–22   grades: Flynn. "needed the steady discipline": Nixon, *RN*, 15. "I'd see him": YN, Palmer, 7. "sitting at the . . . table": YN, Herman Brannon, 6. "head down, plodding": YN, Otterman, 17. "always in a hurry": Jackson, 57. invariably Nixon: YN, Perry, 17. "old place . . . in the corner": YN, Stout.

122   "superficial": West, *Hide and Seek*, 190.

123   Paul Smith "climbing" *et seq.*: YN, Otterman, 17; Hornaday, 9–10. "Cross of Gold": YN, Smith, 16. "the aliveness of it": YN, Ellis, 13–14. "behind it all": YN, Hornaday, 9–10. "very liberal": YN, Wray, 17. "gone assiduously through . . . deeply . . . involved": Kornitzer, 99.

123–24   Teggart's "book of caution": Jackson, 58. "analytical": YN, Smith, 2. "a brute": Jackson, 58. "always so brief . . . fast, if you can": YN, Smith, 2–3.

124   Upton's influence: Rothmann interview. "pretty salty": YN, Triggs and Gibbs, 12. "hated the ground"; "you know ain't true": Morgan transcripts. "And we did . . . Upton and Nixon . . . together": YN, Ingrum, 10.

125   "victim of . . . magic": *Current Biography, 1944*, 510. "would not be complete . . . became a Tolstoyan": Nixon, *RN*, 15. "middle-aged gentleman": *The Acropolis, 1931*, WCA. "deep voice . . . old man's face": Abrahamsen, 98. "tried to convert": Morgan transcript.

125–26   "a good cry": Upton interview, UU. "outstanding performance": QC, November, 18, 1932. "with a surety": *The Acropolis, 1933*, WCA. "Now, there are tricks": Kornitzer, 107. "loved the stage": Brodie, 115. "never coached": Morgan transcripts.

126   "nervous fits": Morgan transcripts.

126   "legs would give out": Nixon to Ross Rasmussen, June 4, 1957, Whittier College File, VPA. "marvelous . . . instinctive rapport": Mazlish, 62. "getting to an audience": Upton interview, UU. "didn't hurt his ego": Morgan transcripts. "as genius or . . . destined for greatness": WDN, January 18, 1969; Kornitzer, 104.

126–27   "typical American Quaker": Mazo, 26. "pure in heart"; "closest": Upton interview, UU. "iconoclast": Nixon, *RN*, 15–16.

127   "everything that he did": YN, Hornaday, 30. "I dropped the issue": Kornitzer, 238. turns down religious society: YN, Hornaday, 15.

127   "a growing tendency": Kornitzer, 61–62.

128–29   "What Can I Believe": Nixon, *RN*, 17.

129   "You have to be . . . careful": YN, Smith, 12.

130   "settle down": YN, K. Ball, 6. "impossible handwriting": Morgan transcripts. "some of the men didn't like": YN, Stout.

130   "May I make this . . . clear": YN, Hornaday, 5. "deadly rival": QC, October 2, 1931. "Sweeney was much better": YN, Stout. "father would always": YN, Ball, 2. "convinced free-trader": Nixon, *RN*, 17.

131   "not a . . . boisterous place": Nixon, *RN*, 18. "fluttering feminine hearts": QC, October 21, 1932.

131   "Blizzards, mix-ups": *The Acropolis, 1933*, WCA. "Nixon overwhelmed us": Taylor interview, UU; *The "Y" News* (Brigham Young University), January 26, 1933.

131–32   "merciless opponent": WDN, January 18, 1969. "opponent off-balance . . . learned his lesson": Gardner, 56. "get mad": Kornitzer, 112. "pour it on" *et seq.*: Brodie, 107; YN, Stout.

132   "come out suddenly": YN, K. Ball, 5. "never . . . unguarded": YN, Hornaday, 16. "going to the bow-wows": Morgan transcripts. "quoted from a blank paper": Abrahamsen, 111.

132-33   "all bones": YN, Triggs and Gibbs, 63. "undersized fellas": Newman [author's notes]. "He just nearly died": YN, Parsons, 14.

133   "If he could have run well": Newman [author's notes]. "guts": Morgan transcripts. "The harder you hit him": Jackson, 56. "I don't know why you do this": Kornitzer, 110.

133-34   "can't . . . remember Dick in bull sessions": Newman [author's notes]. "just a little remote": YN, Wood Glover, 9. "Dick's father . . . watching": Triggs and Gibbs, 39. "keyed up . . . whether Dick played or not": Newman interview, UU. "father and son": YN, Triggs and Gibbs, 61.

134   jumped in jalopies: YN, Hornaday, 13. "kicked around as a kid": YN, Triggs and Gibbs, 40. "willing to pay the price"; "Chief drove the fellows": Schulte, 189. "You know who a good loser is?": Nixon, *Public Papers, 1971*, 836. "You must get angry": Nixon, *Six Crises*, 402.

134-35   "I'll leave you girls alone": YN, Triggs and Gibbs, 51. "That's all he knew": YN, Ingrum, 6. "You ought to come out": Nixon, *Public Papers, 1971*, 836. "once out you can't quit": Newman [author's notes]. "pleasure . . . putting on a wet uniform": Schulte, 189. "some underhanded act": Kornitzer, 109. "tremendous roar": Alsop, *Nixon and Rockefeller*, 227.

135   "make Dick look good": Schulte, 187. "never saw anybody play harder": YN, Wunder, 7.

135-36   "my happiest memories"; "I admired him more": Nixon, *RN*, 19. "chicken dinner and Dick . . . played": YN, Wood Glover, 5. "enjoyed being around it": YN, Wood Glover, 3. "contact with those people": YN, Ingrum, 26.

136   "all having a rough time": YN, Wood Glover, 6. "families all camped around": YN, West, 10. "vagrancy" arrests; "Unemployment is a crime": McWilliams, 292.

136-37   "couple of hundred bucks": YN, West, 7. "I'll shoot to kill him": YN, Hadley Marshburn, 4. "good old Quaker . . . shoot any intruder": YN, Smith, 17–18.

137   "not all that serious": QC, October 16, 1931. "if you can bring in a dollar or two": YN, Hornaday, 13. "It was that close": Morgan transcripts.

137   student memories of poverty: Schulte, 195; Morgan transcripts; YN, Hornaday and Stout. "If you had fifty cents": YN, Wunder, 4.

137   "Dick got what he needed": YN, West, 10–11. huge Thanksgiving dinners: YN, Paldanius, 2. "lots of credit extended": YN, Mendenhall, 11–12. "We had to carry a lot of people": Alsop transcript.

137-38   "how deeply I felt": Nixon, *Public Papers, 1970*, 1124–25. "full of laughs and jokes": YN, West, 11, 28; see also Merle West interview, UU. "one out of fifty": YN, Lindstrom, 14. "half a dozen cars": YN, Halliday, 12. "one of the fortunate few": YN, Perry, 4.

138   "none of us had a tux": YN, Farnham, 18. "loaning me his new tuxedo": Spaulding correspondence.

138   "considered rich": Jessamyn West interview, UU.

138-39   "one of the things . . . used to argue about": Alsop transcript. "certain families": Kornitzer, 75.

139   shoplifter: Gardner, 63–64; H. Nixon; see also Wills, 163–64.

139   "isn't the gushy type"; "He'd get me to buy it": H. Nixon. "press his shirt": YN, Parsons, 14. "anything . . . but Richard's shirts": H. Nixon. Several relatives were enlisted to do his ironing if they happened to be around the house or store. See YN, Paldanius, 39. "everything was being done": Hough interview, UU.

139-40   "so cruel, so loud-mouthed": Jessamyn West interview, UU. "angry . . . argument with his father": Clough interview, UU.

140 "sophomore with the intellectual look": QC, October 10, 1931. "not conceited": QC, March 18, 1932. "wouldn't say . . . hail-fellow": Morgan transcripts. "intensely dislike or intensely like": Schulte, 218. "not the real friendly type": YN, Wunder, 1.

140–41 "always a tense person": YN, Triggs and Gibbs, 63. good "listener": YN, Perry, 13. "he ended it": YN, Ingrum, 8. "laying down the line": Triggs and Gibbs, 102. "he was stuffy": Morgan transcripts. "a kind of power attempt . . . [never] had self-confidence": YN, Perry, 21. "ruthless cocksureness": Kornitzer, 100.

141 no "close friends": Morgan transcripts. "probably me": Morgan transcripts. "just pals": YN, Halliday, 12.

141–42 "damn strong woman": Nunes interview, UU. "dignity of a true lady": *The Acropolis, 1934*, WCA. "made a handsome couple": Morgan transcripts. "matched intellectually": YN, Netzley, 11.

142 "why do you go out with him?": Morgan transcripts. "He wasn't sexy": YN, Triggs and Gibbs, 74. "Oh, Dick, come off it": Jackson, 56. "supposed to be having fun": Spaulding, 62. "no close boyfriends," *et seq.*: Ola's recollections are drawn from Morgan, "Whittier '34;" Morgan transcripts; Shearer; Jobe interview, UU; David; Abrahamsen; Jackson.

143 "her mother and father felt strongly": Abrahamsen, 104–5.

143 "combative . . . nasty temper": Mazlish, 63.

144 "Nixon more than enjoying": QC, May 5, 1933.

144 "accommodation date": YN, Sheldon Beeson, 13. "where the fire was": Triggs and Gibbs, 75. "have to needle Dick": Schulte, 193. "not in demand": Kornitzer, 102.

144–45 "embarrassed as he was": YN, Elizabeth Glover, 8. "wasn't one you'd find downtown": YN, Burchell, 12. "a lot of semi-dirty jokes": YN, West, 22. "with a broad smile": QC, April 21, 1933. "He felt comfortable with her": Abrahamsen, 102. "tacit agreement": David, 57. "foregone conclusion": David, 57. "all of us . . . expected": Shearer. "never really knew him": Jackson, 54a.

145–46 rode his own horse irrepressibly: see YN, Paldanius, 37–39 and Timberlake. tries to buy house; Harold's coming and going: see YN, West and Wildermuth.

146 "insisted on coming home"; "knew he was going to die": YN, Wildermuth, 18. "just gasping for breath": YN, West, 21. "sign of the last stages": YN, Palmer, 15. "One by one": Nixon, *RN*, 11.

146 "dropped everything": Nixon, *RN*, 12. "He loved . . . beauty": Abrahamsen, 90–91. his brother's voice: Nixon, *RN*, 12. "down, down, down": YN, West, 21, who also describes the trailer, but says the Nixons had it specially built for the trip.

146–47 "He barely had the strength": Nixon, *RN*, 12. "until we meet in heaven": Abrahamsen, 91. "crying uncontrollably": Nixon, *RN*, 12.

147 "a deep effect on him": H. Nixon. "fatalistic": Jackson, 56. Palmer (YN, Palmer, 7) recalled the family now all the more worried about Richard's sleepless nights of studying. College friends thought him "very closely observed for many years because he might be carrying the disease": YN, Triggs and Gibbs, 61.

147 "high hopes for him": Kornitzer, 60. "Why . . . the best and . . . brightest . . . taken first?"; "flower of the family": Jessamyn West interview, UU. "Harold accomplished as much": Abrahamsen, 90–91.

148 "desperate will to live": Nixon, *RN*, 12. "always incurable": Nixon, *RN*, 11. In fact, there were numerous recoveries among those under strict care, as

would be the case with Jessamyn West and others. "more than we could afford": Nixon, *Public Papers, 1970*, 1124; *Public Papers, 1974*, 127. one epitaph: Morrow interview.

148–49   "He didn't care about . . . popularity": YN, Hornaday, 34. "seemed to get dragged": Mazo, 43. "wanted to be president": Jobe interview, UU. "fireball": WDN(I).

149–50   "to hell with Oxy" *et seq.*: see YN, Soeberg, 14; Chisler, 9; Gaudio, 4; Hornaday, 19 ff.

150   "bringing a Negro": YN, Triggs and Gibbs, 92; see also YN, George. "My policy": QC, April 29, 1932. "unusually quiet": QC, May 6, 1932. "as large and gaudy a privy": de Toledano, 26.

151   "sort of a police force": YN, Hornaday, 23–24. "menial tasks": Schulte, 193. "logical steps": YN, Harris, 8.

151   "He couldn't stay": YN, Smith, 25; Hoyt, 209. "all they could eat": YN, Olive Marshburn, 10.

152   "no secret. . . . The logical man": QC, April 21, 1933.

152   "foregone conclusion": YN, Stout. "real organized fight": YN, Wunder, 7.

152   "students' choice . . . Thomson . . . has a better personality": QC, April 23, 1933.

153   "quite a bit of competition": Kornitzer, 101.

153   "didn't stand a chance . . . talked him out of giving up": Kornitzer, 103.

153–54   "heavy campaigning": QC, May 5, 1933. "If elected president": QC, May 5, 1933.

154   "There are none so blind": QC, October 10, 1930. "Why, it's terrible . . . went round and round": YN, Parsons, 12–13.

155   "not just the ones that might belong": YN, Wunder, 4. "a tremendous ability": YN, Merton Wray, 7. "dangerous platform": YN, Stout. "hedges planted": YN, K. Ball, 7.

155–56   "Nixon . . . a hard man to beat": QC, May 5, 1933. "banded together": YN, Burchell, 14.

156   "swung [the] election": Jobe interview, UU. "unusually quiet": QC, May 12, 1933.

156   "Dick Nixon . . . unscathed": *The Acropolis, 1934*, WCA. "necessarily low-keyed": Nixon, *RN*, 18. "he was smart": Morgan transcripts. "this . . . surprised me . . . a real smart politician": WDN(I). "a bitter attack": Gardner, 58–59.

156–57   "opportunity of becoming"; "a new deal": QC, May 19, 1933.

157   "I promised": YN, Wunder, 3. "he knew which ones to contact": YN, Soeberg, 11. "Surely . . . it would be better": Nixon, *RN*, 18–19.

157–58   "Think of the nerve": YN, Smith, 3. "we lost a lot of people": YN, George, 5. "have to be beholden": YN, Hornaday, 3.

158   "admirable leadership": QC, November 3, 1933. "he never disclosed": Schulte, 217. "something big": YN, Perry, 16. "become a congressman": YN, Stout. "watch him bristle": Morgan, "Whittier '34." "glad you're back, Nicky": QC, March 2, 1934. "Mr. Magnanimous Nixon"; "Great-Hearted": QC, April 27, 1934, May 4, 1934.

158   "don't think he knows what happened": Morgan transcripts. "all 'round good fellow": *The Acropolis, 1934*, WCA.

159   recommendations for Duke: de Toledano, 26–27; Gardner, 75–78.

159   "wasn't good enough": Jobe interview, UU; Shearer. "I had to call my folks": David, 58; see also Morgan transcripts and Jobe interview, UU. "we aren't going steady": Morgan transcripts.

159–60 "he was joyous, abandoned": Jackson, 57; Abrahamsen, 105. "pink and white disposition": QC, May 17, 1934.

160 Dexter as "radical": Upton interview, UU; Morgan transcripts. "Always progressive": *The Acropolis, 1934*, WCA. "cluster of strong people": Morgan transcripts.

160–61 "my early thinking": Nixon, *RN*, 17. "I didn't know what a prestige college was": Morgan transcripts. "pretty second-rate"; "all quite happy": YN, Stout.

161 "just passed him by": H. Nixon.

Chapter 6. Duke Law, 1934–37

Page

162 "such big plans": YN, Stanley, 3. "medieval cathedral town": Nixon, *RN*, 20.

163 "one thing money could not buy": Kiefer correspondence. "my deepest appreciation": Nixon–Dean Justin Miller, undated letter c. Spring 1934, Student Years File, Duke. "fourteen preachers": *The Duke Chronicle*, November 18, 1976.

163 "he did not eat as regularly": Alsop, *Nixon and Rockefeller*, 235. "reddish-purple sweater": *ibid.*, 237. "None of us had any money": Rubin interview, UU. "all scroungers": Kiefer interview, UU.

164 family means: H. Nixon; Kornitzer, 42, 275. Frank's property: YN, Hadley Marshburn, 3.

164 so "we could keep Dick at Whittier [sic]": LAT, December 16, 1971. "Hand over my wallet": H. Nixon; Kornitzer, 129.

165 counted Phi Beta Kappa keys: Mazo, 29. "You have what it takes": Spaulding, 99. "My memory was a great asset"; "I sometimes despaired": Nixon, *RN*, 20.

165–66 "like . . . martyrs facing the lions"; "first to stand up": Kornitzer, 117. "flat-footed and feet apart": Jackson, 54a.

166 "sad letters": Jackson, 57; Spaulding, 95. "as confused and homesick": Nixon–Oren Mollenkopf, June 26, 1959, Duke University Friends File, VPA.

166 "Without money and . . . friends": Kornitzer, 124. "a kind word": Mollenkopf–Nixon, March 27, 1959, Duke University Friends File, VPA.

167 Cady friendship: *The San Antonio Light*, November 20, 1968; see also miscellaneous clippings, Richard Milhous Nixon papers, Duke.

167 "pushing to help her"; "plight of the waitresses": Rubin interview, UU.

167 "I greatly enjoyed": Nixon–Dean H. C. Horack, June 21, 1935, Student Years File, Duke.

168 "Nothing mushy": Brodie, 123. "love letters": Jobe interview, UU. "Richard was furious": Mazlish, 64; Morgan, "Whittier '34." "you're going to have to learn something": Morgan transcripts. "still keeping Richard on the string": Shearer.

168–69 "I found him with Edward": H. Nixon. long drive back: see YN, Hadley Marshburn, 3, who relates Richard's distraction, and Rubin interview, UU. "as if we would get married": Jobe interview, UU. "he was very upset": Abrahamsen, 106. "ended abruptly": Morgan transcripts. "Gail Jobe . . . took her right away": Triggs and Gibbs, 75.

169 "Nixon wasn't": Morgan transcripts. "Who knows about him?": David, 57.

170 "intestinal theory of jurisprudence": Perdue interview, UU. "essential course": Nixon, *Six Crises*, 297. "into the jungles of . . . Durham" *et seq.*: Gardner, 81–82.

171   "informality . . . friendly": Kiefer correspondence. "personally as well as professionally": Nixon–Horack, June 26, 1936, Student Years File, Duke.

171   "Well, . . . grades must be there" *et seq.*: Albrink and Perdue interviews, UU; *The Charlotte Observer*, July 22, 1973. Author Edwin Hoyt contended that Nixon once privately admitted the break-in, saying that he and not Perdue had been boosted over the transom. See Abrahamsen, 117–19.

171–72   "not . . . as horrendous": Cavers interview, UU. "some kind of punishment": Rubin interview, UU. "simply don't remember": Perdue interview, UU. "I have a legal training": Abrahamsen, 118. "grades . . . sufficiently high": Horack–Nixon, June 12, 1936, Student Years File, Duke.

172   Washington-Baltimore weekend; "never . . . exposed": Kiefer correspondence.

173   "outvoted him": Alsop, *Nixon and Rockefeller*, 231. "eye on a political career": reprinted in the *Raleigh Times*, December 6, 1938. "a great time": Nixon, *RN*, 20. "Changing Rules of Liability": *Law and Contemporary Problems* (Fall 1936): 476–90. See also Nixon's note, "Application of the Inherent Danger Doctrine to Servants of Negligent Independent Contractors," the *Duke Bar Association Journal* (Spring 1936): 115–17.

173–74   ethics paper: "Automobile Accident Litigation; The Lawyer v. the Public," holograph term paper submitted November 30, 1936, Legal Ethics Term Papers, Duke. The paper seems to have been inspired by an article that followed Nixon's in *Law and Contemporary Problems* the same autumn, Robert Monaghan's "The Liability Claim Racket."

174   "active and able": Brodie, 129. small white onions: Cavers interview, UU. "intellectual inferiority complex": Jackson, 57. "limited in humor": Brodie, 126. "a cartoon character": *The Duke Chronicle*, November 18, 1976.

174–75   "at home in the horseplay": Alsop, *Nixon and Rockefeller*, 233. "None . . . overly obscene": Albrink interview, UU. "his uninhibited . . . enjoyment": Kornitzer, 111. "stiff and stilted": Kiefer correspondence. "sort of monastic": Rubin interview, UU.

175–76   "he never stayed longer": Albrink interview, UU. "a few girls I liked": Spaulding, 100. "shot full of rectitude": Jackson, 57. "just amoral": Hunter interview, UU. "such intensity": Alsop, *Nixon and Rockefeller*, 235. "an oddball": Abrahamsen, 121. "basically aloof": Alsop; *Nixon and Rockefeller*, 237.

176   "unpleasing mien": Alsop, *Nixon and Rockefeller*, 237.

176   table tennis incident: Sheldon interview, UU.

176–77   "Social security . . . insecurity": Hoyt, 215; Alsop, *Nixon and Rockefeller*, 233–34. "Dick Nixon as a New Deal supporter": *ibid.*, 230. views on Supreme Court: Kiefer correspondence and interview, UU; Spaulding, 118; Alsop, *Nixon and Rockefeller*, 234.

177   "shocked and disturbed": Alsop, *Nixon and Rockefeller*, 230. "as a moral issue": *ibid.*, 235. "unbending and unyielding": *ibid.*, 236.

177   "some intense discussions": Nixon, *RN*, 21.

177–78   "I wouldn't have a chance": Gardner, 83. "no real campaign": Alsop, *Nixon and Rockefeller*, 231–32. "last person in the class": *ibid.*, 238.

178–79   "ever . . . too much of that": Nixon–Charles H. Young, c. July-August 1937, Student Bar Association Presidential Correspondence, Duke. "Our New Prexy": April 13, 1936 banquet program, H. C. Horack records, Duke. "lonesome . . . popularity": Alsop, *Nixon and Rockefeller*, 229–30.

179   "Dear Grandmother": Kornitzer, 43.

179–80   "almost impossible": Rubin interview, UU. "upper reaches": Nixon, *RN*, 21. "a West Coast prejudice": Perdue interview, UU. "thick, luxurious carpets": Mazo, 30.

180 "a real success": White, 306. "no longer so keen": Nixon, *RN*, 21. "One of our very best students": Horack–James E. Brenner, January 8, 1937, Student Years File, Duke.

181 "finest . . . in character and ability": Spaulding, 106. "do better than that . . . He mentioned the FBI": Jackson, 58. "let down his hair": Alsop, *Nixon and Rockefeller*, 238–39. snapshot: *The Cedar Rapids Gazette*, January 11, 1953.

181 "worked harder . . . Duke University is responsible": Speech at Greensboro, North Carolina, August 17, 1960, *Senate Report*, no. 994, 1961, 2.

Chapter 7. Return to Whittier—Law and Politics, 1937–41

Page

182 "When I got home": Nixon–Charles H. Young, c. July 1937, Student Bar Association correspondence, Duke. Hannah's intervention: Bewley interview, UU. "things . . . importuned": Smith interview, UU. See also Schulte, 153.

182–83 "not . . . a mistake": YN, Smith, 10. Bewley's unanswered calls: YN, Parsons, 10. "make a stab . . . chance to fail": Nixon–Helen Kendall, July 3, 1937, Richard Milhous Nixon papers, Post-Graduation File, Duke. "as if he'd been offered . . . FBI": Perdue interview, UU.

183–84 "had it out with him": YN, Parsons, 10. "I received a very good offer": Nixon–Horack, c. August 1937. "Don't worry": Horack–Nixon, August 10, 1937, both Post-Graduation File, Duke. Flees to study for bar: Marshburn and Bewley interviews, UU.

184 "After several false beginnings"; "I've convinced myself that it is right": Nixon–Horack, October 6, 1937, Post-Graduation File, Duke.

184 "unnerving experience . . . my distress": Nixon, *RN*, 22.

185 swearing-in; toast: Clough interview, UU. "I shall be with . . . Wingert and Bewley": Nixon–Horack, November 3, 1937, Post-Graduation File, Duke. "wealthy residential city": California: Federal Writers' Project Tour Guide (Washington, 1939), 399.

185–86 "Oh, there were class differences"; "terribly gossipy": YN, Loubet, 17, 23. Whittier's isolation: YN, Fantz, 3 and Black, 3. storm drains: YN, Otterman, 23.

186 "smacked of communism": LAT, January 26, 1975.

186–87 "six years' practical experience": one of his campaign ads appeared in QC, October 31, 1930. "We are a cold people": Bewley interview, UU. "very much loved": YN, Loubet, 4.

187–88 Wingert and Bewley: See YN, Loubet. The partners' résumés and financial worth as well as the firm's general standing are summarized in successive editions of Martindale and Hubbell's *Law Directory* of the era: 1937–39 (69th–71st editions).

187 fires maid: YN, Loubet, 29. "upper stratum": YN, Loubet, 3.

188 first impressions of Nixon: WDN(I); Wills, 161–62; Spaulding, 113. "mature good looks": Kornitzer, 127. "I was satisfied": WDN(I). "needed someone badly": Abrahamsen, 122. cleans library: Mazo, 32.

188–89 work habits: WDN(I); Dorn interview, UU; Costello, 28; Wills, 161.

189 "didn't seem . . . a steam roller": YN, Loubet, 28–29. "I can honestly say": Nixon–Horack, May 31, 1938, Post-Graduation File, Duke.

189–92   Schee Case: the surviving original documentation is extensive. See *Schee* v. *Holt* [56 C. A. 2d Dec. 1942], 364–366; *Schee and Force* v. *Wingert and Bewley*, Superior Court of California, Los Angeles County, no. 436435, March 1939; *Schee* v. *Holt et al.*, 132 *Pacific Reporter*, 2d Series, 544–45; and the appeal briefs, 2nd Civil no. 13774, District Court of Appeal, Second Appellate District, State of California, August 1942. In addition, see Irving Wallace, "Research Notes on Richard M. Nixon's First Law Case," unpublished manuscript, UU; Schwartz, Pacht, Paonessa, and Kaufman interviews and correspondence, UU; Abrahamsen, 122–28.

192   "He was terribly upset": Bewley interview, UU; Brodie, 139.

192–93   "butter wouldn't melt": David, 49. "the right stance . . . right voice": Kornitzer, 128. "ahead of the witness": Gardner, 88. "reduce . . . to . . . essentials": Jackson, 58–64. stopwatch: Spaulding, 114. "Go see Dick": YN, Dixon, 17–18. "didn't have . . . bedside manner": Jackson, 64.

193   "embarrassing": Alsop transcript. "tense and morose": Kornitzer, 130. "lost his temper . . . irritated"; "ever lost a case": *ibid.*, 128. "count on . . . one hand": Schulte, 212. not "many cases in those days": YN, Black, 4–5.

194   "I was Mr. Nixon": Nixon, *RN*, 22.

194   "apologize for his father": Bewley interview, UU. "lower middle class . . . on the way back": YN, Loubet, 26.

195   "different sort of day for him": *ibid.*, 11–12.

195–97   accounts of Citra-Frost: Dorn and Bewley interviews, UU; Wills, 160–61. "like a dog": Mazo, 33. $100 paid back: Dorn interview, UU. stockholders laughed it off: Rothmann interview. "disappointed investors": Mazo, 33. "hate his guts": Bewley interview, UU.

197   "making money": H. Nixon.

198   "This tiny little place": YN, Paldanius, 13. For rich descriptions of the La Habra interval, see FNT, November 7, 1968 and a small archive of clips from the *La Habra Star*, August 18, 1939 to January 2, 1942 at CSU; see also YN, Stone, Burch, McCabe, and Roberts.

198   "take advantage of . . . connections": YN, Merton Wray, 11. "well-known to many La Habrans": *La Habra Star*, August 18, 1939.

198   "days on end": YN, Black, 4. "as they often were": "President Nixon located law office in La Habra in 1939," undated article by Doug Coleman in the LASP, CSU.

199   20–30 Club: YN, Fantz, Remley. "self-appointed committee . . . found Dick drunk": Blew correspondence.

199–200   national convention; "he would confide": YN, Black, 6–8.

200   "one office or another": WDN(I).

200–201   posted police: Spaulding, 116. "quite an argument": YN, Merton Wray, 10. "worked on Jap Burch": YN, McCabe, 13, 20. "had a political setup": YN, Stone, 5, 9.

202   "couldn't afford": YN, Stone, 2.

202   "talk about communistic demonstrations": YN, Kepple, 10, 15. "fair-haired boy": YN, Black, 9.

203   "he'd like to go to the . . . Assembly": YN, Burch, 5. Kepple did not know: Kepple, 6. "gave him all the help he could": Bewley interview, UU. "speechmaking": YN, Loubet, 14. "better politician than . . . lawyer": *ibid.*, 13. "They talked about running me": Alsop transcript. "no conscious plans": Nixon–Douglas R. Hayward, May 15, 1961, Committee of 100 File, VPA.

203   "the . . . little theater": Kornitzer, 131.

Chapter 8. Patricia Ryan, 1912–40

204   "wasn't very enthusiastic": YN, Black, 12. "air of permanent resentment": J. Eisenhower, 55.

204–5   "quiet vivaciousness": YN, Cloes, 3. "I could not take my eyes away": Nixon, *RN*, 23. "attentive all evening . . . a date . . . too busy": YN, Cloes, 2–3. "you sit next to him . . . going to marry you": *ibid.*, 3. "to see if he was teasing": J. Eisenhower, 55.

205   "I met this guy": J. Eisenhower, 55. "a sixth sense": Nixon, *RN*, 23.

205   "culturally deprived": YN, Mrs. Merton G. (Marcia) Wray, 7.

206   "luckless speculator": WP, October 9, 1960. "Just sew it up": J. Eisenhower, 32.

206–7   "I detest temper": J. Eisenhower, 21. "You are the happiness": *ibid.*, 25. "She lived in fear": *ibid.*, 20. Born in Elgin, Illinois: see Gardner, 95.

207–8   "Sundays . . . a Seventh-Day Adventist"; "used to beg": YN, Gwinn, 18. "terrified he would sell her": J. Eisenhower, 21. "quite strict": YN, Borden, 4.

208   told to kiss him: J. Eisenhower, 21. "a path . . . we'd run across": YN, Gwinn. "more of a tomboy": YN, Borden, 8. "even by Artesia standards": Brown interview, UU. "very primitive": WP, October 9, 1960.

209   "get out, get out": YN, Borden, 2. "I may be dying": *Time*, February 29, 1960.

209   "Didn't she look beautiful?": YN, Mrs. Merton G. (Marcia) Wray, 5. "sad around the eyes": YN, Conde, 4. "tremendously disciplined": YN, Marcia Wray, 5, who thought "perhaps some of Pat's amazing self-discipline has come from her mother and the Christian Science background."

209–10   "giving her heck": YN, Gwinn, 9. "a cherubic child": YN, Baron, 6.

210   "all her girlish moods": *The 1928 Green and White*, Excelsior High School Yearbook, 64. "not always . . . perfectly groomed": J. Eisenhower, 30. "one dress": YN, Mrs. Merton G. (Marcia) Wray, 7. "afraid to ask her": YN, Gardiner, 5. "very protective": YN, Gortikov, 6. "aloof": YN, McHatton, 3. "a mind of her own"; "you stubborn Irishman!": YN, Borden, 14.

210–11   "She wouldn't get right over it": YN, Borden, 15. "very, very strong": YN, Gortikov, 5, 6. "very ambitious": YN, Griffin, 9. "to run a boardinghouse": *The 1928 Green and White*, 28. "a big ranch": YN, Gwinn, 13. "the real secret of living": J. Eisenhower, 31.

211   "everything started with an education": WP, October 15, 1960.

211–12   "sharp stab": J. Eisenhower, 35. "some heartbreaks": YN, McCormick, 5. "remarkably well": David, 38. "lot of poise": YN, McCormick, 5. "Artesia is unbearable": J. Eisenhower, 39. "clicking stays with me yet": Jessamyn West, "The Real Pat Nixon."

212   "spend my life . . . for the afflicted": J. Eisenhower, 37. "most haunting of my life"; "contract health from me": Jessamyn West, "The Real Pat Nixon."

213   "Al Smith . . . and President Roosevelt": J. Eisenhower, 39. "People stared": WP, October 11, 1960. "rushed her"; "very discriminating": *ibid.* "glad I'm not in their boots": J. Eisenhower, 41. "*restrict you so*": *ibid.*, 38.

213–14   "so thrilled . . . Life is fleeting": *ibid.*, 41. "womanly softness . . . and inner strength": J. Eisenhower, 45. "how tired"; "stood out": *Time*, February 29, 1960.

214–15   "moping around": J. Eisenhower, 44. "any 'right' boys"; "so much beneath the surface": *ibid.*, 45. "knew so damn little": *ibid.*, 44. "I really eyed him": Winzola McLendon, "The Nixons Nobody Knows," *McCall's*, May 1971. "That life is too rough": J. Eisenhower, 40. slammed door: *ibid.*, 46.

215   "the moneyed class"; registration: *ibid.*, 47, 85. Her daughter notes here that Pat had campaigned for Democrat Al Smith in the 1928 presidential election.

216   "looked so perky": WP, October 12, 1960.

216   "vintage Underwoods and Royals"; "had hurt . . . farmers and . . . growers": Jean Lippiatt, "Pat Nixon Was My Typing Teacher," *The Saturday Evening Post*, Summer 1971.

216   "unwritten codes"; "Never talk about anybody": J. Eisenhower, 50–51. "you've got certain trouble": David, 47. "serving the coffee or . . . doing the dishes": *ibid.* "first young teacher"; "a direct look": Lippiatt, "Pat Nixon Was My Typing Teacher," *The Saturday Evening Post*, Summer 1971.

217   "Smile and be pleasant": from a 1970 Ann Landers column, quoted in J. Eisenhower, 53. "Whittier . . . notably free of . . . prejudice": *ibid.*, 52. "Individuality, enthusiasm and pep!": *ibid.*, 53.

218   "properly enter and leave"; "never . . . disclose": WP, October 12, 1960. "I never spent a weekend": J. Eisenhower, 54.

218–19   "hard to work with": YN, Behrens, 2. "I've talked to her": Gardner, 93. "No, I'm not going to do it": YN, Behrens, 2. "always in a semi-rage": J. Eisenhower, 57. "We didn't suspect Richard": H. Nixon.

219   "she did her part nicely": David, 59. "funny": J. Eisenhower, 64. "enigma to Dick's parents": *ibid.*, 57. "That wasn't so": H. Nixon. "a bit unusual": David, 60. "Miss Vagabond" *et seq.*: J. Eisenhower, 56–69, contains excerpts of the subsequent love notes and letters, and is the principal narrative source for the courtship.

219–20   "a little rat": David, 59. "mysteriously wild beauty": J. Eisenhower, 58. "I took *the* walk tonight": *ibid.*, 58.

220   walking aimlessly: David, 60, who writes that Pat Nixon later confirmed "these unique acts of fidelity and perseverance" with the comment, "It's true. But it's mean to report it." "a darling bachelor": J. Eisenhower, 56. "the sort that would appeal": YN, Loubet, 28. "couldn't have been *me* . . . that bad": Schulte, 226. saw no one else: Spaulding, 127. "hot and heavy": YN, Mendenhall, 2.

221   "acting like a sorehead": J. Eisenhower, 59.

221   "no declarations . . . or proposals": *ibid.*

221–22   exchange on clock: J. Eisenhower, 59–60. "I bet you're mad": *ibid.*, 60.

222   "four billion dollars": J. Eisenhower, 61. ice-skating: Dorn interview, UU. increasing closeness: J. Eisenhower, 66ff.

223   "strangely sad": J. Eisenhower, 63. "inadvertently": *ibid.*, 61. "blustery and inarticulate": *ibid.*, 66. "saint with a short temper": Jessamyn West, "The Real Pat Nixon." "help you get the pies ready": H. Nixon. "Pat was chasing Dick": David, 60.

223–24   "wasn't a modern person": J. Eisenhower, 62. "rugged individualist": YN, Sheldon Beeson, 13. "very humble": YN, Mrs. Sheldon (Dorothy) Beeson, 9. "knowing her way around": *ibid.*, 10. "she was ambitious": YN, Timberlake, 18. "handsome in a strong way"; "he was going places": J. Eisenhower, 58.

224–25   "lots of luck"; "love from mother": *ibid.*, 63–64. "Somebody from . . . a better family": YN, Loubet, 21. "she was the one": *ibid.*, 39. "Would like to take you": J. Eisenhower, 66.

225   "for the purpose just suggested": J. Eisenhower, 66. "the finest ideals": *ibid.*, 461. "he still may be funny": *ibid.*, 64.

226   "she was not sure": J. Eisenhower, 66. "broke the romantic spell": *ibid.*, 66. "What are you marrying *him* for?": *ibid.*, 67. "Dick never . . . said": Dorn interview, UU.

226–27   "buys a ring once": David, 62. "squeal with excitement": J. Eisenhower, 68.

227–28   "destiny": J. Eisenhower, 68. "You're going to Richard's wedding": YN, Timberlake, 58–59. "One would . . . expect . . . fancy wedding": YN, Mrs. Sheldon (Dorothy) Beeson, 10.

228   "They had run off": YN, Loubet, 22. "We just went": David, 64. "We're on our honeymoon!": YN, Gardiner, 9.

Chapter 9. Marriage and War, 1940–44

Page

229   early residences: see Esther R. Cramer, "La Habra and the President," unpublished manuscript, CSU; FNT, November 7, 1968; David, 65; J. Eisenhower, 7. $4,800: the total may even have been somewhat more, combining his $3,000 a year from Wingert and Bewley and her teaching salary, estimated as high as $190 a month. See Cramer manuscript cited above; Bewley, UU; Spaulding, 127; Hoyt, 226. Nixon himself (*RN*, 24) reported her salary at $190, and his later pay of $3,200 a year "not nearly so much as Pat and I were making together with her teaching and my law practice," *RN*, 25.

229   rituals: David, 66. "broke my heart": J. Eisenhower, 71.

230   "mostly my friends"; *Beauty and the Beast*: Mazo, 36–37. "Dick would . . . order for everyone": Jackson, 64. "family get-togethers": YN, Muriel Kelly. pearl necklace: H. Nixon.

230–31   "I'd never seen her": WDN(I). "casually"; "one of the reasons": J. Eisenhower, 85.

231   Willkie speeches; Glenn Frank connection: see Nixon, *RN*, 15, 25; Mazo, 43; YN, Stone, 2ff.; YN, Smith; WDN(I).

231–32   campaign for college presidency: Rothmann interview. See also Mazo, 33; Hoyt, 222. "entertained": Gardiner, 33. lobbying: YN, Schuyler, 6–7. "a serious move": Upton interview, UU.

232–33   told Burch: YN, Burch 6. "no reasonable chance": *La Habra Star*, c. May 1940, CSU. tenderfoot badges: *ibid.*, June 12, 1940. rare books: *ibid.*, November 14, 1940. presidency of Association: *ibid.*, May 30, 1941. featured speaker: *ibid.*, August 1, 1941. "grooming him": WDN, January 27, 1942. "no talk of politics": Mazo, 37.

233   ceramic knight: the figure was astride a plunging black charger. "It reminds me of him," she later told a reporter. Helen W. Erskine, "Dick and Pat Nixon," *Colliers*, July 9, 1954. confided in Drowns: Hoyt, 230. "He wasn't interested in staying in Whittier": Dorn interview, UU. "for almost the entire trip": Nixon, *RN*, 25.

233–34   "Dick as . . . Grecian lady"; "horrid existence!": J. Eisenhower, 72–73. law practice in Cuba: Dorn interview, UU; Mazo, 38.

234   not "particularly disturbed"; "side with the Loyalists": Nixon, *RN*, 45. "How excited I was": *ibid.*, 462. "strongly against Stalin": *ibid.*, 45. "We both hoped": *ibid.*, 25. "I had so little": *ibid.*, 462.

234   "wonderful coolness!"; "just a gypsy": J. Eisenhower, 73. "last vacation": Nixon, *RN*, 25.

235   "desperate": Wallace interview. "money . . . not a major consideration": J. Eisenhower, 73. It was "at her urging," Julie writes of her mother, that Nixon answered Ginsberg's letter. "What spirit": *ibid.*, 74. "a snowy fairyland": *ibid.*, 75. "He seemed . . . what we needed": Emerson interview, UU.

235–36   "just one more": Nixon, *RN*, 26. plans return to firm: YN, Loubet, 33. "matter of economics": YN, Black, 10. "secretly relieved": Nixon, *RN*, 25.

236   "Our greatest hopes": Viorst.

236–37   "Heard . . . impossible"; "lucky day": J. Eisenhower, 75.

237   "straining his neck": J. Eisenhower, 75; for Rockwell's recollections, see also WP, October 12, 1960. "walking into utter chaos": Wallace interview. "courage, and imperviousness": Robert E. Sherwood, *Roosevelt and Hopkins* (New York, 1948), 631.

237–38   filled in $2,800: Jacob Beuscher–Stewart Alsop, April 25, 1958, Alsop Papers, LC. Thought he made $12,000: Emerson interview, UU. $5–6,000: Beuscher–Alsop, cited above. "He told me afterward": Kornitzer, 142. salaries: Office of Emergency Management, Pay Roll for Personal Services, February–May 1942, NA. "others with lesser": Nixon, *RN*, 26.

238   "shortage . . . critical": Arthur Burns–Leon Henderson, December 9, 1941; OPA files, Tire Rationing Program, NA (henceforth simply cited as OPA/NA). "lowest point of the war": Robert E. Sherwood, *Roosevelt and Hopkins* (New York, 1948), 631. "part of a bigger cause": Viorst.

239   documentary record: memoranda, correspondence, and other material relating to Nixon's work in the OPA is contained in Record Group 188, The Office of Price Administration, Rationing Records, Legal Division Administration and Organization, Boxes 113–26; Legal Division—Tires, Boxes 153–54; and in Tires and Tubes, Regulation and Administrative Files, Boxes 26–27, and Boxes 450–77, as well as Tires "Correspondence," Boxes 534–40, all National Archives, Washington, D.C. The following citations are given by date from those records.

239   "Report of Work Done": Nixon–Daniel Margolies, January 26, 1942, OPA/NA.

239–40   "no backlog": Nixon–Margolies, February 7, 1942, OPA/NA. "head up" the interpretation unit: Margolies–Thomas Harris, February 14, 1942, OPA/NA. "that the . . . staff be relieved": Nixon–Margolies, February 21, 1942, OPA/NA. "Nixon will see . . . letter . . . mailed": Charles Phillips–J. C. Ray, et. al., February 26, 1942, OPA/NA, which attaches yet another, even more detailed and meticulous diagram hand-written by Richard Nixon and precisely titled "Tentative Mail Routing and Clearance Procedure for Auto Rationing Legal Unit." "designated informally": David Lloyd–Tom Harris, March 10, 1942, OPA/NA.

240–41   "legal mail desk"; "Review . . . tough problems": hand-written notes, attached to Phillips–Ray memoranda, c. March 1942. "questioned by their unit": Aaron Lewittes–Ann Landy Wolf, April 21, 1942, OPA/NA. "splendid right-hand and left-hand": Beuscher–Stewart Alsop, April 25, 1958, Alsop papers, LC.

241   "a real plugger": Viorst. "highly instructive": Beuscher–Harris, May 18, 1942. overtime: hand-written "Progress Report," June 7–12, 1942, OPA/NA. editing of bureaucratic prose: Nixon–Harris, June 27, 1942, OPA/NA. Three days later, Beuscher registered his own and Nixon's complaint about the rigor of the office. "We should be much more hard-boiled about discrepancies between automobile, gasoline and tire eligibility interpretations," he wrote.

"Dick Nixon is at the moment working upon a memorandum on this subject": Beuscher–M. L. Krichman, June 30, 1942, OPA/NA. "considerable burden": Beuscher–Harris, July 13, 1942, OPA/NA.

241 "favorable comment": Beuscher–Harris, July 13, 1942 (under the heading "SPECIAL MATTERS"), OPA/NA.

242 "A grand person": Horack Personal Files, Duke. "uncomfortable among . . . liberals . . . Jews": Viorst. "terribly ill-at-ease": Viorst. "an affinity": Kornitzer, 143.

242–43 trip to Duke: Nixon–Horack, April 23, 1942: Horack Personal Files, Duke. "self-conscious": Hoyt, 231. "the D.C. message": Emerson interview, UU. "Those with political ambitions": Viorst. "family . . . troubled": J. Eisenhower, 76.

243 "I could have been a conscientious objector": A Self Portrait (script of a film prepared for the 1968 Republican Convention, text in Mugar Library, Boston University). "never crossed my mind": Jackson, 64. "Her acquiescence": J. Eisenhower, 75. "mighty uncomfortable": Kornitzer, 139–40. "I have decided to volunteer": Nixon–Horack, April 23, 1942, Horack Personal Files, Duke. "obsessed with their own power": Nixon, RN, 26. "Build a little staff": ibid. "mediocrity of so many"; "people angling for something": Viorst.

243–44 "a great experience": Alsop transcripts. "We learned": Viorst. "getting away with murder": Alsop transcripts.

244 Kennebunkport trip; "so happy there": J. Eisenhower, 76.

244 "things to be prepared for": YN, Black, 10. "lonely ride": J. Eisenhower, 77, which continues to be a main source of their correspondence and impressions for the ensuing period. "the longest I've ever known": ibid. "duck soup": Public Papers, 1971, 426. "chiefs run the Navy"; "I had never stood straighter": ibid. "not graduate with distinction": ibid, 430. "quite a class": ibid, 430.

245 Pat at OPA: "Employment Record of Patricia R. Nixon," General Services Administration Memorandum, January 30, 1970, CSU. "all of me . . . all the time"; "how very much"; "Plum's hand"; "not the Romeo type": J. Eisenhower, 77.

245 "middle of a cornfield": Nixon, RN, 27. "little more than a receptionist": Jerry Szumski, "When the Nixons Lived in Iowa," Des Moines Register, February 8, 1970. "conscientious"; "he wasn't the party type"; "as common as they come": ibid.

245–46 Ottumwa impressions; "head in the air" et seq.: Szumski, cited above.

246 "painful meal": Nixon, RN, 27. "take good care": H. Nixon. "My mother held her sorrow in": Nixon, RN, 28.

246–47 "crackers and soup": Jackson, 68. "He played a quiet game": Kornitzer, 144. theater of the war: see S. E. Smith, editor, United States Navy in World War II (New York, 1966), 426–88; and Samuel Eliot Morison, Breaking the Bismarcks Barrier: 22 July 1942–1 May 1944 (Boston, 1964), 3–26; 225–53; 279–423, passages of which are cited below by the author's name.

247–48 "old and beaten shells": Smith, cited above, 486. "Please say it always"; "You rode along with me": J. Eisenhower, 81. "Always write": ibid., 79.

248 "make up for me": J. Eisenhower, 83. "I'm antisocial I guess": ibid., 79. "less civilized place . . . working on an angle": ibid., 79–80. "pick out the important points": Gardner, 107.

248 "problem we shall face": Nixon–Horack, September 4, 1943, Horack Personal Files, Duke.

249 "Reading everything": J. Eisenhower, 79. pajamas: *ibid.*, 82. "what a waste": *ibid.*, 81. "I have always wanted to read Karl Marx": *ibid.*, 82. "first baby after thirty": *ibid.*, 82–83.

249–50 wartime reading and notes: Hoyt, 233–36.

250 "lack of sleep and the centipedes": Gardner, 103. "Our tent . . . completely destroyed": Nixon, *RN*, 28.

250–51 "koala bears": J. Eisenhower, 82. "very impressed": *ibid.*, 99. "walk right up . . . and kiss you": *ibid.*, 83. "The only real danger": Jackson, 66.

251 "carnage was terrible": Nixon, *RN*, 29.

251–52 "peeled off his shirt": Spaulding, 136–37. "He learned how to get along": YN, Parsons, 10–11.

252 "the real catalyst": Nixon–Douglas R. Hayward, May 15, 1961, Committee of 100 File, VPA. "hold his own": Spaulding, 140. "Nick could swap anything": Spaulding, 137. "meant so much": *Life*, November 20, 1970.

252 "ever lost a cent": Spaulding, 141. "etiquette surrounding them": Nixon, *RN*, 29. winnings: see Jackson, 66; Brodie, 166–68; J. Eisenhower, 83; Spaulding, 137 ff.

253 "instructed that she not be told": Dorn interview, UU. "a wonderful day": J. Eisenhower, 81.

253 "Your job . . . far more important": J. Eisenhower, 79. "Should we live there afterwards?"; "So you are inclined"; "Too many restrictions": *ibid.*, 82.

253 "I will have to admit": *ibid.*, 83.

254 farewell party: Kornitzer, 149. citation: Résumé of Military Service, Robert Finch–Douglas Price, November 19, 1959, VPA.

254 "He was that kind of officer": *Life*, November 20, 1970. "I was overcome with . . . futility of war": Nixon, *RN*, 30.

Chapter 10. Running for Congress, July 1944–June 1946

Page

257 "succeeded where . . . Teapot Dome . . . failed": Daniel Bell, syndicated column, May 24–26, 1943, copy in JVP. "VOORHIS HERO": WP, June 19, 1943. "greatest kind of service": Voorhis, *Confessions*, 192. For Elk Hills in general, see Oil Speeches File, JVP; Voorhis's original address in the *Congressional Record*, May 21, 1943, 78th Congress, First Session; his statement before the House Committee on Public Lands, May 28, 1943, *Hearings to Protect Naval Petroleum Reserve, No. 1*, 17–28, JVP; *Newsweek*, June 28, 1943; *Labor* (Washington, D.C.), May 27, 1943; Voorhis, *Confessions*, 187–92; Bullock, 186–87. Not all the press reaction was favorable. The *Los Angeles Times* attacked the congressman for depriving the people of California of gasoline and thus harming the "war effort."

258–59 "look me in the eye": JV/OH, 3: 4. "living in the Kingdom of God": *The World Tomorrow*, February 15, 1934.

259 "a smug reactionary": *The Nation*, April 21, 1950. "Americanism vs. Socialism": Bullock, 43. "I remember how you stood": Robert Heinlein–Voorhis, November 6, 1946, JVP. "Driven by conscience": Paul Douglas, 237. "Kid Atlas": Bullock, 112. "first in integrity" *et seq.*: see Voorhis's letter to the *Observer*, November 21, 1968, JVP; *Time*, April 26, 1954; "Washington Press Gallery Rates Pacific Coast Legislators," undated release c. 1946, JVP; George Martin–Ben O'Brien, April 3, 1949, JVP.

259–60 "temper rightist blasts": *Time*, February 20, 1939, though the magazine also later called Voorhis himself (November 6, 1939) "a little Leftist." "Wobbly as usual"; "defeats his own purpose": Bullock, 134; Pearson's judgment appeared in his syndicated column July 27, 1940. "student . . . trying to talk sense to drunkards": Goodman, 145.

260 "deep thinking bids fare": *Washington Star News*, July 10, 1943. "they just do not believe it": JV/OH, 4: 28. more than a hundred speeches; saves a fourth of salary: JV/OH, 3: 33, 41.

261 "cancerous superstructure": Bullock, 199.

261 "really brought the wrath": BAN/OH, Elizabeth Snyder, 37, who recalled as well that Democrats "begged" Voorhis in the mid-forties to move and run in more safely Democratic east Los Angeles. "political saint": Paul Douglas, 237, who noted that "seldom has a saint achieved such practical results." "so filled with despair": undated diary entry, Box 34, Folder 3, JVP.

262 visits and gifts: YN, Cato and Funk, 6; Wildermuth, 11; Burbank, 2, Walker, 3–4. "slap down the old fellow": Kornitzer, 147. "blossomed into an extrovert": YN, Heffern, 12. old friends also remembered him already "politicking" with veterans groups: Rothmann interview. "Things on this side": "Dear Al" letter, August 7, 1944, Casoni, 14.

262–63 "chief janitor"; "has my desk been dusted": J. Eisenhower, 84. "idealistic dreamer": Kornitzer, 150.

263 "cheap seats": J. Eisenhower, 61. FDR's death: Nixon, *RN*, 33. sees Eisenhower June 19, 1945: Coughlan, 146.

263 "very conservative . . . conventional": Cobey interview, UU. "I don't know if it will pan out": J. Eisenhower, 85.

264 "It is lovely": Boyer, 141.

264 14,000 strikes: Ceplair and Englund, 207. "something momentous"; "sorrow and doubt": Boyer, 6–7.

264–65 "pall of disgust": Donovan, *Conflict and Crisis*, 229. Broiler and Sizzle: Boyer, 102. "To err": Donovan, *Conflict and Crisis*, 230.

265 "so divided": Donovan, *Conflict and Crisis*, 231.

265–66 "Years of languishing": Ceplair and Englund, 206–7. "Russia abroad . . . labor at home": quoted in Griffith and Theoharis, 78. "Soviet armies . . . on the march": John Cronin–Francis Mathews, March 18, 1946, Mathews Papers, HST. "firing squads": John Sullivan-Francis Mathews, January 21, 1946, Mathews Papers, HST.

266 "bloc of one": Ronald L. Feinman, *Twilight of Progressivism: The Western Republican Senators and the New Deal* (Baltimore, 1981), 7.

266 Johnson's legacy: see George E. Mowry, *The California Progressives* (Berkeley, 1951); John H. Culver and John C. Syer, *Power and Politics in California* (New York, 1980); Royce D. Delmatier, Clarence McIntosh, and Earl Waters, editors, *The Rumble of California Politics* (New York, 1970).

267 "twitch . . . by its nerve ends": Theodore H. White, *Breach of Faith* (New York, 1975), 53. "make tuberculosis popular": Mankiewicz, 66.

268 350,000 jobless: Ceplair and Englund, 89. "vast, inchoate coalition": Mankiewicz, 32. "epilepsy . . . catalepsy": George Creel, *Rebel at Large* (New York, 1947), 282–83. "without gun bearers": Klehr, 1974. "faker and . . . fascist": *ibid.*, 173.

268 anti-Sinclair campaign: Ceplair and Englund, 89–94; McWilliams, 296–99; UCLA/OH, Carey McWilliams.

268 "Nothing is unfair": Ceplair and Englund, 92.

269 "Republican Party, the open shop, and God": Katcher, 35. borrowed silver:

EW/OH, Faries, 30. "you couldn't buy him": EW/OH, Barnes, 32. "No man should be permitted": Katcher, 197. "One leg astride": Richard B. Harvey, *Earl Warren: Governor of California* (New York, 1969), 165–66.

270 "pinkoes and outright Communists": Katcher, 199. "They feared the Democrats more": *ibid.*, 197. "better not ask me": *ibid.*, 170. "monstrous patchwork quilt": SB, November 18, 1948, reporting a meeting of some 500 southern California Republicans deploring Warren's "New Dealism."

270–71 "What would you think of Dick Nixon": YN, Otterman, 26. Perry talks with others: see WDN(I) and YN, Otterman, 25 ff. "if you would like to be a candidate": Nixon, *RN*, 34.

271 "the heady idea": J. Eisenhower, 86. "honored" and "excited": Nixon, *RN*, 34. "If you fellows out there": RN/OH, Jorgensen, 8. "poured some cold water": Nixon, *RN*, 34. "he guessed he was a Republican": "Re: Senator Nixon," memorandum by Herman Perry, c. 1952, Alsop papers, LC; see also Flynn.

271 "Voorhis can be beaten"; "aggressive, vigorous campaign": Nixon, *RN*, 35.

272 "A stodgy reactionary": Bullock, 21. "over fifteen cents in the bank": RN/OH, Day, 3–4. "sunk in a morass": Voorhis–staff, August 18, 1945, JVP.

272–73 "just a rump": RN/OH, Adams, 4. "bitched so much": RN/OH, Day, 19. "all the big shots": RN/OH, Day, 4. "two or three bigwigs . . . in a locked-up room": RN/OH, Day, 3. "endorse ONE candidate": Day–Walter Dexter, October 13, 1945, RDP.

273 "we sure crucified": RN/OH, Day, 17. "looking for a job": RN/OH, Jorgensen, 5. "if this is all": *ibid.* "They asked a lot of people": EW/OH, Barnes, 34. "None . . . appear dangerous": Jack Long–Voorhis, October 6, 1945, JVP.

273 "old Blood and Guts": LAT, October 11, 1945; PSN, October 11, 1945. "keep completely out of politics": PPB, October 12, 1945.

273–74 "I am not certain": Dexter telegram–Day, October 8–9, 1945, RDP. "this district wants to go Republican"; "very powerful interests": Day–Dexter, October 13, 1945, RDP. Dexter asks assurance: RN/OH, Jorgensen, 7.

274 "did not warm up": LAT, October 14, 1945. "If Walter Dexter had lived": APA, November 13, 1968. "seriously being considered": WDN, October 23, 1945.

274 testimonial: YN, Fantz, 14; see also WDN(I).

274 "Whittier . . . interested in suggesting"; "very aggressive individual": H. L. Perry–Lance D. Smith, October 3, 1945, RDP.

275 "spoke very highly of him": Day–Perry, October 12, 1945, RDP. "she knew what she was doing": RN/OH, Jorgensen, 7.

275 ERCO credit card: William G. Key–Kenneth C. Sears, August 18, 1958, Drew Pearson File, VPA, which attaches background documentation on the incident, including testimony from ERCO officials; see also Drew Pearson's column, *Philadelphia Bulletin*, October 30, 1952.

275–76 "still without a candidate": Jack Long–Voorhis, October 18, 1945, JVP. "commencing to fight": Long–Voorhis, October 30, 1945, JVP. "flying here from Baltimore": WDN, PPB, MNP. October 31, 1945.

276 banner and "claque": Blew correspondence. "don't want a dole": WDN, November 2, 1945. "This man is salable merchandise": RN/OH, Day, 5.

277 "Nice guys and sissies": Bullock, 243, 322. "Republican wheelhorse": William L. Roper in *Frontier*, September 1955. "If they shoot": RN/OH, Jorgensen, 3. "We work our ass off": *ibid.*, 52.

277 "far from energetic": RN/OH, Jorgensen, 4. "Why are we having . . . a socialist": *ibid.*, 2. "blueblood": EW/OH, Faries, 102.

278   proxy for Standard Oil: RN/OH, Jorgensen, 8, 33.

278–79   accounts of University Club: RN/OH, Jorgensen, 8–9, 32–33; RN/OH, Day, 5ff; EW/OH, Faries, 102–3ff; EW/OH, Barnes, 90ff.

279   "triumph of private citizens": *Frontier*, September 1955; see especially Bowers and Blair. San Marino "fatcats": Bullock, 117.

279–80   "How much do you need": RN/OH, Jorgensen, 10. "You just didn't turn him down": YN, Schuyler, 8. "real bell sheep": YN, Newman. "Mr. Republican": YN, Otterman, 25. "charnel house of iniquity": Costello, 39. "to put an end": "Re: Senator Nixon," memorandum by Herman Perry, Alsop papers, LC. "tinctured basically with Communism": Perry–Helen W. Steere, March 24, 1954, Herman Perry file, VPA.

280   "It wasn't a Bolshevik": RN/OH, Day, 16. An original list of the Committee is in RDP. "To give bodies to the effort": "The Man I Now Present to You," undated memorandum by Roy O. Day, RDP. "a big horse laugh": *Arcadia Tribune*, October 11, 1945. "hand in glove": RN/OH, Day, 17.

280–81   "I fail to see in him": Day–Dexter, October 13, 1945, RDP. "play 'hard to get' ": *ibid*. "deplored . . . tendency to find fault": WDN, November 3, 1945. "electrifying personality": APA, November 13, 1968.

281   "two definite opinions" *et seq*.: WDN, November 3, 1945.

281   Chotiner's "enthusiasm": Chotiner interview, UU. "A lot of work": RN/OH, Jorgensen, 9. "swamped the . . . regulars": WDN(I). "it looks like a landslide": Day–Nixon, November 12, 1945, RDP.

282   "expressing freely": Day circular, November 15, 1945, RDP. "to dictate the Republican candidate": *Arcadia Tribune*. October 18, 1945. "making it easy": *Monrovia Journal*, November 1, 1945. "Standard Oil . . . to move heaven and earth": *Independent Review*, November 6, 1945. "You will have to hand it": Jack Long–Voorhis, November 5, 1945, JVP. "considered a natural": LAT, November 29, 1945.

282   "nomination's yours!": Nixon, *RN*, 35. "talked until dawn": J. Eisenhower, 86.

282–83   "reputation must be blasted" *et seq*.: Nixon–Day, Mazo, 45, 46. "pored over"; "I was confident": Nixon, *RN*, 35–36.

283   letter to Stassen: Joseph R. Parker–Harold Stassen, December 4, 1945, RDP.

283   "I'm not as conservative . . . not as wild": Kornitzer, 151–52.

284   "realistic foreign policy"; "opposed to class hatred": *San Marino Tribune*, December 27, 1945; WDN, December 21, 1945. "a political animal": YN, Black, 18. "taught . . . ample respect": WDN(I).

284   "so the bankers decided": YN, Merton Wray, 7. "he had sold his soul": YN, Stout.

284   "coldest reception I've ever had": JV/OH, 5:64.

285   "to see that the money is there": RN/OH, Jorgensen, 11. "discussed the events": "Roy P. Crocker's Relationship with President Nixon," memorandum by Crocker dated September 22, 1969, BAN. "Nixon . . . had full control": RN/OH, Jorgensen, 27. "where . . . posters should be placed": Arnold, iii.

285–86   every word and layout: YN, Walker, 10. "we'd run fairly close": RN/OH, Jorgensen, 11. "put up several hundred": Crocker memo cited above, September 22, 1969, BAN. Jorgensen raises $5,000: RN/OH, Jorgensen, 11. "money that would be needed": Hoyt, 239, 242. Hoyt suggests that some of these funds were used to pay for the airplane ticket for Nixon's audition before the committee.

286   "Atom Bomb Dancers": Boyer, 12.

287   "nibbled": JV/OH, 5:80. "one immense flower garden" *et seq.*: Aubrey Drury, *California: An Intimate Guide* (New York, 1947), 97–104. "petty bourgeois": Bullock, 254. "I used to leave . . . strictly alone": JV/OH, 3:38.

287   "bitter-end bigotry": Bullock, 254.

287–88   "today's hot problems": APA, January 6, 1946. "melting-pot": Mankiewicz, 37. "constructive campaign": LAT, February 6, 1946. "governmental controls"; "boys in the backroom": WDN, January 19, 1946; PPB, March 7, 1946.

288   Pomona clubhouse scene: RN/OH, Day, 7; PPB, MNP, WDN February 13, 1945; EW/OH, Barnes, 39. "all the way to the presidency": "The Man I Now Present to You," Day memorandum cited above, RDP. "He didn't need . . . help": RN/OH, Day, 14. suit and shoes: Harmsen correspondence; Day memorandum cited above, RDP.

288   "remember the tie"; "look these people in the face": RN/OH, Day, 7, 9.

288–89   "completely unsophisticated": RN/OH, Crocker, 25. "His strongest point"; "rather than . . . direct contradiction": RN/OH, Day, 9. "only boss I recognize": PPB, March 7, 1946.

289   exchange with Voorhis: Voorhis–Nixon, April 16, 1946, JVP; de Toledano, 49–50. "He had two sitting ducks": RN/OH, Day, 10.

290   "Uncle Herman got them": RN/OH, Jorgensen, 10; Day, 11. "lousy cottage": WP, August 9, 1974.

290   diapers and "foolscap": RN/OH, Day, 11. "six or seven talks a day": J. Eisenhower, 88. "persistent critiques": Nixon, *RN*, 36. "Pat was . . . anxious": Dorn interview, UU. "nervous, uptight": David, 75.

291   "No one cared": J. Eisenhower, 90.

291   Hoepple episode: from a memorandum entitled simply "Hoepple," 1946 Primary Campaign File, JVP. "several hundred dollars": Voorhis–Long, March 28, 1946, JVP. "mean and continuous": Voorhis–Long, April 3, 1946, JVP.

291   "not . . . enough 'meat' ": Chotiner–Nixon, April 1, 1946, Roy Day Personal Files, quoted in Alexander (this material, as much else, was not among the documents deposited by Day and others at Bancroft).

292   "I learned a lot . . . I don't completely respect": RN/OH, Day, 14. "nothing to do with it!": EW/OH, Cunningham, 8. "great contempt": EW/OH, Small, 268.

292   "visions gone sour": Wills, 81.

293   "ENDORSEMENT . . . BY PAC," WDN, April 24, 1946.

293–94   "hoped I wouldn't get it": Voorhis–Long, April 6, 1946, JVP. "mixed bag": Bullock, 248.

294   "fighting . . . every inch": Bullock, 250.

294   "this intelligence field": Klein, 139. "I never sought nor did I receive": clipping in 1946 Primary File, JVP. Voorhis letters: Voorhis–Loren Grey, May 22, 1946; Voorhis–Chester Watson, May 28, 1946, JVP.

294   "He carried the group by storm": W. Earl Emick–Voorhis, May 2, 1946, *Confessions of a Congressman* File, JVP.

294–95   "with the agile perfection" *et seq.*: "Report on Mass Meeting," campaign intelligence memorandum dated May 3, 1946, Primary File, JVP.

295   "at least two writers": Long–Voorhis, March 28, 1946, JVP. "getting any too good response": *ibid.*

296   "radical PAC endorsements": APA, May 18, 1946. "born with a silver spoon": SPR, May 24, 1946.

296   "editorials . . . financed": EW/OH, Faries, 105, 102–4.

296–97   role of *Post-Advocate*: APA, November 13, 1968. "Herb helped us": RN/OH, Jorgensen, 53.

297   "more publicity . . . than has Nixon": Long–Voorhis, April 13, 1946, JVP. "I am afraid": Long–Voorhis, April 25, 1946, JVP. attempted retraction: the scene described in Long–Voorhis, June 24, 1946, JVP. "free readers": Long–Voorhis, May 4, 1946. "paper shortage": *ibid.*

298   "never smiled or stopped": WDN(I).

298   "greatest power of darkness": the view of both Harry Chandler and the *Times* by the *Los Angeles Record*, as quoted in Marshall Berges, *The Life and Times of Los Angeles* (New York, 1984), 48. "paper devoid of fairness and justice": Halberstam, 167.

299   "ingratiating . . . cynical"; "dealt in intrigue": Berges, *Life and Times*, cited above.

299–300   "kiss his ring": Halberstam, 170. "serious . . . gawky young fellow" *et seq.*: Kornitzer, 160. "fatherly relationship": Halberstam, 363–64.

300   "extraordinary man on our hands": Kornitzer, 160. "a winner": LAT, May 17, 1946. "best candidate": LAT, May 19, 1946.

301   "a comer": Kornitzer, 160. "circumvent the rules": *Frontier*, September 1955.

301   "mailed FIRST CLASS": "Newsgram for All Nixon-For-Congress Campaign Chairmen," c. May 4, 1946, RDP.

301   ad tactics: "Newsgram" cited above. "crack . . . church following": *ibid.*

302   campaign brochures: copies of the various versions are in Duke, JVP, and RDP. "politicians who spend thousands": Kinnett advertising in JVP.

302–3   "totalitarian ideologies of the New Deal": APA, May 31, 1946. "no personal quarrel . . . day of reckoning": MNP, PPB, June 2–3, 1946.

303–4   "I feel they deserve it" *et seq.*: Nixon–Day, undated, RDP.

304   campaign spending: "Candidate's Campaign Statement of Receipts and Expenditures," Richard M. Nixon, June 4, 1946, CSA. "fighting two-fisted": PPB, June 7, 1946.

304–5   "Story is . . . paid women": confidential memorandum, June 13, 1946, EWP. "greedy-minded people": Long–Voorhis, May 14, 1946, JVP.

305   "ready for the 'fray' ": Voorhis, *Confessions*, 333.

Chapter 11. First Victory, June–November 1946

Page

306   "his wife praised and braced him": David, 76–77. "a wise man . . . smooth": RN/OH, Jorgensen, 14–15. campaign payments: see RN/OH, Jorgensen, 22, 26–27; Crocker, 27; Adams, 6; some, though by no means all, expenditures were recorded in the Primary and General "Candidate's Campaign Statement of Receipts and Expenditures," Richard M. Nixon, June 4, 1946 and November 5, 1946, CSA. hiring three assemblymen: "Roy P. Crocker's Relationship with President Nixon," memorandum of September 22, 1969, RDP.

307   press secreatry: Arnold, 31. "harsh . . . hurtful battle": J. Eisenhower, 92. "called in to help": RN/OH, Crocker, 27; Crocker reports that Chotiner was also summoned "at my suggestion."

308   "Whittier Republican Club": see Affidavit of Receipts and Expenditures, "Candidate's Campaign Statement": cited above, November 5, 1946, CSA. "They were friendly": RN/OH, Day, 28.

308   Morton *et al.*: RN/OH, Jorgensen, x, 34; EW/OH, Call, 18, 20; Faries, 102–

3; Fry interview. "big war chest": see especially Charles B. Voorhis–Jerry Voorhis, April 10, 1944, relating contacts of the congressman's father, himself a former oil man, with sources in the industry. "Oil Interests Aid in Jerry Voorhis' Defeat," *The Cooperator* (New York), November 25, 1946. "unlimited sums of money": *ibid.*

308–9   "a good talk with Harry March": J. Paull Marshall–Nixon, February 20, 1946, VPA. March and tidelands "Principal pleader": see *Second Issue*, September 1945, 34, JVP.

309   "I won't take it this way": LAT, July 26, 1974. $12,000 for campaign: Edward S. Shattuck–Earl Warren, August 17, 1946, attaching "confidential summary of proposed and recommended budgets," EWP.

309–10   "man who made up the minds": EW/OH, Faries, 73. "we could always raise": EW/OH, Call, 18. movie connections: RN/OH, Jorgensen, 63–64. northern California money: Rothmann interview.

310   corporate levies; "Send it to my office in cash" *et seq.*: William F. Ackerman–Fawn Brodie, January 2, 1979, incorporating Ackerman's "journal notes"; see also Ackerman correspondence, April 10, 18, and 26, 1979, UU.

311   Hoover money: Herbert Hoover Oral History Project, G. Keith Funston; John D. M. Hamilton, HH. See also Richard Norton Smith, *An Uncommon Man: The Triumph of Herbert Hoover* (New York, 1984), 360–61. "you've got it": EW/OH, Faries, 72.

311   Adams offer: Nixon, *Six Crises*, 424.

311–12   "vaguely liberal ideas": Smith, 483–84. "interested . . . your campaign to liberalize": Nixon–Harold Stassen, May 20, 1946, VPA. responses: Stassen–Nixon, May 24, June 14, 1946, VPA. "help this Nixon kid": Pierce Butler III interview; see also JV/OH 5:38, registering Voorhis's own eventual knowledge of the far-flung Democratic contributions to his opponent. Learning of Stassen's support, his GOP presidential rival, Thomas Dewey, promptly arranged his own surrogate donations to Nixon, in this case $100 from New York congressman Leonard Hall; see Hall interview, UU.

312–13   "committed to the Soviet Union": Caute, 26. "ended all doubts": Boyer, 102.

313   Lockwood-Shackelford letter: Crocker–Nixon, June 20, 1946, BAN. "brand of Americanism": LAT, June 13, 1946.

313   Eaton's "kickoff": EW/OH, Barnes, 40–42; RN/OH, Jorgensen, iv, PPB, WND, July 29, 1946. "the sky clanged with it": campaign aide Zan Thompson's reminiscence in the *Daily Pilot* (Orange County), August 11, 1974. "under way with speed": LAT, August 10, 1946. "his radical theories": MNP, August 22, 1946.

313–14   editorials as news stories: APA, August 22–23, 1946; WDN, August 29, 1946; APA, November 13, 1968.

314   "neutral" stance; fired and evicted: JV/OH, 5:51; see also Bourne. "no special strings": Wilber Jerger, "The Real Nixon Story," *Los Angeles Free Press*, October 4, 1956, 1. "red paint thrown": Dorn interview, UU. thimbles: RN/OH, Jorgensen, 58; Arnold, 2. "the remarkable impression": Paul Bullock–Voorhis, August 26, 1946, JVP.

314   "a matter of record" *et seq.*: the ad and related stories are in the general campaign file, JVP; see also APA, September 11, 1946. "NIXONITES OFFER PROOF," PPB, September 11, 1946.

315   "some joint meetings": Voorhis–Long, May 11, 1946, JVP. "a boy like Nixon": Long–Voorhis, June 11, 1946, JVP. "not be wise to . . . openly challenge": Voorhis–Long, June 14, 1946, JVP.

316   "couldn't bring myself to refuse": JV/OH, 4:39; 3:24. "reluctant and uncertain"; "enthusiastic"; "had some qualms": Bullock, 256.

316   only if speaks last; no one tells Voorhis: Bullock, 256. studies Voorhis; took down shorthand: Dorn interview, UU. "very smart": RN/OH, Day, 11; see also Nixon, *RN*, 38–39.

317   Voorhis retraction: Bullock, 257; JV/OH, 5:10, 21.

317   "No recalled event": Bullock, 258. "We always had a few persons": RN/OH, Day, i, an organized claque that Pat Nixon recalled as "all our volunteers": J. Eisenhower, 91. "diamonded": Bullock, 271; Voorhis, *Confessions*, 342. FACTS ABOUT JERRY VOORHIS: see *Confessions* File, JVP.

317–18   "all-out tirade": Bullock, 259. "earnest political speech": Mankiewicz, 41. "thunderous"; "short, pithy simplifications": Bullock, 259. "no labor leader"; "scored a hit": LAT, September 14, 1946; see also APA, September 14, 1946.

318   question periods: Bullock, 260; Voorhis, *Confessions*, 337. "peculiar ideas": Nixon, *RN*, 37–38. "In long strides": Bowers and Blair. "Voorhis . . . so wrought": RN/OH, Jorgensen, 13.

318–19   Voorhis "mumbled": Bullock, 260. "the same thing, virtually": LAT, September 18, 1946. "out of character": *ibid.* "this disturbed me": JV/OH, 5:25.

319   "made my point": Nixon, *RN*, 39. "fuzzy . . . uncertain": Bullock, 261. Hoepple appearance: *ibid.* "transparently political": Bullock, "Rabbits and Radicals," *Southern California Quarterly*, fall 1973, 338. "a little hysterical": RN/OH, Jorgensen, 13. "he cut you to pieces": de Toledano, 52; Costello, 57.

319–20   "resounding success": J. Eisenhower, 90. "some debating tactic . . . half-truths, innuendos"; "have to do this": YN, Stout.

320   "applauded enthusiastically": APA, September 14, 1946. "those . . . in high official places . . . un-American elements": PPB; WDN, September 17, 1946.

320   "leftist taint": LAT, September 18, 1946. "THE TRUTH COMES OUT!": PPB, September 19, 1946; SPR, September 20, 1946. "some dirt to throw": MNP, September 19, 1946. "whatever qualified endorsement": *Independent* (Pasadena), September 20, 1946; APA, September 19, 1946.

321   "all endorsements . . . by the PAC": MNP, September 19, 1946. Whittier debate: *Whittier Reporter*, September 23, 1946; PPB, September 21, 1946.

321–22   "some reservations"; Chotiner's advice: Nixon, *RN*, 39.

322   "subject to communistic influences" *et seq.*: handwritten notes, Campaign and *Confessions* Files, JVP. JV/OH 4:4; 5:39. See also Voorhis–Ernest K. Lindley, April 22, 1960; Voorhis–William Lee Miller, March 9, 1956, JVP. "lagging behind": Arnold, 2.

322–23   "Beginning to make known": Arnold, 32. "race . . . very close": Verne Scoggins–Earl Warren, September 30, 1946, memorandum, Miscellaneous Political File, EWP. rejection through Palmer; "a slow burn": Arnold, 31.

323   Arnold letter *et seq.*: the relevant documents, including original letters to Voorhis and others, are found in Personal, Miscellaneous, and Federal Legislation Files, January–June 1946, EWP and CSA. Ross Marshall's intercession: Verne Scoggins–Warren memorandum, October 15, 1946, U.S. Congress file, EWP.

324   "not, willy nilly, communists": Katcher, 203. "disliked the . . . campaign": M. F. Small, "The Country Editor," unpublished manuscript, 268, BAN. "ever . . . said anything nice": EW/OH, Jones, 29.

324   "such enthusiastic support": YN, Kepple, 9. "walked precincts": Zan Thompson, *Daily Pilot* (Orange County), August 11, 1974. "relentless vigil": Kornitzer, 155.

324–25   typical campaign days: see WDN(I); MNP, October 10, 1946; *Los Angeles*

Examiner, October 14, 1946; WDN, October 2, 1946; MNP, October 2, 1946. "PRO-RUSSIAN VOTES": MNP, October 3, 1946. "I do not question": EMH, October 4, 1946. "Jerry is not a communist but": APA, October 8, 1946.

325 "huge slush fund": MNP, October 12, 1946; WDN, October 11, 1946. "*TRUTH* about the PAC": PPB, October 21, 1946.

326 "DON'T BE FOOLED AGAIN": CAC, October 18, 1946.

326–27 "100,000 communists": SFC, October 14, 1946. "Communist Infiltration": Griffith and Theoharis, 80–81. "Americanism or communism"; "Red sympathizer": the ads and flyers are among campaign material in JVP, as well as California Republican Assembly files, UCLA.

327 "domestic rabbits": CAC, October 11, 1946. "OPA . . . shot through with . . . left-wingers": MNP, October 19, 1946.

327–28 third debate: LAT, October 12, 1946; JV/OH, 4:39; 5:25; see also Brodie, 18. "You're trying to represent me": JV/OH, 5:65–66; see also Arnold, 2. Monrovia debate: PPB, October 31, 1968; LAT, October 24, 1946; MNP, October 24, 1946; WDN, October 24, 1946. "One had to be a rabbit": Nixon, *RN*, 40.

328 Voorhis stays up all night: see *Confessions*, 339–40; Bullock, 266ff.

328 lockout: see Paul Bullock's calculation of ads and coverage in seven district papers, Bullock, 338–39. With other papers of the twelfth included, the disparity would be even greater. "donated": RN/OH, Jorgensen, 83. "work . . . by the hour": *ibid.* "American, American": *ibid.* "all over the place": JV/OH, 5:37.

328–29 radio spots: Dixon interview, UU. "League For Good Government": dated September 30, 1946 and mailed to every tavern in the district, the copy is in the Campaign File, JVP. "NO MEAT": copy in Campaign File, JVP; see also PPB, October 17, 1946, with the notice that it was not "Roy O. Day of Pomona" but "a Major Day in the Republican Headquarters" who placed the cards in local meat markets. "increase the ceiling price": *Confessions*, 324; see also *Chicago Daily News*, November 1, 1958. cost them their credit lines; employees ordered: *Confessions* File, JVP.

329 answer "Nixon for Congress": Bullock, 277. "conclusive action": EMH, October 18, 1946. "solution": JV/OH, 5:49. "lower tax rates": see *What Nixon Said*, 265, JFK.

329–30 joins NAACP: Colgate Prentice–L. A. Bennett, July 15, 1959, Racial Question File, VPA. Ku Klux Klan *et seq.*: see manuscript notes and documents, *Confessions* File, JVP. "Local Jewish . . . Plot": Campaign File, JVP.

330 "DECEPTION . . . HAS NO PLACE"; Exhibits A through H: flyers and ads in Campaign Files, JVP.

330 "They hold all the cards"; "what goes on underneath": handwritten speech notes, Campaign Files, JVP.

330–31 San Gabriel debate: APA, October 29, 1946; *Temple City Press Times*, November 1, 1946. "he was whipped": RN/OH, Day, 10. "He pauses, breathes heavily": *San Gabriel Sun*, October 30, 1946.

331 "How Jerry and Vito Voted": APA, November 2, 1946; MNP, October 29, 1946. "MOSCOW . . . KISS OF DEATH": MNP, October 30, 1946; "sinister fraud": SPR, November 1, 1946. bull horns "upset" Nixon: RN/OH, Day, 25. "a lot of oil company money": PPB, October 31, 1946.

331–32 "War Veterans' . . . League": "The Voorhis Program," Campaign File, JVP; see also WDN, November 1, 1946. contributions of $370/$1000: LAT, November 7, 1946; *Azusa Herald*, November 7, 1946.

332 Fitts statement: APA, November 2, 1946; Bullock, 275. air time refused: see page 44 of Voorhis's handwritten manuscript, *Confessions* File, JVP.

332 Call campaign: JV/OH, 5:4, 46–47: YN, Merton Wray, 8; Remley interview, UU; APA, November 13, 1968; Bullock; 275–76; Helen Douglas, *A Full Life*, 244.

332–33 "impenetrable wall": JV/OH, 5:78. "only the bat-blind": *Los Angeles Herald*, November 2, 1946. "no reactionary in his thinking": LAT, November 3, 1946.

333 "AGAINST NEW DEAL COMMUNISM": *Los Angeles Examiner*, November 4, 1946. "last-minute . . . scurrilous attacks": JV/OH, 5:47; Voorhis's handwritten manuscript, 44, *Confessions* File, JVP. placards appear overnight: Bullock, 278. "I was leading": unpublished manuscript, *Six Crises* File, VPA.

333–34 "watch the things . . . broken": Voorhis, *Confessions*, 344. "The people want a new approach": *Los Angeles Examiner*, November 7, 1946. at the *Times*: Lally Weymouth, "The Word from Mama Buff", *Esquire*, November, 1977, 202–4. "mandate for Americanism": *Los Angeles Herald*, November 7, 1946. "profound effect": *Los Angeles Examiner*, November 6, 1946.

334 "mantle of the White House": J. Eisenhower, 402.

335 "grass-roots campaign": Nixon, *RN*, 41.

335–36 "I can well appreciate": Nixon–John F. Selle, August 8, 1955. Jerry Voorhis File, VPA. "scarcely ever a man": Alsop transcript. "damn fool incumbent": Bourne; Halberstam, 461.

336 "broken and discouraged": Helen Douglas, *A Full Life*, 244. "until their hearts are broken": Voorhis, *Confession of Faith* (New York, 1978), 32. "Oh what a dirty campaign": John V. Coffield–Carson, November 18, 1946, JVP. "to tear down another's reputation": Cora Harry–Voorhis, November 8, 1946, JVP. "There was a lot of material": *Confessions* File, JVP. 1981 interview: Bourne.

336–37 "peripheral but heated issue": Nixon, *RN*, 39. "nothing in the record": Robert H. Finch–Harry W. Gardiner, March 16, 1959, Jerry Voorhis File, VPA. "designed to hurt Nixon": Mazo, 49. "My opponent had . . . the endorsement": *Observer* interview reprinted in *Chicago Sun-Times*, November 18, 1968. "Voorhis had the endorsement": J. Eisenhower, 91.

337 money: Bullock–Voorhis letters (based on interviews with Harrison McCall and Roy Day before their death or incapacity), JVP; handwritten notes, Campaign File, JVP, in which Voorhis records *inter alia* a conversation with "Art Cruse—Treasurer of Nixon campaign [who] agreed that Roy Day's estimate of $32,000 is about correct." See also "Candidate's Campaign Statement of Receipts and Expenditures," Richard M. Nixon, November 5, 1946, CSA; Bowers and Blair; Pat Nixon, "I Say He's a Wonderful Guy." Steve Zetterberg, Voorhis aide and subsequent congressional candidate, later found local twelfth-district Republicans "a little resentful" at all the Nixon money in 1946 "from outside of California": JV/OH, 5:39–40.

Chapter 12. The House, 1947–48

Page

338 "I'm telling you fellows": WDN(I).

338–39 "our pride and joy": *Temple City Times*, November 14, 1946. "he would confide"; "future President": YN, Black, 8. Frank packs; customs search: J. Eisenhower, 93ff.

339–40 Mayflower Hotel: WP, December 17, 1946. finances: by Nixon's own later accounting; see de Toledano, 56; Mazo, 40; Spaulding, 176; Kornitzer, 200–201; Chapter 23 below.

340 "the right words": see Voorhis's handwritten manuscript, 61, *Confessions* File, JVP. letter and meeting: Voorhis, *Confessions*, 347ff; JV/OH, 5:54, Bullock, 283.

341 "I had to win": Bullock, 280. "now a Republican country!": Oshinsky, 53. "wrathful counter-revolution": Goldman, 57. "They were determined": Oshinsky, 53.

341 dismisses Agriculture: Arnold, 5.

342 "remove the Red menace": O'Reilly, 104. "choice assignment": Joe Martin, 194. "promising future"; "rest assured": Kornitzer, 163.

342 Californians lobby; "high recommendation": Joe Martin, 194. "smarten it up": Nixon, *RN*, 44. "politically dangerous": Arnold, 5.

343 "considerable reluctance": Nixon, *RN*, 44–45. "powerful influence": Costello, 182.

343 "No one . . . who did not wish": Joe Martin, 194.

343 "to smash the labor bosses": de Toledano, 58; Costello, 179. Scranton "report": see NYT, February 18, 1947; SFC, February 18, 1947. "a principal architect": Arnold, 6.

344 "labor baron" *et seq.*: *Congressional Record*, April 16, 1947, 3545. "exultant shouts": Donovan, *Conflict and Crisis*, 299. "The Truth About the New Labor Law": Costello, 185–86.

344–45 maiden speech: *Congressional Record*, February 18, 1947, 1129–30.

345 "a quality of steel": *Newsweek*, March 3, 1947. "can't be . . . commies but . . . leanings": Nixon–Dick Cantwell, March 10, 1947, Casoni, 16. "liberties with the facts": Goodman, 201.

346 "uncouth, undignified": Chambers, 536. "narrow-minded, petty": Carr, 213. "so handicapped by . . . vulgarity": quoted in Reeves, 210.

347 "strong prejudices and . . . bitter . . . partisanship": Carr, 227. "deep prejudices . . . narrow horizons": *ibid.*, 235. "I am from Tulane": *ibid.*, 241.

347 Rankin: see O'Reilly, 8ff; Goodman, 205–7; Levitt and Levitt, 34; NYT, August 15, 1948. "worst collection . . . assembled": Reedy interview, UU.

348 "like ladies to the interior decorator": Goodman, 37, 44.

348 "no . . . relevant talents": Carr, 252. "dedicated and fanatical man": *ibid.*, 263. "continually revolting": *St. Louis Post-Dispatch*, October 21, 1947.

348 "he did not like"; "well-known liberals": Carr, 268.

349 "zealot"; "obvious errors": Carr, 269. "grubby men": E. J. Kahn, Jr., *The China Hands* (New York, 1975), 7.

350 "Put Kersten in Congress": Oshinsky, 39. "some good information" *et seq.*: Charles J. Kersten–Peter H. Irons, May 15, 1972, Kersten papers, MU. "Fordham men": Caute, 109. "wastage of taxes": *ibid.*, 108.

350–51 "really taught him": Wills, 35. "like bugging the confessional": Irons interview.

352 *"The Problem of American Communism"* *et seq.*: copy in Francis P. Matthews Papers, HST.

352 "130 communists": WP, March 11–12, 1946. "educational" campaign: Theoharis: 270–71.

352–53 "about certain communists": Wills, 36. "a communist and a liberal": Memorandum of Conference with Mr. G. Howland Shaw, October 24, 1949, AHP. Cronin-Mandel-Kohlberg *et seq.*: Keeley, 196–98.

353 "unimpeachable": Cronin, *The Problem of American Communism*, 50, HST, cited above.

354 "scare hell": Boyer 102–3.

354 "archbishop . . . lay brothers": Goodman, 207. Hoover testimony; "any one area": statement of J. Edgar Hoover . . . before Committee on Un-American Activities, March 26, 1947, Eleanor Bantecou Papers, HST.

354 "Oh, he's the one": Demaris, 117.

354–55 "time of the toad": Dalton Trumbo's title; see Isserman, 244ff. "fear of God": quoted in a Lowell Mellett column, December 29, 1948, HGD. "It will be sensational": WS, July 30, 1947.

355 "anticommunist" films: Goodman, 219. wins contempt citations: *ibid.*, 234.

355 "like hot coals": Ceplair and Englund, 340.

356 "last possible moment": Arnold, 21.

356–57 "such long hours": J. Eisenhower, 93ff. "jocks and imbibers": Cannon. car- pool with Ford: Arnold, 6. "small power nexus": Costello, 181.

357 Donald Jackson: see O'Reilly, 8; Kornitzer, 161–62.

357 McKeesport debate: *McKeesport Daily News*, April 22, 1947; Eric F. Goldman, "The 1947 Kennedy-Nixon 'Tube City' debate," *Saturday Review*, October 16, 1976. "too different": Nixon, *RN*, 43. rake's note: Kennedy Pre-Presi- dential Personal File, JFK.

358 Herter dinner party: J. Eisenhower, 94.

358 "standing there"; "a feeling": Reedy interview, UU.

359 Atkins's photos: see Arnold. "arch character assassin": Nixon–"Dear Col- league" circular, August 1, 1947, Drew Pearson File, VPA.

360 "influence"; "no fixer": Bowers and Blair. "all invitations"; "takes a $500 . . . bite": *ibid.*

360 "drive . . . ambition"; "very proud": YN, Loubet, 20.

361 "obscure": Costello, 179. "I never had the faintest idea": Reedy interview, UU.

361 House record: see "The Public Record of Richard M. Nixon," "Special Report," *Congressional Quarterly*, March 11, 1960; "voting record of Richard Nixon" and "Summary of Richard Nixon's Voting Record": Voting Record File, VPA; "Highlights of the Nixon Record in Congress," Democratic National Committee, Research Division compilation, July 28, 1952, JVP; Nixon-Pedia, Vol. 1: "Handcuffed to a Negative Image," 1947–60, issued by Committee to Re-elect Governor Brown, UCLA; "Vice-President's Record, Stands Ex- amined," *Congressional Quarterly News Features*, August 16, 1956; *Fortnight*, August 4, 1952.

361–62 mimeographed "poll": Gardner, 132. "no conspicuous effort": Costello, 182.

362 "blush for shame": Bowers and Blair. "unthinkable": LAT, August 26, 1947. "completely political man": Robert Coughlan manuscript, William P. Rogers Papers, DDE.

363 "hard and serious workers": NYT, August 27, 1947; Spaulding, 183. visit to Truman: Nixon, *RN*, 43–44.

363 "no junket": Gardner, 124. send-off and hearing aid: Nixon, *RN*, 7. "sub- jected . . . to a skillful . . . program": *ibid.*, 48.

364 "tottering": *ibid.*, 49.

364 "make Henry Wallace . . . piker" *et seq.*: Nixon, *RN*, 50; see also Gardner, 126.

364 atrocities: Hoyt, 253; Gardner, 125ff. "young, vigorous": Nixon, *RN*, 50–51. "soon be reenacted": *ibid.*, 51. "true and brutal face": *ibid.*, 50. Compare his accounts of Trieste, a quarter century apart, in Gardner, 125–26, and *RN*, 50–51, which he embellishes.

365 "a thrill to visit": H. Nixon. "truckload": Nixon, *RN*, 51. "unique in . . . legislative history": Harry Bayard Price, *The Marshall Plan and Its Meaning* (New York, 1955), 54.

365 Herter contacts: see Allen Dulles–Franklin Lindsay, March 20 and April 14, 1948, Allen Dulles Papers, Princeton; and Allen Dulles–Nixon, February 20, 1961, Allen Dulles File, VPA. "lessons" *et seq.*: Nixon, *RN*, 51–52.

366 "I see no reason": Hoyt, 252. "good cure for . . . skeptics": LAT, October 16, 1947. whirlwind speeches: see LAT, October 22, 24, 26, 1947; Julie Eisenhower, 97, notes as well how her father "crusaded" on the issue in his district.

366 "enhancing my popularity": Nixon, *RN*, 51.

367 charades: Jones interview, UU; see also Brodie, 336. "quick smile and it's over" *et seq.*: Mrs. Moore's recollections appeared in WP and LAT, December 20, 1972. "promote a real closeness": Faber, 33.

367 $40,000-a-year business: Gardner, 17. property: see the enumeration by Representative Norris Poulson, January 6, 1953, *Congressional Record Appendix*, A97. ranch-style home: WDN(I). country club investors: YN, Stone, 3. See also Hoyt, 250.

368 "I had already": WP, October 13, 1960. "begun to despair"; "scorned complainers": J. Eisenhower, 97.

368 "great things"; "stunned": *ibid.*

369 "Congressional candidates . . . left out": Hoyt, 254.

369 "they did not think he could win": *ibid.* whitewashed "N's": YN, Newsom, 12.

370 "outstanding young man": WDN, January 22, 24, 1948; Gardner, 134.

370 "Many reputable . . . leaders"; "all out to get Nixon": Roy Day–E. G. Stahlman, February 14, 1948; RDP. "never . . . heavyweight" *et seq.*: RN/OH, Jorgensen, 20, 16–17.

371 "solemn warning": Goldman, 78. "TOTALITARIAN CANDIDATES": WDN, February 7, 1948.

371 "dormant and uninspired": Paul Bullock–Jerry Voorhis, February 27, 1948, JVP. "other . . . Democrats"; "out of desperation": LAT, November 9, 1972.

371 "sound" Jewish: Zetterberg interview, UU. little box: SZ/OH, 2. fall on ice: see LAT, February 14, 1948 ff. "even with pictures": SZ/OH, 23. attacks Clark: WDN, March 3, 1948.

372 filing for primary: LAT, March 13, 1948. "WHITTIER NARROWS": LAT, March 18, 1948.

373 "NIXON'S SILENCE": SZ/OH, 24. For his initial opposition to the dam, including public courtship of the El Monte opponents, see LAT, June 28, 1947, October 26, 1947, January 25, 1948. "I called on him": Kornitzer, 156.

373 "compromise": LAT, March 18, 1948; see also Bullock, 339: SZ/OH, 24–25.

373–74 "Some startling reports": LAT, April 8, 1948.

374 "weakest links": Goodman, 243. "There is no evidence": *ibid.*, 248.

374–75 Harriman wire: LAT, March 7, 1948. "Congress is entitled": *Washington Times-Herald*, March 11, 1948, a newspaper, Goodman notes, that HUAC frequently "made use of."

375 "I was not a member": Nixon–Douglas Maggs, March 16, 1948, Dean's Correspondence File, Duke; see also Condon File, VPA.

375–76 "shameful": see Bert and Peter Andrews, 76. "When Cong. can't get info.": handwritten notes, c. April, 1948, Condon File, VPA. "delinquent teenagers": Goodman, 250, who added "and as risky for anybody in the neighborhood."

376 "walk where ambition led": Goodman, 250.

376 "to curb or control": see Mundt-Nixon Bill File, VPA, especially James P. Gleason's "Memo on Chronology of Mundt-Nixon Internal Security Legislation," July 29, 1952.

376–77 "dignity and intelligence": Carr, 230. "Bill to Tie Reds' Hands": LAT, May 2, 1948. "political proscription": Costello, 189. "spike . . . loose charges": Costello, 188–89. "busily looking for ways": Goodman, 242.

377 investigate "forgeries": LAT, May 16, 1948.

377   "method of Hitler and Stalin": NYHT, May 18, 1948.

378   "such a rush": Sullivan, 44.

378   Stassen-Dewey debate: see NYHT, LAT, NYT, May 18, 1948.

379   "be blamed by all hands"; "commie line": Nixon–Roy Day, May 17, 1948, RDP. "prominent Democrats": WDN, May 3, 1948. "untiring efforts": *ibid.*, May 11, 1948.

379–80   "Fellow Democrats": reproduced in LAT, November 9, 1972. thought Nixon Democrat: *ibid.* "most fearless": LAT, May 18, 1948. "in Azusa too!": reprinted in *Congressional Record Appendix*, May 19, 1948, A3131.

380–81   "characteristic . . . manner": LAT, May 23, 1948. "wished that he . . . died": Brodie, 504. pay raise: WDN, May 24, 1948. office poll: WDN, May 28, 1948. "fearless champion of Democratic principles": *ibid.*

381   "Your Congressman": SZ/OH, 29. "Take God into the polls"; "my deal with Nixon": Steve Zetterberg–*Time, Inc.*, December 22, 1953, HGD.

381   campaign spending: see "Candidate's Campaign Statement of Receipts and Expenditures," Stephen I. Zetterberg, June 1, 1948, Richard M. Nixon, June 1, 1948, CSA; SZ/OH, 20; see also Zetterberg–*Time* letter cited above.

381–82   "Something less than . . . ardent": Arnold, 34, 38.

382   Julie's birth: J. Eisenhower, 98.

Chapter 13. The Case I, August 1948

Page

383   "squeezed oranges": Demaris, 124.

383–84   "difference between the FBI and the attorney general": FBI Memo, Nichols–Tolson, August 27, 1948, HUAC Files, MU; see also O'Reilly, 105. "Hoover's ghost": Demaris, 63–64. "before I got them": Tom Clark Oral History, 210–11, HST. files to HUAC: O'Reilly, 106. "baseless rumor-mongering": Levitt and Levitt, 102–3. "now free to proceed": Thomas–Mundt, July 26, 1948, KMP.

384–85   "Nutmeg Mata Hari": A. J. Leibling's characterization, in Goodman, 257–58. "wrong people"; "valley of the shadow": Goodman, 259. "if . . . corroborated": Cooke, 53–54.

385   "campaign of vilification": Stripling, 94. "keep the heat on": Levitt and Levitt, 34. See Zeligs, 7, for the media buildup.

385–86   "He's ready": Stripling, 97. "consult the floor": Lionel Trilling in *The New York Review of Books*, April 17, 1975. "most disheveled": Nixon, *RN*, 52–53.

386   Chambers's background: see his own *Witness* as well as Weinstein, *Perjury*, and Zeligs.

386   "devastation of empty sockets": *New York Review of Books*, April 17, 1975.

387   "Raskolnikov and . . . Jesus Christ": Goodman, 275.

387   "apathetic about involving others": Weinstein, *Perjury*, 324.

387–88   meeting with Berle: Berle's original notes are set out in FBI Field Report by Ludwig W. R. Oberndorf, January 31, 1949, 13–17, HST; see also Weinstein, *Perjury*, 63–67; Levine, *Eyewitness to History*, 193–95, 209–10; and Berle's diary, Beatrice Bishop Berle and Travis Jacobs, editors, *Navigating the Rapids, 1918–1971* (New York, 1973), 249–50.

388   Berle's check: Weinstein, *Perjury*, 329–30. "go fuck himself": Farago interview, UU.

388   "on the President's desk": FBI Memo, Wacks–Foxworth, August 18, 1941, HST. "By then I was certain": Chambers, 492. Dies episode: see FBI Memo,

Pennington–Ladd, February 3, 1949, MU; Weinstein, *Perjury*, 330. Mandel–Allen episode: FBI Field Report, November 22, 1941, HST.

389   Chambers's first interview; "history, hypothesis, or deduction": FBI letter, Foxworth–Hoover, May 14, 1942, HST.

389   "bumbling operation": Demaris, 115. See the Bureau's own secret chronology on "Delinquencies Noted" in handling of the Chambers information: FBI Memo, December 29, 1948, HST. story circulated: Weinstein, *Perjury*, 331; see also Theoharis, 256–61; and State Department monitoring of Winchell broadcasts, Klaus–Panuch Memorandum October 1, 1946, H. Hubert Wilson Papers, Princeton.

390   Murphy's memorandum and leak to Cronin: see Walter–FBI Memo, March 20, 1945; FBI Memo, Nichols–Tolson, October 10, 1947; FBI Memo, Ladd–Hoover, October 18, 1947; FBI Memo, Tamm–Hoover, November 1, 1957, all HST. The FBI was struck early with the incestuous relationships among Chambers and his contacts, noting that Murphy and Mandel were "very close friends," as well as the ties between HUAC, the conservative press, and Cronin. A detailed accounting of the Cronin leaks is in FBI Memo, Ladd–Hoover, November 25, 1953, HST. "tears streaming down": FBI Letter, Conroy–Hoover, June 26, 1945.

390   Gouzenko-Bentley reports: see Weinstein, *Perjury*, 355–57; Theoharis, 268–70. "accurate": see "Summary Memorandum of November 27, 1945 'Soviet Espionage in the United States,' " HST; sent to the White House and elsewhere, the original memo contained several pages on the Chambers allegations; see Weinstein, 357ff and FBI Memo, "Soviet Espionage in the United States," November 27, 1945, HST. "bigger and bigger": Demaris, 115.

391   "one high American officer": see Klaus–Panuch Memo, October 1, 1946, H. Hubert Wilson Papers, Princeton.

391   "high and trusted officials": Theoharis, 280, 282. Hearst reporter: see O'Reilly, 329. "open secret": Chambers, 493.

392   "most influential communist": Cronin, "The Problem of American Communism in 1945," 49, 37.

392   "Nixon memo": O'Reilly, 332. Nixon aware: O'Reilly, 107.

392–93   OSS/CIA leaks to Nixon: Kohn, 42–43. "told Mr. Nixon": John Chabot Smith, 145. "stacked deck": Weinstein, "Nixon vs. Hiss," 76.

393–94   "Almost exactly nine years ago" *et seq.*, HUAC 1, 564–66. "Hell, why is this?": Weinstein, "Nixon vs. Hiss," 76.

394   Chambers's testimony in public: see John Chabot Smith, 162. voice broke: Andrews, 46. "This one incident": Mazo, 52.

394–95   "as was Alger Hiss"; "purpose . . . not primarily espionage" *et seq.*: HUAC 1, 566–86, containing Chambers's complete testimony. Stripling ready with files: see Cooke, 57. "the first time": Nixon, *Six Crises*, 4.

395   "He cried?"; "very fond": Cooke, 58.

395   this sort of thing in Mississippi: Zeligs, 11; see also John Chabot Smith, 168.

395–96   "one of its eventual objectives"; lost moment: Carr, 117.

396   "courage and good patriotism"; "splendid witness": Cooke, 59. "TIME EDITOR CHARGES": Weinstein, *Perjury*, 6.

397   "No lark more blithe": Zeligs, 159. "I know of no one": *ibid.*, 161.

397   "simultaneously in . . . *Social Register*": Goldman, 104.

397   Hiss's background: as for Chambers, see Zeligs, and Weinstein, *Perjury*; also T. Hiss, and A. Hiss, *Recollections of a Life* (New York, 1988).

397–98   "DO NOT TAKE THIS FATAL STEP": T. Hiss, 50. "self-assertive woman": Marbury, 79.

398–99 "his neat coat": Stripling, 111. "no respect": Weinstein, "Nixon vs. Hiss," 77. "what shits they were": T. Hiss, 131. cartoon: WP, August 5, 1948. "deny unqualifiedly": HUAC 1, 642–43, carries his opening statement.

399 "Is it necessary?" *et seq.*: HUAC 1, 642–59, for Hiss's questioning and testimony. face reddens: Andrews, 51. "rather insolent": Andrews, 52. "impressive": Nixon, *Six Crises*, 6.

399 given photo: John Chabot Smith, 174.

399–400 "never smiled"; "never took his eyes off": Cooke, 61, 64. "virtuoso performance": Nixon, *Six Crises*, 7. asks Mandel if alias: *ibid.*, 8. "moment of rare innocence": Cooke, 63.

400 closing exchange: Andrews, 55. "sit sourly": Cooke, 64. "much too careful": Mazo, 55. "too mouthy": Chambers, 555. "He had the day": Nixon, *Six Crises*, 9.

401 "a dreadful man": John Chabot Smith, 180, Weinstein, 9.

401 "incurable drunkard": Chambers, 547. "going to kill . . . Committee": Nixon, *Six Crises*, 9.

401 "shaking with anger"; "stands convicted": Nixon, *Six Crises*, 9.

401 Truman's "red herring": *Washington Star News*, August 5, 1948 .

401–2 "state of shock"; "We're ruined": Nixon, *Six Crises*, 10. "quite apparent . . . taken in": Nixon, "Memorandum on the Hiss-Chambers Case," undated, Hiss-Chambers File, Ralph de Toledano Papers, HI. (Cited hereafter as "Memorandum on Hiss-Chambers.")

402 "Let's wash our hands": Nixon, *Six Crises*, 10. "a public confession" *et seq.*: *ibid.*, 10–11; Nixon, "Memorandum on Hiss-Chambers," cited above. "hopping mad": Andrews, 59.

402–3 "no action": Nixon, *Six Crises*, 10. "*prima facie* perjury": Stripling, 116. "show"; "too sensitive" *et seq.*: Nixon, "Memorandum on Hiss-Chambers." "vaguely dissatisfied": Stripling, 116. "calculated . . . campaign": Nixon, *Six Crises*, 11. Mandel's "simple procedure": Chambers, 558.

403 "I had put myself": Nixon, *Six Crises*, 11. "No one . . . more aware": *ibid.*, 13.

404 "a personal thing": Weinstein, *Perjury*, 17. "big leagues now": Weinstein, "Nixon vs. Hiss," 79.

404 "sense of relief": Hiss–Dulles, August 5, 1948; Dulles–Jessup, August 9, 1948, both JFD.

404–5 "RED HERRING": NYT, August 6, 1948. "twilight zone"; "failed to . . . justify": WP, August 6, 1948. "fury and vehemence": Nixon, *Six Crises*, 14.

405 "taken in"; "obligation": Nixon, *Six Crises*, 15.

405 Hummer–Cronin–Nixon: Weinstein, "Nixon vs. Hiss," 76; Theoharis, 274.

405–6 "little optimism": Stripling, 117. "personal and confidential": see O'Reilly, 108; FBI Memo, Nichols–Tolson, September 7, 1948, MU.

406 "mysterious witness . . . to 'crack wide open' ": NYHT, August 6, 1948; see also Reuben, *The Honorable Mr. Nixon*, 25. "my . . . intimate knowledge": Chambers, 560. "as well prepared": Nixon, *Six Crises*, 15. "shuffling"; "air of fret"; "Mandel hovered": Chambers, 558. "workmanlike curiosity": Cooke, 66.

406–7 Chambers's Foley Square testimony: HUAC 1, 661–72.

407 "dazzled by detail": Stripling, 119. "either he knew Hiss or . . . made . . . study": Nixon, "Memorandum on Hiss-Chambers," cited above. "personal ring of truth"; "he had to train himself": Nixon, *Six Crises*, 16.

408   "some motive we do not know"; "fine family": Nixon, *Six Crises*, 18. dis-
       crepancies; gap in record: John Chabot Smith, 186–89.

408   "usurping the function": WP, August 7, 1948.

409   "get no assistance whatever": Nixon, "The Hiss Case—a Lesson for the
       American People," reprint of House speech, January 26, 1950, Alger Hiss
       File, VPA. "seldom cool": Stripling, 119. questioning of Perlo and Silverman:
       Goodman, 262–65.

409–10 "ineffable bad taste": Goodman, 266. Nixon's retort to White: Cooke, 58.

410–11 "to avoid publicity"; "a man he really knew": Andrews, 62. visit to Chambers:
       see *ibid.*, and Nixon's account in *Six Crises*, 21–23, though the latter somewhat
       confuses the narrative and does not identify this first visit to Westminster as
       happening on August 9.

411   "I knew from personal experience": Nixon, *Six Crises*, 23. "I became certain":
       Andrews, 62.

411–12 Rogers's background: see Joseph M. Harvey's biographical series in BG,
       August 14–26, 1960; Richard L. Wilson, "Nixon's Best Friend," *Look*, May
       10, 1960; *Rochester Times Union*, January 9, 1954; John Osborn, "Strategist-
       In-Chief For Desegregation," *Life*, November 10, 1958. "I'll never have to
       prove": R. Smith, 245.

412   "little niceties"; "lily pad operation": Anthony Lewis, "Close-up of Our
       Lawyer in Chief," *New York Times Magazine*, April 6, 1958. "I don't
       think . . . any doubt" *et seq.*: from Rogers's version of the meeting, *Rochester
       Times Union*, January 9, 1954.

412   "moral impression": Kornitzer, 170–71. "basically not a confident man":
       transcript of Rogers interview with Bela Kornitzer, March 27, 1959, William
       P. Rogers Papers, DDE.

413   "A big gun": Kersten–Earl Mazo, July 11, 1958, Charles J. Kersten Papers,
       MU. "Dewey campaign . . . grateful": Nixon, *RN*, 56.

414   "torn between loyalty and duty" *et seq.*: Mundt told the story on a Washington
       television program, reported in WP, July 30, 1962. "this tangled web of
       evidence": Mundt–Brownell, August 13, 1948, KMP. "Peurifoy . . .
       absolutely satisfied": John Foster Dulles, "Memorandum for Confiden-
       tial Files," Carnegie Endowment, March 18, 1948, JFD. In 1945, the same
       Peurifoy had even complained to Alger Hiss about FBI leaks to the
       Republicans. "Hoover must have decided that Truman is going to get
       licked . . . I hate to turn over any security stuff to them because it's going
       to get leaked." See T. Hiss, 123ff for this and other bureaucratic machinations
       in the State Department.

414–15 friendly Congressmen lobbying HUAC for Hiss: see Dulles's copy of John-
       ston–Hiss, August 10, 1948, JFD. "expected Carnegie . . . support": Ker-
       sten–Mazo, July 11, 1958, Charles J. Kersten Papers, MU.

415   "almost impossible to believe": Nixon, *Six Crises*, 21; see also Allen Dulles's
       account of the meeting that "hot evening": Allen Dulles–Malcolm Muir, May
       4, 1950, JFD. "courage and integrity": Nixon, *Six Crises*, 21. Dulles advises
       Hiss against confrontation; HUAC "jurisdiction": see Zeligs, 10; John Chabot
       Smith, 193.

416   "back of an old envelope": Kersten–Mazo, July 11, 1958, Charles J. Kersten
       Papers, MU. Like other salient points in the narrative, Nixon's several ac-
       counts of the case omit the Levine visit. Levine's list: see Weinstein, *Perjury*,
       329.

416   "If you became convinced": Andrews, x. For Andrews's earlier clash with
       Hiss, see T. Hiss, 116. "sparred around"; "free to use": Andrews, 72–73.

417 "sixth sense"; "He's holding something back": Nixon, *Six Crises*, 23, who again confuses the dates of the Stripling and Andrews visits to Chambers. "Chambers . . . knows exactly": from a Stripling statement to the FBI. See FBI Memo, Nichols–Tolson, December 20, 1948, HST. "sauntered down"; "listless . . . skeptical": Andrews, 226. "some blunt questions" *et seq.*: Andrews, 73–74.

417–18 "grilled him": Nixon, *Six Crises*, 23. "one of his 'trances' ": Andrews, 75. "for any evil reason": from a Chambers–Andrews letter, quoted in Andrews, 226. "his arm under Mrs. Hiss's neck": *ibid*, 76.

418 "helluva story": Andrews, ii. lecture on "careless methods" *et seq.*: *ibid.*, 76–77.

418 Andrews as adviser: Kornitzer, 178. "every rat hole": Andrews, 77.

419 "fingerprints on slick paper": FBI Memo, Nichols–Tolson, August 18, 1948, AHP.

419 "during this period . . . definite conclusion": Nixon, "Memorandum on Hiss-Chambers," cited above.

419–20 "unable to find a flaw": Associated Press dispatch, August 14, 1948; see also Reuben, *The Honorable Mr. Nixon*, 32. "to assure convictions": see Theoharis, 280. "SLOW TO ACT": *Life*, August 16, 1948. "make that fellow president": Halberstam, 366.

420–25 Hiss testimony August 16: HUAC 1, 935–74.

422 "the gospel truth": John Chabot Smith, 203.

423 "I was the only member . . . who . . . knew": Nixon, "Memorandum on Hiss-Chambers."

424 "compulsive need"; "very quality": see Zeligs, 227.

424 cold silence; *Time* feature: Zeligs, 229.

424 "one further factor": Nixon, "Memorandum on Hiss-Chambers."

425 "When Chambers answered . . . case . . . broken": *ibid*. "lying son of a bitch": Weinstein, "Nixon vs. Hiss," 78.

425–26 leaks: see Andrews, 90; Levitt and Levitt, 42. Significant elements of the secret hearing on August 16, including Hiss's refusal to take a lie detector test, appeared in NYHT, August 17, 1948. "several hours": Nixon, *Six Crises*, 29–30. "before Hiss could build up": Mazo, 57. "flush him": Nixon, *RN*, 61. "victim of tyranny": Thomas L. Stokes, quoted in John Chabot Smith, 213.

426 "same conclusion": Nixon, *RN*, 61. "listless and undecided" *et seq.*: Chambers, 600.

427 scene: Audubon prints: Nixon, *Six Crises*, 31. McDowell calls Hiss: John Chabot Smith, 213. call to Harvard Club, *ibid.*, 215.

427–30 Commodore Hotel testimony: HUAC 1, 975–1000.

428 "tempted to bite": Nixon, *RN*, 62. In a memo written for a sympathetic author (Mazo, 58–59), Nixon wrote more emphatically, "I wondered why Chambers didn't reach out and bite his finger."

429 "hardly keep a straight face": Nixon, *Six Crises*, 33.

429 "This oracular statement": A. Hiss, *In the Court of Public Opinion*, 90.

430 "shaking his fist": Nixon, *RN*, 63. "pricked with a hot needle": Nixon, *Six Crises*, 36.

431 "naked and desperate scramble": Cooke, 74. "Alger behaved very badly": see Weinstein, 38. "I imagined myself in his place": Nixon, *Six Crises*, 37. "Hi-ya, Mistah Crawz-li?": Chambers, 615. "vindicated and I personally would receive credit": Nixon, *Six Crises*, 37.

431 "tuned in . . . play-by-play": see Ray Erwin, "Reporter Practices, Preaches

'Digging,' " *Editor and Publisher*, December 22, 1956. Nixon leaks: see NYT and NYHT, August 18, 1948. "lasted for over three hours": Weinstein, *Perjury*, 39. Chambers's dinner with Luce: see Chambers, 617. Hiss's calls and press conference: John Chabot Smith, 227–28.

432   Nixon hearings August 18: see HUAC 1, 1001–23.

432   "tired"; "battle won"; "she was a woman": Nixon, *Six Crises*, 38.

432–33   "demurely"; "our common Quaker background": Nixon, *Six Crises*, 38. "nervous and frightened": *ibid.* "another step": NYT, August 23, 1948. "a more fanatical communist": Nixon, *Six Crises*, 38.

433   "I could not go through another"; "for your own sake": Chambers, 618.

433–34   "If there is anything else": Chambers, 618. "liked and trusted"; "very small creature": *ibid.* "numerous calls": see again FBI Memo, Nichols–Tolson, August 18, 1948, AHP.

434   Nixon hearings August 20 and 24: see HUAC 1, 1015–75.

434–35   "a man possessed": Levitt and Levitt, 55–56. "eighteen to twenty hours a day" *et seq.*: Nixon, *Six Crises*, 39–41. "almost frightening": J. Eisenhower, 100. sleeping pill: Nixon, *Six Crises*, 41.

435   "day of infernal heat"; "cameras buzzed": Cooke, 85.

435–37   hearing of August 25: HUAC 1, 1075–1206. "the most watchful . . . straining at the leash": Cooke, 87.

436   "disgust on the dais": Andrews, 127.

436   "thoroughly destroyed": John Chabot Smith, 233.

437   "too biased . . . too many ends left loose": WP, August 26, 1948. "evasive testimony"; "forthright and emphatic": see "Interim Report on Hearing Regarding Communist Espionage in the United States Government," House of Representatives, Committee on Un-American Activities, August 28, 1948.

437–38   "the really dangerous ones": NYT, August 30, 1948.

438   "whether . . . Hiss or Chambers": see George Elsey memorandum to Clark Clifford, August 27, 1948, George M. Elsey Papers, HST. "trouble was . . . Hoover": see White House Aide Eben Ayers's diary, August 31, 1948, Eben Ayers Papers, HST. "This is Mr. Hiss's young son": Chambers, 709.

438   "never volunteer information": Chambers, 709.

438   *Meet the Press*: see "Whittaker Chambers Meets the Press": *American Mercury*, February 1949. "crossed the bridge": Chambers, 711. "damned outrage": *ibid.*, 712. "soft-pedal . . . red herring": NYHT, September 1, 1948. Gallup Poll: WP, August 29, 1948.

439   "Are you convinced": Levine, *Eyewitness to History*, 204.

Chapter 14. The Case II, September–December 1948

Page

440–41   letter to Andrews: Nixon–Andrews, September 7, 1948, Alger Hiss File, VPA.

440–44   letter to Dulles: Nixon–John Foster Dulles, September 7, 1948, marked "PERSONAL & CONFIDENTIAL"; Nixon–Dulles, September 7, 1948, marked "PERSONAL," both JFD.

444   Dulles replies: John Foster Dulles–Nixon, September 9, 1948; Dulles–Nixon, September 9, 1948, marked "PERSONAL," JFD.

444   Endowment politics: see John Chabot Smith, 234, and the copies to Dulles of Hiss's supportive letters, August 9–September 2, 1948, JFD. "no intimate

association": John Foster Dulles Memorandum for Herbert Brownell, Jr. and Files, August 20, 1948, JFD. "With understandable bitterness," as one book put it, Hiss later commented of the Endowment chairman, "John Foster Dulles was not only advising me on how to proceed in my defense, but was simultaneously advising Nixon and the House Committee on how to prosecute me as well." See Levitt and Levitt, 25. "it does strike me as curious": Eisenhower–James T. Shotwell, September 21, 1948, JFD.

445   "skeletons in the closet": WDN, September 23, 1948. "he lauded . . . FBI"; "important new developments": *San Francisco Examiner*, September 23, 1948.

445–46   Pearson column: *Los Angeles Daily News*, September 20, 1948. "investigate immediately": Nixon telegram to Arnold, September 21, 1948, Drew Pearson File, VPA. "further unfair treatment": Arnold memorandum to Nixon, September 22, 1948, Pearson File, VPA.

446–47   call to Nichols: FBI Memo, Nichols–Tolson, September 29, 1948, AHP.

447–48   "Well, Alger"; "each day of delay": cited by Levitt and Levitt, 68. "similar charges against political and academic figures"; "advised . . . to go slow": Marbury, 85. "reputation . . . irretrievably destroyed": Marbury, 88. "skeletons . . . would certainly be discovered"; "impression . . . she felt . . . responsible": *ibid*.

448   "I welcome Mr. Hiss's daring suit": Chambers, 722. "a program of education": WDN, October 15, 1948.

448   "progress reports"; Humphrey "promising": see WDN, October 25–31, 1948.

449   "the honor of making you known": Reid–Nixon, September 28, 1948, Helen Reid Papers, HST. "carried away the laurels": Reid–Nixon, November 2, 1948, Helen Reid Papers, HST. "Code" for HUAC: Costello, 199.

449   Harvard Club meeting: see "Memorandum for File," October 19, 1948, Hiss Personal, AHP.

449–50   "Democrats . . . given up hope": WDN, October 25, 1948. "We're losing . . . throwing it away"; "Earl Warren . . . sitting on his butt": Arnold, 36.

450   "unduly biased": Arnold, 36. "No one . . . except Harry S Truman": *Newsweek*, November 8, 1948. "He wasn't . . . looking under beds": R. Smith, 507. "fleck it lightly": *ibid.*, 508. "which might face you": John Foster Dulles cable, "TOP SECRET FOR DEWEY, ALLEN DULLES EYES ONLY," September 24, 1948, JFD. Truman quips: *Newsweek*, November 8, 1948.

450–51   dark "skepticism": Arnold, 37. "He escaped interment": *Fortnight*, December 31, 1948. "No searching analysis": Irwin Ross, *The Loneliest Campaign* (New York, 1969), 245.

451   "Dewey felt it was not proper": Nixon, *Six Crises*, 45–46. "I love Democrats": Kornitzer, 179.

452   Thomas takes the Fifth: see Goodman, 284. "a 'comer' with no place to go": Nixon, *RN*, 72.

452   "I think . . . Truman has won"; "some way to punish me": Chambers, 750.

452   "no stomach for battle": Levine, *Eyewitness to History*, 205. Chambers's grand jury testimony October 14: see Weinstein, *Perjury*, 177; Chambers, 724. "no action": NYT, October 14, 1948.

453   "the business of filching": Isaac Don Levine, "The Inside Story of Our Soviet Underworld," part 2, *Plain Talk*, October 1948. "My hair stood up"; "never heard of fetishes": Levitt and Levitt, 70, see also Zeligs, 234.

453–54   Chambers's deposition: see Marbury, 92–93; Weinstein, *Perjury*, 170–72. "wet on a lollipop": Chambers, 733. "had better get it": *ibid.*, 735. "better left unexplored": Chambers, 375.

454 "a mood of deep depression": Nixon, *Six Crises*, 46.

454–55 "nothing . . . I could do"; "interfere with our vacation": Nixon, *Six Crises*, 46.

455 "boil him in oil": Chambers, 793. "incredibly alone . . . Nixon was busy": *ibid.*, 735.

455 "PLEASE HAVE MY THINGS READY" *et seq.*: Weinstein, *Perjury*, 172 ff. "good God": Chambers, 736.

455–56 "with a flourish": Marbury, 93. "for reasons of friendship": Weinstein, *Perjury*, 174–75.

456 "weight of God's purpose": Chambers, 747.

456 litany of documents: see Weinstein, *Perjury*, 257 ff and Chambers, 749. "devastating effect": Marbury, 94.

456–57 "Mr. Hiss agreed," *et seq.*: John Chabot Smith, 245. "that appalling day": *ibid.*, 247.

457 "total confusion": Weinstein, "Nixon vs. Hiss," 147. similarity of handwritten and typed notes: see Weinstein, *Perjury*, 241–50, 255–63.

457–58 "nothing to lose": Marbury, 95.

458 "charges against Chambers": FBI Memo, Ladd–Hoover, November 23, 1948, HST. "sincere affection": FBI Memo, Special Agent in Charge, Baltimore–Hoover, November 25, 1948, HST. "quite likely"; "truth would prevail"; "best possible way": Marbury, 97. "went into a panic": T. Hiss, 137.

458–59 "any other documents": FBI Memo, Fletcher–Ladd, December 2, 1948, HST. "very startling information": WP, Decmeber 1, 1948. "about to die": *Washington Daily News*, December 1, 1948. "going down the drain": Stripling, 141.

459 "a deliberate leak": Andrews, 174. "this is too hot" *et seq.*: *ibid.*, 174–75. "something had happened": Chambers, 751.

460 "dropped a hint": Marbury, 99. Vazzana reveals documents: see Weinstein, "Nixon vs. Hiss," 144–47, and also Stripling, 141–43, who was the first to tell at least part of the story.

460–61 "nervous and highly irritable" *et seq.*: Weinstein, *Perjury*, 188.

461 "I have a hunch"; "rueful air": Andrews, 175. "if it'll shut your mouth, I'll go": Weinstein, *Perjury*, 188. "Playing a long hunch": Nixon, *Six Crises*, 47.

461–62 "another generation"; "stuffed raven": see Stripling, 143–44 for the investigator's vivid description of the meeting. "trying to avoid a topic": *ibid.* "what I have been afraid of": Nixon, *Six Crises*, 47. "why you're here" *et seq.*: Stripling, 143–44.

462 "You keep . . . second bombshell": Nixon, *Six Crises*, 47. "never took his eyes off": Chambers, 752, who for some reason simply omits Nixon's presence in his account of the conversation.

462–63 "You will understand this": Stripling, 140–41. "photographic technicians?": Stripling, 144. "what do you think he's got?"; "a damn thing": Weinstein, "Nixon vs. Hiss," 147.

463 "the heart to tell Pat": Nixon, *Six Crises*, 48. explains "predicament" to Stripling: *ibid.*

463–64 December 1 call to Nichols: FBI Memo, Nichols–Tolson, December 2, 1948, AHP. Characteristically, Hoover did not pass along Nixon's crucial intelligence to his superiors in the Justice Department.

464 "You were too nice": Andrews, 175–76. "I could not understand" *et seq.*: Nixon, *RN*, 68.

465 Congressman "in high spirits" *et seq.*: William "Fishbait" Miller, as told to Frances Spatz Leighton, *Fishbait: The Memoirs of the Congressional Doorkeeper* (Englewood Cliffs, N.J., 1977), 41–42.

465–66   "I mean *everything*": Andrews, 176; see also Nixon, *RN*, 68. "Get what you can . . . and sit tight": Stripling, 145.

466   "GET OFF HOOK": Andrews, cable to Dulles, December 2, 1948, JFD.

466   "clinching evidence"; "like a kid": Weinstein, *Perjury*, 193. "the indispensable disclosure": Chambers, 739–40.

467   Hiss "investigators" might "ransack": Chambers, 752. "art of concealment": *ibid.*, 753. Stripling serves subpoena: see Stripling, 145; Chambers, 753–54.

467   "playing around with my girlfriend"; "locate the typewriter": the note and Chambers's suggestion are contained in FBI Field Report, March 10, 1949, HST; see also Weinstein, *Perjury*, 185. "an eternity": Stripling, 145.

468   "INFORMATION HERE": Andrews, 179.

468   "what you are looking for": Chambers, 754. "final bathos": Cooke, 92. "Dick Tracy?"; "I don't think . . . any good": Stripling, 146.

469   "I tossed away the top": Chambers, 754. killing frosts: Harlan Vinnedge correspondence; see also Vinnedge–Hiss, July 1, and August 3, 1974, AHP. Chambers even notes (751) that "because of a late start," the pumpkins were "still green." "HAVE ADVISED STRIPLING": Andrews, 179.

469–70   "DEPARTMENT OF STATE": Stripling, 146–47. "SECOND BOMBSHELL": Nixon, *Six Crises*, 48. Compare Stripling's rather different version of the cable: Stripling, 147. "Here we go again": Nixon, *Six Crises*, 48.

470   "DOCUMENTS INCREDIBLY HOT": Andrews, 179.

470–71   photograph of staff: see Goodman, 382ff. "real affection and admiration": FBI Field Report, December 4, 1948, HST.

471   "such a vast network": see Andrews, 177–78; the December 4 statement is also in KMP. "heard nothing . . . advised *at once*": FBI Memo, Fletcher–Ladd, December 4, 1948, HST; see Weinstein, *Perjury*, 185–86. "to leave the ship": Andrews, 180.

471–72   Coast Guard Flight: I am indebted to Harlan Vinnedge for his meticulous research into the flight to and from the *Panama*, including the correction of most previous accounts; Vinnedge correspondence, attaching Bridge Log of *Panama*, December 5, 1948, and Vinnedge correspondence with the late William Arnold and Larry L. Davis, Coast Guard pilot of the PBM. "hardly able to believe": J. Eisenhower, 101. "no longer . . . one man's word"; "by far the most important": see Reuben, *The Honorable Mr. Nixon*, 78.

472–73   "a joke?"; "a crazy man": Nixon, *Six Crises*, 49. "broken our code": Stripling, 148. "No . . . code . . . any difficulty": Kahn interview. Kahn tells the story (*The Codebreakers*, London, 1973) of a retiring U.S. Foreign Service officer who gave a farewell speech in Gray Code, which a sizable audience "followed with ease." The night before Pearl Harbor, Roosevelt penned a note to Cordell Hull: "Shoot this to Grew . . . can go in Gray . . . don't mind if it gets picked up."

473   "one quick look": Andrews, 184. "greatest treason conspiracy" *et seq.*: NYHT, December 7, 1948. learns of possible Chambers indictment: see Nixon, "The Hiss Case—A Lesson for the American People," reprint of House speech, January 26, 1950, Alger Hiss File, VPA. "blame . . . Mr. Chambers": Goodman, 279. "let the chips fall": Weinstein, *Perjury*, 185.

473   "I'm filing . . . in pumpkins": Andrews, 182. "concoction": Tom Clark, Oral History, 191, HST. "flabbergasted": Stripling, 148.

474–75   "record assembly"; "I have read the record carefully": NYT, December 7, 1948.

475–77   film crisis: Weinstein, "Nixon vs. Hiss," 151ff., cited above, and *Perjury*, 272–73, relates the most complete version; see also Stripling, 148–50; Nixon, *Six Crises*, 54–56.

476 "harshest tone": Andrews, 188. "Nixon . . . one of the few friends who really understood": Chambers, 768, who remembered Nixon's voice as "harsh with . . . just anger."

477 "checking into every aspect": Andrews, 189.

477–78 "What took them so long?"; "special prosecutor": see NYHT and WP, December 7, 1948. "table-thumping": Reuben, *The Honorable Mr. Nixon*, 81.

478 "air . . . so blue": Chambers, 771. Nixon describes the "violent verbal battle" and eventual compromise in *Six Crises*, 56–57. "pointless pain": Chambers, 770. "You mistrusted me": Stripling, 151. "Are you *sure*": *ibid.*

478 "my testimony . . . the truth"; "world hates a quitter": Chambers, 774–75. "now on another plane": *ibid.*, 773.

479 "from unimpeachable sources": Levitt and Levitt, 95–96. "systematic and surreptitious looting": testimony of December 7 and 8 is in HUAC 2, 1386–1428; see also Andrews, 191.

479 "before any . . . other people": NYT, December 9, 1948. "Nixon . . . out to embarrass the Bureau": FBI Memo, Ladd–Hoover, December 8, 1948, AHP. Hoover was now only too ready to exploit Nixon's apparent independence of the FBI, noting at the bottom of the Ladd memo, "Advise A. G. by memo. H." "very anxious" to get "specimens"; "extremely mad at the attorney general": FBI Memo, Ladd–Hoover, December 9, 1948, AHP. "approaching President Truman": FBI Memo, Whitson–Fletcher, December 9, 1948, AHP.

480 approach to Lovett: FBI Memo, Keay–Ladd, December 13, 1948, AHP. "not open to . . . doubts": NYHT, December 13, 1948. editorial reaction: see Andrews, 195–98.

480 "not even the immense power": Nixon, *Six Crises*, 59.

481 "indispensable ordeal": see Weinstein, *Perjury*, 276–77. "calm, pudgy little man": *Time*, December 13, 1948. "would be no indictment": Andrews, 196–97.

481 "CONFLICT OF STATEMENTS": Andrews, 198. "new calfskin briefcase": *ibid.*, 199.

481 "Rankin nearly had a fit"; "his own responsibility": FBI Letter, Hood–Hoover, March 30, 1949, AHP.

482 "He did not want to be abhorrent": FBI Memo, Ladd–Hoover, December 13, 1948, AHP.

482–83 "The indictment . . . a whitewash": NYHT, December 14, 1948. "expected . . . out the window": Zeligs, 360. "end up with an indictment": FBI Memo, December 14, 1948, HST. "furnished the link": Reuben, *The Honorable Mr. Nixon*, 88.

483 "in an amazing manner": T. J. Donegan teletype to Hoover, December 14, 1948, HST. "Until the day I die": Nixon, *Six Crises*, 60. "great sense of relief": *ibid.* "vindicates . . . many long months": Goodman, 280. "a politically inspired matter": Zeligs, 362.

484 "as they jump out of windows" *et seq.*: Goodman, 282–83.

484–85 "the Committee has made mistakes": WS, December 19, 1948. "the most startling disclosures": see both *Annual Report of the Committee on Un-American Activities to the United States House of Representatives*, December 31, 1948; and *Soviet Espionage within the United States Government*, HUAC Report, December 31, 1948. "He is on the side of the Bureau": FBI Memo, Nichols–Tolson, January 14, 1949, AHP.

485 "political babe": *Fortnight*, December 31, 1948.

Chapter 15. The Case III, 1949

Page

486   "loosed within American life": Goldman, 113. Inaugural scene: *ibid.*, 91. "tells all his secrets": *ibid.*, 101.

487   "against any aggressor": Goldman, 135. "Same old runaround": FBI Memo, Laughlin–Fletcher, January 4, 1949, HST.

487   offers microfilm to Hiss's attorneys: Levitt and Levitt, 319. "far too drastic": Associated Press Dispatch, January 18, 1949, Alger Hiss File, VPA.

487–88   "his extensive knowledge": WP, January 17, 1949. holds on to microfilm: FBI Letter, Hood–Hoover, March 30, 1949, AHP.

488   Chambers confesses homosexuality: FBI Memo, Fletcher–Ladd, February 18, 1949; Hoover–Clark, March 1, 1949, HST; see also Weinstein, *Perjury*, 118–19, 399. "incensed, angry . . . agitated"; "attorney general . . . could be impeached": FBI Memo, Hottel–Hoover, March 31, 1949, AHP. "Chambers still sees . . . Nixon": FBI Memo, Ladd–Hoover, April 7, 1949, AHP; see also FBI Memo, Nichols–Tolson, March 30, 1949, AHP.

488–89   threat to Hobson: see Zeligs, 407–8, on what Hobson called "polite blackmail" (FBI reports, like HUAC and Washington gossip, had soon begun to allude to some "perverted" relations between Chambers and either Hiss or his stepson: see FBI Memo, Mohr–Tolson, June 1, 1949, HST.). "but a hair's breadth"; "Perfidy and terror": the letters are attached to an FBI report to Hoover, May 23, 1949, HST.

489–90   "Unclean, unclean!": see Weinstein, *Perjury*, 415. "some interesting information": Mundt–Levine, June 10, 1949, KMP. "as to how the judge functions": FBI Memo, Nichols–Tolson, June 13, 1949, AHP.

490   "Dick has a heck of a lot at stake": Lasky–Murphy, undated, c. June, 1949, AHP. (The Lasky–Murphy, Nixon–Lasky correspondence comes from FBI and Justice Department files released under Freedom of Information suits.) "appreciation for the 'excellent' job": Lasky–Murphy, undated, AHP. Nixon memo: Nixon–Lasky, undated, AHP.

490–91   Wadleigh hoped Hiss would "come clean under pressure": FBI Memo, Nichols–Tolson, June 28, 1949, AHP; see also FBI Memo, Fletcher–Ladd, June 28, 1949, AHP.

491   Nixon questions for Hiss: Nixon–Lasky, undated, AHP.

491–92   Levine's visit to Murphy: Levine, *Eyewitness to History*, 209. jurors threatened; Lasky et al. publish transcripts: see Levitt and Levitt, 145–46; Weinstein, *Perjury*, 469. *The New York Journal American* published names and addresses of the pro-Hiss jurors with reports that they had been threatened. See Caute, 61. "prejudice . . . people will be shocked": John Chabot Smith, 357.

492   "nothing bad . . . to Mr. Hiss": Levitt and Levitt, 147–48. "A handful of administration apologists": Goodman, 311; see also Carr, 234; *Newsweek*, July 18–25, 1949.

492–93   " 'left-wing' . . . League of Women Voters"; "prosecuted": FBI Memo, Hottel–Hoover, July 11, 1949. "visibly shaken": Levine, *Eyewitness to History*, 209. "unwise . . . out on a limb": Theoharis, 327.

493   "that it be kept quiet": Levitt and Levitt, 319.

494   "not to permit you": Weinstein, *Perjury*, 413. "has been identified": Levitt and Levitt, 191–92.

495   "230099 . . . between March, 1929 . . . August, 1930": Levitt and Levitt, 189. "sale . . . 1932": *ibid.*

495   "how he could sell": Levitt and Levitt, 194. "unrelability" "no . . . short-ages": *ibid.*

496   "We will corroborate": WP, June 2, 1949. "The typewriter . . . was used to type the evidence": FBI Report, "Re: Woodstock Typewriter," October 27, 1949, HST. "These specimens . . . same typewriter": FBI Memo, Branigan–Sullivan, April 2, 1962, AHP.

496   "No identity . . . attempted or needed": Levitt and Levitt, 195. "never had any information": the sworn affidavit is attached to FBI Memo, Branigan–Sullivan, April 2, 1962, AHP.

496–97   "If you think"; "horrifying cynicism": Levitt and Levitt, 209.

497   "virtually no security": Zeligs, 367.

497–98   "NEVER be acquitted" *et seq.*: Lasky–Nixon, January 1, 1950, Victor Lasky File, VPA. "common man's resistance": Cooke, 305. "Binger . . . unethical charges": FBI Memo, Nichols–Tolson, January 11, 1950, AHP. "slight" communist record: Levitt and Levitt, 161. "typed on that machine"; "Our man said": *ibid.*, 195. "this is the typewriter": *ibid.*, 319.

498–99   "one Irish name": Caute, 109. "all illusion"; "every possible assistance" *et seq.*: Sullivan, 95.

499   "a vindication": WS, January 22, 1950. "keep the public from knowing": Weinstein, *Perjury*, 510.

499   "your patience and persistence": Nixon, RN, 69. "to crow over": Weinstein, *Perjury*, 510.

499–500   "I do not intend to turn my back": Dean Acheson, *Present at the Creation: My Years in the State Department* (New York, 1969), 360. "courageous . . . unnecessary gift": Goldman, 134. "disgusting": Levitt and Levitt, 294. "Traitors in . . . high councils": *ibid.*, 135.

500–502   January 26, 1950 speech: Nixon, "The Hiss Case," cited above.

502–3   McCarthy's Wheeling speech: see Reeves, 210–23; Oshinsky, 103–14. Reuben, *The Honorable Mr. Nixon*, xi–xii.

503–4   "Tell me, Senator": Goldman, 144. HUAC's growth: see Goodman, 287; Stripling, 23, who records "more than 1,000,000 names, records, dossiers." "intolerable situation"; "HUAC . . . headlines": FBI Memo, Ladd–Hoover, March 28, 1950, HUAC File, MU. On another memo and with considerable irony (Ladd–Hoover, April 26, 1950, HUAC File, MU), J. Edgar had penned about the Committee's now eclipsing publicity, "I have little hope that anything will be done as headlines mean more to them than ultimate security."

504   "shyster and subversive": O'Reilly, 135. Nixon warns of Guild: see FBI Memo, Hottel–Hoover, December 13, 1949, MU. In late January, 1950, Nixon had asked HUAC to investigate the Guild and had gone to some pains to publicize his request. See O'Reilly, 137–38. "activities against the FBI": *ibid.*, 137. "June Mail": for this and myriad other measures against "Bureau Enemies," see O'Reilly, 130–94; Theoharis, 21–77.

504–5   "not primarily . . . espionage"; "promotion . . . left tendencies": Earl Latham, in his *Communist Controversy in Washington*, quoted in Goodman, 280–81. no spy conviction post-Hiss: Levitt and Levitt, 307. "the only congressman": Goodman, 285.

505   "beyond any reasonable doubt": from a speech to the "Pumpkin Papers Irregulars," a club of students of the case, *Phoenix Gazette*, January 15, 1986. "turned . . . toward me"; "one of most controversial figures": Nixon, *RN*, 71.

505   "utterly unprincipled"; "Bigamy": Nixon, *Six Crises*, 70.

506   "reason people . . . gone after Daddy"; "irreparable crack": J. Eisenhower, 101–2.

506 "he, more than any other": Goodman, 285.

507 Kohlberg–Eisenhower contact: see Keeley, 224. Nixon's letter, according to the Kohlbergs, spoke of the general in the most enthusiastic terms.

507 "Chinkapin eyes": Alfred Steinberg, *Sam Rayburn* (New York, 1975), 279–80.

507 "had his weaknesses"; "subsoil of the Russian revolution": Levine, *Eyewitness to History*, 211–12.

508 "the requisite energy": Nixon, *Six Crises*, 70. "pure bullshit": Weinstein, "Nixon vs. Hiss," 147. "I went through . . . and we won": from White House conversations cited by O'Reilly, 9.

509 "triumph of due process"; "principled . . . anticommunism": Theoharis, 319.

509 *coram nobis*: see Edith Tiger, editor, *In Re Alger Hiss*, vols. 1 and 2 (New York, 1979, 1980). "inexcusably careless" *et seq.*: William A. Reuben, *Footnote on an Historic Case* (New York, 1983), which contains the annotated text of Judge Owen's opinion.

509–10 "more than . . . truth"; "less": T. Hiss, 135, although, added the judge, he "couldn't say the same for Mrs. Hiss." "could believe that creep": Levitt and Levitt, 301. "familiar territory"; "shock to discover": *ibid.*, 308. "special guilts": quoted in *ibid.*

510 "paternal attitude": Levitt and Levitt, 299. "ass-end-of-history"; "piss-poor job": Demaris, 116.

511 "language of McCarthy": Carey McWilliams, "The Witch Hunt's New Phase," *New Statesman* and *Nation*, October 27, 1951. For Schlesinger's correspondence with Mundt, see Hiss and Personal Files, KMP. "His ego cried": Levine, *Eyewitness to History*, 211.

511 "when I took up my little sling": Chambers, 741.

511–12 "somewhere in a vague area": Nixon, *Six Crises*, 67. "he is always 'Nixie' ": Chambers, 793.

512 "enemy territory": see Chambers–Nixon, May 9, 1952, Whittaker Chambers File, VPA. "fat repulsive": Nixon, "Plea for an Anti-Communist Faith": *Saturday Review*, May 28, 1952.

512 "race with catastrophe": *Saturday Review*, June 14, 1952. "give them . . . more rope": William F. Buckley, Jr., editor, *Odyssey of a Friend: Whittaker Chambers' Letters to William F. Buckley, Jr., 1954–1961* (New York, 1970), 79.

Chapter 16. Maneuvers, November 1948–December 1949

Page

515 "What a relief!": Carey McWilliams, *California: The Great Exception* (New York, 1949), 20–21. (Cited below as McWilliams, *California*) "toward . . . promised land": *ibid.*

515–16 growth of California: see SFC, March 26, 1950; NYT, July 30, 1950; Louis H. Bean, "America's Fastest Growing Area," *Frontier*, September 1, 1950; "no other . . . migration": "Earl Warren (His Record)," undated press release of the Governor's office, c. 1949, EWP and Earl Warren File, VPA. "substantial redistribution": McWilliams, *California*, 8.

516–17 "People simply fill up": McWilliams, *California*, 22. "the highest" rates; "unparalleled shortages": William Harding, "High Stakes in California," *New Republic*, December 26, 1949. "low, gray pall": McWilliams, *California*, 245.

517 "still . . . pacesetter"; "this tiger": McWilliams, *California*, 24.

517 "outdoor hothouse": McWilliams, *California*, 319.

518 "phantom army": McWilliams, *California*, 169. "Out of . . . shacks they come": Robert Ellis, "Misery in the Valley," *Frontier*, May 1, 1950.

518–19 infamous Cottonwood: McWilliams, *California*, 169. "the shoes": SFC, March 26, 1948. starvation, infections: Ellis in *Frontier*, cited above. "Billion Dollars in Sunshine"; eleven infants starved: Roscoe Fleming, "Grapes of Wrath: 1950 Version," *Frontier*, January 1, 1950. See also Fleming's "The 'Hidden' People," *Frontier*, March 15, 1950. "Hunger, sickness . . . misery": James McClatchy in the *Fresno Bee*, quoted in *Frontier*, May 1, 1956. "cycle of destitution": NYT, March 17, 1950. "American DP's": Fleming, "Grapes of Wrath," *Frontier*, January 1, 1950.

519 "largest . . . line of slums in . . . Americas": *New Republic*, December 26, 1949. "not bear . . . scrutiny": McWilliams, *California*, 160.

519 "Di Giorgio . . . Tiffany's": SFC quoted in Carey McWilliams, *Factories in the Field* (Santa Barbara, 1971). strike broken: see McWilliams's *California*, 165ff. (The California Legislature's Committee on Un-American Activities found the violence justified by "Communist" influence behind the strike.) "vigorous and curative action": the organization's own phrase. "police power": McWilliams, *California*, 162. See also Ceplair and Englund, 90ff. "I believe in treating the pickers like they do in Mississippi," announced Forrest Riley in 1950, one of the state's largest cotton growers and a leading member of the Associated Farmers: *Frontier*, May 1, 1950.

519–20 landlords of Valley: see Congressional Record, May 7, 1959, S7669–7670 for representative patterns of ownership in Kern County; also HGD/OH, Douglas, 179–80; Harding, "High Stakes," cited above. "industry and agriculture are one": McWilliams, *California*, 163.

520 Central Valley Project: see H. I. Lewis, "The Central Valley Project," *Frontier*, September, 1951; Robert R. Brunn, "Irrigation . . . Looms as Vital Issue in California," *Christian Science Monitor*, January 4, 1950; Clayton R. Koppes, "Public Water, Private Land: Origins of the Acreage Limitation Controversy," *Pacific Historical Review*, November 1978; Robert de Roos, *The Thirsty Land* (Palo Alto, 1948). "impermanence"; "social cohesion": Koppes, "Public Water, Private Land," cited above; the original study, published by a Special Senate Committee on Small Business, is contained in Walter Goldschmidt, *As You Sow* (New York, 1947).

521 "force communism"; "Remember . . . Japanese": *Dinuba Sentinel*, April 10, 1947. "confiscation": HGD/OH, Arthur Goldschmidt, 58.

521 tidelands: for an informative contemporary account, see Ernest R. Bartley, "The Tidelands Oil Controversy," *The Western Political Quarterly*, March 1949. "satisfactory . . . with state officials": RN/OH, Crocker, 9. "far . . . cheaper to buy": *Los Angeles Daily News* labor editor Ernest Brashear in *New Republic*, September 1, 1952.

521 Pauley on funeral train: Engler, 345. "one kind word": recalled by the redoubtable Harold Ickes before a Senate Committee, *ibid.*, 409.

521 "Amorphous and unpredictable": Harding, "High Stakes," cited above.

522 "grayish . . . handsome": *New Republic*, February 15, 1939. For Downey's career, see *Current Biography* 1949, 172–73; and his obituary, NYT, October 27, 1961.

522 "substantial holdings": see Senate Commerce Committee, *Hearings on Rivers and Harbors Omnibus Bill, California Central Valley Project*, 78 Cong., 2nd Session (1944). "planning and plotting": Downey's words in Koppes, "Public Water, Private Land," cited above. "a real phobia": EW/OH, Carter, 164. "by the little people": *Frontier*, February 15, 1950.

523 "could expect reelection": *New Republic*, December 26, 1949.

523–24 "rendering a real service": Nixon–Downey, January 20, 1948, Sheridan Downey Papers, BAN. "willing to risk defeat": Arnold, iv. "too slow . . . went for broke": Willard R. Espy–Fawn Brodie, November 8, 1979, UU.

524 "well aware . . . shifts in the mood": J. Eisenhower, 104. "early . . . secret ambition": Arnold, iv.

524 polling: see Nixon–"Dear Friend" circular, February 22, 1949, California Republican Assembly Files, UCLA. 150,000 in 1949: see *Christian Science Monitor*, February 13, 1950. confidential "Analysis"; "overcome": Sherrill Halbert Additions, Political General File, UCLA.

525 "didn't think . . . smart": YN, Kepple, 13. "urged me not to run": Alsop transcript. "independently wealthy": YN, Stone, 9.

525 "vitally important backer": J. Eisenhower, 104.

525–26 "I recognized . . . worth": Nixon, *RN*, 72. "Pollyannaish whistling"; "palmiest days of New Deal" *et seq.*: LAT, April 21, 1949. emerges with support: RN/OH, Crocker, 4.

526 "wishy-washy": *Hollywood Citizen-News*, December 17, 1948. "Sacramento hotels are filled": Katcher, 240.

526–27 "Attar of Partisanship"; "box of starch": LAT, December 25, 1948.

527 "send . . . back again and again"; "Only talk"; "some . . . interested": RN/OH, Jorgensen, 36.

527–28 meeting with Mattei *et al.*; return on *Lark*; "we're going to go": RN/OH, Jorgensen, 37–38. "He got the same reaction there," Jorgensen said of the Southern California money.

528 "Who the hell's": RN/OH, Jorgensen, 38. "Why not . . . Chotiner?": *ibid.*, 39. "without . . . authorization": LAT, May 21, 1949.

528 "open hostility": Spaulding, 263.

528–29 meeting with Perry *et al.*: RN/OH, Day, 35–36; Mazo, 69.

530 Hillings's backdrop; "the champion": see BAN/OH, Hillings, 30–31.

530 "let it roll"; "a quiet groundwork": Nixon–Hillings, June 8, 1949; July 20, 1949, Personal Friends in District File, VPA.

531 "risk is worth taking": Nixon, *RN*, 72.

531–32 "I came around"; early work: RN/OH, Jorgensen, 38–45. "a little cool": RN/OH, Crocker, 3. "Kyle . . . with us": RN/OH, Jorgensen, 45. Palmer claims he suggested campaign: Halberstam, 369.

532–33 "hard work and loyalty": Clayton–Brennan, July 3, 1946, Warren 1946 Campaign File, CSA. hiring Chotiner: RN/OH, Jorgensen, 38–40.

533 $100,000 as campaign cost: see Brashear. "our Committee of Twenty": see EW/OH, Faries, 15; HGD/OH, Meyers, 228. pledges of $30,000: Alexander, 25. "He could be President": EW/OH, Faries, 15.

533–34 YR endorsement: LAT, September 15, 1949. "infiltration . . . intrigue": LAT, September 18, 1949. return to fanfare: LAT, September 30, 1949. "I have to pray": Mac St. Johns interview. "get . . . people talking": Murray Chotiner, "Fundamentals of Campaign Organization," lecture delivered at Republican National Committee Campaign School, Washington, D.C., September 7–10, 1955, 6a.

534 "made up . . . mind"; "tired of Sen. Downey": LAT, September 30, 1949. Darby meeting: RN/OH, Jorgensen, 42–43.

534 "backstage efforts": WDN, October 7, 1949.

535 Warren "not . . . interested": AP dispatch, Sacramento, October 8, 1949, HGD. "definitely decided to file": Kornitzer, 181.

535–36 Ebell Club announcement and speech: see LAT, November 4, 1949; *News-*

week, January 9, 1950. "upper middle class"; "man who made"; "happiest lady": *Rosemead Review*, November 10, 1949.

536 campaign office: RN/OH, Jorgensen, 40ff.

536 "virile, young": LAT, November 17, 1949. "Avoid overemphasizing": Alexander, 29.

537 "every bloomin' one": *Rosemead Review*, November 10, 1949. "we wanted her": Spaulding, 270.

Chapter 17. Primaries, January–June 1950

Page

538 For Helen Gahagan's background, see *Collier's*, September 23, 1944; *New York Post*, July 19, 1944; *PM*, October 1, 1944; her entries in *International Motion Picture Almanac*, 1937–38 and *Who's Who in the Theatre*, 1959; official biographies and chronologies, Box 203, HGD; HGD/OH, Chavoor; as well as her own memoir, *A Full Life*. "of some means": Douglas, *A Full Life*, 5. "Helen *is* . . . ten most": *Current Biography, 1944*, 167.

538–39 "thousands . . . in boxcars": quoted in *Current Biography, 1944*, 168. "Helen, for heaven's sake": HGD/OH, Douglas, 53. "strongest . . . Helen had": HGD/OH, Meyers, 238–39.

539 "smoke-filled rooms": *New York Post*, July 19, 1944.

540 "I've never been afraid": from a 1935 interview, quoted in LAT, June 29, 1980.

540 "reported leftist support"; "a political gypsy": LAT, June 29, 1980. "put Port Said to shame": Ed Lybeck (Douglas's campaign manager), "Present Situation in the Fourteenth California District," c. 1944, Lybeck Papers, UCLA and 1944 Campaign File, HGD. "I just love . . . Negro people": Douglas, *A Full Life*, 253.

540 "You don't have a million": HGD/OH, Cahn, 198.

541 "Soviet Union . . . fear and danger": Douglas, "Why I Voted for Arms for Europe": *New Republic*, August 29, 1949. "support any government": HGD/OH, Douglas, 168.

541 "She agonized": HDG/OH, Chavoor, 328. "incompetence, corruption . . . oppression": Douglas, *A Full Life*, 256. "Nixon watching me": *ibid.*, 259.

542 "bearpit sessions": Douglas, *ibid.*, 280. "persuasive poison": statement in Un-American Activities Committee, February 27, 1946, HGD.

542 "My Democratic Credo": House Speech, March 29, 1946, HGD; see also HGD/OH, Douglas, 328–34.

542–43 "gentleman . . . addressing *me?*": HGD/OH, Douglas, 135. "Red Gulch": HGD/OH, Chavoor, 272.

543 Voorhis, Douglas: "The Washington Press Gallery Rates Pacific Coast Legislators," undated release, c. 1945–46, Personal File, HGD. "twelve smartest" *et seq.*: "Fact Sheet," 1950, Campaign File, HGD.

543 "property registered": Ed Lybeck, "14th District in the 1948 Election," Lybeck Papers, UCLA. "little glamorpuss": *The Jeffersonian Democrat* (Los Angeles), September 1, 1948. "sleeps with a Jew": HGD/OH, Meyers, 216. "lose out on lots of roles": *Pittsburgh Press*, November 21, 1948. "dirtiest campaign since 1934": Lybeck, "14th District in the 1948 Election," cited above. Lybeck appraisal: Lybeck, "Present Situation in the Fourteenth California District," cited above.

544 "a glowing fire": Marian Wolcott, "Biographical Information on Helen Ga-

hagan," HGD. "without making people mad": HGD/OH, Harding, 98. strength and weakness: for staff and Congressional peer perspectives on what one called aptly "a complex gal," see HGD/OH, Chavoor, Holifield, Barbee, Myers, and Harding, as well as Lybeck–Chavoor letters, March 3, 1948–August 29, 1949, Lybeck Papers, UCLA.

544   "frustrated . . . heartsick": Douglas, *A Full Life*, 271. See also HGD/OH, Barbee, 10.

544–45   "vicious tactics": Douglas, *A Full Life*, 276. "well known": *ibid.* "Somebody has to do it": HGD/OH, Chavoor, 307. "no halfway houses": Lybeck–Chavoor, July 7, 1949, Lybeck Papers, UCLA.

545   "I'd rather lose you": Lybeck–Douglas, July 22, 1949, Lybeck Papers, UCLA. "cross of no-gold": Douglas, *A Full Life*, 288.

545   "That's not the issue": Douglas, *A Full Life*, 291.

545   "anything . . . you can't have" *et seq.*: HGD/OH, Douglas, 181; Douglas, *A Full Life*, 294–95. "My sense of security": *ibid.*, 292. "hell-bent for election": EW/OH, Carter, 160. By 1949 Douglas was the last member of the California Congressional delegation opposed to the cession of the tidelands. See Mankiewicz, 48–49, who notes support of the oil industry position by "every politician of both parties, except Douglas and Voorhis."

545–46   "Her entry brightened": Nixon, *RN*, 72. "do not try to sell": Murray Chotiner, "Fundamentals of Campaign Organization," lecture delivered at Republican National Committee Campaign School, Washington, D.C., September 7–10, 1955, 21a.

546   press "survey": a copy of the exhaustive document, part of it under *Chotiner-Faries*, October 24, 1949, is in Earl Warren's 1950 campaign files, CSA.

546   "boss man": RN/OH, Jorgensen, 41. "hand-carrying him": EW/OH, McCormac, 193.

546–47   tells Warren to run separate campaigns: EW/OH, Mellon, 23; Pollack, 119–20. "Warren wasn't having": EW/OH, McCormac, 193.

547   "I trust you realize": RN/OH, Dinkelspiel, 33. "pro": *ibid.*, 14. "overall planner": *ibid.*, 25.

547–48   "We hope . . . of further service": Dinkelspiel–Nixon, November 2, 1949, BAN; see also RN/OH, Dinkelspiel, 21–22. "*I do not care for . . . others*"; "many instances": *ibid.*, 28. "highest integrity": *ibid.*, 36.

549   six to three vote for Houser: RN/OH, Dinkelspiel, 30. "Nixon for U.S. Senator": LAT, January 29, 1950. "tape was very effective"; "most prestigious": RN/OH, Dinkelspiel, 30–31. See also "Pebble Beach Meeting," January 10, 1950, Gordon X. Richmond Memorandum, California Republican Assembly, Sherrill Halbert Addition, UCLA; Nixon–Worth Brown, February 4, 1950, California Republican Assembly Collection, UCLA.

549   "a talk with Fred": RN/OH, Jorgensen, 43.

549–50   Darby gambit: see Brashear, 1; Halberstam, 369–70; Alexander, 27; EW/OH, Hansen, 58.

550   "got their advice"; "reluctantly backed off": RN/OH, Crocker, 2. Meyers and Levitt: *Newsweek*, June 5, 1950.

550   "Black brows . . . frown": *San Francisco News*, February 11, 1950. "Republican through and through": FNT, February 13, 1950. "inevitably to war": *San Francisco Call-Bulletin*, February 10, 1950.

550   "neither show off nor . . . blusterer": LAT, February 19, 1950. "get rid of the Jew-Communists": Shannon and Katcher, part 4, October 3, 1952.

551   surplus food: LAHE, March 8, 1950. "fight any move": LAHE, March 11, 1950.

551   "bipartisan . . . advisers": LAT, March 26, 1950; "impartial . . . commission": SFC, March 24, 1950.

551 absent from Wood's million names: see *New York Daily News*, March 24, 1950.

551 "stone wall": Arnold, 11. "what it's all about": Dinkelspiel–Nixon, March 1, 1950, BAN. See also RN/OH, Dinkelspiel, 32.

552 "Why don't you erect": *Manhattan Beach Messenger*, November 17, 1949. "They didn't want Nixon": EW/OH, Carter, 168. "very nasty"; "quite hostile": *ibid.*, 104.

552 "dynamite" *et seq.*: *Independent Review*, December 9, 1949. "Oil money . . . on railroad gondolas": HGD/OH, Meyers, 226. "shut off money": *Willows* (California) *Journal*, February 24, 1950, from a Douglas press conference in Washington scarcely reported by California papers.

553 "grinding, sputtering": SDU, March 2, 1950.

553 "gentle . . . simple . . . sharp-tongued . . . scolding": LAT, March 23, 1950.

553 "left-wing": LAT, March 28, 1950. Downey withdraws: HGD/OH, Rogers, 114. "cheap gimmick:" Spaulding, 268. "missed no opportunity": Douglas, *A Full Life*, 299.

553–54 "never . . . personal": LAT, March 30, 1950. "big boost": SDU, April 2, 1950.

554 "If my entrance": Manchester Boddy–Sheridan Downey telegram, March 29, 1950, Sheridan Downey Papers, BAN.

554 "book-salesman . . . metaphysical": *The Nation*, September 1, 1945. For Boddy's colorful background, see also *Fortnight*, April 14, 1950; Robert A. Rosenstone, "Manchester Boddy and the L.A. Daily News," *California Historical Society Quarterly*, December 1970; Robert C. Brownell, "Manchester Boddy," *Frontier*, May 15, 1950; "The Mind of Manchester Boddy," excerpts from his writing in the *Daily News*, 1946–1950, Lybeck Papers, UCLA. Edison loan, oil money, Hearst subsidy: see Sheldon Sackett telegram to Helen Douglas, October 31, 1955, HGD. Sackett was an Oregon publisher and radio station owner who learned of the extraordinary financial backing in an attempt to purchase the *Daily News. The Nation* in 1945 had reported the Southern California Edison aid "long rumored" –if not support from "the company itself, then some of its officers and influential stock holders."

555 "a man to be true": *Fortnight*, April 14, 1950. Columns on Proust and Plato: *Fortnight*, April 14, 1950. "unpredictable, erratic": *The Nation*, September 1, 1945.

555 "lion tamer": EW/OH, Carter, 169. "a personal friend": Douglas, *A Full Life*, 293. "one of California's great women": SDU, April 2, 1950, reporting a recent Boddy endorsement from the *Daily News*. "crippling blow": Douglas, *A Full Life*, 298.

555–56 "nice unadulterated fascism": *CIO News* (San Francisco), April 5, 1950. stops and placards; "commodious" wagon: NYT, April 16, 1950; see also J. Eisenhower, 105; Abrahamsen, 158.

556 "socialize . . . water supply"; "phony issue": LAT, April 4, 1950. "extremists"; "more vicious than the OPA": SB, April 11, 1950.

556–57 "a magnificent speech": Scobie, 119.

557 twenty-one addresses, twenty-one days: *Oakland Tribune*, April 13, 1950. Drown quoted: LAT, April 11, 1950. "something that he'd dug up": RN/OH, Day, 23. "no opinion concerning . . . validity": SFC, April 16, 1950. "wild unsubstantiated charges": SFC, April 6, 1950.

557–58 embargo, attack; "Godless . . . 'supermen' ": LAHE, April 17, 1950; *Santa Barbara News-Press*, April 21, 1950; WDN, April 21, 1950. "There's no use . . . anything else": RN/OH, Dinkelspiel, 43. "Number-One Target":

LAHE, April 19, 1950. "gnawing into . . . heart": *ibid.*, April 21, 1950. "Russia would wage war": WDN, April 21, 1950. Native Sons, other audiences: LAT, April 29, 1950; WDN, April 22, 1950.

558 "offensive": LAT, April 26, 1950. Long Beach rally: *Long Beach Independent*, April 28, 1950. "Commies": as *Fortnight* later reported the pickets, May 26, 1950. "If I knew": J. Eisenhower, 108.

558 "communists are in his corner": NYT, September 20, 1949; see also Theoharis, 194–95. "coup": SFC, May 2, 1950.

558–59 Smathers victory: Theoharis, 196–98; see also Ralph McGill, "Can He Purge Senator Pepper?" *Saturday Evening Post*, April 22, 1950; *New Republic*, May 15, 1950; and records of the campaign, Claude Pepper Papers, NA. "Nixon Jubilant": LAHE, May 3, 1950. "carefully studied": *Miami Herald*, August 20, 1972.

559 "chosen associates": *Santa Monica Evening Outlook*, May 18, 1950. "Marc and Gahagan": LAT, May 19, 1950. "pink fringe": *Santa Ana Register*, May 19, 1950. "Florida won a battle": LAT, May 13, 1950.

559–60 "actress and housewife": LAHE, May 18, 1950. "almost casual approach": *The Marysville Democrat*, May 10, 1950. "San Francisco does not want you": *Los Angeles Mirror*, May 17, 1950; SFC, May 17, 1950; *San Francisco Call Bulletin*, May 17, 1950. "bewildered . . . in shock": HGD/OH, Douglas, 201; Douglas, *A Full Life*, 314.

560 "sweep the Republican primary"; "slap her around": LAT, May 18, 1950.

560 "scarcely aware . . . too busy": Douglas, *A Full Life*, 297.

560–61 "utter nonsense": APA, May 1, 1950. "One Communist . . . through Monrovia": MNP, May 2, 1950. "every Democrat . . . a Communist": *San Diego Tribune Sun*, May 6, 1950; SFC, May 9, 1950.

561 "so many evil-minded persons": John McCormack–Helen Douglas, May 9, 1950, HGD. "such pipsqueaks": *San Diego Journal*, May 6, 1950. "peewee": rhetoric that quickly spread back to the Nixon camp. See Nixon, *RN*, 77.

561–62 "viciously personal": ibid., 76. "I'll castrate her!": Arnold, 12–13. "name-calling contest with a woman"; "doing our job": Spaulding, 270. "haphazard . . . organization": HGD/OH, Rogers, 117. "teamed up with . . . Marcantonio": see *Berkeley Gazette*, May 15, 1950; LAT, May 16, 1950; *Fresno Bee*, May 16, 1950; *Oceanside Blade-Tribune*, May 16, 1950 and *Alameda Times Star*, May 17, 1950.

562 USC dousing: see *Daily Trojan* (USC), May 17–19, 1950; LAT, May 17, 1950. "Nixon knew everything": Dixon interview, UU.

562 "blackout": *New York Post*, May 21, 1950. "suppression of news": Judge Isaac Pacht, quoted in *ibid*. "so distressed": see *Los Angeles Daily News*, May 8, 1950.

562 "shows little hard work": *Concord* (California) *Transcript*, May 26, 1950. "political dynamite": *Sacramento Union*, May 24, 1950.

562–63 "powerful private oil interests": *Chicago Sun Times*, May 27, 1950. "comfort to Soviet tyranny": *Bakersfield Californian*, June 2, 1950; *Arcadia Tribune*, June 1, 1950. "red-hots": *Riverside Enterprise*, May 30, 1950; LAT, June 5, 1950. "I despise these little men": *CIO News* (San Francisco), June 5, 1950. "no longer . . . a movie star": *Sunday News* (Hollywood), June 4, 1950.

563 "eyes of the nation": Brennen circular, June 2, 1950, Warren Congressional Files, CSA. "the truth, the light and the way": LAT, May 21, 1950.

563 "Democrats for Nixon": LAT, May 28, 1950. "As One Democrat to Another": a copy of the flyer is in the Nixon Campaign File, HGD.

564   "sere and yellow age": LAHE, April 19, 1950. "I don't think money can buy": SB, May 12, 1950. "never even met Nixon"; "He despised the man's politics . . . ethics": HGD/OH, Rogers, 119–20. "die-hard reactionary": SB, June 2, 1950; see also *Los Angeles Daily News*, June 5, 1950, which reproduced Nixon's flyer as well as his latest affidavit of voter registration as a Republican, and denounced the "viciously false circular." "Campaign Trickery"; "Tricky Dick": *Los Angeles Daily News*, June 5, 1950.

564–65   "commies really don't like it": *Chicago Tribune*, June 2, 1950. "on our way to victory": LAT, June 7, 1950. "won't be . . . personalities": SFC, 1950. "I'll do it for her": LAHE, June 8, 1950.

565   "riding high . . . blinded ourselves": HGD/OH, Lustig, 195.

565   "beautiful red dress"; "pinko lady": LAHE, June 9, 1950. "linking . . . with . . . Moscow": Drew Pearson's "Merry-Go-Round," WP, June 8, 1950.

Chapter 18. General Election, June–December 1950

Page

566   "Now we have a woman": RN/OH, Jorgensen, 45. "he had to be very circumspect": Arnold, 11. "not appear ungallant": Nixon, *RN*, 75. "several advance men"; "We worked the hell out of him": RN/OH, Jorgensen, 46.

567   "our suspicions were right": Jorgensen, 47. "don't waste the money"; "things which you can talk about": Murray Chotiner, "Fundamentals of Campaign Organization," lecture delivered at Republican National Committee Campaign School, Washington, D.C., September 7–10, 1955, 15a. this communist thing"; "It was his time": RN/OH, Jorgensen, 44. "about labor and agriculture": Chotiner, "Fundamentals," 8a. "If your candidate should . . . say 'I have been told' ": Chotiner, "Fundamentals," 7a. "A perfectionist"; "everything himself": Spaulding, 272.

567   "be either the candidate or the manager": Mazo, 70. "a lot of homework before": YN, Kepple, 14. "better . . . not to know": de Toledano, 103. "He knew": Richard St. Johns interview.

568   Crocker and large landowners: RN/OH, Crocker ii, 7; see also YN, Schuyler, 6, who was later assigned to deal with smaller farmers. "considerable newspaper advertising": RN/OH, Dinkelspiel, 18. "lean your way": RN/OH, Crocker, 5. "cases and cases": Chotiner interview, UU. "great deal of radio": RN/OH, Dinkelspiel, 18.

568   red, white, and blue: RN/OH, Jorgensen, 57. "the worst designed": Chotiner, "Fundamentals," 22a, cited above. Fourteen hundred billboards": Jean Begeman, "Million Dollar Senators," *New Republic*, April 9, 1951. "catch . . . tourist trade": *ibid.* "garden . . . billboards": Douglas, *A Full Life*, 328.

568–69   "Flying Squadrons"; "planted there . . . to embarrass": RN/OH, Crocker, 14. Dinkelspiel omits: RN/OH, Dinkelspiel, 38. "Committee, committee": RN/OH, Jorgensen, 61.

569   "I was playing a violin": LAT, June 17, 1950.

569–70   June 24, 1950: see Donovan, *Tumultuous Years*, 188–89; Goldman, 145. Nixon on loyalty oath: *Santa Barbara News-Press*, April 21, 1950.

570   "turning back . . . out of the question": Donovan, *Tumultuous Years*, 206.

570–71   "I am a Quaker": Costello, 32–33. "reign of terror": LAT, July 13, 1950. "complete . . . mobilization": LAT, August 2, 1950. "stab in the back": LAT, August 15, 1950.

571   "panic . . . in California": Douglas, *A Full Life*, 302. "we were very fearful": HGD/OH, Lustig, 83. "only foothold we have": WP, July 29, 1950.

571   Korean aid votes: see Costello, 67. "political madman"; "Nixon's whining": "Speech of Congresswoman Helen Gahagan Douglas, National Convention, International Oil Workers of America, Long Beach, California, August 18, 1950," HGD; LAT, August 19, 1950; *Harbor Area Journal* (San Pedro), August 24, 1950.

572   "Her sudden zeal": LAT, July 30, 1950. "She made the fatal mistake": Chotiner, "Fundamentals," 13a, cited above

572–73   contributors to Nixon campaign: see D. V. Nicholson–Charles J. Hagerty, Deputy Secretary of State of California, November 21, 1950, enclosing Receipts and Expenditures, United Republican Finance Committee of California (Northern California Division), and Nixon for U.S. Senator Sub-Committee, CSA; "Candidate's Campaign Statement of Receipts and Expenditures," Richard Nixon, June 6, 1950 and November 7, 1950, CSA. Biographies are variously drawn from *Who's Who in California, 1958* (Los Angeles, 1959); *Who's Who, 1950–; Poor's Register of Directors and Executives, 1950–.*

573   "one of our first supporters": *Forbes*, August 15, 1975.

573–74   "sources . . . available to Nixon": Katcher, 260. "surprised to see each other": EW/OH, Faries, 15. "oil money . . . rallied": HGD/OH, Meyers, 230. "sure things": Reeves, 318–19.

574   "His eyes lit up": Kornitzer, 183. "oil money . . . through that little group": HGD/OH, Meyers, 234.

574–75   "always helping": RN/OH, Jorgensen, 64. Kennedy gives a thousand dollars: Arnold, 14; Nixon, *RN*, 75; see also David E. Koskoff, *Joseph P. Kennedy: A Life and Times* (Englewood Cliffs, N.J., 1974), 410; NYHT, September 29, 1963.

575   handing out hundred-dollar bills; "didn't seem . . . important": McCullah St. Johns interview. "always asking for money" *et seq.*: EW/OH, Faries, 92.

575   "choice between Roosevelt and Hitler": NYT, December 26, 1962.

575–76   "kept Senator": Pearson, *Diaries*, 476. "blackmail": NYT, December 26, 1962. "besieged me": "Internal Revenue Investigation," *Hearings, Subcommittee of Committee on Ways and Means*, House of Representatives, 82nd Congress, 2nd Session, Part 4, 2932. "very firm vote": *ibid.* "capacity to keep his mouth shut": *ibid.*, 2937. "influence peddler": see Pearson, *Diaries*, 178. "gambler-lobbyist-fixer": see Max Lowenthal–Truman, September 18, 1952, President's Secretary's Files, HST. Nixon denies Grunewald: NYT, March 21, 1950.

576   "hardly be doubted": Alexander, 39. Grunewald confessions: see Pearson (*Diaries*, 329–31, 479, 481), who recorded that Grunewald's daughter was later "threatening to shoot . . . Bill Rogers."

577   "two places from the bottom" *et seq.*: Nixon, *RN*, 81–82.

578   "personal attachment": BAN/OH, Ziffren, 38. Downey rebuffs Truman: Mazo, 71; Douglas, *A Full Life*, 308.

578   "oil people . . . for Nixon . . . Democrats": HGD/OH, Meyers, 237. "oil . . . controlled": Ziffren interview, UU. registration of "all communists": *Los Angeles Daily News*, August 23, 1950. Nixon ahead: *Life*, August 28, 1950. "so-called liberalism": *Newsweek*, August 28, 1950. "Now, don't make . . . mistake": Douglas, *A Full Life*, 303–4. film on "communist infiltration": see draft letter, August 28–29, 1950, Personal Statements File, HGD.

578–79   "You know what I'm going to do": HGD/OH, Chavoor, 318. colleagues warn; vote: *ibid.*, 317–330; Douglas, *A Full Life*, 304–5. "I will not be stampeded": statement of Congresswoman Helen Gahagan Douglas on Mundt-Nixon Bill [sic], *Congressional Record*, August 29, 1950, HGD. "How does it feel": HGD/OH, Douglas, 165.

579   "untiring service"; "smiled at Nixon": LAT, August 30, 1950. "worst was over": Douglas, *A Full Life*, 308.

579–80   "pink lady": the original release is in Nixon Campaign File, HGD; see also LAT, August 30, 1950.

580   "red-hot broadside": LAT, August 30, 1950. "all-out mobilization": LAHE, August 31, 1950. (The paper had advertised the broadcast as an ostensible news story the day before.) "354 times exactly": undated release, "Congressman Richard Nixon For United States Senator," c. September 1–7, 1950, Nixon Campaign File, HGD.

580–81   mimeographed sheet: "Voting Record of Helen Gahagan Douglas on Significant Measures Involving Un-American Activities . . ." c. July 24, 1950, Lybeck Papers, UCLA. Pink Sheet: copies are in Nixon Campaign File, HGD, BAN, and HGD/OH, Douglas, 335.

581–82   "for some reason or other": Chotiner, "Fundamentals," 19a, cited above. the voting record: see Costello, 65–66; *Frontier*, August, 1958; Robert Coughlan, "A Debate, Pro and Con, Subject: Richard Nixon," *Life* manuscript, VPA; Morris H. Rubin, "The Case against Nixon," *The Progressive*, November 1960. Alsop comparison: see Alsop transcript.

581–82   "my campaign . . . issued"; "mordant comment": Nixon, *RN*, 74. "her record": Arnold, 11. "No lies": RN/OH, Jorgensen, 47. influence of "color": Chotiner, "Fundamentals," 19a, cited above.

582   "not a smear": Chotiner, "Fundamentals," 12a, cited above. "he bent over backwards": Arnold, 12. Pink Sheet handed out: see Beatrice Stern–Evelyn Chavoor, June 13, 1958, Post-Election Files, HGD, for a recollection of the Pink Sheet being distributed at small-town picnics. "more requests": Chotiner, "Fundamentals," 19a. "didn't feel . . . proper": RN/OH, Dinkelspiel. "smearing distortion": Klein, 79.

582   "kept her pinned": Nixon, *RN*, 75. "frightened more easily": HGD/OH, Lindsley, 142. "never . . . complete . . . record": Chotiner, "Fundamentals," 23a, cited above.

582–83   "not even loyal": *Long Beach Independent*, August 28, 1950. "aid and comfort to communism": SDU, August 31, 1950. "generally found voting": see Douglas, *A Full Life*, 309; Mankiewicz, 51. "pointing up the real issues": Nixon–Edmond Coblentz, September 5, 1950, E. D. Coblentz Papers, BAN.

583   "set the record straight"; "always off-balance": Douglas, *A Full Life*, 310. "just . . . ridiculous": *ibid.*, 321.

583   "flaming liberal": LAT, September 7, 1950. "pleasing to . . . Kremlin": LAT, September 17, 1950. "We do not say she . . . Communist": LAT, September 13, 1950.

583–84   "with a bang": Chotiner, "Fundamentals," 4b, cited above. campaign sweep: LAT, September 10, 1950. "calm and reassuring": Douglas, *A Full Life*, 311.

584–85   "unusual situation" *et seq.*: " 'Kickoff' speech of Congressman Richard M. Nixon," September 18, 1950, Nixon Campaign File, HGD.

585   back in basin: LAT, September 20, 1950. "speak for herself": APA, September 20, 1950. "gales of laughter"; "wild applause": LAHE, September 21, 1950. ovation: LAT, September 21, 1950. "publicly allied": LAHE, September 21, 1950. "Douglas-Marcantonio Axis": LAT, September 23, 1950.

585–86   Democrats for Nixon "best-known": LAT, September 29, 1950; see also Scobie, 120. "no longer . . . aggregations": George Creel, *Rebel At Large* (New York, 1947), 375. "We didn't have to recruit": RN/OH, Jorgensen, 59. "very secretly": George Creel–Thomas Storke, September 21, 1950, Thomas Storke Papers, BAN. Downey's discreet letters: YN, Goeske, 2, 30–31.

586   Boddy backs Nixon: *Oakland Tribune*, September 29, 1950. "think it was running": Chotiner, "Fundamentals," 14a–15a, cited above. "set of . . . has-beens": Carey McWilliams, "Bungling in California," *New Republic*, November 4, 1950. "narrow . . . partisanship": LAT, October 1, 1950. "True in May": copy in Box 204, File 8, HGD. "Is Helen Douglas a Democrat?": Box 194, File 4, HGD.

587   "a Republican?": Douglas–Peter Edsen, September 19, 1956, postelection files, HGD. "frightening crisis": Douglas, *A Full Life*, 315. "fully determined": *ibid.*, 316. "Don't say I sent it": HGD/OH, Douglas, 190. "path of tanks": Douglas, *A Full Life*, 312.

587–88   "quiet boss" *et seq.*: Dixon interview, UU. "an evil person": Chotiner interview, UU. "his thinking": RN/OH, Jorgensen, 40. "Nixon a genius": Jack Chotiner interview.

588   "only man . . . listened to": McCullah St. Johns interview. "I've said everything": EW/OH, Hansen, 65. "hired person": Richard St. Johns interview. "impossible . . . get close": McCullah St. Johns interview. "caste system": Dixon interview, UU.

589   "coattail riders": EW/OH, Faries, 93. "temporize": LAT, September 4, 1950. "how bad . . . she was": Sherwood interview, UU. "always . . . to Kyle's": Ziffren interview, UU.

589   "as good as . . . FBI": Richard St. Johns interview. "He couldn't stand ladies": *ibid.* See also Clements's obituary, NYT, December 7, 1974. NAM publicists: Carey McWilliams, "Bungling in California," *New Republic*, November 4, 1950.

590   "Independent Voters" *et seq.*: see Charles Wertenbaker, "The China Lobby," *The Reporter*, Part I, April 15, Part II, April 29, 1952 (cited below as Wertenbaker). "for the China account": Wertenbaker, I, 20.

590   "pushed aside": de Toledano, 108. "deliver Nixon": Wertenbaker, I, 20.

590–91   "failure to aid free China": see LAT, October 17, 1950. "great haters": Dixon interview, UU.

590   "couldn't stand": Adela Rogers St. Johns interview, UU.

591–92   Adela Rogers St. Johns: Richard and McCullah St. Johns interviews. "mollified her": de Toledano, 114.

592   "He was furious": St. Johns interview, UU.

592   "the group around him": Dixon interview, UU. "what we do with them" *et seq.*: Dorothy Cox memo to Nixon, October 9, 1950, Adela Rogers St. Johns File, VPA.

592–93   "cursed like a pirate": St. Johns interview, UU. "he'd had a tantrum": Sherwood interview, UU. "scared shit": Richard St. Johns interview. "gratefully": David, 88. "several times a day": J. Eisenhower, 104.

593–94   "recoiled from . . . shrillness": J. Eisenhower, 107. "heard them all": David, 90–93. "the effect . . . on Pat": Brodie, 244. "like . . . telling a dog": Dixon and Sherwood interviews, UU. "damned well ready": McCullah St. Johns interview.

594   "so curtly": Dixon interview, UU. "very mad for him": Sherwood interview, UU. "waspy and stung" *et seq.*: Richard St. Johns interview. "got her to go away": Richard St. Johns interview. "hated politics": McCullah St. Johns interview.

594   "race still . . . close": SFC, October 12, 1950.

595   "a thinned-down, tired-looking" *et seq.*: *San Francisco News*, October 28, 1950.

595–96 "I'd case the crowd": RN/OH, Day, 25. "really upset": *ibid.*, 26.

596   "wife of . . . communist sympathizer": RN/OH, Day, 30. "a big show": Arnold, 12.

596   "We ought to get . . . word" *et seq.*: RN/OH, Day, 24–25.

597   "plugging Nixon's candidacy": *Gilroy Evening Dispatch*, October 17, 1950. "Ask the basket cases" *et seq.*: see Richard M. Fried, *Men Against McCarthy* (New York, 1976), 100; Wills, 89; Mankiewicz, 56. "Let Your Conscience": LAT, October 11, 1950.

597   United Press buries story: see *Gilroy Evening Dispatch*, October 17, 1950. "complimentary remarks": *Los Angeles Mirror*, October 6, 1950: see also WS, October 12, 1950.

597–98 "liabilities": APA, May 5, 1950. "nuisance": see Eben Ayers Diary, September 15, 1950, HST. Truman abandons plans: LAHE, September 22, 1950. "furriners": *Los Angeles Mirror*, October 6, 1950.

598   "drinking bourbon": HGD/OH, Meyers, 235. McGrath incident: LAT, October 17, 20, 1950. "setting . . . record on its ear": LAT, October 19, 1950. JFK visit: Congressman Kennedy was in California the week of October 3–10, 1950. See Kennedy–Mary Davis, October 3, 1950, Washington Office, Personal Correspondence File, JFK.

598   "vilest of graffiti": J. N. Moses–Jerry Voorhis, March 2, 1972, enclosing clipping from *San Luis Obispo Telegram Tribune*, JVP. "admitted she was a communist": Sue Lilienthal, "Republican Techniques in the 1950 California Senatorial Race . . . ," manuscript appended to HGD/OH, Chavoor, 358ff. "pink . . . to her underwear": see HGD/OH, Meyers, 228; Douglas, *A Full Life*, 327; Dan Rather and Gary Paul Gates, *The Palace Guard* (New York, 1974), 114. sexual allusions: Halberstam, 370.

599   "whispering campaign": HGD/OH, Hogan, 418. "my friend"; "movie Jews"; "wife of a Jew": Shannon and Katcher, iv.; Costello, 70–71; Lilienthal. (cited above), HGD/OH, Chavoor, 360; Douglas, *A Full Life*, 326–27.

599   "considerable prompting": Mankiewicz, 56. "I am ONE candidate": *Los Angeles Sentinel*, August 31, 1950. "Alger Hiss's pet": see Gerald L. K. Smith Rally advertisement, Box 188, File 4, HGD. "Did You Know": Douglas, *A Full Life*, 326. "Helen Hesselberg Douglas": a copy of the postcard is in Box 205, file H, HGD.

599   "an underlying accusation": RN/OH, Dinkelspiel, 46.

599–600 "the most race-baiting": EW/OH, Carter, 171. "mudslide": Douglas, *A Full Life*, 317. "political disease"; "deeply believe in . . . democratic": see "Statement of Melvyn Douglas October 18, 1950," Campaign Files, HGD, undated manuscript, "Melvyn and I . . . ," *ibid.*

600   Douglas workers turn over car: Newman interview, UU.

600   "slapped her": HGD/OH, Chavoor, 311.

600   "young men in dark shirts": LAT, October 17, 1950; Mazo, 75; Nixon, *RN*, 77. "DON'T BE CONFUSED": *Los Angeles Mirror*, November 3, 1950. "BEAR FALSE WITNESS": *Los Angeles Daily News*, November 1, 1950. "sacrilegious": see Brodie, 242; Nixon, *RN*, 76. "dark shirt he wore": LAT, October 17, 1950. "counterproductive": Mankiewicz, 55.

601   veritable bribe: BAN/OH, Ziffren, 36. "left-handed": Carey McWilliams, "Bungling in California," *The Nation*, November 4, 1950. "fantastically inept campaign": *ibid.*

601   "tugging and pulling": HGD/OH, Meyers, 212, 241. "campaign . . . like a calm center": Douglas, *A Full Life*, 319.

601–2   "didn't vote for her": HGD/OH, Meyers, 229–30. Zasu Pitts's "pink lady": HGD/OH,Chavoor, 309. "I'm trying to help a Senator [sic]": Anne Edwards, *Early Reagan: The Rise to Power* (New York, 1987), 417–18. "Ronald Reagan worked hard": Douglas, *A Full Life*, 323.

602   "You sense it": RN/OH, Jorgensen, 60. Fifty-dollar-an-hour skywriters: Jean Begeman, "Million Dollar Senators," *New Republic*, April 9, 1951.

602   "tens of thousands": HGD/OH, Douglas, 186. "we got ahold": RN/OH, Day, 24. "when we have this": Evelyn Chavoor–Beatrice Stern, June 9, 1958, HGD; HGD/OH, Chavoor, 312, 359; see also Chavoor–Selig Harrison, June 3, 1958; Beatrice Stern–Evelyn Chavoor, June 13, 1958; all HGD on various and vivid memories of the episode.

602   "Meet Richard Nixon": copy in Box 204, File 8, HGD. "takeoff on *Life*": Chotiner, "Fundamentals," 18a, cited above. wooed by Wallace: Box Unp., File 12, HGD. toilet bowl: Box 188, File 4, HGD.

602–3   radio and television themes: Jamieson, 76.

603   "consider her a traitor": *The Hemet News*, October 21, 1950. "terrible things": Douglas, *A Full Life*, 324. stoning and bodyguards: *ibid.*, 332–33.

603   "haven't made you afraid": Douglas, *A Full Life*, 320–21. loans threatened: *ibid.*, 335. "in a war: HGD/OH, Douglas, 170.

604   "evils of communism": HGD/OH, Douglas, 184. See also HGD/OH, Dudley, 74; Mankiewicz, 57. "the woman running": Douglas, *A Full Life*, 322. "name . . . mentioned with communism's": Beatrice Stern–Evelyn Chavoor, June 13, 1958, HGD.

604   diocesan lawyers and bulletin boards: HGD/OH, Lustig, 185. "A Message": HGD/OH, Douglas, 184. "fallen-away catholic": J. Eisenhower, 109. Protestants take up anticommunist fervor: see LAT, September 23, 1950. "California is not France": Mankiewicz, 57.

604   "Nixon does not say": Elmer Davis's transcript of October 30, 1950 is in the "Helen Douglas-Communist Issue" File, Mankiewicz Papers, JFK.

604–5   "to steal reason": *Milwaukee Journal*, October 22, 1950. "nothing too vicious": WP, October 28, 1950. "stuck my neck out": Pearson, *Diaries*, 135–36.

605   calculate endorsements: see "California newspapers which might be sympathic to HGD," undated memo, Box Unp., File B, HGD. Finney's articles: see *San Francisco News*, October 5 and 6, 1950. Nixon's rebuttal to Finney: *San Francisco News*, October 27, 1950. "no witch hunter": October 19, 1950. "avoided . . . illiberal excesses": SFC, October 21, 1950.

606   "NIXON IS LOSING": Bob–George, October 16, 1950, Nixon Campaign File, HGD. "take off the gloves": LAT, October 24, 1950. "somewhat sketchy . . . education": LAT, October 25, 1950. polls predict victory: see *San Francisco News*, October 27, 1950.

606   Creel headlines: LAHE, October 29, 1950: LAT, October 29, 1950.

606–7   "NIXON LIFE STORY": LAHE, October 29, 1950. Field poll: LAT, October 30, 1950; SFC, October 30, 1950. flyers: HGD/OH, Douglas, 211. "anyplace . . . person has to wait": Chotiner, "Fundamentals," 20a, cited above. "EVERY COMMUNIST . . . FOR MRS. DOUGLAS"; "Communist League of Negro Women": see "The Nixon Story": Francis Keesling Papers, SU; see also Oshinsky, 177.

607   "all-time low"; "darling of . . . parlor pinks": LAT, October 31, 1950; see also LAHE, October 31, 1950. "explanation": LAT, November 2, 1950. "Flying Squadron" appeal: LAT, October 30, 1950. The story asked for "women who are willing to ring doorbells, telephone and write their friends," listing over a dozen organizing centers in Southern California alone. mass

mailing: see *Los Angeles Daily News*, November 3, 1950, noting the "dodgers he [Nixon] is sending out like he did in the primary." Another mass mailed postcard was addressed "As Democrat to Democrat," saying Douglas's election would be a "major disaster." See Box 204, File 8, HGD. "PRIZES GALORE": copy in Box 204, File 7, HGD. "gave comfort": Mankiewicz, 53. counter "smear": see, for example, LAT, November 1 and 2, 1950.

608   "rousing climax": LAT, November 2, 1950. rally: LAHE, November 3, 1950; Nixon, *RN*, 77.

608   "cloak-and-dagger . . . production": *Frontier*, December, 1950. "ROUGH ON RATS": LAHE, November 3, 1950. Drawn by Karl Hubenthal, a copy is in Box 184, File 12, HGD.

608–9   "No, Dick": see Katcher, 257–61; Pollack, 119. Chandler dinner party: EW/OH, Cunningham, 31. "pressure for Warren": EW/OH, Hansen, 64. "let Nixon take care of himself": Pollack, 120.

609   Warren never praises Hiss case: Arnold, 39. Brown and Roosevelt compete: see EW/OH, Kent, 9–10; Mazo, 72; Douglas, *A Full Life*, 303ff.

609   "grotesquely unfair": Katcher, 260. Holt questions; "I hope and pray": see SDU, November 4, 1950; Douglas, *A Full Life*, 325; Katcher, 261. Chotiner to Mailliard: EW/OH, Mailliard, 32. "no intention of being coy": LAT, November 5, 1950.

609–10   "pretty good bet": LAT, November 5, 1950. "scurrilous attack"; "he wants to destroy": M. F. Small, "The Country Editor," 268–69, unpublished manuscript, BAN.

610   "did you know": HGD/OH, Lustig, 187; Douglas, 231–32; Douglas, *A Full Life*, 332. See also M. S. Novik–Philip Stern, May 2, 1956, Post-Election File, HGD. "just going down telephone books": HGD/OH, Lustig, 187. 500,000 calls: Maurice Revnes–Douglas, July 15, 1973, HGD; see also HGD/OH, Douglas, 231–32; Hogan, 419. "We knew it was going to happen": HGD/OH, Lindsley, 143.

610   "mood . . . ugly": Douglas, *A Full Life*, 333. "most California papers": *Los Angeles Mirror*, November 3, 1950. "Tricky Dick"; "Shame! Shame!": see SFC, November 3, 1950; SDU, November 4, 1950.

610   "M'ARTHUR IN THREAT": LAT, November 6, 1950.

611   television appearance: see J. Eisenhower, 110; de Toledano, 113. "terrible time relaxing": McCullah St. Johns interview; see also RN/OH, Day, 34. melancholy; "sure . . . defeated": see de Toledano, 115; Hoyt, 262; Spaulding, 279.

611–12   "no difference between them": BAN/OH, Healey, 324. "Dick was so exuberant": Spaulding, 279. "desolate scene": Douglas, *A Full Life*, 335. "CONSOLES . . . STAFF": HGD/OH, Barbee, 19. "deeply hurt": HGD/OH, Hogan, 419. "Oh, Mrs. Douglas": HGD/OH, Chavoor, 325–26.

612   "loss" of China: *U.S. News and World Report*, November 17, 1950. "back into mother-in-law's apartment": Ruth Lybeck–Douglas, undated, c. November 10, 1950, Post-Election File, HGD. "it hurt, yes": RN/OH, Crocker, 16. "it was just enough": EW/OH, McNitt, 11.

612–13   "greatest good"; "brilliant campaign": Mazo, 79. "we are all gratified": Allen Dulles–Nixon, November 15, 1950, Allen Dulles Papers, Princeton. "splendid leadership": Stassen telegram to Nixon, December 1, 1950, Stassen File, VPA. "personally very happy": John P. Mallan, "Massachusetts: Liberal and Corrupt," *New Republic*, October 13, 1952. "glad to . . . see Nixon win": Paul B. Fay, Jr., *The Pleasure of His Company* (New York, 1963), 62.

613   "despicable back-street . . . campaigning": William L. Roper, "The Third Man," *Frontier*, August, 1960. "a housecleaning": Theoharis, 216. "mandate

for McCarthy": Richard Fried, "The 1950 Campaign," in Theoharis, 221. "symbolism . . . escaped him": Reeves, 346.

613–14 early appointment; supports judicial appointees: see LAT, November 23, 1950.

614 swearing-in: LAT, December 5, 1950.

614 "stirring statements": Engler, 394. "don't . . . need us": *ibid.*

615 "dapper little man": Carey McWilliams, "Bungling in California," *The Nation*, November 4, 1950. "They did the smearing": Harry Flannery, "Red Smear in California," *Commonweal*, December 8, 1950. "dirtiest in state history": see *Labor News*, October 19, 1962.

615 Stanford study: LAT, January 26, 1951. a thousand dollars in advertising: see UCLA *Daily Bruin*, November 6, 1950; Pearson's "Washington Merry-Go-Round," WP, November 4, 1950; see also Brashear I.

615–16 $4,209 vs. $42,757: LAHE, November 4, 1950, under the head, "Douglas Outspent Nixon by Big Sum." "war chest": LAT, November 13, 1950. $2,020: *Newsweek*, November 13, 1950. California accounting: see "Candidate's Campaign Statement of Receipts and Expenditures," Richard Nixon, November 7, 1950, CSA; Aylett Cotton–Secretary of State, November 21, 1950; D. V. Nicholson–Secretary of State, November 21, 1950, both with attachments, CSA. Financing of Douglas and Warren: see Brashear I.

616 "around $50,000": Alexander, 40. statewide mailing: Jean Begeman, "Million Dollar Senators," *New Republic*, April 9, 1951. $350,000 as cost of mailing: Douglas, *A Full Life*, 339. $1.6 million on campaign: Begeman, cited above. "at least $1 million": Brashear I.

616 "We gave . . . woman a rough time": RN/OH, Jorgensen, 56. "We never accused her": quoted from a previous interview, NYT, January 31, 1974.

616–17 "kicked hell out of . . . Helen G.": Day–Nixon, undated note, c. November 1961, Day Files, VPA. "added an embellishment": Mazo, 74. "only . . . the facts": Kornitzer, 184. "taken from his hands": de Toledano, 109. "Douglas started": Alsop, 144. "Nixon's pallid version": quoted in J. Eisenhower, 107. "don't have to tell you": for the transcript, see *Chicago Sun-Times*, November 18, 1968.

617 "I was a very young man": Costello, 74.

617–18 "no basis in fact": William G. Key–George J. Burger, Jr., May 26, 1958, Jerry Voorhis File, VPA. "The impression . . . she was pro-communist" *et seq.*: "The Douglas Campaign," material prepared by Nora de Toledano refuting charges, Pearson File, VPA. See also Nixon–Staff, July 7, 1958, *ibid.* "tightly organized bands": Nixon, *RN*, 73. Boddy "despised": *ibid.*, 74. "never questioned . . . patriotism": *ibid.*, 76.

618 "stridency"; "anyone . . . will find": *ibid.*, 78. "He hadn't touched me": Douglas, *A Full Life*, 334–35. "Let me think about it": Pearson, *Diaries*, 199.

618–19 "appointment would cause considerable controversy": Nixon–Faries, January 13, 1951, Faries File, VPA. "don't forget Nixon": HGD/OH, Douglas, 213. "He killed me politically": *ibid.*, 217. "I wanted to forget": Douglas, *A Full Life*, 337. "truly vicious": Douglas–Lea, October 31, 1952, Post Election File, HGD. "innuendo and distortion": *New York Post*, October 26, 1956. "without intellectual stature": notes for a diary, November 9, 1960 (Box 205, File 7), HGD.

619–20 "did not want . . . Senate": Douglas–James Adams, January 9, 1959; Douglas-Communism File, Mankiewicz Papers, JFK. "no attack"; "annoyance rather than hardship": Douglas–Realini, May 26, 1962, Post-Election File, HGD. rotten eggs: BG, October 24, 1960. "His enemies . . . increased": Spaulding, 280. "I've never gotten over": HGD/OH, Barbee, 19.

620 "I will not break bread": Brodie, 244. "technical compliance": Clayton R. Koppes, "Public Water, Private Land," *Pacific Historical Review*, November 1978, 625.

620–21 thought Marcantonio "sincere": Mazo, 76. "beat that bitch": Klein, 80. Marcantonio's death; "species becoming extinct": Alan Schaffer, *Vito Marcantonio; Radical in Congress* (Syracuse, 1966), 211, 214.

Chapter 19. The Senate, 1951–52

Page

625–26 Sulgrave Club incident: Reeves, 348–49; Oshinsky, 179–81; Thomas, 215–17; Mazo, 128.

627 "you should not have shown": Perry–Nixon, December 14, 1950, Herman Perry File, VPA.

627 "aura of scandal": see Donovan's *Tumultuous Years*, 114–31. "crude . . . features": Caute, 541.

628 "tacit ally": Costello, 206. "four horsemen": SFC, January 26, 1951. "Black Silence": *Frontier*, April 1952; see also James F. Simon, *Independent Journey: The Life of William O. Douglas* (New York, 1980), 291–98.

628 speeches: see "Speaking Engagements, 1951," Speeches File, 1951–52, VPA. "caught up": Nixon, *RN*, 78. "fund-raising": J. Eisenhower, 112. honoraria: Richard Wilson, "Is Nixon Fit to Be President?" *Look*, February 24, 1953, 42. "a few friends": Nixon–Perry, February 15, 1951, Herman Perry File, VPA.

629 "against Red China": LAT, January 28, 1951. "bear . . . proportional share": "Broadcast of Senator Richard Nixon Over CBS—January 9, 1951," Press Releases File, 1951–52, VPA. "will to resist": "Radio Talk over Station KFI, March 4, 1951": *ibid*. Nixon promptly circulated the text to the office staff, "to be acquainted with my views on public questions": Nixon Staff File, March 5, 1951, VPA. "go on the offensive": LAT, March 20, 1951. "man of the hour": LAT, February 12, 1951.

629–30 "In my experience": St. Johns–Nixon, March 26, 1951, Adela Rogers St. Johns File, VPA.

630 "repeating the error": LAT, March 31, 1951. Truman hung in effigy *et seq.*: see Katcher, 266.

630–31 "five hundred telegrams . . . uninspired" *et seq.*: for his remarks, see Congressional Record-Senate, April 11, 1951, 3649–55.

631 "victory, not appeasement": Associated Press dispatch, May 5, 1951, Speeches File, 1951–1952, VPA.

631 "vicious smear campaigns": "Statement of Senator Richard Nixon," April 22, 1951, Releases File, VPA; see also LAT, April 23, 1951. "political security of the administration": *ibid*. at odds with Dewey and Warren: see R. Smith, 576–77, and Katcher, 266.

632 "show up on the surface": Perry–Nixon, November 13, 1950, Herman Perry File, VPA.

633 "we all knew the fund": EW/OH, McCormac, 190–91. "on several occasions": Humphreys–Sherman Adams, February 7, 1959, Sherman Adams Papers, DDE.

633 "year-round campaign": Mazo, 94. "American Gothic character": Robert Coughlan manuscript, DDE.

633–34   "arrangements to finance": Mazo, 94. "look after the fund": Smith–Arthur Crites, September 25, 1951, Roy Day Papers, BAN. uses of money: *ibid.*

634–35   "So it was worked out": Mazo, 95. "a group of us here": Smith–Crites, cited above. "He had advanced so quickly": Kornitzer, 189. "criticism . . . completely disarmed": Mazo, 93.

635   "any claim on . . . senator's . . . interest": Smith–Crites, cited above. "Nobody . . . drawing . . . salary": *ibid.* "not to be furnished": RN/OH, Adams, 8. "Dick will . . . be very appreciative": Smith–Crites, cited above.

635   budget: Elmo H. Conley–Sherman Adams, September 23, 1952, Roy Day Papers, BAN; see also *U.S. News and World Report*, October 3, 1952. "seeking . . . all the time": EW/OH, McCormac.

635   "send in a few checks": Smith–Hoblick, August 21, 1951, Dana Smith File, VPA.

635–36   "few hundred"; "several thousand": Nixon, *RN*, 92. raised $16,000, spent $12,000: see Smith–Derre and Dolan, October 30, 1951, Dana Smith File, VPA. "abbreviated 'Who's Who' ": NYT, September 21, 1952.

636–37   contributors to Fund: see *U.S. News and World Report*, October 3, 1952; *Washington Times Herald*, June 15, 1953; NYT, September 21, 1952.

636   "supported . . . from the start": Smith–Crites, cited above.

637   "which we all believe in": Smith–Crites, cited above.

638   spending: see Price Waterhouse & Co., Sherman Adams audit report, September 23, 1952; and Elmo Conley–Adams, September 23, 1952, Roy Day Papers, BAN, and Paul Hoffman Papers, HST.

638   Perry solicits stamp money: see Perry–Nixon, December 9, 10, and 12, 1951; Nixon–Perry, December 12, 1951, Herman Perry File, VPA. Among the donors for mail money were old Whittier friends Douglas Ferguson and Tolbert Moorhead.

638   "tremendously indebted to our special group": Mazo, 97. "time . . . for . . . showdown" *et seq.*: *ibid.*, 96–97.

639   "see us through the summer": Mazo, 97.

639–40   Irwin background and duties: Irwin correspondence. "primary function": Dorothy Cox memorandum to Irwin, Arnold, Gleason, March 30, 1951, Staff Memoranda, 1951–52, VPA.

640   Rose Mary Woods: see Nora Ephron, "Rose Mary Woods—the Lady or the Tiger?" *New York*, March 18, 1974. "A special . . . breed": Helen Dudar in the *New York Post*, quoted in Ephron, cited above. Nixon's devoted office women, some of whom were to go on with him to higher office, would later be known among Washington correspondents as "The Nunnery": see LAT, March 14, 1960. "careful never to cross": J. Eisenhower, 110–11.

641   "very efficient staff": Knight–Nixon, March 9, 1951, Goodwin Knight File, VPA. "They complain": Perry–Nixon, April 14, 1951, Herman Perry File, VPA. "careful spot check": Nixon memorandum to Irwin, Arnold, Gleason, March 27, 1951, Staff Memoranda, 1951–52, VPA.

641   "pet phrases": Cox–Gleason, March 28, 1951, Staff Memoranda, 1951–52, VPA. "feel . . . brush-off"; "crackpots": Cox–Irwin, Arnold, Gleason, March 30, 1951, Staff Memoranda, 1951–52, VPA.

641   "Under no circumstances": Nixon–Irwin, Arnold, Gleason, April 3, 1951, Staff Memoranda, 1951–52, VPA. "on top of your desk": Nixon–Staff, August 6, 1951, Staff Memoranda, 1951–52, VPA. work late: Nixon–Staff, July 23, 1951, Staff Memoranda 1951–52, VPA. "I cannot emphasize too strongly": Nixon–Arnold, Irwin, Gleason, April 4, 1951, Staff Memoranda, VPA.

642   "never to accept any gift": Nixon–Staff, December 17, 1951, Staff Memoranda, 1951–52, VPA. "supporter cards": Nixon–Staff, June 11, 1952, Staff Memoranda, 1951–52, VPA.

642   casual "P.S.": Woods–Gaunt, March 20, 1952, Staff Memoranda, 1951–52, VPA.

642   "These goddamned chiselers": Donovan, *Tumultuous Years*, 337; for the scandals in general, see *ibid.*, 333–39; and Fletcher Knebel and Jack Wilson, "The Scandalous Years," *Look*, May 22, 1951.

642–43   "as roundly abused": Fletcher Knebel and Jack Wilson, "The Scandalous Years," cited above. "eye of a hurricane": Nixon, *RN*, 79.

643   "classifying . . . [with] no justification"; "toward a . . . dictatorship": statement, October 8, 1951, Releases File, 1951–52, VPA. "clean-up squad": SFC, December 12, 1951.

643   "The basic issue": see *Frontier*, September 1955. "Consternation": "The Public Record of Richard M. Nixon," *Congressional Quarterly*, March 11, 1960, 379. "house cleaning": LAT, November 7, 1951.

644   "lion in the way": Roper. "champion of integrity": Costello, 215.

644   "crazy as hell": see "Richard Nixon," a memorandum of biography and public statements, Paul Hoffman Papers, HST. "a man of the world": LAT, April 9, 1951.

644–45   "soft" policies and "betrayals": see LAT, May 25, 1951; June 9, 1951. "professional Red-baiting": LAT, November 13, 1951. Hughes tribute; "subversion must be wiped out": LAT, April 3, 1952.

645   "only a perfunctory interest": Phil Corbin, "Why Senator Nixon?" *Frontier*, September 1952.

645   "Dick . . . a relaxed manner": Klein–Arnold, December 11, 1951, Herbert Klein File, VPA.

645–46   "Nowhere in the land": Nixon–Dear Editor, September 26, 1951, Murray Chotiner File, VPA. "suppressed" Brewster story; "Paper Curtain": Roper.

646–47   excess steel for schools: LAT, November 29, 1951. water wars: see LAT, November 30, 1951. "to your interest": W. C. Cheverton–Nixon, December 21, 1951, Herman Perry File, VPA. "splendid . . . history"; "staunch friend": Lincoln Quarberg–Nixon, August 6, 1951, Releases File, 1951–52, VPA.

647   "practical and political considerations": Nixon–Perry, December 19, 1951, Herman Perry File, VPA.

647   Richard Nixon Chair: see Perry–Nixon, July 2, 1951; Nixon–Perry, July 7, 1951, Herman Perry File, VPA.

648   Malaxa case: for general background, see "The Malaxa Case," *Congressional Record-Senate*, October 12, 1962, A7629–31; *Congressional Record-House*, October 5, 1962, 21482–84; WP, February 19, 1952; Malaxa File, "Smears and Special Cases File," VPA. Drew Pearson and Jack Anderson, *U.S.A. Second Class Power* (New York, 1958), 279–81. "financial mainstay": quoted by Senator Estes Kefauver, *Congressional Record*, October 12, 1962, A7630.

648–49   "swell job": Bewley–Arnold, September 10, 1951, Malaxa File, VPA. "a plant important": Knowland and Nixon–Manly Fleischmann, September 14, 1951, Malaxa File, VPA. Malaxa "personally indispensable": *Congressional Record*, October 5, 1962, 21483. colloquy: *ibid.*, 21482ff. Bewley, Knoop and Nixon: see Bewley correspondence with Arnold, September 10, 1951 *et seq.*, Malaxa File, VPA.

649   "any information . . . about Malaxa": Bewley Memorandum to Rose Woods, December 16, 1955, Malaxa File, VPA.

649–50   Smith tax case: see *St. Louis Post-Dispatch*, September 23, 1952. "appreciate anything . . . Embassy might . . . do": NYT, October 30, 1952, January 30, 1953; *Miami Herald*, September 26, 1952. See the traffic on the incident between the U.S. Embassy, Havana and the Department of State: Operations Memorandum, Havana–Washington, September 19, 1952; Havana–Washington cable, September 29, 1952; Operations Memorandum, Havana–Washington, February 2, 1953; Memorandum of Conversation, Washington, September 29, 1952, all NA.

650   Camp Roberts oil: Pearson and Anderson, *U.S.A.*, 290ff, cited above; see also S-1029 in the record of bills introduced, 82nd Congress, 1st session. use of frank: *Washington Times Herald*, June 15, 1953.

650   cheese quota: compare Kornitzer, 190–91 and Pearson and Anderson, *U.S.A.*, 292, cited above.

650   antipublic housing: see Costello, 216–17.

650–52   Senate voting record: see "The Public Record of Richard M. Nixon," *Congressional Quarterly*, March 11, 1960; Voting Record File, VPA; de Toledano, 117–26; Costello, 218–28.

651   "indifference to policy": Richard Rovere, *The Eisenhower Years* (New York, 1956), 302. "bottled up": Pearson and Anderson, *U.S.A.*, 297.

652   "remarkably tightfisted illiberality": Costello, 228.

652–53   "suckered us": EW/OH, McCormac, 194.

653   "substantial down payment": Nixon–Perry, February 15, 1951, Herman Perry File, VPA.

653   new house: see NYT, September 23, 1952; *Fortnight*, August 4, 1952. The property transactions are also traced in various memoranda and telephone call notes, "Veterans Exemption Matter," Drew Pearson File, VPA. "bright California look" *et seq.*: J. Eisenhower, 111; Hoyt, 263. "any person of the Semitic race": see *California Jewish Press*, undated clip, Box 184, File 12, HGD; see also "Dick Nixon Speaks Out on Restrictive Covenants," Roy Day papers, BAN; Pearson and Anderson, *U.S.A.*, 287, 299, cited above.

653   house on Anaconda: see *Fortnight*, August 4, 1952. tax returns: see Wilson, "Is Nixon Fit?" cited above. "you will have word very soon": Rogers–Nixon, June 3, 1952, William Rogers File, VPA.

654   "almost hermitlike": Phil Corbin, "Why Senator Nixon?": *Frontier*, September 1952.

654   "severe back and neck pains": J. Eisenhower, 111. "misery, tension . . . unhappiness": Arnold Hutschnecker, *The Drive to Power* (New York, 1974), 4. "I liked it": Helen Worden Erskine, "Dick and Pat Nixon," *Collier's*, July 9, 1954.

655   "The collector": see "The Florida of Richard Nixon" *et seq.*, *Newsday*, October 6, 11, 12, 13, 1971; Greene interview, UU.

655   "Dick is on the verge" *et seq.*: Jeff Gerth, "Richard M. Nixon and Organized Crime," *Penthouse*, July 1974; see also Gerth's "Nixon and the Mafia," *Sundance*, November–December 1972. "how much influence": U.S. Senate, Hearings, "Watergate and Related Activities: The Hughes-Rebozo Investigation," 93rd Congress, 2nd session, 11513. "Words cannot express": Nixon–Danner, January 9, 1952, Florida-Personal File, VPA. "Bob Nixon": *Vero Beach Press Journal*, January 3, 1952. "assumed name": Smathers–Nixon, January 14, 1952, Florida-Personal File, VPA.

Chapter 20. Positioning, May 1951–June 1952

Page

657 "acquaint . . . with his plans": Chotiner–McCormac, July 3, 1951, EW/OH, McCormac, 3a. "governor on the spot": Perry–Nixon, July 26, 1951. Herman Perry Files, VPA. "ambitions set on . . . governor": Katcher, 283.

658 "The Tafts": Jeffrey Hart, *When the Going Was Good: American Life in the Fifties* (New York, 1982), 288. "wrong for the times": Lodge, 75.

659 "rare combination": Trohan, 279. "How in the world": R. Smith, 578.

659 "very proud"; "abrasive": Nixon, *RN*, 82.

660 McKinley Day Dinner: Nixon, *RN*, 83. Shroyer approaches; "quite sympathetic": Kornitzer, 287–88; Mazo, 83.

660 "I don't say": Costello, 92 "His most ardent supporter": Nixon, *RN*, 79.

661 "His manner is genial": Arthur Krock, "Impressions of the President—and the Man," *New York Times Magazine*, June 23, 1957.

661 "obscure, unknown": Cook, xxiii. "P. D. Eisenhauer": Eric Larrabee, *Commander in Chief: Franklin Delano Roosevelt, His Lieutenants, and Their War* (New York, 1987), 421 (cited hereafter as Larrabee, *Commander*). "a continuation of all I've been doing": Dwight D. Eisenhower Personal Diaries, January 21, 1953, DDE. "study and self-discipline": Larrabee, *Commander*, 412, cited above.

661–62 Nye Committee irony: see Cook, xxiii–iv. "with such subtlety": Larrabee, *Commander*, 419–20, cited above.

662 "a mixture of extremes": quoted in Cook, 77.

662 "militant liberal": Cook, xxvi. "no difference": Eisenhower Personal Diaries, January 1, 1950, DDE. "they know where to find me": *The Reporter*, August 5, 1952. "most covert President": Cook, xvi. "tiny splinter group": quoted in *ibid*, x.

663 "grand $18,761": Cook, 79. "They impressed him": *ibid.*, 69. "I am truly anxious to go": Eisenhower–W. Alton Jones, Novermber 19, 1948, DDE. "excerpts . . . of *Fortune*'s . . . 500": Cook, 74

663–64 "You might have . . . spectacle": Eisenhower–Walter Bedell Smith, September 18, 1947, DDE.

664 Taft meeting; "forever . . . out of the political scene": quoted in Hart, *When the Going Was Good*, 63-65, cited above.

665 "any day": Department of the Army cable to SACEUR, Paris, May 9, 1951. Pre-Presidential Files, DDE.

665 "personal victory": LAT, May 12, 1951. "maintain silence": Eisenhower–Lucius Clay, April 6, 1951, Personal Papers, DDE.

665–66 "What we need over here" *et seq.*: Nixon, *RN*, 81–82. "Not once . . . overstepped": D. Eisenhower, 46.

666–67 "icy blue eyes . . . steel": Nixon, *RN*, 376–77. "very interesting experience": Costello, 76. "much encouraged"; "senator was unable to determine": LAT, May 23, 1951.

667 "last chance": LAT, May 27, 1951. "big shots": Lodge, 78. "only man . . . Nixon": James Bassett Diary, 121, UU.

668 "stalking horse": see Bernard Shanley, "Preface to Eisenhower Memoirs," unpublished manuscript, Bernard Shanley Papers, DDE. "delaying action": Eisenhower Library Oral History, Bernard Shanley, 5, DDE. "counterirritant": R. Smith, 570. statement of principle: Bernard Shanley Diary, 474–75, Bernard Shanley Papers, DDE.

668   "We have lost"; "best sell": LAT, June 29, 1951.

668   "strange blend": Richard Reinhardt, "The Bohemian Club," *American Heritage* 31, no. 4 (June–July, 1980): 82–91. "saturated with sunshine": C. D. Jackson quoted in Cook, 73.

668–70   Slater at Grove: Ellis Slater Diary, July 21–28, 1951, "Bohemian Grove," DDE; see also Ellis Slater's *The Ike I Knew* (privately published, 1980).

670   "No man": Hart, *When the Going Was Good*, 66, cited above.

670–71   "hell of a lot of money": R. Smith, 579. "gentle, reasonable": Lodge, 81. "everybody feeling good": Cook, 141. "devastating frankness": Lodge, 81. "doing his best"; "squirm": Cook, 141.

671   "corpse at every funeral"; "enigma": Cook, 141. Patton diary incident: Trohan, 270.

671   "Warren's bruised feelings": R. Smith, 581.

671–72   "fifth column": R. Smith, 595. Rabb as liaison: see Kornitzer, 224; Lodge, 85. Herman monitors: see Press Release File, 1951–52, VPA. "Long before anyone": Klein, 138.

672   "broke all ten"; "not . . . American way"; "disgraceful thing": Katcher, 267–68. "measly flashlight": *ibid.*, 265. "many leaves forward": *ibid.*, 269.

673   "he never gave up": quoted in Katcher, 270. "Nixon . . . along with us": EW/OH, McCormac, 40. "usual tactics": *San Francisco Call Bulletin*, August 3, 1951. resolution on "creeping socialism": EW/OH, McCormac, 12.

673–74   "your extraordinary accomplishments": Knowland telegram to County Chairmen, November 7, 1952, EW/OH, McCormac, 4–6.

674   "somewhat cautious": LAT, November 14, 1951. "surprisingly large support" *et seq.*: LAT, November 15, 1951.

674   "put the heat on"; "he was evasive" *et seq.*: EW/OH, McCormac, 3, 116.

675   "They opened him up": Warren, 253. " I took a strong dislike": *Oakland Tribune*, November 13, 18, 1951.

675–76   "every special interest": Katcher, 277. "might as well . . . Joe Stalin"; "Warren didn't understand": EW/OH, McCormac, 73, 34, 40.

676   "Nixon was an honorable man": EW/OH, McCormac, 111.

676   "he couldn't lose"; Taft "had assurances"; "cut his throat": *ibid.*, 41, 49.

677   "Hardly a day": Perry–Nixon, November 26, 1951, Herman Perry File, VPA. "an hour with MacArthur . . . Hoover": Nixon–Perry, December 12, 1951, Herman Perry File, VPA. Stassen offers vice presidency: see Shanley Oral History, 11, DDE; Wills, 95; Mazo, 144–45. Smith for Ike; Hoffman meeting: see Nixon–Knowland, December 13, 1951, Knowland File, VPA; *Independent Review*, September 26, 1952; *Santa Fe New Mexican*, September 24, 1952.

677   "rat-killing": EW/OH, McCormac, 116.

677–78   "very confidential" letter: Shanley–Nixon, January 10, 1952, Harold Stassen File, VPA. "new policy": LAT, January 17, 1952. "quit fighting each other": "The Issues for 1952," February 26, 1952, Releases File, 1951–52, VPA. "without tipping your hand": Perry–Nixon, January 16, 1952.

678   "convince the nation": LAT, February 13, 1952. "reluctantly joined"; "any other candidate": LAT, February 22, 1952.

678   "if Eisenhower is not . . . candidate"; "close to your vest": see Perry–Nixon, March 26, 1952, Herman Perry File, VPA.

679   "last carefree vacation": J. Eisenhower, 112. Honolulu statements: *Hilo Tribune Herald*, April 5, 1952; *Honolulu Star Bulletin*, April 5, 30, 1952. "He owes it to his party": LAT, April 17, 1952. "support of Democrats"; "suspect among Republican leaders": LAT, April 28, 1952.

679   Crocker thought clear: RN/OH, Crocker, 20. "strongest dark horses": Nixon–Day, April 22, 1952, Roy Day File, VPA.

679–80   "sniffle once or twice": Lodge, 99; Hart, *When the Going Was Good*, 66, cited above. "not gremlins": R. Smith, 582.

680   threat of MacArthur: R. Smith, 582. "best clerk"; "bootlickers"; "vindictive": Cook, 105. "pushed Dick around": Perry–Nixon, March 10, 1952, Herman Perry File, VPA. "no better than neutral": Katcher, 282. *"drive a bargain"*: Perry–Nixon, handwritten note, c. May 2, 3, 1952, Herman Perry File, VPA.

680–81   pledge: see Pollack, 135; Robert W. Kenny, "The Crisis Nixon Forgot," *Frontier*, April 1962 (cited hereafter as Kenny, *Crisis*). "pretty sure to win": Nixon–Perry, March 19, 1952, Herman Perry File, VPA. "if . . . not been tied down": Perry–Nixon, May 5, 1952, Herman Perry File, VPA. "arm-twisting": see Katcher, 288; Henderson, 381. "to have him satisfied": EW/OH, Warren, 279.

681–82   "I am immodest enough": Katcher, 282. "atheistic . . . socialistic program": LAHE, May 9, 1952. "Despite honest disagreement": LAT, May 19, 1952.

682   "so much abuse": EW/OH, Hotchkis, 45. "We are in . . . danger": statement, c. April–May 1952, Releases File, 1951–52, VPA. "Werdel . . . would be chosen": Perry–D'Aule–Nixon, May 2, 1952, Herman Perry File, VPA.

682–83   "If you have to": Perry–Nixon, handwritten note, c. May 2, 3, 1952, Herman Perry File, VPA. "I do not intend": Nixon–Perry, May 5, 1952, Herman Perry File, VPA. "up-and-coming young senator": Drew Pearson and Jack Anderson, *U.S.A., Second Class Power* (New York, 1958), 278; see also Costello, 84.

683   "I faced a major test": Nixon, *RN*, 83–84.

683   "keyed up": Nixon, *Six Crises*, 299. speech: see Nixon, *RN*, 84; Costello, 80.

683–84   "Make me a promise": for the original version, see Nixon–Dewey, January 15, 1961, Thomas Dewey File, VPA. See also Nixon, *Six Crises*, 299; R. Smith, 584. "not the first time": Nixon, *Six Crises*, 299.

684   twenty-fourth-floor suite *et seq.*: Nixon–Dewey, January 15, 1961, cited above; R. Smith, 584.

684   "Everybody . . . I respected": Mazo, 83–84.

684–85   "subtle constraint": Lyon, 473. "best running mate" *et seq.*: Henderson, 383–84; Mazo, 83; Costello, 84. Mayflower meeting: Nixon, *RN*, 84.

685   letter to Dulles: Nixon–Dulles, May 22, 1952, JFD.

685–86   Ike's appeal: LAT, May 18, 1952. Lodge offer: Parmet, 92. "first thing I knew": Press Conference 70, transcript, May 31, 1955, DDE.

686–87   "moral outrage": R. Smith, 587. Mineral Wells: see *ibid*, 586–87; Parmet, 74–77.

687   "Taft delegates . . . preferred": Katcher, 292. "element of phoniness": *The Reporter*, August 5, 1952.

687   "what about 'fair play'?": R. Smith, 590. "Some way . . . found": Lodge, 108.

688   "at the proper time"; "hope to eliminate": *Oakland Tribune*, May 22, 1952.

688   Warren lashes back: Katcher, 284–85. "heat is on": Perry–Nixon, May 28, 1952, Herman Perry File, VPA. "little frantic": EW/OH, McCormac, 179–80. "I think you will agree": Nixon–Perry, June 6, 1952, Herman Perry File, VPA.

689   "anyone who knows me" *et seq.*: Katcher, 285.

689   "close to writing off": Katcher, 285. "I sometimes wonder": Helen Noid–Nixon, June 9, 1952, Herman Perry File, VPA. whispering campaign: EW/OH, McCormac, 118.

690   "great job": Nixon–Hancock, June 6, 1952, Harvey Hancock File, VPA.

690 "without your support": Perry–Nixon, June 4, 1952, Herman Perry File, VPA. "little gossip": *ibid.*, June 4, 1952.

690 "better . . . on the inside": Nixon–Perry, June 6, 1952, Herman Perry File, VPA. "California's more promising figure": quoted in Katcher, 286. "likely prospect": *The Oregonian* (Portland), May 17, 1952.

690 "part of a Roman Senator": Theodore H. White, "The Gentlemen from California," *Collier's*, February 3, 1956.

691 "Warren all the way": Costello, 58; Katcher, 287.

691 "a national figure": LAT, June 8, 1952. "Bill Knowland . . . proper person": Nixon–Perry, *Personal and Confidential*, June 16, 1952, Herman Perry File, VPA.

691 "by proper manipulation": Perry–Nixon, June 12, 1952, Herman Perry File, VPA.

691–92 poll: Nixon–Dear Friend, June 11, 1952, Earl Warren File, VPA.

692 "No one else in the office": Nixon–Budlong, June 18, 1952, California Campaign File, VPA.

692 "Some . . . eager beavers": LAT, June 20. 1952.

692–93 "infuriated": Pollack, 136. "stab in the back": Henderson, 385. "not consistent with the oath": Warren, 251. "deeply troubled"; "finished as . . . man of honor": Katcher, 288–89. "no penalty": *ibid.*

693 "if . . . time should come": LAT, June 21, 1952. "rumors": *ibid.*, June 24, 1952.

693–94 "aloofness with perfection"; "two weeks before Chicago": R. Smith, 595; Lodge, 110; Mazo, 84. "press for Knowland": SB, June 25, 1952. "I will not need . . . services": Nixon–Staff, June 11, 1952, VPA. "close to your vest": Perry–Nixon, July 7, 1952, Herman Perry File, VPA.

Chapter 21. Convention, July 1952

Page

695–96 amphitheater setting: NYT, June 30, 1952. "two massive forces": John Bartlow Martin, 581.

696–97 "he will be glad to serve": Knowland–Warren, June 13, 1952, Personal Political File, EWP. "more than a stray thought": R. Smith, 589.

697 "soundings with state leaders": Costello, 86. "There is nothing to compromise": NYT, June 30, 1952. "Negroes . . . left the Republican Party": NYT, July 2, 1952.

697–98 "my own judgment": EW/OH, Faries, 98. "It was desirable": Lodge, 110. "not in the same social strata": EW/OH, Faries, 99ff. "You've got about nineteen": EW/OH, Faries, 6.

698–99 "an immense effort": Lodge, 107. "by the indignation expressed": NYT, July 12, 1952. "highest standards of honor" *et seq.*: NYT, July 3, 1952.

699 "forced into a trap": Henderson, 387. "Eisenhower people had 'stolen' ": Parmet, 81–82; see also Pollack, 139. "our wildest dreams": Lodge, 112. "blow" to Taft: NYT and LAT, July 3, 1952. "Ike the Kike": Charles Franklin confidential memoranda to David Bell, "The Money Changers at the Ballot Box" and "The Big Money Men behind Eisenhower," October 25, 1952, Adlai Stevenson Papers, Princeton.

699–700 "complete integrity and fair play": NYT, July 3, 1952.

700–701   Knowland as "outstanding candidate": LAT, July 3, 1952. "prime mover": SFC, July 3, 1952. Faries reports to Warren: EW/OH, Faries, 7. "had no idea": EW/OH, Powers, 39.

701   "it would be the senior senator": Henderson, 389. "Warren didn't have a chance": Chotiner's account of the meeting is in Katcher, 290–91.

702   Athens Club meeting; "misgivings" *et seq.*; "if a man gave his word": EW/OH, Faries, 2–4, 94.

702   "last-minute substitutions": EW/OH, Faries, 18, 94. The delegate list is found in Official Report of the Proceedings, 25th Republican National Convention, Governor's Political File, CSA. "wanted *him* to be president": RN/OH, Crocker, 23.

702–3   "I felt very badly": EW/OH, Faries, 18.

703   Chotiner's assignment: Verne Scoggins memorandum, June 12, 1952, Personal Political Miscellaneous File, CSA. "Anyone who'll wear 'em": NYT, July 2, 1952.

703–4   "Warren's attempt to be fair": EW/OH, Mellon, 23. "we had to watch Nixon": GK/OH, Polland, 10. "if there was any special task": "Republican National Convention: Notes of Paul H. Davis," HI. Davis's account was deposited at Stanford with the instruction, "To be opened only after the deaths of Dwight D. Eisenhower and Earl Warren." "hotter than the hinges of hell": RN/OH, Jorgensen, 69.

704   "The most fundamental things" *et seq.*: NYT, July 4, 1952; Weaver, 180. "walking into an oven"; "baked all night": RN/OH, Jorgensen, 69. "exhilarated": Weaver, 180.

704–5   "wasn't anything phony": Pollack, 130. "I hope Bill don't": EW/OH, Powers, 34. "splinter meetings"; cold silence; Katcher, 290.

705–6   "You stay up all night": RN/OH, Jorgensen, 69. "a question of honor": NYT, July 5, 1952. "quite a bit of feeling between them": EW/OH, Powers, 34.

706   "If he wants to see Dick": Katcher, 290.

706   "Gee, that sounds good": Parmet, 84. "don't you see": Trohan, 279.

706   "our group was running the campaign": Lodge, 113. "would not reject"; "third person": NYT, July 5, 1952.

707   "Eisenhower . . . very strong" *et seq.*: RN/OH, Jorgensen, 69–70. "It was his feeling"; "pleasant and casual": Katcher, 290. "a report on preconvention": NYT, July 5, 1952. "if any of his friends got out of line": Warren, 251.

707–8   "supporting him one hundred percent": EW/OH, Mellon, 27. "the precise moment": Theodore White, "The Gentlemen from California," *Collier's*, February 3, 1956. "thought *he* was the candidate"; "ridiculous": Weaver, 182. "Warren . . . little if any chance": RN/OH, Dinkelspiel, 2.

708–9   "left at the post": Costello, 86. "Taft fraud"; "moral issues": *Independent Review*, October 31, 1952. "that would be all right": EW/OH, Mellon, 28. "throw its strength to Eisenhower" *et seq.*: RN/OH, Dinkelspiel, 3. "If they acted quickly": Henderson, 392; *Oakland Tribune*, July 5, 1952; SFC, July 4, 1952.

709   "Some of those . . . importuned": Warren, 251. "people were running around": EW/OH, Mellon, 28. "If you're on the front end": RN/OH, Jorgensen, 69. "A hullabaloo": R. Smith, 671.

709   "where the Eisenhower votes were": EW/OH, Mellon, 30.

710   "They were working on Nixon": EW/OH, Mellon, 9.

710   "kept hammering"; "arguments . . . so loud"; "We don't give a damn": *ibid.*, EW/OH, Mellon, 31, 28.

710   "fairness and openness" *et seq.*: NYT, July 6, 1952.

711 "furtively": Pollack, 135; EW/OH, Jones, 20. "Eisenhower for President" banners: GK/OH, Polland, 10; Pollack, 137; Katcher, 291. "Thou Shalt Not Steal"; "most impressive display": Patterson, 551.

711–12 "didn't want . . . an out-and-out fight": BAN/OH, Hagerty, 13. "assurances . . . from California": Lodge, 239. "where we could gather . . . reports": RN/OH, Jorgensen, 75. "Nixon meetings": EW/OH, Faries, 16.

712 "Nixon had one of his stooges": EW/OH, McCormac, 125. "practically every night": EW/OH, Faries, 16. "great train robbery": Pollack, 136. "mad as hell": Katcher, 291; Pollack, 137. "to entice California votes": Robert Kenny, "The Crisis Nixon Forgot," *Frontier*, April 1962. "How do you account for him": EW/OH, Hansen, 89.

712–13 "We may never" *et seq.*: J. Eisenhower, 114; NYT, July 12, 1952. "high drama . . . blunt orders": R. Smith, 590. "Why no. I wouldn't do that" *et seq.*: EW/OH, Faries, 12.

713 "This is the way"; "fearing for . . . paychecks": R. Smith, 590. SHOE: Charles Franklin–David Bell, "The Big Money Men behind Eisenhower," October 25, 1952, Adlai Stevenson Papers, Princeton. "a thousand bucks a vote": EW/OH, McCormac, 124.

713 "working California": R. Smith, 671.

713–14 "Is Murray there?" EW/OH, Hansen, 65; see also Scoggins memorandum, June 12, 1952, CSA, cited above.

714 "His people . . . did everything": GK/OH, Polland, 10.

714 "not speaking to Nixon": Pearson, *Diaries*, 396. "bandwagon jumper": *ibid.*, 392; see also Mankiewicz, 61.

714–15 "rushed" to microphone *et seq.*: Costello, 87–88; Katcher, 292; Brodie, 253. "every bit of influence": EW/OH, Mellon, 8.

715 "his delegation"; "vote your conscience": EW/OH, Mellon, 9, 26. "last chance"; "He knew how . . . bound to go": Katcher, 293.

715–16 "We had delegates": GK/OH, Polland, 12. "Nixon used that": *ibid.* "suspiciously upholding . . . Taft": Parmet, 87.

716 "Of solemn mien"; "another way" *et seq.*: Lodge, 115–17.

717 "sudden and vividly to open": Lodge, 119. "two conventions": EW/OH, Hagerty, 11, 16. "lesson in . . . politics": NYT, July 12, 1952. "crassly maneuvered": Pollack, 137. "unpredictable consequences": Lodge, 120. "alternative . . . surrender": NYT, November 25, 1959.

717–18 "Neither Warren nor I": NYT, July 8, 1952. "Imagine my surprise": Warren, 252. Chotiner–Brownell talks: see Henderson, 395.

718 "Headquarters does not want"; "When . . . Warren learned": *Independent Review*, October 31, 1952; Brodie, 254. orders to bar Nixon: Costello, 88.

718 "I saw Dick . . . first night": Mazo, 87; see also Kornitzer, 224.

718 "gory majesty": R. Smith, 591.

719 Warren–Davis meeting: "Republican National Convention, Notes of Paul H. Davis," HI, cited above.

719–20 Davis–Eisenhower meeting: "Republican National Convention, Notes of Paul H. Davis," HI, cited above.

720 "continued undercover sniping": WP, May 17, 1962. "my assignment in '52" *et seq.*: RN/OH, Day, 38ff. Hagerty "reports"; "very active": EW/OH, Hagerty, 14.

720 "up on the mountaintop": Pearson, 216. "no doubt . . . swing *his* vote": EW/OH, Manolis, 2.

721 "selling . . . those . . . on the fence": GK/OH, Polland, 13. reception at Knickerbocker: EW/OH, Faries, 16.

721–22   "He only scowled": Adams, 34. "clear knowledge . . . junior senator": Parmet, 93. "He is being boomed": SFC, July 9, 1952. John Knight report: *Chicago Daily News*, July 9, 1952. "went into a huddle": Kornitzer, 211. "no discussion of a Vice President"; "strategic denial": NYT, July 10, 1952.

722   "nothing of any movement": LAT, July 10, 1952. "first time": *ibid.* sends out for copies; "probably . . . the last time": see Nixon, *RN*, 85. "Man Friday": see J. Eisenhower, 114. "One communist": Parmet, 95. "complete sanction": *ibid.*, 97–98.

722–23   Dirksen's speech: see R. Smith, 593; NYHT, July 10–11, 1952, NYT, July 10–11, 1952. "shook their fists": Lodge, 112. "as though . . . a pickpocket"; "despotic manner": Warren, 252. "fearful rebuke": R. Smith, 593.

723   "key vote": NYT, November 25, 1959. only "realistic": RN/OH, Dinkelspiel, 5.

723   "THE MOST COLD-BLOODED": NYT, July 11, 1952. "This is my last chance" *et seq.*: Warren, 252–53; EW/OH, Mellon, 31; NYT, July 11, 1952.

723–24   "Oh, my!": EW/OH, Hansen, 83. "emissaries beat a path": NYT, July 11, 1952. "kingmakers": EW/OH, Stassen, 3. "feeling sorry for him"; "You have to hock your soul": Pearson, 217; WP, May 17, 1962.

724   "stand firm and not . . . dismayed" *et seq.*: NYT, July 11, 1952.

724–25   "The governor pointedly ignored" *et seq.*: *San Francisco Examiner*, July 13, 1952; NYT, July 11, 1952.

725   "so bitter"; "We had . . . worked out": GK/OH, Polland, 11ff.

725–26   "I had to work": EW/OH, Faries, 90. "supremely confident": *Independent Review*, October 31, 1952. Brownell, Clay, Dewey agree: Cook, 142. "What do we do next, Herb?": Pearson, 217.

726   Brownell-Eisenhower dinner: Adams, 43; R. Smith, 596; Lyon, 446, who places the dinner Wednesday night, though with much the same substance.

726   "give him . . . candid opinion" *et seq.*: Mazo, 87–88; see also R. Smith, 596.

727   "Concluding . . . my work was finished": "Republican National Convention, Notes of Paul H. Davis," HI, cited above.

727–28   talk with Pat; "anxious to talk" *et seq.*: J. Eisenhower, 114–15; Nixon, RN, 85–86; David, 94; Mazo, 88. "Dick, you're a junior senator": Mazo, 88.

728   "Senator Nixon's name": NYT, July 10, 11, 1952; see also LAT, July 11, 1952; Henderson, 393; Costello, 89.

728   "lot of misinformation": NYT, July 12, 1952.

728–29   "We don't want them": R. Smith, 596. "healing party wounds"; "*that* nomination": see EW/OH, Faries, 22; Adams, 34; SFC, July 12, 1952.

729   "I've got to . . . phone Earl": EW/OH, Faries, 22. "Here we go": R. Smith, 594.

729   "I can take it" *et seq.*: Patterson, 564. "forced smiles": NYT, July 12, 1952. "beautiful maneuver": GK/OH, Polland, 13. "left behind": see *San Francisco Examiner*, July 13, 1952. "patsy for anybody": EW/OH, Warren, 283.

730   "last one out": NYT, July 12, 1952. "too much to bear": Patterson, 564. "dazed elation": Sulzberger, 772. "got to talk to Herb": NYT, July 12, 1952. "agreed . . . Nixon": Sulzberger, 772.

730–31   "Slats told you . . . last year": Ellis Slater, *The Ike I Knew* (privately published, 1980), 22. "Dick . . . all decided": EW/OH, Faries, 73. "awful tough on Bill" *et seq.*: *ibid.*, 24.

731   "already a *fait accompli*": Warren, 254. "ward committee . . . candidate for alderman": Adams, 43–44. "No deals": Herbert A. Trask, "How Lightning

Struck Nixon," *St. Louis Post-Dispatch*, September 28, 1952, one of the more colorful and complete accounts of the meeting. "by no means obvious": Adams, 43. Alexander Smith and Eisenhower-Taft ticket: see Eisenhower Library Oral History, Sherman Adams, 73–78, DDE; Adams, 44.

731–32   Sprague vetos Taft: Patterson, 565. "wipe their feet on": Eisenhower Oral History, Adams, 75, cited above, DDE. "We didn't want sponsors": *St. Louis Post-Dispatch*, September 28, 1952. "What about . . . Nixon?": R. Smith, 597. "He was well-liked": *St. Louis Post-Dispatch*, September 28, 1952.

732   "prepared to make a fight": Costello, 90. "bustle and scraping": Adams, 44. "same haphazard system": *St. Louis Post-Dispatch*, September 28, 1952. "keep a smile on her face": R. Smith, 597.

733   call to Nixon: Nixon, *RN*, 87–88; Mazo, 89. "calm and pensive": *ibid.*; Brodie, 256.

733   "one of the last to learn": J. Eisenhower, 115; Brodie, 256. "tremendously surprised"; "He has done as much": NYT, July 12. 1952.

733   "Congratulations, Chief" *et seq.*: J. Eisenhower, 116. talk with Eisenhower: Nixon, *RN*, 87–88; Mazo, 90; Adams, 26.

733–34   "proud and happy": Nixon, *RN*, 89. "that dirty son of a bitch": GK/OH, Polland, 11. Bricker; "taken aback": Nixon, *RN*, 89. "rather had taken a beating": EW/OH, McCormac, 8.

734–35   seconding speeches: *Official Report of the Proceedings of the Twenty-fifth Republican National Convention* (Washington, 1952), 417–21.

735   nomination scene: *Proceedings*, 417–21, cited above. convention floor interview: Halberstam, 317. "I am amazed": NYT, July 12, 1952. "never been on . . . payroll": *ibid.* repeat kiss: J. Eisenhower, 116. "fill any and all vacancies": *Proceedings*, cited above.

735–36   "for the first time": Nixon, *RN*, 89. acceptance: see *Proceedings*, cited above, 423 ff. "too wild": Nixon, *RN*, 90. "destroying the forces of communism": NYT, July 12, 1952. "NIXON RETRIEVES": LAT, July 12, 1952.

736   "without benefit of deals": NYT, July 12, 1952.

Chapter 22. Campaign Interval, July–September, 1952

Page

737   "shouts of rage": J. Eisenhower, 115. "vote for my daddy": LAT, July 12, 1952. Pat's biography: Republican National Committee, "Biographical Facts about Mrs. Richard Nixon," August, 1952, Campaign Material File, VPA. "deeply religious"; "rarely smokes": *Time*, July 21, 1952.

738   "just like a dream"; "snap": see Coughlan manuscript, William Rogers Papers, DDE. "I really didn't want": J. Eisenhower, 116. "he hates Dick": LAT, July 12, 1952.

738–39   "Insiders understood": Reeves, 424. "while they all knew" *et seq.*: Nixon, *RN*, 90.

739   "friendly chat": NYT, July 13, 1952. "little man in a big hurry"; "mean and vindictive": Costello, 7. "power of the . . . financial interest": NYT, November 25, 1959.

739–40   "difficult . . . to categorize," *The Reporter*, August 5, 1952.

740   meeting with Stassen men: Shanley diary, 459–60, Bernard Shanley Papers, DDE.

740   "castrate . . . Chotiner"; "Dewey . . . toughest": R. Smith, 603.

740–41   "I am happy": SB, July 12, 1952. "excellent choice": *Oakland Tribune*, July 14, 1952.

741   "If Nixon had not double-crossed": *Independent Review*, October 31, 1952. "I was for . . . Warren, period": *Fresno Bee*, October 15, 1962. budget shortage: see EW/OH, Hotchkis, 45. "bitterness . . . tremendous": *San Francisco Examiner*, July 13, 1952. "synonymous with treachery": Lyon, 446. "I'd rather lose with Taft": *San Francisco Examiner*, July 13, 1952. "cooled markedly": Warren, 254.

741   "absolutely no use for Nixon": EW/OH, Rodda, 32. "violations of criminal law and ethical conduct": G. Edward White, *Earl Warren: A Public Life* (New York, 1982), 142.

742   Bassett: see LAT, August 26, 1952. "seemed to have good counsel": Bassett interview, UU. Ted Rogers: "relatively easy material": see LAT, August 27, 1952; Halberstam, 463; *St. Louis Post-Dispatch*, September 28, 1952.

743   "fearful . . . could not keep pace": Kornitzer, 224. "same old deal": NYT, July 27, 1952. "Nattily dressed" *et seq.*: LAT, July 28, 1952.

743–44   Whittier homecoming; "rejoicing at your success" *et seq.*: LAT, July 29, 1952. It was advertised by the *Times* as "the biggest event in the history of Whittier": LAT, July 24, 1952. "They stood . . . the mother . . . Pat": *Long Beach Press-Telegram*, July 29, 1952.

745   "He believes in . . . younger people": LAT, July 30, 1952.

745   "Americans . . . communists and socialists": Godfrey Lehman, "Campaign of Fear," *Frontier*, July 1952.

745   "door wide open . . . in the South": LAT, July 30, 1952. "belong to anybody": LAT, July 31, 1952.

745–46   "Nixon and Chotiner . . . locking it up" *et seq.*: Humphreys–Adams, January 14, 1959, Sherman Adams Papers, DDE.

746–47   Malibu dinner: LAT, August 3, 1952; see also Brashear I.

747   "candidate of the people"; "military superiority to win": LAT, SB, August 4, 1952. "anything untoward": Lasky–Nixon, undated, c. August 1952, Victor Lasky File, VPA. "we are pretty fortunate": Nixon–Lasky, August 15, 1952, Victor Lasky File, VPA. "see you at the White House": Perry–Nixon, August 4, 1952, Herman Perry File, VPA.

748   "insinuations of anti-Semitism": LAT, August 19, 1952. Compare *The California Jewish Voice* (Los Angeles), August 8, 1952. Dewey dispatches Katzen: R. Smith, 598. "civil liberties . . . major theme": Hoffman–Nixon, August 20, 1952, Paul Hoffman Papers, HST. "intends to do so": Chotiner–Hoffman, August 26, 1952, Paul Hoffman Papers, HST.

748   interview with Roberts: *Kansas City Times and Star*, August 22–23, 1952; see also Costello, 96.

748   "causing the issue of McCarthyism": NYT, August 22, 1952.

749   "full awareness of the sensitivity"; "I want to make it clear": NYT, August 23, 1952.

749   Eisenhower statement: Reeves, 436–37.

749   "You would never have had 'McCarthyism' ": LAT, August 26, 1952. "What can we do"; "Hollywood Committee": Reeves, 436, 430.

750   "strangers when they meet": Ernest Brashear, "Who Is Richard Nixon, I and II," *New Republic*, September 1 and 8, 1952. "hard, narrow, ambitious": LAT, November 10, 1968. "I say . . . a Wonderful Guy": *Saturday Evening Post*, September 6, 1952.

751   "dry creek": *New York World Telegram and Sun*, August 25, 1952. "possible . . . to lose it": Hughes, 29.

751–52   If he has . . . such a plan": LAT, August 25, 1952. "real swinging": LAT, September 1, 1952. "If the record . . . smears": NYT, September 3, 1952. "tired relic": NYT, September 4, 1952. attacks: NYHT, September 8, 1952; NYT, September 3, 4, 1952; SFC, September 7, 1952; LAT, September 5, 1952.

752   "sidesaddle Adlai": *Newsweek*, September 15, 1952. "gales of giggles": NYT, September 3, 1952. "not deserving . . . nor qualified": SFC, September 7, 1952. "a veritable masterpiece": William Lee Miller, "The Debating Career of Richard M. Nixon," *The Reporter*, April 19, 1956.

752–53   "difference of degree": Goldman, 223. "Eisenhower disdained and ignored" *et seq.*: Hughes, 30–31. "Of all those absent": *ibid.*, 36–37.

753   Warren-Eisenhower meeting: Warren, 255.

754   "filled with superlatives": Herter–Nixon, September 9, 1952. Christian Herter File, VPA. "never forgive me": Nixon–Herter, September 15, 1952, Christian Herter File, VPA. "aura of a command post"; "I was to hammer" *et seq.*: Nixon, *Six Crises*, 76–77. polls: *Newsweek*, September 29, 1952; SB, September 18, 1952.

755   "I certainly never dreamed": Nixon–Dear Friend, September 13, 1952, Thomas Storke Papers, BAN.

755   "large beautiful beds": LAT, September 18, 1952. "The requirements": Brennan–Warren, September 12, 1952, Personal Political File, CSA. "carried away": Nixon, *RN*, 91. send-off program: Roy Day Papers, BAN. The complete fifty-three-page itinerary and program is in the Robert Fenton Craig Papers, UCLA.

755–56   Nixon's speech: LAT, September 18, 1952; NYT, September 18, 1952. sore throat: Nixon, *Six Crises*, 78. "red-gold hair glistened": J. Eisenhower, 118. "path to glory": Mazo, 99. "The *Dick Nixon Special*": program, Roy Day Papers, BAN.

Chapter 23. Campaign in Crisis I, September 18–21, 1952

Page

757   "wealthy landowner" *et seq.*: see Green's own account of how the story unfolded, *Independent Review*, September 26, 1952.

758   other reporters: Green, *Independent Review*, September 26, 1952. Of the three, Green apparently knew only "Ernie Brashear" of the *Daily News*. The *New York Post* reporter he later identified as "Leo Catcher." *Daily News* hesitates: see Costello, 198. "political stunt": Nixon, *RN*, 93.

758–59   "what is this 'fund' " *et seq.*: Nixon, *Six Crises*, 74. "nursery rhyme in a sea": Mazo, 97.

759   "all wrong" *et seq.*: Nixon, *Six Crises*, 75; *RN*, 92–93. Edson's call; "other states": *Chicago Daily News*, September 18, 1952.

759–60   Smith and reporters: Costello, 99–100.

760   "That's probably . . . Edson": Nixon, *Six Crises*, 78. "it might cause trouble": Mazo, 99.

761   "scrupulously careful"; "I don't see"; "ridiculous": Nixon, *Six Crises*, 80; Mazo, 99–100

761–62   Edson story: see *Chicago Daily News*, September 18, 1952. story all but censored: see Rowse, 9, 13ff., 123–28.

762   "suppressed its own story": Costello, 100. "We've been paying"; "heartbeat away"; Di Giorgio money: Katcher interview, UU. "SECRET . . . TRUST"

et seq.: *New York Post*, September 18, 1952. "masterpiece of distortion": Nixon, *Six Crises*, 81.

762   "Leo . . . son of a bitch": Katcher interview, UU. "Numerous publishers": *New York Post*, September 22, 1952. "MYSTERY ANGELS": *New York World-Telegram and Sun*, September 18, 1952, on page 23.

763   "lied to, double-talked"; "band of cutthroats": EW/OH, McCormac, 187.

763–64   "we're going to take care of you" *et seq.*: EW/OH, McCormac, 189–90. tries to arrange call to Ike: *ibid.*, 192. upbraids Drown: Nixon, *Six Crises*, 81. "in the weeds": EW/OH, McCormac, 192. press barred from car: Mazo, 100.

764–65   "seemed made of springs": Harold Lavine, *Smoke-Filled Rooms* (New York, 1970), 10. See Lavine, 1–14 and Raymond Moley's Foreword, vii–xii, for brief descriptions of Humphreys's background. "Never a secret . . . wholesome": Humphreys–Adams, February 7, 1959, Sherman Adams Papers, DDE.

765   "filthy maneuver": AP dispatch, 1:02 P.M., September 18, 1952; see "Introduction" on Fund, Robert Humphreys Papers, DDE. "taking it . . . casually"; "bigger than we dreamed": Humphreys–Adams, February 7, 1959, DDE. "morally wrong": *Chicago Sun-Times*, September 19, 1952.

765   "lost their sense of public morals": NYT, September 19, 1952. "ominous": Humphreys–Adams, February 7, 1959, DDE. "threatened to demolish": Hughes, 38. Dewey telegram: R. Smith, 600. "solid front": Humphreys–Adams, February 7, 1959, DDE.

766   "We never comment on . . . *Post*": Lyon, 454. "Their man . . . too new": *ibid.* Summerfield calls for "explanation": NYT, September 20, 1952. "jolt"; "turmoil": *Des Moines Register*, September 19, 1952.

767   first statement: NYHT, September 19, 1952; Nixon, *Six Crises*, 82.

767–68   "boning up": Nixon, *Six Crises*, 82. "Editors were in no hurry": Rowse, 123. "most of . . . front"; "lost in the back"; "Attack . . . more news": Nixon, *Six Crises*, 82.

768   "PASADENA DISCLOSES": PSN, September 18, 1952. "gloomy and angry": Mazo, 102.

769   "attempt to . . . smear": Associated Press dispatch, *Pittsburgh Post-Gazette*, September 19, 1952. "I don't talk on politics": SB, September 19, 1952.

769   "the same left-wing elements" *et seq.*: NYT, September 20, 1952.

769   "When I turned off the light": Nixon, *Six Crises*, 82–83.

769–70   "buzzing": *New York Post*, September 22, 1952. "terrible turmoil": Shanley Diary, 510, Bernard Shanley Papers, DDE.

770   "not be allowed to end": NYT, September 20, 1952.

770–71   "calmest person" *et seq.*: Cutler, 284–85. "staggered and shaken": Hughes, 38.

771   "I have long admired": NYT, September 20, 1952.

771–72   "even made a small dent" *et seq.*: Humphreys–Adams, February 7, 1959, DDE.

772   "subsidized front man": SB, September 19, 1952.

772–74   Marysville speech: NYT, September 20, 1952. See also combined wire-services accounts in *Kansas City Star*, September 19, 1952; *Time*, September 29, 1952. The Nixon recollections are from *Six Crises*, 83–84.

772   "The Alger Hiss crowd": *Newsweek*, September 29, 1952.

774   "I walked back . . . feeling better": Nixon, *Six Crises*, 84.

774–75   Chico station: NYT, September 20, 1952.

775   "It may be assumed" *et seq.*: NYT, September 20, 1952.

775   Seaton call: NYT, September 20, 21, 1952; *Newsweek*, September 29, 1952; Mazo, 104. "clear to me": Nixon, *RN*, 94.

775   Red Bluff and Redding: NYT, September 20, 1952; Associated Press wire copy, September 19, 1952, Robert Humphreys Papers, DDE.

775–76   "I used it throughout": Nixon, *Six Crises*, 84. staff in tears: *ibid*. California tax inquiry: UP dispatch, September 19, 1952; see SB, September 20, 1952.

776   "professional and business people": Nixon, *Six Crises*, 84. "unbearable"; "almost frantic": J. Eisenhower, 118.

776   "opportunity to enrich": NYT, September 20, 1952.

777   "We have often heard the shout": *St. Joseph* (Missouri) *News-Press*, September 19, 1952. "DONATE HERE": *Life*, September 29, 1952. "If you're tired": NYT, September 20, 1952. "public-spirited citizens": *Kansas City Star*, September 19, 1952. "some advisers": the *Star*'s Duke Shoop from the train; see *Kansas City Star*, September 19, 1952, and the morning *Kansas City Times*, September 20, 1952. "sharply divided": Associated Press dispatch, September 19, 1952; see *Boston Post*, September 20, 1952 and Humphreys's "Introduction," Robert Humphreys Papers, DDE.

777–78   Eisenhower's Kansas City speech: NYT, September 20, 21, 1952. "dropping Nixon . . . never mentioned": see Humphreys, "Introduction," DDE, cited above.

778   call to Knowland: Lyon, 454; Wills, 100. "will be overcome": NYT, September 20, 1952. Ike fitful: Lyon, 455.

778   "atmosphere of gloom": AP dispatch, September 19, 1952; see *New York Daily Mirror*, September 20, 1952.

778–79   staff meeting; "not in the least discouraged": Nixon, *Six Crises*, 84–85.

779   "offer of withdrawal"; "ill-advised": NYHT, September 20, 1952.

779–80   "exemplifies . . . unethical conduct": WP, September 20, 1952. "forced" smile and "Cave Men": Mazo, 106. "any comment?": Nixon, *Six Crises*, 85.

780   "as much of a jolt": Nixon, *RN*, 94. "blockbuster"; "people around Eisenhower": Nixon, *Six Crises*, 86.

780   meets Chotiner, Rogers; "struck with the enormity" *et seq.*: Nixon, *Six Crises*, 86–87; *RN*, 94–95; Wills, 100.

781   "good front"; "You can't think": Nixon, *Six Crises*, 87. "if you get off": Alsop transcript, LC.

781–82   editorials: all cited papers are dated September 20, 1952; see also NYT, September 21, 1952 for various excerpts.

782   "polite anarchy": *Time*, September 29, 1952.

782   "Nixon on TV" *et seq.*: Humphreys–Adams, February 7, 1959, DDE.

783   "Without a full knowledge": Eisenhower–Robinson, September 20, 1952, "En Route St. Louis," Pre-Presidential Files, DDE.

783   "let down": NYT, September 21, 1952. "keep . . . chins up": R. Smith, 600.

783   call to Hoffman; "immediate investigation"; "bad idea": see Adams's and Humphreys's handwritten notes on Hoffman, c. September 20, 1952, Adams Papers, DDE; also Adams, 45, D. Eisenhower, 67.

784   "mixture of emotions"; Clay "angry": Hughes, 38–39. "the building . . . to enormous proportions": Humphreys, "Introduction," DDE, cited above.

784   Clay holds back: Lyon, 455; R. Smith, 600.

784   "like a prison": Nixon, *Six Crises*, 88.

785   Eugene placards, speech, and melee: Alsop transcript, LC; NYT, September 20, 21, 1952; Jamieson, 70; Mazo, 106–7; Kornitzer, 194; Nixon, *Six Crises*, 88–89; Brodie, 280.

785   "fund . . . established . . . to carry on my fight": NYT, September 21, 1952; Nixon, *Six Crises*, 90–91.

786 "this friend"; "that friend"; "dump-Nixon movement" *et seq.*: Nixon, *Six Crises*, 88.

786-87 partisan reactions: NYT, September 21, 1952; LAT, September 21, 1952; Nixon, *Six Crises*, 89–90; *RN*, 95.

787 Taft response: *Christian Science Monitor*, September 22, 1952; Nixon, *Six Crises*, 89. "He was not so naïve": *ibid.*, 90.

787 "Condemnation . . . wrong": LAT, September 21, 1952. "considering . . . wrong decision": Nixon, *Six Crises*, 90. "smelled a rat": *ibid.*

787 Humphreys's tip from Chicago; "rumors": Humphreys–Adams, February 7, 1959, DDE; see also John Bartlow Martin, 691.

787-88 "constantly . . . to my mother": Brodie, 278. "very disgusted"; "no . . . reason for it": YN, Johnson. "bouts of weeping": Nixon, *RN*, 109.

788 Hagerty announces fifty-fifty split; "how close . . . to a decision": NYT, September 21, 1952; Lyon, 455.

788 Ike "on background"; "equivocal smiles" *et seq.*: NYT, September 21, 23, 1952; Goldman, 226; Lyon, 456.

789 "hound's tooth"; "Just what . . . means": NYT, September 21, 1952. "If Nixon has to go": Adams, 45. "Nixon . . . liability": Eisenhower–Nixon Research Service telegram to Adams, September 20, 1952, Sherman Adams Papers, DDE. "jeering attitude": LAT, September 22, 1952.

789-90 "Make it clear. . . . Nail [the] bastards" *et seq.*: Humphreys's handwritten notes in Humphreys and Adams Papers, DDE, cited above; Humphreys–Adams, February 7, 1959, DDE, cited above.

790 "reckless belligerent": *Time*, September 29, 1952. Salem: NYT, September 21, 1952.

790 pickets at Benson Hotel: Nixon, *RN*, 96; NYT, September 21, 1952; "tight-lipped and gray-faced": *Time*, September 29, 1952.

790-91 "not going to be fobbed off": Nixon, *RN*, 96. "It can't be happening" *et seq.*: J. Eisenhower, 119; see also David, 104.

791 "our little group . . . dismayed" *et seq.*: Nixon, *Six Crises*, 92–93. "as furious": Lyon, 456.

792 Grant High School speech; "faith in the . . . people": NYT, September 22, 1952. "Don't quit": Nixon, *Six Crises*, 93. "hearty approval": LAT, September 22, 1952.

793 "sugar-coated reports": Nixon, *Six Crises*, 93. "completely shaken": Hoyt, 274.

793-94 reports and advice: Nixon, *Six Crises*, 93–96.

794-95 "My heart wasn't in it"; "without interruption": Humphreys–Adams, February 7, 1959, DDE, cited above. "shoot their wad": Nixon, *Six Crises*, 96. "If Dick is off": Mazo, 109; see also Nixon, *RN*, 97.

795 "affect the future" *et seq.*: Nixon, *Six Crises*, 96–97.

795 "*Who's Who*" *et seq.*: NYT, September 21, 1952.

796 "deprive this nation": "NOTE: In a conversation between Tex McCrary and Bernard Baruch . . ." September 21, 1952, Sherman Adams Papers, DDE.

796 "mistake in judgment": NYT, September, 22, 1952. "NO . . . WISHFUL THINK-ING" *et seq.*: Eisenhower-Nixon Research Service telegram to Adams, September 21, 1952, Adams Papers, DDE. "loaded for *bear*": Adams note, Sherman Adams Papers, DDE.

797 "long day of argument": Cutler, 285.

797 Burroughs reports: Robert Burroughs–Eisenhower and Adams, September 22, 1952, Sherman Adams Papers, DDE.

798 "bombarded": D. Eisenhower, 65–66. "impartial umpire": Cutler, 285ff.

798   Humphreys's flight: Humphreys–Adams, February 7, 1959, DDE, cited above.

799   "long day of ordeal": Nixon, *Six Crises*, 97. Riley and Bewley; "ready to throw in the sponge" *et seq.*: see YN, Newsom; Kornitzer, 93; Nixon, *Six Crises*, 98.

799–800   "political religion": NYT, September 22, 1952. "changed man": Kornitzer, 193. "controlled . . . temper"; "bitterness": *ibid.* "Aroused Citizens of Whittier" *et seq.*: NYT, September 22, 1952; LAT, September 22, 1952. "It's nice to know": *Life*, September 29, 1952. "a bit 'hysterical' ": NYT, September 22, 1952.

800   call to Dewey: R. Smith, 600, a call Nixon himself does not report. "cracking with emotion"; "age a lifetime": J. Eisenhower, 120.

800   "enemies"; "gloat": Alsop transcript, LC.

801–2   Stassen telegram: Stassen telegram to Nixon, September 21, 1952, Stassen File, VPA. "severe blow": Nixon, *Six Crises*, 98. "you ought to!": Alsop transcript, LC.

802   "I watched every moment": Kornitzer, 192–93.

802   "girls are okay"; "broke down"; "state of mind"; "total despair": Kornitzer, 192–93.

802–3   "I will not crawl": Mazo, 110. "risk his own future": *ibid.*

803   Dewey's call; "hanging jury": Nixon, *Six Crises*, 98–99; *RN*, 97; Wills, 102; R. Smith, 600–601; Mazo, 109.

804   Summerfield call: NYT, September 26, 1952. "last speech": Mazo, 109.

804–5   Humphreys in St. Louis; "unanimous . . . thrown off"; "hot and heavy" *et seq.*: Humphreys–Adams, February 7, 1959, DDE, cited above.

805–7   Eisenhower's call: Nixon, *Six Crises*, 99–101; *RN*, 97–99; D. Eisenhower, 67; Lyon, 457; Alsop transcript, LC; Mazo, 110.

807–8   "resolved the dilemma" *et seq.*: Nixon, *Six Crises*, 100–101. "scarred her deeply"; "We both know": Nixon, *RN*, 98–99. painful neck: see J. Eisenhower, 120.

808–9   "in Everett's behalf": Humphreys–Adams, February 7, 1959, DDE, cited above. Batten, Barton and network: Lyon, 458. fix time after Berle show: Mazo, 111. "I realize . . . misrepresented": LAT, September 22, 1952.

809   meet press: NYT, September 22, 23, 1952. "I've come down to announce": *ibid.* "jumped out of his skin": Nixon, *Six Crises*, 101.

809   "staying on ticket?" "truthful answer": Nixon, *Six Crises*, 101.

809   "Give me . . . time"; "decision was up to Ike": *Time*, September 29, 1952.

Chapter 24. Campaign in Crisis II, September 22–24, 1952

Page

810–11   "not provided" *et seq.*: NYHT, September 22, 1952. "blunts and dilutes": Robinson telegram to Eisenhower via Thomas Stephens, September 22, 1952, Wm. Robinson Papers, DDE.

811   "Overwhelmingly against": Georgia Youth for Eisenhower telegram to Edward Bermingham, September 22, 1952, Sherman Adams Papers, DDE. "Nixon is as expendable": Roy Blount and Grover Hall telegram to E. J. Birmingham [sic], September 21, 1952, Adams Papers, DDE.

811–12   "likely to hurt"; "disgruntled Warren Republican": NYT, September 22, 1952. Lodge, Clay favor withdrawal: NYT, September 24, 1952. Humphreys's "dozen": Humphreys–Adams, February 7, 1959, DDE. "Nixon . . . far better"; "general agreement": *ibid.*

812   Eisenhower's press briefing; "I do not want to nag": NYT, September 23, 1952. threat to Pearson: see Eisenhower-Nixon Research Service telegram to Adams, September 22, 1952, Adams Papers, DDE.

813   "shades . . . carefully lowered" et seq.: Adams, 45–46.

813   "deserted by so many" et seq.: Nixon, Six Crises, 102. "something to hide": Nixon, RN, 99.

813–14   "lay out for everyone" et seq.: Nixon, Six Crises, 103–4. "a kind of malicious pleasure": Alsop transcript, LC.

814   Los Angeles welcome: NYT, September 23, 1952; J. Eisenhower, 121; Nixon, Six Crises, 104.

814–15   leaks; "thrown to wolves": NYT, September 23, 1952; Klein, 372. "excruciating pain": J. Eisenhower, 121. "nobody at all": see Mazo, 111. "building . . . audience"; "round-the-clock research": Nixon, Six Crises, 103.

815   exposure of Stevenson fund: see Rowse, 8; Nixon, RN, 100. "otherwise . . . at your throat": Nixon, Six Crises, 106. "suitable Lincoln quotes": Wills, 105; Nixon, Six Crises, 103.

815–16   "where . . . Dicky Boy": St. Louis Post-Dispatch, September 23, 1952. Justice investigation: NYT, September 22, 23, 1952. coverage of Stevenson: see Rowse, 102–3, 124.

816   "We busted the story": Humphreys–Adams, February 7, 1959, DDE, cited above.

816–17   "Stevenson . . . recovery": Eisenhower-Nixon Research Service–James C. Hagerty for Eisenhower, September 23, 1952, Adams Papers, DDE. "disturbing"; "nothing to indicate"; misgivings": R. Smith, 601–2. "absolutely clean": My report on the Fund . . . ," undated transcript, Paul Hoffman Papers, HST. Hoffman doesn't see findings: see Conley–Hoffman, September 24, 1952, Paul Hoffman Papers, HST. "out of existence": D. Eisenhower, 67. The "same $11,000" collected since the Convention may account for Katcher's "second fund."

817–18   Humphreys to Cleveland; meeting at Carter Hotel: Humphreys–Adams, February 7, 1959, DDE, cited above; see also Lyon, 458ff.

818   Eisenhower–Hall–Dewey order to resign: R. Smith, 601–2; George Shapiro, Dewey's respected counsel, confirmed later that the call from the campaign train came "at Ike's request."

819   "Only when . . . without notes": Nixon, Six Crises, 107. "Edgy and short-tempered" et seq.: ibid., 107–9. "front-row seats"; "I overruled them all": ibid, 107.

819–21   audit and legal report: Price Waterhouse–Sherman Adams; Elmo Conley for Gibson, Dunn and Crutcher–Adams, September 23, 1952, Roy Day Papers, BAN; also Paul Hoffman Papers, HST.

821   "great weight . . . with Eisenhower's associates": Nixon, Six Crises, 108.

821–23   call from Dewey: Nixon, Six Crises, 109–11; RN, 102; D. Eisenhower, 68; R. Smith, 601–3; Wills, 105–6; Mazo, 114–16.

823–24   "Dick, a good . . . manager" et seq.: Nixon, Six Crises, 112; Mazo, 116. "like a rock": Alsop transcripts, LC. "last mile": Nixon, Six Crises, 112; RN, 103.

824–25   meeting in Cleveland: Humphreys–Adams, February 7, 1959, DDE, cited above; see also Alsop, Nixon and Rockefeller, 69.

825   "a giant free balloon": Cutler, 285.

825–26   "grim-faced": Newsweek, October 6, 1952. "Keep it simple": see St. Louis Post-Dispatch, September 28, 1952; Goldman, 227.

826   "nondescript room": Nixon, RN, 103. "Many viewers . . . moved": James A. Kearns in the St. Louis Post-Dispatch, September 28, 1952. For Nixon's

description of the studio and preparations, see *Six Crises*, 112–13; also J. Eisenhower, 120. "doggedly . . . directed motions"; "clasping . . . handkerchief": *ibid.*

826–27 "to feel she is here": Brodie, 282. Rogers draws line: Halberstam, 464. "when I'm finished": Jamieson, 78. "completely on his own": Kornitzer, 194. "I just don't think": Nixon, *Six Crises*, 113.

827–35 the speech: the original notes were reproduced in Richard Wilson, "Is Nixon Fit to Be President?" *Look*, February 24, 1953; the delivered text in NYT, LAHE, *St. Louis Globe-Democrat*, and other papers, September 24, 1952. Nixon's own feelings are described in *Six Crises*, 113–17, and *RN*, 103–4.

827 Hannah "shuddered"; "grateful": H. Nixon.

831 "didn't think I could take it": Kornitzer, 205; Hoyt, 277. "unblinking, thinly smiling"; "I didn't know": Coughlan manuscript, William Rogers Papers, DDE.

833 "Ike got what Dick was getting at": Lyon, 460; Alsop, *Nixon and Rockefeller*, 65; Wills, 108.

834 "No, and you never have been": H. Nixon.

835 "emotional daze"; "I'm sorry": Jamieson, 78; Mazo, 118; Nixon, *RN*, 104.

835 "money's worth": D. Eisenhower, 68. "honest man": Adams, 46.

835–36 Cleveland crowd: *Cleveland News*, September 24, 1952; Lyon, 461; *Newsweek*, October 6, 1952. "complete about-face": Humphreys–Adams, February 17, 1959, Sherman Adams Papers, DDE. "bending the grass": Cutler, 286.

836 "I'm sorry I had to rush"; "fix them" *et seq.*: Nixon, *Six Crises*, 117.

836–37 "I was a failure": J. Eisenhower, 124. "Let's get out of here": Coughlan manuscript, William Rogers Papers, DDE. "not an easy speech": LAHE, September 24, 1952. "hit in the dog world"; "sick with the certainty": Hughes, 40. "Pat . . . pleased": Nixon, *Six Crises*, 118.

837 "expertly stage-managed": Lyon, 461. Ike prepares speech: Humphreys–Adams, February 17, 1959, DDE, cited above. "rewrite it": *Life*, October 6, 1952.

837–38 Eisenhower's Cleveland speech: NYT, September 24, 1952; Adams, 47.

838–39 "voiced no judgment": Hughes, 41. "darts . . . at the National Committee": Lyon, 461.

839 "mobbed" candidate: J. Eisenhower, 124. "we waited tensely": Klein, 138.

839 "greatest production": Coughlan manuscript, William Rogers Papers, DDE. "could not make . . . decision": Nixon, *Six Crises*, 120. "shock and rage": Hughes, 40. "exploded": Hoyt, 270. "despair, then anger": J. Eisenhower, 124. "not going to crawl": *Newsweek*, October 6, 1952. "What more": David, 109. "completely unreasonable" *et seq.*: Nixon, *Six Crises*, 120; *RN*, 105–6.

840 "I don't blame him": Nixon, *RN*, 106. "Chotiner . . . insisted": Nixon, *Six Crises*, 121. wire to Eisenhower; "shocked": Mazo, 120; Adams, 47.

840 "insolence . . . depth": Lyon, 462–63.

841 Humphreys–Chotiner conversation: Humphreys–Adams, February 17, 1959, DDE; Nixon, *Six Crises*, 121; Alsop, *Nixon and Rockefeller*, 68.

841 "Let the bastards wait": Klein, 138.

841–42 Andrews's call: Nixon, *Six Crises*, 122; *RN*, 106.

842 "We haven't begun to fight": NYT, September 25, 1952. "wouldn't get off": Humphreys–Adams, February 17, 1959, DDE, cited above.

842–43 Humphreys's notes: "Making A President . . . ," Robert Humphreys Papers, DDE.

843 "clutching . . . to our breasts": Humphreys–Adams, February 17, 1959, DDE. Drown in Missoula: J. Eisenhower, 125. "taut and knotted": *Life*, October 6, 1952.

844 response to speech: the wires are in WCA, as are a number of Whittier College Master's theses on the phenomenon. See especially Robert W. O'Brien and Elizabeth J. Jones, *The Night Nixon Spoke: A Study of Political Effectiveness* (Los Alamitos, 1976). "one of us": O'Brien and Jones, *The Night Nixon Spoke*, 9, cited above.

844 "flood"; "composure": NYT, September 24, 25, 26, 1952.

844–45 "superb": NYT, September 26, 1952. "silly": R. Smith, 602. "national hero": NYT, September 25, 1952. "CLIP THIS": *New York Journal American*, September 24, 1952. "Without a trace": LAHE, September 24, 1952. contributions to Smith: NYT, September 25, 1952.

845 Lodge's phone: NYT, September 24, 1952. "old-time revival": *Independent Review*, October 3, 1952. "a slick production": Lyon, 460.

846 "somewhat mollified" *et seq.*: Humphreys–Adams, February 17, 1959, DDE; Lyon, 462.

846 "If the ticket had been headed": Alsop, *Nixon and Rockefeller*, 70. "eyed its crest": Hughes, 39; Adams, 48. "everything . . . all right": Humphreys–Adams, February 17, 1959, DDE, cited above.

846–47 "I love my country"; "clean it up": NYT, September 25, 1952. "victory ride": Nixon, *Six Crises*, 123.

847 Eisenhower's greeting: see especially the Associated Press account in *Milwaukee Journal*, September 25, 1952; see also Nixon, *RN*, 106; J. Eisenhower, 125; Mazo, 121. "looking gracious": Wills, 113.

847–48 "Forget it": Nixon, *Six Crises*, 123. "blithely talked": Nixon, *RN*, 106; see also Adams, 49. Mamie and Pat: J. Eisenhower, 125.

848–49 speeches in Wheeling: NYT, September 25, 1952.

849–50 "I had exhausted all": Nixon, *Six Crises*, 124. "This is just like war, General": Nixon, *RN*, 107. "she would hate politics": *ibid.*, 108.

850 "a long time": David, 109. "deep scar": Nixon, *Six Crises*, 128. "suddenly old": Nixon, *RN*, 108. "Nixon won this one": *Milwaukee Journal*, September 25, 1952.

Chapter 25. Aftermath, September 1952–January 1953

Page

851 "bobby-soxers . . . film star"; "they demand it": NYT, September 26, 1952. "No, no": NYT, September 28, 1952.

851–52 "unimpressed"; Stevenson's accounting: John Bartlow Martin, 693, 694–703.

852 "to point out the gaps": Chotiner–Humphreys, October 1, 1952, Sherman Adams Papers, DDE.

852 "equating his fund to Nixon's": John Bartlow Martin, 703. "with kid gloves": Nixon, *RN*, 100.

852–53 "shot in the arm" *et seq.*: NYT, September 29, 1952.

853 "nation saw a little man": quoted in Goldman, 231.

853 "Order of the Hound's Tooth": Nixon, *Six Crises*, 125. "only thing . . . saved my career": *ibid.*

853 "Chapman's friend": Klein, 138.

854 "how he took over!": *St. Louis Post-Dispatch*, September 27, 1952. Lippmann's "disturbing experience": *Chicago Sun Times*, September 26, 1952. "courageous, four-square": Eisenhower–Dear Friend, September 30, 1952, EW/OH, McCormac, 184.

854–55 "negotiate" with Nixon; "acid comments"; "Nixon and Eisenhower": Eisenhower-Nixon Research Service–James C. Hagerty, for Eisenhower, September 27, 1952. Sherman Adams Papers, DDE. (The summaries were now also being addressed to "Murray Chotiner, Senator Nixon's Headquarters.") "just one thing left out": Shanley Diary, September 26, 1952, 516, Bernard Shanley Papers, DDE. "ever wholly trust . . . again": Lyon, 462.

855 "much detachment": Hughes, 40. "tough as nails": Alsop, *Nixon and Rockefeller*, 68–69. "no use for the press": Bassett interview, UU. "Fuck 'em": Halberstam, 465.

855–56 "He had done it his way": Halberstam, 464. "all but . . . hopelessly prejudiced": *Chicago Sun-Times*, September 27, 1952. "more in his own pocket": *St. Louis Post-Dispatch*, September 27, 1952.

856 Williams's series; "not a bad sum": see SB, September 26, 30, October 1, 10, 1952.

856 "irrevocably placed himself": *Commonweal*, October 10, 1952. "moral confusion and ethical relativism": *Christian Century*, October 8, 1952. "he has yet to comprehend": Rovere, 62.

856–57 "Whittier Citizens Committee": see Nixon Post Campaign File, JVP.

857 "again bumping into": *The Reporter*, October 14, 1952.

857 "gutter politics": NYT, October 1, 1952.

857–58 franking story; Nixon "unavailable": NYT and *San Francisco News*, October 3, 1952. "Know your enemy": NYT, October 5, 1952. New York appearances: NYT, October 6, 1952. "for what any good citizen": LAT, October 15, 1952. "AWOL"; "Truman's stoodge"; "spineless school"; "State Department pink": NYT, October 7, 8, 10, 1952.

858–59 "I charge . . . buried record will show": October 18, 1952, quoted in Kornitzer, 230. "*The People's Daily World*": Nixon–Chotiner, Bassett, Chotiner File, VPA.

859 "all-American team": *Newsweek*, October 13, 1952. "heckled by experts": LAT, October 15, 1952. "masterful performer": LAT, October 23, 1952. "If Stevenson . . . taken in": *ibid.*, October 24, 1952. Stevenson's response: see NYT, October 24, 1952.

859–60 FBI leaks: see FBI Memo, Ladd–Hoover, October 9, 1952, AHP; O'Reilly, 110; Levitt and Levitt, 6–7. "to make . . . flesh creep": WP, October 14, 1952; see Costello, 115–116. "Please clear up": FBI Memo, Belmont—Ladd, October 14, 1952, AHP. "sons-of-bitches . . . out to get me": Weinstein, 510–11.

860 "Bundles for Nixon": see H. Allen Smith–Chotiner, October 10, 1952; W. E. Walk, Jr.–Chotiner, October 1, 1952; Chotiner–Brennan, October 1, 1952; W. E. Walk, Jr.–Nixon, September 29, 1952, all Smears and Special Cases File, VPA.

860–61 occasional messages: see "Messages from Everett Walker," October 14, 1952, DDE. "aroused"; "real danger": BG, October 12, 1952. "event gave warning": Hughes, 41–43.

861 "the speech": see LAT, October 29, 1952. "make sure nobody shot him"; "garbage": Bassett interview, UU. "ogre-monger"; "oldest young man": *ibid.*

861–62 "Dick and Pat smiles": Bassett interview, UU. "the finest young couple": LAT, October 26, 1952. "traitors to the high principles": LAT, October 28, 1952; see also 1952 Campaign Clip File, HST. The United Press version omitted the word "traitor." "College of Cowardly": LAT, October 31, 1952. "perfect foil"; "regret . . . those attacks": Nixon, *RN*, 110. "definition of a cynic": Nixon, *RN*, 111. "really loathed": John Bartlow Martin, 693.

862   real-estate charges: see *Chicago Sun-Times*, October 29, 1952. Nixon's response: statement, October 29, 1952, Smears and Special Cases File, VPA. Pearson's false report: see *Los Angeles Daily News*, October 30, 1952. libel suit: J. Eisenhower, 127. threatening letter: Blase A. Bonpane–Pearson, February 1, 1952, Smears and Special Cases File, VPA. demands retractions; warnings: see Nixon wires to ABC, Carter Products, Thomas F. Harrington of Ted Bates Advertising Agency, Sullivan–Stauffer–Colwell, Bayles Advertising, November 2, 1952, Smears and Special Cases File, VPA.

862–63   "filched": Pearson, 225. "Forgetful critics": Nixon, *RN*, 109. "When we're elected": Costello, 6. "gang of roughnecks": Pearson, 227.

863   "our own county": Nixon telegram to Adams, October 31, 1952, Sherman Adams Papers, VPA.

863   "better Vice President": Nixon, *RN*, 112. "wild" scene at Ambassador: LAT, November 5, 1952. "deadly quiet": John Bartlow Martin, 756.

864   "identify . . . with a tradition": Hughes, 46. "Where, Oh, Where": Goldman, 234.

864   "just what the doctor ordered": Nixon–Rebozo, November 28, 1952, Charles "Bebe" Rebozo File, VPA. Smathers-Fulbright proposal: LAT, November 9, 1952.

864–65   "I have no further ambition": LAT, January 21, 1953. "E. Howard Hunt": the card is in the Mexico City Trip File, VPA.

865   "Steps are being taken": Chotiner–Emetia Brady, November 18, 1952, Smears and Special Cases File, VPA. "full of hope": J. Eisenhower, 131. "I am not going to wear": YN, Parsons, 7.

866   "You have gone far": Nixon, *RN*, 117.

Select Bibliography

Books and Articles

Abrahamsen, M.D., David. *Nixon vs. Nixon*. New York: Farrar, Straus & Giroux, 1977.

Adams, Sherman. *Firsthand Report*. New York: Popular Library, 1962.

Alexander, Margarita Fraser. "The Political Campaigns of Richard Milhous Nixon in California," Master's Thesis in History, University of Southern California, 1966.

Alsop, Stewart. "The Mystery of Richard Nixon," *Saturday Evening Post*, July 12, 1958.

——— *Nixon and Rockefeller*. New York: Doubleday, 1960.

——— "A Talk with Nixon," complete text of 1958 interview with Richard Nixon, Stewart Alsop Papers, Library of Congress. (Cited as Alsop transcript.)

Andrews, Bert, and Andrews, Peter. *A Tragedy of History: A Journalist's Confidential Role in the Hiss-Chambers Case*. Washington: R. B. Luce, 1962.

Arnold, Benjamin F., and Clark, Artilissa Dorland. *History of Whittier*. Whittier: Western Printing Corp., 1933.

Arnold, William A. *Back When It All Began: The Early Nixon Years*. New York: Vantage Press, 1975.

Bourne, Tom. "Nixon's First Victim," *Reader: Los Angeles's Free Weekly*, January 9, 1981.

Bowers, Lynn, and Blair, Dorothy. "How to Pick a Congressman," *Saturday Evening Post*, March 19, 1949.

Boyer, Paul. *By the Bomb's Early Light: American Thought and Culture at the Dawn of the Atomic Age*. New York: Pantheon, 1985.

Brashear, Ernest. "Who Is Richard Nixon?" *New Republic*, Part I, September 1, 1952; Part II, September 8, 1952. (Cited as Brashear I and II.)

Brodie, Fawn M. *Richard Nixon: The Shaping of His Character*. Cambridge, Mass.: Harvard University Press, 1983.

961

Bullock, Paul. *Jerry Voorhis: The Idealist as Politician*. New York: Vantage Press, 1978.

Butz, March D. *Yorba Linda, Its History*. Covina: Taylor Publishing Company, 1979.

Cannon, Lou. "The Forces That Forged the Future," *The Washington Post*, August 9, 1974.

Carr, Robert K. *The House Committee on Un-American Activities, 1945–1950*. Ithaca, N.Y.: Cornell University Press, 1952.

Casoni, Frederick. Autograph Collection. Rockville Centre, N.Y.: Kuil Lithograph and Publishing Company, 1982.

Caute, David. *The Great Fear*. New York: Simon & Schuster, 1978.

Ceplair, Larry, and Englund, Steven. *The Inquisition in Hollywood: Politics in the Film Community, 1930–1960*. Garden City, N.Y.: Doubleday, 1980.

Chambers, Whittaker. *Witness*. New York: Random House, 1952.

Cook, Blanche Weisen. *The Declassified Eisenhower*. New York: Penguin, 1984.

Cooke, Alistair. *Generation on Trial*. New York: Knopf, 1950.

Cooper, Charles W. *The A. Wardman Story*. Whittier: Whittier College Press, 1961.

Costello, William. *The Facts about Nixon: An Unauthorized Biography*. New York: Viking, 1960.

Coughlan, Robert. "Richard Nixon," unedited *Life* manuscript, November 10, 1953. William P. Rogers Papers, Dwight D. Eisenhower Presidential Library.

——— "Success Story of a Vice President," *Life*, December 14, 1953.

Cronin, S.S., Rev. John. "The Problem of American Communism in 1945: Facts and Recommendations: A Confidential Study for Private Circulation," Francis P. Mathews Papers, Harry S Truman Presidential Library.

Cutler, Robert. *No Time for Rest*. Boston: Atlantic Monthly Press, 1966.

David, Lester. *Lonely Lady of San Clemente: The Story of Pat Nixon*. New York: Berkley Books, 1979.

Demaris, Ovid. *The Director*. New York: Harper's Magazine Press, 1975.

de Toledano, Ralph. *One Man Alone: Richard Nixon*. New York: Funk & Wagnalls, 1969.

Donovan, Robert J. *Conflict and Crisis: The Presidency of Harry S. Truman, 1945–1948*. New York: Norton, 1977.

——— *Tumultuous Years: The Presidency of Harry S. Truman, 1949–1953*. New York: Norton, 1982.

Douglas, Helen Gahagan. *A Full Life*. New York: Doubleday, 1982.

Douglas, Paul H. *In the Fulness of Time*. New York: Harcourt Brace Jovanovich, 1972.

Eisenhower, Dwight David. *Mandate for Change, 1953–1956*. Garden City, N.Y.: Doubleday, 1963.

Eisenhower, Julie Nixon. *Pat Nixon: The Untold Story*. New York: Simon & Schuster, 1986.

Engler, Robert. *The Politics of Oil*. Chicago: University of Chicago Press, 1961.

Faber, Doris. *The Presidents' Mothers*. New York: St. Martin's, 1976.

Flynn, William. "Richard Nixon's Life Story," *Kansas City Star*, October 30–November 6, 1955 (reprinted from the *Boston Globe*).

Gardner, Richard. "Fighting Quaker: The Story of Richard Nixon," unpublished manuscript, Whittier College Special Collections.

Goldman, Eric. *The Crucial Decade*. New York: Knopf, 1956.

Goodman, Walter. *The Committee.* New York: Farrar, Straus & Giroux, 1968.

Griffith, Robert, and Theoharis, Athan, editors, *The Specter: Original Essays on the Cold War and the Origins of McCarthyism.* New York: New Viewpoints Press, 1974.

Halberstam, David. *The Powers That Be.* New York: Dell, 1980.

Heizer, Robert F., and Almquist, Alan F. *The Other Californians.* Berkeley: University of California Press, 1971.

Henderson, Lloyd Ray. "Earl Warren and California Politics," Ph.D. Dissertation in History, University of California at Berkeley, 1965.

Hiss, Alger. *In The Court of Public Opinion.* New York: Knopf, 1957.

―――― *Recollections of a Life.* New York: Holt, 1988.

Hiss, Tony. *Laughing Last.* Boston: Houghton Mifflin, 1976.

Hoyt, Edwin P. *The Nixons: An American Family.* New York: Random House, 1972.

Hughes, Emmet. *Ordeal of Power.* New York: Atheneum, 1963.

Isserman, Maurice. *Which Side Were You On?: The American Communist Party during the Second World War.* Middletown, Conn.: Wesleyan University Press, 1982.

Jackson, Donald. "The Young Nixon," *Life,* November 6, 1970.

Jamieson, Kathleen Hall. *Packaging the Presidency.* New York: Oxford University Press, 1984.

Jerger, Wilbur. "The Real Nixon Story," *Los Angeles Free Press,* October 4, 1956.

Kahrl, William L. *Water and Power.* Berkeley: University of California Press, 1981.

Katcher, Leo. *Earl Warren: A Political Biography.* New York: McGraw-Hill, 1967.

Keeley, Joseph. *The China Lobby Man.* New Rochelle, N.Y.: Arlington House, 1969.

Klehr, Harvey. *The Heyday of American Communism: The Depression Decade.* New York: Basic Books, 1984.

Klein, Herbert. *Making It Perfectly Clear.* Garden City, N.Y.: Doubleday, 1980.

Kornitzer, Bela. *The Real Nixon.* New York: Rand McNally, 1960.

La Shana, David C. *Quakers in California.* Newberg, Or.: Barclay Press, 1969.

Levine, Isaac Don. *Eyewitness to History.* New York: Hawthorn Books, 1973.

Levitt, Morton, and Levitt, Michael. *Tissue of Lies: Nixon vs. Hiss.* New York: McGraw-Hill, 1979.

Lodge, Henry Cabot. *The Storm Has Many Eyes.* New York: Norton, 1973.

Lyon, Peter. *Eisenhower: Portrait of the Hero.* Boston: Little, Brown, 1974.

McWilliams, Carey. *Southern California: An Island on the Land.* Salt Lake City: Peregrine Smith Books, 1983.

Mankiewicz, Frank. *Perfectly Clear: Nixon from Whittier to Watergate.* New York: Quadrangle Books, 1973.

Marbury, William. "The Hiss-Chambers Libel Suit," *Maryland Law Review* 4 (1982): 77–102.

Martin, Joe. As Told to Robert J. Donovan. *My First Fifty Years in Politics.* New York: McGraw-Hill, 1960.

Martin, John Bartlow. *Adlai Stevenson of Illinois.* New York: Anchor Books, 1977.

Mazlish, Bruce. *In Search of Nixon.* Baltimore: Penguin, 1972.

Mazo, Earl. *Richard Nixon: A Political and Personal Portrait.* New York: Avon Books, 1960.

Moore, James B. "The Town," unpublished manuscript, Whittier College Archives and Nixon Special Collections, California State University, Fullerton.

Morgan, Lael. "Whittier '34: Most Likely to Succeed," *Los Angeles Times WEST Magazine,* May 10, 1970.

Nixon, Hannah. As Told To Flora Rheta Schreiber. "Richard Nixon: A Mother's Story," *Good Housekeeping*, June, 1960.

Nixon, Patricia. As Told To Joe Alex Morris. "I Say He's A Wonderful Guy," *Saturday Evening Post*, September 6, 1952.

Nixon, Richard Milhous. *RN: The Memoirs of Richard Nixon*. New York: Grosset and Dunlap, 1978.

———— *Six Crises*. New York: Doubleday, 1962.

Olmsted, Roger, and Wollenberg, Charles, editors. *Neither Separate Nor Equal: Race and Racism in California*. California Historical Society, 1971.

O'Reilly, Kenneth. *Hoover and the Un-Americans: The FBI, HUAC and the Red Menace*. Philadelphia: Temple University Press, 1983.

Oshinsky, David M. *A Conspiracy So Immense: The World of Joe McCarthy*. New York: Free Press, 1983.

Parmet, Herbert S. *Eisenhower and the American Crusades*. New York: Macmillan, 1972.

Patterson, James T. *Mr. Republican: A Biography of Robert A. Taft*. Boston: Houghton Mifflin, 1972.

Pearson, Drew. Edited by Tyler Abell. *Diaries*. New York: Holt, Rinehart & Winston, 1974.

Pollack, Jack Harrison. *Earl Warren: The Judge Who Changed America*. Englewood Cliffs, N.J.: Prentice-Hall, 1979.

Public Papers of the Presidents, 1969–1974, 5 vols., Washington, Government Printing Office, 1971–75.

Reeves, Thomas C. *The Life and Times of Joe McCarthy*. New York: Stein & Day, 1982.

Reuben, William A. *Footnote on an Historic Case*. New York: The Nation Institute, 1983.

———— *The Honorable Mr. Nixon*. New York: Action Books, 1960.

Roper, William L. "The Man Who Might Be President," *Frontier*, September 1955, 7–12.

Rovere, Richard H. "Nixon: Most Likely to Succeed," *Harper's*, 1955.

Rowse, Arthur Edward. *Slanted News: A Case Study of the Nixon and Stevenson Fund Stories*. Boston: Beacon Press, 1957.

Schulte, Renee K., editor. *The Young Nixon: An Oral History*. Van Nuys: California State University, Fullerton, Oral History Program, 1978.

Scobie, Ingrid Winther. "Helen Gahagan Douglas and Her 1950 Senate Race with Richard M. Nixon," *Southern California Quarterly* (Spring 1976): 113–26.

Shannon, William V., and Katcher, Leo. "The Story of 'Poor Richard' Nixon," *New York Post*, parts 1–4, September 30–October 3, 1952.

Shearer, Lloyd. "Richard Nixon and Ola-Florence Welch: 'Everyone Expected Them to Get Married,' " *Parade*, June 28, 1970.

Sibley, George. "The Desert Empire," *Harper's*, October 1977.

Smith, John Chabot. *Alger Hiss: The True Story*. New York: Penguin, 1977.

Smith, Marie. "The Pat Nixon Story," *The Washington Post*, October 9–14, 1960.

Smith, Richard Norton. *Thomas E. Dewey and His Times*. New York: Simon and Schuster, 1982.

Smythe, William E. *The Conquest of Arid America*. New York: Macmillan, 1911.

Spaulding, Henry D. *The Nixon Nobody Knows*. Middle Village, N.Y.: Jonathan David Publishers, 1972.

Stripling, Robert E. Edited By Bob Considine. *The Red Plot against America*. Drexel Hill, Penn.: Bell Publishing, 1949.

Sullivan, William. With Bill Brown. *The Bureau*. New York: Pinnacle Books, 1982.

Sulzberger, C. L. *A Long Row of Candles*. New York: Macmillan, 1969.

Theoharis, Athan, editor. *Beyond the Hiss Case: The FBI, Congress, and the Cold War*. Philadelphia: Temple University Press, 1982.

Thomas, Lately. *When Even Angels Wept: The Senator Joseph McCarthy Affair*. New York: Morrow, 1973.

Trohan, Walter. *Political Animals: Memoirs of a Sentimental Cynic*. Garden City, N.Y.: Doubleday, 1975.

U.S. Congress, House Committee on Un-American Activities, Hearings Regarding Communist Espionage in the United States Government, July–September 1948. Washington: Government Printing Office, 1948. (HUAC 1)

U.S. Congress, House Committee on Un-American Activities, Hearings Regarding Communist Espionage in the United States Government, Part 2, December 1948. Washington: Government Printing Office, 1949. (HUAC 2)

Viorst, Milton, "Nixon of the O.P.A.," *New York Times Magazine*, October 3, 1971.

Voorhis, Jerry. *Confessions of a Congressman*. Garden City, N.Y.: Doubleday, 1947.

Warren, Earl. *The Memoirs of Earl Warren*. Garden City, N.Y.: Doubleday, 1977.

Weaver, John D. *Warren: The Man, The Court, The Era*. Boston: Little, Brown, 1968.

Weinstein, Allen. *Perjury: The Hiss-Chambers Case*. New York: Knopf, 1978.

———. "Nixon vs. Hiss," *Esquire*, November 1975.

West, Jessamyn. *Hide and Seek*. New York: Harcourt Brace Jovanovich, 1973.

———. "The Real Pat Nixon," *Good Housekeeping*, February 1971.

White, Theodore H. *Breach of Faith*. New York: Atheneum, 1975.

Wills, Garry. *Nixon Agonistes*. New York: Signet, 1971.

Zeligs, M.D., Myer A. *Friendship and Fratricide*. New York: Viking, 1967.

Principal Manuscript Collections and Private Papers

Sherman Adams Papers, Dwight D. Eisenhower Presidential Library

Stewart Alsop Papers, Library of Congress

Archives and Special Collections, University of Southern California

Eban Ayers Papers, Harry S. Truman Presidential Library

Leslie Baird papers, Goleta, Cal. (Private Collection)

Eleanor Bontecou Papers, Harry S. Truman Presidential Library

California Republican Assembly Collection, UCLA

California Republican Associates Archives, Los Angeles

College Archives and Richard Nixon Special Collection, Whittier College

Paul H. Davis Papers, Hoover Institution, Stanford

Roy O. Day Papers, Bancroft Library, University of California at Berkeley

Democratic National Committee Records, John F. Kennedy Presidential Library

Ralph de Toledano Papers, Hoover Institution, Stanford University

Helen Gahagan Douglas Papers, Carl Albert Center, University of Oklahoma

Sheridan Downey Papers, Bancroft Library, University of California at Berkeley

Duke University Law School Archives

Allen Dulles Papers, Princeton University

Bibliography

John Foster Dulles Papers, Princeton University
George M. Elsey Papers, Harry S. Truman Presidential Library
Sherrill Halbert Papers, UCLA
Alger Hiss Papers, Harvard University Law School
Paul Hoffman Papers, Harry S. Truman Presidential Library
Robert Humphreys Papers, Dwight D. Eisenhower Presidential Library
Charles Kersten Papers, Marquette University
Goodwin C. Knight Papers, Stanford University
Isaac Don Levine Papers, Hoover Institution, Stanford University
David D. Lloyd Papers, Harry S. Truman Presidential Library
Ruth and Ed Lybeck Papers, UCLA
Francis Matthews Papers, Harry S. Truman Presidential Library
Karl Mundt Papers, Dakota State College
Richard Nixon Pre-Presidential Papers, National Archives, Laguna Niguel, Cal.
Richard Nixon Special Collection, California State University at Fullerton
Records of the Office of Price Administration, National Archives, Washington
William Robinson Papers, Dwight D. Eisenhower Presidential Library
William P. Rogers Papers, Dwight D. Eisenhower Presidential Library
Bernard Shanley Papers, Dwight D. Eisenhower Presidential Library
Adlai Stevenson Papers, Princeton University
Horace Jeremiah Voorhis Papers, Claremont Colleges
Earl Warren Papers, California State Archives, Sacramento
Stephen Zetterberg Papers, Claremont, Cal. (Private Collection)

Interviews

(Young Nixon) Richard M. Nixon Project, Oral History Program, California State University, Fullerton: Muriel Adams, Marcelina Arroues, Mrs. Charles Ball, Rev. Charles Ball, Kenneth Ball, Marietta Malcolmson Baron, Myra Ware Barton, William H. Barton, Mildred Beard, Jane Milhous Beeson, Sheldon Beeson, Mrs. Sheldon Beeson, Hortense Behrens, L. Wallace Black, Myrtle Raine Borden, William T. Boyce, Rowe Boyer, Jane Parsonson Brakensiek, Edith Brannon, Mr. and Mrs. Herman Brannon, J. Douglas Brannon, Alta Brennon, Raymond Burbank, J. W. Burch, Bruce Burchell, Ollis O. Burdg, Ralph F. Burnight, Blanche Burum, Martha Cato and Wilma Funk, John Chapin, Earl H. Chapman, Irvin C. Chapman, George Chisler, Elizabeth A. Cloes, Ellen C. Cochran, Rev. Eugene Coffin, Marian S. Conde, Mr. and Mrs. G. Hoyt Corbit, Charlotte Craig, Virginia S. Critchfield, David W. Cromwell, Joanne B. Dale, Vincent L. Dauser, Guy Dixon, Helen Dryer, William H. Duncan, Rev. E. Ezra Ellis, Joyce F. Ernstberger, Donald Fantz, Robert Farnham, Douglas Ferguson, Lois T. Findley, Herman Fink, Howard Frampton, Donald F. Franz, Ella Furnas and Blanche McClure, Charles Gallaher, Mary Bell Gardiner, Grant M. Garman, Joseph E. Gaudio, Mr. and Mrs. Richard R. Gauldin, Nathaniel George, Elizabeth Rees Glover, Wood Glover, Janet L. Goeske, George Gortikov, James J. Grieves, Carman D. Griffin, Louise R. Gwinn, Albert Haendiges, Robert R. Halliday, C. Richard Harris, Dick S. Heffern, Eloise Hilberg, Marian W. Hodge, Heber Holloway, Blanche Potter Holmes, William H. D. Hornaday, Emmett Ingrum, Yoneko Dobashi Iwatsuru, Sheldon G. Jackson, Rev. George

Jenkins, Fred Johnson, Louis Jones, George Kellogg, Glen Kelly, Muriel Kelly, Regina Duncan Kemp, Charles Kendle, Gerald Kepple, Marjorie Hildreth Knighton, Dr. I. N. Kraushaar, William Krueger, Helen S. Letts, E. V. and Patricia Lindstrom, Wayne Long, Judith Wingert Loubet, Harold A. McCabe, C. Robert McCormick, Gordon McHatton, Hadley Marshburn, Murle Marshburn, Mr. and Mrs. Oscar Marshburn, Theodore F. Marshburn, Barbara Mashburn, Mildred Sillivan Mendenhall, Mable O. Meyers, Charles L. Milhous, Dorothy Z. Milhous, William A. Milhous, Vivian Cox Montgomery, Morton Morehouse, Leona Stine Myler, Ralph Navarro, Byron Netzley, A. C. Newsom, Mattie Newsom, John C. Neyer, Ray Nichols, Mrs. Ray Nichols, Lyle Otterman, Elizabeth Timberlake Paldanius, Ralph Palmer, Lucille Parsons, Hubert Perry, Tom Phelan, Richard Philippi, Saragrace F. Philippi, Mrs. Cecil Pickering, Forest Randall, Mrs. Irene M. Randall, C. Arthur Remley, Mary Elizabeth Rez, Nellamena Roach, Mrs. Benjamin Roberts, Howard Rupard, Paul Ryan, Edwin Sanders, Manville Saxton, Harry A. Schuyler, H. Glenn Shaffer, Gerald Shaw, George Shoals, Ralph C. Shook, Carl F. Siegmund, Mr. and Mrs. Robert Sillivan, Mary G. Skidmore, Paul S. Smith, William Soeberg, Ed Sowers, Harold Space, Richard Spaulding, Frances Stanley, Felix Stein, Dr. and Mrs. Harold Stone, Osmyn Stout (tape only), Phil and Jeri Studebaker, Albert and Myrtle Stuelke, Ada Sutton, Lyall Sutton, Setsuko Tani, Madeline Thomas, Edith Milhous Timberlake, Frances Timberlake, Phillip H. Timberlake, Catherine Travaglia, Dean Triggs and Robert Gibbs, G. Ellis Triggs, Ralph Veady, Lura Waldrup, Harold Walker, Ed Warner, Herb Warner, Samuel Warren, Merle West, Bessie T. Wickersham, Floyd Wildermuth, H. Esther Williams, Winifred Winget, Keith Wood, Merton G. Wray, Mrs. Merton G. Wray, Marygene Marshburn Wright, Ed Wunder, Harriet Nixon Yates

Horace Jeremiah Voorhis Oral History Project, Claremont Colleges: H. Jeremiah Voorhis, Volumes I–V, Stephen Zetterberg

Oral History Program, University of California at Los Angeles: Dorothy Healey, Volumes I–III, Patrick J. Hillings, Carey McWilliams, Paul Ziffren

Helen Gahagan Douglas Component of the California Women Political Leaders Oral History Project, The Bancroft Library, University of California at Berkeley: Juanita E. Barbee, Rachel S. Bell, Albert S. Cahn, Margery Cahn, Evelyn Chavoor, Lucy Kramer Cohen, Helen Gahagan Douglas, Tilford E. Dudley, India T. Edwards, Arthur Goldschmidt, Elizabeth Wickenden Goldschmidt, Leo Goodman, Kenneth R. Harding, Charles Hogan, Chester A. Holifield, Mary Keyserling, Byron F. Lindsley, Helen Lustig, Alvin P. Meyers, Philip J. Noel-Baker, Frank Rogers

Earl Warren Oral History Project, The Bancroft Library, University of California at Berkeley: Stanley N. Barnes, Edmund G. Brown, Herbert Brownell, Asa Call, Oliver J. Carter, Florence McChesney Clifton, Robert Clifton, Thomas J. Cunningham, Murray Draper, McIntyre Faries, James Hagerty, Victor Hansen, Patrick J. Hillings, Preston Hotchkis, Walter P. Jones, Robert Kenny, Roger Kent, William F. Knowland, Thomas H. Kuchel, Keith McCormac, Rollin Lee McNitt, William S. Mailliard, Paul Manolis, Thomas J. Mellon, Herbert L. Phillips, Langdon Post, Harold Powers, Richard Rodda, James Roosevelt, Verne Scoggins, Merrell F. Small, Harold Stassen, Earl Warren

Richard M. Nixon in the Warren Era, Earl Warren Oral History Project, The Bancroft Library, University of California at Berkeley: Earl Adams, Roy P. Crocker, Roy O. Day, John Walton Dinkelspiel, Frank E. Jorgensen

Governmental History Documentation Project, Goodwin Knight/Edmund Brown, Sr. Era, University of California at Berkeley: Emelyn Knowland Jewett, Estelle Knowland Johnson, Paul Manolis, Milton R. Polland

Fawn McKay Brodie Research Collection, The Marriott Library, Special Collections, University of Utah, Salt Lake City: Frederick Albrink, Patricia Alsop, Richard Arena, James Bassett, Thomas Bewley, Wallace Black, Jesse Lynch Brandt, Kathleen Brown, Mrs. Grace Bumpus, David Cavers, Kenneth Chotiner, Marshall Clough, Jr., James Cobey, Tom Dixon, Evlyn Dorn, Thomas Emerson, Elizabeth Eidson Evans, Ladislas Farago, Helen Rose Lynch Gay, Robert Greene, Leonard Hall, Verna Hough, Phoebe Howard, Ola Welch Jobe, Mildred Jackson Johns, W. T. and Molly Mason Jones, Leo Katcher, Leonard Kaufman, Richard Kiefer, Olive and Oscar Marshburn, Wallace J. Newman, Roy Newsom, Mrs. John Nunes, Jerry Pacht, A. J. Paonessa, William Perdue, George Reedy, Vita Remley, Edward Rubin, Adela Rogers St. Johns, Mrs. Milton Sanden, Francis Schwartz, Ethel Farley Hunter Sheldon, Mrs. Georgia Sherwood, Paul Smith, Weldon Taylor, Albert Upton, Jessamyn West, Merle West, Virginia Williams, Steven Zetterberg, Mr. and Mrs. Paul Ziffren

Transcripts of Interviews by Lael Morgan (for "Whittier '34," Los Angeles Times WEST Magazine, May 10, 1970), deposited in Special Nixon Collection, California State University, Fullerton (cited as Morgan transcripts): Kenneth Ball, Joanne Brown Dale, Wood Glover, Jr., C. Richard Harris, Clint Harris, Gail Jobe and Ola Florence Welch Jobe, Regina Duncan Kemp, Marjorie Hildreth Knighton, Camella Vincent Simmons, Richard Spaulding, Richard Thomson, Dr. Albert Upton, Keith Wood, Ed Wunder

Harry S. Truman Presidential Library Oral History Project: Tom Clark

Dwight D. Eisenhower Presidential Library Oral History Project: Sherman Adams, Bernard Shanley

Herbert Hoover Presidential Library Oral History Project: G. Keith Funston, John D. M. Hamilton

Additional Personal Interviews and Correspondence: Patricia Alsop, Richard Arena, Mrs. William A. Arnold, Leslie Baird, Mrs. James Bassett, Philip G. Blew, Jesse Lynch Brandt, Paul Bullock, Pierce Butler III, David Cavers, Jack Chotiner, Charles Cooper, Mrs. Leonidas Dotson, John R. Erickson, Amelia Fry, Hon. Barry Goldwater, Lillian Rosse Goodrich, Fred Harmsen, Richard F. Harris, Robert Hartmann, Ethel Farley Hunter, Peter Irons, John J. Irwin, Emelyn Knowland Jewett, Estelle Knowland Johnson, David Kahn, Paul Keye, Richard

W. Kiefer, Howard Kohn, Mrs. Isaac Don Levine, Morton R. Lewis, Susan McClintock, Paul T. McNutt, Max McPherson, Paul G. Manolis, Bernard C. Meyer, William Morrow, Jocelyn Moss, Edith Nunes, Francis Herbert Obetz, James Phelan, George Reedy, John Rothmann, Budge Ruffner, Elaine St. Johns, McCullah St. Johns, Richard Rogers St. Johns, Isabelle M. Sheller, Richard Norton Smith, Richard H. Spaulding, Joseph Spear, Ralph de Toledano, Harlan H. Vinnedge, H. J. Voorhis, Jr., Frank Waldrop, Jerry L. Wallace, Earl Warren, Jr., Allen Weinstein, Steven Zetterberg

INDEX

Note: *References to RN refer to Richard Nixon.*

Shattuck, Edward, 673
Shaw, Gerald, 58, 62
Shaw, Virginia, 62
　recollections of, 54, 55–56, 58, 63,
　67, 92–93
Sheen, Monsignor Fulton J., 350
Sheller, Lynn, 91–92
Sherwood, Georgia, 589, 593
Sherwood, Robert, 237, 238
Shockney, Henrietta, 41
Shook, Ralph, 42, 51, 52, 54, 61, 65
Shoreham Hotel, 367
Shroyer, Tom, 660
Shuler, Reverend Robert, 87
Signal Oil, 308
Silberberg, Mendel, 310, 574, 746
Silvermaster, Nathan Gregory, 385, 409
Sinclair, Upton, 16–17, 202, 259, 268,
　299, 522, 554–55, 585–86, 615
Sirica, John J., 738
Sisters of Charity Seton Hospital, 212,
　213, 214
Six Crises (Nixon), 395, 461, 505, 508,
　511–12, 819
Skidmore, Stephen, 65
Slater, Ellis, 668, 672, 730
Small, M. F., 292, 324
Small, Pop, 609–10
Small Town Girl, 214
Smathers, George, 558, 559, 560, 590,
　655–56, 864
Smedley, Gordon, 592
Smith, Al, 213
Smith, Alexander, 731
Smith, C. Arnholt, 573, 675
Smith, Dana, 310, 528, 546
　described, 633
　as Eisenhower fund-raiser, 677, 678,
　688
　help from RN, 649–50, 815, 816, 862
　RN's Fund and, 632–39, 649, 651,
　654, 657, 817, 845
　disclosure of, 757–62, 764, 766,
　768, 770–76, 783, 785, 795–96,
　810, 819–21
　Vice-Presidential campaign and, 744,
　746
Smith, Gerald L. K., 550, 593, 599
Smith, H. Allen, 589

Smith, Hulet P., 637
Smith, J. A., 677
Smith, Margaret Chase, 628
Smith, Paul, 70, 79, 99, 116, 122, 126,
　129, 137, 160, 188, 194, 231,
　232, 605, 743
　described, 123
　Lincoln quote, 815, 819
　as president of Whittier College, 647
　on RN, 123–24, 157, 159, 182
Smith, Richard Norton, 686, 718
Smith, Walker, 637
Smith, William French, 798
Smythe, William, 3
Socialism, 660
Social Security, 176, 177, 361, 362
Society of Friends, see Quakers
Soeberg, William, 149, 157
Solbert, Oscar, 796, 816, 854
Songs O'Cheer, 49, 61
Southern California Edison, 280, 554
Southern California Petroleum Corpo-
　ration, 636
Southern　California　Republican
　Women, 326
Southern Pacific Railroad, 2, 4, 5, 520,
　572
South Korea, 541, 571, 572
　see also Korean War
South Pacific Air Transport Command
　units (SCAT), 247, 250, 254
South Pasadenans, Incorporated, 287
South Pasadena Review, 297
Soviet Union:
　Cold War with, 264, 265, 354, 665–
　66
　German invasion of, 234, 249
　testing of atomic bomb, 493
Spanish Civil War, 234
Sparkman, John, 754, 769, 773, 774,
　786, 832, 833, 851, 852
Spaulding, Richard, 124, 138, 145
Spellman, Francis Cardinal, 333, 350
Spencer, A. Kenneth, 274
Spensers, 860
Spingarn, Stephen, 390, 510–11
Sprague, Russell, 684, 717, 731, 732,
　844
Stalin, Joseph, 234, 341